P9-BXZ-565

OXFORD PAPERBACK REFERENCE

The Concise Oxford Dictionary of the
Christian Church

Dr E. A. Livingstone is the editor of the third edition of
The Oxford Dictionary of the Christian Church, on which
this concise volume is based. She was responsible for
the organization of the International Conferences on
Patristic Studies from 1971 to 1995 and edited the
proceedings. For services to patristic scholarship she
was made an MBE.

Oxford Paperback Reference

The most authoritative and up-to-date reference books for both students and the general reader.

The Concise Oxford Dictionary of the

Christian Church

SECOND EDITION

E. A. LIVINGSTONE

OXFORD
UNIVERSITY PRESS

OXFORD
UNIVERSITY PRESS

Great Clarendon Street, Oxford OX2 6DP

Oxford University Press is a department of the University of Oxford.
It furthers the University's objective of excellence in research, scholarship,
and education by publishing worldwide in

Oxford New York

Auckland Bangkok Buenos Aires Cape Town Chennai
Dar es Salaam Delhi Hong Kong Istanbul Karachi Kolkata
Kuala Lumpur Madrid Melbourne Mexico City Mumbai Nairobi
São Paulo Shanghai Taipei Tokyo Toronto

Oxford is a registered trade mark of Oxford University Press
in the UK and in certain other countries

Published in the United States
by Oxford University Press Inc., New York

© E. A. Livingstone 1977, 2000

The moral rights of the author have been asserted
Database right Oxford University Press (makers)

First published in hardback and paperback 1977
Reissued in new covers 1996
This edition published 2000

All rights reserved. No part of this publication may be reproduced,
stored in a retrieval system, or transmitted, in any form or by any means,
without the prior permission in writing of Oxford University Press,
or as expressly permitted by law, or under terms agreed with the appropriate
reprographics rights organization. Enquiries concerning reproduction
outside the scope of the above should be sent to the Rights Department,
Oxford University Press, at the address above

You must not circulate this book in any other binding or cover
and you must impose this same condition on any acquirer

British Library Cataloguing in Publication Data
Data available

Library of Congress Cataloging in Publication Data
Data available
ISBN 0-19-280057-4

6

Typeset in Swift
by RefineCatch Limited, Bungay, Suffolk
Printed in Great Britain by
Clays Ltd, St Ives plc

Preface

The first edition of the *Concise Oxford Dictionary of the Christian Church* was based on the second edition of F. L. Cross's *Oxford Dictionary of the Christian Church* (published in 1974); this second edition of the *Concise* depends on the extensively revised third edition of the parent volume, published in 1997, with some additional material and revision reflecting more recent events. It aims to provide basic information in an accessible form for those who do not need, or perhaps cannot afford, the parent volume. Further information and lists of books in which a subject may be pursued are normally contained in the corresponding article there. As in the main dictionary, in order to save space 'man' is used to denote both men and women collectively, except where there is a need to distinguish between the sexes, as in the entry 'Adam'. In the absence of an agreed modern translation of the Bible, references and quotations are usually those of the Authorized Version. Modern liturgical developments in the Church of England are described in terms of the *Alternative Service Book 1980*; this will technically be superseded later in 2000 by a new book called *Common Worship*, which marks a further stage in revision, but the *Alternative Service Book* and its supplementary material marked the real break from the *Book of Common Prayer*, which had been used for centuries.

It is my pleasant duty to thank the many people who have answered questions or made suggestions in the light of the publication of the third edition of the parent volume. I am particularly indebted to Dr B. W. Ball, the Revd Dr Michael Bourdeaux, Dr S. P. Brock, Dr J. P. B. Dobbs, the Revd Dr P. S. Fiddes, the Very Revd Protopresbyter Dr Columba Graham Flegg, Professor Andrew Louth, the Revd R. C. Morgan, the Revd Dr Robert Ombres, OP, the Revd Dr S. J. Pix, the Revd John Rees, Dr J. J. Smith, the Very Revd Dr Simon Tugwell, OP, and Mr P. A. Ward Jones, who all supplied new articles or substantial material for revision of existing ones, and for guidance on specific points to Mrs Sheila Allcock, Mrs Marjorie J. Crossley, Dr N. R. M. de Lange, Dr E. T. Dubois, Canon Peter Eaton, the Very Revd Dr A. Eszer, OP, the Revd Nicky Gumbel, Dr David Hilliard, Dr P. M. Joyce, Dr Elaine Kaye, Prof. D. N. J. MacCulloch, Mrs Deirdre Martin, Herr Dieter Messner, Prof. N. F. Palmer, Baroness Park, the Revd Prof. R. W. Pfaff, the Revd Dr H. D. Rack, Prof. D. A. F. M. Russell, Prof. Richard Sharpe, Dom Henry Wansbrough, the Revd Prof. M. F. Wiles, and Dr J. R. C. Wright; also to the staff of the Amana Society, the Bodleian Library, and the Shaker Library. I am also grateful to Mrs Janet Foot, who read both the galley and the page proofs, to Miss Nicola Bion, Mr Angus Phillips, and Miss Helen Cox, my successive editors at the Oxford University Press; and for various suggestions to Mrs Malgorzata Colquhoun.

25 March 2000   E. A. L.

Abbreviations

(A) The most common abbreviations, used throughout the book

Abp.	Archbishop
AD	anno Domini
ASB	*Alternative Service Book 1980
AV	Authorized Version (i.e. King James Version, 1611) of the Bible
BC	before Christ
BCP	Book of *Common Prayer
Bl	Blessed
Bp.	Bishop
BVM	Blessed Virgin *Mary
Card.	Cardinal
C of E	*Church of England
cent.	century
CW	*Common Worship
Emp.	Emperor
Ep.	Epistle
fl.	*floruit* (Lat., 'flourished')
Fr.	French
Ger.	German
Ital.	Italian
JB	Jerusalem Bible (Eng. tr., 1966)
Lat.	Latin
LXX	*Septuagint
MS	manuscript
NEB	New English Bible (NT, 1961; OT and Apocrypha, 1970)
NJB	New Jerusalem Bible (1985)
NRSV	New Revised Standard Version (1989) of the Bible
NT	New Testament
OT	Old Testament
Patr.	Patriarch
q.v.	quod vide (Lat., 'which see')
RC	Roman Catholic
REB	Revised English Bible (1989)
RSV	Revised Standard Version (NT, 1946; OT, 1952; Apocrypha, 1957)
Russ.	Russian
RV	[English] Revised Version (NT, 1881; OT, 1885; Apocrypha, 1895)
Sp.	Spanish
St	Saint
tr.	translation
Ven.	Venerable
Vulg.	*Vulgate

An asterisk (*) preceding a word indicates a relevant article in the *Dictionary* under that (or a closely similar) heading.

(B) Biblical books (given in the order of the AV)

(Names used in the Vulgate and/or derived versions are given in brackets where they differ substantially from those of the AV)

OLD TESTAMENT

Gen.	Genesis
Exod.	Exodus
Lev.	Leviticus
Num.	Numbers
Deut.	Deuteronomy
Jos.	Joshua
Jgs.	Judges
Ruth	Ruth
1, 2 Sam. (1, 2 Reg.)	1, 2 Samuel (1, 2 Regum or Reigns)
1, 2 Kgs. (3, 4 Reg.)	1, 2 Kings (3, 4 Regum or Reigns)
1, 2 Chron. (1, 2 Paralip.)	1, 2 Chronicles (1, 2 Paralipomenon)
Ez. (1 Esd.)	Ezra (1 Esdras)
Neh. (2 Esd.)	Nehemiah (2 Esdras)
Est.	Esther
Job	Job
Pss.	Psalms
Prov.	Proverbs
Eccles.	Ecclesiastes
Song of Songs (Cant.)	Song of Songs (Canticles)
Is. (Es.)	Isaiah (Esaias)
Jer.	Jeremiah
Lam.	Lamentations
Ezek.	Ezekiel
Dan.	Daniel
Hos.	Hosea
Joel	Joel
Am.	Amos
Obad.	Obadiah
Jon.	Jonah
Mic.	Micah
Nah.	Nahum
Hab.	Habakkuk
Zeph. (Soph.)	Zephaniah (Sophonias)
Hag.	Haggai
Zech.	Zechariah
Mal.	Malachi

APOCRYPHA

1, 2 Esd. (3, 4 Esd.)	1, 2 Esdras (3, 4 Esdras)
Tob.	Tobit
Judith	Judith
Rest of Est.	Rest of Esther
Wisd. Sol.	Wisdom of Solomon
Ecclus. (Sirach)	Ecclesiasticus (Sirach)
Bar.	Baruch
S. of III Ch.	Song of the Three Children
Sus.	Susanna

Bel	Bel and the Dragon [Serpent or Snake]
Pr. Man.	Prayer of Manasses
1, 2 Macc.	1, 2 Maccabees

NEW TESTAMENT

Mt.	Matthew
Mk.	Mark
Lk.	Luke
Jn.	John
Acts	Acts of the Apostles
Rom.	Romans
1, 2 Cor.	1, 2 Corinthians
Gal.	Galatians
Eph.	Ephesians
Phil.	Philippians
Col.	Colossians
1, 2 Thess.	1, 2 Thessalonians
1, 2 Tim.	1, 2 Timothy
Tit.	Titus
Philem.	Philemon
Heb.	Hebrews
Jas.	James
1, 2 Pet.	1, 2 Peter
1, 2, 3 Jn.	1, 2, 3 John
Jude	Jude
Rev. (Apoc.)	Revelation (Apocalypse)

A

Aaron. In Hebrew tradition *Moses' brother. He was assigned to Moses as his assistant (Exod. 4: 14), and later he and his descendants were appointed priests (Exod. 28 f.). In Christian theology he is a *type of Christ.

Abailard. See ABELARD.

Abba. The Aramaic word for 'Father', used by Christ.

abbé. A French term, originally restricted to the *abbot of a monastery, but in modern times applied to secular clerics in general.

abbess. The head of certain autonomous houses of nuns. The title is used among *Benedictines, *Cistercians, *Trappists, *Poor Clares, and some *canonesses. The earliest known instance is in 514. In the Middle Ages wide powers were claimed by some abbesses, but the Council of *Trent put an end to most special prerogatives.

Abbo, St (c.945–1004), or 'Abbon', Abbot of *Fleury from 988. He supported the *Cluniac reform and was killed in a revolt occasioned by the reform of the priory of La Réole in Gascony. His letters are a valuable source for the relations between France and the Papacy. He also wrote on logic, mathematics, and astronomy, and an Epitome of the Lives of the Popes. Feast day, 13 Nov.

abbot. In the W. Church the official title of the head of certain monasteries of monks or monastic *Congregations belonging to the *Benedictine, *Cistercian, or *Trappist families, and of some houses of certain orders of *Canons Regular. According to the Rule of St *Benedict, the abbot is to be regarded as the father of his monastic family and has far-reaching powers in the government of his house. Nowadays abbots are elected by the monks of the abbey; they receive a liturgical blessing and may be invested with a *ring, *mitre, and *crosier.

Abbot, Ezra (1819–84), American biblical scholar. A *Unitarian by belief, from 1856 he held posts at Harvard University. He was one of the original members of the American NT Revision Company in charge of the RV, and his judgement was influential.

Abbot, George (1562–1633), Abp. of *Canterbury from 1611. He became Master of University College, Oxford, in 1597. His *Puritan sympathies brought him into conflict with the rising party of *High Churchmen in the University, but he won *James I's favour by his mission to *Scotland (1608), in which he persuaded the *Presbyterians of the lawfulness of episcopacy. Preferment followed. As archbishop he was severe on RCs and partial to *Calvinists at home and abroad. He encouraged the King's attempt to secure the dismissal of C. *Vorstius as an *Arminian from his chair at *Leiden and he ensured that England was represented at the Synod of *Dort (1618). The strong line which he took over the Essex nullity suit (1613) won him respect and a temporary popularity. In 1621 he accidentally shot a gamekeeper and his position was considered to have become irregular; James decided in his favour and he resumed his duties. He crowned *Charles I but had little influence in his reign.

abbreviator. A former official of the Roman chancery, whose principal duty was the preparation of letters and writs for the *collation of Church dignities. He was so named from the excessive abbreviations employed in Papal documents.

Abel. According to Gen. 4: 2 the second son of *Adam and *Eve. He was killed by his brother Cain, who was jealous that Abel's sacrifice had been accepted by God, whereas his own was rejected. In Christian tradition he is regarded as a *type of Christ because of the innocence of his life, his accepted sacrifice, and his violent death.

Abelard, Peter (1079–1142/3), philosopher and theologian. (**Abailard**, used by some scholars, is probably nearer the original form of his name than the traditional spelling.) He lectured at *Paris in dialectics and then in theology until the tragic issue of his love-affair with Héloïse caused him to retire to the monastery of *St-Denis in 1117/8. *Roscelin and others then attacked the orthodoxy of his teaching on the Trinity, and he was condemned unheard at the Council of *Soissons (1121). He returned to St-Denis, but his outspoken criticism of the legends of St *Dionysius (the patron of the abbey) led to his flight. He set up an oratory called the Paraclete, near Troyes, where Héloïse later became abbess of a house of nuns. In 1127 Abelard became Abbot of St-Gildas, but by 1136 he was again teaching in Paris. In 1140 St *Bernard denounced his teaching and several propositions from his writings were condemned at the Council of *Sens.

His extensive writings include *Sic et Non*, a collection of apparently conflicting excerpts from the Bible and the Fathers on a number of questions, intended to help the reader to reconcile the contradictions by making him aware of the difference between authority itself and the different forms in which it is expressed; the *Theologia Summi Boni*, in which he sought to show how the doctrine of the Trinity might be understood by way of 'analogies provided by human reason'; and several well-known hymns, among them 'O quanta qualia' ('O what the joy and the glory must be'). His philosophical and theological doctrines were largely determined by his early interest in *universals. He maintained that only individuals could be described as things ('res'), and that language represented an abstraction from these things. The 'vox' or 'nomen' of language could not be considered a thing, but only a concept, because the qualities shared by individuals are not in themselves things, but the results of a mental act. Later he gave more importance to the question of meaning in language. The understanding of the thing, which is required for words to have meaning, is at least in part (he said) a true understanding of the thing as it was conceived in the mind of God. In his *Ethics* he argued that sin consisted not in any action, but in contempt for the wishes of God. His aim was not simply to set faith against reason but rather to question the content of faith in order to gain a fuller perception of it. Many later authors took up his method and his influence is evident in the history of *scholasticism.

Abercius, Inscription of. The Greek epi-taph of Abercius Marcellus, Bp. of Hieropolis (d. *c.*200), now in the *Vatican Museum. Apparently set up by Abercius over his future tomb, it testifies to the universality of the *Eucharist. The 'Life of Abercius', which incorporates the text of the inscription and attributes to Abercius a 'Book of Teaching', is later (probably 4th cent.).

Abgar, Legend of. According to tradition, Abgar V, King of *Edessa (4 BC–7 AD and 13–50), being ill, wrote to Christ asking Him to visit and heal him; in reply Christ promised that after His Ascension He would send a disciple to cure the King and preach the Gospel to his people. In *Eusebius the letter is followed by an account of the mission of *Thaddeus, who heals the King and converts many of the inhabitants of the city. According to the 'Pilgrimage of *Egeria', Christ's letter was preserved at Edessa.

abjuration. The act of renouncing an idea, person, or thing to which one has previously adhered. In the past, RC canon law defined it as the external retractation, made before witnesses, of errors contrary to Catholic faith and unity. From 1857 to 1967 a form of abjuration was imposed on those received into the RC Church from other bodies, and the Greek Church has set forms of abjuration for converts from *Judaism and *Islam as well as from other Christian denominations.

Abjuration, Oath of. An oath renouncing the Stuart dynasty and the temporal power of the Pope, imposed in 1702 on all who took civil, military, or spiritual office. It was replaced in 1858 by a new form of the Oath of *Allegiance.

ablutions. (1) The washing of fingers and *chalice by the celebrant after Communion in the Eucharist. The ceremony became part of the Eucharistic rite in the 10th or 11th cent.; details have varied. (2) In the RC Church the rinsing of the mouth with wine after reception of the Blessed Sacrament by the new priests in the Ordination Mass, customary until 1968, and a similar rinsing with water formerly common at the Communion of the Sick. A similar custom exists in the E., where in many places communicants receive unconsecrated wine after Communion in the Liturgy.

abortion. See CONTRACEPTION, PROCREATION, AND ABORTION, ETHICS OF.

Abraham (or **Abram**), OT *Patriarch. His story is told in Gen. 11: 26–25: 18. Having moved from Ur of the Chaldees to Haran, he set out for the land of Canaan in response to a Divine command. God promised him a son by his wife Sarai (Sarah) and an innumerable posterity. After the birth of *Isaac, Abraham's faith was put to a severe test by a command to sacrifice his son. When he showed his readiness for this act of obedience, a ram was substituted and Abraham was rewarded by a formal renewal of God's promises.

Scholarly opinion is divided both about the historicity and date of the Abraham tradition. The Church, however, has always recognized in Abraham a spiritual ancestor on account of his faith and obedience in leaving his homeland. His willingness to sacrifice his son furnished a model of perfect obedience to the will of God and came to prefigure the death of Christ.

Abraham, Apocalypse of. An apocryphal writing, perhaps dating from the 1st cent. AD. It describes *Abraham's conversion from idolatry and a series of visions seen by him in the heavens. It shows Christian influence, but the opening part is based on Jewish traditions.

Abraham, Testament of. An apocryphal Greek writing describing how *Abraham, taken to heaven by the Archangel *Michael, has a vision of the two roads leading to hell and paradise; he is brought back to earth and finally borne by the Angel of Death to paradise. It may date from the 2nd cent. AD, but opinions differ about its date and whether its author was a Christian or a Jew.

Absolute Idealism. 'Idealism' is the name sometimes given to philosophical theories according to which reality is mental or spiritual (ideal from 'idea') rather than material or independent of mind. 'Absolute Idealism' is distinguished from 'Subjective Idealism'. Whereas 'Subjective Idealism' is typically understood as holding that the only reality is ideas in the human mind, 'Absolute Idealism' says that there is significant reality outside the human mind.

absolution. The formal act of a bishop or priest pronouncing the forgiveness of sins by Christ to penitent sinners. A formula of absolution is included in many liturgical acts of worship, but according to traditional Catholic belief, *mortal (or grave) sins are normally absolved only in the Sacrament of *Penance. The need for a formal absolution by an ordained minister is commonly denied among Protestants who generally do not ascribe any sacramental force to such an absolution. The indicative form of absolution ('I absolve you') is used in the W. for individuals; the precatory form, in which the priest formally prays that God will absolve an individual or congregation, is used for absolutions in the course of the liturgy and in the E. also for individuals.

Absolutions of the Dead. The service in the RC Church formerly said after the *Requiem Mass before the body was taken from the church. It consisted of prayers for the departed soul and the aspersing and censing of the body. In 1969 it was replaced by a final commendation, which includes a short address, aspersing and censing of the body, a collect, and a chant.

abstinence. A penitential practice, consisting in abstaining from the use of certain kinds of food. Among RCs abstinence from flesh-meat has traditionally been observed on nearly all *Fridays and certain other occasions. In 1966 the number of penitential days was reduced and Episcopal Conferences were empowered to substitute for abstinence other forms of penance, particularly works of charity or piety. In the E. Church the practice is more rigid. There are about 150 days of abstinence in the year, and fish, eggs, milk, cheese, oil, and wine, as well as meat, are forbidden. See also FASTS AND FASTING.

Abuna. The Patriarch of the *Ethiopian Church.

Abyssinian Church. See ETHIOPIAN CHURCH.

Acacian schism. A temporary schism (482–519) between Rome and the East which began while Acacius was Patr. of Constantinople (471–89). It arose out of the *Henoticon.

Acacius of Caesarea (d. 365), *Arian theologian. He succeeded *Eusebius in the see of *Caesarea (in Palestine) in 341, but was pronounced deposed by the Council of *Sardica (343). In 359 he proposed a *Homoean Creed at the Council of *Seleucia. He signed the Creed of *Nicaea in 363 but returned to Arianism and was deposed in 365. His followers ('Acacians') were a distinct and important theological party between 357 and 361.

Acarie, Mme (1566–1618), Bl 'Mary of the Incarnation'. Barbe Jeanne Avrillot, though anxious to join the *Poor Clares, in 1584 married Pierre Acarie. They had six children. Their house was a centre of charitable works and intense spirituality; Mme Acarie experienced visions and *ecstasies. She took part in establishing the first house of the Reformed *Carmelites in France in 1604. She also helped to bring the *Ursulines to Paris and supported P. de *Bérulle in the foundation of the *Oratorians. After her husband's death in 1613, she joined the Carmelites as a lay sister. Feast day, 18 Apr.

Acathistus (Gk. 'not sitting', because it was sung standing), a famous Greek liturgical hymn in honour of the BVM. It may be the work of St *Romanos 'Melodos', but the authorship is disputed.

Acceptants. Those who 'accepted' the bull '*Unigenitus' (1713) in the *Jansenist controversy. See also APELLANTS.

Accession Service. The form of prayer for use on the anniversary of the accession of the reigning British sovereign, printed at the end of the BCP.

accident. In medieval philosophy, an entity whose essential nature it is to inhere in another entity as a subject (*ens in alio*). It is thus contrasted with a substance (*ens per se*). The term has played an important part in Eucharistic doctrine, since the *Schoolmen evolved the theory of 'accidents without a subject' to elucidate the mystery of the Presence. The concept was used to explain how, after the changing of the substances of the bread and wine into those of the Body and Blood of Christ, the accidents of the former, e.g. quantity, colour, etc., continued to exist and be perceptible by the senses. See also TRANSUBSTANTIATION.

accidie (Greek for 'negligence', 'indifference'). By the early 5th cent. the word had become a technical term in Christian asceticism, signifying a state of restlessness and inability either to work or to pray. It is accounted one of the '*seven deadly sins'.

accommodation. In theology, the adaptation of a text or teaching to altered circumstances. The word is used: (1) Especially by RCs to connote the giving to a text of Scripture a meaning not intended by the writer, e.g. the reference of Pharaoh's words 'Go unto Joseph' (Gen. 41: 55) to the Lord's foster father. (2) By 18th-cent. liberal German theologians to expound the mode of Divine communication through the Bible. Thus Christ's words or assumptions about the authorship of parts of the OT, or about the objective reality of demon-possession, are explained as the deliberate adjustment of His ideas to contemporary Judaism. (3) In a more general sense of the teaching by Christians of only part of the truth for the sake of prudence, or of the modification of the form of Christian teaching to secure its more ready acceptance. A notable instance of accommodation in this sense was the practice of *Jesuit missionaries in *China of using the word *t'ien* for God and of allowing converts to continue in practices akin to ancestor-worship.

Aceldama. 'The field of blood', a piece of land near *Jerusalem, so named (1) according to Mt. 27: 8, because it was bought with the price of the Lord's blood; but (2) according to Acts 1: 18 f., because it was the scene of *Judas Iscariot's end.

Acoemetae (literally 'sleepless ones'). A celebrated body of Orthodox monks. Abbot Alexander established at *Constantinople (*c*.400) a religious house whose monks were to observe absolute poverty, do no manual work, and keep up perpetual psalmody in alternating choirs. The monks were subsequently transferred to the modern Tchiboukli, where they were first called 'Acoemetae'. They defended orthodoxy against the *Monophysites, but later fell into the *Nestorian heresy, for which they were excommunicated by Pope John II in 534. By the 12th cent. they were back in Constantinople.

acolyte. The first in rank of the two Lesser Ministries in the RC Church. Until 1972 acolytes formed one of the four *Minor Orders. First mentioned *c*.251, they were specially dedicated to the service of the altar, administering Communion both inside and outside Mass. With the *subdeacon, they absorbed most of the functions of the other Minor Orders at Mass and Baptism. Since 1972 the acolyte may be a layman.

Acquaviva, Claudius. See AQUIVIVA, CLAUDIO.

act, human. In moral theology the term denotes the free and voluntary action of a human being done with knowledge and attention. To such acts alone can moral praise or blame be accorded.

Acta Apostolicae Sedis. From 1909 the official gazette of the *Vatican.

Acta Sanctorum. The celebrated series of lives of the saints, arranged in the order of their feasts in the ecclesiastical year, which was begun by the *Bollandists in the 17th cent. By 1925 it had reached 10 Nov.

action. A name once applied to the whole Mass and later restricted to the *Canon of the Mass as the ultimate sacrificial action.

Action Française. A French political movement, founded in 1898 at the height of the Dreyfus affair. In 1926 it was condemned by *Pius XI on the grounds of extreme nationalism and a cynical misappropriation of Catholic doctrine. The last issue of its newspaper *L'Action Française* appeared in 1944.

action sermon. Among Scottish *Presbyterians, the sermon preached before the administration of the *Lord's Supper.

Acton, John. See AYTON, JOHN.

Acton, John Emerich Edward Dalberg, first Baron Acton (1834–1902), historian. In 1859 he became editor of the RC *Rambler; under the threat of a Papal veto he suspended it in 1864. He sought to resist the movement towards *Ultramontanism in the RC Church. In 1869 he went to Rome to organize resistance to the definition of Papal *Infallibility at the *Vatican Council, collaborating with J. J. I. von *Döllinger in publishing the series of letters under the signature '*Quirinus'. From 1895 he was Regius Professor of Modern History at Cambridge.

ACTS. See CHURCHES TOGETHER.

Acts of the Apostles. The fifth Book of the NT. It outlines the mission of the Church from the *Ascension of Christ to St *Paul's visit to Rome, *c.*AD 62. It is generally admitted to be the work of St *Luke (q.v.). Its composition is variously dated, but most critics would probably settle for the 80s.

This is late enough to allow for the idealized picture of the nascent Church, but prior to systematic *persecution by the Roman authorities. The so-called 'We-sections' (16: 10–17; 20: 5–15; 21: 1–18; 27: 1–28: 16) may have come from the author's travel-diary, revealing him as an eye-witness of many of the events he related; alternatively, the use of the first person may derive from one of his sources or from his desire to achieve vividness in his narrative.

The Book emphasizes the Divine origin of Christianity. The Apostles affirm that Jesus is the *Messiah, proclaimed as such by His Resurrection. Salvation is offered through Him, though it is less clearly associated with His death than it is by Paul. Belief in the Divine status of Christ is reflected, notably in the title 'Lord'. According to Acts the Church from the beginning had her own rites of *Baptism for the remission of sins (2: 38) and of the 'breaking of bread' (2: 42; the term used for the Eucharist). It seems to have been governed at first only by Apostles, to whom the 'Seven' were added later (6: 1–6), as well as *presbyters and *bishops, the latter two not yet distinguished. The picture of the Church given in Acts is probably substantially reliable, however partial.

Acts of the Martyrs. The most reliable accounts of early Christian martyrdoms are those (few) which follow the official reports of the trials. The so-called 'Passions' were written by Christian authors and based on eye-witness accounts; later versions often embellished with miraculous material. A third category belong to the realm of legend, with probably no historical kernel whatever.

Acts of Sts Paul and Thecla; Acts of St Peter; etc. See PAUL AND THECLA, ACTS OF STS; PETER, ACTS OF ST, etc.

Actual Sin. A sin which is the outcome of a free personal act of the human will. In Christian theology it is contrasted with *Original Sin. See also SIN.

Actus Purus (Lat., 'Pure Actuality'). The Scholastic term used (e.g. by St *Thomas Aquinas) to characterize the nature of God and distinguish Him from His creatures.

Adalbert of Bremen (*c.*1000–72), Abp. of Bremen-Hamburg from 1043. He was an energetic promoter of missionary activities, especially in the Nordic countries, and planned to become Patriarch of the North. In 1053 *Leo nominated him Papal Vicar and Legate. His last years were darkened by the invasion of pagan Wends who destroyed Hamburg in 1071–2.

Adam. According to the Biblical story, the first human being. In Genesis there are two accounts of his creation. In 1: 26–31, he was created on the sixth day, made in the image and likeness of God, commanded to multiply, and given dominion over the earth. Gen. 2: 5–7 assigns his creation to the time when the earth was still void. *Eve, we are told, was created from Adam's rib. When they had disobeyed God's command by eating the forbidden fruit (the *Fall), they were expelled from the Garden of Eden, and on Adam was imposed toilsome labour and on Eve the pains of childbirth. Traditional theology has utilized the Scriptural statements about Adam in its doctrine of man and his relation to God. See SECOND ADAM.

Adam of Marsh (d. c.1258), English theologian. Becoming a *Franciscan in 1232/3, from c.1247 he was regent of the Franciscan house of studies in *Oxford. Apart from his work as a scholar, he exercised great influence on English political and social life.

Adam of St-Victor (12th cent.), *sequence writer and composer. He was long thought to have been a Breton who entered the abbey of St-Victor in Paris (see VICTORINES) c.1130 and died between 1177 and 1192. He has recently been identified with the Adam who was Precentor of the cathedral of *Notre-Dame by 1107, entered the abbey of St-Victor after 1133 and died in 1146. It is not certain which of some 60 sequences surviving from 12th-cent. Paris are Adam's work, but he probably wrote a core of the early texts and some of the melodies.

Adam, Karl (1878–1966), German Catholic theologian. He combined a liberal and modern outlook with full Catholic orthodoxy, exercising wide influence over a lay public. His best-known work was *Das Wesen des Katholizismus* (1924; Eng. tr., 1929).

Adamantius. The name of the orthodox protagonist in the 4th-cent. dialogue *De recta in Deum fidei*, and commonly supposed

to be its author. It is a disputation first with two disciples of *Marcion and then with followers of *Bardesanes and *Valentinus.

Adamites. A small early Christian sect who aimed at returning to man's primitive innocence by the practice of nudity.

Adamnan, St. The older form of the name St Adomnán (q.v.).

Adamson, Patrick (1537–92), Abp. of St Andrews from 1576. He became involved in controversy with the *Presbyterian party. He won the support of *James VI (I), but his disfavour with the *General Assembly increased and his *Declaration of the King's Majesty's Intention and Meaning towards the late Acts of Parliament* (1585) provoked much hostility. His character and opinions were attacked at the Synod of Fife (1586), which excommunicated him.

Addai. The traditional founder of the Church at *Edessa. In Syriac tradition he was one of the 72 (or 70) disciples of Lk. 10: 1. According to the *Doctrine of *Addai* he was sent by St *Thomas the Apostle to heal King *Abgar. *Eusebius identifies him with *Thaddeus.

Addai, Doctrine of. A Syriac writing which describes how King *Abgar was brought into contact with Christ and *Addai was sent from *Edessa to convert him. In its present form it dates from the early 5th cent. and incorporates the more recent legend of the *Invention of the Cross by Protonice, described as the wife of the Emp. Claudius (d. AD 54).

Addai and Mari, Liturgy of. The Syriac Liturgy which is still the normal rite of the *Church of the East and the *Chaldeans. It probably originated in *Edessa and may go back to the 3rd cent. The most notable feature of the Anaphora in its original form is the address to Christ (not to God the Father). The Institution Narrative is absent in most MSS; it is disputed whether this was an original feature.

Adelard of Bath (12th cent.), English *Scholastic philosopher. In his main work, *De Eodem et Diverso*, he tried to reconcile the *Platonic and *Aristotelian doctrines of *universals, holding that the universal and the particular were identical, and distinct only in our mode of apprehending them.

Adeste Fideles. An anonymous Christmas hymn, probably written in the 17th or 18th cent., of French or German authorship. The common English translation is 'O come, all ye faithful'.

Adhémar de Monteil (d. 1098), Bp. of Le Puy from some time between 1080 and 1087. In 1095 *Urban II summoned the Council of *Clermont from Le Puy and made Adhémar his representative on the First *Crusade. Adhémar's death diminished any likelihood of Papal control of the Franks in the East.

Adherents. In the Church of *Scotland, baptized persons who, although non-communicants, are intimately connected with the congregation.

Adiaphorists. A party in German Protestantism which held that certain rules and actions were matters of indifference. The first controversy on the subject broke out in connection with the *Leipzig Interim (1548). One side declared certain Catholic practices such as *Confirmation and the veneration of *saints 'adiaphora', i.e. matters on which concessions might be made without prejudice to Protestant doctrine. The other side stressed the dangers to integral *Lutheranism of these concessions. The controversy was ended only by the Formula of *Concord (1577), which ruled that in times of persecution concessions should not be made, but otherwise ceremonies not commanded or forbidden by Scripture might be altered according to the decisions of individual Churches. Another controversy broke out in the late 17th cent. between the *Pietists, who declared all worldly pleasures such as theatres to be sinful, and the orthodox Lutherans, who held them to be indifferent and therefore permitted.

ad Limina Apostolorum (Lat., 'to the thresholds of the Apostles'). Pilgrimages 'ad Limina Apostolorum', *sc.* to the tombs of St *Peter and St *Paul, were popular in the Middle Ages. In modern times the term ordinarily denotes the visits which RC bishops are required to pay to Rome to venerate the tombs of the Apostles and to report to the Pope on the state of their dioceses.

Admission to Candidacy for Ordination of Deacons and Priests. In the RC Church, a rite introduced in 1972 when the orders of *acolyte and *lector ceased to be a stage on the way to the priesthood. Either during Mass or in the course of some other service involving 'the proclamation of God's word', the candidates are presented to the bishop, who examines them and prays for them.

Admission to Holy Communion Measure 1972. This allows the General Synod of the C of E to provide for the admission to Communion of those who have been baptized but not confirmed, including communicant members of other Churches.

Admonition to Parliament, An (1572). A *Puritan manifesto demanding a non-episcopal constitution for the English Church. It was issued anonymously, but responsibility for it was probably correctly attributed to two London clergymen, Thomas Wilcox and John *Field.

Ado, Martyrology of. The *martyrology compiled between 853 and 860 by St Ado (*c*.800–75), later Abp. of Vienne. Its plan and arrangement were the model for later martyrologies.

Adomnán, St (*c*.624–704), also 'Adamnan', and in Ireland, 'Eunan', Abbot of *Iona from 679. Unable to persuade the monks of Iona to accept the Roman dating of *Easter, in 692 he went to Ireland, where he promoted the Roman usage. He also proposed a law to protect non-combatants in war; it was accepted at the Synod of Birr (697) and periodically enforced as the 'Law of Adomnán'. His Life of St *Columba is of great historical value. He also wrote *De Locis Sanctis*, an account of a visit to the Holy Land by Arculf, a bishop from Gaul. Feast day, 23 Sept.

Adonai (Hebrew for 'Lord'). Divine name often used in the OT. Jews also read it for the unutterable name of *Yahweh, which in the Hebrew Bible is usually pointed with the vowel-signs proper to Adonai. In the Christian liturgy the term is applied to Christ in one of the *O-Antiphons.

Adoptianism. (1) The heresy, originating in Spain in the 8th cent., according to which Christ, in His humanity, is not the true, but only the adopted, Son of God. *Elipandus, Abp. of Toledo, arguing against *Migetius, drew a sharp distinction between the humanity of Christ ('of the seed of David') and His Divine Sonship, and maintained that the human Jesus was only the adopted Son of God. Elipandus was supported by the Spanish bishops, especially *Felix of Urgel, but after he died the heresy disappeared. It was revived in a modified form in the 12th cent. by *Abelard, *Gilbert de la Porrée, and others. (2) The term (usually spelt 'Adoptionism') has also been used of the heretical stream in early Greek theology which regarded Christ as a man gifted with Divine powers.

adoration. In strict terminology 'adoration' denotes an act of worship due to God alone. In early times the word was sometimes used loosely to include the veneration paid to persons and objects of a sacred character. After the *Iconoclastic Controversy a distinction came to be accepted between *'latria', the adoration of God, and *'dulia', the veneration of created things.

Adoro Te devote, or, more correctly, 'Adoro devote'. Eucharistic hymn attributed to St *Thomas Aquinas, though his authorship has been contested. The common English translation is 'Thee we adore, O hidden Saviour'.

Advent (Lat. *Adventus*, 'coming', i.e. of Christ). The ecclesiastical season immediately before *Christmas. In the W. it begins on the Sunday nearest St *Andrew's Day (30 Nov.); in the E. in the middle of Nov. Though fasting is no longer ordered in the W., Advent is observed as a penitential season, in preparation not only for Christmas but also for the *Second Coming of Christ.

Adventists. Various groups which hold in common that the *Second Coming of Christ is imminent. As a denomination they date from 1831 in the USA. The original body, the 'Evangelical Adventists', have died out; the chief denominations are now the 'Advent Christians' and the '*Seventh-day Adventists'.

Advertisements, book of. The abbreviated title of a book issued by Abp. M. *Parker in 1556. Among other things it ordered the use of the *surplice at the Eucharist and kneeling at the reception of Communion. It is disputed whether this book is to be understood as the 'other order' mentioned in the Act of *Uniformity of 1559. See VESTIARIAN CONTROVERSY.

advowson. The right of appointing a clergyman to a parish or other ecclesiastical benefice. Advowsons may be held by the diocesan bishop or some other person (known as the 'patron'). A patron, who may be an individual or a corporation, clerical or lay, presents the candidate to the bishop for *institution and *induction; the latter may for due cause reject the nominee. Advowson in the C of E is a property right which can pass by gift, inheritance, or (until 1923) by sale. Since the Patronage (Benefices) Measure 1986, however, only communicant members of the C of E or a Church in communion with it can exercise the right of patronage, and nominations require the consent of the bishop and representatives of the *Parochial Church Council.

Aegidius. The Latin form of *Giles (q.v.).

Aelfheah, St. See ALPHEGE, ST.

Aelfric (*c*.955–*c*.1020), the 'Grammarian'. Trained at *Winchester under *Ethelwold, in 1005 he became first Abbot of Eynsham. He wrote two sets of homilies in English which gained notoriety at the time of the Reformation, as he not only used language which excluded the doctrine of the *Immaculate Conception of the BVM but was supposed to have maintained a doctrine of the Eucharist incompatible with *transubstantiation. He composed the earliest Latin grammar in any vernacular language, besides a third series of sermons on 'Lives of the Saints' and other works. His greatest claim to fame was his provision of books of literary merit for the rural clergy in their own tongue.

Aelia Capitolina. The new city which the Emp. Hadrian built *c*.130 on the site of *Jerusalem (destroyed AD 70).

Aelred, St. See AILRED, ST.

Aeneas of Gaza (d. 518), Christian *Neoplatonist. In his *Theophrastus* he defended the immortality of the soul and the resurrection of the body, but rejected such tenets of *Platonism as conflicted with orthodox Christian doctrine.

Aeneas Silvius Piccolomini. See PIUS II.

aer. A veil used in the E. Church to cover the *chalice and *paten during the Liturgy.

Aerius (4th cent.), presbyter of Pontus. He was originally an associate of *Eustathius, Bp. of Sebaste, but later they quarrelled. He taught that the observance of *Easter was a Jewish superstition; that prescribed fasts were wrong; and that it is useless to pray and give alms for the dead. His followers (Aerians) died out soon after his death.

Aeterni Patris (1879). The encyclical of *Leo XIII commending to the Church the study of philosophy, and especially the work of St *Thomas Aquinas.

Aetius (d. *c*.366), *Arian sophist. He was a dialectician at *Alexandria and was made a bishop by the Arians. He and his followers (*Anomoeans) asserted that the Son, being begotten, was in essence unlike the Father, the Ingenerate. His *Syntagmation* is preserved by *Epiphanius and in a few fragments elsewhere.

affective prayer. A kind of prayer in which the emphasis is on making aspirations of love towards God, rather than on formulating petitions or engaging in discursive reflection.

affinity. In *moral theology, relationship created by marriage. It is held to form an impediment to subsequent marriage between one party and certain blood relations of the other. In the C of E the sphere of affinity is regulated by the 'Table of *Kindred and Affinity'.

affirmation. In English civil law, a solemn declaration in place of an *oath made by those who have conscientious objection to being sworn, either because of their religious conviction or because they have no religious belief.

affusion. The method of *Baptism now ordinarily practised in the W. Church whereby water is poured over the head of the candidate. It did not become general until the later Middle Ages, *immersion and *submersion being the usual methods in earlier times. See also ASPERSION.

Africa, Christianity in. Apart from Egypt and the Mediterranean coast (Roman 'Africa', on which see the next entry), Christianity had by the 4th cent. penetrated to *Nubia (where it died out in the 16th cent.) and *Ethiopia, but it did not spread further south until the era of Portuguese expansion in the late-15th cent. In the 16th and 17th cents. it penetrated into the *Congo kingdom and took root in the Portuguese colony of *Angola, but at the end of the 18th cent. Christianity was restricted to a few coastal areas.

A new era began with the settlements of *Black Christians from Nova Scotia in *Sierra Leone in 1787 and the missionary advance inland from Cape Town beginning with the arrival there of J. T. *van der Kemp in 1799. New missionary societies (the *LMS, the *CMS, the *Holy Ghost Fathers, the *White Fathers, etc.) began work in many parts of Africa, though, apart from the extreme south and the Horn, the interior was hardly touched before the last quarter of the 19th cent. The missions founded in 1875 on Lake *Malawi and in 1877 in *Uganda mark a new beginning. In the next 30 years, with the political 'Scramble for Africa', missions were established almost everywhere and Churches grew. In general missionary activity benefited from the conditions of colonial rule, but some missionaries voiced criticism of abuses and in the later colonial period relations were often strained (e.g. in *Zimbabwe, *Mozambique, and *South Africa). Since political independence they have varied.

From the 1890s African Christians in some countries began to reject missionary control and some aspects of missionary teaching and to form independent Churches. Some of these resulted from secession from a mission Church, remaining broadly similar to the body that had been left. Others were the result of the activity of a 'prophet' such as W. W. *Harris or S. *Kimbangu. Their number has increased greatly in the 20th cent. Their character varies, but most are concerned with *spiritual healing, including a traditional African interpretation of sickness in terms of spirit possession and *witchcraft.

The mainstream Churches mostly moved from White missionary to indigenous Black leadership about the time of the political independence of the countries concerned. Since then (*c*.1960) the growth of all the Churches has been prodigious.

Africa, the Church in Roman. It is not known how Christianity reached Roman

'Africa' (roughly Tripoli, Tunisia, Algeria, and Morocco), but by the end of the 2nd cent. the Church was organized and widespread. *Persecution under the Emp. *Decius (250) temporarily weakened the Church, leading to controversy over the readmission of lapsed members and to the *Novatianist schism. The 4th cent. saw the struggle with *Donatism, the rise of St *Augustine, the growth of *monasticism, African resistance to Papal claims, and a series of African Councils, whose canons were incorporated into both E. and W. *canon law. Such achievements were ended by the Vandal invaders (429), whose *Arian kings normally repressed Catholic Christianity. The reconquest (534) under *Justinian restored orthodoxy, but the Arab conquest at the end of the 7th cent. reduced the Church to a shadow.

African Independent Churches. See AFRICA, CHRISTIANITY IN, paragraph 3.

African Missions, Society of. A RC society of priests and lay brothers dedicated to the evangelization of Africa and people of African origin. Founded at Lyons by Melchior de Marion Brésillac in 1856, its first missions were in *Sierra Leone and *Nigeria. In the USA its members work among Black and Hispanic Americans.

Africanus, Sextus Julius. See JULIUS AFRICANUS, SEXTUS.

Agabus, St, a prophet mentioned in Acts (11: 28 and 21: 10). In the E. Church he is held to be one of the seventy mentioned in Lk. 10: 1. Feast day, in the E., 8 Apr.; in the W., 13 Feb.

agape (1). The Greek word for love. In the *Septuagint it is used to cover love in all its senses. In the NT it acquired a special connotation; in Christian usage agape (ἀγάπη) denotes spiritual and unselfish love, contrasted with eros (ἔρως), carnal love. It was translated into Latin by *caritas*; hence the original meaning of 'charity' in English.

(2) The term is also applied to the common religious meal which seems to have been in use in the early Church in close relation to the Eucharist. Since 1986 the C of E has allowed an Agape within the Eucharist on *Maundy Thursday.

(3) In the 18th cent. the Agape was introduced among various *Pietist communities, including the *Moravians, and 'Love Feasts'

became an established feature of *Methodism until the mid-19th cent. In the 20th cent. it has been used as a means of reconciling Christians of different traditions in a liturgical rite distinct from the Eucharist.

Agapemone, Church of the, English sect. It was founded by H. J. Prince (1811–99), who, as a curate in Somerset, with his rector started a revivalist movement. Both left the C of E and in 1849 opened the 'Agapemone' or 'Abode of Love' in the village of Spaxton. His followers believed Prince to be a Divine being and their licentiousness led to grave scandal. The sect disappeared early in the 20th cent.

Agapetus, St (d. 536), Pope from 535. A defender of orthodoxy, he deposed Anthimus, the *Monophysite Patr. of Constantinople, and consecrated *Mennas as his successor. Feast day, in the E., 17 Apr.; in the W., 20 Sept.

Agatha, St. A virgin martyred at Catania in Sicily. Her name occurs in the *Canon of the Mass and two early churches at Rome were dedicated to her. The *acts of her martyrdom are legendary. Feast day, 5 Feb.

Agathangelos. The reputed author of a 'History of the Armenians'. This gives an account of the conversion of *Armenia and the life of St *Gregory the Illuminator (q.v.), whom the author claims as a contemporary. 'Agathangelos' may be only a pseudonym of an Armenian Christian proclaiming to his countrymen the 'good tidings' of their conversion.

Agatho (c. 577–681), Pope from 678. In 680 he held a council at Rome against the *Monothelites. He also took up the cause of *Wilfrid of York against *Theodore, Abp. of Canterbury. Feast day, 10 Jan.

Agde, Council of (506). A council held at Agde in S. France under the presidency of *Caesarius of Arles; 47 genuine canons are preserved.

age, canonical. The age, fixed by *canon law, at which a person becomes capable of undertaking special duties, etc. The term is used especially in connection with *ordination.

age of reason. The age at which a child may be supposed to be capable of discerning right from wrong and therefore of being responsible for his conduct. In RC moral theology this is held to be reached at about 7 years.

Agenda (Lat., 'things to be performed'). The term has been used for matters of religious practice as opposed to those of belief; for the central part of the Eucharist; and for prescribed forms of service.

aggiornamento (Ital., 'renewal'). A word connected with the pontificate of *John XXIII, denoting a fresh presentation of the faith, as well as a recognition of the natural rights of man and support for freedom of worship and the welfare state.

Agios o Theos (Gk., 'Holy God'). A Greek anthem which has survived untranslated in the RC *Good Friday liturgy.

Agnellus of Pisa, Bl (c.1194–1236), founder of the English *Franciscan Province. According to tradition, he was received into the Order by St *Francis. Sent to England in 1224, he established friaries at *Canterbury, London, and *Oxford and engaged R. *Grosseteste to teach in the Oxford friary, which soon became a centre of learning. Feast day, 10 Sept. (formerly, 13 Mar.).

Agnellus, Andreas (c.800–c.845), historian of *Ravenna. His *Liber Pontificalis Ecclesiae Ravennatis* traces the history of the see from St *Apollinaris to his own age. It embodies valuable information about contemporary buildings and customs.

Agnes, St. The legends of her martyrdom vary and nothing certain is known about the date or manner of her death. A *basilica was built at Rome on the site of her remains c.350, and her name occurs in the Roman *Canon of the Mass. In art she is represented by a lamb, doubtless because of the similarity between 'agnus' (Lat., 'lamb') and 'Agnes', and the *pallium, made from the wool of two lambs, is blessed on her feast (21 Jan.).

Agnoetae. A *Monophysite sect whose members attributed ignorance to the human soul of Christ. Founded by Themistius, a 6th-cent. deacon of *Alexandria, they are also known as 'Themistians'. Most Monophysites rejected their teaching.

agnosticism. As commonly understood, the view that we cannot know whether there is a God or not.

Agnus Dei (Lat., 'Lamb of God'). (1) The formula beginning with the words 'O Lamb of God' recited in the liturgy of the W. Church shortly before the Communion. (2) A wax medallion bearing the figure of a lamb, blessed by the Pope in the first year of his pontificate and every 7th year afterwards.

Agobard (c.769–840), Abp. of Lyons from 816. He was a versatile scholar. He attacked the excessive veneration of *images, trial by *ordeal, and belief in *witchcraft. He also wrote against the Adoptionist views of *Felix of Urgel; he may have written against the liturgical speculations of *Amalarius of Metz, but his authorship of the work in question has been challenged.

Agonizants. A religious order devoted to the needs of the sick and dying. It was founded by St *Camillus de Lellis in 1586.

Agrapha ('unwritten [sayings]'). A name given to the sayings of Christ not recorded in the four canonical Gospels. One occurs in Acts (20: 35), others in the *apocryphal Gospels, especially the Gospel of *Thomas, and in the writings of the Fathers.

Agricola, Johann (c.1494–1566), German Protestant. He was a pupil and follower of M. *Luther, but his *antinomian views brought him into conflict first with P. *Melanchthon and then with Luther. In 1540 he moved to Berlin, where he published a recantation which ended the conflict, at least officially. Johann II, Elector of Brandenburg, appointed him *General-Superintendent; he was associated with the preparation of the *Augsburg Interim of 1548 and supported the traditional Lutherans against the *Adiaphorists.

Agrippa von Nettesheim, Heinrich Cornelius (1486–1535), scholar and adventurer. His career included appointments as physician to Louis of Savoy (1524), historiographer to *Charles V (1529), and a place in the entourage of *Hermann of Wied (1532–5). His fierce criticism of ecclesiastical abuses was qualified by protestations of loyalty to the Catholic Church. His *De Oculta Philosophia* (written c.1510; publd., 1531) seeks to recover what he believed to have been an ancient tradition of secret magical wisdom which encompassed all branches of knowledge and was in harmony with, and ultimately derived from,

Divine revelation. His *De Incertitudine* (1530) was a work of profound scepticism; it attacked *Scholasticism, denied the power of reason to attain truth, and made revelation the only source of truth.

Aidan, St (d. 651), Irish monk of *Iona and Bp. of *Lindisfarne. He was sent from Iona at the request of *Oswald, King of Northumbria, and consecrated bishop in 635. He established his headquarters at Lindisfarne and made long journeys to the mainland; the practices he taught were those of the *Celtic Churches. Feast day, 31 Aug.

Ailred, St (1109–67), also 'Aelred', Abbot of *Rievaulx. The son of a Saxon priest, he entered the *Cistercian house at Rievaulx *c.*1133, became Abbot of Revesby in 1143 and Abbot of Rievaulx in 1147. His extensive spiritual writings show similarity of interest and attitude with those of St *Bernard and *William of St-Thierry; his devotion is marked by a strong attachment to the suffering humanity of Christ. His works include the *Speculum Caritatis, De Spirituali Amicitia*, and a Life of *Edward the Confessor. Two collections of sermons have in recent times been attributed to him. Feast day, 12 Jan.; also 3 Mar.

aisle. The extension of the *nave of a church made by piercing its side walls with a series of arches and building an extension with a separate and lower roof. The word is often, but quite wrongly, used of a gangway up the centre of the nave or elsewhere.

Aksum. See AXUM.

Alacoque, St Margaret Mary. See MARGARET MARY ALACOQUE, ST.

Alan (or **Alain**) **of Lille** (d. 1203), poet, theologian, and preacher. He probably studied and taught at Paris *c.*1150-*c.*1185. Later he moved to the South of France and towards the end of his life entered the abbey of *Cîteaux. His early theological writings include the incomplete *Summa Quoniam homines*, the *Regulae caelestis iuris*, in which he tries to state theological truths in a series of rules or axioms, and the allegorical poem *Anticlaudianus* (1182–3). He later compiled a dictionary of Biblical terms with literal, moral, and allegorical interpretations, an *Ars praedicandi*, to which was attached a set of 27 model sermons, and a *Liber poeni-*

tentialis, the earliest medieval manual for confessors.

Alane, Alexander. See ALESIUS, A.

Alaric (*c.*370?–410), Visigothic leader. Of noble family, until 395 he combined a prominent position in the Gothic world with high office in the Imperial army; after the death of *Theodosius I, he sought a more important and regular place in the Empire and, on being frustrated, turned to violence. He besieged Rome in 408 and 409 before entering and sacking it in 410. This event prompted St *Augustine's *City of God*.

à Lasco, John. See LASKI, JOHN.

alb. A white linen garment, reaching from the neck to the ankles, with tight-fitting sleeves and held in at the waist by a girdle, worn by the ministers at Mass.

Alban, St. The first British martyr. A pagan of Verulamium (now *St Albans), he was converted and baptized by a fugitive priest whom he sheltered. When the Emperor sent soldiers to search the house, Alban disguised himself in the priest's cloak, was arrested, and condemned to death. His martyrdom almost certainly took place under Septimius Severus (*c.*209), not under *Diocletian. Feast day, 22 June (dropped from the RC calendar in 1969; now observed locally on 20 June); 17 June in the BCP.

Albania, Christianity in. Christianity probably reached Albania early, but with the fall of the W. Empire in the 5th and 6th cents. its influence was largely destroyed. In the Dark Ages the Albanians were partly conquered by Slavs. In the 9th cent. some were incorporated into the *Bulgarian kingdom, adhering to E.*Orthodoxy, and in the 11th cent. they came under *Serbian sway. At the time of the schism between the E. and W. Churches, some transferred their allegiance from Constantinople to Rome. After the Turks finally subjugated Albania in 1521, there was much apostasy. In 1913 Albania became independent and the Orthodox Church became *autocephalous in 1922. Under Communist rule after 1945 all places of worship were closed, but the outward practice of religion was allowed again in 1991.

Albert of Brandenburg (1490–1545), Cardinal Abp. and Elector of Mainz. In 1517 he was charged with the publication in Saxony and Brandenburg of the *indulgence for *St Peter's, Rome; he secured the services of J. *Tetzel to preach it. He was a man of liberal views and a friend of the humanists. Having temporized during the *Peasants' War (1525), he threw in his lot with the German Catholic princes. He was a resolute defender of the Papacy, though he discouraged extreme measures against the Protestants.

Albert of Prussia (1490–1568). The last Grand Master of the *Teutonic Order and first Hohenzollern Duke of Prussia. He was converted to Protestantism and in 1525 succeeded in making Prussia a hereditary duchy. A strict form of *Lutheranism was established in his dominions.

Albert the Great (d. 1280, over 80 years old), *Dominican theologian, philosopher, and scientist. He studied theology at *Cologne, taught at various Dominican houses, and from 1245 to 1248 held one of the Dominican chairs in the university of *Paris. In 1248 he was sent back to Cologne to take charge of the new international Dominican house of studies. Here he lectured on the works of *Dionysius the Pseudo-Areopagite and on the new, complete translation of *Aristotle's *Ethics*. In 1256 he visited the Papal Court and there conducted a disputation against the doctrine of the non-intellectual nature of the intellect attributed to *Averroes. In 1260 he became Bp. of Ratisbon, but was allowed to resign in 1262. He was teaching at Cologne in 1277 when he intervened to prevent the condemnation in Paris of *Thomas Aquinas, his former pupil.

Albert taught at a time when many theologians were reacting against the new Aristotelianism mediated by Arab and Jewish commentators, and particularly against some of the philosophical tenets of Aristotle himself. Albert's commentaries cover almost the whole Aristotelian corpus and some pseudepigrapha such as the *Liber de Causis*. He aimed at making the physics, metaphysics, and mathematics of Aristotle intelligible to the Latins. He exercised a profound influence on Thomas Aquinas and remained influential among philosophers. His popular fame rested largely on works falsely ascribed to him. Feast day, 15 Nov.

Albigenses. A medieval term for the inhabitants of parts of S. France applied to the heretics who were strong there in the late-12th and early-13th cents. They were a branch of the *Cathars. They were condemned by successive councils from 1165 onwards, and *Innocent III authorized a *Crusade against them. The N. French forces were opposed not only by those who sympathized with heresy but a large part of S. French society. In 1233 the *Inquisition began effective action against the heretics and by 1300 few survived. For their beliefs, see CATHARS.

Albright Brethren. See EVANGELICAL CHURCH.

Alcuin (c.740–804), a major figure in the *Carolingian Renaissance. Educated at the cathedral school at *York, after meeting *Charlemagne in 781, he joined his court. From 796 he was Abbot of St Martin's, Tours. He had a talent for teaching and both at court and at Tours he played an important part in developing the resources of contemporary ecclesiastical culture. He produced a major work on the doctrine of the *Trinity, three treatises against the *Adoptianism of *Felix of Urgel, Lives of various saints, poems, and educational manuals. He also revised the Roman *lectionary and adapted the *Gregorian Sacramentary for use in Gaul. Feast day in the American BCP (1979), 20 Mar.

Aldhelm, St (d. 709), Abbot of Malmesbury and then from 705 first Bp. of *Sherborne. He took a prominent part in the reforming movement initiated by Abp. *Theodore and *Hadrian the African; he founded some monasteries and several churches. Much of his Latin writing survives. Feast day, 25 May.

Aleander, Girolamo (1480–1542), humanist scholar. *Leo X appointed him one of two Papal envoys commissioned to present M. *Luther with the bull ''Exsurge Domine' and to negotiate with the Emperor for support against him. At the Diet of *Worms (1521) he denounced Luther and demanded his condemnation without trial. In 1524 he was made Abp. of Brindisi and in 1538 a cardinal.

Alembert, Jean Le Rond D'. See D'ALEMBERT, JEAN LE ROND.

aleph (א). The first letter of the Hebrew alphabet. Textual critics use it to denote the *Codex Sinaiticus.

Alesius, Alexander (1500–65), also 'Aless' or 'Alane', Scottish *Lutheran divine. As a canon of St Andrews, he was selected to confute Patrick *Hamilton, but was won over by his arguments and steadfastness at the stake (1528). Soon afterwards he preached a sermon attacking the morals of the clergy. He was imprisoned but escaped to Germany, where he signed the *Augsburg Confession. For a short time he was lecturer in divinity at Cambridge; in 1540 he became professor of theology at Frankfurt-on-Oder. He wrote many exegetical and controversial works.

Alexander, St (d. 328), Bp. of *Alexandria from 312. He was concerned in putting down the *Melitian and *Arian schisms. He excommunicated *Arius, one of his presbyters, c.321, and took a leading part in the Council of *Nicaea. Feast day, in the W., 26 Feb.; in the Greek Church, 29 May; in the *Coptic Church, 22 Apr.

Alexander II (d. 1073), Pope from 1061. He had been Bp. of Lucca. Elected Pope with the support of Hildebrand (later *Gregory VII), he was enthroned without the support of the Emp. *Henry IV, who had an antipope (Honorius II) elected. Generally recognized as Pope from 1064, Alexander tried to realize the ideals of the reforming party. He renewed the decrees against *simony and enforcing clerical *celibacy, laid down regulations for the freedom of episcopal elections, and legislated on *matrimony, and took strong action to enforce these measures. His blessing was given to *William I's invasion of England.

Alexander III (d. 1181), Pope from 1159. During the 17-year schism occasioned by the establishment of an antipope (Victor IV) supported by the Emp. *Frederick I, Alexander lived mainly in France. Here he came into contact with Henry II of England over the *Becket affair. Though embarrassed by the archbishop, he was firm in imposing penance for his murder. In 1179 he assembled the Third *Lateran Council (q.v.). He encouraged the scholastic revival of the 12th cent., but it is unlikely that he wrote the 'Decretum' of *Gratian or the 'Sententiae Rolandi' long ascribed to him.

Alexander V (c.1339–1410), Pope from 1409. Peter of Candia (Crete) became a *Franciscan and lectured at Paris; from 1386 he held a succession of bishoprics. At the Council of *Pisa he was unanimously elected to fill the Papal chair presumed vacant; he died 10 months later.

Alexander VI (1431–1503), Pope from 1492. Rodrigo Borgia's election was secured largely through bribery. The most notable acts of his pontificate were the series dividing the New World between *Spain and *Portugal (1493–4), his prosecution and execution of G. *Savonarola (1498), the crusade against the Moors (1499–1500), and the *Jubilee of 1500.

Alexander VII (1599–1667), Pope from 1655. As a theologian he held strongly anti-*Jansenist views, and to make Jansenist subterfuge impossible, in 1656 he condemned the five propositions from the *Augustinus in the sense in which C. O. *Jansen had meant them. In this he was supported by Louis XIV of France, but later, when Louis threatened to invade the *States of the Church, Alexander had to sign the humiliating peace of Pisa (1664). In 1665 and 1666 he condemned several *Probabilist propositions, though not the system as a whole.

Alexander VIII (1610–91), Pope from 1689. He effected a reconciliation with Louis XIV of France, who in 1690 returned *Avignon and Venaissin. In 1690 he condemned the Four *Gallican Articles of 1682 and 31 propositions of C. O. *Jansen.

Alexander of Hales (c.1186–1245), theologian. He studied arts and theology at *Paris, becoming a doctor c.1220/1. He took the fateful step of using the Sentences of *Peter Lombard, instead of the Bible, as the basic text for his lectures on theology. In 1236 he joined the *Franciscan Order, but retained his chair. He is regarded as the founder of the Franciscan school of theology, but the Summa theologica which goes under his name is only partly his. He had some part in the composition of an Expositio in Regulam S. Francisci (1242), popularly known as 'The Four Masters'.

Alexander of Lycopolis (3rd cent.), writer against *Manichaeism. He praises the simplicity and efficacy of Christian philosophy and contrasts it with the illogical and contradictory doctrines of Manichaeism.

Alexander, Michael Solomon (1799–1845), first Anglican bishop in *Jerusalem (from 1841). See also JERUSALEM, ANGLICAN BISHOPRIC IN.

Alexandre, Noel (1639–1724), *Dominican Church historian. His *Selecta Historiae Ecclesiasticae Capita* (26 vols., 1676–86) is a work of great erudition; because of the *Gallican sympathies seen in some volumes, it was placed on the *Index.

Alexandria. An important city in the Roman Empire, Alexandria in Egypt was a centre of both Hellenism and Judaism. The foundation of the Church is traditionally ascribed to St *Mark. It won fame as a centre of Christian thought through the work of *Clement and *Origen. Its ecclesiastical importance increased in the 4th and 5th cents., especially under its bishops *Athanasius and *Cyril. It was later diminished by the rise of *Constantinople, further reduced by the adherence of most Egyptian Christians to the *Monophysites, and virtually destroyed by the Persian and Arab invasions of the 7th cent. At the division of the E. and W. Churches, Alexandria remained on the side of the Constantinople. See also COPTIC CHURCH.

Alexandrian text. An early form of the Greek text of the NT, now frequently equated with the *Neutral text.

Alexandrian theology. A modern designation for a style of theology associated with the Church of *Alexandria. It is particularly used (in contrast to *Antiochene theology) of forms of belief which emphasized the Divine nature of Christ and the unity of His person. In their exegesis of Scripture the Alexandrians were drawn to mystical and *allegorical exposition, in contrast with the literal and historical method of Antioch. See also CATECHETICAL SCHOOL OF ALEXANDRIA.

Alfred the Great (849–99), King of Wessex from 871. Apart from his defeat of the Danes, which contributed to the maintenance of Christianity in England, he is memorable for his promotion of ecclesiastical reform and the revival of learning. With a band of scholars he translated into English a number of popular Latin works,

including the 'Pastoral Rule' [commonly called 'Pastoral Care'] of *Gregory the Great and the 'Consolation of Philosophy' by *Boethius; at his instigation Werferth, Bp. of *Worcester, translated Gregory's 'Dialogues'. He was regarded as the pattern of a Christian king. Feast day, 26 Oct.

aliturgical days. Days on which the Eucharist may not be celebrated. In the RC Church *Good Friday and *Holy Saturday are the only such days; there are many more in the E. Church.

All Saints' Day. The feast, now kept in the W. on 1 Nov., to celebrate all Christian saints, known or unknown. It was apparently originally kept on the first Sunday after *Pentecost, as it still is in the E. Its observance on 1 Nov. dates from the time of Gregory III (d. 741), who on that day dedicated a chapel to 'All the Saints'.

All Souls' Day. The commemoration of the souls of the faithful departed on 2 Nov., the day after *All Saints' Day. Its observance became universal through the influence of *Odilo of Cluny (d. 1049). In the C of E it was dropped at the Reformation, but provision is made for it in many modern Anglican liturgies.

Allah. An Arabic word used as the name of God by all Muslims and in some circumstances by Arabic-speaking Christians.

Allamano, Bl Giuseppe (1851–1926), founder of the *Consolata Missionaries. In 1880 he was appointed guardian of a Marian shrine in Turin. On recovering from a severe illness in 1891, he vowed to found a missionary society for priests and laymen. He did this in 1901 and founded a missionary congregation for women in 1910, directing both until his death. Feast day, 16 Feb.

Allatius, Leo (1587/8–1669), Greek RC theologian. He was custodian of the *Vatican library from 1661. In various books he tried to show the unity in essential doctrine of the Orthodox and RC Churches.

Allegiance, Oath of. The oath of fidelity and true allegiance to the Sovereign taken by holders of clerical office in the C of E.

allegory. In Christian exegesis, one of the traditional ways of interpreting Scripture in distinction to the literal or historical sense. The Greek word comes from ancient literary theory and is defined as 'speaking one thing and signifying something other than what is said'. From the first Christians applied allegory to the OT to make it yield a Christian meaning. St *Paul used the term (Gal. 4: 24) to point to the relationship between the old Israel and the Church. *Origen, who is regarded as the great exponent of allegory, distinguished a threefold literal, moral, and spiritual sense, but in practice usually worked with a two-fold distinction between letter and spirit, history and deeper allegorical meaning, as did most of the Fathers. Concern to safe-guard the literal, historic meaning of the biblical text led to criticism of allegory in the patristic period by *Antiochene theologians and later by the Reformers. In modern times there has been renewed appreciation of patristic allegory, often called 'typology'. See also EXEGESIS.

Alleluia (Heb., 'Praise ye Yah'), a liturgical expression of praise. It occurs in the Bible (e.g. in Pss. 111–17) and it was early taken into the liturgy of the Church. In the W. it is omitted from the Mass and Office during Lent, and as an expression of joy it is used especially frequently in *Paschaltide. In the E. Alleluias occur with special frequency during the Lenten services.

Alleluyatic Sequence. A name given to the hymn 'Cantemus cuncti melodium' ('The strain upraise of joy and praise') because of its frequent repetition of 'Alleluia'. It dates from the early 10th cent.

Allen, Roland (1863–1947), missionary theorist. He joined the North China Mission of the *SPG in 1895, but left Beijing in 1903 when his health broke down. He wrote widely, contrasting the local and indigen-ous character of the NT Churches, expand-ing 'by the unexhorted and unorganized activity of individual members ... explain-ing to others the Gospel they had found for themselves', with modern missions which, he felt, imposed foreign direction, kept financial control, and established an alien-ated professional ministry.

Allen, William (1532–94), Cardinal from 1587. Forced to flee from England in 1565, he concentrated on training RC mission priests for the conversion of England; he founded colleges at *Douai (1568) and Rome (1575–8) and encouraged the foundation at Valladolid (1589). The *Douai version of the Bible was produced under his inspiration.

Allestree, Richard (1619–81), probably the author of 'The *Whole Duty of Man'. Under the Commonwealth he helped to continue C of E services in a private house; from 1663 to 1679 he was Regius Professor of Divinity at Oxford.

almoner. An officer, often in holy orders, who has the duty of distributing alms.

almuce (or **amice).** An item of ecclesi-astical dress, usually a cape lined with fur, worn in some religious orders.

Alogi. A group of heretics in Asia Minor (*c*.AD 170). They seem to have opposed *Montanism and to have ascribed Jn. and Rev. to *Cerinthus.

Aloysius Gonzaga, St (1568–91), patron of RC youth. After a few years at court he entered the *Jesuit novitiate in 1585. He died when 23, a victim of his labours among the plague-stricken at Rome. Feast day, 21 June.

alpha and omega (A and Ω). The first and last letters of the Greek alphabet, used to denote God's eternity and infinitude.

Alpha courses are structured introduc-tions to the Christian faith conducted under the aegis of Holy Trinity Brompton, a leading *evangelical Anglican church in London. Started in 1977, they are designed primarily for non-Churchgoers.

Alphege, St (954–1012), also **Aelfheah**, Abp. of *Canterbury from 1006. He was mur-dered by the Danes because he would not ransom himself at the expense of his poor tenants, and was therefore regarded as a martyr. Feast day, 19 Apr.

Alphonsus Liguori, St (1696–1787), founder of the *Redemptorists and moral theo-logian. Alfonso Maria dei Liguori practised at the bar before he was ordained in 1726. He became a close friend of Tommaso Fal-coia, who had taken part in the foundation of a house of nuns at Scala, near Amalfi. When Falcoia became Bp. of Castellam-mare in 1730, Alphonsus moved to Scala and in 1731 reorganized the nuns (the first 'Redemptoristines'). In 1732 he founded the 'Congregation of the Most Holy Redeemer' or 'Redemptorists' for men in a house nearby. Falcoia was technically their director until his death (1743), when Alphonsus was formally elected Superior-General. In 1762 he reluctantly accepted the see of Sant' Agata dei Goti, which he resigned in 1775.

Alphonsus sought to commend the Gospel to a sceptical age by gentle and direct methods, believing that the rigorism of the contemporary confessional repelled rather than won back sinners. He set out his ideals in his celebrated *Theologia Moralis* (1753–5). In the debate on how far it is allowable to follow any 'probable' opinion in matters of conduct, he developed a system known as '*Equiprobabilism' (q.v.). His devotional writings were popular, though their exuberance made them a target of criticism. Feast day, 1 (formerly 2) Aug.

altar. The word was used of the Eucharistic table from early times. It was disliked by the Reformers, who associated it with the doctrine of the *sacrifice of the Mass.

The earliest altars were doubtless of wood, being tables in private houses, and it was perhaps the custom of celebrating the Eucharist on the tombs of the martyrs which led to the introduction of stone altars. After the persecutions bodies of martyrs were placed under altars, and until 1977 the RC Church required the enclosure of relics in all altars. It was long customary to have only one altar in a church, but in the W. the custom of saying private Masses caused others to be added, the original one then being known as the 'high altar'. Altars were long placed against the east wall of the church, but the earlier free-standing position has now been largely restored. See also WESTWARD POSITION.

altar lights. The custom of placing on the altar two candles flanking an altar cross is attested c.1175. The number of candles used has varied, and in the RC Church they may now be placed either on the altar or on the floor around it. In the C of E the legality of altar lights was contested in the 19th cent., but allowed in 1890.

altar rails. Rails to protect the altar from profanation were widely introduced in English churches in the early years of *Elizabeth I, when the *rood screens and their protecting doors were removed. Disliked by the *Puritans, they came back at the Restoration in 1660.

Alternative Services. The Prayer Book (Alternative and Other) Services Measure 1965 provided that for a limited period the services of the C of E might follow forms sanctioned by the *Church Assembly (later by the General *Synod) as well as the BCP. The Church of England (*Worship and Doctrine) Measure 1974 allows the use of such services on a permanent basis. After 3 series of separate services had been used experimentally, the complete Alternative Service Book 1980 was authorized. In modern English, it includes 2 forms of Eucharistic rite, (optional) short forms of Morning and Evening Prayer, and a *Calendar with many new names. A revision, entitled *Common Worship, published in 2000, has now superseded it.

Alumbrados (also *Illuminati*, i.e. 'enlightened'). Loosely knit groups of spiritual persons who lived a retired life of prayer and contemplation in 16th-cent. Spain. It is unclear whether several of them were unorthodox, but some alumbrados were certainly spiritually unbalanced and were treated severely by the *Inquisition; others have been canonized.

Amalarius of Metz (c.780–850/1), liturgical scholar. A prominent figure in the *Carolingian Renaissance, in 835 he was appointed to administer the see of Lyons after the temporary deposition of Abp. *Agobard. His *De ecclesiasticis officiis*, which was partly an attempt to further the fusion of Roman and *Gallican liturgical practices, exercised great influence in the Middle Ages. Its explanations of ritual are sometimes fanciful, and at the Synod of *Quiercy in 838 parts of it were pronounced heretical and he was removed from Lyons.

Amalric (d. c.1207), scholastic philosopher. He taught at *Paris. He maintained that God was the one essence underlying all created beings and that those who remain in the love of God cannot sin. His theses were condemned in 1210.

Amana Society. A small Christian sect, also known as the Community of True Inspiration. It originated in Germany in 1714. A large part of the body sailed to America in 1842 and in 1855 settled at Amana, Iowa. Their settlements were organized on a communal basis until the Amana Society was converted into a modified joint stock company in 1932. The Amana Church Society, which then became a separate legal entity, in 1998 had c.450 adult members.

Amandus, St (d. c.675), Apostle of Flanders. In 628, having been consecrated bishop without a fixed see, he began active missionary work in Flanders and Carinthia. He founded two monasteries, one at Ghent and one at Elnon, which was afterwards known as St-Amand. Feast day, 6 Feb.

ambo. A raised platform in a Christian *basilica, from which the Scriptures could be read and other public parts of the liturgy conducted. After the 14th cent. ambos were superseded by *lecterns and *pulpits, but in some places they have been reintroduced in modern times.

Ambrose, St (c.339-97), Bp. of Milan and one of the four traditional *Doctors of the Church. He was governor of Aemilia-Liguria, when in 373 or 374, on the death of the *Arian bishop, *Auxentius, the Milanese laity demanded that Ambrose should succeed him, though he had not yet been baptized. As bishop he was famous as a preacher and was a zealous upholder of orthodoxy against Arianism. He was partly responsible for the conversion of *Augustine (386). He exercised a remarkable degree of authority in his dealings with successive Emperors, excommunicating *Theodosius for a massacre in 390, and he maintained the independence of the Church from the civil power. Apart from the *De Sacramentis (q.v.), his most notable work was a treatise on Christian ethics. He also wrote Latin *hymns (q.v.), and it was through his influence that hymns became an integral part of the liturgy of the W. Church. Feast day, 7 Dec.; in the BCP calendar, 4 Apr.

Ambrose, Isaac (1604-64), English *Puritan. Ordained priest before 1627, he held various cures. In 1641 he adopted *Presbyterianism. He served on the committee for the ejection of 'scandalous, ignorant and insufficient ministers' in Lancashire and was himself ejected in 1662. After an illness he determined to write a devotional description of what the Lord had done for his soul: Looking unto Jesus (1658).

Ambrosian rite. The rite used in the old archiepiscopal province of Milan, and one of the few non-Roman rites which survive in the RC Church. It takes its name from St *Ambrose, Bp. of Milan, but there is no evidence of any connection with him. It differs from the Roman rite in a number of minor points, e.g. the *Offertory comes before and not after the Creed. The Missal was revised in 1976 and the Breviary in 1983.

The Ambrosian chant is characterized by its tendency to greater melodic elaboration and modal freedom when compared with the *Gregorian.

Ambrosiaster. The name given since 1690 to the author of a set of Latin commentaries on the 13 Epp. of St *Paul, ascribed in all the manuscripts but one, and by most medieval authors, to St *Ambrose. This ascription is now universally denied.

ambulatory. The 'walking-space' created when an apsidal sanctuary in certain churches of the Norman period is surrounded by continuous *aisles.

AMDG. The initial letters of 'Ad Maiorem Dei Gloriam', 'to the greater glory of God'.

Amen. A Hebrew word meaning 'verily', used to express assent at the end of religious formulas, especially prayers.

Americanism. A movement propagated especially among American RCs at the end of the 19th cent., which aimed at adapting the external life of the Church to supposed modern cultural ideals. Its adherents stressed the 'active' virtues (humanitarianism, etc.) and urged that the Church should relax the rigour of her requirements on converts and minimize the points of difference between RCs and other Christians. It was condemned in 1899.

Ames, William (1576-1633), English *Calvinist theologian. At Cambridge he became an extreme *Puritan. He took a prominent part in the *Remonstrant controversies in the Netherlands and in 1622 he became professor of theology at Franeker. His chief work, De Conscientia (1632), is one of the first Protestant treatises on *casuistry and was long held in high repute for its incisive decisions.

amice. A square or oblong linen cloth, with strings attached, which in the W. Church may be worn round the neck by the celebrant of the Eucharist and by other ministers who wear the *alb. See also ALMUCE.

Amish (or **Amish Mennonites**), a small conservative group in the USA and Canada which originated in a division among the *Swiss Brethren under the leadership of Jakob Ammann (c.1656—before 1720). They were distinguished by their more frequent celebration of the Lord's Supper, during which they washed each other's feet, by their shunning of those who had been excommunicated, and by their 'plain dress'. Most of them migrated to N. America in the 18th and 19th cents. Here the majority belong to the Old Order Amish Mennonite Church. In doctrine and Church order they differ little from the *Mennonites, but they use 'Pennsylvania Dutch' (German) in their services.

Ammon, St (d. c.350) (also **Amum**), Egyptian hermit. He is mentioned by St *Athanasius in his life of St *Antony. Feast day, 4 Oct.

Ammonas, St (d. before 396), Egyptian hermit. He became a disciple of St *Antony and succeeded him as leader of the monastery of Pispir after his death. Some of his sayings are preserved in the *Apothegmata Patrum, and a collection of 14 letters is ascribed to him. Feast day, 16 Jan.

Ammonian Sections. See EUSEBIAN CANONS AND SECTIONS.

Ammonius Saccas (c.175–242), an Alexandrian, reputed to be the founder of *Neoplatonism. He was highly regarded as a teacher and appears to have influenced *Plotinus.

Amos, Book of. Amos was the earliest of the canonical prophets of the OT; he is said to have prophesied between 760 and 750 BC. He claimed that his prophetic inspiration derived from a direct call from God while he was a shepherd. The main theme of his message was that increasing affluence among the leaders of Israelite society had produced an unjust social order in which the poor were exploited, and that in consequence God would put an end to Israel's special status by causing the nation's downfall. The 'day of the Lord' would be a day of darkness and despair.

Amphilochius, St (c.340–95), Bp. of Iconium from 373. A cousin of *Gregory Nazianzus,

he was president of the Council of Side (390) which excommunicated the *Messalians. His *Iambics for Seleucus* contains a list of books of the Bible, important for the history of the *canon. Feast day, 23 Nov.

Ampleforth Abbey, N. Yorks. An English *Benedictine Abbey, founded in 1802 with a nucleus of monks from Dieulouard in Lorraine. The community claims continuity with the Benedictines of *Westminster Abbey.

ampulla. A globular vessel for holding liquid. The term is used of: (1) bottle-shaped vessels, usually of glass, found at tombs in the *catacombs, and previously thought to contain the blood of martyrs; (2) vessels of baked clay used to preserve oil from lights burnt in *martyria*; (3) vessels used for the sacramental oils. The most famous is that supposed to have been brought by a dove at the prayers of St *Remigius for the Baptism of *Clovis. The 'Sainte Ampoule' preserved at *Reims is known to have been used for the coronation of French kings from 1131 to the Revolution.

Amsdorf, Nikolaus von (1483–1565), *Lutheran theologian. He joined M. *Luther in 1517 and accompanied him to the Disputation of *Leipzig (1519) and the Diet of *Worms (1521). In 1524 he went to Magdeburg to lead the Protestant opposition to the Catholic clergy and to reform the services on Lutheran lines. He objected to the *Leipzig Interim (1548) and became one of the leaders of the *Gnesio-Lutheran party opposed to the *Adiaphorists. Against G.*Major and others, he maintained that good works were not only useless but actually harmful.

Amsterdam Assembly (1948). The Assembly of Church leaders in Amsterdam which formally constituted the '*World Council of Churches'.

Amyraut, Moïse (1596–1644), French Protestant theologian. From 1626 he was minister at Saumur and lecturer at the Protestant Academy there, becoming Principal in 1641. In his *Brief Traitté de la predestination* (1634) he taught that Christ had been sent into the world to redeem all people, provided they had faith, not just those predestined for salvation. He was tried for heresy at the Protestant Synod of Alençon in 1637, but escaped condemnation.

Anabaptists. The comprehensive designation of various closely related groups who, holding that infant *Baptism was no true Baptism, refused to allow their children to be baptized and reinstituted the Baptism of believers in the 16th cent. The main groups were: (1) Thomas *Müntzer and the *Zwickau Prophets, who appeared in *Wittenberg in 1521. (2) The *Swiss Brethren, who reintroduced believers' Baptism as the basis of Christian fellowship at Zurich in 1525; unlike Müntzer they preached non-resistance and rejected Christian participation in the magistracy. (3) Communities which found asylum in Moravia and, under the leadership of Jacob Hutter (d. 1536), established settlements based on common ownership of property. Their descendants, known as 'Hutterites' or 'Hutterite Brethren', survive in Canada and the USA. (4) The South German Anabaptists, who shared the eschatological and spiritual interests of Hans Hut (d. 1527), but, especially under the leadership of Pilgram Marpeck (d. 1556) moderated their views in line with those of the Swiss Brethren. (5) Melchiorites or Hoffmanites, that is, Anabaptists influenced by Melchior *Hoffmann, mainly in NW Germany and the Low Countries. (6) A group of Anabaptist refugees in Münster who in 1533–5 attempted to establish a Kingdom of Saints; their excesses brought disrepute on the movement. (7) The *Mennonites (q.v.).

The Anabaptists were denounced by M. *Luther, U. *Zwingli, and J. *Calvin and persecuted by both RCs and Protestants. There were Anabaptists in England by 1534. They probably influenced the early *Separatists and *Brownists.

Anacletus, St (1st cent.), Bp. of Rome. He is probably to be identified with 'Cletus'. He followed St *Linus (the successor of St *Peter) and preceded St *Clement of Rome. Feast day of St Cletus, 26 Apr., dropped in 1969.

analogy. In common modern usage the word signifies a resemblance or similarity between objects of discourse. More technically analogy is a linguistic and semantic phenomenon which occurs when one word bears different but related meanings, as in the expressions a healthy diet and a healthy complexion. In theology it helps to explain how one can significantly refer to God by means of words more usually used of creatures. Thus one can meaningfully say that 'God is wise' and 'Solomon is wise', even though the wisdom of God is incomprehensible. The use of analogy in talking about God allows us to employ arguments about Him which abide by common rules of logic and proceed by means of terms for which there is already some (non-theological) meaning. The recognition that our discourse about God can be analogical is a corrective to *anthropomorphism or any tendency to imply that God is the same kind of thing as any nameable creature.

Analogy of Religion, The (1736). J.*Butler's famous book seeks to show both that Christianity is not unreasonable and that both Natural and Revealed Religion are positively reasonable. He argues that various objections to particular religious beliefs are not decisive, since similar objections can be raised with respect to non-religious beliefs concerning nature. The balance of probability points to the truth of both Natural and Revealed Religion whose propositions are of practical importance.

Anamnesis. The commemoration of the Passion, Resurrection, and Ascension of Christ, which in most liturgies is included in the *Eucharistic Prayer after the Words of *Institution.

Anaphora. The name used in the E. Church of the central prayer in the Eucharistic liturgy, known in the W. as the *Eucharistic Prayer (q.v.).

Anastasia, St (c.304), martyr. She was apparently killed at Sirmium in Pannonia, whence her relics were translated by *Gennadius to *Constantinople. From here her cultus spread to the church in Rome near the Imperial Palace known as the *titulus Anastasiae* (perhaps from its founder); the dedication was then understood of the Sirmian saint. Feast day in the W. until 1969, 25 Dec.; in the E., 22 Dec.

Anastasis (Gk., 'resurrection'). The term is used both of the resurrection of Christ and of that of mankind in general.

Anastasius, St (d. c.700), Abbot of the monastery of St Catherine on Mount *Sinai. He is believed to have attacked *Monophysitism at *Alexandria as early as 640 and it is chiefly against this heresy that his main work, the *Hodegos* (*Guide*), is directed. Feast day in the E., 21 Apr.

Anastasius I (d. 598), Patr. of *Antioch 559–70 and 593–8. A critic of *Justinian I's *aphthartodocetism, he was deposed by Justinian II and spent 23 years in exile. A key figure in the dogmatic discussions of the time, he wrote treatises against a tritheist, on the Trinity and Incarnation, on the providence of God, and on problems of biblical interpretation. He defended the creed of *Chalcedon, but tried to close the gap with the *Monophysites.

Anastasius Bibliothecarius (9th cent.), scholar. He was the best Greek scholar of his age in the W. and became Papal librarian (hence his title). He attended the final session of the Eighth *Oecumenical Council (867) and in 871 translated its Acts into Latin. In 873 he translated those of the Seventh Council (787).

anathema. The word means 'separated' or 'accursed'. In the OT it was used of 'things devoted to God', that is not for common use, and later came to involve for people exclusion from the community and loss of goods. St *Paul used it of separation from the Christian community. Anathematization, which became the regular procedure against heretics, was distinguished from *excommunication; whereas the latter involved only exclusion from the *sacraments and worship, the former was complete separation from the body of the faithful. The distinction gradually lost its meaning and since 1983 the term has had no official application in the penal code of the RC Church.

Anatolius, St (d. *c*.282), Bp. of Laodicea from 268. A teacher and senator of *Alexandria before his consecration, he was learned. His writings include a treatise on the date of *Easter and a work on the Elements of Arithmetic. Feast day, 3 July.

Anatolius (*c*.400–458), Patr. of *Constantinople. A native of *Alexandria, he was sent by St *Cyril to Constantinople and elected bishop when *Flavian was deposed in 449. Pope *Leo I demanded that he should condemn *Eutyches and *Nestorius and endorse the *Tome of Leo; Anatolius agreed in 450. He seems to have encouraged the Emp. *Marcian to summon the Council of

*Chalcedon and had some part in formulating the Definition of *Chalcedon.

anchorite (*m.*), **anchoress** (*f.*). A person who withdraws from the world to live a solitary life of silence, prayer, and mortification. The word is used especially of one who lives in confined quarters (his 'cell').

Ancient of Days. A designation of God found in Dan. 7 (AV and RV).

Ancren(e) Riwle (or **Ancrene Wisse**). An early 13th-cent. 'Rule' or 'Guide for Anchoresses', written in English. It was originally composed for three well-born sisters and later revised by the author for a larger group of recluses. The identity of the author is uncertain, but his style is clear, lively and rhetorically accomplished. The 'Rule' was widely copied and adapted for other communities of men and women.

Ancyra (also **Angora**, now Ankara, Turkey). Among the more important early Church synods held here were those of: (1) 314, which dealt with the reconciliation of the lapsed and those who had committed other offences; and (2) 358. A council of *Semiarians who asserted that the Son was 'like in substance' to the Father.

Andreae, Jacob (1528–90), *Lutheran theologian. He was Professor of Theology in the University of *Tubingen from 1561. He took part in various negotiations between RCs and Lutherans, but above all he strove to secure harmony among the Lutheran Churches. He was one of the authors of the Formula of *Concord (1577).

Andrew, St, *Apostle. He was the brother of St *Peter, and several incidents are recorded of him in the Gospels. *Eusebius states that he later went to Scythia. According to an unreliable tradition, he was crucified at Patras in Greece in 60. The earliest evidence for the form of the cross taking the shape of an X dates from the 10th cent. He is the patron saint of Scotland, Greece, and Russia. Feast day, 30 Nov.

Andrew, Acts of St. An apocryphal book, probably dating from the late-2nd cent., of which there is an epitome by *Gregory of Tours. It depicts the apostle imprisoned at Patras in Greece. The 'Martyrdom of St Andrew', a variant text of part of the work, describes his death by crucifixion, but without mention of the 'St Andrew's cross'.

Andrew of Crete, St (c.660–740), theologian. He became Abp. of Gortyna in Crete c.692. In the early stages of the *Iconoclastic controversy, he defended the veneration of icons. He wrote many hymns, notably a series of *canons, a form of composition which he is said to have invented. Feast day in the E., 4 July.

Andrew of St-Victor (d. 1175), biblical exegete. A canon of St-Victor in Paris (see VICTORINES), he became Abbot of Wigmore in Herefordshire. In his commentaries he used Jewish sources and concentrated on the literal sense of Scripture to an extent not found elsewhere in the Middle Ages.

Andrewes, Lancelot (1555–1626), Bp. successively of *Chichester (from 1605), *Ely (1609), and *Winchester (1619). He attended the *Hampton Court Conference (1604) and was one of the translators of the AV. When *James I's defence of the Oath of Allegiance was attacked by St Robert *Bellarmine, Andrewes wrote a vigorous and able reply, and in 1617 he accompanied James to Scotland in an attempt to persuade the Scots to accept episcopacy. Theologically he was one of the main influences in the formation of a distinctively Anglican theology, which, in reaction from the rigidity of *Puritanism, was to be reasonable in outlook and Catholic in tone. In his lifetime his fame rested on his preaching; the first collection of his sermons was published in 1629. His famous *Preces Privatae* was a collection of prayers gradually compiled for his own use. Feast day, 25 or 26 Sept. in different parts of the Anglican Communion, the divergence reflecting uncertainty over the date of his death.

angel. In the Bible angels are represented as an innumerable multitude of beings intermediate between God and man (e.g. Gen. 32: 1 f.). They form the heavenly court (Is. 6), and particular angels are mentioned as performing God's commands for nations and individuals (e.g. Dan. 10: 13 and 12: 1). Christ seems to have sanctioned the popular belief; a number of His sayings (e.g. Mt. 16: 27; 18: 10; and 26: 53) refer to angels. The NT writers represent Him as surrounded by angels at all the most important points in His life.

In the first centuries of the Church interest in angels was comparatively peripheral; it largely centred on the question of angelic orders raised by the two enumerations in Eph. 1: 21 and Col. 1: 16. In *Dionysius the Pseudo-Areopagite's *Celestial Hierarchies* they are arranged in three hierarchies of three choirs each. In the Middle Ages there was speculation and controversy over detailed points, e.g. their substantiality, form, and nature. In general, Catholic Christianity teaches the existence of angels and enjoins a cult similar to that given to the saints. Protestants have shrunk from definition and in modern times the whole concept of such supernatural beings has been challenged. See also GUARDIAN ANGELS.

Angela of Foligno, Bl (c.1248–1309), Umbrian mystic. After the death of her husband, she became a *Franciscan tertiary. The account of her frequent visions, circulated as *Liber Visionum et Instructionum*, reflects early Franciscan piety at its highest. Feast day, 4 Jan.

Angela Merici, St (1470/75–1540), foundress of the *Ursulines. After a period of blindness, in 1535 she founded at Brescia a religious community of women, which she named after St *Ursula. Feast day, 27 Jan.

Angelic Doctor, the. St *Thomas Aquinas.

Angelic Hymn. The *Gloria in excelsis*.

Angelico, Bl Fra (1395/1400–1455), Giovanni da Fiesole, painter. He entered the *Dominican Order between 1417 and 1423. In the 1430s he was active in Cortona, where some of his greatest pictures still are. The earliest evidence of his presence at San Marco in Florence dates from 1441. His work here included the high altarpiece in the church and the frescoed decoration of the cells, cloisters and corridors of the convent. Between 1446 and 1449 he painted four fresco cycles in chapels at the *Vatican. His great artistic achievement was in his narrative power and use of brilliant colours; many of the most memorable images in Christian art were conceived by him. Feast day, 18 Feb.

Angels of the Churches. The angels of the seven Churches mentioned in Rev. 1–3.

Angelus. In the W. Church, the devotion consisting in the repetition three times daily (early morning, noon, and evening) of three *Ave Marias with *versicles and a *collect as a memorial of the Incarnation. A bell is rung three times for each Ave and nine times for the collect.

Angelus Silesius (1624–77) (**Johann Scheffler**), mystical poet and controversialist. The son of a *Lutheran Polish noble, he became a RC in 1653. His chief fame lies in his mystical poems *Heilige Seelenlust* (1657) and *Der Cherubinische Wandersmann* (1675; 1st edn., with different title, 1657).

Anglican chant. The music of the Psalms as widely used in the Anglican Communion. It consists of a tune in barred music, harmonized, in which the first part of each half-verse is sung on a reciting note, and the concluding words fitted to a tune in metrical rhythm.

Anglican Communion. The Church in communion with, and recognizing the leadership of, the see of *Canterbury. It consists of the *Church of England (the only part retaining state *establishment), independent Churches or Provinces throughout most of the world, and a few 'extraprovincial' dioceses under the jurisdiction of the Abp. of Canterbury or another Anglican Primate or his see.

For the first 250 years after the *Reformation, the Anglican Communion, except for the Episcopal Church of *Scotland (disestablished in 1689) consisted solely of the one (state) Church of England, Ireland, and Wales. Priests working overseas were placed under the jurisdiction of the Bp. of London. After the consecration of S. *Seabury by Scottish bishops in 1784, an Act of Parliament was passed in 1786 making possible the consecration in England of bishops for sees in other parts of the world. Further American bishops were consecrated by the English Archbishops and in 1789 the *Episcopal Church in the United States of America became an autonomous body in communion with the see of Canterbury. In 1787 the first colonial bishop was consecrated, with jurisdiction over British N. America. Bishoprics were established in *India (1814), *Australia (1836), *New Zealand (1841), and other parts of the British Empire. Provincial organization began in 1835, and gradually complete independence of the jurisdiction of the Canterbury was secured by those dioceses with provincial organization; by the second

half of the 20th cent. this extended almost everywhere. In Britain the Church of *Ireland was disestablished in 1869 and that of *Wales in 1920. Overseas Churches within the British Empire were disestablished in the 19th and 20th cents. Outside the British Empire a few Anglican sees were founded, e.g. in *China, *Japan, and South America.

Anglican bishops meet periodically as a body at the *Lambeth Conference (q.v.). In 1969 the Anglican Consultative Council, which includes clerical and lay as well as episcopal representatives from each Church or Province, was established as an advisory body. The Primates have met regularly since 1979.

See also ANGLICANISM.

Anglican Evangelical Group Movement. An association of Anglican clergy and laity who held *Liberal Evangelical views. It began in 1906 as a private society with the title 'Group Brotherhood', becoming a public body in 1923. It was formally terminated in 1967.

Anglicanism. The word properly denotes the system of doctrine and practice of those Christians who are in communion with the see of *Canterbury, but it is used especially of that system in so far as it claims to possess a religious and theological outlook distinguishable from that of other Christian communities. As a doctrinal system it took shape in the reign of *Elizabeth I. Its formularies, including the Book of *Common Prayer, the *Ordinal, the *Thirty-Nine Articles, and the Books of *Homilies, became the basis of Anglican self-understanding, preaching, and doctrine. In the 17th cent. the C of E confirmed her rejection of the claims of Rome and refused to adopt the theological and ecclesiastical systems of the Continental Reformers. The historic episcopate was preserved, though many did not regard it as of Divine institution. The extent of legitimate change was held to be limited by appeal to Scripture as containing all things necessary to salvation. Truth was to be sought from the joint testimony of Scripture and ecclesiastical authority, which in its turn was to be based on the tradition of the first four centuries.

At the Restoration in 1660, the dominant party comprised *High Churchmen, who stressed the continuity of the C of E with its

Catholic roots. The *Cambridge Platonists (1633–88) and their successors emphasized devotional religion as well as a conservative respect for the wisdom of the past. Their immediate heritage was a *latitudinarianism which gained strength in the early 18th cent.; it emphasized practical Christian living, morality, and a distrust of enthusiasm. The emergence of *Evangelicalism among Anglicans in Britain and the USA in the later 18th cent. may be seen in part as a reaction against this trend. The *Oxford Movement (q.v.) sought to restore to Anglicanism a sense of its roots and sacramental life as part of the Catholic Church. By the mid-20th cent. many of the practices advocated by its leaders had been accepted.

Until 1948 *Lambeth Conferences had regarded the BCP as a bond in the *Anglican Communion; with minor revisions it was used throughout the world in some language or other. In the second half of the 20th cent. there has been liturgical experimentation and almost every Province has produced a different Prayer Book. The increasing proportion of Anglicans in non-English-speaking countries contributes to the challenge of maintaining a unity of ethos in contemporary Anglicanism. The ordination of *women to the priesthood and episcopate in some Provinces and not in others has strained the bounds of comprehensiveness of Anglicanism and highlighted questions of *authority.

Anglican-Methodist Conversations. On the basis of a suggestion by G. *Fisher in 1946 that unity between the C of E and the Free Churches might be achieved if the latter would accept episcopacy, the *Methodist Conference and the *Convocations of Canterbury and York in 1955 agreed to enter conversations. The final report was published in 1968, in two parts: *The Ordinal* and *The Scheme*. It was accepted by the Methodist Conference but failed to gain the necessary majority in the Convocations in 1969 and in the General Synod in 1972. New talks were initiated in 1995.

Anglican Ordinations. Until the subject was removed from public discussion in the RC Church by *Leo XIII's bull '*Apostolicae Curae' (1896), there was diversity of opinion in that Church about the validity of Anglican *Orders. The grounds on which their validity was attacked fall into two classes: (1) attacks on the historical continuity of the laying-on of hands; and (2) attacks on the *Ordinal introduced under *Edward VI as either defective in *intention or invalidated by the omission of the Tradition of the *Instruments and other rites. Neither ground is now generally accepted, and in recent times the refusal of the RC Church to recognize the validity of Anglican Orders has been seen as a serious impediment in ecumenical relations.

Anglican-Roman Catholic International Commission (ARCIC). A joint commission of the RC Church and the *Anglican Communion, intended to further the goal of visible unity between the two bodies. Set up after a meeting in 1966 between Pope *Paul VI and M. *Ramsey, Abp. of Canterbury, the Commission held a series of residential meetings (known as 'Conversations') and produced 'Agreed Statements' on 'Eucharistic Doctrine' (1971), 'Ministry and Ordination' (1973), and 'Authority in the Church' (1976). The 1988 *Lambeth Conference held that the first two statements were 'consonant in substance with the faith of Anglicans', but called for further study of questions concerning Papal primacy. The formal RC response in 1991 judged that 'differences or ambiguities' remained. Meanwhile a new Commission (ARCIC II) was established in 1982.

Anglo-Catholicism. The term 'Anglo-Catholic' is commonly used of that section or party within the Anglican Communion which stems from the *Tractarian Movement of the 1830s. Anglo-Catholics hold a high doctrine of the Church and Sacraments; they attach importance to the '*apostolic succession', that is to an episcopal order derived from the Apostles; to the historic continuity of the C of E with the earliest centuries; and to the Church's ultimate independence of the State.

The original Tractarians were concerned with doctrine, and they revived *religious communities and various practices of personal discipline such as the use of auricular *confession and *fasting; they were not much interested in ceremonial. Later Anglo-Catholics came to be regarded as preoccupied with the externals of worship and were known as 'ritualists'. Despite opposition, many of the practices they advocated (e.g. the use of *candles) spread throughout the C of E, and the increased frequency of celebrations of the Eucharist has owed much to their influence. See also OXFORD MOVEMENT.

Anglo-Saxon Church. The Church in England from the end of the 6th cent. to the Norman Conquest (1066). In 597 the Roman mission of St *Augustine landed in Thanet in the south and sees were quickly set up at *Canterbury, London, *Rochester, and *York. In the north, St *Aidan established himself at *Lindisfarne c.635. For a time the work of the missions was hindered by disputes over differences in such customs as the date of observing Easter, but after the Synod of *Whitby (664), union between the north and the south was gradually achieved. In 669 *Theodore of Tarsus arrived as Abp. of Canterbury and began his great work of reform and organization. The Danish invasions were a blow to the Church, although the victory of *Alfred secured the nominal acceptance of Christianity by the invaders. In the 10th cent. reforms were initiated by St *Dunstan and St *Ethelwold, and closer contact with the Continent was established. In the Anglo-Saxon Church monasticism was strong, and most of the evangelization was done by monks. There were also particularly close links between the Church and State. The conversion of a district usually began in the royal palace; bishoprics were conterminous with tribal areas, and it is often difficult to decide whether a particular assembly was primarily ecclesiastical or secular.

Angola, Christianity in. The *Portuguese colony of Angola dates from 1576. From 1596 it was placed within the newly established (RC) diocese of San Salvador, comprising the *Congo kingdom and Angola. Despite the demoralization of the slave trade, and long periods when there was no bishop, the Church survived; areas in Angola are the only part of sub-Saharan Africa where there has been a continuous local Church since the 16th cent., though by the mid-19th cent. there were few priests. In 1865 French *Holy Ghost Fathers took responsibility for the mission and the Church began to revive. Protestant activity, based in Britain and America, began later in the 19th cent. The Independence of Angola in 1975 was followed by civil war, in which *Baptists and *Methodists were often linked with forces opposed to the government, with RCs being more sympathetic to the Marxist rulers. About half the population belongs to the RC Church and under a quarter to Protestant denominations.

Anima Christi (Lat., 'Soul of Christ'), the well-known prayer, beginning 'Soul of Christ, sanctify me', often used as a private Eucharistic devotion. It appears to date from the early 14th cent.

Annas. The Jewish *High Priest from AD 6 (or 7) to 15 and father-in-law of *Caiaphas. According to Jn. 18: 13 Christ was brought before Annas before being sent on to Caiaphas.

annates. The first year's revenue of an ecclesiastical benefice, paid to the Papal curia. In England payment was transferred to the Crown in 1535. They were assigned to '*Queen Anne's Bounty' in 1704 and abolished in 1926.

Anne, St, Mother of the BVM. Her name (not found in the Bible) and the legend of her life occur in the *Protevangelium of James (2nd cent.). Her cult developed in the Middle Ages and was an object of attack by M. *Luther and other Reformers. Feast day in the W., 26 July; in the E., 25 July.

Anne (1665–1714), Queen of Great Britain and Ireland from 1702. The second daughter of *James II, she continued to be brought up as an Anglican after her father had become a RC. She created '*Queen Anne's Bounty' for the clergy (1704). By exercising her right to nominate bishops, she introduced a *High Church and Tory element to the Bench and she supported the *Occasional Conformity Bill (introduced 1702; passed 1711).

Anne Boleyn (?1501–36), second Queen of *Henry VIII. She began living openly with Henry in 1531 and became pregnant in 1532. After a secret marriage in Jan. 1533, she was crowned Queen. She gave birth to the future *Elizabeth I; her next child in 1536 was stillborn. She was accused of adultery, Abp. T. *Cranmer declared her marriage to Henry null, and she was executed. Apart from her importance in precipitating the 'divorce' crisis, she played a major role in advancing reformers to positions of power in the Church.

Annexed Book, the. The actual BCP annexed to the Act of *Uniformity of 1662, which prescribed the use of 'true and perfect copies' of it.

Anno Domini (Lat., 'in the year of the Lord'). The current system of dating by 'AD', based on the traditional date of the birth of Christ, was devised by *Dionysius Exiguus (6th cent.). It is now commonly held that the actual birth was several years earlier.

Annunciation of the BVM. The feast, observed on 25 Mar. ('Lady Day'), commemorates the announcement of the Incarnation by the angel *Gabriel to the BVM and the conception of Christ in her womb (Lk. 1: 26–38). In the RC Church it is now called the 'Annunciation of the Lord'.

anointing. A ceremonial action to separate persons and things from profane use and to obtain for them the infusion of Divine grace. In the OT priests and kings are anointed, and the future deliverer is designated the 'Anointed One' or '*Messiah' (q.v.). The Church from early times used sacramental anointing in the rites of *Baptism, *Confirmation, and *Ordination, as well as in the consecration of churches, bells, altars, etc. See also CHRISM, UNCTION, and CORONATION RITE IN ENGLAND.

Anomoeans. 4th-cent. exponents of a doctrine akin to *Arianism, now often called 'Neo-Arians'. They held that the Son, being begotten, was in essence unlike the Father, the Unbegotten. Their leaders were *Aetius and *Eunomius.

Anselm, St (c.1033–1109), Abp. of *Canterbury from 1093. He had been Abbot of *Bec. He had various disputes with William II and in 1098 he went to Rome. He first learnt of the Papal decrees against lay *investiture in 1099; when the new king, Henry I, recalled him to England in 1100, he insisted on observing the decrees without compromise. In 1103 he went again to Rome and remained in exile until 1107, when the Pope and the King agreed to a compromise behind his back.

Both as a philosopher and a theologian, Anselm has a foremost place among medieval thinkers. Unlike his predecessors, he preferred to defend the truth by intellectual reasoning instead of employing Scriptural and patristic authorities. The object of his *Monologion* was to establish the being of God solely on rational grounds. In the *Prologion* this reasoning was given the more systematic form of the *ontological argument. If we mean by God (as Anselm held that we do) 'that than which nothing greater can be thought', then we cannot think of this entity except as existing; for, if it did not exist, it would not be 'that than which nothing greater can be thought'. His *Cur Deus Homo* was the most considerable contribution to the theology of the *Atonement in the Middle Ages. He interpreted the doctrine in terms of the satisfaction which is needed to restore the universal harmony of the Creation dislocated by sin; he repudiated the notion that the Devil had rights over fallen man which it was a leading purpose of the Cross to satisfy. Anselm saw in faith the precondition of the right use of reason, but it is our duty to exercise our minds in apprehending revealed truth. Feast day, 21 Apr.

Anselm of Laon (d. 1117), theologian. He taught in the cathedral school at Laon. His lectures on the Bible discussed points of interest as they arose; after his death these lectures were reworked and enlarged into systematic *Summae*. He was traditionalist in his views, but his methods were new. The corpus of his work is not settled, but he certainly arranged commentaries on the Psalter, the Pauline Epp., and Jn., which are the foundation of the *Glossa Ordinaria.

Anselm of Lucca, St (c.1035–86). Nominated to the see of Lucca in 1073, he was driven out by partisans of the Emp. *Henry IV, probably late in 1080. From then he was *Gregory VII's standing legate in Lombardy. He made a collection of canons (c.1083) and wrote a treatise in support of Gregory against the antipope. Feast day, 18 Mar.

Anskar, St (801–65), or **Ansgar**, the 'Apostle of the North'. A monk of *Corbie, he went to Corvey in Westphalia and then to *Denmark and *Sweden, where he built the first Christian church. About 832 he became Bp. of Hamburg and c.848 Abp. of Bremen. Feast day, 3 Feb.

ante-chapel. The western end of certain medieval college chapels.

Ante-Communion. In the C of E the earlier part of the service of Holy Communion down to and including the Prayer for the Church Militant, especially when used without the remainder of the service.

Antelapsarianism. See SUPRALAPSARIANISM.

antependium. A vesture or *frontal which hangs in front of the altar.

anthem. The Anglicized form of the word *antiphon, it is commonly applied to sacred vocal music usually set to scriptural words. The BCP provides for an anthem after the third collect at Morning and Evening Prayer. In many modern Anglican liturgies, 'a canticle, psalm, hymn or anthem' may be sung before the Gospel and at various other points in the Eucharist.

Anthony, St. See ANTONY, ST.

anthropology. In its more exact sense the word designates the study of man as contrasted, e.g. with that of God or of angels. It enables the Christian apologist to exhibit the true nature of man against views which represent him as an economic unit or a mass of psychological reflexes. In popular usage 'anthropology' is used of the science which studies the life and environment of primitive man, and more recently, of the study of man in society (social anthropology).

anthropomorphism. In theology, the attribution to God of human characteristics. Discussion of its propriety has often centred around the concept of *analogy.

anthroposophy. A system evolved by R. *Steiner, based on the premiss that the human soul can, of its own power, contact the spiritual world. The concepts of reincarnation and karma are central to it. It acknowledges Christ as a cosmic being, but its understanding of Him is very different from that of orthodox Christianity.

Antiburgher. See BURGHER.

Antichrist. The prince of Christ's enemies. In the NT he is referred to by name only in 1 and 2 Jn. (where he is identified with those who deny the Incarnation), but many see him in the strange beasts of Rev. and in the 'man of sin' in 2 Thess. 2: 3–10. Some have connected Antichrist not with a person but with an evil principle; others have seen in Antichrist a reference to some historical person (e.g. *Nero).

Anticlericalism. A liberal movement in politics and religion which affected many parts of Europe and Latin America in the 19th and 20th cents. It was directed against the RC Church as a State religion, claiming a monopoly of religious truth and political power. The French Revolution was a breakthrough for anticlericalism. After 1815 the identification of the RC Church with reactionary regimes and conservative social élites drove many liberals and democrats to anticlericalism. It came in waves, notably after the revolutions of 1830 in *France and *Belgium, the triumphs of the Liberals in *Portugal (1834) and *Spain (1836), and the Portuguese Revolution of 1910. In Latin America anticlericalism was rife in *Mexico after the Revolution of 1910. The movement towards national unification was a second force behind anticlericalism; the loyalty of Catholic clergy and laity to Rome was seen by national state-builders as a challenge to the sovereign state. Italy, in particular, could not be unified until the temporal power of the Papacy had been eliminated (1870). The Papacy's accommodation with totalitarian governments in Italy, Germany, and France meant that the return of liberal and democratic regimes in W. Europe after 1944 was marked by a certain resurgence of anticlericalism. See also ASSOCIATIONS, LAW OF.

Antididagma. The reply issued in 1544 by the cathedral chapter of *Cologne to the plan set out by Abp. *Hermann of Wied to reform Catholic practices.

antidoron (Gk., 'instead of the gift'). The remains of the loaves from which the Eucharistic Bread is cut in the E. Church. It is distributed at the end of the Liturgy, in theory only to those who have not received Communion, but in fact to all present.

antilegomena. The name given by *Eusebius of Caesarea to those Scriptural books whose claim to be considered part of the NT Canon was disputed.

Anti-Marcionite Prologues. The short introductory prologues prefixed to the Gospels of Mk., Lk., and Jn. in some 40 MSS. of the *Vulgate. They are no longer thought to have been directed against *Marcion.

antiminsion, also **antimension.** In the E. Church a silk or linen cloth, containing relics; it was originally intended for use when there was no consecrated altar, but it is now used like a W. *corporal.

antinomianism. A general name for the view that Christians are by grace set free from the need to observe any moral law. Various *Gnostic sects held that, as matter was sharply opposed to spirit, bodily actions were indifferent and therefore licentiousness was admissible. At the Reformation antinomian teaching was revived, e.g. by the *Anabaptists, as following from the *Lutheran doctrine of *justification by faith.

Antioch. In size and importance Antioch in Syria was the third city of the Roman Empire. A Christian community existed here from early days and it was here that the followers of Christ were first called 'Christians' (Acts 11: 26). According to tradition St *Peter was the first bishop. By the 4th cent. the see ranked after *Rome and *Alexandria as the third patriarchal see of Christendom. The rise in power of *Constantinople and the erection of *Jerusalem into a Patriarchate reduced the importance of Antioch, which was further diminished by the *Nestorian and *Monophysite schisms. See also the following entries.

Antioch, Council of (341). The Council was held on the occasion of the consecration of *Constantine's 'Golden Church' at Antioch. Four creeds were put forward to replace that of *Nicaea. The 25 (mainly disciplinary) 'Canons of Antioch' were long thought to have been the work of this Council but are now generally held to belong to a Council held at Antioch in 330.

Antiochene theology. A modern designation for a style of theology associated with the Church at *Antioch, contrasted with *Alexandrine theology. In scriptural exegesis it placed more emphasis on the literal and historical sense of the biblical text. In its Christological teaching, stress was laid on the humanity of Christ and the reality of His moral choices. To achieve this, and to preserve the impassibility of His Divine nature, the unity of His person was described in a looser way than in Alexandrian theology. It was primarily this difference which was at the heart of the *Nestorian controversy.

Antiochus Epiphanes (d. 164 BC), King of Syria from 175 BC. In 169 BC he attacked *Jerusalem and despoiled the *Temple; in 167 BC Jewish customs were forbidden, the Temple was defiled, and pagan cults instituted. This led to the *Maccabean revolt.

antiphon (originally 'something sung alternately by two choirs'). In the W. Church, sentences, usually from the Bible, recited before and after the *Psalms and *Canticles in the Divine *Office. The name is also used of the four Anthems of the BVM, one of which is sung after *Compline. In the E. Church the word is applied to various chants sung antiphonally.

Antiphonal, also **Antiphonary**. Originally the liturgical book in the W. Church containing the parts of the *Office and *Mass which were sung by the choir antiphonally. In later times the Office and Mass portions were separated and in current usage the word is restricted to the former.

antipope. A person set up as Bp. of Rome in opposition to the person holding the see or held to be lawfully elected to it.

antisemitism. See JEWS, CHRISTIAN ATTITUDES TO.

Antitrinitarianism. Various professedly Christian systems which agree only in rejecting the doctrine of the *Trinity. Antitrinitarians have included *Ebionites, upholders of *Subordinationism, Monarchian *Modalists, *Arians, and in modern times *Unitarians.

Antonelli, Giacomo (1806–76), Cardinal Secretary of State. In 1848 he arranged the flight of *Pius IX to Gaeta and after his return to Rome in 1850 became virtually the temporal ruler of the city until 1870. He opposed the convening of the First *Vatican Council, and then advised the Pope to drop the *Infallibility question.

Antonians. Several communities claiming the patronage of, or descent from, St *Antony of Egypt: (1) the original disciples of St Antony; (2) a congregation founded by Gaston de Dauphiné in 1095, known as the 'Hospital Brothers of St Antony'; (3) an order in the *Armenian Church founded in the 17th cent. to maintain the connection with the RC Church; (4) a congregation founded in Flanders in 1615.

Antoninus, St (1389–1459), Abp. of Florence. He became a *Dominican in 1404/5 and was among those who sought to restore the primitive observances and austerity of the Order. His appointment as Abp. of Florence in 1446 is said to have been made on the advice of Fra *Angelico. He became the counsellor of popes and statesmen. He was also a distinguished theological writer. He held that money invested in business was true capital and that it was therefore not necessarily wrong to receive interest. Feast day, 10 May.

Antony, St, of Egypt (251?–356), hermit. About 269 he gave away his possessions and devoted himself to a life of asceticism, and c.285 retired completely to the desert, to the 'Outer Mountain' at Pispir, where he is said to have fought with demons in the guise of wild beasts. About 305 he came out of his solitude to organize his disciples into a community of hermits living under a rule, though with much less common life than the later religious orders had. About 310 he retired again into solitude to his 'Inner Mountain' (near the Red Sea), but he later exerted influence in support of the *Nicene party, in which he was associated with St *Athanasius. Feast day, 17 Jan.

Antony, St, of Padua (1188/95–1231), *Franciscan friar. When he was 15 he joined the *Augustinian canons. He was deeply moved when the relics of some Franciscans killed in Morocco were brought to Coimbra in 1220; he obtained his release, joined the Franciscans and sailed for Morocco late in 1220, but was forced by illness to return to Europe. When called upon to preach at an ordination, his unexpected eloquence and learning were discovered. He was appointed the first lector in theology in the Franciscan Order and held a series of other offices. Regarded as a worker of miracles, he is chiefly invoked for the return of lost property, possibly because of the incident of a novice who ran away with a Psalter he was using and was forced by an alarming apparition to return it. Feast day, 13 June.

apatheia. A Greek word meaning 'impassibility' or 'passionlessness', used in ascetic theology in the E. Church. When applied to God, it is used in its literal sense, but it is also used as a technical term for human perfection, denoting mastery of the passions or serenity.

Apelles (2nd cent.), founder of a *Gnostic sect. Originally a disciple of *Marcion, he modified his dualism in an attempt to defend a less *Docetic doctrine of the Person of Christ. Christ, he held, came down from the good God, who was not himself the creator of the world, however, and really lived and suffered in a body miraculously formed out of the elements.

Aphrahat (early 4th cent.), the first of the Syriac Church Fathers. He was an ascetic, evidently holding high ecclesiastical office. His *Demonstrations* (inaccurately known as his *Homilies*) were completed between 337 and 345. The first 22 give a survey of Christian faith, the last being an appendix. They throw valuable light on early Christianity in Iran and on the text of the NT.

Aphthartodocetae. An extreme *Monophysite group led by *Julian, Bp. of Halicarnassus. They taught that from the moment of the incarnation the earthly body of Christ was in its nature incorruptible, impassible, and immortal, though this fact did not preclude Him from accepting suffering and death as a free act of will.

Apiarius. A priest in proconsular Africa who was deposed for misconduct. The incident is important in connection with the growth of Papal jurisdiction. Apiarius appealed to Pope *Zosimus (417–18), who ordered his reinstatement. A Council at *Carthage in 419 then forbade appeals beyond the sea.

Apocalyptic literature. The word 'apocalypse' means a 'revelation' or 'unveiling', so an apocalyptic book claims to reveal things which are normally hidden or to reveal the future. The Jewish Apocalyptic books belong approximately to the period from 200 BC to AD 200 and deal with the end of the present order or with the next world.

Apocalyptic literature proper begins with the Book of *Daniel, probably written during the persecution of *Antiochus Epiphanes (175–164 BC), though there are apocalyptic tendencies in some of the prophetic writings with their references to the approaching 'day of the Lord'. The Apocalyptic writings are almost always pseudonymous and written in the names of Israel's past heroes. The Jewish Apocalyptic writings outside the OT include 1 and 2 *Enoch, *Baruch II, 4 Ezra (2 *Esdras), the Assumption of *Moses, *Jubilees, the

Ascension of *Isaiah, and the *Testaments of the Twelve Patriarchs. The main Christian Apocalypses are *Revelation and the (non-canonical) Apocalypse of *Peter.

Apocatastasis. The Greek name for the doctrine that ultimately all free moral creatures—angels, men, and devils—will be saved. It was condemned in the first anathema against *Origenism, probably put out by the Council of Constantinople in 543. The doctrine, which has modern defenders, is also known as *Universalism.

apocrisarius. An ecclesiastical deputy or other official of high rank. (1) The envoys used by the Patriarchs as diplomatic representatives in other patriarchal cities or at imperial courts. (2) Senior court chaplains of the Frankish courts.

Apocrypha, the (Gk., 'the hidden [things]'). The biblical Books received by the early Church as part of the Greek version of the OT, but not included in the Hebrew Bible. Their position in Christian usage has been ambiguous. In the *Vulgate and versions derived from it they are mostly part of the OT; but in the AV, RV, NEB, and other non-RC versions they form a separate section between the OT and NT, or are omitted altogether. They comprise (in the order of the AV): 1 and 2 *Esdras, *Tobit, *Judith, the Rest of *Esther, the *Wisdom of Solomon, *Ecclesiasticus, *Baruch with the Epistle of *Jeremy, the *Song of the Three Children, the History of *Susanna, *Bel and the Dragon, the Prayer of *Manasses, and 1 and 2 *Maccabees.

The Church received these writings from Hellenistic Judaism. In the *Septuagint (LXX), which incorporated all except 2 Esdras, they are in no way differentiated from other parts of the OT. They date from the period 300 BC–AD 100 approximately, and mostly from 200 BC to AD 70, i.e. before the definite separation of the Church from Judaism. When the Hebrew *Canon of Scripture was settled (perhaps around AD 100), the Hebrew text of the excluded Books ceased to be copied. The Greek, on the other hand, survived because of its use by Christians who at first received all Books of the LXX equally as Scripture.

In the 4th cent. many of the Greek Fathers came to recognize a distinction between those Books of the LXX which were canonical in Hebrew and the rest. St *Jerome accepted the distinction and introduced the term 'apocrypha' for the latter class. With few exceptions the W. continued to regard all the LXX Books as equally canonical. In the E. opinion varied, but at the Synod of *Jerusalem in 1672 it was decided that Tob., Judith, Ecclus., and Wisd. were alone to be regarded as canonical. At the Reformation Protestant leaders refused the status of inspired Scripture to those Books of the Vulgate not found in the Hebrew Canon. The Council of *Trent (1548) confirmed the full canonicity of the Books, except 1 and 2 Esdras and the Prayer of Manasses, which were then placed in an appendix to the Vulgate; this ruling was repeated at the First *Vatican Council in 1870. In the C of E the *Thirty-Nine Articles say that the Apocryphal Books should be read for 'example of life and instruction of manners', but not used to establish doctrine. Parts of them have been included in successive C of E lectionaries. They are regarded with suspicion by the *Presbyterians and other English Nonconformists, and so frequently omitted from English Bibles, though their value as historical sources has been increasingly recognized in modern times.

Apocryphal New Testament. A modern title for various early Christian books outside the *Canon of the NT which are similar in form or content to the corresponding canonical Scriptures. The epithet 'apocryphal' does not of itself convey the modern sense of fictitious invention.

Many apocryphal Gospels exist. Some may embody trustworthy traditions, but this applies only to the earliest, such as the Gospel of *Thomas. Others were clearly intended to support heretical views, while a third group aimed at satisfying popular curiosity about the childhood of Christ or His post-Resurrection life.

The most important Acts are those of Sts *Peter, *Paul, *John, *Andrew, and *Thomas, all probably 2nd cent. Their subject-matter is made up partly of stories parallel to and perhaps inspired by the Acts of the Apostles, partly credible oral tradition, partly evident romance. Nearly all reflect heretical influences.

There were numerous epistles and other writings such as that of Paul to the *Laodiceans and many *apocalypses besides Revelation.

Apodeipnon. In the E. Church the late evening liturgical service, which is the counterpart of W. *Compline.

Apollinaris, St (date unknown), first Bp. of *Ravenna and according to St Peter *Chrysologus a martyr. Feast day, 23 July.

Apollinarius, Claudius (2nd cent.), Bp. of Hierapolis and an *Apologist. His writings, all lost, included a 'Defence of the Faith', presented to *Marcus Aurelius. Feast day, 8 Jan.

Apollinarius and **Apollinarianism,** the heresy which denied the completeness of Christ's manhood. Apollinarius (or Apollinaris) (c.310–c.390), who was an upholder of orthodoxy against the *Arians, became Bp. of Laodicea c.360. His Christological teaching does not appear to have been the object of criticism until late in his career, but it was condemned by synods in Rome in 374–80 and by the Council of *Constantinople in 381. He seceded from the Church c.375. Most of his extensive writings have been lost and those that survive have been preserved under the names of other authors or in a fragmentary state.

Convinced that only the unchangeable Divine Logos could be the saviour of man with his inherently changeable and fallible mind or soul, Apollinarius denied the presence of a human mind or soul in Christ. While this enabled him to stress the unity of Godhead and flesh in the person of Christ and to repudiate any conception of moral development in His life, it carried the implication that Christ's manhood was not complete. The fundamental objection raised by Catholic orthodoxy is that if there is no complete manhood in Christ, He could not redeem the whole of human nature, but only its physical elements.

Apollonius of Tyana (d.c.98), Neopythagorean philosopher. Anti-Christian writers composed biographies of him which consciously paralleled the Gospel life of Christ.

Apollos. A 'learned' Jew of *Alexandria, apparently already a Christian, though 'knowing only the baptism of John [the Baptist]' (Acts 18: 24–5). M. *Luther and others have argued that he was the author of the Epistle to the *Hebrews.

apologetics. The defence by argument of Christian belief and of the Christian way against alternatives and against criticism. There is a long tradition of such activity from St *Paul's speech on the *Areopagus, the 2nd-cent. *Apologists, and St *Thomas Aquinas. Objections to apologetics were raised by K. *Barth, who insisted that the Gospel's basis in revelation alone yielded no common ground for a defence of Christianity by natural reason. This view has been widely disputed by theologians, both Protestant (e.g. P. *Tillich) and RC (e.g. H. *Küng), for whom man's reason cannot be regarded as wholly corrupt and for whom the natural world, especially human nature, provide rationally defensible intimations of transcendence.

Apologia pro vita sua (1864), J. H. *Newman's 'history of [his] religious opinions' down to his reception into the RC Church in 1845. It was provoked by a gibe of C. *Kingsley in *Macmillan's Magazine* for Jan. 1864.

Apologists. The name given to the Christian writers who (c.120–220) first addressed themselves to the task of making a reasoned defence and recommendation of their faith to outsiders. They include *Aristides, *Justin Martyr, *Athenagoras, *Tatian, *Theophilus, and *Tertullian. They had to contend with both pagan philosophy and the general outlook which it influenced and specifically Jewish objections. Their method was to present Christianity as politically harmless and morally and culturally superior to paganism.

Apolysis. The concluding blessing in E. rites.

apophatic theology, or negative theology. A way of approaching God by denying that any of our concepts can be properly affirmed of Him. It is contrasted with affirmative and symbolic theology. The soul rejects all ideas and images of God and enters the 'darkness that is beyond understanding', where it is 'wholly united with the Ineffable' (*Dionysius the Pseudo-Areopagite). The roots of apophatic theology may be seen in the ban on *images in parts of the OT and a similar rejection of *anthropomorphism by Greek philosophers. In the W. Church apophatic theology tends to be seen as an affirmation of the inadequacy of human understanding in matters Divine. In the E. Church it is seen as an affirmation that the essence of God is unknowable, though He makes Himself known to us through His energies.

Apophthegmata Patrum. Collections of sayings of, or brief stories about, Egyptian monks, known in English as 'Sayings of the Desert Fathers'. The material dates from the 4th–5th cents. and vividly conveys the spirit of early desert spirituality.

apostasy. The abandonment of Christianity. Until 1983 the term was used in the RC Church also of public defection from the RC Church and of desertion by a professed religious who had taken perpetual vows.

aposticha. In the E. Church, brief liturgical hymns or *stichera attached to verses from the Psalter.

Apostle. (1) A title given in the early Church to some of its leaders (1 Cor. 12: 28), especially missionaries, and at Heb. 3: 1 to Christ Himself. The origin and significance of the term is disputed, but some reference to being sent (Gk. ἀποστέλλω, 'I send') is certain. St *Paul claimed the title for himself (Rom. 1: 1 etc.) on the basis of a commission from the Risen Christ, and used it of others, including St *James, the Lord's Brother (Gal. 1: 19). It is used, most often by St *Luke, of the twelve disciples whose names are recorded in Mk. 3: 14–19, Mt. 10: 2–4, and Lk. 6: 13–16, the slight variations perhaps indicating uncertainty rather than fluctuating membership of the group or different names for the same person. The title later came to be restricted to the twelve. In modern usage the term is sometimes applied to the leader of the first Christian mission to a country, e.g. St *Patrick, the 'Apostle of Ireland'. See also APOSTOLIC SUCCESSION.

(2) A name given to the *Epistle read at the Eucharist in the E.Church.

(3) An official of the *Catholic Apostolic Church.

Apostle of the Gentiles. A title given to St *Paul (cf. Gal.2: 7).

Apostles' Creed. A statement of faith used in the W. Church. Like other early *Creeds, it falls into three sections concerned with God the Father, Jesus Christ, and the Holy Spirit. Its title is first found in a letter of St *Ambrose, c.390, by which time the legend of its joint composition by the Apostles was

current. By the early Middle Ages it was everywhere employed at Baptism in the W., and between the 7th and 9th cents. it secured a place in the daily offices.

Apostolic Age. A modern title for the first period in the history of the Church, falling approximately within the lifetime of the *Apostles.

Apostolic Canons. A series of 85 canons attributed to the Apostles; they form the concluding chapter of the '*Apostolic Constitutions'. They mostly deal with the responsibilities and moral conduct of the clergy. The first 50 were translated into Latin by *Dionysius Exiguus and so became part of the *canon law of the W. Church.

Apostolic Church Order. An early Christian document containing regulations on ecclesiastical practice and moral discipline. Its contents are ascribed to various Apostles, but it was probably composed, in Greek, in Egypt c.300.

Apostolic Constitutions. A collection of ecclesiastical laws dating from c.350–80 and almost certainly of Syrian provenance. There has been much speculation about the compiler, who was clearly an *Arian, perhaps *Julian the 'Arian'.

Apostolic Delegate. A person appointed by the Pope to keep the *Vatican informed of ecclesiastical affairs in the territory assigned to him.

Apostolic Fathers. A title given since the 17th cent. to those Fathers of the age immediately after the NT period whose works survive in whole or part. They are *Clement of Rome, *Ignatius, *Hermas, *Polycarp, and *Papias, and the authors of the 'Epistle of *Barnabas', the 'Epistle to *Diognetus', 2 Clement, and the '*Didache'.

Apostolic See. The see of Rome, so called because of its traditional association with the Apostles St *Peter and St *Paul.

apostolic succession. The method whereby the ministry of the Church is held to be derived from Christ through the *apostles by a continuous succession; it has usually been associated with an assertion that the succession has been maintained by a series of *bishops. The continuity of the succession, emphasized by *Clement of Rome before the end of the 1st cent., has occasionally been disputed; the necessity of it, widely taught within the historic Church, is denied by most Protestants and asserted only with qualifications by some other theologians. Doubts about the continuity of the apostolic succession were among the reasons leading to the condemnation of *Anglican Orders (q.v.) by Rome in 1896. More recently the maintenance of the 'historic episcopate' has been an issue in schemes of *reunion involving Anglicans and other bodies.

Apostolic Tradition, The. A liturgical treatise now generally held to be the work of St *Hippolytus (d.c.236), containing a detailed description of rites and practices which are alleged to be traditional. It includes rites of *Ordination and *Baptism, and a *Eucharistic Prayer which was used as a basis of the second Eucharistic Prayer in the 1970 RC Missal. Written in Greek, it survives in Latin and Oriental translations.

Apostolicae Curae (1896). *Leo XIII's Bull declaring *Anglican Orders invalid.

Apostolici (Lat., 'Apostolics'). The bodies to whom the title has been applied, by themselves or others, include: (1) some *Gnostic communities of the 2nd–4th cents.; (2) an ascetic body which flourished in the 12th cent. around *Cologne and at Périgueux in France; (3) a sect originating at Parma in 1260, which drew its inspiration from *Franciscan teaching on poverty and was condemned in 1286 and 1291; (4) certain *Anabaptist sects.

Apostolicity. One of the four characteristics of the Church set forth in the *Nicene Creed. On a Catholic view the word means identifiable with the Apostles by succession (see APOSTOLIC SUCCESSION) and continuity of doctrine, to which RCs would add communion with the 'see of Peter'. By Protestants the word is generally understood to mean 'primitive', as contrasted with post-apostolic corruptions. See also NOTES OF THE CHURCH.

apotheosis. The assimilation of a man to a god. Greeks and Romans made no firm distinction between gods and men, and from at least the 4th cent. BC cults were rendered to rulers as if to gods, though it does not appear that they were credited with supernatural powers. The Christians' refusal to take part in the cult of Roman emperors has sometimes been seen as a reason for their persecution by the government, but implausibly, since participation was not legally obligatory on any subject. See also DEIFICATION.

apparitor. An officer chosen by an ecclesiastical judge to summon persons to appear before, and to execute the decrees of, his court.

appeals. Appeals by clergy and laity to authorities higher than their diocesan bishops were based on Roman civil law and regulated by several councils. In England from the time of Henry II successive kings had tried to limit appeals to Rome; they were finally abolished in 1534 by *Henry VIII, who made the Court of *Delegates the final arbiter in ecclesiastical causes. Appeals in the C of E are now governed by the *Ecclesiastical Jurisdiction Measure 1963.

Appellants. (1) The 31 RC secular priests who in 1598–9 appealed to Rome for the cancellation of the appointment of G. *Blackwell as *archpriest and superior of the mission. The original Appeal failed, but after further Appeals in 1601 and 1602 Blackwell was reprimanded.
(2) The name given to those of *Jansenist and *Gallican sentiments who rejected the condemnation by '*Unigenitus' (1713) of 101 propositions from P. *Quesnel's *Reflexions morales*. In 1717 four bishops appealed against the Papal Bull to the next General Council; they were soon joined by other bishops, the *Sorbonne, and some clergy. In 1718 *Clement XI formally condemned and excommunicated them.

Appian Way. The road constructed by the censor Appius Claudius Caecus in 312 BC from Rome to S. Italy. St *Paul, travelling on the Appian Way, was met by groups of Christians at Appii Forum and Three Taverns (Acts 28: 15).

appropriation. The practice of annexing to a monastery, college, or other spiritual body the *tithes and profits of a parish. It was then usually necessary to endow and appoint a *vicar to perform the parochial duties. See also IMPROPRIATION.

apron. The shortened form of *cassock which is part of the distinctive dress of

Anglican bishops, deans, and archdeacons. It is now seldom worn.

apse. A semicircular or polygonal eastern end to a chancel. It was a universal feature of the primitive *basilican type of church architecture. The altar stood on the chord of the apse, with seats for the bishop and presbyters in the curved space behind.

APUC ('Association for the Promotion of the Unity of Christendom'). A society formed in 1857 to further the cause of reunion, especially between the C of E and the RC Church. RCs had to withdraw in 1864 and it was disbanded in 1921.

Aquarians. An early sect or sects which used water instead of wine in the Eucharist.

Aquaviva, Claudio (1543–1615), fifth General of the *Jesuits from 1581. Under his leadership the Society was consolidated both in respect of its internal structures and its characteristic approach to ministry. Its membership increased from *c*.5,000 to *c*.13,000. The '*Ratio Studiorum' (q.v.) was completed, as well as a set of guidelines (or 'Directory') for the use of the *Spiritual Exercises*. He also overcame a number of attempts to change the Society's form of government which were instigated by Spanish Jesuits with powerful support.

Aquila, St. See PRISCILLA, ST.

Aquila, Version of. A Greek version of the OT. It was the work of Aquila, who became a proselyte to Judaism and learnt Hebrew from the *Rabbis; he used this knowledge to make a revision of the *Septuagint, bringing it into line with the official Hebrew text. His translation, which was probably finished *c*.140, is very literal.

Aquileia, on the Adriatic coast, became an important city during the late Roman Empire. According to legend it was evangelized by St *Mark, but the beginnings of the Church cannot be traced beyond the 3rd cent. In 381 its bishop, Valerian, appears as *metropolitan of the Churches in the area and under him and his successor, *Chromatius, Aquileia was a centre of learning. The floor of the basilica (rebuilt in the 11th cent.) is covered with early 4th-cent. mosaics.

Aquinas, St Thomas. See THOMAS AQUINAS, ST.

Aramaic. The Semitic language which was the vernacular in Palestine in the time of Christ and which He almost certainly used. In later OT times it increasingly ousted *Hebrew as the spoken language of Palestine, and a few sections of the OT are written in it. By NT times Aramaic paraphrases of Scripture (*Targums) were issued to satisfy the needs of the people. Many passages in the NT reflect Aramaic modes of thought and occasionally Aramaic words are preserved (e.g. Mk. 5: 41).

Arator (6th cent.), Christian Latin poet. He left the imperial service to become a subdeacon at Rome, where he was associated with Pope *Vigilius. His *De actibus apostolorum*, a version of the Book of Acts in hexameters, provides an elaborate exegesis of the symbolic meaning in the biblical narrative. It was widely studied.

archaeology, Christian. The phrase commonly denotes the study of the monuments, as distinct from the documents, of early Christianity for the light they can throw on the thought and religious life of the Church, especially in the first six centuries. The beginnings of Christian archaeology are associated with explorations of the Roman *catacombs in the late 16th and early 17th centuries, and Rome remained the main focus of attention for the next 250 years. Since the beginning of the 20th cent. research has spread to areas outside Rome and now encompasses the whole of the ancient Mediterranean world, including N. Africa. In Britain especially, there has been a trend towards including the excavation and scientific study of Christian sites of the medieval period within the field of Christian archaeology.

The main classes of monuments studied are *cemeteries, buildings (chiefly churches, *baptisteries, and *monasteries), sculpture, paintings, *mosaics, textiles, liturgical apparatus, and miscellaneous objects such as *lamps, medals, and *rings. The study of such material provides information that could not be obtained from literary records alone, particularly with regard to the lives of the lower social classes of Christian society and the ordinary routine of Christian observance.

archangel (Gk., 'chief *angel'). In Christian tradition *Michael and *Gabriel are reckoned among the archangels.

archbishop. The title, applied in the 4th–5th cents. to *patriarchs and holders of other outstanding sees, came to be extended to all *metropolitans having jurisdiction over an ecclesiastical province.

Archbishops' Council. A body set up by the *National Institutions Measure 1998 to focus the leadership and co-ordinate the central structures of the C of E. It brings together a number of functions previously performed by various committees of the *Church Commissioners and the General *Synod. It reports annually to the General Synod, and it may introduce legislation into the synodical process. Its membership comprises the Abps. of *Canterbury and *York; a number of elected officers and members of the General Synod representing each of its Houses, including the *Proluctors of the *Convocations; one Church Estates Commissioner; and up to six further members appointed by the Archbishops in consultation with the General Synod.

archdeacon. In the Anglican Communion, a cleric having administrative authority delegated to him by the bishop; the territory assigned to him is known as his archdeaconry and gives him a territorial title, e.g. 'Archdeacon of Lindsey'. The duties normally include general disciplinary supervision of the clergy and care over the temporal administration of ecclesiastical property. An archdeacon was originally the chief of the *deacons who assisted diocesan bishops in their work.

archdiocese. A diocese of which the holder is *ex-officio* *archbishop, e.g. *Canterbury, or in the RC Church *Westminster.

Arches Court of Canterbury. The Court of the province of *Canterbury which formerly met in *Bow Church ('S.Maria de Arcibus'). It now has no original jurisdiction but hears appeals from the diocesan *Consistory Courts within the province in cases not involving doctrine, ritual, or ceremonial.

archimandrite. In the E. Church the term originally meant either the head of one religious house or the head of a group of monasteries; today it is used simply as a title of honour for an unmarried priest.

archpriest. In early times the title was given to the senior presbyter of a city who performed many of the bishop's liturgical and governmental functions in his absence or during a vacancy; in the countryside it was given to the cleric who presided over the group of parishes which united for the Sunday Eucharist and other functions previously performed by the bishop. In the RC Church it was given to the superior in charge of the secular priests from foreign seminaries sent to England between 1598 and 1621. The dispute between the *Appellants (1) and G.*Blackwell is known as the 'Archpriest Controversy'. In the Orthodox Church the title survives as one of honour; it is the highest rank which a married priest can attain.

arcosolium. An arched burial niche of the Roman period, built or excavated above or below ground, and particularly those dug in the galleries of the *catacombs. Bodies were placed in tombs cut into the niche; they were also sometimes placed on or under a stone slab which divided the niche horizontally and sometimes served as an altar.

area bishop. In the C of E, an unofficial designation of a *suffragan bishop to whom certain powers have been legally delegated by the diocesan bishop when a diocese has been divided into areas under the Dioceses Measure 1978.

Areopagite, the. *Dionysius (6), so named from a wrong identification with the Dionysius converted by St *Paul's speech on the *Areopagus (Acts 17: 34).

Areopagus (Greek for 'Mars' Hill'). A spur of land near the western end of the Acropolis in Athens. The name was also applied to an oligarchical council which met on the hill. It is not clear whether, when St *Paul was brought to the Areopagus to explain his teaching (Acts 17: 19), it was before the court or whether the place was merely chosen as convenient for a meeting.

Argentina, Christianity in. Christianity was brought to Argentina by the *Franciscans, who arrived in 1539, followed by the *Jesuits some 40 years later. When the former Spanish colony became independent in 1816, RCism remained the State religion, and the RC Church claims a membership of 25 million, over 90 per cent of the population. There is, however, a shortage of priests and a strong body of *anticlerical feeling in the country. Protestant Churches, who began missionary work in the 19th cent., constitute just under 3 per cent of the population. Of these the *Pentecostals form the largest group.

Arianism. The main heresy which denied the full Divinity of Christ, so called after its author, *Arius. Arius seems to have held that the Son of God was not eternal but created by the Father from nothing as an instrument for the creation of the world; He was therefore not God by nature, but a creature susceptible of change, even though He differed from other creatures in being the one direct creation of God; His dignity as Son of God was given Him by the Father on account of his foreseen righteousness. Earlier scholars saw this teaching as an adulteration of Christian faith by pagan philosophical concerns; recently it has been argued that a major objective of the Arians was to distinguish the Divinity of the Father from that of the Son in order to avoid ascribing the limitations of the Incarnate Son to the full Divinity which they attributed only to the Father.

The teaching of Arius, though condemned by a synod at *Alexandria (c.320), spread until *Constantine, anxious for peace in the Empire, called a General Council which met at *Nicaea in 325. The Council, largely under the leadership of *Athanasius, defined the Catholic faith in the coeternity and coequality of the Father and the Son; the famous term '*homoousios' was used to express their consubstantiality. Constantine, at first a supporter of the Nicene faith, soon wavered, and in 350 Constantius, an avowed Arian, became sole ruler. Among the Arians three main groups emerged: the '*Anomoeans', also known in modern times as 'Neo-Arians', pressed the differences between the Father and the Son; the '*Homoeans' tried to avoid dogmatic precision by affirming that the Son is similar to the Father 'according to the Scriptures'; the '*Semiarians' favoured the term 'homoiousios' as expressing both the similarity and the distinction between the first two Persons of the Trinity. A Homoean formula, drawn up by a Council of *Sirmium (357), was accepted by a double Council of E. and W. bishops which met at

Seleucia and *Ariminum respectively in 359. This crowning victory of Arianism frightened the Semiarians into the ranks of orthodoxy, and with the death of Constantius (361) Arianism lost its chief supporter. In 362 Athanasius held a Council which helped to unite a wide spectrum of opponents of Arianism. In the W. Arius had little direct influence, though for some time a more straightforward biblical form of *subordinationism was a powerful force there. The brilliant expositions of the Nicene faith by the *Cappadocian Fathers prepared the way for the final victory of orthodoxy at the Council of *Constantinople in 381.

Driven from the Empire, Arianism retained a hold among the Teutonic tribes, which prevented their assimilation with their Catholic subjects when they overran most of the W. Empire and caused persecutions in Spain and N. Africa. The conversion of the Franks to Catholicism (496) was the prelude to the disappearance of Arianism.

aridity or **dryness**. The term is used to refer either generally to a lack of conscious fervour and delight in the Christian life as a whole or more specifically to a lack of fervour and delight in prayer and other spiritual exercises. When due to factors outside a person's control, spiritual writers agree that it provides an occasion to recall one's own weakness and to appreciate that the service of God does not depend on felt consolations; regular Christian practices should not be abandoned.

Ariminum and Seleucia, Synods of. Two synods to which the Emp. Constantius summoned the bishops of the East and West respectively in 359 to deal with the *Arian dispute. Although the majority at Ariminum (Rimini) were orthodox, under imperial pressure they subscribed to an Arianizing Creed. This was also accepted at Seleucia.

Aristeas, Letter of. A Jewish pseudepigraphical letter which contains a legend of how the LXX came to be miraculously written. Its composition has been variously dated between 200 BC and AD 33.

Aristides (2nd cent.) of Athens, Christian philosopher and *Apologist. In an 'Apology' presented either to the Emp. Hadrian in 124 or to Antoninus Pius (d. 161), Aristides sought to defend the existence and eternity of God, and to show that Christians had a fuller understanding of His nature than the barbarians, Greeks, or Jews, and that they alone live according to His precepts.

Aristion (1st cent.). According to *Papias (as reported by *Eusebius), he was a primary authority, with *John the Presbyter, for the traditions about the Lord.

Aristo of Pella (c.140), *Apologist. He apparently wrote a (lost) 'Disputation'; in it Jason, a baptized Jew, converts Papiscus, a fellow Jew, by proving the fulfilment of the Messianic prophecies in Christ.

Aristobulus, St. In Rom. 16: 10 St *Paul sent greetings to the 'household of Aristobulus'. According to a Spanish legend he became Bp. of Britonia (modern Mondoñedo) in Spain. Feast day, 30 or 31 Oct. He has sometimes been identified with the Aristobulus who, according to the Greek *menologies, was one of the seventy disciples (Lk. 10: 1), a brother of St *Barnabas and father-in-law of St *Peter. Feast day, 15 or 16 Mar.

Aristotle (384–322 BC), philosopher. He was a member of the group which gathered round *Plato in Athens. He was later tutor to the future Alexander the Great. On his return to Athens, though he did not sever his connection with the Academy, he opened a rival school at the Lyceum in 335.

Though he was a disciple of Plato, his philosophical position was very different. Whereas Plato set out from a world of 'ideas', Aristotle asserted that an idea exists only as expressed in the individual object. Thus he held that, so far from there being an idea 'tree' possessing existence in its own right, it is the union of the 'form' tree with 'matter' which makes the real individual tree. This view required a theory of causation to account for the conjunction of form and matter, and Aristotle was thus led to postulate a 'First Cause', though he did not hold this supreme cause to be personal in the Christian sense.

Aristotle's philosophy was regarded with suspicion in the early Church, largely because it was thought to lead to a materialistic view of the world. Aristotle was conceived as diametrically opposed to Plato, who was held in high esteem. In the W. knowledge of his works was gradually recovered between the 9th and 13th centuries. Some of his scientific works were transmitted indirectly through Arabic translations and were therefore theologically suspect. Even though such great Christian philosophers as St *Albertus Magnus and St *Thomas Aquinas built their systems on an avowedly Aristotelian basis, it was only in 1879 with the commendation of Thomistic Aristotelianism in the encyclical '*Aeterni Patris' that the suspicion was entirely dissipated.

Arius (d. 336), heresiarch. Probably born in Libya between c.260 and 280, he was ordained in *Alexandria and put in charge of one of the main churches there. About 319 he came forward as a champion of subordinationist teaching about the Person of Christ; he was condemned by a Council at Alexandria and excommunicated. The Council of *Nicaea (325) also condemned him. Owing to the influence at court of *Eusebius of Nicomedia, he was recalled from exile probably c.334. He died suddenly in Constantinople. See also ARIANISM.

Ark. (1) The Ark which *Noah built to preserve life during the *Flood (q.v.).

(2) The Ark of the Covenant, the most sacred religious symbol of the Hebrew people and believed to represent the Presence of God. It was in the form of a wooden rectangular box, overlaid with gold inside and out. According to the traditional accounts the Israelites carried the Ark from the time of the *Exodus into the land of *Canaan. In Solomon's *Temple its home was the 'Holy of Holies', which the *High Priest alone entered once a year. It was apparently captured when *Jerusalem fell to the Babylonians c.586 BC and nothing further is known of its history.

The Christian Fathers interpreted the Ark of Noah as typifying the Church, the Ark of the Covenant as a symbol of the Lord.

Arles, Synods of. Among the more important were those of: 314, summoned by *Constantine to deal with the *Donatist schism; 353, an *Arianizing Council; 1234, against the *Albigensian heresy; and 1263, which condemned the doctrines of *Joachim of Fiore.

Armagh. Archiepiscopal see in the North of *Ireland. According to tradition, it was founded by St *Patrick, and from the 7th cent. it was the most powerful Church in Ireland. The English conquest of Ireland, with government centred in *Dublin, diminished Armagh's independence. In 1552 the first Protestant bishop was appointed, and henceforth there was both a Protestant and a RC succession.

Armagh, Book of. A 9th cent. vellum codex now in *Trinity College, Dublin. It contains a collection of documents relating to St *Patrick, a complete non-*Vulgate Latin NT, and a copy of the Life of St *Martin of Tours by *Sulpicius Severus. Written in 807-8, it was treated as a relic of St Patrick and used for the swearing of oaths.

Armenia, Christianity in. The Armenians were converted by *Gregory the Illuminator, who in 314 was consecrated bishop by the Metropolitan of Caesarea in Cappadocia. In 374 the Armenians repudiated their dependence on the Church of Caesarea. In the early part of the 5th cent. St *Isaac the Great and St *Mesrob increased the strength of the Church by inventing a national script, and the Bible and Liturgy were translated into Armenian. Owing to wars, the Armenians were not represented at the Council of *Chalcedon (451), but in 555 the Armenian Church repudiated that Council and has since been reputed *Monophysite. The Armenians of Little Armenia (or Cilicia, an independent kingdom from the end of the 12th cent. to 1375) accepted union with Rome in 1307 and this was confirmed at the Council of *Florence (1438-9). The Armenians of Greater Armenia sent representatives to the Council of Florence, which issued the famous instruction 'Pro Armenis' on the Sacraments, but the union thus achieved had little effect and an independent line of patriarchs was re-established in 1441.

There are thought to be some 5 million Armenians of whom the majority profess allegiance to the Armenian Church, and c.100,000 are in communion with Rome. The dogmas of the Armenian Church are similar to those of the E. Orthodox Church, and the liturgy substantially that of St *Basil in classical Armenian.

armill. One of the British *Coronation regalia. The word means a bracelet, but in the *Liber Regalis and elsewhere it has been applied to a garment resembling a *stole

and held to signify the quasi-priestly character of the anointed king. At the coronation of Elizabeth II (1953) the use of armills in the form of bracelets was restored, the stole royal being given immediately afterwards.

Arminianism. Jacobus Arminius (Jakob Hermansz or Harmensz, 1560-1609) was a Dutch Reformed theologian, ordained in 1588. Study of the Epistle to the *Romans led him to doubt the Calvinistic doctrine of *predestination. In 1603 he was appointed professor at *Leiden and he was immediately drawn into controversy with F. *Gomar. He obtained possession of his chair only after a disputation in which he cleared himself of charges of *Pelagianism and *Socinianism. He tried, unsuccessfully, to obtain the revision of the *Belgic Confession and *Heidelberg Catechism.

Arminian doctrines, formally set out in the *Remonstrance of 1610, were a theological reaction against the deterministic logic of *Calvinism. The Arminians insisted that the Divine sovereignty was compatible with a real human free will; that Christ had died for all and not only for the elect; and that both the *Supralapsarian and the *Sublapsarian views of predestination were unbiblical. The Arminians were condemned at the Synod of *Dort (1618-19); many of them were banished and others persecuted. As representatives of a more liberal school of theology than the strict Calvinists, however, they influenced the formation of modern Protestant theology. The anti-Calvinist trend in 17th-cent. English theology was termed 'Arminian' by its opponents, though it is doubtful if Arminius' teaching had much direct influence in this case.

Arnauld, Antoine (1612-94), French theologian and philosopher. A brother of Angelique *Arnauld (see following entry), from 1638 he was in touch with *Saint-Cyran and in 1641 he retired to *Port-Royal. His book De la fréquente communion (1643), with its stress on the need for a thorough preparation for Communion and its emphasis on the right dispositions, did much to propagate *Jansenist principles among a wide public. From 1644 he was the acknowledged leader of the Jansenists. An attack on *Jesuit method in the confessional led to his being censured by the *Sorbonne in

1656 and solemnly degraded; after the '*Peace of the Church' of 1668, his doctorate was restored. With P. *Nicole he then began a major treatise against the *Calvinists, *La Perpétuité de la foi catholique touchant l'Eucharistie* (1669–74).

Arnauld, Jacqueline Marie Angélique (1591–1661), 'Mère Angélique'. A sister of Antoine *Arnauld, she became Abbess of *Port-Royal in 1602. She shared without protest in the relaxed discipline of the house until she was converted by a sermon in 1608. She promptly introduced drastic reforms. The community increased and in 1625 she moved it to a larger house in Paris. Differences with Sébastien Zamet, Bp. of Langres, led her to resign as Abbess in 1630 but after the election of her sister Agnes as Abbess in 1636, she again exercised (indirect) power. She came under the influence of *Saint-Cyran, under whom the community became an enthusiastic upholder of *Jansenist principles and practice. From 1642 to 1654 she was again Abbess.

Arndt, Johann (1555–1621), *Lutheran theologian and mystical writer. He is chiefly remembered for his *Vier Bücher vom wahren Christentum* (1606); against the penal theory of the *Atonement, he dwelt on the work of Christ in the heart of man.

Arnobius (3rd–4th cent.), Christian apologist. In his *Adversus Nationes* he defended the consonance of the Christian religion with the best pagan philosophy.

Arnobius Junior (5th cent.), a monk, probably of African origin, who left an account of a debate between himself and an Egyptian *Monophysite. He also wrote allegorizing 'Commentaries' on the Psalms and notes on the Gospels. The '*Praedestinatus' has sometimes been ascribed to him.

Arnold of Brescia (d. 1155), reformer. A *canon regular, *c.*1139 he had to leave Brescia after taking part in a conflict between the bishop and reformers. In France he supported Peter *Abelard and at the Council of *Sens (1140) he was condemned with him. He went to Rome in 1146/7. After a brief reconciliation with the Church, he backed the senate in its rejection of the temporal dominion of the Pope; he was excommunicated in 1148 and later captured by the Emp. *Frederick Barbarossa

and hanged. It is probable that he discouraged his followers from receiving the sacraments from priests guilty of *simony, but like other reformers of the time, he was mainly concerned to revive the ideal of apostolic poverty. He developed this into an assault on the possession of worldly goods and the exercise of secular authority by the Church.

Arnold, Gottfried (1666–1714), German Protestant theologian and devotional writer. His main work, the *Unparteiische Kirchen- und Ketzer-Historie* (1699–1700), is important as a history of Protestant mysticism and for its use of out-of-the-way documents. After 1701 he applied himself increasingly to pastoral work, and his writings of this period are devotional. He is also well known as a hymn-writer.

Arnold, Matthew (1822–88), poet and literary critic. The eldest son of T. *Arnold, from 1851 to 1883 he was a Government Inspector of Schools; from 1857 to 1867 he was also Professor of Poetry at Oxford. He held that religion should be concerned with conduct and not speculation. Christianity stressed personal rather than national conduct and suffused morality with emotion and so with happiness.

Arnold, Thomas (1795–1842), Headmaster of Rugby from 1828 to 1841. He fostered a system of education based on a foundation of religious training, seeking to educate the sons of middle-class parents into a high sense of duty, of public service, and of the importance of personal character. He objected to the *Tractarians on the ground of their ecclesiasticism; he was a founder of the *Broad Church movement.

Arnulf, St (*c.*580–*c.*640), Bp. of Metz. He rose to high position in the court of Austrasia. About 614 he was consecrated Bp. of Metz and from 623 he played a large part in the government of the Ardennes. He later retired to a deserted place for prayer. Married before his consecration, he was an ancestor of the Carolingian kings of France. Feast day, 18 July or 16 Aug.

ars praedicandi (Lat., 'the art of preaching'). The medieval *artes praedicandi* provided instruction in the composition of sermons either as an adjunct to a collection of sermons or as a manual which circulated with other aids for the preacher. The genre received its distinctive form in the 12th cent., the first major example being that by *Alan of Lille.

Artemon (also **Artemas**) (3rd cent.), *Adoptionist heretic. *Eusebius of Caesarea says that *Paul of Samosata revived his heresy and that the '*Little Labyrinth' was directed against his teaching.

Articles. See FORTY-TWO ARTICLES; IRISH ARTICLES; LAMBETH ARTICLES; ORGANIC ARTICLES; SIX ARTICLES; TEN ARTICLES; THIRTY-NINE ARTICLES; TWELVE ARTICLES.

artophorion. In the E. Church, the *tabernacle on the altar in which the Blessed Sacrament is reserved; also the small portable ones used for taking Communion to the sick.

Arundel, Thomas (1353–1414), Abp. successively of *York and *Canterbury. He was a prominent politician, several times Chancellor of England. He strenuously opposed the *Lollards, holding a provincial council against them at Oxford in 1408. The Constitutions he issued in 1409 were designed to ensure orthodoxy.

Asaph, St (late 6th cent.), Welsh saint. According to a 12th-cent. reference, he was a disciple of St *Kentigern, and, when the latter returned to Scotland, succeeded him as head of the monastery of Llanelwy (later called *St Asaph) and became the first Welsh bishop of the see. Feast day 5 (formerly 11) May.

Asbury, Francis (1745–1816). One of the first *Methodist bishops in America. He was sent to America by J. *Wesley in 1771. When the American Methodists became a separate organization in 1784, he and Thomas *Coke became joint superintendents. His *Journal* is historically valuable.

Ascension of Christ. The statement in the Creeds that Christ 'ascended into heaven' is based mainly on Acts 1: 1–9 where, after 40 days of appearances, the Risen Lord speaks to the Apostles and is then taken up in a cloud. The reference to the Apostles' return to *Jerusalem from the Mount of *Olives (Acts 1: 12) gave rise to the tradition that it took place there. Lk.24: 50–53 by contrast seems to imply that this withdrawal of Christ into Heaven occurred at *Bethany on the evening of the day of the Resurrection.

Behind St *Luke's narrative stands the conviction of the early Church that God had vindicated Jesus after His crucifixion. The Ascension marks the close of the post-Resurrection appearances and signifies the rule of Christ in the present (cf. 1 Cor. 15: 25). Doctrinally it implies Christ's humanity being taken into Heaven. Ascension Day, kept on the 6th Thursday, i.e. the 40th day, after Easter, is one of the chief feasts of the Christian year.

Ascent of Mount Carmel, The. The title of a treatise by St *John of the Cross.

ascetical theology. See SPIRITUALITY and PURGATIVE, ILLUMINATIVE, AND UNITIVE WAYS.

asceticism. The term, derived from the Greek word for 'exercise' or 'training', denotes (1) practices employed to combat vices and develop virtues and (2) the renunciation of various facets of customary social life and comfort or the adoption of painful conditions for religious reasons. In the NT there are repeated exhortations to self-denial. In the early Church many ascetic practices seem to have been common, including renunciation of marriage, home, and property; some ascetics practised extreme forms of fasting and self-deprivation. The theoretical foundations of Christian asceticism were developed by *Clement of Alexandria and *Origen. Taking over from the *Stoics the idea of ascetic action as a purification of the soul from its passions, they saw it as a necessary means for loving God more perfectly and for attaining to contemplation. Origen also stresses its value as a preparation for martyrdom. The Desert Fathers from the late 3rd cent. and the subsequent monastic tradition tended to favour a more temporate external asceticism and to lay more stress on interior abnegation and cultivation of virtues. In the Middle Ages, with the growing devotion to the humanity of Christ, asceticism became increasingly inspired by a desire for conformation to His sufferings. This led to more violent forms of asceticism, such as flagellation and the wearing of hair-shirts and chains. At the end of the Middle Ages there was a twofold reaction: various movements stressed the interior life and questioned the value of external ascetic observances, and the Protestant Reformers, with their insistence on *justification by faith, denied the propriety of many conventional works of penance. The ascetical idea, however, was upheld in the RC Church. Among the *Puritans asceticism, in the negative sense of abstinence from particular pleasures and recreations, was widely upheld. In a more positive sense it also found a place in *Methodism and among the *Tractarians and their successors. According to its classical Christian exponents, asceticism is not an end in itself but essentially a preparation for the life of union with God.

Ash Wednesday. The first day of *Lent. At one time public penitents were ceremoniously admitted to begin their *penance on this day; when this discipline was dropped, the general penance of the congregation took its place. This was symbolized by the imposition of ashes on the heads of clergy and people, a rite still ordered in the Roman Missal and now restored in many parts of the Anglican Communion.

Aske, Robert (d. 1537), leader of the '*Pilgrimage of Grace'. In 1536 he put himself at the head of the 'Pilgrimage' when rebellion broke out in Yorkshire. After treating with the royal leaders, in 1537 he returned northward with a promise of the redress of grievances. After a fresh outbreak of violence Aske was seized, condemned for treason, and hanged in chains.

Askew (or **Ayscough), Anne** (1521–46), Protestant martyr. In 1545 she was arrested on account of her beliefs about the Eucharist. She refused to recant or, even under torture, to incriminate leading Protestants at Court. She was burnt at *Smithfield.

Asperges. In the W. Church the sprinkling of *holy water over the altar and people after the entrance rite at Mass on Sundays.

aspersion. The method of *Baptism whereby the candidate is merely sprinkled with the baptismal water. It is held to be permissible only in exceptional cases.

aspirant. One who aspires to a vocation to the *religious life.

Assemblies of God. The name taken by many autonomous but usually loosely-associated national groupings of individual *Pentecostal Churches, virtually forming a denomination within Pentecostalism. The earliest was formed in the USA in 1914.

Assemblies of the French Clergy. The quinquennial meetings of representatives of the French RC clergy which were an established institution from the end of the 16th cent. until the French Revolution. The 'extraordinary' Assembly of 1682 approved the *Gallican Articles.

Assent, Declaration of. A declaration of assent to the *Thirty-Nine Articles, the Book of *Common Prayer and the *Ordinal (described as the 'historic formularies' of the C of E) which is required of all bishops, clergy, readers, and lay workers of the C of E as a condition of taking office.

Assisi. A city in the Umbrian Hills, famous as the birthplace of St *Francis. The remains of St Francis and St *Clare rest in two of its basilicas. The *Portiuncula chapel is in a basilica in the plain below Assisi.

Associations, Law of. The French law of 1901 which enlarged trade-union rights but also required all religious orders which should have requested authorization under a decree of 1804, but had not done so, to regularize their position. Under the Radical government which came to power after the 1902 elections, religious orders which had not requested authorization were closed forthwith, and those which requested authorization, apart from females engaged in charitable work, were refused it in 1903. In 1904 all religious were banned from teaching in France.

Assumption of the BVM. The belief that the BVM, 'having completed her earthly life, was in body and soul assumed into heavenly glory' (definition, 1950). The belief was unknown in the early Church; it first appears in certain NT apocrypha dating from the 4th cent. The doctrine was formulated in orthodox circles in the West by *Gregory of Tours (d. 594); it seems to have been widely known by the end of the 7th cent. and it was defended by various *Schoolmen. In 1950 *Pius XII defined it. In the E. Church belief in the corporal assumption is general, though in less precise terms than those of the RC definition.

The date on which the feast of the Assumption is celebrated (15 Aug.) is probably connected with the dedication of some church to the BVM. In the C of E the feast disappeared from the BCP in 1549, but it is now observed in many places. In parts of the Anglican Communion 15 Aug. is kept as the main feast of the BVM, though without reference to the Assumption.

Assumptionists (Augustinians of the Assumption). A religious congregation founded at Nîmes in 1845. Its members follow a modification of the *Augustinian rule. Their work includes the care of asylums and schools, the dissemination of literature, and missionary work.

Assyrian Christians. A name adopted in modern times by members of the *Church of the East (q.v.) who claim descent from the ancient Assyrians. Their Patriarch is now officially styled 'Catholicos Patriarch of the Assyrian Church'. More recently the term 'Assyrian' has sometimes been adopted by members of the *Syrian Orthodox Church abroad.

asteriscus. A utensil placed over the bread during the Byzantine Liturgy to keep it from contact with the veil that covers it. It is removed at the *Sanctus.

Asterius (d. after 341), the 'Sophist', *Arian theologian. He was present at the Council of Antioch in 341. Fragments of his works are preserved by St *Athanasius (from his *Syntagmation*) and by *Marcellus of Ancyra. Homilies on the Psalms ascribed to him have been recovered in modern times, though some scholars think these are the work of another Asterius.

Astruc, Jean (1684–1766), physician and Pentateuchal critic. In his (anonymous) *Conjectures sur les Mémoires originaux dont il paroît que Moyse s'est servi pour composer le Livre de la Genèse* (1753) he maintained that in its present form the Book of *Genesis was a piecing together of earlier documents.

asylum, right of. See SANCTUARY.

Athanasian Creed. A profession of faith which has been widely used in W. Christendom. It expounds the doctrines of the *Trinity and *Incarnation, adding a list of the most important events in the Lord's life; it includes *anathemas against those who do not believe its affirmations. The attribution to St *Athanasius has been generally abandoned, chiefly on the ground that it contains doctrinal expressions which arose only in later controversies. It was probably composed after 428.

Athanasius, St (*c.*296–373), Bp. of *Alexandria. He was secretary to *Alexander, Bp. of Alexandria, and accompanied him to the Council of *Nicaea (325), succeeding him as bishop in 328. He incurred the enmity of the powerful *Arianizing party, who secured his exile from Alexandria on a number of occasions between 336 and 366.

In his *De Incarnatione* he expounds how God the Word (*Logos), by His union with mankind, restored to fallen man the *image of God, and by His death and resurrection overcame death. Many scholars date this work before *c.*318; others place it some 15–20 years later. As bishop Athanasius was the greatest and most consistent theological opponent of *Arianism. Between 339 and 359 he wrote a series of works in defence of the true Divinity of the Son. From *c.*361 he worked to reconcile the *Semiarian party to the Nicene term '*homoousios' ('of one substance'). He also argued for the Divinity of the Holy Spirit in his *Epistles to Serapion*. As the friend of *Pachomius and *Serapion, and closely linked with (perhaps the biographer of) *Antony, he aided the ascetic movement in Egypt and was the first to introduce knowledge of monasticism to the West. Feast day, 2 May.

Athanasius (the Athonite), St (*c.*920–1003). He became a monk in Bithynia but migrated to Mount *Athos, where he established the first of its famous monasteries (961). He became Abbot-General of the communities on the Mount, of which 58 existed when he died. Feast day, 5 July.

atheism now normally means disbelief in God. Until the expression '*agnosticism' came into general use in the 19th cent., 'atheist' was used of those who thought the existence of God an unprovable thesis. Of such there are three main groups: philosophical agnostics, materialists, and pantheists, any of whom may be atheist, but need not be. For instance, the philosophical agnostic normally says that the evidence is not sufficient to compel us either to assert or deny the existence of God, but it is only if he adds that the assertion of God's existence is not merely rash but meaningless that he is strictly to be called an atheist. Modern atheism is usually seen by its adherents as a way of safeguarding an affirmation of human freedom and man's ability to control his own destiny. Paradoxically 'atheism' is regarded by some Christian theologians (e.g. J. *Moltmann) as a legitimate means of avoiding positing God as one entity among others, an infinite Being encroaching on finite beings.

Athelstan (c.894–939), King of England from 927. He was recognized as King of the Mercians on his father's death in 924 and by 927 had so extended his rule that he was the first king of all England. He was a generous benefactor of the Church and during his reign contacts were established with rulers and ecclesiastics on the Continent.

Athenagoras (2nd cent.), *Apologist. His 'Apology' or 'Supplication', addressed c.177 to *Marcus Aurelius and his son, sought to rebut the current calumnies against the Christians, namely *atheism, Thyestian banquets, and Oedipean incest. A treatise 'On the Resurrection' is ascribed to him, but this attribution has been challenged.

Athenagoras (1886–1972), Patr. of *Constantinople from 1948. His attempts to secure closer co-operation between the Churches of the *Orthodox communion bore fruit in the Panorthodox Conferences which met on his initiative in Rhodes in 1961 and the following years. In the field of ecumenical relations his most striking achievements were his meeting with Pope *Paul VI in Jerusalem in 1964 and the revocation of the anathemas between the RC and Orthodox Churches in 1965.

Athens. By the 1st cent. AD the city was important only for its schools of philosophy. It was visited by St *Paul, but his preaching seems to have met with little response (Acts 17: 16–34). There was a Christian community in Athens in the 2nd cent. It appears to have been one of the earliest centres of a philosophical interpretation of Christianity, though its schools were closed by *Justinian in 529 for their support of paganism. Soon afterwards the Parthenon and other temples were converted into churches.

Athos, Mount. The peninsula off the coast of Greece which terminates in Mount Athos has long been the property of the monasteries of the E. *Orthodox Church. The first monastic settlement was founded by St *Athanasius the Athonite in 961.

There are now 20 virtually independent monasteries, though matters of common concern are settled by a council. No women are allowed on the peninsula.

Atonement ('at-one-ment'). In Christian theology, man's reconciliation with God through the sacrificial death of Christ.

The need for such reconciliation is implicit in the OT conception of God's absolute righteousness; its achievement is represented as dependent on an act of God Himself, whether by the appointment of a sacrificial system by which uncleanness might be purged, or by the giving of a new covenant. In the NT Christ is reported as speaking of giving His life as 'a ransom for many' (Mk. 10: 45); in the earliest Christian teaching His death is proclaimed to be 'for our sins' (1 Cor. 15: 3).

The Fathers developed the doctrine of the NT but posed new questions. For *Origen, the death of Christ was the ransom paid to Satan, who had acquired rights over man by the *Fall. St *Athanasius held that God the Son, by taking our nature upon Him, had effected a change in human nature as such. The general patristic teaching is that Christ is our representative, not our substitute, and that the effect of His suffering, obedience, and resurrection extends to the whole of humanity and beyond. In the 11th–12th cents., with *Anselm's *Cur Deus Homo, the emphasis shifted. The role of Satan gave way to the idea of the satisfaction due to God for sin. The death of Christ was then seen not as a ransom paid to the devil but as a debt paid to the Father. At the *Reformation M. *Luther rejected the satisfaction theory and taught that Christ, in bearing by voluntary substitution the punishment due to man, was reckoned by God a sinner in man's place. In reaction against the exaggerations of this 'penal theory' arose the doctrine, defended by the *Socinians, which denied the objective efficacy of the Crucifixion and looked upon the death of Christ primarily as an example to His followers. In 1930, however, G. *Aulen defended the traditional theme of Christ's victory as the 'classic idea' of redemption and *Barthian theology has renewed stress on the Cross as the centre of the Christian creed.

Atonement, Day of. The annual Jewish fast day designed to cleanse the people from sin and to re-establish good relations between God and His chosen ones. Much of the ritual ordered in the OT has necessarily lapsed, but the day is still widely observed by Jews with fasting and prayer. Its Hebrew name is 'Yom Kippur'.

atrium. The main court in a Roman house. The word is also used of the forecourt attached to early Christian churches; it usually consisted of a colonnaded quadrangle with a fountain in the middle.

Atterbury, Francis (1662–1732), Bp. of *Rochester, 1713–23. In his (anonymous) *Letter of a Convocation Man* (1697) and his *Rights and Privileges of an English Convocation* (1700) he was the champion of *Convocation against the Crown and of the inferior clergy against the bishops. In 1723 he was deprived of office and exiled for alleged complicity in a Jacobite plot.

Atticus (d. 425), Patr. of *Constantinople from 406. Though a bitter opponent of St John *Chrysostom, he realized that the quarrel with Rome over Chrysostom's condemnation weakened the prestige of his see; he re-established communion with Rome and restored Chrysostom's name to the *diptychs. At the request of *Aurelius, Bp. of Carthage, he repelled *Pelagians. In the E. Church he is venerated as a saint. Feast days, 8 Jan. and 11 Oct.

Attila (d. 453), King of the Huns from *c*.433. He invaded Gaul in 451. In 452 he turned to Italy, ravaging its northern cities. Unreliable sources say that he was persuaded to leave Rome in peace by *Leo I.

attrition. The sorrow for sin which proceeds from the fear of punishment or a sense of the ugliness of sin. It is contrasted with *contrition, which is held to proceed from the love of God.

Auburn Declaration. A statement of the principal doctrines of the American *Presbyterians of the 'New School' which was accepted at Auburn, New York State, in 1837, and made the theological basis on which the 'New School' was organized as a separate body.

Audiani. A 4th-cent. rigorist sect, founded by Audius; it separated from the Church on the ground that the clergy were too secularized.

Audience, Court of. Formerly an ecclesiastical court of the Province of *Canterbury in which the Archbishop exercised his *legatine authority. In the 17th cent. it was superseded by the Court of *Arches.

audiences, pontifical. Receptions given by the Pope to visitors to Rome and officials having business with the Holy See.

audientes (Lat., 'hearers'). In the early Church, those who belonged to the first stage of the *catechumenate.

Audrey, St. See ETHELDREDA, ST.

Aufklärung (Ger., 'Enlightenment'). A movement of thought which appeared in a particularly clear-cut form in 18th-cent. Germany. It combined opposition to all supernatural religion and belief in the sufficiency of human reason with a desire to promote human happiness in this life. One of its ideals was religious toleration. See also ENLIGHTENMENT.

Augsburg, Confession of (1530). The *Lutheran confession of faith presented to the Emp. *Charles V at the Diet of Augsburg in 1530. Its language is studiously moderate. The first part epitomizes the essential Lutheran doctrines; the second reviews abuses for which remedy is sought.

The original text of the Confession (the so-called 'Invariata') remains a standard of faith in Lutheran Churches. A revised text issued by P. *Melanchthon in 1540 (the 'Variata') is accepted by the Reformed (Calvinist) Churches in some parts of Germany.

Augsburg, Interim of. The doctrinal formula accepted at the Diet of Augsburg in 1548 as the provisional basis of a religious settlement between Catholics and Protestants; it was intended to last until the Council of *Trent reached a final settlement. It conceded to the Protestants clerical marriage and *communion in both kinds.

Augsburg, Peace of (1555). The settlement of religious affairs in the German Empire reached between Ferdinand I and the Electors at Augsburg in 1555. It recognized the existence of Catholicism and Lutheranism (but not Calvinism), providing that in each land subjects should follow the religion of their rulers.

Augustine, St, of Canterbury (d. between 604 and 609), first Abp. of *Canterbury. Sent from Rome by *Gregory I, Augustine landed in Kent in 597; within a few months Christianity was formally adopted by *Ethelbert, King of Kent, whose wife was already a Christian. In 604 he sent *Justus to preach west of the R. Medway and *Mellitus to work among the East Saxons. Feast day, 26 May; in the RC Church since 1969, 27 May.

Augustine, St, of Hippo (354–430), Bp. of Hippo Regius (modern Annaba, on the coast of Algeria). Through his Christian mother (St *Monica) he was made a *catechumen in infancy. In adolescence he lost his faith, and at the age of 17 he took a concubine, with whom he lived for 15 years. About 374 he adopted *Manichaeism, which retained his loose allegiance as he passed through successive teaching posts at Carthage, Rome, and Milan. There various factors contributed to a religious crisis and in 387 he was baptized by St *Ambrose. He returned to Africa in 388 and established an ascetic lay community at Thagaste. In 391, on a visit to Hippo, he was unwillingly ordained priest. Probably in the summer of 395 he became co-adjutor bishop and was in sole charge after Valerian's death soon afterwards.

Augustine's consecration as bishop was controversial, not least on account of his Manichaean past, and in the next three years he wrote his deeply anti-Manichaean *Confessions* (q.v.). His opposition to *Donatism helped to win the confidence of the Catholic community. He invited Donatist bishops to debate the central issue of unity versus holiness, and he sought to induce his colleagues to recognize the sacraments conferred by Donatists. To this end he developed the distinction between *validity (q.v.) and efficacy.

Augustine wrote a vast body of works against *Pelagius, who in 405 had been scandalized by a quotation from his *Confessions* which he felt destroyed human responsibility. Pelagius held that, while grace is needed to carry out God's commands, the agent of a moral action has a part to play. Augustine argued that without grace there could be no faith, no act of good will; the consequences of Adam's *fall had made humanity corrupt and selfish; therefore the grace needed is more than external instruction and has to be the love of God poured into the passive heart, so that humanity is enabled to do right because it

is then enjoyable. Nevertheless, though Baptism is the sacrament of the remission of sins both actual and 'original' (i.e. corporately transmitted from Adam), no believer attains perfection, being tied by the body's desires. The sexual instinct is never without some flaw of egotism, even if procreative marriage makes good use of it. That salvation is wholly by grace is the logic of *predestination: by an eternal decree antecedent to merit God has shown His mercy in choosing a minority of souls who are granted the gift of perseverance.

Augustine's other main works include *The City of God*, which appeared in instalments between 416 and 422. It is a massive vindication of Christianity against pagan critics who held the sack of Rome in 410 was due to the abandonment of the old gods. The central theme of *On the Trinity*, written between 399 and 419, is that there is nothing irrational in the notion of being one and three, since being, knowing, and willing are all constitutive of human personality. His Tractates on St John's Gospel, his Sermons and Rule (on which see following entry) embody the heart of his religion: his yearning for God and his profound sense of the ecclesial community. Near the end of his life he composed a review of his writings (*Retractationes*), partly correcting and partly defending himself. His influence on subsequent W. theology has been immense. Feast day, 28 Aug.

Augustine of Hippo, Rule of St. A monastic Rule which exists in three main forms, two for men and one for women; their relationship is disputed. As there is no reference to a rule in St *Augustine's *Retractationes*, his authorship has been doubted. The Rule was little known until it was adopted by the *Augustinian Canons at the end of the 11th cent. It was later accepted by the *Dominicans, the *Augustinian Hermits, and various other orders.

Augustinian Canons, also known as **Austin** or **Regular Canons.** In the mid-11th cent. various communities of clerics in N. Italy and S. France sought to live a common life of poverty, celibacy, and obedience. Their way of life was approved at *Lateran synods in 1059 and 1063. By the early 12th cent. members of these communities, which had spread throughout W. Europe, came to be known as 'Regular Canons';

they had also generally adopted the Rule of St *Augustine. A regular canon thus became synonymous with an Augustinian canon, i.e. one who follows the Rule of St Augustine. Independent Augustinian congregations were also founded, including the *Victorines and *Premonstratensians.

Augustinian Hermits or **Friars.** A religious order living under the Rule of St *Augustine. It was formed in 1256 by the union of various congregations of hermits and became widely established in W. Europe. It was to a reformed congregation of this order that M.*Luther belonged. Though they suffered badly from the effects of the Reformation and the secularization of later times, they still survive, notably in Europe, N. and S. America, and the *Philippines.

Augustinians of the Assumption. See ASSUMPTIONISTS.

Augustinus. The treatise by C. O. *Jansen on grace and human nature, published in 1640. See also JANSENISM.

Aulén, Gustaf (1879–1977), Bp. of Strängnäs from 1933 to 1952. He was one of the leaders of the *Motivsforschung* school, which sought to see the essential truth behind a doctrine rather than stress the form in which it was presented. In his work on the *Atonement (1930; abridged Eng.tr., 1931) he defended a modified version of the 'ransom to the devil' theory. His later writings stressed the elements of coherence and continuity in doctrine, and the historical trustworthiness of the Gospel record.

aumbry. A recess in the wall of a church or sacristy in which in medieval times sacred vessels, books, and occasionally the reserved Sacrament were kept.

Aurelius, St (d. *c.*430), Bp. of *Carthage from *c.*391. He presided over a series of African councils and was held in honour by St *Augustine. Feast day, 20 July.

aureole. In sacred pictures, the background of gold which sometimes surrounds a figure, as distinct from the 'nimbus' (or *halo) which covers only the head.

auricular confession. Confession of sins to God in the hearing of a priest. See also PENANCE.

Ausonius (*c.*310–*c.*395), Roman poet. Decimus Magnus Ausonius was raised to the consulship in 379. Some of his poems suggest that he made some profession of Christianity. He wrote to *Paulinus of Nola (in verse), trying to dissuade him from becoming a monk.

Austin. An older English form of '*Augustine'.

Australia, Christianity in. When the British Government formed a penal colony in New South Wales in 1788, the C of E was given a favoured status. The colonial government, however, also encouraged the worship of other denominations and from the 1820s paid their clergy. The large number of RC convicts were served, first by convict priests, then by official chaplains, and after 1833 by missionary priests who included W. B.*Ullathorne and J. P. Polding, a *Downside monk who became the first RC bishop in 1835. *Congregationalists, *Methodists, *Presbyterians (mainly Scottish free settlers) and *Baptists came. In 1836 South Australia was established as a separate colony to encourage the free settlement of dissenters, among whom were *Lutheran refugees from Prussia. The various denominational missions to the Aboriginal people had little initial success.

In the second half of the 19th cent. the spread of secular views led to the withdrawal of state aid for religion. During the 1870s state school systems were established to provide 'free, compulsory and secular' education, and after 1880 evangelical piety declined. By the early 20th cent. most denominations had a majority of Australian-born clergy, for whom they established theological colleges. After 1918 there was a change of emphasis from denominational issues to wider social concerns. Councils of Churches were established in various states; they pursued matters of public morality and social need, but seldom seldom theological questions.

After 1945 denominational traditions became more consciously Australian, and in 1981 the C of E became the Anglican Church in Australia. In 1977 the Methodist Church, most Congregationalists, and a majority of Presbyterians joined to form the Uniting Church in Australia. Migration brought large numbers of RCs, especially from Italy, and Greek and Russian Orthodox. In the 1996 census 27 per cent of Australians declared themselves RC, 22 per cent Anglican, and 7 per cent Uniting Church.

authority. The power or right to persuade individuals or groups to obey precepts or recommendations. In the State, the coercive power of the government can ensure compliance, and when the Church was identified with organized society, Church authority was enforced with temporal penalties. In the Christian community authority now operates on the ground of an appeal to *conscience, with the understanding that deviation from what is acceptable to the community, in faith or morals, may entail exclusion or spiritual censure.

For Christians the ultimate authority is God, revealed in Jesus Christ. The NT writings presuppose the authority of Jesus and of the Christian community's interpretation of His teaching. In the Church, however, there have been tensions of various kinds. Whereas Orthodox and Anglicans think of major Councils as decision-making bodies, for RCs they are expressions of Christian opinion to advise the Pope who gives the authoritative ruling.

Authorized Version of the Bible. See BIBLE, ENGLISH VERSIONS (3).

auto de fe (Sp., 'the delivery of sentence in matters of faith'). The ceremony of the Spanish *Inquisition at which, after a Procession, Mass, and Sermon, sentences were read and executed. Those sentenced to death were handed over to the secular authority and until 1781 burnt at the stake.

auto sacramental. Spanish religious plays, somewhat analogous to the English *morality plays. Their classical period was the 15th–16th cents., when they were always associated with the feast of *Corpus Christi; in their later development they took the form of allegorical treatments of the mystery of the Eucharist. They were prohibited in 1765.

autocephalous. The term was used in the early Church of bishops who were under no superior authority and thus were independent of both *Metropolitan and *Patriarch, and of those directly dependent on the Patriarch without intermediate reference to a Metropolitan. It is currently used of those national Churches of the E. Orthodox Church which are governed by their own synods.

Auxentius (d. 373/4), Bp. of Milan from 355. He was the most prominent supporter of *Arianism in the West. Despite condemnation for heresy at Councils at Paris (360) and Rome (372), he held his see until his death. He was succeeded by St *Ambrose.

Avancini, Nikola (1611–86), *Jesuit ascetic writer and theologian. His *De Vita et Doctrina Jesu Christi ex Quattuor Evangelistis Collecta* (1665), a collection of terse and pithy daily meditations, was translated into many languages and widely used.

Ave Maria. The Latin form of 'Hail Mary' (q.v.).

Ave Maris Stella. A popular Marian hymn, dating at least from the 9th cent. One English translation begins 'Hail Thou Star of Ocean'.

Ave Verum Corpus. A short anonymous Eucharistic hymn, probably dating from the 14th cent. One English translation begins 'Hail true body, Born of the Virgin Mary'.

Averroism. Averroes (Ibn Rushd, 1126–98) was from an important Muslim family of Córdoba in Spain. From 1182 to 1195 he was chief physician to the caliph at Marrakesh. His fame rests on his Commentaries on *Aristotle. According to Averroes God, the Prime Mover, is entirely separated from the world, while the celestial spheres are intelligences emanating from God in a descending series until they reach man. He also taught the eternity and potentiality of matter and the unity of the human intellect, i.e. that only one intellect exists for the whole human race, in which every individual participates, to the exclusion of personal immortality.

The theories of Averroes became known in Catholic Europe c.1230, but they were not immediately understood. In 1256 Pope Alexander IV instructed *Albert the Great to investigate Averroes's teaching on the unity of the intellect. In Paris *Siger of Brabant expounded Averroist theories which were attacked by St *Thomas Aquinas, and in 1270 the Bp. of Paris condemned 13 errors arising from Averroist teaching. After 1277 Averroism ceased to be taught in the University of Paris, though it infiltrated again in the 14th cent. and survived in Italy until the Renaissance.

Avesta. The sacred books of the *Zoroastrians which set forth the theology and religious system of the ancient Iranians.

Avicebron or **Avicebrol** (c.1020–c.1060), the Latin name of the Spanish Jewish philosopher Solomon Ibn Gabirol. St *Thomas Aquinas wrote a work against his view that the distinction between matter and form applied in the non-material as well as the material world. His main work, the *Fons Vitae*, written in Arabic, was in its Latin translation popular in the Middle Ages.

Avicenna (980–1037), Muslim philosopher. He held that there was a hierarchy of emanations from the Godhead which mediate between God and man. He distinguished, in the usual Aristotelian fashion, between necessary and contingent being, holding that God was necessary and the universe contingent; but between the two he set the world of ideas, which he held to be necessary, not of itself but because God had made it so. He exercised great influence on the early *Schoolmen.

Avignon. From 1309 to 1377 Avignon was the residence ('*Babylonian Captivity') of the Popes, though it did not become Papal property until 1348, when Clement VI bought it from the Queen of Naples.

Avitus, St (d. c.518), Bp. of Vienne from c.490. Of Roman senatorial family, he succeeded to the see on the death of his father. He exercised an enduring influence on the ecclesiastical life of Burgundy and won the *Arian King Sigismund to the acceptance of Catholic orthodoxy. Feast day, 5 Feb.

Axum (or **Aksum)** in N. *Ethiopia. In the early 6th cent. it emerged as a major Christian power, and even after the disappearance of the kingdom of Axum in the 7th cent. the Churches retained their prestige throughout Ethiopia until the 20th cent.

Ayliffe, John (1676–1732), English jurist. His *Parergon Iuris Canonici Anglicani* (1726), arranged alphabetically, remains a treatise of high authority.

Ayton, John (d. before 1350), or Acton, English canonist. He wrote a commentary on the 'Constitutions' of the Papal legates Otto and Ottobon which was printed in the 1496 and later editions of W. *Lyndwood's *Provinciale*.

Azymites. The name given to the W. Church by the Easterns at the time of the Schism of 1054, with reference to their use in the Eucharist of unleavened bread. See also BREAD, LEAVENED AND UNLEAVENED.

Baal. The word was used especially of the Semitic deities who were held to produce agricultural and animal fertility. The Hebrew Prophets had constantly to resist attempts to fuse the worship of God with that of the local Baalim.

Babel, Tower of. According to Gen. 11: 1–9, the tower reaching to heaven, the presumptuous construction of which was frustrated by God through confusion of languages among its builders.

Babylas, St (d. c.250), Bp. of *Antioch from c.240. St John *Chrysostom relates that he refused an emperor access to a church on the ground of an unrepented crime. He was imprisoned in the *Decian persecution and died in bonds. Feast day in the W., 24 Jan.; in the E., 4 Sept.

Babylonian captivity. The captivity in Babylon to which a significant part of the population of Judah was deported in two batches c.597 and c.586 BC. The expression is also used metaphorically of the exile of the Popes to *Avignon from 1309 to 1377.

Bach, Johann Sebastian (1685–1750), German composer. He was *cantor at the Lutheran Thomaskirche at Leipzig from 1723 until his death. His works include two great settings of the Passion (according to St John, 1724; according to St Matthew, 1727), which intersperse the Gospel narrative with arias and chorales to produce large-scale *oratorio Passions; the 'Magnificat'; the 'Christmas Oratorio' (a series of six cantatas for the Christmas season), and the Mass in B Minor. This last is too monumental for liturgical use. His music has transcended denominational boundaries.

Bacon, Francis (1561–1626), philosopher. Under *James I he held various offices, in 1618 becoming Lord Chancellor and Lord Verulam. In 1621 he confessed to bribery and corruption, ending his public career.

In his *Advancement of Learning* (1605) and *Novum Organum* (written c.1608, pub., 1620) Bacon stressed two characteristics of natural knowledge: almost unprecedently, he held that knowledge was cumulative, that it is possible to enlarge rather than simply preserve the wisdom of the past; and he insisted that the sort of knowledge that should be pursued is for practical ends, as the indispensable means to the 'relief of man's estate'. *The New Atlantis* (1627, posthumous) embodies his conception of natural enquiry as a cooperative undertaking. His *Essays*, mainly worldly moralizing, appeared with additions in each new edition (1597, 1612, and 1625); that on 'Atheism' first came out in 1612.

Bacon held that by natural knowledge we can establish the existence of God, but that we have to depend on revelation for knowledge of His nature, action, and purposes. He took the rational soul to be implanted in the human body by God, thus securing its immortality.

Bacon, Roger (c.1214/20–1292 or later), English philosopher. His earliest writings are a series of *quaestiones* on works attributed to *Aristotle. He then turned to the study of languages, mathematics, and natural sciences. About 1257 he entered the *Franciscan Order, probably in Oxford. In Paris he had the chance to expound his ideas on the defects in western education to a priest who was in 1265 to become Pope Clement IV. The Pope bade him dispatch to Rome an account of his doctrines 'secretly and without delay'. Bacon set to work and in late 1267 or early 1268 sent the Pope an encyclopaedic work in seven parts known as the 'Opus maius', in which he outlined the causes which had hindered the progress of philosophy among the Latins and had weakened W. Christendom in its struggle against *Islam. The work also stressed the importance of the study of languages for a proper understanding of the Bible, and the value of mathematics, optics, the natural sciences, and moral philosophy in strengthening W. Christendom. Two shorter works, the 'Opus minus' and the 'Opus tertium', were partly synopses and partly elaborations of sections of the 'Opus maius'. The death of Clement IV in 1268 ended any hope of Papal commendation of his ideas. In 1277 he is said to have been condemned by the General of the Franciscan Order for 'suspect novelties' and 'dangerous doctrine'; the background of the condemnation is not known.

Bagot, Richard (1782–1854), Bp. of *Oxford (1829–45) and *Bath and Wells (1845–54). At Oxford after the publication of *Tract 90* he induced J. H. *Newman to cease issuing the tracts but in 1842 he defended the *Tractarians while denouncing their 'lamentable want of judgement'. The last months of his life were taken up with a controversy with G. A. *Denison on Eucharistic doctrine.

Baillie, John (1886–1960), Scottish theologian. From 1934 to 1956 he was Professor of Divinity at Edinburgh and latterly also Principal of New College. His numerous publications were marked by loyalty to the substance of the Christian faith, despite unease at some of its traditional formulations, and avoidance of philosophical and theological extremes. They include *And the Life Everlasting* (1934), *A Diary of Private Prayer* (1936), and *The Sense of the Presence of God* (1962).

His brother, **Donald Macpherson Baillie** (1887–1954), won international acclaim for his *God was in Christ* (1948).

Bainbridge, Christopher (c.1464–1514), Abp. of *York from 1508. *Henry VIII sent him to Rome as ambassador in 1509. In 1511 *Julius II, having made him a cardinal, entrusted to him a military expedition against Ferrara. He died of poison administered by one of his chaplains.

Baius, Michel (1513–89), Flemish theologian. Despite an earlier censure by the *Sorbonne, he was one of the representatives of the University of Louvain at the Council of *Trent. A papal bull of 1567 condemned various propositions from his writings without mentioning him by name. He made a formal recantation.

The main principles of 'Baianism' were: (1) that in the primitive state, innocence was not a supernatural gift of God to man but the necessary complement of human nature itself; (2) that *original sin is not merely a privation of grace but habitual *concupiscence, transmitted by heredity, and so even in unconscious children is a sin or moral evil of itself; and (3) that the sole work of *redemption is to enable us to recover the gifts of original innocence and live moral lives; this end is achieved by the substitution of charity for concupiscence as the motive for each meritorious act. The grace conferred by redemption is thus not considered to be supernatural.

Baker, Augustine (1575–1641), *Benedictine writer. *Sancta Sophia, or Holy Wisdom* (1657) is a posthumous collection of his ascetical writings; it expounds the way of contemplation. He also wrote on the history of the Benedictine Order in England.

Baker, Sir Henry Williams, Bart. (1821–77), hymn-writer. From 1851 he was Vicar of Monkland, near Leominster. His many hymns include 'The King of Love my Shepherd is' and 'Lord, Thy Word abideth'. He compiled the original edition of *Hymns, Ancient and Modern* (1861).

baldachino. A canopy used to cover an altar, also called umbraculum or *ciborium. It may be made of wood, stone, or metal, in which case it is supported on pillars, or of silk or velvet, when it is suspended from the ceiling or attached to the wall. The word is also used for the canopy over a bishop's throne, over statues, and of the movable canopy carried in processions, e.g. of the Blessed Sacrament.

Baldwin (d. 1190), Abp. of *Canterbury. He was a *Cistercian monk at Forde in Devonshire before he was made Bp. of *Worcester in 1180. In 1184 he was translated to Canterbury. His plans to found a college of secular canons at Hackington, near Canterbury, and later at *Lambeth, led to a dispute with the monks of Christ Church, which culminated in a struggle in the Papal court at Rome. In 1188 he held a metropolitical visitation of the Welsh dioceses, so affirming the jurisdiction of Canterbury in *Wales. He died on the Third *Crusade.

Bale, John (1495–1563), Bp. of Ossory. A *Carmelite from the age of 11, he was converted to Protestantism c.1533. He then defended the Reformation, writing earthily Protestant plays. In 1552, when nominated Bp. of Ossory, he aroused controversy by refusing to be consecrated by the traditional rite and insisting on the use of the BCP. Genuine, if partisan, scholarship is reflected in his *Illustrium Maioris Britanniae Scriptorum . . . Summarium* (1548), a pioneering attempt at British bibliography.

Balfour, Arthur James (1848–1930), British philosopher and statesman, Prime Minister (1902–5), and Foreign Secretary (1916–19). His *Defence of Philosophic Doubt* (1879), despite its title, endeavours to show that the ultimate convictions of mankind rest on the non-rational ground of religious faith. His *Foundations of Belief* (1895) attracted wide attention in view of his eminence as a statesman.

Ball, John (d. 1381), priest. In 1366 he was accused of preaching *Wycliffite doctrines on property and later imprisoned. During Wat Tyler's insurrection (1381) he was freed by the rebels from the Abp. of *Canterbury's prison at Maidstone. He incited the populace to kill those who opposed social equality and was present at the death of Abp. *Simon of Sudbury. He was executed as a traitor.

Ballerini, Pietro (1698–1769), patristic scholar. He was commissioned by *Benedict XIV to prepare an edition of the works of *Leo the Great to replace that of P. *Quesnel, which was tainted with *Gallicanism. This edition (1753–7), published in conjunction with his brother Girolamo, has remained the standard text. The joint work of the brothers included editions of the works of St *Zeno, St *Antoninus, and *Ratherius.

Balsamon, Theodore (c.1140–after 1195), Greek canonist. His *Scholia* consists of: (1) a commentary on the 'Nomocanon' of *Photius and (2) one of the principal collections of *canon law in the East.

Balthasar, Hans Urs von (1905–88), Swiss theologian. In 1929 he became a *Jesuit. From 1940 to 1948 he was university chaplain at Basle. Here he met Adrienne von Speyr, a medical doctor and mystic; he became the amanuensis of her visions and editor of her works. In 1950 he left the Jesuits to set up a Secular *Institute under her inspiration. He was nominated a cardinal in 1988 but died before admitted to the office.

His literary output was enormous and varied. His greatest achievement lay in his incomplete *Herrlichkeit* (1961–9; Eng. tr., *The Glory of the Lord*, 1982–91) and its subsidiary volumes. God's glory was seen as the central concept of the biblical revelation, primarily beautiful, then also true and good. This concept broadens the basis of theology by uniting knowledge and love in contemplation.

Baltimore, Councils of. A series of ecclesiastical councils at Baltimore, Maryland, three plenary (1852–84) and ten provincial (1829–69), by which many details of the administration and discipline of the RC Church in the USA were settled.

Baluze, Étienne (1630–1718), ecclesiastical historian and canonist. His works include an edition of the letters of *Innocent III (1682; incomplete), *Conciliorum Nova Collectio* (1683), and *Vitae Paparum Avenionensium* (1693: put on the *Index for alleged *Gallicanism).

Bancroft, Richard (1544–1610), Abp. of *Canterbury. He was an outspoken opponent not only of *Puritanism but also of *Presbyterianism. In 1597 he became Bp. of London, and on account of J. *Whitgift's age and incapacity had virtually archiepiscopal power. He played a leading part in the *Hampton Court Conference, where he took an uncompromising position. Later in 1604 he was translated to Canterbury. The *canons passed by the *Convocations

of Canterbury and York in 1604 and 1606 were largely his work.

Báñez, Domingo (1528–1604), Spanish *Dominican theologian. From 1580 he held the chief professorship at Salamanca. He was an exponent of the traditional Scholastic theology and took part in the Jesuit–Dominican controversy on *grace which led to the appointment of the 'Congregatio *de Auxiliis'. He became the director and confessor of St *Teresa of Ávila.

Bangor. Of the many places of this name, the best known are:
(1) 'Bangor Fawr' on the NW coast of Wales, opposite Anglesey. Traditionally, the see was supposed to have been founded by St *Deiniol (d. c.584). See also BANGORIAN CONTROVERSY.
(2) 'Bangor Iscoed' in Wrexham. The site of one of the greatest monasteries in Wales.
(3) Bangor in Co. Down, N. Ireland. St *Comgall founded an abbey in 555 or 559. It was the original home of St *Columbanus and St *Gall. The Antiphonary of Bangor was written here between 680 and 691; it is the only surviving liturgical authority for the choir office of the early Irish Church.

Bangorian Controversy. The dispute which followed a sermon preached by B. *Hoadly, Bp. of *Bangor, before George I in 1717. The sermon sought to show that the Gospels afford no warrant for any visible Church authority. To save Hoadly from synodical condemnation, the King prorogued *Convocation, which did not meet again, except formally, until 1852.

banns of marriage. The custom of announcing a forthcoming marriage during Divine Service seems to have been developed in the early Middle Ages to prevent *consanguinity. The BCP regards the publication of banns as the normal prelude to marriage; they must be published in church on three Sundays preceding the marriage. See also MARRIAGE LICENCES.

Baptism. The *sacramental rite, involving the use of water, by which a candidate is admitted to the Church. It is clear that it goes back to the earliest days from the many references in Acts and in the Epistles of St *Paul. Traditionally it has been held that Christ Himself instituted the sacrament, but how far He made His intentions explicit, or indeed envisaged the Church as a continuing institution, is now disputed.

Baptism has been in the name of Father, Son, and Holy Spirit at least since the end of the 1st cent. In the early Church it was normally administered by *immersion. The rite, at which the bishop usually presided, included the laying on of *hands and anointing, and culminated in the Eucharist. (For the later division of these ceremonies in the W., see CONFIRMATION.) In the first four or five cents. it was common to defer Baptism until death was thought to be imminent because of the responsibilities attached to it.

The theology of Baptism was elucidated by the 3rd-cent. controversy over the *validity of Baptism administered by heretics. Largely through the influence of St *Augustine, it came to be accepted that the validity of sacraments depended on the use of the correct form, regardless of the faith or worthiness of the minister. Against the *Pelagians Augustine maintained that one of the chief effects of Baptism was the removal of the stain of *Original Sin on the soul which bars even the new-born child from Heaven. He also held that the Holy Spirit produced in Baptism an effect independent of sanctifying grace; it could not be destroyed and was not to be repeated. In the 16th cent. various aspects of Catholic teaching were rejected by the Reformers. M. *Luther sought to combine belief in the necessity of Baptism with his doctrine of *justification by faith alone; for him Baptism was a promise of Divine grace after which a man's sins are no longer imputed to him. U. *Zwingli denied the necessity of Baptism, seeing in it only a sign admitting man to the Christian community. J. *Calvin taught that it was efficacious only for the elect, since they alone had the faith without which it was worthless. The BCP preserved the traditional Catholic teaching. At the Council of *Trent, the RC Church stressed that Baptism is not merely a sign of grace, but actually contains and confers it on those who put no obstacle in its way.

The forms of the rite used in the RC Church are the most elaborate found in the W. In the case of children it includes an undertaking from the parents that the child shall be brought up in the Christian faith, a prayer of *exorcism, blessing of water, renunciation of evil by parents and *godparents and a declaration of faith,

Baptism by immersion or *affusion with the Trinitarian formula, and anointing with *chrism. The child's father, godfather, or someone else, holds a candle lit from the *Paschal Candle. The Baptism of Adults is not very different, except for the omission of the chrismation; it is followed immediately by Confirmation. The C of E rite is similar but simpler. In CW, renunciation of evil is followed by the signing of each candidate with the cross, blessing of water, and Baptism by immersion or affusion, using the Trinitarian formula. A lighted candle may be given to the newly baptized. In the Orthodox Church, the rite for the admission to the catechumenate, consisting of exorcisms, the renunciation of Satan and profession of faith, is followed by the rite of Baptism proper, in which water and oil are blessed, the candidate is anointed with oil, immersed three times in water, and clothed with a white garment. Chrismation follows immediately and, if possible, Communion is given at the same time to the newly baptized.

'Baptism, Eucharist and Ministry' (BEM). A major statement on these subjects was approved by the *Faith and Order Commission of the *World Council of Churches at Lima in Peru in 1982. Virtually all confessional bodies (including the RC Church) was represented. The text expressly affirms convergence, not consensus sufficient to remove all division; the restoration of unity is seen as a gradual process.

'baptism in the Holy Spirit'. A doctrine now best known in its Pentecostal form. Pentecostals generally claim that the believer is empowered for Christian witness through a unique action of Christ (cf. Mk. 1: 8), distinct from conversion or sacramental *Baptism ('water baptism'). They maintain that, as the Holy Spirit fell on the first Apostles, so those summoned to be likewise 'filled' (cf. Acts 2: 4) are 'baptized with the Holy Spirit' (cf. Acts 11: 15 f.), and that the normal outward sign of this 'baptism' is their breaking into tongues (i.e. *glossolalia) (cf. Acts 10: 44–7). This teaching has been accepted in a modified form by many members of the *Charismatic Renewal Movement in the main Churches.

Baptism of Christ. The event is recorded by the first three Evangelists and implied in Jn. Even generally sceptical critics accept that Jesus Christ came to hear St *John the Baptist and received baptism at his hands. Mk. 1: 10–11 tells of a vision of the heavens opening and a Divine Voice declaring His Sonship. Later writers reflect perplexity that the sinless Son of God should undergo a baptism of repentance, and at the hands of a subordinate figure.

baptistery. The building or part of the church in which *Baptism is administered. From the 3rd cent. onwards the baptistery was often a separate building west of the church and polygonal in shape. The spread of *Infant Baptism led to the increasing use of *fonts placed within the church, often at the west end.

Baptists. One of the largest Protestant communions. Its origins in modern times are usually attributed to the action of John *Smyth, a *Separatist exile in Amsterdam, who in 1609 reinstituted the Baptism of committed believers as the basis of fellowship of a gathered Church. The first Baptist Church in England consisted of members of Smyth's congregation who had returned to London in 1612 under the leadership of Thomas *Helwys. The Churches which sprang from this were *Arminian in theology and came to be known as '*General Baptists'. In 1633 the adoption of believers' Baptism by a group of *Calvinistic London Separatists gave rise to '*Particular Baptist' Churches in many parts of the the country. Many Baptists were associated with the more radical spiritual and political movements of the 17th cent., but after the *Restoration they moved close to the *Presbyterians and *Independents and became recognized as one of the *Three Denominations of Protestant Dissenters. In the 18th cent. many 'General Baptists' came under *Unitarian influences, but under the stimulus of the *Evangelical Revival a 'New Connexion' was formed in 1770; it maintained a vigorous life and a century later united with the main stream of Baptist life. The Baptist Missionary Society, founded in 1792, initiated the modern missionary expansion among Protestant Churches. In the 19th cent. Baptists generally became less rigidly Calvinistic and most Baptist Churches welcomed all believers to Communion. The increase in numbers more than kept pace with the growth in population, but in Britain there has been a marked decline in the second half of the 20th cent.

In America the first Church on Baptist principles was established by Roger *Williams in 1639. In the 18th cent. the *Great Awakening led to the beginnings of rapid and spectacular growth. Baptist preachers were in the van as the frontier was carried westward and in many southern States Baptists became the largest religious community; about two thirds of the members of the *Black Churches in the USA are Baptist. By 1997 there were over 33 million Baptists in N. America. They are organized in several Conventions, the Southern Baptist Convention being the largest and most conservative.

In 1834 a Baptist Church was formed in Hamburg. From this came an extensive Baptist movement in Continental Europe, spreading to Slavic-speaking peoples. Baptists were generally persecuted in Tsarist *Russia, increased in numbers during the early years of the Soviet regime but later suffered from the restrictions on religious freedom. After 1990 they grew significantly and now form the largest Protestant community in countries of the former USSR. In *Australia and *New Zealand Baptist Churches were formed in the early 19th cent. and in the 20th cent. Baptist work expanded in Asia, *Africa and South America. In ecumenical relations Baptists have been hesitant about schemes for organic union because of their concern to preserve their witness to believers' Baptism and the autonomy of the local Church as the 'gathered community', though they have been eager for partnership and co-operation with other Christians. Only 22 Baptist Conventions or Unions are members of the *World Council of Churches, but they comprise about 45 per cent of the world Baptist constituency.

Barabbas. The robber whom (according to Mk. 15: 6–15 and parallels) *Pilate released from prison rather than Christ.

Barbara, St. According to tradition, the daughter of a pagan of Nicomedia who, on being converted to the Christian faith, was handed over by her father to the prefect and martyred. Feast day, 4 Dec., suppressed in the RC Church in 1969.

Barbarossa. See FREDERICK I.

barbe. A title used by the *Waldenses of their preachers.

Barclay, John (1734–98), founder of the '*Bereans' (q.v.) or 'Barclayites'. While he was assistant to A. Dow, the *Presbyterian minister at Fettercairn in Scotland, Barclay published *Rejoice Evermore* (1766), in which he expounded a doctrine of immediate Divine Revelation. He was censured by the Presbytery and not appointed to succeed Dow on his death in 1772. At Edinburgh in 1773 he constituted a new Church, known as the Berean Assembly, from its zeal for the study of the Bible (cf. Acts 17: 10 f.).

Barclay, Robert (1648–90), Scottish *Quaker theologian. He followed his father in becoming a Quaker in 1667. His 'Apology', published in Latin in 1676, was issued in an English version in 1678; its impressive defence of the doctrine of the '*Inner Light' against the sufficiency of external authorities, including the Bible, made it the classic exposition of Quaker principles. Barclay won the favour of the Duke of York (later *James II), and was able to assist W. *Penn in the foundation of Pennsylvania.

Barclay, William (1907–78), NT scholar. From 1947 to 1977 he held teaching posts at Glasgow University. His chief importance lay in his ability to distil the fruits of NT scholarship and communicate the Gospel message to a wide public both in his writing and broadcasting.

Bar Cochba. The leader of a Jewish rebellion in Palestine in AD 132. He claimed to be, and was accepted as, the Messiah.

Bardesanes (154–222), correctly 'Bar-Daisan', regarded by later writers as a heretic. All that is certain about his life is that he was a speculative thinker associated with the court of Abgar VIII at *Edessa. In his 'Dialogue of Destiny' he argued against the determinism of astrologers. His cosmological teaching probably influenced *Mani; his Christology was *docetic and he denied the resurrection of the body.

Bar Hebraeus (1226–86), the usual name of Abû-l-Faraǧ, a *Jacobite bishop and polymath. The son of a Jewish physician, he was converted to Christianity, consecrated bishop in 1246, and in 1264 became *Primate of the East. His works, mostly encyclopaedic in character, were mainly written in *Syriac, a few in Arabic.

Barlaam and Joasaph, Sts, the subjects of a popular legend. Because of a prophecy

that he would be converted to Christianity, Joasaph (or Josaphat), the son of an heathen Indian king, was shut up in a palace so that he should know nothing of the facts or evils of life. Barlaam, a monk, visits him in disguise and converts him to Christianity. The Greek text has traditionally, but apparently wrongly, been ascribed to St *John of Damascus. Feast day, 27 Nov.

Barlow, William (d. 1568), Bp. of *Chichester from 1559. An *Augustinian canon, in the 1530s he was in the royal diplomatic service and gained the favour of *Anne Boleyn. He became Bp. of *St Davids in 1536 and of *Bath and Wells in 1548, resigned on *Mary's accession and on *Elizabeth I's became Bp. of Chichester. As the chief consecrator of Abp. M. *Parker, Barlow's position is at the centre of the controversy over *Anglican ordinations; there is no surviving record of his own consecration, but every indication that it took place regularly under the Catholic ordinal.

Barlow, William (*c*.1565–1613), Bp. successively of *Rochester (from 1605) and *Lincoln (from 1608). He attended the *Hampton Court Conference in 1604; his *Summe and Substance of the Conference ... at Hampton Court* (1604), despite criticism, remains the most satisfactory account. He was one of the translators of the AV.

Barmen Declaration (1934). The statement drawn up at the first Synod of the *Confessing Church at Barmen in Germany to define the beliefs and mission of the Church in the face of the theologically liberal tendencies of the Nazi *German Christians.

Barnabas, St. A Jewish *Levite who became one of the earliest Christian disciples in *Jerusalem. Along with St *Paul, he is called an *Apostle (Acts 14: 14). He introduced Paul to the Apostles after his conversion and went with him on his first 'missionary journey'; later, owing to a dispute over John *Mark, they parted, and Barnabas sailed for *Cyprus. He is the traditional founder of the Cypriot Church and legend asserts that he was martyred at Salamis in AD 61. Feast day, 11 June.

Barnabas, Epistle of. An epistle ascribed to the Apostle *Barnabas, but perhaps written by a Christian of Alexandria some time between 70 and 150. It contains a strong attack on Judaism and claims to find in the OT testimonies for Christianity.

Barnabas, Gospel of. A writing in Italian, apparently dating from the 14th cent., by a native of Italy who had renounced Christianity for *Islam.

Barnabites. A small religious order founded at Milan in 1530. Officially known as the 'Clerks Regular of St Paul', their popular name derives from their church of St Barnabas in Milan.

Barnett, Samuel Augustus (1844–1913), social reformer. From 1873 to 1894 he was vicar of St Jude's, Whitechapel, in London, and from 1884 to 1896 first Warden of Toynbee Hall, which he helped to found. Throughout his life he was active in initiating projects directed to the reform of social conditions on Christian principles and in urging Christians to study them.

Baro, Peter (1534–99), French anti-Calvinist theologian. Compelled to flee from France, in 1574 he was appointed Lady Margaret Professor of Divinity at Cambridge. Here, despite his earlier personal association with J. *Calvin, he became a critic of the more predestinarian of the Calvinist doctrines.

Baronius, Cesare (1538–1607), ecclesiastical historian. A member of the *Oratory, he was made a cardinal in 1596 and in 1597 Librarian of the *Vatican. His main work, the *Annales Ecclesiastici* (12 vols., 1588–1607), is a history of the Church (to 1198), undertaken as a RC reply to the *Centuriators of Magdeburg.

baroque. The ornate style of art and architecture which flourished in Italy in the 17th and early 18th cents., and spread throughout mainland Europe, especially in France and Spain.

Barrington, Shute (1734–1826), Bp. successively of *Llandaff, *Salisbury, and *Durham, he was one of the most influential *prelates of his age. He deprecated any relaxation of the obligation to subscribe to the *Thirty-Nine Articles on the ground that precise articles of faith were indispensable in an Established Church.

Barrow, Henry (c.1550–93), also **Barrowe**, English *Congregationalist. In 1586, when visiting J. *Greenwood in prison, he was detained and kept in confinement until his death. He wrote various works in defence of separatism and congregational independence. In 1590 he was charged with circulating seditious books and three years later was sentenced to be hanged.

Barsanuphius, St (d. 540), ascetical writer. He spent most of his life as a hermit in the region south of Gaza. He exerted much influence on E. spirituality through his correspondence with John of Gaza, a fellow hermit; it is called 'Questions and Answers'. Feast day in the E., 6 Feb.

Barsumas (d. before 496), Bp. of Nisibis in the *Church of the East. He became a keen propagandist for the theology of *Theodore of Mopsuestia. He was instrumental in founding an influential theological school at Nisibis, and, when the school of *Edessa was closed in 489, he welcomed its exiles.

Barth, Karl (1886–1968), Swiss Protestant theologian. He wrote his famous 'Commentary on Romans' (*Der Römerbrief*, '1919', pub. 1918) while he was a pastor of Safenwil (Aargau). In this he revived Pauline and *Reformation themes that had been muted in liberal theology—the sovereignty of God, the finitude and sinfulness of man, *eschatology, and God's judgement on human institutions. In 1921 he became assistant professor at Göttingen and then professor at Münster (1925) and Bonn (1930). With the outbreak of the 'Church Struggle' in Germany (1933), he threw in his lot with the '*Confessing Church'; the *Barmen Declaration (1934) was largely his work. In 1935 he became professor of theology at Basle.

Barth aimed to lead theology away from what he believed to be the fundamentally erroneous 19th-cent. synthesis between theology and culture. Theology was to be based on the Word of God communicated in the Bible. Human reason, he held, has no power to attain to the knowledge of God which is given only in God's gracious revelation in Jesus Christ. This revelation comes from God to man and is contrasted with religion, which is described as man's sinful attempt to grasp God. This outlook rules out *natural theology and makes any dialogue with non-Christian religions virtually impossible.

Apart from many other works, Barth

devoted much of his life to a systematic exposition of his theology on a vast scale. The first volume of *Die kirchliche Dogmatik* (or *Church Dogmatics*, as it is known in English) appeared in 1932; the final section in 1967. The work is the most detailed Protestant exposition of Christian doctrine to have appeared since the Reformation.

Bartholomew, St. One of the twelve Apostles. He has sometimes been identified with *Nathaniel. He may have visited *India. He is traditionally said to have been flayed alive at Albanopolis in Armenia. Feast day in the W., 24 Aug.; in the E., 11 June.

Bartholomew, Gospel of St. An apocryphal Gospel whose existence was known to *Jerome and *Bede. It has perhaps been incorporated into the 'Questions of Bartholomew' which have parallels with the *Gnostic Gospels.

Bartholomew of the Martyrs (1514–90), Dominican theologian. Bartholomew Fernandez owes his name 'of the martyrs' to the church in which he was baptized. From 1559 to 1582 he was Bp. of Braga. At the Council of *Trent he took part in drafting the decrees on the reform of the clergy.

Bartholomew of Pisa (c.1260–1347), *Dominican theologian, famous chiefly for his alphabetically arranged *Summa de Casibus Conscientiae* (1338).

Bartholomew's Day, Massacre of St. The massacre of a large number of *Huguenots which took place on the night of 23–4 Aug. 1572 and the two following days in Paris and other French cities.

Bartholomites. (1) *Armenian*. A community of *Armenian monks who fled from their country in 1296 and settled in 1307 at Genoa, where a church dedicated to St *Bartholomew was built for them. They were suppressed in 1650.

(2) *German*. A congregation of secular priests founded in 1640 to revive the morals and discipline of clergy and laity after the decline due to the *Thirty Years War. They lived in community without vows. They survived until the secularization of the German ecclesiastical states in 1803.

Bartimaeus. The blind beggar healed by Christ on His last journey to Jerusalem (Mk. 10: 46–52).

Bartolommeo, Fra (1475–1517), Florentine painter. A follower of G. *Savonarola, he entered the *Dominican Order in 1500 and was based on San Marco, Florence. His most famous works include the 'Last Judgement' (painted 1499–1500) for S. Maria Nuova (now in the Museo di San Marco) and the 'Lamentation' in the Pitti, both in Florence.

Barton, Elizabeth (c.1506–34), the 'Maid of Kent'. A servant girl, she had trances, claimed to utter prophecies, and became a nun in *Canterbury. Her prophecies then consisted of attacks on *Henry VIII for his intention to divorce his queen. After she had confessed that her trances were feigned, she was executed.

Baruch, Book of. A Book of the *Apocrypha to which is attached the 'Epistle of *Jeremy' (q.v.), the two forming, with *Lamentations, appendices to the Book of *Jeremiah. It consists of an introduction professing to be by Baruch, Jeremiah's secretary, a liturgical confession, a sermon, and a set of canticles. It is generally dated in post-*Maccabean times, possibly after AD 70.

Baruch II. 'The Syrian Apocalypse'. A Jewish work which professes to have been written by Baruch, *Jeremiah's secretary. It was probably written after the fall of *Jerusalem in AD 70 to encourage the Jews after the destruction of the *Temple. It was composed in Greek, but mostly survives only in Syriac.

Baruch III and IV. 'The Greek Apocalypse of Baruch' (traditionally called III Baruch) is an apocryphal work describing the vision of the seven heavens granted to Baruch. It is apparently of Jewish origin but worked over by a Christian hand. It may date from the 2nd cent. 'The Paraleipomena of Jeremiah' or 'The Rest of the Words of Baruch' (traditionally called IV Baruch) deals with the end of Jeremiah's life. It is probably the work of a Jewish Christian and also dates from the 2nd cent. The numbering of III and IV Baruch are sometimes interchanged.

Basel, Confessions and **Council of.** See BASLE, CONFESSIONS and COUNCIL OF.

Basil, St, 'the Great' (c.330–79 [or possibly slightly earlier]), one of the three *Cappadocian Fathers. The brother of St *Gregory of Nyssa, he settled as a hermit near

Neocaesarea in 358; he left his retirement only when called upon by his bishop to defend orthodoxy against the *Arian Emp. Valens. In 370 he became Bp. of Caesarea in Cappadocia. This office involved him in controversies with the extreme Arian party led by *Eunomius, as well as with the *Pneumatomachi, who denied the Divinity of the Holy Spirit.

His writings include a large collection of letters, a treatise 'On the Holy Spirit', and three 'Books against Eunomius'. With St *Gregory of Nazianzus he compiled the '*Philocalia'. He tried to reconcile the *Semiarians to the formula of *Nicaea and to show that their term *Homoiousios* ('like in substance [to the Father]') had the same implications as the Nicene *Homoousios* ('of one substance'). The virtual termination of the Arian controversy after the Council of *Constantinople of 381 is a tribute to his success. He possessed great talent for organization and impressed on E. monasticism the structure and ethos which it has retained ever since. Feast day in the W., 2 Jan. (formerly 14 June, as now in parts of the Anglican Communion); in the E., 1 Jan. See also following entries.

Basil, Liturgy of St. This liturgy exists in two forms, of which the earlier and shorter is the ordinary liturgy of the *Coptic Church. This form has served as a model for modern *Eucharistic Prayers, notably the Third Eucharistic Prayer of the RC Church. For some centuries the longer form was the chief liturgy of the E. Church, but it was eventually superseded, except on a few specified days, by the Liturgy of St *Chrysostom.

Basil, Rule of St. The monastic Rule put forward by St *Basil the Great, which is the basis of the usual Rule followed by religious in the E. Church. The most widespread form of the Rule consists of various Basilian documents put together in the 6th cent., and later expanded; a different form was used by St *Theodore of Studios (d. 826) in his revision of the Rule. While strict, the Rule avoids the extreme asceticism of the hermits of the desert.

Basil of Ancyra (4th cent.), *Arian bishop. Elected to succeed *Marcellus in the see of Ancyra in 336, he was deposed at the Council of *Sardica in 343, but reinstated by Constantius *c.*348. He took part in various Arianizing synods, but his increasing criticism of extreme Arian doctrines led to his removal in 360.

Basil of Seleucia (d. after 468), Abp. of Seleucia by 448. Having condemned *Eutyches in 448, he acquiesced in his rehabilitation at the *Latrocinium in 449, but recanted and signed the *Tome of Leo in 450.

basilica. An early form of church, apparently modelled on a Roman building of the same name. Often approached through an *atrium or outer courtyard, it consisted of a narrow porch (*narthex) leading into the main building. This had a nave and two (or four) *aisles with pillars supporting horizontal architraves and later arches; above these rose the clerestory, pierced with windows. The east end was completed by an arch and semi-circular *apse. The *altar, raised on a platform, stood out from the wall on the chord of the apse; underneath it and partly below floor level was the 'confessio' or chapel which sometimes contained the body of the patron saint. The title 'basilica' is now given by the Pope to certain privileged churches.

Basilides. A theologian of *Gnostic tendencies who taught at *Alexandria in the 2nd cent. His system is difficult to reconstruct, since only fragments of his works survive and conflicting accounts are given. His followers soon formed a separate sect.

Basilikon Doron. A book addressed to his eldest son Henry (d. 1612) by King *James I of England. Its professed purpose was to guide Henry in his duties when he succeeded to the throne, but its real object was to rebuke ministers of religion who meddled in State affairs. Published openly in 1603, it was immediately popular.

Basle, Confessions of. The [first] 'Confession of Basle', compiled by O. *Myconius, was made the basis of the reform introduced at Basle in 1534. It represents a compromise between the positions of M. *Luther and U. *Zwingli. The 'First *Helvetic Confession' of 1536 is sometimes known as the 'Second Confession of Basle'.

Basle, Council of (1431–49). The Council was convened by *Martin V. When the new Pope, *Eugenius IV, dissolved the Council, it disregarded his action and reaffirmed the decrees of the Council of *Constance on the superiority of a *General Council to a Pope. Under political pressure in 1433 the Pope revoked his decision and recognized the Council. In 1437 the *Hussite question was settled against the Papal views by ratification of the 'Compactata', conceding to the Bohemians *Communion in both kinds. In the same year occurred the break with the Orthodox Church over the place of meeting for a council which was intended to unite the E. and W. Churches; Eugenius then transferred the Council to Ferrara. Those who remained at Basle declared him deposed and elected an antipope, Felix V, in 1439. In 1448 they were driven from Basle and in 1449 at Lausanne decreed the Council closed.

The oecumenicity of the Council has been disputed, but most RCs now recognize the first 25 sessions, until the transfer of the Council to Ferrara and *Florence.

Bath and Wells. A see in the Province of *Canterbury, founded c.909 as the diocese of *Wells. Sometime between 1088 and 1091 the see was moved to Bath. *Honorius III authorized the title 'Bath and Wells' in 1219, and in 1245 *Innocent IV ordered that elections should be made alternately in Bath and Wells by the two chapters jointly, with enthronement at the place of election. Since the *dissolution of Bath Abbey in 1540, Wells has been the sole cathedral of the diocese; the abbey-church at Bath has served as a parish church.

Batiffol, Pierre (1861–1929), Church historian, for some time associated with the early *Modernists. His work on the Eucharist (1903) created a storm and he was forced to resign his rectorship of the Institut Catholique at Toulouse. His *Histoire du Bréviaire romain* (1893; Eng. tr., 1912) influenced the revival of liturgical study.

Bauer, Bruno (1809–82), German theologian. He adopted a position even more extreme than that of D. F. *Strauss, attributing the Gospel story to the imagination of a single (2nd-cent.) mind.

Baur, Ferdinand Christian (1792–1860), German Protestant theologian, founder of the *Tübingen School. He taught in Tübingen University from 1826 until his death. From 1835 he was inspired by G. W. F.

*Hegel's theory of historical development; this guided his interpretation of *Gnosticism (1835) and various works on doctrine. He had also recognized the fact of conflict in the early Church and later made this the key to his understanding of early Christianity. In 1835 he denied the Pauline authorship of the *Pastoral Epistles, dating them in the 2nd cent. on account of the historical situation they presuppose. His monograph on St *Paul (1845) went on to deny the authenticity of all the Pauline Epistles except Gal., 1 and 2 Cor., and Rom., and assigned Acts to the later 2nd cent. In his work on the Gospels (1847) he gave the earliest dating to Mt., as representing the Judaizing party, and the latest to Jn., as depicting the final reconciliation. This last Gospel, he argued, reflected the Gnostic and *Montanist controversies of the 2nd cent. and was devoid of historical value. Such views aroused a storm of controversy.

Bavon, St (d. c.653), patron saint of Ghent and Haarlem. Feast days, 10 May, 1 and 9 Aug., and 1 Oct.

Baxter, Richard (1615–91), *Puritan. He was ordained in 1638 but in 1640 rejected belief in episcopacy in its current English form. In 1641 he became curate to the incumbent of Kidderminster; he laboured here until 1660, largely ignoring denominational distinctions. Early in the Civil War he temporarily joined the Parliamentary Army; after leaving it in 1647, he wrote his devotional classic, *The Saints' Everlasting Rest* (1650). He took part in the recall of *Charles II in 1660, but declined to accept the bishopric of *Hereford. He was then not permitted to return to Kidderminster or hold any living. At the *Savoy Conference he presented the *Exceptions to the BCP. Between 1662 and 1687 he suffered persecution. He left nearly 200 writings. They breathe a spirit of unaffected piety and reflect his love of moderation. His hymns include 'Ye holy angels bright'. In CW, feast day, 14 June.

Bay Psalm Book. The metrical version of the Psalms produced at Cambridge, Mass. (popularly known in the USA as 'Bay State'), in 1640. It was the first book to be printed in British America.

Bayle, Pierre (1647–1706), sceptical writer. He was a professor at Rotterdam from 1681 to 1693. He held that religion and morality being independent of one another, all private and social virtues may be equally practised by atheists, and he championed universal toleration. His most famous work was his *Dictionnaire historique et critique* (1695–7).

Bayly, Lewis (d. 1631), the author of *The Practice of Piety* (3rd edn., 1613; the date of its original publication is not known), a work which was popular, especially among *Puritans. From 1616 he was Bp. of *Bangor.

BCMS ('Bible Churchmen's Missionary Society'). A society formed out of the *CMS when a group broke away from the parent body in 1922 in order to assert its fidelity to the traditional doctrines of the *Evangelical party, and in particular to belief in the complete inerrancy of Scripture.

Bea, Augustin (1881–1968), cardinal from 1959. A German *Jesuit, his life was devoted mainly to Biblical scholarship until *John XXIII appointed him President of the newly created Secretariat for Christian Unity in 1960. Bea stressed the importance of the *Baptism of non-RCs and it was largely through his influence that the documents of the Second *Vatican Council described them as 'separated brethren' rather than outside the Church.

bead. Originally the word meant a prayer, but later it was transferred to the small spherical bodies used for 'telling beads' (i.e. counting the beads of a *rosary), and hence also applied e.g. to the parts of a necklace. 'To bid a bead' thus means 'to offer a prayer'.

beadle. In the Church of *Scotland an official appointed by the *session to care for the place of worship and to perform other similar functions.

Beard, Charles (1827–88), *Unitarian minister. He edited the *Theological Review* from 1864 to 1867 and gave the series of Hibbert Lectures for 1883 on *The Reformation*, in which he stressed the humanistic, rather than the definitely theological, aspects of the Reformers' work.

Beatific Vision. The vision of the Divine Being in heaven which, according to Christian theology, is the final destiny of the redeemed. Its nature was the subject of much dispute in the later Middle Ages.

According to some theologians the vision is granted in exceptional circumstances for brief periods in this life.

beatification. In the RC Church, the act by which the Pope permits the public veneration after death of a Catholic in parts of the Church. Such a person receives the title 'Blessed'. See also CANONIZATION.

beating of the bounds. A ceremony common in medieval England and associated with the *Rogationtide procession round the parish. The bounds were solemnly beaten with willow rods, and on occasion boys of the parish were beaten or bumped on the ground. It has been revived in some parishes.

Beatitudes, the. Christ's promise of coming blessings in the '*Sermon on the Mount' (Mt. 5: 3–11) and the 'Sermon on the Plain' (Lk. 6: 20–22).

Beaton (or **Bethune), David** (*c.*1494–1546), Cardinal Abp. of St Andrews. He held high office under James V of Scotland and on his death (1542) made a bid for the regency. He is remembered in Scotland for the trial and condemnation of G. *Wishart, who seems to have been involved in political plotting and designs on Beaton's life. He was assassinated.

Beauduin, Lambert (1873–1960), founder of *Chevetogne. In 1906 he entered the *Benedictine Abbey of Mont-César at Louvain. Here he wrote *La Piété de l'Église* (1914), which popularized the aims of the *Liturgical Movement. After *Pius XI had urged Benedictines to pray for Christian unity, Beauduin founded a monastery of Union at Amay-sur-Meuse (see CHEVETOGNE). He attended Cardinal *Mercier at the *Malines Conversations and in a report expressed his desire that the Anglican Church should be 'united with Rome, not absorbed'; as a result he had to leave Amay in 1928 and in 1930 he was condemned by a Roman tribunal. He returned to his community, by then at Chevetogne, in 1950.

Beaufort, Henry (*c.*1375–1447), Cardinal from 1426. The son of John of Gaunt, declared legitimate in 1397, he became Bp. of *Lincoln in 1398 and of *Winchester in 1404. He attended the Council of *Constance, where he was largely responsible for the election of *Martin V. He played a prominent part in English politics, was several times Chancellor, and from 1424 to 1426 he virtually ruled the country. At Winchester he completed the transformation of the nave of the cathedral.

Beaufort, Margaret. See MARGARET, LADY.

Bec, Abbey of. The abbey of Bec, in Normandy, was founded by Bl Herluin and consecrated in 1041; it was rebuilt on a larger scale in 1060. Its notable monks included *Lanfranc and *Anselm of Canterbury. Bec was taken over by the *Maurists in 1626; it was suppressed in 1790. In 1948 Benedictine life (*Olivetan Congregation) was re-established.

Becket, St Thomas (?1120–70), Abp. of *Canterbury from 1162. He had been Chancellor and an intimate friend of Henry II, and accepted the archbishopric reluctantly. He resigned his chancellorship, and disputes with the king, notably over the trial and punishment of criminous clerks, led Henry in 1163 to require the bishops to sanction the 'ancient customs of the kingdom'. When a code of these customs, the 'Constitutions of *Clarendon', was promulgated in 1164, Becket submitted but soon repented his action. Henry then required him to account for money he had received as Chancellor, and charged him with breaking his promise to observe the Constitutions. His trial and condemnation in the royal court at Northampton led to his flight to France and appeal to *Alexander III. In 1170 he unexpectedly made peace with Henry who promised to make amends for the coronation of his son by the Abp. of *York, while Becket sent Papal letters of suspension to the bishops who had taken part in the ceremony. On his return to England he refused to absolve the bishops unless they would swear to accept penalties the Pope would impose. Henry, in a fit of rage, uttered words which inspired four knights to go to Canterbury and assassinate Becket in his cathedral. The murder provoked indignation and Becket's shrine made Canterbury one of the chief centres of pilgrimage in Christendom. Feast day, 29 Dec.; of his translation, 7 July.

Becon, Thomas (c.1511–67), Protestant Reformer. Ordained priest in 1538, he was arrested for preaching Protestant doctrines and forced to recant in 1541 and in 1543. He held various offices under *Edward VI; under *Mary he was imprisoned and then went abroad. Under *Elizabeth I in 1559 he became a canon of *Canterbury cathedral. His prolific and usually polemical writings enjoyed wide popularity. To the first Book of *Homilies he contributed the one on adultery.

Beda, the. The college at Rome where English candidates for the RC priesthood who have discovered their vocation late in life, including converts from non-Roman ministries who wish to be ordained in the RC Church, are trained.

bede (prayer). An archaic form of *bead.

Bede, St (c.673–735), 'The Venerable', the foremost scholar of Anglo-Saxon England. At the age of 7 he was given as an *oblate to the newly-founded monastery of *Wearmouth; on the foundation of Jarrow in 682 he was transferred there. Apart from brief excursions to *Lindisfarne and *York, he spent the rest of his life at Jarrow.

His pedagogical writings include an alphabetically arranged glossary of Latin words likely to be confused or misunderstood; an account of the principles underlying quantitative verse, and a cursory exposition of natural phenomena such as the motions of planets. All survive in a large number of manuscripts. His De Temporibus was written to explain to his students the principles for calculating the date of *Easter according to the Roman usage adopted at the Synod of *Whitby. A later, more discursive account of Paschal reckoning, De Temporum Ratione, was the most widely studied computistical manual of the Middle Ages. His commentaries on various Books of the Bible were motivated primarily by concern with clarity of exposition; it was this concern that commended them to his contemporaries and successors. He made an extensive revision of the *Hieronymian Martyrology and wrote two lives of St *Cuthbert (one prose and one in verse) which established Cuthbert's cult throughout Europe. His computistical interests led him to the study of chronology; this in turn culminated in the Historia Ecclesiastica Gentis Anglorum (completed in 731), the single most important source for our understanding of early England. Feast day, 25 (formerly 27) May.

Beecher, Lyman (1775–1863), American Protestant minister. He was pastor first of *Presbyterian and then of *Congregational churches. A major figure in American evangelical Protestantism in the period before the Civil War, he was a leader in *revivals (at first he opposed C. G. *Finney and his 'new measures' but later accepted him), a committed advocate of social reform (the *temperance movement and anti-*slavery), and a staunch opponent of *Unitarianism and RCism. In 1835 he was tried for heresy but acquitted by his *presbytery and synod.

Beelzebub (or **Beelzebul).** The name applied to the 'prince of devils' in the Gospels, where Christ's enemies accuse Him of 'casting out devils by Beelzebub' (Mk. 3: 22–6 and parallels), i.e. of acting by the power of, or of being an agent of, the evil one.

Beguines, Beghards. The Beguines were women leading pious, but non-monastic lives, mainly in the late Middle Ages. Living either alone or in communities, they promised to remain celibate while Beguines, but retained the use of private property and were free to change their status and marry. Their male counterparts were the Beghards (usually weavers, dyers or fullers), who had a common purse and held no private property. Found in the Low Countries in the 12th cent., the Beguines became numerous in Germany, France, and other parts of mainland Europe in the 13th and 14th cents. They were criticized by the Church authorities on account of their lack of enclosure and regular status, often coupled with an enthusiastic piety which emphasized their personal relations with God. The Council of *Vienne (1311–12) condemned both Beguines and Beghards. Some Beguines (e.g. M. *Porette) were executed.

Bel. Another form of '*Baal' (q.v.).

Bel and the Dragon (Serpent or **Snake).** Two stories attached to the Book of *Daniel in some Greek MSS of the OT and hence included (as a single item) in the *Apocrypha of the English Bible. They recount exploits of Daniel.

Belgic Confession (1561). A confession of faith of the Reformed Churches drawn up on the basis of the *Gallican Confession. Its adoption in synod at Antwerp in 1566 marked the final acceptance of Calvinist principles in the Netherlands.

Belgium, Christianity in. In the mid-4th cent. the first Bp. of Tongres attended the Councils of *Sardica and *Ariminum, but the area was more lastingly evangelized in the 7th cent. by St *Amandus and St *Eligius. A large number of monasteries were founded and throughout the Middle Ages there was religious fervour which found expression in the movements of *Beguines and Beghards and in the writings of mystics such as J. van *Ruysbroeck and *Hadewijch. After the *Reformation Spanish repression kept what was to be Belgium within the Catholic sphere of influence. In the 17th cent. *Jansenism was the object of bitter controversy. When Belgium became independent of the *Netherlands in 1830, the separation of Church and State was enshrined in the constitution, but tensions have still been reflected in recurrent problems over the financing of Catholic schools and other matters. Belgium is predominantly a RC country, and in modern times the Belgian Church has played an international role, e.g. the part of Card. J. D. *Mercier in the *Malines Conversations and the influence of Card. L. J. Suenens at the Second *Vatican Conference. There are Protestant and Orthodox minorities.

Belial. A Hebrew word probably meaning 'worthlessness', 'wickedness', or 'destruction'. It occurs several times in the OT, usually in combination with a noun, e.g. 'sons of Belial', only once in the NT.

Bell, George Kennedy Allen (1881–1958), Bp. of *Chichester from 1929 to 1958. While he was Dean of *Canterbury (1924–9) visitors' fees were abolished and the *Friends of the Cathedral established. He was one of the leaders of the *Life and Work movement. He supported the *Confessing Church in its struggle against the Nazi government. During the Second World War he criticized the indiscriminate bombing of German cities. After the War his international contacts facilitated the first meeting of the *World Council of Churches in 1948. He supported the Church of *South India and was joint chairman of the *Anglican-Methodist Conversations.

Bellarmine, St Robert (1542–1621), theologian. Roberto Francesco Romolo

Bellarmino became a *Jesuit in 1560. He was made a cardinal in 1599 and from 1602 to 1605 he was Abp. of Capua.

He was a vigorous opponent of Protestantism; his chief work, *Disputationes de Controversiis Christianae Fidei* (1586–93), provides a systematic and clear apologia for the RC position. He took part in the production of the revised edition of the *Vulgate in 1592. His view that the Pope had only an indirect and not a direct power in temporal affairs brought him into disgrace with *Sixtus V. His sympathetic interest in G. *Galileo reflects his reasonableness. Feast day, 17 Sept. (formerly 13 May).

Belloc, Joseph Hilaire Pierre (1870–1953), RC historical writer and critic. He joined G. K. Chesterton and his brother in a series of political broadsides popularly known as 'Chesterbellocs'. He became a well-known figure in journalism, expounding Catholic economic liberalism and upholding the traditional values of European civilization. His historical writings seldom contributed to serious knowledge.

bells. The legend that associates the introduction of bells into Christian worship with *Paulinus of Nola (d. 431) lacks historical foundation. Handbells were much used in areas under *Celtic influence from the 5th to the 9th cents. Hanging bells had come into general use by the 8th cent. Bells are used to summon the people to church and on other occasions, e.g. to announce the death of a parishioner, or for the ringing of the '*Angelus'.

bell-tower. See CAMPANILE.

'beloved disciple'. The anonymous and idealized disciple in Jn. (e.g. 13: 23). He has often been identified with St *John the Apostle, but others have been suggested.

bema. The E. counterpart of the *sanctuary.

Benedicite (Lat., 'Bless ye [the Lord]'). The *canticle or song of praise put into the mouths of Shadrach, Meshach, and Abednego as they stood in the 'fiery furnace' (cf. Dan. 3). It forms part of the '*Song of the Three Children'. It has been used in Christian liturgical worship from early times.

Benedict, St (*c*.480–*c*.550), of Nursia, 'Patriarch of Western monasticism'. The licentiousness of society at Rome led him to withdraw *c*.500 to a cave at *Subiaco to live as a hermit. A community grew up around him and he is said to have established a group of monasteries in the area. Local jealousy prompted him to move, with a small group of monks, to *Monte Casino, *c*.529. Here he elaborated plans for the reform of monasticism and composed his Rule (see BENEDICT, RULE OF ST). He does not seem to have been ordained or to have contemplated founding an order. Feast day, in the W., 11 July (formerly, 21 Mar); in the E., 14 Mar.

Benedict, Rule of St. The monastic Rule drawn up by St *Benedict of Nursia *c*.540 for his monks, mostly laymen, at *Monte Cassino. Drawing freely on earlier Rules, Benedict created a taut, inclusive, and individual directory of the spiritual as well as of the administrative life of a monastery. See also BENEDICTINE ORDER.

Benedict of Aniane, St (*c*.750–821), abbot. In 779 he founded on his own property at Aniane in Languedoc a monastery which became the centre of an extended reform of French monastic houses. His systematization of the *Benedictine Rule received official approval at Synods of Aachen in 816 and 817. He was probably responsible for the '*Hucusque'. Feast day, 11 Feb.

Benedict Biscop, St (*c*.628–689/90), *monk. Of noble Northumbrian ancestry, he became a monk at *Lérins in 666. In 669 he accompanied Abp. *Theodore to *Canterbury. In 674 he founded the monastery of St Peter at *Wearmouth and in 682 that of St Paul at Jarrow. He visited Rome five times and promoted Roman chant and liturgical practice. Feast day, 12 Jan.

Benedict Joseph Labre, St. See LABRE, ST BENEDICT JOSEPH.

Benedict XII (d. 1342), Pope from 1334. Jacques Fournier was the third of the *Avignon Popes. A *Cistercian monk and abbot, as Pope he inaugurated several ecclesiastical reforms. He fought the rapacity of the clergy, forbade the holding of benefices in *commendam except by cardinals, and was a zealous reformer of religious orders. In the political field he was less successful. In 1336 he defined the doctrine that the souls of the just who have no faults to expiate enjoy the *Beatific Vision immediately after death.

Benedict XIII (d. 1423), *antipope at *Avignon from 1394 to 1417. Pedro de Luna took part in the election of *Urban VI, but later supported the antipope Clement VII. He succeeded him, largely because he promised to end the schism, if necessary by abdication. After his enthronement he refused to resign. The Council of *Pisa deposed him in 1409; that of *Constance confirmed his deposition in 1417, and his last adherents then left him.

Benedict XIII (1649–1730), Pope from 1724. A *Dominican, he presided over the provincial Lateran Council of 1725 which tried to reform clerical morals. Also in 1725 he confirmed the bull '*Unigenitus', though he suffered members of his own Order to preach a doctrine of *grace akin to that of the *Jansenists.

Benedict XIV (1675–1758), Pope from 1740. He was an exemplary administrator, conciliatory in his dealings with the secular powers and concerned to strengthen the moral influence of the Papacy. His *De Servorum Dei Beatificatione et Beatorum Canonizatione* (1734–8) remains the classic treatment of the history and procedure of *beatification and *canonization. He also compiled an authoritative work on Diocesan Synods (1748), wrote on the Sacrifice of the Mass (1748), and issued a standard edition of the *Caeremoniale Episcoporum* (1752). He had a real interest in science and learning and founded a number of academies in Rome.

Benedict XV (1854–1922), Pope from 1914. Elected Pope shortly after the outbreak of the 1914–18 War, he protested against inhuman methods of warfare and made strenuous efforts to bring about peace. In 1917 he promulgated a new code of canon law (*Codex Iuris Canonici*) and in an apostolic letter of 1919 he urged missionary bishops to build up a native clergy.

Benedictine Order. St *Benedict of Nursia founded monasteries and wrote a Rule (see BENEDICT, RULE OF ST), but he did not found an order. His Rule was one among several which a monastery might adopt, but in the 7th and 8th cents. it came to be widely followed. In 816–17 *Louis the Pious, assisted by St *Benedict of Aniane, imposed on all

monasteries within the Frankish domain a uniform observance based upon this Rule; monks and nuns in the W. became conscious that they all belonged to the family, or Order, of St Benedict.

In the Middle Ages liturgical observance became more prolonged and manual work less important; monasteries became wealthy and abuses crept in. The fact that each house was autonomous (i.e. had no superior above its own *abbot), made reform difficult. *Cluny (founded in 909) was one of the centres of reform. Several Popes tried to promote reform by establishing general chapters and visitations on the *Cistercian model. In the 15th cent. there were unions of independent monasteries (e.g. the Bursfeld Union in Germany, 1446) and some monastic *congregations were founded in which the autonomy of individual houses was virtually abolished. In the 16th cent. the Reformation ended monastic life in N. Europe and England. The *Enlightenment, the French Revolution, and the anticlerical legislation of the 19th cent. led to the suppression of nearly all Benedictine monasteries, but in the mid-19th cent. there was a revival, with the foundation of *Solesmes (1833) and *Beuron (1883). In 1893 *Leo XIII united all the Benedictine congregations of monks into the Benedictine Confederation, with an Abbot Primate in Rome. This has since been joined by smaller orders following the Benedictine Rule (*Vallombrosians, *Olivetans, *Camaldolese, *Sylvestrines), but not the Cistercians.

Communities of nuns following the Rule of St Benedict date from at least the 7th cent. The Council of *Trent in 1563 imposed on all nuns stricter *enclosure than communities of Benedictines had previously practised. Benedictine sisters, who are not nuns and have less strict rules of enclosure, engage in charitable work (including education) and missionary activity. Most of these communities were founded in the 19th and 20 cents.; they are most common in the USA but there are increasing numbers in Africa.

benedictio mensae. A liturgical form of grace at meals.

benediction. See BLESSING.

Benediction of the Blessed Sacrament. A service in the W. Church culminating in the blessing of the people with the *Reserved Sacrament. It came to be the most common form of evening service in the RC Church before the introduction of Evening Masses after 1953. For details, see EXPOSITION OF THE BLESSED SACRAMENT.

Benedictional. In the W. Church the liturgical book containing certain forms of blessing formerly used by bishops.

Benedictus. The song of thanksgiving (Lk. 1: 68–79) uttered by *Zachariah for the birth of *John the Baptist. In the W. Church it is sung liturgically at *Lauds, whence it was taken over for *Mattins in the BCP.

Benedictus qui venit. The Latin form of Mt. 21: 9: 'Blessed is he that cometh in the name of the Lord'. It is sung or said after the *Sanctus in most ancient liturgies (including the RC); its use is allowed in CW and other modern Anglican rites.

benefice. A term originally used for a grant of land for life as a reward for services, in *canon law it came to imply an ecclesiastical office which prescribed certain duties or conditions for the due discharge of which it provided certain revenues. Holders of parochial benefices in the C of E are known as either *rectors or *vicars. See also ADVOWSON.

Benefit of Clergy. The exemption from trial by a secular court on being charged with felony which was accorded to the clergy in the Middle Ages. The privilege was finally abolished in England in 1827.

Benet, St. An older English form of the name of St *Benedict.

Benet of Canfield (1562–1611), spiritual writer. William Fitch became a RC in 1585 and in 1587 entered the *Capuchin Order in Paris. He returned to England in 1599 and was imprisoned in Wisbech Castle until 1602 or 1603. His *Règle de Perfection* (1610) covers the three forms of God's will: the exterior, in which God's will is actively sought in the circumstances of life; the interior, in which God's will is manifested through inspiration and illumination of the passive soul; and the essential, in which the soul contemplates God's will directly without the aid of intellect or images; this entails the annihilation of the self before God.

Bengel, Johannes Albrecht (1687–1752), *Lutheran NT scholar. His text and critical apparatus of the NT (1734) mark the beginning of scientific work in this field.

Bennett, William James Early (1804–86), Anglican *High Churchman. As priest-in-charge of St Paul's, Knightsbridge, in London, he built St Barnabas's, Pimlico (opened 1850); the advanced ceremonial which he introduced provoked mob rioting. In 1867 a public letter to E. B. *Pusey, in which he dealt with the *Real Presence in the Eucharist, led to a series of legal actions, which showed the inadequacy of the existing courts to deal with matters of doctrine.

ben Sira. The author of *Ecclesiasticus.

Benson, Edward White (1829–96), first Bp. of *Truro (1877–83) and Abp. of *Canterbury (1883–96). He encouraged the establishment of the House of Laymen in 1886, and to deal with the ritual charges brought against E. *King, Bp. of Lincoln, he revived the 'court of the Abp. of Canterbury' (see also LINCOLN JUDGEMENT).

Benson, Richard Meux (1824–1915), founder of the *Society of St John the Evangelist. In 1850 he was appointed Vicar of Cowley, near Oxford. He was about to go to India in 1859 when Bp. S. *Wilberforce persuaded him to remain and take charge of a suburb developing at the Oxford end of his parish. A sermon preached by J. *Keble inspired him to found the Society of St John the Evangelist in 1865.

Berakah. The characteristic Jewish prayer which takes the form of a blessing or thanksgiving to God.

Berdyaev, Nicolas (1874–1948), Russian *existentialist philosopher. From 1922 he lived as an émigré, mainly in Paris. His works portray a philosophical evolution from Marxism to Idealism, and thence to Orthodoxy or would-be Orthodox mysticism. The most theological, *Freedom and the Spirit* (1927; Eng. tr., 1935), sets out his version of religious existentialist or personalist philosophy. He believed that the 'contradictions of modern history' portended a new era of 'divine-human creation'. His critical, nonconformist allegiance to Orthodoxy was combined with moral and social radicalism and an eventual acceptance of post-Revolutionary Russia.

Bereans, also known as **Barclayans** and **Barclayites**. A religious sect founded at Edinburgh in 1773 by J. *Barclay and so called from their zeal in studying the Bible (cf. Acts 17: 10 f.). Berean communities were established in London and Bristol as well as in Scotland, but after Barclay's death (1798) they soon melted away, mainly merging with the *Congregationalists.

Berengar of Tours (c.1010–88), theologian. His family was connected with St Martin's, Tours, and by 1030 he was a canon there. He was archdeacon and treasurer of Angers cathedral, but he returned to Tours and from c.1070 he was 'master of the schools'. Some time after 1080 he retired to a hermitage. He was much criticized for his Eucharistic teaching, against which tractates were written all over Europe. In his reply to that of *Lanfranc (traditionally known as the *De Sacra Coena*, now as *Rescriptum contra Lanfrannum*), he maintains the fact of the *Real Presence but denies that any material change in the elements is needed to explain it.

Berggrav, Eivind (1884–1959), Bp. of Oslo from 1937 to 1950. He soon became a leader of the *Ecumenical Movement. After the Nazi occupation of Norway (1940), he organized resistance; he was arrested in 1941 and remained a prisoner until 1945. He assisted in the foundation of the *World Council of Churches.

Bergson, Henri (1859–1941), French philosopher. Believing that the way to reality was by intuition, Bergson aimed at a radical criticism of all forms of intellectualism. He held that all intellectualist conceptions of reality rest on spatial patterns akin to the diagrams and clock-time of the physicist, which distort the truth and must be abandoned for a new view of time. Reality is evolutionary and progressive, and at the root of moral action lies a 'life force' (*élan vital*). His ideas appealed to many religious thinkers (notably RC *Modernists) who were dissatisfied with the dominating position which traditional theology assigns to the human intellect.

Berkeley, George (1685–1753), philosopher. From 1734 he was Bp. of Cloyne. Berkeley held that when we affirm material things to be real, we mean no more than that they are perceived. Material objects continue to exist when they are not perceived by us solely because they are objects of the thought of God. The only things that exist in a primary sense are spirits, and material objects exist simply in the sense that they are perceived by spirits.

Bernadette, St (1844–79), a peasant girl of *Lourdes. When 14, she received 18 visions of the BVM at the Massabielle Rock, near Lourdes. She later joined the Sisters of Notre-Dame at Nevers. Feast day in France, 18 Feb.

Bernard, St (1090–1153), Abbot of *Clairvaux. In 1112 he entered the monastery of *Cîteaux and three years later was sent to establish a new house at *Clairvaux. He came to exercise an immense influence in ecclesiastical and political affairs. In 1129 at the Synod of Troyes he obtained recognition for the Rule of the *Templars, which he is said to have drawn up. In the disputed Papal election in 1130, he secured the victory of Innocent II; his relation with the Papacy became even closer with the election of a *Cistercian monk and former pupil as *Eugenius III in 1145. In his last years Bernard preached the Second *Crusade.

His best-known work is the unfinished series of sermons on the Song of Songs. In it he ranges from the practical life of the monk to the mystical confrontation between the bridegroom and the bride of the Canticle; by use of *allegory he interprets the bridegroom as Christ and the bride sometimes as the Church, sometimes as himself. Other sermons convey his deepfelt devotion to the BVM. Various treatises single out particular themes of the ascetic life. His letters show his concern with political and moral matters. They did much to prepare and then secure the condemnation of Peter *Abelard at the Council of *Sens (1140). Bernard sought to limit the use of reason in theology, and in his denunciation of the luxury of the *Cluniac way of life to defend the ascetic ideal. In his opposition to the persecution of the Jews, he stood out from his contemporaries. Feast day, 20 Aug.

Bernard of Chartres (c.1080–c.1130), grammarian. A canon of *Chartres, he was a master in the cathedral school from at least c.1114.

Bernard of Cluny (c.1100–c.1150), also called Bernard of Morlás or Morval. He was probably a *Cluniac monk. His poem, *De contemptu mundi*, is the source of 'Jerusalem the Golden'.

Bernardines. The title popularly given to the 'Reformed Congregation of St Bernard', i.e. the Italian branch of the *Feuillants.

Bernardino of Siena, St (1380–1444), *Franciscan reformer. He became a Franciscan friar at the age of 22 and in 1438 was elected Vicar General of the Friars of the Strict *Observance in Italy. He was an eloquent preacher and at the time of his death perhaps the most influential religious force in Italy. He promoted devotion to the *Name of Jesus. Feast day, 20 May.

Berne, Theses of. Ten *Zwinglian theological propositions compiled by two Berne pastors for the disputation on 6–26 Jan. 1528 which had been convened by the City Council. After debate by Catholics and Protestants, they were embodied in a decree which enforced the Reformation in Berne, thus ending the confessional isolation of Zurich within Switzerland.

Bérulle, Pierre de (1575–1629), French diplomat and theologian. After a visit to Spain in 1604, he brought the reformed *Carmelites to Paris, and in 1611 he founded the French *Oratory on the pattern of that established by St *Philip Neri. He negotiated the dispensation necessary for the marriage of *Henrietta Maria to *Charles I in 1625. In 1627 he was made a cardinal. In his main work, *Discours de l'État et des Grandeurs de Jésus* (1623), he expounded his Christocentric spirituality, his devotion to Christ as God-made-man.

Bessarion (1403–72), cardinal, Greek scholar and statesman. In 1437 he was made Metropolitan of Nicaea by the Emp. John VIII Palaeologus, whom he accompanied to the Council of Ferrara-*Florence. He was convinced by the arguments of the Latins and became an advocate of the union of the Greek and Latin Churches. He was made a cardinal in 1439. He fulfilled various ecclesiastical commissions, was nearly elected Pope, and in 1463 *Pius II appointed him Patr. of Constantinople (since 1453 in the hands of the Turks). He translated *Aristotle's *Metaphysics* into Latin and was an enthusiastic patron of scholars.

Bethabara. According to Jn. 1: 28 (AV) the place where *John the Baptist baptized, and thus presumably the site of Christ's *Baptism. Many important MSS. followed by the RV, read '*Bethany beyond Jordan' at this point.

Bethany. The village of *Martha, *Mary, and *Lazarus, *c.*2 miles from *Jerusalem, where Christ lodged during the week before His Passion. Its modern name is 'Azaryah', i.e. 'the place of Lazarus'. 'Bethany beyond Jordan' (Jn. 1: 28 RV) is another village.

Bethel (Heb., 'House of God'). (1) A sanctuary north of *Jerusalem. According to Gen. 28: 10–22, God appeared here in a dream to *Jacob. On the division of the Hebrew Kingdom after the death of *Solomon (*c.*930 BC), the first ruler of the northern kingdom (*Israel) set up a 'golden calf' here; worship continued until 621 BC.

(2) The small town near Bielefeld in Westphalia which gives the popular name to the *Bodelschwinghsche Stiftungen*. These are homes for epileptics, training centres for deaconesses and male nurses, and a college for Protestant theological students.

(3) A name used, especially by some *Methodists and *Baptists, for a place of worship.

Bethesda. A pool at *Jerusalem (Jn. 5: 2) believed to have possessed healing properties connected with a periodical disturbance of the water.

Bethlehem. The small town 5 miles S. of *Jerusalem which was the native city of *David and the birthplace of Christ. It contains the 'Church of the Nativity', built by *Constantine in 330 on the supposed site of Christ's birth; much of the original church survives. For the Council of Bethlehem (1672) see JERUSALEM, SYNOD OF.

Bethlehemites. The name of several religious orders, most of which no longer survive. In 1976 a *Carthusian-inspired order of monks and nuns of Bethlehem was founded in France; they have a special interest in religious art.

Bethphage. A village on the Mount of *Olives near *Bethany.

Bethsaida. A predominantly Gentile village on the E. bank of the *Jordan where it enters the Sea of Galilee; its site has not been identified. It was visited by Christ (Mk. 8: 22). 'Bethsaida of Galilee' (Jn. 12: 21) may have been a different place.

Bethune, David. See BEATON, DAVID.

betrothal. A free promise of future marriage between two persons. In many countries formal betrothal before witnesses is customary, but in England the Church has ceased to exercise any authority in the matter. See also MATRIMONY.

betting and gambling. A gamble is a contract whereby the loss or gain of something of value is wholly dependent on an uncertain event. The morality of gambling, considered as a species of recreation, is disputed. Some hold it to be always illicit, but most Christians regard it as permissible, though open to abuse. It must not be about an unlawful matter, the stake must not be excessive, and it must be for some end other than pure avarice, e.g. recreation.

Beuno, St (d. c.640), Abbot of Clynnog. He is said to have founded monasteries in Herefordshire, but his chief mission work is believed to have been in N. Wales, where his tomb was long venerated at Clynnog Fawr. Feast day, 21 Apr.

Beuron, Abbey of. The mother house of the 'Beuron Congregation' of *Benedictine monks in Hohenzollern, on the upper Danube. The present abbey was constituted in 1863 and the monastic *congregation in 1873, though *Augustinian Canons were established at Beuron in the 11th cent. The abbey became famous through its work in the *Liturgical Movement.

Beveridge, William (1637–1708), Bp. of *St Asaph from 1704. In 1672 he became Vicar of St Peter's, Cornhill, where he had a daily service and Eucharist every Sunday. When T. *Ken was deprived in 1691, Beveridge was offered (but declined) the vacated see of *Bath and Wells. His *Private Thoughts upon Religion* (1709) place him among the spiritual writers of the century.

Beyschlag, Willibald (1823–1900), German Evangelical theologian. A leading exponent of the '*Vermittlungstheologie', he rejected *Chalcedonian Christology. After 1870 he helped to draw up the new constitution for the Prussian Church; he supported the Government in the

*Kulturkampf; and he was one of the chief agents in founding the *Evangelische Bund.

Beza, Theodore (1519–1605), *Calvinist theologian. De Bèze (the original form of his name) came of an old Catholic family in Burgundy. He renounced Catholicism in 1548 and went to *Geneva. He was professor of Greek at Lausanne from 1549 to 1558, when J. *Calvin offered him a professorship at the newly-founded academy at Geneva, a post he held until 1595. In 1561 he took part in the Colloquy of *Poissy. On Calvin's death in 1564 he succeeded him as head of the Geneva Church and leader of the Calvinist movement in Europe. In 1571 he presided over the National Synod of La Rochelle which marked the consolidation of the French Huguenot Church.

In 1559 Beza published his *Confession de la foi chrétienne*, an exposition of Calvinist beliefs, translated into Latin in 1560. In the 1550s and 1560s he disputed with S. *Castellio about free will and defended the orthodox doctrine of the Trinity against L. *Socinus and others. In defence of his view that Christ's Divine (but not His human) nature is present to the faithful in the Eucharist, he produced a series of works against the Lutheran *Ubiquitarians. He is usually thought to have hardened Calvin's doctrine of *predestination by arguing that even the *Fall was part of God's eternal plan; it followed the election of some to salvation and others to damnation, the atoning death of Christ being offered only for the former. His annotated Latin translation of the NT (1556), to which he added the Greek text in 1565, was widely influential; it was used by the translators of the AV. See also CODEX BEZAE.

Bible. The word 'Bible' derives from a Greek word meaning 'books'; as the biblical Books came to be regarded as a unity, the word came to be used as a single noun.

JEWISH SCRIPTURES. The Jews classified their Scriptures into three groups: (1) The Law, which comprised the *Pentateuch (Gen.-Deut.) and was regarded as on a higher level than the rest; (2) The Prophets (Jos., Jgs., 1 and 2 Sam., 1 and 2 Kgs., Is., Jer., Ezek., and the Twelve *Minor Prophets); and (3) The 'Writings', comprising the remaining Books of the English OT, as well as some others, e.g., Tobit, which the Jews later rejected. By the time of Christ Jews recognized the Law and Prophets as Scripture, but the exact compass of the Writings was still undefined. The *canon of the Jewish Scriptures was settled at about the end of the 1st cent. AD, or perhaps rather later.

GREEK OT. Before the Christian era the Hebrew Scriptures had been translated into Greek, including some which were later rejected from the canon. The translation in most general use was the *Septuagint (LXX), and it was in this version that Christians first received the Jewish Bible. The Jewish rejection of certain Books c. AD 100 was at the time unheeded by the Church; later the Books rejected from the Hebrew canon came to be known as the '*Apocrypha' (q.v.).

NT. During the 2nd cent. the Church came to regard some of its own writings, especially those of Apostolic origin, as of equal authority and inspiration to those she had received from Judaism. The canon of the NT, based on the four Gospels and the Epistles of St *Paul, came to existence largely without definition. It was probably formally fixed at Rome in 382 when the Christian OT (based on the LXX) was also defined.

AUTHORITY AND INTERPRETATION. The respect shown by Christ and the early Church to the Scriptures of Judaism form the basis of the Christian attitude to the Bible. The OT Scriptures, regarded as inspired by the Holy Spirit, were seen as a revelation of God and a preparation for the coming of Christ. Many of the OT ordinances were superseded by the Christian revelation, but the OT as a whole retained its authority; its message was completed by the NT, so that the two formed a single and final revelation. Apart from the challenge of *Marcion, this view was accepted by orthodox and heretics alike. The Reformers insisted on the priority of the literal and historical sense over the *allegorical, and appealed to Scripture against ecclesiastical tradition; this stress led to the development of theories of verbal inerrancy, and Catholics and Protestants shared a view of inspiration that insisted on the truth of biblical statements, not only in matters of history, doctrine, and ethics, but also in cosmology and natural science. This position was challenged by *Cartesian philosophy and modern science and in the 18th cent. it was undermined by linguistic, *text-critical, and historical study of the Bible. In 19th-

cent. England geology and evolutionary theories did most to shake biblical authority. Despite bitter controversy, by the end of the 19th cent. *higher criticism was widely accepted in the Protestant Churches of Europe and North America. The suppression of *Modernism by *Pius X and the emergence of *Fundamentalism in the USA were reactions against biblical criticism, but after 1943 RC biblical scholarship progressed more openly and since the Second *Vatican Council has played a major role. Evangelical scholarship has also developed, and newer literary approaches have directed attention away from the more contentious questions of historicity. See also BIBLICAL COMMISSION; BIBLICAL THEOLOGY; FORM CRITICISM; HISTORICAL JESUS, QUEST OF THE; MANUSCRIPTS OF THE BIBLE.

For translation of the Bible into Latin, see OLD LATIN and VULGATE; for other ancient versions see SEPTUAGINT and SYRIAC VERSIONS OF THE BIBLE. For English versions, see following entry.

Bible, English versions. (1) PRE-REFORMATION VERSIONS. There were Anglo-Saxon interlinear glosses of the Gospels and Psalms and translations of portions of the Bible, sometimes abridged. From c.1250 Middle English metrical versions of certain Books, especially Gen., Exod., and the Psalter, were made. In the 14th cent. several anonymous translations of NT Books appeared, apparently under the influence of J. *Wycliffe. The Council of Oxford in 1407 prohibited the making of any fresh translations of the whole or part of the Bible.

(2) THE REFORMATION PERIOD. The first translations made directly from the original languages were the work of W. *Tyndale (q.v.). His NT was printed on the Continent in 1526; it was followed by the *Pentateuch (1529–30), Jonah (1531), and revisions of Gen. and the NT. In 1534 Canterbury *Convocation petitioned *Henry VIII that the whole Bible might be translated into English, and in 1535 Miles *Coverdale (q.v.) published a complete Bible dedicated to the King. He based his rendering on Tyndale's version where available; the other OT Books he translated from the German of M. *Luther and others. His Psalter has remained in use in the BCP version of the Psalms. In 1537 '*Matthew's Bible' appeared, with the King's authorization.

This consisted of Tyndale's Pentateuch, a version of Josh.-2 Chron. made from the Hebrew, probably by Tyndale and not previously published, Tyndale's NT of 1535, and the rest in Coverdale's version. Further revisions of the whole Bible followed: the '*Great Bible' of 1539, the '*Geneva Bible' of 1560 (which used verse divisions), the '*Bishops' Bible' of 1568, and for RCs the *Douai-Reims Bible (qq.v.).

(3) THE AUTHORIZED VERSION. At the *Hampton Court Conference (1604) J. *Rainolds suggested that there should be a new translation of the Bible, and *James I ordered the work. The 54 revisers were instructed to take the Bishops' Bible as their basis, to retain ecclesiastical terms ('Baptism' for 'Washing'), and to exclude marginal notes unless needed to explain Hebrew or Greek words. The result of their work, published in 1611, was a version of great felicity which became the only familiar form of the Bible for generations of English-speaking people. In the USA it is known as the 'King James Version'.

(4) THE REVISED VERSION and AMERICAN STANDARD VERSION. The growth of Biblical scholarship as well as changes in English usage led to increasing dissatisfaction with the AV in the 19th cent. In 1870 the Convocation of Canterbury took the matter up and a committee of revisers was appointed. They were instructed to introduce as few alterations into the text of the AV as possible consistent with faithfulness and to limit the expression of such alterations to the language of the AV and earlier versions. The NT was published in 1881, the OT in 1885, and the *Apocrypha in 1895. The *American Standard Version*, published in 1901, incorporated into the text of the RV those renderings favoured by the American scholars who had co-operated (by correspondence).

(5) MODERN TRANSLATIONS. In the last 100 years, there have been a number of private translations of the NT or the whole Bible, aimed increasingly at making the Bible intelligible to the common man. These have included the NT of R. F. Weymouth (1903); the NT (1913) and OT (1924) of J. *Moffatt; the NT (1945) and OT (1948-9) of R. A. *Knox; *The New Testament in Modern English* (1958; revised 1973) of J. B. Phillips and two versions in non-ecclesiastical English: the *Good News Bible: Today's English Version*, published by the American and other Bible Societies (NT, 1966; whole Bible, 1976), and *The Living Bible*, paraphrased by K. N. Taylor (1971). The most important Biblical translations, however, have been corporate ventures. The *Revised Standard Version* (NT, 1946; OT, 1952; Apocrypha, 1957) is a revision of the *American Standard Version* undertaken by a committee representing the major Protestant Churches of N. America. The revisers took account of current scholarship and changes in language to produce a more accurate version and one free from archaisms, but preserving a dignity suitable for public worship. The RSV is widely used not only in America but in Britain and other English-speaking countries. In 1965 the NT, and in 1966 the whole Bible (in Vulgate order) appeared in a 'Catholic edition' bearing the *imprimatur. In what became known as the 'Common Bible' (1973), designed to appeal to RCs, Protestants and Orthodox, the RSV text was rearranged. A revision of the RSV, the *New Revised Standard Version*, appeared in 1989. This is a direct descendant of the AV and retains much of its solemnity. The *New English Bible* (NT, 1961; whole Bible, 1970) was designed as a new translation of the Bible into contemporary English, to be made from the original languages; it was made under the direction of a Joint Committee of the non-RC Churches of the British Isles, established in 1947 on the initiative of the Church of Scotland. It won only limited acceptance and in 1974 a revision was undertaken by a panel which included RCs. The *Revised English Bible* (1989) is a radical revision of the NEB and is generally more conservative in its treatment of the original text. The *Jerusalem Bible* (1966) is an English parallel of *La Bible de Jérusalem*, a French rendering of the original Hebrew, Greek, and Aramaic texts made by the *Dominicans of the École Biblique in Jerusalem and published in France (1948-54). The English text was made with reference to the original languages and accompanied by revised notes. It follows the Vulgate order but has the traditional (AV/RV) form of Biblical names rather than those of the Douai version (e.g. Hosea, not Osee). Its revision, the *New Jerusalem Bible* (1985) makes use of the new edition of *La Bible de Jérusalem* (1973). It was the first complete English translation to make serious efforts to use inclusive language. The *New American Bible* (1970) was made by members of the

Catholic Biblical Association of America; it is widely used by RCs in the USA. The *New International Version* (1978) is the work of scholars representing a broad range of *evangelical denominations, directed by the New York Bible Society.

Bible Christians. One of the bodies, also known as Bryanites, which made up the *United Methodist Church in 1907. It was founded in 1815 in N. Devon by William O'Bryan, a local preacher of the *Wesleyan Methodist Church who had extended his evangelism beyond the limits of his own circuit. The movement spread rapidly and engaged in missionary work abroad.

Bible Churchmen's Missionary Society. See BCMS.

Bible divisions and references. The division of major sections of the OT (e.g. the *Pentateuch) into Books was associated with the amount of material which would fit on to a single scroll. When the Hebrew was translated into Greek, which takes more space than Hebrew, some Books (e.g. Sam.) were divided into two. Conversely single items were collected into Books. Chapter divisions originated in Christian Bibles. Introduced for ease of reference, they followed various systems, e.g. that of the *Eusebian canons. That in current use is attributed to Stephen *Langton (d. 1228). Verse numbers were first used by Rabbi Nathan in his concordance of the Hebrew Bible in the mid-15th cent. These were used for the OT in the French (1553) and Latin (1555) Bibles printed by Robert Estienne (*Stephanus). For the NT he used his own verse numbers in his 1551 edition. These have remained in use ever since. The *Geneva Bible (1560) was the first English Bible to have numbered verses throughout.

Bible Society, British and Foreign. See BRITISH AND FOREIGN BIBLE SOCIETY.

Biblia Pauperum (Lat., 'the Bible of poor people'). Though also used to describe various short biblical summaries for elementary education, the title came to denote specifically a picture-book in which on each page a set group of figures illustrates a NT antitype flanked by two corresponding OT *types, with short explanatory texts from the Bible and mnemonic verses.

Biblical Commission. A committee of car-dinals was instituted by *Leo XIII in 1902 to further Biblical studies and to safeguard the authority of Scripture against the attacks of exaggerated criticism. In answer to questions it issued a series of conservative *responsa*, such as that on the Mosaic authorship of the *Pentateuch (1906). After 1943 a more liberal attitude prevailed and in 1954 the Commission's secretary declared that *responsa* dealing with literary questions were to be regarded as conditioned by their time. In 1971 the Commission was reorganized as part of the Congregation for the *Doctrine of the Faith; it now consists of 20 scholars who advise the Congregation and Pope on biblical aspects of current issues.

Biblical Theology. An influential movement among biblical scholars in the mid-20th cent. which derived from the thought of K. *Barth and others of similar outlook. Its adherents generally held that: (1) biblical concepts were different in kind from other ideas and that Hebrew thought was preferable to Greek; (2) biblical concepts were still adequate for all essential purposes; (3) God's action in history was the primary medium of revelation; (4) the biblical records were generally historically trustworthy; and (5) the biblical material had an inner coherence which was often represented as centred on key concepts, such as *covenant.

bibliolatry. Excessive veneration for the letter of Scripture, found among certain Protestants.

Bickersteth, Edward (1786–1850), leader of the Anglican *Evangelicals from the death of Charles *Simeon in 1836 until his own. In 1815 he gave up the practice of law and was ordained deacon and priest, before going to Africa on behalf of the *CMS to settle disputes among the missionaries. He was secretary of the CMS from 1824 to 1830, when he became Rector of Watton, Herts. He was one of the founders of the Parker Society and active in the foundation of the *Evangelical Alliance.

Biddle, John (1615–62), English *Unitarian. His 'XII Arguments' against the deity of the Holy Spirit was published in 1647 and ordered to be burnt. After publishing two further anti-Trinitarian tracts, he was saved from sentence of death by his friends among the *Independent Parliamentarians. On the passing of the Act of Oblivion (1652), his adherents began regular Sunday worship. He then published two catechisms and eventually died in prison.

Biel, Gabriel (*c.*1420–95), scholastic philosopher. He joined the *Brethren of the Common Life and in 1479 became provost of the house at Urach. He took part in the foundation of the University of *Tübingen, where he was professor of theology. He was a follower of the *nominalist thought of *William of Ockham. He held that the 'just price' was determined by supply and demand rather than by theological maxims and that the merchant is a useful member of society.

bigamy. (1) A 'second marriage' contracted by a person whose 'first' husband or wife is still alive, when the 'first' marriage has not been declared null. (2) In older usage the term denotes a second marriage after the death of one of the parties of the first marriage. See also DIGAMY.

Bilney, Thomas (*c.*1495–1531), Protestant martyr. He is said to have converted H. *Latimer to the doctrines of the Reformation and to have influenced M. *Parker. In 1531 he was tried for *Lollardy; after recanting and relapsing he was burnt.

bilocation. The presence of a person in more than one place at the same moment.

bination. The celebration of two Masses on the same day by the same priest. In the RC Church no priest may normally celebrate (or concelebrate) Mass more than once a day except on the few occasions, such as *Christmas, when more than one Mass is provided. The local *ordinary may allow priests to celebrate more than once in a day when pastoral necessity requires it.

binding and loosing. The power which Mt. 16: 19 reports that Christ gave to St *Peter and later to all the Apostles (Mt. 18: 18). It seems to be a general authority to exercise discipline over the Church, though some identify it with the power of forgiving or retaining sins (Jn. 20: 23).

Bingham, Joseph (1668–1723), Anglican clergyman. His famous work, the *Origines Ecclesiastiae; or the Antiquities of the Christian Church* (10 vols., 1708–22), with its wealth of systematically arranged information on the

hierarchy, organization, rules, discipline, and calendar of the early Church, has not been superseded.

Binitarianism. The belief that there are only two Persons in the Godhead, involving denial of the deity of the Holy Spirit.

bioethics. The term was coined in 1971 to describe ethical reflection on issues arising within the sphere of the biological and medical sciences. For Christians it is a part of *moral theology and is governed by its principles, including the sacredness of human life, love of neighbour, and respect for the sovereignty of God. For discussion of some branches of bioethics, see CONTRA-CEPTION, PROCREATION, AND ABORTION, ETHICS OF; and DYING, CARE OF THE.

biretta. A hard square cap sometimes worn by clergy in the W. Church.

Birgitta, St. See BRIDGET, ST.

Birinus, St (d. 649/50), first Bp. of *Dorchester, near Oxford, and Apostle of the West Saxons. He was consecrated in Genoa and landed in Wessex in 634. In 635 he converted and baptized King Cynegils, who gave him Dorchester as his episcopal see. Feast day, 3 Dec. (in some places 5 Dec.).

Bischop, Simon. See EPISCOPIUS.

bishop. The highest order of ministers in the Christian Church. In Catholic Christendom (including the *Anglican Communion) bishops are the chief pastors, who individually form a centre of unity in their *dioceses and together embody the unity of the Church, and, by their consecration and power to confer *Orders, witness to the succession of the Church throughout the ages. They normally receive consecration at the hands of a *Metropolitan and two other bishops, and are consecrated to rule a particular diocese in that Metropolitan's *province. In the RC Church the election of a bishop is performed by the Pope. Elsewhere a bishop is usually elected by the *dean and *chapter of the *cathedral of the diocese or some other ecclesiastical body existing for the purpose. In the C of E the *Crown Appointments Committee submits two names to the Prime Minister, who recommends one to the Sovereign; the Sovereign then gives leave to the College of Canons to elect, and nominates the person to be elected. The candidate must be of mature age (30 years in the C of E), have spent a certain period in priest's orders, and be of good character and sound doctrine. The chief duties of a bishop in the W. Church consist in the general oversight of his diocese, in the leadership of his clergy and laity, and in administering those Sacraments which he alone is competent to confer (*Confirmation and Orders). Diocesan bishops may be assisted by other bishops known as *suffragans, auxiliaries, coadjutors, or assistants. In the E. Church the position is similar, except that bishops, unlike other priests, are required to be unmarried (or widowed). From medieval times English bishops have had a seat in the House of Lords, but since 1878 only 26 English bishops have enjoyed this privilege. The number is likely to be reduced. The traditional insignia of a bishop include the throne in his cathedral (*cathedra), *mitre, *pastoral staff, *pectoral cross, and *ring.

The beginnings of the episcopate have long been debated. It seems that at first the terms 'episcopos' and 'presbyter' were used interchangeably (cf. e.g. Acts 20: 17 and 20: 28). But for *Ignatius (early 2nd cent.) bishops, presbyters, and deacons are quite distinct. By the middle of the 2nd cent. the leading centres of Christianity would appear to have had their own bishops and until the Reformation Christianity was everywhere organized on an episcopal basis. After the Reformation the title of bishop was retained in some *Lutheran Churches, but it usually implied no claim to *apostolic succession or any of the peculiar powers deriving therefrom. It is also similarly used in the *Methodist Episcopal Churches in America and Africa.

See also APOSTOLIC SUCCESSION.

Bishops' Bible. An English translation of the Bible compiled at the direction of Abp. M. *Parker and published in 1568. It was a revision of the *Great Bible.

Bishops' Book (1537). Entitled 'The Institution of a Christen Man', it was compiled by a committee of English bishops and clergy. It expounded the *Creed, *Sacraments, *Decalogue, *Lord's Prayer, and *Ave Maria, and dealt with various questions disputed between the C of E and the RC Church. See also KING'S BOOK.

Bishops' Wars. Two brief campaigns in

Scotland in 1639 and 1640. After *Charles I tried to enforce the use of the BCP in Scotland, the Scots rebelled, with the avowed aim of abolishing episcopacy.

Black Churches. Apart from the ancient Churches of *Nubia and *Ethiopia, Black Churches originated in the 18th cent. among the descendants of African slaves in the *United States of America. From the 1740s, evangelical *revivals attracted Blacks to Christianity, perhaps largely because they were allowed to assume active roles as preachers and leaders. By the 1770s Black *Baptists were acting as pastors of separate Black congregations of slave and free members. In the South, Black Churches were restricted and sometimes suppressed because they were thought liable to foment slave rebellion. In the 19th cent., however, slaves regularly held their own religious meetings and in sermon and song identified themselves as a chosen people whom God would free; they generated a distinct religious culture expressed in the *spirituals.

In the North, the abolition of slavery after the Revolution (1776–83) enabled Blacks to exercise religious freedom. Alienated by White discrimination, Blacks in Philadelphia founded two influential churches in 1794; they were followed by others of various denominations. In 1816 the first major Black denomination, the African Methodist Episcopal Church, was formed. Most Black Churches were Protestant. Membership was predominantly female, and, though barred from ordination until the 20th cent., women led home prayer meetings and exercised influence. Blacks began the first American foreign missions in the 1780s. After Emancipation in 1865, Northern missionaries went South to organize Churches among the former slaves and the influx of Southern members enlarged the rolls of Black denominations and made them national in scope. Ex-slaves withdrew from White Churches to found their own. At the end of the 19th cent. Black Church membership reached 2.7 million out of a population of 8.3 million Blacks. In 1895 Black Baptists united to form the National Baptist Convention, soon the largest Black denomination. Blacks joined the new *Holiness and *Pentecostal Churches which emphasized sanctification and speaking in tongues. At the beginning of the 20th cent. rural Blacks in increasing numbers moved into the cities. RCism attracted significant numbers of Black converts, primarily by means of the parochial schools. Secular alternatives gradually began to compete, but the Church has remained a central institution for Black social, cultural, and political life.

In Britain Black Churches have a substantial presence in urban areas. After 1945 a large number of Black people from the Caribbean were recruited for work. Many who came first were from mainstream Churches, but, feeling unwelcome in the English congregations, came to disregard denominational loyalties. Later immigrants came largely from Holiness or Pentecostal backgrounds. They felt alienated from what they regarded as nominal Christianity. The regrouping of individuals around denominational loyalties within the Holiness-Pentecostal stream provided not only a common bond in worship but also some social and cultural cohesion for Afro-Caribbeans of various denominations. There are also Black Churches among the *Seventh-day Adventists and the emerging African Christian groups.

Black Friars. A popular name for the *Dominicans, so called from the black cloaks worn over their white habits.

Black Letter Days. The lesser (mainly non-biblical) Saints' Days (printed in black), as distinct from the major festivals, which used to appear in red in the BCP calendar.

Black Mass. A popular name for: (1) a *Requiem Mass, so called from the custom of using black vestments; (2) a parody of the Mass celebrated with blasphemous intent.

Black Monks. A name given in medieval England to the *Benedictine monks, from their black habits.

Black Rubric. A 19th-cent. name for the 'Declaration on Kneeling' printed at the end of the Holy Communion Service in the BCP. It was inserted in the Book of 1552 without Parliamentary authority. When *rubrics came to be printed in red, the fact that the 'Declaration' was not a rubric was indicated by printing it in black.

Blackwell, George (1547–1612), RC *archpriest. After training at *Douai, he returned to England on the RC mission in

1576. In 1598 he was put in control of the secular clergy and given the title of archpriest. He supported the policy of those (mainly *Jesuits) who wanted to destroy the government of *Elizabeth I against the seculars who aimed at a political *rapprochement* with the Crown. Thirty-one seculars (*Appellants) appealed to Rome in 1598–9; a reply was issued in Blackwell's favour, but after further appeals he was rebuked in 1602. He was imprisoned in 1607 and took the Oath of Allegiance to *James I. He was replaced in 1608.

Blake, William (1757–1827), poet and artist. His works include *Songs of Innocence* (1789); *Songs of Experience* (1794); his poem *Milton* (1804), the proem of which consists of the famous 'Jerusalem', widely used as a national hymn; and his allegorical poem *Jerusalem*. His books were mostly engraved by hand and illustrated by coloured drawings. In the *Illustrations to the Book of Job* (1826) the figures, often of elemental strength and beauty, move in the atmosphere of crude black and white contrasts which give Blake's works their characteristic impression of haunting unreality.

Blandina, St. A slave girl martyred in 177 at Lyons. Feast day in the W., 2 June; in the E., 26 July.

Blasius, St. According to a historically worthless legend he was Bp. of Sebaste in Armenia and martyred in the 4th cent. Feast day in the W., 3 (formerly 15) Feb.; in the E., 11 Feb.

blasphemy. Speech, thought, or action manifesting contempt of God. It may be directed either immediately against God or mediately against the Church or the saints, and it is by its nature a mortal sin. It was previously also a legal offence, but in Britain only scurrillous attacks on Christianity can now be sustained under the blasphemy laws, as calculated to offend believers or cause a breach of the peace.

Blastares, Matthew (fl. 1335), monk of Thessalonica. He composed an alphabetical handbook of *canon law and seems to have been the author of a collection of hymns.

Blemmydes, Nicephorus (1197–?1269), Greek theologian. He took an active part in attempts to unite the E. and W. Churches.

Blessed. See BEATIFICATION.

Blessed Sacrament. A term used of the Eucharist and applied both to the service and to the consecrated elements.

Blessed Virgin, the. See MARY, THE BLESSED VIRGIN.

blessing. The authoritative pronouncement of God's favour. Blessings of people and things are recorded in the OT. In Christian practice blessing finds a frequent place in the liturgy, especially in the blessing of the elements in consecration (so Mt. 26: 26). In many places it is now customary to end all services with a blessing, often given at the altar. The section on blessings in the *Romanum Rituale* (1984) provides forms of blessing for people and objects; these blessings are real services, including biblical readings and intercessions.

Blomfield, Charles James (1786–1857), Bp. of London from 1828. During his episcopate some 200 new chuches were built and consecrated. Both his politics and his Churchmanship appeared inconsistent. He supported the *Jerusalem Bishopric scheme of 1841, but signed the protest against R. D. *Hampden's appointment to the see of *Hereford.

Blondel, David (1590–1655), French ecclesiastical historian. For most of his life he was a country pastor, though in 1650 he succeeded G. J. *Voss at Amsterdam. His *Pseudo-Isidorus et Turrianus Vapulans* (1628) finally discredited the historicity of the *False Decretals.

Blondel, Maurice (1861–1949), French RC philosopher. In *L'Action* (1893; Eng. tr., 1984), his analysis of action led him to conclude that the human will which produces action cannot satisfy itself, because its fundamental desire is never fulfilled by any finite good. From this point of departure he developed an argument for the being of God resting on volition, in the light of which he modified the Scholastic proofs. God imposes Himself on the will as the first principle and the last term; we must therefore 'opt' either for Him or against Him. In his later works Blondel accords a greater place to abstract conceptions and affirms the legitimacy of methodical argumentation, e.g. in the rational proofs of the existence of God. For him, however, it is not that

knowledge of creatures precedes knowledge of God, but rather it is the existence of an obscure yet positive affirmation of God that is the very condition that makes the Aristotelian and Thomist proofs possible. For several years he was closely associated with the leaders of the *Modernist Movement.

Bloxam, John Rouse (1807–91), ceremonialist. A learned ecclesiologist, he was the real originator of the ceremonial revival in the C of E. As J. H. *Newman's curate at Littlemore, he introduced various ornaments which were copied by F. *Oakeley at the Margaret Chapel in London and thence spread into general use.

Blumhardt, Johann Christoph (1805–80), Protestant evangelist. The nephew of Christian Gottlieb Blumhardt, who founded the Protestant 'Basel Mission', in 1838 he became pastor at Möttlingen in Württemberg. His evangelical work attracted attention, largely because of the physical cures which sometimes accompanied it. From 1852 he worked at Bad Boll, near Göppingen, which became an influential centre of missionary work.

Boanerges. The surname given by Christ (Mk. 3: 17) to *James and *John, the sons of Zebedee.

Bobbio. A small town in the Apennines, once the seat of an abbey founded in 612 by St *Columbanus. Its celebrated collection of early MSS included the 'Bobbio Missal' (now in Paris), an important collection of liturgical texts dating from the 8th cent.

Bodley, George Frederick (1827–1907), ecclesiastical architect and designer. In partnership (1869–98) with Thomas Garner, he developed the 19th-cent. English Gothic tradition in a number of outstanding churches in England. His style spread throughout the Anglican Communion. He designed St David's Cathedral, Hobart, Tasmania, and, with Henry Vaughan, the Episcopal Cathedral in *Washington, DC.

Bodmer Papyri. A collection of important MSS, most on papyrus (see PAPYROLOGY), acquired for his library in Geneva by M. Martin Bodmer, mostly in 1956. They include an almost complete MS of Jn. (P. 66) of *c.* AD 200 and a copy of *Melito, 'On the Pasch'.

Body of Christ. (1) The human body which Christ took of the BVM and which, according to Christian theology, was changed but not abandoned at the Resurrection; (2) the Church; (3) the consecrated Bread at the Eucharist; and (4) in its Latin form, '*Corpus Christi', the feast commemorating the institution of the Eucharist; also used as a designation of churches and colleges dedicated in honour of the Eucharist.

Boehme, Jakob (1575–1624), German *Lutheran theosophical writer. He claimed in his writings to describe only what he had learnt by Divine illumination.

According to Boehme God the Father is the 'Ungrund', the indefinable matter of the universe, neither good nor evil, but containing the germ of either, unconscious and impenetrable. This 'abyss' tends to know itself in the Son, who is light and wisdom, and to expand and express itself in the Holy Spirit. The Godhead has two wills, one good and one evil, which drive Him to create nature, which unfolds itself in the seven nature spirits, of which the last is man. The unfolding of creation is revelation, or the birth of God. Man accepts this revelation through faith in Christ and experiences the birth of God in his soul. He will then be a conqueror on earth and will ultimately replace Lucifer, the fallen angel, in the heavenly city. Boehme's writings, which are obscure, had a wide influence.

Boethius, Anicius Manlius Torquatus Severinus (*c.*480–*c.*524), philosopher and statesman. In middle life he began to take an active part in politics and in 522 became 'Master of the Offices' at the Ostrogothic court at *Ravenna. He was charged with treason and judicially murdered.

Boethius made Latin translations of, and commentaries on, *Aristotle's *De Interpretatione* and *Categories* and a commentary on Marius *Victorinus' translation of *Porphyry's *Isagoge*. These were a main source of knowledge of Aristotle in the W. in the early Middle Ages. His most famous work, the *De consolatione philosophiae*, was written in the face of death. In it he offers a vindication of providence, which he reconciles with free will by the doctrine that what is contingent to us is not so to God, who is timeless. Despite the absence of specifically Christian teaching, the moral of this work was clear to medieval commentators;

through philosophy the soul attains to knowledge of the vision of God. Feast day, as 'St Severinus', 23 Oct.

Bogomils. A medieval Balkan sect of *Manichaean origin. They taught that the world and the human body were the work of Satan, only the soul being created by God. The ideals of abstinence from marriage, meat, and wine, and renunciation of all possessions, were practised only by the 'Perfect'; the ordinary faithful might sin but were obliged to obey the Perfect and would receive 'spiritual baptism' on their deathbeds. They held that Christ did not have a human body, but only the appearance of one. They rejected the Sacraments, churches, and relics, but retained a hierarchy of their own.

In the 11th cent. Bogomilism spread rapidly in the Balkans and Asia Minor, and from the mid-12th cent. it exerted a formative influence on the *Cathari in France and Italy. In the 13th cent. its adherents secured a notable success in Dalmatia and especially in Bosnia, where under the name of *Patarines they later became the dominant religious group. After the Turkish conquests, many people adopted *Islam; practically no trace of the heresy remains in the Balkans.

Boharic. A dialect of *Coptic.

Bohemian Brethren, later known as '*Moravian Brethren' and 'Unitas Fratrum'. They were a group of *Utraquists who formally separated from that body in 1467; they stood for a simple and unworldly Christianity. Organized as a Church by Lukáš of Prague (d. 1528), the sect spread rapidly. After 1547 repressive measures were taken against them; many migrated to *Poland, where they allied themselves with the *Calvinists in 1555. Those who remained in Bohemia obtained freedom to practise their cult in 1575, but fixed their principal seat in Moravia; hence their alternative name. They became the leading sector in Bohemian Protestantism, with many rights, but after the Battle of the White Mountain (1620) all Protestants were exiled. In 1721 the remains of the sect accepted an offer of N. L. von *Zinzendorf to join the *Herrnhutter, with whom they amalgamated. They laid special emphasis on Church services, organization, and education; their contribution to Czech literature was considerable, especially through their translation of the Bible (1579–93). They influenced early *Methodism. For their later history, see MORAVIAN BRETHREN.

Bohemond I (*c.*1052–1111), Prince of *Antioch. He led the S. Italian contingent in the First *Crusade. In return for his undertaking to secure the surrender of Antioch, the other leaders promised him possession of the city, which should have been returned to the Emp. Alexius I; he was invested by the new Latin Patriarch of Jerusalem. He was later defeated by the Byzantines and died at Canosa.

Bollandists. The *Jesuit editors of the '*Acta Sanctorum', so called after John van Bolland (1596–1665), the founder and first editor of the work.

Bologna, N. Italy. In the Middle Ages its university (founded in the 12th cent.) was the chief centre in Europe for the study of *canon and civil law.

Bologna, Concordat of (1516). The agreement between *Leo X and Francis I of France which ended the *Pragmatic Sanction of Bourges. The King was given wide rights to nominate ecclesiastics, who were to be confirmed by the Pope.

Bolsec, Hieronymus Hermes (d. 1584), physician and religious controversialist. Originally a *Carmelite friar in Paris, he adopted Protestantism *c.*1545 and then worked as a physician. In *Geneva he came into conflict with J. *Calvin by arguing that *predestination to salvation or reprobation amounted to no more than a person's faith or lack of faith in God. He was banished from Genevan territory. In his last years he returned to the RC faith.

Bolsena, Miracle of. According to the traditional story, a German priest celebrating Mass in the Umbrian town of Bolsena was disturbed by doubts about the *transubstantiation of the bread and wine; these were resolved when he saw blood issue from the consecrated elements and bathe the *corporal.

Bonaventure, St (*c.*1217–74), *Franciscan theologian. Giovanni di Fidanza probably became a Franciscan in 1243. He taught at *Paris. In 1257 he was elected Minister General and he did much to settle internal dissensions in the Order. In 1263 his Life of St *Francis was approved as the official biography. In 1273 he was made Cardinal Bp. of Albano.

As a theologian he remained faithful to the tradition derived from St *Augustine and had less sympathy with *Aristotelian doctrines than did St *Thomas Aquinas. In his *Itinerarium Mentis in Deum* he emphasized the folly of all human reason when compared with the mystical illumination which God sheds on the faithful Christian. His influence as a spiritual writer endured. Feast day, 15 (until 1969, 14) July.

Bonhoeffer, Dietrich (1906–45), German *Lutheran pastor. He sided with the *Confessing Church and signed the *Barmen Declaration in 1934. After serving as chaplain to the Lutheran community in London, he returned to Germany in 1935. He was forbidden by the Nazi government to teach and banned from Berlin. In 1942 he tried to form a link between the Germans opposed to Hitler and the British government. He was arrested in 1943 and hanged in 1945.

His writings have enjoyed wide influence. The best-known, *Widerstand und Ergebung* (1951; Eng. tr. *Letters and Papers from Prison*, 1953), is concerned with the growing secularization of man and the need to speak about God in a secular way. Though writers of the '*Death of God' school took up his idea of religionless Christianity, his teaching represents a search for the beyond in the midst, and a demand for a radical reform of the Church; he sought a form of Christianity capable of dispensing with traditional religion as a prerequisite for biblical faith. In CW, feast day, 9 Apr.

Boniface, St (*c.*675–754), the 'Apostle of Germany'. Wynfrith, as he was originally called, was born in Wessex (at *Crediton, according to tradition). After *Gregory II in 719 commissioned him to preach to the heathen, he converted many of the Hessians and in 722 was consecrated bishop without being given a see. His courage in felling the Oak of Thor at Geismar, near Fritzlar, won many converts. Probably in 732 Gregory III sent him a *pallium and in the following years he laid the foundations of a settled ecclesiastical organization E. of the Rhine. He convened a series of Councils to reform the Frankish Church, and *c.*746 he became Bp. of Mainz. He resigned after a few years to return to Frisia, where he was martyred. Feast day, 5 June.

Boniface I, St (d. 422), Pope from 418. He took a decisive stand against *Pelagianism, restored the rights of the metropolitans in S. Gaul, and secured the prefecture of Illyricum for his own jurisdiction when *Theodosius II tried to transfer it to the obedience of *Constantinople. Feast day, 4 Sept.

Boniface VIII (c.1234–1303), Pope from 1294. His pontificate was dominated by his struggle with Philip the Fair of France. The bull '*Clericis laicos' (1296) forbade extraordinary taxation of the clergy without Papal consent; Philip then stopped the transport of gold and valuables to Rome, and the Pope had to concede to him the right to decide for himself cases of necessity when he might levy taxes. The struggle broke out again in 1301. In his bull '*Unam Sanctam' (1302) Boniface defended the jurisdiction of the Pope over all persons; in 1303 Philip tried to bring Boniface to trial. The Pope prepared a bull of excommunication but was taken prisoner at Anagni; though he was released after three days he was broken in health and soon died. Among his achievements was the compilation of the '*Sext' and the foundation of the Roman University, the 'Sapienza', in 1303.

Boniface of Savoy (d. 1270), Abp. of *Canterbury. The son of a Count of Savoy, he entered the *Carthusian Order as a boy. He was elected Abp. of Canterbury in 1241, but was not enthroned until 1249. His metropolitical visitation met with strong resistance. He spent much time abroad.

Bonn Reunion Conferences. Two conferences held at Bonn in 1874 and 1875 under the presidency of J. J. I. von *Döllinger to foster reunion between Churches which had retained the faith and order of historic Christianity. Their direction was in the hands of the newly separated *Old Catholics.

Bonner, Edmund (c.1500–69), Bp. of London from 1539. Under *Edward VI he opposed the Royal *Injunctions of 1547 and evaded the provisions of the BCP; he was in 1549 deprived and imprisoned for disobeying a Privy Council instruction. Restored under

*Mary in 1553, he was energetic in the reconstruction of Catholic belief and worship and in the conviction of heretics, though his reputation for cruelty may be exaggerated. Under *Elizabeth I he refused to take the Oath of Supremacy in 1559; he spent his last years in prison.

Bonosus (d. c.400). A Bp. of Naïssus (modern Niš) or of *Sardica, who denied the perpetual virginity of the BVM. His followers, the 'Bonosians', survived until the 7th cent.

Book, Annexed, the; Book of Advertisements; of Armagh; of Common Order; of Common Prayer; of Concord; of Kells. See ANNEXED BOOK, THE; ADVERTISEMENTS, BOOK OF; ARMAGH, BOOK OF; COMMON ORDER, BOOK OF; COMMON PRAYER, BOOK OF; CONCORD, FORMULA AND BOOK OF; KELLS, BOOK OF.

book of life. The phrase occurs some 6 times in the NT. The conception of a heavenly register of the elect is based on ideas found in the OT and in 1 *Enoch.

Book of Sports. See SPORTS, BOOK OF.

Books of Discipline. See DISCIPLINE, BOOKS OF.

Booth, William (1829–1912), founder and first General of the *Salvation Army. In 1861 he left the *Methodists and established a revivalist movement of his own, then called the Christian Mission, which undertook evangelistic, social, and rescue work. From 1880, when the Salvation Army spread to the USA, Australia, and Europe, he spent much of his time travelling and addressing meetings.

Bordeaux Pilgrim. The earliest known Christian pilgrim from the W. to the *Holy Land. He made his journey in AD 333–4.

Borgia, Cesare (1475–1507), Italian prince. An illegitimate son of Pope *Alexander VI, he married the sister of the King of Navarre. An able soldier, he was unscrupulous in securing his ends, but once they were conquered, he ruled his subjects with justice and firmness; on him Machiavelli is said to have based his portrait of *The Prince*.

Borgia, St Francis (1510–72), *Jesuit. He succeeded his father as Duke of Gandía in 1543. After the death of his wife he joined the Jesuits; he made his solemn profession in 1548 secretly, with a dispensation regarding poverty for three years. In 1550 he went to Rome, where he made public his membership of the Society of Jesus. He was in charge of the Jesuit provinces of Spain and Portugal from 1554 to 1560; in 1561 he became assistant to D. *Laínez, succeeding him as *General in 1565. The membership of so significant a figure enhanced the prestige of the new Society, and his money and influence were crucial in the establishment of the 'Roman College' (later *Gregorianum). He also inaugurated Jesuit missions in the Spanish American colonies. Feast day, 10 Oct.

Borromeo, St Charles. See CHARLES BORROMEO, ST.

Borrow, George Henry (1803–81), traveller and author of *The Romany Rye* (1857). He was an agent of the *British and Foreign Bible Society and translated portions of Scripture into various little-known languages. *The Bible in Spain* (1843) became popular through its picturesque narrative.

Bosanquet, Bernard (1848–1923), Idealist philosopher. With F. H. *Bradley he was the leading exponent of *Absolute Idealism in England. He conceived of religion as only a stage towards metaphysics and God as no more than the highest of the appearances of the Absolute; the *Incarnation he found meaningless.

Bosco, St John (1815–88), founder of the *Salesian Order. A vision at the age of nine aroused in him a keen interest in winning boys to the Christian faith, and in 1859 near Turin he founded the 'Pious Society of St *Francis de Sales', commonly known as the Salesians. Feast day, 31 Jan.

Bosio, Antonio (c.1575–1629), Italian archaeologist. His *Roma sotterranea* ('1632', really 1634) remained the standard work on the *catacombs until G. B. *de Rossi's researches.

Bossey, Switzerland. An Ecumenical Institute of the *World Council of Churches was opened in 1946 at the Château de Bossey, 12 miles from Geneva.

Bossuet, Jacques-Bénigne (1627–1704), French preacher. In 1669 he was appointed Bp. of Condom and also delivered the first of his great 'Funeral Orations' (on *Henrietta Maria). From 1670 to 1681 he was tutor to the Dauphin, in 1681 becoming Bp. of Meaux. He then took a prominent part in French ecclesiastical affairs. In 1682 he was mainly instrumental in securing the support of the French clergy for the moderate *Gallicanism of the Four *Gallican Articles which he drew up. He approved the revocation of the Edict of *Nantes (1685) and directed various works against the Protestants. In his last years the case of Mme *Guyon led him into a bitter controversy with F. *Fénelon, and Bossuet was mainly responsible for Fénelon's condemnation in 1699. His *Méditations sur l'Évangile* (published 1731) and his *Élévations sur les mystères* (published 1727) are classics of French Catholic devotional literature.

Botulph, St (mid-7th cent.), also **Botolph**, **Botwulf**. According to the Anglo-Saxon Chronicle, in 654 he founded a monastery at Icanhoe (Iken in Suffolk or, less probably, Boston in Lincs.). Feast day, 17 June.

Bourchier, Thomas (c.1410–86), Abp. of *Canterbury from 1454 and Cardinal from 1467. He was much involved in political affairs. In 1457 he took a leading part in the trial of R. *Pecock, Bp. of Chichester.

Bourdaloue, Louis (1632–1704), French preacher. He joined the *Jesuits in 1648. His twelve courses of sermons delivered in Lent and Advent before Louis XIV and his court in and after 1670 earned him a reputation as an outstanding preacher.

Bourignon, Antoinette (1616–80), Flemish enthusiast and mystical writer. She tried to found a new ascetic order, but after 1662 she became estranged from mainstream Christianity. She influenced P. *Poiret, who published her works.

Bousset, Wilhelm (1865–1920), German NT scholar. He investigated the connections of later Judaism and early Christianity with the contemporary Hellenistic religions. The growth of the '*Religionsgeschichtliche Schule' owed much to him.

Bow Church. The church of St Mary-le-Bow (S. Maria de Arcubus) in Cheapside, London, so called from the stone arches of the original 11th-cent. church on the site. The present church was built by C. *Wren. It gave its name to the *Arches Court of Canterbury.

Boyle, Robert (1627–91), scientist. He saw his scientific work as demonstrating the Divine design of nature, and he published treatises emphasizing the harmony between scientific enquiry and the Christian life. He left £50 a year for lectures to confute unbelievers (the 'Boyle Lectures').

Bradford, John (c.1510–55), Protestant martyr. He was ordained deacon in 1550 by N. *Ridley, who made him his chaplain. Soon after *Mary's accession he was imprisoned on a charge of sedition. He defended the doctrine of *predestination against the *Freewillers among his fellow-prisoners before he was burnt at *Smithfield.

Bradley, Francis Herbert (1846–1924), exponent of *Absolute Idealism. His *Appearance and Reality* (1893) was the most original work in British metaphysics in the 19th cent. He argued that everywhere in the fields of natural science, ethics, religion, etc., contradictions are patent and that therefore these realms cannot be conceived of as reality. The only true reality is to be found in an all-inclusive experience, the Absolute, wherein all contradictions, including the gulf between subject and object, are transcended. Theism and personal immortality are rejected.

Bradwardine, Thomas (c.1295–1349), Abp. of *Canterbury. He taught at Oxford before he became chancellor of *St Paul's Cathedral in 1337. He was consecrated Abp. of Canterbury in 1349, but died later in the year.

In his main theological work, *De causa Dei*, Bradwardine sought to build up a theological system on evident propositions. Against the prevalent *Pelagian ideas he insisted on the necessity of grace and the 'irresistible' efficacy of the Divine Will, which lies behind all action, whether necessary or contingent. His writing paved the way for the predestinarian thought of J. *Wycliffe.

Brady, Nicholas. See TATE, NAHUM, AND BRADY, NICHOLAS.

Braga, rite of. The form of the RC rite used in the cathedral of Braga in N. Portugal. It certainly existed by the 14th cent. It was revised in 1924 and 1971.

Bramhall, John (1594–1663), Abp. of *Armagh from 1661. He went to Ireland as Strafford's chaplain in 1633, becoming Bp. of Derry in 1634. He retired to England in 1642 and to the Continent in 1644. He devoted his exile to defending the English Church against attacks, writing against the *Puritans, against the philosophical materialism and determinism of T. *Hobbes, and against the RC Church. As Archbishop, he exercised moderation in enforcing the Conformity Laws.

branch theory of the Church. The theory that, though the Church may have fallen into schism within itself and its several parts be out of communion with each other, each may yet be a 'branch' of the Church of Christ, provided that it holds the faith of the undivided Church and maintains the *apostolic succession.

brasses. Monuments consisting of brass plates, engraved with images or inscriptions, set into stones in the floor or on the walls of a church. Originating in the 13th cent., they were much used until the 16th.

brawling. The offence of creating a disturbance in a church or churchyard.

Bray, Thomas (1656–1730), founder of the *SPCK and *SPG. When an appeal for help with the ecclesiastical organization of Maryland, USA, reached H. *Compton, Bp. of London, the Bishop appointed Bray his commissary. In view of the poverty of the clergy, Bray worked out a scheme for the provision of free libraries in the colony; he promoted a similar project at home. Another of his schemes took shape in the foundation of the SPCK (1698).With others, he founded the SPG as a separate society for foreign missions (1701). Feast day in parts of the Anglican Communion, 15 Feb.

Bray, the Vicar of. The hero of a ballad whose pretended zeal for each new form of established religion from *Charles I to George I assured his tenure of his benefice.

Brazil, Christianity in. The conversion of Brazil was effected mainly by the *Jesuits, who founded the city of São Paulo in 1554. The influx of slaves from Africa, who were forcibly converted to Christianity, produced a synthesis of African religions and Catholicism as a way of preserving the language and culture of the African tribes (Afro-Brazilian rites). Brazil became independent of *Portugal in 1822. With the establishment of the Republic in 1889, the Church was disestablished and freedom of worship guaranteed to all bodies. In recent years Protestantism (especially *Baptists, *Pentecostals, and *Seventh-day Adventists), *Spiritualism, and Afro-Brazilian rites have increased their adherents. RC Brazilian bishops have been active in implementing the 'option for the poor'; many of the pioneers of *Liberation Theology worked within the Basic Christian communities in Brazil.

bread, leavened and unleavened. In the Eucharistic rite most of the E. Churches use leavened bread, whereas Catholics in the W. use unleavened; the divergence became a cause of dissension. In the Anglican Communion the use of either is now permitted, either implicitly or explicitly. Leavened bread is generally used by Nonconformists.

Bread of the Presence. See SHEWBREAD.

Breakspear, Nicholas. See HADRIAN IV.

Breastplate of St Patrick. An Old Irish hymn familiar in the translation beginning 'I bind unto myself today The strong Name of the Trinity'. It has been dated to the early 8th cent. The ascription to St *Patrick is impossible on linguistic grounds.

Breda, Declaration of. The declaration made by *Charles II at Breda in the Netherlands in Apr. 1660, immediately before the Restoration. It promised 'liberty to tender consciences' in matters of religion not affecting the peace of the realm.

Breeches Bible. A popular name for the *Geneva Bible of 1560 from its translation of Gen. 3: 7, where the AV has 'aprons'.

Bremond, Henri (1865–1933), French spiritual writer. His principal work, *Histoire littéraire du sentiment religieux en France* (1916–33 + index, 1936), is a history of French spirituality, chiefly in the 17th cent., in the form of a series of essays on outstanding religious personalities.

Brendan, St (484–577 or 583), also **Brennain**, Abbot of Confert. In his lifetime he was renowned as a navigator, and the anonymous *Navigatio S. Brendani* (probably 8th cent.) describes voyages made by Brendan and 12 monks to various mythical islands in search of an earthly paradise. The

tradition that he founded the monastery of Cluain Fearta (Clonfert, in Co. Galway, Ireland) may well be true. Feast day, 14 May.

Brent, Charles Henry (1862–1929), Anglican *ecumenical leader. Born and trained in Canada, in 1901 Brent became Bp. of the Philippine Islands, where he combated the opium trade, and in 1918 Bp. of Western New York. After the *Edinburgh Conference of 1910 he induced the General Convention of the *Episcopal Church to convene a 'World Conference on *Faith and Order'; when the Conference met at *Lausanne in 1927, Brent was its President. Feast day in the American BCP (1979), 27 Mar.

Brenz, Johann (1499–1570), German Reformer. In 1522 he was appointed Preacher at the church of St Michael in Schwäbisch Hall and from then actively supported the Reformation. In his *Syngramma Suevicum* (1525) he insisted on the Real Presence in the Eucharist and thus ensured the acceptance of the *Lutheran teaching in most of Württemberg. In 1527 he put forward a proposal for a Church Order in Hall which from 1535 began to be adopted throughout Württemberg. He also compiled the *Württemberg Confession. In 1553 he became Provost of the Stiftskirche in Stuttgart.

Brest-Litovsk, Union of, now often called the Union of Brest. The union concluded in 1596 between the *Ukrainian (or Ruthenian) and the RC Churches.

Brethren, Church of the. See TUNKERS.

Brethren of the Common Life. An association founded in the 14th cent. to foster a higher level of Christian life and devotion. The original leader was G. *Groote (q.v.); he demanded no vows but left his disciples free to continue their ordinary vocations. They founded many schools offering excellent free education, and many of their members engaged in copying MSS and later in printing. After Groote's death (1384) the leadership was assumed by *Florentius Radewijns. One group adopted a rule and organized themselves as *Augustinian Canons. The Brethren included I. *Busch, *Thomas à Kempis, and G. *Biel.

Brethren of the Free Spirit. Individuals who apparently believed that they could be entirely liberated from conventional moral norms through attaining perfect union with God. They were first identified by St *Albertus Magnus near Augsburg in the 1270s. The heresy came to be associated with certain *Beguines.

brethren of the Lord. The 'Lord's brethren' referred to in the NT may have been: (1) sons of the BVM and *Joseph, born after Christ; (2) according to St *Jerome, sons of Mary, 'the mother of James and Joses' (Mk. 15: 40), whom he identified with the wife of Clopas and sister of the BVM; (3) sons of Joseph by a former marriage (so the E. Church); or (4) sons of Mary, 'the mother of James and Joses' (not identified with the sister of the BVM), and Clopas, who was perhaps the brother of Joseph.

Brett, Thomas (1667–1744), *Nonjuror. On the accession of George I (1714) he resigned his living; he was received as a Nonjuror by G. *Hickes, after whose death he was consecrated bishop in 1716. He took part in the abortive negotiations for reunion of his party with the Greek Church and he was involved in the controversy over *Usages. His *Dissertation on the Ancient Liturgies* (1720) is still of some value.

Breviary. The liturgical book containing the Psalms, hymns, lessons, prayers, etc., to be recited in the Divine *Office of the RC Church. The various parts were originally contained in different books. To collate the texts needed for the day's office, the *Ordo*, giving the reference and opening words of the texts, was developed in the 11th cent. In the 12th cent. the full texts were added, making the Office book or breviary.

Bride, St. See BRIGIT, ST.

Bridges, Robert Seymour (1844–1930), Poet Laureate from 1913. In 1882 he abandoned medicine for literature and music. *The Testament of Beauty* (1929) is a philosophical poem which seeks to reconcile scientific knowledge with Christian faith. In the *Yattendon Hymnal* (1895–9) he revived many fine 16th- and 17th-cent. melodies; his work was drawn on in the *English Hymnal*. He also published the first collected edition of the *Poems* of G. M. *Hopkins.

Bridget (Birgitta) of Sweden, St (c.1303–73), founder of the *Bridgettine Order. She married early and had 8 children. After the death of her husband, she appears to have had a series of revelations which led her to urge the Pope to return to Rome from *Avignon. She also received detailed instructions about the foundation of a new religious order (see next entry). From 1349 she lived mainly in Rome. Her *Revelations* were valued in the Middle Ages. Feast day, 23 July (formerly 8 Oct.).

Bridgettine Order, also known as the 'Brigittine Order'. It was founded by St *Bridget of Sweden, following revelations which she was held to have received. Land for the mother house at Vadstena was granted in 1346 and the order approved in a bull of 1370. Its members were organized in double monasteries, with priests and lay brothers acting as chaplains and assistants to a larger number of nuns. Though segregated, they shared a church. The male branch died out in 1842; the female religious still maintain a few houses.

Bridgewater Treatises. Eight treatises, published between 1833 and 1836, on various aspects of the 'power, wisdom, and goodness of God, as manifested in the Creation'. F. H. Egerton, 8th Earl of Bridgewater (d. 1829), left £8,000 for the purpose.

briefs, Church. Warrants (usually royal, but sometimes issued by bishops or archbishops) authorizing collections for specific charitable purposes. In England after the Reformation Church briefs were the successors to Papal briefs (see BULL). They were read out in church. The process was suppressed in 1828.

Briggs, Charles Augustus (1841–1913), OT scholar. He held professorships at the *Union Theological Seminary, New York. An exponent of *Higher Criticism, he was one of the editors of the *International Critical Commentaries* and also of the standard Hebrew *Lexicon*.

Brigit, St (perhaps 5th–6th cent.), 'Bride'. Though she is greatly venerated in *Ireland, the traditions about her are conflicting; she may never have lived and may represent the pagan goddess Brig Christianized. One tradition connects her with Faughard, near Dundalk, where she is said to have been born; another with Kildare, where she is honoured as patron and founder. Feast day, 1 Feb.

Brigittine Order. See BRIDGETTINE ORDER.

British and Foreign Bible Society. One of the largest Bible Societies. An inter-denominational body, it was founded in London in 1804 for the printing and distribution of Bibles at home and abroad. It has published translations of the Bible (excluding the *Apocrypha) in many languages.

British Council of Churches. An organization created in 1942 to further common Christian action and promote the cause of unity among the Churches of Great Britain and Ireland. On the foundation of the *World Council of Churches in 1948, it became an 'Associated Council'. Its membership increased over the years, and from 1965 the RCs sent observers to its meetings. In 1990 it was succeeded by the *Council of Churches for Britain and Ireland. See also CHRISTIAN AID.

Britten, Edward Benjamin (1913–76), English composer. In 1947 he settled at Aldeburgh, Suffolk, where he established the famous festival. In the *War Requiem*, written for the celebrations connected with the dedication of *Coventry Cathedral (1962), he juxtaposed poems of Wilfred Owen (who died in the 1914–18 War) with the traditional Latin text. Apart from settings for the *Te Deum* and *Jubilate*, the *Missa Brevis* for the trebles of *Westminister Cathedral (1959), and the *cantata *Rejoice in the Lamb* (1943), he wrote little music specifically for use in Church services, but he was preoccupied with cruelty and the plight of the innocent 'outsider'.

broadcasting, religious. The use of electronic means of communication to transmit radio programmes dealing with religion predates the beginning of regular broadcasting in the 1920s; in 1912 R. E. Fessenden transmitted a Christmas Eve service to ships off the E. coast of America. When regular broadcasting began on both sides of the Atlantic, the religious potential was recognized, but its context, control, and content developed differently in the USA and Europe.

In the USA the first licensed radio station, KDKA, broadcast a religious service in 1921, and in 1924 the first radio station launched under religious auspices, KFUO ('keep forward, upward, onward') began broadcasting. In 1927 the Federal Radio Commission was set up; licensing policy became less permissive and the number of Church-owned stations fell. When the main radio networks were established, the religious broadcasts they transmitted were 'mainstream' Christian. Evangelical Protestant denominations bought radio time from commerical stations; they learnt to make programmes that appealed to large audiences and attracted funds. In Europe, where there were few commercial stations, religious proselytizing by radio was either forbidden or frowned on, but religious broadcasting developed its own momentum. The *Netherlands acknowledged religious differences by creating a balanced system of public broadcasting, with four services based on religion: two Protestant and two RC. In Britain Christianity was afforded a special place in broadcasting, and the BBC, which began operating in 1922, set up a 'Sunday Committee' in 1923. The establishment of a Central Religious Advisory Committee was significant in that it included not only Anglicans and Nonconformists but also RCs, and it supervised broadcasting on weekdays as well as Sundays. In Italy, the RC Church was strong enough to ensure that there was no Protestant religious broadcasting on State radio before 1944.

In the USA, the emergence of radio personalities who broadcast religious messages, was carried over into television. A number of them became involved in political, as well as religious, controversy. In 1950 Billy *Graham's 'Hour of Decision' was first televised on a major network, but it was paid evangelical broadcasting that came to dominate what was increasingly thought of as a market, international as well as American. In Europe the advent of television opened up opportunities for religious broadcasting in various countries, including *France, where the first televised RC Mass was broadcast on Christmas Eve 1948.

Religious broadcasting by the BBC has generally been 'mainstream' on both television and radio, but in 1954 'people's religious programmes' were introduced on television. With the advent of competition from commercial companies in 1955, the number of experiments increased. In the

1970s more emphasis was placed on religious broadcasting as a forum, and attempts have been made to meet the religious interests of those outside the Churches.

Broad Church. A popular term, coined on the analogy of *High Church and *Low Church, for those of the C of E who objected to positive definitions in theology and sought to interpret the Anglican formularies in a broad and liberal sense.

broad stole. A broad band of material formerly worn like a *stole by the deacon during parts of *High Mass in certain penitential seasons.

Brooks, Phillips (1835–93), Bp. of Massachusetts in the *Episcopal Church from 1891. He was the most celebrated American preacher of his day. He wrote the carol 'O little town of Bethlehem'. Feast day in the American BCP (1979), 23 Jan.

Brother Lawrence of the Resurrection **(Nicolas Herman)** (c.1614–1691), *Carmelite lay brother and mystic. His writings, published after his death as *Maximes spirituelles* (1692) and *Mœurs et entretiens de F. Laurent* (1694), recommend an elevated form of prayer consisting in the simple practice of the presence of God, whether by the imagination or the intellect.

Brothers Hospitallers. The Order, whose members are mostly laymen, developed out of the work for the sick of St *John of God (d. 1550). In 1572 *Pius V approved the Order, which adopted the *Augustinian Rule.

brothers. See BRETHREN.

Browne, George (d. c.1556), Abp. of *Dublin. An English *Augustinian friar, as Provincial of his Order he was charged by *Henry VIII in 1534 with part in a visitation of the friars which included administering the Oath of *Supremacy. In 1536 he was appointed Abp. of Dublin. He took part in the suppression of the Irish monasteries, and under *Edward VI he became the leader of the Irish clergy who accepted the new religion. In 1554, under *Mary, he was deprived of his see, presumably because he was married.

Browne, Robert (c.1550–1633), *Puritan separatist. A relative of William Cecil, Lord Burghley, he came under the influence of T. *Cartright and in 1581 established an independent congregation at *Norwich. He was promptly imprisoned. Freed through Cecil's intervention, he migrated with his flock to Middelburg in the Netherlands. He soon fell out with many of them. Returning to England, he made a formal submission to the C of E and became Master of St Olav's School, *Southwark, in 1586, though he still seems to have ministered to separatist congregations. In 1591 he received episcopal ordination and became Rector of Thorpe Achurch, Northants. He exercised an important influence on the beginnings of *Congregationalism, whose early members were often called 'Brownists'.

Browne, Sir Thomas (1605–82), physician, natural historian, antiquary, and moralist. In *Religio Medici* (1642) he expounded his reconciliation of devout belief in the Word of God with empiricism when reading the Book of Nature. *Pseudodoxia Epidemica* (1646), examines various accepted beliefs in the light of reason and experience. The twin tracts, *Hydriotaphia* and *The Garden of Cyrus* (published together, 1658) are meditations on death and resurrection in the form of treatises on burial customs.

Brownists. See BROWNE, ROBERT.

Brunner, Emil (1889–1966), Swiss *dialectical theologian. From 1922 to 1953 he taught mainly at Zurich. He supported K. *Barth in opposing theological liberalism, but he was sharply divided from him by the influence of M. *Buber and by his acceptance of the concept of *natural theology, by which a limited knowledge of God may be gained from creation. This, though it did not, like revelation, provide a personal meeting, was a necessary condition of Christian thought. His works include *Der Mittler* (1927; Eng. tr., *The Mediator*, 1934) and *Das Gebot und die Ordnungen* (1932; Eng. tr., *The Divine Imperative*, 1937).

Bruno, St (c.925–65), Abp. of *Cologne from 953. The third son of Henry I of Germany, he played a leading role in the government of his brother, Otto I. Feast day, 11 Oct.

Bruno, St (c.1032–1101), founder of the *Carthusian Order. He became head of the cathedral school at *Reims c.1057. Soon after 1080 he turned to the religious life.

After a short time under the direction of St *Robert of Molesme, he went with six companions into the mountainous district near Grenoble, where he laid the foundations of the Carthusian Order (1084). In 1090 he was summoned to Italy by his former pupil, Pope *Urban II. He refused the archbishopric of Reggio, retired to Calabria, and founded the monastery of La Torre, where he died. Feast day, 6 Oct.

Bruno, Giordano (1548–1600), Italian philosopher. In 1562 he joined the *Dominican Order at Naples, but on being censured for unorthodoxy he fled in 1576. In 1592 he was captured by emissaries of the *Inquisition and was kept in confinement until he was burnt at the stake. He was a fierce opponent of *Aristotelian doctrines and an admirer of N. *Copernicus. His enthusiasm for nature led him to hold an extreme form of *pantheistic immanentism.

Bruys, Pierre de. See PETER DE BRUYS.

Bryanites. See BIBLE CHRISTIANS.

Buber, Martin (1878–1965), Jewish religious thinker. A native of Vienna, he took part in the Zionist movement. He was deprived of his professorship at Frankfurt in 1933; in 1938 he became professor at the Hebrew University at Jerusalem.

Buber's best-known work, which influenced both Christian theologians and the German Youth Movement, was a small treatise, *Ich und Du* (1923; Eng. trs., *I and Thou*, 1937 and 1970). This contrasts the 'I-Thou' relationship, in which the other is granted its full reality, with the 'I-It' relationship, in which the other is subjected to my needs and purposes.

Bucer, Martin (1491–1551), Protestant Reformer, also spelled **Butzer**. A *Dominican, he adopted *Lutheranism in 1521 and settled in Strasbourg, where he was given charge of a parish. He took part in the *Marburg Colloquy (1529) and various other unsuccessful conferences between Catholics and Protestants, and he helped *Hermann of Wied in his vain attempt to introduce Reformed doctrines at *Cologne. His Eucharistic doctrine is usually held to be mid-way between that of M. *Luther and U. *Zwingli. In 1549 he came to England at T. *Cranmer's invitation and was made Regius Professor of Divinity at *Cambridge.

He influenced parts of the Anglican *Ordinal.

Buchanan, George (1506–82), Scottish scholar and man of letters. While teaching in *Portugal, he came under suspicion of heresy for his satires on the contemporary Church, was imprisoned by the *Inquisition, and moved from humanism of the *Erasmian type to Protestantism. Returning to Scotland in 1561, he was *Moderator of the General Assembly of the Kirk in 1567. Though tutor to both *Mary, Queen of Scots, and James VI (*James I of England), he rejected the doctrine of the *Divine Right of Kings and regarded the people as the source of political power.

Buchman, Frank Nathan Daniel (1878–1961), founder of the *Oxford Group (q.v.). He served as a *Lutheran minister and undertook social work in America before resigning in a spirit of disillusionment. On a visit to England he attended a *Keswick Convention and experienced conversion. He visited India and the Far East, and in 1920 he went to Cambridge. Some Cambridge undergraduates joined him in visiting Oxford, and out of this visit the Group movement grew. In the 1930s he travelled widely. In 1938 in London he called for *Moral Rearmament, a development of the work which stressed the role of individuals in spiritually transforming society.

Buckfast Abbey, Devon. The first abbey was founded in 1018. Ceded to the Abbot of *Savigny in 1136, it adopted the Rule of *Cîteaux in 1147 and remained *Cistercian until its *dissolution in 1539. A private house was built on the site in the 19th cent. and to this the exiled French monks from the abbey of La-Pierre-qui-Vire came in 1882. The present abbey church was consecrated in 1932.

Bugenhagen, Johann (1485–1558), *Lutheran theologian. He played a leading part in the organization of Lutheran Church life in N. Germany and *Denmark. The 'Brunswick Church Order' of 1528 was mainly his work. In 1537 he went to Denmark; here he rearranged ecclesiastical affairs on a Protestant basis, himself consecrating seven men as superintendents or 'bishops'. The Danish Church thus lost the *Apostolic Succession.

bugia (also **scotula**, **palmatorium**). A portable candlestick with lighted candle sometimes held beside a RC bishop when he reads certain prayers.

Bulgakov, Sergius (1871–1944), Russian theologian. Expelled from Russia after the 1917 Revolution, he was Dean of the Orthodox Theological Academy in Paris from 1925 until his death. He was widely known in W. Europe and America through his participation in the *Ecumenical Movement. Theologically he is best known for his contributions to Sophiology, a body of thought which seeks to solve the problems of the relation between God and the world by the concept of the Divine *Wisdom or *sophia*.

Bulgaria, Christianity in. The official introduction of Christianity into Bulgaria occurred in 864–5, with the Baptism of Prince Boris. Missionaries from both E. and W. were at work; c.870 Boris decided in favour of the E. Church. Under Tsar Simeon (893–927) the Bulgarian Church became *autocephalous, but during the Turkish period it became increasingly subject to Constantinople, finally losing all trace of independence in 1767. On attaining political independence in 1870, the Bulgarians created an autocephalous *Exarchate, but were excommunicated by the Patriarch of Constantinople in 1872 for nationalism; the schism continued until 1945. In 1953 the Metropolitan of Sofia assumed the title of *Patriarch and was so recognized by the *Oecumenical Patriarch in 1961.

bull. A written mandate of the Pope of a more serious and weighty kind than a 'brief'.

Bull, George (1634–1710), Bp. of *St Davids from 1705. He was a staunch *High Churchman. His *Harmonia Apostolica* (1669–70) was an attack on the more Protestant theories of *justification. His celebrated *Defensio Fidei Nicaenae* (1685) maintained, against D. *Petavius, that the teaching of the pre-Nicene Fathers on the Trinity agreed with that of orthodox theologians of Nicene and post-Nicene times. Bull received the unusual tribute of the formal thanks of the French clergy.

bullarium. A collection of Papal *bulls and other similar documents.

Bullinger, Heinrich (1504–75), Swiss Reformer. Convinced of the primary importance of the Bible, he adopted *Lutheranism and later Zwinglianism. In 1531 he succeeded U. *Zwingli as the Chief Pastor at Zurich. Within Switzerland, he played a leading role in drawing up the first and second *Helvetic Confessions (1536 and 1566) and the *Consensus Tigurinus* (1549); these provided a national basis for the Reformation and prevented it from becoming merely a cantonal phenomenon. Abroad he combatted the Lutheran doctrine of the Eucharist and refuted *Anabaptist theology. He saw no basic distinction between the Christian State and the Christian Church and considered that the norms for a Christian society had been established by God in the OT: from this *covenant theology it followed that the jurisdiction of the civil authority extended to ecclesiastical matters, and, though *predestination was still of prime importance, God's election was binding in history only so far as men kept the conditions of the covenant.

Bultmann, Rudolf (1884–1976), NT scholar and theologian. He was a professor at *Marburg from 1921 until he retired in 1951. He carried the methods of *Form Criticism to the point where any historical value in the *Synoptic Gospels was called into question. In his *Jesus* (1926; Eng. tr., *Jesus and the Word*, 1934), he presented the mission of Jesus as summoning His followers to a decision. Bultmann combined his biblical scholarship with the *dialectical theology of K. *Barth and the Lutheran doctrine of *justification by faith alone to make an almost complete hiatus between history and faith, leaving only the bare fact of Christ crucified as necessary for Christian faith. He regarded St *Paul and the author of Jn. as the only genuine theologians of the NT, because they offer an interpretation of human existence and see talk of God, Christ, and salvation, in terms of the individual's changed self-understanding effected by the proclaimed Word or *kerygma. Narrowing the theological focus in this way involved criticizing the cosmological elements in the NT as 'myth', and it was his programme of *demythologizing the NT which in the 1940s and 1950s made Bultmann notorious. Latterly his aim to make the Christian message intelligible in the modern world has been more widely respected.

Bunting, Jabez (1779–1858), Wesleyan *Methodist minister. In 1835 he became president of the first Wesleyan Theological College, established at Hoxton in London. His main work was to transform the Methodist society into a Church, with a sound organization, independent of the C of E.

Bunyan, John (1628–88), author of *The *Pilgrim's Progress*. Few facts about his life are known. Born of poor parents, he took part in the Civil War on the Parliamentary side (1644–6), and *c*.1649 married a woman of piety. In 1653 he joined an *Independent congregation at Bedford; he was formally recognized as a preacher in 1657. After the *Restoration he spent most of the years 1660–72 in Bedford gaol. During and after his imprisonment he wrote extensively. His chief works are his autobiography, *Grace Abounding to the Chief of Sinners* (1666); *The Pilgrim's Progress* (q.v.); and *The Holy War* (1682). For Bunyan the world was exclusively the scene of a spiritual warfare and nothing mattered save the salvation of the soul. Feast day in CW, 30 Aug.

Burchard (*c*.965–1025), Bp. of Worms in Germany from 1000. Between *c*.1008 and 1012 he compiled his *Decretum*, a collection of *canon law, which exercised great influence in the 11th and 12th cents.

Burckard (or Burchard), John (d. 1506), Papal Master of Ceremonies from 1483. His main work was a detailed set of rubrics for *Low Mass, the *Ordo servandus*, published in 1502, which was the basis of the *Ritus Celebrandi* of 1570. It was the first attempt to lay down the ceremonial for this form of Mass.

Burdett-Coutts, Angela Georgina (1814–1906), heiress and philanthropist. She inherited her wealth from Thomas Coutts, the banker. Her benefactions to the C of E included the building and endowment of a number of churches and the endowment of the Anglican bishoprics of Cape Town, Adelaide, and British Columbia.

Burgher. A member of the group in the Scottish Secession Church which in 1747 defended the lawfulness of the religious clause in the civil Burgess Oath and thus separated from the Antiburghers, who denied it.

Burgundio of Pisa (*c*.1110–93), lawyer. He translated into Latin the works of St *John of Damascus and other Greek fathers.

burial services. Burial is the traditional Christian method of disposing of the dead. At first burials were occasions of joy; from about the 8th cent., when the prevalence of nominal Christianity made such joy not always fitting, the service became 'black' and the prayers petitions for speedy purification. By the later Middle Ages the burial itself, with committal prayers, was preceded overnight by *Vespers, after which *Mattins and *Lauds (*Dirge) were said in the night, and in the morning a *Requiem Mass. The 1969 RC *Ordo Exsequiarum* provides various alternative forms, in some cases allowing all the funeral rites, including the Mass, to take place in the house of the deceased. In the BCP the Dirge in a modified form (sentences, Psalm, and lesson) is ordered, followed by committal prayers at the graveside. Modern Anglican liturgies make changes in phrasing, allow different Psalms and lessons, and provide for an (optional) Eucharist. They also recognize *cremation and sometimes include a form for the burial of ashes. In the Orthodox Church the burial service includes the *contakion 'Give rest, O Christ, to Thy servant' and an *epistle and *gospel. The coffin is normally left open and those present kiss the body. See also DEAD, PRAYERS FOR THE, and REQUIEM MASS.

Burma, Christianity in. Italian *Barnabites founded a mission in Burma in 1722; from 1830 this was transferred to other RC religious orders. The first permanent *Baptist mission came from the USA under Adoniram *Judson in 1813. Anglican missionary activity began in 1859, *Methodist in 1879. Christianity gained few converts from Burmese of Buddhist background, but had some success among the Karens, Kachins, and other tribal minorities. A RC hierarchy was created in 1955. The Anglican Church, formerly part of the Church of India, Burma, and Ceylon, became a separate Province in 1970. The largest Christian body is the Burma Baptist Convention. Since independence in 1948 Burma has been ruled mainly by a military-socialist government and in 1966 foreign missionaries had to leave.

Burnet, Gilbert (1643–1715), Bp. of *Salisbury from 1689. He tried, unsuccessfully, to carry through plans which would allow for the incorporation of Nonconformists in the C of E. His episcopate was a model of zeal and activity. His writings include his *History of My Own Time* (1723–34).

burning. Burning alive was a penalty for certain criminal offences in late Roman and early Germanic law and was subsequently adopted in most W. European penal codes. The burning of convicted heretics was a medieval development. In 1022 Robert II of France burned some ten convicted heretics at Orléans, and burning subsequently became the normal penalty for heresy throughout the W. Initially such executions were carried out against the wishes of the Church authorities, but in 1184 Pope Lucius III decreed that unrepentant heretics should be handed over to the secular authorities for punishment and this practice was followed by the *Inquisition from its inception. By 1298 all rulers punished heresy by burning. In England the Crown claimed the right to issue a writ to order the burning of condemned heretics. The act *De Haeretico Comburendo* (1401) gave statutory force to the burning of heretics; it was repealed in 1533, restored by *Mary, and again repealed in 1558. *Elizabeth I and *James I ordered heretics to be burnt for *Arianism and *Anabaptism. The last such burning took place in 1610. In the rest of Europe burning for heresy declined in the 17th cent. and even in *Spain and its dependencies became rare. Burning was the penalty for *witchcraft in Catholic and some Protestant countries, including *Scotland; the last burning for witchcraft in the British Isles took place at Dornoch in 1727. In parts of Europe witches were burned until at least the 1750s.

burning bush, the. The scene of *Moses' call, where the Angel of God appeared 'in a flame of fire out of the midst of a bush' (Exod. 3: 2–4).

Burrough, Edward (*c.*1634–63), *Quaker. After hearing G. *Fox preaching in 1652, Burrough joined the *Friends and began preaching himself. He was arrested in 1662 and died in prison.

burse. A cover consisting of two squares of stiffened material in which until 1970 the rubrics of the RC Missal ordered that the *corporal should be kept. Though no longer required, it is still widely used in RC and Anglican churches.

Busch, Jan (1399–*c.*1480), one of the principal *Brethren of the Common Life. He took a prominent part in reforming monasteries in the spirit of the Council of *Basle and for a time worked in co-operation with *Nicholas of Cusa. He wrote a history of the Brethren's house at *Windesheim.

Bushnell, Horace (1802–76), American *Congregationalist. Pastor to a church in Hartford, Conn., from 1833 to 1859, he was a pioneer of liberal theology in New England. On the ground that language was essentially symbolic, he held that while the doctrine of the Trinity might be true for man in that God was experienced under three different aspects, it did not provide real information as to the inner nature of the Godhead or require the existence of eternal distinctions in His Being.

Butler, Alban (1710–73), author of the work commonly known as *The Lives of the Saints* (1756–9). The lives are arranged according to the Church calendar. Butler was a mission priest in England (1746–66), and then President of the English College at *St-Omer.

Butler, Joseph (1692–1752), Bp. of *Durham. From 1718 to 1726 he was preacher at the *Rolls Chapel (London), where he delivered the sermons which won him his reputation. In 1726 he obtained the rich benefice of Stanhope, Co. Durham, where he prepared his famous *Analogy of Religion* (1736; q.v.). In 1738 he became Bp. of Bristol; in 1750 he was translated to Durham.

Butler ranks among the greatest exponents of natural theology and ethics in England since the Reformation. He held that morality consisted in living in accordance with one's nature, and that the primary constituent principles in human nature were self-love, benevolence, and conscience. True benevolence was strictly disinterested. To conscience attached a supreme authority. The principles of morality were intuitively evident and errors of moral judgement arose only from superstition and self-deception. Belief in Providence convinced Butler that in the end the dictates of conscience and the demands of self-love will be found to have pointed to the same conclusion. In the American BCP (1979) and CW, feast day, 16 June.

Butler, Josephine Elizabeth (1828–1906), social reformer. Her main interest was in the reclamation of prostitutes and the suppression of the 'white slave' trade. Her activity was based on a life of almost continuous prayer, in which she took as her model St *Catherine of Siena, of whom she published a Life in 1878. In CW, feast day, 30 May.

Butler, William John (1818–94), Dean of *Lincoln from 1885. In 1846 he became Vicar of Wantage. Through a long incumbency he trained many curates and in 1848 he founded St Mary's Sisterhood, which, as the Community of St Mary the Virgin (CSMV), has grown into one of the largest of the Anglican *religious communities.

Butterfield, William (1814–1900), architect. He was a keen Churchman who came under the influence of the *Oxford Movement. He built a number of churches, including All Saints', Margaret Street, London, Keble College, Oxford, and the Anglican cathedrals at Perth, Adelaide, and Melbourne in Australia.

Byrd, William (1543–1623), English composer. He became organist of *Lincoln Cathedral in 1563; in 1570 he was sworn as a Gentleman of the *Chapel Royal, where he became organist with T. *Tallis. He was a practising RC, but was not thereby prevented from executing his duties. Besides his three superb Masses, two books of *Gradualia*, and other music for the Latin rite, he set to music the Preces and Responses and Litany of the English liturgy and composed at least two complete services for Morning and Evening prayer, two other Evening Services, and a number of anthems, including 'Sing Joyfully'.

Byrhtferth (d. c.1020), scholar. A monk of Ramsey Abbey, he left a substantial body of computistical, hagiographical, and historical writings, including a computus and commentary on it known as the *Enchiridion*, a Life of St *Oswald, Abp. of York, and a *Historia regum*, treating of English history to the reign of *Alfred. This last was long attributed to *Simeon of Durham. He is the only Anglo-Saxon author whose range of interests is comparable to *Bede's.

Byzantine rite. The liturgical rite of the E. *Orthodox Church, so called because it was used in *Constantinople (anciently the city of Byzantium).

Byzantine text of the NT. The form of the Greek NT which became standard in the Greek-speaking Church; it is now generally known as the 'Lucianic Text' (q.v.).

Byzantium. See CONSTANTINOPLE.

Cabasilas, St Nicholas (b. c.1322), Byzantine mystical writer. In a set of discourses 'Concerning the Life in Christ' he explained how, through *Baptism, *Confirmation, and the *Eucharist, spiritual union with Christ was to be achieved. He also wrote an 'Interpretation of the Divine Liturgy'. Feast day in the E., 20 June.

Cabbala. See KABBALA.

Cadbury, Henry Joel (1883–1974), American NT scholar. He was Professor of Divinity at Harvard from 1934 to 1954. A *form critic and a pioneer of *redaction criticism, in his works on Lk. and Acts he virtually demolished the contention that St *Luke's writing showed specifically medical interests. He was a member of the panel which produced the *Revised Standard Version* of the NT (see BIBLE, ENGLISH VERSIONS, 5). After his retirement he revised two standard works on the history of Quakerism and throughout his life played a leading role in the work of the *Quakers.

Caecilian (d. before 343), Bp. of *Carthage from 311 or perhaps 307. His importance lies in his part in the opening stages of the *Donatist controversy. The rigorist party at Carthage consecrated a rival bishop, urging that Caecilian's consecration was invalid on the ground that he had been consecrated by a '*traditor'.

Caedmon (d. *c*.680), the earliest English Christian poet. According to *Bede, Caedmon was a labourer at the monastery of Whitby, who received in a vision the gift of composing verses in praise of God; he then became a monk and turned the Scriptures into verse.

Caeremoniale Episcoporum. In the RC Church, the book ordering the liturgical celebrations of a bishop. The *Caeremoniale Episcoporum* issued in 1600, with some changes, remained in force until the Second *Vatican Council (1962–5). A new *Caeremoniale Episcoporum* was issued in 1984.

Caeremoniale Romanum. A Latin service book dealing with the ceremonies of the Papal court.

Caerularius, Michael. See MICHAEL CERULARIUS.

Caesar. The word was virtually a title of the Roman emperors in the 1st–3rd cents. AD. To the inhabitants of Palestine and the provinces it denoted the imperial throne rather than the person occupying it.

Caesarea (Palestine). A city on the coast north of Jaffa, it was rebuilt by *Herod the Great and renamed in honour of the Emp. Augustus (*c*.13 BC). In the course of a visit by St *Peter, the Holy Spirit was here first given to the Gentiles (Acts 10: 44 f.). St *Paul was imprisoned here for two years (Acts 23: 23; 24: 27). The home of *Origen from 231, Caesarea became noted as a seat of learning. The city was important during the *Crusades, but was demolished in 1265.

Caesarea Philippi, now Banias, at the foot of Mount Hermon. The scene of St *Peter's confession of Christ's *Messiahship.

Caesrean text. A form of the Greek text of the NT (comparable to the *Western and *Alexandrian texts) which B. H. *Streeter

claimed to have identified on the basis of the peculiarities of the text of Mk. used by *Origen after his move to *Caesarea in Palestine in 231.

Caesarius, St (*c*.470–542), Abp. of Arles from 502. He had been a monk at *Lérins. He took an important part in the ecclesiastical administration of S. Gaul and was largely instrumental in securing the condemnation of *Semipelagianism at the Council of *Orange in 529. A number of his sermons, along with two monastic Rules, have survived. The *Statuta Ecclesiae Antiqua* has sometimes been attributed to him, almost certainly mistakenly. Feast day, 27 Aug.

Caesarius of Heisterbach (*c*.1180–1240), ecclesiastical writer. In 1199 he entered the *Cistercian monastery at Heisterbach (in the vicinity of Bonn). His *Dialogus Miraculorum* (*c*.1219–23) is a collection of spiritual anecdotes written for the edification of novices. He also wrote 8 books (not all extant) 'On Miracles' and a Life of St *Elizabeth of Hungary.

Caesaropapism. The system whereby an absolute monarch has supreme control over the Church within his dominions and exercises it even in matters (e.g. doctrine) normally reserved to ecclesiastical authority. The term is most generally used of the authority exercised by the Byzantine emperors over the E. patriarchates.

Caiaphas. The Jewish *High Priest before whom Christ was tried (Mt. 26: 3, etc.).

Cainites. A *Gnostic sect which, regarding the God of the OT as responsible for the evil in the world, exalted those who withstood him, e.g. Cain.

Caius. See GAIUS.

Cajetan, St (1480–1547), founder of the *Theatine Order. A priest in Rome, with Pietro Carafa (later *Paul IV) and two others in 1524 he founded the congregation known as the Theatines for clerics bound by vow and living in common, but engaged in pastoral work. Feast day, 8 (formerly 7) Aug.

Cajetan, Thomas de Vio (1469–1534), *Dominican theologian. As *General of his Order (1508–18), Cardinal (1517), and Bp. of Gaeta (1519), he played an important part in ecclesiastical affairs, urging the cause of reform before the *Lateran Council of 1512, reasoning with M. *Luther in 1518, and opposing the projected divorce of *Henry VIII (1530). His commentary on St *Thomas Aquinas's *Summa Theologiae* (1507–22) was the first monument of the 16th-cent. revival of *Thomism.

Calamy, Edmund (1) (1600–66), 'the Elder', English *Presbyterian. He was one of the authors of the composite work *Smectymnuus*. In the *Westminster Assembly of 1643 he tried to defend presbyterianism as a middle way between prelacy and congregationalism. He took a moderate line at the *Savoy Conference but, refusing to conform, was ejected from his preferments in 1662.

Calamy, Edmund (2) (1671–1732), historian of *Nonconformity, grandson of the preceding. His writings throw particular light on the ministers and fellows of colleges ejected in 1662.

calced (Lat. *calceatus*, 'shod'). A term applied to some branches of certain religious orders to distinguish them from their '*discalced' brethren. Thus the unreformed *Carmelites, who wear shoes, are called 'calced' as opposed to the discalced members of the *Teresian reform.

Calderwood, David (1575–1650), Scottish Church historian. He co-operated with A. *Henderson in drawing up the 'Directory of Public *Worship'. His main work, *The True History of the Church of Scotland*, is characterized by anti-*Erastian bias, but is a valuable source of information on ecclesiastical history in Scotland in the 16th and 17th cents.

calefactory. The room in a medieval monastery in which a fire or fires were maintained for the use of the monks. The term is now used for a communal place of recreation in religious houses.

calendar. The calendar in use when Christianity began was that devised by Julius Caesar in 46 BC. In this the length of the year was not quite exactly calculated. The error was rectified by the *Gregorian calendar of 1582 (q.v.).

Beginning the Christian era with the date of the Incarnation was suggested by *Dionysius Exiguus in the 6th cent. and in due course adopted throughout Christendom. Calculations began from 25 Mar. AD 1, the supposed date of the *Annunciation, which was taken as New Year's Day. The Gregorian calendar restored the beginning of the year to 1 Jan.

For the ecclesiastical calendar, see YEAR, LITURGICAL.

Calixtines. The moderate party of the *Hussites of Bohemia and Moravia, also known as *Utraquists. They were so named because they believed that the laity should receive Communion from the chalice (*calix*) as well as in the form of bread.

Calixtus, Pope. See CALLISTUS.

Calixtus, Georg (1586–1656), Protestant theologian. He was professor of theology at Helmstedt from 1614. He tried to build up a theological system (*Syncretism) which would reconcile *Lutherans, *Calvinists, and Catholics on the basis of the Scriptures, the *Apostles' Creed, and the faith of the first five cents.

calling. A technical term for the Divine act whereby those destined for salvation are persuaded to accept the Gospel.

Callistus (or Calixtus) I, St (d. *c*.222), Bp. of *Rome from 217. He was attacked by *Hippolytus for countenancing *Sabellianism and for his laxity, especially in re-admitting to communion those guilty of fornication and adultery, but some of the charges may be discounted. Feast day, 14 Oct.

Callistus (or Calixtus) II (d. 1124), Pope from 1119. He was a strong opponent of lay investiture; during his pontificate the *Investiture Controversy was settled by the Concordat of *Worms (1122). At the *Lateran Council of 1123 he issued a series of decrees on *simony, clerical *celibacy, and the election of bishops.

Callistus (or Calixtus) III (1378–1458), Pope from 1455. Originally a supporter of *Benedict XIII, he induced his successor Clement VIII (antipope, 1423–9) to submit to *Martin V. The main efforts of his Papacy were directed to the organization of a crusade against the Turks, a project to which he had been devoted since the fall of *Constantinople in 1453, but his plans had little success. He annulled the sentence against *Joan of Arc.

Calovius, Abraham (1612–86), German *Lutheran theologian. As a staunch defender of Lutheran orthodoxy he opposed G. *Calixtus's policy for reuniting the Confessions. He also attacked *Socinianism and *Pietism.

caloyer. A designation of Greek monks.

Calvary, Mount. The place of Christ's crucifixion, just outside *Jerusalem.

Calvin, John (1509–64), French Reformer and theologian. His sympathy with the Reformation movement led him to leave Paris in 1533. In 1534 he resigned his ecclesiastical benefices and, under threat of persecution, fled to Basle in 1535. The first (Latin) edition of *Institutes* was published there in 1536. Passing through *Geneva later that year, he was persuaded by G. *Farel to stay and help organize the Reformation in the city. In 1537 he and Farel drew up articles regulating the organization of the Church and worship. Opposition to their imposition of ecclesiastical discipline arose, and when in 1538 Calvin defied the city council's instructions to conform to the (*Zwinglian) religious practices of Berne, he was ordered to leave the city. While pastor to the French congregation at Strasbourg, he produced an enlarged edition of the *Institutes* (1539), a commentary on Romans (1539), and the celebrated letter to Card. *Sadoleto defending the principles of the Reformation. In Sept. 1541 he accepted an invitation from the city council to return to Geneva and spent the next 14 years establishing a theocratic regime. His 'Ecclesiastical Ordinances', adopted by the city council in Nov. 1541, distinguished four ministries of pastors, doctors, elders, and deacons; he introduced the vernacular into the liturgy and placed ecclesiastical discipline in the hands of a *consistory which sought to enforce morality through the threat of temporary excommunication. Despite some opposition, by 1555 Calvin was virtually unimpeded in his promotion of the Reformation. The establishment of the Genevan Academy (1559) provided an international forum for his ideas. He was the most influential writer among the Reformers. See also the following entry.

Calvinism. The theological system of J. *Calvin, especially as formulated by T. *Beza. It is generally accepted by most non-Lutheran Protestant Churches. It shares with *Lutheranism belief in the Bible as the only rule of faith, in the bondage of human free will through sin, and in *justification by faith alone. It is distinguished from Lutheranism primarily by its more radical use of Scripture as a criterion of ecclesiastical doctrine and practice, its stress on *predestination and Divine omnipotence and on the importance of the certainty of salvation to the elect, its modification of Luther's teaching on the Church and sacraments, and its emphasis on the necessity of discipline within the Church. Calvin defended a theocratic polity, subjecting the State to the Church, while M. *Luther had upheld the supremacy of the State. On the Eucharist he attempted a compromise between Luther's belief in the *Real Presence and U. *Zwingli's view of a mere symbolism; his language is ambiguous, but tends towards Zwinglianism.

The most influential document of strict Calvinism was the Second *Helvetic Confession of 1566, which was accepted in many Protestant countries. Calvinism gained considerable influence in *France in the early 1560s; until the Wars of Religion it seemed possible that the *Huguenots might gain political ascendancy. In the *Netherlands Calvinism became the State religion in 1622. It also replaced Lutheranism in parts of Germany, *Romania, and *Hungary. In England its greatest impact was on the *Puritans. Its strongest effect was in *Scotland and in colonial N. America. It suffered setbacks in the 18th and 19th cents., but re-emerged as a major religious force in the 20th cent., particularly through the writings of K. *Barth.

Calvinistic Methodism. The Church which emerged in *Wales through the revivalist preaching of Howel *Harris and others. They had contacts with English *Methodists, but among the leaders of the movement there was no wish to separate from the C of E. The English Calvinistic Methodists, led by G. *Whitefield, were eventually absorbed into *Congregationalism. Separation of the Welsh Calvinistic Methodists from the Established Church began in 1795 as a result of persecution. They were obliged to seek the protection of the *Toleration Act, and their meeting houses were registered as Dissenting Chapels. The first ordination of ministers took place in 1811. The Confession of Faith (based on the *Westminster Confession) was drawn up in 1823 and the *Constitutional Deed* formally completed in 1826. An Act of Parliament in 1933 secured the autonomy in things spiritual of the Calvinistic Methodist Church (also known as the Presbyterian Church of Wales) and a Property Board was established. The Church is Presbyterian in government and mainly Welshspeaking.

Camaldolese. St *Romuald founded a monastery at Camaldoli, near Arezzo, between 1012 and 1023; its ideal was the minimum of communal ties. A hospice which he founded at Fontebuona developed as a *coenobitic house; the two were meant to complement each other. Monastic practice has varied in the different daughter houses.

Câmara, Helder Passoa (1909–99), RC Abp. of Olinda and Recife in *Brazil from 1964 to 1985. A native of Brazil, he was consecrated auxiliary Bp. of Rio de Janeiro in 1952. Here he was instrumental in setting up the Conference of Brazilian Bishops and the Latin American Episcopal Council. He was increasingly concerned about the plight of the destitute in the capital and as Archbishop was outspoken in his condemnation of political injustice. His writings gave him a world-wide reputation.

Cambridge. The city, of Roman origin, had a remarkable number of churches and religious houses by the central Middle Ages. When Cambridgeshire was split from the diocese of *Lincoln in 1109, its first bishop settled at *Ely but the link between Ely and Cambridge was close; it was probably the bishop's clerks who provided hospitality in Cambridge for students escaping riots in Oxford in 1209, and so founded the University of Cambridge. The first college, Peterhouse, was founded in 1284. The university won royal patronage, but until the 15th cent. remained modest in comparison with *Oxford. Many of the leaders of the Reformation came from Cambridge, including Abp. T. *Cranmer, as did leading Anglicans of the 16th and 17th cents. In the 19th cent. it played a part in the *evangelical revival, especially through the influence of C. *Simeon, and later nurtured a series of eminent biblical scholars. See also following entries.

Cambridge Camden Society. A society founded in 1839 by J. M. *Neale and B. *Webb for the study of ecclesiastical art. Renamed the 'Ecclesiological Society' in 1846, it survived until 1868.

Cambridge Platonists. A group of influential philosophical clergymen who flourished at Cambridge between 1633 and 1688. They stood between the *Puritans and the *High Anglicans and advocated tolerance and comprehension within the Church, basing their demand on their conception that reason was the arbiter both of natural and of revealed religion. They held that reason could judge the data of revelation by virtue of the indwelling of God in the mind. They included B. *Whichcote, R. *Cudworth, and H. *More.

Camerarius, Joachim (1500–74), German classical scholar and reformer. He took part in drawing up the Confession of *Augsburg, wrote a Life of P. *Melanchthon, and discussed with Francis I in 1535 and with Maximilian II in 1568 the possibility of reunion between Catholics and Protestants.

Camerlengo. The chamberlain of the Papal court. He presides over the Apostolic Camera (a department of the Roman *Curia) and oversees economic affairs during a vacancy in the Holy See. He also assembles and directs the *conclave.

Cameron, John (d. 1446), Bp. of Glasgow. He was consecrated in 1427. By this date he was already Chancellor of Scotland. In 1427 he supported royal legislation limiting the activities of Scottish benefice-hunters in Rome; he was summoned to Rome in 1429 but the King told the Pope he could not spare his Chancellor. He was part of the official Scottish delegation to the Council of *Basle and arranged for the first visit of a Papal legate in 200 years to take steps to reform the Church in Scotland.

Cameron, John (c.1579–1625), Scottish Protestant theologian. He held academic posts in France and Scotland, but his exalted views on the nature of the secular authority led him into trouble. In his theological works he argued that Christ's action on the will was moral, not physical; he was thus considered by stricter *Calvinists to be inclining to *Pelagianism. His doctrines were accepted by a group of contemporary theologians ('Cameronites').

Cameron, Richard (d. 1680), Scottish *Covenanting leader. He was an eloquent field-preacher in the Covenanting cause. In 1678 he went to the *Netherlands, where he was ordained. Returning to Scotland, in 1680 he joined in the 'Sanquhar Declaration', which disowned allegiance to *Charles II and attacked Covenanters who accepted the royal indulgence then offered.

Cameronians. A term applied to extreme *Covenanters, such as the followers of R. *Cameron, and especially to the *Reformed Presbyterian Church.

Camillus of Lellis, St (1550–1614), founder of the 'Ministers of the Sick'. Reduced to poverty through gambling, he was employed by the *Capuchins at Manfredonia and in 1575 he began to embrace a penitential life. He became a nurse at a hospital in Rome, was ordained priest in 1584, and about the same time established a congregation, whose members take a fourth vow to devote themselves to the material and spiritual care of the sick, especially the plague-stricken. They are also known as 'Camillians' or '*Agonizants'. Feast day, 14 (formerly 18) July.

Camisards. A group of fanatical French Protestants, who rose in revolt in the Cévennes district in 1702 against the rigorous steps taken by Louis XIV to suppress their religion.

Campanella, Tommaso (1568–1639), Italian *Dominican philosopher. His disavowal of *Aristotelian philosophy aroused the hostility of his ecclesiastical superiors, while his suspected complicity in anti-Spanish plots provoked the civil authorities in Naples; he was imprisoned from 1603 to 1629. Anticipating R. *Descartes, Campanella held that individual consciousness was the fundamental fact of experience, and that the existence of God could be deduced from the idea of God in human consciousness.

campanile. A bell-tower or bell-steeple; the name is applied especially to the detached bell-towers which originated in Italy.

Campbell, Alexander (1788–1866), co-founder, with Barton W. Stone (1772–1844), of the *Disciples of Christ. The son of a Seceder *Presbyterian minister from Ire-

land, he settled at Bethany, W. Virginia. He taught that a rational study of the biblical text revealed the essential facts of primitive Christian faith and advocated Christian union on the basis of NT teaching. He left the Presbyterians, holding that creeds should not be made tests of fellowship. In 1812 he joined the *Baptists, but later separated from them. He initiated a revival on the Western Reserve and in 1832 his movement was united with Stone's Christian Connection in Kentucky. By the mid-19th cent. it was one of the largest American denominations. See also DISCIPLES OF CHRIST.

Campbell, John McLeod (1800–72), Scottish theologian. In 1831 he was found guilty of heresy by the *General Assembly and deprived of his cure. He maintained a successful ministry to an independent congregation in Glasgow from 1833 to 1859. The thesis of his main work was that the spiritual context of the sufferings of Christ, rather than their penal character, made atonement for sin.

Campeggio, Lorenzo (1472–1539), Abp. of *Bologna from 1523. He was sent to England in 1518 to try to gain *Henry VIII's support for a crusade against the Turks, and in 1524 Henry made him Bp. of *Salisbury. After work in Germany he returned to England in 1528 in the matter of Henry's projected divorce. He was instructed with T. *Wolsey to settle the question of fact, though the Pope had secretly pledged him to refer the matter to Rome before passing judgement. Failing to satisfy the king, Campeggio left England in 1529.

Campion, St Edmund (1540–81), *Jesuit. He became a Junior Fellow of St John's College, Oxford, in 1557 and was ordained deacon in the C of E in 1569. In 1571 he went to *Douai and was received into the RC Church. He became a Jesuit in 1573 and in 1580 he joined R. *Parsons in the first Jesuit mission to England. He was arrested in 1581, charged with conspiracy against the Crown, and executed. He was among the *Forty Martyrs canonized in 1970.

camp meeting. A religious *revivalist meeting held out of doors and lasting for several days, during which those taking part live in tents or temporary huts. This kind of meeting, first tried in 1799, has most often been used by *Methodists, especially in the USA.

Canaan. The land, later known as Palestine, which the Israelites conquered and occupied in the later part of the second millennium BC, or possibly rather earlier.

Canada, Christianity in. First brought to what is now Canada by Norse colonists from Greenland c.1001, Christianity took permanent root with the arrival of French settlers in Acadia in 1605. They soon set about evangelizing the aboriginal people; Franciscan *Recollects, *Jesuits, the Society of *Saint-Sulpice, and the Society of Foreign Missions in Paris all took part in different areas. After the British conquest (formalized in 1763), *Anglicans, *Methodists and Jesuits were prominent in eastern Canada, while from the 1840s the *CMS and the RC *Oblate Order of Mary Immaculate maintained the largest enterprises in the north and west. The *Moravians began work in Labrador in 1771. Quebec was a strictly RC colony until American and then British immigration brought religious variety. The *SPG and other missionary societies provided clergy. Frontier revivalism appealed to many, leading to the prominence of Methodists in Ontario and *Baptists in the Maritime provinces. An impulse towards union culminated in 1925 in the formation of the United Church of Canada by Methodists, *Congregationalists, and most Presbyterians. Since the 1960s there have been a large number of new liturgies, and the main Protestant (and Anglican) Churches ordain *women. In 1991 45 per cent of the population was RC, 36 per cent divided, in descending order, among United, Anglican, Baptist, *Lutheran, *Pentecostal, and *Orthodox. Conservative Protestant Churches are growing.

candle. The widespread use of candles as ornaments on the *altar seems to have developed from processional lights which were in earlier times placed beside or on the altar. They are lighted during liturgical services and at certain other times. The 1969 RC rite for the Baptism of Children provides that after the Baptism the child's father, godfather, or another person, shall hold a candle lit from the *Paschal Candle, and some modern Anglican liturgies allow for the giving of a lighted candle to a parent or godparent (or to the child) to show that the baptized have passed from darkness to light. The E. Church follows a similar practice. Votive candles are lit before statues or shrines as a personal offering. See also ALTAR LIGHTS.

Candlemas. The feast, now observed on 2 Feb., commemorating the purification of the BVM and the presentation of Christ in the Temple 40 days after His birth (Lk. 2: 22–39). It was kept locally at *Jerusalem from c.350. In 542 *Justinian ordered its observance at *Constantinople; it spread throughout the E. Church and somewhat later in the W. A procession with lighted candles is a distinctive feature of the RC rite.

Canisius, St Peter (1521–97), *Jesuit theologian. He founded a Jesuit colony at *Cologne and attacked the Protestant views of Abp. *Hermann of Wied. From 1549 he worked in Bavaria, Vienna, and Prague. He compiled a number of popular catechisms. In 1556 he became Provincial of Upper Germany and to him more than any other was due the success of the *Counter-Reformation in the S. German lands. Feast day, 21 Dec. (formerly 27 Apr.).

Cano, Melchior (?1509–60), Spanish *Dominican theologian. He took part in the debates on the *Eucharist and on *Penance at the Council of *Trent and later became involved in Spanish politics. He defended the unusual thesis that the consent of the parties is merely the *matter of the sacrament of *matrimony, the *form being the sacerdotal blessing.

canon. The Greek word originally meant a rod or bar; it came to be used of the rules of an art or trade or to signify a list or catalogue. In Christian language it denotes the list of Books regarded by the Church as Scripture (*canon of Scripture); the central part of the Mass (*Canon of the Mass); and the rules concerning the life and discipline of the Church (*canon law).

canon (ecclesiastical title). Though first applied to all clergy on the official staff of a diocese, the word came to be limited to those secular clergy belonging to a cathedral or collegiate church. 'Residentiary canons' form the permanent salaried staff of a cathedral and are primarily responsible for the maintenance of its services, fabric, etc. In the C of E a 'non-residentiary canon' is one who holds an unsalaried post, which entails certain privileges and responsibilities. See also MINOR CANON and PREBENDARY.

canon (hymnological). In the E. Church stanzas of poetry began in the 7th cent. to be inserted between the verses of the biblical *canticles sung during the second part of *Orthros. In most places the text of the canticles (except the *Magnificat) then disappeared, leaving only the sets of odes which are known as the canon.

canon law. The body of ecclesiastical rules or laws imposed by authority in matters of faith, morals, and discipline. Its beginnings may be traced to the practice of convening Councils to settle matters of uncertainty or dispute and their issue of *ad hoc* pronouncements (known as 'canons') on matters of doctrine and discipline. The decrees of influential bishops were another source of ecclesiastical legislation, and special authority attached to the letters of Popes (*Decretals). An important stage in the development of canon law was reached when *Gratian issued his *Decretum* (*c.*1140). Though in essence this was a private collection, such authority was accorded to it that it was supplemented by a series of later collections to form the *Corpus Iuris Canonici* (q.v.), which enjoyed authority until it was overhauled and codified in the *Codex Iuris Canonici* promulgated in 1917. This Code was revised and promulgated anew in 1983. A separate Code for the *Uniat Churches was promulgated in 1990.

In addition to laws regarded as universally binding, there have been others of local authority, such as the Synodical Constitutions of the Province of *Canterbury. See also CANONS, THE.

In the E., under the Byzantine Empire, there was a less clear distinction between the law of the Church and of the State than in the W. Imperial legislation dealt with ecclesiastical matters, and *Justinian decreed that canons had the 'force of law'. The development of specifically ecclesiastical law took the form of commentary on collections of canons (especially the *Nomocanon).

Canon of the Mass. The consecratory prayer of the Mass used practically throughout the RC Church until 1968. A nearly related form is quoted by St *Ambrose (d. 397), and by the time of Pope *Gregory I (590–604) it was virtually fixed.

Originally opening with the *Preface, which came to be regarded as an introduction to the Canon rather than as part of it, it is composed of a series of short prayers, including the Words of *Institution. In a slightly revised form, it is the first of the *Eucharistic Prayers in the 1970 Roman Missal.

canon of Scripture. The term '*canon' gradually acquired a technical meaning for the Books which were officially received as Scripture. It was long thought that the Hebrew Canon of the OT was closed in the second half of the 1st cent. AD, but it has been suggested that there was no defined canon until much later than this and there is discussion as to whether the canon of the OT formed a model for that of the NT or the other way round. The Jews of the *Diaspora regarded as equally inspired certain other Greek Books, most of which are printed in the AV and RV among the *Apocrypha (q.v.). The Four Gospels and the 13 Epistles of St *Paul had been accepted, at least in parts of the Church, as an authoritative witness to the Apostolic teaching by *c.*130; towards the end of the 2nd cent. these NT writings came to be regarded as 'Scripture' on the same footing as the OT. Other NT writings were received more slowly, while some, e.g. the Epistle of *Barnabas, were admitted by individual Churches though rejected by the majority. St *Athanasius in his *Festal Letter* of 367 is the earliest exact reference to the present NT canon. A Council probably held in Rome in 382 gave a complete list of the canonical Books of the OT and NT which is identical with that given at the Council of *Trent.

canoness. The name was first used in the 8th cent. of communities of women who lived in common but did not renounce their property. They were later known as 'secular canonesses' and are now extinct. After the 11th cent. many orders of *canons regular had counterparts for women, whose members were known as 'canonesses regular'; some survive.

canonization. In the RC Church the definitive sentence by which the Pope declares a particular dead person to have already entered into heavenly glory and ordains for the new 'saint' a public cult throughout the Church. In the Orthodox

Church canonizations are usually made by a synod of bishops within a particular *autocephalous Church.

In the early Church bishops controlled the cult of saints within their own dioceses, but the veneration of some saints spread beyond local limits and the resulting problems brought Papal intervention. The first historically attested canonization is that of *Ulrich of Augsburg in 993. About 1170 *Alexander III asserted that no one should be venerated as a saint without the authority of the Roman Church; the assertion became part of W. canon law. Papal authority is now given only after a long legal process beginning at diocesan level and continuing in Rome in the Congregation for the *Causes of Saints. Normally proof of one *miracle since *beatification is required.

Canons, Apostolic. See APOSTOLIC CANONS.

Canons, the. The main body of canonical legislation in the C of E after the Reformation was long the Book of Canons passed by the *Convocation of Canterbury in 1604 and that of York in 1606. The subjects covered included the conduct of Divine service and the administration of the sacraments, the duties and behaviour of clerics, the care of churches, and ecclesiastical courts. Apart from the section of Canon 113 dealing with the *seal of confession (which remained unrepealed), the 17th-cent. canons have now been superseded by a new set, promulgated in two parts, in 1964 and 1969. They cover much the same ground and are revised from time to time by the General *Synod.

canons regular. A body of canons living under rule which originated in the 11th cent. In the 12th cent. they largely adopted the Rule of St *Augustine and have come to be known as *Augustinian Canons (q.v.).

canopy, processional. An awning carried over the Blessed Sacrament in processions, and also formerly over certain ecclesiastical dignitaries, in the RC Church.

Canossa. A castle in N. Italy which was the scene of the submission of *Henry IV of Germany to *Gregory VII. In 1077 Henry, as a penitent, spent three days outside the castle in bitter weather before the Pope restored him to communion.

cantata. A form of musical composition designed to be sung, as opposed to the instrumentally performed sonata. In its sacred context it came in late-17th and early-18th cent. Germany to represent a work in various sections, involving arias and recitatives for single voices, as well as choral sections. In the *Lutheran liturgy it formed a commentary on the Gospel of the day. The term is now used for anything between an extended *anthem to a small-scale *oratorio.

Canterbury. In 597 St *Augustine arrived in Canterbury and established his first church there. He had been instructed to organize England in two provinces, with archbishops at London and *York, but from the first the place of London was taken by Canterbury. Its archbishop is 'Primate of All England'. See also ANGLICAN COMMUNION.

According to *Bede, an existing Roman basilica was consecrated by Augustine as the Cathedral Church of Christ. Destroyed by fire in 1067, the church was rebuilt by *Lanfranc, extended under *Anselm, and consecrated in 1130. After a fire in 1174 the choir was rebuilt in Transitional style; under Abp. *Sudbury the nave was pulled down and rebuilt in Perpendicular style. The chief glory of the cathedral in the Middle Ages was the shrine of St Thomas *Becket, dedicated in 1220.

About 598 a monastery, dedicated to Sts Peter and Paul, was established east of the city to accommodate the bodies of future bishops and kings. In 978 St *Dunstan rededicated the conventual church in honour of Sts Peter and Paul and St Augustine, and the monastery came to be known as St Augustine's. A building on the site opened as a college for missionaries in 1848; it has since been used for various other purposes.

Canterbury cap. A soft cloth cap sometimes worn by English clerical dignitaries and others.

canticle. A song or prayer (normally other than one of the Psalms) derived from the Bible, which is used in the liturgical worship of the Church. In the E. and W. Churches the NT canticles, the *Magnificat and *Nunc Dimittis (and in the W. also the

*Benedictus), are used in the Office every day. The OT canticles prescribed for use in the E. Church are usually omitted; in the W. they vary from day to day. In modern Anglican rites the choice of canticles is more flexible.

Canticle of the Sun, The. A hymn of St *Francis in praise of the Divine revelation in nature.

Canticles, Book of. See SOLOMON, SONG OF.

Cantilupe, St Thomas de (c.1218–82), also **St Thomas of Hereford**, Bp. of *Hereford from 1275. He was Chancellor of Oxford University in 1261 and again in 1273, and for a short time Chancellor of England in 1265. As bishop he combated simoniacal practices and nepotism. His later years were filled with disputes with J. *Pecham (from 1279 Abp. of *Canterbury) over questions of jurisdiction; one of these led to his excommunication in 1282. The fame of his sanctity and the miracles at his tomb nevertheless led to his canonization in 1320. Feast day, originally 2 Oct.; in modern RC calendars, 3 Oct.

cantor. A singer who leads the liturgical music of the Church. In cathedral and monastic churches he sets the pitch of *plainsong by singing the opening words and performs the solo parts of the chant. In modern RC usage the term also denotes the choirmaster who is enjoined to lead the people in singing their part of the Mass. It is also the title of the director of music in a *Lutheran church.

cantoris (Lat., '[the seat] of the cantor'). As the traditional place of the *cantor is on the north side of the choir, the term is used to indicate those who in antiphonal singing sit on that side.

Capernaum. A town near the Sea of Galilee which was a centre for Christ's ministry (Mk.2: 1). It has been identified with Kefar Naḥum (Tell Hûm).

Capistrano, St Giovanni. See GIOVANNI CAPISTRANO, ST.

capital punishment. The infliction of death following judicial sentence. St *Paul appears to recognize its legitimacy (Rom. 13: 1–5), and no religious body as such holds it to be immoral except the Society of *Friends. Individual Christians have some-

times held that it contravenes the 6th *Commandment. Its abolition in many countries in modern times is due, at least in part, to Christian influence.

Capitilavium (Lat., 'washing of the head'), an early medieval name for *Palm Sunday.

Capito, Wolfgang (1478–1541), Protestant Reformer and OT scholar. In 1523 he settled at Strasbourg and became, with M. *Bucer, the city's chief Reformer. With Bucer, he drew up the *Tetrapolitan Confession (1530) and, in 1532, with B. *Haller, he composed the Church ordinance which consolidated the Reformation in Berne. He was exceptionally tolerant towards *Anabaptists and other dissidents.

Capitular Mass. The public Mass said or sung in RC cathedrals and collegiate churches, attended by the whole chapter.

capitulary. (1) A collection of civil statutes; (2) a compilation of previously enacted laws made by bishops for the guidance of clergy and laity in their dioceses; (3) in biblical MSS a brief summary of the contents, put at the head of each Book.

cappa magna. In the RC Church a cloak with a train and hood, the use of which is now confined to bishops.

Cappadocian Fathers, the. St *Basil the Great, St *Gregory of Nazianzus, and St *Gregory of Nyssa (qq.v.).

Capreolus, John (c.1380–1444), *Thomist philosopher and theologian. A *Dominican, he lectured at *Paris and Toulouse. His main work (Defensiones, 1409–32) was a defence of the teaching of St *Thomas Aquinas against numerous attacks; it did much to revive the authority of Thomism.

Captivity Epistles, the. The four epistles—Phil., Col., Eph., and Philem.—believed to have been written by St *Paul in captivity. See entries on individual epistles.

Capuchins. An offshoot of the *Franciscan Order, founded by Matteo di Bassi of Urbino (d. 1552), an *Observant Friar. Its members wear a pointed cowl (capuche). The Rule, drawn up in 1529, re-emphasized the Franciscan ideals of poverty, austerity, and contemplative prayer. Until modern times the Capuchins were the strictest of the Franciscan families.

Carbonari (Ital., 'charcoal-burners'). A secret political society which emerged in Italy in the early 19th cent. They utilized Christian symbolism but rejected Divine revelation and looked to *natural religion as a sufficient basis for virtue and brotherhood.

Cardale, John Bate (1802–77), lawyer and first '*apostle' of the *Catholic Apostolic Church' (from 1832). He became its principal liturgist and 'Pillar of Apostles'.

Cardijn, Joseph-Léon (1882–1967), founder of the *Jocists. He had long been concerned about the alienation from the Church of young workers in industrialized society; after he was appointed assistant priest in a suburb of Brussels in 1912 and put in charge of the Christian social work in the city in 1915, he organized groups of young factory-workers to evangelize their colleagues. In the face of opposition, in 1925 he appealed to *Pius XI who approved the movement, now called 'Jeunesse Ouvrière Chrétienne'; Cardijn spent most of the rest of his life organizing it on a world-wide basis. He attended the Second *Vatican Council as an adviser and in 1965 he was made a cardinal.

cardinal. The title, at first applied to any priest permanently attached to a church, came to be restricted to the clergy of Rome, i.e. the parish priests, the bishops of the *suburbicarian dioceses, and the 7 (later 14) district deacons. These gradually formed a college and became the Pope's immediate counsellors. They assumed the government of the RC Church during a vacancy of the Holy See, and since 1179 the right of electing a Pope has been exclusively theirs.
The three ranks of cardinals originated at different times. The cardinal-priests were the parish clergy of the various Roman churches. Cardinal-deacons had care of the poor of the seven districts of Rome. Cardinal-bishops were created c. the 8th cent., when the increase in Papal business necessitated invoking the help of neighbouring bishops to act from time to time as the Pope's representative. All cardinals must now be in priest's orders and those not already bishops are given episcopal consecration. They are nominated by the Pope. Unless excused or bishops of foreign dioceses, they reside in Rome and act as heads of curial offices and *Roman Congregations and preside over ecclesiastical commissions.

cardinal virtues. The virtues of prudence, temperance, fortitude, and justice. By Christian writers they are contrasted with the *theological virtues.

Carey, William (1761–1834), *Baptist missionary. Baptized as an Anglican, he became convinced of Baptist teaching (1783). Largely through his inspiration the Baptist Missionary Society was founded in 1792, and in 1793 he sailed for *India. He worked on a translation of the NT into Bengali (published 1801), and when Fort William College was opened in Calcutta, he was appointed professor of Sanskrit, Bengali, and Marathi. He translated the whole Bible into Bengali (1809) and the whole or part into 24 other languages or dialects.

Caribbean, Christianity in the. See WEST INDIES, CHRISTIANITY IN THE.

Carlile, Wilson (1847–1942), founder of the *Church Army. After a successful business career, he was ordained in 1880. In 1882 he founded the Church Army, and combined his work as its honorary Chief Secretary with various parochial appointments.

Carlisle. According to *Simeon of Durham, an estate at Carlisle was given to St *Cuthbert when he became Bp. of *Lindisfarne in 685. In 1133 Carlisle became the centre of a new diocese. The church of the priory there, founded c.1122, became the cathedral; it was served by *Augustinian Canons. When the priory was dissolved in 1540, its lands and revenues were used to endow a new cathedral establishment. The cathedral fell into disrepair and five bays of the nave were demolished between 1649 and 1652. Its chief glory is the 14th-cent. East window.

Carlstadt (c.1480–1541), German Reformer, so named from his birthplace. From 1505 he taught at *Wittenberg. In 1518 he supported M. *Luther's criticism of *indulgences and in 1519 he disputed publicly with J. *Eck. He was excommunicated in 1520 and announced his break with the Papacy. In 1521 he celebrated the Eucharist in the vernacular, the first Reformer to do so; he wore no *vestments, abandoned the *Canon of the Mass, made no reference to sacrifice, and communicated the laity in both kinds. His programme of reform at this stage was more radical than Luther's; he came into conflict with him and resigned his academic position in 1523. In 1534 he was appointed preacher at the university church and professor of Hebrew at Basle.

Carmel, Mount. A high ridge near the modern port of Haifa. It was the scene of a contest between *Elijah and the prophets of *Baal (1 Kgs. 18). A church was built there c.AD 500, and a monastery founded by Greek monks. See the following entry.

Carmelites. The 'Order of the Brothers of Our Lady of Mount Carmel' dates from the late 12th cent. A group of *hermits living on Mount *Carmel accepted an austere rule written c.1208 by St Albert, the Latin Patr. of *Jerusalem. By the mid-13th cent. the instability of the Crusader kingdom led some of the hermits to migrate to Europe and in 1247 *Innocent IV allowed foundations not only in desert places but also in towns and cities and made other changes. The Order then grew rapidly. Communities of women, who adapted the Rule of Albert, were associated to the Order and formally incorporated into it in 1432. Also in 1432 *Eugenius approved a second mitigation of the Rule. This, together with the decline in religious observance in the later Middle Ages, led to attempts at reform which were encouraged in the revised constitutions of 1456. After losing the French provinces in the Revolution and its aftermath, the Carmelites have rebuilt their European provinces and expanded in the New and Third World. There are now Carmelite Friars (of the Ancient Observance), *Discalced Carmelite Friars (who look to the '*Teresian Reform' as their inspiration) and Carmelites of Mary Immaculate (founded in India in 1831), enclosed communities of Carmelite Nuns, congregations of active Carmelite Sisters, and *Secular Institutes of lay people.

carnival. The name given in RC countries to the period of feasting immediately before *Lent.

carol. A song of joy, originally accompanying a dance; now applied especially to traditional songs of a religious character. Modern English practice has tended to confine the singing of carols to Christmas-tide and to break down the distinction between hymns and carols.

Caroline Books, the. A treatise compiled c.790–2, which purports to be the work of *Charlemagne. It attacks the *Iconoclastic Council of 754 (for prohibiting images altogether) and *Nicaea II of 787 (for allowing excessive reverence to be paid to them). It was long attributed to *Alcuin but is probably by *Theodulf of Orléans, though Alcuin may have written a small part.

Caroline Divines. The Anglican theologians of the 17th cent., especially as considered as exponents of *High Church principles.

Carolingian Schools. During the reign of *Charlemagne (768–814) there was a lasting intellectual Renaissance. Responsibility for this revival rests largely with Charlemagne himself and his advisers *Alcuin and *Theodulf of Orléans. In 787 Charlemagne issued a *capitulary ordering that in all monasteries and bishops' houses there should be study and 'let those who can, teach'. Later capitularies demanded the establishment of schools. A Palace School was attended by members of the court, children of the nobility, and other laity. Most schools of the period, however, were connected with cathedrals and monasteries. The Carolingian schools were not outstanding for originality of thought, but they restored Latin to the position of a literary language, and their scholars were largely responsible for the formation of a more accurate orthography. They also copied and preserved texts of the classics, both Christian and pagan.

Carpenter, Lant (1780–1840), *Unitarian minister. He sought to foster a more liberal spirit in English Unitarianism. In 1825, when three older societies amalgamated into the British and Foreign Unitarian Association, he was instrumental in expunging from the constitution of the new body a preamble branding Trinitarianism as idolatrous.

Carpocrates (2nd cent.), *Gnostic teacher, probably a native of *Alexandria. His disciples, the 'Carpocratians', who survived until the 4th cent., preached a licentious ethic, the transmigration of souls, and the doctrine that Jesus was born by natural generation.

Carroll, John (1735–1815), first bishop of the RC hierarchy in the USA. A native of Maryland, he was trained at *St-Omer and became a *Jesuit in 1753. When the Jesuits were suppressed in 1773, he returned to America. Partly through the influence of Benjamin Franklin, in 1784 *Pius VI appointed Carroll Superior of the Missions, a step which made the Church of the USA independent of the *Vicars Apostolic in England. In 1789 Carroll was appointed Bp. of Baltimore; in 1808 he was made an archbishop, his diocese being divided into four sees.

Carstares, William (1649–1715), statesman and Scottish *Presbyterian minister. In the Netherlands he met William of Orange, then seeking British agents; he accompanied William to England in 1688 and was his chief adviser of Scottish affairs. A leading figure in the re-establishment of Presbyterianism in *Scotland (1690), he was four times *Moderator of the General Assembly, and he played a large part in securing Scottish acceptance of the Act of Union in 1707.

Carta Caritatis. The 'Charter of Love', so called in opposition to the obligatory charters of the *Cluniac Order, was the document outlining the constitution of the *Cistercian Order. It was presented to Pope *Callistus II in 1119. The final form dates from *c.*1155; the nucleus is probably the work of *Stephen Harding.

Carter, Thomas Thellusson (1808–1901), *Tractarian. As rector of Clewer, near Windsor, in 1849 he founded a House of Mercy for the rescue of fallen women and in 1852 a sisterhood, the Community of St John the Baptist, to look after it.

Cartesianism. The philosophical principles embodied in the teaching of R. *Descartes.

Carthage, Councils of. Early ecclesiastical Councils held at Carthage include: (1) Those under St *Cyprian in 251, 252, 254, 255, and 256. The earlier ones were concerned with the reconciliation of those who had lapsed in the *Decian persecution, the later with the dispute over the re-*baptism of heretics. (2) The long series under *Aurelius from 393 to 424. The most celebrated was that of 419, when the claims of Rome to

exercise jurisdiction over Africa were contested (see APIARIUS).

Carthusian Order. This strictly contemplative order was founded by St *Bruno in 1084 at the *Grande Chartreuse (hence its name). The monks were vowed to silence; each lived in his own cell, working and devoting several hours daily to mental prayer, and meeting for the *Office, conventual Mass, and for meals only on feast days. Between 1121 and 1128, *Guigo I compiled as their Rule the 'Consuetudines Cartusiae', which received Papal approval in 1133. Subsequent elaborations have done little to modify the austerity which characterized the Order from the beginning. At the end of the 18th cent. the Carthusians suffered badly in the French Revolution, and in 1901 they were again driven from the Grande Chartreuse, to which they returned in 1940. The Order includes a few houses of nuns.

cartouche. A type of mural memorial tablet widely introduced into English churches in the 17th and 18th cents.

Cartwright, Thomas (1535–1603), *Puritan. A Fellow of Trinity College, Cambridge, he was appointed Lady Margaret Professor in 1569. He criticized the constitution of the C of E, was deprived of his Professorship in 1570, and went to *Geneva. He returned in 1572 but his defence of the *Admonition to Parliament led to the loss of his Trinity Fellowship. He fled and did not return to England until 1585, though he was given semi-official encouragement to write against the RC Church from 1583. On *James I's accession (1603) he took part in the Puritan petitioning of the new King and seems to have been intended as one of the Puritan spokesmen at the *Hampton Court Conference, but died before it met.

Casel, Odo (1886–1948), liturgist. In 1905 he became a *Benedictine monk at *Maria Laach. He was concerned to expound the theological aspects of the liturgy and saw in the Eucharist a re-enactment of the mysteries of Christ by His Church (*Mysterienlehre*). His teaching is summarized in English in *The Mystery of Christian Worship* (1962).

Cashel, Council of (1172). A council called by Henry II after his invasion of *Ireland. It was attended by Bp. Christian of Lismore as

Papal legate, nearly all the Irish hierarchy, and most leading Churchmen, together with English clergy nominated by the king. The Irish Church was thus seen to recognize Henry's authority. Its constitutions were intended to introduce 12th-cent. discipline to the still very irregular Irish Church.

Cassander, Georg (1513–66), Catholic theologian. He tried to mediate between Catholics and Protestants, advocating concessions by Catholics such as giving Communion in both kinds. In his chief work he sought to show that abuses were no sufficient reason for leaving the RC Church. In 1564 the Emp. Ferdinand I invoked his aid in the official attempt at reunion, but Cassander's endeavour to put a Catholic interpretation on the official Protestant formularies met with disapproval from both sides.

Cassian, John (c.360-after 430), monk. As a young man he joined a monastery at *Bethlehem, but he soon left to study monasticism in Egypt. About 415 he founded two monasteries near Marseilles. His *Institutes* sets out the ordinary rules for the monastic life and discusses the chief hindrances to a monk's perfection; it was taken as the basis of many W. Rules. The *Conferences* take the form of a record of conversations with the leaders of E. monasticism. He shared the unease of many of the monks of Gaul with the extremes of St *Augustine's doctrine of *grace and attacked this doctrine in *Conference* 13; his position was later called *Semipelagianism. Feast day in the E., 29 Feb. (when this occurs).

Cassinese Congregation. A monastic *Congregation of *Benedictine monks which owes its origin to a reform initiated by Ludovico Barbo at Padua in 1409. The aim of the reformers was to overcome the evil of appointing abbots *in* *commendam, and the congregation was characterized until the 20th cent. by the overall authority of the General Chapter and the centralized system of appointing abbots on a temporary basis. It took its present title after the accession of *Monte Cassino in 1504. See also SUBIACO CONGREGATION.

Cassiodorus, Flavius Magnus Aurelius Cassiodorus Senator (c.485/90–c.580), Roman statesman, author, and monastic founder. He held high office under the *Ostrogothic rulers at *Ravenna. In 537,

when Ostrogothic rule collapsed, he withdrew from public life. He went to *Constantinople but in 554 he returned to a pacified Italy and established the monastic community of Vivarium on his estate near Naples. He built up an important library, arranged for the copying of manuscripts, and had Greek texts translated, including the histories of *Socrates, *Sozomen, and *Theodoret which served as the basis of his own *Historia Ecclesiastica Tripartita*.

cassock. The long garment, now usually black, worn by the clergy. It originated in the ankle-length dress which was retained by the clergy when in the 6th cent. shorter garments became normal for secular use. In church an *alb may now be worn instead of a cassock in the RC Church (and in the C of E for Communion). In the W. cassocks of bishops are purple, those of cardinals red, the Pope's white, and in England those of royal chaplains red.

Castel Gandolfo. A small town c.18 miles SE of Rome, which is the site of the Pope's summer residence.

Castellio, Sebastian (1515–63), classical scholar and Protestant theologian. After adopting Protestantism, he studied under J. *Calvin, who procured for him a post in *Geneva in 1541. Theological differences led to a breach with Calvin and Castellio left Geneva in 1545. He worked as a proofreader in Basle until c.1553, when he became professor of Greek in the university. In 1551 he published a translation of the Bible in classical Latin. As well as defending the doctrine of free will, it contained a plea for freedom of worship which was unique among 16th-cent. theologians. He was the instigator (and perhaps the author) of a work condemning the burning of M. *Servetus. His doctrine of religious *toleration received its fullest expression in his *Conseil à la France désolée* (1562).

casuistry. The art or science of bringing general moral principles to bear on particular cases. The introduction of universal private *Penance was the natural cause of the rise of formal casuistry in the Church, and by the 7th cent. '*Penitential Books' were common. From the 16th cent. various systems of casuistry, such as *Probabilism, *Probabiliorism, and *Equiprobabilism, developed in the RC Church.

Caswall, Edward (1814–78), hymn-writer. He was *Perpetual Curate of Stratford-sub-Castle in Wiltshire from 1840 to 1847; in 1847 he became a RC and in 1850 joined the *Oratorians. His many popular translations of Latin hymns include 'Jesu, the very thought of thee'.

catacombs. Burial-places consisting of labyrinths of underground galleries, often of two to five stories with connecting stairs. Within these, bodies were placed in floor-graves or in wall-niches (*loculi*), often holding more than one body, and closed by stone slabs or tiles. Though similar structures have been found in various locations, the most famous and extensive are near *Rome. Like all Roman tombs, they enjoyed legal protection and had to be dug outside the walls of the city. Excavation probably began c.150–200. Some of the earliest catacombs seem to have been dug on private ground, but their ownership and management soon passed to the Church. Families probably held commemorative meals at the catacombs, and by the 4th cent. the Eucharist was often celebrated at the grave of a martyr on the supposed anniversary of his death; the areas surrounding the graves of martyrs were then enlarged and embellished. After the 4th cent. the catacombs gradually fell into disuse and were largely forgotten until the 16th cent.

catafalque. An erection resembling a bier, formerly used at *Requiem Masses to represent the body in its absence. The term is now also used in a general sense of the coffin and its appurtenances.

catechesis. Instruction given to *catechumens preparing for *Baptism, especially in the early Church, and the books containing such instruction. In the RC Church the word is also used for education in faith throughout life.

Catechetical School of Alexandria. A Christian school in *Alexandria, concerned with advanced teaching in theology and with a succession of teachers in charge from the 2nd to the 4th cent., is depicted by *Philip Sidetes (5th cent.) and, with some differences, by *Eusebius of Caesarea; it is not, however, clear that this picture is accurate. It is more probable that there were various individual teachers, and it is uncertain whether advanced teaching continued after *Origen's departure to *Caesarea in 251.

catechism. A popular manual of Christian doctrine. Originally the term was applied to the oral instruction given to children and adults before *Baptism; the name passed to the book containing such instruction. In the Middle Ages prescriptions for catechizing the faithful were frequently issued, and books were produced containing explanations of the *Lord's Prayer and *Creed, lists of mortal sins, etc. The *Reformation brought a flood of new catechisms. M. *Luther's *Kleiner Katechismus* (1529) is still the standard book of the *Lutheran Churches. The *Heidelberg Catechism (1563) occupies a similar position in the *Calvinist communions. The RC Church also produced a number of new catechisms. RCs in England until recently commonly used *A Catechism of Christian Doctrine* (1898), popularly known as the 'Penny Catechism', which is based on a work of R. *Challoner. The desire for a modern manual of doctrine in the RC Church led to the publication of the '*Catechism of the Catholic Church'. See also GENEVA CATECHISM, WESTMINSTER CATECHISMS, and the following entry.

Catechism, Prayer Book. The 'Instruction' in the BCP, in the form of questions and answers, to be learned by candidates for *Confirmation. Though its authorship is uncertain, it was probably largely the work of A. *Nowell.

Catechism of the Catholic Church (1997). A comprehensive account of RC teaching. While covering the various areas of the faith, such as *sacraments and prayer, it also includes material on such modern ethical problems as the sale of organs for transplant surgery. The official Latin text was issued in 1997; a French version had appeared in 1992.

catechist. (1) In the early Church a teacher of *catechumens or a lecturer in a catechetical school. (2) In modern usage occasionally a person appointed to give instruction in Christianity, e.g. to children. (3) In the mission field a native teacher.

catechumens. In the early Church those undergoing training and instruction preparatory to *Baptism. They were assigned a place in the church, but solemnly dismissed before the *Eucharist proper began. There was an elaborate ritual of preparation in the preceding *Lent, with the candidates finally being admitted at the *Paschal Vigil.

In 1962 the catechumenate was restored in the RC Church when provision was made for the elements surviving in the *Rituale Romanum* (enrolment, *exorcisms, pre-baptismal *anointings) to be administered separately. The 1972 Order for the Christian Initiation of Adults made the restored catechumenate a necessary prelude to all adult Baptisms. Various ceremonies, spread over several weeks, mark the different stages.

Catechumens, Mass of the. The first part of the Eucharist, so named because in the early Church it was the part of the service which *catechumens were allowed to attend.

Categorical Imperative. In the ethical theory of I. *Kant, the absolute moral law, given in reason, and therefore binding upon every rational being.

catena (Lat., 'chain'). A word applied to the biblical commentaries dating from the 5th cent. onwards, in which the successive verses of the scriptural text were elucidated by 'chains' of passages derived from previous commentators.

Catharinus, Ambrosius (c.1484–1553), theologian. Lancelot Politi became a *Dominican in 1517, taking the name of two saints of the Order. He was soon employed in controverting *Lutheran teaching. In Siena, he incurred the hostility of his superiors by his attempt to secure their consent to the celebration of the feast of the *Immaculate Conception. He was subsequently freed by *Clement VII from the control of provincial superiors and placed directly under the Master General. In his *Opuscula* (Lyons, 1542) he included treatises on the Immaculate Conception and on *predestination. He distinguished between the 'predestination' of certain special saints who are guaranteed by a special grace against the possibility of damnation, and the 'foreknowledge' by which God knows that some people will be saved, but who remain capable of salvation or damnation throughout their lives, depend-

ing upon whether or not they accept the grace that is freely offered by God to everyone. He rejected with horror the idea that anyone is predestined to damnation. He played a prominent part in the Council of *Trent.

Cathars (Gk., 'pure'). The name was applied to several sects in patristic times, but is used mainly for a large group of dissenters who posed a serious challenge to the Church in the 12th and 13th cents. They were known to their contemporaries under various names: Cathars, *Manichaeans, Bulgari, *Albigenses (in France), and *Patarines (in Italy). Affirming two principles of good and evil, they rejected the flesh and material creation as evil; the purpose of redemption was the liberation of the soul from the flesh. They held that Christ was an angel with a phantom body who consequently neither suffered nor rose again, and whose redemptive work consisted only in teaching man the true doctrine. Rejecting the sacraments, the doctrines of hell, purgatory, and the resurrection of the body, and believing that all matter was bad, they condemned marriage and the use of meat, milk, eggs, and other animal produce. As these ideals were too austere for most people, they distinguished two classes: the 'perfect', who received the 'consolamentum', i.e. baptism of the Holy Spirit by the imposition of hands, and kept the precepts in all their rigour, and ordinary 'believers', who were allowed to lead normal lives but promised to receive the 'consolamentum' when death approached.

Traces of this way of thinking can be found in W. Europe in the early 11th cent. From c.1140 there is clear evidence of their distinctive ideas and organization, and by 1200 they were strong in S. France and Lombardy. The reforms of the Fourth *Lateran Council of 1215 and the emergence of the *Dominican Order were both in part reactions to the threat of heresy, as was the development of the *Inquisition.

cathedra. The bishop's chair or throne in his cathedral. The phrase 'ex cathedra' (i.e. 'from the throne') is used of the pronouncements uttered by the Pope with the full weight of his office; such pronouncements are held by RCs to be *infallible.

cathedral. The church which contains the throne or *cathedra of the bishop of the diocese. It is usually large and of some splendour. It was originally served by the bishop and his household, but responsibility for the cathedral was gradually delegated to a separate body of clergy, which developed into an ecclesiastical corporation or *chapter.

In medieval England, some chapters were secular, some monastic. With the *Dissolution of the Monasteries, the religious foundations came to an end. New constitutions were imposed on the cathedrals previously served by religious; they have become known as 'New Foundations', in contrast with those which, retaining their medieval statutes, are known as 'Old Foundations'. The creation of new English dioceses in modern times has brought a corresponding growth of cathedrals. In most cases an existing church has been used, but in some (e.g. *Liverpool) new buildings have been erected. In the RC Church the restoration of the hierarchy in England in 1850 was followed by the foundation of cathedrals, e.g. at *Westminster.

English cathedrals are now governed by three bodies: the Chapter, consisting of the *dean, the residentiary *canons, and a few other persons, some lay; the College of Canons, composed of the dean, all canons, the *suffragan and full-time stipendiary assistant bishops, and the archdeacons of the diocese; and a Council composed of a lay chairman nominated by the bishop, the dean, and members representing the Chapter, the College of Canons, the cathedral community, and other interests. The cathedral staff also normally includes *minor canons, responsible for rendering the priest's part of the musical services, and a choir consisting of an organist, choirmen (sometimes called 'lay clerks'), and choristers. In the older cathedrals there has been a tradition of high musical performance.

cathedral schools. Schools established in medieval times or later for the education of choristers of cathedral churches. Most of them also admit other, fee-paying pupils.

Catherine, St, of Alexandria. According to tradition she was a virgin martyred in the 4th cent. Legend represents her as of noble family and great learning, who was tied to a wheel, tortured, and beheaded. Her body was said to have been discovered c.800 on Mount *Sinai, whither, her *Acts assert, it was transported by angels after her death. Her symbol is a spiked wheel. Feast day, 25 Nov., suppressed in 1969.

Catherine, St, of Genoa (1447–1510), mystic. Caterina Fieschi was married at the age of 16; she was suddenly converted 10 years later. She began to receive Communion almost daily, and underwent a number of remarkable mental experiences. Her husband helped her in the care of the sick in a hospital in Genoa. Her spiritual doctrine is contained in the *Vita e dottrina* (1551), though perhaps she did not put this account of her visions into their present form. Feast day, 15 Sept.

Catherine, St, de' Ricci (1522–90), *Dominican nun, from 1552 until her death either prioress or subprioress of San Vincenzo, Prato. For some years she underwent periodic raptures, in which she experienced an intense union with Christ's Passion. Feast day, 4 Feb. (until 1971, 13 Feb.).

Catherine, St, of Siena (?1347–80), *Dominican tertiary from the age of 16. Having, as she believed, received a command from Christ to leave her solitude to care for the sick and poor and convert sinners, she was soon called upon to act as a mediator between local factions and in higher matters such as the conflict between Florence and the Holy See. She helped to persuade *Gregory XI to transfer the Papacy from *Avignon back to Rome in 1377. In her writings (letters, prayers, and the synthesis of her teaching known as the *Dialogo*) the central theme is that of Christ crucified; she saw His blood as the supreme sign and pledge of Divine love and the chief motive for ours. Feast day, 29 (formerly 30) Apr.

Catherine, St, of Sweden (1331–81). The daughter of St *Bridget and first abbess of Vadstena, she spent much of her life in Italy obtaining confirmation of the *Bridgettine Order and seeking her mother's *canonization. Feast day, 22 Mar.

Catherine de' Medici (1519–89), Queen-Consort of France from 1547 and Queen-Mother from 1559. In the wars of religion she at first advocated a policy of toleration for political reasons; between 1567 and 1570 she took violent measures against the Protestants; after an interval of mildness she tried to re-establish her position by the murder of G. *Coligny and the Massacre of St *Bartholomew's Day (1572).

Catholic. The word, meaning 'general' or 'universal', has come to have various uses in Christian terminology: (1) Of the universal Church as distinct from local Christian communities. (2) In the sense of 'orthodox', as distinct from 'heretical' or 'schismatical'. (3) Of the undivided Church before the schism between the E. and W., traditionally dated in 1054. Thereafter the W. Church referred to itself as 'catholic', the E. preferring to describe itself as 'orthodox'. (4) Since the *Reformation RCs have come to use it exclusively of themselves. Anglicans and *Old Catholics have also adopted it to cover besides themselves and the RC Church also the E. Orthodox Church in the belief that these Communions together represent the undivided Church of earlier ages. (5) In general it is employed of those Christians who claim to possess a historical and continuous tradition of faith and practice, as opposed to *Protestants who tend to find their ultimate standards in the Bible as interpreted on the principles of the 16th-cent. Reformation.

Catholic Action. Organized religious activity, especially of a social, educational or quasi-political kind, on the part of the RC laity. In 1922 *Pius XI encouraged the creation of flexible organizations for the purpose under the direction of the clergy. Later Papal pronouncements have insisted more on the vocation of every member of the Church to spread the Kingdom of God on earth.

Catholic Apostolic Church. A religious body partly inspired by the teaching of E.*Irving; its members were sometimes called 'Irvingites'. It developed out of a *millenarian circle which had gathered round H. *Drummond at Albury, Surrey, and counted Irving among its members. They believed in the imminence of the Second Coming of Christ, in preparation for which they resolved to re-establish the primitive offices of apostles, prophets, etc. The first 'apostle' (J. B. *Cardale) was called in 1832; the full college of 12 held their first 'council' in 1835. They soon undertook missionary journeys to mainland Europe, Canada, and the USA. After the death of the last

'apostle' in 1901 they dwindled and are now virtually extinct.

Catholic Association. An association founded in 1823 by D. *O'Connell for the defence of RC interests in Ireland. Its influence largely contributed to the passing of the *Catholic Relief Act 1829.

Catholic Emancipation Acts. See CATHOLIC RELIEF ACTS.

Catholic Epistles. A title used properly of the NT Epistles of Jas., 1 and 2 Pet., 1 Jn., and Jude, because they are 'general' and not addressed to specific individuals or Churches. It is usual, however, to include also 2 and 3 Jn. among them.

Catholic Majesty, His. A traditional title of the Kings of *Spain.

Catholic Relief (or Emancipation) Acts. A series of Acts freeing RCs from civil disabilities. By that of 1778 RCs were allowed to own land on taking an oath not involving the denial of their religion; in 1791 RC worship and schools were tolerated. By the Roman Catholic Relief Act 1829 almost all disabilities were removed and RCs were admitted to most public offices.

Catholic Truth Society. A RC society formed in 1884 for the printing of cheap literature of a devotional, educational, or controversial nature.

Catholic University of America. The university was founded at Washington, DC, in 1889. It was originally intended for the higher education of the RC clergy; the laity were admitted in 1905.

Catholicos. A title now restricted to the Patriarchs of the *Armenian and *Georgian Churches and the *Church of the East (in the case of the last two in the form 'Catholicos Patriarch').

Caton, William (1636–65), early *Quaker. An itinerant preacher, he spent a short time in France and visited the *Netherlands. His *Journal* (edited by G. *Fox, 1689) was long read among Friends.

Causes of Saints, Congregation for the. Established in 1969, when the Congregation of *Rites was divided, it deals with *beatification and *canonization procedures, those for declaring '*Doctors of the Church', and with the authentication and preservation of *relics.

Caussade, Jean Pierre de (1675–1751), French ascetic writer. Becoming a *Jesuit in 1693, he travelled widely. His influence did much to rehabilitate mysticism at a time when it was still suffering from the condemnation of *Quietism. In addition to letters of spiritual direction, he wrote a book on prayer. The treatise on abandonment to Divine Providence was taken from papers put together by the *Visitation nuns at Nancy; whether all the material can be ascribed to de Caussade is disputed.

cautel. A rubrical direction for the correct administration of the Sacraments.

Caxton, William (c.1422–91), the first English printer. After some years in commerce, he entered the service of Margaret, Duchess of Burgundy, for whom he made several English translations. Tiring of copying these by hand, he learnt the new art of printing at *Cologne (1471–2) and introduced it at Bruges. In 1476 he set up his press at the Almonry, Westminster. Much of his printing was of religious works.

CCCS ('Colonial [later Commonwealth] and Continental Church Society'). Formed in 1851 by a union of two existing bodies, it was intended to enable *Evangelicals in the C of E to take an active part in the work of Church extension in the British Empire; it later provided chaplains in Continental Europe. In 1979 it became the Intercontinental Church Society.

Cecilia, St (2nd or 3rd cent.), Roman martyr. According to her (apocryphal) acts, she converted both her husband and brother before dying for the Christian faith. Under Paschal I (817-24), her relics were moved from the *catacombs to the church which bears her name in Trastevere in Rome; here her body is said to have been found uncorrupted when the church was repaired in 1599. She is the patroness of Church music. Feast day, 22 Nov.

Cedd, St (d. 664), Bp. of the East Saxons. The brother of St *Chad, he was brought up at *Lindisfarne. He was sent to evangelize Essex and consecrated bishop in 654. He was the founder and first abbot of the abbey of Lastingham, N. Yorks. At the Synod of *Whitby (664) he accepted the Roman Easter. Feast day, 7 Jan.

Cedron (or **Kidron).** The valley or gorge on the E. of *Jerusalem, between the city and the Mount of *Olives. Jn. 18: 1 records that the brook was crossed by Christ on the night before His Passion.

celebret (Lat., 'let him celebrate'). In the RC Church a certificate authorizing its possessor to celebrate the Eucharist.

Celestine I, St (d. 432), Pope from 422. His support for *Apiarius led a Council at *Carthage, c.424, to protest against what the Africans regarded as an infringement of their rights. In 429 he sent *Germanus of Auxerre to Britain to combat *Pelagianism. At a Roman Synod in 430 he formally condemned *Nestorius. Feast day in the E., 8 Apr.; in the W., formerly 6 Apr.; after 1922, 22 July; now suppressed.

Celestine III (c.1106–98), Pope from 1191. He defended *Abelard at the Council of *Sens (1140) and later urged Thomas *Becket to adopt a less intransigent attitude. Elected Pope in his 85th year, his reign was marked by indecision. However, he approved the Orders of Knights *Templar, the *Hospitallers, and the newly formed *Teutonic Order.

Celestine V, St (c.1215–96), Pope from July to Dec. 1294. He became a *Benedictine at the age of 17, but retired to Monte Morrone, where the many disciples who gathered round him became the nucleus of the *Celestine Order. Elected Pope when he was nearly 80, he was naïve and ignorant of procedure and became a tool of Charles II of Naples; he abdicated. He is sometimes known as St Peter Celestine from his baptismal name of Peter. Feast day, 19 May, no longer in the universal calendar.

Celestine Order. A congregation of the *Benedictine Order, founded by the future *Celestine V at Monte Morrone in Central Italy. Established in 1259, the abbey secured Papal approval in 1263 and the Order was recognized in 1275. Its discipline was severe. The last house closed in 1785.

Celestius (5th cent.), heretic. A native of Britain, he was practising as an advocate in Rome when he met *Pelagius. They became convinced that the contemporary low morality could be reformed only by stressing the responsibility of men for their actions, and so began teaching a doctrine of free will that left no room for *grace. Celestius denied that Adam's sin was transmitted to his descendants (*original sin). He migrated to Africa c. 410, was condemned by the 411 Council of *Carthage, and went to *Ephesus. See also PELAGIANISM.

celibacy of the clergy. In the E. Church the legal position has always been that priests and deacons may marry before ordination but not after, and that bishops must be celibate. In the W. Church a legal position was gradually reached by which all the higher clergy were required to be celibate. The earliest canonical enactment is can. 33 of the Council of *Elvira (c.306); in the Middle Ages there were repeated efforts to enforce celibacy on those in Holy Orders. This position is retained in the RC Church, though since the Second *Vatican Council some older married men have been made *deacons and *dispensations are sometimes granted to married clergy received into the RC Church from other Communions. In the C of E the obligation to celibacy was abolished in 1549.

cell. (1) The private room of a *religious of either sex. It usually contains only bare necessities. (2) A monastic house dependent on its mother house. (3) Small groups of Christians who have pledged themselves to intensive work for the propagation of the Christian faith in their secular surroundings.

cella (also **cella coemeterialis**). A small chapel erected in cemeteries in early Christian times.

cellarer. One of the officials in a medieval monastic community. He was responsible for seeing that there was sufficient food and drink to hand, and in practice he was usually in charge of nearly all the monastery's dealings with outside tradesmen.

Celsus (2nd cent.), pagan philosopher. His 'True Discourse' (c.178) is the earliest literary attack on Christianity of which details have survived; most of it is preserved in *Origen's reply. Celsus praised the *Logos doctrine and the Christian moral code, but he objected to the exclusive claims of the Church and appealed to Christians to abandon their religious and political intolerance. He found the doctrines of the Incarnation and Crucifixion repugnant.

Celtic Churches. The Churches of the areas using Celtic languages—Cumbria, *Wales, Cornwall, Brittany, *Ireland, and *Scotland—were not linked by any institutional unity, nor were there any clearly defined practices common to these Churches but distinct from others; nevertheless they all developed from the Church in late-Roman Britain. It was probably through trading links with W. Britain that Christianity was taken to Ireland, so that in 431 *Palladius could be sent as their first bishop 'to the Irish believing in Christ'. Later in the 5th cent., however, when St *Patrick came from Britain, Ireland was still largely pagan, and, apart from his writings, there is no evidence of the Church there until well into the 6th cent. Meanwhile, in Britain the expansion of the mainly pagan Anglo-Saxons pushed the British Churches westward. Their hostility towards the Anglo-Saxons and the mission from Rome was demonstrated by the failure of St *Augustine (of Canterbury) to reach agreement with them.

Certain features have been held to characterize the Celtic Churches, mainly because over them they came into conflict with those who followed different practices which came to prevail in the W.; they include different methods of calculating the date of *Easter and the shape of the *tonsure. Their ecclesiastical structure was less hierarchical than elsewhere; diocesan limits were not defined and monasteries tended to be the centres of ecclesiastical organization. With the coming of the Normans firm diocesan and metropolitan organization was established in all these Churches. See also ANGLO-SAXON CHURCH; CHURCH OF ENGLAND; IRELAND, CHRISTIANITY IN; SCOTLAND, CHRISTIANITY IN; and WALES, CHRISTIANITY IN.

cemetery. A place set apart for the burial of the dead. The Greek from which the word is derived means a 'sleeping-place', and seems to have been used exclusively of Christian burial-grounds.

Cenaculum. The 'upper room' in *Jerusalem in which the *Last Supper was celebrated and the Holy Spirit descended at *Pentecost. The upper room in a structure known as 'David's tomb' is supposed to be the Cenaculum.

cenobites. See COENOBITES.

censer. Another name for a *thurible.

censures, ecclesiastical. See PENALTIES.

Centre Party. The party founded by the Prussian Catholics in 1870–1 to counteract the anti-Catholic policy of the Conservatives and especially of the National Liberals. It was the most effective opponent of Bismarck in the '*Kulturkampf'. With other German parties it was suppressed in 1933. After 1945 its place was taken by the interdenominational Christian Democratic Union.

Centuriators of Magdeburg. The authors of the *Historia Ecclesiae Christi* (1559–74), a history of the Church divided by 'centuries'. This depicted the pure Christianity of the NT as coming progressively under the power of the 'Papal Antichrist' until liberated by M. *Luther.

Cerdo (2nd cent.), Syrian *Gnostic who taught at Rome c.140. He held that the Creator God of the OT was to be distinguished from the Father of Jesus Christ, and that only the soul, not the body, will share in the resurrection.

cere cloth (Lat. *cera*, 'wax'). According to W. usage, a cloth impregnated with wax which is laid on the surface of the altar to prevent the linen cloths above from being soiled, e.g. by the oils used in consecrating the *mensa.

ceremonial. In ecclesiastical usage, the performance of Divine worship with prescribed and formal actions.

Cerinthus (*fl. c.*100), *Gnostic. He is said to have taught that the world was created, not by the supreme God, but either by a *Demiurge (a less exalted being) or by angels. Jesus, he held, began His earthly life as a mere man, though at His Baptism 'the Christ', a higher Divine power, descended upon Him, but departed before the crucifixion.

Cerularius. See MICHAEL CERULARIUS.

Cesarini, Julian (1398–1444), cardinal *in pectore* from 1426, an appointment made public in 1430. In 1431 he was made president of the Council of *Basle. He solemnly inaugurated it on 14 Dec. 1431 and continued his leadership even when it had been dissolved by *Eugenius IV, though seeking to reconcile Pope and Council. After the transfer of the Council to *Florence he took a prominent part in the negotiations for union between the Greek and Roman Churches. He persuaded the king of Hungary to renew war against the Turks; the Christians were totally defeated at Varna, Cesarini being killed, according to some sources, in flight after the battle.

chaburah (cf. Heb. חָבֵר 'friend'). In Jewish practice a group of friends formed for religious purposes. They often shared a common weekly meal, usually on the eves of sabbaths or holy days. It has been argued that Christ and His disciples formed such a chaburah and that the *Last Supper was a chaburah meal.

Chad, St (d. 672), Bp. of *Lichfield. The brother of St *Cedd, he was irregularly made Bp. of *York during St *Wilfrid's absence in France, but on Wilfrid's return he accepted the ruling of Abp. *Theodore and retired to the abbey of Lastingham in 669. Impressed by his humility, later in 669 Theodore regularized his consecration and provided for him to be Bp. of the Mercians. Chad fixed his see at Lichfield. Feast day, 2 Mar.

Chalcedon, Council of (451). The Fourth *Oecumenical Council. It was convoked by the Emp. *Marcian to deal with the heresy of *Eutyches, whom the Council condemned. It then drew up a statement of faith, the so-called Definition of *Chalcedon. Though nearly all the bishops present were Easterns, the W. Church accepted its dogmatic decisions.

Chalcedon, the Definition of. The statement of faith made by the Council of *Chalcedon (451). It reaffirms the *Christological definitions of *Nicaea and *Constantinople and formally repudiates the errors of *Nestorius and *Eutyches. It declares Christ to be one Person in two natures, the Divine of the same substance as the Father, the human of the same substance as us; these are united unconfusedly, unchangeably, indivisibly, and inseparably. By the end of the 7th cent. the Definition had been generally accepted in E. and W., except among the *Oriental Orthodox Churches.

Chaldean Christians. That part of the *Church of the East in communion with the see of Rome. There are two main groups: those of the Middle East and those of *Malabar. As a result of a disputed succession within the Middle Eastern group, a separate line of *Uniat Patriarchs came into existence in 1553 and remained in communion with Rome until 1672. In 1681 a new Uniat line of Patriarchs at Diyarbekr was inaugurated and lasted for over a century. In 1830 the Uniat Patriarchate was again restored, now at Baghdad, with the title 'of Babylon'. For the Indian group, see MALABAR CHRISTIANS.

Chaldee. An obsolete and misleading name for *Aramaic.

chalice. In ecclesiastical usage the cup used to contain the wine consecrated in the Eucharist. The earliest Christian chalices were commonly made of glass; by the 4th cent. the precious metals were general. In the Middle Ages chalices came to have stems which were gradually elongated.

chalice veil. A square of material, normally of the same colour as the Eucharistic vestments, for some centuries used in the W. to cover the *chalice and *paten during the parts of the Mass when they were not in use, i.e. until the *offertory and after the *ablutions. The 1970 Roman Missal makes no mention of the chalice veil.

Challoner, Richard (1691–1781), author of The *Garden of the Soul (q.v.). Of *Presbyterian parents, he became a RC while still a boy. In 1741 he was consecrated at Hammersmith Bishop (*in partibus*) of Debra and coadjutor to the *Vicar Apostolic, whom he succeeded in 1758. He wrote controversial and devotional books and revised the *Douai-Reims translation of the Bible.

Chalmers, James (1841–1901), Scottish *Congregational missionary and explorer. After ordination, in 1866 he sailed for Rarotonga in the *South Pacific. There he did much to make the Church indigenous before sailing for New Guinea in 1877. He slowly won the confidence of the people. He tried also to establish peaceful relations with the peoples of the Fly River region but was brutally killed in the Gulf of Papua.

Chalmers, Thomas (1780–1847), theologian and philanthropist. His chief importance lies in his leadership of the movement for the choice of ministers in the Established Church of *Scotland by the people and the schism which followed its failure in 1843. In that year he left the Established Church with a considerable band of followers and founded the *Free Church of Scotland. See also DISRUPTION.

Chambers, Robert (1802–71), Scottish publisher and author. His *Vestiges of the Natural History of Creation* (1844) was a popular handbook defending an evolutionary theory of man's origin which helped to prepare the public for *Darwinism.

chancel. Originally the part of the church immediately about the altar, now called the 'sanctuary'. When further space was reserved for clergy and choir westward from the sanctuary, the word was applied to this area as well and hence now normally designates the whole area in the main body of the church east of the nave and transepts.

chancellor. In the C of E, the diocesan chancellor is a professional lawyer who is the chief representative of the bishop in the administration of the temporal affairs of his diocese. He is usually the sole president of the *Consistory Court in *faculty cases. He deals with applications for faculties and, through his *surrogates, common *marriage licences. With two clerical and two lay assessors as jury, he hears complaints against clerics under the *Ecclesiastical Jurisdiction Measure 1963, when these do not involve matters of doctrine, ritual, or ceremonial.

In England the title of chancellor is also held by one of the residentiary *canons in *cathedrals of the 'Old Foundation'. He used to be responsible for the cathedral school and library but now often has wider educational functions.

In the RC Church, the diocesan chancellor is primarily responsible for the official archives, but considerable authority is often delegated to him by the bishop.

Chancery, Papal. The name attached in the late 12th cent. to the Pope's secretariat. In the 14th cent. the Chancery exercised quasi-legislative powers, but from the 15th cent. its influence diminished. In 1973 it was abolished and its functions transferred to the Secretariat of State.

Channel Islands, Christianity in the. Christianity was apparently introduced about the 5th–6th cent. After the separation of England and Normandy in 1204, the islands were annexed politically to England. Ecclesiastically they were finally detached from the diocese of Coutances and annexed to *Winchester on the orders of *Elizabeth I in 1568–9. In the 16th cent. *Huguenot and other Protestant refugees induced the islanders to adopt *Presbyterianism, but Anglicanism was imposed in the reign of *James I and has remained the official creed.

Channing, William Ellery (1780–1842), American *Unitarian. He became pastor of a Congregational Church in Boston in 1803. In the schism between liberal and conservative *Congregationalists in the USA, Channing espoused the · liberal or Unitarian cause. From *c.* 1820 he was reckoned a Unitarian, though he disapproved of Unitarianism as a sect.

Chantal, St Jane. See JANE FRANCES DE CHANTAL, ST.

chantry. An endowment for the maintenance of priests to celebrate Mass for the souls of the founder and others nominated by him; the body of priests so endowed; and any chapel in which such Masses were celebrated. The chapel usually took the form of an altar in a space partitioned off within a church or of a building constructed as a 'chantry chapel'. In the 14th and 15th cents. chantries became numerous. Under *Henry VIII the possessions of the chantries were vested in the King for the term of his life in 1545, but wholesale suppression did not take place until the passing of the Dissolution of Colleges Act 1547 under *Edward VI. The chantries had often been educational centres; a few were refounded as schools, sometimes bearing the name of Edward VI.

chapel. The word is used of a variety of sacred buildings which are less than churches. They include: (1) Chapels of private institutions, e.g. schools or hospitals. (2) RC and dissenting places of worship, in distinction from English parish churches. (3) Part of a large church with a separate altar, e.g. a '*Lady Chapel'. (4) A *proprietory chapel (q.v.). See also CHANTRY, ORATORY, and the following entries.

chapel of ease. A chapel subordinate to a mother church, founded for the ease of parishioners in prayers and preaching. Many acquired parochial status and were used for the administration of the Sacraments and for burials.

chapel royal. A private chapel attached to a royal court. In England the Chapel Royal and Royal *Peculiars are not subject to the jurisdiction of the bishop of the diocese in which they are situated but are under that of the sovereign, which is exercised by the 'Dean of the Chapels Royal'.

chaplain. Ordinarily a cleric who performs non-parochial duties. Chaplains are often appointed to monarchs, bishops, and other high ecclesiastical dignitaries; to serve in institutions such as schools, prisons, and embassies abroad; and in the armed forces of most Christian countries.

chaplet. The name given to the three parts into which the devotion of the *Rosary is divided. It consists of five *decades and forms a complete devotion in itself.

Chapman, John (1856–1933), NT and patristic scholar. He became Abbot of *Downside in 1929. His *Spiritual Letters* (1935) are much valued.

chapter. (1) A section of a monastic rule, such as was daily read publicly in religious houses; (2) the assembly of the members of a religious house to hear this reading and for other purposes, and then the members in their corporate capacity; (3) the members of any corporate body responsible for an ecclesiastical institution, especially the *canons of a *cathedral. See also BIBLICAL DIVISIONS AND REFERENCES.

Chapter, Little (or 'Short Reading'). A lesson of a verse or two from the Bible included in each of the Divine *Offices except the *Office of Readings.

chapter house. A building used for meetings of a cathedral or monastic chapter.

character. In Catholic sacramental theology the indelible quality which *Baptism, *Confirmation, and *Ordination are held to imprint upon the soul.

Chardon, Louis (1595–1651), French *Dominican spiritual writer. In *La Croix de Jésus* (1649) he argued that just as the grace given to Christ impelled Him to choose suffering and crucifixion, and even a sense of abandonment by God, so grace in the believer typically leads to crosses and desolation, even if consolations and 'mystical phenomena' may accompany the earlier stages of the spiritual life. Through desolation the soul comes to rely on God alone.

charge. An address delivered by a bishop, archdeacon, or other ecclesiastical person at a *visitation of the clergy under his jurisdiction. Charges are also delivered to ordinands by bishops (and in the *Presbyterian Church by ministers) immediately before *ordination.

charismata (Gk., 'gifts of grace'). The blessings, spiritual and temporal, given to every Christian for the fulfilment of his vocation. In a narrower sense the word is used of the supernatural graces which individual Christians need to perform the specific tasks incumbent on them.

Charismatic Renewal Movement or 'Charismatic Movement', also known as 'Neo-Pentecostalism'. A predominantly lay movement within the main Churches. It originated in *Pentecostalism and, like it, emphasizes group worship and the exercise of the spiritual 'gifts' (*charismata), especially Divine (or *spiritual) healing, and *glossolalia. It began in N. America and dates from *c.*1960. In the RC Church its importance was recognized by representation at the 1987 Rome Synod of Bishops on the Laity. Here it is more structured and theologically conservative than when it first appeared.

charity. The usual AV translation of the Greek word *agape*, elsewhere usually rendered *love (q.v.).

Charlemagne (*c.*742–814), 'Charles the Great', first Emperor (from 800) of what was later to be called the *Holy Roman Empire. A son of *Pepin III, he became sole ruler of the Franks in 771. He extended his kingdom. First he subdued Lombardy, perhaps at the request of *Hadrian I. Then he conducted campaigns against the Saxons (772–85) and the Muslims in Spain (785–801). On Christmas Day 800 he was crowned Emperor by *Leo III in Rome.

At home Charlemagne created a strong central administration and encouraged ecclesiastical reform and learning. He was personally interested in *Adoptianism and *Iconoclasm, the main theological disputes of his day, and in the corrected text of the Bible prepared by *Alcuin. He tried to achieve liturgical uniformity, sought to promote the Roman Mass, and provided for a standard *homiliary and an approved collection of *canon law. His patronage of the scholars who formed the palace 'school' did much to stimulate learning. See also CAROLINGIAN SCHOOLS.

Charles I (1600–49), King of Great Britain and Ireland from 1625. He favoured the party in the Church which was ready to abandon the prevalent *Calvinistic outlook and to welcome a theological position nearer the Catholic tradition. He promoted *High Churchmen, in 1633 appointing W. *Laud Abp. of *Canterbury, and later shared in his unpopularity. The fact that his Queen, *Henrietta Maria, was a RC, added to his difficulties. In *Scotland, his attempt to impose the BCP and to control the government and policy of the Church of Scotland was met in 1638 by the inauguration of the *National Covenant pledging Scotland to *Presbyterianism. The Civil War, which broke out in England in 1642, was largely caused by ecclesiastical differences. By 1648 the defeat of Charles ensured the eclipse of the C of E and temporary triumph of Presbyterianism. His execution was due in part to his refusal to sacrifice episcopacy; it has been seen as *martyrdom. He is commemorated in CW on 30 Jan.

Charles II (1630–85), King of Great Britain and Ireland (in exile) from 1649; restored in 1660. He promised religious toleration in the Declaration of *Breda, and after the Restoration he tried to give effect to it in the *Declarations of Indulgence of 1662 and 1672. The sentiment of the country was, however, exclusively Anglican and led to the passing of the Act of *Uniformity (1662), the *Conventicles Act (1664), the *Five Mile Act (1665), and the *Test Act (1673). The King eventually supported the establishment, but on his deathbed he made a formal profession of the RC faith.

Charles V (1500–58), Emperor. When he was elected in 1519 he held the Netherlands,

Spain and the Spanish Empire, Naples, and the county of Burgundy. The most urgent problem confronting him was the growth of *Lutheranism. The Diet of *Worms (1521) banned M. *Luther, but Charles's other difficulties prevented him from taking consistent action. At the Diet of *Augsburg (1555) the Protestant princes forced upon his brother Ferdinand the principle of '*cuius regio, eius religio'. Charles abdicated in 1555-6.

Charles Borromeo, St (1538-84), Abp. of Milan and cardinal from 1560. He was one of the leaders of the *Counter-Reformation. He influenced the third and last group of sessions of the Council of *Trent. He initiated reform in his diocese: he founded an order of Oblates (modelled on the *Jesuits), established seminars for the education of the clergy, and reorganized a Confraternity of Christian Doctrine for instructing children. His influence was extensive, especially in Switzerland. Feast day, 4 Nov.

Charles Martel (c.690-741), Frankish ruler. An illegitimate son of Pepin II, Mayor of the Palace to the Merovingian kings, he faced opposition, but by 723 his position as *Princeps Francorum* was assured. He conducted campaigns against the Frisians, Saxons, and Bavarians, and defeated an Arab army at the battle of Poitiers in 732.

Charron, Pierre (1541-1603), French preacher and philosopher. Influenced by M. *Montaigne, Charron doubted whether human reason, unaided, could reach any certainty about God and His properties, but he held that the RC Church was the vehicle of revealed truth. His main work, *De la Sagesse* (1601), was put on the *Index.

charterhouse. The English name for a *Carthusian house. The English public school commonly so called was founded on the site of such a house in London.

Charter of Love. See CARTA CARITATIS.

Chartres. This French town has been the seat of a bishop since the 4th cent., with some intervals. The cathedral consists of an 11th cent. crypt and a magnificent Gothic church above it, built and decorated between c.1130 and 1230. Its glories are the stained glass and the stone sculpture on the west front and the porches to the north and south transepts. *Fulbert (d. 1028) taught here, but the idea that Chartres was a major centre of learning in the 12th cent. has been abandoned.

Chartreuse, La Grande. See GRANDE CHARTREUSE, LA.

chasuble. The outermost garment worn by bishops and priests when celebrating the Eucharist, and in the E. Church also at solemn celebrations of the morning and evening offices and on certain other occasions. It derived from the outdoor cloak worn by both sexes in the Graeco-Roman world.

Chateaubriand, François René, Vicomte de (1768-1848), French Romantic writer. He had a distinguished career as a politician. His *Génie du christianisme* (1802) is a brilliant rhetorical defence of Catholic Christianity. He sought to lift Christianity from the discredit into which the destructive work of 18th-cent. rationalist philosophers had brought it by transferring the debate from the plane of reason to that of feeling.

Chaucer, Geoffrey (1343/4-1400), English poet. He fought in France, was captured, ransomed by the King, and entered his service. The *Canterbury Tales* were apparently begun c.1387 and was unfinished when he died. The anti-ecclesiastical satire in the General Prologue is traditional in content and not motivated by any reforming drive; his religious vision of the power of suffering comes in the saints' legends and in the Clerk's Tale of patient Griselda.

Chelsea, Councils of. A series of synods representing the Church in England south of the Humber, held at Chelsea in the late 8th and early 9th cent. That of 787 witnessed the elevation of *Lichfield to archiepiscopal status; that of 816 affirmed and extended bishops' jurisdiction over monasteries.

Chemnitz, Martin (1522-86), *Lutheran theologian. He spent most of his life in Brunswick. He defended M. *Luther's doctrine of the *Real Presence of Christ in the Eucharist, though he deprecated further elaboration as to the mode of the Presence. He attacked the Council of *Trent and wrote an important doctrinal work on the Person of Christ. He took a leading part in drawing up the Formula of *Concord and was one of the main influences in consolidating Lutheran doctrine and practice in the generation after Luther's death.

Cherubicon or 'Cherubic Hymn'. In the E. Church a hymn usually sung during the *Great Entrance.

Cherubim. The Hebrew word, which is plural in form, denotes the second of the nine orders of *angels.

Chester. The city was perhaps the seat of the bishops of Mercia, but for most of the Middle Ages it was not a bishopric. The see was refounded in 1541 by *Henry VIII, who made the church of the dissolved abbey of St *Werburg the cathedral, under a new dedication to Christ and the BVM.

Chester Beatty Papyri. A group of papyrus codices, now in Dublin, most of which were acquired in 1931 by A. Chester Beatty (d. 1968). They include Biblical texts which provide valuable evidence for the Greek Bible, since they are a century or more older than the earliest vellum MSS.

Chevetogne. The *Benedictine community which has been at Chevetogne in Belgium since 1939 was founded in 1925 at Amay-sur-Meuse by L. *Beauduin in response to *Pius XI's request that Benedictines should pray for Christian unity. The community seeks to restore closer relations between the RC and other Churches; it is divided into two groups, the Latin and the Eastern, the one following the W. rite, the other the E. (Greek and Slavonic).

Chicago-Lambeth Articles. See LAMBETH QUADRILATERAL.

Chichele, Henry (?1362–1443), Abp. of *Canterbury from 1414. He was one of the architects of the government's pastoral response to the *Lollard challenge. His resistance to *Martin V's assault on the *Provisors legislation led to the suspension of his legatine powers and other humiliations. He founded All Souls College, Oxford (1438).

Chichester. The see, which was founded at Selsey by St *Wilfrid during his exile from York, was transferred to Chichester (on the site of the Roman city of Regnum) in accordance with the decree of the Council of London of 1075. The cathedral was built in the 12th–13th cents.

Children's Crusade (1212). A popular movement intended to recover *Jerusalem for Christian rule. Marching from *Cologne, the main party reached Genoa, but went no further. The so-called 'children' were perhaps servants, shepherds, and other marginalized people.

Chile, Christianity in. The Spanish invasion of Chile began in 1535; the first missionary priest arrived in 1541. The conversion of the country was not, however, completed until the end of the 17th cent. In 1818 Chile became independent of Spain, but the RC Church continued to be 'protected' and subsidized. In 1925 Church and State were separated. Over 80 per cent of the population are nominally RC. Protestant activity dates from 1821. *Pentecostal Churches have grown phenomenally since the 1960s.

chiliasm. Another name for *Millenarianism.

Chillingworth, William (1602–44), Anglican cleric. He became a RC and went to *Douai in 1630. The next year he returned to England and in 1634 again declared himself a Protestant. His *Religion of Protestants a Safe Way to Salvation* (1638) defended the rights of reason and free inquiry in doctrinal matters, and denied that any Church was infallible.

chimere. A sleeveless garment worn by Anglican bishops and by doctors of divinity.

China, Christianity in. According to legend, St *Thomas the Apostle preached in China. The *Sigan-Fu stone shows that missionaries from the *Church of the East reached China in the 7th cent.; Syriac Christianity survived there until the 14th cent. The first W. mission was that of John of Monte Corvino (c.1294); this was ended by the advent of the Ming dynasty in 1368. The famous mission of the *Jesuits began in 1582. They succeeded in building up a Chinese Christian community, but their method of *accommodation gave rise to controversy, and the subsequent assertion of Papal authority in the 18th cent. antagonized the Emperor. Persecution and imperial decrees banning Christianity followed.

The 19th-cent. missionary movement was faced with the isolationist policy of the Manchu dynasty. The first Protestant missionary, Robert *Morrison, who arrived in Canton in 1807, was able to remain only because he was employed as a translator by the East India Company. In the period 1839–65 the Western powers by military action secured for themselves rights of residence and jurisdiction. Missionaries then came from all the main denominations in Europe and America; they founded churches, schools, and hospitals throughout the country. When the Communists came to power in 1949 Christian institutions were taken over by the State, many churches were closed, and the activities of missionaries were curtailed; most were withdrawn by 1952. The new rulers, wishing to sever links between the Chinese Church and the West, encouraged the organization among Chinese Christians of the 'Three-Self Patriotic Movement' (self-supporting, self-governing, self-propagating). In 1957 RCs were forced to break relations with Rome. In the Cultural Revolution (1966) all religion was virtually outlawed. In 1979 churches began to reopen and in the 1980s restrictions on religious activity were reduced. After the massacre in Beijing in 1989 a more restrictive atmosphere prevailed, but Christianity represented a dynamic force with some appeal.

China Inland Mission (CIM). An interdenominational mission to the interior of *China founded by J. H. *Taylor in 1865. In 1951 it withdrew from China and relocated its work in E. Asia. In 1965 it was renamed the '*Overseas Missionary Fellowship'.

choir (architectural). The part of a church containing the seats of the clergy. In the Roman *basilicas these seats were set round the *apse behind the altar; the choir is now usually included in the *chancel, at its western end.

choir (musical). A body of singers assisting at Divine Service. As early as the 4th cent. such bodies existed, made up of clerics in *minor orders and boys, and by the time of *Gregory I (d. 604) the *Schola Cantorum seems to have been established. About the 12th cent. polyphony began to supplement the *plainsong of the Church and lay singers augmented church choirs. In recent years many churches have replaced or supplemented choirs by informal 'music groups' of singers and instrumentalists.

choir sisters. Nuns under obligation to attend all choir *Offices, as contrasted with *lay sisters who, though living under rule, attended only certain services. The distinction is now largely obsolete.

chorepiscopus. In the early Church a bishop of a country district in full episcopal Orders. He had restricted powers and was wholly subject to the authority of his diocesan. In the E. there were many chorepiscopi in the 4th cent., especially in Asia Minor, but their functions were progressively restricted and by the 13th cent. they had disappeared. In the W. they are first mentioned in 439, were numerous in missionary districts of Germany in the 8th cent., but disappeared in the 12th.

chrism. A mixture of olive oil and balsam used in the ritual of the Greek and Latin Churches. It may be consecrated only by a bishop; in the E. now only by Patriarchs and other heads of *autocephalous Churches. According to present Latin usage, chrism is consecrated on *Maundy Thursday, since 1955 at a special Mass of the Chrism. In the E. chrismation is part of the rite of *Baptism, and is also used for the reconciliation of *apostates and the reception of converts from other Christian Churches. In the W. it is used in Baptism, *Confirmation, and *Holy Orders. In both E. and W. it is used in the consecration of churches and altars.

chrismatory. A small vessel for keeping the three kinds of holy oil, namely oil of the catechumens, oil of the sick, and *chrism.

Christ (Gk., literally the 'Anointed One'). The word is a Greek translation of the Hebrew *Messiah. Originally a title, it soon came to be used by the followers of the risen Jesus as a proper name for their Lord, so that they themselves came to be known as *Christians. See also JESUS CHRIST and CHRISTOLOGY.

Christ the King, Feast of. The feast instituted in the RC Church in 1925 to celebrate the all-embracing authority of Christ. Since 1970 it has been kept on the last Sunday before the beginning of *Advent.

Christ Church, Oxford. A college in the University of *Oxford, founded by T. *Wolsey on the site of the monastery of St *Frideswide as 'Cardinal College'. In 1546 it was reconstituted by *Henry VIII. At the same time the new episcopal see was moved to the church of St Frideswide, which thus became both a cathedral and a college chapel.

Christadelphians. A sect founded in America in 1848 by John Thomas. They hold that the core of the Gospel is belief in the return of Jesus Christ in power to set up a visible theocracy beginning at Jerusalem, and that assurance of this is necessary to salvation.

Christian. The name was originally applied to the followers of Christ by outsiders, according to Acts 11: 26 being first used at *Antioch c.40–4. *Tacitus reports that it was current among the people at Rome at the time of the *Neronian persecution (AD 64) and it was always the official Roman designation of members of the Church; thus in times of persecution it was often the confession or denial of this name that was crucial. It was later adopted by the Church as a designation to distinguish itself from other religions.

Christian Aid. Formerly a division of the *British Council of Churches, it is now an official agent of *Churches Together. It originated in the work of the Ecumenical Refugee Commission set up in 1944. It provides assistance for the poorer nations and for refugees and victims of disaster throughout the world, working with members of the Churches in the areas concerned.

Christian Initiation. See BAPTISM and CONFIRMATION.

Christian Majesty, His Most. A title of the kings of *France.

Christian Science. The tenets of a religious body founded by Mary Baker Eddy (1821–1910), who set out her teaching in *Science and Health* (1875; revised, with *Key to the Scriptures*, 1883). While accepting the historicity of the Gospel accounts of Jesus' birth, death, and bodily resurrection, she drew a distinction between Jesus the man and Christ, the divinity which He manifested. Everything that does not express the nature of God is 'unreal'; evil and sickness have no ultimate reality and are to be destroyed by the subject's becoming aware of God's power and love (rather than by medical treatment). In 1879 the 'Church of

Christ, Scientist' was founded in Boston, Mass., and reorganized on a permanent basis in 1892. Christian Science spread, especially in the English-speaking world and in Germany.

Christian Socialism. A 19th-cent. movement for social reform initiated by members of the C of E. The first phase, beginning in 1848, was an attempt to counter Chartism within the working classes by providing an alternative Christian social critique; the second, from 1877, was more political and aimed to permeate the Church with social radicalism. The establishment of the Working Men's College in 1854 was the work of F. D. *Maurice. Other leaders were J. M. F. *Ludlow, C. *Kingsley, and Thomas Hughes.

Christian stewardship. See STEWARDSHIP.

Christian Year, The. The collection of poems for the Sundays and holy days of the year, published by J. *Keble in 1827.

Christina (1626–89), Queen of Sweden. The only surviving child of *Gustavus Adolphus, she succeeded to the Swedish throne in 1632. Assuming government in 1644, she made it her first aim to end the *Thirty Years War, and she was partly responsible for the Treaty of *Westphalia (1648). She promoted education at home and patronized foreign scholars. She abdicated in 1654. In 1655 she became a RC and settled at Rome.

Christkatholiken. The official name of the *Old Catholics of Switzerland.

Christmas. The commemoration of Christ's nativity. The earliest mention of its being celebrated on 25 Dec. is in the *Philocalian Calendar, which represents Roman practice in 336. The date was probably chosen to oppose the pagan feast of the *Natalis Solis Invicti* by a celebration of the birth of the 'Sun of Righteousness'. Another tradition derived the date of Christmas from that of the *Annunciation, held to have taken place on the same day of the year as the *Crucifixion and calculated as 25 Mar. After the accession of *Constantine, the observance of 25 Dec. in the W. spread from Rome. In the E. the closely related feast of the *Epiphany (6 Jan.) was at first more important; by the later 4th cent. this commemorated the Nativity as well as the *Baptism of Christ. By the mid-5th cent. most of the E. had adopted 25 Dec.

The day is celebrated in the W. rite by three Masses, of the night (normally at midnight), of the dawn, and of the day.

Christocentric. (1) Of systems of theology which maintain that God has never revealed Himself to man except in the Incarnate Christ; they preclude the possibility of *natural religion. (2) More generally, of any set of religious beliefs which is focused on the Person of Christ.

Christology. The study of the Person of Christ, and in particular of the union in Him of the Divine and human natures, and of His significance for Christian faith. In the NT Jesus of Nazareth is presented as a teacher, a prophet, and as *Messiah (the Christ), but such merely human categories were felt to be inadequate; instead of being an interpreter of the Law, Jesus is seen as superseding the Law (Mt. 5: 21–48), and the role in the work of creation that Jewish thought had ascribed to the *Torah or *Wisdom is attributed to Christ, the Son of God, the Word (1 Cor. 8: 6; Heb. 1: 2; Jn. 1: 3).

The idea that in Jesus man encountered the One through whom God had made the universe provided a starting-point for a more philosophical approach to Christology. The *Apologists of the 2nd cent. saw Jesus as the *Logos or Word of God, understood as the source of all order and rationality; in Jesus the Logos united Himself to a human being. For them, however, the Logos was an intermediary between God and the world, distinct from Him. When *Arius (d.336) held that such a subordinate Logos was not the uncreated God but part of the created order, he was opposed by those for whom to say that Jesus was the Logos incarnate was to say in some way that He is God. At the Council of *Nicaea (325) Arius was condemned and it was asserted that the Son of God who became incarnate in Jesus is 'consubstantial with the Father'. Such a clear affirmation of the divinity of Christ provoked debate. The *Alexandrians stressed that in Christ God Himself was living a human life; the *Antiochenes emphasized that in Christ both humanity and divinity co-operated without involving any encroachment on the reality of either nature. After the Council of *Ephesus (431) had rejected *Nestor-

ius' objection to the title of '*Theotokos' ('Mother of God') being applied to the BVM, *Cyril of Alexandria and the moderate Antiochenes reached an agreement enshrined in the 'Formulary of Reunion' (433); this affirmed the unity of Christ and asserted that He is 'consubstantial with the Father in Godhead and consubstantial with us in manhood'. *Eutyches in 447 began to teach that after the union there was one nature and that this nature was not 'consubstantial with us', but this teaching was condemned at the Council of *Chalcedon (451), which asserted that there is 'one Christ ... in two natures, without confusion, without change, without separation'. It also endorsed the Christological teaching of Pope *Leo that there is one subject in Christ, to which, paradoxically, two sets of attributes, Divine and human, are to be ascribed. Neither the Council of Ephesus nor that of Chalcedon secured complete agreement. Those who supported Nestorius rejected the Council of Ephesus and formed a schismatic Church, the *Church of the East. The so-called '*Monophysites' rejected the Chalcedonian Definition. In an effort to secure agreement between the Chalcedonians and the *Oriental Orthodox Churches the 6th cent. 'Neo-Chalcedonians' developed the doctrine of '*Enhypostasia' (q.v.). In the W. the Chalcedonian Definition was generally accepted.

At the *Reformation Christological concern shifted from the question of the two natures of Christ to a more direct analysis of His work in redemption. J. *Calvin stressed the Divine transcendence, while the *Lutheran tradition developed a new Christology of the two states of Christ's humiliation and exaltation in cross and resurrection, in accounting for the biblical stress on historical contingency in the Incarnation. This led to reflection on *kenosis (self-emptying) in Jesus and in God.

After the *Enlightenment a new Christology was produced which tended to see belief in the divinity of Christ as a way of articulating the conviction that the distinctive character of Christian faith in God is that this faith is focused on Jesus of Nazareth. It looked for the divinity of Jesus in the unique quality of His life on earth. In reaction to such an approach the so-called '*dialectical theology' arose. K. *Barth's God is wholly other; in Christ He reveals

Himself as and when He wishes. For R. *Bultmann Jesus is the one who confronts man with an *eschatological message, demanding response. Bultmann's pupils developed a 'New Quest' of the historical Jesus, accepting the importance of *kerygma, but seeking again to relate it to history. J. *Moltmann sees the cross of Christ as the key not just to Christology but to all legitimate talk about God. *Liberation Theology relates the Incarnation to salvation directly in its commitment to love of the poor and dispossessed. See also HISTORICAL JESUS, QUEST OF THE; INCARNATION; and JESUS CHRIST.

Christopher, St (Gk., 'one who carried Christ'). According to tradition, he was martyred in Asia Minor in the 3rd cent. A legend represents him as a giant who earned his living by carrying travellers across a river; one passenger was a small child who caused him to bow beneath his burden as the child was Christ and His weight that of the world. He is the patron of wayfarers; recently he has been adopted by motorists. His feast day in the W., 25 July, was dropped from the Roman calendar in 1969; in the E., 9 May.

Chrodegang, St (d. 766), Bp. of Metz from 742 (possibly from 747). He was chief minister to *Charles Martel and *Pepin III and a leading ecclesiastical reformer. On the death of St *Boniface (754) he assumed responsibility for the ecclesiastical affairs of the Frankish kingdom. In 748 he founded the abbey of *Gorze and he caused the canons of his cathedral to live a community life, drawing up for them the 'rule' that bears his name (c.755). This allowed them to hold private property. He also introduced the Roman chant and liturgy into his diocese. Feast day, 6 May.

Chromatius, St (d. 407), Bp. of *Aquileia from c.388. He was a learned scholar and tried to mediate between St *Jerome and *Rufinus. Some of his sermons have long been known; others have been identified in modern times.

Chronicles, Books of. These OT Books record the history of Israel and Judah from the Creation to the return from Exile (c.539 BC). In the Hebrew Bible they are a single Book; the division goes back to the *Septuagint, where they are called '*Paralipomenon', i.e. 'that which is left over' (from Sam. and Kgs.). The term 'Chronicles' was introduced by St *Jerome, whence it passed into English versions. The work appears to have been written in the latter half of the 4th cent. BC. On its historical value, opinion is divided.

Chronicon Paschale. A Byzantine chronicle, compiled in the early 7th cent., so named because it was based on the Easter reckoning. It extended from the creation of *Adam to AD 630, but not all of it has survived.

Chronographer of AD 354, the. The name given by T. Mommsen to the compiler of an almanac drawn up for the use of Christians at Rome in the 4th cent. The document includes a list of the dates of death of the Bps. of Rome from 255 to 352, a primitive Roman *martyrology, and a list of Roman Bishops from St *Peter to Pope *Liberius (the *Liberian Catalogue).

chronology, biblical. (1) OLD TESTAMENT. It is difficult accurately to date the events narrated, partly because there are few allusions to events known from sources outside the OT, partly because the times given for the duration of events in the Hebrew Bible are not always consistent and there are divergences in the *Septuagint, and partly because of the occasional use of chronological schemes for theological purposes. From the 9th cent. BC the dates of events narrated can be roughly discovered by comparing them with Assyrian and Persian chronologies.

(2) NEW TESTAMENT. Complications are caused by the different methods by which the years of monarchs were reckoned and by the intricacies of the Jewish calendar. According to Mt. 2: 1 Jesus was born 'in the days of *Herod the king' (d. c.4 BC), but according to Lk. 2: 2 during 'the first enrolment made when Quirinus was governor of Syria' (probably AD 6–9). There are similar discrepancies about other events in His life, including the *Crucifixion, for which the most likely dates are AD 30 or 33. However, all are agreed that He 'suffered under Pontius *Pilate', who was prefect of Judaea from AD 26 to 36. The date of St *Paul's conversion is also disputed. The outline of the events recorded is unaffected by these uncertainties.

Chrysippus (c.405–79), 'of Jerusalem', ecclesiastical writer. He became guardian of the Holy Cross at the Church of the *Holy Sepulchre. His few surviving works include four panegyrics.

Chrysogonus, St. According to legend he was arrested in Rome during *Diocletian's persecution and slain at *Aquileia. From the 6th cent. he was supposed to have been the spiritual director of St *Anastasia, with whom he is held to have corresponded on the behaviour of Christians towards their pagan spouses. Feast day in the E., 22 Dec.; in the W., formerly 24 Nov., now suppressed.

Chrysologus, St Peter (c.400–450), Bp. of *Ravenna. His episcopate coincided with *Galla Placidia's time in Ravenna, and he shared her enthusiasm for ambitious building projects. A large number of sermons attributed to him survives, but little else. In a letter to *Eutyches he asserted the need to adhere to the see of Rome in matters of faith. Feast day, 30 July (formerly 4 Dec.).

chrysom. The 'chrism-robe' put on a child at Baptism, as a symbol of the cleansing of its sin. It may originally have been a cloth put over the head to prevent the *chrism from being rubbed off. In the C of E its use disappeared in 1552, but is allowed in CW. In the RC Church it survived.

Chrysostom, Pseudo-. Many sermons have been falsely ascribed to St John *Chrysostom; of special interest are those by representatives of heretical movements from which little else survives: three paschal homilies which have been attributed to *Apollinaris; two homilies for the octave of Easter which seem to be *Anomoean; and the *Opus Imperfectum in Matthaeum*, a series of Latin homilies by an *Arian bishop of the 5th or 6th cent.

Chrysostom, St John (c.347–407), Bp. of *Constantinople. He studied at *Antioch and later (c.373) became a hermit. Made deacon in 381 and priest in 386, he was specially charged with the task of preaching ('Chrysostom' means 'golden-mouthed'). His famous series of sermons 'On the Statues' was given in 387 after a riot at Antioch in which the Imperial statues were overthrown. His homilies on Books of the Bible establish his title as the greatest

Christian expositor. These works combine a great facility for seeing the spiritual meaning of an author with an equal ability for immediate practical application. He was, however, opposed to the *allegorical exegesis of Scripture and stressed the importance of the literal sense. In 398 he was made Patr. of Constantinople. He incurred the hostility of the Empress Eudoxia. When he sheltered the *Tall Brothers, who had fled from Egypt after the condemnation of *Origenism, *Theophilus, Patr. of Alexandria, took the opportunity to humiliate the see of Constantinople. At the Synod of the *Oak (403), which was packed by Theophilus, Chrysostom was condemned and deposed. Though recalled by the Court, his plain speaking antagonized the Empress and on a technicality he was exiled. Feast day in the W., 13 Sept. (formerly 27 Jan., also observed in parts of the Anglican Communion); in the E., 13 Nov. See also preceding and following entries.

Chrysostom, Liturgy of St. The normal liturgy used in the E. Orthodox Church except on a few days in the year. In its present form it is much later than the time of St *Chrysostom. Most scholars question the grounds for associating it with him at all, but parallels in his works have led in recent times to a defence of the connection. It probably owed its influence to being the liturgy of the imperial capital.

Chrysostom, The Prayer of St. The prayer in the BCP was drawn by T. *Cranmer from the Liturgy of St *Chrysostom. Its authorship is unknown.

Church. The word denotes both a church building and the Christian community, local or universal. The origins of the Church as a sect within 1st cent. Judaism lie in the Lord's choice of 12 disciples (called *Apostles). Their mission was initially to Israel, but soon after the Resurrection *Gentiles began to join the Greek-speaking Jewish Christians. St *Paul's Gentile mission laid the foundations for the Gentile Christianity which became dominant after the fall of *Jerusalem in 70 and the expulsion of Jewish Christians from *synagogues in the 80s. From the outset the Church never considered itself a voluntary organization; it constituted the faithful remnant of God's people who had recognized the coming of the *Messiah and it soon understood its mission in universal terms. After the deaths of St *James (the Great), St *Peter and Paul in the 60s, and the marginalization of Jewish Christianity, new structures were developed. The essence of the Church was later epitomized in the traditional '*notes of the Church', namely unity, holiness, catholicity, and apostolicity. As teaching the Apostles' doctrine and historically descended from them, the Church is apostolic. Its membership, its orders of ministers, and its unity are established by participation in visible sacraments, i.e. those of *Baptism and Confirmation, of Holy *Orders, and the *Eucharist, respectively. After the split between the E. and W., the RC and E. Orthodox Church each maintained the other was in *schism (q.v.) and that itself was the historical manifestation of the visible Church. In addition to the visible Church on earth, there exists the invisible Church of the faithful departed.

The *Reformation led to a reformulation of the idea of the Church. It sought to proclaim its being in terms of the Word of God rather than in sacramental relationships. Among Protestants, two doctrines gained wide acceptance: (1) that the Church is a visible body and in the Divine intention one throughout the world, but that in view of the errors and corruptions which have arisen it is justified within a particular nation in reforming itself, even if this involves a breach of visible unity; (2) that the true Church is an invisible body of the saved whose membership is known only to God. Most holders of this view maintained that it was desirable that the Church should possess an outward organization, membership of which should correspond as far as possible with that of the invisible Church. Some Protestants held that visible unity should be secured in each nation by an '*established religion' determined by the ruler; others regarded unity of organization between Christian communities as unnecessary.

In modern times among Catholics, Protestants, and Orthodox there has been fresh interest in the theology of the Church. In the early part of the 20th cent. this vision of the Church focused on the Pauline notion of the Body of Christ; in the second half of the century increased stress was laid on the Church as sacramental, an idea emphasized by Orthodox theologians who see the community gathered to celebrate the Eucharist with its bishop as the primary manifestation of the Church. This has affinities with the concept of the Church as centred in each congregation that has characterized *Congregational and other Protestant Churches. In the RC Church a less institutional and juridical view than had been normal in that communion found expression in the Second *Vatican Council's Constitution on the Church, *Lumen Gentium* (1965), in which the Church is seen primarily as the People of God.

Church Army. An Anglican society of lay *evangelists founded in 1882 by Wilson *Carlisle, on lines broadly similar to those of the *Salvation Army. It represents a wide spectrum of churchmanship. Besides evangelism, it undertakes social work.

Church Assembly. This body, officially the National Assembly of the Church of England, was established by the *Convocations in 1919; in 1970 it was superseded by the General *Synod. It consisted of a House of Bishops; a House of Clergy; and a House of Laity elected by representative electors of the Diocesan Conferences. It prepared ecclesiastical measures for transmission to Parliament under powers provided by the Church of England Assembly (Powers) Act 1919 (the *Enabling Act).

Church Association. A society founded in 1865 by several Evangelical Churchmen to maintain the Protestant ideals of faith and worship in the C of E. In 1950 it became (with the National Church League) the Church Society.

Church Commissioners for England. The body formed in 1948 by the amalgamation of the *Ecclesiastical Commissioners and *Queen Anne's Bounty. It has been responsible for managing many of the C of E's historic assets. By the *National Institutions Measure 1998 the number of the Commissioners was reduced from 95 to 33 and a number of its functions, including some financial responsibilities, passed to the *Archbishops' Council.

Church Hymnary, The. The authorized hymnal of most of the *Presbyterian Churches in Britain. It was issued in 1898 and revised in 1927 and 1973.

Church Meeting. The regular assembly of all members of a *Congregational or *Baptist Church for Church administration, the admission of members, the election of officers, and the exercise of discipline.

Church Mission Society. See CMS.

Church's Ministry among the Jews. The common name since 1962 of the body founded in 1809 as the 'London Society for Promoting Christianity among the Jews'. Originally interdenominational, it became an Anglican society in 1815.

Church of England. The presence of British bishops at the Council of *Arles in 314 is evidence of the existence of an organized Church. British Christians were driven into the western parts of Britain by the Anglo-Saxons, who were converted by *Celtic missionaries from Ireland and *Scotland, and by the mission of St *Augustine of Canterbury sent from Rome (597). Unification and organization of the *Anglo-Saxon Church was achieved under *Theodore of Tarsus, who summoned national ecclesiastical councils, divided dioceses, and encouraged learning. After a period of decline, Abp. *Dunstan, St *Ethelwold, and St *Oswald initiated reform of the monasteries and cathedral chapters in accordance with contemporary European models. After the conquest by *William I, the Norman age saw the removal of episcopal sees from remote villages to cities, the beginning of an outburst of building activity, and the reorganization of ecclesiastical administration. Most important of all, the royal separation of the ecclesiastical and civil courts opened the way for the entrance of the Roman *canon law, the chief agent of Papal control in the W. Church. There were a number of disputes between the Church and State, notably about *investiture and the limits of the royal power, but by the 13th cent. Papal power in England had become very great. Soon, however, with the accentuation of national self-consciousness on the one hand, and the Papal scandals of the *Babylonian captivity and the *Great Schism on the other, the exactions and policy of the Roman see became the subject of increasing criticism in England; there was, for instance, legislation to curtail the Papal practice of diverting the income of English benefices for the support of foreign ecclesiastics.

When in the 16th cent. the Tudor monarchs deemed it expedient to measure their strength against the Papacy, many elements in the nation were ready to support them. Evidence of religious yearning was represented among the learned by the humanist revolt against *Scholasticism and among the literate by the purchase of newly-printed religious books and the expansion of domestic piety. The occasion of the Reformation was the famous 'divorce' of *Henry VIII. The *Convocations acknowledged the King to be the Supreme Head on earth of the Church of England, and a series of laws severed the financial, judicial, and administrative bonds between England and Rome. The monasteries were dissolved. Under *Edward VI, Abp. T. *Cranmer produced the First and Second Books of *Common Prayer in 1549 and 1552. The advance to Protestantism was reversed under *Mary. Upon the accession of *Elizabeth I the Papal obedience was again repudiated, the Crown assumed the title of 'Supreme Governor', the second BCP with some changes became the service-book of the C of E, and the *Thirty-Nine Articles its doctrinal formulary. The Elizabethan attempt to achieve a comprehensive national settlement was challenged both by RCs, who were sustained by missionary priests from Continental colleges, and Protestants who strove for change from within the Church. Under *Charles I the ascendency of W. *Laud and his endeavours to secure a higher standard of order in the Church sharpened *Puritan criticism and made episcopacy and Anglicanism a subject of conflict in the Civil Wars. The victory of Parliament led first to a *Presbyterian reform and then to *Independency. With the Restoration of *Charles II, the C of E again became the established Church and repressive measures were taken against dissenters. *James II's attack on the C of E was largely responsible for his downfall.

After the Revolution of 1688, the C of E, weakened by the secession of the *Nonjurors, settled to a period of quiescence. A limited toleration pacified the dissenters, theological disputes became unpopular, and the alliance of Church and State was a mutually defensive pact against all subversive forces. The *Methodist revival was the parent both of a new Christian body and of Anglican *Evangelicalism.

*Latitudinarianism dominated the intellectual atmosphere until well into the 19th cent., which witnessed the foundation of new parishes and bishoprics and much administrative reform. The *Oxford Movement laid new emphasis on the Catholic character of the established Church, but ceremonial novelties led to litigation and dispute. The Church of England Assembly (Powers) Act 1919 (the *Enabling Act) gave to the *Church Assembly the power to prepare legislation for consideration by Parliament; in 1927 and 1928 Parliament rejected a revised BCP. Since the end of the Second World War (1945) there has been considerable change. Lengthy negotiations for union with the Methodist Church proved abortive in 1972 (see ANGLICAN-METHODIST CONVERSATIONS), as did an attempt to establish a covenant with the Free Churches (1982; see REUNION), but since 1972 members of other Churches have been free to receive Communion in Anglican churches. The introduction of *Synodical Government in 1970 gave a voice to the laity in legislation in most areas. Prayer Book revision culminated in the publication of the *Alternative Service Book 1980; this was facilitated by the Church of England (*Worship and Doctrine) Measure 1974, which gave the C of E liberty, within certain safeguards, to order its own worship without reference to Parliament. Since 1976 through the *Crown Appointments Commission, the Church has had a dominant voice in the choice of its bishops. In order to prevent serious defections after the ordination of *women as priests (1994), provision was made for three provincial bishops to minister in those parishes unwilling to accept the ministration of bishops who had been involved in the ordination of a woman.

See also ANGLICAN COMMUNION and ANGLICANISM.

Church of the East (or *Assyrian Church of the East), often misleadingly called the *Nestorian Church. The Church in Mesopotamia (roughly modern Iraq) was outside the Roman Empire and took no part in the great Councils, though the Creed and Canons of *Nicaea (325), affirming the Divinity of Christ, were formally accepted in 410. The Council of *Ephesus (431), and especially the title '*Theotokos' for the BVM, is rejected. Attitudes to the Definition of *Chalcedon are ambivalent, because of a different understanding of the term *hypostasis. The liturgical language is Syriac.

In the 4th–5th cent. the Church suffered intermittent persecution. A monastic revival in the 6th cent. led to a large number of new foundations and by the early 7th cent. missionaries from the Church of the East had reached *China. By the end of Sassanian rule (651) Christians constituted an important religious minority. The Church of the East suffered drastic losses in the 14th cent., after the conversion of the Mongol dynasty to *Islam in 1295. In the mid-16th cent. it was divided by the creation of a separate *Uniat line of Patriarchs (see CHALDEAN CHRISTIANS). Several missions were sent from the West in the 19th cent. In the 20th cent. the Church of the East suffered as a result of political developments, and its members are now scattered in many parts of the world, especially the USA; only about 30,000 remain in the Middle East. Since 1968 there has been a schism, with one Catholicos resident in Baghdad, the other in the USA.

Church Pastoral Aid Society. See CPAS.

Church Sisters. In the Church of *Scotland women specially set apart to help in parochial work. They have now been merged in an order of *Deaconesses.

Church Society. See CHURCH ASSOCIATION.

Church Times. A weekly religious newspaper dating from 1863. It was founded to propagate *Anglo-Catholic principles but now occupies a position of central Churchmanship in the C of E.

Church Union. An Anglican association formed in 1934 by the amalgamation of the *English Church Union and the Anglo-Catholic Congress.

Church Unity Octave. An *octave of prayer observed since 1908 from 18 to 25 Jan. by a group of Anglican High Churchmen and others for the visible reunion of the Church. Under P. I. *Couturier it evolved into the widely observed 'Week of Prayer for Christian Unity'.

Churches of Christ. See DISCIPLES OF CHRIST.

Churches Together. The Council of Churches for Britain and Ireland in 1990 succeeded the *British Council of Churches, taking its present name in 1999. It embraces a wider spectrum of Christian traditions than the British Council of Churches did, and co-ordinates the work of the new national *ecumenical bodies—Churches Together in England, ACTS (Action of Churches Together in Scotland), CYTUN (Churches Together in Wales)—and the Irish ecumenical bodies.

Churching of Women. The form of thanksgiving which Christian women make after childbirth. The BCP Office, which is based on the *Sarum rite, is intended to precede Holy Communion. CW provides a service of 'Thanksgiving for the Gift of a Child' (either by birth or adoption). It is intended to involve the whole family. The RC rite, which used to be similar to that of the BCP, has been replaced by a blessing of the mother at the end of the *baptismal service.

Churchmen's Union. See MODERN CHURCH PEOPLE'S UNION.

churchwardens. In the C of E two churchwardens are chosen annually by the incumbent and parishioners. They represent the laity and are responsible for the movable property in the church.

churchyard. Properly the ground in which a church stands. The word is often used as though it were equivalent to '*cemetery'.

ciborium. (1) A chalice-shaped vessel, with a lid, used to contain the Sacramental Bread of the Eucharist. (2) A canopy over the altar, more usually in the W. termed a *baldachino.

Cimabue (d. 1302 or later), the usual name of Cenni di Pepo, Florentine painter. He worked in Rome and also in the church of S. Francesco, *Assisi, particularly in the transepts and apse of the Upper Church, and also in the apse of Pisa cathedral.

Circumcellions. Bands of predatory peasants who flourished in N. Africa in the 4th cent. and became linked with the *Donatists.

circumcision. Though circumcision had long been in use as a religious rite among the Jews, it was abandoned at an early date by nearly the whole Church. In St *Paul's Epistles 'the circumcision' is used substantively of the Jewish people.

Circumcision, Feast of the. The feast traditionally kept on 1 Jan., the 8th day of *Christmas, in commemoration of Christ's circumcision. The observance dates from the mid-6th cent. Since it is recorded that when He was circumcised, the Lord was given the name Jesus (Lk. 2: 22), many modern Anglican liturgies call the feast the Naming of Jesus. In the RC Church 1 Jan. is now called the 'Solemnity of Holy Mary, the Mother of God'.

circumincession, also **circuminsession.** In Christian theology the technical term for the interpenetration of the Three Persons of the Trinity.

Cisneros, Francisco Ximénez de. See XIMÉNEZ DE CISNEROS, FRANCISCO.

Cistercian Order. The Order was founded at *Cîteaux in 1098 by St *Robert of Molesme and others who wanted a form of *Benedictinism stricter and more primitive than any then existing. After some precarious years St *Bernard arrived as a novice in 1112, and the Order spread rapidly.

The Cisterican life was one of secluded communal intercession and adoration. Houses were erected only in remote situations; churches were plain, and manual work given its primitive prominence. The constitution developed in the 12th cent., and its basic documents (including the *Carta Caritatis) took shape gradually in the process. A founding abbey had permanent oversight over abbeys which it founded; this was achieved through visitation by the abbot to ensure observance and discipline. Daughter-abbeys could make foundations of their own; thus lines of filiation developed. Cîteaux itself was visited by the abbots of its eldest daughters (the 'protoabbots'). All Cistercian abbots were obliged to attend an annual General Chapter; in this was vested legislative, executive and judicial authority over the whole Order.

Starting with Castile in the 15th cent., foreign houses formed national congregations outside the control of Cîteaux. In the 17th cent. Cistercians, like other orders, were divided between reformers (the Strict Observance), who rejected all mitigations of the Rule, and those, led by Cîteaux, who wanted a minimum of change (the Common Observance).

In the 18th cent. Cistercians in the Austro-Hungarian Empire survived the *Josephine edicts only by undertaking educational and parochial responsibilities. Soon afterwards the French Revolution destroyed not only all houses in France and the neighbouring lands, but also the structure of central authority. Government hostility to monastic life in the 19th cent. and wars and other crises in the 20th, led to massive closures and expulsions. The Abbot General of the Common Observance now presides over a union of about a dozen congregations of differing patterns of life.

The extinction of Cîteaux and the proto-abbeys in 1790/91 left *la Trappe as the only French male community of any order to survive. Twenty-four monks fled to Switzerland; they soon attracted recruits and founded communities in various countries. Some of these followed A.-J. le B. de *Rancé's original reform, others the even more rigorous regime adopted by the Trappists in Switzerland, only partly relaxed when they returned to France. In 1892 the three Trappist congregations were united and in 1893 recognized as a new independent order; in 1902, after Cîteaux became their mother house, they were designated the Cistercian Order of the Strict Observance or Reformed Cistercians. This Order is not the continuation of the Strict Observance destroyed in 1791, but the lineal descendant of de Rancé's reform of 1664 at la Trappe. Worldwide expansion strained the practice of uniformity, and under the new constitutions approved in 1990, cultural differences are recognized, but the regime of the Trappists remains austere. The two separate Cistercian Orders co-operate.

citation. A summons to appear before a court of justice, especially an ecclesiastical court.

Cîteaux. The mother house of the *Cistercian Order in Burgundy. Expropriated in the French Revolution, Cîteaux was acquired in 1898 by the newly independent order formed from *Trappist congregations united in 1893.

Civil Constitution of the Clergy (1790). The legislative measures passed by the Constituent Assembly during the French Revolution to reorganize the Church in France. Salaries of the clergy were to be paid by the State, bishops and *curés* were to be elected by the more prosperous local citizens, and the Papal power of confirming nominations to the episcopate was transferred to the metropolitans. On 27 Nov. 1790 the Assembly imposed an oath to the Civil Constitution on all priests wishing to retain ecclesiastical office. About half the parish clergy accepted it. See also CONSTITUTIONAL CHURCH.

Clairvaux. The fourth house of the *Cistercian Order, founded by St *Bernard in 1115. The community was broken up and the property taken over by the French State in 1790.

clandestinity. The celebration of marriages without the cognizance of proper authority. Attempts to deal with the abuse, which was widespread in the Middle Ages, were made by both Catholics and Protestants in the 16th cent. The Reformers generally held that marriages without parental consent were null and void. RC canonists were ambivalent until the Council of *Trent in 1563 ruled that, though clandestine marriages were proper marriages, in future such marriages would be held to be null; all marriages were to be made before the parish priest (or another priest) and two other witnesses. In the C of E publicity is secured by the publication of *banns, the issue of a *marriage licence or the certification of a superintendent registrar, and the requirement of witnesses to the ceremony. Clandestinity is, however, commonly held not to void a marriage.

Clapham Sect. An informal group of wealthy Anglican *Evangelicals, many of whose members lived near Clapham and worshipped in its parish church. They included J. Venn, Rector of Clapham (1792–1813), Z. *Macaulay, and W. *Wilberforce. They supported the campaign against the *slave-trade, extension of missionary enterprise, the formation of the *British and Foreign Bible Society, the establishment of a model colony in *Sierra Leone, and the extension of *Sunday Schools.

Clapton Sect. See HACKNEY PHALANX.

Clare, St (1193/4–1253), foundress of the *Poor Clares. About 1212 she gave up her possessions and joined St *Francis at the

*Portiuncula. He placed her in a *Benedictine community before moving her to San Damiano outside the walls of *Assisi; when other women wishing to live on Franciscan lines joined her, she was made abbess (c.1215), a position she held until she died. Feast day 11 (formerly 12) Aug.

Clarendon, Constitutions of. A schedule of sixteen clauses put forward by Henry II as a statement of English customs under his grandfather, to regulate the relations between ecclesiastical and lay jurisdiction and other matters. They were produced at the Council of Clarendon (1164) for the assent of Thomas *Becket, who refused to affix his seal to the document. *Alexander III condemned various clauses and a long dispute followed.

Clarke, Samuel (1675–1729), Anglican clergyman. In 1704 and 1705 he delivered two sets of *Boyle Lectures in defence of rational theology against the empiricism of J. *Locke. Though a critic of the *Deists, he sympathized with some aspects of their teaching. His *Scripture-Doctrine of the Trinity* (1712), which had *Unitarian leanings, aroused criticism in Convocation, though no formal retraction was imposed.

Clarkson, Thomas (1760–1846), anti-slave-trade agitator. In 1787 he was involved in the establishment of a Christian settlement for poor Blacks in *Sierra Leone and, with some leading *Quakers and with W. *Wilberforce, he formed a group which pressed in the House of Commons for the abolition of the slave-trade in the British Empire (achieved in 1807).

class meeting. A meeting, usually weekly, of small sections of each *Methodist congregation, at which contributions to Church funds are paid, and inquiry is made into the conduct and spiritual progress of individual members.

Claudel, Paul Louis Charles (1868–1955), French RC author and diplomat. His chief claim to fame rests on his plays, which revivified the French theatre; their central theme was the consecration of the world to God in Christ. His poems rank with the finest Christian poetry of his time.

Claudianus Mamertus (d. c.474), Christian philosopher. The younger brother of St *Mamertus, he became a monk. In his *De Statu Animae* (c.470), he defended the doctrine that the soul was immaterial against *Faustus of Riez, who held that the soul, as a created substance, was of corporeal and extended character.

Claudius (d. after 827), Bp. of Turin from c.817. He made a series of attacks on image-worship, relics, the adoration of the Cross, and every visible sign of Christ's life, as well as on pilgrimages and the intercession of saints. He was also famous for his biblical commentaries. A number of works formerly attributed to other authors have recently been ascribed to him.

clausura. (1) The practice of separating a part of a religious house to the exclusion of those of the opposite sex to the community, and sometimes even to lay persons of the same sex; and (2) the portion so enclosed.

Clayton, John (1709–73), one of the first *Methodists. At Oxford he was a member of the ''*Holy Club' founded by the *Wesleys. In 1740 he became chaplain, and in 1760 a Fellow, of the Manchester Collegiate Church.

Clement of Alexandria. See after Pope CLEMENT XIV.

Clement of Rome, St (*fl.* c.96), Bp. of Rome. He appears in the early succession lists as the second or third bishop after St *Peter, but as there is no evidence for monarchical episcopacy in Rome so early, the meaning of this evidence is not clear. Besides the spurious '*Clementine Literature' (q.v.), two 'Epistles to the Corinthians' have been ascribed to him. The former (I Clement) is genuine. It was written c.96 in the name of the Roman Church to deal with strife in the Church at *Corinth, where certain presbyters had been deposed; it insisted that the deposed presbyters must be reinstated and legitimate superiors obeyed. It affords valuable evidence on the state of the ministry at the time. The so-called 'Second Epistle of Clement' is really a homily, assigned on stylistic grounds to another author. The earliest surviving Christian sermon, it sets out in general terms the character of the Christian life. According to one tradition, Clement was banished to the Crimea and forced to work in the mines; he was bound to an anchor and thrown into the Black Sea. Feast day in the W., 23 Nov.; in the E., 24 or 25 Nov.

Clement V (1264–1314), Pope from 1305. Bertrand de Got came of an influential French family. His policy was largely subservient to French influence, which increased when he fixed the Papal residence at *Avignon in 1309. He acquiesced in Philip the Fair's attack on the *Templars, suppressing the Order at the Council of *Vienne (1311); though the Pope assigned the Templars' property to the *Hospitallers, Philip managed to get most of their possessions. Clement added the '*Clementines' to the canon law.

Clement VI (1291–1352), Pope from 1342. Pierre Roger was elected Pope at *Avignon. His French sympathies hindered his efforts to make peace between England and France, and, together with his lavish use of Papal provisions, led to anti-Papal legislation in England, notably the first Statute of *Provisors (1351). Like his predecessor, he refused to confirm the election as Emperor of Louis of Bavaria and he appointed Charles of Bohemia (Charles IV) King of the Romans in 1346. In Italy he faced turmoil in Naples under his ward, Queen Joanna, and popular revolt in Rome led by Cola di *Rienzo in 1347. He strengthened the Papal establishment at Avignon by buying the city from Joanna of Naples and trying to make it the intellectual nucleus of Christendom. He was celebrated as a preacher and theologian, and he protected the Jews.

Clement VII (1478–1534), Pope from 1523. Though personally blameless in character, his lack of courage caused his pontificate to be marked by shifty diplomacy and intrigue. He tried to steer a middle course between the conflicting aims of Francis I of France and the Emp. *Charles V, and he irresolutely procrastinated over the 'divorce' of *Henry VIII. His failure to foster the movement for reform within the Church encouraged the spread of Protestantism during his pontificate.

Clement VIII (c.1536–1605), Pope from 1592. It was his policy to secure the representation of all the conflicting influences in the *curia, and especially to limit that of Spain. He supported the Catholic League against *Henry of Navarre, but also negotiated with him, so that in 1595 Henry became a RC. Clement issued new editions of the *Vulgate, *Missal, and *Breviary.

Clement XI (1649–1721), Pope from 1700. In the political sphere he met with little success, and in the Treaty of Utrecht (1713) his rights in Sardinia and elsewhere were ignored. His condemnation of *Jansenism in '*Vineam Domini Sabaoth' (1705) was followed by the condemnation of P. *Quesnel's work in 1708 and by '*Unigenitus' (1713). In the dispute between the *Dominicans and the *Jesuits over the Chinese Rites, he supported the *Holy Office which censured the opinion of the Jesuits. In 1708 he made the feast of the *Immaculate Conception of the BVM one of obligation throughout the Church.

Clement XIII (1693–1769), Pope from 1758. The main preoccupation of his pontificate was the storm over the *Jesuits. When the Parlement of Paris demanded drastic changes in their constitution in 1761, Clement refused. Nearly all French Jesuits had to go into exile in 1764; the Pope replied by issuing a bull praising the work of the Jesuits (1765). The demand of the ambassadors of Spain, Naples, and France in 1769 for the destruction of the Society is thought to have hastened Clement's death.

Clement XIV (1705–74), Pope from 1769. He was elected after a stormy conclave, the Bourbon courts having decided to recognize only a Pope ready to suppress the *Jesuits. His chief aim was to preserve peace with the Catholic powers in order to gain their support against the growing irreligion; under pressure he issued a brief suppressing the Society of Jesus in 1773. The former Papal possessions of *Avignon and Benevento were restored, but in France a royal commission continued suppressing religious houses, and in Portugal the secular authorities interfered in ecclesiastical affairs and education.

Clement of Alexandria (c.150–c.215), theologian. He was a pupil of *Pantaenus in *Alexandria, assumed the role of teacher (c.190), but fled from Alexandria in the *persecution (c.202). His surviving writings include the *Protrepticus*, or an 'Exhortation to the Greeks'; the *Paedagogus*, on Christian life and manners, and eight Books of *Stromateis*, or 'Miscellanies' (though the last

Book seems to be a misplaced fragment on logic). His work represents an attempt to meet the charge that Christianity is a religion for the ignorant. He treads a middle way between heretical *Gnosticism which had intellectual pretensions and a religion of simple faith, seeing in Christianity the fulfilment both of the OT Scriptures and of Greek philosophy. He depicts the *Logos as exposing the error and immorality of Greek religion and leading people, through Baptism, to the true religion of Christianity; he applies the term 'gnostic' to the Christian who has attained to the deeper understanding of the Logos. The ultimate goal of the Christian life is presented as *deification. Clement's name appears in earlier martyrologies under 4 Dec., but *Clement VIII excised it on the grounds of the doubtful orthodoxy of some of his writings. In the American BCP (1979), feast day, 5 Dec.

Clement Mary Hofbauer, St. See HOFBAUER, ST CLEMENT MARY.

Clementine Literature. A number of apocryphal works circulated in the early Church under the name of St *Clement of Rome, but by convention the term 'Clementines' is restricted to three of them.

(1) The *Clementine Homilies* is a religious and philosophical romance which Clement is supposed to have sent from Rome to *James, the Lord's brother, preceded by two letters from St *Peter and Clement also addressed to James, and instructions for the correct use of the work. They describe Clement's travels in the East, when he met Peter and witnessed his conflict with *Simon Magus.

(2) The *Clementine Recognitions* resemble the 'Homilies' and the narrative goes over much of the same ground, with additional details about the vicissitudes of various members of Clement's family and their reunion after their 'recognition' (hence the title) by Peter.

(3) Two Greek *Epitomies* of the above. They are evidently later and introduce an account of Clement's martyrdom.

It is generally thought that the 'Homilies' and 'Recognitions' depend on a common lost source, which probably dated from the early 3rd cent. The 'Homilies' belong to the 4th cent. and betray *Arian sympathies. The 'Recognitions' appear to be later; they

survive mainly in a Latin translation by *Rufinus.

Clementines. In canon law the collection of *Decretals issued by *Clement V in 1314. It contains the Decretals of *Boniface VIII, Urban IV, and Clement himself. It was the last item officially embodied in the '*Corpus Iuris Canonici'.

Cleopas. One of the two disciples to whom the risen Christ appeared on the road to *Emmaus.

Clerical Disabilities Act 1870. The Act which allows a cleric of the C of E after resigning his preferments to execute a Deed of Relinquishment and thereby regain such civil rights as he lost through being a clergyman.

Clerical State, Admission to the. See ADMISSION TO CANDIDACY FOR ORDINATION OF DEACONS AND PRIESTS.

Clerical Subscription Act 1865. The Act changing the form of declaration made by Anglican clergy on ordination and on accepting preferment. Acknowledgement of the Royal Supremacy was no longer required, and only a general assent to the *Thirty-Nine Articles was demanded. In 1975 the form of assent was made even less rigid. See also ASSENT, DECLARATION OF.

Clericis Laicos. The bull issued by *Boniface VIII in 1296 forbidding any cleric to pay ecclesiastical revenues to laymen without Papal approval, and any layman to receive such payments.

Clerk in Holy Orders. A designation, chiefly legal and formal, for a bishop, priest, or deacon in the C of E.

Clerk of the Closet. In the C of E the cleric who presides over the Royal College of Chaplains. He presents bishops to the Sovereign when they do homage after consecration.

clerks regular. A term applied to certain bodies of RC clergy, bound under religious vows, who live in community and engage in active pastoral work. Such regular clerks originated in the 16th cent. through the efforts of various bands of clerics to perfect their work by the stimulus of ordered discipline. They include the *Theatines (founded 1524), the *Barnabites (1530), and the *Jesuits (1534).

Clermont, Council of (1095). It was summoned by *Urban II for the reform of the Church and the preaching of the First *Crusade. Besides proclaiming remission of all penances for those who went to Jerusalem to free the Church of God, it passed numerous canons.

Cletus, St. See ANACLETUS, ST.

Clifford, John (1836–1923), British *Baptist minister. He became President of the Baptist Union in 1888 and from 1905 to 1911 he was President of the World Baptist Alliance. He led the movement for 'passive resistance' to A. J. *Balfour's Education Act of 1902, which he held to be injurious to Nonconformist interests.

Climacus, St John. See JOHN CLIMACUS, ST.

Clitherow, St Margaret (c.1556–1586), the 'martyr of York'. She became a RC when 18. In 1586 she was arrested and charged with harbouring priests. To save her children from having to witness against her, she refused to plead, and was crushed to death. She was among the *Forty Martyrs of England and Wales canonized in 1970.

cloister. An enclosed space which normally forms the central part of a monastery or other religious building. The term is also used in general for a Religious House and for the Religious Life.

Close, Francis (1797–1882), Dean of *Carlisle from 1856 to 1881. He was previously, from 1826, incumbent of Cheltenham. Here his sermons made him one of the best-known *Evangelical preachers. In 1847 he founded the colleges of St Paul and St Mary in Cheltenham.

Clotilde, St (474–545), Frankish queen. In 492 or 493 she married *Clovis (q.v.), whom she at once tried to convert to Christianity. After his death in 511 she retired to the abbey of St *Martin at Tours. Feast day, 3 June.

Cloud of Unknowing, The. An anonymous English mystical treatise of the 14th cent. The author insists that, in this life, God cannot be grasped by the intellect; between Him and us there is always a 'cloud of unknowing' which can be pierced only by a 'sharp dart of love'.

Clovesho, Councils of. A series of synods representing the Church of England south of the Humber, held between the late 7th and early 9th cent. That of 747 ordered adherence to the Roman liturgical rite; that of 803 abolished the archiepiscopal status of *Lichfield. The site of Clovesho is unknown.

Clovis (c.466–511), King of the Franks. By inheritance he became King of the Salian Franks in 481; by conquest he expanded his domain to include much of Roman Gaul and other territory. The decisive event of his career was his conversion to Christianity and his Baptism. The date of this is given by *Gregory of Tours as 496, but modern critics suggest 503, 506, or 508 as more likely.

Cluny, Cluniacs. The monastery of Cluny, in Burgundy, was founded in 909/10. The high standard of monastic observance from an early stage led to the adoption of its customs by other houses, old and new. The objects of the reform included a return to the strict *Benedictine Rule, especially as expounded by St *Benedict of Aniane, cultivation of personal spiritual life, stress on the choir *office (which tended to grow to excessive length) and the splendour and solemnity of worship generally, with a corresponding reduction in manual labour. It seems clear that the Cluniac houses were not welded into a system until the time of *Odilo (abbot, 994–1048) and *Hugh (abbot, 1049–1109). Under Hugh the number of Cluniac houses exceeded 1,000, with control highly centralized. Cluny then exercised great influence on the life of the Church and largely inspired the reforms associated with *Gregory VII. In the later Middle Ages its influence declined, though the monastery survived until 1790.

CMS. The 'Church Mission Society', founded in 1799, was the first C of E society to send missionaries to the indigenous populations of Africa and Asia. Its theology has always been *Evangelical.

coadjutor-bishop. A bishop appointed to assist a diocesan bishop, often with the right of succession to the see at the next vacancy. The office is common in the RC Church and in the *Episcopal Church in the USA.

coarb. In Ireland, the 'heir' or successor of a saint who founded a church.

Coat of Christ, Holy. See HOLY COAT.

Cocceius, Johannes (1603–69), Johann Koch, dogmatic theologian. He was born in Bremen and taught there and at Franeker before he moved to *Leiden in 1650. He sought to expound dogmatic theology on a purely biblical basis, but, although professedly a *Calvinist, he objected both to the Calvinist spirit and the scholastic orthodoxy of his day. He interpreted the relation between God and man in terms of a personal covenant; his system thus became known as *Föderaltheologie*.

Cochlaeus, Johannes (1479–1552), RC controversialist. He had a strong sympathy with the *Platonist and humanist revival of the Renaissance. He engaged in writing against M. *Luther, but the bitter tone of his polemic won little favour.

co-consecrator. A bishop who assists the chief consecrator in the laying-on of hands at the making of a bishop.

COCU. See CONSULTATION ON CHURCH UNION.

Codex Alexandrinus ('A'). The early 5th-cent. MS of the Greek Bible which Cyril *Lucar offered to *James I; it is now in the British Library. It also contains the two (so-called) Epistles of *Clement.

Codex Amiatinus. The oldest extant MS of the Latin *Vulgate. It was written at *Wearmouth or Jarrow between *c.*690 and 700. From the 9th or 10th cent. the MS was in the monastery of Monte Amiata, hence its name; in 1782 it passed to the Laurentian Library in Florence.

Codex Bezae ('D'). This bilingual (Latin and Greek) MS of the Gospels and Acts, with a fragment of the Latin of 3 Jn., is the chief uncial representative of the so-called *Western text. Written between the 4th and 6th cent., it was presented to the University of Cambridge by T. *Beza.

Codex Ephraemi ('C'). A 5th-cent. Greek MS of the Bible now at Paris. It was converted into a *palimpsest by a covering of writings by St *Ephraem Syrus.

Codex Iuris Canonici (CIC). The code of *canon law in force in the (Latin) RC Church since 1918. In view of the unwieldy nature of the material of RC canon law, a code was compiled and promulgated in 1917, to come into force in 1918. A new code was promulgated in 1983, with a separate code for the *Uniat Churches promulgated in 1990.

Codex Sinaiticus ('א'). A MS of the Greek Bible, probably written in the 4th cent., which was discovered by C.*Tischendorf in the monastery of St Catherine on Mount *Sinai. He presented most of the MS to the Tsar of Russia; in 1933 the Soviet Government sold this to the Trustees of the British Museum. (43 leaves are in Leipzig; 15 more were found in St Catherine's monastery in 1975.) The MS contains about half the OT, the whole NT, the 'Epistle of *Barnabas', and part of the 'Shepherd' of *Hermas. The NT readings are one of the chief witnesses to the *Neutral or *Alexandrian text.

Codex Vaticanus ('B'). A 4th-cent. MS of the Greek Bible, now in the *Vatican Library, where it has been since at least 1481. It was extensively restored in the 15th cent., with most of Gen. copied from another Vatican MS. The *Pastorals are totally missing. The NT readings are one of the chief witnesses to the *Neutral or *Alexandrian text.

Codrington, Christopher (1668–1710), soldier and colonial administrator. He left estates to found in Barbados a college of medicine and divinity, whose members were to do missionary work in the *West Indies. The Codrington Missionary Training College was built in 1714–42.

coenobite. A religious in vows who lives in a community (as opposed to a *hermit). The term is also used in a technical sense of *anchorites who occupy separate dwellings and observe a rule of silence, but live otherwise as a community of *monks in a common enclosure. See also LAVRA.

Coffin, Charles (1676–1749), hymn-writer. In 1718 he became rector of the University of Paris. He published a collection of Latin hymns in 1727; several of them are well known in English versions, e.g. 'On Jordan's banks the Baptist's cry'.

cogito ergo sum (Lat., 'I think, therefore I am'). The primary datum of truth accepted by R. *Descartes, on the ground that, however much a man doubted, he could never think away himself as the doubting subject.

Coke, Thomas (1747–1814), pioneer of *Methodist missions. In 1784 J. *Wesley 'ordained' him as Superintendent (or 'Bishop') of the Methodist Episcopal Church formed at a conference in Baltimore later that year. Coke divided his time between the American Church and the *West Indian missions which he initiated.

Colenso, John William (1814–83), Bp. of Natal from 1853. Storms of protest were aroused by his commentary on Romans (1861), with its denial of eternal punishment and rejection of much traditional sacramental theology, and by his papers on the *Pentateuch and *Joshua, which challenged the traditional authorship and the accuracy of these Books; in 1863 he was declared deposed by his Metropolitan, Robert *Gray. Colenso appealed to the *Judicial Committee of the Privy Council, which ruled in his favour (1865) on the ground that the Letters Patent appointing him preceded those appointing Gray. Hence, though solemnly excommunicated by Gray, who consecrated another bishop, Colenso maintained his position and by a series of judicial decisions obtained the cathedral and endowment of the see. The schism in Natal was formally ended only in 1911.

Coleridge, Samuel Taylor (1772–1834), poet and thinker. He published the *Lyrical Ballads*, with W.*Wordsworth, in 1798, his most famous contribution being 'The Ancient Mariner'. Soon afterwards he wrote the last of his great poems, including the second part of 'Christabel' (1800) and the 'Ode to Dejection' (1802).

Coleridge preached the need of man for a spiritual interpretation of life and the universe against a fossilized Protestant orthodoxy as well as against the materialist and rationalist trends of his age. His conviction that Christianity is primarily ethical led him to believe in the possibility of a unification of Christendom on a wide basis of common tenets.

Colet, John (1466?–1519), Dean of *St Paul's from 1504. He learnt Greek in Italy. On his return he constantly inveighed against ecclesiastical abuses and, though he never challenged the doctrines of the Church, he was often suspected of heresy. He spent part of a large fortune in re-founding St Paul's School, where 153 boys could gain the rudiments of education, be brought up in a sound Christian way, and be taught Greek as well as Latin.

Colettines. A branch of the *Poor Clares founded by St Colette (1381–1447), a native of Corbie in Picardy who was canonized in 1807 (feast day, 6 Mar.).

Coligny, Gaspard de (1519–72), *Huguenot. He was converted to *Calvinism in 1560 and in 1569 he became the recognized leader of the Huguenot cause. His influence at court led the French to aid the Netherlands in their revolt. He was killed in the Massacre of St *Bartholomew's Day.

collation. (1) The light meal allowed on days of fasting in addition to the main meal; (2) the lives of the *Fathers, especially as arranged for reading in monasteries; and (3) *institution to an ecclesiastical benefice when the *ordinary is himself the patron (i.e. when presentation and institution are one and the same act).

collect. The short form of prayer constructed (with variations in detail) from (1) an invocation, (2) a petition, and (3) a pleading of Christ's name or an ascription of glory to God. The prayers later known as *Secrets and *Post-Communions are structurally indistinguishable, but the term 'collect' in the Eucharistic rite is normally confined to the prayer (or prayers) which immediately precedes the lections. Such prayers were familiar by the 5th cent. They secured a place in the daily *Offices as well as in the Eucharist.

Collegialism. The thesis that the Church and State are purely voluntary associations (*collegia*) in which supreme authority rests with the body of the members, and that the civil magistrate has no other relations with the Church than those which he has with other voluntary associations.

collegiality. A word used in a theological context to signify that the bishops constitute a body, of which each is a part, and not a mere collection of individuals. In the RC Church, the concept found some expression in the establishment of the Synod of Bishops in 1965.

collegiate church. A church which is endowed for a body of canons and/or prebendaries (the 'chapter'), but is not, like a *cathedral, a bishop's see.

Collier, Jeremy (1650–1726), English *Nonjuror. In 1696 he was outlawed for giving absolution on the scaffold to two attempted assassins of William III, but he returned to London in 1697. In 1713 he was consecrated as a 'bishop of the Nonjurors' and he joined in their attempt at reunion with the Orthodox Church. He was largely responsible for the production of the Nonjurors' Communion Office of 1718.

Collins, Anthony (1676–1729), English *Deist. His main work, *A Discourse of Freethinking* (1713) argued that free inquiry was the only means of attaining to the truth and was commanded by Scripture. It was designed as a defence of Deism and provoked replies by many Churchmen.

Colluthus (4th cent.), schismatic priest of *Alexandria. During the episcopate of St *Alexander (312–28) he assumed the power of conferring orders, though only a presbyter. In 324 he was deposed.

Collyridians. A 4th-cent. sect, which apparently originated in Thrace and consisted mainly of women, who offered an idolatrous cult to the BVM.

Colman, St (d. 676), leader of the *Celtic party in Northumbria. He became Bp. of *Lindisfarne in 661. At the Synod of *Whitby (664) he unsuccessfully pleaded for the retention of such customs as the Celtic date for Easter and the Celtic *tonsure. He afterwards left Lindisfarne for a monastery in Ireland. Feast day, 11 Feb.

Cologne. The see was founded in or before the reign of *Constantine (d. 337). In the 11th–12th cents. the Abps. of Cologne became important secular princes and in 1356 were recognized as imperial electors. The cathedral dates from the 13th–15th and the 19th cents., and contains the shrine of the *Magi.

Colombini, Bl Giovanni (1304–67), founder of the *Gesuati. A wealthy merchant of Siena, he was moved by reading a Life of St *Mary of Egypt when he was about 50. He then devoted himself to the service of the poor and sick, later persuading his wife to accept separation. When his example was followed by other young nobles, the city authorities exiled him; he was recalled when an epidemic broke out. In 1367 he and his followers were formally constituted into the congregation of the Gesuati. Feast day, 31 July.

Colonial and Continental Church Society. See CCCS.

Colosseum. The name by which the 'Flavian Amphitheatre' at Rome has been known since about the 8th cent. Completed c.AD 80, it has been venerated as the scene of many early martyrdoms; the truth of this tradition has been questioned.

Colossians, Epistle to the. A letter included in the NT, traditionally held to have been written by St *Paul when he was in prison, probably in *Rome, possibly in *Ephesus; many modern critics attribute it to an early follower of Paul. The Church at Colossae, in western Turkey, had been founded not by Paul but by Epaphras. The primary purpose of the epistle was to recall its readers to faith in Christ as their all-sufficient Redeemer and Lord.

colours, liturgical. A sequence of colours at different seasons of the ecclesiastical year for vestments and other liturgical objects is first found in the use of the *Augustinian Canons at *Jerusalem in the early 12th cent. The standard sequence in the W. Church (white, red, green, purple, and black) was established much later. There are no definite rules about colours in the E. Church.

Columba, St (c.521–97), Abbot of *Iona and missionary. Of Irish royal lineage, after the battle of Cúl-drebene (561), for which he was held partly responsible, he sailed to Britain as a pilgrim and founded a monastery on Iona. In 574 he anointed Aedán mac Gabráin King of the Scots of Dalriada, and in 575 he attended the convention of the kings at Druim Cett in Ireland. He founded the monastery of Durrow in Ireland. Feast day, 9 June.

Columbanus, St (d. 615), abbot and missionary. An Irish monk of *Bangor, he left Ireland c.590 on perpetual *pilgrimage and sailed to Gaul. Here he set up monasteries at Annegray and *Luxeuil. His religious fervour and encouragement of private

*Penance helped to respiritualize an area where Christianity was at a low ebb, but his adherence to the customs of the Irish Church aroused opposition. With his companions he was expelled from Gaul in 610 and eventually settled at *Bobbio. His surviving works include letters, sermons, and the Monks' Rule; the Communal Rule and Penitential ascribed to him are also substantially his. Feast day, 23 Nov.

Comboni, Bl [Antonio] Daniele (1831–81), first RC Bishop of Central Africa and founder of the *Verona Fathers. In 1854 he was ordained priest for the African mission in the Institute founded at Verona by Nicholas Massa and later became Vice-Rector of its African colleges. In 1864 he conceived his 'Plan for the Regeneration of Africa'; its basic idea was to 'save Africa with Africa'. In 1867, when the Mazza Institute gave up its African work, he founded the Missionary Institute for Africa, commonly known as the Verona Fathers. At the First *Vatican Council (1870) he presented a 'Petition on behalf of the Black Populations of Central Africa'. In 1872 he founded the Institute of the Missionary Sisters of Verona. He was appointed *Vicar Apostolic of Central Africa in 1877. He was involved in the struggle against *slavery. Feast day, 10 Oct.

Comboni Missionaries. See VERONA FATHERS.

Comenius, Johannes Amos (in Czech, Jan Amos Komensky) (1592–1670), educationalist. He belonged to the *Bohemian Brethren (Moravian) and was minister at Fulnek and later at Lissa in Poland. After the destruction of Lissa in 1656, he found refuge in the Netherlands.

His educational ideas were influenced by his personal religious experience. Hoping for a Utopian Church which would unite all religions in Christian love, he regarded education as the means to its fulfilment; the development of character on Christian lines, rather than learning, was to be the ultimate aim. His ideas have influenced modern pedagogy. Since the 1890s interest in his religious and philosophical thought has revived.

Comes (Lat., *Liber comitis*, *Liber comicus*, *Liber commicus*), a book containing the passages to be read at Mass as *Epistles, or containing both Epistles and *Gospels. Originally a collection of complete readings, the terms came to be used for lists containing only references to the passages to be read.

Comfortable Words, the. Four short passages from the NT which the BCP instructs the celebrant to read at the Holy Communion after the Absolution of the people. In CW their use is required in the Holy Communion, Order Two, but is optional elsewhere.

Comforter, the. A Johannine title of the Holy Spirit.

Comgall, St (d. *c*.600), Abbot of *Bangor (Co. Down), is one of the the best-attested founders of monastic churches in 6th-cent. Ireland. The 7th-cent. Life of St. *Columbanus by Jonas of Bobbio describes Columbanus's years of study with Comgall; his virtues are praised in a hymn preserved in the late-7th-cent. Antiphonary of Bangor. Feast day, 10 May.

commandery. Among the *Hospitallers an estate or manor in the charge of a member of the Order.

Commandments, the Ten. Precepts divinely revealed to *Moses on Mt. *Sinai and engraved on two tablets of stone. The text is preserved in two closely similar versions (Exod. 20: 1–17 and Deut. 5: 6–21). Their dating has been a matter of controversy. It is now regarded as an open question, with many critics accepting the possibility that in a primitive form they may go back to Moses himself.

The Ten Commandments have played a substantial part in the teaching of the Church. By the time of St *Augustine they had gained a prominent place in the instruction of *catechumens; they again came to the fore in the development of the penitential system in the 9th cent. and in the popular teaching of the 16th-cent. Reformers. In the 1552 BCP their recitation was introduced into the Communion Service, but in modern practice they are usually omitted or replaced by the *Kyrie Eleison or by the Lord's Great Commandments (Mk. 12: 29–31); provision is made for these and other alternatives in CW.

Commandments (or Precepts) of the Church. Certain moral and ecclesiastical precepts imposed by the RC Church on all its members. The *Catechism of the Catholic Church (1997) lists five: to attend Mass on

Sundays and *Feasts of Obligation; to go to confession (see PENANCE) at least once a year; to receive Communion during the Easter season; to keep holy the Feasts of Obligation; and to observe the days of *fasting and abstinence. To these is added the duty of providing for the material needs of the Church.

commemoration. In W. liturgical practice, when two feasts fall on the same day, until recently that of the lesser rank was 'commemorated' by including some of its prayers after the corresponding prayers of the feast being observed.

commendam. An individual (who could be a layman) was said to hold an ecclesiastical benefice *in commendam* when its revenues were granted to him temporarily during a vacancy. Gradually the term came to be restricted to benefices which a bishop or other dignitary held more or less permanently along with his see.

Commendatio morientium (Lat., 'Commendation of the dying'). The prayers prescribed in the W. Church to be said at the bedside of a dying person. It was formerly called 'Commendatio Animae'.

Commination. The service drawn up by the compilers of the BCP for use on *Ash Wednesday and other days appointed by the *ordinary. It consists of an exhortation (in the course of which the Curses against various classes of evil-doers are recited), Ps. 51, suffrages, and prayers.

Commodian, Christian Latin poet. He is generally held to have flourished in Africa in the mid-3rd cent., but some have dated him later, e.g. in the 5th cent. in S. Gaul. He was a convert from paganism. Two of his poems have survived.

Common Life, Brethren of the. See BRETHREN OF THE COMMON LIFE.

Common of the Saints. Those parts of the *Missal and *Breviary containing the offices of such saints as do not have an individual office (a '*proper') of their own.

Common Order, Book of. (1) The directory of worship drawn up by J. *Knox in 1556 for the English Protestant congregation in *Geneva. Appointed for use in *Scotland by the *General Assembly in 1562, it was replaced by the *Westminster Assembly's 'Directory of Public *Worship' in 1645.

(2) In modern times the title has been revived for various service-books, none of them mandatory, used in Scotland by Churches of the *Presbyterian tradition. Following the union of the Church of Scotland and the *United Free Church in 1929, the 1940 *Book of Common Order* was authorized by the General Assembly. The 1979 *Book of Common Order* was a revision of the 1940 Book. In 1994 a new book, called *Common Order*, was published.

Common Prayer, The Book of. The official service-book of the C of E containing the daily offices of *Morning and *Evening Prayer, the forms for the administration of the *Sacraments and other rites, the *Psalter, and (since 1552) the *Ordinal. The book was compiled because of the desire of T. *Cranmer and others to reform, simplify, and condense the Latin services of the medieval Church and to produce in English a simple, convenient, and comprehensive volume as an authoritative guide for priest and people.

The First BCP was issued in 1549 and its use ordered by the first Act of *Uniformity. In doctrine and ritual it was a compromise between the old and new schools and pleased neither. Revision in the light of Protestant criticism led to the issue of the Second BCP in 1552. After the reign of *Mary, this was reissued, with a few alterations, as the Elizabethan BCP of 1559. Under the Commonwealth, the BCP was officially superseded by the Directory of Public *Worship (1645), but after the *Restoration, the 1662 Act of Uniformity authorized a BCP revised by *Convocation. The most important change was the introduction of the AV for the Epistles and Gospels. This 1662 Book remained almost unchanged until modern times. However, in the face of ritual controversies in the late-19th cent., a new Book (whose use was to be wholly permissive) was drawn up and passed by the Convocations and *Church Assembly but rejected by the House of Commons in 1927 and again, after some amendments, in 1928. In 1955 the Abps. of Canterbury and York appointed a Liturgical Commission to prepare a revision which, after a period of authorized experimentation with individual services, led to the acceptance in 1980 of the *Alternative Service Book (q.v.).

Outside England the BCP underwent numerous revisions. The Scottish (Episcopalian) Communion Office of 1764 influenced the American BCP of 1789. Elsewhere the English 1662 Book was used until the Church of *Ireland, freed by disestablishment from the Act of Uniformity, in 1877 produced its own BCP, a conservative revision in a Protestant direction. In the early 20th cent., revisions of the BCP were issued in *Canada (1922), the *United States of America (1928), and Scotland (1929). In other parts of the Anglican Communion the BCP or parts of it were generally translated into local languages, though in some areas different forms of the Communion Service appeared in the first half of the 20th cent. Until 1948 *Lambeth Conferences viewed the BCP as a bond of the Anglican Communion and it was only after 1958 that encouragement was given to provincial revisions.

In the 1960s modern English was introduced into the Anglican liturgy and new experimental rites addressed God as 'you' rather than 'Thou'. As in the C of E, the revision of individual services was followed by the issue of a single Book; in some provinces its use is mandatory; in others it is an alternative to the BCP, though in practice tending to replace it.

Commonwealth and Continental Church Society. See CCCS.

Common Worship. The title of the services designed to supersede the ASB in Advent 2000. For details see p. 644.

Communicantes. A section of the RC *Canon of the Mass (and of the First Eucharistic Prayer), so named from its opening word in the Latin text; it comes shortly before the Words of *Institution.

communicatio idiomatum (Lat., 'interchange of the properties'). The doctrine that, while the human and Divine natures in Christ were distinct, the attributes of the one may be predicated of the other in view of their union in His Person.

Communion, frequency of. On a possible interpretation of Acts 2: 46 the apostolic community communicated daily; from other passages in the NT and 2nd-cent. writers it seems that members of the local Churches all communicated at the Sunday Eucharist. Later, though attendance at the Liturgy was general, communion became infrequent. The Fourth *Lateran Council (1215) ordered that all Christians should communicate at least once a year. Nearly all post-medieval revivals, Catholic and Protestant, have sought to increase frequency of communion. In the RC Church the relaxation of the *Eucharistic fast was directed to this end, and in the second half of the 20th cent. communion was sometimes allowed for the second time on the same day, e.g. at a *Nuptial Mass. Weekly communion is common among the devout laity of the RC Church and the C of E; in religious communities and among a small proportion of the laity daily communion is normal. The same change from infrequent communion (not more than once a month) to weekly (or more frequent) communion occurred in the E. Orthodox and many Protestant non-episcopal Churches during the 20th century.

Communion, The Order of the (1548). A form for administering Communion, drawn up in English, and originally interpolated into the Latin Mass between the Communion of the priest and that of the people. Its essential parts were an exhortation, a brief address to the intending communicants, the General Confession and Absolution, the *Comfortable Words, the Prayer of *Humble Access, the Words of Administration (for both kinds), and the Blessing. Its contents passed into the BCP.

Communion anthem or antiphon. In the RC Mass the short passage said or sung during the administration of the communion.

Communion in both kinds. The custom of receiving Communion under the two species of bread and wine was general until about the 12th cent., though there were a few exceptions. By the 13th cent. in the W. the chalice was restricted to the celebrant. The legitimacy of the practice was denied by the *Hussites. The 16th-cent. Reformers also insisted that Communion in both kinds alone had Scriptural warrant, and the practice was adopted in all Protestant Churches, including the C of E. In the RC Church the Council of *Trent ruled that the existing practice was justified by the doctrine of *concomitance, but since the Second *Vatican Council provisions have been made for general reception in both kinds. See also INTINCTION and UTRAQUISM.

Communion of Saints. Part of the 9th article of the *Apostles' Creed. It is usually interpreted as the spiritual union existing between each Christian and Christ, and so between every Christian whether in *Heaven, *Purgatory, or on earth.

Communion plate. In the RC Church, a plate of silver or metal gilt formerly held under the chin of the communicant as he received the Sacrament. The term is also used collectively of the vessels used in the celebration of the Eucharist, which are often plated with gold.

Communion Sunday. A Sunday on which the Holy Communion is celebrated.

Communion table. The table at which the Holy Communion is celebrated. In the C of E the term is used especially by *Low Churchmen, *High Churchmen preferring the word '*altar'.

Communion tokens. Metal tokens which served as certificates of fitness for admission to the Communion. They were used mainly in the Church of *Scotland, where their place has been largely taken by printed cards on which the names of the communicants are written.

Communion under both species. See COMMUNION IN BOTH KINDS.

Community of the Resurrection. This Anglican community was founded at Oxford in 1892 by C. *Gore. It moved to Mirfield, Yorks., in 1898. The Community conducts a college for the training of ordinands and engages in pastoral and educational work in South Africa.

comparative religion. The branch of study which investigates by scientific and historical methods the religions of the world and their mutual relations. Its successful pursuit as a science rests on the universality of religion and the frequent recurrence of certain patterns of religious experience in widely separated ethnological and social groups. It studies the conditions under which these various forms of religious behaviour manifest themselves, the processes of their growth, and the part they play in the cultures and traditions to which they belong. It is not concerned with ques-

tions of ultimate validity. It has posed problems for Christian faith by its recognition that much that was thought to be exclusive to the Christian tradition is held in common with other world religions; on the other hand it has brought out the distinctiveness of some elements in Christianity. It has also brought Christian apologists a deeper understanding of other religions and has influenced missionary methods.

competentes (Lat., 'those qualified'). In the early Church *catechumens in the final stage of preparation for *Baptism.

Compline. The last of the canonical day-hours (see OFFICE, DIVINE) of the W. Church, said before retiring for the night. Various forms had evolved by the 4th cent.; Ps. 91 occurs in most of them, and usually also Pss. 4 and 134. A hymn and the *Nunc Dimittis (not taken into the *Benedictine rite until 1977) were soon added. Much of Compline was incorporated into the *Evensong of the BCP.

Complutensian Polyglot. The first *polyglot edition of the whole Bible, begun in 1502 at the expense of Card. F. *Ximénes de Cisneros, who assembled a group of scholars at Alcalá (Lat. 'Complutum'), where the Bible was printed, 1514–17.

Compostela (properly 'Santiago [i.e. 'St James'] de Compostela') in NW Spain, traditionally supposed to be the burial-place of St *James the Apostle. It has been the seat of a bishop since the 9th cent., and is a centre of pilgrimage. See also SANTIAGO, ORDER OF.

comprecation. The intercession which the saints are believed to make on behalf of the rest of the Church. The word is also loosely used of requests to God for the intercession of saints.

Compton, Henry (1632–1713), Bp. of London from 1675. He was tutor to the princesses Mary and Anne, but his anti-papal attitude brought him into disfavour with *James II, and he was restrained from the exercise of his spiritual functions on the ground of his failure to suspend J. *Sharp for his anti-Roman sermons. He officiated at the coronation of William III and supported the project for comprehension and the *Toleration Act.

Comte, Auguste (1798–1857), founder of

French *Positivism and of the 'Religion of Humanity'. The foundation of his system is the law of the three stages—the theological, the metaphysical, and the 'positive'—which constitute the phases of development of the human race as well as of its individual members. In the theological and metaphysical stages the human mind seeks a cause or essence to explain phenomena, but in the third or positive phase explanation is discovered in a law. Comte advocated the organization of mankind in one vast system in which altruism was to conquer egoism. Thinking this possible only on a religious basis, he constructed a new kind of religion, with humanity in the place of God, and a cultus mainly borrowed from Catholicism.

concelebration. The joint celebration of the Eucharist by a number of priests. The practice was probably common in the early Church. In the RC Church it was restored in 1963; here it is required that all concelebrating priests recite the central part of the Canon together. In the E. Church concelebration survived, though in modern times the Canon is usually said by the celebrant alone.

Conception of the BVM. See IMMACULATE CONCEPTION OF THE BVM.

Conciliar theory. The doctrine that supreme authority in the Church lies with a *General Council. The movement associated with the theory culminated in the 15th cent., but the foundations of it were laid in the early 13th, when canonists found difficulty in reconciling the increasing claims of Papal authority with the theoretical possibility of a heretical Pope. The outbreak of the *Great Schism in 1378 raised the question of authority in an acute form. In 1380 *Conrad of Gelnhausen advocated the summoning of a General Council, arguing that the absence of a single recognized Pope left the duty of convening it to the *cardinals. In the early sessions of the Council of *Constance it was claimed that the power of the Council came directly from Christ, but the very success of the Council in ending the schism weakened the position of the conciliarists. *Pius II in 1460 specifically forbade appeals from the Pope to a future General Council, and after the 15th cent. support for the Conciliar theory waned.

conclave. The closed apartment in which the *cardinals are confined during the process of electing a new Pope. The word 'conclave' is also loosely applied to the meeting itself, either on this occasion or, more loosely, of the cardinals for any purpose.

concomitance. The doctrine that in the Eucharist the Body and Blood of Christ are present in each of the consecrated species. See also COMMUNION IN BOTH KINDS.

Concord, Formula (1577) and **Book (1580) of**. The 'Formula of Concord' was the last classical *Lutheran formula of faith; the 'Book of Concord' is a definitive collection of the chief confessional documents of Lutheranism. In the face of internal disagreements within Lutheranism, in 1567 J. *Andreae was commissioned to produce a union formula. The Swabian Concord of 1573 in a revised form was combined with the Maulbronn Formula of 1576, produced by another group of Lutheran theologians and then edited by Andreae to produce the Solid Declaration and an Epitome, which together constitute the Formula of Concord. It appeals to Scripture, the early Fathers, the *Apostles', *Nicene and *Athanasian Creeds, the *Augsburg Confession of 1530 (to which P. *Melanchthon's 'Treatise on the Power and Primacy of the Pope' was appended in 1537) and its Apology (1531), the *Schmalkaldic Articles (1537), and M. *Luther's two catechisms (1529). The Formula itself and these documents (with Scripture and the Fathers represented by extracts in an appendix) formed the basis of the Book of Concord, which was published in German in 1580, and in Latin in 1584.

concordance. An alphabetical list of words in the Bible giving, for each appearance of a word, its location and a brief context. The first such list, a concordance to the *Vulgate, was produced in the 13th cent. by *Dominicans in Paris as a tool for writing sermons. In the first stage only locations were listed; later 8–10 word contexts were provided; before 1286 a one-volume version, with briefer contexts, was completed. Printed in 1474, it remained in use until modern times. A concordance of the Hebrew OT was compiled in 1437–45 and published in 1523; one to the Greek NT appeared in 1546, and one to the *Septuagint in 1607. The first concordance in

English was that to M. *Coverdale's translation of the NT by T. Gybson (1535); that to the whole Bible was made by J. *Merbecke (1550). The most important English concordance to the AV was that by A. *Cruden (1737). There are concordances to modern versions of the Bible.

concordat. An agreement between the civil and ecclesiastical authorities on some matter of concern to both parties.

Concordat of 1801. The agreement concluded between *Pius VII and Napoleon Bonaparte which led to the formal restoration of the RC Church in France.

Concordia Regularis. See REGULARIS CONCORDIA.

concupiscence. In moral theology the inordinate desire for temporal ends which has its seat in the senses. Catholic theology in general holds concupiscence to be the result of *Original Sin, rather than a part of it, and regards it as 'material for the exercise of virtue', since it provides reason and will with opportunities to resist the disordered movements of the senses. Protestant theology looks upon concupiscence itself as sin and its existence as an offence against God.

concurrence. The falling on consecutive days of ecclesiastical feasts or other days to be observed, so that the Second *Vespers or *Evensong of the first coincided with the First Vespers or Evensong of the second. The complicated rules which used to govern the use of collects etc. in such situations in the RC Church no longer apply.

concursus divinus (Lat., 'Divine concourse'). A technical term for the co-operation of the *grace of God with the actions of finite creatures.

condignity. In the Scholastic theology of *grace, those actions which fallen man performs as a Christian in conscious reliance on the Holy Spirit are held to merit the grace of God 'by condignity' (*gratia de condigno*), i.e. as from a debtor.

conditional immortality. The theory that immortality is not a necessary attribute of the soul as a separate entity from the body, but rather that it is bestowed on the whole being at the Last Day and is conditional on the believer's faith in Christ or, in modern times, on his behaviour during life. The idea found renewed favour in the 19th cent. as a means of accounting for the fate of the impenitently wicked without accepting either the orthodox doctrine of eternal punishment or the theory that all free moral creatures will ultimately be saved (*apocatastasis or universalism). It was recently revived by some *Evangelicals, who hold that annihilation follows a period of torment in Hell.

Condren, Charles de (1588–1641), French theologian. He entered the *Oratory in 1617 and in 1629 succeeded P. de *Bérulle as Superior-General. He was much sought after as a spiritual director. His letters were posthumously published in 1642, and *L'Idée du sacerdoce*, put together by his followers, in 1677 (Eng. tr., 1906).

Confessing (or **Confessional) Church.** The group of German Evangelical Christians most actively opposed to the '*German Christian' Church Movement sponsored by the Nazis. It consisted of the 'Pastors Emergency League' founded in 1933 under the leadership of M. *Niemöller, the Lutheran *Landeskirchen* which had not succumbed to the 'German Christians', and a strong parish movement particularly in W. Germany. In 1934 it began to establish its own canonical authorities in areas where the official administration was 'German Christian'; it also issued the *Barmen Declaration (1934). The outbreak of war in 1939 made further open resistance impossible. At the end of the war in 1945 leaders of the Confessing Church made a 'Declaration of Guilt' to a delegation of the provisional *World Council of Churches. In 1948 the '*Evangelical Church in Germany' was founded from a federation of all the regional Lutheran, Reformed, and United Churches in Germany; the Confessing Church continued to be an active movement, though no longer claiming to be the only Church government.

Confessio Augustana, Confessio Helvetica, Confessio Scotica. See AUGSBURG, HELVETIC, and SCOTTISH CONFESSION.

confession. (1) The tomb of a *martyr or '*confessor'; the structure or shrine built around such a tomb; or the church in which a martyr is buried. (2) The profession of faith by a martyr or confessor, and so in general a declaration of religious belief; the term is used particularly of the Protestant professions of the 16th and 17th cents. From this sense derives its use for a communion or religious body. (3) An acknowledgement of sin, made either in general terms by a congregation during liturgical worship or by an individual penitent in private or *auricular confession. See also ABSOLUTION and PENANCE.

Confessions of St Augustine, The. The anti-*Manichaean prose-poem written by St *Augustine c.398–400. The title means both 'confessing' in the biblical sense of praising God, and also avowal of faults. Books 1–9 are autobiographical; the last four deal with memory, time, creation, and Gen. 1 as an allegory of the Church.

confessor. (1) In the early Church one who suffered for confessing his or her faith, but only to an extent which did not involve martyrdom. Later the word was applied loosely to holy men and ultimately to those pronounced such by the Pope. (2) A priest who hears (especially private) confessions.

Confirmation. In Sacramental theology, the rite whereby the grace of the Holy Spirit is conveyed in a fuller measure to those who have already received it in some degree at *Baptism.

Many theologians have seen instances of Confirmation in references to the laying on of *hands in the NT (e.g. Acts 8: 14–17), but in all the early evidence it is hard to discern the precise relationship between the various elements which were associated with initiation into the fullness of the Christian life. In the early 3rd cent. the laying on of hands and anointing with oil are depicted as an integral part of the Baptismal liturgy. In the mid-3rd cent. they are distinguished from the actual Baptism, and by the 4th cent. Confirmation, whether conferred by anointing or laying on of hands, was in the W. Church frequently a separate rite. As the number of candidates seeking admission to the Church made it impossible for the bishop to baptize them all in person, the parish clergy came regularly to administer Baptism and the part of the bishop in the initiation ceremonies was deferred until the next episcopal visitation, when candidates could be presented to the bishop for Confirmation. In the E. Church

the practice of conferring Confirmation at the same time was retained. This was achieved by confining the bishop's part to the consecration of the oil used for anointing. The oil is then conveyed to the parish priest who performs the rite of Confirmation as occasion requires.

The theological significance of the rite has been, and still is, disputed. Some regard it as an integral part of, and in its effects indistinguishable from, Baptism; others as conveying a new gift of the Spirit, especially the grace necessary to strengthen the candidate in his conflict with evil.

Since the later Middle Ages the normal practice in the RC Church has been to confirm as soon as convenient after the seventh birthday, but since 1971 the possibility of a later age has been envisaged. Confirmation is normally administered during Mass. After the homily the candidates renew their Baptismal promises; the bishop, extending his hands over them, prays that they may receive the Holy Spirit and then traces the *sign of the Cross with *chrism on the forehead of each. In some cases priests can now confirm on their own with chrism blessed by the bishop, e.g. when receiving converts from another Communion.

At the Reformation the C of E continued the medieval practice, though the use of oil ceased in 1549 and the sign of the Cross in 1552. CW provides a shorter formula of administration than the BCP, but requires the bishop to address each candidate by name. According to the BCP no one is to be admitted to Communion until he is confirmed or 'ready and desirous to be confirmed', but since 1972 baptized members of other Churches have been admitted. Confirmation has traditionally been preceded by a formal course of instruction.

The rite is also in use among *Lutherans and some other Protestant bodies.

Confiteor (Lat., 'I confess'). One of the forms of confession used in the RC Church. It is so called from the first word of the Latin text.

confraternity. See FRATERNITIES.

Congar, Georges-Yves (1904–95), French *Dominican theologian. He developed a passionate interest in ecclesiology and *ecumenism. In a controversial article he ascribed the alienation of French culture from the Church to the latter's 'disfigured face'. He wrote a number of books on the nature of the Church, in 1950 appealing for a reform of its structures by a 'return to the sources'. The publication of an article in support of the 'worker-priest' movement in France led in 1954 to his being forbidden to teach. With the election of *John XXIII in 1958, the situation changed. Congar was appointed theological consultor to the preparatory commission of the Second *Vatican Council and influenced many of its documents. In 1969 he became a member of the Pontifical International Theological Commission and in 1994 a *cardinal.

congé d'élire (Fr., 'permission to elect [a bishop]'). In 1214 King *John agreed that bishops in England should be elected by the dean and chapter of the cathedral, but royal permission, the *congé d'élire*, was to be secured first and the election confirmed by Royal Assent. Since the Reformation the *congé d'élire* has been accompanied by a 'letter missive' requiring the dean and chapter to elect the person named therein by the Sovereign.

Congo, Democratic Republic of the, Christianity in. In the late 19th cent. this huge area of central Africa was formed into a single country, known as the Congo Independent State, mainly through the efforts of Leopold II, king of the Belgians. Exploration was followed by missionary endeavour. In 1878 the Baptist Missionary Society began work in the Lower Congo region; in 1880 the *White Fathers founded a mission in the east of the country. Other missions, British, American, and Swedish followed. From the mid-1890s King Leopold's policy of financing the Independent State through a trading monopoly enforced with brutality made missionary work difficult and provoked protest from Protestant missionaries; the ensuing international agitation led to Belgium's annexation of the Congo in 1908. There was close co operation between the government and the RC Belgian missionaries, who were granted extensive privileges. Only in 1946 did the Protestants obtain equal treatment. The alliance between the RC Church and the State was weakened in the 1950s when there was a socialist government in Brussels. Independent African Churches and prophetic movements, which had been banned since the trial of

Simon *Kimbangu in 1921, came into the open.

After Independence in 1960 there was much resentment against the missionaries. Under the authoritarian State (called Zaire from 1971 to 1998), the Churches were largely Africanized and in 1965 by presidential decree only three Churches were recognized: the RC Church (by far the largest); the 'Church of Christ in Zaire' (a loose federation of mission-founded Protestant Churches); and the Kimbanguists, to which the Greek Orthodox Church was added later.

See also following entry.

Congo, Kingdom of, Christianity in. A *Portuguese expedition reached the ancient Congo kingdom in 1483. In 1491 the king and one of his sons was baptized; the king reverted to paganism but the son, who did not, on the death of his father became king himself as Afonso I (1506–43). Both he and his successors appealed for more priests, and the *Jesuits opened a college in San Salvador in 1625. In 1645 a *Capuchin mission arrived and for the next 150 years Capuchins worked in the country. After the defeat of Antonio I by the Portuguese in 1665, the kingdom largely disintegrated. Church life continued in the western province of Soyo, but in the course of the 18th cent. the supply of missionaries failed; Christian life was sustained only by the *maestri*, catechist interpreters who led the Church in the absence of a priest. Nevertheless, when British *Baptist missionaries reached San Salvador in the 1870s, the king who welcomed them still thought of himself as a Christian. For the later history, see previous entry and ANGOLA.

Congregation of the Lord (also **Congregation of Christ** or simply **the Congregation).** The title assumed by the Scottish Reformers who supported J.*Knox.

congregation, monastic. A group of monasteries united under a superior, usually known as the Abbot President or Abbot General. The purpose of the union is to foster good discipline, but individual monasteries remain independent.

Congregation, Religious. Those Religious *Institutes of Consecrated Life in the RC Church whose members take simple *vows were, until 1983, designated Religious Congregations, in contrast to Religious Orders, in which solemn vows are taken. The terminology is no longer officially recognized.

Congregationalism. The form of Church polity which rests on the independence and autonomy of each local Church. It has been held that the system is primitive and represents the earliest form of Church order. Modern Congregationalism, however, dates from the Reformation. As early as 1550 there is evidence of men and women meeting together to preach the Word of God and administer the Sacraments as *Separatists from the national Church. When it was clear that *Elizabeth I did not intend a drastic reform of the Church, the number of such companies increased. R. *Browne, insisting that these 'gathered churches', bound under God by covenant, should be independent of the State and have the right to govern themselves, laid down the lines of essential Congregationalism. From the 1580s Brownists (as outsiders called them) increased in number and the somewhat amorphous Separatism became more clearly defined Congregationalism; Churches were formed in *Norwich, London, and elsewhere. The movement was driven underground by persecution. Some Separatists migrated to the *Netherlands and ultimately to the *United States of America, where Congregationalism was influential in shaping both religion and politics. In England the Independents (as they were called) formed the backbone of O. *Cromwell's army, and they defended their position at the *Westminster Assembly and restated their principles in the *Savoy Declaration of 1658. The 1662 Act of *Uniformity made Nonconformists of Independents and *Presbyterians alike, though the *Toleration Act 1688 gave them the right to exist. Attempts to fuse these two types of Church at this time were unsuccessful, mainly because of theological differences. Being excluded from the ancient universities, the Independents set up Dissenting Academies and played a leading part in the foundation of London University. A product of the *Evangelical Revival was the indigenous growth of Congregationalism in Scotland.

The independency of the Congregational Churches did not involve them in complete isolation. They recognized the bond of a common faith and order and in time formed County Associations for mutual intercourse and support. The Congregational Union of Scotland was formed in 1812; that of England and Wales in 1832. These Unions had no legislative authority but served to advise the Churches and express their common mind. In 1972 the greater part of the Congregational Church in England and Wales united with the Presbyterian Church of England to form the *United Reformed Church. In the USA most of the Congregational Christian Churches in 1957 joined with the Evangelical and Reformed Churches to form the *United Church of Christ, and Congregationalists have been involved in modern unions in other parts of the world (see REUNION).

Congregations, Roman. See ROMAN CONGREGATIONS.

congruism. The doctrine that God confers *grace for the performance of good works (*gratia de congruo*) in accordance with such human circumstances as He sees will be most favourable to its use.

Conrad of Gelnhausen (*c.*1320–90), theologian, first Chancellor of the University of Heidelberg. From the outbreak of the *Great Schism (1378), he was an advocate of the *Conciliar theory. His thought is based on an appeal to the underlying authority of the Church understood as the whole congregation of the faithful as opposed simply to the Pope and his Curia. In his *Epistola Concordiae* (1380) he argued for the summoning of a General Council by the *cardinals on behalf of the universal Church, even without the Pope.

Conrad of Marburg (*c.*1180–1233), *Inquisitor. He was charged with reforming missions in Germany and won the confidence of the Landgrave Ludwig IV of Thuringia; in 1225 he became the director and confessor of his wife, St *Elizabeth. In 1231 he was appointed the first Papal Inquisitor in Germany, with absolute power over heretics. He exercised his authority ruthlessly and was murdered.

Consalvi, Ercole (1757–1824), Italian statesman. He entered the Papal service early and in 1800 was created cardinal and made Secretary of State. He was chiefly responsible for the negotiation of the *Concordat of 1801. He represented the

Pope at the Congress of Vienna (1815) and secured the restoration of the Papal States.

consanguinity, blood-relationship. Within certain degrees it renders marriage not only unlawful but null and void. See also KINDRED OF AFFINITY, TABLE OF, and PROHIBITED DEGREES.

conscience. The word now denotes the capacity for judging the rightness of actions, whether in general or in particular. Christians are agreed that it is unique to man and that its effectiveness is increased by experience and through *grace.

Western medieval theologians differed as to whether the source of moral discernment lay in the affections and will, or in practical reason. The Reformers reacted against the idea of an uncorrupted natural power to discern good and evil untouched by the *Fall and emphasized the dependence of the Christian conscience on faith. More recent thinkers have been divided on the reality and authority of conscience. Some have tended to discard the concept and speak only of moral judgment; others (e.g. Bp. J. *Butler) have seen in conscience a kind of moral sense in the exercise of which man becomes aware of a Being higher than himself. According to I. *Kant conscience is the awareness of the universal claim of the moral dictates of reason (the *Categorical Imperative). Religion is the recognition of this claim as the will of God, and it is by following the dictates of conscience that man realizes his independence of conventional and social codes. Modern psychology regards conscience as the activity of the super-ego, which is formed in childhood and represses drives that are socially unacceptable. Nevertheless, a critical attitude to social pressures, combined with the sense that man's freedom implies some sort of ultimate autonomy, has meant that the notion of conscience has seemed useful when an individual's sense of value conflicts with those imposed by the State or society. Moral theologians have stressed the need for conscience to be informed by attention to the teaching of Scripture and the Church; conscience thus informed is to be followed.

consecration. The separation of a thing or person for Divine service. The term is used: (1) Of the Eucharist, for the act whereby the bread and wine become the Body and Blood of Christ; (2) Of clergy and laity professing the *counsels of perfection through vows or other bonds recognized by the Church. It was formerly also used for the making of bishops, who are now said to be ordained rather than consecrated (see ORDERS and ORDINAL) and of churches and altars, now said to be dedicated rather than consecrated (see DEDICATION OF CHURCHES).

Consecration, the Prayer of. The central prayer in the Eucharistic rite of the BCP.

Consensus Genevensis (1552). J. *Calvin's reformulation of his teaching on *predestination. Directed primarily against A. *Pighi, it was also intended to combat H. H. *Bolsec and other Protestants who had attacked Calvin's doctrine.

Consensus Tigurinus (Lat., 'the Zurich Agreement'). The formula of faith agreed upon in 1549 by the representatives of Protestants of French and German Switzerland. They were primarily concerned to set forth a doctrine of the Eucharist which conformed with *Calvinist principles and was free from the objections which the *Zwinglians felt to *consubstantiation.

Conservative Evangelicalism. See EVANGELICALISM.

consignatorium. The room or building in which the bishop used to confirm the newly baptized by 'signing' them with the *chrism.

consistory. In the RC Church the consistory is the assembly of *cardinals, convoked by the Pope and meeting under his presidency. An ordinary consistory, to which only those cardinals resident in Rome need be summoned, is held when the Pope wishes to consult them or to perform some solemn act, such as conferring the *pallium; extraordinary consistories, to which all cardinals are summoned, take place when serious matters suggest it.

In the C of E the Consistory Court is the bishop's court for the administration of ecclesiastical law in his diocese. It is the court of first instance in *faculty cases and in proceedings against clerics not involving doctrine, ritual, or ceremonial ('conduct cases'). Where the *chancellor certifies that disciplinary proceedings involve a point of doctrine, ritual, or ceremonial, they become a 'reserved case', and go immediately to the *Court of Ecclesiastical Causes Reserved.

In many *Presbyterian Churches, the Consistory Court is the name given to the court corresponding to the *Kirk session (q.v.) in Scotland.

Consolata Missionaries, a RC missionary congregation of men and women founded at Turin in 1901 and 1910 respectively by Bl Giuseppe *Allamano. It received final official approval in 1923. It is characterized by devotion to the BVM 'Consolata' ('Virgin of Consolation').

Constance, Council of (1414–18), The Council was convoked by *John XXIII at the instigation of the Emp. Sigismund. Its purpose was to end the *Great Schism, reform the Church, and combat heresy.

In 1414 there were three Popes: Gregory XII in the line of *Urban VI; *Benedict XIII, the successor of Clement VII of Avignon; and John XXIII, who was in the line inaugurated at the Council of *Pisa. John offered to resign if his rivals would do the same. He then left Constance in disguise on 20 Mar. 1415. The Council then passed the decree 'Haec Sancta'; this declared that the Council held its power direct from Christ and that everyone, even the Pope, was bound to obey it. John was brought back and deposed on 29 May 1415. Gregory abdicated on 4 July, though only after his representative had reconvoked the Council. After various political manœuvres, on 26 July 1417 Benedict was deposed. By a special procedure, Oddo Colonna was elected Pope on 11 Nov. 1417; he took the name of *Martin V.

Reform of the Church presented difficulties, and many of the aspirations of the individual Nations were settled by *concordats. In its attempts to combat heresy the Council condemned over 200 propositions of J. *Wycliffe; John *Huss, who came to Constance under a safe-conduct from the Emperor, was condemned as a heretic and burnt, as was *Jerome of Prague.

The Council is usually reckoned as the 16th *Oecumenical Council, but opinions differ as to whether its oecumenicity dates from the beginning, from Gregory's reconvocation, or from Martin's election. Its importance lay in its ending of the schism and in its crystallizing and diffusing of ideas about authority in general and especially about authority in the Church.

Constantine the Great (d. 337), Roman Emperor. The son of the Emp. Constantius Chlorus and St *Helena, he was proclaimed Emperor at *York in 306, and became senior ruler of the Empire after the battle of the *Milvian Bridge (312). Following instructions received (according to *Lactantius) in a dream, Constantine had fought under the sign of the Cross; he attributed his victory to the Christian God and soon afterwards toleration and imperial favour were given to Christianity.

Constantine's policy was to unite the Church and State by the closest possible ties. In 313 the *Donatists appealed to him to settle their controversy with the Church in Africa. He heard the case himself in 316 and gave judgement against the Donatists. When rioting followed, he reinforced his verdict with repressive measures, but was unable to end the schism. A similar appeal from the contending parties led him to summon the Council of *Nicaea (325) to settle the *Arian dispute.

After his victory at Chrysopolis (324) had made him sole Emperor, Constantine fixed his capital at Byzantium (rebuilt and inaugurated as '*Constantinople' in 330). He had to deal cautiously with paganism, which remained influential among his subjects, but his commitment to Christianity is clear in his policy and legislation, even though he was not baptized until just before his death (deferment of *Baptism was then common). In 321 he ordered that Sunday should be a public holiday, and he liberally endowed Christian church building, especially in Palestine, Rome, and Constantinople. Legend has added much to history, including among its embellishments the '*Donation of Constantine'. In the E. he is venerated as a saint; feast day (with St *Helena), 21 May.

Constantinople. In 330 *Constantine inaugurated Constantinople as his capital on the site of the Greek city of Byzantium. It remained the capital of the E. Empire until it fell to the Turks in 1453.

Byzantium had a Christian community at least from the 2nd cent., and Constantinople was a Christian city from its inauguration. In 381 its Bishop was given honorary pre-eminence after the Bp. of Rome; in 451, though the Pope objected, patriarchal powers were formally conferred on him. Constantinople was challenged by *Alexandria for supremacy in the East, but by the

6th. cent. the Patr. of Constantinople was recognized as the *Oecumenical Patriarch in the East. Estrangement from Rome developed, leading to the final breach between the Catholic West and Orthodox East, usually assigned to the year 1054.

Constantinople, First Council of (381). It was convened by *Theodosius I to unite the E. Church at the end of the *Arian controversy. It came to be regarded as the Second *Oecumenical Council, even though no W. bishops were present. The work of the Council of *Nicaea on the doctrine of Christ was ratified, and the humanity of Christ was safeguarded by condemning *Apollinarianism. The so-called Niceno-Constantinopolitan Creed (see NICENE CREED), traditionally ascribed to this Council, was probably not drawn up by it, but it may well have been endorsed by it.

Constantinople, Second Council of (553). The Fifth *Oecumenical Council, convoked by the Emp. *Justinian to settle the controversy over the *Three Chapters (q.v.). The Council, attended mainly by E. bishops, condemned the Three Chapters and anathematized their authors. Meanwhile Pope *Vigilius, who refused to attend the Council, drew up the so-called 'Constitutum'; this condemned 60 propositions of *Theodore of Mopsuestia but refused to anathematize his person, on the ground that he had not been condemned at *Ephesus (431) or *Chalcedon (451) and that it was not the custom of the Church to condemn the dead. Pressed by the Emperor, Vigilius finally agreed to accept the Council and annulled his former decisions in favour of the Three Chapters.

Constantinople, Third Council of (680–81). The Sixth *Oecumenical Council, convoked to settle the *Monothelite controversy in the E. Church. The Council, attended by delegates of Pope *Agatho, condemned the Monothelitic formulas and their adherents, and proclaimed the existence of two wills in Christ, Divine and human, to be the orthodox faith.

Constantinopolitan Creed. See NICENE CREED.

Constitutional Church. The State Church set up during the French Revolution by the *Civil Constitution of the Clergy (1790). Its clergy were those who took the oath prescribed by the Constituent Assembly. The Constitutional Church was ended by the *Concordat of 1801.

consubstantial. Of one and the same substance. The word is used especially of the eternal relationship which subsists between the Three Persons of the Trinity.

consubstantiation. In the doctrine of the Eucharist, the belief that after the consecration the substances of both the Body and Blood of Christ and of the bread and wine co-exist in union with each other.

Consuetudinary. See CUSTOMARY.

Consultation on Church Union (COCU). A Church union negotiating committee of the American Churches of the Protestant and Anglican traditions. Set up in 1962, in 1970 it put forward a draft *Plan of Union*, envisaging organic unity among the Churches involved. The responses to this proposal led the participating Churches to redefine their goal as a relationship of full communion among the various traditions. In 2002 they formed 'Churches Uniting in Christ', recognising the authenticity of each, but leaving negotiations over any reconciliation of ministries for the future.

contakion. In the E. Church a hymn composed in a series of strophes and intended for liturgical use.

Contarini, Gasparo (1483–1542), cardinal. An adherent of the New Learning, he became famous as a theologian. Though only a layman, he was made a cardinal in 1535. In 1536 he was put on a commission which was to prepare the way for the Council (of *Trent) and at the Conference of *Ratisbon (1541) he took an active part in this last attempt to secure union with the *Lutherans. His mystical experience of 1511 antedated M. *Luther's famous *Turmerlebnis* by several years.

contemplation, contemplative life. The Latin *contemplatio*, like its Greek equivalent, primarily means looking at things, either with the eyes or with the mind; in either case it can be contrasted with doing things. *Gregory the Great gave a classic definition of the contemplative life as one devoted exclusively to the love of God; he also argued that we know God precisely in loving Him.

In the later Middle Ages there was a tendency to conflate the notions of meditation, prayer, and contemplation around the idea of an intense love of God, felt in the affections. This led to the notion of contemplation as a form of prayer, and so to 'contemplative prayer', distinguished by St *Teresa of Ávila and St *John of the Cross from '*mental prayer' or meditation. They defined it as being a supernatural state of prayer, in which the exercise of the natural powers of the mind and will is suspended.

In modern times 'contemplative life' is equated with the life of members of strictly enclosed religious orders, such as the *Carthusians and *Carmelite nuns.

contraception, procreation, and abortion, ethics of. The principles applied by Christians to moral problems associated with procreation are the sacredness of human life, love of neighbour, and respect for the sovereignty and providence of God. On the basis of these principles early Christian thinkers were united in their condemnation of infanticide and abortion, in contrast to their pagan contemporaries. The general patristic condemnation of contraception was also shaped by insistence on the integrity of the OT teaching that procreation within marriage was good, combined with reasoning (paralleled in *Stoic thought) that asserted the unnaturalness of a sexual act which did not have procreation as its end.

These prohibitions dominated Christian teaching until recent times when there has been some questioning of traditional attitudes to contraception and abortion. The 1930 *Lambeth Conference expressed qualified acceptance of the propriety of artificial contraception. A similar change of view has prevailed in the mainstream Protestant Churches and finds some support among RC moralists. The official teaching of the RC Church remains that affirmed by *Pius XI in 1930 condemning any use of marriage 'in the exercise of which the act, by human effort, is deprived of its natural power of procreating life'. The so-called 'rhythm-method' is the only form of contraception officially sanctioned in the RC Church. In the E. Orthodox Church it appears that individually-given advice varies in different areas.

Responses to technological advances aimed at the alleviation of infertility reflect similar differences. RC pronouncements have condemned artificial insemination by the husband and *in vitro* fertilization as contrary to *natural law, in that they separate the procreative and unitive aspects of sexual intercourse, and that they fail to respect the dignity of the human act that procreation ought to be. Other moralists, including some RCs, argue that, while a Christian marriage must be open to the goods for which it was ordained (in W. tradition, the procreative, unitive, and sacramental), it can be so even if each individual sexual act is not. They thus regard artificial insemination by the husband and *in vitro* fertilization (like contraception) as in principle acceptable in enabling marriage to achieve one of its goods. Procedures involving donated material, on the other hand, are open to the objection that they allow procreation to take place outside marriage. Surrogacy (where a fertilized egg is carried to term on behalf of a couple who have contributed one or both parts of the genetic material) is acceptable to few, if any, moral theologians of any denomination.

On questions of abortion, there have also been some changes in attitude. Where modern surgery makes it possible, by aborting a foetus, to save the life of a woman which would be endangered by the birth of a child, some Christians regard abortion as permissible. Some also accept abortion where the mother's interests or those of her family are seriously threatened, and civil law in many countries allows this. The RC Church, however, maintains that any abortion as an end in itself ('direct abortion') is sinful, though an operation which may incidentally involve an abortion (an 'indirect abortion'), is permissible; thus the removal of a cancerous womb may be considered licit. The RC belief that 'from the time when the ovum is fertilized, a human life is begun' is the basis for its condemnation of direct abortion and of the use of human embryos and foetuses for experimentation or in the treatment of disease. Among Christians (and others) there is no agreement as to when life begins.

Contra-Remonstrantie. The counter-declaration in which in 1611 the more rigid Dutch *Calvinists stated their objections to the *Arminian '*Remonstrance'. It included a statement of belief in the unconditional *predestination of some souls to damnation.

contrition. A form of interior repentance or sorrow for sin. Moral theologians hold that to be real it must have its grounds in the love of God, and hence distinguish it from *attrition, an imperfect sorrow for sin, inspired by such lower motives as the fear of punishment.

convent. In ecclesiastical usage either the building in which a body of religious live together, or the religious community itself. Historically applied to the domicile of religious of either sex, in English the term is now usually restricted to those of women.

Conventicles Act 1664. This declared illegal all meetings of more than five persons (in addition to the household) for worship other than that prescribed in the BCP.

Conventual Mass. The public Mass sung (or occasionally said) in religious communities in which the Divine *Office is publicly recited.

Conventuals. The branch of the *Franciscan Order which allowed adaptations and mitigations to the Rule of St *Francis and the use of Papal privileges, including those permitting the accumulation of property. The term is also used of a similar division among the *Carmelites.

conversi. A name widely used of *lay brothers in monasteries.

Conversion of St Paul, Feast of the. The feast, kept on 25 Jan., is peculiar to the W.; it is of *Gallican origin.

Convocations of Canterbury and York. The two ancient provincial assemblies of the clergy of the C of E, dating from *Anglo-Saxon times. They originally consisted only of prelates, but in 1225 Stephen *Langton also summoned *proctors for the cathedral and monastic chapters. From 1283 the Convocation of Canterbury included representatives of the clergy of each diocese and cathedral chapter. At first the bishops and lower clergy sat together, but since the 15th cent. they have sat as separate Houses.

From an early date these assemblies were the means by which the clergy taxed themselves, but in 1664 the Convocations surrendered the right of making their own grants to the King; they ceased to be licensed for business. In the course of the *Bangorian Controversy they were prorogued by Royal Writ. Their meetings were then purely formal until the Convocation of Canterbury in 1852, and that of York in 1861, began discussing business again. Joint sittings of the two Convocations were initiated at the beginning of the 20th cent. By the *Synodical Government Measure 1969 nearly all the functions of Convocation, including the power to legislate by *canon, were transferred to the General Synod, though provision was made for each Convocation to meet separately and matters before the General Synod concerning doctrine and worship can be referred to them for separate consideration if they so require.

Convulsionaries. Adherents of a prophetic sect which evolved from a movement initiated by supposedly miraculous phenomena in 1731 at the tomb of a *Jansenist in Paris. They were mainly Jansenist *Appellants against the bull '*Unigenitus'.

Cooper, Thomas (d. 1594), also 'Cowper', Bp. successively of *Lincoln (1571) and *Winchester (1584). A man of great learning, in 1562 he answered an attack on J. *Jewel's *Apology*. He also wrote against the *Marprelate tracts and was himself attacked, especially in *Hay any Work for Cooper*.

Coornhert, Dirck Volckertszoon (1522–90), Dutch theologian. He defended liberalism against the strongly *Calvinist doctrines then current in the Netherlands. He rejected the idea of a visible Church and maintained the sufficiency of a faith inspired by the Bible and the *Apostles' Creed. Denying any doctrine of *original sin, he urged the need for interior piety. The *Arminians and the *Pietists owed something to his influence.

cope. A semicircular cloak worn at certain liturgical functions in the W. Church where the *chasuble is not used. In the Middle Ages it was widely used as a ceremonial choir habit by communities on feasts. In the C of E the 1604 *Canons ordered the use of a cope by the celebrant at the Holy Communion in cathedrals and collegiate churches. It was widely revived in the 19th cent.

Copernicus, Nicholas (1473–1543), astronomer. From 1495 he held a canonry in Frauenburg (NE Poland) and lived there from 1510. By 1514 he had written a short treatise, the *Commentariolus* (first published in 1878), sketching out a new system of astronomy in which the sun rather than the earth was the centre of the universe, and the earth one of the planets revolving round it. This was given mature expression in his *De revolutionibus orbium caelestium* (1543). Theological objections were muted at first, but when the issues were popularized by G. *Galileo, religious debate became intense and in 1616 the *De revolutionibus* was put on the *Index.

Coptic (language). Coptic was the language usually spoken by the native populace of Egypt from about the middle of the 3rd to the 10th cent. AD and is still that of the liturgy of the *Coptic Church. In essence it is the language of ancient Egypt, into which a large number of Greek words have been incorporated, and it is written in an alphabet akin to that of the Greeks.

Coptic Church. One of the *Oriental Orthodox Churches. According to tradition the Church in Egypt was founded by St *Mark; *Alexandria was one of the chief sees in the early Church. The Egyptian Church suffered severely in the persecution under *Diocletian. In the 4th cent. *monasticism was founded in Egypt by St *Antony and others. Most of the Copts rejected the Council of *Chalcedon's Definition of the two natures in the incarnate Christ and became increasingly isolated from the rest of Christendom. The Orthodox (*Melchite) body established in Alexandria received little support from the native population. In Upper Egypt, however, there was a rapid development of monasticism. In the 7th cent. the Copts were conquered by the Arabs, whose rule has lasted to the present day. Outside Egypt there are Coptic dioceses at *Jerusalem, in the *Sudan, *Kenya, *France, and the USA. The *Ethiopian Church is an autonomous daughter of the Egyptian Church. There is also a small *Uniat Coptic Church dating from 1741, when Athanasius, the Coptic Bishop of Jerusalem, joined the RC Church.

Corbie. This celebrated monastery, east of Amiens, was founded from *Luxeuil *c.*660. It possessed a fine library and one of the most important *Carolingian schools.

Cordeliers. A name given in France to the *Franciscan *Observantines from the knotted cord which they wore round the waist. It was assumed by a political party during the French Revolution.

Corinth. In NT times Corinth (in modern Greece) was the capital of a Roman province and a commercially important city. The Church there was established by St *Paul *c.*50. It included prominent Jewish converts but appears to have consisted largely of Gentiles. It seems to have contained some who prided themselves on their intellect, and certainly many from the poorer classes, including slaves. See also CLEMENT OF ROME and following entries.

Corinthians, Epistles to the. These two NT letters of St *Paul were probably written from *Ephesus and Macedonia, *c.*52–56. 1 Corinthians, occasioned by news which Paul had received from the Church at *Corinth, deals with a variety of subjects. The sections on the *Eucharist (10: 16 ff., 11: 20 ff.), on love (*agape*) (13), and on the Resurrection (15) are among the most important in the NT. In 2 Corinthians the main topic is the authority and ministry of the Christian *apostle. Some scholars think that chs. 8–9 were originally separate letters and that chs. 10–13 belonged to a different epistle.

Corinthians, Third Epistle to the. An apocryphal letter written in reply to an equally apocryphal letter from the Church of *Corinth. The two are sometimes incorporated in the 'Acts of *Paul' (*c.*170).

Cornelius (d. 253), Bp. of Rome from 251. Elected after the Papacy had been vacant for 14 months, he was faced with opposition from the *Novatianist schismatics, who objected to his relatively lenient policy towards those who had lapsed during the *persecutions. He died in exile, traditionally a martyr. Feast day, 16 Sept.

Cornelius a Lapide (1567–1637), Cornelis Cornelissen van den Steen, Flemish biblical exegete. He became a *Jesuit in 1592. In 1616 he was called to Rome; there he completed his commentaries covering all the Canonical Books except Job and the Psalms.

Coronation of Our Lady. The final triumph of the BVM in heaven, wherein she is crowned by Christ. It is the subject of the last *Glorious Mystery of the *Rosary.

Coronation rite in England. It falls into three parts: (1) the promises made by the sovereign and his acclamation by the people; (2) the consecration and anointing of the sovereign; (3) the vesting, coronation, and enthronement, followed by the homage and the sovereign's Communion.

The earliest surviving rite for the coronation of an English king dates from the 9th cent. It was amplified by the time of the coronation of *Edgar in 973 and has since undergone further modifications, the most elaborate form being that in the *Liber Regalis, used in 1308. For the coronation of *James I in 1603 it was translated into English and the Eucharist generally brought into line with the BCP. An oath in defence of Protestantism was added in 1689.

corporal. In W. liturgical usage a piece of linen on which the bread and wine are placed and consecrated in the *Eucharist.

corporal works of mercy. Traditionally they are (1) feeding the hungry; (2) giving drink to the thirsty; (3) clothing the naked; (4) harbouring strangers; (5) visiting the sick; (6) ministering to prisoners; (7) burying the dead. See also SPIRITUAL WORKS OF MERCY.

Corporation Act 1661. The Act requiring members of municipal corporations to take an oath abjuring rebellion against the king, declaring the *Solemn League and Covenant null and unlawful, and affirming that they had received Communion according to the rites of the C of E in the year preceding their election.

Corpus Christi, Feast of, since 1970 officially called 'Festum Corporis et Sanguinis Christi' in the RC Church. The feast commemorating the institution and gift of the *Eucharist, observed in the W. Church on the Thursday after *Trinity Sunday. The institution of the feast was largely due to the influence of Bl *Juliana (d. 1258). Its observance was ordered by Pope Urban IV in 1264 and became universal in the W. in

the 14th cent. The services of the day have traditionally, and probably correctly, been attributed to St *Thomas Aquinas.

Corpus Iuris Canonici. The chief collection of *canon law in the W. Church before the promulgation of the *Codex Iuris Canonici in 1917. It was composed of the 'Decretum' of *Gratian, a private collection of canons of Councils, decrees of Popes, and other material; 5 books of *Decretals, collected by *Raymond of Peñafort at the command of *Gregory IX, who added his authority to that already possessed by the component parts; the '*Sext', a sixth book added to the Decretals of Gregory IX by *Boniface VIII; the '*Clementines', compiled by *Clement V and promulgated after his death by *John XXII; the '*Extravagantes' of John XXII; and the 'Extravagantes Communes', the decress of various Popes between 1261 and 1484.

correctoria (Lat., 'correctories'). (1) Books containing sets of variant readings for 'correcting' the corrupted text of the Latin *Vulgate Bible. (2) Polemical writings criticizing or defending the teaching of St *Thomas Aquinas after the Paris and Oxford condemnations of 1277.

corrody. Originally the right possessed by some benefactors of religious houses or their nominees to board and lodging within them, the term was applied to pensions and other allowances made by the monastery to those who had served its needs or had secured a corrody by payment.

Cosin, John (1594–1672), Bp. of *Durham. His famous *Collection of Private Devotions* (1627) was compiled for the use of Queen *Henrietta Maria's English maids of honour. The Long Parliament deprived him of all his benefices and in 1644 he was ejected from the Mastership of Peterhouse, Cambridge. He went to Paris, where he was chaplain to the C of E members of the Queen's household. At the Restoration (1660) he became Bp. of Durham. He attended the *Savoy Conference in 1661 and influenced the subsequent revision of the BCP. His translation of the '*Veni Creator' was included in the *Ordinal. See also DURHAM BOOK.

Cosmas and Damian, Sts, patron saints of physicians. According to tradition, the twin brothers practised their profession without claiming any reward from their patients. Both are supposed to have suffered martyrdom. Feast day in the E., 1 July (also 1 Nov.); in the W., 26 (formerly 27) Sept.

Cosmas Indicopleustes (i.e. 'Cosmas, the Indian navigator', mid-6th cent.). He was a merchant of *Alexandria, who may have become a monk. His 'Christian Topography' (c.547) attacks the Ptolemaic system in favour of various astronomical doctrines intended to harmonize with a literal understanding of the Bible; its chief value lies in its geographical information, especially on *Sri Lanka, and its witness to the spread of Christianity.

Cosmas Melodus, St (c.675–c.751), author of Greek liturgical hymns. He was adopted by the father of St *John of Damascus; early in the 8th cent. he entered the *Lavra of St Sabas nr. Jerusalem, and in 735 he became Bp. of Maïuma nr. Gaza. His most famous works are his '*canons', odes in honour of the great Christian feasts, of which 14 are incorporated in the liturgical books of the E. Church. Feast day in the E., 14 Oct.

Cosmocrator (Gk., 'Ruler of the World'). The word, taken from pagan religious vocabulary, came to be used as a technical term for Satan, e.g. by the *Gnostics and *Marcion.

Cosmological Argument. A family of arguments which hold that the existence of the world or universe (as opposed to its character) must be caused by God. In some forms the argument maintains that God must be postulated as a cause of the world's beginning; other forms suggest that the existence of the world implies the existence of God whether or not the world had a beginning.

cosmology. The part of *metaphysics which deals with the world, considered as a totality of phenomena in time and space.

cotta. A shortened form of *surplice, formerly widely used in the RC Church.

Council. A formal meeting of bishops and representatives of several Churches convened for the purpose of regulating doctrine or discipline. General or *Oecumenical Councils are assemblies of bishops representing the whole Church, and their decrees are held to possess the highest authority. See also CONCILIAR THEORY.

Council for World Mission. In 1966 the Congregational Council for World Mission was formed to succeed the *LMS and Commonwealth Missionary Society. When the *United Reformed Church was formed, it was enlarged and in 1973 became the Council for World Mission (Congregational and Reformed), taking its present title in 1977.

Council of Churches for Britain and Ireland. See CHURCHES TOGETHER.

Counsels of Perfection. Traditionally they are: poverty, or renunciation of private (sometimes also communal) property; chastity, or renunciation of marriage; and obedience to the lawful commands of superiors. Since the late Middle Ages they have been regarded as forming the basis of the (technically) *religious life.

Counter-Reformation. The revival of the RC Church in Europe, usually considered as extending from the middle of the 16th cent. to the period of the *Thirty Years' War (1618–48). Though stimulated by Protestant opposition, reform movements within the RC Church had begun almost simultaneously with the *Lutheran schism. The new religious orders of the 1520s (*Capuchins, *Theatines, *Barnabites) preceded the foundation of the *Jesuits, who soon became the spearhead of the movement both within Europe and as a missionary force in America and the East. The definitions of doctrine and various internal reforms accomplished in the last session of the Council of *Trent (1562–3) sealed the triumph of the Papacy both over those Catholics who wished for conciliation with the Protestants and over those French and Spanish bishops who had opposed Papal claims. The Popes of the later 16th cent. took advantage of the peace in Italy to improve discipline within the *Curia and among the episcopate. Spain under *Philip II constituted itself the secular arm of the Counter-Reformation, while the spiritual qualities of the Spanish mystics, the skilful manipulation of the machinery of the Empire, and the conversion of several important princes were among the factors making for success in the late 16th and early 17th cents. Within Europe the greatest triumph of the movement was the reconquest to the Roman obedience of S. Germany and Poland.

Countess of Huntingdon's Connexion.
See HUNTINGDON, SELINA.

Courayer, Pierre François Le (1681–1776),
French theologian. He corresponded with
W. *Wake about the episcopal succession
in the C of E and in 1723 he published a
treatise defending the validity of *Anglican
Ordinations. He was excommunicated in
1728 and fled to England.

Court of Delegates. See DELEGATES,
COURT OF.

Court of Ecclesiastical Causes Reserved.
A C of E court established in 1963. It has
original jurisdiction over offences by clergy
involving doctrine, ritual, or ceremonial,
and it hears appeals from the *Consistory
Courts in *faculty cases involving these
matters.

Court of Faculties; of High Commission.
See FACULTIES, COURT OF; HIGH COMMIS-
SION, COURT OF.

Courtenay, William (c.1342–96), Abp. of
*Canterbury from 1381. The great-grandson
of King Edward I, he rose to high position in
Church and State. An opponent of J.
*Wycliffe, he was responsible for calling
the *Earthquake Synod of 1382, which condemned his doctrines.

Couturier, Paul Irénée (1881–1953),
French priest. He spent most of his life in
Lyons. While staying at Amay-sur-
Meuse (see CHEVETOGNE) his interest in the
*Ecumenical Movement was aroused. He
introduced a Triduum or three-day period
of prayer for Christian unity at Lyons in
1933, followed in 1934 by an octave of
prayer from 18 to 25 Jan. This was a development of the *Church Unity Octave (q.v.).
He engaged in vast correspondence in
connection with his ecumenical work, and
produced and distributed numerous tracts
on prayer for unity.

Covel, John (1638–1722), Master of Christ's
College, Cambridge, from 1688. In 1669 he
was appointed chaplain to the British
Embassy at *Constantinople, and there he
amassed material for his future work. His
Account of the Present Greek Church (1722) was
one of the few books giving information on
the Greek Church before the 19th cent.

covenant. A bond entered into voluntarily
by two parties in which each pledges to do
something for the other. The notion was
used in a range of secular contexts before
being employed as a model for the relationship between God and His people
Israel. As such it became central to the
religion of the OT. The Prophets stressed
that the perfect relationship between God
and man is based on the inward righteousness of the heart, and *Jeremiah looked
forward to a 'new covenant'. In the NT St
*Paul sees this eschatological conception
realized in the sacrificial death of Christ
represented in the Eucharist (1 Cor. 11: 25).
The tradition found in Mk. 14: 24 (and in
the best MSS of Mt. 26: 28) ('This is my
blood of the covenant') echoes Exod. 24: 8
and probably sees the sacrificial death of
Christ in terms of that fundamental covenant with Israel.

Covenant, National. See NATIONAL
COVENANT.

Covenanters. Bodies of *Presbyterians in
Scotland who bound themselves by oath to
maintain the cause of their religion. Various small covenants were signed between
1556 and 1562, leading up to the *King's
Confession of 1581. *Charles I's attempt to
introduce the Scottish Prayer Book of 1637
prompted the *National Covenant of 1638.
After the outbreak of the Civil War the English Parliament made an alliance with the
Scots in terms of the *Solemn League and
Covenant (1643; q.v.). The persecution of
Presbyterians in Scotland between 1661 and
1688 gave rise to further Covenants.

Coventry. A *Benedictine house was
founded at Coventry in 1043 and in 1095
Coventry became the seat of a bishopric.
Though the title of Bp. of Coventry and
*Lichfield (adopted between 1188 and 1198)
remained until 1836, it was only in the 12th
cent. that Coventry was a genuine see
town. The diocese was reconstituted in
1918. The collegiate church of St Michael
(completed in 1433) became the cathedral.
It was largely destroyed in an air raid in
1940. A new cathedral, completely modern
in design, was consecrated in 1962. The
Charred Cross from the old cathedral is an
emblem of the work of reconciliation with
Germany, in which the cathedral authorities have been much involved.

Coverdale, Miles (1487/8–1569), translator
of the Bible. As an *Augustinian friar at

Cambridge, he became an enthusiast for ecclesiastical reform. After preaching against confession and images, he was forced to live abroad. In 1535 he produced on the Continent the first complete English Bible; in 1539, with R. *Grafton, he issued the '*Great Bible'. In 1551 he became Bp. of *Exeter. He went into exile again in *Mary's reign, but under *Elizabeth I he was one of the *Puritan leaders. See also BIBLE, ENGLISH VERSIONS.

cowl. A loose garment worn over the tunic and *scapular by modern *Benedictines and *Cistercians during the liturgy. The hood (usually unattached) which forms part of the habit of most religious orders is sometimes called a 'cowl'.

Cowley Fathers, the. A colloquial name for the priests of the *Society of St John the Evangelist, founded in the neighbourhood of Cowley, near Oxford.

Cowper, Thomas. See COOPER, THOMAS.

Cowper, William (1731–1800), poet and hymn-writer. He was called to the Bar in 1754, but fear of a competitive examination provoked a suicidal mania in 1763 and he was sent to a private lunatic asylum. In 1767 he moved to Olney, Bucks. Here he worked as a lay assistant to the incumbent, John *Newton, at whose request he began writing hymns. He contributed his finest hymns to the 'Olney Collection', published in conjunction with J. Newton in 1779. They include 'God moves in a mysterious way' and 'Hark, my soul! it is the Lord'.

Cox, Richard (c.1500–81), Bp. of *Ely. He sat on the commission which drew up the *King's Book (1543), and he helped to compile the 'Order of *Communion' of 1548 and the BCP of 1549 and 1552. At Oxford he introduced *Peter Martyr and other foreign theologians into the university. He went into exile under *Mary. Under *Elizabeth I he became Bp.of Ely (1559), but he refused to minister in her chapel on account of its crucifix and lights.

CPAS ('Church Pastoral Aid Society'). A society founded in 1836 to assist the work of the C of E by making grants for the stipends of curates and lay workers.

Crakanthorpe, Richard (1567–1624), Anglican clergyman. A learned defender of

*Calvinist principles, he interested himself in the Romanist controversy. His principal work, *Defensio Ecclesiae Anglicanae* (1625; posthumous) was an answer to M. A. *de Dominis's defence of his recantation.

Cranach, Lucas (1472–1553), 'the Elder', German painter. In his youth he was celebrated as a painter of altar-pieces and all his life of portraits. In the early days of the *Reformation, he espoused the *Lutheran cause.

Cranmer, Thomas (1489–1556), Abp. of *Canterbury. Soon after he became a Fellow of Jesus College, Cambridge, he became convinced that specifically English matters were not properly any concern of the Pope. When in 1529 it seemed that *Henry VIII's 'divorce' proceedings were unlikely to succeed, Cranmer played an active part in marshalling University opinion on behalf of the King. On William *Warham's death (1532), Henry arranged for Cranmer to be elected Abp. of Canterbury (consecrated 1533). In 1533 he annulled Catherine of Aragon's marriage with Henry and three years later pronounced a similar judgement on the King's marriage with *Anne Boleyn. He was partly responsible for the '*Ten Articles' and for the dissemination of the Bible in English. Under *Edward VI, in the Book of *Common Prayer of 1549 and again in 1552, he achieved his ambition of revising the Church services and putting them into English. He was largely responsible for the abolition of the old Church ceremonies, the destruction of images, the '*Forty-Two Articles', and an attempt at canon law revision (*Reformatio Legum Ecclesiasticarum*), and he pressed for union with the reforming Churches of Europe. On the accession of *Mary (1553) he was accused of treason, tried, and sentenced, but the Queen spared his life. After being tried for heresy, he made several recantations but renounced them and was burnt at the stake. Feast day in CW, 21 Mar.; in the American BCP, 16 Oct.

Crashaw, Richard (c.1613–49), religious poet. The son of a *Puritan, he came under High Church influence, and in 1644 he was expelled from a fellowship at Peterhouse, Cambridge, on refusing to subscribe to the *National Covenant. He went to France and became a RC. His poetry is filled with a devotion nourished on the Song of Songs and the mysticism of St *Teresa.

Creation. In theology, the notion that the universe was brought into being out of nothing by a free act of God, hence termed the Creator. This teaching is characteristic of the Judaeo-Christian tradition. Though a few Fathers accepted the *Platonic view that in constructing the universe God made use of pre-existing matter, by the end of the 2nd cent. the thesis of creation from nothing (ex nihilo) was almost universally accepted in the Church. It was dogmatically formulated at the Fourth *Lateran Council in 1215 and reaffirmed at the First *Vatican Council in 1870. The changes in the traditional picture of creation brought about by increased knowledge (astronomical, geological, etc.) since the early 19th cent. affect our view of the order and dating of events (and hence also whether the OT can be regarded as a scientific book), but they hardly touch the fundamental notion of creation. Nevertheless, the traditional picture of creation often suggested a single event at the beginning of time; this has largely given way to an understanding of creation as a continuous process through time. Developments in modern physics (relativity, quantum theory, etc.) suggest that the doctrine of creation is an affirmation of the dependence of the created order on God's sustaining and preserving power.

Creationism. The doctrine that God creates from nothing a fresh soul for each individual at or after his conception. It is opposed to *Traducianism, which maintains that the soul is generated with the body, as well as to any doctrine of the soul's pre-existence.

The word is occasionally used also for the doctrine that the world was created and for a literal reading of the biblical accounts of creation.

credence. A small side table, also known as a 'credence table', placed near the altar to hold the bread, wine, and water to be used at the Eucharist, and other accessories of the service.

Crediton. Traditionally regarded as the birthplace of St *Boniface, c.909 Crediton became the see of a bishopric covering Devon and Cornwall. In 1050 the see was moved to *Exeter. Since 1897 Crediton has provided the title of a *suffragan bishop.

credo ut intelligam (Lat., 'I believe so that I may understand'). A formula in which St *Anselm summarized his conception of the relation between faith and knowledge.

creed. A concise, formal, and authorized statement of important points of Christian doctrine. The classical examples are the *Apostles' Creed and the *Nicene Creed. Candidates for Baptism originally accepted short formulas of belief; these gradually became crystallized into creeds. After the Council of Nicaea (325) credal professions of faith came to be used as standards of orthodoxy. The practice of reciting the (Nicene) Creed at the Eucharist arose as a local custom in the E. in the 5th cent.; it was not adopted at Rome until 1014. See also RULE OF FAITH.

Creed, Apostles'; Nicene. See APOSTLES' CREED; NICENE CREED.

Creed of Pius IV. The formula, also known as the **Professio fidei Tridentinae**, published by *Pius IV in 1564. It contains a summary of the doctrines promulgated at the Council of *Trent. It was imposed on holders of ecclesiastical office in the RC Church until 1967, when it was replaced by a shorter and less explicit formula.

Creed of St Athanasius. See ATHANASIAN CREED.

Creeping to the Cross. See VENERATION OF THE CROSS.

Creighton, Mandell (1843–1901), historian and bishop. He was a professor at Cambridge (1884–91), Bp. of *Peterborough (1891–7), and then of London. His History of the Papacy (1882–94) is a clear, dispassionate, and erudite work. His episcopate was marked by statesmanship and tact, especially in dealing with the conflicts between Ritualists and *Kensitites.

cremation. Disposal of the dead by reducing the body to ashes. Belief in the *resurrection of the body made cremation repugnant to the early Christians, and *burial was generally adopted. Cremation was revived in the 19th cent., largely in free-thinking circles. Though normally still forbidden in the Orthodox Church, it has been permitted in the RC Church since

1963; in the C of E its legitimacy was recognized in the 1969 *Canons.

crib. In the W. Church by popular custom a representation of the crib (or manger) in which Christ was laid at His birth, with a model of the Holy Child, is placed in church on Christmas Eve. St *Francis of Assisi is thought to have made the first model of the crib at Greccio in 1223.

Crisis, Theology of. Another name for the *Dialectical Theology of K. *Barth and his disciples, based on various associations of the Greek word κρίσις.

Crispin and **Crispinian, Sts** (c.285), martyrs. According to the purely legendary account of their martyrdom, the two brothers fled from Rome during the *Diocletianic persecution and set up at Soissons as shoemakers, taking only such money as was freely offered them. Feast day, 25 Oct.

critical apparatus. In printed texts, a list of MS readings differing from those in the accepted text. It is commonly printed at the foot of the page. See also TEXTUAL CRITICISM.

Critique of Pure Reason, The. The English title of the treatise in which I. *Kant first set out the principles of his 'Critical Philosophy'. It was published in 1781.

Croce, Benedetto (1866–1952), Italian philosopher. His philosophy is a form of 'Creative Idealism' which concentrates on the forms taken by the life of the Spirit. Of these forms Croce recognized four: 'Intuition' (art), 'Concept' (science, philosophy, and history), 'Individuality' (economics), and 'Universality' (ethics). Religion he held to be a sub-form of Intuition, and Theology an illicit application of Concept, and both only transitory manifestations of the Spirit.

Cromwell, Oliver (1599–1658), Lord Protector. Having been elected MP for Cambridge in 1640, he strongly supported the religious and political views of the *Puritan party, which he combined with the fervent spirituality of the *Independents. When the Civil War broke out (1642), it appeared to him, as to *Charles I, as a religious struggle. He built up a magnificently trained army, which defeated the royal forces. He urged the need to execute the King and was among those who signed Charles I's death warrant. He then ruthlessly put down rebellion in *Ireland and defeated the Scots. In 1653 he dismissed the Long Parliament and was installed as 'Lord Protector'. He ruled England by a series of constitutional experiments, none really successful. Bishops, deans, and cathedral chapters were removed from the C of E and use of the BCP discontinued; parishes survived under a mixed ministry of ordained and unordained ministers. His government, which rested on military force, fell apart at his death. He regarded himself as the instrument of a Divine providence, but his character has been variously assessed.

Cromwell, Thomas (c.1485–1540), created Earl of Essex in 1540. From 1524 T. *Wolsey made use of his legal services; after Wolsey's disgrace (1529) Cromwell entered the King's service and became a strong advocate of Protestantism and the royal supremacy in Church and State. In 1535 he was made Vicar General and Vice-Gerent in Spirituals. He arranged for the visitation and *dissolution of the monasteries between 1536 and 1540, and he acted as the chief intermediary between *Henry VIII and the Reformation Parliament. He issued the *Injunctions of 1536 and 1538, the latter ordering a Bible to be provided in every church. He arranged the marriage of Henry VIII and Anne of Cleves, which was mainly responsible for his fall. He was sentenced for treason and beheaded.

crosier. The staff carried by bishops and sometimes also by abbots and abbesses. In the E. Church it is surmounted by a cross between two serpents. The W. form resembling a shepherd's crook, is due to late symbolism.

Cross, Devotion to the. See EXALTATION, INVENTION, and VENERATION OF THE CROSS.

Crown Appointments Commission. A commission which, under a convention agreed with the leaders of the main political parties in 1976, submits the names of two candidates to the Prime Minister when a diocesan *bishop in the C of E is to be appointed. Besides the Abps. of *Canterbury and *York, it contains representatives of the Houses of Clergy and Laity of the

General *Synod and representatives of the *Vacancy-in-See Committee of the vacant diocese.

Crown of Thorns. One of the instruments of Christ's passion. Its supposed preservation is first mentioned in the 5th cent. In 1239 the relic then at *Constantinople came into the hands of *Louis IX of France, who built the *Sainte-Chapelle to house it.

Crowther, Samuel Adjai (or Ajayi) (c.1809–91), first African Anglican bishop. A member of the Yoruba people, he was captured and sold as a slave. The ship transporting him was arrested and brought to *Sierra Leone, where he came under the care of the *CMS in 1822. After studying at Islington College (the CMS training college in London), he was ordained in 1843 and from 1857 led the Niger Mission with an all African staff. From 1864 he was Bp. of Western Africa beyond the Queen's jurisdiction (jurisdiction over White clergy thus being avoided). In his last years the African Niger Mission was effectively dismantled by European missionaries.

crucifix. A model of the cross, bearing an image of the crucified Lord. Crucifixes are widely used among Catholics as objects of private and public devotion. In the C of E after the Reformation crucifixes were rare before the 19th cent. *Lutherans are the only Protestant body which habitually uses the crucifix. In the E. their place is taken by a flat likeness, i.e. a form of *icon.

crucifixion. Infliction of death by nailing or binding to a cross. It was much used by the Romans as the extreme punishment for slaves, though it might also be inflicted upon any person who could not prove Roman citizenship. The crucifixion of Christ between two thieves is recorded by all four Evangelists.

Cruden, Alexander (1701–70), compiler of the 'Biblical Concordance'. His life was marked by eccentricities bordering on insanity. In 1732 he established a bookshop in London. He began to compile his *concordance of the OT and NT in 1736 and in Nov. 1737 he presented a copy to Queen Caroline.

cruets. Vessels of glass or precious metal in which the wine and water for the *Eucharist are brought to the altar.

Crusades. The primary use of the term is to describe the series of expeditions from W. Europe to the E. Mediterranean, beginning in 1095, which were designed to recover the *Holy Land from Islam and then to retain it in Christian hands, and later to counteract the expanding power of the Ottoman Empire. Crusaders were granted *indulgences and the status of martyr in the event of death.

The history of the Crusades may be divided into three periods.

(1) 1095–1204. The *First Crusade* was solemnly proclaimed by *Urban II at the Council of *Clermont (1095), with the double object of relieving the pressure of the Seljuk Turks on the E. Empire following the Battle of Manzikert (1071) and of freeing the church of *Jerusalem from Muslim control. Several armies set out. *Antioch was captured in 1098 and Jerusalem in 1099. *Godfrey of Bouillon was appointed as the first Latin ruler of Jerusalem; on his death in 1100 his brother Baldwin was crowned King of Jerusalem. During the next 20 years a series of Latin States was established along the E. coast of the Mediterranean. These proved difficult to defend. The *Second Crusade* of 1147, provoked by the fall of *Edessa (1144), was preached by St *Bernard of Clairvaux; it was led by Louis VII of France and Conrad III, King of the Romans. It did not ease the situation and in 1187 Saladin captured Jerusalem. The *Third Crusade* of 1189–92, in which the Emp. *Frederick I, Richard I of England, and Philip II of France all took part, failed to recover Jerusalem. In 1202 the *Fourth Crusade* set out, but it was diverted to *Constantinople, where a Latin Empire was established from 1204 to 1261.

(2) 1204–91. Attempts to defend the remaining W. possessions in Syria continued. Jerusalem was recovered through negotiation by *Frederick II and was in Latin hands from 1229 to 1244. The two largest Crusades were directed against Egypt, but both failed. In 1291 the last remaining possession on the mainland fell. Public opinion in the W. was becoming critical of Papal conduct of Crusading, partly because the concept had been extended to cover expeditions against non-Christians in Europe (e.g. Muslims in Spain), against heretics (e.g. the *Albigensians) and against the political enemies of the Papacy.

(3) AFTER 1291. The recovery of Jerusalem

was now unlikely but the expansion of Ottoman power into E. Europe in the 14th cent. provoked a series of attempts to organize expeditions against it, and Crusading ideas helped to shape the Portuguese and Spanish oceanic expansion in the early 16th cent. In the W. in the 19th and 20th cent. the terms 'Crusade' and 'Crusader' were used for a variety of enterprises, usually in a favourable sense.

See also CHILDREN'S CRUSADE; HOSPITALLERS; TEMPLARS; WAR, CHRISTIAN ATTITUDE TO.

crutched friars (fratres cruciferi). A general name given to several religious congregations, mostly of *canons regular, whose history is obscure. The name comes from their habit of carrying a cross in their hands or having one sewn on the front of their habit. One such community, founded in Flanders (c.1210) by Theodore of Celles, expanded into neighbouring countries; it was almost extinguished in the French Revolution, but has experienced a revival.

crypt. A chamber or vault beneath a church, partly or wholly below ground, often used as a chapel or a burying-place.

Crypto-Calvinism. A term used by the *Gnesio-Lutherans to denigrate the teachings of P. *Melanchthon.

Cudworth, Ralph (1617–88), *Cambridge Platonist. From 1654 he was Master of Christ's College, Cambridge. Perhaps the most distinguished of the Cambridge Platonists, he opposed both religious dogmatism and the atheism of his day. In *The True Intellectual System of the Universe* (1678) he argues that the only real source of knowledge is the Christian religion. Religious truth is embodied in three great principles: the reality of the supreme Divine intelligence and the spiritual world which that intelligence has created, the eternal reality of moral ideas, and the reality of moral freedom and responsibility.

cuius regio, eius religio (Lat., 'In a [prince's] country, the [prince's] religion'). The formula adopted at the Peace of *Augsburg (1555), by which the princes of the Empire were permitted to settle whether the religion of their lands should be RC or Lutheran.

Culdee. The name, meaning 'companion of God', was used: (1) in the 8th and 9th cents. of Irish monks who sought a life of stricter devotion in certain churches; (2) later of clergy forming the cathedral establishment at some churches in Ireland and Scotland before they were replaced by *canons regular in or after the 12th cent.; (3) by the 16th cent. in a debased sense of any monks of Celtic observance.

Cullmann, Oscar (1902–99), NT scholar and theologian. From 1948 to 1972 he was professor simultaneously at Basle and Paris. He was particularly concerned in developing a theory of *Heilsgeschichte*. According to Cullmann what is distinctive in the NT is its view of time and history. Throughout world history there has been a narrow stream of sacred history. This sacred history, whose central point is Jesus Christ, provides the clue to the understanding of general history, which is seen to be linear in form and to run from creation to consummation. His *ecumenical interests were demonstrated in his study of St *Peter.

Cum Occasione. The constitution of *Innocent X in 1653 condemning 5 propositions which embodied the dogmatic substance of *Jansenism.

Cumberland, Richard (1632–1718), Bp. of *Peterborough from 1691 and moral philosopher. In *De legibus naturae* (1672) he maintained that the laws of nature are ethical and immutable, and that their root principle is that of 'Universal Benevolence'. He was the real founder of English *Utilitarianism.

cuneiform. The characters of wedge-shaped components in which ancient Accadian, Persian, and other inscriptions were written.

curate. Properly, a clergyman who has the care ('cure') of a parish, i.e. in England a *rector or *vicar. Such a clergyman is also known as the 'incumbent'. He is chosen by the 'patron' and admitted to the cure of souls by the bishop (see ADVOWSON). In general speech, however, the word now denotes an assistant or unbeneficed clergyman, i.e. one appointed to assist the incumbent, or to take charge of a parish temporarily during a vacancy or while the incumbent is unable to perform his duties ('curate in charge'). Assistant curates are nominated by the incumbent or the bishop, and licensed by the bishop. See also PERPETUAL CURATE.

Cur Deus Homo (Lat., 'Why [did] God [become] man?'). The title of St *Anselm's treatise on the *Atonement.

Curé d'Ars, the, St Jean-Baptiste Marie Vianney (1786–1859). Ordained in 1815, from 1818 he was parish priest at Ars. At first from neighbouring villages and then from far afield all sorts of people sought his counsel and he spent long hours in the confessional. Feast day, 4 (formerly 9) Aug.

Curia. The Papal court and its functionaries, especially those through whom the government of the RC Church is administered. It includes the *Roman Congregations, Tribunals, and Pontifical Councils, and acts with the delegated authority of the Pope. The term is also used in the RC Church of the court of diocesan officials who act on behalf of an individual bishop.

cursive script was the basis of what became a formal book-hand, properly called 'Greek minuscule', which used small rounded ('lower-case') letters, joined together for speed of writing.

Cursor Mundi. An early English poem on the history of the world, probably dating from the early 14th cent. The first six books extend from the Creation to the life of Christ and the Apostles, and the seventh deals with the Last Judgement.

Cusanus, Nicolaus. See NICHOLAS OF CUSA.

Customary (also known as a **Consuetudinary** or **Liber Ordinarius**). The book containing (1) the rites and ceremonies of the services, and/or (2) the rules and customs of discipline, of a particular monastery, cathedral, or religious order.

Cuthbert, St (c.636–87), Bp.of *Lindisfarne. In 651 he became a monk at Melrose. With his abbot he went to found a monastery at *Ripon, but when they refused to conform to Roman usages, they were expelled and returned north. In 664 Cuthbert became Prior of Melrose and later of Lindisfarne. He was allowed to become a hermit on Farne Island, where many sought his counsel. In 685 he was consecrated Bp. of Lindisfarne, but soon withdrew again to Farne. His body

was taken for safety to Chester-le-Street in 883 and in 995 to *Durham, where *sanctuary rights developed around it and his cult became important. Feast day, 20 Mar.

Cynewulf (9th cent.), Anglo-Saxon poet. Four religious poems are certainly his work. The second part of *Christ*, the only part by Cynewulf, celebrates the mystery of the Ascension; *Juliana* is the account of the martyrdom of the saint; *Elene* tells the story of the finding of the True Cross by St *Helena; and *The Fates of the Apostles* is a fragment incorporating legends about the Apostles after their dispersal. Of the author nothing is known. See also DREAM OF THE ROOD.

Cyprian, St (d. 258), Bp. of Carthage, N. Africa. Thascius Caecilianus Cyprianus was a pagan rhetorician converted to Christianity c.246. Within two years he was elected Bp. of Carthage. When the *Decian persecution began (249) he was forced to flee; he returned in 251. He was opposed to the easy reconciliation of Christians who had lapsed from their faith or become *libellatici; two councils (251 and 252) decided that they should be reconciled only after suitable penance and delay. Meanwhile the *Novatian schism gave rise to the controversy over rebaptism. Cyprian demanded the rebaptism of schismatics on the ground that no one outside the Church could administer her Sacraments. The Church at Rome held that both schismatics and heretics could validly administer Baptism. The ensuing correspondence between Cyprian and Pope *Stephen I was significant for later controversy on Papal claims. Persecution cut short the dispute.

Some of Cyprian's writings are of theological importance, especially those dealing with the Church, the ministry, and the Sacraments. His *De Catholicae Ecclesiae Unitate*, on the nature of true unity in the Church in its relation to the episcopate, is held in special esteem. He is commemorated in the BCP calendar on 26 Sept. (through confusion with another Cyprian); in CW on 15 Sept., and in the RC Church on 16 Sept.

Cyprian, St (c.300), a converted magician of *Antioch. According to a probably worthless legend, he was converted while using his magic arts to ensnare a Christian virgin. He became a bishop and was beheaded in the *Diocletianic persecution. Feast day in the E., 2 Oct.; in the W., 26 Sept., dropped in the RC Church in 1969.

Cyprus, Christianity in. Cyprus was evangelized by St *Paul and St *Barnabas (Acts 13). There were three bishops from Cyprus at the Council of *Nicaea (325), and that of *Ephesus in 431 recognized the claims of the Cypriot bishops to independence of the patriarchates; since the 5th cent. the archbishop, or *exarch, has held rank immediately after the five patriarchs. The Cypriots came under Arab rule but were set free in the 10th cent., and at this time the great monasteries were built. The *Crusaders introduced a Latin hierarchy in 1196. The Latin Church was extinguished when the Turks took the island in 1571, but the Greeks were eventually allowed to reconstitute their Church. After British rule was established in 1878, since the bishops and clergy tended to be nationalist leaders, relations with the authorities were often strained; in 1960 Abp. Makarios became the first President of the Republic of Cyprus. Since 1974 much of the island has been occupied by Turks; here churches and monasteries have been closed, demolished, or turned into mosques.

Cyril, St (c.315–87), Bp. of *Jerusalem from c.349. In 357 *Acacius, the *Arian Bp. of *Caesarea, had Cyril banished on the ground of his opposition to Arianism, but the Council of *Seleucia recalled him in 359. Later Cyril's beliefs about the Godhead of Christ became suspect in the opposite quarter because he disliked as man-made the term *Homoousios. The Council of *Antioch in 379 sent St *Gregory of Nyssa to investigate; he reported that the faith of the Church of Jerusalem was sound.

Cyril's most important surviving work is a series of addresses given to candidates for Baptism. The (pre-Lenten) 'Procatechesis' and the 'Catecheses' (given in Lent) were delivered c.350; the 'Mystagogic Catecheses' (given in the week after Easter) came late in his episcopate, unless they are the work of his successor. The series provides much material on the liturgy. Feast day, 18 Mar.

Cyril, St (d. 444), Patr. of *Alexandria from 412. The most important of the many conflicts in which he engaged arose out of the support given by *Nestorius, Patr. of *Constantinople, to a chaplain who objected to the application of the word *Theotokos (the 'one who gave birth to God') to the BVM on the ground that she was the mother of only the humanity of Christ. Cyril defended the contested word in his Paschal letter for 429. He then persuaded Pope *Celestine I to summon a synod at Rome in 430 and condemn Nestorius. Cyril, who had been delegated to act for Celestine, had the condemnation repeated in his own synod at Alexandria and sent Nestorius a letter appending for his acceptance 12 anathemas. At the Council of *Ephesus (431) he had Nestorius deposed before the Antiochene bishops arrived. The Antiochenes held a separate council and deposed Cyril, but in 433 he reached agreement with the moderate Antiochenes.

The most brilliant representative of the *Alexandrian theological tradition, Cyril put into systematic form the classical Greek doctrines of the Trinity and of the Person of Christ. His writings are marked by precision in exposition, accuracy in thought, and skill in reasoning, though they lack elegance. They include letters, exegetical works, treatises on dogmatic theology, and sermons. Feast day in the E., 9 June; in the W., 27 June (formerly, 9 Feb.).

Cyril, St (826–69) and **Methodius, St** (c.815–85), the 'Apostles of the Slavs'. In 862 the two brothers were sent from *Constantinople as missionaries to what is now Moravia. Cyril invented an alphabet (probably *Glagolitic), adopted Slavonic in the liturgy, and circulated a Slavonic version of the Bible. He died in Rome. Methodius was then consecrated bishop and returned to Moravia. He met with resistance from the German bishops and Pope John VIII for a time withdrew permission to use Slavonic as the regular liturgical language. Feast day in the E., 11 May; in the W., 14 Feb. (formerly, 9 Mar. and then 7 July).

Cyril of Scythopolis (b. c.525), Greek monk and hagiographer. He went to *Jerusalem in 543. He was the author of the Lives of seven Palestinian abbots; they are remarkable for their accurate detail.

Cyrillic. The alphabet used by the Slavonic peoples of the E. Church. It was named after St *Cyril, one of the 'Apostles of the Slavs', though *Glagolitic, not Cyrillic, is generally believed to be the alphabet he invented.

CYTUN. See CHURCHES TOGETHER.

Czechoslovak Hussite Church. The title adopted in 1971 by the Czechoslovak Church, whose origins go back to an association of RC priests, called 'Jednota', formed in 1890. They sought the introduction of the Czech language into the liturgy, the abolition of compulsory clerical *celibacy, and participation of the laity in the government of the Church. In 1919, when Czechoslovakia became an independent State, these demands were submitted to Rome. On their rejection, Jednota formed an independent religious body in 1920. It was constituted on *Presbyterian lines.

'D'. A symbol used by scholars who follow the 'documentary thesis' of the origins of the *Pentateuch (q.v.) to denote the source most characteristically represented by the Book of *Deuteronomy.

Daillé, Jean (1594–1670), French Reformed theologian and controversialist. From 1626 until his death he was pastor at Charenton, where the Reformed Church of Paris held its services. He claimed that all Christian doctrines are either stated in Scripture or deducible from it. He also defended M. *Amyraut's teaching that Christ died for all and not only for the elect.

d'Ailly, Pierre (1350/1–1420), French theologian. He taught at *Paris and in 1397 he became Bp. of Cambrai. His main concern was to find a means of ending the *Great Schism. He attended the Council of *Pisa, where he supported the newly elected *Alexander V; he was made a cardinal by his successor, *John XXIII. From 1414 to 1418 he attended the Council of *Constance, where he upheld the *Conciliar Theory, without, however, entirely approving the 'Decrees of Constance'. In 1416 he published his influential *Tractatus super Reformatione Ecclesiae*.

In his doctrinal teaching d'Ailly usually accepted the views of *William of Ockham. He held that the existence of God was not a rationally demonstrable truth, and that sin was not inherently evil but sinful only because God wills it to be so. He maintained that bishops and priests received their jurisdiction directly from Christ and not mediately through the Pope, and that neither Pope nor Council was infallible. His views were developed by the Reformers and influenced *Gallicanism.

Dale, Robert William (1829–95), *Congregational preacher and theologian. He took a leading part in the municipal affairs of Birmingham, where he ministered. He was president of the International Congregational Council in 1891. In *The Atonement* (1875) he maintained a penal doctrine, but sought to emphasize its ethical rather than its forensic aspects.

D'Alembert, Jean Le Rond (1717–83), French mathematician, philosopher, and *Encyclopaedist. He showed mathematical talent and in 1743 he published a treatise in which he developed the mechanical principle known as 'D'Alembert's Principle'. He was drawn into religious disputes by his collaboration in D. *Diderot's *Encyclopédie*, to which he contributed the *Discours préliminaire*, as well as many articles.

dalmatic. The over-tunic worn in the W. Church at Mass by *deacons, and on certain occasions also by bishops. It is ornamented with two coloured strips running from front to back over the shoulders.

Damascus. The ancient capital of Syria. It was on the road from *Jerusalem to Damascus that St *Paul was converted to the Christian faith. A Christian community has existed there continuously from Apostolic times. It is now the seat of the Greek *Orthodox, the Greek Catholic (*Melchite) and *Syrian Orthodox Patriarchs of *Antioch.

Damasus, St (c.304–84), Pope from 366. On the death of *Liberius a conflict broke out between the supporters of Damasus and those of his rival Ursinus, each being elected in a different basilica. The Emp. Valentinian I intervened on behalf of Damasus and banished Ursinus. Damasus was active, by synods and with the help of the imperial power, in suppressing heresy (*Arianism, *Donatism, *Macedonianism, *Luciferians). He strengthened the position of the see of Rome, made provision for the proper housing of the Papal archives and adorned the tombs of the martyrs. At a Council probably held in Rome in 382 he promulgated a Canon of Scriptural Books and he commissioned St *Jerome to revise the Biblical text (see VULGATE). Feast day 4 (formerly 11) Dec. See also FIDES DAMASI and TOME OF DAMASUS.

Damian, St. See COSMAS AND DAMIAN, STS.

Damian, St Peter. See PETER DAMIAN, ST.

Damien, Father (1840–89), leper missionary. Joseph de Veuster became a member of the Picpus Society (Fathers of the Sacred Heart of Jesus and Mary) in 1859, taking in religion the name 'Damien'. He was sent to the Hawaiian Islands in 1863 and in 1873, at his own request, to a settlement of lepers at Molokai. He ministered single-handed to the spiritual and physical needs of 600 lepers. He died of the disease.

damnation. In general, 'condemnation', but especially to eternal loss (*damnum*) in Hell.

Dance of Death. An allegorical subject in European art, in which the figure of Death, usually represented as a skeleton, is shown meeting various characters and leading them all in a dance to the grave.

Daniel, Book of. This OT Book consists of: (a) a narrative section (1–6) describing the experiences of Daniel and his three companions under Nebuchadnezzar and Belshazzar, kings of Babylon, and Darius the Mede; and (b) a series of visions (7–12) which reveal the future destinies of the Jewish people. The traditional belief that

the Book was written in the 6th cent. BC by Daniel, one of the Jewish exiles in Babylon, is now almost universally regarded as untenable. The consensus of modern critical opinion is that it dates from 167 to 164 BC. See also SONG OF THE THREE CHILDREN; SUSANNA, BOOK OF; BEL AND THE DRAGON.

Daniel, St (409–93), *Stylite. A disciple of St *Simeon Stylites, at the age of 51 he took up his position on a pillar four miles from *Constantinople. He lived on it for 33 years, descending only once to rebuke the Emp. Basiliscus for supporting *Monophysitism. Feast day, 11 Dec.

Daniélou, Jean (1905–74), French *Jesuit theologian. From 1943 he was professor at the Institut Catholique in Paris. A *peritus* at the Second *Vatican Council, he was made a cardinal in 1969. He wrote books on *Origen, *Philo, and on the history of Christian doctrine before the Council of *Nicaea, and he was one of the founders of 'Sources Chrétiennes', an important series of editions of patristic and medieval texts with French translations.

Dante Alighieri (1265–1321), poet and philosopher. Dante was born in Florence. He first met his Beatrice in 1274; after her death in 1290, he promised her a poem 'such as had been written for no lady before', a promise fulfilled in the *Divina Commedia. He then studied philosophy, entered politics, and was banished from Florence in 1301. He became a supporter of the Emp. Henry VII, for whom he wrote the De Monarchia; this argued the need for a universal monarchy to achieve the temporal happiness of mankind and the independence of the Empire from the Pope and the Church. Henry's death in 1313 shattered Dante's prospects. The last years of his life were devoted to completing the Divina Commedia (q.v.).

Darboy, Georges (1813–71), Abp. of *Paris from 1863. His *Gallican sympathies and claims to episcopal independence brought him into conflict with Rome; before and during the First *Vatican Council he opposed the definition of Papal *infallibility, though he eventually subscribed to it. When the Commune gained control of Paris in 1871, he was shot.

Darby, John Nelson (1800–82), *Plymouth Brother. He was ordained in the C of E but resigned in 1827 and joined a sect called the 'Brethren', then newly founded by A. N. Groves; this rejected all Church order and outward forms. A quarrel within this body led to a schism; Darby became the leader of the stricter Brethren, who were organized as a separate body ('Darbyites').

D'Arcy, Martin Cyril (1888–1976), *Jesuit philosophical theologian. From 1933 to 1945 he was Master of Campion Hall, Oxford, and from 1945 to 1950 Provincial of the English Province. He expounded Catholic principles and philosophy to a public with less narrowly theological interests.

Dark Ages, the. In W. Europe the period extending from the decay of classical culture (c. the 5th cent.) to the beginning of medieval culture (c. the 11th cent.).

Darwinism. The form of the theory of evolution put forward by Charles Darwin, especially in *The Origin of Species* (1859) and *The Descent of Man* (1871). Darwin held that species of living beings evolve by natural selection, the individuals best adapted to their circumstances being the most likely to survive and propagate.

Davenport, Christopher (c.1595–1680), English RC theologian. Probably while studying at Oxford, he was converted to the RC faith. He became a *Franciscan in 1617 and was chaplain to Queens *Henrietta Maria and Catherine of Braganza. He was on good terms with many Anglican clergy and tried to show that the *Thirty-Nine Articles could be interpreted in conformity with Catholic tradition.

Davenport, John (1597–1670), *Puritan. He was vicar of a London church and then co-pastor of the English church in Amsterdam. He sailed for Boston in 1637 and in 1638 founded the colony of New Haven; here Church membership was obligatory for electors and civil officers. In 1662 he became involved in a controversy over Baptism, connected with the *Half-Way Covenant.

David (probably d. c.970 BC), first king of the Judaean dynasty. His reign is recounted in 1 Sam. 16–1 Kgs. 2 and in the idealized description of 1 Chron. 2 f. and 10–29. He first appears when he is anointed by *Samuel to the future kingship. After his victory over Goliath, the Philistine giant, he was promoted by Saul but subsequently excited his jealousy and fled. On Saul's death he set himself up at Hebron as king of the Judaean tribes and later was accepted also by the Israelites. He made *Jerusalem his capital and reigned there for 33 years. He brought the *Ark to the city, and, according to tradition, planned the building of the *Temple. He is traditionally regarded as the author of the *Psalms, but it is unlikely that more than a fraction of the Psalter is his work.

In Hebrew tradition the name of David occupied a central place. His house and dominion were to stand for ever. But his dynasty lost the allegiance of the northern tribes (Israel) on the death of *Solomon and fell to the Babylonians c.586 BC. The Prophets then looked for the re-establishment of the sovereignty of 'David' (i.e. of the house of David) as part of the deliverance of the nation to be achieved by a future prince of the house. In the NT the evangelists assume the Davidic descent of the *Messiah, and it is as 'Son of David' that the Lord is welcomed to Jerusalem before His Passion. The Fathers regarded David as the *type of Christ.

David, St (d. c.601), patron saint of *Wales. According to legend, he came of noble family, founded 12 monasteries, and settled at Mynyw or Menevia (later called *St Davids), where he established an abbey with a life of extreme asceticism. One of the few historically established facts is that he attended the Synod of Brefi (the modern Llanddewi Brefi) c.560. Feast day, 1 Mar.

David of Augsburg (c.1200–72), German preacher and spiritual writer. Probably a native of Augsburg, he entered the *Franciscan Order at Regensburg; later he was transferred to the newly-founded house at Augsburg. His main Latin works are a three-part treatise *De Compositione*, often ascribed to St *Bernard and to St *Bonaventure, and two letters. The attribution of others is disputed. He is generally regarded as the first author to publish spiritual writings in German; some of these are based on Latin works, some are independent compositions. His teaching is eminently practical.

David of Dinant (fl. 1200), naturalist and philosopher. He probably came from Dinant in Belgium. He described himself as a physician and he wrote a treatise on anatomy. *Innocent III in 1206 called him his 'chaplain'. In 1210 a provincial Council of Sens ordered that his writings be burnt. The surviving fragments show knowledge of the original text of the physical works of *Aristotle; they also set out some startling doctrines. David held that all distinctions in real being are to be explained by a primal possible being, which he identified with the Divine Being. All things, material, intellectual, and spiritual, have one and the same essence, that is God. The circulation of such views in *Paris led to the condemnation there of the study of Aristotle's *Metaphysics* and his works on natural philosophy.

Davidson, Randall Thomas (1848–1930), Abp. of *Canterbury from 1903 until his resignation in 1928. As confidential adviser to Queen Victoria and then as Primate he exercised great influence in the Church and nation. As Archbishop he had to deal with the disestablishment of the Church in *Wales, the controversy following the *Kikuyu conference, the *Enabling Act, the *Malines Conversations, revision of the BCP, and relations with various E. Churches. He presided over the *Lambeth Conferences of 1908 and 1920, and was the first Abp. of Canterbury to make an official visit to the USA and Canada.

Day Hours. Traditionally the services of the Divine *Office other than *Mattins, i.e. *Lauds, *Prime, *Terce, *Sext, *None, *Vespers, and *Compline. For the arrangement of the Offices in the 1971 Breviary, see OFFICE, DIVINE.

Day's Psalter. A popular name for the metrical edition of the Psalms by T. *Sternhold and J. Hopkins printed by John Day from 1562 onwards.

deacon, the rank in the Christian ministry next below the presbyter (priest) and bishop. The institution of the diaconate is traditionally seen in the ordination of the 'seven men of honest report' by the imposition of *hands for the service of the poor and the distribution of alms (Acts 6: 1–6), though the word is not found there. Where it occurs in the NT in a technical sense (Phil. 1: 1, 1 Tim. 3: 8) it is in conjunction with 'bishop'; deacons seem to be assistants to the bishops. In the *Pastoral Epistles the deacons are a separate class of Church officials, charged chiefly with material duties. They first appear in the third place after bishops and presbyters in the Letters of St *Ignatius. In the patristic age, when the office was normally held for life, their functions varied from place to place. Although deacons were (and still are) barred from celebrating the *Eucharist or giving *absolution, they commonly read or chanted the *Epistle and *Gospel, assisted in the distribution of the consecrated elements to the people, and directed the prayers of the laity. In the W. their liturgical functions were curtailed in 595, but their responsibility for collecting and distributing the alms gave them importance, and the *archdeacon, the chief deacon in a given place, became the bishop's principal administrative officer. Their influence diminished in the Middle Ages and in most W. episcopal Churches the diaconate has become only a stage in preparation for the priesthood. The Second *Vatican Council (1962–5), however, envisaged the possibility of restoring a permanent diaconate (which has been retained in the E. Church), and in some countries RC bishops have ordained older married men as deacons, though young men ordained deacon are still bound to *celibacy. At the Reformation the C of E retained the order of deacon. In 1986 it was made open to *women, as was already the case in some other Provinces of the Anglican Communion.

In many Protestant Churches the name is applied to holders of an office in the ministry. In the *Lutheran Church the word denotes an assistant parochial minister, even though in full Lutheran orders. J. *Calvin recognized two classes of deacons, those who administered the alms and those who cared for the sick and poor; these remain the functions of deacons in *Presbyterianism. In the *Baptist and Congregational Churches deacons assist the pastor and distribute the elements at the Communion. See also following entry.

deaconess. A woman officially charged with certain functions in the Church. The practice of women fulfilling the office of *deacon goes back to Apostolic times: St *Paul's mention of Phoebe (οὐσαν διάκονον; Rom. 16: 1) as well as 1 Tim. 3: 11 are usually held to refer to a special office. In the early period the distinction between *widows and deaconesses is obscure, but the office developed in the 3rd and 4th cents. The deaconess assisted in the Baptism of women when, for reasons of propriety, many of the ceremonies could not be performed by a deacon. When adult Baptisms became rare the office declined in importance. Two 6th-cent. councils abrogated it, but in some places deaconesses survived until the 11th cent. In the E. their disappearance was slower. In the 19th cent. the office was revived in a modified form. The first Protestant community of deaconesses was that established at *Kaiserswerth in 1836. In the C of E the Deaconess Community of St Andrew was founded in 1861 and in 1862 the first deaconess was set apart for her work by A. C. *Tait, Bp. of London. The duties assigned to deaconesses came to include saying Morning and Evening Prayer (except the Absolution) and in some circumstances, preaching, baptizing, and conducting funerals. In 1986 women were admitted to the diaconate; there were to be no further admissions to the order of deaconess. See also WOMEN, ORDINATION OF.

dead, prayers for the. Though 2 Macc. 12: 40–5 is the only biblical text in which prayer for the dead is clearly recorded, there is ample evidence for the practice in the inscriptions of the *catacombs and in the early liturgies, as well as in the writings of the Fathers. In the E. Church no limits are placed on such prayer; saints and martyrs, those 'bound in Hades', and pagans are all mentioned. In the W. such prayer was gradually limited to prayer for the 'holy souls', that is souls in *purgatory. The W. Church does not pray for the souls of martyrs and canonized saints because they are believed to be already in possession of beatitude. Nor, it is held, can the damned be helped by our prayers, though who they are is known to God alone. Thus, RC canon law forbids the public offering of Masses for the Dead and funeral rites for various classes of persons unless they have shown signs of repentance before they died. (Private prayers and Masses are, however, allowed.) The Reformers after a time denounced prayer for the dead, partly because they believed it to be without biblical foundation (Macc. was dismissed, since the *Apocrypha no longer ranked as Scripture), and partly through their rejection of the doctrine of purgatory. In the C of E express prayers for the dead disappeared from the BCP in 1552, but they have been

widely used since the mid-19th cent. They are allowed in CW and some (though not all) other modern Anglican liturgies. Prayer for the dead is still avoided by *Evangelicals and in the Free Churches. See also BURIAL SERVICES, REQUIEM, and SUICIDE.

Dead Sea. The inland sea on the border of Israel and Jordan into which the R. *Jordan flows.

Dead Sea Scrolls. The term denotes scrolls and fragments discovered at seven sites on the NW and W. shores of the *Dead Sea, mainly between 1947 and 1960; it is commonly used only of these writings from caves near Qumran. They are referred to by cave number, site, and abbreviated title: 1QH = cave 1, Qumran, *Hodayot*.

From the Qumran caves there are remains of over 750 documents. Some may come from the 3rd cent. BC; most date from c.130 BC to AD 50. They probably once belonged to the library of a Jewish community based on a building at Qumran; many scholars identify this community with the *Essenes.

Almost all the Books of the canonical OT are represented among the scrolls, which are important for reconstructing the history of the OT text. The non-biblical MSS include several apocryphal and pseudepigraphal books already known (e.g. *Enoch, *Jubilees) and many previously unknown. Some MSS seem to relate specifically to the Qumran community, e.g. the Manual of Discipline and various liturgical texts. Others may have been composed elsewhere and copied and edited at Qumran. The scrolls provide evidence for Jewish life and thought at the time when Christianity was born.

deadly sins, seven. See SEVEN DEADLY SINS.

dean. The title of various officials. (1) The dean of a *cathedral controls its services and, with the *chapter, supervises its fabric and property. (2) The heads of the *collegiate churches of *Westminster and other *peculiars which are governed by deans and chapters. (3) The judge in the *Arches Court of Canterbury. (4) In the RC Church the Dean (the head) of the *Sacred College is a *Cardinal Bishop elected by the *suburbicarian cardinals from among their number. (5) The *Lutheran superintendent and the *Calvinist overseer are sometimes styled dean. See also RURAL DEAN.

Dearmer, Percy (1867–1936), writer on religious music and ceremonial. He tried to popularize the adaptation of medieval English ceremonial to the Prayer Book rite, setting out his ideas in *The Parson's Handbook* (1899) and putting them into practice as Vicar of St Mary's, Primrose Hill (1901–15). From 1916 to 1936 he was professor of ecclesiastical art at *King's College, London. He was co-editor of the *English Hymnal* (1906) and *Songs of Praise* (1925).

'Death of God' Theology. A movement in vogue in the 1960s, especially in the USA. The phrase 'God is dead' has been used in various ways. It occurs in a *Good Friday hymn by M. *Luther in reference to the death of Christ. G. W. F. *Hegel used it to mean that Absolute Spirit has given up its transcendence to enter the finite reality of history. Others gave the phrase a cultural sense, meaning that man had reached a stage of civilization in which the concept of God had no relevance. F. W. *Nietzsche held that to achieve their status as autonomous beings men must abolish God and become responsible for the world and creators of moral values. These differences of meaning are reflected in the 'death of God' theologies. G. Vanhanian in a book called *The Death of God* (1961) claimed that in contemporary W. culture God had ceased to be a meaningful factor. Taking up D. *Bonhoeffer's phrase 'religionless Christianity', various theologians tried to produce versions of Christianity without God. Others held that a transcendent God was incompatible with human freedom. See also GOD.

decade. A division of the *Rosary, so called because it consists of ten *Hail Marys, together with the *Lord's Prayer and a *Gloria Patris.

Decalogue. An alternative name for the Ten *Commandments.

decani (Lat., '[the place] of the dean'). As the dean's stall is on the south side of the cathedral, the term is used to indicate those who in antiphonal singing sit on that side of the choir.

Decapolis, the. A region consisting of ten allied cities E. of the *Jordan in biblical Palestine.

Deceased Wife's Sister's Marriage Act 1907. This Act allows the marriage of a widower with his wife's sister. Its provisions, and those of the corresponding Deceased Brother's Widow's Marriage Act 1921, were in conflict with the ecclesiastical law of the C of E until the *Canons were amended in 1946.

Decius (d. 251), Roman Emperor from 249. In 249 he commanded all subjects to sacrifice to the pagan gods and obtain certificates of their obedience. What was perhaps intended as a general act of solidarity with the old religion led to the first *persecution of Christians on an imperial scale.

Declaration against Transubstantiation. A declaration imposed in 1673 on all holders of civil or military office.

Declaration of Assent. See ASSENT, DECLARATION OF.

Declaration of the Sovereign, also known as the 'Royal Declaration'. The oath repudiating the RC faith which Parliament imposed on William and Mary when they came to the throne. It has been taken by all subsequent British sovereigns, though its form was simplified in 1910.

Declarations of Indulgence. Four proclamations by *Charles II and *James II on religious *toleration. The Worcester House Declaration of 1660 granted a temporary indulgence in ceremonial matters. Of the Declarations of Indulgence properly so called, that of 1662 announced Charles II's intention of placing before Parliament a bill allowing him more power to suspend the operation of the penal laws against dissenters from the C of E. The other three, in 1672, 1687, and 1688, suspended the operation of these laws by virtue of the royal prerogative. See also JAMES II.

Declaratory Acts. Two Acts in Scottish *Presbyterian Churches relieving ministers from their obligation to subscribe to every item of the subordinate standards of faith. That of 1879, passed by the *United Presbyterian Church, proclaimed the 'free offer of salvation to men without distinction', affirmed that the damnation of infants and the heathen is not necessarily involved in *election, and that total depravity and foreordination to death must allow for human responsibility. It explicitly upheld liberty of opinion on such matters as the 'six days' in the creation story in Genesis. The 1892 Act, passed by the *Free Church of Scotland, is on similar lines. Both Acts are included among the 'leading documents setting forth the constitution' in the 1929 Basis and Plan of Union of the reunited Church of *Scotland.

Decollation of St John the Baptist. The feast on 29 Aug. commemorating the beheading of St *John the Baptist as related in Mt. 14: 3–12 and Mk. 6: 14–30.

decretals. Papal letters, strictly those in response to a question. They have the force of law within the Pope's jurisdiction. The earliest influential collection was made by *Dionysius Exiguus (c.520). See also FALSE DECRETALS.

Decretum Gelasianum. An early Latin document which includes a list of Books of the Bible. In the MSS it is most frequently attributed to Pope *Gelasius (492–6); it probably dates from the 6th cent. and may have originated in Italy or Gaul.

Dedication, Jewish Feast of the. The feast instituted by *Judas Maccabaeus in 165 BC to commemorate the purification of the *Temple after its defilement by *Antiochus Epiphanes. Modern Jews observe it as 'Hanukkah'; it falls in late Nov. or Dec.

dedication of churches. The earliest recorded instance of the dedication of a Christian church is that of the cathedral at Tyre in 314. For the solemn consecration of permanent churches, an elaborate ritual developed, consisting of six main parts, followed by the Eucharist. According to the 1977 RC Ordo the dedication takes place within the framework of the Mass and includes anointing the altar and walls of the church with *chrism by a bishop. For temporary churches a simpler ceremony of blessing by a priest is provided. Although dedication is intended to be permanent, where a church cannot be used for worship the diocesan bishop may allow it to be used for a secular but not unbecoming purpose.

The Feast of the Dedication is the annual celebration of the day of the dedication of the church. A feast of the dedication of the

Church of the *Holy Sepulchre is described by *Egeria. In the C of E the Feast of Dedication is commonly kept on the first Sunday in October when the date of consecration is not known.

de Dominis, Marco Antonio (c.1560–1624), Abp. of Spalato from 1602 to 1616. Political and personal difficulties led him to resign his see. He was welcomed in England and made Dean of *Windsor in 1617. In his *De Republica Ecclesiastica* he attacked the monarchical government of Rome and defended national Churches. He left England in 1622, was reconciled with Rome, and then wrote against the C of E.

Defender of the Faith. A title conferred on *Henry VIII by *Leo X in 1521 in recognition of his treatise defending the doctrine of the *seven sacraments. In 1544 Parliament recognized the style as an official title of the English monarch; it has been borne by all subsequent sovereigns.

Defender of the Matrimonial Bond. A person whose duty it is to uphold the marriage bond in cases before the RC ecclesiastical courts in which the *nullity or dissolution of a marriage is in dispute.

Defensor (late 7th cent.), monk of Ligugé, near Poitiers. He compiled the *Liber Scintillarum*, an ascetic work which had a wide circulation in the Middle Ages; it was attributed to *Bede and others.

de fide. In Catholic theology, a proposition is said to be *de fide* (or *de fide catholica*) if it has been expressly declared and defined by the Church to be true.

de Foucauld, Charles Eugène (1858–1916), explorer and hermit. After some time in the French army, he explored Morocco. In 1890 he entered a *Trappist monastery, but, desiring greater solitude, he left the Order when the period of his temporary vows was completed in 1897. He was ordained priest in 1901. Soon afterwards he went to Algeria, where he lived as a hermit, first at Beni Abbès and then in the remote Hoggar Mountains and at Tamanrasset. He was assassinated.

He composed rules for communities of 'Little Brothers' and 'Little Sisters', but no companions joined him. In 1933 René Voillaume and four other priests settled on the edge of the Sahara and adopted a monastic way of life based on his first rule. Since 1945 small communities have been established in most parts of the world. While maintaining a contemplative element in their lives, these 'Little Brothers of Jesus' seek to conform to the economic and social milieu in which they live; they mostly earn their living in factories, farms, etc., exercising their influence by sharing the life of those around them. With similar aims, the Little Sisters of the Sacred Heart were founded near Montpellier in 1933, the Little Sisters of Jesus at Touggourt in the Sahara in 1939, to be followed by the Little Brothers and Little Sisters of the Gospel in 1958 and 1965 respectively.

De Haeretico Comburendo. The Latin title of the Suppressions of Heresy Act 1400, passed in 1401. By it, those found guilty of heresy in an ecclesiastical court were to be burnt by the secular authority.

deification, 'becoming God', the normal term for the transforming effect of *grace in Greek patristic and E. *Orthodox theology. 2 Pet. 1: 4 ('that you might become partakers of the Divine nature') provides the only explicit biblical support for the notion, but it is allied to both Pauline and Johannine thought. St *Irenaeus develops the idea that as God shared our life in the Incarnation, so we are destined to share the Divine life and 'become what He is'. The tenet that God through the Incarnation of His Son has called men to share the Divine life in His Son, is reiterated by St *Athanasius and others. In the E. the teaching received its definitive formulation in the work of St *Gregory Palamas, who held that man can be united with the Divine energies, though not with the Divine essence. The language of deification has been less prominent in W. theology, but has remained in liturgical prayers and in the teaching of the mystics.

Deiniol, St (d. c.584), Welsh saint. He is honoured as the founder of the monastery of *Bangor Iscoed and is alleged to have been consecrated first Bp. of Bangor by St *Dubricius in 516. St Deiniol's Library, Hawarden, is a residential library, founded by W. E. *Gladstone. Feast day, 11 Sept.

Deism. A system of natural religion which was developed in England in the late 17th and 18th cents. At first there were various classes of Deists, from those who held that God was the Creator, with no further interest in the world, to those who accepted all the truths of natural religion, including belief in a world to come, but rejected revelation. Gradually all belief in Divine Providence and in rewards and punishments was abandoned, and the chief mark of later Deism was belief in a Creator God whose further intervention in His creation was rejected as derogatory to His omnipotence and unchangeableness. Never widely accepted in England, Deism exercised great influence in France and Germany.

Deissmann, Adolf (1866–1937), German Protestant theologian. He did distinguished pioneer work in biblical philology, making full use of material from the recently discovered *papyri.

de la Taille, Maurice (1872–1933), French *Jesuit theologian. His main work, *Mysterium Fidei* (1921; partial Eng. tr., 1941–50), is a comprehensive study of the Mass. He argues that there is only one real immolation, that on Calvary, to which the *Last Supper looks forward and the Mass looks back.

Delegates, Court of. In England, under the *Submission of the Clergy Act 1533 (passed in 1534), commissioners were appointed to deal with appeals from the Archbishops' courts which until the previous year had gone to Rome; these commissioners came to be known as the Court of Delegates. From 1833 its place has been taken by the *Judicial Committee of the Privy Council.

de Lisle, Ambrose Lisle March Phillipps (1809–78), English writer. Of Anglican parentage, he became a RC in 1824. He was active in furthering reunion between the C of E and Rome; he took part in founding the 'Association for Promoting the Union of Christendom' (*APUC), withdrawing when it was condemned by Rome in 1864.

Delitzsch, Franz Julius (1813–1890), German OT scholar and orientalist. Of pietist *Lutheran background and Jewish descent, he sought to combat anti-Semitism and to further the conversion of Jews. He established at Leipzig an Institutum Judaicum (1886; later Institutum Delitzschianum) and translated the NT into Hebrew (1877). He published a series of commentaries on the OT and wrote extensively on Rabbinic subjects.

della Robbia, Luca (1399/1400–1482), and **Andrea** (1435–1525), Florentine artists. Luca's work includes marble sculptures, the bronze north sacristy door of the cathedral of Florence, and works in enamelled terracotta. These often show white figures on a pale-blue ground, framed by borders of fruit and flowers. That of his nephew Andrea includes the series of medallions with infants for the front of the Foundling Hospital at Florence and numerous Madonnas.

Deluge, the. See FLOOD, THE.

de Maistre, Joseph (1753–1821), French *Ultramontane writer. He was influenced by 18th-cent. rationalism, but after the 1789 Revolution he became a reactionary, who saw in the Church the safeguard of political stability. In his main work, *Du pape* (1819), he argued that the only true basis of society lay in authority, which took the double form of spiritual authority vested in the Papacy and temporal authority in human kings. His ideas contributed to the overthrow of *Gallicanism.

Demetrius, St (d. 231/2), Bp. of *Alexandria from 189. At first he supported *Origen, whom he recognized as head of the *Catechetical School in the city *c.*202. Later, when Origen preached in Palestine while still a layman, Demetrius recalled him and censured his conduct. In 231 he banished him for having been ordained priest irregularly at *Caesarea and soon afterwards deprived him of the priesthood. Feast day in the E., 26 Oct.; in the W., 9 Oct.

Demiurge. The English form of a Greek word meaning 'craftsman', used of the Divine Being by *Plato in his account of the formation of the visible world, and so by Christian writers of God as the Creator of all things. The *Gnostics used the word disparagingly of the inferior deity to whom they ascribed the origin of the material universe, distinguishing him from the supreme God.

demythologizing. A term used from 1941 by R. *Bultmann for his proposal to interpret the NT critically in order to express the theological meaning of its mythological language. He claimed that the biblical three-storied universe, belief in *angels, etc., was incredible in the modern world, and that the Gospel message could be freed from these stumbling blocks. Though he insisted that he was interpreting rather than eliminating myth, his slogan came to be attached to various reductionist interpretations of Christianity.

Denis. An alternative form of *Dionysius.

Denison, George Anthony (1805–96), Archdeacon of Taunton from 1851. Between 1854 and 1858 he was unsuccessfully prosecuted in the civil courts for teaching the doctrine of the *Real Presence in the *Eucharist.

Denmark, Christianity in. Christianity gained a firm footing in the 9th cent., when the Danish chief, Harold, was baptized on a visit to the Frankish king *Louis the Pious, and on his return brought with him St *Anskar. In the 11th cent. Christianity became generally accepted. The Reformation in Denmark took place between 1520 and 1540. A *Lutheran Creed was adopted in 1530 and in 1537 J. *Bugenhagen set up a Lutheran episcopate and introduced a new liturgy. In the 17th cent. the Danish Church suffered from the dry intellectualism of Lutheran 'orthodoxy' and experienced the *Pietist reaction in the late 17th and early 18th cent. A revival of orthodox Lutheranism in the 19th cent. was largely due to N. F. S. *Gruntvig. By laws of 1849 and 1852, which granted complete religious liberty, the Evangelical Lutheran Church was disestablished, though it continues to receive State support. In 1947 Parliament legislated for *women pastors, despite resistance from all but one of the bishops. Danish missions abroad began in 1814; their most extensive work has been done in Greenland.

Denney, James (1856–1917), Scottish *Free Church theologian. He held high office in the *United Free Church and took a leading part in the movement for reunion with the Established Church of *Scotland. Doctrinally he moved from a liberal to an evangelical position.

de Noailles, Louis Antoine (1651–1729), Abp. of *Paris from 1695, created a cardinal in 1700. He was a devoted pastor and an ardent reformer of clerical discipline.

His repeated commendations in 1695 and 1699 of P. *Quesnel's *Réflexions morales* caused him to be suspected of *Jansenism. A staunch *Gallican, he defended the rights of the French bishops in the *Assemblies of the Clergy in 1700, 1704, and 1713, and thereby incurred the antagonism of the *Ultramontanes. In 1718 he appealed against the bull '*Unigenitus'; though forced to sign an acceptance of it in 1728, he had prepared a recantation which was circulated later.

de Nobili, Robert (1577–1656), *Jesuit missionary. He set out for *India in 1603. Observing the influence of the Brahmins in Hindu society, he adopted the penitent lifestyle of a Brahmin Sanyasi. His strategy was criticized, but once his methods were approved by Pope Gregory XV in 1623, he was able to work successfully in S. India.

Denys. An alternative form of *Dionysius.

Deo gratias (Lat., 'Thanks be to God'). A liturgical formula in constant use in the services of the W. Church. During the *Donatist controversy it was a mark of orthodoxy as contrasted with the 'Deo laudes' used by the schismatics.

Deprecatio Gelasii (Lat., 'Intercession of Gelasius'). A Latin litany for the Church universal. The ascription to Pope *Gelasius (492–6) is now generally accepted. He appears to have introduced it into the Roman Mass, possibly at the place where the *Kyrie became established.

De Profundis (Lat., 'Out of the deep'). Ps. 130, so called from its opening words. It is traditionally used in the W. on behalf of the dead.

Der Balyzeh Fragments. A few incomplete pages of a Greek *papyrus codex discovered at Der Balyzeh in Upper Egypt in 1907. They contain liturgical prayers and a (*c.*6th-cent.) Creed. The prayers, which have been variously dated, show the existence of an *Epiclesis before the Words of *Institution.

de Rossi, Giovanni Battista (1822–94), archaeologist and epigrapher. He devoted his life to the excavation and study of the Roman *catacombs, making full use of literary sources to find and interpret archaeological data. At the First *Vatican Council he defended the priority of the Apostolic See and so upheld *infallibility.

De Sacramentis. A short liturgical treatise, almost certainly the work of St *Ambrose (d. 397). Addressed to the newly baptized, it treats of *Baptism, *Confirmation, and the *Eucharist. It is the earliest witness to the Roman *Canon of the Mass in substantially its traditional form.

Descartes, René (1596–1650), French philosopher. He settled in the Netherlands in 1629, publishing the definitive statement of his metaphysics, *Meditationes de Prima Philosophia* in 1641 and the mammoth philosophical and scientific textbook, *Principia Philosophiae* in 1644. In 1649 he became tutor to Queen *Christina of Sweden.

Attracted by the clarity and certainty of mathematics, Descartes aimed to extend its methods to the whole of human knowledge. To this end he designed his method of doubt, 'rejecting everything in which one can imagine the least doubt', so as to arrive at an unshakeable foundation for philosophy. This he finds in the famous '*Cogito ergo sum*' ('I am thinking, therefore I exist'). His proof of God's existence starts from the idea of God which he finds in himself: whatever caused the idea must have all the perfections that are represented in it.

Descent of Christ into Hell, the. Most Christians believe that this article in the Creed refers to the Lord's visit after His death to the realm of existence in which the souls of pre-Christian people waited for the message of the Gospel. It first occurs in 4th-cent. *Arian formularies, from which it spread in the W. and found its way into the *Apostles' Creed.

Desert Fathers. See MONASTICISM.

Determinism. The view that all events (including human actions) are somehow inevitable or necessitated. See also PREDESTINATION.

Deuterocanonical Books, the. An alternative name for the *Apocrypha.

Deutero-Isaiah. The name commonly given to the unknown author of the later chapters of *Isaiah. Earlier critics, believing Is. 40–66 to be a unity, applied the term to the authors of all these chapters; it is now usually restricted to that of 40–55, which date from c.550–539 BC. See also TRITO-ISAIAH.

Deuteronomistic History. The name given by M. *Noth and others to the Books Deut.–2 Kgs., all of which appear to have been compiled on the same editorial principle, i.e. independent units of material have been assembled and set in a framework by an editor or editors who believed that obedience to the Divine commands led to success and disobedience to disaster.

Deuteronomy, Book of. The last Book of the *Pentateuch. It contains *Moses' final utterances, consisting essentially of seven mainly legislative and hortatory addresses (including the Ten *Commandments); it ends with an account of his death.

The distinctive style and diction of Deut. mark it off from the other Pentateuchal Books. According to the traditional view it was written by Moses, but most modern critics assign it in its present form to a much later date, mostly to the 7th cent. BC. They emphasize, however, that it shows evidence of a lengthy literary history.

Deutsche Christen. See GERMAN CHRISTIANS.

Deutsche Theologie. The vernacular title of *Theologia Germanica*.

de Veuster, Joseph. See DAMIEN, FATHER.

devil. In theological terminology the chief of the fallen angels. In the narrative of the *Fall (Gen. 3) the serpent which seduces *Eve has traditionally been considered an embodiment of the devil, and in the Book of Job *Satan acts as a tempter and tormentor, though always in submission to the will of God. In the pseudepigraphical Jewish literature there is a much more developed demonology with traces of pagan influence. In the NT the devil tempts the Lord at the beginning of His public ministry (see TEMPTATION OF CHRIST), and Christ shows his powerlessness over those who resist him. Satan also wanted the disciples, especially St *Peter (Lk. 22: 31–2). At the Last Judgement he and those who belong to him will depart into eternal fire (Mt. 25: 41). An account of the angels' fall is given in Rev. 12: 7–9.

Most of the Fathers held that the fall of the angels was caused by their envy of men,

though others attributed it to pride. In the Middle Ages there was much speculation on the subject. The *Dominicans held that the initial sin of the devil, committed immediately after his creation, consisted in pride, manifested in a desire for a natural beatitude obtained by his own powers. The *Franciscans taught that the devils committed various sins before becoming obstinate in evil, that *Lucifer, their chief, desired equality with God, and that his sin consisted in inordinate love of his own excellence. Since the 16th cent. the traditional teaching has been accepted by most Christians, but there has been a reaction against speculative elaboration.

Devil's Advocate. See PROMOTOR FIDEI.

Devotio Moderna (Lat., 'Modern Devotion'). A revival of spiritual life which originated in the Netherlands at the end of the 14th cent. It stressed the inner life of the individual and encouraged methodical meditation. Among the common people it made its way through associations of secular priests and lay people, called '*Brethren of the Common Life'; among the religious the *Windesheim Canons were its chief representatives.

Devout Life, Introduction to the. The celebrated treatise on the spiritual life by St *Francis de Sales. It deals with the practical problems and obligations of people of social standing, but its teaching is of universal application. It was first published in 1609 (definitive edition 1619).

de Wette, Wilhelm Martin Leberecht (1780–1849), German theologian. His radical rationalism led to his being deprived of his professorship at Berlin; from 1822 he was professor at Basle. Latterly he became more conservative and emphasized the importance of religious experience, but his doubts about the biblical miracles and his reduction of the stories of the Birth, Resurrection, and Ascension of Christ to myths offended the *Pietists.

d'Hulst, Maurice (1841–96), French scholar and priest, and from 1890 first rector of the Institut Catholique at *Paris. At first he was associated with many who later became *Modernists, but after 1893 he became more conservative.

diaconicon. The area to the south of the

sanctuary in a Byzantine church, so called because the *deacons have charge of it. The sacred vessels, vestments, and service-books are kept here.

Diadochus (5th cent.), Bp. of Photike after 451. He wrote (in Greek) 100 'Capita Gnostica' on the means of attaining spiritual perfection; they are one of the earliest witnesses to the devotion which found formal expression in the '*Jesus Prayer'. Various other works have been attributed to him with less certainty.

Dialectical Theology. A name applied to the theological principles of K. *Barth and his school, on the ground that it finds the truth in a dialectic apprehension of God which transcends the 'Yes' and 'No' of the other methods. Its object is to preserve the Absolute of faith from every formulation in cut-and-dried expressions. Rejecting the liberal tradition in modern theology, Barth sought to return to the basic principles of the Reformers, especially J. *Calvin. The stress of Dialectical Theology on the transcendence of God commended it to many theologians of different traditions.

Diamper, Synod of (1599). A synod of the native (St Thomas) Church of *India, held some 12 miles SE of Cochin, which brought into being the *Malabar Uniat Church. *Nestorianism was renounced and complete submission to Rome imposed, though the Liturgy of *Addai and Mari was retained.

Diaspora, Jewish. The Dispersion (διασπορά) of the Jews began with the Assyrian and Babylonian deportations (c.721 and c.597 BC). It eventually spread throughout the Roman Empire, and by NT times there were at least a million Jews in *Alexandria. The Jews of the Diaspora kept in touch with their home country, paying the *Temple taxes and keeping their religion. The Jewish *synagogues in Asia and Asia Minor were the first scenes of Christian preaching.

Diatessaron. The edition of the four Gospels in a continuous narrative, compiled by *Tatian c.150–60. In *Syriac-speaking countries it became the standard text until it gave way to the four separate Gospels in the 5th cent. Its original language was probably Syriac or Greek.

Dibelius, Martin (1883–1947), German NT scholar. He was a pioneer in the method of *Form Criticism, which he applied to the Epistles as well as the Gospels. He supported the *Ecumenical Movement and was a leader of the *Faith and Order Commission.

Dibelius, Otto (1880–1967), *Lutheran Bp. of Berlin. The cousin of M. *Dibelius, he became *General Superintendent of the Kurmark in 1925. He took part in various early conferences of the *Ecumenical Movement. In 1933 he was dismissed from his post and, though put under restraint by the Nazis, worked with the *Confessing Church. In 1945 he became Bp. of Berlin, in 1949 Presiding Bishop of the *Evangelical Church in Germany, and in 1954 a President of the *World Council of Churches.

didache (Greek for 'teaching'). The elements in primitive Christian apologetic of an instructional kind, as contrasted with *kerygma or 'preaching'.

Didache. A short early Christian manual on morals and Church practice. It includes instructions on *Baptism, *fasting, *prayer, the *Eucharist, and how to treat *apostles and *prophets, *bishops, and *deacons. Baptism is to be by *immersion if possible, and two Eucharistic Prayers, of an unusual and primitive kind, are given. The author, date, and place of origin are unknown; most modern scholars now place it in the 1st cent. The community described is probably Syrian.

Didascalia Apostolorum. An early 'Church Order', professedly the 'Catholic Teaching of the Twelve Apostles ... of our Redeemer'. It is addressed to readers in various states of life and deals with miscellaneous subjects, such as penance, liturgical worship, and behaviour during persecution, but the arrangement is disorderly. It is directed especially against Christians who regard the Jewish ceremonial law as still binding. It seems to have been composed in N. Syria in the 3rd cent. Written in Greek, it survives entire only in a Syriac version.

Diderot, Denis (1713–84), French *Encyclopaedist. A publisher's suggestion in 1746 that he should translate Chambers's *Cyclopedia* developed into a project to edit, with J. Le R. *D'Alembert, a new and more ambitious French encyclopedia (see ENCYCLOPAEDISTS). His initial estrangement from the Church may have been partly due to impatience with the sexual restraints which it imposed, but intellectual obstacles increased it. Influenced by the natural religion of the third Earl of Shaftesbury (whose *Inquiry Concerning Virtue* he had translated in 1745), by J. *Locke, and by contemporary scientific inquiry, he moved from rationalist *Deism to a materialist empiricism which dispensed with belief in a deity. Atheism, however, presented him with moral difficulties, and his later writings show a preoccupation with ethical problems.

Didymus. An alternative name for the Apostle St *Thomas.

Didymus the Blind (c.313–98), *Alexandrian theologian. He was a staunch *Nicene in trinitarian theology, but he was condemned as an *Origenist at the Council of *Constantinople in 553, and much of his vast literary output has perished. His 'On the Holy Spirit' (in *Jerome's translation), 'Against the Manichees' (in a mutilated text), and fragments of exegesis have long been known; 'On the Trinity' has been attributed to him since the 18th cent., but this ascription is now challenged. Books 4 and 5 of St *Basil's *Contra Eunomium* are sometimes attributed to him. The discovery in 1941 of a group of papyrus codices near Toura (in Egypt) brought to light his commentaries on Job, Zechariah, and Genesis, as well as other commentaries whose authenticity is less certain.

Dies Irae (Lat., 'Day of Wrath'), the opening words and hence the name of the *sequence in the Mass for the Dead in the W. Church. It is now thought to go back to a rhymed prayer of 12th-cent. *Benedictine origin. Since 1969 its use has been optional.

Dietrich of Nieheim (or of 'Niem') (c.1340–1418), Papal notary. He took a prominent part in the efforts to end the *Great Schism. At the Council of *Constance he renounced *John XXIII and both there and in his writings upheld the *conciliar theory. His historical works, though one-sided, are a valuable source for contemporary events.

digamy. In the early Church, those who married again after the death of their first spouse were regarded with disfavour. The Council of *Nicaea (325) insisted that they should not be excluded from Christian fellowship. The E. Church has always been more severe in the matter than the W., and even now the nuptial blessing is not given in the same form as for a first marriage.

diggers. See FOSSORS.

Diggers (17th cent.). A section of the *Levellers. Believing that Christian principles required a communistic mode of life and the cultivation of crown property and common land, they began digging up waste land in various places in 1649. The movement was suppressed within a year.

dikirion, trikirion. Candles held in candlesticks with two or three branches respectively, used by E. bishops when giving the blessing during a Pontifical Liturgy.

Dilthey, Wilhelm (1833–1911), German philosopher. He was the virtual creator of the philosophy of history in its modern form. He stressed the fundamental differences between the methods of the humanities or 'human sciences' employed in the study of culture, art, religion, etc., and those adopted in the natural sciences. He was much influenced by F. D. E. *Schleiermacher, and like him, he saw the art of understanding as an attempt to recreate the creative process of the writer or artist. He was, however, critical of the possibility of a systematic sociology, holding that the spiritual life was too complicated to be comprehended in formulas. His own studies in religion were especially directed to it as an element in human culture.

diocese. In ecclesiastical usage, normally the territorial unit of administration in the Church. In the RC Church it is defined as 'a portion of the people of God entrusted for pastoral care to a bishop', but it normally comprises a particular area. In the W. Church it is governed by a bishop, with the assistance of the lower clergy and sometimes one or more other bishops; it is usually divided into *parishes. Dioceses are commonly associated to form a *province, over which one of the diocesan bishops presides, with varying powers of intervention in the affairs of other dioceses. In the E. Church the word denotes the area controlled by a *patriarch.

Diocletian (Gaius Aurelius Valerius Diocletianus) (245–313), Roman Emperor from 284 to 305. Proclaimed Emperor by the Army, he created an absolute monarchy, centring all power in himself as the semi-Divine ruler. In 286 he associated Maximian in government as co-Augustus, taking the Eastern Empire himself and giving Maximian the West. In 305 he abdicated, compelling Maximian to take the same step.

For most of his reign Christians seem to have enjoyed tranquillity. In 303 the Great *Persecution broke out. An edict on 23 Feb. enjoined the demolition of churches and the burning of Christian books. Further edicts ordered the clergy and then (early in 304) all subjects to sacrifice to the gods; the punishment for resistance was imprisonment, torture, and in some cases death. The final collapse of the persecution was due to *Constantine's victory at the *Milvian Bridge in 312 and the 'Edict of *Milan' in 313.

Diocletianic Era. The reckoning of time from the year of *Diocletian's accession (AD 284). It is also known as the 'Era of the Martyrs'.

Diodore (d. *c*.390), Bp. of Tarsus from 378. He had combated *Arianism in *Antioch and opposed *Julian the Apostate. In 381 he was named by *Theodosius I one of the bishops communion with whom was a test of orthodoxy. He followed the *Antiochene tradition in theology, insisting on literal and historical exegesis and, against *Apollinarius, on the complete humanity of Christ. Apart from a commentary on the Psalms, only fragments of his writings survive.

Diognetus, the Epistle to. A letter in Greek written by an unknown Christian to an otherwise unknown inquirer. It probably dates from the 2nd or 3rd cent. The author explains why paganism and Judaism cannot be tolerated, describes Christians as the soul of the world, and insists that Christianity is the unique revelation of God.

Dionysius (1) the Areopagite. His conversion by St *Paul at *Athens is recorded in Acts 17: 34. Confusion was caused by attempts to identify with him Dionysius (3) and (6) below.

Dionysius (2) (*c*.170), Bp. of *Corinth. Several of his letters are described by *Eusebius. Feast day in the E., 8 Apr.

Dionysius (3) of Paris, St (*c*.250), also **St Denys**, patron saint of France. According to *Gregory of Tours (6th cent.), he was sent to convert Gaul and, after becoming Bp. of Paris, was martyred. In 626 his remains were translated to *St-Denis. In a 9th-cent. Life he was identified with Dionysius (1) the Areopagite and consequently believed to be the author of the Pseudo-Dionysian writings (6). Feast day, 9 Oct.

Dionysius (4) the Great, St (d. *c*.264), Bp. of *Alexandria from 248. He fled from the city in the *Decian persecution (250) and was banished in that of Valerian (257). He took part in various important controversies. He decided to readmit to the Church those who had lapsed under persecution and, with Pope *Stephen, not to rebaptize heretics and schismatics. He attacked *Sabellianism but was accused of tritheism by Dionysius (5) of Rome, who accepted his defence. Feast day, 17 Nov.

Dionysius (5), St (d. 268), Bp. of Rome from 259. Little is known of him apart from his controversy on *Subordinationism with Dionysius (4) of Alexandria. Feast day, 26 Dec.

Dionysius (6) the Pseudo-Areopagite (*c*.500), mystical theologian. The name given to the author of a body of theological writings to which the supporters of *Severus, Patr. of Antioch, appealed in 533, attributing them to Dionysius (1) of Athens. The author is thought to have written in the early 6th cent., probably in Syria. His extant writings are: the 'Celestial Hierarchy', which explains how the nine orders of angels mediate God to man; the 'Ecclesiastical Hierarchy', which deals with the Sacraments and the orders of clergy and laity; the 'Divine Names', which examines the being and attributes of God; the 'Mystical Theology', which describes the ascent of the soul to God; and ten letters.

The aim of Dionysius' works is the union of the whole created order with God, which union is the final stage of a threefold process of purification, illumination, and perfection or union. One aspect of the way to such union or *deification is concerned with the use of the sensible created order; this embraces both the use of images as metaphors in theology (e.g. 'God is a consuming fire') and the use of material elements in sacramental action. Another aspect concerns the perfecting of our intellectual concepts in their application to God. Both of these reveal that God is beyond symbols and concepts, and this discovery points to '*apophatic' theology, in which the soul, passing beyond the perceptions of the senses as well as the reasoning of the intellect, is united with the 'ray of divine darkness' and comes to know God through unknowing. Because of their supposed apostolic authority, as well as their intrinsic value, these writings exerted a profound influence on medieval theology in both E. and W.

Dionysius (7) Exiguus (d. between 529 and c.556), Scythian monk, famous for his contributions to chronology and *canon law. He seems to have arrived in Rome soon after the death of *Gelasius I (496). When called upon to construct a new Easter cycle, he abandoned the era of *Diocletian and dated the first year in his Easter cycle from the (supposed) year of the Incarnation. The 'Christian Era' was adopted by *Bede; it is that still in use. His corpus of canon law was the first collection to gain wide influence.

Dionysius (8) the Carthusian (Denys van Leeuwen, Denys Ryckel) (1402–71), theologian and mystic. Besides commentaries on the Bible, he edited or commented on the works of *Boethius, *Peter Lombard, *John Climacus, and *Dionysius, the Pseudo-Areopagite, and he wrote on moral theology and ecclesiastical discipline.

Dioscorus (d. 454), Patr. of *Alexandria from 444. He supported *Eutyches and in 449 presided over the '*Latrocinium' at Ephesus, in which *Flavian, Bp. of Constantinople, was deposed. After the reversal of imperial theological policy on the death of the Emp. *Theodosius II in 450, Dioscorus was deposed at the Council of *Chalcedon in 451 and banished by the secular authorities. He is accounted a saint in the *Coptic Church; feast day, 4 Sept.

Dippel, Johann Konrad (1673–1734), German *Pietist. The works written after he became a Pietist emphasized the alleged contrast between Christianity and the Church, between right living and right doctrine, and maintained that the development of Christianity from *Constantine onwards had been one of decline from the ideals of primitive times. The *Lutheran ecclesiastical authorities forbade him to issue further theological publications. He then turned to chemistry and alchemy.

diptychs. The lists of names of living and departed Christians for whom prayer is made in the Greek and Latin Eucharistic Liturgies. In early times the diptychs were recited publicly, and the inclusion or exclusion of a name was held to be a sign of communion or excommunication.

Directory of Church Government, A (1645). An English translation of a Book of Discipline compiled in Latin by W.*Travers. In both English and Latin it circulated in manuscript among the *Puritans. The English version was published in 1645 in the interests of the projected introduction of *Presbyterianism into England.

Dirge. The traditional name for the Office of the Dead. Derived from the former antiphon, 'Dirige Domine Deus..' (Ps. 5: 8), it was originally confined to the morning *Office but came to include the *Vespers sung on the previous evening.

diriment impediment. In RC *canon law, a fact or circumstance relating to a person that makes him or her incapable of contracting a valid marriage. Such impediments include an already existing marriage, holy orders, *affinity, and *consanguinity; those not of Divine law may be dispensed by the ecclesiastical authorities.

discalced (lit. 'unshod'). The term is applied to certain religious orders and congregations whose members wear sandals rather than shoes, e.g. the Discalced *Carmelites and *Passionists.

Disciples, the. A term sometimes used of the 12 *Apostles whose names are recorded in the Gospels.

Disciples of Christ (or Churches of Christ). A religious body which began in the *United States of America among *Presbyterians concerned for evangelism on the American frontier in the 19th cent., particularly Alexander *Campbell and Barton W. Stone (1771–1844). It became a separate communion in 1832. The Churches are congregationally organized, regard the Bible as the only basis of faith, practise believers' Baptism, and celebrate the Lord's Supper every Sunday. Minor theological differences, enhanced by sociological ones, led to the formation of three main groups in the USA after 1906: (1) the Christian Church (Disciples of Christ); (2) the Christian Churches/Churches of Christ; and (3) the Churches of Christ. These divisions are to some extent reflected in other parts of the world, but without the same distinction of name. Disciples have joined in a number of unions; in Britain the majority of the Churches of Christ joined the *United Reformed Church in 1981.

disciplina arcani (Lat., 'discipline of the secret'). The practice ascribed to the early Church of concealing certain theological doctrines and religious usages from *catechumens and pagans.

discipline. The word has several religious connotations: (1) the totality of ecclesiastical laws and customs relating to the religious and moral life of the Church; (2) a system of mortification, e.g. that involved in the religious life (monastic discipline); (3) a scourge of knotted cords, chain, or other instrument used for penitential beating; and (4) as a technical term the word is applied to the *Calvinist polity, which was built up on rigid principles. It is the duty of consistories, formed by elders and pastors, to fix penalties for neglect of religious duties, culminating in excommunication.

Discipline, Books of. The 'First Book of Discipline' (1560) was drawn up by J. *Knox and others as a plan for the ordering and maintenance of the new Scottish Church. It was never enforced.

The so-called 'Second Book of Discipline' (1578), chiefly the work of A. *Melville, was prepared as a manifesto of the stricter *Presbyterians against efforts to restore a modified episcopacy.

discus. In the E. Church the plate on which

the bread of the Eucharist is offered and consecrated.

Dismas. The traditional name of the Good Thief (Lk. 23: 39–43) crucified with Christ.

dispensations. Licences granted by ecclesiastical authority to do something otherwise canonically illegal, or for the remittance of a penalty for breaking such a rule. By the later Middle Ages dispensation had become virtually a papal prerogative, but in 1965 RC diocesan bishops were given ordinary power to dispense from the general laws of the Church in particular cases, except in matters specially reserved for the Pope. Objects of dispensation include matters relating to the ordination of clergy, *vows, marriage, and *divorce. The Church can suspend or abrogate only laws of its own making, not natural or Divine laws. In the C of E the dispensing power of the Pope was transferred to the Abp. of *Canterbury in 1534; it is now used mainly in the granting of special *marriage licences. The *Methodist Conference sometimes grants dispensations allowing a lay person to preside at Holy Communion.

Disruption, the (1843). The split in the Established Church of *Scotland when the *Free Church of Scotland was formed by the secession of 474 (out of 1,203) ministers. See also TEN YEARS' CONFLICT.

Dissenters. In a religious context, those who separate themselves from the communion of the *Established Church. Originally the term included RCs, but it is now usually restricted to Protestant Dissenters.

Dissolution of the Monasteries. Though there was some criticism of the monasteries in the later Middle Ages, *Henry VIII abolished the system for personal motives, including the need to replenish his treasury. The Suppression of Religious Houses Act 1535 (passed in 1536) ordered the suppression of all religious houses having an annual value of less than £200; some 250 were involved. After the defeat of the *Pilgrimage of Grace (1536–7), to which the popularity of the monasteries had contributed, royal agents toured the country to obtain individual surrenders of the remaining monasteries and nunneries. The remaining friaries were suppressed in 1538. The Suppression of Religious Houses Act 1539 completed the process by vesting in the Crown all monasteries that had been or should be surrendered; the last house surrendered in 1540. Apart from the friars, most religious were pensioned. The bulk of the proceeds passed from the Crown to the nobility and gentry, though part was used to found six new dioceses.

Diurnal. The service-book containing the '*Day Hours'.

Dives (Lat., 'rich'). A word which has become a convenient, almost a proper, name for the unnamed rich man in the parable, Lk. 16: 19–31.

Divina Commedia, La. The name commonly given to *Dante's poem describing his vision of the three realms of the world to come, *Inferno, Purgatorio*, and *Paradiso*. In his vision Dante travels for a week in 1300 from a dark forest on this side of the world down through Hell to Satan at the centre of the Earth and up the seven terraces of the mount of Purgatory, an island in the Antipodes opposite Jerusalem, to its summit, the Earthly Paradise, where *Adam and *Eve were created. So far *Virgil has been his guide, but now he meets Beatrice, who conducts him through the nine planetary and stellar spheres to the Empyrean, where St *Bernard of Clairvaux takes her place. St Bernard presents Dante to the BVM, at whose intercession the poet is granted a glimpse of the *Beatific Vision. The date, purpose, and detailed interpretation of the poem are widely disputed.

Divine Praises, the. A series of praises, beginning 'Blessed be God', sometimes said or sung after *Benediction of the Blessed Sacrament before the Host is replaced in the Tabernacle. The nucleus is thought to have been compiled c.1779 by Louis Felici, SJ, to be used in reparation for blasphemy and profanity.

Divine Right of Kings. The doctrine that monarchy is God's chosen form of government, and that rebellion against the monarch is always a sin. Where active obedience to an evil ruler is morally impossible, it is held that passive obedience (i.e. willing acceptance of any penalty imposed for non-compliance) is demanded.

St *Paul's injunction to obey 'the powers that be' (Rom. 13: 1–2) reverberated through the centuries as the mainstay of Christian political quietism, though it was modified by the need to 'obey God rather than men' (Acts 5: 29). After the conversion of *Constantine, Greek theories of divine kingship became Christianized: the Emperor was the earthly image of God's ruling wisdom. Divine attributes were used to describe kings and, in parallel, imperial vocabulary used to describe Christ's kingdom. To the monarch's Godlike nature was added his Christlike nature. Monarchs were quasi-sacerdotal, and *anointings became a normal feature of coronations. With the revival of knowledge of *Aristotle and of Roman law from the 12th cent., the theory of Divine Right became a theological gloss upon Roman jurisprudence and later upon ideas of absolute sovereignty. Divine Right kingship confronted two opposing traditions: the claim to supreme authority by the Church and popular representative institutions. Under the Stuarts the doctrine of Divine right was widely accepted by the Anglican clergy, though *James II's attack on the C of E eroded its support. Those who opposed it accepted that sovereign authority was ordained by God, but insisted that God left people free to choose the form of government, whether monarchy or not.

Divine service. Strictly the term seems to denote the Divine *Office, and hence *Mattins and *Evensong, and not to include Holy Communion, but it is often used loosely for any form of religious service.

Divine Word, Society of the (SVD), a RC religious and missionary congregation of priests and lay brothers. It was founded in 1875 at Steyl in the Netherlands by Bl Arnold Janssen, a German priest who made his foundation outside Germany because of the *Kulturkampf. Officially approved in 1905, it focuses its work 'where the Gospel has not been preached at all, or only insufficiently, and where the local Church is not viable on its own'. In the USA the Society founded the first RC foreign missionary seminary in 1909 at Techny, Illinois, and pioneered the lay *retreat movement. It also initiated the RC apostolate to Black Americans.

Divine Worship, Congregation for. See RITES, CONGREGATION OF SACRED.

divorce. The word is used both of a dissolution of the marriage bond and of legal separation. Since W. *canon law insists on the principle of the indissolubility of marriage, divorce in the first sense is contrary to the canons and formularies of the C of E, and persons divorced in the civil courts may not normally remarry in church. Mitigations to this rule have been proposed by the House of Bishops. In the RC Church a sacramental and consummated marriage can be dissolved only by death, but marriages which are not sacramental (i.e. those not between baptized persons), or are sacramental but not consummated, may be dissolved on various counts. In the second sense (legal separation) W. Canon law permits divorce for grave causes, particularly adultery. In the E. Church divorce in both senses is allowed on many grounds. See also NULLITY.

Dix, Gregory (1901–52), Anglican *Benedictine monk. In his later years he became a well-known figure in the C of E, and an influential controversialist. His most considerable work, *The Shape of the Liturgy* [1945], did much to revive and popularize liturgical studies in the C of E.

Docetism. In the early Church a tendency, rather than a formulated doctrine, which considered the humanity and sufferings of the earthly Christ as apparent rather than real. In some forms it held that Christ miraculously escaped death, e.g. by *Judas Iscariot or *Simon of Cyrene exchanging places with Him just before the Crucifixion. It reached its zenith in the 2nd cent., particularly among the *Gnostics.

Doctors, Scholastic. In later medieval times the outstanding Scholastic teachers and others were often given distinguishing epithets, e.g. *Doctor angelicus* (St *Thomas Aquinas).

Doctors' Commons. A society of ecclesiastical lawyers founded in the late 15th cent. It served as a college of advocates for those practising in the ecclesiastical courts and in the Court of Admiralty. Judges in the Abp. of *Canterbury's courts were usually selected from its members. It virtually ceased in 1857, though it was in legal existence until 1912.

Doctors of the Church. A title regularly given since the Middle Ages to certain Christian theologians of outstanding merit and acknowledged saintliness. Sts *Gregory the Great, *Ambrose, *Augustine, and *Jerome were originally held to be the 'four doctors' *par excellence*; the list has been increased to over 30.

Doctrine in the Church of England (1938). The Report of a Commission on Doctrine set up in 1922 by the Abps. of *Canterbury and *York. It was intended to demonstrate the extent of existing agreement within the C of E, but in the *Convocations it met with hostile criticism.

Doctrine of the Faith, Congregation of the. See HOLY OFFICE.

Dodd, Charles Harold (1884–1973), NT scholar. He held professorships at Manchester and Cambridge. His theory that Christ regarded the *Kingdom of God as having already arrived with His ministry ('realized eschatology') was widely discussed. From 1950 he was General Director of the NEB (see BIBLE, ENGLISH VERSIONS, 5); he played a major part in translating the NT.

Doddridge, Philip (1702–51), *Dissenting cleric and hymn-writer. He entered the Dissenting Academy at Kibworth, Leics. In 1729 the Academy was reconstituted at Northampton under Doddridge, who became minister of an important Dissenting congregation in the town. 'Ordained a presbyter' in 1730 by 8 ministers, 5 of them *Presbyterians, he sought to obliterate party lines and in 1748 suggested an interchange of pulpits with C of E clergy. He welcomed the first stirrings of the *Evangelical Revival, and was among the pioneers of modern missionary enterprise. His many hymns include 'Hark the glad sound! the Saviour comes' and 'O God of Bethel, by Whose hand'.

Dodwell, Henry (1641–1711), 'the elder', theologian. In 1688 he was appointed Camden praelector of ancient history at Oxford. He contended that the replacement of the *Nonjuring bishops was uncanonical and was deprived of his post in 1691 when he refused to take the Oath of Allegiance. He was one of the foremost *Nonjuring apologists.

dogma. In Christianity the term signifies a religious truth established by Divine Revelation and defined by the Church.

Dold, Alban (1882–1960), *Benedictine scholar. Professed at *Beuron in 1903, he worked on liturgical *palimpsests; he elaborated new techniques and developed a photographic process for reading difficult texts by fluorescence.

Dolling, Robert William Radclyffe (1851–1902), *Anglo-Catholic. In 1885 he was put in charge of St Agatha's, Landport, the Winchester College Mission. Here he fought successfully against the evils of slum life. In 1896 opposition to his ceremonial by R. T. *Davidson, then Bp. of Winchester, led to his resignation. He became Vicar of St Saviour's, Poplar.

Döllinger, Johann Joseph Ignaz von (1799–1890), Bavarian Church historian. From 1826 to 1873 he was professor of Church history at Munich. At first he held *Ultramontane views, but he later mistrusted Roman influence. The *Letters of *Janus* (in conjunction with others, 1869) and *Letters of *Quirinus* (1869–70) revealed him as a formidable critic of the First *Vatican Council and of the doctrine of papal *infallibility. After refusing to accept the conciliar decisions, he was excommunicated in 1871. In his later years he largely identified himself with the *Old Catholic Churches and worked for reunion (see BONN REUNION CONFERENCES).

DOM, i.e. **Deo Optimo Maximo** (Lat., 'to God, the Best and Greatest'). Originally a pagan formula addressed to Jupiter, it came to be used with a Christian application over the doors of churches and on sepulchral monuments.

Dom (abbreviation of *Dominus*, 'Master'). A title given to professed monks of the *Benedictine and some other orders.

Dome of the Rock. The Muslim shrine in *Jerusalem, built in the area of the Jewish *Temple. It was completed in 691/2. The rock from which it takes its name is believed in *Islam to be that from which Muhammad ascended to heaven, and by Jews to be that on which *Abraham prepared to sacrifice *Isaac. The shrine is also known as the 'Mosque of Omar'.

Dominic, St (c.1174–1221), founder of the Order of Preachers known as the *Dominican Order. Born in Old Castile, he joined the canons of Osma. In 1203–5 he accom-

panied the new bishop of Osma on two embassies to N. Europe; on their way back to Spain they became involved in the mission against the *Albigensians. A new style of itinerant, mendicant preaching was adopted and in 1215 Dominic, who was a regular member of the mission, was put in charge of its new base at Toulouse. With the support of the local bishop, he founded a permanent community of preachers there. They adopted the Rule of St *Augustine and between 1216 and 1218 were progressively recognized by *Honorius III as a new order. In 1217 Dominic began to disperse his friars to other parts of the world. In 1220 he summoned a General Chapter at *Bologna, where the Order's first constitutions were completed. He also laid the foundations of an order of Dominican nuns. He is traditionally, but wrongly, held to have instituted the *rosary. Feast day, 8 Aug.; formerly 5 Aug. until 1558, then 4 Aug.

Dominican Order or **Order of Preachers,** known in English also as *Black Friars. The Dominicans are officially dedicated to preaching and the good of souls, and study has always occupied a central position. Founded by St *Dominic, the Order took definite shape at the General Chapter at *Bologna in 1220. It adopted not only individual but corporate poverty, owning only its houses and churches; communities were to be supported by alms not revenue. The Order spread throughout Europe and into Asia, and Dominicans followed the Portuguese and Spanish explorers in both the E. and W. hemispheres. During the Reformation and later during successive political upheavals they lost houses and even provinces, but since the revival of the Order during the 19th cent. it has again spread throughout the world.

The intellectual side of the Order's work expanded during the 13th cent., and a complex educational system was established culminating in '*Studia Generalia', usually associated with universities. The adaptation of *Aristotle to Christian philosophy was largely the work of Dominicans, chiefly St *Albertus Magnus and St *Thomas Aquinas. Indiscriminate recruitment after the Black Death and other factors led to a weakening of community life and laxness of observance. In the 14th cent. there were attempts to reform the Order, leading to the establishment of reformed houses and later of reformed congregations and provinces. The prohibition against holding revenue-producing properties was found to be unworkable and was finally abolished by *Sixtus IV in 1475. Dominicans were widely used by the Papacy in the Middle Ages for preaching *Crusades and in some places for staffing the *Inquisition.

There are also cloistered nuns (the Second Order) and fraternities of lay Dominicans (see THIRD ORDER) under the jurisdiction of the Master of the Order; together with autonomous congregations of Dominican sisters engaged in active works, and Secular *Institutes, these form the non-juridical 'Dominican Family'.

Dominis, Marco Antonio de. See DE DOMINIS, MARCO ANTONIO.

Domitian, Titus Flavius (51–96), Roman Emperor from 81. Roman historians ranked him as a tyrant; Christian tradition held him to have been a persecutor. Under his successor, being a Christian was already a capital offence, but this may have been the case continuously since the reign of *Nero. See PERSECUTIONS, EARLY CHRISTIAN.

Domitilla, Flavia (d. *c.* AD 100), Roman matron of the Imperial family. She was banished to the island of Pandateria when her husband, a cousin of *Domitian, was put to death in 95. Both are said to have suffered as Christians, but the claim is open to serious doubt.

Donatello (*c.*1385/6–1466) (**Donato di Niccolò di Betto Bardi**), Italian sculptor. He was born and died in Florence, working on its cathedral on and off for 30 years. He realized that Christian pathos can be expressed by distortion and ugliness, and that physical and spiritual beauty are not the same; his ravaged *Magdalen* (Florence, Baptistery) and other works have a huge emotional appeal. His low reliefs, such as the *Ascension, with the Giving of the Keys* (London, Victoria and Albert Museum), exploit perspective. Later sculptors were all indebted to him.

Donation of Constantine. A document fabricated in the later 8th cent., incorporated in the *False Decretals (*c.*850). It purports to be a record by the Emp. *Constantine of his conversion, profession of faith, and the privileges he conferred on Pope *Sylvester I and his successors. These included primacy over the Churches of *Antioch, *Alexandria, *Constantinople, and *Jerusalem, and dominion over Italy and 'the Western regions'; the Pope was made supreme judge of the clergy and offered the Imperial crown (which he refused). Its falsity was demonstrated in the 15th cent.

Donatism. The Donatists were a schismatic body in the African Church. They refused to accept *Caecilian, Bp. of Carthage, on the ground that his consecrator had been a *traditor* in the *Diocletianic *persecution. The Numidian bishops consecrated Majorinus as a rival to Caecilian; he was succeeded by Donatus, from whom the schism is named. A commission under *Miltiades, Bp. of Rome, investigated the dispute in 313 and decided against the Donatists. The State employed coercion between 316 and 321, and again early in the 5th cent. The schism nevertheless continued until the African Church was destroyed by the Arabs in the 7th–8th cent. The Donatists drew on African regional feeling, Numidian jealousy of Carthage, and economic unrest. Theologically they were rigorists and maintained that they alone formed the Church. They were vigorously opposed by St *Augustine.

Donne, John (1571/2–1631), *Metaphysical poet. In 1598 he became secretary to the Lord Keeper, Sir Thomas Egerton, but he was dismissed in 1602 because of his secret marriage to his master's niece. After repeated failure to find secular employment, he was ordained in 1615. In 1621 he became Dean of *St Paul's.

Donne's secular poetry was mainly written in his youth; his religious poetry belongs mostly to his troubled middle years. He wrote both the famous 'Hymn to God the Father' and his *Devotions upon Emergent Occasions* (1624) during a serious illness in 1623. His sermons are masterpieces of the old formal style of preaching, but his great strength is as a moral theologian, preaching as a sinner who has found mercy to other sinners. Feast day in the American BCP (1979) and CW, 31 Mar.

doorkeeper. The doorkeepers constituted the lowest of the *Minor Orders in the W. Church. They are mentioned in a letter of *c.*251. Their functions were similar to those of a modern verger. In the RC Church the office was abolished in 1972.

Dorchester, Oxon. In 635 St *Oswald, King of Northumbria, and Cynegils, King of the West Saxons, concurred in establishing it as a see, with St *Birinus as bishop. About 1072–3 the see was transferred to *Lincoln. The abbey of *Augustinian Canons, founded in 1140, was suppressed in 1536; the abbey church is now the parish church. In 1939 the bishopric was re-created, suffragan to *Oxford.

Dormition of the BVM. In the E. Church, the Feast of the Falling Asleep (*dormitio*) of the BVM, corresponding to the *Assumption in the W. It is observed on 15 August.

Dorotheus, St (6th cent.), spiritual writer. About 540 he founded a monastery near Gaza, of which he became *archimandrite. For its members he wrote a series of 'Instructions' on the religious life, though not all the 24 items in the edition made in the 9th cent. are his work. He gave a high place to humility, putting it above love.

Dorothy, St, also **Dorothea,** virgin and martyr. According to her legendary *Acta*, she was mocked on her way to execution by a young lawyer, Theophilus, who asked her to send him fruits from the garden to which she was going; later an angel appeared with a basket of apples and roses, which she sent to Theophilus; he ate the fruit and became a Christian and martyr. Feast day, 6 Feb., suppressed in 1969.

dorsal, also **dossal.** A piece of cloth which is sometimes hung at the back of an altar in place of a *reredos.

Dort, Synod of (1618–19). The assembly of the Dutch Reformed Church convened at Dort (Dordrecht) by the States-General to deal with the *Arminian controversy. It passed five articles asserting unconditional election, a limited atonement, the total depravity of man, the irresistibility of grace, and the final perseverance of the saints. It also confirmed the authority of the *Belgic Confession and the *Heidelberg Catechism. As a result some 200 *Remonstrant clergy were deprived.

dorter. A dormitory, especially in a monastery.

Dositheus (2nd cent.), Judaeo-*Gnostic heretic. He came from Samaria and, according to *Origen, claimed to be the Messiah foretold in Deut. 18: 18. A small body of followers survived to the 10th cent. A short work beginning 'The revelation of Dositheus about the three steles of Seth' was discovered at *Nag Hammadi, but it is not clear whether this claims to be the work of this Dositheus.

Dositheus (1641–1707), Patr. of *Jerusalem from 1669. He convened the 1672 Synod of *Jerusalem (q.v.) and he was the main author of its decrees and confession. His patriarchate was marked by various monastic and financial reforms and by his vigorous defence of the Greeks against the Latins, e.g. in the dispute with the *Franciscans over their rights to the Holy Places. He also tried to extend the influence of Hellenism in Russia.

Dostoevsky, Fedor Mikhailovitch (1821–81), Russian novelist. In his lifetime, he was known chiefly as a journalist; his more enduring works were the novels in which he penetrated the recesses of the human mind. They include (in Russian) *Crime and Punishment* (1865–6), *The Idiot* (1869), and *The Brothers Karamazov* (1880). The centre of his religious experience is the consciousness of salvation as the free gift of God to the weak and miserable and the refusal to admit any cooperation between God and man. The result is a complete absence from religion of reason and will, and the moral effort that flows from them. The characters in his novels live entirely by their emotions, of which the foremost is boundless and irrational compassion. His writings had a deep influence both among Russian Orthodox and on the *Dialectical Theology of K. *Barth.

Douai, NE France. Formerly part of the Spanish Netherlands, it was the seat of a university founded by *Philip II in 1562, and it came to house several colleges set up for the benefit of RC students from the British Isles. That founded by W. *Allen became an important seminary for training priests to work in England; its members translated the *Douai-Reims Bible. When the college was suppressed in the French Revolution, its work was continued near Ushaw and at St Edmund's Old Hall, Ware. See also DOWNSIDE ABBEY.

Douai Abbey, Woolhampton, Berks. The English *Benedictine community of St *Edmund the Martyr, founded in Paris in 1615, became a Jacobite centre. After difficulties during the French Revolution, in 1818 the monks moved to the building at *Douai vacated by the community now at *Downside. In 1903 they were expelled from France; taking the name of Douai, they settled at Woolhampton.

Douai-Reims Bible. The version of the Bible used by English-speaking RCs until modern times. It was the work of members of the English College at *Douai. The NT was published in 1582 at Reims (whither the college had temporarily migrated), the OT at Douai in 1609–10. The translation was made from the *Vulgate and is very literal. Modern editions are based on the revision of R. *Challoner in 1749–50.

Double Feasts. The name formerly given in the Roman *Missal and *Breviary to the more important feasts.

double justice. A distinction between two kinds of righteousness drawn by some 16th-cent. theologians in an attempt to explain the mystery of *justification. The traditional distinction between the justice (or righteousness) acquired through *grace and that acquired through good works lay behind M. *Luther's early work, *De duplici justitia* (1519). Various Catholic writers, recognizing some truth in Luther's doctrine of justification by faith, then distinguished between (1) inherent justice acquired through sanctifying grace and/or good works performed in co-operation with grace; and (2) imputed justice acquired through faith when the merits of Christ were imputed to the believer.

double monastery. A religious house for both men and women. The two sexes lived in separate but contiguous establishments, worshipped in distinct parts of a common church, and were ruled by a common superior. Such monasteries are first found in the E. in the last years of the Roman Empire. In the W. they were numerous in 6th- and 7th-cents. France, England, and Germany. Most disappeared in the 9th and 10th cents., but they were revived by some of the smaller monastic orders in the 12th cent.

Double Procession of the Holy Spirit. The doctrine of the W. Church that the Holy Spirit proceeds from the Father and the Son. Against it E. theologians have urged that there must be a single Fount of Divinity in the Godhead; they hold that the Holy Spirit proceeds from the Father 'through the Son'. W. theologians argue that as both Latins and Greeks hold everything common to the Father and the Son except the relationship of Paternity and Sonship, the Spiration of the Holy Spirit, in which this relation is not involved, must be common to both. The question did not become a matter of controversy between the E. and W. Churches until the time of *Photius (864); it was one of the chief points of difficulty at the Council of *Florence. See also FILIOQUE.

Doukhobors (Russian, 'Spirit-fighters'). A Russian sect of uncertain origin. It seems to have arisen among the peasants in the district of Kharkov *c*.1740. The Doukhobors came into conflict with the Russian government, and most of them migrated to Cyprus or Canada; here, after various upheavals, the majority were organized in 1938 into the Union of Spiritual Communities in Christ, also known as the Orthodox Doukhobors. Those who remained in Russia continued to suffer persecution. The Doukhobors believe that God is present in all human beings, who are thus equal, and that Christ was one of a succession of inspired leaders; they reject the Bible, sacraments, and Christian dogma.

dove. The dove is used as a Christian symbol for peace and reconciliation, for the Holy Spirit, for the Church, and for the individual soul regenerated by Baptism. The 'Eucharistic Dove' is a hollow receptacle in the shape of a dove designed to contain the Blessed Sacrament.

Downside Abbey, near Bath. The *Benedictine community traces its origin to a small settlement of English monks at *Douai in 1607. Expelled from Douai in the French Revolution, the monks came to England; in 1814 they settled at Downside.

Dowsing, William (1596–1668), *Puritan iconoclast. He was zealous in carrying out the 1643 order of Parliament for the destruction of ornaments in churches, working in Cambridgeshire and Suffolk.

Doxology. An ascription of glory to the Persons of the Trinity. Besides the *Gloria in Excelsis* (the Greater Doxology) and the *Gloria Patri* (the Lesser Doxology), there are metrical forms appended to some hymns.

Dragonnades (1683–6). Persecutions of the *Huguenots, so named from their being carried out by mounted troops ('dragoons'), who were quartered on them with a view to forcing them to accept Catholicism.

drama. In the first centuries of the Christian era, drama existed only in the form of *spectacula*, which necessarily incurred the hostility of the Church; these traditional pagan shows ended with the destruction of the Roman Empire. In the 10th cent. a new development is indicated by two documents: the Saxon nun *Hrosvit wrote a number of edifying 'comedies' and *Ethelwold described the 'praiseworthy custom' of celebrating the death and resurrection of Christ by a representation, with mime or dialogue, performed in church during or after the liturgical rites. The Resurrection play provided the model for other liturgical dramas which were widely disseminated in Europe until the 16th cent. Vernacular religious drama intended for popular audiences existed as early as the 12th cent., but it was chiefly represented in the 14th and 15th cents. by the English Corpus Christi or *Mystery cycles, the French Passion Plays, and the *Morality genre. At the same time there was a great development of secular drama in all parts of Christendom, but most of the plays were at least ostensibly edifying. Since the 16th cent. drama has generally lost its ecclesiastical connection. The more puritanical of the Reformers tended to repudiate the stage altogether, but most Christians have acquiesced in the establishment of drama as a normal part of social life. The traditional religious plays have survived in some places, e.g. *Oberammergau, and there have been numerous revivals of the medieval Mysteries and Moralities in the 20th cent.

Dream of the Rood, The. An Old English poem which represents the feelings of the Cross during the Crucifixion. The poet is unknown, as are the date and origin of the poem, which was formerly ascribed to *Cynewulf. Some 15 lines of it are carved on the Ruthwell Cross (8th cent.).

Driver, Samuel Rolles (1846–1914), OT and Hebrew scholar. From 1883 he was Regius Professor of Hebrew in Oxford. His sound judgement and caution did much to foster the spread of the critical view of the OT in Britain.

Droste-Vischering, Clemens August von (1773–1845), Abp. of *Cologne. Of noble family, he was elected Abp. in 1835 at the suggestion of the Prussian government, who hoped thereby to reconcile the Catholic nobility to their policy. He came into conflict with the government, first for refusing to approve *Hermesianism and then over *mixed marriages; under pretext of treasonable activities he was imprisoned in 1837. J. J. von *Görres took up his cause in his tract *Athanasius* (1838). He was freed in 1839 and retired to Münster.

Drummond, Henry (1786–1860), politician and one of the founders of the *Catholic Apostolic Church, which developed from the conferences on 'unfulfilled prophecy' which he convened at Albury, Surrey, between 1826 and 1830. In 1833 he became the second of its 'apostles', later being assigned responsibility for Scotland and Switzerland.

Drummond, Henry (1851–97), revivalist. He assisted D. L. *Moody and I. D. Sankey on missions and later conducted missions to several British universities. He was well known as a geologist and explorer.

Drummond, James (1835–1918), *Unitarian clergyman. From 1885 to 1906 he was principal of Manchester New College, first in London and from 1889 at Oxford. He valued Unitarianism for its encouragement of theological freedom rather than for its dogmatic negations. He held that the Resurrection and nature miracles of the Gospels were not *a priori* impossible, though the evidence for affirming them was insufficient.

Dry Mass. An abbreviated form of Mass, common in the late Middle Ages. It was not properly a Mass at all, since the *Offertory, *Canon, and Communion were omitted. It was used, for instance, when a priest wished to say a second Mass on a particular day or if a priest who had not broken his fast was not available.

Dryden, John (1631–1700), poet, dramatist, and controversial writer. Brought up as a *Puritan, he served under O. *Cromwell, but welcomed *Charles II. In 1670 he was appointed poet laureate and royal historiographer. He defended R. *Simon's work on the OT as compatible with Anglican freedom in *Religio Laici* (1682), depicting the C of E as providing a middle way between Rome and fanaticism. After *James II's accession Dryden became a RC, defending his new Church as the 'milk white hind' in the allegorical *Hind and the Panther* (1687).

dryness. See ARIDITY.

dualism. (1) A metaphysical system which holds that good and evil are the product of separate and equally ultimate first causes. (2) The view that in the Incarnate Christ there were not merely two natures but two persons, a human and a Divine.

Dublin. Dublin grew up as a Norse town in the 9th cent. Donatus, its first known bishop, died in 1074. In 1152 Dublin became an archbishopric. St Laurence O'Toole (Abp. 1162–80) made the cathedral chapter into a community of *canons regular. The English invasion of Ireland took place during his archiepiscopate; Dublin became the capital of English government, and subsequent Archbishops until the *Reformation were Englishmen nominated by the Crown. Under *Elizabeth I the (Protestant) Church of Ireland was finally established, and in 1591 *Trinity College was founded to support the settlement. The majority of the population, however, remained RC; Dublin was frequently governed by *vicars-general, but normal diocesan life was resumed under Thomas Troy (Abp. 1786–1823). Under him *Maynooth College was founded, the pro-cathedral begun in 1815, and many schools and religious houses established. Since 1929 Dublin has been the seat of a Papal *nuncio.

Dublin Review. An influential RC quarterly, of which the first issue appeared in 1836. In 1969 it was incorporated into *The Month*, which itself ceased publication in 2001.

Dubourg, Anne (*c.* 1520–59), French Protestant martyr. He became *conseiller-clerc* to the Parlement of Paris in 1557. At Easter 1559 he made his communion with the *Huguenots. A provocative speech in their defence in the Parlement led to his arrest, trial for heresy, and burning at the stake.

Dubricius, St (6th cent.), reputed Bp. of *Llandaff. He seems to have established monastic settlements in S. Wales, but generally the traditions about him do not merit credence. Feast day, 14 Nov.

Du Cange, Charles Dufresne (1610–88), French historian and philologist. His *Glossarium ad scriptores mediae et infimae latinitatis* (1678) remains the main complete dictionary of Late Latin. It was followed in 1688 by a similar work on Low Greek.

Duchesne, Louis (1843–1922), French Church historian. From 1895 he was director of the French school at Rome. He was eminent in the field of Christian archaeology and early Church history, but his sharp critical sense and negative attitude to traditional legends aroused opposition.

Duff, Alexander (1806–78), Scottish *Presbyterian missionary. The first missionary of the Established Church of *Scotland in *India, he reached Calcutta in 1830. He opened a school, which developed into a centre of W. education in India. At the *Disruption (1843), he joined the *Free Church of Scotland, losing all his mission property. He was Chairman of the General Assembly of the Free Church in 1851 (and again in 1873). During his last stay in India (1856–64) he was largely occupied with the foundation of the University of Calcutta.

Dugdale, William (1605–86), author of the *Monasticon Anglicanum* (q.v.). This work was based on the documents collected by Roger Dodsworth, whom Dugdale met in 1638. Soon afterwards, in view of the dreaded civil war, he was commissioned by Sir Christopher Hatton to make exact drafts and records of monuments in the principal churches of England.

Duhm, Bernhard (1847–1928), OT scholar. From 1888 he was a professor at Basle. His main work was on the Prophets. In his commentary on *Isaiah (1892) he separated Is. 56–66 from 40–55 (*Deutero-Isaiah) as a later composition (*Trito-Isaiah) and he argued that the *Servant Songs were not the work of Deutero-Isaiah.

dulia. The reverence which, according to Orthodox and RC theologians, may be paid to the saints; it is contrasted with *latria, which is reserved for God alone.

du Moulin, Pierre (1568–1658), French Reformed theologian. He took a prominent part in religious controversy, upholding a mediating position which irritated Catholics and Calvinists alike.

Dunkers, Dunkards. See TUNKERS.

Duns Scotus, Bl Johannes (c.1265–1308), philosopher. He was probably born near Duns in Berwickshire, Scotland. He became a *Franciscan c.1280, studied arts and theology at *Oxford, and lectured there. It is possible that he also lectured in *Cambridge. He completed his doctoral requirements in *Paris and became a regent master in 1305. In 1307 he moved to *Cologne. His chief work is a commentary on the *Sentences* of *Peter Lombard.

Writing after the condemnation of several *Aristotelian positions by the Abp. of Paris in 1277, Scotus tries to mediate between Aristotelianism and the *Augustinianism associated with *Henry of Ghent. He asserts the radical contingency (nonnecessity) both of created entities and of God's action. He believes that for human will to be free, it must be able to will what it does not in fact choose to will. The intellect offers guidance to the will, but the will can go against the suggestion of reason. Human actions are given moral value only if God commands them. The exception is the act of loving God: that God should be loved is implicit in the word 'God'. Scotus' proof of the existence of God attempts to show that one necessary cause is required to explain the existence of contingent entities. Creatures do not exist necessarily, but have the possibility of being caused; if a creature is capable of being caused, there must be some agent to cause it. He rejects St *Thomas Aquinas's position that individuation is by matter and holds instead that each created thing is given its own form of individuality added to its matter and form. He allows a certain intuitive knowledge of individual things, though he rejects Henry of Ghent's contention that certitude follows only from Divine illumination, and, like Aquinas, holds that certitude derives from necessary principles that are known naturally by the intellect. In theology he stresses the primacy of Christ as the supreme manifestation of God's love,

and holds that the Incarnation would have taken place irrespective of the *Fall. For him, this view entails the doctrine of the *Immaculate Conception of the BVM, which he was the first well-known theologian to defend. Feast day, 8 Nov.

Dunstan, St (c.909–88), Abp. of *Canterbury. He was a monk of *Glastonbury and from c.940 abbot. He reformed the monastery, insisting on the full observance of the *Benedictine Rule. After *Edgar became king of all England, Dunstan was made Abp. of Canterbury (959); together they planned a reform of Church and State. The restoration of regular monastic life in England was in the first instance Dunstan's work; as it got under way much of the initiative passed to St *Ethelwold and St *Oswald. Feast day, 19 May. See also REGULARIS CONCORDIA.

Dupanloup, Félix Antoine Philibert (1802–78), Bp. of Orléans from 1849. He became one of the foremost Catholic educationalists in France and he was active in securing for the Church the right, conceded in 1850, to conduct voluntary schools. At the First *Vatican Council in 1870 he advised the minority to abstain from voting and to withdraw, but he accepted the decision of the Council.

Du Perron, Jacques Davy (1556–1618), French cardinal. The son of a *Calvinist minister, he became a RC in 1577/8. He helped to instruct *Henry IV before his reception into the RC Church (1593) and was sent to Rome to secure his absolution from heresy in 1595. He was involved in a number of controversies, including that with P. *du Plessis-Mornay in 1600. He was made a cardinal in 1604 and appointed Abp. of Sens in 1606. Both in his writings and in his famous 'Harangue' at the Estates General in 1615 he defended the Ultramontane position against the *Gallican.

Dupin, Louis Ellies (1657–1719), *Gallican theologian. The first volumes of his vast *Nouvelle Bibliothèque des Auteurs Ecclésiastiques* (1686–1719) aroused opposition; Dupin was censured by the Abp. of Paris (1693) but continued writing the *Bibliothèque*, which was put on the *Index only in 1757. He took part in a project for union between the Russian and French Churches in 1717, and in 1718 he entered into correspondence with W. *Wake, Abp. of Canterbury, in an equally unsuccessful attempt to achieve union between the Churches of England and France.

du Plessis-Mornay, Philippe (1549–1623), *Huguenot leader. He escaped the Massacre of St *Bartholomew's Day (1572) and acted as a military leader in the Huguenot cause and as diplomatic agent to William of Orange and *Henry of Navarre. In 1589 he became governor of Saumur, where he founded a Protestant academy (1593). Henry IV's conversion (1593) came as a blow to him, but he continued to work for religious toleration and helped to secure the Edict of *Nantes (1598). In 1598 he issued a treatise on the Eucharist. J. D. *Du Perron charged him with misquotations; in a public debate in 1600 Du Perron was defeated, though few misquotations were found. In 1621, when persecution broke out again, he was deprived of his governorship.

Duplex Querela. In the C of E the form of action open to a cleric whom the bishop refuses to institute to a benefice to which he has been presented.

Duppa, Brian (1588–1662), Bp. successively of *Chichester (from 1638), *Salisbury (1641), and *Winchester (1660). From 1645 to 1660 he was one of the leaders of the persecuted Church; he tried to keep the extruded clergy together during the Commonwealth and he held private *ordinations when opportunity offered.

Dura Europos, an ancient city on the R. Euphrates. Excavations have revealed the earliest known Jewish *synagogue (AD 245) and an early Christian church. This was constructed from two rooms of a private house and probably dates from the 240s.

Durandus of Saint-Pourçain (c.1275–1334), *Dominican philosopher. He taught at *Paris; in 1313 he was summoned to be Lector at the Papal Court at *Avignon; later he became a bishop. He was one of the earliest exponents of what came to be called *Nominalism. Rejecting the current doctrine on intelligible and sensible species, he held that the only real entities were individuals and that the search for a principle of individuation was meaningless. In theology he stood for a sharp contrast between faith and reason. He also held that the presence

of Christ in the Eucharist did not preclude the continuing existence of the bread and wine.

Durandus of Troarn (c.1018–88), Abbot of Troarn in Normandy from 1059. A monk of Fécamp, Durandus presents in his *Liber de corpore et sanguine Domini* the Eucharistic doctrine common there in the 1050s.

Durandus, William (c.1230–96), Bp. of Mende from 1285. He was one of the chief medieval canonists. He attended *Gregory X at the Second Council of *Lyons (1274) and probably helped draft its decrees. His *Speculum iudicale* centred on legal procedure; his *Rationale divinorum* is a compendium of liturgical knowledge, with allegorical interpretation. His *Pontifical was taken as a model.

Dürer, Albrecht (1471–1528), German painter and engraver. His religious paintings include some famous altarpieces. His woodcuts, which were widely used as illustrations of the Bible, influenced Italian painters. His engravings are characterized by closely observed landscape backgrounds. Although he never renounced the Catholic faith, he was sympathetic to the *Reformation.

Durham. At the end of the 10th cent. the see of *Lindisfarne was moved to Durham, and a cathedral was begun as a shrine for the relics of St *Cuthbert. Bp. Carilef began building the present cathedral in 1093 and he replaced the secular clergy by a *Benedictine community, which lasted until the *Dissolution in 1540. The Galilee chapel, projecting from the W. end, was built at the end of the Norman period; the Chapel of Nine Altars, with its rose window and elaborate carving, is Early English. The medieval bishops held wide civil jurisdiction, ranking as Counts Palatine; this dignity attached to the see until the time of W. *Van Mildert (Bp. 1826–36). Durham shares with London and *Winchester a rank inferior only to *Canterbury and *York, and its bishop is at present entitled to a seat in the House of Lords immediately he takes possession of his see. The university was founded in 1832.

Durham Book. A copy of the BCP printed in 1619 with MS notes by J. *Cosin and W. *Sancroft designed as a first draft for the revision of 1662. It is in *Durham.

Durie (or Dury), John (1596–1680), Scottish Protestant minister. In Prussia he devised plans for the reunion of the non-RC Churches, especially the *Lutherans and *Calvinists. In 1634 he was ordained priest in the C of E. He continued to travel in the cause of religious unity. At first a royalist in the Civil War, he took up a chaplaincy at Rotterdam in 1643, returning to London in 1645 to take part in drawing up the *Westminster Confession and Catechisms.

Duvergier de Hauranne. See SAINT-CYRAN, ABBÉ DE.

dying, care of the. The spiritual care of the dying has always been a central concern of the Church; it has long made provision for reconciliation through *Penance and for sacramental anointing (see UNCTION) and for the administration of Communion to those facing death (see VIATICUM). The physical care of the sick and dying was one of the activities of the religious orders. In the W., the care of the sick largely passed to secular institutions. It was partly in reaction to the limitations of such care, in which the main thrust is towards prolonging life, that the modern hospice movement developed. This is based on the view that by the proper control of physical pain and distressing symptoms, dying patients are enabled to value and find meaning in what remains of life and perhaps accept death when it becomes inevitable. St Christopher's Hospice in South London opened in 1967; it has had international influence through the founding of other hospices and through the incorporation of the principles of hospice care into medical practice.

In modern times there has also been increased advocacy of so-called euthanasia, a term now used to denote the termination of life on humanitarian grounds, as in the case of incurable illness. Like *suicide, it is incompatible with a proper respect for the sacredness of human life. Christian moralists regard it as illicit, though there is said to be no obligation to pursue burdensome or extraordinary measures to preserve life. Euthanasia was condemned by the RC Church in 1940, 1980, and 1995, and by the General *Synod of the C of E in 1976. Various bills to authorize it in Britain have been defeated. In 1976 the state of California in the USA permitted terminally ill patients there to authorize, by prior directive, the withholding of life-sustaining procedures when death is believed to be imminent. In the *Netherlands, under strictly limited conditions, euthanasia became legal in 2001.

Dykes, John Bacchus (1823–76), writer of hymn-tunes. In 1862 he became vicar of St Oswald's, Durham; here his High Church sympathies led to a long and unhappy conflict with the bishop. His hymn-tunes became popular. They include *Hollingside* ('Jesu, Lover of my soul') and *Dominus regit me* ('The King of Love my Shepherd is').

Dyophysites. A *Monophysite title for the Catholics in reference to the orthodox belief that in the Person of Christ the two separate natures of God and man coexist.

Dyothelites. Those who, as against the *Monothelites, hold the orthodox doctrine that in the Person of Christ there are two distinct wills, the one human and the other Divine.

'E'. A symbol used by scholars who follow the 'documentary hypothesis' of the origins of the *Pentateuch (q.v.) to denote the Eloistic source. It is distinguished from '*J' by its regular use of *'eloihim* ('God') where 'J' uses Yahweh (Jahveh or Jehovah).

Eadmer (*c*.1060–*c*.1128), English historian and theologian. He was a member of the household of St *Anselm. He wrote Lives of Anselm and other English saints (including *Wilfrid and *Dunstan), a history of England covering the period from *c*.1066 to c.1122, and a treatise defending the doctrine of the *Immaculate Conception of the BVM, formerly attributed to Anselm.

Earle, John (c.1601–65), Bp. of *Salisbury from 1663. He gained literary fame by his *Microcosmography* (1628), a pleasant collection of character studies. In 1643 he became Chancellor of Salisbury Cathedral. Deprived by the *Puritans, he accompanied *Charles II in his exile and received rapid promotion at the Restoration. He was tolerant towards Nonconformists.

Earthquake Synod. In 1382 a Synod was held at Blackfriars, London, under Abp. W. *Courtenay; in the course of one meeting the city was shaken by an earthquake. The synod condemned as heretical 24 theses taken from the writings of J. *Wycliffe and took various measures against heresy.

Easter. The Feast of the Resurrection of Christ, the greatest and oldest feast of the Christian Church. In the ancient Church the *catechumens, after watching all (*Holy) Saturday night, were baptized early on Easter Day and received Communion. In both E. and W. the ceremonies were put back to the Saturday. In the RC Church between 1951 and 1955 they were restored to the night of Saturday-Sunday. In the E. Church, in addition to the services on Saturday, Mattins of Easter Sunday begins at Midnight on Saturday-Sunday, and is followed by the Liturgy of Easter Day. See PASCHAL VIGIL SERVICE.

The date of Easter is determined by the Paschal Full Moon, its extreme limits being 21 March and 25 April. For disputes on the computation of Easter see PASCHAL CONTROVERSIES.

Easter Litany. The principal confession of faith of the *Bohemian Brethren. It is based on the *Apostles' Creed, with considerable expansions. It dates from 1749.

Eastern Catholics. See UNIAT CHURCHES.

Eastern Orthodox Church. See ORTHODOX CHURCH.

Eastertide. See PASCHALTIDE.

eastward position. In connection with liturgy, the term denotes the position of the celebrant of the Eucharist standing on the same side of the altar as the people, with his back to them; because of the normal *orientation of churches, in this position he usually faces east.

Ebedjesus (Abdisho'bar Berikha) (d. 1318), Metropolitan of *Armenia. He was the last important theologian of the *Church of the East. His works, in Syriac, include a catalogue of Syriac authors, two compendia of canon law, a theological work called *Margaritha* (the *Pearl*), and the *Paradisus-Eden*, a collection of 50 poems.

Eberlin, Johannes (c.1468–1533), Reformation polemical writer. A Bavarian *Franciscan, he encountered the writings of M. *Luther in 1520 and in 1521 he published 15 pamphlets; the radical social ideas in some of these contributed to the discontent which was to be manifested in the *Peasants' War. After 1552, he became more moderate.

Ebionites. An ascetic sect of Jewish Christians which flourished on the E. of the R. *Jordan in the early years of the Christian era. Their main tenets seem to have been: (1) a 'reduced' doctrine of the Person of Christ, to the effect, e.g., that Jesus was the human son of Joseph and Mary and that the Holy Spirit in the form of a dove lighted on Him at His Baptism, and (2) overemphasis on the binding character of the Mosaic Law. They are said to have rejected the Pauline Epistles and to have used only one Gospel.

Ebionites, Gospel according to the. The name given by modern scholars to the Greek *apocryphal Gospel supposed to have been used by the *Ebionites. *Epiphanius says that the Ebionites 'receive the Gospel according to Matthew' and 'call it the Hebrew Gospel'. It cannot be identified with the canonical Mt., and its relationship, if any, to the 'Gospel according to the *Hebrews' is unclear.

Ecce Homo (Lat., 'Behold the Man!'). The title of a controversial Life of Christ published by Sir John *Seeley in 1865. It depicted the Lord as a moral reformer.

Ecclesiastes. The main theme of this OT Book is the worthlessness and vanity of human life. The title 'Ecclesiastes' is an attempted rendering of the Hebrew title 'Qoheleth'; English versions usually translate this as 'the Preacher'. Though the Book is traditionally ascribed to *Solomon, the subject-matter and linguistic style make it clear that it is the product of a late age in OT history; it was one of the latest Books to be admitted to the Hebrew *canon.

Ecclesiastical Commissioners. The body which from 1835 to 1948 managed the estates and revenues of the C of E. In 1948 it was united with *Queen Anne's Bounty to form the *Church Commissioners for England.

Ecclesiastical Courts Commissions. (1) The Parliamentary Commission set up in 1830 recommended the replacement of the Court of *Delegates by the Privy Council as the final court of appeal in ecclesiastical matters. As a result the *Judicial Committee of the Privy Council was formed in 1833. (2) Another Parliamentary Commission was appointed in 1881, with the immediate object of finding a better way to deal with the ritual controversies. In 1883 it recommended a radical revision of the courts. No legislation followed.

Ecclesiastical Discipline, Royal Commission on. A Commission appointed in 1904 to inquire into 'breaches or neglect of the Law relating to the conduct of Divine Service' in the C of E and to devise remedies. In 1906 it reported that the law was too narrow and that the machinery for discipline had broken down. One of its recommendations led to the proposed Prayer Book which was defeated in Parliament in 1927 and 1928 (see COMMON PRAYER, BOOK OF).

Ecclesiastical Jurisdiction Measure 1963. A measure designed to simplify the ecclesiastical law and jurisdiction of the C of E. It established the *Court of Ecclesiastical Causes Reserved which has original jurisdiction over clergy in matters involving doctrine, ritual, or ceremonial. Other cases (known as 'conduct cases') are heard in the first instance in the *Consistory Courts, with appeal to the Provincial Court.

Ecclesiastical Titles Act 1851. The Act forbidding the assumption by RCs of territorial titles within the United Kingdom. Introduced as a counter-measure to the restoration of the RC hierarchy in 1850, it was a dead-letter; it was repealed in 1871.

ecclesiasticism. (1) Over-attention to the external details of ecclesiastical practice and administration; (2) the point of view which is guided solely by the interests of the Church as an organization.

Ecclesiasticus. A Book of the *Apocrypha, usually reckoned part of the so-called Wisdom Literature. It was written or compiled in Hebrew by Jesus (i.e. Joshua) the son of Sirach of Jerusalem; the translator's prologue also states that the translation into Greek was made by the author's grandson in Egypt after 132 BC. (The first prologue printed in the AV is spurious.) The catalogue of famous men (44–50) and other internal evidence confirm a date some two generations before 132 BC for the original.

ecclesiology. (1) The science of the building and decoration of churches; (2) the theology of the Church, now the more common meaning.

Echternach. The monastery of Echternach in Luxembourg was founded by St *Willibrord in 698. In the early 8th cent. its scriptorium produced a large number of fine MSS; in the 11th cent. it became the royal atelier of the Salian Emperors of Germany.

Eck, Johann (1486–1543), **Johann Maier 'of Eck'** (from his birthplace, Egg an der Günz), German theologian. He came under humanist influences. Until the controversy over *indulgences broke out, he was on good terms with M. *Luther, but in the public debate at Leipzig in 1519 he opposed *Carlstadt and Luther, and he was largely responsible for securing the latter's excommunication. For the rest of his life he took a prominent part in organizing Catholic opposition to German Protestantism.

Eckhart, Meister (c.1260–c.1328), German *Dominican theologian and preacher. He lectured at Paris and was Provincial of the Dominican province of Saxony. As a *Scholastic theologian, he conceived an ambitious speculative and exegetical project, the *Opus Tripartitum*, of which only parts survive. He was famous as a preacher. When he was accused of heretical teaching in 1326 and tried before the court of the Abp. of *Cologne, he appealed to the Pope but died during the proceedings. In 1329 *John XXII condemned 28 propositions as heretical or misleading, but declared that Eckhart had recanted before his death.

Eckhart teaches that we should 'break

through' the complexities of all the particulars which confront us, to reach the simple 'ground' of all reality, where God and the soul are inseparably one, by abstracting from all that is 'this' or 'that', both metaphysically and ascetically. For him, 'abstractedness' is the highest virtue, because it produces the most intimate union with God, from which the Christian life flows as spontaneously as God's own life.

eclecticism. Any system of theology or philosophy which selects elements from different schools or traditions and combines them.

ecphonesis. In the E. Church the concluding words, uttered in an audible voice, of a prayer, the rest of which has been said quietly.

ecstasy. The Greek word ἔκστασις is used to refer to any state of powerful emotion, such that one is 'beside oneself'. Though often used pejoratively, it could be used of someone being raised above himself to consort with the Divine (*Plato) or of prophetic inspiration (*Philo, *Justin, and others). *Plotinus used it in a positive sense to refer to a union with God in which the individual, having passed beyond his mental powers, is no longer quite 'himself'. In the later Middle Ages, ecstasy came to be associated with 'rapture', and both tended to become technical terms referring to a state of more or less complete abstraction from the senses. Under the influence of St *Teresa of Ávila and St *John of the Cross, they were effectively identified and given a specific place in the scheme of spiritual progress.

ectene. In the E. Church a prayer consisting of short petitions said by the deacon to which choir or congregation respond with *Kyrie Eleison.

Ecthesis (Gk. ἔκθεσις, 'a statement of faith'). The formula issued in 638 by the Emp. *Heraclius forbidding the mention of 'energies', whether one or two, in the Person of Christ and asserting that the two Natures were united in a single Will. See MONOTHELITISM.

Ecumenical Councils. See OECUMENICAL COUNCILS.

Ecumenical Movement. The movement in the Church towards the visible union of all believers in Christ. Aspirations for unity can be traced from NT times. The modern ecumenical movement may be dated from the *Edinburgh Conference of 1910, though this owed much to earlier developments. It led to the establishment of the International Missionary Council and thence to the creation in 1925 of the Universal Christian Conference on *Life and Work and of the first World Conference on *Faith and Order which met in *Lausanne in 1927. These two bodies were fused in the *World Council of Churches (q.v.).

The initiative between 1910 and 1927 came mainly from within W. Protestantism. The World Council of Churches, however, from the beginning included some E. *Orthodox and *Oriental Orthodox Churches. In 1961 official RC observers were for the first time permitted to attend the World Council of Churches' Third Assembly; in 1962 non-RC observers were invited to the Second *Vatican Council, and in 1964 the Council's Decree on Ecumenism referred to members of other Churches as 'separated brethren' rather than as outside the Church. Various organic unions among Protestant Churches have taken place (see REUNION) and the multilateral discussions conducted under the auspices of the World Council of Churches are paralleled by bilateral dialogues between world-wide organizations of different denominations. Councils of Churches at regional, national, and local levels now normally include both Orthodox and RCs. Since the late 1960s there has been a marked increase in the participation of non-Western Churches and of women. So far the *Pentecostal Churches (except in Latin America) have taken little part.

Eden, Garden of. The original home of *Adam and *Eve (Gen. 2: 8–3: 24).

Edessa. The present city (now Urfa) was founded in 304 BC. From an early date it was the centre of Syriac-speaking Christianity. It was the home of the 'Persian School' until that was closed in 489 on account of its alleged *Nestorian tendencies, and it has always been a focus of opposition to the Christological teaching of the Council of *Chalcedon. In 641 it fell into the hands of the Arabs, but continued to be an important Christian centre for some centuries. See also ABGAR, LEGEND OF.

Edgar (c.943–75), King of England from 959. He supported the work of monastic reform, appointing St *Dunstan Abp. of Canterbury (959), St *Ethelwold Bp. of Winchester (963), and St *Oswald Bp. of *Worcester (961) and Abp. of *York (971). On his initiative a synodal council was convened at Winchester (c.970), which promulgated the *Regularis Concordia.

Edicts of Milan and **Nantes.** See MILAN, EDICT OF; NANTES, EDICT OF.

Edinburgh Conference (1910). The World Missionary Conference was significant for its presentation of the ideal of world-evangelization and as inaugurating the modern *Ecumenical Movement. By its creation of the International Missionary Council it led to increased co-operation between missionary societies.

Edinburgh Conference (1937). The second World Conference on *Faith and Order. It approved the proposal of a *World Council of Churches.

Edmund, St, of Abingdon (also wrongly **Edmund Rich)** (c.1180–1240), Abp. of *Canterbury from 1233. He tried, boldly but ineffectually, to check royal mismanagement and Papal exactions. In his earlier years he taught the new logic at *Oxford; his association with the University is commemorated in St Edmund Hall. He wrote a devotional treatise, *Speculum Religiosorum*; the vulgate Latin text, which is a translation of one of the Anglo-Norman versions and is commonly known as the *Speculum Ecclesie*, circulated widely. Feast day, 16 Nov.

Edmund Campion, St. See CAMPION, ST EDMUND.

Edmund the Martyr, St (c.840–69), King of East Anglia by 865. In 869 his kingdom was invaded and he was captured by the Danes. He was offered his life if he would share his kingdom with the Danish leader; he refused as a Christian to associate himself with a pagan, was condemned to be made a target of the Danes' archery practice, and finally beheaded. In the 10th cent. his body was translated to Bury St Edmunds, where the abbey became a place of pilgrimage. Feast day, 20 Nov.

Edward, St (c.962–78), king and martyr. The eldest son of *Edgar, King of England, with the support of St *Dunstan, he succeeded him in 975, but was murdered three years later. In 1008 he was officially decreed a martyr. Feast day, 18 Mar.; of his translation, 20 June.

Edward the Confessor, St (c.1005–66), King of England from 1042. His reign was outstandingly peaceful, seriously disturbed only by the rebellion of Earl Godwin and his sons in 1051; their subsequent dominance led to Edward's being succeeded by Harold Godwinson, his brother-in-law. In his later years Edward re-endowed and rebuilt St Peter's Abbey at *Westminster as his mausoleum. His reputation for sanctity developed after the Norman Conquest. Feast day, 13 Oct.

Edward VI (1537–53), King of England from 1547. He was the son of *Henry VIII and Jane Seymour. Having delegated his royal authority to the Privy Council, he was of little account politically. His reign, however, was outstanding ecclesiastically for the many reforms and changes often forced upon the C of E by a government influenced by Continental Protestant theologians. It was marked by the issue of the *Injunctions of 1547, recognition of clerical marriage (1549) and by the Acts of *Uniformity passed in 1549 and 1552 imposing the First and then the Second BCP, and a new *Ordinal (1550).

Edwards, Jonathan (1703–58), American evangelical preacher and *Calvinist theologian. He was ordained to the ministry of the *Congregational church at Northampton, Mass., in 1727, and was drawn into the public arena by his congregation's participation in a series of revivals beginning in 1734. During the *Great Awakening of the 1740s he emerged as the champion of evangelical religion; he preached the necessity of a 'new birth' and in his *Treatise Concerning Religious Affections* (1746) he defended the role of both the will and the intellect in the religious life. In 1750 he was dismissed from his congregation because he insisted on strict standards for admission to Communion. He then served as a missionary to the Indians at Stockbridge, Mass. There he wrote *Freedom of the Will* (1754), as well as works on human depravity and ethics. Freedom, as popularly understood, he rejected, maintaining that self-determination was 'unphilosophical, self-contradictory and absurd' and that the essence of virtue and vice lay 'not in their cause but in their nature'. Regarded as the foremost American theologian and philosopher of the colonial period, Edwards exercised considerable influence through his writings, through a school of disciples known as the 'New England Theologians', and through the expansion of the evangelical movement.

Edwin (c.585–633), Northumbrian king from 616. In 625 he married Ethelburga, daughter of King *Ethelbert, a Christian who came to Northumbria with St *Paulinus as her chaplain. In 627 Edwin was baptized. He appointed Paulinus Bp. of *York and set about building a stone church there. He was killed at the battle of Hatfield Chase.

efficacious grace. In the RC theology of *grace, grace to which free consent is given by the will, so that it always produces its effect. It has been disputed whether the efficacy of such grace depends on the character of the grace or on the fact that it is given under circumstances which God foresees to be congruous with the dispositions of the recipient.

Egbert (d. 766), Abp. of *York. He became Bp. of York c.732, and, on the advice of *Bede, applied for the *pallium in 735. He founded the cathedral school and carried out many reforms. His name is associated with a collection of canons (in its present form not earlier than the 11th cent.), a treatise on Church discipline and a 'Poenitentiale', both added to from later sources. The '*Pontifical' that goes under his name has no connection with him.

Egbert, St (d. 729), Northumbrian hermit. A monk of *Lindisfarne, he went to *Ireland and was influential in organizing the evangelization of Germany; he arranged the mission of St *Willibrord and others. From about 716 he lived on *Iona. Feast day, 24 Apr.

Egede, Hans (1686–1758), the 'Apostle of the Eskimos'. He went as a *Lutheran missionary from Norway to Greenland in 1721. In 1736 he returned to Copenhagen, where he founded a seminary for missionaries to Greenland.

Egeria, Pilgrimage of. The account of a journey by a devout woman to Egypt, the *Holy Land, *Edessa, Asia Minor, and *Constantinople, probably in 381–4. In the first part she records her identification of places with the sites of biblical events; in the second the descriptions are mainly of liturgical matters, especially the services of *Jerusalem and the neighbourhood.

Egerton Papyrus. Two imperfect leaves and a scrap of papyrus in the British Library ('Egerton Papyrus 2') containing passages from a Greek writing akin to, but distinct from, the canonical Gospels. It used to be dated c. AD 150, but is now put nearer 200.

Eginhard. See EINHARD.

Egypt, Christianity in. See COPTIC CHURCH.

Egyptian Church Order. An early name for the *Apostolic Tradition (q.v.).

Egyptians, Gospel according to the. An apocryphal Gospel, written from an ascetic standpoint, probably in Egypt in the early 2nd cent. Only a few quotations from it survive. It has no connection with the 'Gospel of the Egyptians' *Nag Hammadi.

Eighteen Benedictions, the. A group of prayers, now 19, which are recited on weekdays at each of the three services of the Jewish synagogue. Their content dates in part from pre-Christian times.

***Eikon Basilike**, 'The Portraiture of His Sacred Majesty in His Solitudes and Sufferings'. A royalist publication issued just before the death of *Charles I and purporting to be his work.

eileton. In the E. Church, a cloth spread on the altar during the Liturgy. It is the counterpart of the W. *corporal.

Einhard (c.770–840), also **Eginhard**, Frankish historian. One of *Charlemagne's most trusted friends, he is credited with overseeing the building works at Aachen. His writings include a remarkable 'Life of Charlemagne', distinguished by its fresh and accurate presentation of the Emperor's character and rule. He may also have written an epic poem about Charlemagne. His authorship of the so-called 'Annales Einhardi' is no longer accepted.

Einsiedeln. *Benedictine abbey and place of pilgrimage in Switzerland. Previously the dwelling-place of St *Meinrad, the abbey was founded in 934. The library has a valuable collection of MSS.

Ejectors. See TRIERS AND EJECTORS.

elder. A Church officer in the *Presbyterian Church. There are two kinds: (1) 'Teaching elders', whose function is pastoral; (2) 'Ruling elders', lay people often set apart by ordination who assist the pastor in the administration and government of the Church. When the word is used without specification, the latter class is commonly meant. For the office in the early Church, see PRESBYTER.

election. In the vocabulary of theology, an act of the Divine Will exercising itself on creatures, among whom it chooses some in preference to others. In the OT the Divine election bears especially on Israel, the 'Chosen People'; in the NT the place of the Old Israel is taken by the Church. In the teaching of the Fathers and Schoolmen the term plays an important part in connection with *predestination (q.v.). It came to be a matter of dispute, especially among *Calvinists, whether God's election was wholly without relation to faith and works. K. *Barth focused on the assertion that it is primarily in Jesus Christ that election (and reprobation) is realized.

Elevation. At the Eucharist, the lifting up of the sacred elements in turn by the celebrant immediately after he has said the Words of *Institution over them, in order to exhibit them for the people's adoration. The practice of elevating the Host apparently originated early in the 13th cent.; the elevation of the chalice was added later.

Elgar, Sir Edward (1857–1934), English composer. He rose to international fame c.1900 as a composer of choral and orchestral music. His religious works include a setting for J. H. *Newman's *Dream of Gerontius* and the *oratorios *The Apostles* and *The Kingdom*.

El Greco (1541–1614), properly Domenicos Theotocopoulos, painter and sculptor. A native of Crete, by 1577 he was in Toledo, where he seems to have spent the rest of his life. The works of his Spanish period are marked by a quality of mysticism as well as by personal idiosyncrasies. Formal modelling is abandoned as human forms and facial expressions are exaggerated and even distorted to produce an emotional rather than a literal likeness.

Elias. See ELIJAH.

Elias of Cortona (c.1180–1253), *Franciscan. He was one of the earliest companions of St *Francis. In 1232 he became third General of the Franciscan Order; his government was marked by repeated crises and despotic behaviour, and he was deposed by *Gregory IX in 1239. He then supported *Frederick II and was excommunicated and expelled from the Order.

Eligius, St (c.590–660), patron saint of metalworkers. Through his skill in working in precious metals, he rose to high office in the courts of the Frankish kings. He was consecrated Bp. of Noyon in 641 and evangelized Flanders. Feast day, 1 Dec.

Elijah (Gk. form, 'Elias') (9th cent. BC), Hebrew prophet. According to Kgs., he maintained the ascendancy of the worship of God in the face of Canaanite and Phoenician cults, upheld the claims of moral righteousness and social justice, and was translated into heaven. His return was held to be a necessary prelude to the deliverance and restoration of Israel. Feast day, 20 July.

Eliot, Thomas Stearns (1888–1965), poet and critic. An American by birth, he worked in a bank in London. From 1922 to 1939 he edited *The Criterion*. He joined the board of Faber, the publisher, in 1925.

Brought up in the *Unitarian tradition, Eliot passed through a period of agnosticism reflected in his earlier poetry. In 1927 he was baptized in the C of E. Henceforth much of his poetry, culminating in the *Four Quartets* (1935–42), expressed his religious search, his struggle with faith and doubt, and his attempt to find fresh meaning in tradition. His poetical drama was less successful but also tried to communicate something of the dilemmas of faith, notably in *Murder in the Cathedral* (1935; written for the Canterbury Festival). He was deeply interested in the social implications of Christianity.

Elipandus (*c*.717–802), Abp. of Toledo. He was the originator and chief exponent of the *Adoptianist heresy in Spain. His doctrines were condemned as heretical at various synods from 792 onwards, but the Arab domination enabled him to retain his see.

Elizabeth, St. The mother of *John the Baptist and 'cousin' (Lk. 1: 36) of the BVM. According to a few MSS of the NT it was she who spoke the words known as the *Magnificat. Feast day in the W., 5 Nov.; in the E., 5 Sept.

Elizabeth, St, of Hungary, now more generally known as **Elizabeth of Thuringia** (1207–31). The daughter of the King of Hungary, in 1221 she married Ludwig IV, Landgrave of Thuringia. After his death (1227) she was driven from court on the ground that her charities were exhausting the State finances. She settled at Marburg; under the direction of *Conrad of Marburg she gave up her children and led a life of great austerity. Feast day, 17 (formerly 19, as in the American BCP, 1979), Nov.

Elizabeth I (1533–1603), Queen of England from 1558. The daughter of *Henry VIII and *Anne Boleyn, she was placed next in the succession after *Edward VI and *Mary by Act of Parliament. On her accession she tried to break away from the policies that had made Mary unpopular; her own sympathies and supporters were Protestant. In the Parliament of 1559 she tried to achieve a royal supremacy and restoration of the 1552 Book of *Common Prayer; she accepted supreme governorship of the C of E and a slightly amended BCP. She appointed Protestant bishops but made some attempts to conciliate Catholic opinion; she reintroduced a *crucifix in her chapel and tried to insist on the use of traditional *vestments. Later she attempted to limit Protestant preaching; her refusal to consider further structural changes in the Church led to tensions with leading Protestants, including her own bishops.

Although politically cautious, Elizabeth I posed as the patron of Protestants, sending military aid to Protestant rebels abroad. In 1570 she was excommunicated by *Pius V. From 1583 she turned more decisively against English Catholics, partly for fear of plots and partly because the growth of popular Protestantism made conservative concessions less necessary. Persecution of *recusants was vigorous in 1585–91, and in 1587 she allowed the execution of *Mary, Queen of Scots. Her image as Protestant protectress helped her to overcome suspicion of female rule and made anti-popery a powerful national ideology.

Elkesaites. A Jewish sect which arose *c*.AD 116 in Mesopotamia; they took their name from the 'Book of Elkesai' which claimed to contain revelations given to Elkesai ('hidden power') by an angel 96 miles high. In the 3rd cent. this book was taken over by Judaeo-Christians who held beliefs similar to those of the *Ebionites.

Ellerton, John (1826–93), English clergyman. He is remembered for his many hymns, both original compositions and translations. They include 'The day Thou gavest, Lord, is ended'.

Elmo, St (in Spain, 'San Telmo'). The popular name of Bl Peter Gonzalez (*c*.1190–1246). Having joined the *Dominicans, he accompanied Ferdinand III's campaign against the Moors of Andalucia; he spent the last ten years of his life preaching in NW Spain and N. Portugal. He was regarded as the special patron of seafarers; probably for this reason he was given the name of an earlier patron of theirs, St Erasmus, known as Ermo or Elmo, a martyr in the *Diocletianic *persecution. Feast day, 14 Apr.

Elohim. A Hebrew word meaning 'gods'. In the OT it is generally used of the God of Israel, especially frequently in what is commonly reckoned the second oldest *Pentateuchal source (the supposed author of which is therefore referred to by critics as 'the Elohist').

Elvira, Council of. A Spanish Council held early in the 4th cent., traditionally dated *c*.306, probably at Granada. It imposed severe penalties for apostasy and adultery, and required continence of all clergy.

Ely. In 673 St *Etheldreda founded a *double monastery here for monks and nuns. It was destroyed by the Danes in 870, but restored, for monks only, in 970. The see of Ely was formed in 1109; the prior and monks became the *cathedral chapter. At the *Dissolution the prior became dean and eight canonries were founded (1541). The cathedral is famous for its central octagon (1322–8), with its domed roof (known as 'The Lantern', completed in the 1340s) and other 14th cent. work, including the magnificent Lady Chapel.

Ember Days. Four groups each of three days, namely the Wednesday, Friday, and Saturday after St *Lucy (13 Dec.), the first Sunday in *Lent, *Whitsunday, and *Holy Cross Day (14 Sept.) respectively, which have been observed as days of fasting and abstinence in the W. Church. In the RC Church they were replaced in 1969 by days of prayer for various needs at times to be determined by regional conferences of bishops. Originally connected with the crops, from at least the 5th cent. the Ember seasons were associated with *Ordinations, and the association of Ember Days with prayer for ordination candidates is preserved in modern Anglican liturgies even when the usual time for Ordinations has changed. Thus CW places two groups of Ember Days before the Sundays nearest the feasts of St *Peter and St *Michael and All Angels.

Embolism (Gk. for 'intercalation'). In the Roman Mass, the prayer beginning 'Deliver us . . .' inserted between the *Lord's Prayer after the *Canon and the Prayer for Peace. The word is also used (not in a specifically religious sense) to denote the difference of days in the calendar between the lunar year of 354 days and the solar year of 365¼ days.

Embury, Philip (1728–75), one of the earliest *Methodist preachers in America. A native of Ireland, he was converted by J. *Wesley. In 1768 he built the first Methodist church in America, in New York, but in 1770 he moved to Camden, where he founded a Methodist society.

Emerson, Ralph Waldo (1803–82), American essayist, philosopher, and poet. He was a *Unitarian minister at Boston, Mass., from 1829 to 1832. Later he lectured on literature and philosophy at Concord, Mass. His philosophy was founded on a combination of rationalism and mysticism. It appears that fundamentally he believed in 'Transcendentalism'—the doctrine that 'the highest revelation is that God is in every man'. It follows that man contains all

that is needful in himself and that even redemption is to be sought within the soul. At least from the 1840s he had wide influence.

Eminence. A title of honour given to *cardinals.

Emmanuel. See IMMANUEL.

Emmaus. The village in which the Lord made a Resurrection appearance to two disciples (Lk. 24: 13–35). Its site is disputed.

Emmerick, Anna Katharina (1774–1824), ecstatic. She entered an *Augustinian convent in Westphalia in 1802; when this was closed in 1812 she took refuge in a private house, where she had a serious illness. She received the *Stigmata of the Passion on her body. Her 'Meditations on the Passion' and other visions were taken down and published after her death.

Ems, Congress of. A conference attended by representatives of the Abps. of Mainz, Trier, *Cologne, and Salzburg in 1786. It issued the 'Punctation of Ems', which sought to limit Papal intervention in Germany. The project failed to secure the support of the German bishops. See also FEBRONIANISM.

Emser, Hieronymus (1478–1527), RC writer. He engaged in controversy with M. *Luther from 1519 until his death. In 1527 he published a counter-edition to Luther's 'December Bible' of 1522, which it was made to resemble, with introduction and notes added.

Enabling Act. The commonly used name for the Church of England Assembly (Powers) Act 1919. It gave the *Church Assembly power to prepare ecclesiastical measures and, after they were approved by an Ecclesiastical Commission of both Houses of Parliament, present them to Parliament which could accept or reject (but not amend) them. It also gave legal status to *Parochial Church Councils.

Enarxis. In the Byzantine liturgy, the section between the *Proskomide and the *Little Entrance. It consists of three Diaconal Litanies, each followed by Psalms or antiphons sung by the choir, and sometimes ending with the *Beatitudes.

enclosure. See CLAUSURA.

encolpion. An oval medallion worn by bishops in the E. Church. It is suspended from the neck by a chain.

Encratites. A title applied to several groups of early Christians who carried their ascetic practices and doctrines to extremes which were in most cases considered heretical. They commonly rejected the use of wine and meat, and also often of marriage.

encyclical. A circular letter sent to all the churches in a given area. In early times the word might be applied to letters sent out by any bishop, but in modern RC usage it is confined to those of the Pope.

Encyclopaedists. The contributors to the French *Encyclopédie* (28 vols., 1751–72), edited by D. *Diderot and (initially) J. Le R. *D'Alembert. The *Encyclopédie* sets out to review the full extent of human achievement in the arts and sciences from a secular standpoint. The tone is that of rationalist humanism and scepticism about the claims of revealed religion; pleas for religious and political liberty are insinuated into a mass of accurate information. It became a rallying point for opponents of established beliefs and practices in the political and social as well as the religious spheres.

energumen. In ancient Christian literature the term was used of demoniacs and others possessed of abnormal mental and physical states, especially insanity. They received the ministrations of *exorcists.

England, Church of. See CHURCH OF ENGLAND (for history); ANGLICANISM (for theological outlook).

English Church Music, School of. See ROYAL SCHOOL OF CHURCH MUSIC.

English Church Union. A society formed in 1859 as the 'Church of England Protection Society' and renamed in 1860. Its object was to defend and propagate *High Church principles in the C of E. In 1934 it was united with the Anglo-Catholic Congress to form the '*Church Union'.

English College, Rome. The seminary for English candidates for the RC priesthood. Originally founded in 1362 as a hospice for English pilgrims, in 1579 it was refounded as a seminary, whose students had to take an oath to go to England when it should seem good to their superiors.

English Hymnal, The. An Anglican hymn-book, published in 1906, which to some extent reflects the *Anglo-Catholic sympathies of those responsible for its production. In 1986 a revision, designed to meet the needs occasioned by liturgical changes and shifts in custom and feeling, was issued under the title *New English Hymnal*. Both the original edition and the revision include some liturgical matter as well as hymns.

Enhypostasia. The doctrine that, in the incarnate Christ, though the humanity has no 'person' (*hypostasis*) of its own, it is not on that account 'anhypostatic' (deprived of a *hypostasis*), but finds its *hypostasis* in the *hypostasis* of the Logos. Thus the distinguishing features of the particular man who Jesus is, as well as the essential qualities of the species (mankind) to which He belongs, are attributed to the Divine *hypostasis*.

Enlightenment, the. Though the term originated as a translation of the German *Aufklärung*, it is now applied more generally to the movement of ideas which characterized much of 18th-cent. Europe. Its adherents distrusted all authority and tradition in matters of intellectual inquiry, and believed that truth could be obtained only through reason, observation, and experiment. They sought to diffuse knowledge and where possible to further tolerance, justice, and the moral and material welfare of mankind. The movement embraced a vast spectrum of views, and many of its leaders came into conflict with the Church, especially in Catholic countries.

Ennodius, St, Magnus Felix (*c*.473–521), Christian rhetorician and from *c*. 514 Bp. of Pavia. He was twice sent by *Hormisdas on missions to *Constantinople. His numerous writings reflect an attempt to combine a fundamentally pagan culture with the profession of the Christian creed. Feast day, 11 July.

Enoch, OT patriarch. Many legends became attached to his name. See also the following entry.

Enoch, Books of. 1 Enoch, or 'Ethiopic Enoch', so called because it survives in its most complete form in Ethiopic, is one of

the most important Jewish *Pseudepigrapha. It embodies a series of revelations, of which *Enoch is the professed
recipient, on such matters as the origin of
evil, angels, and the nature of *Gehenna
and *Paradise. It is clearly a composite
work. The passages on 'the *Son of Man' in
the 'Parables' or 'Similitudes' (chs. 37–71)
have been widely held to have influenced
the NT writings, but it seems probable that
the section is a later (Christian) insertion
into the Book. Other parts of the Book are
reflected in the NT.

2 Enoch, or 'Slavonic Enoch', or 'The
Book of the Secrets of Enoch', which survives only in Old Church Slavonic (the
language of the Russian Church), has
points of contact with 1 Enoch. About its
origin, date, authorship, and original
language opinions have differed widely.

3 Enoch is a Jewish work dating from
well within the Christian era (perhaps 4th
or 5th cent.). It appears to have traces of
anti-Christian polemic.

enthronization. The rite by which an
archbishop, bishop, or sovereign is put into
possession of his throne. It is normally performed by ceremonially leading him to it
and seating him thereon; in the case of the
sovereign it forms part of the *Coronation
rite. Bishops seem originally to have been
enthroned by the consecrating bishop
immediately after consecration. In the late
12th cent., when bishops were commonly
consecrated outside their cathedrals,
enthronization became a separate rite, and
in the 13th cent. it came to be understood
as the formal assumption of the see. At the
same time *metropolitans began to assign
the task of enthroning bishops to their
*archdeacons.

Entrance, Great; Little. See GREAT
ENTRANCE; LITTLE ENTRANCE.

Enurchus, St (4th cent.), Bp. of Orléans.
Little is known of him. His feast (7 Sept.)
was included in the calendar of the BCP to
mark Queen *Elizabeth I's birthday.

epanokamelavchion. The veil placed on
top of the *kamelavchion and hanging
down at the back, worn by monks and
bishops in the E. Church.

Epaphroditus. A fellow-worker of St *Paul
mentioned in Philippians.

eparchy. In the E. Church, the name for an
ecclesiastical *province. Its head is the
'eparch', often called the 'metropolitan',
who has a veto on the election of bishops in
his eparchy.

Ephesians, Epistle to the. This NT Epistle
was apparently written when its author
was in prison, but considerations of style
and theological emphasis have led scholars
to question whether it is the work of St
*Paul. Since the words 'in Ephesus' in 1: 1
are missing in some MSS, it has been suggested that it was a circular letter in which
the appropriate place-name was inserted in
the copies sent to different Churches.
There are close parallels with Col., and it
has sometimes been held that Eph. is a
working-up of Col. into a more systematic
doctrinal treatise, or even an exposition of
Pauline teaching designed as an introduction to the first collection of his letters.

Ephesus. In NT times Ephesus was the capital of the Proconsular Province of Asia and
an important commercial centre. It was the
scene of important labours of St *Paul and
traditionally the home of the aged St *John
the Apostle. It was one of the *Seven
Churches addressed in Rev. (2: 1–7). See also
the preceding and following entries and
Seven Sleepers of Ephesus.

Ephesus, Council of (431). The third
*Oecumenical Council, summoned by
*Theodosius II in the hope of settling the
*Nestorian controversy. *Cyril of Alexan-
dria opened the Council without waiting
for the Syrian bishops, headed by *John of
Antioch, or for the Papal legates. Nestorius
was deposed, his doctrines condemned,
and the Creed of *Nicaea was reaffirmed.
When they arrived, the Syrian bishops and
others held a rival meeting, but agreement
between John and Cyril was reached in 433.

Ephesus, Robber Council of 499. See
LATROCINIUM.

ephod. An ancient Israelite liturgical
vestment of linen and beaten gold. It was
apparently worn only by the *High Priest,
though a similar garment of linen only was
worn by others (e.g. Samuel and *David).

ephor. In the E. Church, a lay guardian
or protector in whose charge monastic
property was often vested from the 10th
cent. onwards.

Ephphatha. A ceremony in the RC Baptismal rite in which the celebrant, pronouncing the words 'Ephphatha, that is, Be opened' (Mk. 7: 34), touches the ears and mouth of the candidate.

Ephraem Syrus, St (c.306–73), Syrian biblical exegete and hymn-writer. After the cession of Nisibis to Persia in 363 he settled at *Edessa, where most of his extant works were written. His voluminous exegetical, dogmatic, controversial, and ascetical writings are mostly in verse. Over 500 genuine hymns survive; after his death they were arranged into hymn cycles, of which the most famous are those on Faith (including the five 'On the Pearl'), on Paradise, and on Nisibis (the second half of this cycle is concerned with the *Descent of Christ into Hell). Several of his works, in verse as well as prose, were written to combat heretics, notably *Marcion, *Bardesanes, and *Mani. He wrote in Syriac, but his works were translated into Armenian and Greek at an early date. Feast day in the E., 28 Jan.; in the W., formerly 1 Feb., then 18 June, now 9 June (10 June in the American BCP, 1979).

epiclesis. Although the term originally meant 'invocation' and subsequently 'prayer' in general, it is commonly used in Christian writing only for the petition for the consecration of the bread and wine in the Eucharist, and it is usually restricted to the form of this petition which asks the Father to send the Holy Spirit upon the bread and wine and make them into the Body and Blood of Christ.

Early *Eucharistic Prayers, such as that in the *Apostolic Tradition (3rd cent.), have petitions for the descent of the Holy Spirit on the Church's offerings, asking that those who receive the elements may benefit thereby, and also seeking the gathering into one of all present. From the 4th cent. the petition is more specifically for the consecration and transformation of the bread and wine. In the Roman *Canon of the Mass there is no explicit mention of the Holy Spirit. Modern RC Eucharistic Prayers, however, contain two prayers for the operation of the Holy Spirit, the first that the elements be changed and the second in connection with the fruits of Communion. Modern liturgies of other Churches often include prayers invoking the operation of the Holy Spirit on the elements, on the

congregation, or more generally on, or through, the Eucharistic action.

Epictetus (c.50–c.130), *Stoic philosopher. The influence of Christian ideals on Epictetus and vice versa has often been discussed, but the resemblances hardly go beyond similarity of moral temper.

Epicureanism. The system of philosophical ethics founded by the Greek thinker Epicurus (342–270 BC). Epicurus held that the senses, as the source of all our ideas, provided the sole criterion of truth, and he sought the goal of human conduct in pleasure, which he equated with freedom from pain and from fear.

epigonation. In the E. Church, a lozenge-shaped stiffened vestment used by certain ecclesiastical dignitaries.

epimanikia. In the E. Church, cuffs worn by bishops and priests over the ends of the sleeves of the *sticharion, and by deacons over the ends of the sleeves of the cassock.

Epiphanius, St (c.315–403), Bp. of Salamis and Metropolitan of *Cyprus from 367. He was an ardent upholder of the faith of *Nicaea, took part in the *Apollinarian and *Melitian controversies and, after meeting St *Jerome in 382, joined with him in his attack on *Origenism. His 'Panarion' or 'Refutation of all the Heresies' describes and attacks every heresy known to him. Feast day, 12 May.

Epiphany (from the Greek for 'manifestation'). A feast of the Church kept on 6 Jan. It originated in the E., where it has been celebrated in honour of the Lord's Baptism since the 3rd cent., one of its main features being the solemn blessing of water. It was introduced into the W. Church in the 4th cent. Here it became chiefly associated with the manifestation of Christ to the Gentiles in the persons of the *Magi, though the Baptism of Christ and the miracle at Cana (Jn. 2: 1–11) are also mentioned. In 1955 the Sunday after Epiphany became a separate feast of the Baptism in the RC Church.

episcopacy. The system of Church government by bishops.

Episcopal Church in the United States of America. The Church in the *United States of America in communion with the see of *Canterbury. Previously called the

Protestant Episcopal Church in the United States of America, it adopted the new title as an alternative in 1967 and as its official designation in 1979.

The first Anglican church in America was built at Jamestown, Virginia, in 1607; many other congregations were established, all under the jurisdiction of the Bp. of London. It was only after the War of Independence that the Protestant Episcopal Church became an autonomous organization. In 1784 S. *Seabury, who had been elected bishop by the clergy of Connecticut, received episcopal *Orders at the hands of the bishops of the Episcopalian Church in *Scotland. At a General Convention in 1789 a constitution and canons were drawn up and the Book of *Common Prayer revised. During the Civil War of 1861–5, the Church in the southern states formed itself into a separate body, but reconciliation followed the peace of 1865. Since then the Church has expanded at home and abroad, establishing missionary dioceses in many parts of the world. Further revisions of the Prayer Book were made in 1892 and in 1928–9; a new Prayer Book, which became official in 1979, includes services in both traditional and contemporary language.

The constitution of the Church gives the laity a major role in all legislative bodies. Bishops are elected by majority vote of both clerical and lay orders in diocesan conventions. The ultimate governing body is the General Convention. Opposition to its decision in 1976 to permit the ordination of *women to the priesthood, and to a lesser degree to the new Prayer Book, led to the formation of several small schismatic bodies. The consecration in 1989 of the first woman to become a bishop in the Anglican Communion aroused further controversy.

Episcopalian. Properly a member of any Church ruled by bishops, but used especially of the *Anglican Communion.

episcopi vagantes (Lat., 'wandering bishops'). The name given to persons who have been consecrated bishop in an irregular or clandestine manner or who, having been regularly consecrated, have been excommunicated by the Church that consecrated them and are in communion with no recognized see. A man is also included in this group when the number in communion with him is so small that the sect appears to exist solely for his sake.

Episcopius. The assumed name of Simon Bisschop (1583–1643), who systematized the typical tenets of *Arminianism. One of the signatories of the *Remonstrance (1610), he was chief spokesman of the Remonstrants summoned to the Synod of *Dort, and he later drew up a confession of faith for the newly founded Remonstrant Brotherhood. He emphasized the practical nature of Christianity, protested against the current Calvinist teaching on *predestination, stressed the responsibility of man, not God, for sin, and taught a reduced view of the divinity of Christ and a *subordinationist doctrine of the Trinity.

Epistle. It was long customary for two passages of Scripture to be read or sung at the Eucharist; the former came to be known as the 'Epistle', doubtless because it was usually taken from one of the NT Epistles. In 1969 the RC Church restored the earlier practice of including lessons from the OT, and a reading from the non-Gospel part of the NT is no longer always obligatory on weekdays. Similar arrangements are now permitted in the C of E. In the E. Church an Epistle (called '*Apostle') and Gospel are chanted at all sacramental celebrations.

Epistle of the Apostles. See TESTAMENT OF OUR LORD IN GALILEE.

Epistolae Obscurorum Virorum. A famous pamphlet in the dispute between J. *Reuchlin and the *Dominicans of *Cologne. It appeared in two parts (1515 and 1517). It is a bitter satire on the methods of later Scholasticism, on the religious practices of the age, and on many ecclesiastical institutions and doctrines.

epitaphion. In the E. Church, a veil embroidered with the scene of Christ's burial. It is carried in procession on *Good Friday and *Holy Saturday. It remains on the altar until the eve of *Ascension Day.

epitrachelion. The form of the *stole worn by priests in the E. Church.

Equiprobabilism. The moral system defended by St *Alphonsus Liguori. It holds that the stricter course should be followed if the question concerns the cessation of the law, while the laxer course may be pursued if the question is whether the law ever existed.

Erasmus, St. See ELMO, ST.

Erasmus, Desiderius (1446/9–1536), humanist. He became an *Augustinian canon in 1487, but later left his monastery with the agreement of his superiors. For a time he joined Aldus Manutius' 'New Academy' in *Venice, and while there published the *Adagiorum chiliades*, with which he achieved international fame. He was the first teacher of Greek at Cambridge. In 1521 he settled at Basle, in the house of J. *Froben, refusing all offers of official position. When the Reformation was introduced at Basle in 1529, he fled to Freiburg.

Erasmus' *Praise of Folly* (1509) is a bitter satire on monasticism and the corruptions of the Church. In 1516 his celebrated Greek NT appeared, with his own translation into classical Latin. Next to his Greek NT, his most important work was probably his attempt to print reliable texts of the Fathers, though in some cases his own share in the editions perhaps did not go much beyond writing the prefaces. He was the most renowned scholar of his age. Though he paved the way for the Reformation by his satires, he remained loyal to the Church as the safeguard of stability.

Erastianism. The ascendancy of the State over the Church in ecclesiastical matters, so named from the Swiss theologian Thomas Erastus (1524–83). According to Erastus, in a State which professes but one religion the civil authorities have the right and duty to exercise jurisdiction in both civil and ecclesiastical matters. With the growth of the modern secular State the doctrine came to be modified and is now generally understood of the claim of the representatives of the State, whether professing any religion or none, to legislate on religious matters concerning the Established Church. See also ESTABLISHMENT.

Erigena (or more correctly **Eriugena**), John the Scot (*c.*810–*c.*877), philosopher. An Irishman, he became head of the palace school at Laon.

His philosophy is an attempt to reconcile the *Neoplatonist idea of emanation with the Christian idea of creation. In his *Periphyseon* or *De Divisione Naturae*, Erigena argues that Nature should be divided into four categories: first, Nature which is not created, but creates, i.e. God; secondly, Nature which is created and which creates, i.e. the world of primordial causes or Platonic ideas; thirdly, Nature which is created and which does not create, i.e. things perceived through the senses; and lastly, Nature which neither creates nor is created, i.e. God, to whom all things must in the end return. Thus the world was held to begin and end with God. In the 13th cent. this treatise was condemned. Erigena also wrote *De Divina Praedestinatione* against *Gotteshalk. Having a knowledge of Greek which was exceptional for his time, he translated into Latin the writings of *Dionysius the Pseudo-Areopagite and wrote a commentary on his *Celestial Hierarchy*, and translated works of *Maximus the Confessor and *Gregory of Nyssa.

Errington, George (1804–86), English RC prelate. In 1855 he was appointed coadjutor to N. P. S. *Wiseman and titular Abp. of Trebizond, with the right of succession to *Westminster. His relations with Wiseman became strained; he rejected *Pius IX's proposal that he should resign and in 1862 his connections with Westminster were severed by the Pope. He took part in the First *Vatican Council (1869–70), where he was a signatory of the Anti-Infallibility Petition.

Erskine, Ebenezer (1680–1754), leader of the most important 18th-cent. secession from the Church of *Scotland. Minister at Portmoak from 1703 and at Stirling from 1731, he was a notable preacher. A sermon which he preached in 1732 upholding the rights of ordinary Church members in ministerial appointments brought him into conflict with the *General Assembly. He and three other ministers felt obliged to 'make a secession' from the 'prevailing party' in the Established Church, forming an 'associate presbytery' in 1733. In 1740 he was formally deposed from his charge. Despite internal divisions, the Seceders soon became a powerful Evangelical force in Scotland.

Erskine, Thomas (1788–1870), Scottish religious thinker. He developed liberal views, finding the meaning of Christianity mainly in its conformity with man's spiritual and ethical needs. In 1831 he championed J. McLeod *Campbell after his deposition by the General Assembly for teaching the universal atonement.

eschatology, the doctrine of the last things, that is the ultimate destiny both of the individual soul and of the whole created order. When the end of the world expected in the early Church did not take place, it became peripheral to most Christian theology. The concept was gradually individualized and the 'Four Last Things' (death, judgement, Heaven, and Hell) formed the subject of *Advent preaching. In the 19th cent. the discovery of early Jewish *Apocalypses drew attention to the eschatological material in Scripture. More significantly, in 1892 J. *Weiss claimed that Christ Himself spoke primarily of God's final intervention; A. *Schweitzer popularized the view of the centrality of the eschatological element in Christ's teaching. Its extent is now a matter of debate (see JESUS CHRIST). C. H. *Dodd eliminated the futuristic element in the phrase '*kingdom of God' (q.v.) by describing Christ's teaching as 'realized eschatology'. K. *Barth reinterpreted biblical eschatology in terms of the presence of eternity and R. *Bultmann in terms of human existence, both losing its future scope. This has been recovered by J. *Moltmann and by *liberation theologians drawing on modern biblical scholarship and also on Marxist categories. See also PAROUSIA.

Esdras, Books of. 'Esdras' is the Greek and Latin form of *Ezra. The *Septuagint contains Esdras A, a Greek Book based on parts of 2 Chron., Ez., and Neh., with an additional story not in the Hebrew; and Esdras B, a straight rendering of the Hebrew of Ez.–Neh. (treated as one Book). In the current form of the *Vulgate I and II Esdras are St *Jerome's rendering of Ez. and Neh., treated as separate Books; III Esdras is the *Old Latin version of Esdras A, and IV Esdras is another Book not extant in Greek. In 1546 III and IV Esdras were rejected from the RC *Canon and in subsequent editions of the Vulgate they appear as an appendix after the NT. In the *Geneva Bible (1560) and subsequent English versions I and II Esdras of the Vulgate are entitled 'Ezra' (q.v.) and 'Nehemiah', while III and IV Esdras are the '1' and '2' Esdras of the *Apocrypha.

1 ESDRAS (i.e. Esdras A of the LXX, III Esdras of the Vulgate, or *The Greek Ezra*),

recounts the story of Israel from Josiah to Ezra. It is mainly composed of matter taken from the Hebrew canonical Books. It is generally dated between c.200 and 50 BC.

2 ESDRAS (IV Esdras of the Vulgate or *The Ezra-Apocalypse*) is composite.: (*a*) 1–2, an introductory section denouncing the sins of Israel and partly based on the NT; (*b*) 3–14, the 'Ezra-Apocalypse' proper, in which the writer relates his visions and discourses with an angel; this section (the oldest part) is generally dated after AD 70 and not later than the reign of Hadrian (117–38); (*c*) 15–16, an appendix, in some MSS reckoned as 'V Esdras'.

Espen, Zeger Bernhard Van. See VAN ESPEN, ZEGER BERNHARD.

Espousals of the BVM. A feast observed in parts of the RC Church on 23 Jan.

Essays and Reviews (1860). A collection of essays by seven Anglican authors who believed in the necessity of free inquiry in religious matters. The liberalism of the book was denounced by S. *Wilberforce; it was condemned by a meeting of bishops in 1861 and synodically condemned in 1864.

Essenes. A Jewish ascetic sect apparently existing from the 2nd cent. BC to the 2nd cent. AD. Their manner of life was highly organized and communistic. Suggestions that figures in the early Church, including Christ Himself, had Essene connections, are unsubstantiated. Many scholars identify the Essenes with the community of the *Dead Sea Scrolls (q.v.).

Establishment. In ecclesiastical usage, the recognition by the State of a particular Church as that of the State. In OT Judaism and in much of the ancient world, religious observance was part of the civil order, but the first move towards the establishment of the Christian Church dates from the time of *Constantine (d. 337); he not only granted *toleration to Christianity, but he gave the Church a favoured position in the Empire and exercised considerable control over its affairs. After the Reformation the RC Church remained the established religion in much of Europe, but was largely under the controlling influence of the Crown. In Protestant States, as the jurisdiction of the Pope was repudiated, national Churches were established, usually with financial support for the Church by the

State and more direct control over appointments and other matters. By the 18th cent. the whole idea of established Churches was being challenged. The American constitution forbade an establishment of religion on principle. The secularization of society in the 19th and 20th cents. has led to the separation of Church and State and the consequent disestablishment of the Church in parts of Europe. In South America, Asia, and Africa the establishment of independent States normally involved the disestablishment of Churches set up by the former colonial power.

In England the C of E is the established Church. The *Supremacy of the Crown Act 1534 declared *Henry VIII 'the only supreme head on earth of the Church of England'; *Elizabeth I was 'supreme governor', as are her successors. In effect this royal supremacy became by the end of the 17th cent. mainly a parliamentary supremacy. After the Reformation the only way to enact new legislation for the Church was by Act of Parliament. While the situation was modified in 1919, Measures approved by the General *Synod take effect only when they receive the Royal Assent (given only when they are approved by Parliament). Since 1974 the General Assembly has been able to legislate by Canon on forms of worship, but Canons still require the Royal Assent. The Crown also has a wide measure of patronage, including the appointment of bishops, in the case of diocesans after consultation with representatives of the Church. And the Church Courts are the Queen's Courts.

Esther, Book of. This relates how Esther, a Jewess, obtained a position of influence as the consort of Xerxes I, King of Persia (486–65 BC, here called 'Ahasuerus') and used it to save her fellow-countrymen when they were in danger of extermination. A popular romance, it was probably included in the *canon of the OT because it described the institution of *Purim.

Estienne, Henri; Robert. See STEPHANUS.

Eternal City, the. A designation of Rome.

eternal life. In Christianity, not only a life of endless duration but the fullness of life of which the believer becomes possessed here and now through participation in God's eternal being.

Ethelbert, St (d. 616), King of Kent from c.560. He married Bertha, daughter of Charibert, the Frankish king; probably under her influence, he welcomed St *Augustine and the Roman mission in 597, was himself converted, and then supported the cause of Christianity in his realm. Feast day, 24 Feb.; in modern calendars, 25 Feb.

Ethelbert, St (d. c.794), King of the East Angles and martyr. He is said to have been treacherously killed by *Offa or his wife, to whose daughter he was to have been betrothed. He was buried at *Hereford (q.v.). Feast day, 20 May.

Ethelburga, St (d. c.676), abbess. The sister of St Erconwald, Bp. of London, she was the first abbess of his *double monastery at Barking. Feast day, 11 Oct.

Etheldreda, St (d. 679), also **Audrey**, founder of *Ely. The daughter of a Christian king of the East Angles, she was married twice, but consummated neither marriage. She became a nun c.672. In 673 she founded a *double monastery at Ely, of which she was abbess until her death. Feast day, 23 June; of her translation, 17 Oct.

Ethelhard (d. 805), Abp. of *Canterbury. He was elected in 791 but not consecrated until 793. The opposition of the Kentish people to a Mercian archbishop broke into open revolt in 796. After a visit to Rome, Ethelbert obtained the abolition of the archiepiscopal status of *Lichfield; the supremacy of Canterbury over the Mercian sees was acknowledged at the Council of *Clovesho in 803.

Ethelwold, St (c.908–84), Bp. of *Winchester from 963. With St *Dunstan and St *Oswald of Worcester, he effected the revival of English monasticism. The *Regularis Concordia is partly, perhaps mainly, his work. He was probably also the author of an account of the monastic revival of his time, and was responsible for translating the Rule of St *Benedict into English. Feast day, 1 Aug.

Etheria. An alternative form of *Egeria.

Ethical Movement. In 1876 the 'Society for Ethical Culture' was founded in the USA by Felix Adler, to unite those who hold that morality is the fundamental element in religion. A corresponding movement begun in Britain in 1887 won less support.

ethics. See MORAL THEOLOGY.

Ethiopian Church, one of the *Oriental Orthodox Churches. Christianity was introduced into Ethiopia in the 4th cent. by St *Frumentius (q.v.) and Edesius of Tyre, and in the early 6th cent. the kingdom of *Axum in N. Ethiopia became an important Christian power. The advent of *Islam led to the decline of the Ethiopian kingdom from the 7th cent. and to its isolation from the rest of the Christian world. After the restoration of the Solomonic dynasty (claiming descent from the Queen of Sheba and *Solomon) in 1270, the Church was revitalized by the reforms of Tekla Haymanot, the founder of the monastery of Debra Libanos, and missionary work was undertaken in the south. In the 16th and 17th cents. the *Portuguese sent military aid and missionaries. In 1626 King Susenyos gave his formal obedience to the Papacy and abjured '*Monophysitism' on behalf of his people. Public outcry led to his abdication and the expulsion of the *Jesuits. The country became closed to missionary activity until the 19th cent. The head of the Ethiopian Orthodox Church was a metropolitan bishop, or '*Abuna', appointed by the *Coptic Orthodox Patriarch until 1959, when the Church became independent; its head now has the title of Patriarch. The liturgical language is Ge'ez, which died out as a spoken language in the early Middle Ages. Judaic features are a distinctive mark of Ethiopian Christianity. The Ethiopian Bible contains some additional items, such as *Jubilees and 1 *Enoch. There is a small *Uniat Ethiopic Church.

Eucharist. (1) NAME. The title 'Eucharist' (meaning 'thanksgiving') for the central act of Christian worship is explained either because at its institution Christ 'gave thanks' or because the service is the supreme act of Christian thanksgiving. Other names are the 'Holy Communion', the '*Lord's Supper', the '*Mass', and in the E. Church, the 'Divine Liturgy'.

(2) ORIGIN. The institution of the Eucharist is recorded by St *Paul in 1 Cor. 11: 23–5 and in the three *Synoptic Gospels. From Acts it is clear that from a very early date it was a regular part of Christian worship and was held to have been instituted by Christ.

(3) DOCTRINE. That the Eucharist conveyed to the believer the Body and Blood of Christ was universally accepted from the first. The Eucharistic elements were themselves commonly referred to as the Body and Blood. During the *patristic period some theologians wrote as if they believed that the bread and wine persisted after the consecration, others as if they held that they were no longer there; there was no attempt at precise definition. After the controversies arising from assertions by *Paschasius Radbertus in the 9th cent. and *Berengar in the 11th, definition was felt to be desirable. The Fourth *Lateran Council (1215) used the term '*transubstantiation' to assert the Real Presence against the *Cathari. Later in the 13th cent. this teaching was worked out in detail; it was maintained that consecration effected a change in the 'substance' of the Bread and Wine, whereas the 'accidents' (i.e. the outward appearance) remained.

At the Reformation there was much controversy on the subject. M. *Luther defended a doctrine of *consubstantiation, according to which after the consecration both the bread and the wine and the Body and Blood of Christ co-existed. U. *Zwingli affirmed that the Lord's Supper was primarily a memorial rite and that there was no change in the elements. J. *Calvin and his followers held an intermediate position. They denied that any change in the elements took place, but maintained that the faithful received the power or virtue of the Body and Blood of Christ, a doctrine which became known as *virtualism. The ambiguous wording of the BCP has permitted the coexistence of a variety of doctrines in the C of E.

From at least the end of the 1st cent. it was also widely held that the Eucharist was in some sense a sacrifice, though here again definition was gradual. This aspect of Eucharistic doctrine was the centre of discussion in the E. Church, and a Council at *Constantinople in 1157 upheld the teaching that the Liturgy makes present the Sacrifice of Christ that is 'eternally celebrated' upon the 'altar on high'. Among the Reformation theologians there was a tendency to deny the sacrifice or to explain it in an unreal sense. The Council of Trent, on the other hand, affirmed that the Sacrifice of the Mass was propitiatory, that it availed for the living and the dead, and that it did not detract from the sufficiency of the Sacrifice of *Calvary.

In the 20th cent. theologians have emphasized the element of *anamnesis (or memorial) as central to an understanding of the Eucharist. The *Anglican-Roman Catholic International Commission achieved a measure of agreement on the subject by stressing the idea of anamnesis, understood as 'the making effective in the present of an event in the past'. The Eucharist is thus presented as 'a means through which the atoning work of Christ on the cross is proclaimed and made effective in the Church'. The *Liturgical Movement emphasized that the Eucharist is a commemoration of the whole paschal mystery and brought out its relation to the corporate nature of the Church and the role of the laity in its celebration. The Second *Vatican Council also stressed the corporate nature of the Eucharist and the sociological significance of Eucharistic worship expressed in the active participation of the people. See also EUCHARISTIC PRAYERS.

Eucharistic fast. By this is commonly understood complete abstinence from food and drink for a period preceding the reception of Communion. The traditional period of the fast in the W. was from the previous midnight. The observance was taken over by the Reformers, but gradually died out among Protestants, though it was encouraged in the C of E by the *Tractarians. In the RC Church in 1964 the period of the fast was reduced to one hour before receiving Communion. In the E. Church a strict fast is observed from bedtime on the previous day.

Eucharistic Prayers. Forms of the central prayer of the *Eucharist. Until well into the 3rd cent. the bishop, as the normal president at the Eucharist, would have improvised the prayer, and the forms that survive from the early period are probably only possible models. The 4th and 5th cents. saw the composition of the prayers in the liturgies ascribed to St *Basil and St John *Chrysostom. In the W. the Roman *Canon of the Mass was virtually the only Eucharistic Prayer in use from the 6th cent. onwards. At the Reformation *Lutherans suppressed all of the Canon except the *Preface and the Words of *Institution; *Reformed Churches often used those Words as a warrant for celebration and had no equivalent to a Eucharistic Prayer. The BCP rearranged the elements of the Canon, inserting the Communion immediately after the Words of Institution. In 1968 the Congregation of Sacred *Rites provided three new Eucharistic Prayers for use in the RC Church as alternatives to the Canon which became, in a slightly revised form, Eucharistic Prayer I. Further Eucharistic Prayers have since been authorized. Provinces of the Anglican Communion have devised a variety of Eucharistic Prayers and liturgical revision has proceeded in most W. Churches.

Eucharistic Prayers normally include the following elements: a thanksgiving for creation and redemption, including the *Sanctus; the Words of Institution; the *Anamnesis; the *Epiclesis; some form of intercession; and a final doxology.

Eucharistic vestments. In the W. the traditional vestments of the celebrant of the Eucharist are the *alb, *amice, *chasuble, *girdle, *maniple, and *stole. They derive from the secular clothing of Roman citizens in the 2nd cent. In the E. Church the vestments are fundamentally the same, though different in shape. In the C of E they fell into disuse after the Reformation; their revival in the 19th cent. aroused controversy, but the 1969 *Canons permit 'an alb with the customary vestments'. See also COPE, ORNAMENTS RUBRIC, and VESTMENTS.

Euchelaion. See UNCTION.

Eucherius, St (d. *c*.450), Bp. of Lyons. With his wife and sons he entered the monastery of *Lérins. He was elected Bp. of Lyons some time between 432 and 441 (when he attended the Synod of *Orange). He wrote exegetical and ascetical works. Feast day, 16 Nov.

Euchites. Another name for the *Messalians.

Euchologion. In the E. Church the book containing the text and rubrics of the three Eucharistic rites in current use, the invariable parts of the Divine *Office, and the prayers required for the administration of the *Sacraments and *Sacramentals.

Eudes, St John (1601–80), French missioner. He joined the *Oratory in 1623; after spending ten years conducting missions, he withdrew in 1643 and founded at Caen the 'Congregation of Jesus and Mary', an association of priests whose object was to run seminaries. He fostered devotion to the *Sacred Heart of Jesus and sought to give it a theological foundation; he also encouraged devotion to the *Sacred Heart of Mary. Feast day, 19 Aug.

Eudists. The common name for members of the 'Congregation of Jesus and Mary', founded by St John *Eudes. After being almost extinguished in the French Revolution, it was reconstituted in 1826 and is engaged mainly in secondary education.

Eugenius III (d. 1153), *Cistercian, Pope from 1145. He was much influenced by St *Bernard, under whom he had entered *Clairvaux in 1135. In 1147 he commissioned him to preach the Second *Crusade. In 1148 he held synods at *Reims, which dealt with the heresy of *Gilbert de la Porrée and the visions of St *Hildegard, and at Cremona, where he excommunicated *Arnold of Brescia. Feast day, 8 July.

Eugenius IV (1383–1447), Pope from 1431. One of his first acts was to dismiss the Council of *Basle, though when it refused to dissolve he recognized it as canonical in 1433. Relations with the Council remained tense and in 1438, against the wishes of the majority, he transferred it to Ferrara and in 1439 to *Florence. The continuing Council at Basle deposed him and elected an antipope in 1439, but the union of the Greek and Roman Churches which Eugenius concluded at Florence, though short-lived, increased his authority. See also FLORENCE, COUNCIL OF.

Eugippius (c.455–c.535), Abbot of Lucullanum, near Naples. He wrote a Life of St *Severinus (c.511) and a monastic Rule. He also made a collection of extracts from the works of St *Augustine and was probably involved in the revision of the *Vulgate text of the Gospels.

eulogia. In early times the word meant a 'blessing' or 'something blessed'. It was applied to the blessed bread distributed to *catechumens and others after the Mass was ended. See also PAIN BÉNIT.

Eunan, St. See ADOMNÁN, ST.

Eunomius (d. 394), *Arian Bp. of Cyzicus. A pupil of *Aetius, he became Bp. of Cyzicus,

probably in 360, but he resigned a few months later. He died in exile at Dakora.

His main work, an 'Ἀπολογητικός (known as his 'First Apology'), is probably the defence of his doctrine which he made at a synod at Constantinople shortly before he resigned. It was answered by *Basil of Caesarea. Eunomius issued a rejoinder (his 'Second Apology'), probably in 378; *Gregory of Nyssa's Contra Eunomium (c.382) was a reply to this work. Eunomius taught a single supreme Substance, whose simplicity is opposed to all distinction; he denied that the generation of the Son took place within the Divine Nature, but regarded Him as being immediately produced by the Father, from whom He received the creative power which caused Him to resemble the Father. The most prominent feature of his teaching is its stress on the importance of exactitude of doctrine for the life of faith. His chief importance lies in the reaction of the *Cappadocian Fathers, whose doctrines of God and human knowledge of God largely took shape as a critique of his teaching.

Euphemia, St (perhaps 4th cent.), virgin and martyr. She was venerated in the E., especially as patroness of the church where the Council met at *Chalcedon in 451. Feast day, 16 Sept.

Europe, Diocese in. A diocese of the C of E, created in 1980 by the union of the jurisdiction of the Bp. of London in Northern and Central Europe with the former extra-Provincial diocese of Gibraltar (founded in 1842); it is officially known as the Diocese of Gibraltar in Europe.

Eusebian Canons and Sections. The system of tables ('canons') devised by *Eusebius of Caesarea to enable the reader of the Gospels to turn up passages ('sections') in other Gospels parallel to the one before him or containing similar matter. The numbering of the sections was formerly attributed to *Ammonius Saccas.

Eusebius (c.260–c.340), Bp. of *Caesarea by 315. During the *Arian controversy he supported Arius and was condemned by the Council of Antioch (324/5). At the Council of *Nicaea (325) he was reinstated when he produced the baptismal creed of Caesarea as evidence of his orthodoxy; he ultimately accepted the *Nicene Creed, but only halfheartedly, and he continued to oppose *Athanasius.

Eusebius's 'Ecclesiastical History' is the main source for the history of Christianity from the Apostolic Age to his own day. It contains a huge range of material on the E. Church, largely in the form of extracts taken over bodily from earlier writers. His other works include 'The Martyrs of Palestine', an account of the *Diocletianic persecution; a 'Chronicle' or summary of universal history with a table of dates; a 'Life of *Constantine', which, though panegyric, contains valuable historical matter; and the 'Preparation for the Gospel' and the 'Demonstration of the Gospel'. The former of these shows why Christians accept the Hebrew and reject the Greek tradition; the latter attempts to prove Christianity from the OT.

Eusebius (mid-5th cent.), Bp. of Dorylaeum (in modern Turkey) by 448, when he attacked the heresy of *Eutyches at the 'Home Synod' in Constantinople. He was deposed by the *Latrocinium (449), but reinstated after the accession of the Emp. *Marcian (450) and took a prominent part in the Council of *Chalcedon (451).

Eusebius (d. c.359), Bp. of Emesa (modern Homs) in Syria. He was a biblical exegete and writer on doctrinal subjects, of *Semiarian sympathies. Having declined the see of *Alexandria when *Athanasius was deposed in 339, he became Bp. of Emesa soon afterwards. Until modern times, only fragments of his works were known, but some 30 sermons have now been ascribed to him. A (quite different) collection of sermons of Gallican provenance has long gone under the name of 'Eusebius'; these are now believed to be derived from *Faustus of Riez.

Eusebius (d. c.342), Bp. of Nicomedia, the leader of the *Arian party. When *Arius turned to him after his condemnation by *Alexander, Bp. of Alexandria, Eusebius was already Bp. of Nicomedia, and he used his influence at court on Arius' behalf. He was exiled soon after the Council of *Nicaea (325), but on his return in 328/9 he led the struggle against *Athanasius. In 337 he baptized the dying *Constantine. Translated to *Constantinople in 339, in 341 he assembled the Dedication Council at *Antioch which marked the beginning of the ascendancy of Arianism.

Eusebius, St (d. 380), Bp. of Samosata by 360. He supported the election of *Melitius to the see of Antioch and shared his subsequent opposition to *Arianism. In 374 he was exiled for his orthodoxy but was recalled four years later. Feast day in E., 22 June; in the W., 21 June.

Eusebius, St (d. 371), Bp. of Vercelli from 340. He was a strong supporter of orthodoxy in the *Arian controversy. Three letters have survived. A treatise *De Trinitate*, traditionally attributed to *Athanasius, has been ascribed to him, though this ascription is disputed. Feast day, 2 Aug. (until 1969, 16 Dec.).

Eustace, St, also **Eustachius**, patron of the city of Madrid and (with St *Humbert) of hunters. His existence is doubtful. He is said to have been a Roman general, converted by a vision of a stag with a crucifix between its antlers, and to have been roasted to death in a brazen bull. Feast day, 20 Sept. (dropped in the W. in 1969).

Eustathius, St, Bp. of *Antioch from c.324 to c.327. At the Council of *Nicaea (325) he was given a place of honour and on his return to his diocese banished many of his clergy suspected of *Arianism. His uncompromising position brought him into conflict with *Eusebius of Caesarea. He was deposed by a Council at Antioch and banished to Thrace. Of his writings only *de Engastrimutho* (against *Origen) survives complete. Feast day, 16 July.

Eustathius (c.300–after 377), Bp. of Sebaste in Pontus from c.357. He was a pupil of *Arius and throughout his life vacillated in his attitude to the *Nicene cause. He took a prominent part in organizing the *monastic movement. In his later years he furthered the *Macedonian heresy.

Eustochium, St Julia (370–c.419), Roman virgin. With her mother, St *Paula, she came under the influence of St *Jerome. A letter which he addressed to her on virginity created such a stir that they left Rome and settled at *Bethlehem. Feast day, 28 Sept.

Euthalius. The reputed author of a collection of editorial material found in many

MSS of the Greek NT. Attached to the Euthalian prologue to the Pauline Epistles is a 'Martyrium Pauli', apparently dated either 458 or 396, but this may not be by the same author.

euthanasia. See DYING, CARE OF THE.

Euthymius, St (377–473), monk. A native of Armenia, he came to *Jerusalem in 405 and established a *lavra at Khanel-Ahmar c.426. He was loyal to the decisions of the Council of *Chalcedon and he exercised a formative influence upon Palestinian monasticism. Feast day, 20 Jan.

Euthymius (mid-11th cent.), monk of the Peribleptos monastery at *Constantinople. He wrote a polemical work against the Phundagiagitae, a sect of the *Bogomils.

Euthymius Zigabenus (early 12th cent.), Byzantine theologian. Nothing is known of his life except that it was at imperial command that he wrote his *Panoplia Dogmatica*, refuting all heresies. The section (27) on the *Bogomils is, with the work of *Euthymius, monk of the Peribleptos, the main source of information about them. He also wrote extensive biblical commentaries.

Eutyches (c.378–454), heresiarch. He was *archimandrite of a monastery at *Constantinople. His opposition to *Nestorius in 448 led to his being accused of the opposite heresy of confounding the two natures in Christ (see CHRISTOLOGY); he was deposed by *Flavian, Abp. of Constantinople, acquitted at the *Latrocinium (449), and deposed and exiled at the Council of *Chalcedon (451). Eutyches affirmed that there was only one 'nature' in the incarnate Christ and denied that His manhood was consubstantial with ours, a view which was held to be incompatible with our redemption through Him. While the *Oriental Orthodox Churches share his language about 'one nature', they explicitly condemned him for his denial that Christ's human nature was consubstantial with ours. See also MONOPHYSITISM.

Eutychianism. See MONOPHYSITISM.

Evagrius Ponticus (346–99), spiritual writer. He was a noted preacher at *Constantinople. In 382 he set out for the *Nitrian desert, where he spent the rest of his life. He worked out an account of the progress of the monk (or hermit) through *apatheia to contemplation. His works include his 'Monachos' or 'Practicos' (on the spiritual life of the monk); 'Gnostic Chapters' (a more advanced treatment of the same subject), prefaced by a brief work called 'The Gnostic'; a treatise 'On Prayer' (at one time attributed to *Nilus of Ancyra); and *Scholia on various biblical Books only discovered in modern times.

Evagrius Scholasticus (c.536–600), Church historian. His History, extending from 431 to 594, uses good sources.

Evangeliary. (1) A book containing the text of the four Gospels. (2) The liturgical book containing the portions of the Gospel to be read at the Eucharist, arranged according to their place in the ecclesiastical year.

Evangelical Alliance. An interdenominational body formed in London in 1846 to 'associate and concentrate the strength of an enlightened *Protestantism against the encroachments of *Popery and *Puseyism, and to promote the interests of a Scriptural Christianity'. In 1951, at a joint meeting of the American National Association of Evangelicals and the British Evangelical Alliance, the World Evangelical Fellowship was founded on similar principles.

Evangelical Association. See the following entry.

Evangelical Church. A small American Protestant body, also known as the **Albright Brethren** after Jacob Albright (1759–1808). Albright, originally a *Lutheran, associated himself with the *Methodist Episcopal Church. In 1796 he began preaching, but, failing to gain the support of his Methodist leaders, he created for his followers an independent organization, known from 1816 as the Evangelical Association. Internal controversies led to a schism; this was healed in 1922 and the reunited body called itself the Evangelical Church. Through mergers with similar bodies, in 1968 it became a part of the United Methodist Church.

Evangelical Church in Germany (*Evangelische Kirche in Deutschland*). The federation of autonomous Protestant territorial Churches in Germany formed in 1945.

Seven of the 27 member Churches were already united in the Evangelical Church of the Union, which included *Lutheran and *Reformed Churches. Within these Churches there is full sacramental fellowship, but the Lutheran Churches are not yet officially in full communion with them or the other Reformed Churches. In 1948 the Lutheran territorial Churches formed the United Evangelical Lutheran Church of Germany within the Evangelical Church in Germany. Attempts to reach a greater measure of unity among the members of the Evangelical Church in Germany, based on the so-called *Leuenberg Concord of 1973, failed to achieve ratification in all the member Churches.

Evangelical Counsels. See COUNSELS OF PERFECTION.

Evangelicalism. (1) The term 'Evangelical' has been applied since the Reformation to the Protestant Churches generally because of their claim to base their teaching pre-eminently on the Gospel.

(2) In Germany and Switzerland 'Evangelical' was long used of the *Lutheran group of Protestant Churches as contrasted with the *Calvinist ('Reformed') Churches.

(3) In the C of E the term is currently applied to the school which lays special stress on personal conversion and salvation by faith in the atoning death of Christ. The group originated in the 18th cent. and had points of contact with the *Methodist movement. C. *Simeon made Evangelicalism a force at Cambridge and indirectly at other universities and prepared clergy and laity for work in the parishes and overseas. Dislike of their religious earnestness led to opposition, but the piety and humanity of the Evangelicals gradually won them a large following.

From c.1830 Anglican Evangelicalism narrowed and there were divisions, especially over belief in the return of Christ before the millennium. There was, however, general acceptance of belief in the verbal inspiration of the Bible and resistance to the findings of science and biblical criticism.With the stress on personal consecration and world evangelism, social and political reform disappeared from the Evangelical programme.

In the 20th cent. there was a deep division between *Liberal Evangelicals, who accepted the findings of biblical criticism, and Conservative Evangelicals who stood firm on the verbal inspiration of Scripture. The latter group experienced a revival in the latter half of the century. The first National Evangelical Anglican Conference at Keele in 1967 broke the isolation of a century. Since then Conservative Evangelicals have taken a full part in the General *Synod and other councils of the C of E, often working with *Anglo-Catholics to oppose liberalism. There has been new concern for politics and social justice and a more positive attitude to the enjoyment of culture.

Evangelical Union. A religious denomination formed in Scotland in 1843 by James *Morison (q.v.). The Union was an association of independent Churches over whom it exercised no jurisdiction; in 1897 most of the Churches in the Union joined the *Congregational Union of Scotland.

Evangelische Bund (Ger., 'Evangelical League'). An alliance of German Protestants founded in 1866–7 by W. *Beyschlag and others to defend Protestant interests against the growing power of Catholicism.

Evangelische Kirche in Deutschland. See EVANGELICAL CHURCH IN GERMANY.

evangelist. (1) In the NT the word is thrice used of a travelling missionary. Probably no specific office is designated. Certain laymen in Protestant Churches who undertake popular preaching are so called. (2) In a more technical sense, the author of one of the four canonical *Gospels.

Evangelistarium. In the *Orthodox Church, a book of tables indicating the Gospel lections for each year in accordance with the varying date of *Easter.

Evangelium Veritatis (Lat., 'The Gospel of Truth'). A *Gnostic treatise included among the Coptic texts found at *Nag Hammadi. It expounds the mission of Jesus as 'the Word' or 'the Name' of the Father and comments on His death and its significance. It includes some unusual features, such as the attribution of evil to Error, personified as a female figure. Some scholars have identified it with a work of this title referred to by *Irenaeus as having been produced by the disciples of *Valentinus. It is sometimes suggested that it was written by Valentinus himself.

Evanson, Edward (1731–1805), Anglican clergyman. After he had resigned his living, he published the earliest formal attack on the traditional authorship of St *John's Gospel.

Eve. The first woman, the wife of *Adam. In the Genesis story (ch. 2 f.), she is tempted to eat the forbidden fruit of the tree of knowledge; she and Adam disobey, '*fall', and are driven out from *Eden; and Eve is punished with the pain of childbirth. She is an important figure in *Feminist Theology.

Evelyn, John (1620–1706), Anglican diarist. Under the Commonwealth he befriended many of the dispossessed clergy. He enjoyed royal favour under *Charles II and *James II and held various appointments. He played a prominent part in Church affairs, especially in the rebuilding of *St Paul's Cathedral. His *Diary* is an important document for social history.

evening Communion. There are possible references to evening celebrations of the Eucharist in the NT, but it seems that an early hour soon became the usual time. After the Reformation some Protestant Churches celebrated the Lord's Supper in the morning and evening indiscriminately. In the RC Church rules about the *Eucharistic fast were relaxed during the Second World War and evening Masses were permitted in military establishments; they are now common in all churches. In the C of E celebrations of the Eucharist in the evening (introduced in 1852) were a mark of *Low Churchmanship until the mid-20th cent., but are no longer so.

Evening Prayer. See EVENSONG. The name is also sometimes used for the RC evening *Office (Vespers) in the 1971 Breviary.

Evensong. The common name for the C of E service of Evening Prayer. The office in the BCP consists basically of Psalms, a reading from the OT, the *Magnificat, a reading from the NT, the *Nunc Dimittis, the *Apostles' Creed, and prayers. In substance it is a conflation of *Vespers and *Compline. Modern Anglican liturgies have introduced changes, mainly in the direction of curtailment and the provision of alternatives.

Evergetinos, Paul (d. 1054), compiler of an influential monastic *florilegium. After founding a monastery near *Constantinople, *c.*1050 he put together a selection of spiritual texts; it was called by him *Synagoge* but is usually referred to as the *Evergetinon*.

Ewald, Heinrich Georg August (1803–75), German OT theologian and orientalist. His 'Hebrew Grammar' (1827) was a landmark in the history of OT philology, while his History of Israel influenced British scholarship. He exercised a restraining influence on the negative tendencies of OT criticism.

Exaltation of the Cross. The feast in honour of the Cross of Christ, observed on 14 Sept., and also known as 'Holy Cross Day'. In the W. Church it now commemorates the exposition of the supposed true Cross at Jerusalem in 629 after its recovery from the Persians.

examining chaplains. In the C of E the duty of examining candidates for holy orders properly belongs to the *archdeacons, but other ministers are also appointed for this purpose.

exarch. The title of: (1) certain civil governors in the later Roman Empire; (2) certain bishops lower in rank than *patriarchs but having rights over the *metropolitans in one civil diocese.

excardination. In W. canon law the liberation of a cleric from his present *Ordinary with a view to fresh enlistment (*incardination) under a new superior.

ex cathedra. See CATHEDRA.

Exceptions. The list of objections made by the *Puritans at the *Savoy Conference (1661) to the existing BCP (of 1604) with a view to its revision.

Exclusion, Right of. The right formerly claimed by the heads of certain Catholic States to name a particular candidate whom they desired to exclude from being elected Pope. It was annulled in 1904.

Exclusion Controversy. After T. *Oates's announcement of the *Popish Plot, the Whigs tried to exclude James, Duke of York (later *James II), from the succession to the throne. Bills to exclude James were rejected in 1679 and 1680.

excommunication. An ecclesiastical censure which excludes those subject to it from the communion of the faithful and imposes certain other deprivations and disabilities. It does not profess to extend to the union of the soul with God. In the RC Church it is now one of the 'medicinal' *penalties. It is either declared or imposed by an ecclesiastical authority, or incurred automatically, e.g. by procuring an abortion. All excommunicated persons are forbidden to celebrate the Sacraments or receive them (except when in danger of death), to take any ministerial part in public worship, or exercise any ecclesiastical office or act of government. If the excommunication has been imposed or declared, some additional consequences follow. In the C of E the BCP and the 1969 *Canons envisage the possibility of excommunication, but its use is now very rare.

exegesis. The act of explaining a text, in theology usually a sacred text. The purpose may be either to describe the author's meaning or to apply that meaning to a contemporary situation.

Biblical exegesis has been practised from early times by both Jews and Christians. In conflict with *Gnostic exegetes, Christian writers insisted that the meaning must be elucidated in conformity with apostolic tradition. A chiefly *allegorical mode of interpretation was fostered by the *Alexandrian school, while that of *Antioch cultivated the explanation of the literal sense of the Bible. In the W. the *Schoolmen favoured the fourfold method of literal, allegorical, moral, and analogical (or mystical) exegesis; their chief contribution was an increase in the systematization of materials and in logical order. At the Reformation many Protestant theologians rejected the authority of the Church's tradition as a criterion of exegesis, substituting the interior witness of the Holy Spirit. It was among Protestants that literary and historical criticism first came to be practised. It emerged strongly in Germany in the 18th cent. From the beginning of the 19th cent. much attention was given to the origin, nature, and history of individual biblical documents and to the reconstruction of biblical history, including the life of Jesus. With notable exceptions among the *Modernists, RC exegesis until fairly recent times largely ignored or reacted against critical Biblical scholarship, but a new openness and independence is now apparent. See also HERMENEUTICS.

exemplarism. The view of the *Atonement which holds that the value of the death of Christ for us lies purely in the moral example which it sets us of complete love and self-surrender, thus moving our imagination and will to repentance and holiness.

exemption. In an ecclesiastical sense, freedom from control by one's normal superior (usually the bishop of the diocese) and hence in general immediate subjection either to the superior of one's religious house or order, or to the Pope. The term 'exempt' is also applied to dioceses which are not subject to a metropolitan but are directly under the *Holy See. The increasing number of exemptions in the Middle Ages became a cause of friction between the bishops and religious orders; they were restricted by the Council of *Trent. The legal impact of exemption was somewhat changed by the 1983 *Codex Iuris Canonici which subordinated it to the rightful autonomy of life enjoyed by all *Institutes of Consecrated Life.

exequatur (Lat., 'he may perform'). The right, also known as the 'Regium Placet', claimed by certain governments to prevent ecclesiastical enactments of the Roman see from taking automatic effect in their territories.

Exeter. By c.680 a monastery had been established within the walls of the Roman settlement. Although later refounded and restored, it was in decay by 1050 when Bp. Leofric of *Crediton, who combined the dioceses of Devon and Cornwall, converted Exeter into a new see, safe from Viking attack. Of the Norman cathedral only the towers remain; most of the present cathedral is in the decorated style. Notable are the *miserere seats, a clock made at *Glastonbury in 1285, the bishop's throne, and the 14th–15th cent. image screen across the west front.

Exile, the. The phrase is used absolutely of the captivity of the Jews in Babylon from c.586 to c.539 BC.

Existentialism. Certain types of philosophical thinking which share a practical concern for the individually existing person and his freedom. The contemporary movement goes back to S. *Kierkegaard, F. W. *Nietzsche, and E. Husserl, whose *Phenomenology provided a systematic method of describing the universal elements in human consciousness. The main body of Existentialist thinking seems to derive from the discovery of Kierkegaard by philosophers in Germany in the early 20th cent. and from the shattering of cultural values in Europe after the First World War.

The question of a Christian Existentialism has been prominent in Protestant theological debate. Opponents have claimed that Existentialism reduces theology to anthropology, dissolves the historical foundations of Christianity, and treats salvation as only a self-generated decision in favour of authentic existence. Supporters have held that an Existentialist standpoint is implicit in the NT, and that to acknowledge the salvation event as part of history only serves to confirm the radical nature of faith, locating salvation not in external events but in an encounter between God and our personal existence. Existentialism was condemned by the encyclical 'Humani Generis' (1950), but it continued to influence some RC theologians.

Exodus, Book of. This OT Book records the events attending the 'Exodus' (i.e. the release of the Israelites under *Moses from their Egyptian bondage) and the giving of the Law on Mount *Sinai. Its authorship has traditionally been ascribed to Moses. Modern scholars assign the Book to a later time than that of Moses, some holding it to be a composite work, its strata probably having been written between the 9th and 5th cents. BC. The date of the Exodus is also debated, but most scholars favour the 13th cent. BC. The deliverance has throughout Jewish history been regarded as the outstanding instance of God's favour to His chosen people; Christian writers have used the imagery of the *Passover with reference to the sacrifice of Christ on Calvary and of the *Eucharist. In modern times the Exodus has become a symbol of liberation for many groups, from *Black Christians in the USA to *Liberation theologians in Latin America.

ex opere operato. A term used by theologians to express the essentially objective mode of operation of the Sacraments, and its independence of the subjective attitudes of either the minister or the recipient.

exorcism. The practice of expelling evil spirits by means of prayer and set formulas was common among Jews and pagans. From NT times the Church has exorcized persons possessed of an evil spirit. The RC Church provides for such a rite, but restricts its use to priests specifically authorized by the bishop. A revival of the practice of exorcism in the C of E led to the issue of guidelines by the Abp. of *Canterbury in 1975; on the basis of these, diocesan bishops formulated policy for their own dioceses.

Exorcism has also been applied to *catechumens; it is included in the 1972 RC Order for Adult Initiation and the 1969 Order for the Baptism of Infants, though in the latter case it may be omitted. The Baptismal exorcisms are prayers asking for the restraint of the powers of evil.

exorcist. The second of the traditional *Minor Orders. The duties of the exorcist came to include the imposition of hands on '*energumens' and the exorcizing of *catechumens. In the RC Church the office was suppressed in 1972.

expectant, the Church. The body of Christians waiting between earth and heaven, in what is traditionally called *purgatory.

expiation. The atoning or making up for an offence committed against God or one's neighbour. Christianity claims that the only sufficient expiation of human sin is the offering made by Christ of His earthly life and death, and that the merits of this offering are infinite. See also ATONEMENT.

Expiation, Day of. An alternative name for the Day of *Atonement.

Exposition of the Blessed Sacrament. Exposition of the Blessed Sacrament as a service apart from Mass dates from the late 14th cent. In modern RC practice there are two forms of exposition: (1) the solemn form when a large Host is exposed to view in a *monstrance, placed on or above the altar, surrounded by lights and often flowers, and censed; and (2) the simple form in which the *ciborium containing Hosts for Communion is shown at the open doors of the *tabernacle. The rite concludes with the blessing of the people with the Host (veiled in the simple form of exposition). In the past the blessing was often given after only a short period of exposition, in a form of the service known as '*Benediction of the Blessed Sacrament'; it is now forbidden to give the blessing on its own. See also FORTY HOURS' DEVOTION.

Exsurge, Domine. The bull issued by *Leo X in 1520 threatening to excommunicate M.*Luther. Luther broke with the Papacy by publicly burning the bull.

extra-liturgical services. Services for which no fixed form is provided in the authorized liturgical formularies.

Extravagantes. The term, at one time applied to certain officially recognized Papal *decretals which were not included in the 'Decretum' of *Gratian ('extra decretum vagantes'), is now used almost exclusively of the two concluding sections of the *Corpus Iuris Canonici (q.v.).

Extreme Unction. See UNCTION.

Exultet. In the W. liturgy the 'Paschal Proclamation' sung by the deacon standing near the *Paschal Candle on *Holy Saturday, and so named from its opening word.

On the 'Exultet Rolls' the text was divided into sections interspersed with pictures disposed in the reverse way from the text, so that the picture might be the right way up for the congregation when the part of the roll that had been read was slipped over the back of the *ambo.

Exuperius, St (d. after 410), Bp. of Toulouse, to whom *Innocent I addressed an important letter. Feast day, 28 Sept.

Eyck, Hubert and **Jan Van.** See VAN EYCK, HUBERT and JAN.

Ezekiel, Book of. One of the three 'Major' Prophetic Books of the OT. It prophesies

the destruction of *Jerusalem and Judah at the hands of the Babylonians, doom for various foreign nations, and the redemption and restoration of the Jewish people. It ends with a vision of the ideal *theocracy and especially the form and worship of the restored *Temple.

Ezekiel was a Jerusalem priest, probably taken captive to Babylon in 597 BC. His experience there seems to have convinced him of the universality of God's rule. Traditionally the whole Book was regarded as the work of Ezekiel. A majority of scholars now regard the bulk of the Book as coming from Ezekiel, with most of the rest deriving from prophetic circles influenced by the tradition of his words. A few regard only a small part as going back to Ezekiel or question whether he was ever in Babylon at all. The Book had great influence in post-Exilic Israel.

Eznik (5th cent.), Bp. of Bagrevand in *Armenia. He wrote a *Confutation of the Sects* and took part in translating the Armenian version of the Bible.

Ezra. Jewish priest and scribe. His activities are recorded in the Books of *Ezra and Nehemiah and 1 *Esdras. He took measures to ensure the racial purity and distinctiveness of the Jewish people. The traditional date of his arrival in *Jerusalem is 458 BC, but it may have been 428 or 398, making him later than *Nehemiah.

Ezra and **Nehemiah, Books of.** These OT Books continue the story of the Hebrew people begun in *Chronicles. Ez. relates the return of the exiles from Babylon, their efforts to rebuild the *Temple, and *Ezra's mission and work. Neh. relates *Nehemiah's plans for the restoration of *Jerusalem and arrangements for the occupation of the city. Modern scholars generally hold that the compiler of these Books wrote at a date later than that of Ezra and Nehemiah, though opinion is divided as to whether he was also the author of Chron. See also ESDRAS, BOOK OF.

F

Faber, Frederick William (1814–63), *Oratorian. Brought up a *Calvinist, he came under the influence of J. H. *Newman at Oxford and was ordained in the C of E. In 1845 he became a RC. With other converts he formed a small community, which in 1848 joined the Oratory of St *Philip Neri; the next year Faber became head of the London house. He wrote many hymns and devotional books.

Faber, Jacobus (c.1455–1536), also known as **Lefèvre d'Étaples** or **Stapulensis**, French humanist. Two critical essays on St *Mary Magdalene led to his condemnation by the *Sorbonne for heresy in 1521; he had to leave France in 1525. He never accepted the Reformers' main doctrines, and his attitude to the Reformation has been compared with that of *Erasmus. He published the first printed text of the (Latin) *Ignatian Epistles (1498) and a French translation of the *Vulgate (NT, 1523; OT, 1528).

Faber, Johann (1478–1541), Bp. of Vienna from 1530. His friendship with *Erasmus led him at first to sympathize with P. *Melanchthon and U. *Zwingli in their desire for reform, but as the doctrinal cleavage became clear he withdrew his support and defended Catholic orthodoxy.

Fabian, St (d. 250), Bp. of Rome from 236. When the *Decian *persecution broke out in 250, he was among the first to suffer martyrdom. Feast day, 20 Jan.

Fabri, Felix (1438–1502), a learned *Dominican who has left a vivid record of his journeys in 1480 and 1483–4 to Egypt and the Holy Land.

Fabricius, Johannes Albert (1668–1736), German *Lutheran scholar. His *Bibliotheca Graeca* (1705–28), covering the period from Homer to 1453, and a corresponding survey of Latin writing, laid the foundations for subsequent histories of literature. He did important work on the *Apocrypha and in 1716–18 he produced the first edition of the works of *Hippolytus.

Faculties, Court of. The court established in 1534 when the granting of *dispensations, licences, and *faculties in the provinces of *Canterbury and *York was transferred from the Pope to the Abp. of Canterbury.

faculty. A dispensation or licence from an ecclesiastical superior permitting someone to perform an action or occupy a position which without it he could not lawfully do or hold. In 1534 the 'Court of *Faculties' was created to restrain people from suing for dispensations from Rome. Since in every diocese the consecrated lands and buildings and their contents are in the ultimate guardianship of the Bishop, faculties are needed for additions or alterations to churches or churchyards; in such cases they are normally issued by the Bishop's *Chancellor or, since 1991, in uncontested cases by the *Archdeacon.

In the academic world a faculty is an organization for the teaching of a particular subject, so called because it can grant a faculty to receive or supplicate for a degree.

Facundus (6th cent.), Bp. of Hermiane in Africa. In the *Monophysite controversy he was one of the chief supporters of the *Three Chapters. He went to *Constantinople and there in 547–8 he completed a treatise upholding the orthodoxy of *Ibas, *Theodore of Mopsuestia (with some reservations), and *Theodoret. After his return to Africa and the anathematization of the Three Chapters, he defended himself in two further works (c.571).

Fairbairn, Andrew Martin (1838–1912), *Congregational theologian. He was the first principal of Mansfield College, Oxford (1886–1909). After visiting Germany, he warmly advocated theological liberalism. His eloquence, learning and personal character won him a unique position among Congregational ministers of his generation.

faith. The term is used in two distinct senses.

(1) The body of truth ('the Christian faith') to be found in the *Creeds, the definitions of *Councils, etc., and especially in

the Bible. This complex of doctrine is held to embody or to follow from the teaching of Christ and to be wilfully rejected by man only at the peril of his salvation.

(2) To this objective faith is opposed 'subjective' faith. This is the human response to Divine truth, depicted in the NT as involving trust in God rather than intellectual assent. According to orthodox theologians, it is a supernatural, not a natural, act, and is dependent on God's action in the soul. It nevertheless demands an act of will. This voluntaristic movement in the act of faith accounts for the moral quality which it is held to possess and the conviction that wilful unbelief merits the censure of God. In the Middle Ages a distinction was drawn between those truths accessible to the human intellect by the light of natural reason, e.g. the existence of God, and those which could be appropriated only by faith, e.g. belief in the *Trinity. At the Reformation faith received a new emphasis. M. *Luther's teaching on *justification by 'faith alone' stressed the voluntaristic side of faith, in so far as faith was allowed to be a human act at all. The chief moment in it was trust, a supremely personal trust in the atoning work of Christ. The old opposition between faith and knowledge re-emerged in such thinkers as I. *Kant and S. *Kierkegaard, for whom faith is so contrasted with knowledge as to be a subjective attitude without objective content. In the RC Church the Second *Vatican Council initiated a new phase in the inter-confessional exploration of faith. It conceived of the 'truth' of 'the Gospel' in less exclusively propositional terms than previous theologians had done, and it recognized the importance of *conscience, so that people must be called to affirmations of faith willingly.

Faith, Defender of the and **Promoter of the.** See DEFENDER OF THE FAITH and PROMOTOR FIDEI.

Faith, St (d. c.287), virgin and martyr. According to late legend she suffered for the faith at Agen in Aquitaine. Her relics were brought c.855 to the abbey of Conques, which became a famous place of pilgrimage. Feast day, 6 Oct.

Faith and Order. The branch of the *Ecumenical Movement by which Conferences were organized at *Lausanne in 1927 and at *Edinburgh in 1937. It was absorbed into the *World Council of Churches.

Faithful, Mass of the. The part of the *Eucharist from the *Offertory to the end, so called because in early times only the baptized (the faithful) remained for the central part of the service.

falda. A white vestment formerly sometimes worn over the *alb by the Pope.

faldstool. In the RC Church a folding stool used in the *sanctuary by bishops and other prelates when not occupying the throne.

Falk, Paul Ludwig Adalbert (1827–1900), German Liberal politician. From 1872 to 1879 he was Minister of Public Worship and Education, appointed with explicit instructions to defend the State against the Church in the *Kulturkampf. His *May Laws failed because of opposition from orthodox Protestants as well as RCs.

Fall, the. The first act of disobedience of *Adam and *Eve whereby humanity lost its primal innocence. According to Gen. 2 f., Eve, tempted by a serpent, ate the forbidden fruit of the 'tree of the knowledge of good and evil' and induced Adam to do likewise. The punishment was expulsion from the Garden of *Eden, the imposition of toilsome work on Adam and the pains of childbirth on Eve, and the decree of perpetual enmity between the serpent and man. The biblical narrative teaches that sin arose by human choice and that all human life has thereby been radically changed for the worse, so that its actual state is different from that purposed for it by the Creator.

Until modern times the common Christian belief regarded the Fall of Adam and Eve as a historical event. The serpent was identified with the *Devil, a spiritual being who must have been created good and himself previously fallen, and hence the original Fall was inferred to be that of Satan rather than of Adam and Eve. Since all subsequent humanity was believed to have descended from Adam and Eve, the consequences of the Fall were held to affect all mankind by inheritance. While the Greek Fathers tended to minimize the evil done to man by the sin of Adam and stress the responsibility of each individual, the Latins (especially St *Augustine), emphasizing the enormity of Adam's transgression and its consequences for mankind, developed the doctrine of *original sin (q.v.). Though in modern times the concept of the Fall has often been held to be inconsistent with the facts of man's development known to science, orthodox theologians still see in the story of Gen. 2 f. a fundamental truth about man in his relation to God, even if the truth is now held to be there conveyed in legendary form.

False Decretals. A collection of *canon law documents ascribed to '*Isidore Mercator' but really compiled *c.*850, probably in France. In its fullest form it contains three sections, the second and third of which are based on genuine canons of councils and decretals, much interpolated. The first section consists of letters in the names of Popes from *Clement I to *Miltiades (d. 314) and includes the *Donation of Constantine; all are spurious. They show concern for the rights of diocesan bishops against their metropolitans and against the laity, and for Papal supremacy as their guarantee.

Familists. Members of a sect called the 'Family of Love', founded by H. *Nicholas at Emden in 1540. They believed in the '*Inner Light' and the birth of Christ in their souls; they rejected the services and sacraments of the Churches but were advised to conform outwardly to the religion of the State. The sect disappeared in the 17th cent.

fan, liturgical. From at least the 4th cent. fans were sometimes used at the Eucharist to keep insects away from the oblations. Their surviving use in some E. Churches is now purely symbolic.

fanon. The word has been applied to various accessories of religious worship, but it is now confined to the collar-shaped garment until recently worn by the Pope over his *amice when celebrating a solemn pontifical Mass.

Farel, Guillaume (1489–1565), Reformer. He came under the influence of J. *Faber (Stapulensis) and adopted Protestantism in the early 1520s. He prepared the first Protestant liturgy in French and in 1529 published his famous *Sommaire*, a declaration of Protestant belief. He introduced the Ref-

ormation in Neuchâtel in 1530, and with P. *Viret established it in the Canton of Vaud and in 1534–6 in *Geneva. He later returned to Neuchâtel, where he put into practice the Genevan Reformation model.

farmery, another form of 'infirmary', especially of a monastery.

Farrar, Frederic William (1831–1903), Dean of *Canterbury from 1895. A 'Broad Church Evangelical', he had great influence on the religious feeling and culture of the Victorian middle class, especially through his *Life of Christ* (1874) and *Life and Works of St Paul* (1879).

fast. See FASTS AND FASTING.

Fastidius (early 5th cent.), British ecclesiastical writer. *Gennadius calls him a bishop and attributes to him two works, *De vita christiana* and *De viduitate servanda*; their identity is disputed, but they are often thought to be *Pelagian works.

fasts and **fasting.** Fasting, as a penitential discipline, is designed to strengthen the spiritual life by weakening the attractions of sensible pleasures. It was practised in Judaism and apparently recommended by Christ both by example and teaching. In the early Church regular weekly fast days soon developed, notably *Friday and *Wednesday, and for some time in the W. *Saturday. The fast of *Lent came to extend to 40 days before *Easter. The E. Church added three further periods of fasting.

In early times fasting meant complete abstinence from food during the whole or part of the fast day and, in the latter case, a restricted diet. In the E. it is still observed with considerable strictness. In modern RC practice fasting generally means one chief meal with a light '*collation' in the morning and evening. The only universally binding Fast Days in the RC Church now are *Ash Wednesday and *Good Friday. In the C of E the BCP contains a 'Table of the Vigils, Fasts and Days of Abstinence', but no specific instructions are given for the mode of their observance. See also ABSTINENCE.

Father. Originally the title of bishops, the word was later applied to confessors, called in medieval England 'ghostly fathers'. In England all RC priests, whether secular or religious, are now called 'Father'; this usage is also found among Anglo-Catholics.

Fathers, Apostolic; White. See APOSTOLIC FATHERS; WHITE FATHERS.

Fathers of the Church. From the late 4th cent. the title has been used of an indeterminate group of ecclesiastical writers of the past whose authority on doctrinal matters carried special weight; they were held to be characterized by orthodoxy of doctrine, holiness of life, the approval of the Church, and antiquity. The *patristic period is commonly regarded as closing with St *Isidore of Seville in the W. and St *John of Damascus in the East. Among the Orthodox, however, no such limitation is found.

Fatima. A place of pilgrimage in Portugal. In 1917 three illiterate children saw visions of a woman, who declared herself to be 'Our Lady of the Rosary', told them to recite the *Rosary daily, and asked for a chapel to be built in her honour.

Faulhaber, Michael von (1869–1952), German cardinal. He became Abp. of Munich in 1917 and was created cardinal in 1921. In his earlier years he made some important contributions to patristic studies; later he was the leader of the right-wing German Catholics and, though originally impressed by Hitler, he became an outspoken critic of the Nazis.

Faustus of Milevis (4th cent.), *Manichaean propagandist. He won fame at Rome, but when he visited Carthage in 383, *Augustine, himself then a Manichee, found him a fraud.

Faustus of Riez, St (d. *c.*490), theologian. A monk of *Lérins, *c.*460 he became Bp. of Riez (in Provence), but was later driven from his see because of his opposition to the Visigothic king's *Arianizing policy. In his *De Gratia*, he adopted a *Semipelagian position, insisting on the need for human co-operation with Divine grace, and on the initial free will of man, even when in sin, for the acceptance of that grace. A collection of Gallic sermons transmitted under the name of *Eusebius (of Emesa) may be partly based on his work. Feast day, 28 Sept.

Fawkes, Guy (1570–1606), the most famous member of the *Gunpowder Plot conspiracy. He was given the task of firing the gunpowder, but he was arrested while keeping watch.

Fayûm Gospel Fragment. A 3rd-cent. papyrus fragment, discovered in 1882, which contains an imperfect account of the prediction of St *Peter's denial, akin to Mk. 14: 27–30.

feasts, ecclesiastical. These come under three main headings:

(1) *SUNDAYS, the weekly commemoration of the Resurrection.

(2) MOVABLE FEASTS. The most important are *Easter, the annual commemoration of the Resurrection, and *Whitsunday (q.v.). Certain other feasts vary with the date of Easter.

(3) IMMOVABLE FEASTS. The earliest were probably the anniversaries of *martyrs, to which other saints' days were added later. By the 4th cent. various fixed feasts of the Lord, notably *Christmas and the *Epiphany, became generally observed.

See also FESTUM, MEMORIA, SOLEMNITAS, and YEAR, LITURGICAL.

Feasts of Obligation. In the RC Church, feasts of outstanding importance which the laity as well as the clergy are obliged to observe by hearing Mass on the day itself or on the previous evening and by abstaining from 'work or business that would inhibit the worship to be given to God, the joy proper to the Lord's Day, or the due relaxation of mind and body'.

Feathers Tavern Petition (1772). A petition to Parliament for the abolition of subscription to the *Thirty-Nine Articles and its replacement by a simple declaration of belief in the Bible. It was signed at the Feathers Tavern, Strand, London.

Febronianism. The movement in the RC Church in 18th-cent. Germany against the claims of the Papacy, especially in the temporal sphere. In 1763 J. N. von *Hontheim, who had been asked by the three Archbishop-Electors to investigate their grievances against Rome, published his findings under the pen-name 'Justinus Febronius'. The Archbishop-Electors tried unsuccessfully to assert their claims at Bad *Ems in 1786.

Felicity, St (2nd cent.), Roman martyr. According to her *acta*, she was martyred with her seven sons. She may be the Felicity named in the *Canon of the Mass. Feast day, 23 Nov.

Felicity, St (d. 203), African martyr. She was one of the companions of St *Perpetua. Feast day, 7 (formerly 6) Mar.

Felix, St (d. *c*.648), Bp. of Dunwich. After converting the East Anglian prince Sigeberht, then in exile, to Christianity, he successfully preached the Gospel to the heathen in East Anglia. Feast day, 8 Mar.

Felix (d. 818), Bp. of Urgel in Spain and one of the leaders of the *Adoptianist heresy. He was charged as a heretic at the Council of Ratisbon (792) and recanted. He later became convinced of his heresy again and was unmoved by the criticism of his doctrine written by *Alcuin. He was formally accused at the Councils of *Frankfurt (794) and Aachen (799 or 800); at the latter he again recanted.

Fell, John (1625–86), Bp. of *Oxford from 1676. Under the Commonwealth he helped maintain C of E services in a private house, and in 1660 he became Dean of *Christ Church. He largely brought about the re-imposition of Anglican orthodoxy on the University.

Feminist Theology. A theological movement of various strands united in a determination to secure social justice for women. Its origins may be traced to 19th-cent. social campaigns, but it was only after the end of the Second World War (1945), and particularly in the 1980s, that it posed a serious challenge within the Christian tradition. Here the central issue is the unease about associating the female or feminine with the godlike. Since it is agreed that God transcends both sex and gender, feminist theologians argue for a humanly inclusive theology, the 'envisioning' of God in a gender-inclusive way. The stumbling-blocks to attributing the full 'image of God' to women are held to be fourfold; failure to find the feminine in God; insistence that woman is derivative and hence secondary to man; the assumption that woman is characterized by passivity; and the tendency to identify women with bodiliness as opposed to the transcendent mind. It is claimed that the modern acknowledgement of the equal importance of the part of women in human reproduction (where the male was previously considered the primary source) has wide implications, including that of appropriate language for God,

notably metaphors of mother/father. Feminist theologians are also concerned about other groups held to have been devalued, and about complications of race and class. They seek the integration of ethics with theology, especially in relation to such issues as pregnancy-termination, the use of fetal tissue, and artificially assisted human reproduction, and they emphasize the values of which women are culturally the bearers, such as care and interdependence. Feminist theology is influential in ecclesiastical life as a movement in active lay theology and spirituality. See also WOMEN, ORDINATION OF.

Fénelon, François de Salignac de la Mothe (1651–1715), Abp. of Cambrai. From 1678 he was involved with those converted from Protestantism, and in 1689 he was appointed tutor to Louis XIV's grandson. He met Mme *Guyon in 1688; he was impressed by her account of her spiritual experiences and especially by her doctrine of pure love and 'passive prayer'. He long defended her and was therefore implicated when she was censured in 1694. In 1695 he became Abp. of Cambrai and signed the Articles of *Issy condemning *Quietism. In 1697, however, he published *Explication des maximes des saints*, defending the concept of disinterested love. It was attacked by J.-B. *Bossuet and a bitter controversy followed. When 23 propositions from the work were condemned by Pope Innocent XII in 1699, Fénelon submitted. He was much sought after as a spiritual director and his spiritual writing remained influential in the 18th cent.

Feophan the Recluse, St. See THEOPHAN THE RECLUSE, ST.

Ferdinand II (1578–1637), Holy Roman Emperor; one of the main upholders of the *Counter-Reformation. He had already done much to re-establish Catholicism in Inner Austria when he became Emperor in 1619 and set about extirpating Protestantism from all the Habsburg domains. The attempt of the Protestants of Bohemia to replace him with the Calvinist Elector Palatine *Frederick III was repressed, but Ferdinand's decision to punish Frederick broadened the conflict into the *Thirty Years War. After Catholic military successes his 'Edict of Restitution' (1629) ordered Protestants to restore appropriated ecclesiastical property in their dominions; the Protestants rebelled and under *Gustavus Adolphus nearly overthrew the Emperor. See also THIRTY YEARS WAR.

Ferdinand V (1452–1516), 'the Catholic', King of Castile and León and II of Aragon. In 1469 he married his cousin *Isabella, the disputed heiress of the Castilian throne. They defeated her rival and ruled jointly in Castile and later in Aragon, where Ferdinand inherited his father's throne in 1479. As a consequence of his political skills he was enshrined in Machiavelli's *Prince*. For his conquest of the Moors of Granada in 1492 and his zeal for the Spanish *Inquisition, he and Isabella were called the '*Catholic Kings' by *Alexander VI.

feretory. A *shrine in which a saint's relics are deposited and venerated.

feria. While in classical Latin the word means 'feast day' or 'holiday', in ecclesiastical usage it is applied to such days (other than Saturdays and Sundays) on which no feast falls.

Fermentum. In Rome (5th cent.), fragments of the Bread of the Eucharist sent on Sundays from the Papal Mass to presbyters in the parish churches to typify the unity of the faithful in Christ.

Ferrandus (d. before April 548), deacon of the Church of *Carthage. His *Breviatio canonum* is an epitome of canons of early Councils.

Ferrar, Nicholas (1592–1637), founder of *Little Gidding. He was elected a Fellow of Clare Hall, Cambridge, was Deputy-Treasurer of the Virginia Company, and was elected a member of Parliament. In 1625 he settled at Little Gidding, where other members of his family joined him to establish a kind of community life in accordance with the principles of the C of E. He was made deacon in 1626. Under his direction the household lived a life of prayer and work under a strict rule. Feast day in CW, 4 Dec.; in the American BCP (1979), 1 Dec.

Ferrara-Florence, Council of. See FLORENCE, COUNCIL OF.

festivals. See FEASTS.

festum (Lat., 'feast'). The name given in current RC liturgical documents to festivals of intermediate importance.

Feuerbach, Ludwig Andreas (1804–72), German philosopher. He sought to recast the teaching of G. W. F. *Hegel in a positivistic sense hostile to Christianity. Rejecting all belief in transcendence, he held that theology and philosophy were properly concerned only with the nature of man.

Feuillants. The reformed *Cistercians of Le Feuillant (near Toulouse) founded in 1577 by Abbot J. de la Barrière, who established in the house a new rule stricter than the original. The Order became independent in 1589 but came to an end during the Napoleonic wars.

Fichte, Johann Gottlieb (1762–1814), Idealist philosopher. He was appointed professor of philosophy at Jena in 1794 but was dismissed for atheism in 1799. From 1809 he was a professor at Berlin.

Fichte held that the objects of our knowledge are the products of the consciousness of the ego. This ego, however, is not the individual 'I', but the Absolute Ego, which can be known only by philosophical intuition. It develops in three phases. In the first it posits itself, in the second it posits a non-ego against itself, and in the last it posits itself as limited by the non-ego. According to Fichte God is the Absolute Ego, 'the living operative moral order'; but He is not to be conceived as personal. True religion consists in 'joyously doing right'. When society has reached a condition in which morality is the norm, the Church will be unnecessary.

Ficino, Marsilio (1433–99), Italian humanist and philosopher. He came under the patronage of Cosimo de' Medici, who wanted to found a Platonic Academy at Florence; Ficino became its head. He studied Greek and embarked on a fresh translation of *Plato (1484). Ficino, who was ordained in 1473, expounded his synthesis of Christianity and Greek mysticism in *De Religione Christiana* (1476). His main philosophical work, *Theologia Platonica de Immortalitate Animorum* (written between 1469 and 1474; published in 1482), was largely based on Plato's *Phaedo*. He also translated into Latin works of *Plotinus, *Porphyry, and *Dionysius the Pseudo-Areopagite.

Fidei Defensor. See DEFENDER OF THE FAITH.

Fideism. Various doctrines which hold in common belief in the incapacity of the intellect to attain to knowledge of divine matters and correspondingly put an excessive emphasis on faith.

Fides Damasi (Lat., 'Faith of Damasus'). An important credal formula, formerly attributed to St *Damasus or St *Jerome, but now thought to have originated in Gaul towards the end of the 5th cent.

Fides Hieronymi (Lat., 'Faith of Jerome'). An early form of the *Apostles' Creed, probably from the late 4th cent. Ascribed in the MSS to St *Jerome, it has also been attributed to *Gregory of Elvira.

Field, Frederick (1801–85), one of the most learned and accurate patristic scholars of the 19th cent. He published important editions of St *Chrysostom's Homilies on Mt. (1839) and on the Pauline Epp. (1849–62) and of *Origen's *Hexapla* (1867–75).

Field, John (1545–88), *Presbyterian propagandist. Ordained priest, uncanonically early, in 1566, he soon became a leading member of an extreme *Puritan group in London and was debarred from preaching for 8 years (1571–9). In 1572 he wrote the bitter 'View of Popish Abuses yet remaining in the English Church' which appeared with T. Wilcox's *Admonition to the Parliament*; both were sentenced to a year's imprisonment. Field was an adept propagandist and organizer, though he failed in his attempt to impose a Presbyterian uniformity on English Puritans.

Field, Richard (1561–1616), Dean of *Gloucester from 1609. He took part in the *Hampton Court Conference (1604). His main work, *Of the Church* (1606–10), argued that the counterpart of the modern RC Church was to be found in early times in the *Donatists, with their claim to exclusiveness and purity.

Fifth Monarchy Men. A fanatical sect of the mid-17th cent. in England whose members aimed at bringing in the 'Fifth Monarchy' (Dan. 2: 44) which should succeed the empires of Assyria, Persia, Greece, and Rome. After unsuccessful risings in 1657 and 1661, their leaders were beheaded and the sect died out.

Figgis, John Neville (1866–1919), Anglican historian and theologian. In 1907 he joined the *Community of the Resurrection. He wrote a number of works on political theory; he was among the first Christian thinkers alive to the dangers to religion and human freedom in the modern omni-competent State.

Filaret. See PHILARET.

Filaster. See PHILASTER.

Filioque (Lat., 'and the Son'). The dogmatic formula expressing the *Double Procession of the Holy Spirit added by the W. Church to the *Nicene Creed immediately after the words 'the Holy Ghost . . . who proceedeth from the Father'. It is first met with as an interpolation at the Third Council of *Toledo (589). From c.800, when the Creed began to be generally chanted in the Eucharist throughout the Frankish Empire, the words became widely familiar. It has been the chief ground of attack by the E. Church on the W. Modern Anglican theologians have often been disposed to agree to dropping the Filioque from the Creed. See DOUBLE PROCESSION.

Finding of the Cross. See INVENTION OF THE CROSS.

Finland, Christianity in. The origins of Christianity in Finland are obscure. It seems clear, however, that by the 12th cent. Finland had received Christianity from *Sweden and *Russia, and in 1220 an independent Church organization was established. *Lutheranism was introduced in 1523. In Karelia (E. Finland) the population remained Orthodox; when Finland came under Russian rule in 1809 the Orthodox Church increased in numbers and influence. By Acts of 1869 and 1889 RCism was tolerated for the first time since 1523, but RCs form a small minority. The National Church of Finland is a Lutheran body, in which episcopal succession was maintained until 1884; it was then lost when all three sees became vacant simultaneously, but it has gradually been recovered with the help of the Church of Sweden. About 90 per cent of the population belong to it. The Orthodox Church of Finland is a second established Church, embracing about 1 per cent of the population.

Finney, Charles Grandison (1792–1875), American evangelist. In 1821 he underwent a conversion experience. He was ordained by the *Presbytery of Oneida, NY, in 1824, and began his rise to prominence as an itinerant revivalist preacher. In 1835 he was appointed Professor of Theology at Oberlin College, Oberlin, Ohio; in 1837, abandoning Presbyterianism, he also became pastor of a *Congregational church in the town. Almost singlehandedly, he transformed *revivalism in America. He popularized so-called 'new measures': 'protracted meetings' (with the cessation of non-religious activity over several days), the 'anxious bench', prayer meetings, public prayer for individuals by name, and a dramatic pulpit style. He became an opponent of *Calvinism and *predestination, espousing a theology of human responsibility and agency in conversion.

Finnian, St (6th cent.). Irish annals distinguish Finnian of Clonard (d. 549) and Finnian of Moville (d. 579). One of them is probably the *Vennianus* who wrote to St *Gildas about monastic discipline and composed the *Poenitentiale Vinniani* used by St *Columbanus. Feast day of Finnian of Clonard, 12 Dec.; Finnian of Molville, 10 Sept.

Fioretti. See LITTLE FLOWERS OF ST FRANCIS.

Firmicus Maternus, Julius (d. after 360), a rhetorician converted to Christianity in adult life. His chief work, *De errore profanarum religionum*, is an appeal to the Emps. Constantius and Constans to destroy the pagan idols by force.

Firmilian, St (d. 268), Bp. of Caesarea in Cappadocia from *c*.230. He supported St *Cyprian against Pope *Stephen I in holding that Baptism could be validly performed only within the Church and that heretics must therefore be 'rebaptized'. He presided over the first of the synods of Antioch held to consider the case of *Paul of Samosata. Feast day in the E., 28 Oct.

First Fridays. The special observance of the first Friday in each month in the RC Church is based on the promise which Christ is supposed to have made to St *Margaret Mary Alacoque that unusual graces would be given to all who received Holy Communion on the first Friday of nine consecutive months.

fish. In Christian art and literature the fish is a symbol of Christ, also sometimes of the newly baptized and of the Eucharist. In modern times some C of E associations willing to help those in need have adopted the symbol of a fish.

From early times fish has taken the place of meat on days of fasting and *abstinence.

Fisher, Geoffrey Francis (1887–1972), Abp. of *Canterbury from 1945 to 1961. As Bp. of London (1939–45) he showed great administrative skill in dealing with the pastoral reorganization necessitated by war damage and as Chairman of the Churches' Main War Damage Committee. In 1946 he preached an influential sermon on *reunion at Cambridge, and in 1960, when he travelled to meet the Oecumenical Patriarch of *Constantinople and Pope *John XXIII, he was the first Abp. of Canterbury to visit the Vatican since 1397. He encouraged the formation of new Provinces and so divested himself of authority over the African and Asian parts of the Anglican Communion.

Fisher, St John (1469–1535), Bp. of *Rochester from 1504. A friend of *Erasmus, he was one of the greatest scholars of his day. Despite a later attribution, he was not the author of *Henry VIII's *Assertio Septem Sacramentorum*, but he wrote important works in defence of Catholic doctrine. When Henry began to seek a divorce from Catherine of Aragon in 1527, Fisher was her foremost defender. He opposed Henry's attacks on the liberties of the English Church, securing the mitigation of *Convocation's first submission to the king as Supreme Head by the insertion of the clause 'as far as the law of Christ allows' (1531). After refusing to take the oath required by the Act of Succession he was imprisoned in the Tower of London (1534). In 1535 he gave his opinion on the royal supremacy to the King in confidence, but he was found guilty of treason and executed. Before his trial *Paul III made him a cardinal. Feast day, formerly 9 July; now, with St Thomas *More, 22 June.

Fisher, Samuel (1605–65), *Quaker. His *Rusticus ad Academicos . . . The Rustick's Alarm to the Rabbies* (1660) is considered the most important Quaker controversial writing of the Commonwealth period.

Fisher the Jesuit (1569–1641), i.e. **John Fisher,** RC controversialist. His real name was Percy. Converted to the RC faith as a young man, he joined the *Jesuits in 1594. On the English mission he made many converts. His Anglican opponents included *James I and W. *Laud.

fistula. A tube, usually of gold or silver, through which the laity occasionally received communion from the chalice in the Middle Ages.

FitzRalph, Richard (c.1295–1360), Abp. of *Armagh from 1347. On visits to the Papal court at *Avignon in 1334–6, he became involved in controversy over the *Beatific Vision and in 1337–44 in controversy with the *Armenians. His final visit, beginning in 1357, was concerned with his attack on the *Mendicant Orders; he maintained that voluntary begging was against the teaching of Christ. In his *De Pauperie Salvatoris* he dealt with the question of evangelical poverty and the connection of dominion, possession and use with the state of grace; it later influenced J. *Wycliffe.

Five Mile Act. The common name for the Nonconformists Act 1665 which prohibited clergymen who had refused to conform to the Act of *Uniformity 1662 from preaching, teaching, or coming within five miles of a city, town, or parish where they had previously officiated, unless they took an oath not to try to alter the government of Church or State.

Flacius, Matthias (1520–75), also known from his birthplace as **Illyricus**, *Lutheran theologian. He was appointed professor of Hebrew at *Wittenberg in 1544. While apparently not a personal friend of M. *Luther, he supported the *Gnesio-Lutheran tendency. In 1548 he tried in vain to unite the theological faculty at Wittenberg against the *Augsburg Interim and left for Magdeburg. There he wrote against the *Adiaphorists. He was a leading force behind the *Centuriators of Magdeburg, but probably not one of the authors.

flagellants. Bands of men who in later medieval times scourged themselves in public processions in penance for the sins of the world. Famine and war, and perhaps

the prophecies of *Joachim of Fiore, produced a conviction of Divine displeasure; in 1260 processions of penance and other activities took place throughout Italy. The movement was spontaneous and embraced all classes. It quickly spread to Germany, France, and the Low Countries, and revived after the Black Death in 1348–9. See also FRATERNITIES.

Flavian, St (d. 449), Patr. of *Constantinople from 446. In 448 at a synod in Constantinople he excommunicated *Eutyches for heretical teaching about the Person of Christ. At the *Latrocinium this decision was reversed; the maltreatment Flavian suffered is said to have caused his death. He was vindicated at the Council of *Chalcedon, which regarded him as a martyr. Feast day in the E., variously 16, 17, 18 Feb. and 12 Nov.; in the W., 18 Feb.

Fléchier, Esprit (1632–1710), French preacher and man of letters. He is chiefly known for his sermons, especially his funeral orations. In 1687 he became Bp. of Nîmes, where he exerted a conciliatory influence in the aftermath of the revocation of the Edict of *Nantes (1685).

Fleming, Richard (d. 1431), Bp. of *Lincoln from 1420. As Junior Proctor at Oxford in 1407, Fleming had *Wycliffite sympathies. He represented the English nation at the Councils of Pavia and Siena in 1423, and impressed *Martin V. In 1427 he founded Lincoln College, Oxford, primarily to train opponents of Wycliffite teaching (which he had since forsworn).

Fletcher, John William (1729–85), Vicar of Madeley in Shropshire. A Swiss by birth and education, he came to England in 1750. Probably in 1753 he joined the *Methodist movement (then still within the C of E). He was ordained in 1757 and in 1760 accepted the living of Madeley. Although he resisted J. *Wesley's desire to designate him as his successor in the leadership of the Methodists, his personal sanctity won him a strong personal influence in the movement.

Fleury. The place owed its celebrity to the (real or supposed) transference hither in the 7th cent. of the remains of Sts *Benedict and *Scholastica from *Monte Cassino and the monastery erected to house them. It is also known as Saint-Benoît-sur-

Loire. The abbey was suppressed in 1790. In 1944 monks returned to Fleury and a new abbey has been built.

Fleury, Claude (1640–1723), ecclesiastical historian. From 1689 he was one of the tutors to Louis XIV's grandsons, and after his death (1715) he was chosen as confessor to the young Louis XV. His chief work is his *Histoire ecclésiastique* (20 vols., 1691–1720), the first large-scale history of the Church, which is held in repute for its learning and judgement.

Flood, the. According to Gen. 6: 5–9: 17, God brought a 'flood of waters' upon the earth 'to destroy all flesh' because of the wickedness of the human race, only *Noah and his family, with specimens of each species of animal life, being preserved in the *Ark to repeople the earth. Parallel flood stories are found in Mesopotamian sources, including the *Gilgamesh Epics, and there is archaeological evidence of such floods.

Florence, Council of (1438–45). This was a continuation of the Council at *Basle, which *Eugenius IV transferred to Ferrara (1438–9), Florence (1439–43) and then Rome (1443–5). Its chief object was reunion with the Greek Church, which sought support from the W. against the Turks. The main points of controversy were the *Double Procession of the Holy Spirit, the use of unleavened *bread for the Eucharist, the doctrine of *purgatory, and the primacy of the Pope. The *Filioque clause presented particular difficulty. After the Council had moved to Florence, *Bessarion addressed to the Greek synod his 'Oratio Dogmatica', urging that the Double Procession was taught more or less explicitly by both Latin and Greek Fathers. Eventually the Greeks accepted statements on the disputed issues. These were incorporated into the Decree of Union signed on 5 July 1439. After the Greeks had left, the Council continued in session. The superiority of the Pope over Councils was affirmed. Union was established with the *Armenians in 1439, with the *Copts in 1442, and with various other E. Churches.

The union with the Greeks was challenged by popular sentiment in Constantinople. The city was captured by the Turks in 1453 and the union ceased. That with Armenia lasted until 1475. The importance of the Council lies in its definition of doctrine and in the principle it established for Church union—unity of faith with diversity of rite.

Florentius Radewijns (1350–1400), one of the earliest members of the *Brethren of the Common Life. On G. *Groote's death in 1384 he became head of the community which he had founded at Deventer. Under his influence the monastery at *Windesheim was founded in 1387.

florilegium. A collection of passages from the writings of previous authors. Special interest attaches to the Greek *patristic florilegia. Besides those composed of excerpts from commentaries on the Bible (known as *catenae), a number of dogmatic florilegia, compiled from the 5th cent. onwards, have survived. They were often drawn up to establish the orthodoxy or heterodoxy of individual theologians, and many were incorporated in the *acta* of councils. Latin florilegia were well established from the 5th cent. Their material is patristic, supplemented by excerpts from *Carolingian and later from 12th-cent. authors. The early Latin florilegia were dogmatic and ascetic. In the later Middle Ages florilegia became preaching tools.

Florovsky, George (1893–1979), Russian theologian. He left Russia in 1920 and in 1926 became a professor at the Orthodox Theological Academy of St Sergius in Paris. Moving to the USA in 1948, he held professorial chairs at Harvard and Princeton. He wrote (mainly in Russian) on the Greek Fathers and published a study of Russian religious thought. He was active in the *Ecumenical Movement.

Florus (d. *c.*860), deacon of Lyons and a canon of the cathedral church. When *Amalarius tried to make changes in the liturgy, Florus attacked him in a number of works, including the *Expositio Missae*. In the controversy over *predestination, he defended *Gottschalk. He also compiled various Expositions on the Pauline Epistles, based on the writings of different Fathers.

Flüe, Nikolaus von. See NICHOLAS OF FLÜE.

Focolare, the (Ital., 'hearth'). A lay movement, predominantly RC but with ecumenical membership and aspirations. Officially styled 'Opera di Maria' ('Work of Mary'), it was founded at Trent, N. Italy, by Chiara Lubich in 1943. It received Papal approval in 1962 and its statutes were sanctioned in 1990. It includes both celibate and married people, and seeks unity through dialogue between Churches, with other religions, and with contemporary culture.

folded chasuble. A form of the *chasuble, pinned up in front, formerly worn in the W. Church by the *deacon and *subdeacon at High Mass in penitential seasons.

Foliot, Gilbert (c.1110–87), Bp. of London. A monk of *Cluny, he became Bp. of *Hereford in 1148. He was a candidate for the Archbishopric of *Canterbury in 1162, and with T. *Becket's support he was translated to London in 1163. When Henry II quarrelled with Becket, Foliot supported the King. After Becket's flight (1164), Foliot, as Dean of the Province of Canterbury, operated as its acting-head until Becket excommunicated him for recalcitrance (1169). The next year Becket reanimated the excommunication (which had been lifted on Papal authority), and reinforced it by suspension because Foliot had taken part in the coronation of the King's son in derogation of the rights of the Church of Canterbury. Becket on his return to England refused to absolve him; Foliot then went to the King's court in Normandy and took part in the discussions which led to Becket's murder. After purging himself of complicity, he was released from excommunication (1171) and suspension (1172) and resumed a leading position in the English Church.

font. Receptacle for baptismal water, in the W. normally made of stone. In early times, it was a large basin below ground level in which the candidate stood while water was poured over him, but when *affusion became the prevalent form of Baptism in the W., fonts became smaller and higher. In the E. a portable font, usually made of metal, is now used.

Fontevrault, Order of. A 'double order' of monks and nuns, living under the rule of one abbess, though in separate convents. The abbey of Fontevrault in France was founded in 1100 by Bl Robert d'Arbrissel. It disappeared in the French Revolution but was revived as an order for women only in 1806.

fool in Christ. See SALOS.

Fools, Feast of. A mock religious festival widely celebrated in the Middle Ages on or about 1 Jan., especially in France.

foot-washing. See PEDILAVIUM.

Forbes, Alexander Penrose (1817–75), Bp. of Brechin from 1848, the 'Scottish Pusey'. He laboured to further *Tractarian principles in Scotland; his defence of the doctrine of the *Real Presence in his primary charge, delivered in 1857, led to his censure by the college of bishops.

form. The word is literally synonymous with 'shape', but philosophers use it in a wider sense. For *Plato a form was an eternal transcendent prototype which acted as a pattern for each sort of earthly reality. *Aristotle held that forms existed only within things themselves, making them what they are and (in living things) controlling their development. St *Augustine adopted the Middle *Platonic understanding of forms as thoughts of the Divine mind which find expression in created reality. In the Middle Ages Aristotle's distinction between form and matter was revived and given an extended use, while various distinctions were elaborated. In the theology of the *Sacraments the form is held to consist of the words which give significance to the sacramental use to which the matter is being put; thus in Baptism the matter of the Sacrament is water, whereas the form consists of the Trinitarian formula employed.

formal sin. A sinful act which is both wrong in itself and known by the person committing it to be wrong.

Form Criticism. As applied especially to the Bible, the attempt to discover the origin and trace the history of particular passages by analysis of their structural forms. It entails three distinct processes: (1) the analysis of the material into their separate units, the form of which is held to have been generally fixed in the process of transmission from mouth to mouth; (2) the recovery of the earlier history of these forms; and (3) the ascertainment of the historical setting which determined the various forms.

The method was developed in connection with the OT but its most notable use has been upon the oral traditions behind the *Synoptic Gospels. The main classes of form which emerge are: (1) *Paradigms (i.e. models for preachers). These are short stories culminating in a saying of Jesus; (2) Miracle Stories; (3) Sayings; and (4) Historical Narratives and Legends (i.e. narrative material). It is widely agreed that the needs of the Church helped to mould the traditions about Jesus; more controversial is the claim that they were created in this context or that their use in the Church can be inferred from their literary form.

Formosus (c.816–96), Pope from 891. He acted constructively towards the E. Church, proposing a compromise solution to the question of *Photius's ordinations. After his death the party opposed to him in Imperial politics charged him with usurping the Holy See, and a synod convened by Pope Stephen VI in 897 declared him deposed. Later Popes reversed the decision.

Formula Missae et Communionis. The reformed Communion Service put out by M. *Luther in 1523. Latin was retained, but the central part of the rite was drastically altered to exclude any suggestion of the doctrine of the Eucharistic sacrifice.

Formula of Concord. See CONCORD, FORMULA OF.

Forsyth, Peter Taylor (1848–1921), *Congregational minister and theologian. He became Principal of Hackney College, Hampstead, in 1901. In early life he was a liberal in theology, but he later modified his attitude because of a deep sense of the need for *Atonement through the Cross.

Fortescue, Adrian (1874–1923), writer. In 1907 he became the RC parish priest at Letchworth, where he built a church which he made a centre of liturgical life. His *Ceremonies of the Roman Rite* (1918) was long a widely used directory of ceremonial practice.

Fortunatus, Venantius. See VENANTIUS FORTUNATUS.

Forty Hours' Devotion. A RC devotion in which the Blessed Sacrament is exposed (see EXPOSITION) for a period of c.40 hours, and the faithful pray before it by turns. In its present form the devotion began in Italy in the 16th cent.

Forty Martyrs of England and Wales. Forty English and Welsh RCs put to death by the State between 1535 and 1680. In 1960 the promoters of the causes of those who had been executed in this period decided to concentrate on a select number, termed the Forty Martyrs. The Roman authorities agreed to accept proof of two miracles for the whole group instead of for each member of it. The Forty Martyrs were canonized in 1970. Feast day, 25 Oct.

Forty-Two Articles. The collection of Anglican doctrinal formulae issued in 1553. They formed the basis of the *Thirty-Nine Articles.

forum (Lat., 'place of public assembly', hence 'judicial tribunal'). In *moral theology the term is applied to the exercise by the Church of her judicial power. A distinction is made between the 'internal forum', where, especially in the Sacrament of *Penance, judgement is given on matters which relate to the spiritual good of the individual, and the 'external forum', e.g. the ecclesiastical courts, where the public good of the Church is in question.

Fosdick, Harry Emerson (1878–1969), American *Baptist minister. From 1926 to 1946 he was minister of the Baptist Riverside Church, New York. He wrote widely from an evangelical liberal point of view.

fossors, grave-diggers. In early Christian times they were regarded as inferior clergy, and in the late 4th and early 5th cents. they formed powerful corporations controlling the management of the *catacombs.

Foucauld, Charles Eugène de. See DE FOUCAULD, CHARLES EUGÈNE.

Foundations. A theological symposium, published in 1912. It professed to be a 'statement of Christian belief in terms of modern thought'. It was controversial and initially influential.

Fountains Abbey. An abbey near Ripon, founded from *York in 1132; it became *Cistercian in 1133. Extensive ruins of the church and cloister buildings survive.

Fox, George (1624–91), founder of the Society of *Friends. The son of a Leicestershire weaver, in 1643 he felt a call to abandon all ties of family and friendship and spent the next years travelling. In 1646 he gave up attendance at church, relying on the *Inner (or Inward) Light of Christ. He began to preach in 1647, teaching that truth is primarily to be found in the inner voice of God speaking to the soul. He was often imprisoned but attracted followers whom he began to form into a stable organization. He undertook missionary journeys to the West Indies and North America as well as Germany and the Netherlands. His *Journal* was published in 1694.

Foxe, John (1516–87), martyrologist. On *Mary's accession, Foxe fled to the Continent. He wrote a history of the Christian persecutions, first issued in Latin at Strasbourg in 1554. An expanded English version appeared in 1563 as the *Acts and Monuments of matters happening in the Church*, commonly known as 'Foxe's Book of Martyrs'. Its main object was to extol the heroism of the Protestant martyrs of Mary's reign. It retains major historical value, despite the obvious bias of Foxe's commentary.

Foxe, Richard (? 1448–1528), Bp. of *Winchester from 1501. His ecclesiastical appointments were intended mainly to provide him with financial means while he engaged in diplomatic work; from 1511 he was gradually superseded by T. *Wolsey. He founded Corpus Christi College, Oxford, in 1515–16.

Fra Angelico; Fra Bartolommeo. See ANGELICO, BL FRA; BARTHOLOMMEO, FRA.

Fraction. The formal breaking of the bread which in all Eucharistic liturgies takes place before the Communion. It goes back to Christ's action at the *Last Supper and was a sufficiently striking element in the primitive rite to make the 'breaking of bread' a regular name for the Eucharist. The precise manner and moment of the Fraction varies in different liturgies.

France, Christianity in. Christianity seems to have been introduced into Gaul in the 2nd cent. by missionaries from Asia Minor. The Christian community at Lyons suffered *persecution in 177. A Gallic episcopate was established between c.250 and 313; a synod of the W. Church at *Arles in 314 included 14 Gallic bishops and the next century saw the definitive organization of the Gallo-Roman Church. Though the occupation of S. Gaul by *Arian Visigoths does not seem to have disrupted the lives of the Catholic bishops, the conversion of the Frankish king *Clovis to Catholicism and his conquest of Gaul opened the way for a close relationship between the Church and the secular rulers. Under *Pepin III, who secured the throne definitively in 751, his son *Charlemagne, and his successors, there was legislation touching all aspects of Church life. The Frankish Church was notable for its regularization of the liturgy, the development of ecclesiastical chant, and an influential revision of the *Vulgate text of the Bible. The close relationship of the Frankish rulers and the Papacy was expressed dramatically in the coronation of Charlemagne as Emperor in 800. The co-operation of Church and State continued after Hugh Capet in 987 succeeded the last Carolingian ruler in France. The *Investiture Contest saw no open clash with the Papacy over the king's claim to confer on bishops the *ring and *crozier; two reforming Popes, *Urban II and *Callistus II, were Frenchmen; and France was the homeland of the *Crusades and of *Cluniac and *Cistercian monasticism. After the spread of the *Albigensians in S. France, the Albigensian Crusades (1209–29) enabled the monarchy to assimilate Languedoc into the Frankish kingdom.

Under Philip IV (reigned 1285–1314) Papal power and prestige was damaged by the imprisonment of *Boniface VIII by Philip's agents in 1303. The election of *Clement V in 1305 was followed by the moving of the Papal court to *Avignon, within French territory. So far from being a French captivity of the Papacy, however, France was raided for benefices in the expansion of Papal 'provisions'. *Gallicanism took form as Church Councils tried to deprive the Pope of his control over benefices and taxation as a means to end the *Great Schism of 1378.

The Concordat of *Bologna (1516), by conceding to the French Crown the right to nominate to major benefices, disposed her monarchs to seek accommodation rather than a break with Rome. It also dictated the (unsuccessful) strategy of J. *Calvin and T. *Beza, which aimed to capture the support of the Crown so that the whole Gallican Church could be transformed on Protestant principles. Until the adoption of the RC faith by *Henry IV in 1593 the *Huguenots hoped this might be achieved. They gained limited protection under the Edict of *Nantes (1598), but this was eroded and finally removed by the Revocation of the Edict of Nantes (1685). Their numbers declined and RC Christianity was invigorated by post-Tridentine piety. Louis XIV (reigned 1643–1715) affirmed the power of the Crown not only against the Protestants but also against the Papacy, inducing the clergy to publish the *Gallican Articles in 1682. He also struck out against the *Jansenists, destroying their spiritual centre at *Port-Royal and encouraging the designs of the *Jesuits. Though religious practice was almost universal except in the towns, intellectually the Church could make only a halting reply to criticism (e.g. from *Voltaire and J. J. *Rousseau), and it was the target of *anticlericalism on account of its wealth. In the Revolution of 1789, Church property was sold, *tithe abolished, and the taking of monastic vows ended. The *Civil Constitution of the Clergy (1790) set up the *Constitutional Church. The *Concordat of 1801 (q.v.) 'restored the altars', increased the prestige of the Papacy, and weakened the Gallican spirit of the French clergy. From then *Ultramontanism became a force, moving towards its triumph at the First *Vatican Council (1870). In the 19th cent. Calvinism revived somewhat, though weakened by a split between orthodox, moderates, and liberals in 1872.

The identification of many Churchmen with the régime of Napoleon III and later proposals for a royalist restoration led politicians of the Third Republic to adopt anti-clerical policies and various acts weakened the influence of the Church. In the early 20th cent. most religious orders were expelled from France and in 1905 the Church and State were separated. The State grant to the Church ceased and with it all recognition of the Church as an institution. During the First World War French clergy fought alongside the laity and the estrangement of many French people from the Church was diminished. Unobtrusively the religious orders returned and the interwar years were marked by moderation in the relations between the Church and State. Catholic scholarship flourished and remained vigorous for some years after the end of the Second World War, with French *Dominicans in Jerusalem producing the

first scholarly Catholic translation of Scripture (1948–54; the 'Jerusalem Bible'). The activities of worker-priests in the 1940s and 1950s were designed to counter the loss of the working-classes to the Church in the 19th cent. In 1984 Catholics were able to defeat plans of the Socialist Government to integrate Church schools into the State system, and in the 1980s the Church established two *broadcasting stations. In the late 1990s, a large majority of the population still described themselves as RC, but only some 7–8 per cent practised their religion.

Frances of Rome, St (1384–1440), foundress of the *Oblates Regular of St Benedict. Though anxious to enter the religious life, she married and was an exemplary wife and mother. In 1425 she founded a society of pious women, not under strict vows, to help the poor; after her husband's death (1436) she entered the community and became its superior. *Pius XI declared her patroness of motorists. Feast day, 9 Mar.

Francis of Assisi, St (1181/2–1226), founder of the *Franciscan Order. The son of a rich merchant of Assisi, in 1202 he was taken prisoner in a border skirmish and held captive for a year. Setting off for war again in 1204, he was directed by a vision to return home. On a pilgrimage to Rome he exchanged clothes with a beggar and spent the day begging. When he returned to Assisi, he broke with his old companions, was disowned by his father, overcame his fear of leprosy by embracing a leper, and devoted himself to repairing a church which was in ruins. About 1208 when attending Mass he heard the Lord's words read, bidding His disciples to leave all (Mt. 10: 7–19), and took them as a personal call. He soon gathered a band of followers. When their number reached 12, he drew up a simple rule ('Regula Primitiva') and on a visit to Rome in 1209 secured for it the oral approval of *Innocent III. On his return he sent out friars in pairs to preach; they called themselves 'friars minor' and increased rapidly. In 1212 his ideals were accepted by St *Clare, who founded a similar society for women. Failing to reach Africa because of illness, Francis was probably at the Fourth *Lateran Council (1215) where his Order escaped the command to adopt an existing rule. In 1219 he went to

Egypt, leaving two vicars in charge of the Order. To correct abuses, with the help of the future *Gregory IX, he codified his original rule into what became known as the 'Regula Prima'; *Honorius III in 1223 approved a revised form of this, known as the 'Regula Bullata'. Later in 1223 Francis arranged for apparently the first Christmas *crib to be made. He received the gift of the *Stigmata in 1224. His generosity, his simple faith, his passionate devotion, his love of nature, and his deep humility have made him one of the most popular saints in modern times. Feast day, 4 Oct. (commemoration of the Stigmata, 17 Sept.). See also CANTICLE OF THE SUN and LITTLE FLOWERS OF ST FRANCIS.

Francis Borgia, St. See BORGIA, ST FRANCIS.

Francis of Paola, St (1416–1507), founder of the Order of *Minims and patron of Italian seafarers. As a boy, he spent a year with the *Franciscans. In 1431 he began to live as a hermit, first in a cave near the Tyrrhenian Sea and then in a nearby forest. He was joined by others c.1435 and became the spiritual guide of a group of hermits; from c.1452 he began to live with them in community. Other foundations followed. Feast day, 2 Apr.

Francis de Sales, St (1567–1622), a leader of the *Counter-Reformation. Despite attractive offers of secular employment, he felt a strong vocation to holy orders; in 1593 he was ordained priest and made Provost of Geneva. He won many *Calvinists to Catholicism. In 1599 he was nominated Coadjutor-Bishop of Geneva, but was not consecrated until he succeeded to the see in 1602. He met St *Jane Frances de Chantal in 1604, and with her founded the *Visitation Order in 1610. His most famous works, the *Introduction to the* *Devout Life* (1609) and the *Treatise on the Love of God* (1616; designed for those more advanced in the spiritual life) were adapted from instructions given to individuals. Feast day, 24 (formerly 27) Jan.

Francis Xavier, St (1506–52), 'Apostle of the Indies' and 'of *Japan', and an original member of the *Jesuits. Of aristocratic Spanish-Basque family, in 1534 with St *Ignatius Loyola and five others he made a vow of poverty and service in the Holy Land or wherever the Pope should send them. In response to a petition for Jesuits from the Portuguese ambassador to *Paul III, Xavier sailed from Lisbon in 1541. In 1542 he reached Goa, which he made his headquarters. He went on to Travancore, Malacca, the Molucca Islands and *Sri Lanka. In 1549 he landed in *Japan, where he founded a Church which endured through great persecution. He died on his way to *China. His work is remarkable for the extent of his journeys and the large number of his converts. Feast day, 3 Dec.

Franciscan Order. The Order of Friars Minor was founded by St *Francis of Assisi in 1209 when he gave his followers their first rule, now lost. This rule was recast in 1221 and brought into its final form in 1223, when *Honorius III confirmed it by bull (whence it is known as 'Regula bullata'). Its distinguishing feature is insistence on complete poverty not only for individual friars but corporately for the Order. With the spread of the Order two factions developed: the '*Spirituals' (q.v.), who insisted on a literal interpretation of the rule, and the majority who preferred a more moderate view. In 1317–18 the question was decided against the stricter party by two bulls of *John XXII which allowed the Order corporate ownership of property. Many of the Spirituals fled, and during the 14th cent. laxity increased. A return to poverty was brought about by the '*Observants' (q.v.), who gained ecclesiastical recognition in 1415 when the Council of *Constance granted their French province separate provincials and in 1443 *Eugenius IV provided them with a separate Vicar General; in 1517 they were separated from the '*Conventuals' and declared the true Order of St Francis. Another reform led to the establishment of the *Capuchins, whose rule was drawn up in 1529. In the 17th and 18th cents. reform parties sprang up again. Of these the chief were the 'Reformati', the *Recollects, and the *Discalced, who lived according to their own statutes though remaining under the same General. At the end of the 19th cent. the Order gained new vigour by the reunion of its different branches, confirmed in 1897.

To the Franciscan friars are attached a Second Order of contemplative nuns (the *Poor Clares) and a *Third Order (q.v.), now divided into Regular and Secular Tertiaries.

In the C of E a group inspired by Franciscan ideals settled near Cerne Abbas in Dorset in 1921. In 1931 they took vows and were constituted a religious community. There are also small Anglican communities for women.

Franck, Sebastian (*c*.1499–*c*.1542), German humanist and radical reformer. He became a *Lutheran in the 1520s and held pastoral appointments from 1526. Soon he became disenchanted with the work and moved into the printing trade. His radical ideas led to his expulsion from Strasbourg in 1531 and from Ulm in 1539. He promoted a form of undogmatic Christianity which was equally offensive to Catholics and Protestants.

Francke, August Hermann (1663–1727), German *Pietist and educationalist. He was already attracted to a pietistic form of religion when he came into contact with P. J. *Spener. In 1691 he was appointed professor of Greek and Oriental languages at Halle and also pastor of Glaucha, near Halle. In 1696 he founded his 'Paedagogium' and his orphanage; both grew and a publishing house and dispensary were soon added. His theology was similar to that of Spener, but he placed more emphasis on the need for an inner religious struggle. The strict ethical code which he tried to impose gave his form of Pietism a legalistic turn which influenced the development of Pietism, especially in North and Central Germany.

Franckforter, Der. An alternative name for the *Theologia Germanica*.

Frankfurt, Councils of. The best-known of the many councils held at Frankfurt am Main was that called by *Charlemagne in 794 to condemn the *Adoptianist heresy.

Franzelin, Johann Baptist (1816–86), Austrian *Jesuit. He took a prominent part in the preparations for the First *Vatican Council, and he was made a cardinal in 1876. He was a man of great learning and wrote a number of dogmatic treatises.

frater. The hall of a monastery or friary used for meals or refreshment.

fraternities. In the Middle Ages fraternities of many kinds were founded in the Church to meet the religious and social needs of clergy and laity. Their primary purpose was to secure for their members mutual support in death through Masses and prayers, as well as intercessions in sickness, etc. They also provided in material ways for such contingencies as death and natural disasters, and by social gatherings promoted fellowship and recreation. They developed rapidly from Carolingian times. Until the 13th cent. they were usually local (either rural or urban) or affiliated to an abbey; thereafter they catered for burgeoning forms of lay piety and included such movements as the *flagellants, who were concerned to counter heresy and sodomy as well as to appease civil strife and relieve poverty. Many fraternities were associated with orders of *Mendicant Friars; these were often not attached to any particular locality.

Fraticelli. Originally a term of contempt for heretical *Franciscans, it was applied to two groups, both mainly confined to Italy and extinct by 1500. The *Fraticelli de Paupere Vita* were followers of Angelo Clareno (d. 1337); the *Fraticelli de Opinione*, followers of Michael de Cesena (d. 1342), were organized as a Church with their own bishops, priests, and women preachers.

Frederick I (Barbarossa) (*c*.1122–90), German king and Emperor. Elected King by the German princes in 1152, he secured peace in Germany partly by allowing his cousin, Henry the Lion, a virtually free hand in the north-east. In Italy he was constrained by the treaty of Constance which he concluded with *Eugenius III in 1153 and renewed with *Hadrian IV in 1155; after his coronation as Emperor in 1155 tension between Frederick and Hadrian increased. When, at the Papal election of 1159 two Popes emerged, Frederick in 1160 recognized the minority candidate, Victor IV, against *Alexander III. After his defeat at Legnano in 1176 he was faced with the need to make concessions either to the Lombard League or to Alexander III; he preferred to submit to the Pope. In Germany Henry the Lion rebelled, but after his overthrow in 1181, Frederick became an awe-inspiring figure; his power was increased by the marriage of his son to the heiress of the Norman kingdom of Sicily in 1188. In 1189 he set off on a *Crusade, but was drowned in Cilicia.

Frederick II (1194–1250), Holy Roman Emperor and King of Sicily. The son of the Emp. Henry VI (d. 1197), he grew up in Palermo. When his guardian, *Innocent III, needed his help against the Guelph Emp. Otto IV, Frederick was able to regain his lost family position north of the Alps. At his coronation in 1215 he took the cross of a *crusader, but kept postponing his departure. Excommunicated by *Gregory IX, he set out in 1228. He regained *Jerusalem by agreement with the Sultan. Back in Italy he extracted absolution from the Pope in 1230. He crushed a rebellion in Germany and soon afterwards opened an offensive against the Lombard communes; the inevitable breach with the Papacy followed. Gregory again excommunicated Frederick and released his subjects from obedience to him in 1239. Frederick secured the election of *Innocent IV in 1243, but Innocent in 1245 declared him guilty of *heresy and *sacrilege and deposed him. His rule became increasingly messianic and his enemies branded him as *antichrist.

Frederick III (1463–1525), Elector of Saxony from 1486, surnamed 'the Wise'. From the outset he was interested in humanist education and Church reform. In 1502 he founded the University of *Wittenberg and later invited M. *Luther and P. *Melanchthon to teach there. When Luther was cited to Rome in 1518, Frederick tried to have the matter settled in Germany, and when the *Diet of *Worms (1521) outlawed Luther, he arranged safe custody for him at the *Wartburg. How far he accepted Lutheran doctrine is disputed.

Frederick III (1515–76), Elector Palatine of the Rhine from 1559, surnamed 'the Pious'. Through his wife he became well-disposed towards the *Reformation, though she was more inclined to *Lutheranism, he to *Calvinism. At first he tried to compromise, but his publication of the *Heidelberg Catechism in 1563 put the Palatinate into the Calvinist camp.

Free Church Federal Council. In 1892 a National Free Church Council was formed, with a loose network of local councils affiliated to it. In 1919, the Federal Council of the Evangelical Free Churches was organized, with membership on an officially approved representative basis. The two bodies united in 1940 to form the Free Church Federal Council.

Free Church of England. A small Protestant body which originated in a dispute in 1843 between H. *Phillpotts, Bp. of Exeter, and one of his clergy, James Shore. It received definite shape in 1863 in association with the Countess of *Huntingdon's Connexion. In 1927 it united with the Reformed Episcopal Church, a similar group which had separated from the *Episcopal Church in the United States of America in 1873.

Free Church of Scotland. The religious body formed at the *Disruption (1843) by the separation of nearly a third of the ministers and members of the Church of *Scotland. In 1900 it joined with the *United Presbyterian Church to form the *United Free Church.

Free Churches; Free Spirit, Brethren of the. See NONCONFORMITY; BRETHREN OF THE FREE SPIRIT.

Freemasonry. The origins of the Freemasons probably go back to the 12th cent. when the English masons established a religious fraternity to guard the secrets of their craft. This brotherhood was abolished in 1547 but later reorganized for social and educational purposes, and in the 18th cent. became a stronghold of *Deism. Freemasonry (no longer connected with stonemasons) spread from England to other countries. In the Latin countries the Masonic Lodges were hostile to the Church and religion; in England and the Germanic countries they for the most part professed an undogmatic Christianity. The hostility of Latin Freemasonry to religion has led to its repeated condemnation by the RC Church and members of the E. Orthodox Church are forbidden to become Freemasons.

Freer Logion. A passage added to the text of Mt. 16: 14 in the 5th-cent. Greek codex 'W' (in the Freer Museum, Washington) which includes a saying attributed to the Risen Christ.

freewill offerings. In ancient *Israel's sacrificial system one of the three forms of peace offering (Lev. 7: 11–18) was so named because it went beyond what legal demands required. In modern times the term has been applied to a method of Church finance.

Freewillers. A group of religious radicals active in SE England from the 1540s to the 1560s. They proclaimed the importance of free will in gaining salvation and advocated religious *toleration.

frequency of Communion. See COMMUNION, FREQUENCY OF.

Frere, Walter Howard (1863–1938), Bp. of *Truro from 1923 to 1935. A member of the *Community of the Resurrection (from 1892), he took part in the *Malines Conversations and was an authority on liturgical matters.

friar. The popular title of a member of one of the *Mendicant Orders founded in the Middle Ages.

Friday. Friday is widely kept as a weekly commemoration of Christ's Passion, being traditionally observed by *abstinence from meat, or other acts of penitence or charity. See also FIRST FRIDAYS, GOOD FRIDAY, and PAENITEMINI.

Frideswide, St (d. traditionally 735, but 727 according to the oldest source), patron saint of the city and university of *Oxford. According to a 12th-cent. Life, she was the daughter of Didanus, 'King of Oxford', and became abbess of a convent founded by her father in Oxford. A monastery bearing her name existed in Oxford in 1002; her shrine became a place of pilgrimage. The monastery was suppressed by T. *Wolsey in 1525, but the church became the cathedral of the new diocese of Oxford in 1546. Feast day, 19 Oct.

Friends, Religious Society of, commonly known as *Quakers. A body with Christian foundations, originally called 'Children of the Light', 'Friends in (or of) the Truth', or 'Friends'. In parts of the USA 'Friends' Church' is usual.

The Quaker movement arose out of the religious ferment of the mid-17th cent. G. *Fox, its leader, emphasized the immediacy of Christ's teaching within each person and held that to this ordained ministers and consecrated buildings were irrelevant. By 1655 Quakers had spread throughout Britain and Ireland and to the Continent of Europe, and in 1682 W. *Penn founded Pennsylvania as a 'Holy Experiment' on Quaker principles. Their refusal to take *oaths, pay *tithes, or show deference to social superiors led to widespread persecution in Britain before the passing of the *Toleration Act 1688. In America a split occurred in 1827–8 as a result of the teaching of E. *Hicks, whose emphasis on 'Christ within' seemed to undervalue the authority of Scripture and the historic Christ. In Britain there were three minor secessions in the 19th cent.

The religious beliefs of the 17th-cent. Friends were set out by R. *Barclay. Modern Friends continue to affirm their belief in the *Inner (or Inward) Light and the direct experience of God's Spirit. They have no set liturgy, creeds, or ordained ministers, and no *sacraments as such, though they believe in a spiritual baptism and communion. (In parts of the USA and elsewhere silent worship with spontaneous ministry has been replaced by prepared forms, often led by a paid pastor.) Their organization is based on a system of interrelated 'Meetings for Church Affairs'. In Britain this involves Monthly Meetings, General Meetings, a Yearly Meeting, and a Meeting for Sufferings (a standing representative body responsible for the care of matters affecting Friends in Britain). In their Meetings, Friends seek to discern God's will, and the 'clerk' records the 'sense of the Meeting'; no decisions are taken by voting. Each of the world's Yearly Meetings is autonomous, but they are linked through the World Committee for Consultation (established in 1937).

Until the middle of the 19th cent. Friends, like other Nonconformists, were excluded from the Universities in England, and many sought to express their convictions in commerce, banking, and industry. Their refusal to take up arms and their commitment to social and educational progress, penal reform, the promotion of peace and justice and, especially in the 20th cent., international relief, has earned them wide respect.

Friends of God. See GOTTESFREUNDE.

Frith, John (c.1503–33), Protestant martyr. A junior canon of 'Cardinal College' (*Christ Church), Oxford, he was imprisoned for heresy in 1528 but escaped to the Continent, where he assisted W. *Tyndale. On his return in 1532 he was arrested and condemned to death for denying that *purgatory and *transubstantiation were necessary dogmas.

Froben, Johann (*c.*1460–1527), printer and scholar. He started a printing press in Basle in 1491, and began publishing on his own in 1512. His press was renowned for the quality of its type and high standards of accuracy. *Erasmus moved into his house *c.*1513 and prepared a series of editions for his press, including the first edition of the Greek NT (1516) and the works of several of the Fathers.

Froissart, Jean (*c.*1335–*c.*1404), French chronicler. From 1382 until his death he was chaplain to the count of Blois and canon of Chimay. His *Chroniques* relate the history of the more considerable European countries between 1325 and 1400, most of it being based on eye-witness accounts.

frontal. The panel of embroidered cloth, or in some cases wood or metal, ornamented with carving or enamel, placed in front of the altar. It is usually changeable, its colour agreeing with the liturgical colour of the season or day.

Froude, Richard Hurrell (1803–36), *Tractarian. A Fellow of Oriel College, Oxford, he collaborated with J. H. *Newman and J. *Keble in the early stages of the *Oxford Movement. His *Remains* (posthumously published, 1838–9), which were largely extracts from private diaries, created a storm by their strictures on the Reformers and their disclosure of his own practices.

Fructuosus, St (d. 259), Bp. of Tarragona. With two deacons he was arrested and burnt at the stake. Feast day, 21 Jan.

Frumentius, St (*c.*300–*c.*380), 'Apostle of the Ethiopians'. According to *Rufinus, he was captured by 'barbarians' on his way back from 'India', taken before his captors' king, and helped in governing the country. He engaged in missionary work and was consecrated Bp. of *Axum by St *Athanasius. Feast day among the Greeks, 30 Nov.; among the *Copts, 18 Dec.; in the W., 27 Oct.

Fry, Elizabeth (1780–1845), *Quaker prison reformer. The daughter of John Gurney,

in 1800 she married John Fry, a London merchant and a 'Plain Quaker'. In 1811 she is recorded as an approved 'minister' in the Society of Friends. In 1813 her interest was aroused in the state of the prisons and she devoted herself to the welfare of female prisoners in Newgate. She campaigned for the separation of the sexes, classification of criminals, female supervisions of women, and the provision of secular and religious instruction. Feast day in CW, 12 Oct.

Fulbert, St (*c.*970–1028), Bp. of *Chartres from 1006. By 1004 he was a deacon at Chartres and teaching in the cathedral school. His main surviving writing is a collection of over 100 letters and 24 poems; the former are concerned mainly with politics and administration, the latter range from schoolroom mnemonics and anecdotes to autobiography and prayers. Also attributed to him, with varying degrees of security, are several sermons and further poems, including the Easter hymn 'Chorus Novae Ierusalem' ('Ye choirs of New Jerusalem'). Feast day, 10 Apr.

Fulda. The abbey of Fulda in Hesse was founded in 744 by a disciple of St *Boniface, whose tomb made it a place of pilgrimage. Under *Rabanus Maurus it was one of the foremost centres of Christian culture. The abbey was finally secularized in 1803.

Fulgentius, St (468–533, or perhaps *c.*462–527), Bp. of Ruspe in N. Africa from *c.*507 (or 502). He suffered persecution from the *Arian king, Thrasamund. Soon after he became bishop he was banished to Sardinia. He returned to Africa *c.*515 (or 510) for a debate with the Arian clergy, was banished again two years later, and finally returned in 523. He wrote treatises against Arianism and *Pelagianism. Feast day, 1 Jan.

Fulke, William (1538–89), *Puritan theologian. As a Fellow of St John's College, Cambridge, he became involved in the *Vestiarian controversy; he was for a time expelled. He benefited from the patronage of the Earl of Leicester and in 1578 was elected Master of Pembroke Hall. His attack on the *Reims version of the NT led to its becoming widely known in England.

Fuller, Andrew (1754–1815), *Baptist minister. *The Gospel worthy of all Acceptation* [1785] was directed against the extreme form of *Calvinism which allowed 'nothing spiritually good to be the duty of the unregenerate'. In 1792 he became the first secretary of the Baptist Missionary Society.

Fuller, Thomas (1608–61), Anglican historian. He held various benefices and managed to escape deprivation under O. *Cromwell. His witty and popular style won him a wide reputation. His best-known works are his *Church-History of Britain* (1655) and his *Worthies of England* (1662).

Fundamentalism. A movement in various Protestant bodies reacting against evolutionary theories, liberal theology, and biblical criticism. It began in the late-19th cent. and developed after the First World War (1914–18), especially in the USA. A series of Bible Conferences of Conservative Protestants was held in various parts of America; that of Niagara in 1895 issued a statement containing what came to be known as the 'five points of fundamentalism', namely the verbal inerrancy of Scripture, the Divinity of Jesus Christ, the *Virgin Birth, a substitutionary theory of the *Atonement, and the physical and bodily return of Christ. In 1919 the World's Christian Fundamentals Association was founded and soon several Protestant denominations in the USA were divided into Fundamentalist and Modernist wings. The controversy attracted attention in 1925 when a school-teacher of Dayton, Tenn., was convicted of violating the state law by teaching biological evolution.

In a wider sense the term is applied to other religious and political groups (e.g. 'Muslim Fundamentalism'); since 1950 these have grown in strength, generally supporting conservative social positions. In some areas they are reinforced by a *charismatic tendency.

funeral services. See BURIAL SERVICES.

Gabbatha. According to Jn. 19: 13 the place in *Jerusalem where *Pilate sat in judgement on Christ. The site of Pilate's official residence, where Gabbatha was, has not been conclusively identified.

Gabirol, Solomon Ibn. See AVICEBRON.

Gabriel. One of the seven *archangels. He figures in Dan., foretells the birth of *John the Baptist, and announces the conception of the Lord to the BVM. Feast day, in the E., 26 Mar.; in the W., formerly 24 Mar.; now, with *Michael and *Raphael, 29 Sept.

Gabriel Severus (c.1540–1616), theologian. He was consecrated Metropolitan of Philadelphia, now Ala-Shehr, in Asia Minor, in 1577. As the see was in Turkish hands he acted as bishop to the Greek Christians in Venice. His best-known work is a defence of the custom of venerating the Eucharistic elements at the *Great Entrance.

Gairdner, William Henry Temple (1873–1928), missionary. He went to Cairo as a *CMS missionary in 1898. He studied Arabic and Islamics and threw himself into the reorganization of the Arabic Anglican Church, determined to make it a spiritual home for converted Muslims.

Gaius, also **Caius** (early 3rd cent.), Roman presbyter. He rejected Jn. and Rev., holding them to be the work of *Cerinthus (see ALOGI). His reference to the 'trophies of apostles' has been one of the key texts in discussions about the excavations under *St Peter's, Rome.

Galatians, Epistle to the. St *Paul apparently wrote this letter from *Ephesus or Macedonia to his Galatian converts on receiving news of a movement requiring them to keep all the commandments of the Jewish Law and thereby (as he thought) imperilling the whole value of their faith in Christ. It is universally recognized as genuine. It may have been addressed to Christians in the country of Galatia in the interior of Asia Minor, which had been peopled by Gauls in the 3rd cent. BC (the traditional 'North Galatian' view); alternatively 'Galatia' may refer to the Roman province of Galatia, which covered a wider area (the 'South Galatian' view). Either way there are problems about relating the events in Paul's life recorded in Gal. 1f. with Acts. On one view the Epistle is dated in 50 or a little earlier, making it the earliest of Paul's letters, but most scholars prefer a date in the mid-50s.

Gale, Thomas (c.1635–1702), antiquary. From 1697 he was Dean of *York. He edited the *Historiae Anglicanae Scriptores Quinque* (1687) and *Historiae Britannicae Scriptores* (1691); both are valuable sources for the history of medieval England.

Galerius (d. 311), Roman Emperor. He became *Diocletian's co-adjutor ('Caesar') in the E. in 293 and succeeded him in 305. According to Christian writers, he inspired the *persecution initiated in 303. Unable to enforce his dominance in the W., he issued an edict of *toleration in 311.

Galgani, St Gemma (1878–1903), Italian *stigmatic. Ill-health prevented her from becoming a *Passionist nun. She enjoyed frequent ecstasies, and received the stigmata and marks of scourging intermittently between 1899 and 1901. Feast day, 11 Apr.

Galilee. (1) Originally the term was applied only to part of the tribe of Naphtali, but in NT times it denoted all the district of N. Palestine from the Mediterranean to the *Jordan. It was the scene of most of the Lord's earlier life and of much of His ministry.

(2) In medieval cathedrals an outer porch or chapel.

Galilei, Galileo (1564–1642), mathematician and scientist, usually known as 'Galileo'. As professor of mathematics at Pisa and then Padua, he developed ideas on a new science of motion that can be seen as leading to Newtonian physics. In 1609 he heard of a new instrument (later known as the telescope) and embarked on a systematic observation of the heavens; he used the results in works published in 1610 and 1613 to support a heliocentric *Copernican cosmology. In 1610 he moved to Florence. Soon the theological significance of Copernicanism for the first time became a matter of concern, and in 1616 the *Holy Office asserted that to maintain the immobility and centrality of the sun as opposed to that of the earth was heretical. Apparently under the impression that he could then discuss the new system provided he treated it as hypothetical, Galileo published a new work on the subject in 1632. He was summoned before the *Inquisition, made to recant, and spent the rest of his life under house arrest. In 1992 *John Paul II endorsed the report of a commission admitting the 'subjective error' of Galileo's judges.

Gall, St (c.550–c.650), missionary. A follower of St *Columbanus, when Columbanus went to Italy in 612, Gall remained in what is now Switzerland, living mainly as a hermit. The monastery of St Gallen was founded c.719 on the site of his hermitage. Feast day, 16 Oct.

Galla Placidia (c.390–450), Roman Empress. The daughter of *Theodosius I, on the accession of her son as Valentinian III (425), she acted as regent. She supported Pope *Leo III in the *Eutychian controversy.

Gallia Christiana. A documentary account of the bishoprics, bishops, abbeys, and abbots of France. It derives from a work of this title published in 1626; a later edition (1656) has been revised and continued.

Gallican Articles, the Four. The claims made by an *Assembly of the French clergy in 1682. They denied that the Pope had dominion over things temporal and affirmed that kings are not subject to the Church in civil matters; they reaffirmed the authority of a General Council over the Pope; insisted that the ancient liberties of the French Church were inviolable; and asserted that the judgement of the Pope was not irreformable. See also GALLICANISM.

Gallican chant. The music of the early *Gallican rite has not survived and nothing certain of its nature is known.

Gallican Confession. The *Confession de foi* or *Confessio Gallicana*, adopted by the First National Synod of Protestants at Paris in 1559. In substance it was an epitome of J. *Calvin's central doctrines.

Gallican Psalter. St *Jerome's revision of the Latin Psalter made *c.*392 on the basis of the *Hexaplaric Greek text of the LXX. It became popular in Gaul (hence the name 'Gallican'), and came to be used in public worship throughout the W. Church.

Gallican rite. The term is used with three meanings: (1) for the liturgical forms used in Gaul before the adoption of the Roman rite under *Charlemagne; (2) loosely, for all non-Roman rites in the early W. Church; and (3) for the 'neo-Gallican' liturgies of the 17th and 18th cents.

It is not known why the rites of N. Italy, Gaul, *Spain, and the *Celtic Churches in early times differed from that of Rome. The rite in Gaul may have been indigenous and developed with the introduction of prayers varying according to the Church calendar. In the Mass the order of the various items differed somewhat from that of the Roman rite; the *Canon, apart from the Words of *Institution, varied with the season, and there was sometimes a form of *epiclesis. In Baptism there was an additional rite of *Pedilavium. Ordinations seem to have included a public ceremony for the *Minor Orders which was taken over by Rome.

Gallicanism. The collective name for the body of doctrine which asserted the more or less complete freedom of the RC Church, especially in France, from the ecclesiastical authority of the Papacy. In the 14th and 15th cents. the main question at issue was the claim of the French Church to a privileged position in relation to the Papacy. In the Concordat of *Bologna (1516) the Pope conceded the right of the French king to nominate to bishoprics and other high ecclesiastical offices. In 1663 the *Sorbonne published a declaration, in substance reaffirmed by an *Assembly of the French clergy in 1682 in the formula known as the Four *Gallican Articles (q.v.). Gallican principles were preached in the 18th cent. by the *Jansenists, and were codified and pro-

claimed at the Synod of *Pistoia (1786). In the 19th cent. there was a renascence of *Ultramontanism in France, and the definition of Papal *infallibility at the First *Vatican Council (1869–70) made Gallicanism incompatible with Roman Catholicism.

Gallio, Lucius Junius. The brother of *Seneca, he was the Proconsul of Achaia (in AD 52) before whom St *Paul was accused at *Corinth (Acts 18: 12).

Gallus, Thomas. See THOMAS GALLUS.

Gamaliel. The Jewish rabbi who was the teacher of St *Paul in his pre-Christian days. His tolerant views were exemplified in his attitude to St *Peter and his companions (Acts 5: 34–40).

gambling. See BETTING AND GAMBLING.

Gandolphy, Peter (1779–1821), *Jesuit preacher. He made many converts at the Spanish Chapel in London. In 1812 he issued *A Liturgy*, modelled on the Anglican BCP; he was accused of heresy and, though vindicated, retired to his family home.

Gangra, Council of. A Council at Gangra in Paphlagonia, *c.*341, passed 20 canons directed against false asceticism. To these was added an epilogue, often called 'canon 21', on the true nature of asceticism.

Gansfort, Wessel. See WESSEL.

Garden of Eden; Garden of Gethsemane. See EDEN, GARDEN OF; GETHSEMANE, GARDEN OF.

Garden of the Soul, The. The influential 'Manual of Spiritual Exercises and Instructions for Christians who, living in the world, aspire to Devotion', compiled by R. *Challoner and first published in 1740.

Gardiner, Stephen (*c.*1497–1555), Bp. of *Winchester from 1531. He was employed in negotiations with Rome for annulling *Henry VIII's marriage to Catherine of Aragon, and in 1533 he acted as an assessor in the court which declared the marriage null and void. For a time he accepted the royal supremacy but he opposed the Reformist influence of T. *Cromwell. He was imprisoned under *Edward VI and deprived of his bishopric but restored by *Mary and became Lord High Chancellor.

Garnet or **Garnett, Henry** (1555–1606), English *Jesuit. He was sent on the English Mission in 1586 and became Superior of it in 1587. He was arrested and executed, some months after the *Gunpowder Plot, for not having revealed his knowledge of it.

Gascoigne, Thomas (1403–58), English scholar. He declined nearly all ecclesiastical office to devote himself to scholarly pursuits at *Oxford. Though hostile to *Wycliffite influences, he denounced ecclesiastical abuses. His main work was a theological dictionary.

Gasquet, Francis Aidan (1846–1929), cardinal from 1914. He was elected Prior of *Downside in 1878. In 1896 he went to Rome, where he was a member of the Commission on *Anglican Ordinations. He took part in the election of *Benedict XV (1914), countering anti-British propaganda. His writings, though often inaccurate, increased knowledge of English monasticism.

Gauden, John (1605–62), Bp. successively of *Exeter (1660) and *Worcester (1662). In the early days of the Civil War his sympathies were with Parliament, but later he changed his views. He published controversial works against the *Puritans and was probably the author of the *Eikon Basilike (q.v.).

Gaudentius, St (4th–5th cent.), Bp. of Brescia by 397. In 404–5 he went to *Constantinople to plead on behalf of St John *Chrysostom, without avail. Feast day, 25 Oct.

Gaunilo, Count. The 11th-cent. *Benedictine monk who, in the guise of the 'fool', criticized the validity of the *Ontological Argument for the existence of God used by *Anselm in his *Proslogion*.

Gavanti, Bartolommeo (1569–1638), *Barnabite liturgist. He took part in the reform of the *Breviary and *Missal under Popes *Clement VIII and *Urban VIII.

Geddes, Jenny. According to tradition, the vegetable-seller who in 1637 threw her stool at the head of the Bp. of Edinburgh in St Giles' Cathedral when the Scottish Prayer Book was used for the first time.

Gehenna. A valley outside *Jerusalem. From early times it was a place of human sacrifice and in later Jewish thought it was regarded as a Divinely appointed place of punishment for apostates and other great sinners. Hence in NT times the word is used for the final place of torment for the wicked after the Last Judgement.

Geiler von Kaisersberg, Johann (1445–1510), 'the German *Savonarola'. He held teaching posts at Freiburg and Basle, but his reforming interests led him to abandon academic work. From 1478 he held the office of cathedral preacher at Strasbourg. Despite his austere moral ideals and his denunciation of the vices of all classes, he won and held his hearers. He demanded reform but never seems to have contemplated leaving the Church.

Gelasian Decree, the. See DECRETUM GELASIANUM.

Gelasian Sacramentary. The term is used both of a particular MS (Vat. Reg. Lat. 316) and of the class of sacramentaries to which it belongs. The Vatican MS dates from the mid-8th cent. The ascription of the text to Pope *Gelasius is mistaken.

Gelasius, St (d. 496), Pope from 492. He upheld the primacy of the Roman see against *Constantinople during the *Acacian Schism. To rebut the *Manichaean abhorrence of wine, he insisted on the Eucharist being received in both kinds. He also laid down that Ordinations should be at what later came to be called the *Ember seasons. He wrote a treatise on the Two Natures in Christ. Although the *Gelasian Sacramentary and the *Decretum Gelasianum have been wrongly attributed to him, some of his work may be traced in the *Leonine Sacramentary. Feast day, 21 Nov.

Gelasius (d. 395), Bp. of *Caesarea in Palestine from c.367. As a convinced *Nicene, he was ousted from his see for a time in the reign of Valens. He wrote a continuation of the 'Ecclesiastical History' of *Eusebius, a treatise against the *Anomoeans, and an 'Expositio Symboli'.

Gelasius of Cyzicus (*fl.* 475), ecclesiastical historian. He wrote a 'Syntagma', or collection of the *Acta* of the Council of *Nicaea (325), to refute the *Monophysite claim that their faith was identical with that of the Nicene Fathers.

Gellert, Christian Fürchtegott (1715–69), German poet. He wrote many hymns which became popular with *Lutherans and RCs. They include 'Jesus lives! thy terrors now'.

Gematria. A method of interpretation employed by the Rabbis to extract hidden meanings from words. It depended on the fact that every Hebrew letter possessed a numerical value and it was thus possible by counting the value of the letters in a Hebrew word to assign to it a numerical value. The method was occasionally used by early Christians. In Rev. 13: 18 the *number of the beast is given as 666, which is the numerical equivalent of the Hebrew words for 'Nero Caesar'.

Gemistus Plethon, Georgius (c.1355–1452), scholar. From the beginning of the 15th cent. he lived in Mistra in the Peloponnese. He had a great veneration for the teaching of *Plato, and when, in 1438–9, he attended the Council of *Florence as one of the E. spokesmen, he was welcomed by some of the Italian humanists. His 'Laws' was modelled on that of Plato. He also wrote in defence of the E. doctrine of the *Procession of the Holy Spirit.

Gemma Galgani, St. See GALGANI, ST GEMMA.

genealogies of Christ. Mt. and Lk. contain (somewhat differing) genealogies of Christ; they are intended to emphasize that He belonged to the House of *David.

General. The usual name for the head of a religious order or *congregation, now officially styled *institutes of consecrated life. It is commonly combined with a noun. Thus the *Franciscans have a 'Minister General' and the *Jesuits, *Redemptorists, and others a 'Superior General'.

General Assembly. The highest court of a Church in *Presbyterianism.

General Baptists. As contrasted with the *Particular Baptists, those *Baptists whose theology was *Arminian and whose polity allied with that of the *Presbyterians. To this group belonged the earliest English Baptists, led by T. *Helwys. After many General Baptist Churches had moved towards *Unitarianism, a New Connection was formed in 1770. This group united with the Particular Baptists in 1891.

General Chapter. A canonical meeting of the heads and representatives of a religious order or *congregation, especially to elect new superiors and deal with business concerning the whole order.

General Confession. (1) In the BCP the Confession at the beginning of *Mattins and *Evensong said by the whole congregation. (2) A private confession where the penitent (exceptionally) resolves to confess all his past sins and not only those since his last confession.

General Councils. See OECUMENICAL COUNCILS.

General Judgement, the, also **the Last Judgement.** In contrast with the so-called *Particular Judgement on souls immediately after death, in Christian theology the General Judgement after the Resurrection of the Dead is held to be the occasion of God's final sentence on humanity, as well as His verdict on each individual.

General Superintendent. Formerly the highest ecclesiastical office in many German Protestant Churches. In modern times the title has often been replaced in the W. provinces by that of Präses, and in the E. a Bishop of Berlin has been set up over the General Superintendents.

General Thanksgiving. In the BCP the first of the thanksgivings 'to be used before the two final prayers of the Litany or of Morning and Evening Prayer', so named to distinguish it from the particular thanksgivings ('for rain', etc.) which follow.

General Theological Seminary, New York City. The largest training centre for clergy in the *Episcopal Church in the USA. It was founded in 1817.

Genesis, Book of. The opening Book of the OT. It contains the story of the beginnings of the universe and the early history of the human race. It includes accounts of the *Creation, *Fall, *Flood, the call of *Abraham, and the story of Joseph's captivity in Egypt and the prosperity of his family there. The Book has traditionally been held to be the work of *Moses, but most modern scholars believe either that it is a composite structure made up of materials from sources which can be traced also in other Books of the Pentateuch or that, together with the rest of the Pentateuch, it forms a unified composition from a period much later than that of Moses.

Geneva. The foundation of a Christian community in Geneva dates from *c.*350; by the end of the 4th cent. it was the centre of a diocese. In 1162 the Emp. *Frederick I conferred secular authority on the Bp. of Geneva. Increasing prosperity led the merchants to press for Geneva to be constituted a city-state; in 1387 Bp. Adhémar Fabri granted the city its franchise, while retaining the basic powers of the prince-bishop. The beginnings of the *Reformation in Geneva are linked with a political rebellion against the remaining powers of the prince-bishop from 1513 onwards. The preaching of G. *Farel, P. *Viret, and Antoine Froment gave a confessional basis to the movement and led to the abolition of the Mass in 1535. In 1536 the Reformation was officially adopted by edict and the city-state was separated from the RC diocese. J. *Calvin introduced the *Presbyterian system of Church government, carrying out most of his reforms in 1541/2. In 1559 he founded the Genevan Academy, primarily to train clergy. After a period of stagnation and rigidity in the 17th cent., more liberal tendencies appeared in the 18th cent. and *Lutherans were granted freedom of worship in 1707. The annexation of the city by Napoleon in 1799 led to the official recognition of RC worship for the first time since 1535. After the withdrawal of French troops in 1815, the city and its dependencies became a canton of the Swiss confederation. In 1907 the Calvinist Church was separated from the State.

Geneva is the seat of several international ecclesiastical organizations, including the *World Council of Churches. In a historical context, Geneva is regarded as the centre of Presbyterianism and is used to denote the system in the same way as Rome is used to designate the RC Church.

Geneva Bible. The English translation of the Bible first published at Geneva in 1560, and widely used for about a century. See also BIBLE, ENGLISH VERSIONS.

Geneva gown. The black preaching-gown worn by the early *Reformed ministers, loose-fitting and with full sleeves. It is still worn by *Presbyterians and other *Calvinists.

Genevan Catechism. Two formulas of J. *Calvin. (1) *Catechismus Genevensis Prior*, a compendium of doctrine based on the *Institutes*, issued in French in 1537. With it were associated other documents, including a Confession by G. *Farel which was imposed on the citizens of *Geneva, but the relationship of the documents is not clear. (2) *Catechismus Genevensis*, a catechism in the form of question and answer, published in French in 1542 and reissued with a Latin translation in 1545. It became one of the basic documents of the Genevan ecclesiastical State.

Geneviève, St (*c.*422–*c.*500), chief patroness of *Paris. According to her Life, she consecrated herself to God at the age of 7, took the veil at 15, and led a life of mortification. Her intercession is said to have diverted the Huns under *Attila from Paris in 451. Feast day, 3 Jan.

geniza. The room attached to a *synagogue used to house MS books unfit for use in worship, e.g. worn-out copies of Scripture, and heretical works.

Gennadius I (d. 471), Patr. of *Constantinople from 458. In his earlier years he opposed the *Christological teaching of St *Cyril of Alexandria. He wrote biblical commentaries and dogmatic works. Feast day in the E., 17 Nov.; in the W., 25 Aug.

Gennadius II. See GEORGE SCHOLARIUS.

Gennadius of Marseilles (*fl.* 470), presbyter and ecclesiastical historian. His *De Viris Illustribus* is a continuation of *Jerome's book of the same name; its bibliographical information is invaluable. He is almost certainly also the author of an early recension of the *Liber ecclesiasticorum dogmatum*, a theological compendium which circulated widely. The *Statuta Ecclesiae Antiqua* has sometimes been attributed to him.

Gennesaret. A district on the W. shore of the Sea of *Galilee.

Gentile, Giovanni (1875–1944), Italian philosopher. An early Fascist, as Minister of Education (1922–4) he reintroduced the teaching of Catholicism in State schools. He developed his Idealist philosophy in conjunction with B. *Croce. Reality, which was fundamentally historical, was the idea as realized in the human mind. God was the 'transcendent pure thinking'; religion was a complete intuition of life, and the Catholic form of it was especially suited to the needs of the Italian people.

Gentiles. A biblical term usually denoting non-Jews.

genuflexion. A momentary kneeling on the right knee, with the body erect, used in the W. Church as a ceremonial reverence when passing before the Blessed Sacrament and on certain other occasions.

Geoffrey of Monmouth (d. 1154), Bp. of *St Asaph and pseudo-historian. His *Historia Regum Britanniae* claims to trace the history of Britain from Brutus, great-grandson of Aeneas, to Cadwaladr in the 7th cent. AD. It includes a substantial (and imaginary) account of the reign of King Arthur. His fabulous description of the ecclesiastical affairs in his court, and of the archbishoprics of London, York, and Caerleon, influenced 12th-cent. ecclesiastical politics.

George, St, patron saint of England and martyr. Little is known of him, though his historical existence is now generally accepted. It is not improbable that he suffered martyrdom at or near Lydda before the time of *Constantine (d. 337). His cult did not become popular until the 6th cent.; the slaying of the dragon was first attributed to him in the late 12th cent. His rank as patron of England probably dates from the reign of Edward III, who founded the Order of the Garter under St George's patronage (*c.*1347). Feast day, 23 Apr.

George (*c.*640–724), 'Bishop of the Arabs'. He became bishop of the Arab nomads in Mesopotamia in 686. His writings are one of the main sources for the history of *Syriac Christianity.

George of Cappadocia (4th cent.), extreme *Arian bishop. He was intruded into the see of *Alexandria in 357 and held it until he was murdered in 361. Some elements of his martyrdom passed into the legends about St *George.

George Hamartolos (9th cent.), 'George the Sinner', also 'George the Monk', Byzantine historian. He wrote a *Chronicon Syntomon*, extending from the Creation to AD 842. Though coloured by his hatred of

*Iconoclasm, it is an important source for the period immediately before *Photius.

George Scholarius (*c.*1405–*c.*1472), Patr. of *Constantinople. At the Council of *Florence in 1439 he supported the scheme for reunion, but later he opposed all such projects. He became a monk *c.*1450, taking the name of 'Gennadius'. After the capture of Constantinople, in 1454 the Sultan made him Patriarch as 'Gennadius II'. He was a prolific writer and translated the works of St *Thomas Aquinas into Greek.

George Syncellus (*fl.* *c.*800), Byzantine historian. He was the *syncellus of *Tarasius, Patr. of *Constantinople. He wrote an important 'Chronicle', extending from the Creation to the time of *Diocletian, continued after his death to AD 813.

Georgia, Church of. The preaching of a Christian slave-woman from Cappadocia led to the conversion of the Iberian royal house *c.*350, and so to the adoption of Christianity as the religion of the country. At first dependent on the Patriarchate of *Antioch, the Georgian Church became *autocephalous in the 8th cent. In 1811 it was absorbed by the Church of *Russia; it regained its autocephalous status in 1917, though it was not recognized by the Soviet authorities or the Russian Church until 1943. It was a focus of nationalist opposition and suffered severe persecution, but since 1977 there has been a revival.

Georgian Version. The earliest version of the NT into the Georgian language dates from the 6th cent.: it was apparently made from the *Armenian.

Gerald de Barri; Gerald of Wales. See GIRALDUS CAMBRENSIS.

Gerhard, Johann (1582–1637), *Lutheran theologian. He taught theology at Jena from 1616 until his death. His massive *Loci Theologici* (1610–22), which reintroduced scholastic methodology and terminology into Reformation dogmatics, became a standard compendium of Lutheran orthodoxy.

Gerhard Zerbolt of Zutphen (1367–98), a member of the *Brethren of the Common Life. He became a priest and librarian of the house at Deventer, and was remarkable for his learning and skill as a director of souls.

One of his writings influenced the '*Spiritual Exercises' of St *Ignatius Loyola.

Gerhardt, Paul (1607–76), German *Lutheran hymn-writer. He held important pastoral offices. Though in his theology he was an uncompromising Lutheran, he was susceptible to the influence of Catholic mysticism, and one of his hymns, 'O sacred head, sore wounded', is based on the 'Salve caput cruentatum' attributed to St *Bernard. Many of his hymns are widely known.

Gerhoh of Reichersberg (1092/3–1169), *Augustinian Canon. He became 'magister scholarum' of the cathedral school of Augsburg c.1118, but had to leave his post because of his opposition to the simoniacal bishop. He joined the Augustinian canons at Rottenbuch and in 1132 became Provost of their house at Reichersberg. He was often sent on embassies to Rome, but his zeal for reform aroused hostility and he was even accused of heresy. In 1166 he was banned by the Emp. *Frederick I and had to flee from his monastery because he refused to support the Imperialist antipope. In his famous De Investigatione Antichristi (1160/62) he advocated a clearer definition of the spheres of Papal and Imperial power.

Germain, St. See GERMANUS, ST.

German Baptists. See TUNKERS.

German-Christians (Deutsche Christen). A Protestant group which tried to bring about a synthesis between Nazism and Christianity. In 1933 they gained a majority in the Church elections and L. Müller, their most prominent member, became *Reichsbischof of the German Evangelical Church. His attempt to introduce an 'Aryan paragraph' (excluding Jews from being clergymen or Church officials) into Reich Church law and his incorporation of the Evangelical Youth into the 'Hitler Jugend' alienated the embryonic '*Confessing Church' and he was virtually superseded by the appointment of Hanns Kerrl as Minister for Church Affairs in 1935. Nevertheless, the 'German-Christians' retained the official leadership of more than half the German Landeskirchen during the Second World War. After it the more extreme members disappeared from public view; others seceded from the Landeskirchen to join in a free Church.

Germanus, St (d. 437/48), Bp. of Auxerre probably for 30 years. *Prosper of Aquitaine records that he was sent to Britain in 429 by *Celestine I to quell *Pelagianism. His Life portrays him as an ascetic bishop of considerable standing; it mentions two visits to Britain and a journey to *Ravenna. Feast day, 31 July.

Germanus, St (c.496–576), Bp. of *Paris from 555. A monk before he became bishop, he tried to check the licence of the Frankish kings and to stop the perpetual civil wars. The church of *St-Germain-des-Prés stands on the site of his tomb. Feast day, 28 May; of his translation, 25 July.

Two letters, almost certainly wrongly attributed to him, were used by earlier scholars in their reconstruction of the *Gallican rite. They were probably written in S. France, c.700.

Germanus, St (c.640–c.733), Patr. of *Constantinople. He was head of the clergy of *Hagia Sophia and probably played some part in the Third Council of *Constantinople (680) and the *Trullan Synod (692). He was Metropolitan of Cyzicus before he was elected Patriarch in 715; soon afterwards he anathematized the *Monothelites. In 725 the Emp. *Leo III issued his first edict against the veneration of *icons (see ICONOCLASTIC CONTROVERSY); Germanus resisted and was forced to resign in 730. He wrote three treatises, dogmatic letters, and sermons fostering the cult of the BVM. He is probably also the author of a work interpreting the contemporary Byzantine liturgy, and of some fine liturgical poems. Feast day, 12 May.

Germany, Christianity in. See CONFESSING CHURCH; EVANGELICAL CHURCH IN GERMANY; GERMAN-CHRISTIANS; HOLY ROMAN EMPIRE; LUTHERANISM; REFORMATION; and THIRTY YEARS WAR.

Gerontius, The Dream of. A poem by J. H. *Newman, first issued in 1865. It is a vision of a just soul leaving the body at death and its subsequent conversation with the angels.

Gerson, Jean le Charlier de (1363–1429), French Churchman and spiritual writer. He studied at *Paris, becoming a doctor of theology and in 1395 Chancellor of the University. He worked for the reform of the Church from within and the ending of the *Great Schism; the return of France to the obedience of *Benedict XIII was largely due to his work. In 1415 he went to the Council of *Constance. He asserted the superiority of a General Council over the Pope and demanded that doctors of theology should have a voice in it together with the bishops. He also took part in drawing up the Four Articles of Constance.

Gerson developed the *Conciliar theory, but without rejecting the primacy of the Pope. In moral theology he accepted the extreme *Nominalist doctrine, according to which nothing is sinful in itself, but the sinfulness or goodness of an action depends solely on the will of God. His mystical teaching had marked *Augustinian tendencies; he consciously opposed the spiritual teaching of the 'antiqui' to the dry intellectualist activities of the Nominalist 'moderni', who threatened to convert theology into mere dialectics. The chief of his many treatises devoted to the spiritual life is *The Mountain of Contemplation* (1397). Both his Conciliar views and his mystical teaching were immensely influential. The attribution to him of the '*Imitation of Christ' has generally been abandoned.

Gertrude, St (1) (629–59), abbess. The daughter of Pepin the Elder, she became first abbess of the convent founded by her mother at Nivelles in Belgium. Feast day, 17 Mar.

Gertrude, St (2), **'the Great'** (1256–c.1302), German mystic. Entrusted as a child to the nuns of Helfta in Thuringia, at 25 she experienced a conversion and then led a life of contemplation. She was associated with *Mechthild of Magdeburg and St Mechthild of Hackenborn. Her *Legatus Divinae Pietatis* (of which only the second book was written by her, the other four being based on notes) is one of the major literary products of Christian mysticism. She was an early exponent of devotion to the *Sacred Heart and is the patroness of the *West Indies. Feast day, 16 Nov.

Gervasius and **Protasius, Sts,** protomartyrs of Milan. Nothing certain is known of them. In 386 St *Ambrose, obeying a 'presentiment', dug in search of relics; two skeletons were recognized as the remains of these martyrs and transferred to a new church, where miraculous healings are said to have taken place. Feast day, 19 June.

Gesuati (or, officially, **Clerici apostolici S. Hieronymi).** A congregation of laymen founded c.1360 by Bl John *Colombini. They secured Papal approbation in 1367 on condition that they established proper monasteries. The congregation was dissolved in 1668.

Gethsemane, Garden of. The garden, just outside *Jerusalem, to which the Lord retired after the Last Supper and which was the scene of His agony and betrayal.

Geulincx, Arnold (1624–69), philosopher. He was deprived of his professorship at Louvain in 1658 because of his attacks on *Scholasticism and monasticism. He then went to *Leiden and became a *Calvinist.

Starting from R. *Descartes' distinction between body and thought, Geulincx developed the theory known as *Occasionalism. He denied any action of bodies on bodies or bodies on spirits or spirits on bodies, and consequently of all movements produced by our will. God is the sole cause of all movement and thought. Man can achieve nothing of himself. God, however, is wholly inaccessible to man, and to lead the moral life man must turn to the Divine in himself, i.e. the human reason by which he participates in the Divine nature.

Ghana, Christianity in. Christian activity dates from the arrival of the Portuguese on the coast in 1471, but RCs were a small minority when the Dutch took over the Portuguese interests in 1642. Sustained missionary work began when the Swiss-based Basel Mission entered the Danish trading sector in 1828. Other missions followed. Favoured by the increasingly dominant British, they prospered in the Fante south; Ashante was more resistant, and British conquest in 1896 probably stiffened opposition to Christianity. RC missions returned, beginning with the Society of *African Missions in 1880. During the First World War missionaries from Continental Europe were expelled, but Church membership increased under local leadership. Preachers without missionary tutelage caused large movements towards Christianity. Where Christianity had already been established, Churches stressing prophecy and healing developed, incorporating elements of traditional culture. Contemporary Ghanaian Christianity is strong in the South, limited in the North. There are new denominations and *charismatic and para-church movements, in addition to the historic Churches deriving from the older missions.

Ghéon, Henri, pseudonym of Henri-Léon Vangeon (1875–1944), French Catholic writer. He tried to build up a Christian theatre, producing his own plays and working with a company of young RCs which he founded in 1924. Many of his works dealt with the lives of saints and other sacred themes; their deliberate naïvety of tone sought to reproduce the atmosphere of medieval hagiography. His biographies appealed to a wide public.

ghetto. In former times the street or quarter of a city in which the Jewish population customarily lived. Now the word is loosely used of any close settlement of a minority group.

Gibbon, Edward (1737–94), historian of the later Roman Empire. He conceived the plan of the *Decline and Fall of the Roman Empire* in Rome in 1764. It appeared between 1776 and 1788. It is unchallenged as a history on a grand scale, but its hostile attitude to the Church aroused controversy.

Giberti, Gian Matteo (1495–1543), Bp. of *Verona from 1524. He was one of the leading advocates in Italy of ecclesiastical reform who prepared the way for the Council of *Trent.

Gibraltar in Europe, Diocese of. See EUROPE, DIOCESE IN.

Gibson, Edmund (1669–1748), Bp. of London. One of the fruits of his intervention in the Convocation controversy, in which he opposed F. *Atterbury, was his *Synodus Anglicana; or the Constitution and Proceedings of an Anglican Convocation* (1702), a standard manual. His *Codex Iuris Ecclesiastici Anglicani* (1713) is still the most complete collection of English ecclesiastical statutes. A High Church Whig, he became Bp. of *Lincoln in 1716 and of London in 1723. Here he promoted the welfare of the American colonists, then under his jurisdiction.

Gidding, Little. See LITTLE GIDDING.

Gideon Bibles. Bibles placed in hotel bedrooms, prison cells, hospitals and other places by an organization of Christian business and professional men and their wives. The Gideons were founded by a group of commercial travellers in Janesville, Wisconsin, in 1899; they took their name from Gideon, whose victory against great odds is recorded in Jgs. 6: 11–7: 25. In 1908 they pledged themselves to place Bibles in every hotel in the USA. In 1947 the Gideons International Extension Committee was formed; they are now established all over the English-speaking world.

Gifford Lectures. A series of lectures delivered in Scottish universities under the foundation of Adam Gifford, Lord Gifford (1820–87), for promoting and diffusing the knowledge of God and the foundation of ethics. The first course was given in 1888.

Gilbert de la Porrée (d. 1154), biblical commentator and theologian. Born *c.*1080 or slightly later, he taught at *Paris before becoming Bp. of Poitiers in 1142. He wrote commentaries on the Psalter and Pauline Epistles, but he is chiefly remembered for that on the theological *opuscula* of *Boethius. The language used in this work on how to reconcile the statements 'God is one' and 'God is three' aroused opposition, and Gilbert was summoned to appear before the Council of Reims in 1148. Despite pressure from St *Bernard, there was no formal condemnation. His followers were known as the Porretani.

Gilbert of Sempringham, St (*c.*1083–1189), founder of the Gilbertine Order. As parish priest at Sempringham in Lincolnshire, he encouraged seven women to adopt a rule of life founded on a *Cistercian model and received their profession. Lay brothers and sisters were soon associated with them, and their numbers grew. The Cistercians having declined to govern communities of women, Gilbert entrusted their direction to *Augustinian Canons; the communities then took the form of *double monasteries. Feast day, 4 Feb.

Gildas, St (6th cent.), British monk and historian. His *De Excidio et Conquestu Britanniae* (apparently written in S. Wales) is primarily a denunciation of the evils which accompanied the subversion of sub-Roman Britain by the invading pagan English between *c.*450 and *c.*550. He is the only contemporary writer to have attempted a general survey of British history in this period. Feast day, 29 Jan.

Giles, St (? 8th cent.), patron of cripples, beggars, and blacksmiths. According to a 10th-cent. Life, he was an Athenian who became a hermit near the mouth of the Rhône; here he lived on herbs and the milk of a hind. Flavius Wamba, king of the Visigoths, hunted the hind to Giles's abode and, impressed by his holiness, built him a monastery. The town of St-Gilles, which grew up near his grave, became a place of pilgrimage. Feast day, 1 Sept.

Giles of Rome (c.1243/7–1316), philosopher. Born in Rome, he became an *Augustinian Hermit at *Paris. He was made Abp. of Bourges in 1295. His many writings include commentaries on works of *Aristotle and on *Peter Lombard's 'Sentences'; treatises against the *Averroists, on *angels, and on *Original Sin. The most popular, his *De Regimine Principum*, was written for his pupil, the future King Philip the Fair. His *De Summi Pontificis Potestate* may have been the foundation of *Boniface VIII's bull '*Unam Sanctam'.

Gilgamesh, Epics of. The Babylonian Gilgamesh Epic is a long narrative poem known from tablets and fragments dating from c.1800 to c.300 BC. Behind it lie five Sumerian Gilgamesh Epics. The story centres on Gilgamesh's fear of death and the death of his friend Enkidu. The *flood story in the Babylonian Epic is echoed in Gen. 6–9.

Gill, Arthur Eric Rowton (1882–1940), sculptor, letterist, and wood-engraver. He joined the RC Church in 1913. As a stone carver he excelled in producing inscriptions and small objects such as crucifixes and holy-water stoups. In his art he sought to express a Christian vision of the created order (his appreciation of which included an unembarrassed celebration of erotic love).

Gilpin, Bernard (1517–84), 'Apostle of the North'. A great-nephew of C. *Tunstall, he disapproved of the doctrinal changes under *Edward VI. Tunstall made him Archdeacon of Durham, almost certainly in 1556, but his attacks on clerical corruption led to trouble with the Marian Church authorities. He was offered, but declined, preferment under *Elizabeth I. He made long and successful missionary journeys in the North of England, collecting a large following, including some *Puritans.

Gilson, Étienne (1884–1978), *Thomist philosopher. He held professorships in France and, after he retired, at the Pontifical Institute of Mediaeval Studies in Toronto. From 1959 he lived mainly in France. His earliest work was on R. *Descartes, but most of his life was devoted to the study of medieval philosophy; he wrote on different aspects of this and on key figures.

Gioberti, Vincenzo (1801–52), Italian politician and philosopher. Banished from Italy in 1834, he taught in Brussels, where he published most of his philosophical works. Returning to Italy in 1847, in 1849 he became briefly a member of the Cabinet of Victor Emmanuel II. His philosophical ideas were *Ontologistic. He held that there was an exact correspondence between the orders of being and knowing and that the human mind directly perceived the absolute necessary Being, God, the creative cause of all existence and the source of human knowledge.

Giotto (c.1267–1337), the usual name for Ambrogiotto di Bondone, painter. Little is known of his life; he was employed by King Robert of Naples, c.1329–33, and in 1334 he was appointed surveyor of the cathedral at Florence. He broke away from the rigid formality characteristic of late Byzantine art in Italy and introduced a new sense of dramatic realism. Though it is disputed whether he designed the cycle of frescoes in the Upper Church at *Assisi, he was certainly responsible for those in the Arena Chapel at Padua and the Peruzzi and Bardi Chapels of Santa Croce in Florence; all demonstrate his concern for naturalism and his genius for narrative and characterization.

Giovanni Capistrano, St (1386–1456), friar. Taken prisoner in war, he had a vision of St *Francis; on his release he joined the *Franciscans in 1416. He took part in the General Chapter which met at Assisi in 1430 to secure union of the *Conventuals and the *Observants, and on several occasions he was Vicar-General of the Order. In 1451 he was sent to Austria to help combat the *Hussites. In Hungary, with Hunyady, he raised an army which defeated Turks in 1456. Feast day, 23 Oct. (formerly 28 Mar.).

Giraldus Cambrensis (c.1146–1223), **Gerald de Barri**, historian. From c.1175 to 1203 he was Archdeacon of Brecon. He was twice elected Bp. of *St Davids, but failed to obtain consecration. His historical works are amusing and vivid, but the facts are sometimes exaggerated.

girdle. As an article of liturgical attire, a usual accompaniment of the *alb, and hence one of the six *Eucharistic vestments.

Glabrio, Manius Acilius, consul in AD 91. Ordered by *Domitian to fight with wild beasts in the amphitheatre, he was then banished and executed in 95. The idea that he was a Christian is probably mistaken.

Gladstone, William Ewart (1809–98), British statesman. Brought up as an *Evangelical, he became a *High Churchman. In 1854 he supported G. A. *Denison, who was prosecuted for teaching the *Real Presence. In 1867 he became leader of the Liberal Party. He fought the next general election on the issue of the disestablishment of the Church of *Ireland, which he carried through as Prime Minister in 1869. In 1874 he opposed Abp. A. C. *Tait's *Public Worship Bill in the interests of the liberty of the C of E, and in the same year he published several bitter attacks on the RC Church, especially on the decrees of the First *Vatican Council. He was responsible for the foundation of many sees in the growing British Empire. He defended the doctrine of *conditional immortality in *Studies Subsidiary to the Works of Bishop Butler* (1896).

Glagolitic. The Slavonic alphabet generally thought to have been devised by St *Cyril, the Apostle of the Slavs.

Glanvill, Joseph (1636–80), religious writer. In 1666 he became rector of the Abbey Church, Bath. He was an early member of the Royal Society (elected in 1664). In various writings he tried to show that evidence derived from physical phenomena supported religious belief.

Glasites (also **Sandemanians),** a small Scottish sect named after John Glas and his son-in-law Robert Sandeman. Glas, who was ordained in 1719 as minister of Tealing, near Dundee, came to hold that the exist-

ence of a State Church was unscriptural and challenged the basis of the Presbyterian establishment. He was deposed in 1730. He established independent congregations among his (mainly poor) followers, for whom unordained elders conducted communion services. Leadership gradually passed to Sandeman, who in *Letters on Theron and Aspasio* (1757) attacked the *Calvinist teaching that God imputes the righteous acts of Christ to individual Christians, holding rather that a reasoned faith was the only basis for a proper relationship with God and the attainment of salvation.

Glastonbury Abbey, Somerset. Originally a *Celtic foundation, under St *Dunstan Glastonbury became an important educational and religious centre. Between 1129 and 1139 *William of Malmesbury wrote a history of the abbey; a 13th-cent. revision of this work records the legends associating Glastonbury with *Joseph of Arimathaea, King Arthur, and St *Patrick. The abbey was suppressed in 1539. The 'Glastonbury Thorn' was a Levantine hawthorn, around which several legends collected; it was cut down under O. *Cromwell, but descendants of it remain.

glebe. In English and Scots ecclesiastical law, the land devoted to the maintenance of the incumbent of the parish. The term now excludes the parsonage house and the land occupied with it. In 1978 ownership of glebe land in England was transferred from the incumbent to the Diocesan Board of Finance. In Scotland glebe was vested in the General Trustees of the Church by Act of Parliament in 1925.

Gloria in excelsis. The initial words in Latin, and hence the common designation, of the hymn 'Glory be to God on high', etc. Its date and authorship are unknown. In the 4th cent. it formed part of morning prayers, and it is still recited in the Orthodox *Orthros. In the W. Church its main use is in the Eucharist.

Gloria Patri. The first words of the Lesser *Doxology ('Glory be to the Father', etc.), an ascription of praise to the Trinity. Its use at the end of Psalms dates from the 4th century.

Glorious Mysteries, the Five. The third *chaplet of the *Rosary, consisting of: (1) the *Resurrection; (2) the *Ascension; (3)

the Descent of the Holy Spirit; (4) the *Assumption of the BVM; and (5) the *Coronation of the BVM.

Glos(s)a Ordinaria. The standard medieval commentary on the Bible, known also as the **Glos(s)a Communis** or simply the **Glos(s)a**. It was drawn up chiefly from extracts from the Fathers, and was arranged in the form of marginal and linear glosses. Its composition was begun in the school of *Anselm of Laon, who was responsible for the Gloss on the Pss., Pauline Epp., and Jn. The whole Bible was covered by about the mid-12th cent.

glossolalia. Speaking in 'tongues', a form of ecstatic speech, sometimes believed to be supernaturally initiated. Glossolalia was a common phenomenon in NT times (cf. Acts 10: 46; 1 Cor. 14). What most authorities believe to be a similar or identical experience has been encountered in many religious revivals and plays a prominent part in modern *Pentecostalism and in the *Charismatic Renewal Movement.

Gloucester. A religious house was founded here in 681 and converted into a college of secular priests in 823. It was refounded as a *Benedictine monastery by *Wulfstan, Abp. of York, in 1017. The present (cathedral) church was begun in 1089. It is notable for the Perpendicular panelling superimposed on the Norman pillars in the choir, and for the cloisters, with their early fan tracery (before 1377). The monastery was suppressed in 1540. The diocese was founded in 1541, with the abbey church as the cathedral.

gloves, liturgical. In the W. Church liturgical gloves may be worn by the Pope and certain others during a *Pontifical Mass; their use ceased to be obligatory in 1968.

Gnesio-Lutherans. A modern name for the party of strict *Lutherans, led by N. von *Amsdorf and M. *Flacius, who opposed the *Leipzig Interim put forward by Duke Maurice of Saxony in 1548. See ADIA-PHORISTS.

Gnosticism. A complex religious movement which in its Christian form came into prominence in the 2nd cent. In Christianity, Gnosticism first appeared as a school (or schools) of thought within the Church,

but by the end of the 2nd cent. the Gnostics had mostly become separate sects. Different forms were developed by particular teachers, such as *Valentinus, *Basilides, and *Marcion, but some features are common to the movement as a whole. A central importance was attached to 'gnosis', the supposedly revealed knowledge of God and of the origin and destiny of mankind, by means of which the spiritual element in man could receive redemption. The source of this special 'gnosis' was held to be either the Apostles, from whom it was derived by a secret tradition, or a direct revelation given to the founder of the sect. Gnostic teaching distinguished between the *Demiurge or 'creator god' and the supreme and unknowable Divine Being. From the latter the Demiurge was derived by a series of emanations or 'aeons'. It was he who was the immediate source of creation and ruled the world, which was therefore imperfect and antagonistic to what was truly spiritual. But into the constitution of some men there had entered a seed or spark of Divine spiritual substance, and through 'gnosis' and the rites associated with it this spiritual element might be rescued from its evil material environment. The function of Christ was to come as the emissary of the supreme God, bringing 'gnosis'. As a Divine Being He neither assumed a properly human body nor died, but either temporarily inhabited a human being, Jesus, or assumed a phantasmal human appearance.

Gnosticism in various forms long persisted. The sect of the *Manichees, founded by Mani in the 3rd cent., survived until the 13th; meanwhile the possibly related sects of *Albigensians and *Cathars had appeared in France, Germany, and Italy. The *Mandaeans still survive. See also NAG HAMMADI.

Goar, Jacques (1601–54), French *Dominican liturgist. The most important of his works is the Εὐχολόγιον *sive Rituale Graecorum* (Paris, 1647; ed. 2, Venice, 1730). It contains the rites of the Greek Liturgy, Offices, Sacramentaries, etc., with Latin translations and notes; it is the basis of all subsequent research in the field.

God. The word is used both as a common noun, e.g. in polytheism, where a number of supposed existences claim belief, worship, and service, and as a proper name, e.g. in *monotheism, where there can be only one such existence. Christianity affirms that God is a *Trinity, consisting of 'three persons in one substance', the Father being the Source of all existence, the Son the Eternal Object of the Father's love and the Mediator of that love in creation and redemption, and the Holy Spirit the Bond of Union between the Father and the Son.

In the OT account of the Divine revelation to *Moses, God makes Himself known in the name '*Yahweh' ('I am who I am') as the unique God who tolerates no rival. The Prophets developed the different aspects of God. Whilst for many in Israel Yahweh remained pre-eminently a national God, the idea of God as saviour of the Gentiles as well as the Jews had an important place, especially during and after the Exile (Is. 49: 6; Jonah). In the events recorded in the NT a new revelation was given. This was made through Jesus Christ, the Incarnate Son, who revealed God as the Father of all men, whose infinite goodness had no need to manifest itself in material recompenses.

In the patristic age the development of the doctrine of God was determined by the data of Scripture, controversies with pagans, Jews, and heretics, and by the Greek philosophy which was the foundation of the education of most of the Fathers. Their wide speculations were gathered into a synthesis in the works of St *Augustine, who gives several proofs for the existence of God, e.g. from contingency, from the order and beauty of the world, and from the moral argument of conscience. The Divine transcendence was stressed particularly by *Dionysius the *Pseudo-Areopagite; he saw God as beyond Being and most surely reached by *apophatic theology, where concepts and images are denied and God known by unknowing. His translator, John Scottus *Erigena, held that by reason God is known as the cause of all things, but not as what He is; a higher knowledge of Him is possible by contemplation, but even here only through theophanies which He grants to angels and believers.

One of the concerns of the Schoolmen was to investigate the Divine Nature by the method of rational proof, without direct appeal to revelation. St *Anselm was the author of the *Ontological Argument for His being. St *Thomas Aquinas rejected this but elaborated his own five-fold proof for the existence of God (*Quinque Viae). Trying to hold a balance between an anthropomorphic conception of God and an exaggerated transcendence, he developed the idea that there are three ways of conceiving God—by affirmation, negation, and eminence. Thus, while His goodness (way of affirmation) is asserted, He may also be called 'not good', i.e. not good in the way a man is called good (way of negation), and 'super-good', i.e. above all human ideas of goodness (way of eminence).

The shattering personal experiences of the Reformers was reflected in their intensely personal experience of God. M. *Luther directed a tirade against the speculative theology of the Schools; J. *Calvin emphasized His majesty and transcendence. Subsequent theology has veered between emphasis on His transcendence and His *immanence, often expressed in *pantheistic terms.

A decisive attack on natural theology was made by I. *Kant, who in his *Critique of Pure Reason* (1781) sought to prove the impossibility of any rational proof of the existence of God; for him the only valid proof was from morality ('I had to remove knowledge to make way for faith'). The step from the refusal of any metaphysical basis for belief in God to resting the belief on feeling was made by F. D. E. *Schleiermacher. All religious statements must be derived not from logic but from personal experience and the origin of belief in God be sought in the feeling of dependence, common to human beings.

In the early 20th cent. there was a reaffirmation of the Divine transcendence. In Protestant theology it was associated particularly with the name of K. *Barth. In RC theology it had its counterpart in the revival of Scholastic teaching. The so-called '*death of God' theology in the 1960s reflected a widespread dissatisfaction with philosophical Theism, some of which was inspired by reflection on the 'silence of God' during the Nazi attempt to exterminate the Jews (the *Holocaust). *Process theologians sought to reconstruct the concept of God; by depicting Him as in some sense developing through His intercourse with the created world, they presented Him as both transcendent and immanent, eternal and temporal, impassible and passible. Reflection on the silence of God during the Holocaust also lies behind the doctrine of God who suffers in the theology of J. *Moltmann and E. Jüngel.

'God Save the King/Queen'. The British National anthem. There is some evidence that the words were put into substantially their present form for use in the RC chapel of *James II. The tune also seems to be a 17th-cent. recasting of earlier phrases.

godchildren. See GODPARENTS.

Godfrey of Bouillon (d. 1100), *Crusader. A member of the family of the counts of Bologne and duke of Lower Lorraine, he set off on the First Crusade in 1096 and led the assault which captured *Jerusalem in 1099. He was elected first Christian ruler of the city. He was one of several important princes on the Crusade, but has been depicted as its hero.

godparents, also **sponsors.** Witnesses to a *Baptism who assume responsibilities for the Christian upbringing of the newly baptized. In the case of infant Baptism they also make the promises of renunciation, faith, and obedience in the child's name.

Gog and Magog. In Rev. 20: 8 they are two powers under the domination of Satan. In the OT they appear together in Ezek. 38–9, where Gog is described as the prince of various groups which invade the land of Israel. In later *apocalyptic and *rabbinic literature they are conventional figures for those opposed to the people of God. The wooden statues of Gog and Magog at the Guildhall, London (destroyed in 1940), represented two giants of medieval legend.

Golden Calf. An object of worship set up (a) by the Israelites in the wilderness (Exod. 32) and (b) by King Jeroboam I (1 Kgs. 12: 28).

Golden Legend. A collection of saints' Lives and short treatises on the Christian festivals compiled by *James of Voragine. It was completed by 1265. Intended as a source-book for preachers, it became popular with a wider audience.

Golden Number. The number of any year in the Metonic cycle (devised in 432 BC by the Athenian astronomer Meton); it is used in computing the date of *Easter.

Golden Rose. An ornament of gold and gems in the form of a rose which is blessed by the Pope on the Fourth Sunday in Lent and may afterwards be presented as a mark of favour to an individual or community.

Golden Rule. A (modern) name for the precept 'Whatever you wish that men would do to you, do so to them' (Mt. 7: 12).

Golden Sequence. The *Sequence for *Whitsunday, '*Veni, Sancte Spiritus'.

Golgotha. The Hebrew form of *Calvary.

Gomar, Francis (1563–1641), Dutch *Calvinist. In 1594 he was appointed professor of theology at *Leiden. Here he became an upholder of rigid Calvinist principles and engaged in a prolonged controversy with J. *Arminius. At the Synod of *Dort (1618–19) he was among the chief opponents of Arminianism but failed to win majority support for his *Supralapsarian view of *predestination. He was one of the official revisers of the Dutch OT.

Gonzales, St Peter. See ELMO, ST.

Good Friday. The Friday before *Easter, kept as the anniversary of the Crucifixion. It is a day of fast, abstinence, and penance.

The present RC rite consists of: lessons and prayers, with the singing of the Passion according to Jn.; the *Veneration of the Cross, with the chanting of the *Reproaches and *Trisagion; and a General Communion of the people with Hosts reserved on *Maundy Thursday (see PRE-SANCTIFIED, MASS OF THE). The C of E provides for a normal celebration of the Eucharist, but until recently this rarely happened. In modern Anglicanism a form of service akin to the current RC rite has been fairly widely adopted. Of the extra-liturgical devotions the best known is the *Three Hour Service. In Continental Protestantism Good Friday is often a special day for the administration of the Lord's Supper. In the *Orthodox Church *Vespers ends with the solemn veneration of the *epitaphion, and *Mattins of Holy Saturday (on Good Friday night) finishes with a symbolic burial service of Christ.

Good Samaritan. The *Samaritan of the parable in Lk. 10: 30–7 who tended the traveller who had fallen among thieves.

Good Shepherd. A title of Christ based especially on His discourse in Jn. 10: 7–18 and on the parable of the Good Shepherd (Lk. 15: 3–7).

Gorcum Martyrs. A group of 19 RC priests put to death by the *Calvinists after the capture of Gorcum (S. Holland) by the *Gueux in 1572. Feast day, 9 July.

Gordon Riots (also No Popery Riots). The riots which broke out in London in 1780 when a mob, headed by Lord George Gordon, marched to Parliament with a petition for the repeal of the *Catholic Relief Act of 1778.

Gordon's Calvary. A site outside the north wall of *Jerusalem held by some archaeologists to be the place of Christ's Crucifixion. The name derives from General C. G. Gordon, one of its advocates.

Gore, Charles (1853–1932), Bp. of Oxford, 1911–19. The first principal of Pusey House, Oxford (1884–93), he defended the Catholic doctrine of episcopacy in *The Ministry of the Christian Church* (1888), and edited *Lux Mundi* (1889). His independent mind and strength of character brought a new strand into the *Anglo-Catholic Movement. He was also involved in the foundation of the *Community of the Resurrection. In 1902 he became Bp. of *Worcester, and in 1905 the first Bp. of Birmingham. Here he was highly successful. He was less happy after his translation to Oxford.

Gorgonia, St (d. *c.*370), sister of St *Gregory of Nazianzus. An incident in her life has sometimes (but probably wrongly) been taken as an early instance of devotion to the Reserved Sacrament. Feast day, in the E., 23 Feb.; in W., 9 Dec.

Gorham Case. In 1847 the Revd G. C. Gorham was presented to the vicarage of Brampford Speke. The Bp. of *Exeter, H. *Phillpotts, found him unsound on the doctrine of baptismal regeneration and refused to institute him. Gorham appealed to the *Judicial Committee of the Privy Council, which, attributing to him a view which he did not hold, declared it to be not contrary to the doctrine of the C of E. The decision caused controversy and many defections to the RC Church.

Görres, Johann Joseph von (1776–1848), German Catholic writer. After various adventures, he returned to the RC faith in 1824, and in 1827 he was offered a professorship at Munich; here he became the centre of a circle of RC scholars including J. J. I. von *Döllinger and J. A. *Möhler. When in 1837 the Abp. of *Cologne, C. A. von *Droste-Vischering, was deposed and imprisoned by the Prussian government, Görres took up his cause in his tract *Athanasius* (1838), which brought all Catholic Germany to the defence of the Church. His writings gave an impetus to the study of the mystics and contributed to the spread of Catholic ideas in Germany.

Gorton, Samuel (*c.*1592–1677), founder of the 'Gortonites'. A London clothier, *c.*1636 he sailed for Boston, Mass., in the hope of enjoying complete religious liberty, but there he encountered difficulties with the civil authorities. He came to hold many unorthodox doctrines, e.g. he denied that of the *Trinity and professed belief in *conditional immortality. His followers survived as a sect until the 18th cent.

Gorze, a monastery near Metz, founded in 748 by St *Chrodegang. After difficulties in the 9th cent., it was revived and built up by Adalbero I, Bp. of Metz (929–62), and became a centre of monastic reform. It has become customary to describe the observances which it promoted as 'Gorzian' in contrast with those of *Cluny. Its leaders put themselves at the disposal of patrons, both lay and episcopal, who invited them to take charge of and reform monasteries in their domains. Such houses did not form a network of institutions; they were associated chiefly by bonds of confraternity and mutual prayer.

Goscelin (d. after 1107), English hagiographer. A *Benedictine monk at St-Omer, in 1058 he entered the service of Herman, then Bp. of Ramsbury (later Bp. of *Sherborne and then of *Salisbury). He fell into disfavour with Herman's successor and seems to have stayed in a succession of religious houses, writing the Lives of local saints. From *c.*1090 he was at St Augustine's, *Canterbury.

Gospel ('good news'). (1) The central content of the Christian revelation, the glad tidings of redemption. St *Paul's use of the word without explanation in writing to believers in *Rome whom he did not know suggests that the Christian sense was already current. (2) The title of the books in which the Christian Gospel is set forth. This usage may derive from the title line of Mk. (1: 1). As there can be only one Gospel, 2nd-cent. superscriptions called the Church's books 'The Gospel *according* to Matthew', etc. The unique authority of Mt., Mk., Lk., and Jn. was becoming established in the second half of the 2nd cent. (3) The word is also used of the so-called *apocryphal Gospels written in the 2nd cent. and later outside the Church. They are clearly historically inferior to the canonical Gospels, whose authority they never seriously challenged in the Church.

Gospel (in the Liturgy). In the Eucharistic rite the reading from the Gospel proper to each Mass. It always occupies the last place (i.e. after the *Epistle and other readings, if any) as the position of honour. In the *Orthodox Church Gospels are also solemnly chanted at various other services.

Gospel Music. Religious music of a *revivalist nature, which originated in the USA in the second half of the 19th cent. Its texts emphasize the themes of personal salvation and the anticipation of heavenly joys; its music is largely derived stylistically from popular secular music. Developing from *spirituals and Sunday School hymnody, it manifested itself in the hymn-singing and other music associated with the crusades of D. L. *Moody and I. D. Sankey. Its most characteristic feature is the use of a refrain at the end of each verse. In the *Black Churches from the early 20th cent. it took a more radical form, incorporating elements of ragtime, jazz, blues, and similar styles, and much 'call and response' interaction between those leading the singing and the congregation. Its performance may involve anything from a solo singer with guitar or instrumental group to full scale 'gospel choirs', with or without congregational participation. This Black style of Gospel Music has spread throughout the *Pentecostal and other charismatically inspired Churches world-wide.

Gospel of Truth. See EVANGELIUM VERITATIS.

Gospeller. The person who sings or reads the Gospel in the *Eucharist.

Gother (more correctly **Goter), John** (d.

1704), RC controversialist. Of *Presbyterian family, he became a RC and in 1668 entered the English College at Lisbon. He was sent to England in 1682. In 1685 he published the first part of *A Papist Misrepresented and Represented*, the second and third parts following in 1687. It evoked many replies. His translation of the Roman Missal (published in 1718) was apparently the first English version of the complete text.

Gothic Version. The Greek Bible was apparently translated into the Gothic language by *Ulphilas (d. 383), but only part survives.

Gothic vestments. Eucharistic *vestments of medieval style and pattern, the *stole and *maniple being long and narrow, and the *chasuble circular, or nearly so, when laid out flat.

Gottesfreunde (Ger., 'God's friends'). The adherents of an informal movement of mystical piety, centring upon the Rhineland and Switzerland in the 14th cent. They stressed inner transformation rather than the external forms of religion.

Gotthard, St (960/61–1038), Bp. of Hildesheim from 1022. He made his monastic profession at Niederaltaich in 991, becoming abbot in 996. The Emp. Henry I commissioned him to reform many of the monasteries in Upper Germany. The St Gotthard Pass in the Alps is said to take its name from a former chapel dedicated to him on the summit. Feast day, 4 May.

Gottschalk (*c*.804–*c*.869), heterodox theologian. Entered as an *oblate at *Fulda, he later sought to leave the monastic life. He elaborated an extreme doctrine of *predestination, according to which the chosen are predestined to blessedness but others to eternal fire, though not to sin. He was ordained by a *chorepiscopus and propagated his views in Italy and the Balkans. In 848 he returned to Germany and at the Synod of Mainz his teaching was condemned. He was sent to *Hincmar, Abp. of Reims, and at the Synod of *Quiercy in 849 he was again condemned, deprived of his orders, and sentenced to imprisonment. He replied to a pastoral letter of Hincmar with the statement of his views known as the 'Confessio prolixior'. He also defended the use of the phrase 'trina deitas' against Hincmar.

grace. In Christian theology, the supernatural assistance of God bestowed upon a rational being with a view to his sanctification. While the need for this aid is generally admitted, the manner of it has been the subject of much discussion.

The theology of grace first emerged clearly in the controversy between St *Augustine and *Pelagius. Augustine regarded man, since the *Fall, as totally evil and deserving of damnation; by himself fallen man could only sin, and grace was necessary for the performance of all good actions. Pelagius, on the other hand, held that man was free to choose the good and able to take the initial steps to salvation by his own efforts; grace was given that the commands of God might be more easily fulfilled. Though the logical inference of Augustine's teaching was *predestination to damnation as well as to salvation, he himself sought to safeguard man's free will by various distinctions such as that between prevenient grace (i.e. grace antecedent to conversion) and subsequent grace, in which the Divine energy co-operates with man after his conversion. No such systematic development took place in the E. Church which continued to emphasize both the necessity of grace and the reality of human free will, and resisted the notion of predestination. Such ideas are reflected in the teaching of John *Cassian, whose doctrine of grace was seen in the W. as an attempt to mediate between Augustine and Pelagius, and hence dubbed '*Semipelagianism'. Cassian, while accepting Augustine's teaching on *original sin, rejected total depravity, irresistible grace, and unconditional predestination. Though grace was universally necessary, the will remained free at all stages. The Second Council of *Orange (529) attempted to settle the question on an Augustinian basis, with modifications; prevenient grace was held to be rendered necessary by the Fall, but emphasis was laid on human co-operation after conversion, and predestination to damnation was anathematized. The debate on the relationship of grace and free will continued, becoming acute in the controversy surrounding *Gottschalk. In the 13th cent. St *Thomas Aquinas distinguished 'habitual grace' (which is held

to be normally conveyed through the Sacraments), from 'actual grace' (which may exist in the unbaptized), while *Duns Scotus emphasized the timelessness of God in relation to the theology of grace. The Reformers returned to a more rigid Augustinianism. J. *Calvin taught absolute predestination and added the doctrine of the indefectibility of grace. This teaching was challenged by J. Arminius and his followers (see ARMINIANISM). In the post-Reformation RC Church there have been two main controversies, that associated with the teaching of L. de *Molina and the *Jansenist controversy.

The exact relationship between the giving of grace and the reception of the Sacraments has given rise to similar problems. In the 20th cent. there were various attempts to cut through the complexities of the W. doctrine of grace, including the assertion of the primacy of the notion of uncreated grace (the Holy Spirit Himself) over the various classifications of created grace (the effects of the Spirit's operation).

Grace, Pilgrimage of. See PILGRIMAGE OF GRACE.

Grace at Meals. The custom of giving thanks before and after food is not exclusively Christian. Various fixed forms are recited audibly in religious houses, colleges, and schools.

gradine. A ledge above and behind the altar upon which the cross, candlesticks, etc. are sometimes placed.

Gradual. In the W. Church, the *responsary, usually from the Psalms, sung immediately after the first Scriptural reading in the Eucharist. Since 1969 a responsorial Psalm has often taken its place.

Gradual Psalms. Pss. 120–34, each of which bears in Hebrew a title rendered by St *Jerome 'canticum graduum' (AV 'A Song of Degrees'; RV 'A Song of Ascents'; REB 'a song of the ascents'). Various explanations of the title have been offered.

graffiti (Ital.). Ancient inscriptions which are roughly scratched and not properly carved. Christian graffiti are numerous, especially in the *catacombs of Rome.

Grafton, Richard (c.1507–73), printer. An enthusiastic supporter of the Reformation, *c.*1536 he arranged with E. *Whitchurch for the printing at Antwerp of *Matthew's Bible (1537). He was then responsible for the printing of the *Great Bible at Paris; when this was suspended by the *Sorbonne, he escaped to England. He also printed the 1549 and 1552 BCP.

Graham, 'Billy' (William Franklin Graham) (1918–), American evangelist. He experienced conversion at the age of 16 and entered the Southern *Baptist ministry in 1943. He began his first major evangelistic campaign in Los Angeles in 1949, and in 1950 the Billy Graham Evangelistic Association was formed. Thereafter he toured the world, becoming well known for his 'stadium campaigns' in which he addressed huge crowds. In later years he made full use of modern technology, including *broadcasting and satellite links.

Grail, the Holy. In medieval romances, a vessel possessing spiritual powers and affording, under certain conditions, mystical benefits to its beholders. It is sometimes identified with the cup used by Christ at the *Last Supper.

Grande Chartreuse, La. The mother house of the *Carthusian Order, some 15 miles north of Grenoble.

Grandmont, Order of. A French religious order, founded by St Stephen of Muret (*c.*1054–1124/5), with its mother-house at Grandmont in Normandy. The discipline was originally severe, but it became increasingly lax. The Order came to an end before the French Revolution.

Gratian (d. by *c.*1160), canon lawyer. Practically nothing is known of his life. His *Concordantia Discordantium Canonum*, known as his *Decretum*, is a collection of patristic texts, conciliar decrees, and Papal pronouncements, presented within the framework of a treatise designed to resolve contradictions in his sources. It was used as an authority in the practice of the Papal *curia and formed part of the *Corpus Iuris Canonici*.

Gratry, Auguste Joseph Alphonse (1805–72), French Catholic apologist. He was concerned with the revival of Church life in France and took a prominent part in the restoration of the *Oratory. His many books sought to present the Christian faith to educated opinion.

gravamen (med. Lat., a 'grievance'). A memorandum sent from the Lower to the Upper House of *Convocation with a view to securing a remedy.

grave-diggers. See FOSSORS.

Gray, Robert (1809–72), Bp. of Cape Town from 1847 and Metropolitan of the Anglican Province of *South Africa from 1853. In 1861 he suspended from cure of souls Mr. Long, a clergyman who contended that the Letters Patent appointing Gray gave him no authority to summon him to synods; the decision of the *Judicial Committee of the Privy Council in Long's favour was of constitutional importance because it ended the legal contention that the C of E as a body established by law extended to all the dominions of the Crown. In 1863 J. W. *Colenso, Bp. of Natal, was presented on a charge of heresy to Gray, who deposed and then excommunicated him; his sentence was reversed by the Judicial Committee of the Privy Council who held that Gray's Letters Patent could grant him no coercive authority over Colenso, whose appointment antedated them.

Great Awakening, the. A widespread religious revival in the USA. Beginning among the Dutch Reformed Churches *c.*1726, it spread to the *Presbyterians and *Congregationalists and reached its zenith in New England in the 1740s. It was closely associated with the preaching of J. *Edwards and G. *Whitefield. A similar revival in the late 18th and early 19th cents. is known as the 'Second Great Awakening' and one in the period *c.*1875–1914 as the 'Third Great Awakening'.

Great Bible. The edition of the English Bible which T. *Cromwell in 1538 ordered to be set up in every parish church. It was not issued until 1539. It was the work of M. *Coverdale.

Great Entrance. In the E. Church, the solemn procession before the *Offertory at which the Eucharistic bread and wine are carried from the *prothesis to the *altar.

Great Schism. The term is used of:
  (1) The breach between East and West, traditionally dated 1054, when Cardinal *Humbert excommunicated *Michael

Cerularius and the latter excommunicated the Western legates. Negotiations continued over a long period. The formal repudiation of the Union of *Florence by the Synod of Constantinople in 1484 marks the final breach. The division remains, though the anathemas of 1054 were nullified in 1965.

(2) The period 1378–1417, during which W. Christendom was divided by the creation of antipopes. The Council of *Constance ended the schism with the election of *Martin V.

Greater Antiphons. See O-ANTIPHONS.

Greece, Christianity in. Christianity was preached in Greece in the first cent., principally by St *Paul. In the *Iconoclastic Controversy the Greeks stood firm in the cause of the images. During the Frankish occupation from 1204 onwards, though the Church was subject to a RC archbishop, it retained its E. character and its hold on the people. When the Turks became masters of Greece in the 15th cent., they favoured the Greek clergy. In the War of Independence it was Abp. Germanus of Patras who raised the standard of revolt in 1821. The Greek Church asserted its independence from *Constantinople in 1833 and was formally recognized as *autocephalous in 1850. The clergy are paid by the State, but since 1974 Church-State links have been weakened. See also ORTHODOX CHURCH.

Greek (biblical and patristic). The basis of the Greek of both the *Septuagint and the NT is the Hellenistic Greek (known as the Κοινή or 'Common' dialect) which spread over the Near East as a result of the conquests of Alexander the Great (d. 323 BC). This was a simplified form of Attic Greek, with some contributions from other dialects. There are, however, differences between writers. In the LXX, the *Pentateuch and Is. are in literary Hellenistic Greek; the other Prophets, Pss., Chron., and most of Sam. and Kgs. are nearer to the vernacular. Some of the later books (Dan., 1 Esd., Est., Job, Prov., Wisd.) are deliberately artistic in style. In the NT, *Luke is the most literary writer, then St *Paul and the author of Heb. At the other end of the scale, Rev. is in an uneducated vernacular Greek, frequently ungrammatical.

For the first three cents. Christian writers were generally not influenced by pagan lit-erature. When Christianity became the religion of the Empire, Christians shared the education of the Greek world. A deliberate cultivation of Attic models and a conscious elaboration of style coloured patristic Greek, especially the works of John *Chrysostom and *Gregory of Nazianzus. The language was also progressively affected by modifications in the meanings of words necessitated by the requirements of Christian theology and philosophy.

Green, Thomas Hill (1836–82), philosopher. From 1866 he taught in Oxford. He sought to rethink and propagate in England the idealistic doctrines of I. *Kant and G. W. F. *Hegel. He held that the analysis of consciousness showed that reality was an organic whole and not a mere aggregate; that the evidence of art, morality, and religion all pointed to the spiritual nature of reality; that God, the eternal consciousness, was realized in each individual person; and that, since personality alone gave meaning to the evolutionary process, the permanence and immortality of the individual were assured.

Greenwood, John (c.1560–93), a leader of the early *Separatists. He either found or created the 'Ancient Church' in a house in St Paul's churchyard, London. He was imprisoned in 1587. With H. *Barrow, he wrote many pamphlets. Both were hanged.

Gregorian Calendar. The calendar as reformed in 1582 by *Gregory XIII and now in use in most of the Christian world. The calendar devised by Julius Caesar (46 BC) did not correspond exactly to the period taken by the earth to go round the sun, and an error of 10 days had accumulated. Protestant countries were reluctant to introduce the Gregorian calendar, and it was not adopted in England until 1752.

Gregorian chant. See PLAINSONG.

Gregorian Sacramentary. The name given to a family of Sacramentaries traditionally ascribed to *Gregory I (590–604). The most important of these is the book sent by *Hadrian I to *Charlemagne. The deficiencies in this book were made good from *Gelasian service-books current in Gaul. From a fusion of these two sources, 'Gregorian' and 'Gelasian', the later Roman Missal is derived. The ascription to Gregory I of the book sent by Hadrian cannot be taken literally, as it contained a Mass for his feast, but it has been shown to include material composed by him.

Gregorian Water. In W. usage, solemnly blessed water formerly used in the consecration of churches and altars. It is so named from the formula used in blessing it being attributed to Pope *Gregory I.

Gregorianum. The *Jesuit university at Rome. It was founded in 1551 as the 'Collegium Romanum' by St *Ignatius Loyola and in 1582–4 endowed by Pope *Gregory XIII and constituted a university.

Gregory I, St (c.540–604) (**Gregory the Great**), Pope from 590. He was Prefect of Rome in 573. He then devoted his wealth to the relief of the poor and monastic foundations, entering one of the monasteries which he had founded. When he became Pope, Italy was in a bad way. He made a separate peace with the Lombards in 592–3, setting aside the authority of the Emperor's representative. He also undertook various initiatives in matters affecting the civil administration and military defence of Italy. He refused to recognize the title of '*Oecumenical Patriarch' adopted by the Patr. of Constantinople. One of the achievements of his pontificate was the mission to England, for which he selected St *Augustine (later of Canterbury) with monks from his own monastery.

Gregory's *Liber Regulae Pastoralis* sets out directions for the pastoral life of a bishop. The *Dialogues* (traditionally and almost certainly correctly ascribed to him) relate the lives and miracles of Italian saints, including St *Benedict. He also wrote commentaries on Job and other Books of the OT, and Homilies on the Gospels. 854 letters survive. His theology was dominated by the ideal of the contemplative life, and some of his stories about the fate of souls after death played a part in the development of the doctrine of *purgatory. He promoted monasticism, made important changes in the liturgy, fostered the development of liturgical music, and gave the Roman '*Schola Cantorum' its definite form. His pontificate did much to establish the idea that the Papacy was the supreme authority in the Church. Feast day in the W., 3 Sept. (formerly 12 Mar., still observed in the E.).

Gregory II, St (669–731), Pope from 715. He was confronted with danger from the Saracens, against whom he had the walls of Rome repaired, and the paganism of the German tribes. To them in 719 he sent St *Boniface, aided by British monks and nuns. In the *Iconoclastic controversy he rebuked the Emp. *Leo III in 727, without, however, countenancing the planned revolt of Italy. Feast day, 13 Feb.

Gregory VII, St (d. 1085), Pope from 1073. Hildebrand was probably born c.1015; certainly not later than 1034. Educated in a monastery at Rome, he took monastic vows. He was chaplain to Pope Gregory VI and after the accession of *Leo IX (1049) exercised great influence. As Pope, he extended his work for the reform and moral revival of the Church by issuing decrees against the *simony and incontinence of the clergy in 1074. These measures, which were enforced by Papal legates, were strongly opposed, especially in France and Germany. In Germany *Henry IV, threatened with excommunication and deposition, held two synods which declared the Pope deposed (1076). Gregory then deposed and excommunicated Henry and freed his subjects from their oath of allegiance. Henry submitted to the Pope at *Canossa in 1077, did penance, and was absolved from his censures. The German princes nevertheless elected Rudolf of Rheinfelden as German king. Gregory did not recognize him until 1080, when he again excommunicated Henry, who had not fulfilled the promises made at Canossa. Henry set up an antipope and took Rome in 1084. Gregory was freed by Norman troops but died at Salerno. Feast day, 25 May.

Gregory IX (c.1148–1241), Pope from 1227. He excommunicated *Frederick II for his delay in fulfilling his promise to go on a *crusade, and when he sailed unreconciled in 1228, proclaimed an *interdict over his land and wherever he went. In 1230 he agreed to a treaty with the Emperor, but in 1239 he excommunicated him again and died while Frederick was besieging Rome.

A friend of St *Francis of Assisi, he became Protector of the *Franciscan Order in 1220, and it was largely from *Dominicans and Franciscans that he recruited the full-time *Inquisitors appointed from c.1233. In 1230 he commissioned *Raymond of Peñafort to collect the Papal *decretals of the last 100 years in the so-called 'Liber Extra' (published in 1234).

Gregory X (1210–76), Pope from 1271. He recognized Rudolf of Habsburg as Emperor, inducing Alfonso of Castile to resign his claims to the German throne. At the Second Council of *Lyons (1274) the Greek Emp. Michael Paleologus made his submission to the Pope, though the reunion was short-lived. Among the innovations of his pontificate was the introduction in 1274 of the *conclave in papal elections.

Gregory XI (1329–78), Pope from 1370. Elected Pope at *Avignon, he was persuaded to return to Italy by St *Catherine of Siena. He entered Rome in 1377 but could not end the disturbances. He condemned the teaching of J. *Wycliffe (1377). The *Great Schism followed his death.

Gregory XIII (1502–85), Pope from 1572. His pontificate was notable for its pro-Spanish temporal policy and its vigorous promotion of the *Counter-Reformation. He was committed to implementing the decrees of the Council of *Trent, and established numerous *seminaries, entrusting many of them to the *Jesuits, who also received from him a monopoly of missions to *China and *Japan. He approved St Philip Neri's *Oratorians (1575) and the Discalced *Carmelites (1580). He also promulgated the *Gregorian Calendar.

Gregory XVI (1765–1846), Pope from 1831. Soon after his election revolution broke out in the Papal states and was quelled only by the intervention of Austria. The troubles continued, and for most of his pontificate Gregory's relations with foreign powers remained strained. He condemned Liberalism in the person of F. R. de *Lamennais (1834) and also the semi-rationalistic theology of G. *Hermes (1835). In the field of foreign missions, he erected new bishoprics and vicariates and encouraged the formation of a native clergy.

Gregory Dialogus, St. A title of Pope *Gregory I.

Gregory of Elvira, St (d. after 392), Bp. of Elvira, near Granada. An intransigent opponent of *Arianism, he supported the refusal of *Lucifer of Cagliari to pardon those who had 'Arianized' at the Council of *Ariminum (359), and after Lucifer's death

he became the leader of the Luciferians. Now recognized as an important theologian, his writings are generally agreed to include the *Tractatus Origenis, Homilies on the Song of Songs, and De Fide, a doctrinal work refuting Arianism. Feast day, 24 Apr.

Gregory the Illuminator, St (c.240–?332), 'Apostle of *Armenia'. Apparently brought up as a Christian while in exile in Cappadocia, after his return to Armenia he converted the King, Tiridates (289–?330), to the Christian faith. He was consecrated bishop (*Catholicos), and the episcopate remained for some generations in his family. Feast day, 30 Sept.; in the American BCP (1979), 23 Mar.

Gregory of Nazianzus, St (329/30–389/90), '*Cappadocian Father'. The son of the Bp. of Nazianzus in Cappadocia, he studied at Athens. He then adopted the monastic life. About 372 he was consecrated Bp. of Sasima, a village in Cappadocia, and assisted his father as suffragan. In 379 he was summoned to *Constantinople, where his preaching helped to restore the *Nicene faith. In 381 he was appointed Bp. of Constantinople, but he retired in the same year. His writings include his 'Five Theological Orations', which contain an elaborate treatment of the doctrine of the Holy Spirit; the *Philocalia, which he compiled with St *Basil; letters against *Apollinarianism; and poems. Feast day, in the E., 25 Jan.; in the W., 2 Jan. (formerly 9 May, as in the American BCP, 1979).

Gregory of Nyssa, St (c.330–c.395), '*Cappadocian Father'. The brother of St *Basil, he entered a monastery. He was consecrated Bp. of Nyssa in Cappadocia c.371, deposed by the *Arians in 376, but regained his see in 378.

His chief theological works are polemical treatises against *Eunomius, *Apollinarius, and the *Tritheistic teaching of a certain Ablabius. In his 'Catechetical Orations' he expounded the doctrines of the Trinity, Incarnation, and Redemption, and the Sacraments of Baptism and the Eucharist for those whose duty it was to instruct *catechumens. His exegetical works deal especially with the mystical sense of Scripture. He also wrote 'On Virginity', a spiritual guide for monks entitled De Instituto Christiano (almost certainly influenced by the 'Great Letter' of *Macarius/Simeon), and a Life of his sister, St *Macrina. He was an ardent defender of the *Nicene doctrine of the Trinity, and he distinguished carefully between the generation of the Son and the procession of the Holy Spirit. In his account of the *Atonement he uses, perhaps for the first time, the simile of the fish-hook by which the devil was baited. Feast day, in the E., 10 Jan.; in the W., 9 Mar.

Gregory Palamas, St (c.1296–1359), Greek theologian and exponent of *Hesychasm. He was a monk of Mt *Athos. In 1337 he became involved in controversy with Barlaam, a monk from Calabria, who stated the doctrine of God's unknowability in an extreme form. In answer to Barlaam's attack on the contemplative practices of the Hesychasts, Gregory wrote the *Triads in defence of the Holy Hesychasts*. He later produced a more succinct exposition of his theology, the *One Hundred and Fifty Chapters*. He argued that the physical exercises used by the Hesychasts in prayer, as well as their claim to see the Divine Light with their bodily eyes, could be defended in virtue of the biblical notion of man as a single whole, body and soul together. In 1347 he was consecrated Abp. of *Thessalonica. Feast day in the E., 14 Nov.; also the second Sunday in Lent.

Gregory of Rimini (d. 1358), philosopher. An *Augustinian Hermit, he taught at *Paris. His philosophy carried further the *Nominalist teaching of *William of Ockham. In theology he was thoroughly *Augustinian; he held that unbaptized infants incur eternal damnation.

Gregory Thaumaturgus, St (c.213–c.270), Church Father. He was converted to Christianity by *Origen in *Caesarea. Soon after his return to Neocaesarea in Pontus, his native city, he became its bishop. In 264–5 he took part in the first Synod of Antioch against *Paul of Samosata; he also fought against *Sabellianism and *Tritheism. The wealth of miracles attributed to him, and to which he owes his surname of Thaumaturgus or wonder-worker, testify to the strength of his character. Only a few of the writings attributed to him are genuine; they include his Ecthesis or Creed and the so-called 'Canonical Letter', which contains information on the penitential discipline of the early Church. Feast day, 17 Nov.

Gregory of Tours, St (538/9–94), Bp. of Tours from 573 and historian. His *Historia Francorum* covers the period from the Creation up to 591, from 575 in detail; this work is of prime importance for the history of France. His hagiographical *Miraculorum Libri* are of less historical value. Feast day, 17 Nov.

gremial. According to W. usage, a cloth spread by the bishop upon his lap when seated during parts of the Mass to prevent his hands from soiling the vestments.

Grey Friars. Friars of the *Franciscan Order, so named from the colour of their habits (now generally brown).

Grey Nuns. A name given to Sisters of Charity in various countries. The best known are those founded by Madame d'Youville (Ven. Marie-Marguerite Dufrost de Lajemmerais) at Montreal in 1737 as a small community of ladies who devoted themselves to the care of the sick.

Griesbach, Johann Jakob (1745–1812), NT scholar. From 1775 he was professor of the New Testament at Jena. In 1775–7 he published an edition of the Greek NT in which, for the first time in Germany, the '*Textus Receptus' was abandoned, and thereby laid the foundations of all subsequent work on the Greek text. His theory that St *Mark was the latest of the *Synoptic Evangelists was revived in the 20th cent., but is accepted by few scholars.

Grignion de Montfort, St Louis-Marie (1673–1716), priest. In 1704 he began giving missions in W. France. His *Traité de la vraie dévotion à la Sainte Vierge* (recovered in 1842) has exercised a powerful influence on RC devotion. Feast day, 28 Apr.

Grimshaw, William (1708–63), *perpetual curate of Haworth, W. Yorks, from 1742. He invited to his pulpit *Methodists and *Evangelicals and engaged in itinerant preaching, as well as assisting J. *Wesley in supervising Methodist societies in the north of England. His clear sincerity led his diocesan to tolerate his behaviour.

Grindal, Edmund (?1519–83), Abp. of *Canterbury. He was chaplain to *Edward VI, went into exile under *Mary, became Bp. of London in 1559, Abp. of *York in 1570, and Abp. of Canterbury in 1575. On his refusal to suppress *Puritan 'prophesy-ings', in 1577 he was suspended from his jurisdictional, but not from his spiritual, functions; his resignation was under negotiation when he died.

Grocyn, William (?1449–1519), English Renaissance scholar. He studied Greek and Latin in Florence from 1488 to 1490/91, when he returned to Oxford to give the first public lectures in Greek. His learning was much admired, and he had a remarkable collection of Greek MSS. He used to be thought conservative in his religious views, but the evidence is inconclusive.

Groote (or Grote), Geert (1340–84), founder of the '*Brethren of the Common Life'. In 1374 he was converted from luxury to a simple life; in 1379 he became a missionary preacher in the diocese of Utrecht. His outspoken criticism of abuses led to his licence as a preacher being withdrawn in 1383, but his appeal against the sentence was never answered. He gathered round him friends who lived a quasi-monastic life at Deventer and became the nucleus of the Brethren of the Common Life.

Gropper, Johann (1503–59), theologian. After attending a synod (1536) called by *Hermann, Abp. of *Cologne, to combat the teaching of the Reformers, Gropper drew up an *Enchiridion* in which he put forward an early form of the doctrine of '*double justice'. At the time it was well received as a possible basis for reconciliation. He took part in the Conference at *Ratisbon in 1541. When the Abp. of Cologne became a Protestant, Gropper secured his deposition and the restoration of Catholicism in Cologne.

Grosseteste, Robert (c.1170–1253), Bp. of *Lincoln. Little is known of his early life. By 1225 he was lecturing on theology at Oxford; about 1230 he gave up his position as university lecturer to become the first *lector* to the recently established community of *Franciscans outside the city walls of Oxford. In 1235 he became Bp. of Lincoln.

Until 1225 he was mainly occupied with scientific studies. His most important work in this field was a commentary on *Aristotle's *Posterior Analytics*. Between c.1225 and 1235 he produced most of his theological works, notably the *Hexaemeron, De Decem Mandatis, De Cessatione Legalium*, and commentaries on the Psalms and Galatians. He also acquired a competence in Greek hitherto almost unparalleled in the W. As bishop he employed a group of scholars to carry through large enterprises of translation from Greek to Latin; these included the works of *Dionysius the Pseudo-Areopagite and commentaries on them and the *Ethics* of Aristotle with commentaries. He also translated part of the works of St *John of Damascus, St *Basil, the newly-discovered *Testaments of the Twelve Patriarchs, and the Greek lexicon ascribed to *Suidas.

In his episcopal work he showed energy and dedication. He promoted political action against the intrusion of royal and Papal officials into parochial benefices. He made a famous appeal in person on the subject to *Innocent IV at Lyons in 1250. He denounced the abuses of power by Papal officials, the curia, and the Pope himself, proposing reforms. Feast day in the American BCP (1979) and CW, 9 Oct.

Grote, Geert. See GROOTE, GEERT.

Grotius, Hugo (1583–1645), Huig de Groot, Dutch jurist and theologian. From an early age he held various State offices. Theologically he sided with the *Arminians, but he supported moderation and in 1614 drafted a *Resolution for Peace in the Church*. In 1619 he was sentenced to life imprisonment but escaped and in 1621 settled in *Paris. In 1635 Queen *Christina made him Swedish Ambassador to France.

Grotius's main religious work was the *De Veritate Religionis Christianae* (published in Dutch verse in 1622; in Latin in 1627). Designed as a handbook for missionaries, it sought to uphold the evidences of natural theology and to establish the superiority of the Christian faith to all other creeds. His *De Jure Belli ac Pacis* (1625) severed law from theology, fixing the principle of justice in the unalterable Law of Nature, which has its source in man as a human being. It earned him the title of 'Father of International Law'.

Grottaferrata. The site of a Greek Orthodox monastery near Rome, founded in 1004. It came under Latinizing influences, but in 1881 *Leo XIII re-established a purely Byzantine rite.

Grou, Jean-Nicolas (1731–1803), French *Jesuit. From 1792 he lived in England. He is known chiefly for his spiritual writings.

group ministry. In the C of E, a number of neighbouring parishes may be grouped together and the incumbent of each benefice has, besides the care of his own benefice, the legal authority to assist the incumbents of other benefices in the group.

Group Movement. See OXFORD GROUP.

Grundtvig, Nikolai Fredrik Severin (1783–1872), Danish religious leader. From 1839 until his death he was preacher at the Vartov Hospital in Copenhagen; in 1861 he was given the title and rank of a 'Bishop'. In 1824 he started a reforming movement in Danish *Lutheranism ('Grundtvigianism'), attacking the rationalism and State domination of religion.

Grünewald, Matthias (c.1475–1528), German painter, known in his lifetime as Mathis Gothart Nithart. The most famous work attributed to him is the altar-piece of Isenheim, now in Colmar. The Crucifixion is portrayed with cruel realism, with St *John the Baptist pointing to the Cross.

Gualbert, St John. See JOHN GUALBERT, ST.

Guarantees, Law of. The law passed in 1871 to regulate relations between the first government of the new kingdom of Italy and the Papacy.

guardian. The superior of a *Franciscan friary.

guardian angels. The belief that God assigns to every man an angel to guard him in body and soul was common to the pagan and Jewish world, though it is not clearly formulated in the OT. In the NT the belief is reflected in Acts 12: 15 and confirmed, in the case of children, by the Lord (Mt. 18: 10). Though in general accepted by the Fathers, it was first clearly defined by *Honorius 'of Autun' (12th cent.); he held that each soul was entrusted to an angel at the moment it was introduced into the body. The function of guardian angels is the protection of body and soul and the presentation of prayers to God (Rev. 8: 3f.). Feast day, 2 Oct.

guardian of the spiritualities. In the C of E, when a bishopric is vacant, the archbishop of the province provides for its administration, usually by authorizing a *suffragan bishop to act on his behalf. In this capacity the archbishop is described as 'guardian of the spiritualities'.

Gudule, St (d. c.710), patroness of Brussels. She is said to have belonged to a noble family of Brabant and to have devoted herself to prayer and charitable deeds. Feast day, 8 Jan.

Guéranger, Prosper Louis Pascal (1805–75), *Benedictine monk. With a view to re-establishing the Benedictine Order in France, he bought the priory of *Solesmes in 1832, opened it in 1833, and in 1837 became its first abbot. He was keenly interested in liturgical matters.

Guest, Edmund (1518–77), Bp. of *Salisbury from 1571. His *Treatise against the Privy Mass* (1548) repudiated the Eucharistic Sacrifice and adoration of the consecrated elements, and in 1549 he spoke against *transubstantiation. Under *Mary he remained in hiding. In 1560 he became Bp. of *Rochester. He played a prominent part in the 1563 debate on the revision of the *Forty-Two Articles, and it was he who devised the statement (incorporated into the *Thirty-Nine Articles) that the 'Body of Christ is given, taken and eaten in the Supper, only after an heavenly and spiritual manner.'

Gueux (Fr., 'ragamuffins'). Originally those who petitioned Margaret of Parma against the *Inquisition in 1566; then other Protestant bodies who opposed the Spaniards in the Low Countries.

Gui, Bernard (c.1261–1331), *Dominican historian. He was appointed *inquisitor of Toulouse in 1307 and Bp. of Lodève in 1324. He is remembered chiefly for his contribution to the history of the Dominican Order.

Guibert of Nogent (c.1053/65–c.1125), Abbot of Nogent, near Laon, from 1104. He opposed *Berengar's Eucharistic teaching. He wrote *Moralia* on Genesis, prefaced by an essay on biblical interpretation and preaching; a tract 'On the Incarnation against the Jews'; a history of the first *Crusade; an astonishing attack on the abuse of *relics; and an autobiography.

Guigo I (1083–1136), fifth prior of the *Grande Chartreuse from 1109. Soon after

1109 he began a collection of 'thoughts' (*Meditationes*) which has been compared with the *Pensées* of B. *Pascal. Under him the Grande Chartreuse began to have daughter-houses; partly to meet their needs he compiled the *Carthusian *Customary between 1121 and 1128.

Guigo II (d. prob. 1188), ninth prior of the *Grande Chartreuse from some time after 1173 to 1180. His *Scala Claustralium* ('Ladder of Monks'), with its programme of reading, meditation, prayer, and contemplation, contributed to later, more systematic, notions of the spiritual life.

Gunkel, Hermann (1862–1932), Protestant theologian. He held academic posts in Germany. He was a leading member of the *Religionsgeschichtliche Schule and a pioneer of *Form Criticism. He worked out the method in his commentary on Genesis (1901) and then extended it to the Psalms. He concluded that Hebrew religious poetry had a long history and that its forms had taken shape in oral tradition at a comparatively early date and become fully developed before the *Exile.

Gunning, Peter (1614–84), Bp. successively of *Chichester (from 1669) and *Ely (from 1675). He ministered to Anglican congregations during the Commonwealth, and at the Restoration he received rapid promotion. He took a leading part in the *Savoy Conference.

Gunpowder Plot (1605). The attempt to blow up the Houses of Parliament and destroy the King, Lords, and Commons together, in the hope that the RCs would then be able to seize the government. The plot was revealed.

Günther, Anton (1783–1863), religious philosopher. He spent most of his life in Vienna. He held that human reason could prove scientifically the mysteries of the Trinity and Incarnation, and that there was no cleavage between natural and supernatural truth. He also held that the dogmas of the Church were liable to revision in the light of fuller knowledge.

Gustav-Adolf-Verein, since 1946 called the 'Gustav-Adolf-Werk'. A German Protestant society to aid weaker sister Churches in Catholic areas. It was founded in 1832 to commemorate the bicentenary of *Gusta-

vus Adolphus's death, but it did not become important until the court preacher Karl Zimmermann amalgamated it with a similar society of his own in 1842.

Gustavus II Adolphus (1594–1632), King of *Sweden from 1611. He made peace with Denmark in 1613 and with Russia in 1617, and began a war against the Catholic Vasas of Poland in 1621. After repeated defeats he concluded a six-year truce in 1629. In 1630 his fear of the increasing Imperial power in the Baltic led him to intervene in the *Thirty Years War. He obtained help from France, but was at first opposed by the German Protestant princes, most of whom joined him after his victory at Breitenfeld (1631). He penetrated deep into W. and S. Germany. He was killed in battle at Lützen.

Gutenberg, Johann (c.1396–1468), inventor of printing. He was a native of Mainz. By c.1449 he seems to have possessed movable metal type cast in separate letters and had invented a typecasting machine. He printed the *Mazarin Bible (q.v.).

Guthlac, St (? 673–714), hermit. Of royal blood, he was a monk at Repton. He later migrated to an island in the Fens, where he lived a life of severe asceticism. The Guthlac Roll (now in the British Library) consists of drawings depicting his life. Feast day, 11 Apr. (in some calendars, 12 Apr.).

Guthrie, James (c.1612–61), Scottish *Presbyterian minister. He excommunicated General J. Middleton as an enemy of the *National Covenant and made him do public penance in 1650. In 1654 the English Council of State appointed Guthrie one of the *Triers. After the Restoration he was arraigned for treason and hanged.

Guthrie, Thomas (1803–73), Scottish *Presbyterian minister and social reformer. A supporter of the Evangelical party during the *Ten Years' Conflict, he 'came out' at the *Disruption (1843) and was remarkably successful in raising money for manses for ministers of the Free Church. From 1847 he engaged in establishing 'Ragged Schools', where poor children could be given a sound education on a Protestant basis. In his later years he advocated a national, rather than a denominational, scheme of education for Scotland, realized in the Education (Scotland) Act 1872.

Guyard (or Guyart), Marie (1599–1672), Bl Marie de l'Incarnation. Though drawn to the religious life, in 1617 she married C. J. Martin (d. 1620) and had a son. In 1631 she entered the *Ursuline convent at Tours. She was among those who accepted an invitation to form a convent at Quebec in 1639; she became its first superior. She was the recipient of visions from childhood. Feast day, 30 Apr.

Guyon, Madame (1648–1717), French *Quietist. Jeanne Marie Bouvier de la Mothe in 1664 married Jacques Guyon. After his death (1676) she came under the influence of a *Barnabite priest with whom she toured France. They were suspected of heresy and immorality and imprisoned. Mme Guyon was released through the efforts of Mme de Maintenon. From 1688 she corresponded with F. *Fénelon, who found her mystical experiences authentic. J. B. *Bossuet, however, distrusted her illuminism and wrote her a doctrinal letter in 1694. She requested a theological Commission to clear her of the suspicion of heresy, but the Conference of *Issy (1695) condemned her writings. She taught complete detachment from the world, indifference to suffering and misfortune, self-abasement, and submission to God's will in pure love.

Habakkuk, Book of. *Minor Prophet. Habakkuk complains of oppression and lawlessness; God answers that punishment is imminent in the invasion by the Chaldeans, who will themselves fall through pride and idolatry. Ch. 3 describes a vision of God coming to deliver His people.

The Book is probably to be dated in the late 7th or early 6th cent. BC. Most critics agree that ch. 3 is an independent addition. The Book's central message, that 'the just shall live by his faith' (2: 4), has played an important part in Christian thought.

habit (religious dress). The distinctive outward sign of the religious life. A habit is worn by members of the old orders (monks, friars, and nuns); it normally consists of a tunic, belt or girdle, *scapular, hood for men and veil for women, and a cloak. In modern times drastic changes have been made in some orders.

Hackney Phalanx. A loosely defined group of Anglican *High Churchmen in the early 19th cent. associated with J. J. Watson, Rector of Hackney, and H. H. Norris, Rector of South Hackney. They are sometimes known as the 'Clapton Sect' (from the home of one of them).

Hades. The place of waiting of departed spirits before judgement, visited by Christ after the Crucifixion. See also DESCENT OF CHRIST INTO HELL.

Hadewijch, 13th-cent. contemplative writer. She spoke the dialect of Brabant and probably belonged to a community of *Beguines. Her *Visions* (treatises in the form of letters), *Poems in Stanzas* and *Poems in Couplets* all treat of the union of the soul with God who transcends all union. Though her 'love mysticism' (*Brautmystik*) was in the tradition of St *Bernard, she was pre-eminent in assimilating this and adapting the concepts and terminology of courtly love for Christian ends. Some of her *Poems in Couplets* (25–9) are now attributed to a follower, 'Hadewijch II'; the authorship of others (17–24) is disputed.

Hadrian I (d. 795), Pope from 772. By persuading *Charlemagne to conquer Lombardy (774) and depose its king, Hadrian freed the Papacy from a long-standing menace. He also enlisted Charlemagne's help in suppressing *Adoptianism and supported his efforts to achieve unity in liturgy and canon law. See also GREGORIAN SACRAMENTARY.

Hadrian IV (*c.*1100–59), Nicholas Break-spear, Pope from 1154; the only Englishman to hold the Papacy. He secured the execution of *Arnold of Brescia and exacted full homage from *Frederick I (Barbarossa) before consenting to crown him. His claim that the Emperor held his crown as a *beneficium* from the Pope precipitated a quarrel which became acute under *Alexander III. The authenticity of his Bull granting the overlordship of *Ireland to Henry II of England, though long disputed, is now generally accepted.

Hadrian VI (1459–1523), Pope from 1522. He was tutor to the future *Charles V and from 1516 the virtual ruler of Spain. As Pope his main aims were to reform the *Curia, reconcile the European princes, check the spread of Protestantism, and deliver Europe from the menace of the Turks. His efforts at reform were frustrated and Rhodes fell in Oct. 1522.

Hadrian the African, St (d. 709/10), monk. Having declined Pope *Vitalian's offer of the see of *Canterbury, he was instrumental in securing the appointment for *Theodore of Tarsus. He set off for England with him in 668 and became the abbot of the monastery of Sts Peter and Paul (later St Augustine's), Canterbury, and master of the school. A man of learning, he fostered education. Feast day, 9 Jan.

Hagenau, Conference of. The gathering convened by *Charles V in 1540 to discuss the points in dispute between the Catholics and Protestants in Germany. It broke up without positive result.

Haggadah (Heb., 'narrative'). In Judaism: (1) the ritual of reading prayers that accompany the *Passover meal; (2) those parts of the traditional literature (*Midrash and *Talmud) not comprehended under the heading *Halachah, in particular tales and legends about biblical and rabbinic figures.

Haggai, Book of. *Minor Prophet. The Book, dated in the second year of Darius, i.e. 520–519 BC, consists of four discourses concerned to promote the rebuilding of the *Temple. The fourth (2: 21–24), promising Zerubbabel victory over his enemies, has traditionally been regarded as a reference to the *Messiah.

Hagia Sophia. The church at *Constantinople, dedicated to the 'Holy *Wisdom' (i.e. the Person of Christ), was built under *Justinian and consecrated in 538. Its chief feature is the huge dome which crowns the basilica. In 1453 the Turks converted the church into a mosque and its mosaics were covered up and partly destroyed. Discovered during restoration work, they were restored in the 20th cent. Since 1935 the church has been a museum.

Hagiographa (Gk., 'sacred writings'). A title applied to the third division of the OT canonical Scriptures, i.e. all Books not belonging to the 'Law' or the 'Prophets'. The Books comprised are Pss., Prov., Job, Ruth, Lam., Song of Songs, Eccles., Esther, Dan., 1 and 2 Chron., Ezra, and Neh.

hagiography. The writing of the lives of the saints. The primary sources include *martyrologies, *passions, calendars, biographies, and liturgical texts. The critical examination of these writings has been especially fostered by the *Bollandists.

hagiology. The literature dealing with the lives and legends of the saints and their cult.

Hagios o Theos. See AGIOS O THEOS.

hagioscope, also 'squint'. An opening in the chancel walls of some churches to permit worshippers to see the *Elevation at Mass.

Hail Mary. A form of prayer to the BVM, based on the greetings of *Gabriel (Lk. 1: 28) and *Elizabeth (Lk. 1: 42). In its modern W. form, it is as follows: (1) 'Hail Mary, full of grace, the Lord is with you: Blessed art thou among women, and blessed is the fruit of thy womb, Jesus'; (2) 'Holy Mary, Mother of God, pray for us sinners now and in the hour of our death'. A slightly different form is used in the Orthodox Church.

hair-shirt. A shirt made of cloth woven from hair, worn as a means of discipline.

Halachah (Heb., 'that by which one walks'). In rabbinic Judaism, the body of teaching which has a direct practical application, in contrast to *Haggadah.

Hales, Alexander of. See ALEXANDER OF HALES.

Half-Way Covenant, the. A doctrine current in 17th- and 18th-cent. American *Congregationalism which was held to express the relationship to God of those (especially baptized) members of the community who had had no describable religious experience.

Halifax, Charles Lindley Wood (1839–1934), Second Viscount Halifax. A *High Churchman, he was associated with the foundation of *SSJE in 1865, and as President of the *English Church Union (1868–1919 and 1927–34) he was involved in most of the ecclesiastical controversies of his time. Friendship with E. F. Portal led him to promote reunion between the C of E and the RC Church; with Portal he was responsible for initiating conversations in 1894–6 (terminated by *Apostolicae Curae). After the *Lambeth Appeal of 1920, he reopened the matter with Cardinal D. J. *Mercier, with whom he arranged the *Malines Conversations (q.v.).

Hall, Joseph (1574–1656), Bp. of *Norwich. He attended the Synod of *Dort as one of *James I's representatives. In 1627 he became Bp. of *Exeter. When the bishops were attacked in Parliament in 1640, Hall defended his order. He was translated to Norwich in 1641, but his income was impounded by Parliament and he lived in poverty.

Hall, Robert (1764–1831), *Baptist. He became an influential preacher in Bristol (1785–90 and 1826–31), Cambridge (1791–1806), and Leicester (1807–25).

Hallel (Heb., 'praise'). A name given by the Jews to Pss. 113–18. They are used at most of the main Jewish festivals and during the *Passover meal; they may have been the hymn sung by Christ and the Apostles at the *Last Supper (Mt. 26: 30).

Hallelujah. See ALLELUIA.

Haller, Berchtold (1492–1536), Reformer. He became a canon of Berne in 1520. From 1521 he was in contact with U. *Zwingli. He took part in the Disputations of Baden (1526) and *Berne (1528), collaborating in the composition of a Protestant liturgy and the reformatory edict of 1528. From 1532 he was the acknowledged religious leader of Berne.

halo (or nimbus). A circle of light round the head or, more rarely, the whole body. In Christian art its use was at first restricted to Christ, but from the 5th cent. it was extended to the BVM, angels, and saints, and later to other important persons. In modern RC practice a halo is allowed only for persons canonized or beatified or whose cult has been otherwise approved.

Hamann, Johann Georg (1730–88), religious thinker. He was one of the fathers of the German 'Storm and Stress' movement. He insisted on the importance of inner experience in matters of religion, proclaimed the rights of the individual personality, and attacked the rationalism of the *Enlightenment. In *Golgatha und Scheblimini!* (1784) he upheld Christianity as the historical revelation of the Triune God, of Atonement, and of Redemption.

Hamilton, John (1511–71), Abp. of St Andrews and Primate of Scotland from 1547. He was one of the most influential opponents of Protestantism. He held synods to reform the morals of the clergy and the religious education of the laity; the chief result was the compilation of a catechism in the vernacular known by his name (1552). In 1560 he protested against the acceptance by Parliament of J. *Knox's confession of faith. He was imprisoned in 1563, but released at the intervention of Queen *Mary. After her flight he was pronounced a traitor and hanged.

Hamilton, Patrick (c.1504–28), Scottish Protestant proto-martyr. He was attracted to M. *Luther's writings and visited *Wittenberg and *Marburg. On his return to Scotland he converted A. *Alesius, who had been deputed to convince him of his errors. He was charged with heresy and burnt.

Hamilton, Walter Kerr (1808–69), Bp. of *Salisbury from 1854 and the first *Tractarian to become a diocesan bishop in England. In 1861–4 he prosecuted R. *Williams (a contributor to *Essays and Reviews*), whose benefice was in his diocese.

Hammond, Henry (1605–60), Anglican clergyman. In 1633 he became rector of Penshurst, Kent, where he instituted daily services in church and a monthly celebration of the Eucharist. In 1645 he was appointed Chaplain in Ordinary to

*Charles I, whom he attended until his imprisonment in 1647. Under the Commonwealth he devoted himself to relieving the needs of the deprived clergy and raising funds to train future ordinands. His commentary on the Books of the NT (1653) is a pioneer work of biblical criticism. He also helped B. *Walton in the compilation of his Polyglot Bible.

Hampden, Renn Dickson (1793–1868), Bp. of *Hereford from 1848. In his Bampton lectures on *Scholastic Philosophy* in 1832 he expounded a view of Christianity in which its dogmatic elements were much reduced. Strong opposition was aroused by his appointment as a bishop.

Hampden Court Conference (1604). The conference between the English bishops and the *Puritan leaders to consider the Puritan demands for reform of the Church set out in the *Millenary Petition. The Puritans won only minor concessions.

Handel, George Frideric (1685–1759), musical composer. He was born in Germany, spent some time in Italy, but from 1712 lived mainly in London. He is regarded as the originator of the English *oratorio, with its prominent role for the chorus. Most of his oratorios were originally performed in the theatre, but without scenery or theatrical dress. The most famous, *Messiah* (1741; first performed 1742) is atypical in being non-dramatic. His other religious works include the anthem 'Zadok the priest', sung at every English coronation since 1727.

hands, imposition of. A ritual gesture which figures prominently in the Bible and in the life of the Church. In the Bible its predominant use is as a manner of blessing (e.g. Gen. 48), though in some cases an element of commission may be implied. It was used by Christ in many of His healing miracles. Some of the references in Acts have traditionally been taken as examples of *Confirmation and *Ordination. While the significance of these texts is open to question, the placing of the bishop's hand on the head of each candidate has come to be the central act of both these sacraments. The priest lays his hands on the sick person in the RC rite of *Unction and in some modern Anglican rites for the *Visitation of the Sick.

Hannington, James (1847–85), missionary. In 1884 he was consecrated first Bp. of Eastern Equatorial Africa. He was murdered by natives of *Uganda. Feast day in parts of the Anglican Communion, 29 Oct.

Hardenberg, Albert (c.1510–74), Reformer. He entered the monastery of Aduard c.1527. He later came into contact with J. *Laski and other Reformers, whom he openly joined in 1542. He went to *Cologne to help Abp. *Hermann of Wied, took part in the Diets of *Speyer (1544) and *Worms (1545), and in 1547 was appointed cathedral preacher at Bremen; he was expelled from this post in 1561 for his denial of the *Lutheran doctrine on the Lord's Supper. From 1567 he was preacher at Emden.

Harding, St Stephen. See STEPHEN HARDING, ST.

Hardouin, Jean (1646–1729), French *Jesuit. He is chiefly remembered for his edition of the texts of the ecclesiastical councils from NT times onwards.

Hare, Julius Charles (1795–1855), *Broad Churchman. Through travel in Germany he came under the influence of German theologians and men of letters; he introduced many German ideas into English theology. In 1840 he became Archdeacon of Lewes.

Harklean Version. A revision of the *Philoxenian Syriac Version of the NT made by Thomas of Harkel in 616.

Harless, Gottlieb Christoph Adolph von (1806–79), theologian. He held high academic positions and was one of the most influential representatives of *Lutheran orthodoxy in his generation. In 1852 he became president of the supreme consistory of Bavaria, where he reorganized the State Church.

Harmony Society. A communist sect, founded in Württemberg by J. G. Rapp (1757–1847). The community settled in the USA; it was dissolved in 1905.

Harms, Claus (1778–1855), *Lutheran theologian. He became provost of St Nicolai at Kiel in 1835. He is remembered chiefly for his defence of Lutheran theology at a time when its distinctive elements were threatened by the movement for uniting the Protestant confessions in Prussia.

Harnack, Adolf (1851–1930), German Church historian and theologian. From 1888 to 1921 he was a professor at Berlin. He was probably the most outstanding *patristic scholar of his generation, dealing especially with the pre-Nicene period. He aroused conservative opposition by his critical attitude to traditional Christian dogma and by his emphasis on the moral aspects of Christianity to the exclusion of the doctrinal. He also published notable studies on the *Synoptic problem.

Harris, Howel(l) (1714–73), one of the founders of Welsh *Calvinistic Methodism. After a conversion experience in 1735, he began an itinerant lay ministry in Powys, organizing his converts into religious 'societies'. Because of differences with others in the Welsh Methodist movement, he separated from it in 1750. He set up a religious community at Trevecca and in the 1760s was involved in the establishment of the Countess of *Huntingdon's college nearby. He remained an Anglican all his life.

Harris, William Wadé (c.1860–1929), West African evangelist known as 'Prophet Harris'. He belonged to the Glebo people of Liberia. Of *Methodist background, he trained as a *catechist in the Episcopal Church. In 1910, while imprisoned for anti-government activity, he became convinced of his calling as a prophet, and during 17 months in 1913–15 he preached across the Ivory Coast and through *Ghana, proclaiming the coming judgement of Christ and calling on all to abandon the traditional fetishes. White-robed, bearing a cross and a Bible, and accompanied by women singers, he was an impressive figure; he baptized large numbers and made a great impact.

Harrison, Frederic (1831–1923), English *Positivist. In his earlier years he was a member of the C of E, but he came under the influence of A. *Comte and embraced Positivism in 1870. He became the recognized leader in England of that school of thought.

Harrowing of Hell. The medieval English term for the defeat of the powers of evil at the *Descent of Christ into Hell after His death.

Hartmann, Eduard von (1842–1906). German philosopher. He saw in the 'Unconscious' an all-pervasive monistic principle which was at once will and presentation and also the ground of evolutionary development. Christianity, which was only a stage along the way to the religion of Absolute Spirit, was dead and its gravedigger was modern Protestantism.

Harvest Thanksgiving. In Britain an unofficial religious festival of thanksgiving for the fruits of the earth, usually observed on a Sunday in Sept. or Oct., after the ingathering of the harvest. An annual festival had become common by the mid-19th cent., and a parochial thanksgiving replaced the traditional Harvest Home. Various modern Anglican liturgies provide a set of collects, Psalms, and biblical readings for use on this day.

Hasmonaeans. The family name of the *Maccabees.

Hastings, James (1852–1922), Scottish *Presbyterian minister. He is famous as the editor of the *Dictionary of the Bible* (1898–1904), the *Encyclopaedia of Religion and Ethics* (1908–26), and other religious encyclopaedic works.

Hat, Cardinal's. See RED HAT.

Hatfield, Council of (679). This Council of the English Church, which met under Abp. *Theodore at Hatfield (or perhaps Heathfield), repudiated *Monothelitism, accepted the decrees of the first five General Councils, and affirmed its belief in the *Double Procession of the Holy Spirit.

Hauranne, Jean Duvergier de. See SAINT-CYRAN.

Hawkins, Edward (1789–1882), Provost of Oriel College, Oxford, 1828–74. He was influential in weaning J. H. *Newman from his early *Evangelicalism, but later stopped him from receiving tutorial pupils. In 1841 he drew up the condemnation of *Tract 90 by the Oxford Heads of Houses.

Haymo of Faversham (d. 1244), *Franciscan. Born at Faversham in Kent, he entered the Franciscan Order, probably in 1226. He took a leading part in the deposition of *Elias and was elected General of the Order in 1240. His works include an order for private and conventual Mass on ferias and notes for a ceremonial.

Headlam, Arthur Cayley (1862–1947), Bp. of *Gloucester 1923–45. He previously held high academic offices. A central Churchman who disliked all ecclesiastical parties (*Anglo-Catholics, *Evangelicals, and *Modernists), he was one of the most influential English prelates in his time.

hearse. (1) A triangular frame on a stand, holding 15 candles, formerly used at *Tenebrae. (2) Various funeral furnishings, now usually the car bearing the coffin.

heart. In the Bible the heart usually designates the whole personality, though here the emphasis is on the activities of reason and will rather than on the emotions. In Christian spirituality the heart is regarded as the organ for the love of God. See also SACRED HEART.

Heaven. In Christian theology the dwelling-place of God and the angels, and ultimately of all the redeemed, wherein they receive their eternal reward. In the Bible it is conceived as above the sky.

It is the distinctive Christian hope and belief that all faithful disciples (and not merely exceptional human beings) will, through Christ's victory, eventually reign with Him in glory. This may be thought of as attained at the end of history, but it is also believed that even before the general resurrection some at least of the redeemed are with Christ, i.e. in Heaven. According to Catholic doctrine, these are the souls who, having died in a state of grace and been purged of their stains in *purgatory, have passed to Heaven, where they enjoy perfect bliss, but (except for the BVM) such souls await re-union with their bodies until the general *resurrection of the dead. Modern theologians stress the quality of the life of Heaven rather than any details.

hebdomadarian. In cathedral churches and monasteries the priest who presides at the Eucharist and Divine Office, normally for a week at a time.

Heber, Reginald (1783–1826), Bp. of Calcutta from 1823. He is best known for his hymns, which include 'Holy, holy, holy, Lord God Almighty' and 'From Greenland's icy mountains'.

Hebrew (people). The inhabitants of Palestine, who entered the land with the *Patriarchs and *Moses. They generally spoke of themselves as 'Israelites'; the term 'Hebrew' was largely used of them by others.

Hebrew (tongue). The Semitic language in which practically all the OT was written. In the NT period spoken Hebrew had largely been replaced by *Aramaic, but Hebrew survived as a written language and has been revived as the official language of the modern State of Israel. In the NT 'Hebrew' may denote either classical Hebrew or the colloquial Aramaic dialect of Palestine.

Apart from brief inscriptions, the only surviving classical Hebrew literature is the OT itself. The vocabulary is small, the style is simple and direct. The earliest Hebrew was written in a form of ancient Phoenician script, running from right to left, which was also the ancestor of the Greek alphabet and of our own. During the Babylonian captivity (c.586–c.538 BC) this gave way to an Aramaizing form of the same script, from which the so-called 'Assyrian' or 'square' script was developed. This alphabet consisted of 22 signs for consonants. The absence of vowels was remedied first by using certain of the existing consonants to represent both vowels and consonants, and later by the development of a system of strokes and dots known as *vowel points.

Hebrews, Epistle to the. Traditionally included among the letters of St *Paul, this Epistle, unlike most others in the NT, does not contain the name of the writer or of those addressed; the traditional title is probably an inference from its contents. The Epistle asserts the finality of the Christian dispensation and its superiority to the Old Covenant. Its theological teaching, notably on the Person of Christ, reaches a level unsurpassed in the NT.

From an early date it was received at *Alexandria as Pauline. In the W. it was known to *Clement of Rome, but not quoted as Pauline or certainly canonical until the 4th–5th cent. Modern scholars consider that internal evidence marks it as non-Pauline. Both its author and its intended readers were apparently familiar with Jewish worship, but it is disputed whether it was addressed to converts from Judaism or to Gentiles. A date before AD 70 has been supported by several scholars; the majority argue for a date under *Domitian (81–96).

Hebrews, Gospel according to the. An *apocryphal Gospel used by Jewish Christians. It has been variously identified with the 'Gospel according to the *Ebionites' or an Aramaic Gospel used by the *Nazarenes, but the relationship between the various Jewish Christian Gospels is unclear. The surviving fragments contain some Dominical sayings not recorded in the canonical Gospels; it may preserve traditions of historical value.

Hebron, one of the oldest cities in the world. It was chosen by *Abraham as his nomadic home when he arrived in Palestine (Gen. 13: 18) and is the scene of various events recorded in the OT.

Hecker, Isaac Thomas (1819–88), founder of the *Paulists. He became a RC in 1844, entered the novitiate of the *Redemptorists in Belgium in 1845, and returned to his native New York in 1851. Difficulties having arisen with his Redemptorist superiors, in 1857 he was dispensed from his vows and founded a new congregation for missionary work in the USA which was known as the 'Paulists'. It has been suggested that *Leo XIII's condemnation of *Americanism in 1899 had Hecker in mind.

hedonism. The ethical doctrine which maintains that the proper end of all moral action is pleasure.

Hefele, Karl Joseph (1809–93), Church historian. From 1869 he was Bp. of Rottenburg. He had an important part in the preparations for the First *Vatican Council, at which he opposed the definition of Papal *Infallibility. His main work was his history of the ecclesiastical councils (completed by J. Hergenrother, 1855–90).

Hegel, Georg Wilhelm Friedrich (1770–1831), German Idealist philosopher. In 1818 he succeeded J. G. *Fichte as professor of philosophy at Berlin. The distinctive character of his system lay in his attempt to present all philosophical problems and concepts in an evolutionary perspective. For Hegel no idea has an unchanging and eternal validity, but it discloses its meaning in the continuous process of its development; a process in which contrasts and oppositions become intelligible through an identity within which they are related, even if only as opposites. Moreover the antitheses which thought apprehends are also constitutive of reality. Development is the outcome of a dialectical 'movement' in which a *thesis* is succeeded by an *antithesis*, the ensuing conflict resulting in the two being brought together on a higher plane as a *synthesis*. The ultimate resolution of all differences, both in thought and reality, is attained in the Absolute. This evolutionary view of the universe comprehends not only the natural sciences, but also the humanities, since truth lies not in individual disciplines but in the whole. Although Hegel regarded himself as a Christian, in his philosophy of religion he sees religious ideas as a figurative representation of truths which philosophy restates in conceptual and fully rational terms.

He exercised a vast influence on later thought, including that of Karl Marx. In Britain his followers included T. H. *Green, through whom Idealism exercised a profound influence on English religious philosophy in the years 1885 to 1920.

Hegesippus, St (2nd cent.), Church historian. He wrote five Books of 'Memoirs' against the *Gnostics. It appears that he drew up a 'succession list' of the early bishops of Rome; it has been argued that the list in *Epiphanius (*Haer.* 27. 6) is a reproduction of this. If so, it is the earliest witness to the names of the first Roman bishops. Feast day, 7 Apr.

hegumenos. A title in the E. for the ruler of a monastery.

Heidegger, Martin (1889–1976), German *existentialist philosopher. He was a professor at Freiburg from 1929 to 1951. He elaborated a metaphysic of the human person. In *Sein und Zeit* (1927; Eng. tr., *Being and Time*, 1962) he uncovers man's temporal being in order to focus on Being in its unity and totality. Man's personal existence (*Dasein*: literally 'there-ness') is a unique transcendent possibility, which is rooted in immediate, temporal relationships. Authentic existence, facing nothingness, is lived out only in the full acceptance of death. In his later works it seems that Being is intuitively grasped rather than philosophically explored.

Heidelberg Catechism. The confession of faith compiled in 1562 by Z. *Ursinus and

K. Olevian at the instance of the Elector *Frederick III, and accepted in 1563 as the standard of doctrine in the Palatinate.

Heiler, Friedrich (1892–1967), German religious writer. As a RC he studied Catholic theology, but in 1919 he joined the *Lutheran Church at *Uppsala. He was appointed a professor at *Marburg in 1922. He became the organizer of a German High Church movement and even founded an Evangelical Order of Franciscan *Tertiaries. His principal work, *Das Gebet* (1918; abridged Eng. tr., *Prayer*, 1932) is a comprehensive historical analysis of the subject.

Heim, Karl (1874–1958), *Lutheran theologian. In 1920 he became a professor at *Tübingen. He was a leading opponent of the (pagan) German Faith Movement. In theology he stressed the contrast of faith and reason and emphasized the transcendence of faith.

Heiric of Auxerre (841–876/7), teacher and hagiographer. He entered the monastery of St *Germanus at Auxerre as an oblate when he was about 7. After studying elsewhere he taught at Auxerre until his death. His chief work is a metrical life of Germanus.

heirmos. The opening stanza in each ode of the *canon.

Helena, St (c.255–c.330), also **Helen**, mother of the Emp. *Constantine. Abandoned by her husband, she was accorded a position of honour on Constantine's accession. She zealously supported the Christian cause. In 326 she visited the Holy Land, where she founded basilicas on the Mount of *Olives and at *Bethlehem. According to later tradition she discovered the Cross on which Christ was crucified. Feast day in the W., formerly 18 Aug.; in the E. and in CW, 21 May.

Heliand. An Old Saxon Biblical poem. It is based on *Tatian's harmony of the Gospels and written in alliterative verse. The Latin 'Praefatio' states that it was written at the order of *Louis I (the 'Pious') for the benefit of his recently converted Saxon subjects.

Hell. The word is used in English translations of the Bible to represent both the Hebrew '*Sheol', the place of the departed, and the Greek '*Gehenna', the place of punishment for the wicked after death. In Christian theology it normally signifies the place or state to which unrepentant sinners are held to pass, by God's final judgement, after this life. According to traditional Scholastic theology, souls in hell experience both the *poena damni*, i.e. exclusion from God's presence and loss of contact with Him, and a certain *poena sensus*, denoted in the Bible by fire and usually interpreted as an external agent tormenting them. Modern theology stresses that hell is but the logical consequence of ultimate adherence to the soul's own will and rejection of the will of God which necessarily separates the soul from God, and hence from all possibility of happiness.

Helvetic Confessions. The First Helvetic Confession was compiled at Basle in 1536 by H. *Bullinger and others as a uniform confession of faith for the whole of German-speaking Switzerland. The Second Helvetic Confession was the work of Bullinger, issued in 1566 in response to a request from the Elector-Palatine *Frederick III, who had announced his adhesion to *Calvinism. It soon won acceptance not only among the Swiss Protestant Churches but among other 'Reformed' (i.e. Calvinists) outside Switzerland.

Helvidius (4th cent.). A Latin theologian who was attacked by St *Jerome for his denial of the perpetual virginity of the BVM.

Helwys, Thomas (c.1550–c.1616), English *Baptist. Having migrated to the Netherlands with J. *Smyth in 1608, he became convinced that 'Infant Baptism' was invalid, and he joined Smyth's separatist community, the first Baptist Church to come into existence. In 1612 he returned to London, where he founded the first *General Baptist congregation in England. His *Declaration of the Mystery of Iniquity* (1611–12) contained an early plea for universal religious toleration.

Hemerobaptists. A Jewish sect for which daily ablution was an essential part of religion.

Hemmerlin, Felix, also **Hemerli** (c.1388–c.1460), reformer. A native of Zurich, in 1421 he became provost of St Ursus at Solothurn, where he revised the statutes of his collegiate clergy. He also advocated reforms of all kinds and attacked the *Mendicant Orders and the *Lollards. In his later years he was involved in politics and lost his ecclesiastical offices.

Henderson, Alexander (*c*.1583–1646), Scottish Covenanting leader. He was mainly responsible for drafting the *National Covenant of 1638, and during the *Bishops' Wars of 1639–40 he was the recognized leader of the Scottish *Presbyterians. He prepared the draft of the *Solemn League and Covenant for both Scotland and England (1643) and of the Directory for *Public Worship (1644).

Henotheism. A primitive form of faith which recognizes the existence of several gods, but regards one particular god as the deity of the family or tribe; makes him the centre of its worship; and for practical purposes neglects the existence of other gods. Modern scholars commonly hold that the early Hebrew faith took this form.

Henoticon. The theological formula put forward in 482 to secure union between the *Monophysites and the Orthodox, and sponsored by the Emp. *Zeno. Widely accepted in the E., but never countenanced at Rome, it provoked the *Acacian schism.

Henricians. A medieval heretical sect which arose in the 12th cent. under the inspiration of *Henry of Lausanne.

Henrietta Maria (1609–69), Queen. She married *Charles I in 1625, on condition that the penal laws against RCs were suspended and she be allowed free exercise of her religion. She was unpopular.

Henry II, St (972–1024), German King and Emperor. He became King in 1002; he was crowned Emperor in 1014. He frequently interfered in the affairs of the Church, but he commonly had the political support of Rome. In his later years he encouraged the monastic reform movement centred on the abbey of *Gorze. Later legend saw in him a monarch of outstanding piety and asceticism. Feast day, 13 (formerly 15) July.

Henry IV (1050–1106), German King and Emperor. He succeeded to the throne in 1056. His reign was troubled by rebellious Saxon princes and by the reforms of *Gregory VII (q.v.). Having conquered the Saxons in 1075, Henry refused obedience to the Pope and answered his threat of excommunication by declaring Gregory deposed. Gregory then released Henry's subjects from their oath of allegiance; the Saxons rose again and the princes refused obedience unless Henry was reconciled to the Pope. He submitted to the Pope at *Canossa in 1077. In 1080 he was again excommunicated; he set up an antipope who crowned him Emperor in 1084.

Henry IV (1553–1610), King of France. Brought up a Protestant, he became King of Navarre in 1572. He took part in the wars of religion on the Protestant side. In 1589 he inherited the crown of France; despite military victory, he was not recognized as king until he became a RC in 1593. In 1598 he issued the Edict of *Nantes, granting freedom of worship to Protestants in certain places. He was assassinated.

Henry VI (1421–71), King of England. Succeeding Henry V in 1422, he was crowned King of England in 1429 and of France in 1431. Difficulties in France increased and England was unsettled by personal rivalries. The birth of a son excluded Richard, Duke of York, from the succession, but when Henry fell into a depressive stupor in 1453, York became Protector. Relations between them deteriorated into civil war in 1459, and Henry was taken prisoner. On being freed, he lived as an exile in Scotland, but in 1465 he was captured, imprisoned and eventually murdered. He was a deeply religious man. He founded Eton College and King's College, Cambridge.

Henry VIII (1491–1547), King of England from 1509. When M. *Luther's ideas began to influence the English universities, Henry agreed to a demonstration of official orthodoxy. The *Assertio Septem Sacramentorum* (1521), for which Henry took the credit, earned him the title ''*Defender of the Faith'. In 1527 he began taking steps to procure the annulment of his marriage with Catherine of Aragon. He argued that Catherine's former marriage to his late brother invalidated his union with her, despite the *dispensation given by *Julius II. In 1529 pleadings on the marriage were heard in London before T. *Wolsey and L. *Campeggio, but *Clement VII revoked the case to Rome. In Nov. 1529 Henry summoned Parliament. In 1530–31 a charge of *praemunire* against the whole clergy (for illegal exercise of ecclesiastical jurisdiction) was used to extract from *Convocation a fine and limited acceptance of Henry's claims for England's jurisdictional independence from Rome. In 1532 the payment of *Annates Act 1531, which was conditional, threatened to cut off Papal revenues from England. A House of Commons petition was used to secure the '*Submission of the Clergy' from a rump Convocation. These measures, however, did little to forward the cause of Henry's marriage to *Anne Boleyn. The death of W. *Warham in Aug. 1532 allowed Henry to appoint T. *Cranmer as Abp. of Canterbury. In Dec. 1532 Anne became pregnant; in Jan. 1533 Henry secretly married her. In Apr. Parliament forbade appeals to Rome in temporal cases, such as marriage. Cranmer annulled Henry's marriage to Catherine and pronounced that to Anne valid, and crowned Anne Queen. After Clement had threatened to excommunicate Henry unless he returned to Catherine, a Succession Act in 1534 imposed a national oath recognizing his marriage to Anne and entailing the Crown on its children, and a *Supremacy Act declared Henry 'supreme head' of the English Church. The most eminent of these who denied the royal supremacy (T. *More and J. *Fisher) were executed. Henry began the *dissolution of the monasteries in 1536, negotiated with *Lutheran princes, and supported the *Ten Articles (1536). The *Pilgrimage of Grace in Oct. 1536 showed that there was hostility to change, at least in the north. In 1537 Henry refused to give full official sanction to the *Bishops' Book and began his own more conservative revision, which became the *King's Book (1543). The *Six Articles (1539) reaffirmed Catholic doctrine. In his later years he tried to maintain a balance in religion. See also REFORMATION.

Henry of Blois (d. 1171), Bp. of *Winchester from 1129. He was the grandson of *William I ('the Conqueror') and brother of King Stephen. On the death of William of Corbeil (1136) he hoped for the see of *Canterbury, but after *Theobald's consecration in 1139, Pope Innocent II gave Henry a legatine commission, which made him in some ways Theobald's superior. Henry then sought the elevation of Winchester into an archiepiscopal see. After Stephen's death (1154), his position under Henry II was insecure and in the *Becket controversy he did what he could for the Archbishop. He was a great builder and founded the Hospital of St Cross at Winchester.

Henry of Ghent (d. 1293), theologian. A master of *Paris by 1276, he combined an active university teaching career with ecclesiastical offices. He was an outspoken critic of the privileges granted to the *Mendicant Orders. Between 1276 and 1292 he produced extensive *Quodlibeta, his Summa, Quaestiones ordinariae, and probably also the questions on *Aristotle's Physics and the commentary on the Hexaemeron attributed to him. He was the chief representative among the secular clergy of neo-Augustinianism. He stressed God's omnipotence, His free will in creation, the existence of exemplar ideas or possible essences, man's need for Divine illumination to attain true cognition, and the primacy of will over reason in human action.

Henry of Lausanne (d. after 1145), sectarian. An itinerant preacher, c.1116 he gave the Lenten sermons at Le Mans by permission of the bishop. He was expelled from the diocese because he carried anti-clericalism to the point of heresy; he continued his activities in S. France. According to St *Bernard, he denied the objective efficacy of the Sacraments.

Henry of Susa. See HOSTIENSIS.

Henry Suso, Bl (c.1295–1366), German spiritual writer. He entered the *Dominican house at Constance at the age of 13; five years later he adopted rigid standards. Studying at *Cologne, he was influenced by *Eckhart. In 1330 tension within the Order led to his being deprived of his teaching position, but he preached widely in Switzerland and the Upper Rhine area. His main work, 'The Little Book of Eternal Wisdom' or 'Clock of Wisdom', is a practical, warmly devotional, book of meditations. It was written in two versions, German and Latin. Feast day, 23 Jan. (formerly 2 Mar.; then 15 Feb.).

Henson, Herbert Hensley (1863–1947), Bp. of *Hereford (1918–20) and then of *Durham (1920–39). His nomination to the see of Hereford aroused protest on account of his doctrinal position, especially his attitude to the *Virgin Birth and *miracles; a crisis was averted when Abp. R. T. *Davidson and Henson issued a joint statement in which Henson appeared to retract his earlier views. Until Parliament rejected the revised Prayer Book (1927–8), he was a strong advocate of the *Establishment; he then sought freedom for the Church from State control.

heortology. The study of the origin, history, and meaning of the festivals and seasons of the ecclesiastical *year.

Heptateuch. A name sometimes used for the first seven books of the OT on account of their supposed unity.

Heracleon (*fl. c.*145–80), *Gnostic teacher. He wrote a commentary on St *John's Gospel. The 'Tractate on the Three Natures' found at *Nag Hammadi is sometimes attributed to him.

Heraclius (575–641), Byzantine Emperor from 610/11. In 629 he brought back to *Jerusalem the Cross which the Persians had removed in 614. In an attempt to secure doctrinal unity he issued the '*Ecthesis' (q.v.) in 638.

Herbert, Edward (1582–1648), first Lord Herbert of Cherbury; philosopher and poet. He held that the essence of religion lay in five innate ideas: that there is a God; that He ought to be worshipped; that virtue is the chief element in this worship; that repentance for sin is a duty; and that there is another life of rewards and punishments. He was a forerunner of the English *Deists.

Herbert, George (1593–1633), poet. A brother of the preceding, he seemed marked out for the career of a courtier. The death of *James I and the influence of N. *Ferrar led him to study divinity. In 1630 he was ordained and became rector of Fugglestone with Bemerton, near *Salisbury.

His most famous prose work, *A Priest to the Temple; or the Country Parson* (1652), outlines a sober and well-balanced ideal of the English clergyman. His collection of poems, entitled *The Temple*, was entrusted to Ferrar on his deathbed and published in 1633. Herbert was a man of deep religious conviction and remarkable poetic gifts. His compositions in current use as hymns include 'The God of love my Shepherd is' and 'Let all the world in every corner sing'.

Feast day in parts of the Anglican Communion, 27 Feb.

Hereford. The see was founded in 676 by Putta, Bp. of *Rochester, who had fled from the heathen invaders of his diocese. St *Ethelbert, King of the East Angles, was buried in the cathedral and, with the BVM, designated its joint patron. The main part of the present cathedral dates from 1079–1110. In 1786 the west end collapsed, carrying part of the nave with it. The Hereford *Mappa Mundi* (late-13th cent.) shows the world as a circle with *Jerusalem at the centre, the whole lying under a portrayal of the Last Judgement.

Hereford, Nicholas. See NICHOLAS HEREFORD.

heresiarch. The originator of a heresy or the founder of a heretical sect.

heresy. The formal denial or doubt of any defined doctrine of the Catholic faith. From early days the Church claimed teaching authority and consequently condemned heresy. The need to rebut heresy has sometimes stimulated the formulation of orthodox Christian doctrine.

In the early centuries heresy was mainly a matter of erroneous attempts to understand the nature of the Person of Christ, of the Trinity, or both. After the Church had become a structured and wealthy institution, many of the heretical movements were inspired by a desire to return to what was seen as the simplicity of the apostolic Church; they often came to reject the Sacraments as well as other institutions of the Church. The *Inquisition was established to secure the conversion of heretics, and punished the obdurate.

According to RC canon law, heresy is defined as the obstinate denial or doubt, after Baptism, of a truth 'which must be believed with divine and catholic faith'. This 'formal heresy' is a grave sin involving automatic excommunication. 'Material heresy', the holding of heretical doctrines 'in good faith', e.g. by those brought up in heretical surroundings, constitutes neither crime nor sin.

Herimannus Contractus (1013–1054), **Hermann the Lame**, poet and chronicler. A monk of *Reichenau, he wrote on a wide range of subjects. His works include many hymns and antiphons, but the attribution to him of the '*Salve Regina' and the 'Alma Redemptoris Mater' rests on insufficient evidence. His 'Chronicon' is valuable for its record of contemporary history.

heritor. In *Scotland heritors were the owners of heritable property in a parish to whom descended the obligation to pay the *teinds to the minister and keep the parish church and manse in repair. An Act of Parliament in 1925 provided for the termination of their rights and duties.

Herman, Emma (1874–1923), writer. The wife of a *Presbyterian minister, she spent part of her life in Constantinople and Sydney. Later she joined the C of E. Her chief works were *The Meaning and Value of Mysticism* (1915) and *Creative Prayer* (1921).

Hermann of Reichenau. See HERIMANNUS CONTRACTUS.

Hermann of Wied (1477–1552), reformer. He became Abp.-Elector of *Cologne in 1515. In his earlier years he was hostile to the Protestant movement, but *c.* 1539 he set out to create a parallel movement within the Catholic Church. His increasing adhesion to the Protestant cause led to his excommunication and deposition in 1546. His proposals for reform influenced the compilers of the BCP.

Hermas (2nd cent.), author of 'The Shepherd', accounted one of the '*Apostolic Fathers'. A Christian slave, he was freed, married, became a rich merchant, and then in a *persecution lost all his property.
'The Shepherd' is divided into three parts: 5 'Visions', in which a matron appears to Hermas representing the Church; 12 'Mandates', in which Hermas gives his teaching on Christian behaviour and virtues; and 10 'Similitudes', in which various Christian principles are represented under a series of images. The work inculcates the need for penance and the possibility of the forgiveness of post-Baptismal sin. Though Hermas says that he was a contemporary of St *Clement of Rome, the *Muratorian Canon attributes his work to a brother of *Pius I, and many scholars thus date it between 140 and 155.

hermeneutics. The science of the methods of *exegesis. Whereas exegesis is usually the act of explaining a text, hermeneutics is the science or art by which exegetical procedures are devised. In theology hermeneutical theory arises out of awareness of the ambiguity of a sacred text and the consequent analysis of the art of understanding. The Protestant emphasis on the importance of Scripture and belief in the possibility of comprehending it, encouraged reflection on the act of understanding, as well as a return to more literal exegesis. In modern times F. D. E. *Schleiermacher gave new prominence to the act of correctly understanding all human utterance and thereby subsumed biblical hermeneutics into a general theory of interpretation. Subsequently interpretation rather than perception has been seen as the fundamental mode of man's relation to the world, and some theologians regard hermeneutics, rather than metaphysics, as the central task of Christian theology.

Hermesianism. The system of philosophical and theological doctrines taught by Georg Hermes (1775–1831), professor of theology at Münster. Holding that our only certain knowledge was of ideas actually present in the mind, he taught that the criterion of objective truth must be found in our subjective beliefs. He held that, starting from this principle, the existence of God could be proved by theoretical reason, and that the possibility of supernatural revelation could then be demonstrated.

Hermetic books. A collection of Greek and Latin religious and philosophical writings ascribed to Hermes Trismegistus, a later name for the Egyptian God Thoth, who was believed to be the father and protector of all knowledge. They probably date from the mid-1st to the late-3rd cent. AD.

Hermias (date uncertain), Christian philosophical writer. He is known only as the author of a small treatise, the 'Irrisio' or 'Mockery of the Heathen Philosophers'. Modern scholars assign him to various dates between the 2nd and 6th cents.

hermit. One who from religious motives has retired into a solitary life. Christian hermits began to abound in Egypt and the surrounding areas in the late-3rd cent. In the W. they died out after the *Counter-Reformation, though much of their tradition is retained in some monastic orders. In the 20th cent. hermits again appeared in both the RC and Anglican

Churches. In the E. they survived without interruption.

Herod family. *Herod the Great* was appointed King of the Jews by the Romans in 40 BC; he ruled from 37 to 4 BC. Christ was born during his reign. On his death his territory was divided between his sons: *Archelaus*, as ethnarch of Judaea, Idumaea, and Samaria, who was deposed in AD 6; *Antipas*, as tetrarch of *Galilee and Peraea, the 'Herod the tetrach' of the Gospels (4 BC–AD 39) who beheaded *John the Baptist; and *Philip*, as tetrarch of the remaining territory (4 BC–AD 33/4). *Agrippa I*, Herod the Great's grandson, succeeded to all these territories between 37 and 41; he ruled until 44 and is the 'King Herod' of Acts. His son, *Agrippa II* (ruled from *c.*50–93 or 100) was the 'King Agrippa' before whom St *Paul appeared.

Herodians. A party mentioned in the Gospels as hostile to Christ. They were presumably partisans of the *Herod family.

Herrmann, Wilhelm (1846–1922), theologian. In 1879 he became professor of systematic theology at *Marburg. Though he regarded the Gospels as in some sense the record of a historical personality, he insisted that the Church should teach only those facts about Christ which will act upon man, e.g. His moral teaching, as distinguished from His Virgin Birth.

Herrnhut. A village some 40 miles east of Dresden, built and settled in 1722 by a group of *Moravian Brethren on a site presented by N. L. von *Zinzendorf.

Hertford, Council of (672 or 673). A Council of bishops held under *Theodore, Abp. of Canterbury, to promote the reorganization of the English Church. It issued 10 canons, concerned especially with the rights and duties of clerics and monks. This was the first occasion on which the English Church acted as a unity.

Hesperinos. See VESPERS.

Hesychasm. In the E. Church, the tradition of inner, mystical prayer, associated particularly with the monks of Mt *Athos. The Hesychasts attached special importance to unceasing recitation of the *Jesus Prayer. They recommended a particular bodily posture, with breathing controlled to keep time with the recitation of the prayer. Their immediate aim was to secure what they termed 'the union of the mind with the heart', so that their prayer became 'prayer of the heart'. This leads, in those chosen by God, to the vision of the Divine Light, which, it was believed, can be seen with the material eyes of the body.

Hesychius (*fl. c.*300), biblical textual critic. According to *Jerome, he revised the text of the LXX in the light of the Hebrew.

Hesychius of Jerusalem, St (5th cent.), Greek ecclesiastical writer and exegete. In early life he was a monk, but little else is known of his career. He was alive and supporting the *Alexandrians in the controversies leading up to the Council of *Chalcedon (451). He is said to have commented on the whole Bible. Most of the long commentary on Pss., formerly attributed to St *Athanasius, is probably his work. Feast day in the Greek Church, 28 Mar.

Hexaemeron. The account of the creation of the universe in six days in Gen. 1; also patristic commentaries on this narrative.

Hexapla. The edition of the OT produced by *Origen, in which the Hebrew text, the Hebrew text transliterated into Greek characters, and the four Greek versions of *Aquila, *Symmachus, the *Septuagint (in a revised text with critical signs), and *Theodotion were arranged in parallel columns. For some sections of the OT, up to three further Greek versions were added, making nine columns in all.

Hexateuch. The name given by J. *Wellhausen and others to the first six books of the OT in the belief that they were compiled from a single set of literary sources.

Heylyn, Peter (1600–62), Anglican controversialist. His championship of *High Church views attracted the notice of W. *Laud. *Charles I made him a prebendary of *Westminster (1631), and other preferments followed. In the 1630s he became the official apologist for the Laudian reforms: his *History of the Sabbath* (1636) defended anti-*sabbatarianism and in other works he upheld the requirement that the *Communion table (or altar) be placed at the east end of the Church and refuted charges of innovation. Under the Commonwealth his controversial writings led to trouble. At the Restoration he worked for the reinstatement of the C of E and particularly for the revival of the *Convocations.

Hibbert, Robert (1770–1849), founder of the Hibbert Trust. He employed a *Unitarian minister for the benefit of the slaves on his estate in Jamaica. In 1847 he founded the Hibbert Trust 'for the spread of Christianity in its most simple and intelligible form' and the 'unfettered exercise of the right of private judgement in matters of religion'; its aims are anti-Trinitarian.

Hickes, George (1642–1715), *Nonjuring bishop. He became Dean of *Worcester in 1683. In 1689 he refused to take the oaths to William and Mary and in 1690 he was deprived of his deanery. In 1694 he was consecrated titular Bp. of Thetford by the Nonjurors, and after the death of W. Lloyd (1709) was their acknowledged leader. In order to continue the Nonjuring succession, he consecrated three bishops in 1713.

Hicks, Elias (1748–1830), American *Quaker. He took up the cause of the Negroes. He opposed the creation of any credal basis for Quakerism, notably in his *Doctrinal Epistle* (1824), in which he protested against insistence on the orthodox doctrines on the Person of Christ and the *Atonement. A schism ensued (1827–8) at Philadelphia and elsewhere between his followers (the 'Liberal Branch' or 'Hicksites') and the orthodox.

Hieracas of Leontopolis (2nd–3rd cent.), a leader of the monastic movement in Egypt. He upheld the pre-existence of souls and the spiritual nature of the resurrection body; *Peter of Alexandria's condemnation of *Origenism may have been directed against him. None of his writings survive.

hierarchy. The word has been used since patristic times of the ordained body of Christian clergy. RC theologians used to distinguish between the hierarchy of order and that of pastoral government, but since the Second *Vatican Council the hierarchical constitution of the Church has been seen differently. First there is the supreme Church authority enjoyed by the

Pope and college of bishops, with power over the universal Church, and secondly there are particular Churches and their groupings. Only those in holy orders are capable of the power of government or jurisdiction. The threefold hierarchical order of bishops, priests, and deacons has been retained in the Anglican Communion in common with the RC and E. Churches.

Hieronymian Martyrology. A *martyrology composed in Italy in the mid-5th cent. It is so named from a statement in the correspondence preceding the text that its compilation was the work of St *Jerome.

Hieronymus. The Latin form of *Jerome.

Hierusalem. A Latinized form of *Jerusalem.

High Altar. The main altar of a church, traditionally standing in the centre of the east end.

High Churchmen. A term coined in the 17th cent. to describe those members of the C of E who emphasized its historical continuity as a branch of the Catholic Church and upheld 'high' conceptions of the rights of the monarchy and episcopacy and of the nature of the sacraments. The existence of such a school can be traced to Elizabethan times; it flourished under the Stuarts. The accession of William of Orange (1689) violated the principle of indefeasible hereditary succession (see DIVINE RIGHT OF KINGS) and precipitated the schism of the *Nonjurors, though many of them continued to work with conforming High Churchmen to promote piety and defend the C of E against the spreading heterodoxy and toleration of Protestant dissenters. High Churchmen initially shared the concern of the *Oxford Movement at the erosion of the Church's privileges after 1828, but many were soon alienated by what they regarded as its tendency to divisiveness and innovation. See also ANGLO-CATHOLICISM.

High Commission, Court of. From 1549 ecclesiastical commissions to check heresy and enforce the prescribed forms of public worship were often appointed in England. The term 'High Commission' began to appear *c.*1570 and was normally employed after 1580, a development corresponding with the elevation of an *ad hoc* commission into a permanent court. It became the normal court of appeal from the ancient ecclesiastical courts in doctrinal and disciplinary cases. It was abolished in 1641.

High Mass (Missa solemnis). In the W. long the normal, though not the most usual, form of the Mass. Its essential feature was the presence of the *deacon and *subdeacon assisting the celebrant. Since the Second *Vatican Council the term has disappeared from RC official documents.

'High Places', the. In the OT the local (usually hill-top) sanctuaries other than *Jerusalem at which God was worshipped with sacrifice in early times. Worship at these sites, which had Canaanite affinities, was denounced by many of the Prophets; the 'high places' were destroyed in 621 BC.

High Prayers. A title for the service in certain Oxford college chapels on great festivals.

High Priest. In the OT the head of the *Levitical priesthood whose institution is described in Exod. 28. His chief function was the superintendence of the Temple worship, and it was his special prerogative to offer the Liturgy on the Day of *Atonement. In post-exilic times he was the head of the Jewish State as well as the chief religious functionary.

Higher Criticism. The critical study of the literary methods and sources used by the authors of (especially) biblical Books, in distinction from *Textual ('Lower') Criticism, which is concerned solely with recovering the text as it left its author's hands.

Hilarion, St (*c*.291–371), the founder of the *anchoritic life in Palestine. He was converted to Christianity at *Alexandria, and under the influence of St *Antony retired for a short time to the Egyptian desert as a hermit. In 306 he returned to Palestine, where he lived a life of extreme asceticism near Gaza. Feast day, 21 Oct.

Hilary of Arles, St (*c*.401–49), Bp. of Arles. A monk of *Lérins, he became Bp. of the metropolitan see of Arles *c.* 430, and presided over several councils. In 444, by deposing a bishop, he seems to have exceeded his rights, and Pope *Leo I deprived Arles of its metropolitan jurisdiction and obtained from the Emperor a

decree granting Rome supreme authority over the Church in Gaul. Feast day, 5 May.

Hilary of Poitiers, St (*c*.315–67/8), the foremost Latin theologian of his age. A convert from paganism, he was elected Bp. of Poitiers *c*.350. He became involved in the *Arian disputes and, probably as a result of his defence of Catholic teaching, in 356 was exiled for 4 years by the Emp. Constantius. In 359 he defended the cause of orthodoxy at the Council of *Seleucia. His main works are a treatise *De Trinitate* (against the Arians); *De Synodis*, valuable for the doctrinal history of the period; and the so-called *Opus Historicum*. He is the earliest known writer of *hymns in the W. Church. Feast day, 13 Jan. (before 1969, 14 Jan. in the RC Church).

Hilda, St (614–80), Abbess of Whitby. Descended from the Northumbrian royal line, in 657 she founded a *double monastery at Whitby; it grew in fame and influence. At the Synod of *Whitby (664) she sided with St *Colman in his defence of the Celtic customs. Feast day, 17 Nov.; 18 Nov. in the American BCP (1979); 19 Nov. in CW.

Hildebert of Lavardin (1056–1133), poet and canonist. Elected Bp. of Le Mans in 1096, he continued the building of his cathedral (consecrated in 1120), expelled *Henry of Lausanne from his diocese, and probably took part in the First *Lateran Council of 1123. In 1125 he became Abp. of Tours. He is famous chiefly for his literary works, which were regarded as a model of elegant style in the Middle Ages. Not all those attributed to him are genuine.

Hildebrand. See GREGORY VII.

Hildegard of Bingen, St (1098–1179), Abbess of Rupertsberg, near Bingen. Born of a noble family and apparently subject to supernatural religious experiences from early childhood, at the age of 8 she was entrusted to the care of Bl Jutta, a recluse attached to the *Benedictine monastery of Disibodenberg. On Jutta's death in 1136, she succeeded her as Abbess of the community which had gathered round her. She moved the community to Rupertsberg.

Her *Scivias* (probably intended as an abbreviation of 'scito vias [viventis luminis]'), dictated between 1141 and 1151, record 26 visions; they show her conception of salvation-history leading to the Last Judgement. It was followed by the *Liber vitae meritorum*, devoted to a disputation of the virtues and vices and her vision of the joys and torments with which they are rewarded in the afterlife, and the *Liber divinorum operum*, containing visions of the cosmos, earth, and created things. An important element in the *Scivias* is a body of dramatic songs, also used in her musical play, the *Ordo virtutum*. Her other works include musical compositions and two medical treatises. Feast day, 17 Sept.

Hilton, Walter (*c*.1343–96), English contemplative writer. One of a circle of clerks associated with T. *Arundel both at *Ely and *York, after a period as a hermit, *c.* 1386 he became an *Augustinian canon at Thurgarton Priory, Notts. His main work is the *Scale of Perfection* or *Scala Perfectionis*, written in English. This describes the renewal of the defaced image of God in the soul, first by 'reforming in faith' and then by 'reforming in feeling'. Between these stages is the 'luminous darkness' of mortification, the transition from disordered self-love to love of God. He wrote various other works in English, translated *Eight Chapters on Perfection* from Spanish, and wrote academic works in Latin.

Hincmar (*c*.806–82), Abp. of *Reims from 845. He opposed Lothair, King of Lorraine, when he wanted to divorce his wife, and he strove to defend his metropolitan rights both against his own bishops and against the Pope. After Lothair's death (869) he crowned Charles the Bald at Metz, despite Papal objections.

Though not a speculative theologian, Hincmar took a prominent part in the controversy with *Gottschalk on *predestination. He himself wrote against Gottschalk and he called upon John Scottus *Erigena for help. Another dispute with Gottschalk and *Ratramnus arose when Hincmar changed the words 'Trina Deitas' in one of the Vespers hymns to 'Summa Deitas', because he suspected the former phrase of *tritheism.

Hinnom, Valley of. The literal meaning of *Gehenna (q.v.).

Hinsley, Arthur (1865–1943), Abp. of *Westminster from 1935 and cardinal from 1937. He founded the '*Sword of the Spirit' in 1940 and became widely known through his leadership of English RCs in the early part of the Second World War.

Hippo, Council of (393). A council of the Catholic (i.e. non-*Donatist) Church in Latin Africa. A *breviarium* of its canons passed into general canon law.

Hippolytus, St (*c*.170–*c*.236), theologian. He was a presbyter at Rome, apparently of some importance. Under *Callistus (217–22), whom he regarded as a heretic, he seems to have allowed himself to be elected as a rival Bp. of Rome and continued to attack Callistus' successors. In the *persecution of the Emp. Maximin, Hippolytus and Pope Pontianus (230–5) were exiled together to Sardinia. The bodies of both were brought back to Rome in 236. Feast day in the E., 30 Jan.; in the W., 13 Aug.

A list of several of Hippolytus' writings, as well as his Easter tables, were discovered on a statue found in Rome in 1551. Many other works are listed by *Eusebius of Caesarea and St *Jerome. His main work is the 'Refutation of all Heresies' published in 1851 under the title 'Philosophumena'. In this Hippolytus expresses his trinitarian theology in a form of *Logos doctrine, distinguishing between two states of the Word, the one immanent and eternal, the other external and temporal as the Father's voice. Containing in Himself all the Father's ideas, the Word is able to actualize them as the Father's creative agent. The 'Refutation' also illustrates his opposition to the mitigation of the penitential system necessitated by the influx of pagan converts.

The attribution of the '*Apostolic Tradition' to Hippolytus is now generally accepted. Other works usually attributed to him include various biblical commentaries, a discourse against the followers of *Noetus, and a *Chronicon*. Differences of style and theology between the 'Refutation' and the *Contra Noetum* have led some scholars to divide the works between two authors and sometimes to postulate a second Hippolytus, perhaps an E. bishop.

Hippolytus, Canons of St. A collection of canons, probably compiled between 336 and 340. They are dependent on the '*Apostolic Tradition' of *Hippolytus, to whom they were attributed.

Hispana Collection. A collection of canons and *decretals, so called because of its Spanish origin. In its earliest form, which a persistent if disputed tradition links with *Isidore of Seville, it consists of the canons of various councils ending with that of *Toledo in 633, followed by decretals of Popes from *Damasus to *Gregory I.

Historical Jesus, Quest of the. The English translation of A. *Schweitzer's *Von Reimarus zu Wrede* (1906) was published as *The Quest of the Historical Jesus* (1910), and this title has provided a label for the post-*Enlightenment attempts to reconstruct the life and teaching of Jesus of Nazareth by critical historical methods.

The conclusions of the pioneer work of H. S. *Reimarus became known when G. E. *Lessing published the *Wolfenbüttel fragments in 1774–8. The subsequent challenge to the historicity of the Gospels by D. F. *Strauss in his *Leben Jesu* (1835) set Gospel criticism on its modern course. The floodgates of attempts to portray Jesus simply as a human person were opened by J. E. *Renan in 1863. This became the central task of later liberal Protestantism in Germany and of the *Social Gospel movement in America. Despite the repudiation of the quest by K. *Barth and R. *Bultmann, it was renewed by some of the latter's pupils in the 1950s (the 'New Quest'), and outside the Bultmann school continued without a break. See also JESUS CHRIST.

History of Religion School. See RELIGIONS-GESCHICHTLICHE SCHULE.

Hoadly, Benjamin (1676–1761), Bp. successively of *Bangor (1716), *Hereford (1721), *Salisbury (1723), and *Winchester (1734). He was the leader of the *Low Church clergy favoured by the Whigs. His sermon in 1717 on 'The Nature of the Kingdom or Church of Christ' provoked the *Bangorian Controversy.

Hobbes, Thomas (1588–1679), English philosopher. He displeased both Royalists and Parliamentarians by holding that, although sovereignty is ultimately derived from the people, it is transferred to the monarch by implicit contract, so that while the power of the sovereign is absolute, it is not of *Divine Right. From 1640 to 1651 he was in exile. On his return to England he published the *Leviathan* (1651), a philo-

sophical exposition of political absolutism. His teaching cut at the root of ethics, as it left no room for any genuine distinction between good and evil.

Hocktide. The second Monday and Tuesday after *Easter.

Hodge, Charles (1797–1878), *Presbyterian theologian. He taught at Princeton nearly all his life. Though not an original thinker, he had a great influence and following.

Hofbauer, St Clement Mary (1751–1820), the 'Apostle of Vienna'. The son of a grazier and butcher, he joined the *Redemptorists in 1784. Unable to found a house in Vienna because of the anti-religious *Josephinist legislation, he went to Warsaw. When he was driven from Warsaw by Napoleon in 1808, he returned to Vienna. Here his influence extended from the highest to the lowest, counteracting the effects of Josephinism and the *Enlightenment. Feast day, 15 Mar.

Høffding, Harald (1843–1931), Danish philosopher. While he upheld a spiritual interpretation of the universe, he denied that there were sufficient theoretical grounds for applying the notions 'cause' or 'personality' to the Absolute or for affirming (or denying) belief in personal immortality. He described his position as 'critical monism'.

Hoffmann or **Hoffman, Melchior** (c.1500–c.1543), German *Anabaptist. He joined the *Lutherans and became a lay preacher in 1523. He became increasingly imbued with eschatological ideas and finally joined the Anabaptists at Strasbourg. He preached in various places, returning to Strasbourg in 1533 to await the Last Day. He was imprisoned for life. The 'Melchiorites' survived him as a distinct party among the Anabaptists.

Hofmann, Johann Christian Konrad von (1810–77), German *Lutheran theologian. From 1845 he was professor of theology at Erlangen. He aimed at being an uncompromising exponent of Lutheran doctrine. His disciples became known as the 'Erlangen School'.

Hohenheim. See PARACELSUS.

Holcot, Robert (d. 1349), *Scholastic theologian. He entered the *Dominican Order and studied and taught at *Oxford. By 1343 he had been transferred to Northampton, where he is said to have died nursing the sick during the plague. His commentary on the *Sentences* circulated widely. Working in Oxford at a time when the impact of *William of Ockham was fresh and it was difficult to maintain that a fully demonstrable proof could be found for God's existence or His creation of the world, Holcot was reduced to saying that God communicates to men of goodwill sufficient knowledge of Himself for salvation. In his biblical commentaries the main emphasis is on the application of the text for preaching.

Holidays of Obligation. See FEASTS OF OBLIGATION.

Holiness Code, also **Law of Holiness.** The collection of legal material in Lev. 17–26, so named by A. Klostermann in 1877. There are indications that it is a product of the Exile in *Babylon.

Holiness, His. A title of Patriarchs in the E. Church and of the Pope in the W.

Holiness Movement. A predominantly American religious movement which centres on the belief that complete sanctification takes place instantaneously in a single crisis experience. It arose in the mid-19th cent., primarily in the *Methodist Church. It was promoted from 1835 by Phoebe Palmer, a Methodist lay leader. The movement reached a wider public through Holiness Camp Meetings, beginning in 1867 at Vineland, New Jersey. Though still mainly Methodist, it spread to other Protestant Churches. In the last two decades of the 19th cent. tensions between the Holiness advocates and Methodist bishops led to seceding groups forming new Holiness denominations. Of these the largest are the Church of the Nazarene, which emerged as a distinct denomination in the USA in 1908, and the Church of God (Anderson, Ind.), which traces its origins to 1881.

The movement modified Wesleyan teaching by emphasizing *revivalist techniques of invitation, decision, and testimony, and by insistence on visible evidence. By the late 19th cent. physical healing was commonly expected, and the experience of sanctification was called '*baptism with (or sometimes of) the Holy Spirit'. Divided by the rise of *Pentecostal-

ism in the early 20th cent., the surviving Holiness groups became less exuberant. Holiness denominations in Britain are small.

Holland, Christianity in. See NETHERLANDS, CHRISTIANITY IN THE.

Holland, Henry Scott (1847–1918), theologian and preacher. He was a canon of *St Paul's (1884–1910) and then Regius Professor of Divinity at Oxford. He was keenly interested in relating Christian principles to social and economic problems, and with C. *Gore in 1889 founded the Christian Social Union. He wrote the hymn 'Judge eternal, throned in splendour'.

Holocaust. A sacrifice completely consumed by fire, and thus a perfect sacrifice. Less accurately, the word is also used of a sacrifice with many victims. Since the 1950s it has come to be applied absolutely ('the Holocaust') to the Nazi persecution of European Jews between 1933 and 1945; this culminated in the attempt to exterminate them in the gas chambers of concentration camps in E. Europe.

Holste, Lucas (1596–1661), *Vatican Librarian. Converted to RCism in 1625–6, he received Queen *Christina of Sweden's public abjuration of Protestantism at Innsbruck in 1655. He was an erudite scholar.

Holtzmann, Heinrich Julius (1832–1910), German Protestant theologian and biblical critic. He defended the *Marcan hypothesis and argued for a psychological development in the Lord's self-consciousness.

Holy Alliance. The declaration signed in 1815 by the sovereigns of Russia, Austria, and Prussia, and later by others, declaring that henceforth the relations of the Powers would be based on 'the sublime truths which the Holy Religion of our Saviour teaches'.

Holy City, the. *Jerusalem.

Holy Club. The nickname given to the group of '*Methodists' which John *Wesley formed at Oxford in 1729 for the deepening of personal religion.

Holy Coat. Since the 12th cent., both the cathedral at Trier and the parish church at Argenteuil have claimed possession of Christ's 'coat without seam' (Jn. 19: 23).

Holy Cross Day. The name given in various Anglican calendars to 14 Sept., also known as the Feast of the '*Exaltation of the Cross' (q.v.).

Holy Days of Obligation. See FEASTS OF OBLIGATION.

Holy Door, the. The door in the façade of *St Peter's, Rome, nearest to the *Vatican Palace. Normally sealed with brickwork, it is opened during the *Holy Year for the passage of those wishing to gain the *Indulgence of the Holy Year.

Holy Family, the. The Infant Jesus, His Mother (the BVM), and His foster-father (St *Joseph). The cult of the Holy Family as such became popular in the RC Church in the 17th cent. A Feast of the Holy Family is kept on the First Sunday after Christmas.

Holy Father, the Most. A title of the Pope.

Holy Ghost. An alternative title for the *Holy Spirit.

Holy Ghost Fathers (or **Spiritans).** The Congregation of the Holy Ghost was founded in Paris in 1703 for the training of priests. After it had been given official approval in 1734, it became concerned with missionary work, particularly in the French colonies. In 1848, at the request of *Pius IX, François Marie Paul Libermann merged it with his own Congregation of the Immaculate Heart of Mary, founded in 1841 for the evangelization of Black ex-slaves, and reorganized it. The Holy Ghost Fathers were pioneers of RC missionary work in E. and W. Africa.

Holy Innocents. The children of *Bethlehem, 'from two years old and under', according to the account in Mt. (2: 16–18) massacred by *Herod the Great in an attempt to destroy the Infant Jesus. Their death is commemorated on 28 Dec. in the W. (29 Dec. in the E.).

Holy Island; Holy Lance. See LINDISFARNE; LANCE, HOLY.

Holy Land, the. A name given to Palestine/Israel with reference to its having been the scene of the *Incarnation and to the sacred sites there.

Holy Mountain, the. Mount *Athos.

Holy Name of Jesus. See NAME OF JESUS.

Holy Office. The *Roman Congregation established in connection with the *Inquisition in 1542 to deal with heresy internationally. In 1965 it became the 'Congregation for the Doctrine of the Faith' and was charged with the positive function of promoting as well as safeguarding sound doctrine. Since 1988 its title has been the 'Congregation of the Doctrine of the Faith'.

Holy Orders. The higher grades of Christian ministry, i.e. those of *bishop, *priest, and *deacon.

Holy Places, the. The places in Palestine/Israel to which pilgrimage is made on account of their traditional association with biblical events.

Holy Roman Empire. *Charlemagne was crowned as universal Roman Emperor by Pope *Leo in 800, though he claimed only to rule the W. section, leaving the E. empire to continue at *Constantinople until 1453. After his son, the imperial title was held by W. rulers of diminishing territorial power until it lapsed in 924. In 962 Otto I of Germany was crowned Emperor in Rome by *John XII; his successors of the Saxon, Salian, and Hohenstaufen dynasties held the title until 1254. The expression 'holy empire' was used from 1157 by *Frederick I as a counterpart to the spiritual jurisdiction of the Papacy, and the term 'Holy Roman Empire' came to be applied to the territories governed by the Emperor. From 1440 the title was held by rulers of the Habsburg dynasty, the empire being known as 'the Holy Roman Empire of the German nation'. The dignity was abolished by Napoleon I in 1806.

Holy Saturday. The day before *Easter Sunday. It commemorates the resting of Christ's body in the tomb. See PASCHAL VIGIL SERVICE.

Holy See. The term commonly denotes the Papacy.

Holy Sepulchre. The rock cave in *Jerusalem where, according to early tradition, Christ was buried and rose from the dead. The first church on the site was dedicated c.335. Among later churches was that built by the *Crusaders, which also covered the neighbouring holy places, including *Calvary. The present church dates largely from 1810. It has several chapels and shrines in which different Christian bodies have rights; their liturgies take place simultaneously on Sunday mornings, and each celebrates its *Holy Week rites according to its own calendar.

Holy Shroud. A relic preserved at Turin and long venerated as the winding-sheet in which Christ's body was wrapped for burial (Mt. 27: 59 etc.). Carbon-dating tests in 1988 indicated a date between 1260 and 1390 for the flax from which it is woven.

Holy Spirit. In Christian theology, the Third Person of the *Trinity, distinct from, but consubstantial, coequal, and coeternal with, the Father and the Son, and in the fullest sense God.

Christian theologians point to a gradual unfolding of the doctrine in the OT, where the notion of 'Spirit' plays a large part as an instrument of Divine action. The Spirit of God is already operative at the Creation. He was bestowed on those appointed to convey Divine truth, and in the future times of fulfilled hope there would be an extension of the Spirit's activities and powers. Although Jesus said little about the Spirit, the Resurrection faith of His disciples was strongly marked by the experience of the Spirit and they interpreted this as God's gift at the dawn of the coming age. This conviction is epitomized in the quotation of Joel 2: 28–32 in the Acts account of St *Peter's speech on the day of *Pentecost after the dramatic outpouring of the Spirit on the disciples. On occasion the Apostles convey the Spirit by the laying on of *hands. The Gospels present Jesus as empowered by the Spirit at His baptism and driven by the Spirit into the wilderness, as well as claiming the operation of the Spirit at His conception.

The OT view of this intermittently active but impersonal power of God undergoes two developments in the NT. The Spirit is held to be given to all members at their *Baptism, and in the epistles of St *Paul and in Jn. the concept is personalized and given ethical content. In Jn. 14–16 the Spirit is 'another Comforter', distinct from Jesus, but performing similar works and making present what Jesus said and did. Paul can associate the Spirit so closely with Jesus that they are almost identified. Possessing the Spirit unites believers with the Lord and has moral implications.

Though implicit in the NT, the doctrine of the Spirit was not fully elaborated for some centuries. From 360 it became a matter of controversy. The *Macedonians, while maintaining the Divinity of the Son, denied that of the Spirit. At the Council of *Constantinople in 381 this heresy was finally repudiated and the full doctrine of the Spirit received authoritative acceptance in the Church. For differences between E. and W. doctrines, see DOUBLE PROCESSION and FILIOQUE. See also CHARISMATIC RENEWAL MOVEMENT and PENTECOSTALISM.

Holy Synod. From 1721 to 1917 the supreme organ of government in the *Russian Orthodox Church. It was a committee of bishops and clergy established by Peter the Great.

Holy Water. Water which has been blessed for certain specific religious purposes. It is used for blessings, dedications, exorcisms, and for ceremonial cleansing on entering a church, as well as in the W. at the *Asperges.

Holy Week. The week preceding *Easter, observed as a period of devotion to the Passion of Christ. For the current ceremonies proper to each day, see PALM SUNDAY, MAUNDY THURSDAY, GOOD FRIDAY, and PASCHAL VIGIL SERVICE.

Holy Year. A year during which the Pope grants a special *Indulgence, the so-called Jubilee, to all who visit Rome, on certain conditions. It was instituted in 1300 by *Boniface VIII, who meant it to be celebrated every 100 years; the interval was settled at 25 years in 1470.

In addition to the regular Holy Years, in the 20th cent. there were special ones of two kinds: Holy Years of Redemption celebrating the Crucifixion and Resurrection of Christ (conventionally dated 33 AD) and Marian Years celebrating the centenary of the definition of the *Immaculate Conception and the presumed bimillenary of the birth of the BVM (in 1987–88).

Homberg, Synod of. A synod convoked by *Philip, Landgraf of Hesse, in 1526 to establish a constitution on Protestant principles for the Church of his domains. It appointed a committee to draw up a Church Order for Hesse; the document which it issued, however, insisted on the independence of each congregation and was never promulgated.

homiliary. A collection of homilies arranged according to the ecclesiastical calendar for reading at *Mattins.

Homilies, Books of. A collection of 12 prescribed homilies, drawn up for the use of disaffected and unlearned clergy, was issued under the authority of *Edward VI's Council in 1547. A 'Second Book' with 21 further homilies was issued under *Elizabeth I, in its final form in 1571. The Homilies retain a measure of authority in view of the references to them in the *Thirty-Nine Articles.

Homoeans. The *Arian party which came into existence c.355 under the leadership of *Acacius, Bp. of Caesarea. They sought to confine discussion of the Person of Christ to the assertion that He was like (Gk. ὅμοιος, 'like') the Father.

Homoousion (Gk., 'of one substance'; rendered in Lat. *consubstantialis*). The term used in the *Nicene Creed to express the relations of the Father and the Son within the Godhead and originally designed to exclude *Arianism. Some theologians preferred the term 'Homoiousion' ('of like substance'), which was held to leave more room for distinctions within the Godhead.

homosexuality. In the OT the only definite references to homosexual behaviour are the story of Sodom in Gen. 19: 4–11, the probably dependent incident recorded in Jgs. 19, and in Lev. 18: 22 and 20: 13. In the NT it is condemned in 1 Cor.6: 9–11, 1 Tim. 1: 10, and most influentially in Rom. 1: 27 which many moralists have seen as supporting the view that homosexuality is, with other sexual acts which are not procreative, contrary to *Natural Law.

Patristic, medieval, and later Christian moralists accepted this judgement, and it is only in modern times that some have argued that it is the quality of a relationship, be it homosexual or heterosexual, that determines its moral value. In 1991 the House of Bishops of the General Synod of the C of E issued a report which did not reject homosexual activity in permanent relationships among the laity, but insisted that the clergy had a special responsibility to maintain the biblical ideal. The 1998

*Lambeth Conference, however, expressed the belief that for all Christians 'abstinence is right for those not called to marriage'.

Honoratus, St (d. 429/30), Bp. of Arles. Of consular family, he was converted to Christianity. He settled on the island of *Lérins, where he founded the famous monastery (c.410). In 427 or 428 he became Bp. of Arles. Feast day, 16 Jan.

Honorius I (d. 638), Pope from 625. He interested himself in the Christianization of the Anglo-Saxons, and he ended the schism of the patriarchs of *Aquileia-Grado. However, his action in the *Monothelite controversy was one of the arguments against Papal *Infallibility. About 634 *Sergius, Patr. of Constantinople, wrote to him about the question of 'one energy' in Christ. This formula, while confessing the two natures, attributed only one mode of activity—that of the Divine Word—to the Incarnate Christ. It had been found useful in reconciling the *Monophysites, but was strenuously opposed by *Sophronius of Jerusalem. Honorius sent Sergius a favourable reply, in which he used the unfortunate expression 'one will' in Christ. This formula was utilized in the '*Ecthesis', and Honorius himself was anathematized at the Third Council of *Constantinople in 681.

Honorius III (d. 1227), Pope from 1216. Succeeding *Innocent III, he was involved in implementing his predecessor's policy and the decrees of the Fourth *Lateran Council. He crowned the Emp. *Frederick II in 1220 and took a prominent part in the political affairs of Europe. He approved the *Dominican, *Franciscan, and *Carmelite Orders and fostered the growth of their *Third Orders. He was the author of the *Liber Censuum (q.v.).

Honorius 'of Autun' (early 12th cent.), popular theologian. The view that 'Augustodunensis', used by Honorius of himself, refers to Autun, has been abandoned, but no agreed alternative has been found. He probably lived for a time in England, later in S. Germany as a monk, perhaps a recluse. He was a prolific writer. Wide and lasting popularity were enjoyed by his *Elucidarium*, one of the earliest surveys of Christian doctrine, and by his *Imago mundi*, a compendium of cosmology and geography. He was not an original thinker.

Hontheim, Johann Nikolaus von (1701–90), founder of *Febronianism. In 1742 he began an investigation, on behalf of the German Archbishop-Electors, of the historical position of the Papacy; in 1763, under the pseudonym 'Justinus Febronius', he published his conclusions, *De statu ecclesiae et legitima potestate Romani Pontificis*. Because of its *Gallican tendencies the book was placed on the *Index in 1764. In 1778 Hontheim made a formal retractation.

Hooker, Richard (*c*.1554–1600), the foremost apologist of the ecclesiastical settlement of *Elizabeth I.

His treatise *Of the Laws of Ecclesiastical Polity* (1593–1662) was designed to justify the constitutional structure of the Elizabethan Church, but it embodied a broadly conceived philosophical theology. His opposition to the *Puritans, who held that whatever was not commanded in Scripture was unlawful, led him to elaborate a theory of law, based on the 'absolute' fundamental of natural law. This natural law is the expression of God's supreme reason, and everything, including the Bible, must be interpreted in the light of it. But the permanence of law does not preclude development of detail. The Church is an organic, not a static, institution, and methods of Church government and administration will change according to circumstance. Hence the C of E, though reformed, possesses continuity with the medieval Church. Feast day in parts of the Anglican Communion, 3 Nov.

Hooper, John (*c*.1495–1555), Protestant martyr. In 1550 he was nominated to the see of *Gloucester; he accepted only when the reference to angels and saints had been omitted from the Oath of Supremacy and after prolonged hesitation about the lawfulness of episcopal vestments. On *Mary's accession he was imprisoned, and in 1555 he was tried for heresy and burnt. He was an exponent of extreme *Zwinglian Protestantism and influenced the *Puritans through his writings.

hope. One of the three *theological virtues. In its widest sense it may be defined as the desire and search for a future good, difficult but not impossible of attainment. As a Christian virtue its primary end, its motive, and its author is God Himself.

Hopkins, Gerard Manley (1844–89), poet. He became a RC in 1866 and joined the *Jesuits in 1868. He was almost unknown as a poet in his life-time, and the preservation of his MSS is due to R. *Bridges, who edited them in 1918. His works, of which the most ambitious is *The Wreck of the Deutschland*, are marked by intensity of feeling, freedom in rhythm, and individual use of words.

Hormisdas, St (d. 523), Pope from 514. His chief importance lies in his healing of the *Acacian schism. In 519 he secured the signature of John, Patr. of *Constantinople, and afterwards of some 250 E. bishops, to a dogmatic formula in which the *Chalcedonian Definition and Leo's *Tome were accepted, Acacius and other heretics condemned, and the authority of the Roman see emphasized. Feast day, 6 Aug.

Horne, George (1730–92), Bp. of *Norwich from 1790. Though an adherent of *High Church principles, he was in sympathy with the spiritual earnestness of the *Methodists and refused to forbid J. *Wesley to preach in his diocese.

Horologion. In the E. Church the liturgical book containing the recurrent portions of the ecclesiastical *Office throughout the year.

Horsley, Samuel (1733–1806), Bp. successively of *St Davids (1788), *Rochester (1793), and *St Asaph (1802). He is famous chiefly for his controversy with J. *Priestley over the doctrines of the Trinity and Christ's Divinity; he defended the traditional view that the pre-Nicene Church was unanimous in its theology of the Lord's consubstantiality with the Father.

Hort, Fenton John Anthony (1828–92), NT scholar. From 1878 he held professorships at Cambridge. He worked, in conjunction with B. F. *Westcott, on an edition of the Greek text of the NT almost continuously from 1852 until its publication in 1881. It is remarkable for its accuracy and the sobriety of its judgements. He then worked on the RV of Wisdom and 2 Macc.

Hosanna. The Greek form of the Hebrew petition 'Save, we beseech Thee'. It was used by the multitudes when they greeted the Lord on His triumphal entry into Jerusalem on *Palm Sunday, and was early introduced into the Christian liturgy.

Hosea, Book of. *Minor Prophet. While Hosea condemns the injustice in Israelite society, his condemnation of Israel centres on his opposition to the syncretistic worship of the sanctuaries, where Canaanite religious traditions had overlaid or perhaps replaced the more austere religion of Israel. He is among the earliest biblical writers to use close human relationships as an illustration of the relationship between God and man, and his realization of God's character of love paved the way for the Jewish and Christian teaching on the Fatherhood of God. While sharing *Amos's conviction that God would punish Israel, Hosea believed that God's love would not allow Him to cast off Israel for good. He prophesied before c.721 BC.

Hosius or **Ossius** (c.256–357/8), Bp. of Córdoba from c.295. He seems to have been *Constantine's ecclesiastical adviser from 313 to 325. In the early stages of the *Arian struggle he was sent to *Alexandria to investigate and it was apparently as a result of his report that the Emperor summoned the Council of *Nicaea (325). He played an important part in this Council and presided over the anti-Arian Council of *Sardica in 343. His support of St *Athanasius led to his banishment in 355. At the Synod of *Sirmium (357) he signed the 'Blasphemy' and was allowed to return to his diocese.

Hosius or in Polish **Hozjusz**, **Stanislaus** (1504–79), Polish cardinal. In 1551 he became Bp. of Ermland (in Polish Warmia), where one of his main tasks was to combat Protestantism. In his chief work, the *Confessio Catholicae Fidei Christiana* (1552–3), he tried to prove that Catholicism and Christianity were identical. In 1560 *Pius IV appointed him nuncio to the Emp. Ferdinand I, and in this capacity he prepared the reopening of the Council of *Trent. In 1561 he was created cardinal and appointed Papal legate at Trent, where he played a leading part in the doctrinal discussions.

Hoskyns, Sir Edwyn Clement (1884–1937), biblical scholar. From 1919 he was Dean of Chapel of Corpus Christi College, Cambridge. In his contribution to *Essays Catholic and Critical* (1926) he argued that the so-called 'historical Jesus' of Liberal Protestantism was unhistorical. Besides writing on the NT, he translated K. *Barth's *Commentary on Romans* (1933).

Hosmer, Frederick Lucian (1840–1929), American hymn writer. He was ordained in the *Unitarian ministry in 1869. His hymns had a wide appeal, especially among adherents of the emancipated liberal theology of the late-19th cent. They include 'Thy Kingdom come, On bended knee'.

hospice movement. See DYING, CARE OF THE.

Hospitallers, also **Knights Hospitaller**. Their full title, 'Knights of the Order of the Hospital of St John of Jerusalem' derives from the dedication to St *John the Baptist of the hospital at Jerusalem which was their headquarters in the late-11th cent. After 1310 they were also known as the **Knights of Rhodes** and from 1530 as the **Knights of Malta**.

About 1080 a hospice for pilgrims was established in Jerusalem. After the success of the *Crusaders in 1099, the Order developed and obtained Papal sanction. Its original concern was the care of the sick poor, but in the 12th cent. it developed a wing of brother knights, probably in imitation of the *Templars. They shared both the success and the failures of the Crusaders. After the fall of Acre (1291) they escaped to Cyprus and later conquered Rhodes (1309). They defended Rhodes against the Turks in 1480 but were defeated in 1522. In 1530 they received the island of Malta from *Charles V. They took part in the battle of *Lepanto in 1571 but declined in the 17th and 18th cents., surrendering Malta to Napoleon in 1798. (In 1998 they were granted a castle on the island.) The Order now devotes itself mainly to the maintenance of hospitals.

In England their property was sequestrated in 1540. In the 1820s the French Knights of Malta re-established an English branch on a mainly Anglican basis; it was constituted an order of chivalry in 1888. It was responsible for the foundation of the St John Ambulance Association in 1877 and the St John Ambulance Brigade in 1888.

hospitals. Christian hospitals were founded from the 4th cent. onwards and became numerous in the Middle Ages, when they were commonly associated with monastic orders. Most medieval hospitals in England were almshouses for the aged.

Host. A sacrificial victim, and so the consecrated Bread in the *Eucharist, regarded as the Sacrifice of the Body of Christ.

Hostiensis (c.1200–71), canonist. Henry de Bartholomaeis or Henry de Susa was commonly known as Hostiensis because he was Cardinal-Bishop of Ostia from 1262. His main works are his *Summa*, which provides a synopsis of canon and Roman law designed for practical use, and the vast *Apparatus* or *Lectura* on the Decretals of *Gregory IX.

Hours, Canonical. The times of daily prayer laid down in the Divine *Office and especially the services to be recited at them.

Housel. A medieval English name for the Eucharist. The 'housling cloth' was the (late medieval) long white linen cloth spread before, or held by, communicants at the time of receiving the Sacrament.

Howard, John (c.1726–90), prison reformer. A man of Evangelical piety, in 1773 he became High Sheriff of Bedford; what he saw of the afflictions of both tried and untried prisoners in the country gaol inspired him to work for reform. He secured official salaries for gaolers; he travelled widely visiting prisons and quarantine hospitals, and wrote *The State of the Prisons* (1777). The Howard League for Penal Reform, a small influential voluntary body, was founded in his memory in 1866.

Howe, John (1630–1705), *Puritan. In 1652 he was ordained by the rector of Winwick, whom he regarded as a 'primitive bishop'. In 1654 he became incumbent of Great Torrington, Devon, from which he was ejected in 1662. In 1676 he became co-pastor of the *Presbyterian congregation at Haberdashers' Hall in London. He headed the deputation of Nonconformist ministers who congratulated William III in 1689. His standpoint inclined to *Latitudinarianism, and he tried to unite the Presbyterians and *Congregationalists.

Howells, Herbert Norman (1892–1983), English composer. He is known chiefly for his choral and organ Church music, notably a series of settings written for specific cathedral and collegiate churches. His anthems include 'Like as the hart' and 'O pray for the peace of Jerusalem'.

Howley, William (1766–1848), Abp. of *Canterbury from 1828. He was the last of the 'Prince-Archbishops', the revenues of his see coming under the control of the *Ecclesiastical Commissioners on his death. At first he supported the *Oxford Movement, but he lost sympathy with it.

Hrosvit or **Hrotsvitha** (10th cent.), poet. She was a *canoness of the abbey of Gandersheim in Saxony. She wrote 8 poems on saints, 6 plays, and an unfinished panegyric on the Ottos. Her plays were designed to oppose to Terence's representations of the frailty of women the chastity of Christian virgins and penitents.

Huber, Samuel (c.1547–1624), Protestant controversialist. He was banished from Switzerland in 1588 after asserting the universality of Christ's atonement. He later signed the Formula of *Concord and for a time held office in the *Lutheran Church in Germany, until this too found his teaching about the atonement too extreme.

Hubert, St (c.657–727), 'Apostle of the Ardennes'. He succeeded St *Lambert as Bp. of Tongeren/Maastricht in 705/6; in 717/8 he transferred the see to Liège. The story that when hunting he saw a stag with a crucifix between its antlers is not found before the 15th cent. Feast day, 3 Nov.

Hubert Walter (d. 1205), Abp. of *Canterbury. He became Bp. of *Salisbury in 1189. In 1190 he accompanied Abp. *Baldwin on the Third *Crusade. He became Abp. of Canterbury in 1193 as Richard I's nominee, negotiated his release from captivity and organized his ransom. In the king's absence, he ruled England, with the office of justiciar, from Dec. 1193 to July 1198. In 1195 he was also made Papal legate for England and Wales. His legatine commission lapsed on the death of *Celestine III in 1198 and he resigned the justiciarship, but he continued to exert unequalled authority and influence in Church and State. He became chancellor in 1199.

Hubmaier, Balthasar (? 1485–1528), German *Anabaptist. In 1521 he became parish priest at Waldshut; here he came into contact with the Swiss Reformers, allied himself openly with U. *Zwingli in 1523, and introduced the Reformation. By 1525, however, he had abandoned Zwinglian doctrines for those of the Anabaptists. He soon became entangled in the *Peasants' War and may have been the author of the *Twelve Articles. He was burnt at Vienna.

Hucusque. The opening word of the preface to the supplement to the *sacramentary sent by *Hadrian I to *Charlemagne and often used to designate the supplement. This sets out to remedy the deficiencies of the sacramentary. It is widely held to be the work of St *Benedict of Aniane. See also GREGORIAN SACRAMENTARY.

Huddleston, Ernest Urban Trevor (1913–98), Abp. of the Anglican Province of the Indian Ocean. He joined the *Community of the Resurrection in 1941 and was sent to work in the African townships of the area now known as Soweto. He was later Bp. of Masasi, Tanzania (1960–68), of E. Stepney in London (1968–78), and Bp. of Mauritius and Abp. of the Province of the Indian Ocean (1978–83). He was closely involved in the struggle of the African people against apartheid and author of *Naught for Your Comfort* (1956).

Hügel, Friedrich von. See VON HÜGEL, FRIEDRICH.

Hugh, St (1024–1109), Abbot of *Cluny from 1049. *Leo IX took Hugh into his confidence and as adviser to nine Popes he exercised a dominating influence on ecclesiastical and political affairs. He took part in securing the condemnation of *Berengar of Tours (1050) and encouraged *Gregory VII's efforts at reform. Under Hugh the monastery reached a position never surpassed; in 1095 *Urban II in person consecrated the high altar of the new basilica at Cluny, then the largest church in Christendom. Feast day, 29 Apr.

Hugh, St (c.1140–1200), Bp. of *Lincoln from 1186. He became a *Carthusian at the *Grande Chartreuse when he was about 25; c.1180 King Henry II secured his services as prior of Witham, the first Carthusian house in England. As bishop he administered his diocese well and showed a courageous independence of the king. He was revered for his holiness and his tomb became a place of pilgrimage. Feast day, 17 Nov.

Hugh of St-Victor (d. 1142), theologian. Little is known of his life except that c.1115 he entered St-Victor, an Augustinian house of canons in Paris (see VICTORINES). He wrote on grammar, geometry, and philosophy; the *Didascalion*, which is a guide to the study of the *artes* and of theology; biblical commentaries; a commentary on *Dionysius the Pseudo-Areopagite's *Celestial Hierarchy*; a treatise on the Sacraments; and works on spirituality. In all these fields he made a distinctive contribution, with no parade of learning or claims to originality.

Hughes, Hugh Price (1847–1902), *Methodist minister. He was among the first Nonconformist leaders to espouse the cause of '*Christian Socialism'. He became a spokesman for 'the Nonconformist Conscience', for demands that the State should intervene to uphold a code of Christian practice. In 1885 he started the *Methodist Times*, a weekly which became a leading organ of Nonconformist opinion. He worked to secure co-operation between Nonconformist bodies and in 1896 became first President of the National Council of the Evangelical Free Churches.

Huguenots, the *Calvinist French Protestants. The name probably derives from *Eidgenossen* (Ger. 'confederates', i.e. those admitted to the Swiss Confederation, Gallicanized in Geneva as *eigenotz*). At its first Synod in Paris (1539) the French Protestant Church formally organized itself on a Calvinist basis. The movement was resisted by the family of the Guises who came to power in 1539. By 1561, however, the Huguenots were a sizeable national minority, and after the Colloquy of *Poissy they obtained a measure of freedom to practise their religion. They were seen as a danger to the State and the ensuing wars of religion (1562–94) were fought between Catholics and Huguenots. In 1598 *Henry IV, by the Edict of *Nantes granted them freedom of worship and other rights; after the fall of their fortress of La Rochelle in 1628 they lost their political rights; their freedom was increasingly curtailed and the Edict of Nantes revoked in 1685. Many were forced to accept Catholicism or fled from France. After the failure of the rebellion of the *Camisards in 1702–3, the influence of the Huguenots in France was negligible; only in 1802 was the legal standing of their Church re-established. In 1909 they combined with non-Calvinist bodies to form the Protestant Federation of France.

Hulst, Maurice d'. See D'HULST, MAURICE.

Humanae Vitae (1968), the encyclical of *Paul VI condemning *abortion and all forms of birth control except the 'rhythm method'. See also CONTRACEPTION, PRO-CREATION, AND ABORTION, ETHICS OF.

Humbert of Romans (d. 1277), Master of the *Dominican Order from 1254 to 1263. He studied in *Paris and joined the Order there in 1224. He made definitive contributions to the final codification of the Dominican liturgy and to the organization of the Dominican nuns. He was responsible for the recognition of philosophical studies in the intellectual life of the Order and for the completion of its academic structure, and he skilfully steered it through the worst of the anti-mendicant controversy. His *Opus Tripartitum* was written for Pope *Gregory X as a preparatory document for the Second Council of *Lyons; the comments on the schism between Catholics and Orthodox were a factor in medieval and even modern attempts at ecumenism.

Humbert of Silva Candida (d. 1061), ecclesiastical reformer and statesman. A monk of Moyenmoutier, he came to Rome with *Leo IX in 1049; by Feb. 1051 he was Cardinal-Bishop of Silva Candida. He was deeply involved in the negotiations with *Michael Cerularius, Patr. of *Constantinople. He wrote a treatise against *simony in reply to *Peter Damian; it contains the first attack on the practice of lay *investiture. See also GREAT SCHISM (1).

Humble Access, the Prayer of. The prayer in the BCP Communion service which opens with the words 'We do not presume to come to this thy Table'. It was composed for the 'Order of the *Communion' of 1548. It has been variously placed in Anglican liturgies.

Hume, Basil. See HUME, GEORGE BASIL.

Hume, David (1711–76), Scottish philosopher and historian. He reduced reason to a product of experience. All perceptions of the human mind are either impressions of experience or ideas, i.e. faded copies of these impressions. But whereas the relations between ideas can be known with certainty, the facts of reality cannot be established beyond an appearance of probability. Causality is not a concept of logic, but a result of habit and association, impressed on our imagination, and the human soul itself is but a sum of perceptions connected by association. Hence there is no such science as metaphysics; and belief in the existence of God and of the physical world, though a practical necessity, cannot be proved by reason. Our moral life is dominated by the passions, which determine our will and actions. By reducing all cognition to single perceptions and by ruling out any purely intellectual faculty for recording and sifting them, Hume destroyed all real knowledge and taught pure scepticism. In his famous 'Essay on Miracles' he argued that reports of miracles should always be doubted, since miracles are, by definition, highly unlikely.

Hume, George Basil (1923–99), English cardinal. Educated at *Ampleforth College, he joined the *Benedictine community there in 1941 and was elected Abbot in 1963. In 1976 he was nominated Abp. of *Westminster and made a cardinal. He quickly became a national leader, and during his time at Westminster, the RC Church in England entered the mainstream of national life.

humeral veil. In the W. Church, a silk shawl laid round the shoulders serving to cover the hands. At *High Mass the *subdeacon used to hold the *paten with it. It is still worn by the celebrant in processions of the Blessed Sacrament and at *Benediction.

Humiliati. An Italian penitential movement. Its adherents devoted themselves to mortification, the care of the sick, and preaching; in 1184 they were condemned for their disobedience to the hierarchy. *Innocent III in 1201 reorganized them in the form of three orders, governed by a single general chapter: the first order consisted of double monasteries of canons and nuns, the second of houses of celibate lay men and women, the third of married people living at home. The first two were assimilated to the *mendicant orders; the third disappeared in the 14th cent.

humility. Originally denoting low estate and the cowed attitude associated with it, in Judaism and Christianity the word acquired positive connotations. Understood as submissiveness before God, it came to be regarded as a virtue, as Christ 'humbled himself and became obedient unto death' (Phil.2: 8). St *Thomas Aquinas thought of it as involving moderation of ambition to keep it within the bounds appointed for each individual by God. M. *Luther regarded it as the joyful acceptance of God's will, and modern Protestant moralists identify it as complete resignation to our dependence on God.

Hundred Chapters, Council of the. See RUSSIA, CHRISTIANITY IN.

Hungary, Christianity in. The preaching of Christianity in the 4th cent. left no permanent impression; in the 9th and 10th cents. Christianity spread in both its E. and W. forms, the W. Church prevailing. A formal constitution for the Church was laid down in 1001 by King (St) *Stephen, who established episcopal sees. State control of Church affairs has always been strong; it was consolidated under Maria Theresa (1740–80) and Joseph II (1780–90), who dissolved a third of the monasteries (see JOSEPHINISM). The RC Church, however, maintained great influence over political affairs until 1945; it suffered persecution under the Communist regime, though the situation was improving even before its overthrow in 1989.

In the 16th cent. most of Hungary was won over to the Reformation. The RC Church regained the western part, but in the eastern part, despite intermittent persecution, Protestantism remained strong, especially in its *Calvinist form.

Hunt, William Holman (1827–1910), Pre-Raphaelite painter. In 1848 Hunt, with D. G. *Rossetti, founded the Pre-Raphaelite Brotherhood. In 1854 Hunt completed his famous *Light of the World*, representing the Lord knocking at the door of the soul. The original is in Keble College, Oxford; a larger version, begun in 1899, is in *St Paul's Cathedral. All his art is imbued with strong religious feeling.

hunting. Though generally held to be lawful for the laity, hunting was forbidden to the clergy by a series of Gallic councils beginning with that of *Agde (506), whose ruling passed into the '*Corpus Iuris Canonici'. In the Middle Ages a distinction was made between 'quiet' and 'noisy' hunting, and it was widely thought that only the latter was forbidden to the clergy. The 1983 Code of RC Canon Law makes no mention of the subject. In modern times hunting by laity and clergy alike has sometimes been condemned on humanitarian grounds.

Huntingdon, Selina, Countess of (1707–91), Selina Hastings, foundress of the body of *Calvinistic Methodists known as 'the Countess of Huntingdon's Connexion'. She joined the *Wesleys' Methodist society in 1739. She supported Methodist ministers by constituting them her *chaplains, but her contention that she could, as a peeress, appoint to the rank of chaplain as many priests of the C of E as she wished, and employ them publicly, was disallowed by the consistory court of London in 1779. She then registered her chapels as dissenting places of worship under the *Toleration Act; she formed them into an association in 1790. Many of her followers were absorbed into *Congregationalism and by 1998 there were only 800 adult members.

Huss, John (c.1372–1415), in Czech **Jan Hus**, Bohemian Reformer. Having been ordained priest in 1400, he soon became a well-known preacher at the 'Bethlehem Chapel' in Prague. When the writings of J. *Wycliffe became known in Bohemia, Huss was attracted to his political doctrines and was sympathetic to his teaching on *predestination and the Church of the elect. At first he was encouraged by the Abp. of Prague, Sbinko von Hasenburg, but soon his violent sermons on the morals of the clergy provoked hostility and he was forbidden to preach. In the course of the dispute between rival candidates for the Papacy, the king in 1409 gave control of the University of Prague to the 'Czech' nation, which became a stronghold of Wycliffite doctrines, with Huss as Rector. Isolated, Abp. Sbinko soon transferred his allegiance to *Alexander V, who ordered the destruction of Wycliffite books and, to curb Huss's influence, the cessation of preaching in private chapels; in 1411 *John XXIII excommunicated Huss. Opinion moved against Huss and the king removed him from Prague; he took refuge with the Czech nobility and devoted himself to writing his main work, *De Ecclesia* (1413), part of which was taken directly from

Wycliffe. Having appealed from the decision of the Papal curia to a General Council, he went to the Council of *Constance with a safe-conduct from the Emp. Sigismund. He was imprisoned and burnt.

By his death Huss became a national hero. Various grievances among the Czechs of Bohemia overflowed into a movement of protest which assumed Huss's name. By the Four Articles of Prague (1420) the Hussites laid down a programme of secularization, *Utraquism, vernacular liturgy, and ecclesiastical reform which in important ways anticipated the *Reformation. During the Hussite Wars (1420–34) they were able to implement much of this in Bohemia; it left a lasting legacy in the sect of the *Bohemian Brethren.

Hutchinson, John (1674–1737), author. In his *Moses's Principia* (1724) Hutchinson expounded a system of biblical philosophy, maintaining that Hebrew was the primitive language of mankind which, if rightly interpreted, gave the key to all knowledge. Its theories were developed by a circle of predominantly *High Church Anglicans called the 'Hutchinsonians'. In their sacramental and mystical interpretation of orthodox Christianity, they are often seen as precursors of the *Oxford Movement.

Hutten, Ulrich von (1488–1523), German humanist and controversialist. He left the monastery of *Fulda in 1505, visited various universities, and engaged in military service. About 1515 he became a contributor to the *Epistolae Obscurorum Virorum*. From 1519 he devoted his life to the propagation of M. *Luther's reformation, in which he saw the instrument for the deliverance of Germany from the power of Rome. He wrote a series of treatises in German and Latin for this purpose. At the end of his life U. *Zwingli gave him refuge.

Hutterites. See ANABAPTISTS.

Hutton, Richard Holt (1826–97), religious writer. He trained for the *Unitarian ministry but became a member of the C of E. In 1861 he was offered the joint-editorship and proprietorship of the *Spectator*, which he used as a pulpit from which to challenge, on Christian principles, the regnant agnosticism of J. S. Mill and T. H. *Huxley.

Huxley, Thomas Henry (1825–95), biolo-

gist. In 1860 he had a memorable passage of words with S. *Wilberforce, Bp. of Oxford, on the subject of evolution. He defended the view that man descended from the lower animal world in his *Evidence as to Man's Place in Nature* (1863) and in a lecture on 'The Physical Basis of Life' in 1863 he discussed a form of *agnosticism. Man, he argued, cannot know the nature of either spirit or matter; metaphysics is impossible; and man's primary duty in life is the relief of misery and ignorance. While he stressed the merits of scientific education, he held that it should be supplemented by study of the Bible as the only means by which religious feeling, the basis of moral conduct, could be sustained. In a study of D. *Hume (1879) he discussed miracles, which he declined to reject out of hand.

Huysmans, Joris Karl (1848–1907), French Catholic novelist. He was a member of the French Ministry of the Interior, but his main claim to fame lay in his literary work, which reflected his interest in religious art, ritual, and mysticism.

Hyacinth, St (d. 1257), 'Apostle of *Poland'. Born in NE Poland, he went to Italy and there joined the *Dominican Order *c*.1220. He was put in charge of a group of Dominicans sent to Poland; he founded priories at Cracow (1223) and Gdańsk (*c*.1225), and devoted himself to missionary work. The story of his extensive labours in Scandinavia lacks historical foundation. Feast day, 17 (formerly 16) Aug.

Hydroparastatae. An alternative name for the *Aquarians.

hylozoism. The doctrine that all matter is endowed with life.

Hymnary. The medieval liturgical book of the W. rite which contained the metrical hymns of the Divine *Office arranged according to the liturgical year.

hymns. Sacred poetry set to music has always formed part of Christian worship. At first OT texts, especially the Psalms, were used, but at an early date distinctively Christian compositions, e.g. the *Magnificat, appeared, and what seem to be quotations from early hymns are found in various places in the NT. The use of hymns is mentioned by several of the early Fathers, and the '*Phos Hilaron' is among those dating from pre-Nicene times. From the 4th cent. hymns were employed not only to celebrate the Christian mysteries, but also to promote or refute heresy, e.g. in the *Arian controversy. Although from the 5th cent. some Christians held that no words other than those of Scripture should be allowed in the liturgy, *troparia (single-stanza hymns) are found in E. service books of the period; they were later joined together to form *contakia and *canons.

Latin hymns appear later than Greek, the real impetus coming from St *Ambrose. Though only three hymns can certainly be ascribed to him, he laid down the line of development of Latin hymnody as simple, devotional, and direct, and it was through his influence that hymns became a recognized and integral part of the public worship of the W. Church. Although hymns were not admitted into the Roman *Office until the 12th cent., the development came to be towards an ordered sequence for use at different times and seasons.

Throughout the Middle Ages hymns were written in the vernacular, but they were largely the work of those outside the main religious stream. With the *Reformation the situation changed. *Lutheranism had a wealth of new hymns written in German by M. *Luther himself and later by P. *Gerhardt. *Calvinism, on the other hand, would tolerate nothing but the words of Scripture in its services; hence the Psalms were put into *metrical versions (q.v.). In the C of E hymns virtually disappeared from the service-books, mainly it seems, because T. *Cranmer lacked 'the grace and facility' to render Latin hymns well in English.

Modern hymn-writing and hymn-singing were mainly the creation of the 18th cent. A prominent part was taken by I. *Watts, whose hymns were written to express the spiritual experience of the singer. They were followed by the works of John and Charles *Wesley. The practice of singing hymns was encouraged by the *Methodists and spread among the *Evangelical party in the C of E. In America the Negro *spirituals were a powerful factor in the Second *Great Awakening of 1797–1805. By the early 19th cent. prejudice against the use of hymns in the C of E was dying, and R. *Heber's collection of *Hymns Written and adapted to the Weekly Church Services of the

Year* (1827) helped to break down the hostility to hymns outside Evangelical circles. A further influence in fostering the use of hymns came from the *Oxford Movement; hymns of the ancient and medieval Church were employed to emphasize the antiquity and Catholicity of the Church. The publication of various collections of old and new hymns followed; the most widely used were probably *Hymns, Ancient and Modern (1861) and The *English Hymnal (1906). The 1980s saw a number of new C of E hymn books, including revisions of the two last named. Among RCs a demand for popular hymns in the 19th cent. was met by such writers as F. W. *Faber. After the Second *Vatican Council hymns became widely used at Mass, and are no longer confined to those by RC authors. Apart from the *Quakers, all other English-speaking Churches have assigned an important place to hymns as being an integral part of Christian worship, rather than an adjunct to it. Over the years they have issued collections of hymns authorized for use in their own services, e.g. The *Church Hymnary (1898) of the Scottish and other *Presbyterians and The Baptist Church Hymnal (1900), and, like the C of E, have produced revisions and new books in recent years. There have also been hymnals compiled for particular types of community, such as schools, and a few non-denominational books, notably *Songs of Praise (1925) and the Australian Hymn Book (1977), better known as With One Voice (1979). Some modern hymns make use of popular linguistic and musical idiom, but the traditional language of classical hymns is usually retained.

Hymns, Ancient and Modern (1861). A hymnal, edited by H. W. *Baker, which drew freely on ancient and modern sources and incorporated many of the traditional *Office hymns (often in translations by J. M. *Neale). The music assisted its popularity. There were revisions in 1950 and 1983.

Hypapante. The name used in the E. Church for the feast of *Candlemas.

Hypatia (c.375–415), philosopher. She was the glory of the *Neoplatonist School of *Alexandria. On the suspicion that she had set the pagan prefect of Alexandria against the Christians, she was attacked by a Christian mob and killed.

hyperdulia. The special veneration paid to the BVM on account of her eminent dignity as Mother of God.

hypostasis. The Greek word (literally, 'substance') had various meanings. In popular language it was used for 'objective reality' as opposed to 'illusion'. In early Christian writers it was used to denote 'being' or 'substantive reality' and not distinguished in meaning from ousia (οὐσία, Greek for 'being'). From the mid-4th cent., however, it was contrasted with ousia and used to mean 'individual reality', especially in Trinitarian and Christological contexts.

The formula 'Three Hypostaseis in one Ousia' came to be accepted as an epitome of the orthodox doctrine of the Trinity.

Hypostatic Union. The union of the Divine and human natures in the One Person ('Hypostasis') of Jesus Christ. The doctrine was formally accepted by the Church in the Definition of *Chalcedon (451).

Hypsistarians. A 4th-cent. sect whose members refused to worship God as 'Father', but revered Him as the 'All Ruler and Highest'.

I

Iamblichus (c.250–c.330), the chief *Neoplatonist of the Syrian school. He held an elaborate theory of mediation between the spiritual and physical worlds, radically modifying the doctrine of *Plotinus by duplicating the Plotinian One and distinguishing between its transcendental and creative aspects. This distinction lies at the basis of the negative (or *apophatic) and affirmative theologies which have differentiated E. and W. theology.

Ibas, Bp. of *Edessa, 435–49 and 451–7. In the *Christological controversies he took a mediating position between the dualistic teaching of the *Nestorians and the *Alexandrian position of St *Cyril. He was deposed by the *Latrocinium and restored at the Council of *Chalcedon, but his only surviving work, a letter addressed to one Mari in 433, was condemned by *Justinian. See also THREE CHAPTERS.

Iceland, Christianity in. Christianity reached Iceland from *Norway c.980 and was accepted by the ruling council in 999/1000. The medieval Church was under the administrative jurisdiction of Bremen, then of *Lund, and finally of Trondheim (Nidaros). At the *Reformation Iceland followed *Denmark, to whose rule she had been subject since c.1380, in adopting *Lutheranism. In modern times there has been a revival of Church life; there was a new translation of the Bible in 1981.

Ichabod, the son of Phinehas and grandson of the priest Eli. The name means 'The glory has departed' (1 Sam. 4: 21); hence its use as an exclamation.

icon. Icons are flat pictures, usually painted in egg tempora on wood, but also wrought in mosaic, ivory, and other materials, to represent Christ, the BVM, or another saint, which are venerated in the E. Church. As it is believed that through them the saints exercise their beneficent powers, they preside at all important events of human life and are held to be powerful channels of grace. See also the following entry and IMAGES.

Iconoclastic Controversy. The controversy on the veneration of *icons which agitated the Greek Church from c.725 to 842. In 726 the Emp. *Leo III published a decree declaring all images idols and ordering their destruction. Disturbances followed persecution, especially of the monks who were the chief defenders of the icons. In 753 the Emp. Constantine V called the

Synod of Hieria, which alleged that, by representing only the humanity of Christ, the icon-worshippers either divided His unity as the *Nestorians or confounded the two natures as the *Monophysites, and declared that the icons of the BVM and the saints were idols and ordered their destruction. Persecution increased. It abated under Leo IV (775–80), and after his death the Empress Irene, regent for her son, reversed the policy of her predecessors. The Second Council of *Nicaea in 787 undid the work of the Synod of Hieria, defined the degree of veneration to be paid to icons, and decreed their restoration throughout the country.

The outbreak of the 'Second Iconoclastic Controversy' took place in 814 under Leo V the Armenian, who removed icons from churches and public buildings; the Patr. *Nicephorus was deposed (815), and St *Theodore of Studios was sent into exile. Persecution ended only with the death of the Emp. Theophilus in 842. His widow, Theodora, caused Methodius to be elected patriarch in 843 and on the first Sunday in Lent a feast was celebrated in honour of the icons; it has since been kept in the E. Church as the 'Feast of *Orthodoxy.'

iconography, Christian. The earliest Christian art was mainly symbolical: Christ was represented by a *fish or as a young shepherd, the Church by a ship. It was soon possible to detect a difference of emphasis in the E. and W., the E. stressing the liturgical function of art, whereas the W. regarded art as providing pictorial illustrations of biblical events and religious doctrines. Byzantine churches often exhibit a planned system of stylized and didactic decoration covering the whole interior. In the W., partly under the influence of the growing devotion to Christ's humanity, a new realistic, less symbolic style of art began to develop from the 12th cent. While individualism had some play, art commonly conformed to a pattern determined by the Church. In the 14th cent. religious art grew less intellectual and more emotional; in the 15th cent. it became frankly realistic and picturesque. See also ICON.

iconostasis. The screen which, in Byzantine churches, separates the sanctuary from the nave.

idiorrhythmic. A term applied to certain monasteries on Mount *Athos, which used to allow considerable freedom to their monks, including the right to possess personal property.

Idiot, the. The pseudonym of a medieval spiritual writer. He is generally identified as Raymundus Jordanus, a French *Augustinian Canon who flourished c.1381.

Ignatius, Father. Joseph Leycester Lyne (1837–1908), mission preacher. Aiming to revive the *Benedictine Order in the Anglican Church, in 1869 he acquired a site for his monastery at Capel-y-ffin, near Llanthony. A deacon since 1860, in 1898 he was ordained priest by J. R. *Vilatte.

Ignatius, St (c.35–c.107), Bp. of *Antioch. Nothing is known of his life except that he was taken under guard from Antioch to Rome. He was received at *Smyrna by St *Polycarp, and from there he wrote to the Churches of *Ephesus, Magnesia, and Tralles letters of encouragement, and to the Church of Rome begging them not to deprive him of martyrdom by intervening with the authorities. At Troas he wrote to the Churches of *Philadelphia and Smyrna and to Polycarp. The *Colosseum is the traditional place of his martyrdom.

Ignatius insists on the reality of both the Divinity and the Humanity of Christ, whose life is continued in the *Eucharist. The best safeguard of the unity of the Christian faith is the *bishop, without whose authority neither the Eucharist nor marriage may be celebrated. Feast day: 17 Oct. in the RC Church (formerly 1 Feb.), some Anglican calendars, and at Antioch; 20 Dec. in the Greek Church.

Ignatius Loyola, St (probably 1491–1556), founder of the *Jesuits. Of noble Spanish family, he embarked on a military career, but was wounded in 1521. He hung up his sword at *Montserrat. During a year at Manresa (1522–3), he underwent a series of spiritual experiences from which he derived many of the insights contained in the *Spiritual Exercises (q.v.). After a visit to Jerusalem, he studied in Spain and France (1524–35). In 1534 he and six companions made a vow of lifelong poverty and service to others, either in the Holy Land or, if that was not possible, wherever the Pope should send them. Turkish attacks prevented them from sailing for Jerusalem. Outside

Rome Ignatius had a vision of himself being accepted as a servant by Christ, at the Father's request. In 1540 the group was constituted as the Society of Jesus, with Ignatius as its first General. His aim was to rekindle religious fervour and practice in the Church through a more efficacious ministry. He also gave priority to missionary work outside Europe and, after 1548, to education. Feast day, 31 July.

IHS. A monogram from the name of Jesus, formed by abbreviating the corresponding Greek word which in *uncials is written ΙΗΣΟΥΣ.

Ildefonsus, St (c.607–67), Abp. of Toledo from 657. He is said to have written many works, but only four survive. One is a vigorous assertion of the privileges of the BVM; one is on *Baptism, another on the spiritual life of the soul after Baptism, and the fourth, *De Viris Illustribus*, is an important source for the history of the Spanish Church in the 7th cent. Feast day, 23 Jan.

Illingworth, John Richardson (1848–1915), Anglican clergyman. His rectory at Longworth was the centre of the *Lux Mundi* group.

Illtyd or **Illtud, St** (5th–6th cent.), Welsh saint. He was abbot of a large monastery, which he is said to have founded; it was probably Llantwit Major in the Vale of Glamorgan. Feast day, 6 Nov.

Illuminati. A name applied to several bodies of religious enthusiasts, including (1) the *Alumbrados; (2) the *Rosicrucians; and (3) a masonic sect founded in Bavaria in 1776 by Adam Weishaupt. Repudiating the claims of all existing religious bodies, they professed themselves to be those in whom alone the 'illuminating' grace of Christ resided. They were banished from Bavaria in 1784 but survived elsewhere.

illuminative way. The intermediate stage of the spiritual life. See PURGATIVE, ILLUMINATIVE, AND UNITIVE WAYS.

Illyricus. See FLACIUS, MATTHIAS.

Image of God. According to Gen. 1: 26 f., man was made in the image and after the likeness of God. Some of the Fathers regarded the 'image' as referring to man's original condition and 'likeness' to his final state of glory; others made no such distinc-

tion. The *Fall involved either the loss of the 'likeness' or damage to, or destruction of, the 'image'. For all Baptism was seen as an indispensable step in the restoration of the image-likeness. In what the image consists was disputed; most located it in human free will. The 16th cent. Reformers expressed their doctrine of man's total depravity by asserting that the image was utterly lost as a result of the Fall.

images. The use of any representation of men, animals or plants was prohibited in the Mosaic Law (Exod. 20: 4) because of the dangers of idolatry. Though images are mentioned in other parts of the OT, it seems that from the time of the *Maccabees the Palestinian Jews observed the prohibition strictly, at least as far as the *Temple was concerned.

The earliest known Christian pictures are paintings in the *catacombs, some from the 2nd cent. After the period of the *persecutions, sacred images came to play an important part in the cultus, especially in the E. This was justified by stressing the theological significance of the Incarnation in which God had become visible by taking human nature. Since the settlement of the *Iconoclastic Controversy, *icons have continued to be an integral element in Orthodox religion. In the W. the veneration of images, which included statues, made slower progress. It was given a doctrinal basis by St *Thomas Aquinas on the lines laid down by E. theologians, that is that the honour paid to the image passes to its prototype. At the *Reformation the use of images was opposed by most of the Reformers, especially the followers of U. *Zwingli and J. *Calvin, who were followed by the *Puritans. The *Lutherans were more tolerant of the practice and keep a *crucifix on their altars.

Imago Dei. Latin for the *Image of God.

Imitation of Christ, The. A manual of spiritual devotion designed to instruct the Christian how to seek perfection by following Christ as his model. It was put into circulation in 1418 and has traditionally been attributed to *Thomas à Kempis; attempts since the 17th cent. to assign it to other writers have failed to win general assent.

Immaculate Conception of the BVM. The dogma that 'from the first moment of her conception the Blessed Virgin Mary was . . . kept free from all stain of original sin' was defined by *Pius IX in 1854. The doctrine was a matter of dispute throughout the Middle Ages, but was generally accepted by RCs from the 16th cent. It has not been endorsed by E. theologians, mainly because they do not share the W. conception of *original sin. The feast, approved by Pope *Sixtus IV in 1476, is kept on 8 Dec. (In the E. the Feast of the Conception of the BVM is kept on 9 Dec.)

Immanence, Divine. The omnipresence of God in His universe. The doctrine is a necessary constituent of the Christian conception of God.

Immanuel or **Emmanuel** (Heb., 'With us [is] God'). The word occurs in Is. 7: 14 and 8: 8, but it is not clear to whom it refers. In Mt. 1: 23 the prophecy is interpreted with reference to the birth of Christ.

immersion. A method of *Baptism, whereby part of the candidate's body is submerged in the baptismal water which is poured over the remainder. It is still found in E. Church. In the W. it has largely been replaced by *affusion, though it is still officially encouraged in the Anglican and RC Churches.

immolation. An act of sacrificial offering. The word has occupied an important place in modern Eucharistic theology.

immortality. Though not a specifically Christian doctrine, the hope of immortality is an integral element in Christian belief. In pre-Christian times Greek philosophers had inferred the existence of the soul before birth and its survival of death, and had regarded the body as a prison-house from which death brought the release of the soul into a fuller existence. Early Hebrew thought about the next world hardly went beyond the conception of a shadowy existence in *Sheol, but in later pre-Christian Judaism a greater sense of the reality of the future life developed. The essential shape which the doctrine assumed in Christianity arose from the fact of Christ's *Resurrection. No longer was the highest destiny of man seen as the survival of an immortal soul, but as a life of union with the risen Christ which would reach completion only with the reunion of soul and body. Since the late-18th cent. the traditional arguments have been challenged, notably by I. *Kant; he held that it was beyond the competence of 'theoretical reason' to establish the soul's immortality or otherwise, but he argued that it could be established on the ground of moral experience, i.e. through 'practical reason'. The abiding character of the moral law and the manifest injustices of the present life were a sure index that there was a purer life in which these injustices would be remedied. A similar line of argument has been adopted by many modern apologists. See also RESURRECTION OF THE DEAD and CONDITIONAL IMMORTALITY.

Impanation. A term applied to certain doctrines of the Eucharist which were designed to safeguard a belief in the *Real Presence while denying the destruction of the natural elements.

impassibility of God. Orthodox theology has commonly held that God is not subject to suffering caused by action from without, changing emotions from within, or feelings of pain or pleasure caused by another being. In Christianity there is, however, tension between the idea of the immutability, perfection, and all-sufficiency of God, which would seem to exclude all passion, and the central conviction that God in His essence is love, and that His nature is revealed in the Incarnate Christ, not least in His Passion. Some modern theologians therefore question whether it is legitimate to speak unreservedly of God's impassibility. In the 20th cent. Divine impassibility has been challenged by philosophers as incoherent, by *Process theologians as a relic of an outmoded metaphysics, and by J. *Moltmann and others as a blasphemous irrelevance in the light of modern suffering under totalitarian regimes.

impediment. In *canon law, an obstacle standing in the way of a properly constituted marriage. In RC canon law until 1983 impediments were either 'impedient' or 'diriment'. The former, which prohibited a marriage but did not invalidate it if contracted despite the impediment, no longer exists; the latter renders such a marriage null and void. See DIRIMENT IMPEDIMENT.

imposition of hands. See HANDS, IMPOSITION OF.

imprecatory Psalms. Psalms which in whole or part invoke the Divine vengeance (e.g. Ps. 58). They are often omitted in public worship.

imprimatur (Lat., 'let it be printed'). The certification that a book has been passed for publication by the appropriate authority. In England various licensing laws in the 16th and 17th cents. required an imprimatur from a civil or ecclesiastical authority for the printing or importation of books. In the RC Church certification by the local *Ordinary that certain kinds of books and other writings are free from doctrinal or moral error is required before their publication.

Improperia. The Latin name of the *Reproaches.

impropriation. The assignment or annexation of an ecclesiastical benefice, for the use of its property, to a lay proprietor or corporation. At the *Dissolution many benefices which had been *appropriated to monasteries, were impropriated by '*lay rectors'; where the monastery was exempt from the requirement to endow a *vicar, the lay rector inherited this privilege and appointed a *perpetual curate to discharge the spiritual duties of their benefices.

imputation. According to classical Protestant theologies of *justification, the righteousness of Christ is imputed or reckoned to the believer in order that he may be justified on its basis. In contrast, according to RC doctrine the believer is justified on the basis of an imparted or infused righteousness, intrinsic to his person.

In Coena Domini (Lat., 'On the Lord's Supper'). A series of excommunications of specified offenders against faith and morals which were issued in the form of a Papal bull. Its publication came to be confined to *Maundy Thursday (hence its name); the practice was abrogated in 1869.

in commendam. See COMMENDAM.

incardination. In W. canon law, the permanent enlistment of a cleric under the jurisdiction of a new *Ordinary.

Incarnation. The Christian doctrine of the Incarnation affirms that the eternal Son of God took flesh from His human mother and that the historical Christ is at once fully God and fully man. It asserts an abiding union in Christ's Person of Godhead and manhood without the integrity or permanence of either being impaired, and it assigns the beginnings of this union to a definite and known date in human history.

The doctrine took shape under the influence of the controversies of the 4th–5th cents. (see CHRISTOLOGY); it was formally defined at the Council of *Chalcedon in 451. Within the limits of the Chalcedonian Definition, however, discussion continued. In the Middle Ages a much disputed (but never settled) point was whether the Incarnation would have occurred but for the *Fall.

The doctrine of the Incarnation raises questions of the relation of time and eternity, of finitude and infinity. Some modern theologians have seen in it the religious expression of the essential relatedness of man and God. Others have sought to interpret it in terms of moral value, and have seen the essence of Christ's Divinity in the conformity of His human will with that of God. Some have even questioned the appropriateness of the concept of Incarnation for expressing the salvific significance of Jesus.

incense. Incense is used in many religious rites, the smoke being considered symbolic of prayer. There is no clear evidence of its Christian use until the last quarter of the 4th cent. The incensing of the altar, church, people, etc., is first recorded in the late 5th cent. in the E. and in the W. in the 9th cent. In the W. incense was long used only at solemn services, but since 1969 it has been more widely permitted, e.g. at any Eucharist. In the E. it is used at most services.

incubation. The practice of sleeping in churches or their precincts in expectation of visions, revelations, and healing from disease. Of pagan origin, the custom came to be associated with particular churches.

incumbent. In the C of E the holder of a parochial charge, i.e. a *rector, *vicar, or (until 1968) a *perpetual curate.

Independents. Another name for the *Congregationalists.

Index Librorum Prohibitorum (Lat., 'List of prohibited books'), in short 'the Index'.

The official list of books issued by the RC Church which its members were normally forbidden to read or possess. The first Index was issued in 1557 by the Congregation of the Inquisition (see HOLY OFFICE). In 1966 the Index ceased to have the force of ecclesiastical law, with attached censures, but is said to retain its moral force.

India, Pakistan, and Bangladesh, Christianity in. There are some ambiguous references to Christianity in India (and possibly Pakistan) in the 4th cent., but the earliest clear testimony is the assertion of *Cosmas Indicopleustes that there were Christians in India before 550. For the history of the Thomas Christians, see MALABAR CHRISTIANS.

W. Christianity was brought to India by the Portuguese in 1498. Attempts to evangelize the inhabitants of the country as a whole date from the arrival of the *Jesuits in 1542. Under the *padroado* (or royal patronage) grants of the Pope, *Portugal claimed the right to nominate all bishops and missionaries in the East. It became clear that Portugal could not fulfil these obligations, and in 1637 the *Propaganda in Rome consecrated a Brahman as *Vicar Apostolic for the non-Portuguese regions of India. Though the policy of choosing Indians for the post lapsed, Vicars Apostolic were appointed in increasing numbers. In 1886 *Leo XIII created a regular hierarchy for India and the future Pakistan.

From 1660 the English and later the Dutch were in the Indian subcontinent. They were mainly concerned with the spiritual care of their own people. Protestant missionary work began seriously in 1706, when King Frederick IV of Denmark founded a mission to work in his territory of Tranquebar in S. India. In 1793 the first English missionary, W. *Carey, landed in Bengal. Since the East India Company opposed missionary activity, Carey established his mission in the Danish territory of Serampore. At the revision of the East India Company's charter in 1813, *Evangelical opinion secured the insertion of provision for a bishopric of Calcutta and freedom for missionary enterprise. The *CMS sent missionaries, and Anglican clergy came in large numbers. By the end of the 19th cent. there were also numerous missionaries from the USA and Continental Europe, and in the second half of the 19th cent. strenu-

ous efforts were made to convert the aboriginal people. A native Indian ministry was formed through the ordination of those trained in their own language and with no knowledge of English; the first such ordination took place in 1850. In 1930 the Anglican Church in India, which had hitherto been a part of the C of E, acquired independence as the Church of India, Burma, and Ceylon (Pakistan was added to the title in 1947).

Co-operation among the non-RC Churches in India dates from 1855. A series of conferences led to the formation in 1908 of the South India United Church (*Presbyterian and *Congregational), the first transconfessional union of modern times. Out of this grew the movement which led in 1947 to the formation of the Church of *South India. A parallel movement led to the formation of the Churches of *North India (1970) and of *Pakistan (1970).

When the former British India became independent in 1947, the country was divided into the predominantly Hindu state of India and the mainly Muslim state of Pakistan, of which the eastern part became independent as Bangladesh in 1971. Religious liberty is written into the constitution of all three states, but conversions are discouraged and in India restrictions were soon placed on foreign missionaries. Nevertheless, after Islam Christianity forms the second largest minority religion, with c.2.5 per cent of the population. In Pakistan there was originally less hostility towards missionaries from the Commonwealth, but since 1969 the government has exercised increasing control over Christian institutions, and Christians have felt their position threatened. They form c.1.5 per cent of the population.

Indicopleustes, Cosmas. See COSMAS INDICOPLEUSTES.

Indonesia, Christianity in. Christianity was effectively brought to Indonesia by the Portuguese maritime trading empire in the 16th cent. *Franciscans from *Portugal established themselves in the Moluccas in 1534. After the Dutch replaced the Portuguese in the Indonesian archipelago in the 17th cent., the RC Church dwindled; for the next 200 years the Dutch Reformed Church was the only officially recognized Church within the sphere of influence of the Dutch

East India Company, which brought clergy from the *Netherlands for its employees. In the 19th and early 20th cents. Dutch and German missionaries of various denominations were active and both Protestants and RCs received financial aid from the Dutch colonial government. To avoid conflict the Dutch authorities assigned different bodies to separate areas. Dutch rule and European missionary enterprise were disrupted by the Japanese occupation (1942–5). In 1949 the new nation of Indonesia came into existence. Protestantism and RCism are officially recognized religions. Christians form about 10 per cent of the population.

induction. The final stage in the appointment of a new *incumbent. After the priest has been *instituted by the bishop, he is inducted to his *benefice, usually by the *archdeacon, who places his hand on the key of the church door and causes him to toll the bell. The legal effect is to give him possession of the temporalities and control of the parish.

indulgences. The remission by the Church of the temporal penalty due to forgiven sin, in virtue of the merits of Christ and the saints. The practice of granting indulgences presupposes that sin must have a penalty either on earth or in *purgatory, even after the sinner has been reconciled to God by penitence and *absolution; that through the *Communion of Saints all Christians can share in the merits of Christ's saving work and in the merits of the saints; and that the Church can administer the benefit of these merits.

In the early Church the intercession of confessors and those awaiting martyrdom was allowed by the ecclesiastical authorities to shorten the canonical discipline of those under *penance; with the development of the doctrine of purgatory in the W., canonical penance came to be considered as a substitute for temporal punishment in purgatory, and from there followed the belief that the prayers and merits of the saints availed to shorten such punishment, even for sins which did not require canonical penance. Later alternative works were permitted instead of the prescribed penances, and the merits of Christ and the saints applied to make up the deficiency. From the 12th cent. the granting of indulgences became common.

The considerable abuses which developed in the later Middle Ages, such as the sale of indulgences, were the immediate cause of the *Reformation. In 1967 *Paul VI revised the practical application of the traditional doctrine in order to make it clear that the Church's object was not merely to help the faithful to make due satisfaction for their sins, but chiefly to induce them to a greater fervour of charity. Indulgences are no longer reckoned in days and years; they simply supplement, and to the same degree, the remission which the person performing the indulgenced action has already gained by the charity and contrition with which he does it. See also PLENARY INDULGENCE.

indult. A faculty granted by the Pope or some other ecclesiastical authority to deviate from the common law of the Church.

Industrial Christian Fellowship. An Anglican organization which seeks to present the Christian faith to the world of industry by missions to industrial workers and by relating the theory and practice of Christianity to industry. It was formed in 1918 by the fusion of two earlier bodies.

infallibility. Inability to err in teaching revealed truth. While many Christians maintain that the Church is infallible, on the basis of such texts as Jn. 16: 13, various beliefs have been held as to the seat where such infallibility rests. At the First *Vatican Council (1870) the RC Church declared that the Pope was infallible when he defined that a doctrine concerning faith or morals was part of the deposit of Divine revelation handed down from apostolic tradition.

Infancy Gospels. The apocryphal stories about the birth and childhood of Christ which were early put into circulation.

Infant Baptism. Although from the first *Baptism was the universal means of entry into the Christian community, the NT contains no specific authority for its administration to infants. Since at least the 3rd cent., however, children born to Christian parents have been baptized in infancy. In the 16th cent. the practice ('paedobaptism') was rejected by the *Anabaptists, and since the 17th cent. also by the *Baptists (and later by the *Disciples of Christ).

In the NT the children of Christians are regarded as themselves Christian, and where the Baptism of households is mentioned, children may have been baptized along with adults. The *Apostolic Tradition* explicitly states that little children are to be baptized first, and if they cannot answer for themselves a member of the family is to do so on their behalf. *Origen refers to the Baptism of infants as an established practice, and *Terullian argued against it (witnessing to its existence). Even in the 4th cent. not all children of Christian parents were baptized in infancy (St *Basil and St *Gregory of Nazianzus were baptized in their twenties) but about this time the Baptism of children became increasingly normal. With the toleration of Christianity under *Constantine, Baptism no longer entailed risks of persecution, and as the Church became identified with the State in the 5th cent., Baptism came to be regarded as a rite of passage connected with birth.

According to Catholic theology the Baptism of infants conveys the essential gift of regeneration. Those who reject it do so on the grounds that it lacks NT warrant and that as a mere ceremony (not a *sacrament) it can convey no benefit to its unconscious recipient. In modern times there has also been some reconsideration of the traditional practice in view of the fact that many who bring their children to be baptized are themselves only nominally Christian, and the 1969 RC Order for the Baptism of Infants acknowledges that in some cases Baptism should be delayed. See also BAPTISM.

infidel. A person who has a positive disbelief in every form of the Christian faith.

infirmarian. In a religious house, the person in charge of the sick-quarters.

Infralapsarianism. See SUBLAPSARIANISM.

Inge, William Ralph (1860–1954), Dean of *St Paul's from 1911 to 1934. His sympathies with *Platonic spirituality found expression in a series of theological and devotional writings, including *Christian Mysticism* (1899) and *The Philosophy of Plotinus* (1918). His grasp of the tastes and prejudices of the English mind, his provocative manner of writing, and his pure English style made him one of the best-known Churchmen of his generation.

inhibition. An episcopal order suspending

from the performance of his office an *incumbent whose conduct makes such action advisable.

initiation. See BAPTISM.

Injunctions, Royal. A set of Tudor orders on ecclesiastical affairs, including those of: (1) *Henry VIII in 1536 requiring the clergy to observe the anti-papal laws, abandon various practices, and teach their people the *Lord's Prayer, etc., in English; (2) Henry VIII in 1538 providing for the setting up of the *Great Bible in all churches; (3) *Edward VI in 1547 requiring the provision of the *Paraphrases* of *Erasmus as well as the Bible in all parishes, banning processions, and ordering that the *Litany be said or sung in English; (4) *Mary in 1554 requiring that married priests be removed or divorced and that clerics ordained 'after the new sort' should have 'that thing which wanted in them before' supplied; (5) *Elizabeth I in 1559 which substantially re-enacted the Injunctions of 1547, with their extreme anti-Romanism toned down, and adding others on how services should be conducted and other matters.

Inner (or Inward) Light. The Divine light in every individual which is held to guide and bring those who accept it into union with God and each other. The concept is characteristic of the Society of *Friends.

Innere Mission. The term covers all voluntary religious, charitable, and social work organized within the Protestant Churches in Germany, apart from parish work. The central organization of the mission dates from 1848; in 1957 it was united with the *Hilfswerk*, an organ of the *Evangelical Church in Germany established in 1945 to relieve distress and make contact with those alienated from the Church.

Innocent I, St (d. 417), Pope from 402. He made more substantial claims for the Papacy than any of his predecessors, insisting that major causes of dispute should be brought for judgement to Rome. In the controversy with *Celestius, *Pelagius, and their supporters, he endorsed the doctrines propounded by the African Councils. His famous letter to Decentius, Bp. of Eugubium, is important for the history of the *Canon of the Mass; it also speaks of *Confirmation as reserved for bishops and mentions the rites of *Unction and *Penance. Feast day, 28 July (dropped in 1969).

Innocent III (1160/61–1216), Pope from 1198. In making the right of the Papacy to interfere in secular affairs depend upon its duty to control the moral conduct of rulers and upon the theory of Papal feudal overlordship, Innocent was enabled by the circumstances of the age and his own personality to make theory and practice coincide to an extent unparalleled before or since. The Emp. Henry VI having died in 1197, Innocent pressed claims to examine as well as to crown the person elected as Emperor; he then supported rival candidates in turn; *Frederick II was elected on condition that he did homage to the Pope for Sicily. In France Innocent compelled Philip Augustus to be reconciled to his Queen. The quarrel over the appointment of Stephen *Langton to the see of *Canterbury led to the submission of King *John of England, who recognized Innocent as his feudal overlord. Elsewhere also the Pope extended his influence. He patronized the new orders of friars, the *Franciscans and the *Dominicans. The *Lateran Council of 1215 was the culminating event of his reign. He was the first Pope regularly to use the title 'Vicar of Christ'.

Innocent IV (d. 1254), Pope from 1243. He was the most outstanding *canon lawyer ever to become Pope, and he wrote a major commentary on the *Decretals, known as the 'Apparatus'. Having tried unsuccessfully to resolve the dispute with *Frederick II which he had inherited, at the Council of *Lyons in 1245 he excommunicated and deposed him, and continued the struggle against his son. Under the pressure of financial needs he extended the system of *provisions, and he authorized the use of torture by the *Inquisition.

Innocent X (1574–1655), Pope from 1644. Elected in spite of opposition from the French court, he supported the protest of his legate against the Peace of *Westphalia (1648), and he condemned five propositions from the *Augustinus of C. O. *Jansen in the bull '*Cum Occasione' (1653).

Innocent XI, Bl (1611–89), Pope from 1676. He struggled against the absolutism of Louis XIV in Church affairs, disapproving of the revocation in 1685 of the Edict of *Nantes; he also opposed *Gallicanism. He similarly disapproved of *James II's measures to restore RCism in England. He condemned 65 *Laxist propositions in 1679 and 68 *Quietist propositions in 1687. Feast day, 12 Aug.

Innocents, Holy. See HOLY INNOCENTS.

Inopportunists. Those who at the First *Vatican Council opposed the definition of Papal *infallibility on the ground that the moment was 'not opportune'.

Inquisition, the. An ecclesiastical tribunal concerned with the detection and prosecution of heresy. In 1184 Pope Lucius III ordered that bishops should make inquisition (inquiry) for heresy in their dioceses and hand over those who would not recant to the secular authorities for punishment. This episcopal inquisition proved ineffective, and in order to deal with *Catharism c.1233 *Gregory IX appointed full-time Papal inquisitors, drawn mainly from the *Dominican and *Franciscan Orders. They were appointed only in areas where heresy was rife and lay rulers were prepared to enforce their decrees. They examined suspects in secret; the accused were not normally told of the charges against them, and lawyers were reluctant to defend such cases for fear of being accused of abetting heresy. Those who recanted were given legally enforceable penances. Unrepentant heretics were handed over to the secular authorities for punishment in accordance with the law of the State; this normally meant *burning at the stake. Such cases were exceptional. After the medieval Inquisition had become moribund in the 15th cent., it was remodelled by *Paul III (see HOLY OFFICE). This Roman Inquisition contributed to the eradication of incipient Protestantism in the Italian peninsula by the end of the 16th cent., but it was only in the Papal States that it exercised undisputed power.

In the Iberian peninsula the Inquisition took a different form. *Ferdinand V and *Isabella, concerned about the problem of only nominally converted Jews in Castile, in 1478 obtained permission from *Sixtus IV to set up a new Inquisition, backed by royal authority. Activated in 1480, the Spanish Inquisition was a highly centralized organization, in due course established in all lands subject to the Spanish monarchy, except Naples. In the 16th cent. it turned its attention to the 'Moriscos' (nominally converted Muslims), the *Alumbrados, and Protestants. Its methods were derived from those of its medieval predecessor. It was finally abolished in 1834.

In 1515 Manuel I of *Portugal asked leave to establish an Inquisition in Portugal along the lines of the Spanish Inquisition. Despite Papal opposition, the Portuguese Inquisition was set up in 1536 and in 1561 extended to Goa. It was abolished in 1821.

inscriptions, early Christian. If the well-known SATOR word square (a cryptogram of doubtful interpretation) is Christian, the examples found at Pompeii (destroyed in 79) must be the earliest extant Christian inscriptions. 3rd-cent. inscriptions are fairly common in the Roman *catacombs and from the 4th cent. they are very common in Rome, N. Africa, Syria, and Asia Minor.

In contrast to pagan inscriptions, Christian inscriptions give little personal detail. They are valuable *en masse* as evidence of the texture of the community and the expansion of the Church, and bear witness to the beliefs of rank-and-file Christians of the period.

installation. The formal induction of a canon or prebendary to a seat or stall in a cathedral or collegiate church.

Instantius (late-4th cent.), a Spanish bishop who supported *Priscillian. He may have been the author of one or more of 11 treatises ascribed to Priscillian.

Institute of Consecrated Life. See INSTITUTES OF CONSECRATED LIFE.

Institutes, The. The abbreviated English title of J. *Calvin's *Institutio Religionis Christianae*. The first edition was published in Latin in 1536; the definitive edition in 1559 (in Latin) and 1560 (in French). It sets out Calvin's characteristic views on (1) God the creator, (2) God the redeemer, (3) the nature, means of appropriation, and effects of *grace; and (4) the Church, ministry, and sacraments.

Institutes of Consecrated Life. The technical term now used in official RC documents for ecclesiastical societies in which members make profession of the evangelical *counsels of perfection. It covers Religious Institutes (still popularly called 'religious orders') and Secular Institutes. Members of Religious Institutes take public *vows and live a common life. Those whose members take solemn vows are known as Orders; those whose members take simple vows as *Congregations. Members of Secular Institutes bind themselves to follow the evangelical counsels and dedicate themselves to the sanctification of the world, while living in it, either in families or groups, or alone.

institution. The admission by a bishop of a new *incumbent into the spiritual care of a *parish.

Institution, the Words of. The words 'This is My Body' and 'This is My Blood' used by Christ in instituting the *Eucharist. In the W. it has been commonly held that these words in the liturgy effect the consecration of the elements.

Instruments, Tradition of the. The solemn delivery to those being ordained of the instruments characteristic of their ministry. In the RC Church deacons receive the Gospel Book and priests the *paten with bread and the *chalice. The Anglican *Ordinal attached to the 1662 BCP directs that a NT be delivered to deacons and a Bible to priests. In some modern Anglican liturgies the delivery of the chalice and paten to priests has been restored or is allowed.

insufflation. The action of breathing upon a person or thing to symbolize the influence of the Holy Spirit. The RC Church still has a rite of insufflation in connection with the consecration of *chrism and until recently also for that of baptismal water. In the Orthodox and some other E. rites an insufflation figures in all Baptisms.

intention. (1) In moral theology, an act of free will directed to the attainment of an end. Such intention may be 'actual' if one wills with conscious attention; 'virtual' if one continues to will in virtue of a previous decision, though at the time not consciously aware of it; or 'habitual' if all voluntary action has ceased but without the original decision being revoked. The intention influences the morality of an action. (2) In the administration of the Sacraments, the purpose of doing what the Church does. Such intention on the part of the minister is essential. (3) The special object, material or spiritual, for which a prayer of *intercession is made. (4) In *Scholastic theories of knowledge the term was sometimes used of the objects of knowledge in so far as they are present to the knowing consciousness.

intercession. Petitionary prayer on behalf of others. In an extended sense, according to Catholic theology intercession can also be made by offering on behalf of others meritorious acts performed or *indulgences obtained for the sake of some specified intention.

Intercontinental Church Society or '**Intercon**'. See CCCS.

interdict. An ecclesiastical *penalty in the RC Church excluding the faithful from participation in spiritual things, but without loss of Communion of the Church. In the past interdicts were of various kinds, some being attached to particular people, others to places. The chief effect of the latter was the cessation of the administration of the sacraments and all solemn services in the areas concerned, though some exceptions were permitted. The 1983 *Codex Iuris Canonici* makes no mention of interdicts attached to places. An interdict now resembles *excommunication, but with less severe consequences; it forbids liturgical activities but does not affect governmental functions or personal income.

Inter-Faith dialogue. See THEOLOGY OF RELIGIONS.

Interim rite. The Order of Holy Communion in the C of E proposed in 1931 by Bp. A. Chandler after the rejection of the proposed BCP of 1927–8.

International Bible Students' Association. A corporation established by C. T. *Russell to deal with the affairs of his followers, called 'Bible Students', outside the USA. It is partly responsible for the British *Jehovah's Witnesses.

interstices. The spaces of time which, by *canon law, must elapse between the conferment of different *Orders in the Christian ministry upon the same person.

intinction. In liturgical use, the practice of absorbing some consecrated or unconsecrated wine into the Eucharistic bread before Communion. In the Communion of the sick the consecrated bread was sometimes moistened with unconsecrated wine to make consumption easier. More usually, the word is applied to the practice whereby the Host is immersed in the consecrated wine and administered with a communion spoon, as is still customary in the E. Church; or the Host may be marked with consecrated wine, either by dipping it into the chalice or with a *fistula or spoon, a process that can also be used in *reservation.

All forms of intinction had virtually disappeared in the W. by c.1200. In modern times the practice of dipping the Host into the consecrated wine has been sporadically revived in the Anglican Communion both for reservation and as a means of giving Communion to the sick; in the 1980s it became generally available in some Anglican churches and was recognized in a statement of the Abps. of *Canterbury and York in 1989. In the RC Church it was authorized in 1965 as one of the ways of receiving Communion in both kinds.

Introit. In the W. Church, the opening act of worship in the Mass. Originally it consisted of a whole Psalm, sung with *antiphon and *Gloria Patri; later only a part of the Psalm was sung and in the RC Church some other chant may now be substituted. Introits were dropped from the BCP in 1552 but their use in the C of E was widely revived unofficially in the 19th cent. and the ASB provided for a hymn, canticle, or Psalm at the entry of the ministers; CW mentions only a hymn.

Invention of the Cross. According to legend the crosses of Christ and the two robbers were found (Lat. *inventae*) by St *Helena, that of Christ being identified by a miracle. In the Greek Church the Finding of the Cross was originally commemorated on 14 Sept., now the feast of the *Exaltation of the Cross. In the W. it was commemorated on 3 May, until the feast was suppressed in the RC Church in 1961.

Investiture Controversy. A term often applied to the long series of disputes between popes and emperors from the future Emp. *Henry IV's withdrawal of obedience from *Gregory VII in 1076 to the Concordat of *Worms in 1122, and also used of the contemporary Papal disputes with the Anglo-Norman and French kings. The issue of investiture concerned the kings' right to confer on bishops and abbots the *ring and *crosier that were their symbols of office. Lay investiture was forbidden by Gregory VII, perhaps in 1075, certainly in 1078, but it became the central issue only from 1100. In England the matter became acute under St *Anselm, who refused to do homage to Henry I or to consecrate bishops who had received lay investiture. A compromise was reached at Bec in 1105 and ratified in 1107, and a tacit understanding was apparently reached in France in 1107. A formal settlement in the Empire was achieved by the Concordat of Worms (1122, q.v.). The lay ruler ceased to invest with ring and staff but continued to bestow the temporalities and to receive homage either before or after the consecration.

invincible ignorance. A term in *moral theology denoting ignorance of a kind which cannot be removed by serious moral effort. It excuses from sin because, being involuntary, it can involve no intention to break the law of God.

Invitatory. In liturgical usage, an invitation to pray (e.g. 'Let us pray'). The term is used particularly of the *Venite, with its *antiphon, which normally stand at the beginning of the first *Office of the day. The antiphon (itself sometimes termed the Invitatory) varies with the season.

invocation of the saints. See SAINTS, DEVOTION TO THE.

IODG. See UIODG.

Iona. A small island in the Hebrides which was given to St *Columba by the local king soon after he came to *Scotland in 563. On it Columba founded a monastery from which missionaries were sent to Scotland and N. England. The monastery became famous for its learning and artistic achievement. In 1203 it was reorganized under the *Benedictine rule.

The Iona Community was founded in 1938 by G. F. *MacLeod to express the theology of the Incarnation in social terms, using the restoration of the conventual buildings of the abbey (completed in 1966) as the symbol of its purpose. Its members,

originally drawn mainly from the Church of Scotland, lived in community on Iona for three months in the year in preparation for work in Scottish industrial areas and in the mission field. Nowadays membership of the Community is ecumenical and the period of residence on Iona more flexible. The Community has taken a leading part in the peace movement.

iota. The Greek letter ι, the smallest letter of that alphabet.

Ireland, Christianity in. Christianity spread to Ireland from Gaul and Britain in the 4th cent. The first firm date is the statement in the Chronicle of Prosper Tiro for 431 that *Celestine I sent *Palladius 'as their first bishop to the Irish believing in Christ'. The second 5th-cent. source, the writings of St *Patrick, provide no clear picture of the Church in Ireland. Until the 7th cent. relations between Ireland and the other *Celtic Churches were close, and for another 500 years the Irish Church retained a structure that lacked metropolitan jurisdiction. Some of the monastic foundations grew into great self-governing communities. Places such as *Armagh and Cork became towns under the jurisdiction of the head of the church, often a layman, and many such churches and their estates were controlled by ecclesiastical dynasties. The establishment of Viking towns, especially *Dublin, opened a way for change. In the 11th cent. the Norse settlers became Christian, and their Churches sought links with the English Church. Three national synods in the 12th cent. established diocesan organization, and new religious orders flourished, especially the *Cistercians. However, many of the older churches declined, and the attempt to impose clerical *celibacy and canonical marriage largely failed. The Anglo-Norman invasion of 1169, and the colonial occupation of much of eastern Ireland, gave rise to a divided Church. In the 15th cent. the clergy were lax, secular control of churches far advanced, and pastoral care was poor.

Under *Henry VIII most of the clergy and laity in contact with the government gave nominal assent to the Irish Act of Supremacy 1537 and in 1560 the Church of Ireland was established by the Irish Parliament, but the *Reformation at first made little headway outside the areas controlled by Dublin or recently settled from England or Scotland. In the early 17th cent. the strength of Protestantism increased, aided by the influx of English and Scottish clergy, the establishment in 1592 of *Trinity College, Dublin, and the promulgation of the *Irish Articles (1615). At the same time, a revitalized Catholicism strengthened its hold on the indigenous population. In 1618 a resident RC hierarchy for a time replaced the *vicars apostolic who had been appointed since 1591. Thereafter Catholicism has remained the religion of the majority in Ireland, increasingly linked with ethnicity and cultural identity. The apparent links between Catholicism and rebellion in Ireland, demonstrated in the uprising of 1641, led to measures specifically directed against RCs; the Catholic revival under *James II and his subsequent defeat prompted the extension of discriminatory measures which after 1704 hit Protestant dissenters as well as RCs and tried to confine political office and ownership of land to members of the Church of Ireland.

Scottish settlers in east Ulster had spread *Presbyterianism in the 17th cent., and in 1690 they organized themselves under the Synod of Ulster. There were also groups of English Presbyterians, *Independents, *Baptists, and *Quakers arriving from England in the 1650s, followed by refugees from France and the Rhineland. In the 18th cent. the Church of Ireland felt equally threatened by the RC majority and the Protestant dissenters. The rebellion of 1798 deepened religious distrust. The Act of Union of 1800 confirmed the position of the Church of Ireland as the established Church and the success of D. *O'Connell in mobilizing the RC masses in demanding Catholic emancipation (granted in 1829) united Anglicans and Dissenters in support of the Union. Famine and emigration radically reduced the RC population in the 19th cent., but a series of reforming bishops revitalized Catholicism and built up a vigorous *Ultramontane Church.

The Church of Ireland was disestablished in 1869. The General Synod became the governing body of the Church. The BCP was revised in 1878 and in 1924–6, and an Alternative Prayer Book was authorized in 1984.

After the partition of Ireland in 1922, the legislation of the Free State (later Republic) reflected the ethos of the RC majority. The Constitution of 1938 recognized both the Protestant and the Jewish communities, even though until 1972 it acknowledged the special position of the RC Church as the guardian of the faith of the majority. In Northern Ireland the RCs, who comprised over a third of the population, were never reconciled to the partition and their discontent over discrimination was one of the causes of the conflict that erupted in 1968/9. Despite underlying distrust between the Churches, the length and violence of that conflict pushed them to co-operation in seeking a solution to it.

Irenaeus, St (c.130–c.200). Bp. of Lyons from c.178. He is generally supposed to have been a native of *Smyrna, and both in his life and thought he forms a link between E. and W. His main work, the *Adversus Omnes Haereses*, is a detailed attack on *Gnosticism, which then posed a serious threat to the Church. In modern times a second work, *The Demonstration of the Apostolic Preaching*, has been found in an Armenian translation. Irenaeus is the first great Catholic theologian. He opposed Gnosticism, not by setting up a rival Christian Gnosis, but by emphasizing the traditional elements in the Church, especially the episcopate, Scripture, and the religious and theological tradition. He developed a doctrine of the 'recapitulation' or summary, of human evolution in the Incarnate Christ, thereby giving a positive value of its own to Christ's manhood. Feast day in the W., 28 June; in the E., 23 Aug.

Irish Articles. The 104 articles of faith adopted by the Church of *Ireland in 1615 at its first Convocation. Apparently compiled by J. *Ussher, they were more *Calvinistic than the *Thirty-Nine Articles of the C of E (accepted in Ireland in 1635).

Iron Crown, of Lombardy. A crown made for Theodelinda, widow of Authoris, King of Lombardy, and presented in 594 to the Duke of Turin, from whom it passed to the recent royal house of Italy. The inner circlet of iron is said to have been made from a nail of the true Cross.

Irving, Edward (1792–1834), Scottish minister associated with the origins of the *Catholic Apostolic Church (q.v.). In 1822 he became minister of the Caledonian chapel in Hatton Garden, London. He turned to *millenarian ideas and came into contact with the circle of H. *Drummond. In 1830 the London Presbytery removed him from its fellowship; after disturbances of a revivalist character at the church in Regent Square, where Irving was now minister, he was expelled in 1832. His supporters moved to a building in Newman Street which, until 1853, was the centre of the Catholic Apostolic Church in London. Irving was deprived of his orders by the Church of Scotland, but ordained to the episcopate in the Catholic Apostolic Church in 1833.

Isaac, OT *Patriarch. He was the Divinely promised son of *Abraham and Sarah after a long childless marriage. To try Abraham's faith God asked Isaac in sacrifice, but, satisfied with the obedience of father and son, accepted a ram instead (Gen. 22). By Christians the sacrifice of Isaac is seen as prefiguring the Passion of Christ.

Isaac the Great, St (c.350–438), *Catholicos of the *Armenian Church from c.389. By gaining from *Constantinople recognition of the metropolitical rights of the Armenian Church, he ended its dependence on Caesarea in Cappadocia. He fostered a national Armenian literature, with St *Mesrob translating much of the Bible. Feast days in the Armenian Church, 9 Sept. and 25 Nov.

Isaac of Nineveh (d. c.700), also 'Isaac the Syrian', monastic writer. About 676 he was made Bp. of Nineveh by the *Catholicos of the *Church of the East, but he soon retired to live in solitude in Khuzistan. His writings on ascetic subjects continue to influence *Athonite and *Coptic monasticism. Feast day in the E., 28 Jan.

Isaac of Stella (c.1100–c.1178), *Cistercian monk. Of English origin, by 1147 he was abbot of Stella (NE of Poitiers). Probably in 1167 he left Stella to set up a monastery on the Île de Ré, off the French coast near La Rochelle. Fifty-seven sermons and two treatises survive. He developed an understanding of the soul's ascent to God whereby, through a purification of love, the *intelligentia* or *mens* attains union with God in an act of intuitive knowledge.

Isabella I of Castile (1451–1504), Queen. The daughter of the king of Castile and León, in 1469 she married *Ferdinand, heir to the throne of Aragon. On the death of her half-brother in 1474, she succesfully challenged the claims of his daughter to the throne. Once established, she and her husband initiated a series of reforms which strengthened the royal power and they recovered Granada and Lower Navarre. She laid the basis for overseas expansion by annexing the Canary Islands and funding Columbus' explorations. She and Ferdinand, who were named the 'Catholic Kings' by *Alexander VI, insisted on religious unity in their kingdoms at home and abroad. They established the Spanish *Inquisition and organized the evangelization of the American Indians.

Isaiah, Hebrew prophet. He was influential at the court of the kings of Judah, especially over foreign affairs. Called to the prophetic office c.740 BC, he continued his work until the Assyrian invasion of Judah in 701 BC. According to tradition he was martyred. He asserted the supremacy of God, emphasized His moral demands, and stressed the Divine holiness, giving to this conception an ethical content. From NT times the so-called Messianic passages in the prophecies ascribed to Isaiah (especially 9: 2–7 and 11: 1–9) have been referred by Christian writers to the historic Christ, but it is disputed how far these can be attributed to the Prophet himself. See also the following entries.

Isaiah, Ascension of. An apocryphal work well known in the early Church. The first part (chs. 1–5) describes the circumstances of Isaiah's martyrdom; the second (chs. 6–11) his ascent in ecstasy through the heavens and the revelations made to him. The work is now thought to be of Christian origin, the first part dating from the 2nd cent., the second from the late 1st.

Isaiah, Book of. Traditionally the whole of this OT Book has been ascribed to *Isaiah, but only parts of the earlier chapters have any claim to be his. The Book falls into three sections.

(1) Chs. 1–35. The parts most probably by Isaiah are the greater part of chs. 1–12, 16–22, and 28–32. Apart from the Prophet's inaugural vision (6), these prophecies mainly concern the political situation in Judah under Syrian pressure in 740–700 BC.

(2) Chs. 36–9. A section mainly taken from 2 Kings.

(3) Chs. 40–66. These chapters appear to be later than the two previous sections. Modern scholars ascribe chs. 40–55 to '*Deutero-Isaiah' and chs. 56–66 to '*Trito-Isaiah'. The theme is Israel's redemption and her mission to the world. See also ISAIAH and SERVANT SONGS.

Iscariot. See JUDAS ISCARIOT.

Isho'dad of Merv (9th cent.), Bp. of Hedatta (on the R. Tigris) in the *Church of the East. He wrote commentaries in Syriac on the whole of the OT and NT.

Isidore, St (d. *c*.440), of Pelusium, ascetic. He was probably a teacher in the church of Pelusium before he retired to a nearby monastery. An admirer of the *Cappadocian Fathers and of St John *Chrysostom, he corresponded with *Cyril of Alexandria during the Third Council of *Ephesus (431). Over 2000 items of his correspondence have survived. Feast day in the E., 4 Feb.

Isidore, St (*c*.560–636), Bp. of Seville and Metropolitan of Baetica from *c*.600. He used his ecclesiastical position to strengthen the Visigothic monarchy, and it can be argued that he evolved the concept of a Spanish Church and united Hispano-Gallic State independent of external authority. He presided over the Fourth Council of *Toledo (633) and is traditionally associated with the development of the *Hispana Collection of conciliar acts. His influence did much to secure the acceptance of the *Filioque clause in the W.

His works were a storehouse of information freely used by medieval authors. The most important, the *Etymologiae*, is an encyclopaedia covering both secular and religious subjects. It is organized on the principle that etymologies usually give information on the things to which the words refer. Derived and often fanciful, it is a valuable source for the learning and thought of the time. His *De Ecclesiasticis Officiis* is a useful source for the *Mozarabic liturgy. Feast day, 4 Apr. See also following entry.

Isidore Mercator. The pseudonym adopted by the author of the *False Decretals, suggesting a connection (if not identity) with St *Isidore of Seville.

Islam. The religion preached by Muhammad (probably *c*.570–632), the adherent of which is called a Muslim. It is the religion of the majority of the inhabitants of the northern half of Africa, the Middle East, Pakistan, Bangladesh, Malaysia, *Indonesia, and Papua-New Guinea; there are substantial Muslim minorities in several European countries, *Russia, the Caucasus and Central Asia, *India, and *China.

The central dogmas of Islam are the absolute unity of God (*Allah) and the prophethood of Muhammad. The main Islam practices are confession of the unity of God and the mission of Muhammad, ritual prayer five times a day, alms-giving, fasting during the month of Ramadan, and pilgrimage to Mecca.

Islam is seen as the aboriginal religion, from which Judaism and Christianity are deviations. At several points in history God has sent prophets, the first of whom was *Adam, the last Muhammad; *Abraham, *Moses, and Jesus are all recognized. In Muslim belief Jesus, though born of a virgin, is created and not begotten; and His crucifixion was only apparent (cf. *Docetism). In the E., Christian writers reacted promptly to the rise of Islam, some with anti-Muslim polemic, some being conciliatory. W. scholars first took an interest in Islam and Arabic thought in the 10th cent., and from the 12th cent. Islamic logic and metaphysics exercised a profound influence on W. medieval philosophers and theologians.

The Arab conquests of the 7th–8th cents. subjected large communities of Christians (and Jews) to Muslim rule. Unlike pagans, they were recognized as 'people of the book', and in return for payment were awarded protected status and permitted to retain their religion and laws. They usually suffered fiscal, legal, and social oppression, but rarely violent persecution. In modern Arab states this tolerance is sometimes threatened by an upsurge of revivalist Islam, e.g. in Iran and the *Sudan.

Israel. The Hebrew nation, thought of as descending from the Patriarch Israel (*Jacob). In their history of the period of the Monarchy the biblical writers normally used Israel (in contrast to *Judah) of the *ten northern tribes, i.e. of those who attached themselves to Jeroboam I after the death of *Solomon. In a theological sense the word was used of the whole nation (South as well as North), especially in their covenant-relation with God. In the NT it was transferred to the Church.

The modern Jewish State established in 1948 bears the name Israel.

Issy, Articles of (1695). The 34 articles drawn up at Issy, near *Paris, by the commission assembled by J.-B. *Bossuet to examine the works of Mme *Guyon. They condemned certain *Quietist teachings.

Istanbul. The Turkish name for *Constantinople.

Italo-Greeks. The Greek communities descended from (1) Greek settlers in Sicily and S. Italy in Byzantine times; (2) later Greek colonies established in Italian seaports; and (3) Greek and Albanian refugees from the Muslim invasion. Their status is *Uniat.

Ite, missa est. The normal concluding formula of the Roman Mass, meaning 'Go, you are dismissed'. Since 1969 it has been

omitted when another liturgical function follows.

Itinerarium. A brief office formerly included in the *Breviary and prescribed for recitation by clerics about to start a journey.

Ives, St (? 7th cent.). Ostensibly a British bishop of Persian origin who came to Britain via Rome and preached in Cambridgeshire. His cult began when his alleged bones were discovered at St Ives, Cambs., in 1001. Feast days, 24 Apr. and 10 June. The town of St Ives in Cornwall seems to be named after another saint.

Ivo, St (c.1040–1115), Bp. of *Chartres from 1090. He was the most learned canonist of his age, and his three treatises, the *Collectio Tripartita*, the *Decretum*, and the *Panormia*, exercised a determining influence on the development of canon law. Feast day, 20 or 23 May.

Iznik. The modern name of *Nicaea, now only a village in Turkey.

J

'J'. A symbol used by scholars who follow the 'documentary thesis' of the origins of the *Pentateuch; it denotes the Jahvistic (Yahwistic or Jehovistic) source. It is marked by its simple narrative style and *anthropomorphism and by its use of the Divine name *Yahweh even before its revelation to *Moses in Exod. 3: 14 f.

Jabneh. See JAMNIA.

Jacob, OT *Patriarch. The son of *Isaac, he deprived his brother Esau of his birthright by an elaborate ruse and fled to Haran in Mesopotamia. On his way back to Canaan he wrestled with a mysterious Divine stranger and received the name of '*Israel'. The twelve tribes of Israel took their names from those of his sons.

Jacob Baradaeus (c.500–78), after whom the name 'Jacobite' was given to the *Syrian Orthodox Church. He spent 15 years at *Constantinople. When the *Monophysite king of the Ghassanids asked for a bishop c.542, Jacob was secretly consecrated Bp. of *Edessa; he spent the rest of his life clandestinely ordaining clergy and helping to establish a separate hierarchy. Feast day in the Syrian Orthodox Church, 31 July.

Jacob of Edessa (c.640–708), *Syrian Orthodox scholar. In 684 he became Bp. of *Edessa, but withdrew from his see in under five years. He knew some Hebrew as well as Greek, and produced a revision of some Books of the *Peshitta OT. His writings include a continuation of *Eusebius' 'Chronicle' to AD 692, many *scholia on the Bible, and translations of some of the works of *Severus of Antioch. Feast day in the Syrian Orthodox Church, 31 May.

Jacob of Nisibis, St (early 4th cent.), Bp. of Nisibis. He was always a prominent figure in Syriac Church tradition, and in later times he acquired a reputation for learning, ability, and holiness. He was present at the Council of *Nicaea (325); according to *Theodoret he opposed *Arius, but Theodoret's account contains anachronisms. Feast day, 15 July.

Jacob of Sarug (or **Serugh)** (c.451–521), Syriac ecclesiastical writer. He became Bp. of Batnae in NW. Syria in 519. His chief writing was a series of metrical homilies, mainly on biblical themes, which earned him the title 'The Flute of the Holy Spirit'. His doctrinal position has been a matter of dispute in modern times; most recent scholars see him as disapproving of *Dyophysite Christology. Feast day in the *Syrian Orthodox Church, 29 Nov.

Jacob of Voragine. See JAMES OF VORAGINE.

Jacobins. The *Dominicans in France so called from their Paris house in the rue St-Jacques. In 1789 the house was acquired by the revolutionary political club which thence assumed the name.

Jacobites. An alternative name for the *Syrian Orthodox, after *Jacob Baradaeus.

Jacobus. See JAMES.

Jacopone da Todi (Jacopo Benedetti) (c.1230–1306), *Franciscan poet. He became a Franciscan *lay-brother c.1278. In 1294 he and some others were given permission by *Celestine V to live in a separate community, observing the rule of the Order in its original strictness. This decision was reversed in 1298 and Jacopone as one of the *Spirituals was imprisoned until 1303. He wrote exquisite and deeply devotional poems (*Laude*) in Latin and the Umbrian dialect. They have traditionally, but probably mistakenly, been thought to include the *Stabat Mater*. Feast day (local), 25 Dec.

Jahweh. An alternative form of *Yahweh.

Jairus. A 'ruler of the synagogue' whose daughter Christ restored to life (Mk. 5: 21–43).

James. The normal English form of the Latin *Jacobus*, which represents one form of the Hebrew name transliterated into English as Jacob. In English versions of the Bible the form 'Jacob' is retained in the OT and those passages of the NT which refer to the OT patriarch.

James, St, 'the Lord's brother' (Mk. 6: 3 and parallels). The natural interpretation of the NT evidence implies that he was the son of the BVM and St *Joseph, but see BRETHREN OF THE LORD. From an early date he was, with St *Peter, a leader of the Church at *Jerusalem, and after Peter had left Jerusalem, James appears as the chief authority. According to *Clement of Alexandria he was chosen 'bishop of Jerusalem'; *Hegesippus says that he was put to death in AD 62. Feast day in the E., 23 Oct.; also in the American BCP (1979). See also JAMES, APOCALYPSES OF, and following entries.

James, St, 'the Great', Apostle. The elder brother of St *John, he belonged to the privileged group of disciples who were present at the raising of *Jairus' daughter, the *Transfiguration, and the Agony in *Gethsemane. James was the first of the Twelve Apostles to suffer martyrdom, being beheaded in AD 44. The tradition that he preached in *Spain has been almost universally abandoned. Feast day in the E., 30 Apr.; in the W., 25 July.

James, St, 'the Less'. The title derives from the description of 'James the less' in Mk. 15: 40, but it is commonly applied to James, the son of Alphaeus (Mk. 3: 18 etc.), one of the Twelve Apostles, who is thus identified with the James of Mk. 15: 40. The epithet is probably attached to the Apostle only to distinguish him from St James 'the Great' (of the previous entry). Feast day in the E., 9 Oct.; in the W., with the Apostle St *Philip, formerly 1 May and still so in the BCP; in the RC Church transferred to 11 May in 1955 and to 3 May in 1969.

James, Apocalypses of. Two short *Gnostic works found at *Nag Hammadi. They embody dialogues between Christ and *James, the Lord's brother.

James, Apocryphal Epistle of. A probably *Gnostic work found at *Nag Hammadi. It begins in the form of a letter but soon passes into a description of a discourse given by the risen Christ to *Peter and *James, the Lord's brother (ostensibly the writer). It probably dates from the mid-2nd cent.

James, Book of. An apocryphal *Infancy Gospel, consisting mainly of an embellished account of the events connected with Christ's birth as related in Lk. 1 f. Professing to be by *James, the Lord's brother, it seems to date from the 2nd cent.

James, Epistle of St. This NT Book, in the form of a letter by 'James, a servant of God and of the Lord Jesus Christ, to the twelve tribes of the Diaspora', stands first among the *Catholic Epistles. It is written in a clear forceful style, using good Greek, and is almost entirely moral in content. The traditional view that the author was *James, the Lord's brother, has to meet formidable objections, none of which is quite conclusive. In any case, it seems likely that the Epistle was composed before AD 95, and some scholars argue for a very early date, c.AD 50.

James, Liturgy of St. This liturgy, extant in a Greek and a Syriac form, is traditionally ascribed to St *James, the Lord's brother. Its use by the *Syrian Orthodox Church (which became a separate body after the Council of *Chalcedon in 451), as well as by the main Orthodox Churches, show that it cannot be later than the mid-5th cent.

James I (1566–1625), King of England and VI of Scotland. He became King of Scotland in 1567 on the abdication of his mother, *Mary, Queen of Scots, and he succeeded to the English throne on *Elizabeth I's death (1603) by virtue of his mother's descent from Henry VII. On his way to London he was presented by the *Puritans with the *Millenary Petition. He heard their case at the *Hampton Court Conference (1604); he offered concessions, but he also expressed his opposition to *Presbyterianism and upheld the connection between the *Divine Right of Kings and *Apostolic Succession. He authorized a new translation of the Bible (the '*Authorized Version' of 1611). He favoured lenient treatment for RCs, though the *Gunpowder Plot (1605) provoked stricter laws against the *Recusants. During his reign the influence of the clergy at court increased. In Scotland in

1610 he persuaded the Assembly of the Church to agree to the introduction of episcopacy and eventually got the Articles of *Perth accepted. In 1618 he issued the Book of *Sports, approving lawful games on Sunday.

James II (1633–1701), King of England and VII of Scotland, 1685–8. The second son of *Charles I, c.1670 he became a RC. Subsequent attempts to exclude him from the succession were defeated. At the beginning of his reign he supported the C of E, but soon he claimed power to dispense from the *Test Act and appointed RCs to high office, and in 1687 and 1688 he issued *Declarations of Indulgence. The refusal of W. *Sancroft and six other bishops to publish the second of these Declarations from the pulpit led to the Trial of the *Seven Bishops. James's promise once again to uphold the rights of the C of E did not stop William, Prince of Orange, and the Whigs from deposing him, and he fled to France. He later tried to recover *Ireland but was defeated in 1690.

James Baradaeus. See JACOB BARADAEUS.

James the Deacon (7th cent.), companion of St *Paulinus, Bp. of *York. He remained in the North of England when Paulinus returned to Kent in 633, and on the restoration of Christianity in Northumbria he took an active part in spreading the Gospel.

James of Edessa, James of Nisibis, James of Sarug. See JACOB OF EDESSA, etc.

James of Voragine (or **Varagine)** (c.1230–98), author of the '*Golden Legend'. He entered the *Dominican Order in 1244 and held various offices before he reluctantly became Abp. of Genoa in 1292. Besides the 'Golden Legend', he wrote a history of Genoa and a series of sermons, including the *Mariale*, in which the material is arranged alphabetically under the various attributes and titles of the BVM. Feast day, 13 July.

James, William (1842–1910), *Pragmatist philosopher. A professor at Harvard, he held that we have a 'right to believe in' the existence of God (because it makes us 'better off'), but no scientific certainty of the validity of that belief. In *The Varieties of Religious Experience* (1902) he drew the now familiar distinction between 'once born' and 'twice born' religious types, and made a scientific analysis of conversion.

Jamnia or **Jabneh,** a city *c.*13 miles south of Joppa. After the fall of *Jerusalem (AD 70), an assembly of Jewish religious teachers was established there. The subjects discussed by the rabbis apparently included the status of certain biblical Books, but there is no evidence to support the suggestion that a particular synod, held here *c.*100, settled the limits of the OT *canon.

Jane Frances de Chantal, St (1572–1641), foundress of the Order of the *Visitation. On the death of her husband in 1601, she took a vow of chastity. With the help of St *Francis de Sales (her spiritual director), she founded the first house of the Visitation at Annecy in 1610. Leaving her 14-year-old son, she joined the Order and spent the rest of her life organizing it. Feast day, 12 Dec. (formerly, 21 Aug.).

Jannes and Jambres. Two reputed Egyptian magicians who imitated the miracles performed by *Moses (Exod. 7 ff.).

Jansen, Cornelius Otto (1585–1638), author of the *Augustinus. He became a director of a newly founded college at Louvain in 1617. In 1628 he began writing the *Augustinus*, after reading St *Augustine's works many times; it was published posthumously in 1640. In 1636 he was consecrated Bp. of Ypres. See also JANSENISM.

Jansenism. Dogmatically, Jansenism is summed up in five propositions derived in substance from the *Augustinus* (1640) of C. O. *Jansen and condemned as heretical by *Innocent X. Their sense is that without a special *grace from God, the performance of His commands is impossible to men, and that the operation of grace is irresistible; hence man is the victim of either a natural or a supernatural determinism, limited only by not being coercive.

The first generation of Jansenists were disciples of *Saint-Cyran, Jansen's friend and collaborator. This party of 'Cyranists', which included the convent of *Port-Royal, was already in existence in 1638. After Saint-Cyran's death in 1643, Antoine *Arnauld became their leader; his writings defined the directions of the movement. These were the defence of St *Augustine's theology of grace as interpreted by Jansen; a rigorist tendency in all matters of ecclesiastical discipline; and hostility to *Probabilism.

In 1653 Innocent X condemned five propositions as summarizing the Jansenist position. The Jansenists sought to evade the condemnation by admitting that the propositions condemned were heretical, but declaring them to be unrepresentative of Jansen's doctrine; this distinction was disallowed by *Alexander VII (1656). In 1668 the Jansenists were persuaded into a qualified submission, but the movement continued to gain sympathizers. P. *Quesnel's *Réflexions morales* (1693), in which some tenets of Jansenism were reaffirmed, was condemned in the bull '*Unigenitus' (1713). In France the Jansenists then faced periodic persecution. In the *Netherlands Jansenism was tolerated, and in 1723 the Dutch Jansenists nominated a Bishop of Utrecht, consecrated in 1724, thus creating a schism (see OLD CATHOLICS). They also remained strong in Tuscany.

Januarius, St, Bp. of Benevento, patron saint of Naples. He probably died in the *Diocletianic persecution. The alleged 'liquefaction' of his blood, preserved in a glass phial, is believed to take place on about 18 occasions each year. Feast day in the E., 21 Apr.; in the W., 19 Sept.

Janus. The pseudonym over which J. J. I. von *Döllinger and others in 1869 published a series of letters attacking the *Syllabus Errorum.

Japan, Christianity in. St *Francis Xavier brought Christianity to Japan in 1549. Despite intermittent persecution from 1596 onwards, thousands of Christians in small communities kept the faith alive. A Franco-Japanese treaty in 1859 allowed freedom of worship to foreigners; it was followed by the arrival of fresh RC missionaries, Anglicans, and *Presbyterians. In 1861 a mission came from the Russian *Orthodox Church; this founded a community whose numbers were exceeded only by the RCs. In 1877 the various Presbyterian bodies began an amalgamation which was completed in 1891 and the different Anglican missions united to form the 'Nippon Sei Ko Kwai' (Holy Catholic Church of Japan) in 1887. At first conversions were aided by the thirst of young Japanese for W. education, but by

1890 a reaction towards national self-reliance had set in. The outbreak of war with the USA and Britain in 1941 led to the removal of all European bishops and clergy, and the government tried to force all non-RC Christians into a single Protestant Church, the United Church of Christ in Japan (the 'Kyodan'). After the defeat of Japan in 1945, State-Shintoism was disestablished and freedom of religion granted. The Anglicans, *Lutherans, and several other groups withdrew from the 'Kyodan', but it remains the largest Protestant body in Japan. The 'Nippon Sei Ko Kwai' was reconstituted under a Japanese episcopate. In 1990 Christians numbered about 1 per cent of the population.

Jarrow. See WEARMOUTH AND JARROW.

Jaspers, Karl (1883–1969), German philosopher. He developed a Christian *Existentialism. He put religion and philosophy in contrast, and stressed the limits of science, notably in its ability to reach the self. This self is the ground of all existence and especially characterized by the need for self-communication. Jaspers repudiated the exclusive claims of Christ, though in his last works he seems to have accorded Him a special position.

Jassy, Synod of (1642). A synod of the Orthodox Church which met at Jassy (in modern *Romania). Including representatives of both the Greek and Slav Orthodox Churches, it condemned the *Calvinist teachings of Cyril *Lucar and ratified (a somewhat emended text of) Peter *Mogila's *Orthodox Confession*.

Jean-Baptiste Marie Vianney, St. See CURÉ D'ARS, THE.

Jehoshaphat, the Valley of. On the basis of Joel 3: 2 and 12, the traditional scene of the Lord's Coming Judgement. Since the 4th cent. AD the name has been used of the valley separating *Jerusalem from the Mount of *Olives.

Jehovah. A form of the Hebrew Divine Name. See TETRAGRAMMATON.

Jehovah's Witnesses. The popular name since 1931 for the Watch Tower Bible and Tract Society which traces its origins to the *Adventist teaching of C. T. *Russell (q.v.). His main claim was that Jesus Christ had returned invisibly to earth in 1874 to prepare for the Kingdom of God which was expected to materialize in 1914. His successor, J. F. *Rutherford, turned his followers into a '*theocratic' organization, demanding from its members exclusive commitment and indifference to the world. His criticism of political ideologies led to clashes with governments. The most visible symbols of the Jehovah's Witnesses are their Kingdom Halls, their door-to-door ministry, and the public sale of their magazines *The Watchtower* and *Awake!* They are also distinctive in their taboo against blood transfusions, their own translations of the Bible, and their refusal to honour symbols of nationhood.

Jeremiah (7th–6th cent. BC), prophet of Judah. He proclaimed the coming destruction of *Jerusalem and the *Temple, counselled submission to the Babylonians, and suffered during the siege of Jerusalem. After the destruction of the city (c.586), he was left free to live in Judah, but the Jews forced him to flee with them to Egypt. According to tradition he was stoned to death. His sufferings and prophecy of the destruction of Jerusalem have been interpreted as figures of the life of Christ, and the W. Church has used the Books of *Jeremiah and *Lamentations (ascribed to Jeremiah) in her Offices for *Passiontide.

Jeremiah, Book of. Jewish tradition and NT quotations ascribe this OT Book to *Jeremiah, but many modern critics attribute a great part of it to editors. The promises of restitution and the giving of a New Covenant (chs. 30 and 31) are often thought to come from scribes living in the time of the *Exile or soon afterwards; the so-called Oracles to the Nations are also often denied to Jeremiah, especially the prophecy against Babylon (chs. 50 and 51), which contradicts the policy of submission advocated in other parts of the Book. There are striking differences between the *Septuagint and the *Massoretic texts which may arise from the amalgamation of two collections of prophecies. In ch. 36 we are told that the prophecies were written down by *Baruch, read to the king and burnt by him, and then written again with additional material.

The Prophet extols both the transcendence and the justice of God, who condemns His people because they have abandoned righteousness. His sense of Divine justice causes Jeremiah's astonishment at seeing the wicked prosper, and here for the first time in the OT is raised the problem of the good fortune of sinners and the sufferings of the just. The most striking feature of the Book is the New Covenant (31: 31–4) which God will make with His people and in which the Gentiles too will participate (16: 19–21).

Jeremiah, Lamentations of. See LAMEN-TATIONS OF JEREMIAH.

Jeremy, Epistle of, or **Letter of Jeremiah.** A short item in the OT *Apocrypha. In what purports to be a letter, *Jeremiah declaims to the exiles in Babylon against the folly of idol-worship. It was probably written in Greek in the 3rd or 2nd cent. BC. In the *Vulgate and some English Bibles it appears as Bar. 6.

Jericho. A town in Palestine, north-east of *Jerusalem.

Jerome, St (c.345–420), biblical scholar. He was born near *Aquileia. About 374 he set off for Palestine. He spent some time in *Antioch and then lived for four or five years as a hermit in the Syrian desert; here he learnt Hebrew. From 382 to 385 he was in Rome, where he acted as secretary to Pope *Damasus and successfully preached asceticism (see MELANIA; PAULA). In 386 he settled in *Bethlehem, where he ruled over a newly-founded monastery.

Jerome's scholarship was unsurpassed in the early Church. His greatest achievement was his translation of most of the Bible into Latin from the original languages (see VUL-GATE). He also wrote many biblical commentaries. He advocated that the Church should accept the Hebrew *Canon of Scripture, excluding the Books which came to be called the *Apocrypha. He translated and continued *Eusebius's 'Chronicle', compiled a bibliography of ecclesiastical writers (*De Viris Illustribus*), and translated into Latin works by *Origen and *Didymus. He attacked *Arianism, *Pelagianism, and *Origenism. Some of his letters advocate extreme asceticism. Feast day, 30 Sept. See also PSALTER.

Jerome Emiliani, St (1481–1537), founder of the *Somaschi. A native of *Venice, ordained priest in 1518, he devoted his life

to work among the poor and afflicted, founding orphanages, hospitals, and houses for fallen women. In 1532 he founded a society to foster this work. Feast day, 8 Feb. (formerly, 20 July).

Jerome of Prague (c.1370–1416), Bohemian Reformer and friend of J. *Huss. Probably a native of Prague, he studied at *Oxford, whence he brought back writings of J. *Wycliffe. On his return to Prague in 1407 he took an active part in the religious controversies and became a leader of the nationalist university students. He followed Huss to *Constance in 1415. After Huss's death, under pressure he read a document anathematizing the teaching of Wycliffe and Huss and accepting the authority of the Pope and Council. The sincerity of this abjuration was suspect and his trial resumed in 1416. He took back his abjuration and was burnt at the stake.

Jerusalem, the capital of Judah, the site of its religious sanctuary (the *Temple), and as such the 'Holy City'. Archaeological evidence indicates that part of the site was inhabited as early as c.3000 BC. About 1000 BC the Jebusite stronghold known as 'Zion' was captured by *David, who made Jerusalem the capital of the United Monarchy. *Solomon built the Temple and enlarged the city. About 597 BC and again c.586 BC it was captured and devastated by Nebuchadnezzar, and many of its inhabitants were deported to Babylon. The return from the *Exile was followed, after some years, by the rebuilding of the Temple in 520–515 BC (the 'Second Temple'). After the Exile the Jews were an ecclesiastically governed State under the suzerainty of various foreign powers. There was a short dynasty of priest-kings at the end of the *Maccabean wars, but after the conquest by Pompey in 63 BC the country was ruled, directly or indirectly, from Rome. The Jews rebelled in AD 66; Jerusalem was besieged for four years, and when it fell in 70, the city, including the Temple, was destroyed. It was refounded as a Gentile city under the name of *Aelia Capitolina in 135.

The Christian history of the city begins with the short ministry of the Lord, culminating in His Crucifixion and Resurrection. The Apostles lived and taught in Jerusalem for some time after *Pentecost and met in Jerusalem for the first Christian council (Acts 15; *c.* AD 49). It was not, however, until the visit of St *Helena (*c.*326) and the beginning of the fashion of venerating holy places that Jerusalem became important as a Christian centre. The see, previously suffragan to *Caesarea, was granted patriarchal dignity at the Council of *Chalcedon (451), but it never attained the prestige of the other patriarchates. The Christian centre of the city is the Church of the *Holy Sepulchre. The present city covers only part of that of NT times. The traditional sites of *Calvary and the Holy Sepulchre lie in an area outside the walls of the town of *Herod the Great, but within those built by Herod Agrippa some 14 years after the Crucifixion, and are therefore within the present Old City.

Jerusalem, Anglican Bishopric in. In 1841 a bishopric was set up in *Jerusalem by the joint efforts of England and Prussia to serve Anglicans and Protestants in the Middle East. The bishop was to be nominated by England and Prussia alternately. The scheme collapsed in 1886; since then the see has been maintained by the Anglicans alone.

Jerusalem, Knights of St John in. See HOSPITALLERS.

Jerusalem, Synod of (1672). A synod of the Orthodox Church held in the Basilica of the Nativity at *Bethlehem (hence also known as the 'Synod of Bethlehem'). It sought to repudiate the movement fostered by Cyril *Lucar towards accommodation with *Calvinism and, along with the Synod of *Jassy (1642), marked the closest approximation of E. Orthodoxy to *Tridentine Catholicism. In addition to doctrinal articles, it declared that 2 Esdras, Tobit, Judith, Wisdom, Ecclus., the Song of the Three Children, Susanna, Bel and the Dragon, and 1-3 Maccabees are to be accounted canonical.

Jesse window. A window whose design is based on the descent of Jesus from the royal line of *David, usually in the form of a tree springing from Jesse (David's father) and ending in Jesus or the Virgin and Child, with the intermediary descendants placed on scrolls of branching foliage.

Jesu, Dulcis Memoria. The late-12th cent. poem familiar through translations of sections of it in the English hymns 'Jesu, the very thought of Thee' and 'Jesu! the very thought is sweet'. It has traditionally been ascribed to St *Bernard, but is probably the work of an English *Cistercian. See also ROSY SEQUENCE.

Jesuits. The Society of Jesus, founded by St *Ignatius Loyola (q.v.), was approved by *Paul III in 1540. Beyond securing the spiritual benefit of its members, its aim was to labour 'for the propagation of the faith' and the promotion of Christian piety, especially through the '*Spiritual Exercises'. Its most characteristic institutions were the humanist schools opened throughout the world from 1548. It was not founded to oppose the *Reformation, but by 1550 it began to be intensively engaged with the situation in Germany and then with similar situations elsewhere.

Peculiar to Jesuits is a special vow to travel for ministry wherever the Pope may order. They were quickly established in *India, *Japan, and *Brazil. Other features pointing to their missionary and ministerial character include the vow not to accept any position in the hierarchy except under constraint by the Pope, the absence of any distinctive habit, and freedom from any obligation to recite the *Office in choir.

The Society grew rapidly and by the early 17th cent. seemed secure in Europe and the mission field. In 1623 a province was formed in England, where St Edmund *Campion and R. *Parsons had been sent in 1580. In the later 17th cent., however, the Jesuits met with serious opposition within the RC Church. The *Jansenists attacked them for their lax casuistry, and they came under fire over the question of *accommodation in the Chinese Rites controversy. A combination of their opponents led to their expulsion from *France in 1764; in 1759 they were banished from *Portugal and in 1767 5,000 Jesuits were deported from Spain and its Empire. In 1773 *Clement XIV suppressed the Society. In Austria and Germany, however, Jesuits were allowed to teach, and they were protected by Frederick II of Prussia and the Emp. Catherine of Russia. They also survived in England, and the mission in Maryland, USA (founded in 1634) continued almost unaffected. Elsewhere they gradually re-established themselves and in 1814 the Society was formally restored by *Pius VII. They now operate in most countries of the world. They are responsible for numerous institutions in Rome (including the Vatican Radio Station), schools and academic centres in many parts of the world, and the supply of priests in hundreds of parishes.

Jesus. The Greek form of the Hebrew Joshua. By Divine command the name was given to the Infant Christ. See also NAME OF JESUS.

Jesus Christ. Jesus of *Nazareth is called by His followers '*Christ', i.e. (God's) *Messiah or anointed one. He was apparently born shortly before the death in 4 BC of *Herod the Great and was executed in or around AD 30 after condemnation by Pontius *Pilate (on dates, see CHRONOLOGY, BIBLICAL).

The Gospel of St *Mark (c.AD 70) reports His *Baptism by St *John the Baptist, His *Temptation in the desert, and a ministry of preaching, teaching, and healing in *Galilee and *Judaea. The narrative centres on a *Transfiguration. Jesus chose twelve disciples (*Apostles) and attracted other supporters. The religious leadership was hostile and finally handed Him over to Pilate for trial and *crucifixion. He was buried but the tomb was found empty and a 'young man' announced that He had been raised. Mark's narrative is generally followed by the Gospels of St *Matthew and St *Luke, with expansions, including accounts of the *Resurrection appearances and (in Luke-Acts) the *Ascension. The author of St *John's Gospel clearly had access to a different narrative tradition which gave more prominence to Jesus' activity in Judaea. He portrays Jesus as the man from heaven who is barely touched by human weakness or pain, but he is clear that Jesus was a human being, whose mother *Mary and *brethren were known, and who suffered an ignominious death on a cross outside *Jerusalem.

Little is known of Jesus' early life. His 'presumed father', St *Joseph, does not appear during the ministry and was perhaps dead by then. The birth narratives are partly modelled on Scripture. Matthew's *genealogy established the messianic identity of Jesus as son of *David and son of God; Luke's prelude roots God's saving intervention on behalf of both *Gentiles and Israel in biblical tradition and so reinforces the Church's identity as God's

multiracial people. All four Gospels reflect the importance of John the Baptist. The ministries of Jesus and John perhaps overlapped, but there are differences between their message and activity. Both included a note of Divine judgement in their *eschatological proclamation, but in His certainty of the nearness of God's rule, Jesus stressed the positive role of what this meant for the poor, hungry, suffering, and the lost sheep of the house of Israel.

The forms of this preaching are more easily analysed than its content. Jesus' remembered words consist largely of *parables and aphorisms. Using this-worldly realities, He proclaimed the will of God with prophetic and more than prophetic authority; He spoke and acted with an immediacy grounded in His consciousness of an intimate relationship with God, whom He addressed as Father (*Abba). While debates on the interpretation of the *Sabbath laws were common, Jesus' extraordinary powers provoked controversy when He healed someone on the Sabbath. His sense of God's will and the intention of the law led Him to criticize the traditions of scribal interpretation and perhaps to sit lightly to the laws on purity. Conversely, His prohibition of *divorce was stricter than that in *Deuteronomy. The most important symbol by which He expressed His religious meaning was God's rule or kingship, often rendered in English as 'the *Kingdom of God'. It is not, however, clear how He understood the coming of God's rule or what kind of eschatological transformation He envisaged. His deeds and words expressed God's providence, love, judgement, and forgiveness and the symbol of sovereignty is qualified by that of fatherhood in Jesus' speaking of God.

The potentially political implications of the 'Kingdom of God' have sometimes been taken to suggest that Jesus was a political national messiah, but it is unlikely that He intended the phrase in an anti-Roman sense. A political motivation for the crucifixion can, however, accommodate the strongly attested claim that the *Sadducean high priestly leaders and their associates in Jerusalem (not the *Pharisees or the Jewish people in general) were responsible for handing Jesus over to the Roman authorities for trial and execution around the time of the *Passover. Jesus attracted crowds, and fears that that enthusiasm might lead to Roman intervention could explain His arrest. The fact that His followers were not arrested with Him suggests that the movement was not perceived as a serious political threat.

How exactly Jesus understood what the evangelists have interpreted in their different ways is uncertain, but He evidently understood Himself to be playing a decisive role in God's saving work and it became clear that this would involve suffering. His execution on a political charge and the inscription over His cross may have helped to crystallize the disciples' growing conviction that He was, or was destined to become, the Christ. But the decisive factor was what they believed had followed His death. They described it as resurrection and understood it to signify His vindication by God. See also CHRISTOLOGY.

Jesus Movement (or Jesus Revolution). A popular term of the late 1960s and early 1970s for the amorphous movement of relatively spontaneous groupings, normally fervent, *evangelical, and *fundamentalist, which emerged in the youth culture of the period, beginning in California. The 'Jesus people' distrusted the established Churches; many adopted *Pentecostal practices and teaching.

Jesus Prayer. The prayer 'Lord Jesus Christ, Son of God, have mercy upon me', which is widely used in the *Orthodox Church. It is first found in a work of the 6th–7th cent.

Jeu, Books of. Two *Gnostic treatises ascribed to *Enoch.

Jewel, John (1522–71), Bp. of Salisbury from 1560. One of the intellectual leaders on the Reforming party, under *Mary he fled to the Continent. After his consecration, he was a strong supporter of the Anglican settlement against both RCs and *Puritans. His celebrated defence of the C of E, the *Apologia Ecclesiae Anglicanae* (1562), argued that a general Reformation had been necessary, that reform by such a body as the Council of *Trent was impossible, and that local Churches had the right to legislate through provincial synods.

Jewish people. See JUDAISM.

Jews, Christian attitudes to. Christianity shares much common ground with Judaism. *Jesus Christ was a Jew, as were the earliest members of the Church. The foundation for the separation of Christianity from Judaism was laid by St *Paul's practice of not requiring *Gentile converts to Christianity to be circumcised and his contention that their new covenant relationship with God was based on faith in God, not works of the law. The persecution of Jewish Christians and their expulsion from the *synagogue caused bitterness. All four Gospels tend to exonerate the Roman power that crucified Jesus by shifting blame to the Jewish authorities, and from the early 2nd cent. Christian writers put forward a negative image of the Jews. Ecclesiastical councils legislated to end social and religious contact with the Jews, except for purposes of converting them, and the triumph of the Church in the Roman Empire led to a similar tendency in imperial legislation. Nevertheless, measures aimed at the forcible extinction of Judaism were rare in the first six centuries. In the early 7th cent. the Baptism of all Jews was decreed in several countries (*Spain in 613, the Byzantine Empire and *France in 632), and the position of Jews was circumscribed. From the time of the First *Crusade there were violent attacks on Jews and in some places whole communities were massacred. The Fourth *Lateran Council (1215) imposed the wearing of distinctive dress so that Jews could be distinguished from Christians. Massacres were succeeded by expulsions from various countries and by 1500 most of Europe was free of Jews; those that remained lived under severe restrictions under both Catholics and Protestants. At the same time efforts were made to convert them, sometimes by threats of death; those who were converted and their descendants were subjected to discriminatory measures, especially in Spain and *Portugal. In the 18th cent., under the influence of the *Enlightenment, efforts were made to improve the conditions of the Jews, often opposed by Churchmen. Meanwhile new missions arose directed specifically at Jews. Antisemitism, an anti-Jewish political movement originating in the later 19th cent., exploited many of the traditional Christian arguments and counted on Christian support (both RC and Protestant). It was favoured in various forms by Christian movements in Austria, Germany (see

GERMAN CHRISTIANS), France, and elsewhere; many prominent Christians opposed it.

After the *Holocaust a new era opened. In 1947 a conference was convened under the auspices of the newly-formed International Conference of Christians and Jews; it issued a list of 'ten points' aimed at eradicating anti-Judaism from Christian teaching. The *World Council of Churches in 1948 and the Second *Vatican Council in 1965 both condemned antisemitism directed against Jews. In most of the main Churches attempts are being made to foster relations between Christians and Jews, to heal the wounds of the past, and to revise those teachings which are recognized as having been harmful.

Jiménez de Cisneros, Francisco. See XIMÉNEZ DE CISNEROS, FRANCISCO.

Joachim, St. The husband of St *Anne and father of the BVM. He is first mentioned in the 'Book of *James' (2nd cent.). Feast day (with St Anne), in the W. since 1969, 26 July; in the E., 9 Sept.

Joachim of Fiore (c.1135–1202), biblical exegete and mystic. A monk of the monastery of Corazzo, he was elected abbot in 1177. He relinquished this office to lead a more contemplative life, in 1196 finally receiving Papal permission to establish his own congregation in the Sila mountains.

The central doctrine of his main works is a Trinitarian conception of the whole of history, viewed in three periods. The first, characterized by the 'Ordo conjugatorum', was the age of the Father in which mankind lived under the Law until the end of the OT dispensation; the second, characterized by the 'Ordo clericorum', is that of the Son which is lived under grace and covers the NT dispensation; the third, that of the 'Ordo monachorum' or 'contemplantium', is the age of the Spirit which will be lived in the liberty of the 'Spiritualis Intellectus' proceeding from the OT and NT. This last age would see the rise of new religious orders to convert the whole world and usher in the 'Ecclesia Spiritualis'. After his death, Joachim's ideas were carried to revolutionary conclusions, notably by certain *Franciscans and *Fraticelli.

Joan, Pope. The legend that a woman, in male disguise, was elected Pope c.1100 and

died after giving birth to a child, first appeared in the 13th cent. It is without foundation.

Joan of Arc, St (1412–31), the 'Maid of Orléans'. The daughter of a peasant, in 1425 she experienced the first of the supernatural visitations, which she described as a voice accompanied by a blaze of light. Her 'voices' revealed to Joan her mission to save France. In 1429 she convinced the (unconsecrated) king (Charles VII) of their genuineness. Clad in a suit of white armour, she led an expedition which relieved Orléans, and then persuaded Charles to proceed to *Reims for his coronation. In 1430 she was taken prisoner by Burgundian troops, sold to the English, and charged with witchcraft and heresy. After trial by an ecclesiastical court, she was burnt. A revision of her trial in 1456 declared her to have been unjustly condemned. Canonized in 1920, she is the second patron of France. Feast day, 30 May.

Joasaph, St. See BARLAAM AND JOASAPH, STS.

Job, Book of. The main portion of this OT Book consists of a discussion between Job and his three friends. Its subject is the problem of innocent suffering. Job rejects the traditional view that suffering is the result of sin, since he has no doubt of his own innocence. No final solution to the problem is offered, apart from emphasis on the omnipotence of God. The Book probably dates from c.400 BC.

Jocists. The association of factory workers in the RC Church known as **Jeunesse Ouvrière Chrétienne (JOC)** or 'Young Christian Workers'. The movement grew out of the groups gathered by J.-L. *Cardijn in and around Brussels after the 1914–18 war and received Papal approbation in 1925. In 1926 it spread to France and has expanded worldwide. It encourages young workers to develop their self-awareness and to take responsibility for converting colleagues.

Joel, Book of. *Minor Prophet. The first section of the Book (1: 1–2: 17) tells of a plague of locusts, and against this background depicts the approaching Day of the Lord with its call to repentance; the rest foretells the future outpouring of the Spirit on all flesh, the final salvation of Judah, and the destruction of foreign nations.

Johannine Comma (also known as the 'Three Witnesses'). An interpolation in the text of 1 Jn. 5: 7 f., namely the words in italic in the following passage from the AV: 'For there are three that bear record *in heaven, the Father, the Word, and the Holy Ghost, and these Three are One. And there are three that bear witness in earth*, the Spirit, and the Water, and the Blood, and these three agree in one'. They are omitted in scholarly modern translations.

John, St, Apostle. According to tradition, the author of the Fourth Gospel, of *Revelation, and of three of the *Catholic Epistles. Together with his brother St *James and St *Peter, he belonged to the inner group of disciples who were present at the raising of *Jairus's daughter, the *Transfiguration, and the Agony in *Gethsemane. In Acts he is several times mentioned with Peter, and he was present at the Apostles' council in *Jerusalem (Gal. 2: 9).

In the Fourth Gospel John is never mentioned by name, but tradition identifies him with the disciple 'whom Jesus loved', who reclined on His bosom at the Last Supper, to whom He entrusted His Mother at the foot of the Cross, who ran with Peter to the tomb on the morning of the Resurrection, and who recognized the Lord at the Sea of Tiberias. The identification of the '*beloved disciple' with John has been contested in modern times.

According to tradition, John settled at *Ephesus, was exiled to *Patmos, where he wrote Rev., and returned to Ephesus and there wrote the Gospel and Epistles. Feast day in the E., 26 Sept. (also 8 May); in the W., 27 Dec. See also following entries.

John, Acts of. An early Greek apocryphal treatise describing events in the life of the Apostle St *John. A fragment, discovered in 1886, contains an account of Christ's passion in *Docetic language, and a hymn known in modern times as the 'Hymn of Jesus'.

John, Apocryphon of. A Coptic document known since 1896 of which three further copies were found at *Nag Hammadi. It takes the form of a dialogue between Christ and the Apostle St *John. It is important for the early history of *Gnosticism.

John, Epistles of St. Three NT Epistles which tradition ascribes to St *John, the Apostle and author of the Fourth Gospel. Modern scholars who defend the apostolic authorship of the Gospel commonly also admit that of the First Epistle; among those who reject it, opinion is divided. The Second and Third Epistles were not generally admitted as authentic in antiquity, and many modern critics assign them to a different author from that of the First Epistle.

The First Epistle reflects many of the themes of the Fourth Gospel, and the writer stresses the continuity of Christian tradition and experience. 'False brethren' are denounced for denying that Jesus Christ 'has come in the flesh', as well as for flouting the demands of righteousness and love. The author urges the ideal of sinless perfection in language that suggests that Christians cannot, and presumably do not, sin, but there are equally emphatic statements that we do sin, and need and receive forgiveness. Some scholars infer that there must have been more than one writer; others ascribe the awkwardness to the need to attack contradictory positions. The Second Epistle insists on the need to profess right doctrine and avoid communion with the teachers of error and the Third on hospitality.

On 1 Jn. 5: 7 f. see JOHANNINE COMMA.

John, Gospel of St. The Fourth Gospel was already in existence early in the 2nd cent. The tradition that it was written by St *John the Apostle goes back at least to the end of the 2nd cent.; it is attested by St *Irenaeus, who perhaps derived his information from St *Polycarp. Polycarp may, however, have been referring to another John, namely *John the Presbyter. The Gospel is not a plain account of the Lord's *miracles and teaching, but rather a deeply meditated representation of His Person and doctrine; direct apostolic authorship therefore seems unlikely. Good sources or historical traditions at many points are probable, and the author claims to be witnessing to what 'we' have seen (1: 14).

The Fourth Gospel differs widely from the *Synoptics in content, style, and outlook. For instance, the Lord's ministry extends over three *Passovers and alternates between *Jerusalem and *Galilee; the expulsion of the money-changers from the *Temple is placed not at the close but at the beginning of His ministry; and the *Last Supper is not a Passover Meal. There is no mention of some important events such as the institution of the *Eucharist, and no *parables of the familiar kind. On the other hand John includes some incidents, such as the Raising of *Lazarus, about which the Synoptics say nothing. Above all, Jesus speaks openly and frequently of His unique Sonship to God and His saving mission, whereas in the Synoptics such claims are rare.

The structure is clear: (1) the Prologue (1: 1–18), in which Jesus is presented as the eternal Word (*Logos) of God; (2) the public ministry (1: 19–12: 50); (3) private teaching and prayer to the Father at the Last Supper (13–17); and (4) narrative of the Crucifixion and Resurrection (18–21). Chapter 21 is probably an appendix, and the so-called '*pericope adulterae' (7: 53–8: 11) was not part of the original text.

The central teaching is Christological. Jesus is the eternal Son of God, who has been given everything the Father has, including authority to give life and execute judgement. His deeds and words are regularly rejected or misunderstood by His opponents, but to those who accept and believe they are the revelation of God. His message and mission for the salvation of all of humanity are expounded in terms of 'light' and 'life'. The Christian teaching that salvation is dependent on the death (and resurrection) of Christ is spelt out, and special emphasis is put on the gift of the *Holy Spirit consequent on these events.

John XII (d. 964), Pope from 955. The son of a ruler of Rome, he became Pope when he was 18. He appealed to Otto I of Germany to help him against the rulers of N. Italy, King Berengar II and his son. In 962 he crowned Otto Roman Emperor. Otto issued the 'Privilegium Ottonis' recognizing the Papal territories in central Italy, but then demanded their allegiance to himself. John engineered a revolt among the imperial troops and sought aid from Berengar and the Byzantines. In 963 Otto presided over a synod in Rome which deposed John and elected in his place a layman (Leo VIII); he also issued a revised form of the 'Privilegium Ottonis' requiring that a newly elected Pope should take an oath of fealty to the Emperor before consecration. In 964 John returned to Rome and deprived Leo but was killed soon afterwards.

John XXI (d. 1277), Pope from 1276. Peter of Spain was born in Lisbon, probably not later than c.1205. In 1273 he was elected Abp. of Braga and created Cardinal Bishop of Frascati; in this capacity he attended the Second Council of *Lyons (1274). As Pope he was concerned to preserve the union with the Greek Church achieved at Lyons, and in 1277 he required the Bp. of *Paris to report to him those who were teaching errors prejudicial to the faith.

Peter of Spain's *Tractatus* or *Summulae logicales* was probably composed in N. Spain in the early 1230s; it is the most influential medieval manual on logic. He also wrote other works on logic and medicine and was among the first to comment on various works of *Aristotle.

John XXII (1249–1334), Pope from 1316. He set out to transfer the Papacy to *Avignon, where he resided, gathering around him craftsmen and scholars. He became involved in the difficulties threatening to split the *Franciscan Order; in 1317 he dissolved the party of the *Spirituals, whose doctrines he denounced as heretical. Soon afterwards he condemned the thesis that the poverty of Christ and the Apostles was absolute, and several of the Franciscans fled to Louis of Bavaria, who supported them. In 1324 the Pope declared Louis a heretic, and a literary feud ensued. Louis seized Rome and in 1328 established an antipope, who submitted, however, in 1330.

An expert canonist, in 1317 John promulgated the *Clementines, the last official book of the *Corpus Iuris Canonici, but a collection of his own decrees later achieved similar status as the *Extravagantes Johannis XXII. He reorganized the *Curia and put the Papal finances on a sound footing. The authorship of the '*Anima Christi' has been assigned to him.

John XXIII (d. 1419), *Antipope to *Benedict XIII and Gregory XII from 1410 to 1415. He was crowned Pope in 1410, but the validity of his election has been contested as being simoniacal. Of the three Popes then existing he had most supporters. In 1413 he convoked a General Council to end the *Great Schism; it met at *Constance. He soon fled from Constance to deprive the Council of authority. He was brought back by force and deposed in 1415.

John XXIII, Bl (1881–1963), Pope from 1958. Angelo Giuseppe Roncalli came of a large peasant family near Bergamo. In 1925 he became Bp. of Areopolis and *Vicar Apostolic to Bulgaria; in 1934 he was appointed Apostolic Delegate to Turkey and Greece; while in the Balkans he established good relations with the Orthodox. In 1944 he was sent as Papal Nuncio to *Paris, and in 1953 he was created a cardinal and later in the year Patr. of *Venice.

Elected Pope at the age of 77, he proposed to the cardinals three undertakings: a diocesan synod for Rome, an oecumenical council for the Church, and a revision of the code of *canon law. The synod was held in 1960 and dealt with local problems. The Second *Vatican Council (q.v.) was the most important event in his pontificate. He attributed the idea of convening it to the inspiration of the Holy Spirit, and he gave to the Council the task of renewing the religious life of the Church; it was to express the substance of the faith in new language and bring up to date its discipline and organization, with the ultimate aim of the unity of all Christians. In 1960 he set up the Secretariat for Promoting Christian Unity and invited to the Council observers from other Churches. He opened and closed the first session of the Council, once intervening to encourage those in favour of change. In 1961 the RC Church was for the first time represented at an Assembly of the *World Council of Churches. Throughout his pontificate there was a feeling that there was a desire in the RC Church to soften the obstacles to reunion with other Christian bodies, while he sought to improve relations with *Judaism by removing from the *Good Friday liturgy the passages which caused most offence.

John of Antioch (d. 441), Bp. of *Antioch from 429 and leader of the moderate Easterns in the *Nestorian controversy. After *Cyril of Alexandria had condemned Nestorius at the Council of *Ephesus (q.v.; 431), John held a counter-council which condemned Cyril and vindicated Nestorius. In 433 he was reconciled with Cyril.

John of Apamea (flourished early 5th cent.), Syriac spiritual writer, also known as John the Solitary. His writings include a 'Dialogue on the Soul'.

John of Ávila, St (1499/1500–69), 'Apostle of Andalusia'. Ordained in 1526, his plan to go to *Mexico as a missionary failed, partly probably because of difficulties arising from his Jewish ancestry. He preached throughout Andalusia. In 1531 he was denounced to the *Inquisition in Seville and kept prisoner for a year.

His concern with the need to improve the quality of the parish clergy and the pastoral care they gave, and to instruct lay people in the Christian faith, led him to establish colleges or schools for the laity and clergy. He conducted a wide correspondence with those seeking spiritual guidance. His one major spiritual work (*Audi, filia*), written for a young aristocratic nun in the mid-1530s, in its developed form expounds the way of perfection for all Christians. It urges confident trust in God and meditation on the sufferings and merits of Christ, through which man finds pardon. The definitive edition appeared posthumously in 1574. Feast day, 10 May.

John the Baptist, St, the 'Forerunner of Christ'. According to Lk. (1: 5–25), he was the son of *Zachariah and *Elizabeth, his birth being foretold by an angel. All four Gospels record his appearance *c.*AD 27 as a preacher on the banks of the *Jordan, demanding repentance and baptism from his hearers. Christ Himself was among those baptized by him. John's denunciation of *Herod Antipas for his marriage led to his imprisonment and death (Mt. 14: 1–12). His continued influence is attested in Acts (18: 25), and outside the NT he is mentioned by *Josephus. The Feast of his Nativity (24 June) is of more solemnity than that of his death ('Decollation'; 29 Aug.).

John Baptist de La Salle, St (1651–1719), founder of the Institute of the Brothers of Christian Schools. A canon of *Reims from 1667, he was ordained in 1678 and in 1679 assisted in the opening of two free schools in Reims. He became interested in fostering religious principles in the teachers, a group of whom lived in his house. In 1683 he resigned his canonry and devoted himself to training his community. In 1699 he opened in Paris the first Sunday Schools giving technical and religious instruction to the sons of artisans. Later schools were started in other parts of France and beyond. In 1690 he decided against including priests in the Institute and in 1694 he drew up the first rule. Feast day, 7 Apr. (formerly 15 May).

John of Beverley, St (d. 721), Bp. of *York. A monk of Whitby, he was consecrated Bp. of Hexham c.687. In 705 he was translated to York, then being claimed by *Wilfrid. Before his death he retired to the abbey which he had founded at Beverley. A cult developed in England. Feast days, 7 May (death) and 25 Oct. (translation of relics).

John Bosco; John Capistran; John Capreolus; John Chrysostom. See BOSCO, ST JOHN; GIOVANNI CAPISTRANO, ST; CAPREOLUS, JOHN; and CHRYSOSTOM, ST JOHN.

John Climacus, St (c.570–c.649), ascetic and spiritual writer, so called after his famous 'Ladder' (Κλῖμαξ). He arrived at Mt *Sinai as a novice when he was 16 and became Abbot. His 'Ladder of Paradise' or 'Ladder of Divine Ascent' treats of monastic virtues and vices and the nature of complete dispassionateness (*apatheia), which is upheld as the ideal of Christian perfection. Feast day, 30 Mar. (in the E. also the 4th Sunday in Lent).

John of the Cross (1), St (1542–91), Spanish mystic and joint founder of the Discalced *Carmelites. He became a Carmelite in 1563. He was dissatisfied with the prevalent laxity of the Order and with St *Teresa's aid he brought her Reform to include friars. After the anti-Reformist General Chapter of the Calced Carmelites (i.e. of the Mitigated Observance) in 1575, he was imprisoned in 1577. He escaped after nine months, and the separation of the Calced and Discalced Carmelites was effected in 1579–80. John became Prior of Granada in 1582 and of Segovia in 1588. He incurred the hostility of the Vicar General of the Discalced Carmelites, was banished to Andalusia in 1591, and died after a severe illness.

His extensive writings on the mystical life consist of commentaries which he built up on three of his poems, which are among the greatest in Spanish. The *Spiritual Canticle* treatise expounds its rich imagery in terms of the *purgative, illuminative, and unitive ways. It is less systematic than the *Ascent of Mount Carmel* and the *Dark Night of the Soul* (a single unfinished treatise) which deals with the purgation of the soul through the 'night of the senses' and the 'night of the spirit'. These nights have an active and passive aspect: actively the soul detaches itself from dependence on things of the senses (including sensible devotion) and adheres in faith to God alone; passively, God acts to fit it for the transforming Union with Himself, described in the *Living Flame*. Though presented in schematic form, these nights are not consecutive phases but complementary parts of a single process, the purifying of the soul for transformation and participation in God. Feast day, 14 Dec. (formerly 24 Nov.).

John of the Cross (2) (c.1505–c.1560), *Dominican spiritual writer. In 1538 he was sent with a group of other Spanish friars to help reform the Dominican Order in *Portugal; he spent the rest of his life there. His main work was a 'Dialogue on the Necessity of Vocal Prayer'. Against the prevalent spirituality of *recollection, he argues that the spiritual life consists in the serious, deliberate practice of the virtues and not in interior devotional fervour.

John of Dalyatha (8th cent.), spiritual writer. A member of the *Church of the East, he lived as a monk in various monasteries in NW Iraq; for a time he was a hermit in the mountains of Dalyatha. Since he belonged to monastic circles mistakenly accused of *Messalianism and *Sabellianism, his writings were condemned in 786. Some 25 Discourses, 50 letters, and a set of 'Kephalaia on Knowledge' survive.

John of Damascus, St (c.655–c.750), Greek theologian. Born of a Christian family of *Damascus, like his father, he held a position of importance at the court of the Caliph. He resigned his office c.725 and became a monk at the monastery of St Sabas near *Jerusalem, where he was ordained. He was a strong defender of *images in the *Iconoclastic Controversy.

His most important work, the *Fount of Wisdom*, is divided into three parts dealing with philosophy, heresies, and the Orthodox faith ('De Fide Orthodoxa'). This last is a comprehensive presentation of the teaching of the Greek Fathers on the main Christian doctrines, especially the Trinity, Creation, and the Incarnation. His other great work, the *Sacra Parallela*, preserved only in fragments, is a vast compilation of scriptural and patristic texts on the Christian moral and ascetical life. He also wrote a commentary on the Pauline Epistles, homilies, and poems; some of these are used as English hymns, e.g. 'Come, ye faithful, raise the strain'. The 'Life of *Barlaam and Joasaph' (q.v.), traditionally ascribed to him, is probably not his work. He exercised great influence on later theology. Feast day, 4 Dec. (in the W., formerly 27 Mar.).

John (1167–1216), King of England from 1199. The youngest son of Henry II, he conspired against both his father and Richard I, but was nevertheless named by the latter as his successor. On his accession he was recognized by England and Normandy and in 1202 defeated Anjou and Brittany, who urged the claims of his nephew Arthur (whom John murdered in 1203). In the following years he lost most of his French possessions. When *Innocent III appointed Stephen *Langton archbishop of Canterbury (1207), John refused to recognize him; in 1208 England was placed under an *interdict, and in 1209 John was excommunicated. Unsure of his barons, threatened with deposition by the Pope and invasion from France, John submitted in 1213, placing England and Ireland under the suzerainty of the Papacy. In 1215 the barons obtained the grant of Magna Carta. John soon regretted his action and civil war broke out. He died, leaving his kingdom in confusion.

John of Ephesus (c.507–86), *Syrian Orthodox historian. In 542 he was sent to convert the pagans in the region of *Ephesus, of which he was consecrated bishop by *Jacob Baradaeus. His *Ecclesiastical History*, of which only the third part survives complete, covers the period 571–85.

John Eudes, St. See EUDES, ST JOHN.

John the Faster, St (d. 595), John IV, Patriarch of *Constantinople from 582. In 588 he assumed the challenging title of 'Oecumenical Patriarch'; despite protests from Popes Pelagius II and *Gregory I, John bequeathed the title to his successors. The manual for confessors attributed to him is not earlier than the 9th cent. Feast day in the E., 2 Sept.

John Fisher, St; John of Gaza. See FISHER, ST JOHN; BARSANUPHIUS, ST.

John of God, St (1495–1550), founder of the 'Order of Charity for the Service of the Sick' or '*Brothers Hospitallers'. After serving as a soldier, in middle age he changed his mode of life and tried to spread the faith by hawking tracts in Spain. In 1538 he was

converted to a life of sanctity by St *John of Ávila, who directed his energies to the care of the sick and poor. Feast day, 8 Mar.

John the Grammarian (flourished c.515), theologian. He was an early representative of *Neo-Chalcedonianism. Fragments of a defence of the *Chalcedonian Definition preserved in *Severus of Antioch's response to it and works against the *Monophysites and *Manichees survive.

John Gualbert, St (d. 1073), founder of the *Vallumbrosan Order. He entered a *Benedictine monastery near Florence, but, disturbed by a *simoniacal election, withdrew c.1036 and eventually settled at Vallombrosa. Here he collected a body of monks who followed a strict observance of the Benedictine Rule under the conditions of a semi-hermit life. He made provision for *conversi whose labours freed the monks from manual work. Feast day, 12 July.

John Lateran, Church of St. See LATERAN BASILICA.

John Malalas (c.490–c.575), i.e. 'John Rhetor', Byzantine chronicler. He has sometimes been identified with *John Scholasticus, but it is more likely that he was a civil servant. His 'Chronography' covered the period from Creation to 565 or perhaps 574, but survives only to 563.

John Mark, St. See MARK, ST.

John of Matha, St (d. 1213), founder of the *Trinitarian Order. He was a native of Provence, founded his order for the redemption of captives, and died at Rome. Feast day, 8 Feb.

John Moschus. See MOSCHUS, JOHN.

John of Nepomuk, St (c.1340–93), Bohemian martyr. As Vicar General of the Archdiocese of Prague, he resisted the attempts of King Wenceslas IV to suppress an abbey. By the King's order he was drowned in the Vltava (Moldau), but his recovered body became the centre of a cult during the *Counter-Reformation. Feast day, 16 May.

John of Parma, Bl (1209–89), *Franciscan. Elected Minister General in 1247, he tried to restore the original asceticism and discipline of the Order, while recognizing the need to adapt. He lived simply, but did not impose his austerity on others, and it seems that it was his sympathy towards *Joachim of Fiore rather than his views on poverty that led to accusations of heresy in Rome. He resigned in 1257, nominating St *Bonaventure as his successor. Feast day, 20 Mar.

John and Paul, Sts. Two Roman martyrs of the 4th cent. of whom virtually nothing is known. Their names figure in the Roman *Canon of the Mass. Feast day, 26 June.

John Paul I (1912–78), Pope from 26 Aug. to 28 Sept. 1978. Albino Luciani was ordained Bp. of Vittorio Veneto by *John XXIII in 1958; in 1969 *Paul VI nominated him Patr. of *Venice and in 1973 created him a cardinal. At Venice he acted as host to five ecumenical conferences. His election as Pope was unexpected; it appears that a majority of the cardinals were anxious for a new style of Pope, without curial connexions but with pastoral experience. After 33 days he died of a heart attack. Vatican ineptitude allowed the spread of rumours of foul play.

John Paul II (1920–), Pope from 1978. Karol Wojtyła, the son of a Polish soldier, was born in an industrial town near Cracow. He became titular Bp. of Ombi and auxiliary to the Administrator Apostolic of Cracow in 1958, Abp. of Cracow in 1964, and a cardinal in 1967. He attended the Second *Vatican Council and sat on several post-Conciliar Commissions.

He was the first Slav to become Pope and the first non-Italian since 1523. In 1979 he went to *Mexico to open the Latin American Bishops' Conference at Puebla; he set the pattern for his later foreign visits, kissing the ground of the country and celebrating Mass in front of vast crowds. He subsequently visited over 100 countries, including Britain (1982). He is credited with a crucial role in the collapse of Communism, which spread from *Poland. In 1989 he received the President of the USSR at the Vatican; soon afterwards the *Uniat Church was restored in the Soviet Union.

His pontificate has been marked by a concern for orthodoxy. He has declined to make any concessions in the Church's attitude to *contraception, abortion, and *homosexuality, repeatedly reaffirming the traditional position. In 1994 he declared that the Church had no authority to confer priestly ordination on *women, teaching

that was defined as *infallible in 1995. A universal *Catechism of the Catholic Church was issued in 1997.

Visiting the *World Council of Churches in 1984 he spoke of the *ecumenical movement as irreversible, though he rejected intercommunion as a means of attaining unity of faith. He especially promoted good relations with the *Orthodox, but the re-emergence of Catholicism in E. Europe in the late 1980s led to difficulties. Relations with the C of E also suffered setbacks. A 'Directory for the Application of Principles and Norms on Ecumenism', issued in 1993, encouraged, but defined limits to, RC participation in ecumenical activity. He fostered good relations with other world religions, especially *Islam and *Judaism.

He reorganized the *Curia and continued to internationalize both the Curia and the college of Cardinals. He promulgated the new *Codex Iuris Canonici* in 1983 and in 1990 the first ever Code of canon law for the Uniats.

John Philoponus (c.490–c.570), philosopher and *Monophysite theologian. A Christian from childhood, he lived in *Alexandria. His philosophical works include commentaries on *Aristotle and an attack on *Proclus. Among his theological works are the *De Opificio Mundi* and 'The Arbiter'. His Christology was close to that of *Severus of Antioch, and his Trinitarian theology was condemned as *tritheist at the Third Council of *Constantinople (680–81).

John the Presbyter. The term 'the Presbyter' ('elder') is applied to himself by the author of 2 and 3 Jn., and *Papias refers to a 'John the Presbyter'. Some scholars think that Papias's evidence suggests the existence at *Ephesus of a second John besides St *John the Apostle. Of those who hold this view some attribute to the Presbyter the Fourth Gospel and the Johannine Epistles; others 2 and 3 Jn. and possibly Rev. The '*beloved disciple' is variously identified with the Apostle and the Presbyter. 'The Presbyter' may have been a local designation at Ephesus for the Apostle.

John of Ragusa (c.1395–1443), theologian. John Stojković was a native of Ragusa (now Dubrovnik) who became a *Dominican at an early age. In 1431 *Martin V sent him to the Council of *Basle as Papal theologian, and from 1435 to 1437 he acted as legate of the Council to Constantinople in order to gain the Greeks for union with Rome. In Constantinople he assembled an important collection of MSS, which he bequeathed to the Dominican house at Basle; some of them were used as printer's copy by *Erasmus for the first edition of the Greek NT.

John of St Thomas (1589–1644), Spanish theologian. John Poinsot entered the *Dominican Order in 1609, taking the name 'John of St Thomas' to express his devotion to the teaching of St *Thomas Aquinas. His major works are the *Cursus Philosophicus* (1631–5) and the *Cursus Theologicus*, commenting on Aquinas's *Summa Theologiae* (1637–67). He took into account not only Aquinas's conclusions, but also the arguments by which he reached them.

John of Salisbury (*c*.1115–80), humanist. From 1147 he was a member of the household of *Theobald, Abp. of *Canterbury, and on his death entered the service of his successor, Thomas *Becket, whom he supported in his quarrel with Henry II. In 1176 he became Bp. of *Chartres.

His chief writings are the *Policraticus*, a survey of courtly life with a discussion of political problems, and the *Metalogicon*, a defence of the study of grammar, rhetoric, and logic. His *Historia Pontificalis*, covering the years 1148–51, deals chiefly with the affairs of the Papal court. His letters are an important source for the history of the contest between Becket and Henry II.

John Scholasticus (d. 577), John III, Patr. of *Constantinople from 565. Before he became patriarch he made a collection of canons ('Synagoge'), which he later enlarged; it became one of the primary sources of E. *canon law.

John the Scot; John the Solitary. See ERIGENA; JOHN OF APAMEA.

John of Wesel (John Rucherat or Ruchrat) (*c*.1400–81), ecclesiastical reformer. He became cathedral preacher at Worms in 1463. Charged with preaching *Hussite doctrines on the Church and Sacraments, he was deposed from his office in 1447 and in 1479 tried before the *Inquisition. After recanting he was imprisoned for life. His writings include a 'Commentary on the Sentences', a treatise against *indul-

gences, and a work on the *Immaculate Conception.

Johnson, Samuel (1709–84), author, lexicographer, and controversialist. A devout *High Churchman, he ascribed his conversion as a young man to reading W. *Law's *Serious Call*. He wrote various works besides his *Dictionary of the English Language* (1755).

The American hymn-writer **Samuel Johnson** (1822–82) is not to be confused with the lexicographer.

Joinville, Jean de (*c*.1224–1319), French historian. He accompanied *Louis IX to Egypt and Palestine on the *Crusade in 1248 and with him was taken prisoner. He was one of the witnesses for Louis's canonization and he wrote a famous Life of the king.

Jonah, Book of. *Minor Prophet. The Book relates the Divine call to Jonah to go to Nineveh and preach repentance, his attempt to escape by sea, his being thrown overboard and swallowed by a fish, his deliverance after three days, and the success of his mission. Most of the Book is assigned by critics to the post-*Exilic period. The 'sign of Jonah' (Mt. 12: 39 etc.) is interpreted as a prophecy of Christ's resurrection.

Jonas, Justus (1493–1555), originally 'Jodocus Koch', German Reformer. An admirer of *Erasmus and M. *Luther, he accompanied the latter to *Worms in 1521. From 1523 to 1533 he was dean of the faculty of theology at *Wittenberg and he took a leading part in the Protestant cause. He translated the German works of Luther and P. *Melanchthon into Latin and the Latin works into German.

Jones, Griffith (1683–1761), founder of the Welsh circulating schools. He was rector of Llanddowror from 1716. In 1730 he began to found his 'circulating schools' for adults and children, with travelling teachers who instructed their pupils in reading the Welsh Bible.

Jones, Inigo (1573–1652), the first British classical architect. He studied the work of Andrea Palladio (d. 1580) in Italy. His significance as a designer of churches lies in his use of classical forms based on the ancient temple, in contrast to the contemporary Gothic style. His ecclesiastical work includes the Queen's Chapel at St

James's Palace and St Paul's, Covent Garden.

Jones, Rufus Matthew (1863–1948), American *Quaker. His many works include *Studies in Mystical Religion* (1909).

Jones, William, 'of Nayland' (1726–1800), Anglican clergyman. In 1777 he became *perpetual curate of Nayland, Suffolk, whence his traditional epithet. He tried to keep alive the High Church traditions of the *Nonjurors. In *The Catholic Doctrine of the Trinity* (1756) he sought to prove from scriptural texts that the doctrine of the *Trinity is contained in the Bible.

Jordan, River. Formed from the waters of four streams which converge, the Jordan flows through the 'Sea of Galilee' and eventually enters the *Dead Sea. By their passage of the Jordan the Hebrews first entered the Promised Land (Jos. 3: 16); St *John the Baptist preached on its banks, and Christ was among those baptized in its waters (Mt. 3: 13). The Jordan became an emblem of the achievement of purity (especially in Baptism) and of the last hindrance to man's final blessedness.

Josaphat, St (1580 or 1584–1623). John Kunsevich, who was Abp. of Polotsk from 1618, was the first saint of the E. Church to be formally canonized by the RC Church. He did much to restore ecclesiastical life where there was still unrest following the Union of *Brest-Litovsk; he was killed by a rival faction. Feast day, now 12 Nov.

Joseph, St, husband of the BVM. Both Mt. and Lk. state that Mary was 'betrothed' to him at the time of the Lord's birth, but both emphasize her virginity. He was a pious Jew of Davidic descent and, according to Mt. 13: 55, a carpenter. Christ grew up in his household at Nazareth for at least twelve years (Lk. 2: 42 and 51). In the 'Book of *James' he is said to have been old at the time of his marriage to Mary, and as a pattern of holiness he is the subject of various legends. The veneration of him originated in the E. and developed comparatively late in the W. Church. Feast day in the E., the first Sunday after Christmas; in the W., 19 Mar.; in the RC Church he is also commemorated as St Joseph the Worker on 1 May (no longer obligatory).

Joseph of Arimathaea, St. The 'counsellor' who after the Crucifixion requested from *Pilate the body of Christ and gave it burial. The story that he came to England with the Holy Grail and built a church at *Glastonbury is not found before the 13th cent. Feast day in the E. and in the American BCP (1979), 31 July; in the W., 17 Mar.

Joseph Calasanctius, St (1557–1648), founder of the *Piarists. José de Calasanz was ordained in 1583 and held various positions in Spain. He went to Rome in 1592, intending to seek a well-endowed benefice, but he was moved by the condition of the children in the poorer parts of Rome and decided to devote himself to their Christian education. In 1597 he opened what L. von Pastor claims was the first free public school in Europe. To give permanence to the work he established a religious order, the Piarists (q.v.). In his schools (called 'Pious Schools'), Catholic, Protestant, and Jewish children were admitted on equal terms. Feast day, 25 (formerly 27) Aug.

Joseph of Cupertino, St (1603–63), *Franciscan friar. The son of a poor carpenter, he became a *Capuchin lay brother. When the Capuchins dismissed him because of his awkwardness, the *Conventual Franciscans at La Grotella, near Cupertino, accepted him as a *tertiary. He was ordained priest in 1628. For the rest of his life he experienced *ecstasies which were remarkable for the levitation which accompanied them. Feast day, 18 Sept., suppressed in 1969.

Joseph the Hymnographer, St (c.810–86), Greek hymn-writer. He left *Constantinople for Rome during the *Iconoclastic Controversy, but was captured by pirates and spent some years in slavery. He eventually escaped and c.850 established a monastery at Constantinople. He is said to have composed 1,000 *canons. Feast day in the E. Church, 3 Apr.

Joseph of Volokolamsk, St (1439/40–1515), Russian monastic reformer. After some years of monastic life, he instituted a strict reform and founded the monastery of Volokolamsk, near Moscow. Unlike *Nil Sorsky, he welcomed gifts, and he created a large community with a rigorous life of obedience, work, and lengthy liturgical services. Feast day, 9 Sept.

Josephinism. The principles which actuated the ecclesiastical reforms of Joseph II, Holy Roman Emperor from 1765 to 1790. They included religious toleration, the right of the State to regulate ecclesiastical affairs, irrespective of Rome, and the restriction of the powers of the Papacy within spiritual limits, as laid down by *Febronius.

Josephus, Flavius (c.37–c.100), Jewish historian. He was a native of Palestine and a *Pharisee. In 66 he took part in the Jewish War. After being taken prisoner, he won Vespasian's favour by prophesying that he would become emperor, and during the siege of *Jerusalem he acted as interpreter to Titus. He returned with Titus to Rome and devoted himself to literary work. His *Jewish War* opens with a summary of events from the time of *Antiochus Epiphanes to the outbreak of the war; the latter part is largely an eye-witness account. His *Antiquities of the Jews* traces the history of the Jews from the Creation to the beginning of the Jewish War. The reference to Christ as 'a wise man, if indeed one should call him a man' (18.3.3) in its present form is not authentic; it seems that Josephus mentioned Christ, but that his original reference was recast by an early Christian writer.

Joshua, Book of. This OT Book traces the history of the Israelites from the death of *Moses to that of his successor, Joshua, and reports the entry into and conquest of Palestine, its partition among the twelve tribes, and Joshua's last speeches. Though some of its sources may go back to the 9th cent. BC, the Book probably did not reach its present form until the 6th cent. or later.

Jovian (c.332–64), Roman Emperor from June 363 to Feb. 364. After the death of the Emp. *Julian, Jovian was chosen Emperor by the troops and forced to conclude a humiliating peace with Persia. In theological disputes he supported orthodoxy and received St *Athanasius.

Jovinian (d. c.405), an unorthodox monk condemned by synods at Rome and Milan. He denied that virginity was a higher state than marriage and that abstinence was better than thankful eating. He did not believe in the perpetual virginity of the BVM.

Jowett, Benjamin (1817–93), Master of Balliol College, Oxford, from 1870. He was a keen liberal in theology. His essay on 'The Interpretation of Scripture' in *Essays and Reviews* (1860) was one of the most debated items in the book; his orthodoxy was henceforth suspect and he ceased to write on theological subjects. His most important work was his translation of *Plato (1871).

Joyful Mysteries, the five. The first chaplet of the *rosary, consisting of (1) the *Annunciation, (2) the *Visitation, (3) the Nativity of Christ, (4) the *Presentation of Christ in the Temple, and (5) the Finding of the Child Jesus in the Temple.

jube. The rood loft dividing the nave of a church from the choir.

Jubilate (Lat., 'O be joyful'). The first word of Ps. 100, to which it gives its name. At Morning Prayer it is provided as an alternative to the *Benedictus in the BCP; CW allows its use as an opening canticle.

Jubilee, Year of. (1) According to the *Mosaic law (Lev. 25) a year occurring every 50 years, when Jewish slaves regained their freedom and land reverted to its former owners: it is questionable how far the law was actually observed in OT times. (2) In the RC Church a '*Holy Year' (q.v.).

Jubilees, Book of. An apocryphal Jewish work, also called 'The Little Genesis'. It purports to have been delivered by God to *Moses on Mt *Sinai. It reinterprets the contents of Gen. and part of Exod. Its purpose appears to be to show that the Law, with its prescriptions about feasts, the *Sabbath, etc., goes back to patriarchal times. The Book is generally dated in the 2nd cent. BC.

Judaea. In Christ's time the term normally meant the most southern of the three districts (*Galilee, *Samaria, and Judaea) into which Palestine, west of the *Jordan, was divided, but it could be used in a wider sense of the whole of Palestine.

Judah. The tribe of Judah was the most powerful of the twelve tribes of *Israel. After the death of *Solomon (c.930 BC), Judah, with Benjamin, formed a separate kingdom (known as the kingdom of Judah), which outlasted that of the ten northern tribes. See also following entry.

Judaism. The faith and practice of the Jewish people. The word is derived from the name of *Judah, the biblical Southern Kingdom which ended with the *Babylonian captivity (c.586 BC). In modern scholarship the term is used of the faith and practice of Jews from this time, though in a wider sense Judaism may be said to go back to the *Patriarchs many centuries earlier (see ISRAEL). There are c.13 million Jews, half living in North and South America, and about a quarter each in Europe and Asia. Only in Israel, established as a Jewish State in 1948, do they constitute more than a small element in the population.

Until AD 70 Jewish religious life centred on the *Temple in Jerusalem, with its hereditary priesthood and its daily rituals and annual celebrations involving animal and vegetable offerings. By the end of the period there was some criticism of the Temple and its priestly establishment, and the ever-increasing *diaspora meant that pilgrimage to Jerusalem was beyond the aspirations of many Jews. The local *synagogue became the place for public gatherings for Scriptural study and religious teaching, and possibly also for worship. After the destruction of the Temple by the Romans in AD 70 the sacrificial form of worship ceased. Authority, both religious and to some extent secular, was concentrated in the hands of the *rabbis, and a new style of leadership emerged. Rabbinic Judaism spread to most parts of the Jewish world. Its classical written text is the *Talmud, but rabbinic literature includes also the *Midrashim, various medieval biblical commentaries, and works of *Halachah.

From the beginning of the *Enlightenment in the 17th cent., rabbinic orthodoxy found it increasingly difficult to resist challenges emanating from the contemporary situation, and the powers of the rabbis were weakened. Hasidism, a revivalist movement, swept through E. European Jewry in the period 1730–1830. In W. Europe various modernist movements emerged in the 19th cent., laying the foundations of the best-known religious denominations in W. Judaism today: Liberalism, Reform, Conservatism, and Orthodoxy (sometimes termed 'neo-Orthodoxy' or 'modern Orthodoxy' to distinguish it from the various forms of traditional Judaism which are still strong in Israel and elsewhere). Contemporary Judaism is also marked by the rise of political antisemitism in Europe, the Russian progroms and subsequent mass migration of Jews from Russia, the racial persecution of Jews in Nazi Germany and the *Holocaust, the creation of the State of Israel, and the conflict between Israel and the countries of the Arab League.

Theology is less central to Judaism than to Christianity, but there is a broad acceptance of the idea of a single, unique, incorporeal God, who created the world, acts in it, and will eventually redeem it, and who revealed His will in the *Torah and elsewhere. Jewish worship traditionally consists of readings from the Torah, Prophets, Psalms, hymns, and set prayers. Movements for liturgical reform have resulted in considerable revision and in the introduction of vernacular languages into the synagogue.

See also JEWS, CHRISTIAN ATTITUDES TO THE.

Judaizers. In the early Church, Jewish Christians who regarded the OT Levitical laws as still binding on all Christians.

Judas Iscariot. The Apostle who betrayed Christ to the Jewish authorities. His death is recorded in three places (Mt. 27: 3–5, Acts 1: 16–20, and in *Papias), but only the account in Mt. is unequivocal in seeing it as *suicide.

Judas Maccabaeus (d. 161 BC), leader of the Jews in the revolt against the Seleucid king of Syria. He won a series of victories in 166–164 and in 163 gained full religious liberty from Antiochus V Eupator (164–2). He successfully negotiated with Rome for help, but before the results of his mission were known he was killed in battle.

Jude, St, *Apostle. He is generally identified, at least in the W., with the author of the NT Epistle of *Jude. The apocryphal 'Passion of *Simon and Jude' describes the preaching and martyrdom of the two Apostles in Iran. In the RC Church Jude is invoked in circumstances of special difficulty. Feast day in the E., 19 June; in the W., with St Simon, 25 Oct.

Jude, Epistle of St. One of the *Catholic Epistles of the NT. It purports to have been written by 'Jude . . . brother of James', who is commonly identified with the Apostle

*Jude. The aim of the Epistle is to combat the spread of dangerous doctrine. The date of its composition is uncertain.

Judgement, General (Particular). See GENERAL (PARTICULAR) JUDGEMENT.

Judges, Book of. This OT Book traces the history of the Israelites from Joshua's death to the beginning of the monarchy, describing incidents connected with the conquest of Palestine, and woven round the names of several leaders ('judges') who ruled the country before the time of Saul. Though it professes to be a sequel to the Book of *Joshua, it covers the same period, probably giving a more accurate picture.

Judicial Committee of the Privy Council. A Court of Appeal established in 1833 by an Act of Parliament to regularize the extensive ecclesiastical jurisdiction of the King in Council. Under the *Ecclesiastical Jurisdiction Measure 1963, it ceased to have any jurisdiction in cases of discipline, but it still hears *faculty appeals in cases not involving doctrine, ritual or ceremonial. It also hears appeals against schemes proposed under certain other Measures.

Judith, Book of. This Book of the *Apocrypha relates how, when Nebuchadnezzar sent his general Holofernes to punish the Jews, Judith made her way to the camp of Holofernes, captivated him by her charms, and then cut off his head. The Assyrians subsequently fled in panic. The Book is wildly unhistorical; the name 'Judith' means 'Jewess' and she appears to personify faithful and resistant Israel. It probably dates from the *Maccabean period.

Judson, Adoniram (1788–1850), American missionary to *Burma. He came to England to confer with the *LMS and was ordained a *Congregational minister in 1812. On reaching Serampore he became a *Baptist. He was refused permission to continue working in the territories of the East India Company and in 1813 he went to Rangoon, where he began to translate the Bible into Burmese. He met with success working among the Karens.

Julian the Apostate (332–63), 'Flavius Claudius Julianus', Roman Emperor from 361. A nephew of *Constantine, he was won to *Neoplatonism and initiated into the Eleusinian mysteries. In 355 he was presented to the army as Caesar and in 360 proclaimed Emperor by the troops. After the Emp. Constantius II's death (361), Julian, now sole Emperor, embarked on ambitious reforms. He aimed to degrade Christianity and promote paganism by every means short of open persecution. In 362 he set out for a campaign against the Persians. In Asia Minor and Syria his strict discipline and anti-Christian policy were unpopular; he was struck by an arrow and died. Most of his treatise *Adversus Christianos* can be recovered from *Cyril of Alexandria's refutation of it.

Julian the 'Arian' (4th cent.), theologian. Many passages in *catenae previously ascribed to *Julian of Halicarnassus are now thought to come from the 4th cent. and to betray an *Arian provenance. In 1973 D. Hagedorn ascribed a reconstructed commentary on Job to Julian the 'Arian', whom he argued may also be the compiler of the *Apostolic Constitutions* and responsible for the long recension of the letters of St *Ignatius (i.e. the interpolations).

Julian of Eclanum (c.386–454), *Pelagian theologian. He became Bp. of Eclanum in Apulia in 416 but, on his refusal in 417 to subscribe *Zosimus' condemnation of Pelagianism, he was deprived of his see and banished. Considerable portions of his *Ad Turbantium* and *Ad Florum* are preserved in St *Augustine's replies; they are a powerful indictment of Augustine's doctrine of the total depravity of fallen man. In the 20th cent. various exegetical works were ascribed to him, as well as a Latin translation of *Theodore of Mopsuestia's commentary on the Psalms.

Julian of Halicarnassus (d. after 518), Bp. of Halicarnassus in Caria. On the accession of the Emp. Justin I (518) he was deposed because of his refusal to accept the Christological teaching of the Council of *Chalcedon and took refuge in *Alexandria. In the *Aphthartodocetic controversy he upheld the incorruptibility of the body of Christ. Fragments of his work are preserved in *Severus of Antioch's polemic against him. The commentary on Job formerly ascribed to him seems to be the work of *Julian the 'Arian'.

Julian of Norwich (c.1342–after 1416), English spiritual writer. Little is known of her

life except that by 1394 she was an
*anchoress, probably at St Julian's church,
*Norwich. She records that in May 1373 she
received a revelation consisting of 15
'showings' (and one more the next day).
Her book, now commonly known as *Show-
ings* or *Revelation(s) of Divine Love*, survives in
a 'Short Text', probably written soon after
1373, and a 'Long Text', completed at the
earliest in 1393. The kernel of her message
is God's love. In Christ's Passion she finds
the key to understanding all that is wrong
in this world as somehow part of God's
purpose in creating human beings who can
become capable of union with God. Feast
day in parts of the Anglican Communion, 8
May.

Julian of Toledo, St (*c*.644–90), Abp. of
Toledo. Born into a converted Jewish family, he was consecrated Bp. of Toledo in 680.
He consolidated the position of Toledo as
the most important metropolitan see in
Spain; he revived the tradition of holding
national councils there and asserted the
right of Spanish bishops to independent
judgement in matters of theological
debate. His works include a defence of his
*Christology against the criticism of Pope
Benedict II, a refutation of the Jewish belief
that Christ had not yet come, and a treatment of the *Last Things. Feast day, 8 Mar.

Juliana of Liège, Bl (*c*.1192–1258), champion
of the Feast of *Corpus Christi. Professed in
an *Augustinian convent near Liège, she
experienced visions and tried to bring
about the establishment of a feast of Corpus Christi. In 1230 she became superior,
but was soon forced to leave the convent
and took refuge in Liège. Here she secured
the interest of James Pantaléon, then Archdeacon of Liège, who after her death as
Pope Urban IV instituted the feast (in 1264).
Feast day, 5 Apr.

Jülicher, Adolf (1857–1938), NT scholar. He
was professor of theology at *Marburg
from 1889 to 1923. He insisted that the
Lord's *parables must be understood as real
similes, not as allegories, and he worked on
the *Old Latin versions of the NT.

Julius I, St (d. 352), Pope from 337. In the
*Arian struggle he was a supporter of
orthodoxy, sheltering *Marcellus of Ancyra
and *Athanasius. In 342–3 he convoked the
Council of *Sardica, which pronounced

Athanasius the rightful occupant of his
see. Because of the appellate jurisdiction
allowed by the Council to Julius as Bp. of
Rome, his name became famous in connection with the rise of the Papal claims. Feast
day, 12 Apr.

Julius II (1443–1513), Pope from 1503. He
was the nephew of *Sixtus IV, who created
him a cardinal. The main achievement of
his pontificate was the restoration and
enlargement of the temporal power of the
Papacy. He conducted various campaigns in
Italy, defeating *Venice with the aid of
France. In 1511 he founded the Holy League
against France. Louis XII replied by calling a
Council at Pisa to depose the Pope in 1511;
the Pope called the Fifth *Lateran Council
and won the Emp. Maximilian to his side.
   Julius II was a patron of Renaissance art.
His *indulgence for the rebuilding of *St
Peter's was later the occasion of M.
*Luther's 95 Theses.

Julius III (1487–1555), Pope from 1550. In
1545 he opened the Council of *Trent as its
first president and Papal legate and played
a part in its transference to Bologna in 1547.
As Pope in 1551 he commanded the Council
to resume its sessions, but had to suspend
it the following year because of political
difficulties. On the death of *Edward VI in
1553, he sent R. *Pole to England with
far-reaching powers.

Julius Africanus, Sextus (*c*.180–*c*.250),
Christian writer. He was perhaps originally
a Jew. He enjoyed close relations with the
royal house of *Edessa and he went on a
successful embassy from *Emmaus to the
Emp. Heliogabalus (218–22). His chief work
was a 'History of the World' to AD 217, of
which fragments are preserved in other
writers. He held that the world would last
for 6,000 years from the Creation and that
the birth of Christ took place in the year
5500.

Jumièges, *Benedictine abbey 17 miles
west of Rouen. Founded by St *Philibert
c.654, it became one of the cultural centres
of N. Europe. In the 17th cent. it was linked
to the *Maurist reform.

Jumpers. A nickname for the Welsh
*Calvinistic Methodists.

Jung Codex. One of the MSS discovered at
*Nag-Hammadi. It was acquired in 1952 by

the Jung Institute for Analytical Psychology at Zurich. It is now in Cairo.

Jurieu, Pierre (1637–1713), French *Calvinist controversialist. In 1674 he became professor of theology and Hebrew at the Protestant Academy at Sedan; when this was closed in 1681 he became minister in the Walloon church at Rotterdam. His *Traité de la dévotion* (1675; Eng. tr., 1692) had a huge circulation. His many works of controversy are energetic and not always orthodox. His *Traité de la puissance de l'Église* (1677) uses juridical arguments to vindicate the Calvinist view of authority in the Church. A tireless worker for all aspects of the Calvinist cause, he dominated the French refugee community in the *Netherlands. His *Lettres pastorales*, published fortnightly from 1686 to 1689, record the suffering and constancy of the Protestants in France.

jus devolutum. In the Church of *Scotland, the right devolving on a *Presbytery to elect a minister to a vacant charge when the congregation after nine months has failed to make an appointment.

justification. In dogmatic theology, the event or process by which man is made or declared to be righteous in the sight of God. The Latin *justificare*, from which the English word derives, etymologically implies the meaning 'to make righteous' (*justum facere*), and this interpretation remained unchallenged until the *Reformation. It was then argued that in the NT the equivalent Greek word (δικαίωσις) and its cognates reflect Hebrew usage and are to be understood as legal metaphors signifying 'vindication' or 'declaring [someone] to be righteous'. In classical *Protestant theology, 'justification' was interpreted as God 'declaring man to be righteous', and it was distinguished from sanctification, in which man is 'made righteous'. In both *Lutheranism and *Calvinism, justification is seen as an act of God, effected without man's co-operation; according to the RC Church it requires man's co-operation. A further difference concerns the formal cause of justification, which Protestants held to be the imputed righteousness of Christ, and the Council of *Trent defined as the inherent or imparted righteousness of Christ.

Justin Martyr, St (*c.*100–*c.*165), *Apologist.

Born of pagan parents, he was converted to Christianity *c.*130. He continued as a philosopher, now teaching Christianity, first at *Ephesus and later in *Rome. His 'First Apology' (*c.*155) was addressed to the Emp. Antonius Pius and his adopted sons; the 'Second Apology', apparently written soon after the accession of *Marcus Aurelius (161), was addressed to the Senate. Justin and some of his disciples were denounced as Christians *c.*165 and on refusing to sacrifice were beheaded.

Besides rebutting the charges of *atheism and immorality, Justin and the other Apologists argued that Christianity was a true philosophy, in comparison with which other philosophies were either false or shadows of the truth fulfilled in Christ. In support of this argument Justin developed his doctrine of the 'generative' or 'germinative' Word, who had sown the seed of truth in all men and had become incarnate in Christ. He used his doctrine of the *Logos to explain why Christians, while remaining *monotheists, worshipped Jesus Christ, regarding Him as an incarnation of the Logos, 'in second place' to God. The 'Dialogue with Trypho the Jew' argues that the fulfilment of the OT prophecies in Christ proves the transitoriness of the Old Covenant and the vocation of the Gentiles to take the place of Israel. A number of other works have circulated under Justin's name, all spurious. Feast day, 1 June; in the W. formerly 14 Apr.

Justinian I (483–565), Roman Emperor from 527. He reconquered N. Africa and Italy; he built many *basilicas at *Constantinople (including *Hagia Sophia), *Ravenna, and elsewhere; and he issued a new legal Code (see next entry). As the champion of orthodoxy he persecuted the *Montanists and closed the philosophical schools at *Athens in 529. His efforts to reconcile the *Monophysites issued in the *Three Chapters controversy.

Justinian, Code of. This revision of the *Theodosian Code was issued by *Justinian in 529. It was supplemented by further constitutions known as 'Novellae' and by the 'Digest' and 'Institutes of Justinian'; together they constituted the *Corpus Iuris Civilis*, which became the authoritative statement of Roman law, gradually accepted throughout W. Europe. The Code strongly influenced the development of W. *canon law.

Justus, St (d. *c*.627), Abp. of *Canterbury from 624. He was sent to England in 601 in *Gregory I's second band of missionaries and made first Bp. of *Rochester in 604. He consecrated St *Paulinus for mission work in Northumbria. Feast day, 10 Nov.

Juvenal (d. 458), Bp. of *Jerusalem from *c*.422. His main ambition seems to have been to make Jerusalem into a '*Patriarchal see'. He sided with *Cyril of Alexandria against *Nestorius at the Council of *Ephesus in 431, but he failed to gain Cyril's support for his claims. In the *Eutychian controversy he supported *Dioscorus at the *Latrocinium in 449 but at the Council of *Chalcedon (451) he voted for his condemnation. This Council recognized Jerusalem as a Patriarchal see with jurisdiction over Palestine. In parts of the E. Church he is revered as a saint; feast day, 2 July.

Juvencus, Caius Vettius Aquilinus (4th cent.), poet. A Spanish presbyter of noble descent, *c*.330 he wrote a Life of Christ in some 3,200 lines of hexameter verse. It is based mainly on Mt., supplemented by the infancy narratives from Lk. and some of the early chapters of Jn.

Juxon, William (1582–1663), Abp. of *Canterbury from 1660. He succeeded W. *Laud as Bp. of London in 1633. Though known to be a *High Churchman, he was widely trusted. He attended *Charles I at his execution; he was deprived of his bishopric but otherwise unmolested under the Commonwealth. He survived only three years as archbishop.

Kabbala. A system of Jewish *theosophy which, by the use of an esoteric method of interpreting the OT, was believed to reveal to its initiates hidden doctrines. A Christian form flourished in the 15th–16th cents.

Kagawa, Toyohiko (1888–1960), Japanese social reformer. Of a wealthy Buddhist family, after his conversion to Christianity he studied at the *Presbyterian seminary at Kobe and at Princeton. Returning to Japan in 1917, he devoted himself to the improvement of social conditions. After the Second World War he was a leader in the movement for democracy in Japan.

Kähler, Martin (1835–1912), *Lutheran theologian. He is remembered chiefly for a pamphlet entitled *Der sogenannte historische Jesus* (1892; extended 1896), in which he attacked the 19th-cent. attempts to reconstruct the life of the *historical Jesus.

Kaiserswerth. The band of Protestant *deaconesses in this Rhineland town was founded in 1836 to meet the need of the reformed Churches for an organization of women devoted to nursing and education. The house trains deaconesses who devote themselves to the care of the sick and poor, to teaching, or to parish work.

kamelavchion. The black cylindrical hat worn by monks and clergy in the E. Church.

Kant, Immanuel (1724–1804), German philosopher. He spent his whole life in Prussia; from 1770 he was Professor of Logic at Königsberg. He first expounded his 'Critical Philosophy' in his *Critique of Pure Reason* (*Der Kritik der reinen Vernunft*, 1781); he applied the same principles to other problems in his later works.

It seems that Kant's main object was to discover a definitive rationale for the admitted validity of mathematics and natural science. He argued that it was the understanding (*Verstand*) which prescribed to nature her laws. The validity of the causal law ('every event has a cause') rests not on some constraining principle in the external world of nature, but in the fact that consciousness is so constituted that it cannot but so interpret the empirical data which it receives. Knowledge is thus the result of a synthesis between an intellectual act and what is presented to the mind from without. In holding that all knowledge required an ingredient derived from nature, Kant cut at the root of traditional metaphysics, with its claim to provide knowledge of subjects which transcend nature. The traditional proofs of the existence of God were all invalidated. But while insisting that Natural Theology was an illusion, Kant believed that the stern voice of conscience in man assures him of truths which reason is impotent to establish. The sense of duty assures us of freedom. Correlative with this belief in freedom is belief in immortality and a Divine Being, since the maladjustment of virtue and happiness in this world require a righteous God who will vindicate the claims of justice, and another world for His operation. Kant defined religion as the recognition of our duties as Divine commands; there is no place, he held, for mystical experience, no need for a personal redeemer, and no place (as in traditional Christianity) for the historical as such. His thought had immense influence.

katavasia. In the E. Church the concluding stanza of an ode of the *canon.

Karlstadt. See CARLSTADT.

kathisma. The Byzantine Psalter is divided into twenty sections; the term 'kathisma' is used to designate both these sections and the brief liturgical hymn sung at the end of each of them during *Orthros.

Keble, John (1792–1866), *Tractarian leader. The son of John Keble, vicar of Coln St Aldwyn, he resigned his post as tutor at Oriel College, Oxford, in 1823 to assist his father in the cure of his parish. Here he wrote the poems which he published in 1827 as The *Christian Year. In 1831 he was elected Professor of Poetry at Oxford. He became increasingly conscious of the dangers threatening the C of E from the reforming and liberal movements, and on 14 July 1833 he preached before the University an assize sermon on *National Apostasy. He took a leading part in the

*Oxford Movement, contributing several of the Tracts for the Times. He worked closely with E. B. *Pusey to keep the High Church movement steadily attached to the C of E. From 1836 he was vicar of Hursley, near Winchester. Keble College, Oxford, was founded in his memory. Feast day in parts of the Anglican Communion, 29 May or 14 July.

Kedron. An alternative form of *Cedron.

Keith, George (c.1638–1716), 'Christian Quaker'. He trained for the *Presbyterian ministry, but in 1663 became a *Quaker. He went to America in 1684, as Surveyor General of the colony of East Jersey. He was critical of much that he considered lax in the discipline and teaching of the American Quakers and of their belief in the 'sufficiency of thy light within'; when disowned by them he gathered followers whom he called 'Christian Quakers'. He returned to England in 1693, conformed to the C of E in 1700, and was one of the first missionaries sent to America by the *SPG.

Kells, Book of. A finely ornamented Latin MS of the Gospels, dating from c.800. It was long thought to have been written at Kells (Caenannus Mór) in Co. Meath, but it may have been brought there from elsewhere. It is now in *Trinity College, Dublin.

Kempe, Margery (c.1373–after 1438), author of the Book of Margery Kempe. About 1393 she married John Kempe, a burgess of Lynn, by whom she had 14 children. She received several visions after a period of madness, and she and her husband went on a pilgrimage to *Canterbury. Her denunciation of all pleasure aroused opposition and accusations of *Lollardy. She visited the Holy Land in 1413, *Compostela in 1417, and Norway and Danzig in 1433. Her Book describes her travels and mystical experiences. Only one MS is known to exist; it was acquired by the British Library in 1980.

Kempis, Thomas à. See THOMAS À KEMPIS.

Ken, Thomas (1637–1711), *Nonjuror. In 1683 he refused the use of his house to Nell Gwyn, the royal mistress; *Charles II respected his boldness and in 1684 appointed him Bp. of *Bath and Wells. Ken was one of the *Seven Bishops who refused to read *James II's *Declaration of Indulgence in 1688, but he declined to take the oath to William and Mary and was deposed from his see. He opposed the consecration of further Nonjuring bishops. His writings include the hymns 'Awake my soul, and with the sun' and 'Glory to Thee, my God, this night'. Feast day in the American BCP (1979), 21 Mar; in CW, 8 June.

Kenites. An obscure Semitic clan listed among the pre-Israelite inhabitants of the land in Gen. 15: 19.

Kennett, White (1660–1728), Bp. of *Peterborough from 1718. He was an active supporter of the Revolution of 1689, became a leading *Low Churchman, and in the *Bangorian Controversy he opposed the proceedings against B. *Hoadly. He was a keen antiquarian.

kenotic theories. Certain theories concerned to explain the condescension involved in the Incarnation. The title comes from the Greek verb (κενόω) in Phil. 2: 7, translated in the RV '*emptied* himself'. Some 19th-cent. *Lutheran theologians held that the Divine Son abandoned His attributes of deity in order to become man; other scholars maintained that within the sphere of the Incarnation the deity so restrained its activity as to allow the existence in the Lord of a limited and genuinely human consciousness. Traditional orthodoxy has generally admitted a self-emptying of the Lord's deity only in the sense that, while remaining unimpaired, it accepted union with a physically limited humanity.

Kensit, John (1853–1902), Protestant propagandist. He started the City Protestant bookshop in Paternoster Row in London in 1885 and in 1890 he became secretary of the newly founded 'Protestant Truth Society'. From 1898 he organized resistance to the growth of 'ritualism' in the dioceses of London and Liverpool, causing friction and disturbance wherever he went.

Kent, Maid of. See BARTON, ELIZABETH.

Kentigern, St (d. *c.*612), also known as **St Mungo**, missionary. According to a 12th-cent. Life, he was the grandson of a British prince in S. Scotland, became a bishop of the Britons of Strathclyde, and founded the Church of Glasgow. He is said to have preached in Wales and Cumbria. His reputed tomb is in Glasgow cathedral. Feast day, 13 Jan.

Kenya, Christianity in. Modern Christianity in Kenya dates from 1844, when a *CMS missionary settled near Mombasa, but little progress was made until the 1870s. A settlement for freed slaves established at Freretown, near Mombasa, prospered, and the first Kenyans were ordained in 1885. When the Uganda Railway, begun in 1896, gave access to the central highland, RC and Protestant missionaries increased in number. The Kikuyu of Central Kenya were suspicious of the missionaries whom they saw as allies of the White settlers, and the settlers regarded them as pro-African. In 1929 controversy arose over the attempt of some Protestant missions to get the practice of clitoridectomy outlawed; many Kikuyu left the mission churches and schools and started their own free of missionary control. In the Mau Mau uprising of 1952 some Christians refused to take the secret Mau Mau oath and were killed; they are commemorated in the Anglican cathedral at Murang'a. After independence in 1964 there was a huge influx into the Churches. The RC and Anglican are the largest, but independent Church movements have grown and multiplied. By 1980 over 70 per cent of the population claimed to be Christian.

Kepler, Johann (1571–1630), German astronomer. In 1613 at the Diet of Ratisbon he defended the *Gregorian calendar against the attacks of his fellow-Protestants. His fame is chiefly due to his discovery of the three laws of planetary motion. He held the world to be an order expressing the being of God Himself.

kerygma (the Greek word for 'preaching'). The element of proclamation in Christian apologetic, as contrasted with '*didache' or its instructional aspects.

Keswick Convention. An annual gathering of *Evangelical Christians from 1875.

Ketteler, Wilhelm Emmanuel von (1811–77), Bp. of Mainz from 1850 and a pioneer in modern Catholic social thought. Preaching at the episcopal conference at Fulda in 1869, he drew attention to the contradictions between economic liberalism and Christian principles. At the First *Vatican Council (1869–70) he opposed the definition of Papal *infallibility on the ground that its promulgation was 'inopportune'.

He also opposed the *Kulturkampf, championing the freedom of the RC Church in Germany from State control.

Kettlewell, John (1653–95), devotional writer and *Nonjuror. During the revolution of 1689 he preached against rebellion under any pretext and in 1690 he was deprived of his living. His *Practical Believer* (1687) was widely read.

Kevin, St (d. 618), also 'Coemgen', the founder and abbot of Glendalough in Co. Wicklow, which became one of the chief centres of pilgrimage in Ireland. The sources for his life are late and untrustworthy. Feast day, 3 June.

Khomiakov, Alexis Stepanovich (1804–60), Russian philosophical theologian. He was one of the founders of the Slavophile movement which he tried to build up on Orthodox Christianity. Over against the RC ('unity without freedom') and the Protestant ('freedom without unity') conceptions of the Church, Khomiakov saw in the Orthodox Church an organic society of which Christ was the Head and the Holy Spirit the Soul and whose essence was 'freedom in the spirit at one with itself'. Of this Church the essential quality was inward holiness, and those who partook of it could be saved even though not in external communion with it. Khomiakov's conception of the Church (often summed up in the term '*sobornost') has influenced Orthodox ecclesiology, Greek as well as Russian.

Kiddush. The Jewish ceremony of the sanctification of the *Sabbath or other holy day. It takes place at the evening meal on the eve of the day in question, when the head of the household says the 'Kiddush' or 'Blessing' of the day over a cup of wine and water. It has been argued that Christ's blessing of the cup at the *Last Supper was the Kiddush of the *Passover.

Kidron. See CEDRON.

Kierkegaard, Søren Aabye (1813–55), Danish philosopher. Of wealthy *Lutheran family, he spent almost all his life in Copenhagen. To the prevailing *Hegelian philosophy, he opposed his own '*Existential' dialectics, pointing out what was involved in the position of man 'existing before God'. Though deeply original, his thought reflects its Lutheran ancestry in its opposition of faith to reason and the stress laid on the relation of the individual soul to God almost to the exclusion of the idea of a Christian community. His oft-repeated statement that 'truth is subjectivity', links truth with the existing subject instead of with its object, and so, in the last resort, makes its communication to other subjects impossible. He drew the theological consequences from this position by denying the possibility of an objective system of doctrinal truths.

Kikuyu. The village in *Kenya where a Missionary Conference of Anglicans, Presbyterians, and other Protestants was held in 1913. A federation of the constituent Churches was proposed.

Kilham, Alexander (1762–98), *Methodist. After J. *Wesley's death (1791) he became the leader of the radical wing of the movement and advocated complete separation from the C of E and lay representation in all Church courts. He was expelled by the Methodist Conference in 1797 and in 1798 founded the *Methodist New Connexion.

Kilian, St (d. c.689), 'Apostle of Franconia'. A native of *Ireland, he was probably already a bishop when he went as a missionary to the Franks and established his headquarters at Würzburg. He made many converts. Feast day, 8 July.

Kilwardby, Robert (d. 1279), Abp. of *Canterbury from 1273 to 1278, when he was made a *cardinal and translated to Porto in Italy. He had been a Master of Arts at *Paris, entered the *Dominican Order, and studied theology at *Oxford. In 1277 he visited Oxford and in conjunction with the Masters of the University condemned 30 propositions in grammar, logic, and natural philosophy. Some of the condemnations were directed mainly against views maintained by St *Thomas Aquinas on the unity of form. Kilwardby's own works include the 'De ortu scientiarum', a classification of knowledge largely based on *Aristotle; a commentary on the 'Sentences' of *Peter Lombard; and treatises on relation, time, imagination, and conscience.

Kimbangu, Simon (c.1889–1951), Church founder. A member of the *Baptist Church in the Democratic Republic of the *Congo, he was baptized in 1915. After experiencing a visionary calling in Kinshasa, he returned to his village home at Nkamba; here his healing ministry drew vast crowds. He was arrested on a charge of sedition and sentenced to death (commuted to life imprisonment). Many of his followers were arrested and taken to other parts of the Congo; his movement continued underground until the 1950s when a legal Church (Église de Jésus-Christ sur la Terre par le prophète Simon Kimbangu) was established. It claims some millions of members and was admitted to the *World Council of Churches in 1969.

Kindred and Affinity, Table of. The list, published by Abp. M. *Parker in 1563 and customarily printed at the end of the BCP, is based on the degrees of intermarriage prohibited in Lev. 18. It was amended slightly in 1946 and again in 1969, when adopted children were added.

King, Edward (1829–1910), Bp. of *Lincoln from 1885. He was a devout *Tractarian High Churchman. In 1888 a 'ritual prosecution' was brought against him by the *Church Association; the verdict in 1890 was substantially in his favour (see LINCOLN JUDGEMENT). Feast day in CW, 8 Mar.

King, Martin Luther (1929–68), *Black *Baptist minister and champion of civil rights in the USA. As pastor of a church in Montgomery, Alabama, he became involved in the struggle over segregation and in 1955 he organized a year-long boycott of buses by Blacks. In 1959 he resigned his pastorship and devoted himself mainly to the civil rights movement. He believed that the reconciliation of the Black to the White population was as important as that of the Whites to the Blacks. He was assassinated in 1968. In 1986 the third Monday in January was made a federal holiday in the USA in commemoration of his birthday.

King, William (1650–1729), Abp. of *Dublin from 1703. He energetically promoted the spiritual and temporal welfare of the Church of *Ireland: he was passed over for the primacy because of his Whig sympathies. His *De Origine Mali* (1702; Eng. tr., 1731) seeks to reconcile the existence of evil with the conception of an omnipotent and beneficent God.

King James Version. A title used, especially in America, for the English translation of the Bible commonly known elsewhere as the Authorized Version (1611) (see BIBLE, ENGLISH VERSIONS, 3).

King's Book. The name commonly given to *A Necessary Doctrine and Erudition for any Christian Man*, put forth by *Henry VIII in 1543. It was based on the *Bishops' Book of 1537, but for the most part its theology was a reaction in a Catholic direction.

King's Books. See VALOR ECCLESIASTICUS.

King's College, London. The College, incorporated in 1829, was designed as an Anglican counterweight to the undenominational University College, London, which had been established in 1827. From 1908 to 1980 the theological department had a separate identity from the rest of the College, but has now been reintegrated. The College is a constituent part of the University of London.

King's Confession. The Protestant statement of belief drawn up by John Craig in 1581 when it was feared that Popery might be revived in Scotland. It was signed by King *James (VI of Scotland); hence its common designation. It formed the basis of the *National Covenant of 1638.

King's evil, touching for the. The tradition that there existed some virtue in the royal touch for healing the 'King's evil', or scrofula, can be traced back to the 11th cent. In England Queen *Anne was the last sovereign to perform the ceremony.

Kingdom of God. The conception of the Kingdom of God (or in Mt. the 'Kingdom of Heaven') is a central element in the teaching of Jesus Christ. Its origins lie in the OT. God's reign was expected to bring with it order and justice, thus manifesting His purpose in creation. When the Jews lacked political autonomy, the Kingdom became linked with ideas about the future manifestation of Divine sovereignty in history. In the inter-testamental period, the coming of God's reign was seen as involving the overthrow of the powers opposed to God and the transfer of power to Israel or to God's agent, the *Messiah.

According to Mk. (1: 15) the ministry of Jesus began with the proclamation of the imminence of the Kingdom. Occasionally the Gospels suggest that it may be already present (e.g. Lk. 17: 21). Entry into the Kingdom is a present possibility, but it demands patterns of behaviour which contrast with the current perceptions of the nature of human dominion (Mk. 10: 13–27). There is, however, little explicit teaching on the nature of the Kingdom. Throughout the *Synoptics, Jesus uses *parables to illustrate the meaning of God's Kingdom, its novelty, and its demands. There are hints that He may have expected its arrival within a generation (Mk. 9: 1). The journey to *Jerusalem, the triumphant entry and the incident in the *Temple have sometimes been taken to suggest that there may have been a political component in Jesus' understanding of the Kingdom of God as well as in the reasons for His arrest and execution. See JESUS CHRIST.

Throughout the NT and early Patristic period it was expected that the coming of the Kingdom would take place in this world. By the 3rd cent. belief in the imminence of the *Parousia was fading and St *Augustine argued that the Kingdom of God was a supernatural entity whose presence could be only dimly perceived in the time between the first and second coming of Christ. *Joachim of Fiore's interpretation of Rev. reopened the possibility of a visible establishment of the Kingdom of God in this world. Much modern political theology has also refused to accept the view that the Kingdom is utterly transcendent and has tried to find a place for human endeavour in its establishment. See also ESCHATOLOGY, LIBERATION THEOLOGY, MILLENARIANISM, and PAROUSIA.

Kings, Books of. The two OT Books of Kings were originally a single Book, which was divided by the Greek translators, who grouped them with the Books of *Samuel and called all four the 'Books of the Reigns'. This method of designation (1–4 Reg.) was printed in the headlines of the Clementine edition of the *Vulgate and has survived in some RC translations.

The narrative covers the reign of *Solomon and the building of the *Temple, the history of the two separate kingdoms of *Judah and *Israel after their division on Solomon's death to the fall of Israel to Assyria c.721 BC; thereafter it is concerned solely with Judah, ending with the fall of *Jerusalem c.586 BC. Events of religious significance are described in detail,

whereas those of the highest political importance are passed over cursorily.

Kingship of Christ, Feast of the. See CHRIST THE KING, FEAST OF.

Kingsley, Charles (1819–75), social reformer and novelist. In 1844 he became vicar of Eversley, Hants, where he spent most of the rest of his life. He was a leading spirit in the *Christian Socialist Movement, but he looked to educational and sanitary reform rather than political change for improvement in the condition of the people. He was at first the main pamphleteer of the group, writing under the pseudonym 'Parson Lot'. Averse to all forms of asceticism, he was a critic of *Tractarian ideals. An ill-considered jibe at J. H. *Newman in 1863 led to the publication of the latter's *Apologia. His own works include *Westward Ho!* (1855), *The Heroes* (1856), and *The Water-Babies* (1863).

Kirk. The Scottish equivalent of 'Church'.

Kirk session (also known as the **session).** The lowest court in the Church of *Scotland and other *Presbyterian Churches.

Kiss of Peace (also **Pax),** the mutual greeting of the faithful in the Eucharistic Liturgy, as a sign of their love and union. It is first mentioned by St *Justin Martyr. Originally an actual kiss, the form of the Peace has been modified in all rites. In recent years hand-shaking has become common in the W. In E. Orthodox practice a Kiss of Peace is also exchanged by the whole congregation at the end of Easter Mattins (which forms part of the midnight vigil; see PASCHAL VIGIL SERVICE).

Kittel, Gerhard (1888–1948), German Protestant theologian. He worked from 1928 until his death on the *Theologisches Wörterbuch zum Neuen Testament* (9 vols., 1933–73; Eng. tr., 1964–76), editing the first four volumes; its purpose was to show the meanings which Greek words took on in the NT. His early work on the relationship of primitive Christianity to Palestinian Judaism led to a consideration of the status of Jews in contemporary Germany and lent scholarly support to Nazi anti-Semitism.

Klopstock, Friedrich Gottlieb (1724–1803), German poet. He spent many years in Denmark, where King Frederick V gave him a pension to enable him to complete

Der Messias. This poem, of nearly twenty thousand lines, deals with the Passion and forty days after the Resurrection. It not only describes events on earth, but introduces hosts of angels and devils, even the Trinity itself appearing, giving to every event and action its deeper significance.

Klosterneuburg, a monastery of *Augustinian canons near Vienna, founded not later than 1108. It possesses great art treasures and a valuable library. In the 20th cent. it became noted for its support of the *Liturgical Movement.

Kneeling, Declaration on. See BLACK RUBRIC.

Knights Hospitaller; Knights of Malta; and Knights of Rhodes. See HOSPITALLERS.

Knights Templar. See TEMPLARS.

Knox, Edmund Arbuthnott (1847–1937), Bp. of Manchester from 1903 to 1921. He was one of the most prominent *Evangelicals of his generation, a great preacher (famed for his missions on the Blackpool sands), and an advocate of Church schools.

Knox, John (*c.*1513–72), Scottish Reformer. Having embraced the principles of the Reformation, he became preacher at St Andrews in 1547. In 1551 he was made chaplain to *Edward VI and as such assisted in the revision of the Second BCP. On *Mary's accession he fled to the Continent and in 1556 he accepted a call to the English church at *Geneva. Here he published *The First Blast of the Trumpet against the Monstrous Regiment of Women* (1558) asserting that government by a woman was contrary to the law of nature and to Divine ordinance. He returned to *Scotland in 1559 and became the leader of the Reforming party. He drew up the *Scottish Confession (q.v.) and brought into being a commission which abolished the authority of the Pope in Scotland and forbade the celebration of, and attendance at, Mass. The *First Book of *Discipline* (1560) and the *Book of *Common Order* (qq.v., 1556–64) were largely his work. After *Mary Stuart's return to Scotland in 1561 he came into repeated conflict with the Queen. His principal work is the *History of the Reformation of Religion within the Realm of Scotland* (published in full, 1644).

Knox, Ronald Arbuthnott (1888–1957), Catholic apologist and translator of the Bible. The son of E. A. *Knox, he became a RC in 1917. He was chaplain to the RC undergraduates at Oxford from 1926 to 1939, when he resigned to devote himself to translating the Bible. His version was based on the Latin *Vulgate and aimed at putting the Bible into timeless English. The NT appeared in 1945, the OT in 1949; the whole Bible in one volume in 1955.

Koch, Johann. See COCCEIUS, JOHANNES.

Kolbe, St Maximilian (1894–1941), martyr. Raymond Kolbe was a Pole; he took the name Maximilian on joining the *Franciscans in 1910. In 1922 he set up a magazine to promote Christian teaching and continued publishing after the German occupation of Poland in 1939. He was arrested and sent to Auschwitz in 1941. Here he voluntarily took the place of a young man chosen for death by starvation in reprisal for an attempted escape. Feast day, 14 Aug.

kollyva. In the E. Church a cake blessed during memorial services for the departed and distributed to those present.

Komenský, Jan Amos. See COMENIUS, JOHANNES AMOS.

komvoschinion. In the E. Church, a knotted cord, similar to the W. *rosary.

kontakion. See CONTAKION.

Koran. The sacred book of *Islam, which Muhammad claimed had been revealed to him as the Word of God, through the mediation of the archangel *Gabriel.

Korea, Christianity in. The first Korean Christians were prisoners captured during the Japanese invasions of 1592–8 and taken to *Japan. The second introduction of Christianity was from *China, where Korean envoys encountered *Jesuit missionaries; a Korean was baptized in Beijing in 1784. By the end of the 18th cent. there were several thousand Christians in Korea and in 1831 an apostolic *vicariate was established. Korean Christians were subjected to waves of persecution; 103 of those martyred in 1839–46 and 1866–7 were canonized in 1984. In the 1880s, following treaties between Korea and the W. powers, freedom of religion was granted. From 1884 numerous Protestant missionaries began work in Korea, mainly American *Presbyterians and *Methodists. When Japan, which had annexed Korea in 1910, was defeated in the Second World War, Korea was divided at the 38th degree of latitude. In North Korea the State tried to eradicate religious institutions. Many Christians migrated south; little is known of those that remain.

In South Korea Christianity is vigorous but fragmented. The Holy Spirit Association for the Unification of World Christianity (the 'Moonies'), founded in 1954 by Sun Myung Moon, has spread to other countries. About 30 per cent of the population is Christian; of these over half belong to indigenous denominations.

Kornthal, NW of Stuttgart, *Pietist settlement. It was founded in 1819 as a centre of Pietist life in opposition to the increasing rationalism of the *Lutheran State Church. The lives of its members are minutely regulated; educational institutes and missionary work have been their main achievements. They number *c.*1250.

Krüdener, Barbara Juliana Freifrau von (1764–1824), Russian *Pietist. She influenced the Tsar Alexander I and gained his support for the idea of the *Holy Alliance.

Kulturkampf. The repressive political movement in Germany in the 1870s against the RC Church. In 1871 Bismarck suppressed the Catholic department of the Prussian Ministry of Public Worship and in 1872 appointed P. L. A. *Falk Minister of Public Worship. The *Jesuits were expelled, education brought under State control, and the famous *May Laws (1873) were passed. In view of the strong opposition aroused, Bismarck became convinced that a *concordat would serve the German Empire better. At the end of the 1870s the previous policy was reversed and peace was made with the new Pope, *Leo XIII.

Kung, Hans (1928–), Swiss RC theologian. He was a *peritus* at the Second *Vatican Council and in 1963 became Professor of Dogmatic and Fundamental Theology at Tübingen and director of the newly-established Institute for Ecumenical Research. Disappointed with the progress of the Vatican Council, he became increasingly critical of the Church and outspoken in his protests against Papal encyclicals. This criticism found expression in two books, *Die Kirche* (1967; Eng. tr., *The Church*, 1967) and *Unfehlbar?* (1970; Eng. tr., *Infallible?*, 1971), a trenchant criticism of mod-

ern Papal claims and the Papacy's exercise of authority. Other works were no less controversial, and in 1979 his *missio canonica* (authority to teach as a Catholic theologian) was withdrawn, though he kept his university post until his retirement in 1996.

Kuyper, Abraham (1837–1920), Dutch *Calvinist theologian and politician. In 1879 he founded the Anti-Revolutionary Party with a view to transforming the orthodox Calvinist sector of the population into a political force; to this end he also founded the Free University in Amsterdam (1880). In 1886 he led a secession from the Dutch Reformed Church. In his Stone Lectures at Princeton (published in England under the title *Calvinism*, 1932), he set out his view of Calvinism as a way of life satisfying all contemporary needs and emphasized the notion of 'common grace'.

Kyriale. The Latin liturgical book containing the musical chant for the *Ordinary of the Mass, so called from its opening part, the *Kyrie.

Kyrie eleison (Greek for 'Lord, have mercy'). A prayer for Divine mercy used in the worship of the Church from at least the 4th cent. in the E., and the 6th cent. in the W. In a letter of 598 *Gregory I mentions that at Rome the 'Kyrie eleison' is supplemented by a similar prayer, 'Christe eleison' ('Christ, have mercy'), not found in the East, and the two seem soon to have been placed in what became the traditional place at the beginning of the Mass. The ninefold Kyrie (that is 'Kyrie eleison' recited three times, followed by 'Christe eleison' three times, and 'Kyrie eleison' three times), found in the 8th–9th cent., became the traditional pattern of the Roman Mass until 1970. In the RC Church a sixfold Kyrie (each of the three petitions being said by the celebrant or sung by the choir and repeated by the people as a response) now forms one of the penitential acts at the beginning of Mass, and the Kyrie may also be used as the people's response in the Prayer of the Faithful.

In the C of E the Kyrie in the Eucharist was replaced in the 1552 BCP by the Ten *Commandments, but its use was revived in the 19th cent. and is permitted in modern Anglican liturgies. Its use (in English) at *Mattins, *Evensong, and in the *Litany has been continuous.

Labadists. A small Protestant sect named after Jean de Labadie (1610–74), its founder. They held *Pietist views and were organized on a communistic basis; they survived de Labadie's death by some fifty years.

labarum. The military standard adopted by the Emp. *Constantine. It incorporated a Christian monogram, the Greek letters X and P (the first two letters of ΧΡΙΣΤΟΣ, 'Christ') intersecting.

Laberthonnière, Lucien (1860–1932), RC *Modernist theologian. He developed a pragmatic view of religious truth, called moral dogmatism, which he expounded in *Essais de philosophie religieuse* (1903) and *Le Réalisme chrétien et l'idéalisme grec* (1904); both were put on the *Index.

Labre, St Benedict Joseph (1748–83), pilgrim and mendicant saint. Born near Béthune, he was rejected by the *Trappists and the *Carthusians as unsuitable for community life and found his vocation in a life of solitude and pilgrimage. He visited most of the leading sanctuaries in Europe. Feast day, 16 Apr.

Lacey, Thomas Alexander (1853–1931), canon of *Worcester from 1918. He was an apologist for the *Anglo-Catholic position. He was also devoted to the cause of reunion, and when a Papal commission was examining the validity of *Anglican ordinations in 1896, Lacey supplied much of the material from the Anglican side.

Lachmann, Karl (1793–1851), German philologist and textual critic. He produced two editions of the Greek NT in 1831 and 1842–50, applying to the biblical text the methods of textual criticism in evaluating the variant readings which he had earlier used for classical authors. He was also the first scholar to put the *Marcan hypothesis on a sound footing.

Lacordaire, Henri-Dominique (1802–61), French *Dominican. He was a contributor to F. de *Lamennais's periodical *L'Avenir*, but severed his connexion when it was condemned in 1832. In 1835–6 he gave his first two series of Conferences or sermons at *Notre-Dame; they drew a vast concourse, largely from the intelligentsia. His political liberalism and *Ultramontane theology aroused distrust, however, and he retired to Rome. In 1839 he entered the Dominican Order with the idea of restoring it in France; in 1843 he established at Nancy the first Dominican house in France since the suppression of the Order in 1790, and in 1852 he founded the teaching *Third Order.

Lactantius (c.250–c.325), Christian apologist. Lucius Caelius Firmianus Lactantius was a teacher of rhetoric at Nicomedia. He is generally thought to have been a convert to Christianity. He was tutor to *Constantine's son Crispus. His main surviving works are his *Divinae Institutiones*, which sought to commend Christianity to men of letters and thereby for the first time set out in Latin a systematic account of the Christian attitude to life; *De Opificio Dei*, an attempt to prove the existence of God from the marvels of the human body; *De Ira Dei*, on God's punishment of human crime; and *De Mortibus Persecutorum*, which describes the deaths of the persecutors of the Church.

lacticinia. Milk and foods made from milk, which (as well as meat and eggs) were often forbidden on fast days in the early and medieval Church, as they still are in the E. Church.

Ladislaus (in Hungarian, **László), St** (1040–95), King of *Hungary from 1077. In the *Investiture Controversy he took the side of *Gregory VII and Victor III against the German Emperor, but when *Urban II refused to acknowledge his suzerainty over Croatia, his relations with the Papacy came under strain. He laboured to spread the Christian faith, especially in Croatia and Dalmatia. Feast day, 27 June.

Lady, Our. A common designation among Catholics for the BVM.

Lady Chapel. A chapel dedicated to the BVM when it forms part of a larger church.

Lady Day. The feast of the *Annunciation of the BVM, 25 Mar.

Laetentur Coeli. The opening words of: (1) the Greek Formulary of Union sent in 433 by *Cyril, Patr. of Alexandria, to *John, Bp. of Antioch, embodying the terms of reunion agreed by both parties, after John had previously given qualified support to *Nestorius; and (2) the bull issued by *Eugenius IV in 1439 decreeing the union settled at the Council of *Florence between the E. Orthodox Church and the W.

Lagrange, Marie-Joseph (1855–1938), *Dominican biblical scholar. In 1890 he founded at *Jerusalem the 'École Pratique d'Études Bibliques'. He supported *Leo XIII's efforts to encourage the critical study of the Bible in the RC Church; his own position perhaps approached as near to that of the *Higher Critics as was compatible with Catholic orthodoxy.

Laínez, Diego (1512–65), second *General of the *Jesuits. He helped St *Ignatius Loyola to found the Society of Jesus. He took a prominent part in the Council of *Trent, where he represented the more irreconcilable elements (e.g. on *justification). When Ignatius died (1556) he succeeded him first as 'General-Vicar' and from 1558 as General.

laity. A lay person is a member of the Church who does not belong to the clergy or (in some traditions) to a religious order. Emphasis on the sharp distinction between clergy and laity in the RC Church was modified by the Second *Vatican Council, which stressed the role of the laity as part of the 'people of God' (e.g. in worship) and underlined their vocation to improve the social order. In the C of E an enhanced role was assigned to the laity in the government of the Church by the *Synodical Government Measure 1969.

lamb. The use of a lamb as a symbol of Christ is based on such passages as Jn. 1: 29 and Rev. 5: 12. Sometimes a lamb with or near a cross represented the sacrifice of Christ; sometimes a lamb is depicted standing on Mt *Zion (cf. Rev. 14: 1). Other passages in the NT suggest the representation of Christian believers as sheep, with the Good Shepherd carrying His lambs or standing among them. After the *Trullan Synod in 692 forbade the representation of Christ under the form of a lamb, such imagery was confined to the W. Church. See also AGNUS DEI, PASCHAL LAMB, and PROSPHORA.

Lambert, St (c.635–before 705/6), martyr. He was Bp. of Tongeren/Maastricht from c.670, though exiled from his see for political reasons from c.675 to 682. It seems clear that he suffered a violent death, but the circumstances are differently recorded. Feast day, 17 Sept.; of the 'Translation' (of his remains to Liège in 718), 31 May.

Lambert, François (1486/7–1530), Reformer. He entered the *Franciscan Order at the age of 15, but travelling in Switzerland in 1522, he met U. *Zwingli and left his Order. In 1526 he was called to Hesse by the Landgraf *Philip. He took part in the *Homberg Synod, was charged with the preparation of a Protestant 'Church Order' for Hesse, and in 1527 became professor of theology at *Marburg.

Lambert of Hersfeld. See LAMPERT OF HERSFELD.

Lambeth. For over 700 years Lambeth has been the London residence of the Abps. of *Canterbury. Abp. *Baldwin (1185–90) acquired the manor and manor-house of Lambeth, though it was not described as 'Lambeth Palace' until c.1658. The Library, founded in 1610, has some 2,500 MSS, including the Registers of the archbishops from 1279 to 1928.

Lambeth Appeal. See LAMBETH CONFERENCES.

Lambeth Articles. Nine *Calvinistic propositions compiled at *Lambeth in 1595 by a committee which met under Abp. J. *Whitgift. They were never authorized.

Lambeth Conferences. Assemblies of the bishops of the Anglican Communion held about every ten years under the presidency of the Abp. of *Canterbury, originally in *Lambeth Palace, but since 1978 in the University of Kent at Canterbury. The first Conference was held in 1867, in response to a request from the Synod of the Anglican Church in *Canada, which was concerned about the unsettling effects of the case of Bp. J. W. *Colenso and the publication of *Essays and Reviews*. The idea of a Council

authorized to define doctrine was abandoned, and the resolutions of Lambeth
Conferences, though significant expressions of the opinions of the Anglican episcopate, are not binding. The Conference of
1920 issued an important 'Appeal to All
Christian People' for reunion, which was
sent to the leaders of Christian communities throughout the world. That of
1958 gave guarded approval to family plan-
ning. The 1978 Conference accepted the *de
facto* ordination of *women in some Provinces; that of 1998 affirmed the legitimacy
of the position of those who did not accept
the ordination of women, and it issued an
important statement on *homosexuality
(q.v.).

Lambeth degrees. Degrees in Divinity,
Arts, Law, Medicine, and Music which the
Abp. of *Canterbury may confer in virtue
of the Ecclesiastical Licences Act 1533
(passed in 1534) which gave him many of
the rights which he had previously enjoyed
as '*legatus natus' of the Pope.

Lambeth Opinions. In 1899 the Abps. of
*Canterbury and *York, in response to
questions, gave their opinion at *Lambeth
Palace that the liturgical use of *incense
and the carrying of lights in procession
were 'neither enjoined nor permitted' in
the C of E. Further opinions in 1900 denied
the legality of *Reservation.

Lambeth Quadrilateral, sometimes called
the 'Chicago–Lambeth Quadrilateral'. Four
Articles approved by the *Lambeth Conference of 1888 as stating the essentials for a
reunited Church. They were based on Articles agreed by the General Convention of
the *Episcopal Church in the United States
of America in Chicago in 1886. They deal
with the Bible, the *Apostles' and *Nicene
Creeds, *Baptism and the *Eucharist, and
the episcopate.

Lamennais, Félicité Robert de (1782–1854),
French religious and political writer.
Reluctantly, he was ordained in 1816. In
1818 he published the first volume of his
Essai sur l'indifférence en matière de religion. In
this he developed the principle of authority, which he equated with the 'raison
générale' or 'sens commun', and maintained that the individual is dependent on
the community for his knowledge of the
truth. Later volumes (1820–3) equated

Catholic Christianity with the religion of
all mankind, denied the supernatural, and
proclaimed subjects freed from their loyalty to temporal sovereigns when rulers
refused to conform their conduct to Christian ideals. To combat the evils of the time
he desired a theocracy, with the Pope as
supreme leader of kings and peoples. The
work was approved by Pope Leo XII, who
possibly intended to make him a cardinal.
Later Lamennais prophesied an impending
revolution and demanded separation both
of the Church and the educational system
from the State, as well as freedom of the
press. In the final issue of his newspaper
L'Avenir, he called for the union of all
freedom-loving men. Convinced that the
Pope would put himself at the head of this
crusade for freedom, he went to Rome in
1832 to defend his ideas before *Gregory
XVI, but they were condemned in the
encyclical 'Mirari vos' (1832). His famous
reply, *Paroles d'un croyant* (1834), which
admitted the authority of the Church in
matters of faith but denied it in the sphere
of politics, was condemned in June 1834.
Lamennais left the Church and all attempts
to reconcile him failed. He was a forerunner of *Modernism.

Lamentations of Jeremiah. This OT Book
deals with the desolation of Judah after the
destruction of *Jerusalem *c.*586 BC. Modern
scholars tend to reject the attribution of
the Book to *Jeremiah, though it probably
originated in his lifetime. Christians commonly interpret it in reference to Christ's
Passion; in the W. it is used in the liturgy of
*Holy Week.

Lammas Day, 1 Aug. In the early English
Church bread made from the first-ripe corn
was blessed at Mass on this day, probably in
thanksgiving for the harvest.

Lampert of Hersfeld (*c.*1024–after 1081),
chronicler. He became a monk at Hersfeld
in 1058, and was the first abbot of Hasun-
gen (Hesse). His *Annals*, which begin with
the creation of the world, are detailed from
1072 to 1077. They were long regarded as
the chief source for the struggle between
*Henry IV and *Gregory VII; their accuracy
was questioned in the 19th cent., but their
value has now been largely rehabilitated.

lamps. These were probably used in Christian worship from the first, as it usually

took place at night. The ceremonial lighting of the evening lamp that accompanied the singing of the '*Phos Hilaron' is attested by St *Basil. From at least the 6th cent. it was customary to burn lights—lamps and later *candles—before shrines and relics (and in the E. before *icons). The burning of a perpetual light before the reserved Sacrament came into general use in the W. in the 13th cent., but was not obligatory before the 16th.

lance (liturgical). In Byzantine rites, a small knife used to cut the Eucharistic bread at the *Proskomide.

Lance, Holy. A relic believed to be the lance mentioned in Jn. 19: 34 as having been used to pierce the Lord's dead body. The first record of its existence dates from the 6th cent. When the Persians captured *Jerusalem in 615, the lance fell into their hands, but its point was saved and brought to *Constantinople. In 1241 this was given to *Louis IX; preserved in the *Sainte-Chapelle, it disappeared at the French Revolution. What is claimed to be another part of the lance was sent by the Turks to the Pope in 1492 and is kept in *St Peter's; its authenticity has always been doubted.

Lanfranc (c.1010–89), scholar and Abp. of *Canterbury from 1070. In 1042 he entered the abbey of *Bec, becoming prior in 1045; in 1063 he became abbot of St Stephen's, Caen. At Bec he commented on the Psalms and Pauline Epistles. His commentary was used by *Anselm of Laon and so passed into the '*Glossa Ordinaria'. His *De Corpore et Sanguine Domini* was the first widely-known criticism of the Eucharistic teaching of *Berengar of Tours. Lanfranc held that the consecrated elements contained the invisible Body and Blood of Christ, but hidden under the species of bread and wine; he approached the doctrine of *transubstantiation.

The first Norman Abp. of Canterbury, Lanfranc was a fine administrator. He restored the demoralized community at Christ Church, Canterbury, rebuilding the cathedral church and providing a set of constitutions for the improved observance of the monastic life. His practical authority in the English Church was demonstrated in the synod of 1075 which transferred the sees of Selsey to *Chichester, *Lichfield to *Chester, and Ramsbury to Old Sarum.

While opposing clerical marriage and concubinage, he still regarded lay *investiture as normal practice. He was thus out of sympathy with *Gregory VII, though he remained loyal to him.

Lang, Cosmo Gordon (1864–1945), Abp. of *York (1908–28) and then of *Canterbury (1928–42). A committed ecumenist, he was chairman of the Reunion committee of the *Lambeth Conference of 1920 which issued the influential 'Appeal to All Christian People', he invited *Old Catholics to attend the Lambeth Conference of 1930, and he visited the *Oecumenical Patriarch in the Phanar in 1939. He played an important part in connection with the abdication of King Edward VIII in 1936.

Langton, Stephen (c.1150/55–1228), Abp. of *Canterbury. He studied in *Paris, where he gained a high reputation as a biblical commentator, preacher, and theologian. In 1207 *Innocent III consecrated him Abp. of Canterbury. King *John's refusal to admit Langton as archbishop kept him out of his see until 1213. His support of baronial grievances against the king cost him the Pope's favour and he was suspended from 1215 until 1218. Under Langton the standards of clerical conduct and rudimentary religious education were raised and the constitutions which he promulgated in his provincial Council at Oxford in 1222 set patterns for the future. He is credited with the division of the Books of the Bible into chapters which, with small modifications, is still in use. He probably wrote the '*Veni Sancte Spiritus'.

Laodicea. A Hellenistic city in the Roman province of Asia. It was the seat of an early Christian community mentioned in Col. 4: 16 and Rev. 3: 14 ff., and a bishopric of some importance for several centuries.

Laodicea, Canons of. A set of 59 4th-cent. canons which were embodied in early collections of ecclesiastical law. Nothing definite is known about the 'Council of Laodicea', but it seems to have taken place after c. 345, probably at least 20 years later. In some texts there is appended a list of the canonical Books (omitting the OT Apocrypha and Rev.); this list is sometimes called canon 60.

Laodiceans, Epistle to the. A letter of St *Paul to Laodicea is mentioned at Col. 4: 16, but has not survived. The Latin apocryphal letter of this name is an artless collection of Paul's own words, doubtless produced to supply the missing letter. It appears to date from the 2nd–4th cent.

Lapide, Cornelius a. See CORNELIUS A LAPIDE.

lapsi (Lat., 'the fallen'). Those who in varying degree denied the Christian faith under persecution. *Apostasy was regarded as the most serious sin a Christian could commit, and was perhaps at first regarded as unforgivable. After the *persecution of 250–51 the Church decided to readmit such persons as showed repentance after *penance and a period of probation. The decision led the *Novatianist rigorists into open schism. See also TRADITORS.

Lardner, Nathaniel (1684–1768), Nonconformist apologist. His work on *The Credibility of the Gospel History* (14 vols., 1727–57) sought to reconcile the discrepancies in the biblical narratives; it is a mine of information for scholars.

La Salette. A village in the Alps where in 1846 a peasant boy and girl saw a vision of the BVM who through them gave 'to all her people' a promise of Divine Mercy after repentance, and also a special secret which was later sent to *Pius IX. In 1852 the first stone of the present church was laid on the scene of the vision, which is a popular centre of pilgrimage.

Las Casas, Bartolomé de (1484–1566), Spanish missionary, the 'Apostle of the Indies'. He went with the Spanish governor to Hispaniola (Haiti) in 1502. He devoted himself to the interests of the Indians by opposing, both in America and at the court of Spain, the cruel methods of exploitation used by the settlers. He joined the *Dominicans in 1522 and from 1543 to 1547 he was Bp. of Chiapa in Mexico. He favoured limited importation of African slaves into America to help the enfeebled Indians, but he was totally opposed to the 'slave trade' and mass importation. His *Destrucción des las Indias* (1552) condemned the horrors perpetrated by the colonists.

Laski or **à Lasco, John** (1499–1560), Protestant Reformer. A Polish nobleman, from 1526 he showed an interest in reforming the Church, while disapproving of M.

*Luther as too extreme. He became Archdeacon of Warsaw in 1538, but was stripped of his ecclesiastical offices on his marriage in 1540; in 1542 he openly broke with the RC Church and was appointed Calvinist minister at Emden. He spent some time in England and is generally thought to have influenced the BCP of 1552.

Lassus, Orlande de (or **Orlando di Lasso)** (c.1532–94), composer. In 1556 he went to Munich as a tenor at the Bavarian court and in 1563 became 'Maestro di Capella' for the rest of his life. Prolific in all forms of vocal music, his technique was equal to that of G. P. da *Palestrina, but his style and range of expression was more varied. His sacred music includes over 60 Masses, 80 settings for the *Magnificat, and some 500 *motets.

Last Gospel. A reading from the Gospels (usually Jn. 1: 1–14) which until 1964 took place at the end of Mass in the W. rite.

Last Judgement. See GENERAL JUDGEMENT.

Last Supper. The final meal of Christ with the Apostles on the night before the Crucifixion. The institution of the *Eucharist is seen in the symbolic acts which He performed with the bread and wine at this meal. These are not mentioned in St *John's Gospel; it alone records the washing of the Apostles' feet (13: 1–11). Traditionally it has been held that the meal was the *Passover, in agreement with the Synoptic Gospels, but Jn. has a different chronology.

Last Things. See ESCHATOLOGY.

Lateran Basilica. The basilica, dedicated to St *John the Baptist (with whom St *John the Apostle is now associated), stands on the site of a palace which belonged to the family of the Laterani. The palace, given to the Church by *Constantine, was the official residence of the Popes from the 4th cent. until they went to *Avignon (1309). It was mostly destroyed by fire in 1308. The new palace, which was at one time a museum of antiquities, now houses the offices of the diocese of Rome. The present church was built under a succession of Popes beginning with *Urban V. It is the cathedral church of Rome.

Lateran Councils. A series of councils held

at the Lateran Palace in Rome from the 7th to the 18th cent.; five of them rank as *oecumenical in the W. Church. The First (1123) ratified the Concordat of *Worms ending the *Investiture contest; the Second (1139) condemned the followers of *Arnold of Brescia; the Third (1179) regulated Papal elections; the Fourth (1215) defined Eucharistic doctrine (for the first time officially using the word '*transubstantiate') and prescribed annual confession; the Fifth (1512–17) invalidated the decrees of the anti-papal Council of Pisa convoked by Louis XII of France.

Lateran Treaty (1929). This treaty between the Italian government and the Holy See settled the position of Rome as the capital of Italy and established the *Vatican City as a sovereign state.

Latimer, Hugh (c.1485–1555), Reformer. In 1522 he was licensed by the University of Cambridge to preach anywhere in England, but his extreme Protestant teaching led to his censure by *Convocation in 1532. When *Henry VIII formally broke with the Papacy in 1534, Latimer became a royal chaplain, and in 1535 he was appointed Bp. of *Worcester. He supported the King in the *Dissolution of the Monasteries. In 1539 he opposed the Act of the *Six Articles and resigned his see. In 1546 he was confined in the Tower, but was released under *Edward VI. In 1548 he preached his famous sermon 'Of the Plough'. On *Mary's accession he was taken, with T. *Cranmer and N. *Ridley, to Oxford to dispute with Catholic theologians. He refused to accept Catholic Eucharistic teaching, was excommunicated and, with Ridley, burnt. Feast day in CW, (with Ridley), in the American BCP (1979), (with Cranmer and Ridley), 16 Oct.

Latin. The language of government and the courts, Latin was also the normal spoken language of many people in the W. provinces of the Roman Empire. It was naturally used as one of the languages of the early Christians, though it was only in the 4th cent. that it superseded Greek. By then Classical Latin had given way to Late Latin and the more popular spoken language had been adopted into literary use. In the late 4th cent. a series of major figures writing in Latin established it as the language of the W. Church: Sts *Hilary, *Ambrose, *Augustine, and *Jerome, whose *Vulgate transla-

tion of the Bible quickly spread throughout the W. Church. In the same period Latin translations were made of Greek theological writers, such as *Origen. From about this time until the *Reformation Latin held a dominant place in the W. For centuries it was not only the language of biblical study, theology, and the liturgy; it was the only language of literacy in much of W. Europe.

With the fragmentation of the W. Empire, spoken Latin increasingly diverged from the written standard as the many Romance dialects of Italian, French, and Spanish emerged. The spread of Christianity beyond the areas of Romance speech, however, meant that Latin was being studied to be written and spoken as the learned language of the Church. Under *Charlemagne strenuous efforts were made to establish a common core to the liturgy and an established pronunciation of Latin for the whole Carolingian Empire. From the 8th to the 13th cent. Latin was used for almost all literary activity in the W. Church; in the late 11th and 12th cent. it was also cultivated as a spoken language in Church courts, schools, and universities.

In the 13th cent. increasing literacy in W. Europe gave rise to a literature in the vernacular, and in the 15th and 16th cent. the use of Latin became increasingly academic. With the Reformation it was all but abandoned for liturgical purposes in the Reformed Churches. The restriction of its use to academic and formal purposes is as apparent in RC as Protestant countries. In official documents in the RC Church the Latin text serves as the authority for vernacular translations worldwide. The Second *Vatican Council declared that the use of Latin was to be maintained in the liturgy, but allowed for some use of the vernacular, which, in the event, has almost entirely displaced Latin.

Latitudinarianism. A term applied opprobriously in the 17th cent. to the outlook of Anglican clerics who remained within the C of E but attached relatively little importance to matters of dogmatic truth, ecclesiastical organization, and liturgical practice.

la Trappe. The abbey near Soligny (Orne) from which the *Trappists take their name. Founded in 1122 as a house of the *Savigny

Order, it joined the *Cistercian Order in 1148. From the early 16th cent. it declined until A. J. de *Rancé introduced the Strict Observance in 1662, and in 1664 initiated a stricter reform of his own. At the time of the French Revolution about a third of the monks chose exile rather than secularization; in 1815 they returned to rebuild their ruined abbey. La Trappe ranks second after *Cîteaux in the Cistercian Order of the Strict Observance.

latria. The fullness of Divine worship which may be paid to God alone.

Latrocinium (i.e. 'Robber Council'). The Council held at *Ephesus in 449. Dominated by *Dioscorus, Patr. of Alexandria, an upholder of *Monophysitism, the Council acquitted *Eutyches of heresy and reinstated him in his monastery. Its decisions were reversed at *Chalcedon in 451.

Latter-day Saints. See MORMONS.

Laud, William (1573–1645), Abp. of *Canterbury from 1633. He had earlier been President of St John's College, Oxford, and Bp. successively of *St Davids (1621), *Bath and Wells (1626), and London (1628). He opposed the prevailing *Calvinist theology and sought to restore something of the pre-Reformation liturgical practice of the C of E. His work on the *High Commission and his efforts to impose liturgical uniformity aroused the intense hostility of the *Puritans. His attempt in 1637 to enforce a new liturgy in *Scotland proved to be a turning point in his career. In 1640 he introduced into *Convocation new *canons proclaiming the *Divine Right of Kings and compelling whole classes of people to swear never to consent to alter the government of the Church; the formula, known as the 'etcetera oath', exposed him to ridicule and had to be suspended at the order of the King. Soon afterwards Laud was impeached by the Long Parliament. He was imprisoned in 1641, tried in 1644, and executed in 1645. Feast day in the American BCP (1979) and CW, 10 Jan.

Lauda Sion. The opening words and hence the name of the *sequence (now optional) composed for the feast of *Corpus Christi by St *Thomas Aquinas. The English translation, 'Laud, O Sion, thy Salvation', is the work of several authors.

Lauds. The morning *Office of the W. Church which before 1911 always included Pss. 148–50, in which the word *Laudate* ('Praise ye . . .') recurs; hence the name. In the BCP parts of Lauds and *Mattins were combined to form Morning Prayer. See also OFFICE, DIVINE.

laura. See LAVRA.

Laurence, St (d. 258), deacon and martyr of Rome. According to tradition, on being asked to deliver up the riches of the Church, he assembled the poor and presented them to the Prefect of Rome, saying, 'These are the treasure of the Church'; he was punished by being roasted to death on a gridiron. The story is widely rejected by modern scholars. Feast day, 10 Aug.

Laurence of Brindisi, St (1559–1619), *Capuchin friar. As chaplain of the Imperial troops, holding a crucifix aloft, he rode before them against the Turks at the battle of Székesfehérvár in 1601. He worked to combat *Lutheranism in Bohemia, Austria, and Germany, and wrote an extensive treatise *Lutheranismi Hypotyposis*. Feast day, 21 (formerly 23) July.

'Lausanne'. The first Conference of the *Ecumenical Movement of '*Faith and Order' held at Lausanne in 1927.

lavabo (Lat., 'I will wash'). The washing of the celebrant's fingers after the offering of the oblations in the Eucharist.

Lavigerie, Charles-Martial Allemand- (1825–92), cardinal. In 1867 he accepted appointment as Abp. of Algiers, with the purpose of evangelizing the African continent. To this end he founded the *White Fathers in 1868 and the *White Sisters in 1869. In 1878 *Leo XIII entrusted him with the organization of RC missions in Central Africa, in 1882 created him a cardinal, and in 1884 revived for him the see of Carthage with the title of primate of Africa. Throughout 1888 he conducted a campaign in European capitals against *slavery.

lavra (Greek for a street or alley). In the early Church a colony of *anchorites who, while living in separate huts, were subject to a single abbot. The oldest lavras were founded in Palestine in the early 4th cent. In modern times the term has been used of important *coenobitic communities.

law, canon. See CANON LAW.

Law, Natural. See NATURAL LAW.

Law, William (1686–1761), *Nonjuror and spiritual writer. He refused to take the Oath of Allegiance on George I's accession and was deprived of his Cambridge Fellowship. From 1740 he lived, in great simplicity, at Kings Cliffe, Northamptonshire.

The most famous of his many works is *A Serious Call to a Devout and Holy Life* (1728), a forceful exhortation to embrace the Christian life in its moral and ascetical fullness; it insists on the exercise of the virtues practised in everyday life, temperance, humility, and self-denial, all animated by the intention to glorify God. The simplicity of its teaching and its vigorous style soon established the book as a classic. Feast day in parts of the Anglican Communion, 9 or 10 Apr.

Lawrence, Brother; Lawrence, St. See BROTHER LAWRENCE; LAURENCE, ST.

Laws, Robert (1851–1934), missionary. Ordained in the *United Presbyterian Church in 1875, he was seconded to the pioneer party of the *Free Church of Scotland 'Livingstonia' mission to the Lake *Malawi area. He was head of that mission from 1878 until he retired in 1927. In 1894 he founded the Overtoun Institute which trained men and women from central and north Malawi and east *Zambia both as pastors and in secular trades. He took part in the union of the missions of the Dutch Reformed Church, the Free Church of Scotland, and the Church of Scotland in 1924 to form the Church of Central Africa Presbyterian.

Laxism. A system in *moral theology which relaxes the obligations of natural and positive law where there is any degree of probability, however slight, in favour of a course of action. Its formulation in the 17th cent. is connected with the appearance of *Probabilism (q.v.). Laxist propositions were condemned in 1679.

lay brother, lay sister. A member of a religious order who is not bound to the recitation of the Divine *Office and is occupied in manual work. The institution originated in the 11th cent. The Second *Vatican Council in 1965 required that lay brothers should be drawn into the heart of the community's life and that, if possible, there should be only one category of nuns.

lay reader. See READER.

lay rector. In the C of E, a lay person who was formerly entitled to receive the rectorial *tithes of a benefice. He has a legal duty to repair the chancel of the church, but in 2001 the Court of Appeal ruled that this obligation contravened the Human Rights Act 2000.

laying on of hands. See HANDS, IMPOSITION OF.

laymen. See LAITY.

Laynez, James. See LAÍNEZ, DIEGO.

Lazarists. The name popularly given to the 'Congregation of the Mission', a congregation of secular priests living under religious vows, founded by St *Vincent de Paul in 1625. The name comes from the priory of St-Lazare, which was Vincent's headquarters in Paris.

Lazarus. The name of two apparently separate figures in the NT. (1) The poor man in Christ's parable of *Dives and Lazarus (Lk. 16: 19–31). (2) The brother of *Martha and Mary. According to Jn. 11: 1–44 Christ raised him from the dead. Some critics have speculated that the story (not mentioned in the Synoptic Gospels) was constructed from the parable. According to E. tradition Lazarus, with Martha, Mary, and others, was put into a leaking boat by the Jews, landed in *Cyprus, and became Bp. of Kition: in later W. tradition he was Bp.of Marseilles. Feast day in the E., the Saturday before *Palm Sunday; in the W., 17 Dec.

Leander, St (*c.*540–*c.*600), Bp. of Seville, probably from 577/8. A leading advocate of Catholic orthodoxy in Spain against the *Arianism of the Visigoths, he converted Prince Hermenegild, and in 589 he presided over the Third Council of *Toledo.

leavened bread. See BREAD, LEAVENED AND UNLEAVENED.

Lebbaeus. An alternative name for *Thaddaeus.

Le Clerc, Jean (1657–1736), *Arminian theologian and biblical scholar. In 1684 he was appointed professor of philosophy at the *Remonstrant College at Amsterdam. A champion of freedom of thought and an enemy of dogmatism, he defended the unlimited rights of reason in the domain of faith. He explained the mysteries of the *Trinity, *Incarnation and *Original Sin on rationalistic lines. He attacked the *Mosaic authorship of the *Pentateuch and held advanced critical views on the inspiration of Scripture, which he denied altogether in parts of the OT.

Leclercq, Henri (1869–1945), *Benedictine scholar. A Belgian by birth, from 1914 he lived in London. He was a prolific writer, especially concerned with the history of Latin Christianity; much of his work is inaccurate. The latter part of the *Diction-naire d'archéologie chrétienne et de liturgie* (ed. by F. *Cabrol and himself, 1903–53) was almost entirely Leclercq's work.

lectern. A bookstand to support liturgical books, often taking the form of an eagle or pelican with outstretched wings.

lectionary. A book containing the extracts from Scripture to be read in public worship. The apportionment of particular extracts for particular days began in the 4th cent. Originally the beginning (*incipit*) and ending (*explicit*) of the passage to be read were noted in the margins of church Bibles, and a 'capitulary', or table of *incipits* and *explicits*, was made for reference, but later the extracts were collected in separate books. Those for the Mass used to be incorporated in the *Missal, but in 1969 a separate lectionary was issued in the RC Church (revised in 1981). The lessons used at *Mattins and *Evensong in the C of E are regulated by a table of readings which is amended from time to time by the General Synod. For weekday Eucharists in CW, the scheme of the RC Church has been adopted.

lector (also **reader**). In the E. and RC Churches, one of the *Minor Orders. In early times the main function of the lector was to read the OT Prophecies, the *Epistle, and in some places the *Gospel. In the RC Church the office was constituted the lower of the two remaining *ministeria* in 1972 and allotted various duties. Only men are eligible for the office, but the duties of the lector may be performed by a man or woman. For the office in the Anglican Communion, see READER.

lecturers. Lecturers were originally ordained stipendiary ministers (often dea-cons), appointed in the century after 1559 by town corporations, parishes, and occasionally by individual laymen, to provide regular frequent preaching. 'Lecturers by combination' were groups of beneficed clergy who would combine to provide a rota of sermons in some central church. Many stipendiary lectureships became a *Puritan device to secure preachers with views of which Puritans could approve.

Ledger, St. See LEODEGAR, ST.

Lee, Frederick George (1832–1902), vicar of All Saints', Lambeth, from 1867 to 1899. He promoted reunion between the C of E and the RC Church, helping to found the *APUC in 1857 and the Order of Corporate Reunion in 1877. He appears to have been secretly consecrated by a prelate in communion with the see of Rome *c*.1877 and took the title of Bp. of *Dorchester (see EPISCOPI VAGANTES). He became a RC in 1901.

Lefèvre d'Étaples, Jacques. See FABER, JACOBUS.

legate, Papal. A personal representative of the *Holy See who has been entrusted with a mission. *Legati missi* are legates sent to carry out particular tasks; those appointed for more exalted occasions came to be known as legates *a latere*, i.e. from the side of the Pope. *Legati nati* were the holders of certain important archbishoprics to whom legatine status was conferred on a stable basis; to some extent these powers survive in the office of certain primates. See also APOSTOLIC DELEGATE and NUNCIO.

Leger, St. See LEODEGAR, ST.

Leibniz, Gottfried Wilhelm (1646–1716), philosopher. From 1673 he was in the service of the family of the Duke of Brunswick-Lüneburg, his chief official duty being to assemble material on the House of Brunswick. He maintained other interests.

According to the *Monadologie* (published 1720), the universe consists of an infinite number of 'monads', i.e. simple substances, and nothing else. These monads, ever active and each different, form a continuously ascending series from the lowest, which is next to nothing, to the highest, which is God. Though Leibniz sometimes described God as the highest of the monads, he could not avoid the difficulties of reconciling the inclusion of God in the monadic series with the Christian view of the Divine transcendence, and in some places he speaks as though God were outside the series and the cause of the monads' existence, or as though they proceeded from Him by 'fulgurations'.

Leiden. To mark its heroic defence against the Spaniards (1574), William of Orange in 1575 gave the city a university. Though it was formally free from Church control, *Calvinist influence was powerful and, strengthened by the foundation of a College for training theological students (1592), Leiden soon became a stronghold of Calvinist orthodoxy and a refuge of the English *Puritans. In the 17th cent. it was the scene of disputes between the *Arminians and the *Gomarists.

Leighton, Robert (1611–84), Bp. of Dunblane (1661–70) and Abp. of Glasgow (1670–74). He accepted a bishopric believing that he had been chosen to bring peace in the conflict between Presbyterianism and Episcopalianism, but he failed in his hopes of accommodating the two systems.

Leipzig, Disputation of (1519). The disputation was provoked by J. *Eck's challenge of *Carlstadt. It began with an academic discussion on grace and free will, but when M. *Luther arrived it turned to the question of the doctrinal authority of the Church. Luther stated that Councils not only may err, but actually have done so.

Leipzig Interim (1548). A more Protestant formula, put forward by Maurice, Elector of Saxony, which was adopted in parts of Germany where the Interim of *Augsburg (q.v.) was not accepted.

Le Neve, John (1679–1741), English antiquary. His *Fasti Ecclesiae Anglicanae* (1716) records the succession of dignitaries in English and Welsh cathedrals.

Lent. The fast of forty days before *Easter. In the first three centuries the period of fasting did not normally exceed two or three days. The first mention of a period of forty days, probably of Lent, dates from AD 325, though the period was long differently reckoned in different Churches. In the W. it now extends from *Ash Wednesday to *Holy Saturday (excluding Sundays).

In the early centuries the observance of the fast was rigid: only one meal a day was allowed, and flesh-meat and fish, and in most places also eggs and *lacticinia, were forbidden. In the W. the fast was gradually relaxed. In the RC Church in 1966 the obligation to fast was restricted to the first day of Lent and *Good Friday. In the E. Church abstinence from meat, fish, eggs, and *lacticinia* is still widely practised.

In the W. Church the penitential character of Lent is reflected in various features of the liturgy, and there is a proper Mass for each day. In the E. Church the celebration of the Eucharist is confined to Saturdays and Sundays; on Wednesdays and Fridays the Liturgy of the *Presanctified is used. The period is also observed as a time of penance by abstention from festivities, by almsgiving, and by devoting more time than usual to religious exercises. In modern times the W. Church has emphasized these aspects rather than physical fasting.

Leo I, St (d. 461), 'Leo the Great', Pope from 440. His Papacy is remarkable for the extent to which he advanced and consolidated the influence of the Roman see. He tried to strengthen the Church by energetic central government and he pressed his claims to jurisdiction in Africa, Spain, and Gaul. He was drawn into E. affairs by the *Eutychian controversy, and his support was coveted by all parties. At the Council of *Chalcedon (451) his legates spoke first, and his *Tome was accepted as a standard of *Christological orthodoxy. He persuaded the Huns to withdraw beyond the Danube (452) and secured concessions when the Vandals took Rome (455). 143 genuine letters and some 97 sermons survive. Feast day in the E., 18 Feb.; in the W., 10 Nov. (formerly, 11 Apr.).

Leo III, St (d. 816), Pope from 795. After being attacked in Rome in 799, Leo fled to *Charlemagne, who provided him with an escort. When Charlemagne came to Rome, the Pope crowned him *Holy Roman Emperor (800). At Charlemagne's instigation he took strong measures against the *Adoptianist heresy. He intervened in the differences between the Abps. of *Canterbury and the Anglo-Saxon kings, and in the E. he encouraged the monks in their opposition to the Emp. Constantine VI. Feast day, 12 Jun.

Leo IV, St (d. 855), Pope from 847. He at once set about repairing the damage done by the Saracens in 846, putting a wall round the part of Rome on the right bank of the Tiber (henceforth the '*Leonine City'). In 850 he crowned Louis, son of Lothair, as co-emperor; he is said to have 'hallowed' *Alfred as future king of England in 853. The *Asperges is ascribed to him. Feast day, 17 July.

Leo IX, St (1002–54), Pope from 1048. He at once began the reform of the Church from its decadence of 150 years and did much to foster a new ideal of the Papacy. At the Easter Synod of 1049 *celibacy was enforced on all the clergy, and soon afterwards various Councils promulgated decrees against *simony and other abuses. At a synod in Rome in 1050 *Berengar of Tours was condemned for his *Eucharistic doctrine. Feast day, 19 Apr.

Leo X (1475–1521), Pope from 1513. Giovanni de' Medici was the second son of Lorenzo 'the Magnificent'. The high hopes placed on him when he was elected were soon disappointed. He squandered the fortune left by *Julius II, and his concern for the independence of the Papal states led him to pursue a shifting political course. He failed to understand what was involved in the revolt of M. *Luther, whom he excommunicated in 1520.

Leo XIII (1810–1903), Pope from 1878. He restored good relations with Germany after the *Kulturkampf, procuring the gradual abolition of the *May Laws in 1886 and 1887. In 1892 he established an Apostolic Delegation in Washington, and he renewed contacts with *Russia and *Japan. The improved relations with Britain found expression in King Edward VII's visit to the Vatican in 1903. Relations with Italy, however, remained strained, and those between the Church and State in *France deteriorated.

His pontificate was important for the lead which he gave on political and social issues. In some notable encyclicals he developed the Christian doctrine of the State; he defined the respective spheres of spiritual and temporal power and emphasized the compatibility of Catholic teaching with a moderate democracy. His most important pronouncement on social questions was '*Rerum Novarum' (q.v.) in

1891. He established the *Biblical Commission in 1902 and gave some encouragement to the new methods of Biblical criticism. He encouraged Anglican aspirations for union and appointed a commission to investigate *Anglican Ordinations, but rejected them as invalid in 1896. He promoted the spiritual life of the Church and encouraged the work of the missions, especially the formation of a native clergy.

Leo III (c.675–741), Byzantine Emperor from 717, 'the Isaurian'. After defeating the Arabs who were besieging *Constantinople in 718, he effected administrative reforms and issued a new code of law. Between 726 and 729 he issued a number of edicts against image worship, thus initiating the *Iconoclastic Controversy.

Leodegar, Ledger, or **Leger, St** (c.616–678/9), Bp. of Autun from 663. He presided over a Council of Autun (date unknown) which recommended the use of the Rule of St *Benedict in all monasteries of the diocese and insisted that the clergy should know the *Athanasian Creed by heart. Though killed in a political struggle, he was soon regarded as a saint and martyr. Feast day, 2 (occasionally 3) Oct.

León, Luis de (1527/8–91), Spanish theologian and poet. He made his profession as an *Augustinian Hermit in 1544 and became a professor at Salamanca in 1561. He was one of the greatest lyric poets of Spain and his polished prose brought a new beauty to the language. His treatise on the duties of a Christian wife (1583) has remained a classic, but his devotional masterpiece is *De los Nombres de Cristo* (1583–95), a dialogue on some of the biblical names of Christ in which he expounds His universal ministry of reconciliation.

Leonard, St (6th cent.), hermit. According to an 11th-cent Life, he was a Frankish nobleman of the court of King *Clovis, whom St *Remigius converted to Christianity. He lived in a cell near Limoges and later founded a monastery. Feast day, 6 Nov.

Leonardo da Vinci (1452–1519), Italian painter and scholar. From 1483 to 1499 he lived at Milan; during this period he executed some of his best-known works, among them the *Last Supper*. This depicts not the institution of the Eucharist but the moment of the announcement of the betrayal. When the French invaded Milan (1499), Leonardo left and began a nomadic life mainly devoted to wide-ranging scientific and scholarly work.

Leonine City. The part of Rome on the right bank of the Tiber, fortified with a wall by Pope *Leo IV in 848-52.

Leonine Prayers. In the RC rite, the prayers which until 1964 were recited in the vernacular by priest and people at the end of Mass. Their ultimate form (three *Hail Marys, the *Salve Regina, a collect, and an invocation of St *Michael) went back to *Leo XIII.

Leonine Sacramentary. The earliest surviving book of Mass prayers according to the Roman rite. It exists in a single 7th-cent. MS preserved at *Verona. Its attribution to Pope *Leo I is arbitrary. It is not a *sacramentary in the proper sense, but a private collection of *libelli. It possesses no *Ordinary or *Canon of the Mass and contains only the variable parts of the liturgy.

Leontius of Byzantium (6th cent.), anti-*Monophysite theologian. He is probably to be distinguished from the Scythian monk of the same name who took part in the *Theopaschite controversy, but practically nothing is known of his life. A staunch upholder of *Chalcedonian Christology, he introduced the notion of *Enhypostasia (q.v.). His main theological work was *Libri III contra Nestorianos et Eutychianos*. See also the following entry.

Leontius of Jerusalem (6th cent.). The name given by modern scholars to the author of the *Contra Monophysitas* and *Contra Nestorianos*, formerly ascribed to *Leontius of Byzantium. His Christology was '*Neo-Chalcedonian' (q.v.).

Lepanto, Battle of (1571). The naval battle in which the 'Christian League' (mainly Venice and Spain) decisively defeated the Turks.

Leporius (5th cent.), monk and later (by 430) priest. He emphasized the distinction between the two natures in Christ at the expense of the unity of His Person. Rebuked by his superiors in Gaul, he went to Africa, where in 418 he publicly confessed his error in a *Libellus Emendationis*.

Lérins. The ancient name of two islands off Cannes, on the smaller of which (now 'St-Honorat') a celebrated monastery was founded by St *Honoratus c. 410.

Leslie, Charles (1650-1722), *Nonjuror. Deprived of his benefice in Ireland, he came to London in 1689. His most celebrated work was an attack on *Deist philosophy, *A Short and Easy Method with the Deists* (1698).

Leslie, John (1527-96), Bp. of Ross from 1566. In 1569 he became *Mary Queen of Scots' ambassador to *Elizabeth I, but in 1571 he was imprisoned for assisting Mary in her projected marriage to the Duke of Norfolk. He was set free in 1573 on condition that he left Britain; on the Continent he continued to further plans in the RC interest. The later part of his *De Origine, Moribus, et Rebus Gestis Scotorum* (Rome, 1578) is an authority for contemporary events.

Lesser Entrance; Lesser Ministries. See LITTLE ENTRANCE; MINOR ORDERS.

Lessing, Gotthold Ephraim (1729-81), a leading figure of the *Enlightenment. He followed a literary career. His interest in theological problems was stimulated by the fragments of H. S. *Reimarus which he edited (1774-8). He saw the essence of religion in a purely humanitarian morality independent of all historical revelation; he embodied his views in the principal figure of his play *Nathan der Weise* (1779), an ideal Jew of serene tolerance, benevolence and generosity, conceived on the lines of enlightened rationalism. His writings laid the foundations of the Protestant Liberalism that was to hold sway in Germany throughout the 19th cent. He rejected Christianity as a historical religion on the ground that 'the accidental truths of history can never become the proof of necessary truths of reason'. He also made some original studies on Gospel origins.

Letters Dimissory. In the C of E the licence which the bishop of a diocese where a candidate for Holy *Orders has his title issues to the bishop of another diocese to perform the ministerial act of Ordination when the former bishop finds it inconvenient to ordain the candidate.

Letters of Business. The document formerly issued by the Crown to the English *Convocations permitting them to prepare *canons on a prescribed subject.

Letters of Orders. A certificate issued to those who have been ordained, bearing the seal and signature of the officiating bishop.

Letters Testimonial. The certificate of 'good life and conversation' which until 1977 a candidate for Ordination in the C of E was required to present to the ordaining bishop. The terminology was changed in 1977 but the principle remains.

Leuenberg Concord. A statement of concord between *Lutheran and *Reformed Churches of E. and W. Europe adopted at Leuenberg in Switzerland in 1973. It revoked 16th-cent. disagreements on various doctrinal points and accepted diversity in worship and Church order.

Levellers. A 17th-cent. English political and religious party. They were opposed to kingship and advocated freedom in religion and a wide extension of the suffrage. The name first occurs in 1647. Their main support was in the Army. After the execution of *Charles I (1649), the Levellers faded out.

Levi, son of Alphaeus. The tax-collector called by Christ to be one of His disciples (Mk. 2: 14). He is apparently to be identified with St *Matthew.

Leviathan. A mythological sea-serpent or dragon mentioned in the Ugaritic texts, the OT, and later Jewish literature. The name was transferred to the devil. T. *Hobbes gave his treatise on 'the matter, form, and power of a Commonwealth' this title.

levirate marriage. The marriage of a man with his brother's widow.

Levites. According to the biblical accounts, members of a tribe descended from Levi, one of the sons of *Jacob, who had been specially set aside as ministers of the sanctuary. Some scholars doubt the existence of such a tribe. In the *Deuteronomic legislation 'priest' and 'Levite' are virtually interchangeable; in the 7th–8th cents. BC 'priest' came to be restricted to those of Levitical descent who could trace their ancestry through Zadok; the Levites were allotted other duties in the *Temple.

Leviticus, Book of. This OT Book consists almost wholly of legislation. Chapters 17–26 form a well-defined unity known as the '*Holiness Code (q.v.). The rest of the Book is not earlier than the 6th cent. BC.

Lewis, Clive Staples (1893–1963), scholar and Christian apologist. He was a Fellow of Magdalen College, Oxford, from 1925 to 1954, when he became a professor at Cambridge. He underwent a gradual conversion experience described in his spiritual autobiography *Surprised by Joy* (1955) and became widely known as a Christian apologist through broadcast talks and through popular religious works, including *The Problem of Pain* (1940) and *The Screwtape Letters* (1942; ostensibly from a senior devil to his nephew, a junior devil). He also published science fiction novels with a Christian flavour and childrens' books, as well as academic works on English literature.

libellatici. Those who during the *Decian persecution (249–51) procured certificates by purchase from the civil authorities stating that they had sacrificed to pagan idols, when no such sacrifice had been made.

Libelli Missarum. Booklets containing the formularies for one or more Masses for a given period for the use of a particular church. They did not include the *Canon, which was fixed, the readings from Scripture, or the parts which were sung. They formed the link between the period of free composition and the organization of fixed formularies in a *Sacramentary.

Liber Censuum. The official register of the Roman Church, which recorded the dues (*census*) payable to the Holy See by institutions such as monasteries, churches, cities, and kingdoms. It was compiled by Cencio Savelli (later *Honorius III).

Liber Comicus. See COMES.

Liber de Causis. A treatise, consisting largely of extracts from *Proclus' 'Elements of Theology', put together in Arabic by an unknown Muslim philosopher *c.*850. Translated into Latin between 1167 and 1187, it circulated as a work of *Aristotle and deeply influenced medieval philosophy.

Liber Pontificalis. A collection of early Papal biographies. Those of the earliest

Popes are short, but from the 4th cent. onwards they tend to increase in size.

Liber Regalis. The Book containing the English *Coronation service introduced for the crowning of Edward II in 1308. It was translated into English for *James I (1603); it was discarded by *James II in 1685.

liberal arts, seven. See SEVEN LIBERAL ARTS.

Liberal Evangelicalism. The outlook of those within the C of E who, while maintaining their spiritual kinship with the *Evangelical Revival, have been concerned to restate old truths in terms felt to be more consonant with modern thought.

liberalism. A general tendency to freedom from bigotry and readiness to welcome new ideas or proposals for reform, with various shades of meaning in a theological context. The 'Liberal Catholics', who formed a distinguished group in the RC Church in the 19th cent., were mainly orthodox theologically, though they favoured political democracy and ecclesiastical reform. 'Liberal Protestantism', on the other hand, developed into an anti-dogmatic and humanitarian reconstruction of the Christian faith which at one time seemed to be gaining ground in nearly all Protestant Churches. The word 'liberalism' is also sometimes used of a belief in secular humanism which is inconsistent with biblical and dogmatic orthodoxy. See also the previous entry.

Liberation Theology. A theological movement that came to prominence in the Conference of Latin American bishops held at Medellín in Colombia in 1968. The term 'liberation' springs from dislike of 'development', which is understood to imply an imposed solution. While there are differences of emphasis among liberation theologians, the salient features of their thought are: (1) a preferential option for the poor, that is the idea that the Church's primary duty in a situation of oppression is to support the poor; (2) liberation is seen as an essential element in salvation, since salvation is concerned with the whole man, not just his spiritual needs; (3) the *Exodus is taken as the biblical paradigm, since individual transformation can come only through social transformation; (4) Christ's apparent lack of involvement in politics is countered by the suggestion that His teaching was highly political or that His confrontation was with social structures; (5) the priority of praxis, that is the conviction that right belief (orthodoxy) can issue only from right action (orthopraxis); (6) the view that structures that coerce are no less violent than the use of physical force. In 1984 the Sacred Congregation of the Doctrine of the Faith was severely critical of various aspects of Liberation Theology; a subsequent Instruction in 1986 was seen by many as more favourable.

The most obvious practical expression of the movement has been the growth of *comunidades eclesiales de base*, small communities of 15–20 families that are led by laymen and try to integrate spiritual and social issues. There are over 70,000 such 'base communities' in *Brazil alone. In their attitude to the use of force positions have ranged from the pacificism of Abp. H. *Câmara to open resort to arms. The movement has influenced both *Black and *Feminist Theology.

Liberian Catalogue. An early list of Popes down to *Liberius (352–66).

Liberius, Pope from 352 to 366. Ordered by the *Arian Emp. Constantius to assent to the condemnation of St *Athanasius as a rebel, Liberius refused and was banished from Rome in 355. In 357 he submitted and in 358 he was allowed to reoccupy his see, having agreed to the deposition of Athanasius and signed a confession of faith which, while not mentioning the *homoousion, is otherwise orthodox.

licences, marriage. See MARRIAGE LICENCES.

Lichfield. The seat of the Mercian diocese under St *Chad, it was an archbishopric from 787 to 803. Despite the nominal removal of the see to *Chester in 1075 and to *Coventry (q.v.) in 1095, Lichfield remained a centre of episcopal administration in the diocese throughout the Middle Ages. The cathedral dates mainly from the 13th cent.

lich-gate. See LYCH-GATE.

Liddell, Henry George (1811–96), lexicographer. He was Dean of *Christ Church, Oxford, from 1855 to 1891. The Greek Lexicon, on which he collaborated with

R. Scott, appeared in a modest form in 1843. It has been repeatedly extended.

Liddon, Henry Parry (1829–90), Canon of *St Paul's from 1870 and from 1870 to 1882 also Dean Ireland's professor of exegesis at Oxford. He exercised great influence at Oxford in face of post-*Tractarian liberalism; throughout his life he exercised a ministry of spiritual direction. He was interested in the *Old Catholics and attended the *Bonn Reunion Conferences. He had an intense admiration for E. B. *Pusey, whose Life he wrote (posthumously published, 1893–7).

Life and Work. The branch of the *Ecumenical Movement concerned with the relation of Christian faith to society, politics, and economics. It held conferences at *Stockholm (1925) and *Oxford (1937). See also WORLD COUNCIL OF CHURCHES.

Light of the World, the. A title of Christ derived from Jn. 8: 12. It is the subject of Holman *Hunt's famous picture.

Lightfoot, John (1602–75), biblical and *rabbinic scholar. He was a member of the *Westminster Assembly, in which he opposed the extreme *Presbyterians. He assisted B. *Walton with the *Polyglot Bible of 1657. His Horae Hebraicae et Talmudicae (1658–78) was designed to show the bearing of Jewish studies on the interpretation of the NT; it is not entirely superseded.

Lightfoot, Joseph Barber (1828–89), Bp. of *Durham from 1879. He held high academic posts at Cambridge and from 1870 to 1880 he was a member of the Company of Revisers of the NT. His critical work on the NT and the Fathers was marked by wide erudition, lucid presentation, freedom from technicalities, and avoidance of sectional controversy. It included commentaries on St Paul's Epistles, an edition of *Clement of Rome (1869), and his famous Ignatius (1885), which disposed of W. *Cureton's suggestion that only the three Epistles in the Syriac recension were genuine.

Ligugé, Defensor of. See DEFENSOR.

Liguori, St Alphonsus. See ALPHONSUS LIGUORI, ST.

Lima Document. See BAPTISM, EUCHARIST AND MINISTRY.

limbo. In Latin theology the abode of souls excluded from the full blessedness of the *Beatific Vision, but not condemned to any other punishment.

Lincoln. A see was established here by Bp. Remigius (d. 1092), who transferred it from *Dorchester, Oxon. It became the largest diocese in England, extending from the Thames to the Humber. The cathedral was begun in 1086 and largely completed by 1300.

Lincoln Judgement. The Judgement given in 1890 by E. W. *Benson, Abp. of *Canterbury, upon complaints against Edward *King, Bp. of *Lincoln, for consecrating the Eucharist in the *eastward position, mixing water and wine in the *chalice, and four other matters. The Judgement upheld the Bishop in the main.

Lindisfarne, the 'Holy Island'. After St *Aidan's arrival in 635, Lindisfarne became a missionary centre and an episcopal see, and the monastic school flourished. The monastery and church were pillaged by the Danes in 793 and again in 875. Earduulf then moved his see to Chester-le-Street; it was transferred to *Durham in 995.

The 'Lindisfarne Gospels' (in the British Library) was written and decorated c.696–8.

Lindsey, Theophilus (1723–1808), *Unitarian. He held various livings in the C of E. He became doubtful about the doctrine of the *Trinity and, stimulated in his unorthodoxy by friendship with J. *Priestley, he joined in the '*Feathers Tavern' petition to Parliament against subscription to the *Thirty-Nine Articles (1772). After its failure he became a Unitarian and from 1774 he conducted services in London.

Lingard, John (1771–1851), English historian. Of an old RC family, he was ordained priest in 1795. In 1811 he went to a country mission where he spent most of the rest of his life writing. The success of his History of England [to 1688] (1819–30) was due to its objectivity, its use of contemporary documents, and the new light in which it viewed such controversial periods as the Reformation. There is some evidence that he was created cardinal in petto in 1826.

Linus, St. According to all the early episcopal lists, Linus was Bp. of Rome after the Apostles *Peter and *Paul. Nothing further is certainly known. Feast day, 23 Sept., suppressed in 1969.

lion. In representations of the story of Daniel in the lions' den (Dan. 6) the lion is conceived as a 'type' of God's redemption of His chosen people. The lion is also a symbol of St *Mark.

Lippi, Fra Filippo (c.1406–69), Italian painter. Brought up as an orphan by the *Carmelites in Florence, he took the habit in 1420, but was released from his vows c.1461 and allowed to marry. His pictures include the *Barbadore Altarpiece* (1437), the *Coronation of the Virgin* (1441), and the fresco cycles in Prato of St *John the Baptist and St *Stephen (1452–65). He influenced the development of devotional art.

Lipsius, Richard Adelbert (1830–92), German Protestant theologian. His works on the *apocryphal acts did much to unravel the problems of this type of literature, and in 1891, with M. Bonnet, he edited what became the standard text.

litany. A form of prayer consisting of a series of petitions or biddings sung or said by a deacon, priest, or cantors, to which the people make fixed responses. It apparently originated at *Antioch in the 4th cent.; it spread to *Constantinople and later to the W. Pope *Gelasius I (492–6) introduced a litanic intercession (the *Deprecatio Gelasii*) into the Mass.

Litany, the BCP. The form of 'general supplication' appointed to be said or sung after *Morning Prayer in the C of E on Sundays, Wednesdays, and Fridays. It is also included, with additional petitions, in the rites of *Ordination.

litany desk. In the C of E, a low movable desk at which the minister kneels to recite the Litany.

Litany of Loreto. A *litany in honour of the BVM, consisting of a series of invocations to her under various honorific titles such as 'Mother of Divine grace', each followed by the request: 'Pray for us'. Its name derives from *Loreto, though it probably did not originate there.

Litany of the Saints. A *litany used in the RC Church. It consists of invocations for mercy and deliverance addressed to the Persons of the Trinity and for intercession

to the BVM and a list of prophets, patriarchs, angels, saints, confessors, and virgins, individually and in classes. Early forms of such a litany are found in the E. from the end of the 3rd cent. and in the W. from the late 5th cent. The list of saints varied until in 1570 it became necessary to obtain Papal licence to differ from the use of Rome. It was revised in 1969, when some modern saints were added.

Literary Criticism. See HIGHER CRITICISM.

literate. In the C of E a cleric who has been admitted to Holy Orders without a university degree.

Little Brothers of Jesus. See DE FOUCAULD, CHARLES EUGÈNE.

Little Entrance. In the E. Church, the procession at the *Liturgy with the *Gospel Book.

Little Flower of Jesus. A popular designation for St *Teresa of Lisieux.

Little Flowers of St Francis (the 'Fioretti'). A collection of stories about St *Francis of Assisi and his companions. It is apparently an anonymous Tuscan translation of part of the Latin 'Acts of the Blessed Francis and his Companions', which was written c.1335, with some other material. The translation dates from c.1375.

Little Gidding. A manor, 11 miles NW of Huntingdon, where the Ferrar family lived under a religious rule in the C of E from 1625 until they were raided by O. *Cromwell's soldiers in 1646. The household consisted of Nicholas *Ferrar, his mother, and the families of his brother and sister. They followed a systematic round of devotion and work, reciting the whole Psalter each day, and engaging in charitable work for the neighbourhood.

Little Labyrinth, The. A lost 3rd-cent. treatise directed against the *Adoptionist heretics *Theodotus and *Artemon. Its authorship is disputed.

Little Office of Our Lady. A brief office in honour of the BVM, modelled on the Divine *Office. First known in the 10th cent., its use spread from the religious orders to the secular clergy. It became the ordinary form of vocal prayer for a number of new congregations of women. In 1953 a revision was approved; this introduced greater variety. See also PRIMER.

Little Offices. Originally these were very short offices, modelled on the *Little Office of Our Lady, and intended for devotional use. In modern times the term has come to denote more elaborate (usually vernacular) forms of prayer, based on the Divine *Office, and intended for corporate as well as individual use. These shortened offices were virtually superseded when the Divine Office was reordered in 1971.

Little Sisters. See DE FOUCAULD, CHARLES EUGÈNE.

Liturgical Movement. A movement aimed at restoring the active participation of the laity in the official worship of the Church. In the RC Church the revival may be traced to P. L. R. *Guéranger, but its main impetus came from *Pius X's direction relating to Church music (1903) and his promotion of frequent Communion. It was fostered by certain *Benedictine abbeys. At about the time of the Second World War in France and slightly later in Germany the momentum of the movement spread beyond the monastic centres into the parishes. The attempt to restore the scrupulous observance of the liturgy in the form in which it had developed was joined by pressure for the reform of the rite itself, in order to bring it more into line with earlier liturgical practice and with contemporary pastoral needs. *Pius XII began a reform of the liturgical rites with the revision of the *Holy Week liturgy in 1951 and 1955. The Second *Vatican Council encouraged the participation of the laity, and legislated for the use of the vernacular and the reform of the rites (a new *Ordo Missae*, lectionary, and calendar appeared in 1969 and a definitive new Missal in 1970; for the new rites of Baptism, Confirmation, etc., see s.vv.). More recently consideration has been given to the possibility of adapting liturgies for use in different parts of the world where different cultures prevail.

In the C of E the Ritualist Movement, inaugurated by the *Tractarians to give a central place to sacramental worship, developed in the early 20th cent. Subsequently there have been changes in the pattern of Sunday worship, with a tendency to replace the various morning services with one 'Parish Communion'; ceremonial designed to stress the corporate aspects of the liturgy has been widely taken over from the RC Church. In other Churches there has been a similar reaction against individualism.

liturgiology. The scientific study of liturgies and related subjects.

Liturgy. The word is used in two senses: (1) of all the prescribed services of the Church, as contrasted with private devotion; and (2) especially in the E. Church, as a title for the *Eucharist. In derived senses it is also used both of the written texts which order services and of the study of these.

Liudprand (*c*.922–*c*.972), or 'Liutprand', Bp. of Cremona. He entered the service of Berengar, ruler of northern Italy, but then transferred his allegiance to the Emp. Otto I, who nominated him Bp. of Cremona in 961 and then employed him on various missions. Liudprand's *Antapodosis* (covering the period 888 to 949) and his *Historia Ottonis* (covering 960–64) are the chief source for the Italian history of the period, though rhetoric and prejudice obscure accuracy and objectivity.

Liverpool Cathedrals. (1) THE ANGLICAN CATHEDRAL was designed by G. G. *Scott in the Romantic Gothic style on a vast scale. The foundation stone was laid in 1904 and work was completed in 1978.

(2) THE RC CATHEDRAL. After two previous designs (by A. W. *Pugin in 1853 and Sir Edwin Lutyens in 1930) were unfinished, a circular and completely modern building, designed by Sir Frederick Gibberd, was consecrated in 1967.

Livingstone, David (1813–73), missionary and explorer. He went to Africa under the auspices of the *LMS and worked as a missionary in the Bechuana country. Reports of his explorations aroused interest in England and he was greeted with enthusiasm on his return in 1856. In 1858 he went back to Africa, no longer technically a missionary, and discovered the lakes of Shirwa and Nyasa, and explored the basin of the Upper Nile. He gave pioneer help to the *UMCA.

Llandaff. Welsh episcopal see, 2 miles north of the centre of Cardiff. The diocese used to cover most of SE Wales, but in 1921 the diocese of Monmouth was formed out of it. Its early history is told in the 'Book of

Llandaff', which is not generally a trustworthy source. When, under the Norman kings, diocesan organization of the Church spread to Wales, the see emerged, with the head of the monastic community as its bishop. In 1107 Bp. Urban recognized the jurisdiction of *Canterbury and in 1120 began to build the cathedral. Largely restored in the 19th cent., it was badly damaged by an air raid in 1941; when it was restored in 1957 an impressive figure of 'Christ in Majesty' by Sir Jacob Epstein was placed high at the east end of the nave.

Llull, Ramon (*c.*1233–*c.*1315), also **Raymond Lull**, missionary and philosopher. He was born in Majorca, then recently recovered from *Islamic rule, and educated as a knight. At the age of 30 he had a vision of Christ crucified; thenceforth he devoted himself to the conversion of Islam. For nine years he remained in Majorca studying Arabic and Christian thought. In a vision on Mt Randa (*c.*1274) the form in which he was to set out his ideas was revealed to him; he worked this out in his 'Art of Finding Truth'. From 1287 he travelled widely, seeking support for his plans. His one practical success was the decree of the Council of *Vienne (1311–2) establishing *studia* of oriental languages in five universities.

In his writing Llull elaborated an approach by which he sought the conversion of Islam and of the Jews by rational argument, without recourse to the authority of Scripture. He tried to relate 'all forms of knowledge ... to the manifestations of God's "Dignities" [i.e. Divine Attributes] in the universe, taking for its point of departure the monotheistic vision common to Judaism, Islam, and Christianity, and their acceptance of a broadly Neoplatonic exemplarist world-picture' (R. D. F. Pring-Mill). His conception of the mystic life centres in the contemplation of the Divine perfections which is achieved by the purification of memory, understanding, and will, and results in action for the greater glory of God.

LMS. The 'London Missionary Society' was founded in 1795 by a body of *Congregationalists, *Anglicans, *Presbyterians, and *Wesleyans who combined to promote Christian missions to the heathen. No form of denominationalism was preached by its members, but decisions about the form of Church government were to be left to those whom they should convert. The Society came to be maintained almost exclusively by Congregationalists, and in 1966 responsibility for its work passed to the (then Congregational) *Council for World Mission.

Locke, John (1632–1704), philosopher. He was secretary to Lord Shaftesbury; on his fall in 1683 Locke fled to the Netherlands. He returned to England after the accession of William and Mary.

Locke was the foremost defender of free inquiry and toleration in the later 17th cent. In the *Letters concerning Toleration* (1689, 1690, and 1692) he pleaded for religious liberty for all except atheists and RCs, whom he excluded as a danger to the State. His ideal was a national Church with an all-embracing creed that made ample allowance for individual opinion, on the ground that human understanding was too limited for one man to impose his beliefs on another. His famous *Essay concerning Human Understanding* ('1690'; in fact published in 1689) attacks the *Platonist conception of 'innate ideas'. The human mind is a *tabula rasa* and all ideas come from experience. Pure reality cannot be grasped by the human mind; consequently there is no sure basis for metaphysics. The spirituality of the soul, though not certain, is at least probable; the existence of God, on the other hand, can be discovered with certainty by reason, and His law gives men their rule of conduct. In *The Reasonableness of Christianity* (1695) Locke maintains that the only secure basis of Christianity is its reasonableness.

loculus. (1) A common type of tomb in the *catacombs, formed as a horizontal rectangular niche. (2) The hole in a fixed altar in which relics were placed before 1977.

logia (Gk., 'sayings'). In NT criticism the term is applied to a supposed collection of the sayings of Christ which circulated in the early Church; this collection is sometimes equated with the lost document '*Q'. The term is also used of the '*Sayings of Jesus' found at *Oxyrhynchus.

Logical Positivism. See POSITIVISM.

Logos (Gk., 'Word' or 'Reason'), used in Christian theology with reference to the Second Person of the Trinity. In the OT

God's word was not only the medium of His communication with men; what God said had creative power, and by the time of the Prophets the Word of the Lord was regarded as having an almost independent existence. In the *Targums the Word was used as a means of speaking of God without using His name. In Hellenistic Judaism the concept of the Logos as an independent *hypostasis was further developed.

In the NT the term in its technical sense is confined to the Johannine writings. In the Prologue to Jn. the Logos is described as God from eternity, the Creative Word, who became incarnate in the man Jesus Christ of Nazareth. Though various antecedents for the Evangelist's ideas have been suggested, his identification of the Logos with the *Messiah was entirely new. In patristic times teaching about the Logos was taken up by St *Ignatius and developed by the *Apologists of the 2nd cent., who saw in it a means of making the Christian teaching compatible with Hellenistic philosophy.

Loisy, Alfred Firmin (1857–1940), French *Modernist biblical scholar. He applied historico-critical methods to the study of the Bible, and in 1893 he was dismissed from his post at the Institut Catholique in Paris. In 1902 he published *L'Évangile et l'Église*. As against A. *Harnack, who sought to base Christianity on the teaching of the historical Jesus apart from later dogmatic accretions, Loisy maintained that its essence was to be sought in the faith of the developed Church as expanded under the guidance of the Spirit. The book was condemned by the Abp. of Paris. In 1903, when Loisy published not only an account of the controversy but also *Le Quatrième Évangile*, *Pius X placed both books on the *Index. Loisy made a formal act of submission and retired to the country. The final breach with the Church came after the Papal acts of 1907 condemning Modernism. Loisy published *Simples Réflexions sur le décret du Saint-Office* Lamentabili (1908) and *Les Évangiles synoptiques* (1907–8); on 7 Mar. 1908 he was excommunicated.

From 1909 to 1930 Loisy was a professor at the Collège de France. He was a prolific writer, but after his break with the Church his work on the NT was generally regarded as erratic. It appears, however, that he was a mystic, with a pastoral sense.

Lollardy. A 'Lollard' was originally a follower of J. *Wycliffe; later the term was applied somewhat vaguely to anyone seriously critical of the Church. The Lollards, following Wycliffe, based their teaching on personal faith, Divine election, and above all the Bible. They commonly attacked clerical *celibacy, *transubstantiation, obligatory oral *confession, *indulgences, and *pilgrimages, and they held that the validity of priestly acts was determined by the priest's moral character.

The movement went through several phases. For about 20 years it enjoyed some academic support, though in 1382 Abp. W. *Courtenay's condemnation of Wycliffe's teaching started to deprive Lollardy of a base at Oxford. Some knights at the court of Richard II also apparently supported Lollardy. In the early 15th cent. rigorous persecution diminished the number of its adherents, and after risings in 1414 (led by Sir John *Oldcastle) and 1431, the movement went underground. It may have declined after the middle of the 15th cent., but apparently revived after c.1490. While it never won over the governing classes in strength, it seems to have contributed to the English Reformation by providing areas and minds receptive to *Lutheranism, and its influence may be traced in the congregational dissent of the 17th cent.

Lombard, Peter. See PETER LOMBARD.

London. See BOW CHURCH, ST PAUL'S CATHEDRAL, WESTMINSTER ABBEY, and WESTMINSTER CATHEDRAL.

London Missionary Society. See LMS.

Longinus, St. The name traditionally given to the soldier who pierced the side of Christ with a spear. It is also sometimes attributed to the centurion who, standing by the Cross, confessed Christ the Son of God, and the two are often confused. Feast day in the W., 15 Mar.; in the E., 16 Oct.

Longland, John (1473–1547), Bp of *Lincoln from 1521. As *Henry VIII's confessor, he took part in furthering the divorce proceedings against Catherine of Aragon.

Longley, Charles Thomas (1794–1868), Abp. of *Canterbury from 1862. As first Bp. of *Ripon (1836–56), he tried to suppress ritualistic practices at E. B. *Pusey's newly built church of St Saviour's, Leeds. As

Archbishop he supported R. *Gray, Bp. of Cape Town, and went as far as he could against J. W. *Colenso without provoking a conflict with the law. He convened the first *Lambeth Conference (1867).

Lopez, Gregory (1615/6–91), the first native Chinese bishop. Of pagan parentage, he embraced Christianity when he grew up. In 1651 he became a *Dominican, and in 1654 he was ordained the first Chinese priest. In 1674 he was offered but declined a bishopric. *Innocent XI overruled his objections in 1679 and ordered him to accept consecration. Now, however, there were difficulties with the Dominican authorities, and Lopez was eventually consecrated in 1685 by Italian *Franciscans. There was no further native RC bishop in China until 1918.

Lord of Hosts. This Divine title occurs in the OT 282 times. Through its translation in some places in the LXX, and thence into Latin as *Deus omnipotens*, it is the direct ancestor of the English 'Almighty God'.

Lord's Day, the. A Christian name for *Sunday.

Lord's Prayer. The prayer beginning 'Our Father', taught by the Lord to His disciples. Mt. 6: 9–13 and Lk. 11: 2–4 give slightly different forms; that in Mt. is universally used by Christians. A concluding doxology was probably added in early times and is found in some later Gospel MSS.

The prayer is usually divided into the address and seven petitions, the first three asking for the glorification of God, the latter four being requests for the chief physical and spiritual needs of man. The meaning of ἐπιούσιος used to describe the bread which is sought (translated 'daily') is uncertain. The prayer has regularly had a place in the Eucharist and the Divine *Office, and has frequently been expounded.

The version of the Lord's Prayer traditionally used by English-speaking Catholics and Protestants alike owed its acceptance to an ordinance of *Henry VIII in 1541. It closely follows the form in W. *Tyndale's version of the NT.

Lord's Supper. A title for the *Eucharist, now used especially by Protestants.

Loreto, near Ancona in Italy, is the site of the Holy House, alleged to have been inhabited by the BVM at the time of the *Annunciation and miraculously transported to Loreto by angels in 1295.

Lossky, Vladimir (1903–58), Russian lay theologian. Expelled from Russia in 1922, he spent most of his life in France. He was a leading exponent of Orthodox thought to the W. world and an opponent of the sophiological doctrines of S. *Bulgakov.

Los von Rom (Ger., 'free from Rome'). An anti-Roman Movement begun in Austria in 1897 and fostered by the Pan-German party, who aimed at the incorporation of an Austria, freed from the Pope, into Germany under the protection of the Protestant Hohenzollern Emperors. Though most of those who left the RC Church became nominally Protestant, the Movement was essentially anti-Christian.

Lou, Tseng-tsiang. See LU, CHENG-HSIANG.

Louis I (778–840), (**the Pious** or **le Débonnaire**). He was the third son of *Charlemagne, who in 781 appointed him king of Aquitaine and in 813 joint emperor. On his accession to the Empire in 814 (on Charlemagne's death), under the direction of St *Benedict of Aniane, he extended his earlier monastic reforms to the whole Frankish kingdom and promulgated major legislation on monasteries in 816–17. His later years were marred by disputes between his sons and their supporters.

Louis IX, St (1214–70), King of France from 1226. Having resolved in 1244 to go on a *Crusade, he sailed in 1248 and captured the Egyptian port of Damietta in 1249. In 1250, however, the crusaders were routed and Louis taken prisoner. He returned to France in 1254, imposed peace on Flanders, and signed treaties with Aragon and England. He embarked on a further crusade in 1270, but died of dysentery at Tunis.

A man of austere and prayerful life, Louis embodied the highest ideals of medieval kingship. He built the *Sainte-Chapelle in Paris for the *Crown of Thorns which he acquired from the Emp. Baldwin II in 1239. Feast day, 25 Aug.

Louis of Granada. See LUIS OF GRANADA.

Lourdes, a place of pilgrimage in France. In 1858 14-year-old *Bernadette Soubirous had visions here of the BVM, who told her that she was the Immaculate Conception. A spring appeared; miraculous healings were reported; and the faithful began to flock to Lourdes. Vast churches have been built and a medical bureau established to investigate the character of the cures. Optional feast of Our Lady of Lourdes, 11 Feb.

love. In Christian theology, the principle of God's action and man's response. In the OT the loving character of God was recognized, notably by *Hosea, but it is only in the NT that the doctrine that love constitutes the essential nature of God was developed. Christ joined the different OT commandments that man should love God and his neighbour, but extended it to cover love of enemies. This Christian love (called in the NT ἀγάπη; see AGAPE) is a matter of will rather than the emotions; its manifestations are described in 1 Cor. 13: 1–8.

Lovedale, a missionary educational centre in the Eastern Cape, *South Africa. In 1824 missionaries from an offshoot of the *LMS founded a mission station in the Tyume valley. In 1841 the Lovedale Institution was inaugurated there. Multiracial and co-educational, it became the leading institution for the training of Africans in the whole of Southern Africa until the Bantu Education Act of 1952 put an end to this work.

Low Churchmen. The group in the C of E which gives a relatively 'low' place to the claims of the episcopate, priesthood, and sacraments, and approximates in its beliefs to those of Protestant Nonconformists.

Low Mass. In the W. Church, the simplified form of Mass which until modern times was the form in most frequent use. In a Low Mass the celebrating priest had no ministers to assist him except a single server, and no part of the service was sung. The term no longer occurs in the RC *Ordo Missae,* which now requires that all Masses celebrated with the people should be community Masses with singing if possible.

Low Sunday. The first Sunday after *Easter.

Lowder, Charles Fuge (1820–80), *Anglo-Catholic priest. As curate of St Barnabas, Pimlico, he was one of the founders in 1855 of the *Society of the Holy Cross. In 1856 he joined the staff of St George's in the East,

where he took a leading part in the first regular mission work in East London. The advanced ceremonial led to riots, but the work expanded and Lowder built the church of St Peter's, London Docks, of which he became vicar. Feast day in CW, 9 Sept.

Loyola, St Ignatius. See IGNATIUS LOYOLA.

Lu, Cheng-hsiang (1871–1949), Chinese statesman and *Benedictine monk. The son of a Protestant catechist, he held various high government offices. He became a RC in 1911. In 1927 he entered the abbey of St-André near Bruges. His intention of returning to the East to establish a Benedictine Congregation in China was frustrated by ill-health. He saw Christianity as the fulfilment of Confucianism, finding St *John's doctrine of the *Logos paralleled by Lao-Tse's teaching of the Tao.

Lubac, Henri de (1896–1991), French *Jesuit theologian. From 1929 he taught at Lyons. A *peritus* at the Second *Vatican Council, he was made a cardinal in 1983. His vast literary output covers a range of subjects, including the Church, grace and the supernatural, the history of *exegesis in the Middle Ages, *Pico della Mirandola, and *Joachim of Fiore. He helped to create the intellectual climate that made the Second Vatican Council possible, largely by opening up the vast spiritual resources of the Catholic tradition which had been cramped by post-Tridentine 'baroque' theology. He was one of the founders of 'Sources Chrétiennes', a series of patristic and medieval texts, with French translation, now involving scholars from all over the world.

Lubbertus, Sibrandus (c.1555–1625), Dutch *Calvinist theologian. From 1585 he was professor of theology at the newly-founded university of Franeker. His prime concern was to counter RC teaching, especially that of R. *Bellarmine, against whom he directed three works. In defence of orthodox Calvinism he also opposed *Socinianism and *Arminianism. He took a prominent part in the Synod of *Dort (1618–9).

Lucar, Cyril (1570–1638), Patr. of *Alexandria (1601–20) and then of *Constantinople (from 1620). His presence at the Synod of *Brest-Litovsk in 1596 had turned him against the RC Church and the *Jesuits, and he became increasingly friendly towards the *Calvinists and the C of E. He presented the *Codex Alexandrinus to *Charles I in 1628. In 1629 a *Confessio Fidei*, with his signature, was published at Geneva; this reinterprets traditional Orthodox faith in Calvinistic terms. He was put to death on a charge of inciting the Cossacks against the Turkish government. His teaching was condemned by various later synods.

Lucian of Antioch, St (d. 312), theologian and martyr. A presbyter of *Antioch, he was an influential teacher, who had both *Arius and *Eusebius of Nicomedia among his pupils; his *subordinationist teaching seems to have been the immediate source of the Arian heresy. He revised the Greek text of the Bible (see LUCIANIC TEXT). Feast day in the E., 15 Oct.; in the W., 7 Jan.

Lucian of Samosata (*c.*115–*c.*200), pagan satirist. He describes the generosity with which Christians looked after Peregrinus, a convert who later apostatized, but scoffs at their simplicity. In another work he confirms the testimony of *Pliny that Christianity had made much progress in Bithynia-Pontus. The *Philopatris,* which purports to be his work, is much later.

Lucianic text. The text of the Greek Bible, as revised by *Lucian of Antioch. It soon became the standard text in Syria, Asia Minor, and *Constantinople, and its NT lies behind the '*Textus Receptus' and AV.

Lucifer (Lat., 'light-bearer'). In Is. 14: 12 (*Vulgate, followed by the AV) an epithet of the King of Babylon. Taking this verse in conjunction with Lk. 10: 18, St *Jerome used the name as a synonym for the devil.

Lucifer (d. 370/71), Bp. of Cagliari. An anti-*Arian theologian, at the first session of the Council of Milan (354) he vehemently opposed the proposal to condemn *Athanasius; his personal altercation with the Emp. Constantius that followed led to his banishment. After the accession of *Julian, he was released (362) and made his way to *Antioch, where by consecrating Paulinus bishop, he created a schism.

Lucina. Several pious women of this name figure in the early traditions of the Roman Church. One of them is said to have had the bodies of St *Peter and St *Paul removed from the *catacombs and that of St Paul

laid in her own property on the *Ostian Way.

Lucius. In legend, the first Christian king of Britain. According to an early form of the story, Lucius asked Pope Eleutherus (174–89) for Christian teachers to be sent to Britain, and he, together with many of his subjects, received Baptism at their hands. The story was later much embellished.

Lucy, St. According to tradition, she was a native of Syracuse who proclaimed her Christian faith by distributing her goods to the poor during the *Diocletianic persecution. She was denounced to the authorities by the man to whom she had been betrothed, and martyred in 303. Feast day, 13 Dec.

Ludlow, John Malcolm Forbes (1821–1911), founder of *Christian Socialism. Called to the bar in 1843, he wrote to F. D. *Maurice from Paris after the Revolution of 1848, insisting that 'the new socialism must be Christianized.' He was largely responsible for promoting the Industrial and Provident Societies Act of 1852, and he co-operated with Maurice in founding the Working Men's College. His influence did much to prevent in England the antagonism between the Church and Socialism which exists in most other countries.

Ludolf of Saxony (*c.*1300–78), also 'Ludolf the *Carthusian', spiritual writer. He entered the *Dominican Order and was a Master of Theology before he joined the Carthusians in 1340. His chief works are a 'Commentary on the Psalms' and his celebrated 'Vita Christi'. The latter is not a biography but a meditation on the life of Christ, with doctrinal, spiritual and moral instructions as well as prayers.

Lugo, John de (1583–1660), Spanish *Jesuit. In Rome he achieved fame as a theologian and was made a cardinal in 1643. He held that God gives light sufficient for salvation to every soul. In his Eucharistic teaching he emphasized the element of destruction as the distinctive characteristic of sacrificial worship, maintaining that in the act of Consecration, Christ's human nature is in some sense 'destroyed' by being changed into a lower state, of which the primary object of its existence is to be consumed as food.

Luis de León. See LEÓN, LUIS DE.

Luis of Granada (1504–88), Spanish spiritual writer. Luis de Sarria was professed as a *Dominican in Granada in 1525. In 1550/51 he was invited by the Cardinal Infante Henry to go to *Portugal, where he spent most of the rest of his life. He refused the archbishopric of Braga, recommending instead *Bartholomew of the Martyrs. His fame rests on his books of spiritual guidance, especially the *Libro de la oración y meditación* ('Book on Prayer and Meditation', 1554) and the *Guía de pecadores* ('Guide for Sinners', 1556–7). He aimed to give spiritual guidance for laymen as well as religious. He attributed great importance to the interior life, to mental as distinct from vocal prayer, and saw outward ceremonies as unimportant compared with the inner religious life.

Luke, St, Evangelist. According to tradition he was the author of Lk. and of *Acts. He was a physician (so Col. 4: 14), and it has been inferred from Col. 4: 11 that he was a Gentile. He apparently accompanied St *Paul on parts of his second and third missionary journeys (Acts 16: 10–17 and 20: 5–21: 18) and went with him to Rome. The *Anti-Marcionite Prologues record a tradition that he was unmarried, wrote his Gospel in Greece, and died at the age of 84. Feast day, 18 Oct. See also following entry.

Luke, Gospel of St. The third of the *Synoptic Gospels. Its attribution to St *Luke is widely accepted. It forms a single work with the *Acts of the Apostles. The prediction of the fall of Jerusalem in more precise terms than in Mt. and Mk. has suggested a date of composition after 70 AD, but this inference has been contested. Most modern scholars hold that the author drew on Mk. and the so-called '*Q'; some think that his second source was Mt. He was perhaps writing for readers outside the Christian circle; he certainly presents his material in the most favourable light from the point of view of the Roman authorities.

The narrative opens with an account of the births of *John the Baptist and of Christ, and then generally follows the same course as Mk. (and Mt.), though it differs at some points. Passages peculiar to Lk. stress the Lord's kindness and human understanding and His care for the outcast and the poor. There are many references to women not found in the other Gospels. Lk. assigns a more prominent place to prayer in the picture of Christ and stresses the activity of the Holy Spirit both in the events of the Lord's life and as the guide and inspiration of the Christian community. An important feature of Lk.–Acts is the insistence that the salvation offered by Christ's life, death, and teaching is addressed to all, and not to the Jews only.

Lull, St (d. 786), Bp. of Mainz. An Anglo-Saxon, he went to Germany and became associated with St *Boniface, who appointed him his successor in the see of Mainz; by a special concession from Pope *Zacharias, Lull was consecrated c.752 and took over Mainz on Boniface's death (754). He did not, however, receive the *pallium until c.781, after *Hadrian I had ordered an examination of him by three Frankish bishops. Feast day, 16 Oct.

Lull, Raymond. See LLULL, RAMON.

Luna, Pedro de. See BENEDICT XIII, ANTIPOPE.

Lund. Apart from one brief break, Lund was the seat of an archbishop from 1104 to 1536. The university dates from 1668. In the 19th cent. the theological faculty stood for a conservative and 'High Church' tradition in contrast to the liberalizing theology of *Uppsala. In 1952 the *Faith and Order Commission of the *World Council of Churches held a conference here which enunciated what became known as the 'Lund Principle': 'Should not our Churches ... act together in all matters, except those in which deep doctrinal differences of opinion compel them to act separately?'

Lupus, Servatus (c.805–62), classical scholar and Abbot of Ferrières from 840. He took an active part in ecclesiastical affairs and his letters are a primary source for the history of his time; they show a remarkable knowledge of classical and patristic authors. His *Liber de tribus questionibus* is a measured, but not unsympathetic, response to the doctrine of double *predestination proposed by *Gottschalk.

Luther, Martin (1483–1546), founder of the German *Reformation. In 1505 he entered a monastery of the *Augustinian Hermits and in 1508 was sent to teach moral philosophy at the newly-founded university of *Wittenberg. He became professor of biblical exegesis here in 1511, retaining this position until his death.

Initially Luther seems to have adopted a form of biblical exegesis and theology of *justification similar to that of *Nominalism, allowing man a definite, if limited, role in his own justification. In the years 1512–19 he came to believe that man is unable to respond to God without Divine grace, and that he can be justified only through faith, by the merits of Christ imputed to him: works and religious observance are irrelevant. This development was apparently linked with what is referred to as the 'Turmerlebnis' ('Tower Experience').

On 31 Oct. 1517 Luther's 95 theses were posted on the door of the castle church in Wittenberg. They were written largely in response to J. *Tetzel's preaching on the *indulgences granted by *Leo X for contributions towards the renovation of *St Peter's, Rome. Although stating little that was exceptional, they came to be viewed as a manifesto for reform. Luther was tried (in his absence) in Rome on charges of heresy and summoned before Card. *Cajetan at Augsburg. He fled to Wittenberg under the protection of the Elector *Frederick III of Saxony. At the *Leipzig Disputation in 1519 Luther confronted J. *Eck; here he denied the primacy of the Pope and the infallibility of General Councils. In 1520 he published three major treatises. The first, addressed to the German princes, laid the foundation for a programme of lay reform by rejecting the distinction between the 'spiritual' and 'temporal' orders and encouraged the princes to abolish tributes to Rome, the *celibacy of the clergy, and many other Catholic practices and institutions. The second criticized the subjection of the laity to the institution of the Church which Luther identified with the denial to the laity of Communion in both kinds, the doctrine of *transubstantiation, and the Sacrifice of the Mass. The third proclaimed the liberation of Christians from the obligation to perform good works. Meanwhile Luther was condemned in the bull 'Exsurge Domine' (12 Jun. 1520); he burnt the bull and was excommunicated in 1521. He was summoned before the Diet of *Worms, refused to recant, and was put under the ban of the Empire. He spent the next eight months at the *Wartburg, where he began his translation of the Bible into German (the NT was published in 1522). After his return to Wittenberg, he discarded his habit in 1524 and married in 1525.

Although his pamphlet advising the princes to wage war against the peasants who had risen in revolt (see PEASANTS' WAR) cost him some popular support, the religious and political situation continued to favour the spread of his views. The Diet of *Speyer (1526) established the right of the princes to organize national Churches. Differences among the Reformers were, however, becoming evident. At the Colloquy of *Marburg (1529) the division between Luther and U. *Zwingli over the nature of the Presence of Christ in the Eucharist proved unbridgeable: Luther argued that after the consecration the substances both of the Body and Blood of Christ and of the bread and wine coexist in union with each other (*consubstantiation), Zwingli that the Presence of Christ was purely symbolic. Though Luther approved of the comparatively conciliatory '*Augsburg Confession' (1530), his final years were darkened by controversy.

Apart from the treatises of 1520, Luther published a large number of works. They include the Small and Large *Catechisms (1529), biblical commentaries, and hymns, many of which are still in use. Some of his ideas were modified by the Lutheran Church after his death (see LUTHERANISM), but in the 20th cent. his '*theologia crucis' was reappropriated.

Lutheranism. A confessional movement within the W. Church tracing its origins to the theology of M. *Luther and the various formulae collected in the Book of *Concord (1580). These writings promote *justification by faith alone as the chief tenet of Lutheranism. Lutherans modified, but generally retained, traditional liturgical forms, placing equal emphasis on preaching and liturgy.

The first systematic presentation of Lutheran theology was P. *Melanchthon's Loci communes (1521). Lutheran 'orthodoxy', which dominated the 17th cent., was elaborated in a scholastic mould which gave it an intellectual cast. The emergence of *Pietism was a reaction against this intellectualism, as well as against confessional strife and the consolidation of State Churches after the *Thirty Years War. The

Pietists appealed to Luther's ideas on the supremacy of Scripture and the personal nature of faith.

In the 16th cent. Lutheranism spread through much of Germany, *Denmark, *Norway, *Sweden, *Finland, and E. Europe (e.g. in *Poland, *Hungary, and Latvia), though in Germany and E. Europe RCism and *Calvinism later reversed or modified the situation. In the 19th cent. the promotion of a union of Reformed (Calvinist) and Lutheran Churches in Prussia (1817), together with the challenge of biblical and historical criticism, stimulated a romantic rediscovery of Luther and a renewed confessionalism. Political events in the first half of the 20th cent. provoked a critique of Luther's 'two kingdoms' ethic, which distinguishes two ways, the spiritual and secular, in which God effects His will in the world. Thus Lutherans in Germany were accused of uncritical accommodation though many Lutherans joined the *Confessing Church. After 1945 Lutheranism in Germany struggled to maintain its identity as it participated in efforts to establish a combined Protestant Church. In 1948 most of the Lutheran regional Churches formed the United Evangelical Lutheran Church of Germany within the *Evangelical Church of Germany (q.v.). In Scandinavia Lutheranism is the officially recognized religion.

Lutheranism came to North America in the 17th cent., but remained small until after 1730 when German immigration surged. In 1742 H. M. *Muhlenburg was sent from Halle to Pittsburgh to organize the Lutheran Church; he established the first Lutheran synod in 1748. Successive waves of immigrants from varied backgrounds led to a proliferation of Lutheran bodies. The history of Lutheranism in North America is marked by struggles for confessional identity and increasingly for visible unity. By 1988 there were three main Lutheran bodies, all the results of amalgamation: the Evangelical Lutheran Church in America, formed in 1988; the Lutheran Church-Missouri Synod, formed in 1971; and the Evangelical Lutheran Church in Canada, formed in 1986.

European missionary efforts, dating from the 18th cent., joined in the 19th cent. by Lutherans from America, established Lutheranism in *India, the *South Pacific and other parts of Asia, in Africa, Latin America, and *Australia. The Lutheran World Convention, formed in 1923, in 1947 developed into the Lutheran World Federation. Lutherans have been involved in a number of ecumenical developments (see REUNION).

Lux Mundi (1889). A collection of essays by a group of Anglicans, edited by C. *Gore. Its acceptance of modern critical views of the OT gave offence to some *High Churchmen.

Luxeuil. The abbey, established *c.*590 by St *Columbanus, soon became the most important in France. Destroyed in 732, it was re-established under *Charlemagne and survived until 1790.

LXX. An abbreviation in common use for the *Septuagint.

lych-gate. The roofed gateway to a churchyard beneath which the coffin is set down to await the arrival of the officiating minister.

lying. A lie is a statement not in accordance with the mind of the speaker, made with the intention of deceiving. Both in the OT and NT the practice of lying is denounced. Theologians have argued whether a lie may ever be lawful, e.g. to save an innocent person's life. Many would admit that conflicts of duty may arise where a lie is the lesser evil, but such cases are exceptional.

Lyndwood, William (*c.*1375–1446), English canonist and from 1442 Bp. of *St Davids. He was closely associated with H. *Chichele in the proceedings against the *Lollards. His *Provinciale* (completed 1430) is a collection of provincial constitutions of the Abps. of *Canterbury from 1222 to 1416, with an extensive gloss and index (completed in 1433). It remains a standard authority on English ecclesiastical law and the text generally used for official purposes.

Lyne, Joseph Leycester. See IGNATIUS, FATHER.

Lyons, First Council of (1245). Reckoned by RCs the 13th *Oecumenical Council, it was convoked by *Innocent IV and attended by bishops mostly from France, Italy, and Spain. It deposed the Emp. *Frederick II. The objections of Frederick's representative, that the accused had not been cited to the Council and that it was irregular for the Pope to be both plaintiff and judge, were overruled.

Lyons, Second Council of (1274). Reckoned by RCs the 14th *Oecumenical Council, it was convoked by * Gregory X mainly to bring about union with the Greek Church. The desire of the Greeks for union arose chiefly out of their fears of Charles of Anjou, who was seeking to become Latin Emp. of Constantinople, and the legates of the Greek Emperor, Michael VIII Paleologus, were ready to submit to Rome. The union achieved ended in 1289. The Council suppressed some of the newly-founded mendicant orders but approved the *Franciscans and *Dominicans.

Mabillon, Jean (1632–1707), *Maurist scholar. He entered the *Benedictine abbey of Saint-Rémy at Reims in 1653, but in 1664 was sent to *Saint-Germain-des-Prés to help edit texts. Probably the most erudite of the Maurists, he produced some 20 folio works, including editions of St *Bernard and of various important liturgical documents.

Macarius of Alexandria, St (d. *c.*394), Egyptian hermit, often confused with St *Macarius of Egypt. He was ordained priest *c.*355 to serve the monks of Kellia. A monastic rule has been ascribed to him, probably erroneously. Feast day in the W., 2 Jan.; in the E., 19 Jan. or 1 May.

Macarius of Egypt, St (*c.*300–*c.*390), 'Macarius the Great'. A native of Egypt, when he was about 30 he founded a colony of monks in the desert of Scetis (Wadi-el-Natrun); it became one of the main centres of Egyptian monasticism. As a supporter of St *Athanasius, he suffered a brief period of exile under his *Arian successor. For the homilies ascribed to him, see MACARIUS/SIMEON. Feast day in the W., 15 Jan.; in the E., 19 Jan. or 9 Mar.

Macarius of Jerusalem, St (d. *c.*334), Bp. of *Jerusalem from *c.*311. He declined to support *Arius, and at the Council of *Nicaea (325) he opposed Arianism. Soon afterwards he was commissioned by *Constantine to build the Church of the *Holy Sepulchre in Jerusalem. Feast day, 10 May.

Macarius Magnes (4th–5th cent.), Christian apologist. His *Apocriticus* attacked the objections which a learned and clever *Neoplatonist (perhaps *Porphyry) had raised against the Christian faith.

Macarius of Moscow, St (1481/2–1563), Metropolitan of Moscow and All Russia from 1542. He embarked on a reform of both the *canon law and liturgical practice of the Russian Church. Feast day, 30 Dec.

Macarius of Moscow (1816–82), Metropolitan of Moscow from 1879. Michael Bulgakov took the name of Macarius when he became a monk. He held academic posts until he was appointed Bp. of Tambov in 1857. His two main works on theology reflect the official doctrinal position which had been imposed on the Russian Church to counteract Protestant influences. He also wrote a history of the Russian Church [to 1667] (12 vols., 1857–82).

Macarius/Simeon (4th–5th cent.), the author of the so-called homilies ascribed in most MSS to St *Macarius of Egypt but in some to a certain Simeon. Some are homilies proper; some are in the form of questions and answers; some are letters. The ascription to Macarius of Egypt is impossible; Syrian provenance is likely. The relation of the homilies to *Messalianism is disputed. Many passages of the Messalians' *Asceticon* (condemned by the Council of *Ephesus in 431) were apparently taken from the homilies, and the 'Simeon', whom some MSS claim as the author, may be Simeon of Mesopotamia, a leader of the Messalians mentioned by *Theodoret. There are, however, also differences, and there are parallels between the homilies and St *Basil of Caesarea and St *Gregory of Nyssa. The teaching of the homilies foreshadows features of *Hesychasm, and they were influential in the monastic spirituality of Eastern Orthodoxy.

Macaulay, Zachary (1768–1838), Anglican *Evangelical philanthropist. Working as a manager of an estate in Jamaica, he was disgusted at the conditions of the slaves. He returned to England in 1792 and made the cause of the abolition of the slave-trade and of *slavery his main concern. He was a member of the '*Clapham Sect'.

Maccabees. The celebrated Jewish family which fostered armed opposition to the introduction of pagan cult into the *Temple at Jerusalem by *Antiochus Epiphanes. The revolt began in 168 BC at Modin, where Mattathias, an aged priest, killed an apostate Jew who was about to offer a pagan sacrifice. The struggle was carried on by his five sons, three of whom, *Judas, Jonathan, and Simon, led the Jews in their struggle.

Maccabees, Books of. Four Books, so called after the hero of the first two, *Judas Maccabaeus, are found in some MSS in the *Septuagint. The first three are included in the *Canon of the E. Church, and the first two in that of the RC Church and the *Apocrypha of (non-RC) English Bibles. 1 Macc. is a history of the Jews from the accession of *Antiochus Epiphanes (175 BC) to the death of Simon Maccabaeus in 135 BC. It describes the desecration of the *Temple and the resistance of Mattathias and his sons. Written probably c.100 BC, it is a primary source for the period. 2 Macc. covers the history of the Maccabaen wars from 176 to 161 BC, ending with Judas Maccabaeus' victory over Nicanor. It is an epitome of a larger work and appears to have been written before 63 BC. 3 Macc. describes the attempt of Ptolemy IV to enter the Sanctuary of the Temple (217 BC), his frustration, and his attempt to take vengeance on the Jews of Egypt. Written between 100 BC and 70 AD, it is probably thus named on the analogy of the events described with those of the Maccabaean period. 4 Macc. is a philosophical treatise on the supremacy of devout reason over the passions, illustrated by examples from the history of the Maccabees.

The Books contain important teaching on *immortality (2 Macc. 7: 9 and 23 and 4 Macc.) and on prayers for the *dead (2 Macc. 12: 43–5).

Maccabees, Feast of the Holy. A feast formerly kept in the W. Church (and still observed in the E.) on 1 Aug. to commemorate the seven brothers whose deaths are described in 2 Macc. 7.

Macedonius (d. c.362), Bp. of *Constantinople from c.342. He supported the *Semiarian cause and defended his position at the Council of *Seleucia in 359. In 360 he was deposed by the *Arian Council of Constantinople. From the end of the 4th cent. he has been regarded as the founder of the '*Pneumatomachi', but it is doubtful how far this association is correct.

Machutus or **Malo, St** (d. c.640), Breton saint. According to tradition, he was trained in the monastic life by St *Brendan, settled opposite the present town of St-Malo, and led an ascetic life. Feast day, 15 Nov.

Mackay, Alexander Murdoch (1849–90), *CMS missionary. He reached *Uganda in 1878. His printing of parts of Scripture in Swahili interested King Mtesa, and he was allowed to carry on missionary work. He soon met with opposition from both RCs and Muslims, and in 1887 he was expelled. He reduced the vernacular of Uganda to writing and translated the Bible into it.

Mackintosh, Hugh Ross (1870–1936), Scottish theologian. In 1904 he was appointed professor of systematic theology at New College, Edinburgh. He sympathized with the Liberal Movement in German Protestant theology and tried to make German teaching better known in Britain.

Mackonochie, Alexander Heriot (1825–87), *Anglo-Catholic leader. By 1862, when he was put in charge of St Alban's, Holborn, he was recognized as an advanced 'ritualist', and from 1867 he was constantly prosecuted by the *Church Association for his ceremonial practices.

Maclaren, Alexander (1826–1910), *Baptist preacher and expositor. He was President of the Baptist Union (1875 and 1901), and he presided over the first Congress of the Baptist World Alliance in 1905.

MacLeod, George Fielden (1895–1991),

founder of the *Iona community. In 1926 he was appointed minister at the fashionable St Cuthbert's Church in Edinburgh, but, despite his popularity there, he accepted an invitation to become minister of Govan Old Parish Church in the slums of Glasgow in 1930. During the 1930s he became a pacifist and a socialist, and an outstanding radio preacher. In 1938 he founded the Iona Community (q.v.). He exercised wide influence and received many honours, being elevated to the House of Lords in 1967.

Macleod, Norman (1812–72), Scottish minister. He was a favourite of Queen Victoria and one of the most prominent and respected parochial ministers of Scotland in the 19th cent.

Macrina, St (c.327–80), sister of St *Basil the Great and of St *Gregory of Nyssa. She is known as 'Macrina the Younger' to distinguish her from 'Macrina the Elder', her paternal grandmother. She established a flourishing religious community on the family estate in Pontus. Feast day, 19 July.

Madauran Martyrs (2nd cent.), the first reputed Christian martyrs in Africa. The four martyrs are supposed to have suffered at Madaura in 180. The earliest reference comes from the 4th cent.

Madeba Map. A map of Palestine and the Near East in coloured mosaics, uncovered in 1896 in the church of Madeba to the east of the *Dead Sea. It almost certainly dates from the 6th cent.

Madonna (Ital., 'My Lady'). A designation of the BVM, used especially with reference to statues and pictures of her.

Maffei, Francesco Scipio (1675–1755), historian. His main historical work centred on his native city of *Verona. In 1712 he rediscovered the *Theodosian Collection (q.v.).

Magdalene, St Mary. See MARY MAGDALENE, ST.

Magdalens. In reference to St *Mary Magdalene, the word has often been applied to reformed prostitutes. In the Middle Ages it was widely adopted as a title by religious communities consisting of penitent women to whom others of blameless life attached themselves.

Magi (Gk. for 'sages' or 'wise men'). The first Gentiles to worship Christ, according to Mt. 2: 1–12. Guided by a star, they came from the East to *Bethlehem with gifts of gold, frankincense, and myrrh. The idea that they were kings appears first in Christian tradition in *Tertullian; *Origen is the first to give their number as three. What are claimed as their relics are enshrined in *Cologne Cathedral. See also EPIPHANY.

Magnificat. The song of praise (so called from the opening word of the Latin text) which the BVM sang when her cousin *Elizabeth greeted her as the mother of the Lord (Lk. 1: 39–55). From an early date it has been the canticle of *Vespers in the W. Church; it was included in *Evensong in the BCP and in modern Anglican liturgies retains its place, though sometimes not on every day of the week. In the E. Church it forms part of the Morning Office. Some scholars argue that Lk. originally attributed it to Elizabeth and not to the BVM.

Magnus, St. (1) Martyr. The supposed existence of a saint of this name occurring in the Roman *martyrology for 19 Aug. seems to have been due to a blunder. (2) of Füssen (d. c.770), Apostle of the Allgäu, Bavaria. His mission was centred on Füssen, where he began to exploit the deposits of iron. Feast day, 6 Sept. (3) (d. 1116), son of Earl Erlin, ruler of the Orkneys. He was captured by the Norwegian king, escaped to Scotland, and later returned to the Orkneys, where he shared the government with his cousin, who treacherously killed him. Feast day, 16 Apr.

Maid of Kent; Maid of Orléans. See BARTON, ELIZABETH; JOAN OF ARC, ST.

Maier, Johannes. See ECK, JOHANN.

Maimonides, Moses (1135–1204), Jewish philosopher, known to Jewish writers as 'Rambam'. A native of Córdoba, he finally settled at Fostat (Old Cairo), where he became head of the Jewish community. He wrote a commentary on the *Mishnah and an extensive *Talmudic code ('Mishneh Torah'). His 'Guide for the Perplexed' (written in Arabic), sought to reconcile the data of the Jewish revelation with the findings of human reason proposed by *Aristotle; it influenced Christian thought in the Middle Ages.

Maistre, Joseph de. See DE MAISTRE, JOSEPH.

Major (or Maier), Georg (1502–74), *Lutheran theologian. He studied under M. *Luther and P. *Melanchthon at *Wittenberg and from 1537 spent most of his life there. He was involved in producing the Wittenberg edition of Luther's works. He is famous chiefly as the protagonist of the 'Majoristic Controversy'. In 1552 he asserted that good works were necessary for salvation. N. von *Amsdorf and other *Gnesio-Lutherans denounced this statement as incompatible with the doctrine of *justification by faith alone. Major then qualified his views, claiming that good works were only a token of justification.

Major Orders. The higher grades of the Christian ministry, in contradistinction from the *Minor Orders (q.v.). The Major Orders are now usually reckoned as those of *bishops, *priests, and *deacons. In the past the *subdiaconate was sometimes accounted a Major Order, the other two then being the diaconate and priesthood (including the episcopate).

Malabar Christians. A title applied in a wider sense to all the Christian communities of the Syrian rite living in Kerala in SW *India (also known as 'Thomas Christians'), and in a narrower sense to the community in communion with Rome (the 'Syro-Malabar Church'). All claim that their Church was founded by St *Thomas the Apostle, but there is no certain evidence that there were Christians in India earlier than the 6th cent. They probably came originally from E. Syria. At the Synod of *Diamper in 1599 they renounced *Nestorius and allied themselves with the RC Church. Though there was a breach with the W. in 1653, about two-thirds of them returned to communion with Rome in 1662. The rest joined the *Syrian Orthodox. At the end of the 19th cent. a reforming group of the Syrian Orthodox constituted themselves the 'Mar Thoma' Church; this has links with the Church of *South India. Another section sought union with Rome and in 1930 the *Malankarese Church came into being. Within the Syrian Orthodox Church in India there are two *Catholicoi, one recognizing the Patriarch in Damascus, the other independent. Since 1907 there has also been a small community again subject to the Patriarch of the *Church of the East.

Malachi, Book of. *Minor Prophet. The author emphasizes the love of God for His people, which is reciprocated only with insincere worship and unworthy practices by the priests, and he announces that a day of judgement will surely come. The language and thought of the Book are of the age following the Exile (i.e. after 538 BC). The prophecy about the messenger who shall prepare the way of the Lord (3: 1) is applied to *John the Baptist (Mk. 1: 2), while the reference to the 'pure offering' in 1: 11 is taken in Christian tradition as a prophecy of the *Eucharist.

Malachy, St (1094–1148), Abp. of *Armagh and an advocate for reform in the Irish Church. When he was nominated Abp. of Armagh in 1129, he was opposed by a rival candidate and not installed until 1134; he resigned in 1137. In 1139 he went to Rome to seek the *pallium for the two metropolitans in Ireland. En route, he met St *Bernard, his future biographer; with four monks from *Clairvaux, he introduced the *Cistercian Order into Ireland. Feast day, 3 Nov.

Malachy, Prophecies of. The so-called Prophecies of Malachy have no connection with St *Malachy apart from their erroneous attribution to him. Contained in a document apparently composed in 1590, they purport to give a motto for every Pope from Celestine II (1143–4) to 'Peter II' at the end of the world.

Malalas, John. See JOHN MALALAS.

Malankarese Church. The group of *Malabar Christians who entered into communion with Rome in 1930.

Malawi, Christianity in. D. *Livingstone reached Lake Malawi in 1859 and the first expedition of the *UMCA arrived in 1861. The *Free Church of Scotland and the Established Church of *Scotland sent out co-operating missions in 1875 and 1876; they were joined by the Cape Synod of the Dutch Reformed Church in 1888. These missions united to form the Church of Central Africa Presbyterian in 1924. The *White Fathers arrived in 1889, to be aided by the *Marists in building up the RC Church in Malawi. The most significant of the African

Independent Churches is the Providence Industrial Mission founded by the nationalist leader John Chilembwe (d. 1915). Of the population of 10 million in 1994, c.7 million were Christian.

Malchion (3rd cent.), *Antiochene presbyter. He was chosen to interrogate *Paul of Samosata at the Council of Antioch (c.270).

Maldonado, Juan (1533–83), Spanish theologian. After becoming a *Jesuit in 1562, he taught in Paris. In 1574 the *Sorbonne attacked his teaching as heretical; though vindicated, he withdrew from Paris. His commentaries on the Gospels (published 1596–7) are held in high repute.

Malebranche, Nicolas (1638–1715), French philosopher. He became an *Oratorian in 1660. His most important works are *Recherche de la vérité* (1674) and *Traité de la nature et de la grâce* (1680). He denied that any action of matter upon mind was possible, and explained sensation as the effect of a new creative act in the mental order to correspond with things in the physical creation ('*Occasionalism').

Malines Conversations. The meetings of a group of Anglican and RC theologians held at Malines in Belgium between 1921 and 1925 under the presidency of Card. D. J. *Mercier. Though there was considerable agreement, the Conversations issued in no tangible result.

Malo, St. See MACHUTUS, ST.

Malta, Knights of. See HOSPITALLERS.

Maltese Cross. A black cross of eight points on a white ground, so named because it was adopted by the Knights of Malta, i.e. the *Hospitallers.

Malvern Conference. The Anglican Conference which met at Malvern in 1941, under the presidency of Abp. W. *Temple, to consider in the light of the Christian faith the crisis confronting civilization. Its 'findings' were especially concerned with the relation of the Church to economic life.

Mamertine Prison. A building in Rome, consisting of two cells in which, according to tradition, St *Peter was imprisoned and converted his gaolers.

Mamertus, St (d. c.475), Bp. of Vienne (the metropolitan see of Gaul) by 463. About 470 he introduced the 'litanies' on the days before *Ascension Day as an act of intercession against earthquakes and other perils, a practice which led later to the institution of the *Rogation Days. Feast day, 11 May.

Man, Isle of. See SODOR AND MAN.

Manasses, Prayer of. This Book of the *Apocrypha consists of a penitential prayer put into the mouth of Manasseh, King of Judah. Its date is uncertain, but it is attested by the 3rd cent. AD. In the E. Church it is recited in *Compline during Lent and on the eves of certain great feasts.

Mandaeans. A *Gnostic sect which survives in S. Iraq and SW Iran. Their origins may go back to a group practising repeated baptisms, living to the east of the R. *Jordan in the 1st and 2nd cent. AD. They hold that man's soul, unwillingly imprisoned in the body and persecuted by demons, will be freed by the redeemer, Manda de Hayyê, the personified 'Knowledge of Life', who was once himself on earth and defeated the powers of darkness. Although Mandaean texts are hostile to Judaism and Christianity, many elements appear to be derived from these sources.

Mande, Hendrik (c.1360–1431), one of the *Brethren of the Common Life. In 1395 he entered the monastery at *Windesheim, where he wrote (in Flemish) several mystical treatises which embodied and developed J. van *Ruysbroeck's ideas.

mandyas. A form of cloak worn by monks and bishops in the E. Church.

Mani (or Manes) and Manichaeism. There are contradictions among the sources, but it appears that Mani (c.216–76) was born near Seleucia-Ctesiphon, the capital of the Persian Empire, and began teaching in 240. Opposition from the *Zoroastrians forced him into exile. He returned in 242, was at first supported and then attacked by Sapor I, and was finally put to death by being flayed alive.

Mani's system was a radical offshoot of the *Gnostic traditions of E. Persia. It was based on a supposed primeval conflict between light and darkness. It taught that the object of the practice of religion was to release the particles of light which Satan had stolen from the world of Light and imprisoned in man's brain, and that Jesus,

Buddha, the Prophets, and Mani had been sent to help in this task. To achieve this release, severe asceticism was practised. Within the sect there was hierarchy of grades professing different standards of austerity: the 'Elect' were supported by the 'Hearers' in their missionary endeavours and in an otherworldly state of perfection.

The sect spread rapidly. It appears to have been established in Egypt before the end of the 3rd cent. and at Rome early in the 4th. In the later 4th cent. Manichaeans were numerous in Africa and for a time included St *Augustine. It is disputed how far Manichaeism influenced the *Albigensians, *Bogomils, and *Paulicians, but it is clear that it survived in Chinese Turkestan to the 10th cent.

maniple. A thin strip of silk formerly worn over the left arm by ministers at Mass.

manna. The food miraculously provided for the *Israelites on their journey from Egypt to the *Holy Land (Exod. 16). It is regarded as a *type of the Christian *Eucharist.

Manners-Sutton, Charles (1755–1828), Abp. of *Canterbury from 1805. He opposed RC emancipation, but favoured concessions to dissenters. He supported many initiatives of the *Hackney Phalanx, presiding over the formation of the *National Society in 1811 and using his influence to secure the foundation of an Anglican episcopate in *India.

Manning, Henry Edward (1809–1892), Abp. of *Westminster. He was ordained in the C of E and in 1841 became Archdeacon of *Chichester. Beginning as an *Evangelical, he gradually swung round to the *Tractarian side and was regarded as a leader of the *Oxford Movement. The *Gorham Judgement destroyed his faith in Anglicanism and in 1851 he became a RC. He was (re-)ordained priest by N. P. S. *Wiseman and founded the Oblates of St *Charles Borromeo, mainly to undertake mission work for the poor of London. In 1865 he succeeded Wiseman as Abp. of Westminster. At the First *Vatican Council he supported the definition of Papal *Infallibility. In 1875 he was made a *cardinal. He was prominent in social work and mediated in the London Dock Strike of 1889.

manse. (1) The dwelling house of a non-conformist minister. (2) In Scotland, also the dwelling house of a minister of the Church of Scotland. (3) In English ecclesiastical law, the parsonage house and *glebe belonging to a benefice, taken together.

Mansel, Henry Longueville (1820–71), Dean of *St Paul's from 1868. In his Bampton Lectures of 1858 on *The Limits of Religious Thought*, he argued that the limitations of the human intellect meant that the truths of religion are not speculative but regulative. God is in Himself unknowable and human knowledge of the nature of God is acquired from supernatural revelation alone. His contentions provoked much criticism.

Mansi, Giovanni Domenico (1692–1769), canonist and, from 1765, Abp. of Lucca. His only considerable original work was his *Tractatus de Casibus et Censuris Reservatis* (1724), but he also issued numerous publications in which his own part usually did not go beyond annotations: the most celebrated was his edition of the Councils.

Mant, Richard (1776–1848), Bp. of Down and Connor from 1823 (with Dromore from 1842). Besides theological works, he wrote some well-known hymns, including 'Bright the vision that delighted'.

Mantegna, Andrea (1431–1506), Italian painter. His series of fresco paintings representing the *Histories of St James and St Christopher* (1448–57) in the church of the Eremitani at Padua (almost completely destroyed in 1944) established his reputation. He is famous for his altar-pieces; in the earlier ones saints are grouped side-by-side; his later ones show originality of composition. The celebrated *Dead Christ* (in the Brera in Milan) is remarkable for its virtuosity in foreshortening the body.

mantelletta. A short cloak reaching to the knees worn by certain dignitaries in the RC Church.

mantellone. A purple cloak of silk or wool until 1969 worn by certain lesser prelates of the Papal court.

mantum. A red cloak of the Pope which from the 11th to the 14th cents. played a part in Papal elections, since investiture with it expressed the transference to the Pope of his right to govern the Church.

Manual Acts. The rubrics of the 1662 BCP require the celebrant at the Holy Communion to take the *paten into his hands, to break the bread, lay his hand upon it, and to perform corresponding acts at the consecration of the wine. In the *Ridsdale case (1875–7) the *Judicial Committee of the Privy Council held that the celebrant must not intentionally stand so as to prevent the congregation from seeing the manual acts.

Manuale (Lat., 'a book of handy size'). In the Middle Ages the usual name for the book containing the forms prescribed for a priest to administer the sacraments.

manuscripts of the Bible. Writing in the ancient world was usually either on papyrus (made from the stems of the papyrus plant; see PAPYROLOGY) or on specially prepared skins of animals ('parchment' or 'vellum'). For lengthy items, including most Books of the Bible, a number of sheets would be joined together to form either a roll or a 'codex' (in which the sheets were first folded in quires and then sewn together as in a modern book).

The earliest part of the OT about the writing of which we have definite information is the Book of *Jeremiah; this is said to have been written on a roll (Jer. 36: 2). It seems that the roll was the normal form of book used by Jews at the time (cf. Ezek. 2: 9) and it continued so until well into Christian times. The evidence of the *Dead Sea Scrolls shows that both parchment and papyrus were used, but that parchment was preferred, particularly for biblical Books. The Jews eventually adopted the codex for private use, but for reading in synagogue they have remained faithful to the parchment roll to the present day.

The first Greek translations of the OT Books are likely to have been written on papyrus, since they seem to have been made in Egypt. The only certain survivals from the pre-Christian era are fragments of two papyrus rolls, both containing parts of Deut. and both dated 2nd–1st cent. BC. The many Christian biblical fragments datable in the 2nd and 3rd cents. AD, whether OT or NT Books, are all from codices. During the 4th cent. there was a tendency for parchment to replace papyrus, at least for MSS written for public reading in church. Such MSS might contain the whole Bible or only part of it; their text is arranged in columns (2, 3 or even 4 to a page); and they were written in the formal *uncial script, roughly equivalent to our capitals. About the 9th cent. a new style of script was introduced (known as 'minuscule'; see CURSIVE SCRIPT); the use of this script made it possible to accommodate the whole of the NT in one convenient volume.

The oldest known Latin biblical MS is the 4th-cent. Codex Vercellensis, a sumptuous volume written in uncial with silver ink on purple parchment, containing an almost complete *Old Latin text of the Gospels. The most ancient complete Bible is the *Codex Amiatinus, written in Northumbria at the end of the 7th cent. As in the East, minuscule types of script were developed, and in the 13th cent. the use of very thin parchment and small writing made it possible to accommodate the whole Bible within single conveniently sized volumes which are termed 'pocket Bibles'.

There are also biblical MSS in *Syriac (many dating from the 5th cent.), *Coptic (dating from as early as the 4th cent.), and other languages. The 'bilingual' MSS are of three kinds: the secondary text is written immediately above the primary text, or the two texts are copied in parallel columns on the same page, or they are arranged to face each other on opposite pages.

For the use of biblical MSS in preparing a text, see TEXTUAL CRITICISM.

maranatha. An Aramaic word, meaning either 'The Lord has come' or more probably 'O Lord, come'.

Marbeck, John. See MERBECKE, JOHN.

Marburg, Colloquy of (1529). A meeting convened by *Philip, Landgraf of Hesse, with a view to uniting the *Lutherans and Zwinglians. It is usually thought that U. *Zwingli, J. *Oecolampadius, and M. *Bucer agreed with M. *Luther and P. *Melanchthon on 14 of the 15 'Marburg Articles' and that the Conference failed only because of Zwingli's refusal to accept the Lutheran doctrine of the *Eucharist, but some historians think that the agreement was only apparent.

Marburg, University of. Founded by *Philip, Landgraf of Hesse, in 1527, it was the first Protestant university established in Europe. Its theological faculty has been famous, especially since the mid-19th cent.

Marca, Pierre de (1594–1662), French canonist. His *De Concordia Sacerdotii et Imperii* (1641) was a defence of *Gallican doctrines; it was put on the *Index. In 1662 Marca was appointed Abp. of *Paris.

Marcan hypothesis, the. The theory that St *Mark's is the earliest of the four Gospels and that in its presentation of the life of Christ the facts are set down with a minimum of disarrangement, interpretation, and embellishment.

Marcellina, St (c.330–c.398), the sister of St *Ambrose. She was consecrated a virgin by Pope *Liberius in 353. Feast day, 17 July.

Marcellus (d. c.374), Bp. of Ancyra and a supporter of the *Homoousion at the Council of *Nicaea. He was deposed from his see in 336, restored in 337, and again expelled c.339. He taught that in the Unity of the Godhead the Son and the Spirit emerged as independent entities only for the purposes of Creation and Redemption; when the redemptive work is achieved they will be resumed into the Divine Unity. The clause in the *Nicene Creed, 'whose kingdom shall have no end', was inserted to combat his teaching.

Marcian (396–457), E. Emperor from 450. He repressed *Monophysitism, personally attending the sixth session of the Council of *Chalcedon (451).

Marcian the Monk (probably late 4th cent.), ascetical writer. He has long been known as the author of three short extracts in the *Florilegium Edessenum*, but in modern times J. Lebon has attributed to him nine other works and identified him with the Marcian who lived in the desert of Chalcis and died c.385. Others have attributed some or all these works to Marcian of Bethlehem who died in 492.

Marcion (d. c.160), heretic. A native of Sinope in Pontus, he made his way to Rome c.140, and attached himself to the local Church; he was excommunicated in 144. He organized his followers in compact communities over a large part of the Empire. By the end of the 3rd cent. most of them had been absorbed in *Manichaeism.

Marcion's central thesis was that the Christian Gospel was wholly a Gospel of Love to the exclusion of Law. He consequently rejected the OT, holding that the Creator God depicted therein had nothing in common with the God of Love revealed by Jesus. This contrast of law and grace, he held, was fully understood only by St *Paul, the Twelve Apostles and the Evangelists being largely blinded to the truth by remnants of Jewish influence. Hence for Marcion the only Canonical Scriptures were ten of the Epistles of St Paul (he either rejected or did not know the *Pastorals) and an edited form of St *Luke's Gospel. His Christology was *Docetic. See also the following entry.

Marcionite Prologues. A set of short introductory prologues to each of the Pauline Epistles which are found in many MSS of the *Vulgate. Most of them probably originated in *Marcionite circles.

Marcosians, the followers of the *Gnostic Marcus, a disciple of *Valentinus. They apparently flourished in the Rhône valley.

Marcus Aurelius (121–80), Roman Emperor from 161. He was a professed *Stoic, though influenced by other philosophies. Under him Christians suffered sporadic *persecution. Some scholars see dark allusions to them in his *Meditations*, and one text (11.3) specifically imputes to them a spirit of refractory opposition; it may be a gloss and no clear view of his opinions on Christianity can be extracted from his writing. A number of 'Apologies' were addressed to him by Christian writers.

Maredsous. The seat of a Belgian *Benedictine abbey, founded in 1872. It is a noted centre of scholarship.

Margaret, St, of Antioch (in Pisidia), also known as St Marina. She is supposed to have been a martyr of the *Diocletianic persecution, but nothing about her is certainly known. She is invoked especially by women in childbirth. Feast day in the W., 20 July; in the E., 17 July.

Margaret, 'The Lady' (1443–1509), Margaret Beaufort, Countess of Richmond and Derby. The mother of King Henry VII, she used her position for religious and educational interests. She founded readerships at Oxford and Cambridge and refounded God's House as Christ's College, Cambridge. Her other foundation, St John's

College, Cambridge, was completed after her death.

Margaret Clitherow, St. See CLITHEROW, ST MARGARET.

Margaret Mary Alacoque, St (1647–90), chief founder of the devotion to the *Sacred Heart (q.v.). In 1671 she entered the *Visitandine Convent at Paray-le-Monial in central France. Between 1673 and 1675 she received several revelations of the Sacred Heart: the chief features of the devotion were to be Holy Communion on the *First Friday of each month, the Holy Hour on Thursdays, and the Feast of the Sacred Heart. Her visions at first were treated as delusions. Feast day, 16 (formerly 17) Oct.

Margaret of Scotland, St (c.1046–93), wife of Malcolm III of Scotland, whom she married in 1070. At her instigation many abuses were reformed, and synods were held to regulate the Lenten fast and Easter Communion. She had great personal piety. Feast day (since 1969), 16 Nov. (formerly 10 and then 8 July).

Marheineke, Philipp Konrad (1780–1846), Protestant theologian. From 1811 he was a professor at Berlin. He sought to invoke the philosophy of G. W. F. *Hegel in support of the Christian faith; the Protestant and Catholic Confessions were to be united in a higher Hegelian synthesis.

Maria Laach. A *Benedictine abbey, c.15 miles NW of Koblenz, founded in 1093. It was suppressed in 1802. The *Jesuits, who had acquired the property in 1862/3, in 1892 sold it to the Benedictines of *Beuron. Maria Laach became a centre of liturgical study and played an influential part in the *Liturgical Movement.

Mariana, Juan (1536–1624), *Spanish *Jesuit. His book *De Rege et Regis Institutione* (1559), justifying *tyrannicide, encouraged the belief that the Jesuits were responsible for the assassination of *Henry IV of France and the *Gunpowder Plot. He also wrote on the history of Spain.

Marianists. The 'Society of Mary' of Bordeaux. This congregation of RC priests and laymen was founded in 1817 by Guillaume-Joseph Chaminade to combat religious indifference. Its members devote themselves mainly to educational work.

Mariavites. A Polish sect, founded in 1906 by J. Kowalski, a priest of Warsaw, and Felicja Kozłowska, a *Tertiary sister, on their excommunication from the RC Church. In 1909 Kowalski was consecrated bishop by the *Old Catholic Bp. of Utrecht, but after a few years of prosperity the sect declined and in 1924 the Old Catholics severed communion with them.

Mariolatry. The erroneous ascription of Divine honours to the BVM. The word is sometimes used abusively by Protestants of what they consider the excessive devotion to the BVM in the RC Church.

Mariology. The systematic study of the person of the BVM and her place in the economy of the *Incarnation.

Marists. The 'Society of Mary' founded at Lyons in 1816 by the Ven. Jean Claude Marie Colin. The congregation comprises priests and lay brothers whose main activities are educational and missionary work. The W. Pacific was allotted to them as their special mission field in 1836.

Maritain, Jacques (1882–1973), French *Thomist philosopher. He became a RC in 1906 and held professorial chairs at Paris, Toronto, and Princeton. In 1970 he became a *Little Brother. In numerous writings he sought to apply the classical doctrines of Thomism to metaphysics and theoretical philosophy, moral, social, and political philosophy, the philosophy of education, history, and culture, and to art and poetry.

Marius Mercator (early 5th cent.), a Latin writer, formerly regarded as of African origin, but more probably born in Italy. He wrote against both the *Nestorians and the *Pelagians, and his works are one of the main sources of our knowledge of Nestorius' doctrines.

Marius Victorinus. See VICTORINUS AFER.

Mark, St, Evangelist. *Papias asserts that Mark, having become the interpreter of St *Peter, set down everything he remembered of the words and actions of the Lord, and Mark is associated with Peter in 1 Pet. 5: 13. He has traditionally (but perhaps unjustifiably) been identified with John Mark, the cousin of St *Barnabas, who set out with Barnabas and St *Paul on their first missionary journey, but turned back;

he later accompanied Barnabas on a mission to *Cyprus and was in Rome with Paul. According to *Eusebius Mark went to *Alexandria and was its first bishop; later tradition associated him with *Venice. Feast day, 25 Apr.

Mark, Gospel of St. *Papias states that the Gospel was written by St *Mark, who drew his information from St *Peter. Later tradition connects the Gospel with Rome. It may have been written by John Mark (see the previous entry); there is no obvious reason why it should have been wrongly attributed to so unimportant a figure, but 'Mark' is a common name. Written in 'koine' or common *Greek, Mk. is the least polished of the Gospels. It was probably written soon after the death of Peter (commonly put in AD 64) and during the siege of *Jerusalem, or perhaps soon after AD 70.

Mk. makes it clear that Jesus is *Messiah and Son of God (1: 1). This truth, known to demons, is disclosed only gradually. After an account of the preaching of St *John the Baptist, the *Baptism and *Temptation of Christ, and His ministry of healing and preaching, a turning-point occurs at 8: 27 ff. with the confession of Peter that Jesus is the Messiah. From this point Mk. describes the burden of the Lord's teaching as the need for the '*Son of Man' to suffer, die, and rise from the dead. The story of the Passion describes the death of Christ as a fulfilment of OT prophecy and as a sacrifice inaugurating the new covenant. The Crucifixion is followed by the Resurrection, but the Gospel ends abruptly at 16: 8. 16: 9–20 is one of two early supplements.

See also MARCAN HYPOTHESIS, MESSIANIC SECRET, and SYNOPTIC PROBLEM.

Mark, Liturgy of St. The traditional Greek Eucharistic Liturgy of the Church of *Alexandria, formerly used by the Egyptian *Melchites. Behind the various forms lies a primitive local Egyptian text in which the great intercessory prayer stood before the *Sanctus and there was no *Benedictus at the end of the Sanctus. Forms in Coptic and Ethiopic are still used in the *Coptic and *Ethiopian Churches.

Mark, Secret Gospel of. A letter ascribed to *Clement of Alexandria, discovered in 1958, warned of a 'secret Gospel of Mark' and quoted from it. The contention that the

quotations go back to an original Aramaic version of Mk., which served as a source for Mk. and Jn., has not found favour.

Mark the Hermit (date disputed; probably early 5th or possibly 6th cent.), ascetical writer. He may have been abbot of a community near Ancyra; later he was a hermit, possibly in Palestine or in Egypt. His writings are mainly practical. His attack on human merit commended him to older Protestant theologians. The treatise *On Fasting*, formerly ascribed to him, is now attributed to *Marcian the Monk.

Marmion, Bl Columba (1858–1923), Abbot of *Maredsous from 1909. An Irishman by birth, he was a gifted spiritual writer and director. His main works originated in series of spiritual addresses.

Marnix, Philipp van (1540–98), Baron de Sainte-Aldegonde, Dutch *Calvinist theologian and statesman. Between 1562 and 1569 he won fame by his Protestant and nationalist writings, of which the most celebrated was the satirical *De biënkorf der heilige roomsche kerche* (1569; Eng. tr., 1579). About 1566–7 he took up arms as an anti-Spanish leader and became a close friend of William the Silent. After 1585 he devoted himself to literary activity, most notably to his Dutch translation of the Psalms.

Maronites. A *Uniat community of Syrian origin, the greater part of whom live in Lebanon. They claim to trace their origin to St Maro, a friend of St *Chrysostom (d. 407), but their existence as a separate community originated in the *Monothelite controversy of the 7th and 8th cent., when they rejected the teaching of the Third Council of *Constantinople that in the Person of Christ there are two wills, one human and the other Divine. Since 1182 they have been in formal communion with the RC Church.

Marot, Clément (c.1497–1544), French poet and translator. His French verse paraphrase of 49 Psalms appeared between 1538 and 1542; it was received with acclaim by the Protestant community and used as a basis by T. *Beza who in 1562 produced the first vernacular Psalter in French.

Marprelate Tracts. A series of violent and often scurrilous *Puritan tracts attacking *episcopacy, issued under the pseudonym of Martin Marprelate in 1588 and 1589.

Marriage. See MATRIMONY.

marriage licences. Licences to dispense with the need for *banns have been granted by bishops since the 14th cent.; the power to issue such licences was confirmed to them by Act of Parliament in 1534. Licences are now normally granted by *surrogates appointed by the diocesan *chancellor. Before a licence is granted one of the parties has to swear that he knows of no impediment to the marriage and that one of the parties has for the past 15 days resided in the parish or chapelry in which the marriage is to be solemnized or that the church or chapel is the usual place of worship of one of the parties. Special licences to marry at any time and in any church, chapel, or other convenient place may be granted by the Abp. of *Canterbury.

Marriott, Charles (1811–58), a leader of the *Tractarian Movement after the secession of J. H. *Newman from the C of E.

Marrow Controversy. A controversy in the Church of *Scotland arising out of the condemnation by the *General Assembly in 1720 of *The Marrow of Modern Divinity*, a book written in 1645 and reissued in 1718. It advocated strongly *Calvinistic doctrines and was held to favour *antinomianism.

Marsh, Herbert (1757–1839), Bp. of *Peterborough from 1819. In Germany he became conversant with the prevalent critical methods, especially as applied to the Gospels, and after his return to Cambridge, he was among the first to popularize these methods in England. He was the foremost English bishop of his age.

Marsiglio (or Marsilius) of Padua (c.1275–1342), scholar. He studied at Padua and then went to Paris. He completed his main work, the *Defensor Pacis*, in 1324. When its authorship became known in 1326, he fled to the excommunicated Emp. Louis of Bavaria. In 1327 *John XXII condemned five propositions from the book and excommunicated its author.

According to the *Defensor Pacis*, the State is the unifying power of society; it derives its authority from the people, who retain the right to censure and depose the Ruler. The Church, on the other hand, has no inherent jurisdiction, spiritual or temporal; all her rights are given her by the State, which may withdraw them at will. Her hierarchy is of human, not Divine, institution; St *Peter was never given the primacy, and the chief authority in ecclesiastical matters is the General Council, which should be composed of priests and laymen. These ideas ran counter to the medieval concept of society.

Martène, Edmond (1654–1739), *Maurist scholar. His main work is the *De antiquis ecclesiae ritibus* (1700–2), a large collection of liturgical texts, with disquisitions on their historical significance.

Martensen, Hans Lassen (1808–84), Danish Protestant theologian. From 1854 he was Bp. of Seeland. His main work, *Den Christelige Dogmatik* (1849; Eng. tr., 1866), rests on the principle of the harmony between faith and knowledge, in the light of which he interpreted the *Lutheran system of doctrine. He is chiefly remembered as S. *Kierkegaard's principal opponent in his attack on the Established Church.

Martha, St. The sister of Mary and *Lazarus. From the incident related in Lk. 10: 38–42, she is commonly regarded as typifying the 'active' Christian life as contrasted with Mary, who typifies the 'contemplative'. According to a medieval legend, Martha, *Mary Magdalene, and Lazarus came to S. France and founded churches at Marseilles and various other places. Feast day in the E., 4 June; in the W., 29 July.

Mar Thoma Church. See MALABAR CHRISTIANS.

Martin, St (d. 397), Bp. of Tours and a patron saint of France. He was born of pagan parents in Hungary, either c.315 or c.336. Forced to adopt his father's profession of soldiering, he gave half his cloak to a naked beggar in Amiens. A subsequent vision of Christ led him to seek Baptism at the age of 18, though he remained in the Roman army until 356. In 360 he joined *Hilary of Poitiers and founded the monastery of Ligugé. Elected Bp. of Tours c.371, he continued to practise and promote monasticism and was active in evangelizing the countryside. *Priscillian's condemnation by a secular court led him to denounce secular interference in Church matters.

Feast day in the W., 11 Nov.; in the E., 12 Nov.

Martin, St (*c.*520–79), Bp. of the metropolitan see of Braga from *c.*570. He was active in furthering the conversion of the Sueves of Galicia, who were *Arians, to Catholicism, and he opposed the Spanish custom of using only one immersion at *Baptism. He wrote several moral treatises, translated a collection of sayings of the Desert Fathers into Latin, and compiled a collection of canons. Feast day, 20 Mar.

Martin I, St (d.655), Pope from 649. He was a vigorous opponent of the *Monothelites. He refused to sign the *Typos of the Emp. Constans II and was eventually arrested, taken to Constantinople, and banished to the Crimea; he died soon afterwards. He is the last Pope who is venerated as a martyr. Feast day, 13 Apr.; in the E. also 20 Sept.; in the W. formerly 12 Nov.

Martin IV (*c.*1210–85), Pope from 1281. He was elected through the influence of Charles of Anjou, on whom he remained dependent throughout his pontificate. With a view to assisting the planned attack on the Greek Empire, in 1281 he excommunicated the Emp. Michael Palaeologus, thus endangering the union of the Latin and Greek Churches achieved at the Council of *Lyons in 1274.

Martin V (1368–1431), Pope. Oddo (Otto) Colonna was unanimously elected Pope at the Council of *Constance in 1417. His reign marked the end of the *Great Schism, the antipope Clement VIII submitting in 1429. He strengthened the papal power by dissolving the Council of Constance in 1418 and that of Pavia and Siena in 1424.

Martin, Gregory (d. 1582), Bible translator. He was a tutor in the household of the Duke of Norfolk; when the Duke was imprisoned he fled to *Douai in 1570. Here he devoted himself to translating the *Vulgate into English. See DOUAI-REIMS BIBLE.

Martineau, James (1805–1900), *Unitarian minister. In 1869 he became Principal of Manchester New College, but continued his pastoral activities. He upheld the theist position against the negations of physical science, and he elaborated the 'Design argument' with the modifications made necessary by the Darwinian theory of evolution. He did much for the organization of Unitarians in England and Ireland.

Martínez de Ripalda, Juan. See RIPALDA, JUAN MARTÍNEZ DE.

Martyn, Henry (1781–1812), Anglican missionary. He became a chaplain of the East India Company at Calcutta in 1805. Besides doing missionary work among the natives, he translated the NT into Hindustani and Persian, the Psalms into Persian, and the BCP into Hindustani. Feast day in the American BCP (1979) and CW, 19 Oct.

martyr. The English word is a transliteration of a Greek one meaning 'witness'. It was used of the Apostles as witnesses of Christ's life and resurrection (e.g. Acts 1: 8), but with the spread of *persecution the term came to be reserved for those who had undergone hardship for the faith, and finally it was restricted to those who had suffered death. They quickly became the focus of veneration in the Church. From early times martyrdom, the 'baptism of blood', was considered the equivalent of normal Baptism where this had not been received. According to RC practice until 1969 relics of martyrs had to be contained in every consecrated altar; this is still the law in the E. Church.

Martyr, Peter. See PETER MARTYR.

martyrium. A church built over the tomb or relics of a *martyr or, occasionally, a church built in honour of a martyr.

martyrology. An official register of Christian martyrs. The earliest are calendars, merely naming the martyr and place of martyrdom under the day of the festival. The later 'historical' martyrologies (e.g. that of *Usuard) add stories from sources of varying value.

Martyrs, Acts of the; Era of the. See ACTS OF THE MARTYRS; DIOCLETIANIC ERA.

Marucchi, Orazio (1852–1931), Italian archaeologist. The *catacombs of Rome were the chief object of his research.

Mary, the Blessed Virgin, the Mother of Christ. In the NT the BVM figures prominently in the birth stories of Mt. 1–2 and especially of Lk. 1–2 (see also VIRGIN BIRTH). Though mentioned several times during Christ's public ministry, she remains mainly in the background; according to Jn. 19: 25

she reappears at the foot of the Cross. In Jerusalem she witnessed the growth of the early Church (Acts 1: 14).

Mary is rarely mentioned in the earliest patristic writings. Her perpetual virginity was first asserted in the apocryphal Book of *James; it was held by St *Athanasius and accepted by orthodox Fathers in the E. and W. from the 5th cent. onwards. The development of Marian doctrine received great impetus at the Council of *Ephesus (431), which upheld the title '*Theotokos'. In the 6th cent. the doctrine of the corporeal *Assumption of the BVM was formulated in orthodox circles by *Gregory of Tours and the Feast became widely observed. Belief in the Assumption seems to have spread without arousing opposition in the pre-Reformation period; it was defined for RCs in 1950. The doctrine of the *Immaculate Conception, on the other hand, was a matter of dispute in the Middle Ages; it was defined for RCs in 1854. In modern times there have been efforts to secure a Papal definition of Mary as 'Mediatrix of All Graces' and 'Co-Redemptrix', but the chapter on Mary added to the Constitution on the Church at the Second *Vatican Council was marked by restraint.

The Marian doctrine of the Orthodox Church is similar to that of RCs, though the corporeal Assumption of the BVM has not been made a dogma and the Immaculate Conception is denied. The Reformers stressed the humility of Mary and attacked her glorification by the RC Church; among all Protestant bodies there was a reaction against excessive devotion to her. In the C of E since the *Oxford Movement some theologians have accorded an important place to the BVM, and German Protestant theologians have been tending to restore an element of Marian doctrine.

Belief in the efficacy of Mary's intercession and hence direct prayer to her is probably very old. It is attested in a papyrus dating from the late 3rd–early 4th cent. Liturgical devotions in the W. came to include the *Little Office of Our Lady as well as the Saturday Mass and Office. Popular piety found expression in the *Hail Mary, *Rosary, *Angelus, and pilgrimages, especially to *Lourdes and *Fatima. In the Orthodox Church Marian devotion is expressed in the *Acathistus hymn and the Theotokia or short prayers to the Theotokos following the invocation of the Trinity which came

into use in the 8th cent. The first Marian feast was a general commemoration, kept in many places on the Sunday before Christmas; this developed into the Feast of the Assumption (15 Aug.). The other major feasts of the BVM are (or were): the (Immaculate) Conception (8 Dec.); the *Nativity (8 Sept.); the *Annunciation (25 Mar.) and the *Purifaction (2 Feb.), both in the RC Church now accounted feasts of Christ; and the *Visitation (2 July; now in the RC Church and some modern Anglican calendars, 31 May). Since 1969 the RC Church has observed 1 Jan. as the 'Solemnity of Holy Mary, Mother of God' (in place of the *Circumcision). Many modern Anglican calendars include a major general feast of the BVM on 15 Aug. (without any reference to the Assumption).

Mary, Gospel of. An apocryphal *Gnostic Gospel, of which 3rd-cent. fragments survive in the original Greek. In it *Mary [Magdalene] describes a vision in which the progress of the Gnostic through the seven planetary spheres is explained.

Mary, Gospel of the Birth of. A medieval apocryphal book describing the birth of the BVM, her life in the *Temple from the age of 3 to 12, her betrothal, the *Annunciation, and the *Virgin Birth of Christ.

Mary of Egypt, St (5th cent.), penitent. After a career of infamy as an actress and courtesan at *Alexandria, she is said to have been converted on the threshold of the *Holy Sepulchre at Jerusalem, fled into the desert E. of Palestine, and lived there in isolation for 47 years. Her story became popular; it forms part of the liturgy for the 5th Sunday in Lent in the Orthodox Churches. Feast days in the E., 5th Sunday in Lent and 1 Apr.; in the W., 2 (also 3 and 9) Apr.

Mary of the Incarnation. See ACARIE, MADAME, and GUYARD, MARIE.

Mary Magdalene, St. A follower of Christ out of whom He is said to have cast 'seven devils' (Lk. 8: 2). She stood by His Cross (Mk. 15: 40); with two other women she discovered the empty tomb (Mk. 16: 1 ff. etc.); and she was granted an appearance of the risen Lord early the same day (Mt. 28: 9; Jn. 20: 11f.). W. tradition long identified her with the 'woman who was a sinner' who anointed Christ's feet (Lk. 7: 37) and with Mary the sister of *Martha, who also anointed Him (Jn. 12: 3), but both identifications have now been abandoned. In several *Gnostic texts she appears as a mediator of revelation or in conversation between the risen Christ and His disciples. According to an early legend in the E. Church she went to *Ephesus and died there; in the W. a legend arose that she came to S. France with Martha and *Lazarus. Feast day, 22 July.

Mary Magdalene de' Pazzi, St (1566–1607), *Carmelite mystic. In the early years after her profession she was severely tried by spiritual desolation and physical suffering, but from 1590 her life became a series of *ecstasies. During these she often gave spiritual counsels which were taken down and published after her death. Feast day, 25 (formerly 29) May.

Mary, Queen of Scots (1542–87). Mary Stuart was crowned Queen in 1543. She went to France for her education and in 1558 she married the Dauphin. After his death she returned to Scotland in 1561. Here nationalist hatred of the pro-French Guise regime had combined with Protestant agitation led by J. *Knox to establish a Protestant-led government. Mary displayed no understanding of her kingdom and dissipated the reserves of loyalty among her subjects. In 1565 she married Lord Darnley, by whom she became the mother of the future *James I (VI of Scotland). In 1567 Darnley was assassinated by the Earl of Bothwell; how far Mary was implicated is disputed. Her marriage with Bothwell was followed by a rising of the Protestant lords. She was imprisoned and later in 1567 she abdicated. In 1568 she escaped and fled to England. *Elizabeth I kept Mary in close captivity. When an unguarded letter implicated her in the Babington Plot, she was executed.

Mary Tudor (1516–58), Queen of England from 1553. The daughter of *Henry VIII and Catherine of Aragon, she was excluded from the succession on the birth of *Elizabeth, but in 1544 she was given second place after *Edward VI. When she became Queen she at first showed leniency to her Protestant subjects, though proscribing their religion, but after the rising of 1554 she resolved to rule more sternly. Her marriage with *Philip II of Spain was much disliked. In 1555 R. *Pole reconciled England to the Papacy. In the same year the heresy laws were restored and the trials for heresy began; T. *Cranmer, H. *Latimer, N. *Ridley, J. *Hooper, and others were burnt. The persecution of Protestants and Mary's inability to have children lost her the affection of the people.

Marys in the NT. Besides (1) the Blessed Virgin *Mary and (2) St *Mary Magdalene, there are: (3) 'The wife of Cleopas' (Jn. 19: 25), who stood by the Cross. (4) 'The mother of James and Joses' (Mk. 15: 40), who stood by the Cross and was a witness to the Empty Tomb (Mk. 16: 1). She may be the same as (3). (5) Mary of Bethany, the sister of *Martha and *Lazarus (Jn. 11: 1 ff.), who sat at Christ's feet when He visited their village (Lk. 10: 38 ff.). She has, unjustifiably, been identified with Mary Magdalene (q.v.). (6) 'The mother of John *Mark' (Acts 12: 12).

Mass (Lat. *missa*). A title for the *Eucharist, now used especially by RCs.

Mass, music for the. The parts of the service sung by the choir or congregation may be divided into chants for (1) the *Ordinary of the Mass (the *Kyrie, *Gloria in Excelsis, *Creed, *Sanctus and *Benedictus qui venit, *Agnus Dei, and *Ite Missa est) in which the words are always the same; and (2) the *Propers, which vary according to the occasion, namely the *Introit, *Gradual (replaced in 1970 by a *responsorial Psalm), *Offertory and *Communion Anthem, and sometimes a *Sequence.

The oldest chant for the Ordinary is little more than an inflective recitative corresponding to that used in the parts of the Mass sung by the officiant. With the growth of polyphony from the 11th cent. onwards, compositions for two or more voices began to appear. In the early 15th cent. the *Sanctus* and *Agnus* occur with a common musical arrangement, to be followed by *Gloria-Credo* pairs; later in the 15th cent. a complete series (or 'Mass-cycle') became common. The full development of polyphony in the 16th cent. led to elaborate settings, such as those of G. P. da *Palestrina and W. *Byrd. In the 18th cent. orchestral settings became popular on the Continent and brought the introduction of music ostensibly designed for the Mass into the concert hall. Against the increasing elaboration of music divorced from the words of the liturgical texts the proponents of the *Liturgical Movement encouraged the revival of *plainchant. In recent times emphasis has been laid on music in which the congregation can take part.

The translation of the liturgy into the vernacular in England in the 16th cent. created a need for new musical settings to fit the new texts; these were supplied by a succession of composers from J. *Merbecke onwards, though until the 19th cent. musical settings for the Eucharist were confined mainly to cathedrals and *collegiate churches. The recent modern-language liturgies have led to the composition of new settings, mainly designed for congregational singing and often employing the idiom of 20th-cent. popular music.

Mass of the Catechumens; Mass of the Faithful. See CATECHUMENS, MASS OF THE; FAITHFUL, MASS OF THE.

Massillon, Jean-Baptiste (1663–1742), French *Oratorian. He was one of the foremost preachers of a great generation, much respected even by the leaders of the *Enlightenment. In 1717 he was nominated Bp. of Clermont; he spent his last years in devoted service to his diocese.

Massoretes. Jewish grammarians who worked on the Hebrew text of the OT between about the 6th and 10th cents. AD. They strove to preserve a biblical text free from accretion, alteration, or corruption by providing marginal notes and instructions for copyists. They also introduced *vowel points and accents to show how the words should be pronounced at a time when Hebrew had ceased to be a living language. The text which derives from their work is known as the 'Massoretic text'.

Master of the Sentences. A title of *Peter Lombard.

material sin. An action which, though in itself ('materially') contrary to Divine law, is not culpable, because the agent acted either in ignorance or under constraint.

Mathew, Arnold Harris (1853–1919), *Old Catholic bishop. In 1908 he received episcopal consecration from the Dutch Old Catholic Church as their archbishop in Great Britain, but he was repudiated in 1910 on the ground that his consecration had been obtained under a misconception of the extent of his following in England. He left irregular episcopal successions of *episcopi vagantes.

Mathurins. Another name for members of the *Trinitarian Order (q.v.).

Matins. See MATTINS.

Matrimony. Christian marriage differs from earlier practice and from modern secular usage most notably in the dignity it has sought for the woman and the life-long nature it ascribes to the marriage bond. Early Hebrew law, which was founded on marriage by purchase, assigned a low status to the woman, who could be divorced for some 'indecency' (Deut. 24: 1 RSV). In His teaching about matrimony Christ was concerned to restore it to its original place in God's plan of creation (Mk. 10: 6–9; Mt. 19: 4–6). He insisted therefore that *divorce was contrary to God's will. Mk. 5: 31 f. (unlike Lk. 16: 18) and Mt. 19: 9 (unlike Mk. 10: 11), however, assume that He intended an exception in cases of unchastity, implying His agreement with Deut. 24: 1. Remarriage is excluded to underline the Divine intention that the union should be for life. Unlike other Jewish thinkers, Christ also saw a place for celibacy for the sake of the *Kingdom of God (Mt. 19: 10–12). While acknowledging the Lord's opposition to divorce (1 Cor. 7: 10), St *Paul's pastoral practice permitted separation (1 Cor. 7: 11) and in some circumstances apparently freedom to remarry (1 Cor. 7: 15). This became the basis of the so-called *Pauline Privilege developed (and widened) in RC moral theology. Paul teaches the equality of men and women in Christ (Gal. 3: 28), but at 1 Cor. 11: 3–12 he echoes the patriarchal assumptions of his Jewish background and Graeco-Roman context.

The purposes of matrimony have traditionally been understood as fidelity, the procreation of children, and the union of the parties in the marriage. The procreative, often understood as the primary end, demands that the good of children be put before other considerations. It has also led many Christians to repudiate all artificial methods of family limitation (see CONTRACEPTION, PROCREATION AND ABORTION, ETHICS OF). In the W. marriage came to be regarded as a *Sacrament, unique in that the parties are the ministers, and the priest only the appointed witness.

The rite of marriage consists of two parts: the betrothal and the marriage proper. The betrothal consists of the giving of a *ring (or the exchange of rings) and the joining of hands. It also includes the making of vows. The marriage service is essentially a service of blessing; from the time of *Tertullian it included a celebration of the Eucharist (*Nuptial Mass). The Nuptial Mass was often replaced even in the medieval Church by a service of blessing in front of the altar, and this arrangement is preserved in Protestant Churches. In the E. Church, the marriage service preserves an Epistle and Gospel, the couple are given crowns (representing the crowns of martyrs) and then share a cup of wine.

It was only in the 11th cent. that the claim of the Church to exercise exclusive jurisdiction in matrimonial cases was conceded. In England, however, civil marriage was established in 1836 and in 1857 the jurisdiction of the ecclesiastical courts in matrimonial cases was abolished. Subsequent legislation provided ever-widening grounds for divorce until the Divorce Reform Act 1969 made the 'irretrievable breakdown' of marriage the sole criterion. Similar developments have taken place in other countries. While civil legislation has not affected the belief of the Church, in the RC Church there has been an increase in the number of petitions for *nullity ; these are heard in Church courts. In some parts of the Anglican Communion after a civil divorce another marriage in church is allowed; in other Provinces a blessing is sometimes given after a civil marriage and both parties are subsequently admitted to Communion. In the Orthodox Church divorce has been tolerated since Byzantine times, though a different ceremony is used for second and third marriages.

See also AFFINITY, BANNS OF MARRIAGE, DIVORCE, MARRIAGE LICENCES, and CELIBACY OF THE CLERGY.

matter. In medieval philosophy, the stuff underlying all material existence before it is determined and actualized by *form (q.v.). The *Schoolmen applied this *Aristotelian concept to Sacramental theology.

Matthew, St, Apostle. He is described in Mt. 10: 3 as a *publican. The call of Matthew by Christ is recorded in Mt. 9: 9 (in the parallel passages in Mk. and Lk. the name of the person called is given as 'Levi'). According to *Papias he made a collection of Christ's sayings in Hebrew, and he is traditionally held to be the author of the First Gospel (see the following entry). Feast day in the E., 16 Nov.; in the W., 21 Sept.

Matthew, Gospel of St. Traditionally held to be the oldest of the four Gospels, it stands first in the NT *Canon. It was probably written *c.*AD 80–90. Though since the 2nd cent. it has been attributed to St *Matthew the Apostle, it is unlikely that it was written by an eye-witness. Most scholars hold that the author drew on Mk., which he expanded with other sources, especially '*Q'. He begins with a *Genealogy of Christ and 'Infancy Narrative'. He interpolates long sections of 'discourse' in the Marcan framework and rearranges the narrative to bring together similar material which is in parallel passages dispersed in Lk. Christ is presented as the fulfilment of prophecy and the true interpreter of the Jewish law. The special commission given to St *Peter (16: 17–20) has proved highly influential. Of the *Synoptic Gospels it is the most suitable for public reading.

Matthew of Aquasparta (*c.*1240–1302), *Franciscan theologian. In 1287 he became General of his Order and in 1288 a *cardinal. He stood high in the confidence of *Boniface VIII. His writings include sermons and biblical commentaries, a commentary on the *Sentences, *quodlibets* and *quaestiones disputatae*. He was a disciple of St *Bonaventure, though in some ways he looked forward to *Duns Scotus.

Matthew Paris (*c.*1200–59), chronicler. He entered the *Benedictine monastery of *St Albans in 1217. His *Chronica Majora*, a history of the world from the Creation to 1259, is a valuable source for contemporary events.

Matthew's Bible. An edition of the English Bible issued in 1537. 'Thomas Matthew', the name of its supposed editor, was an alias for John *Rogers (q.v.).

Matthias, St, Apostle. According to the tradition preserved in Acts 1: 15–26, he was chosen by lot to fill the vacancy in the Twelve left by the treachery of *Judas Iscariot. He is not mentioned elsewhere in the Bible. Feast day in the W., 14 May (formerly 24 or, in leap years, 25 Feb.; 24 Feb. is still observed in some Anglican Churches); in the E. Church, 9 Aug.

Matthias, Gospel of St. A lost apocryphal Gospel mentioned by some early Fathers.

Mattins. It was originally the morning service in the primitive round of daily prayer. Later it was preceded by an early morning *Vigil. In the W. the name was eventually attached to the Vigil or night part of the *Office, the older morning prayer becoming known as *Lauds. Its main components were Ps. 95 (the *Invitatory), a hymn, Psalms, readings (usually from the Bible, the Fathers, or Lives of saints), and the *Te Deum. In 1971 it was replaced by the *Office of Readings.

In the C of E the name is used for the service of 'Morning Prayer'. The structure of the BCP Office is similar to that of *Evensong. Elements come from the medieval Office of Mattins, from Lauds, and from *Prime. Modern Anglican liturgies allow alternative *Canticles and other variations.

Mattins of Bruges. The massacre of the French lodged in Bruges by the Flemish inhabitants at daybreak on 18 May 1302.

Maundy Thursday. The Thursday before *Easter, so called from the *mandatum novum* ('new commandment') given on this day (Jn. 13: 34). Its special commemoration of the Lord's Institution of the *Eucharist is attested by the 4th cent. In the RC Church since 1955 the Maundy Thursday Mass has been celebrated in the evening. It is marked by a number of special features, including the ceremony of foot-washing (see PEDILAVIUM), and all present are expected to receive Communion from Hosts consecrated at this Mass. After it the Hosts needed for the Liturgy of *Good Friday (see PRESANCTIFIED, MASS OF THE) are taken in procession to the Altar of *Repose, where a watch is kept for some hours. In cathedral churches the Holy Oils are blessed at a special *Chrism Mass in the morning. Similar ceremonies have now been authorized in the C of E. The royal 'Maundy Ceremony' is an abbreviated survival of the Pedilavium.

Maur, St (6th cent.), disciple of St *Benedict of Nursia. He is said to have made his way to France in 543 and founded the abbey of Glanfeuil (afterwards St-Maur-sur-Loire). Feast day, 15 Jan.

Maurice, St, leader of the *Theban Legion. According to a 5th-cent. source, a legion from the Thebaïd, composed wholly of Christians, was taken to Gaul; when they refused to sacrifice, they were massacred during the *Diocletianic persecution. Feast day, 22 Sept.

Maurice, Frederick Denison (1805–72), *Christian Socialist. The son of a *Unitarian minister, he gradually accepted the Anglican faith and was ordained in 1834. In 1846 he became Professor of Theology at the newly-created Theological School at *King's College, London. He was moved by the political events of 1848 and became interested in the application of Christian principles to social reform; acquaintance with J. M. F. *Ludlow led to the formation of the Christian Socialists (q.v.). Maurice's orthodoxy was constantly under suspicion and he was dismissed from King's College when his *Theological Essays* (1853) provoked a crisis; in one of these he attacked the popular view of the endlessness of future punishment and maintained that in the NT 'eternity' had nothing to do with time. In 1866 he became Knightsbridge Professor of Moral Philosophy at Cambridge. Feast day in the American BCP (1979) and CW, 1 Apr.

Maurists. The *Benedictine monks of the *Congregation of St-*Maur. This was founded in 1618 to represent in France the reform initiated in the Abbey of Saint-Vanne (Lorraine) in 1600; it received Papal approval in 1621. The literary and historical work, for which the Congregation is famous, was largely centred at *Saint-Germain-des-Prés. The Congregation was dissolved in 1818.

Maximilian, St (d. 295), martyr. It is recorded that he was executed at Theveste in Numidia because he refused to serve in the Roman army. Feast day, 12 Mar.

Maximus, St (d. 408/23), Bp. of Turin. Over 100 of his sermons survive; they throw light on the history of the liturgy and the continuation of paganism in N. Italy. Feast day, 25 June.

Maximus the Confessor, St (c.580–662), Greek theologian and ascetical writer. He was Imperial Secretary under the Emp.

*Heraclius. Having become a monk c.614, he fled to Africa during the Persian invasion (626). From c.640 he was a determined opponent of *Monothelitism, and he had a share in its condemnation at the Lateran Council of 649. He was taken to *Constantinople in 653 and, refusing adherence to the '*Typos' of Constans II, he was banished to Thrace.

Maximus wrote on doctrinal, ascetical, exegetical and liturgical subjects. He held that the purpose of history was the Incarnation of the Son of God and the *deification of man, which consisted in the restoration of the image of God. Man, created in an incorruptible nature devoid of passion, caused evil to come into the world by his desire for pleasure, which destroyed the dominion of reason over the senses; hence Christ had to redeem the race by pain to restore the equilibrium. Through the Incarnate Word man is not only freed from ignorance but given the power to practise virtue. The goal of human life, obtained through abnegation, is union with God by charity. Feast day in the W., 13 Aug.; in the E., 21 Jan. (also 13 Aug.).

Maximus the Cynic (4th cent.), intruded Bp. of *Constantinople. After a disreputable career at *Alexandria, in 379 he went to Constantinople. One night in 380 when *Gregory of Nazianzus was ill, Maximus was consecrated to the see. The Council of *Constantinople in 381 declared that he 'neither is nor was a bishop'. For a short time he was supported in the W. He professed to combine belief in the Cynic philosophy with profession of the Nicene faith.

Maximus the Greek, St (c.1470–1556), monk. Michael Trivolis was a monk on Mt *Athos by 1505/6. In response to a request in 1516 from the Muscovite ruler for a competent scholar to translate works from Greek into Slavonic, he was sent to Moscow. Besides translations, he produced works on theology, philosophy, statecraft, and social problems. Involved in various disputes, he was sentenced to terms of imprisonment and solitary confinement. Feast day, 21 Jan.

Max Müller, Friedrich (1823–1900), comparative philologist and religious writer. A German by birth, he went to Oxford in 1848 to supervise the printing of the first edition of the Rig-Veda. He soon held senior office in the university. In 1875 he undertook the editing of *The Sacred Books of the East*, a series of translations of E. religious classics in 51 volumes. He also wrote on the comparative study of religion.

May Laws. The legislation associated with Bismarck's *Kulturkampf*. The laws, passed in May 1873, were directed against the RC Church in Germany.

Mayne, St Cuthbert (1544–77), the first RC seminary priest executed in England. At Oxford he came under the influence of E. *Campion and became a RC. After ordination at *Douai, in 1576 he was sent on the English Mission and became chaplain to a landowner in Cornwall. He was discovered and sentenced to death. He was among the *Forty Martyrs of England and Wales canonized in 1970.

Maynooth College. The 'Royal Catholic College' at Maynooth, c.15 miles from Dublin, was established by the Irish Parliament in 1795 for the education of the RC clergy for Ireland. Since 1869 it has been a Pontifical University and since 1910 also a College of the National University of Ireland.

Mazarin, Jules (1602–61), statesman. In the service of *Urban VIII, he went to *Avignon. In 1639 he became a naturalized Frenchman and in 1640 entered the service of Louis XIII, at whose instigation he was made a cardinal in 1641. In 1642 he succeeded A. J. du P. *Richelieu as chief minister; he practically ruled France until his death. At the Peace of *Westphalia (1648) he enlarged France's territory, but he could not prevent the country's economic crisis or the civil wars of the Fronde (1648–53). He pursued a policy of reconciliation towards the *Huguenots. He continued the war with Spain and eventually secured the victorious Treaty of the Pyrenees (1659).

Mazarin Bible. A Latin Bible so called from a copy in the library of Card. *Mazarin. It is also known as the 'Gutenberg Bible', after J. *Gutenberg, its printer, and as the '42-line Bible', from the number of lines in each column. It is the earliest full-length book ever printed, probably in 1453–5; it was certainly complete by 1456.

Mazdaism. See ZOROASTRIANISM.

Mazzolini, Sylvester. See PRIERIAS, SYLVESTER.

Mechitarists. A community of *Uniat Armenian monks founded at *Constantinople in 1701. They were driven out by the Turks in 1703 and eventually in 1717 settled on the island of San Lazzaro, *Venice. Another section of the community later established itself at Vienna. Both communities have issued important Armenian works from their printing houses.

Mechthild of Magdeburg (c.1207–82 or somewhat later), author of a book of mystical revelations. Of noble Saxon family, she became a *Beguine at Magdeburg. The various books of her visions, entitled *Das fliessende Licht der Gottheit* ('The Flowing Light of the Godhead'), were written down between c.1250 and 1282; they contain dialogues with the Lord, bridal mysticism, and trinitarian theology and eschatology. About 1270 she became a nun at the *Cistercian-inspired convent of Helfta, where she made contact with St Mechthild of Hackenborn (with whom she has often been confused) and with St *Gertrude the Great.

Mede, Joseph (1586–1638), also 'Mead', English biblical scholar. His best-known work, *Clavis Apocalyptica* (1627), interprets Rev. on the principle that its visions form a whole in chronological order; the Day of Judgement is a period of a thousand years of peace for the Church on earth.

Medina, Bartolomé (1527–80), Spanish *Dominican theologian. He has been called the 'Father of *Probabilism' (q.v.). In his commentary on St *Thomas Aquinas's *Summa Theologiae*, he defends the view that where there are two opinions, both of which are probable, though in an unequal degree, the less probable may be followed.

meditation. In Christian tradition the term has been used of: (1) the recitation or memorizing of biblical texts; (2) keeping religious truths in mind during the day; (3) thinking about things, whether the emphasis is on intellectual rigour, acuteness of perception, or devotional fervour; and (4) the application of the mind and often the imagination to the truths of the faith, and especially to episodes in the life of Christ, with a view to stirring an affective response. In this last sense it came to be regarded as part of prayer and was distinguished from *contemplation. In modern times forms of meditation have been

adopted from Eastern non-Christian religions, often involving the abandonment of deliberate thought rather than focusing on a specific object.

Meinrad, St (d. 861), Patron of *Einsiedeln. A monk at *Reichenau, he sought greater austerity and settled at the spot where Einsiedeln ('hermitage') now stands. He was put to death by two ruffians to whom he had given hospitality. Feast day, 21 Jan.

Meissen Agreement. See REUNION.

Melanchthon, Philipp (1497–1560), German Reformer. In 1518 he became professor of Greek at *Wittenberg, where he both influenced M. *Luther and was influenced by him. In 1521 he found himself at the head of the Reformation movement while Luther was confined at the *Wartburg. One of the most erudite and intellectually powerful figures of his age, Melanchthon was closer than Luther to Catholic teaching on the Law and free will, but his concern to prevent further divisions made him more open to *Zwinglian and *Calvinist doctrines on the Eucharist. He took part in the Diet of *Speyer (1529), the *Marburg Colloquy (1529), and the Diet of Augsburg (1530), where he was the chief architect of the *Augsburg Confession. In 1537, however, he objected to the overt condemnation of the Papacy in the *Schmalkaldic Articles. At the Catholic-Protestant Conferences of *Worms (1540–41) and *Ratisbon (1541) he and M. *Bucer tried hard to unite the Churches. In his later years he was largely concerned with the organization of the Church in Saxony on a semi-episcopal basis and with the *adiaphorist controversy. His characteristic teaching on free will, namely that the human will can co-operate with the Holy Spirit and with the grace of God in the act of conversion (known as *synergism), received its definitive formulation in the 1535 edition of his *Loci communes* (1st edn. 1521).

Melanesian Brotherhood. An Anglican religious order of evangelists who take the traditional vows of poverty, chastity, and obedience, but normally for a limited period. It was founded in 1925 by a Solomon Islander, Ini Kopuria.

Melania. (1) 'The Elder' (c.342–c.410), a wealthy Roman matron. On the death of her husband, she adopted an ascetic life, left Rome, and founded a double monastery with *Rufinus of Aquileia on the Mount of *Olives. (2) Her granddaughter, St Melania 'the Younger' (c.385–438/9), with her husband joined St *Jerome at Bethlehem; she founded another monastery on the Mount of Olives. Feast day, 31 Dec.

Melchiorites. See HOFFMANN, MELCHIOR.

Melchites or **Melkites.** Those Christians of Syria and Egypt who, refusing *Monophysitism and accepting the Definition of *Chalcedon (451), remained in communion with the see of *Constantinople. Today the term is applied to the Christians of the Byzantine rite (particularly the *Uniats, but to a lesser degree the Orthodox also) belonging to the Patriarchates of *Antioch, *Jerusalem, and *Alexandria.

Melchizedek. According to Gen. 14: 18, the 'King of Salem' and 'Priest of the Most High God' who offered *Abraham bread and wine as he returned from battle. The author of Heb. (6: 20, 7: 1 ff.) regarded his priesthood as prefiguring that of Christ; another Christian tradition has seen in his offering a *type of the *Eucharist.

Melitian Schisms. (1) Melitius, Bp. of Lycopolis in Egypt, regarded as too lax the terms laid down c.306 by *Peter, Bp. of Alexandria, for the return of those who had lapsed under persecution. He created disturbances, was excommunicated by Peter, and founded a schismatic Church with clergy of his own ordination. A small body of Melitians seems to have survived until the 8th cent. (2) See the next entry.

Melitius, St (d. 381), Bp. of *Antioch from 360. In the course of the *Arian controversy he was exiled several times, being finally restored in 378. He presided over the Council of *Constantinople in 381. The schism at Antioch called by his name arose when the supporters of *Eustathius (Bp. of Antioch c.324–c.327) secured the consecration of one Paulinus in 362; it lasted until after Melitius' death. Feast day, 12 Feb.

Melito, St (d. c.190), Bp. of Sardis. Little is known about his life. He was a prolific writer, but only fragments of his works were known until 1940, when one preserved on *papyrus was published. The main theme of the *Peri Pascha* ('On the

Pasch') is the new *Pasch inaugurated by Christ. In it there is much polemic against the Jews and an anti-*Gnostic insistence on the true humanity of Christ. Feast day, 1 Apr.

Mellitus, St (d. 624), Abp. of *Canterbury from 619. Sent to England by *Gregory I in 601, he was consecrated bishop for the East Saxons in 604. Feast day, 24 Apr.

Melville, Andrew (1545–1622), Scottish *Presbyterian theologian. He held senior positions in the universities of Glasgow and St Andrews; his educational reforms were of some importance. He also took an active part in attacking what was left of the Scottish episcopal system, and in 1575 he was entrusted with drawing up the Second Book of *Discipline (q.v.). As *Moderator of the General Assembly in 1582, he prosecuted R. Montgomery, one of the '*tulchan' bishops. On this and other occasions he incurred the hostility of *James I. He was confined to the Tower in 1607, but released in 1611 on being offered a professorial chair at Sedan.

Memling or **Memlinc, Hans** (c.1440–94), painter. Of German origin, he was registered as a citizen of Bruges by 1465. His paintings, which are notable for their colour and harmony, include the Donne Triptych in the National Gallery, London, as well as Madonnas and other altarpieces.

Memorare. A widely used intercessory prayer addressed to the BVM. It has commonly been ascribed to St *Bernard of Clairvaux, but its real author is unknown. The most popular English version begins 'Remember, O most loving Virgin Mary'.

memoria (Lat., commonly translated 'memorial'). The name given in current RC liturgical documents to the least important of the three categories of *feast.

Memoriale Rituum. An obsolete liturgical book containing rites for *Candlemas, *Ash Wednesday, *Palm Sunday, and the last three days of *Holy Week in the shortened form previously used in smaller RC parish churches.

Menaion. In the E. Church, each of the twelve liturgical books (one for each month) which contain the variable parts of the Divine *Office for the immovable feasts.

Menas, St (*c.*3rd–4th cent.), Egyptian martyr. He was probably born and martyred in Egypt, but his story was apparently fused with that of a soldier executed in Phrygia under *Diocletian, possibly another Menas, possibly St Gordian. His reputed birthplace, SW of Lake Mareotis, became a pilgrimage centre. Feast day, 11 Nov.

Menas, St (d. 552), Patr. of *Constantinople from 536. At the beginning of the *Three Chapters' Controversy (543) he subscribed to the Imperial Edict and forced his suffragans to do the same. On their complaining to Pope *Vigilius, Menas was excommunicated for a short time in 547 and 551. Feast day, 25 Aug.

Mendicant Friars. Members of those orders which were forbidden to own property in common; they work or beg for their living and are not bound to one convent. In the Middle Ages their activities were carried out mainly in towns; their exemption from episcopal jurisdiction and extensive faculties for preaching and hearing confessions aroused great hostility.

Mennonites, the followers of Menno Simons (1496–1561), a parish priest in Dutch Friesland who renounced his connection with the RC Church in 1536 and joined the *Anabaptists. He preached believers' Baptism, a connectional type of Church organization with emphasis on the responsibilities and rights of the local congregation, rejection of Christian participation in the magistracy, and non-resistance. In the 17th and 18th cents. the Mennonites became numerous and influential in the Netherlands. In 1990 the total number of Mennonites was said to be over 856,500.

Menologion. In the E. Church, a liturgical book containing the Lives of the saints, arranged by months throughout the ecclesiastical year (beginning with Sept.).

mensa (Lat., 'table'). In early Christian times the word was used of the stone tablets set over or near a grave, and apparently used for receiving food for meals in memory of the deceased. It is also in common use to designate the flat stone (or other material) which forms the top of an *altar.

mental prayer. The phrase has been used with a variety of meanings, but it normally denotes discursive *meditation, as opposed to *contemplation.

mental reservation. The conflict which may arise between the duty of telling the truth and that of keeping a secret has led to the development of the doctrine of mental reservation. RC moral theologians distinguish between 'strict' and 'wide' mental reservation. In the former a qualification is added mentally which alters the statement pronounced, so that the hearer is necessarily deceived; it has been thought that it was this form that was condemned by *Innocent XI in 1679. In the 'wide mental reservation' words are used which are susceptible of more than one interpretation, without the speaker's giving an indication of the sense in which he uses them.

Merbecke or **Marbeck, John** (d. *c.*1585), English musician. Appointed organist at St George's Chapel, *Windsor, in 1541, he was condemned to death for heresy in 1543 because he had written the first *concordance to the English Bible. He was, however, pardoned. In 1550 he produced his *Book of Common Prayer Noted*, in which he composed plainchant-style music for *Edward VI's first (1549) liturgy. This was revived in the 19th cent.

Mercator, Marius. See MARIUS MERCATOR.

Mercedarians. A religious order of men founded by St *Peter Nolasco to assist in ransoming Christians captured by the Moors; it was confirmed by *Gregory IX in 1235. Its main work was collecting alms and raising money from its own properties for ransoming captives, but its members also travelled in Muslim lands to negotiate the release of Christians. Since the 19th cent. the Order has undertaken educational, charitable, and missionary work.

Mercersburg Theology. An American school of thought, which opposed both the emotionalism and the rationalism of the mid-19th cent. by emphasizing the importance of doctrine. While it upheld the teaching of the Reformers, it saw this in relation to patristic and subsequent thought. The name derives from the town of Mercersburg in Pennsylvania, in which Marshall College and the Theological Seminary of the German Reformed Church were situated. The movement came into prominence with the publication of J. W. *Nevin's *The Anxious Bench* (1843), which attacked current methods of *revivalist preaching.

Mercier, Désiré Joseph(1851–1926), Belgian philosopher and prelate. As a professor at Louvain, he was an ardent supporter of the *Thomist revival. In 1906 he was made Abp. of Malines and in 1907 created a cardinal. In his Lenten Pastoral for 1908 he denounced G. *Tyrrell. He was the leading spirit on the RC side in the *Malines Conversations.

mercy, works of. See CORPORAL WORKS OF MERCY, SPIRITUAL WORKS OF MERCY.

mercy-seat. In the Jewish *Temple, the covering of solid gold laid on the '*Ark of the Covenant' which was conceived to be God's resting-place.

merit. In theology 'merit' designates man's right to be rewarded for a work done for God. The conception has its foundation in the Bible; in both the OT and the NT rewards are promised to the just for their good works. The theology of merit was elaborated by the *Schoolmen, who distinguished between *condign merit, which confers a claim to a reward due in justice for services rendered, and *congruous merit, which may claim the reward only on grounds of fitness. The traditional doctrine was repudiated by the Reformers, especially M. *Luther, who taught the sinfulness of all human works, whether done before or after *justification.

Merry del Val, Rafael (1865–1930), cardinal. Singled out by *Leo XIII for Papal service, he was secretary of the commission which pronounced against *Anglican Ordinations (1896). In 1903 he was made cardinal and Secretary of State by *Pius X, with whose intransigent policy he became identified. He had a strong pastoral sense.

Mersch, Émile (1890–1940), *Jesuit theologian. He sought to construct a theological synthesis in terms of the 'Mystical Body of Christ'. He traced the doctrine of the Church through history and expounded it from a systematic standpoint.

Mersenne, Marin (1588–1648), French philosopher, scientist, and theologian. His place in the history of modern philosophy rests on the links which he forged with many of the leading French philosophers and scientists of his day. He did much to prevent the new scientific movement from developing in an anti-religious direction.

Merton, Thomas (1915–68), *Trappist monk and writer. Converted to RCism in the USA, in 1941 he joined the Trappists at Gethsemani Abbey in Kentucky. His autobiography, *The Seven Storey Mountain* (1948; published in England as *Elected Silence*, 1949) presented monastic spirituality to a wide audience. His later works echo the changes in modern RCism, leading to a greater openness to other traditions and concern for the moral dilemmas of modern man. He eventually sought the life of a *hermit.

Mesonyktikon. The Midnight *Office in the E. Church.

Mesrob, St (*c.*361–439), *Armenian ecclesiastic and translator. Over a long period he was coadjutor-bishop to the Catholicos *Isaac; on his death he acted as *locum tenens*, but died within six months. He tried to eliminate all traces of Syriac institutions from Armenian life. He composed for the Armenians an alphabet which was adopted in 406, and translated the NT and Proverbs in the Armenian Bible issued *c.*410. Feast days, 19 Feb. and 25 Nov.

Messalians, also known as **Euchites**, a sect apparently originating in Mesopotamia in the 4th cent. They spread to Syria, Asia Minor, Thrace, and Egypt, and were condemned at the Council of *Ephesus in 431, but survived until the 7th cent. They held that in consequence of *Adam's sin everyone had a demon substantially united with his soul, and that this demon, which was not expelled by Baptism, was liberated only by concentrated and ceaseless prayer; this aimed at eliminating all passion and desire.

Messiah (Heb. for 'anointed'). A person invested by God with special powers and functions. It was rendered in Greek by χριστός, from which '*Christ' derives.

In the OT the term could be applied to anyone set apart for a special function, such as the priest in Lev. 4: 3, but it was used more particularly of the king, who was conceived as anointed by Divine command; as 'the Lord's anointed' his person was sacrosanct (1 Sam. 24: 6). Later the whole *Davidic dynasty was seen as specially chosen by God, and the hope that a king who should be both 'the Lord's anointed' and 'the son of David' never died out.

In the NT, Jewish expectations of a

deliverer are echoed at Lk. 24: 21 and Acts 1: 6, and at Mt. 2: 2–4 where, using the absolute form not found in early Judaism, Jesus is called 'the Christ' (AV) or 'the Messiah' (modern translations commonly render the word thus when the Greek has a definite article, and leave it as 'Christ' where there is no such article). The expectation that the deliverer would be descended from David is present both in the *genealogies and in such titles as 'Son of David'. The inscription on the Cross confirms that Jesus was executed as a Messianic figure, but it is unclear whether He Himself defined His role in these terms. In Mk., at a central point St *Peter confesses Jesus as Messiah (8: 29), but the disciples are silenced and His identity is revealed only at His Passion (14: 61 f.) and in His death (15: 39). In the letters of St *Paul the title 'Christ' (or 'Messiah') is already on the way to becoming simply a name. See also CHRISTOLOGY, JESUS CHRIST, and MESSIANIC SECRET.

Messianic Secret. The phrase was given currency by W. *Wrede who in 1901 argued that Jesus' silencing of the demoniacs and the secrecy about His *messianic identity in Mk. were not historical reminiscences but arose out of a tension between the early Church's post-resurrection messianic belief and the historical reality of Jesus' ministry and self-understanding.

Metaphrast, the. A traditional name for *Simeon Metaphrastes.

Metaphysical Poets. A group of 17th-cent. poets including J. *Donne, G. *Herbert, R. *Crashaw, Henry *Vaughan, St Robert *Southwell, F. *Quarles, and T. *Traherne. The term was originally used in a pejorative sense, implying a pretentious display of learning, strained images, and wit leading to wilful obscurity, but since the end of the 19th cent. their positive qualities have won admiration.

metaphysics. The name given by the Greek editors of *Aristotle to his 'First Philosophy', and by analogy to treatises on cognate subjects; it originally merely indicated the position of the books on the subject in the Aristotelian *corpus*: after (*meta*) the *Physics*. The scope of metaphysical enquiry is hard to define. To Aristotelians it is the study of being as such; to idealists that of the ultimate implication of experience; to modern realists, that of the most pervasive features of reality (self-consistency, spatial and temporal relatedness, causality, etc.). Several currents in modern philosophy have cast doubts on the validity of metaphysics. Christian theology has tended to take a realist metaphysics for granted, but it has not been immune from the influence of contemporary philosophy.

metempsychosis. The doctrine that souls migrate from one body to another until complete purification has been reached. It is found in various religions, but it is fundamentally at variance with the Christian doctrine of the resurrection of the body.

Methodism. The system of religious faith and practice promoted by John and Charles *Wesley and their followers. In the 18th cent. the term was often used loosely of evangelicals of all sorts, but since the organization of Wesley's movement as a separate denomination, the name has been confined to members of this Church and others derived from it. See the following entry.

Methodist Churches. In 1784 J.*Wesley (q.v.) made provision for the continuance as a corporate body of the 'Yearly Conference of the People called Methodists' by nominating 100 persons whom he declared to be its members and laying down the method by which their successors were to be appointed. The Conference had power to appoint preachers to the various 'Preaching Houses' (later 'chapels'), the ownership of which was vested in boards of trustees. When Wesley died in 1791 the future relations of Methodism with the C of E were a matter of dispute, but the 'Plan of Pacification' adopted by the Conference of 1795 led to the administration of Baptism and Holy Communion in Methodist chapels and the declaration that the admission of a preacher to 'full connexion with the Conference' conferred ministerial rights. Ordination by the imposition of the hands of ministers was adopted again in 1836.

The secession of the *Methodist New Connexion in 1797 was small. In the first half of the 19th cent. there were secessions of the bodies who became the *Primitive Methodist Church, the *Bible Christians, and the Wesleyan Methodist Association and the Wesleyan Reformers, some of whom joined together in 1857 as the *United Methodist Free Churches. In 1907 the Methodist New Connexion, the Bible Christians, and the United Methodist Free Churches came together to form the *United Methodist Church; in 1932 this united with the original or 'Wesleyan' Methodist Church and the Primitive Methodist Church to form the Methodist Church in Great Britain. The United Methodists and the Wesley Reform Union remain separate bodies.

The organization of the Methodist Church is virtually presbyterian, the supreme authority being the Conference, which consists of equal numbers of ministers and laymen. According to a system peculiar to Methodism, 'All members [of the Methodist Church] shall have their names entered on a Class Book, shall be placed under the pastoral care of a Class Leader, and shall receive a Quarterly Ticket of Membership'. The weekly *class-meeting for 'fellowship in Christian experience' has been a valuable institution.

In 1784 Wesley 'set apart' T. *Coke and others for N. America. With the growth of the USA, Methodist numbers increased rapidly. After the Civil War there were two main Methodist Churches, one in the North and one in the South; they were reunited in 1939. In 1968 the Methodist Church of the United States was joined by the Evangelical United Brethren to form the United Methodist Church; there are still also a number of smaller Methodist bodies. American Methodism is largely 'episcopal' in possessing superintendents who are called bishops, though claiming no episcopal Orders in the Catholic sense. There are Methodist Churches in most parts of the world, many under separate Conferences. Those in *Canada, *South India, *Zambia, and *Australia have entered their respective United Churches, while in Continental Europe Methodists have united with other Protestants in *Belgium, *Spain, and *France. In 1997 Methodist members numbered over 33 million, of whom 13.7 million were in the USA and c.400,000 in Britain. See also ANGLICAN-METHODIST CONVERSATIONS.

Methodist New Connexion. The group of Methodists who in 1797 seceded from the Wesleyan *Methodist Church and in the union of 1907 were incorporated in the *United Methodist Church. The secession was led by A. *Kilham; the differences concerned the representation of the laity in the ruling courts of the Church and the exclusion of any use of Anglican worship.

Methodius and Cyril, Sts. See CYRIL, ST, AND METHODIUS, ST.

Methodius of Olympus, St (d. c.311), bishop in Lycia. Little is known of his life. He was apparently put to death in the *Diocletianic persecution. Only a small part of his extensive writing survives. The 'Symposium [Banquet], or On Chastity', also known as the 'Banquet of the Ten Virgins', extols virginity. In a treatise on the Resurrection, he took issue with *Origen and upheld the identity of the resurrection body with that worn in this life. His work on Free Will is a defence of human liberty against the fatalism of the *Gnostics. Feast day in the W., 18 Sept.; in the E., 20 June.

Methuselah. The eighth in the list of antediluvian patriarchs in Gen. 5 and the longest-lived (969 years; Gen. 5: 27).

metrical psalters. At the Reformation metrical psalmody was introduced in the Low Countries and in the French and Swiss Reformed Churches as a more biblical form of musical worship than the German *Lutheran hymns. In England under *Edward VI metrical versions of the Psalms were published by T. *Sternhold and others. Of the many later English versions the most widely used was that of N. *Tate and N. Brady (1696). After the mid-19th cent. the use of metrical psalters declined in England, but in Scotland has remained a characteristic feature of national worship.

Metrophanes Critopoulos (1589–1639), Patr. of *Alexandria from 1636. A Greek monk of Mt *Athos, he was sent by Cyril *Lucar to study theology in England. In 1638 he signed the anathemas pronounced against Lucar for Calvinism.

metropolitan. The title of a bishop exercising provincial powers. His duties include the summoning and presidency of provincial synods, the visitation of dioceses, the care of vacant sees, some share in the appointment and consecration of his *suffragan bishops, and some disciplinary powers over them. Metropolitans now commonly have the titles of *archbishop and *primate.

Mexico, Christianity in. The pre-Spanish

Aztec empire of Mexico appears to have had vague traditions of biblical and Christian ideas, but their source cannot be traced. Within five years of the first Spanish invasion (1519) *Franciscan and other RC missionaries arrived. Conversions were numerous, if not always entirely voluntary, and much paganism remained under an outward profession of Christianity. Mexican independence was won in 1821, but the Church's influence remained strong until the mid-19th cent., when Church and State were separated and all ecclesiastical property was nationalized. Under the 1917 constitution, Church schools were closed and the number of priests strictly regulated. Further conflict between Church and State arose in 1926, but by 1929 a *modus vivendi* had been achieved. In 1992 amendments to the constitution recognized Churches of all denominations as legal entities, with the right to hold property, and legalized the presence of foreign clergy.

Micah, Book of. *Minor Prophet. The author after whom this OT Book is named appears to have lived in the 8th cent. BC and begun to prophesy before the fall of *Samaria (c.721). Chs. 1–3 are generally accepted as his work; they foretell the destruction of Samaria and *Jerusalem. Most critics regard the rest of the Book as later. Chs 4–5 predict the regeneration of the people and the advent of a *Messiah; chs. 6–7 are mainly occupied with a dispute between God and His people. The complaints of God in Mic. 6: 3–5 form the model of the *Reproaches in the *Good Friday liturgy of the W. Church.

Michael the Archangel, St. In Dan. (10: 13 ff. and 12: 1) he is represented as the helper of the Chosen People; in Jude (v. 9) disputing with the devil over the body of *Moses; and in Rev. (12: 7–9) fighting the dragon. He also plays an important part in the *apocryphal literature. In the Church he was early regarded as the helper of Christian armies against the heathen and as a protector of individual Christians against the devil, especially at the hour of death. Feast day in the W., 29 Sept.; in the E., 8 Nov.

Michael Cerularius (d. 1058), Patr. of *Constantinople from 1043. The beginning of the schism between the E. and W. Churches is conventionally dated in his patriarchate. He was himself anti-Latin in outlook, attacking the *Filioque and the use of unleavened *bread in the Eucharist. The attempted mediation between the E. Emperor and the delegation led by Card. *Humbert of Silva Candida failed; the Latins excommunicated the Easterns; Cerularius anathematized the Latins (1054).

Michael the Syrian (1126–99), *Syrian Orthodox Patr. of *Antioch from 1166. His chronicle preserves many Syriac sources now lost and affords evidence for the history of the Syriac Orthodox Church and for the *Crusades.

Michaelis, Johann David (1717–91), German Protestant theologian. He is important mainly for his work on Hebrew and Arabic and on the early versions of the Bible. His treatment of the legislation of the *Pentateuch as a human achievement had far-reaching influence on the development of German biblical criticism.

Michelangelo (1475–1564), Italian artist. In 1496 Michelangelo Buonarroti went to Rome, where he carved a *Pietà* (finished in 1500) in which Christian austerity and classic beauty are harmonized. He carved his famous *David* (1501–4) during a temporary stay in Florence. Between 1508 and 1512 he painted the celebrated frescoes on the ceiling of the *Sistine Chapel. He also painted the *Last Judgement* on the altar wall (1534–41). He remained in Papal employment and was entrusted with the direction of the building of *St Peter's.

Micrologus. An 11th-cent. Roman Massbook, which provides evidence for the development of the W. liturgy. It was probably the work of Bernhold of Constance (c.1054–1100), a monk of Schaffhausen.

Middle Ages, the. The era preceding the Renaissance, now usually taken to date from c.1100, and extending to the end of the 15th cent.

Middleton, Thomas Fanshawe (1769–1822), first Bp. of Calcutta from 1814. His episcopate witnessed a great advance in Church life, including the foundation of the Bishop's College at Calcutta in 1820.

Midrash (Heb., 'investigation/study [sc. of Scripture]'). The term is commonly applied to the whole tradition of Jewish biblical exegesis, but it primarily denotes *rabbinic interpretation of the Bible as it flourished in Palestine and, to a lesser extent, in Babylonia, from the 2nd to the 8th cent. AD. In all the midrashic texts, Scripture is seen as the primary source of all wisdom and truth; it originated in the mind of God and so is inerrant and totally coherent. The aims of the expositor are to explain apparent errors, harmonize contradictions, and draw out the teaching of the Law and apply it to Jewish life. To this end he may resort to extreme techniques of text-manipulation. Despite the chronological problem, the rabbinic Midrashim have been used to elucidate NT exegesis of the OT, and they shed light on the works of *Origen and St *Jerome.

Migetius (8th cent.), Spanish heretic. He seems to have taught that God was revealed successively in *David (as Father), in Jesus (as Son), and in St *Paul (as Holy Ghost).

Migne, Jacques-Paul (1800–75), editor and publisher of theological literature. He published a vast collection of religious texts and dictionaries, notably the *Patrologia Latina*, a corpus of Latin ecclesiastical writers up to *Innocent III (221 vols., 1844–64), and the *Patrologia Graeca*, of Greek writers to 1439 (162 vols., 1857–66); these collections remain a standard means of citation.

Milan, Edict of. The document so called is a circular of 313 to provincial governors issued by the Emp. Licinius. In accordance with an agreement made with *Constantine at Milan, he extended to the E. provinces freedom of worship for all, including Christians, and the restitution of possessions lost by the Churches since the persecution of 303. See also PERSECUTIONS, EARLY CHRISTIAN.

Milanese rite. See AMBROSIAN RITE.

Mildred, St (*c.*700), Abbess of Minster-in-Thanet. Apparently the daughter of St Ermenburga, foundress of the nunnery at Minster, she entered her mother's convent and succeeded her as abbess. In the 11th cent. there were disputes about her relics. Feast day, 20 Feb. (formerly 13 July).

Milíč, Jan (*c.*1325–74), the most important of the pre-*Hussite reformers in Bohemia and Moravia. He held office in the Imperial chancery, but abandoned his temporal interests before the end of 1363 and preached vigorously against the vices of the clergy. In the later 1360s he was imprisoned by the *Inquisition at Rome, but died at Avignon under suspicion of heresy.

militant, the Church. The body of Christians still on earth, as distinct from those in *Purgatory and those in *Heaven.

Millenarianism. Belief in a future 'millennium', i.e. a 1,000-year period of blessedness. The main source of the concept within Christianity is Rev. 20. Some of its adherents hold that it will follow the Second Coming of Christ; others that it will precede the Advent and prepare the way for it.

In the early Church Millenarianism is found mainly among the *Gnostics and *Montanists, though it was also accepted by some of the early Fathers. In the Middle Ages the chief exponent of millenarian themes was *Joachim of Fiore. At the *Reformation many *Anabaptists, as well as the *Bohemian Brethren, were millenarians, and millenarian beliefs were widely held in 16th- and 17th-cent. English Protestantism. In Germany the millenarian view gained currency in the *Pietist movement of the 17th and 18th cents. In the 19th cent. new advocates of apocalyptic and millenarian ideas arose in the USA and in Britain, among them the *Irvingites, *Plymouth Brethren, and *Adventists, these last reviving the idea of a heavenly millennium after the Second Coming. In the 20th cent. the indigenous Churches of Asia, Africa, and South America produced a variety of millenarian beliefs. In 1944 the *Holy Office gave a ruling against millenarianism, and the major Christian bodies have treated the subject with reserve.

Millenary Petition. The petition presented in 1603 by the *Puritans to *James I, in which they prayed to be relieved from their 'common burden of human rites and ceremonies'. It was the immediate occasion of the *Hampton Court Conference (q.v.).

Mill Hill Missionaries, officially 'St Joseph's Society for Foreign Missions', a RC missionary society of secular priests and lay brothers devoted to the propagation of the Gospel among unevangelized peoples. It was founded in 1866 at Mill Hill, in NW London, by H. *Vaughan. It played an important role in *Uganda when a British

Protectorate was established in 1894. It also works in other parts of Africa and elsewhere.

Milman, Henry Hart (1791–1868), Dean of *St Paul's from 1849. His *History of the Jews* (1829) aroused criticism by the way in which it handled the OT narrative; it treated the Jews as an oriental tribe and attached little weight to the miraculous. His well-known *History of Latin Christianity* (1855) fostered intelligent study of medieval life and institutions.

Milner, John (1752–1826), RC apologist. From 1803 he was titular Bp. of Castabala and *Vicar Apostolic of the Midland District in England. His main work, *The End of Religious Controversy* (written 1801–2; published 1818), forcefully presented the RC case in a series of letters.

Miltiades, St (d. 314), Pope from 310 or 311. His pontificate is remarkable for *Constantine's victory over Maxentius and the issue of the so-called 'Edict of *Milan'. Miltiades held a Council which condemned *Donatism. Feast day, 10 Dec.

Miltitz, Carl von (c.1480–1529), Papal nuncio. After Card. T. de V. *Cajetan's failure to silence M. *Luther, Miltitz was chosen to take the *Golden Rose to *Frederick III, Elector of Saxony, and try to win his support against Luther. He took it upon himself to negotiate a compromise, and at a meeting at Altenburg in 1519, Luther agreed to refrain from further action pending reference of the matter to a German bishop. Miltitz proceeded to Leipzig, where, in the hope of restraining the movement, he disavowed J. *Tetzel, but two further meetings with Luther proved fruitless.

Milton, John (1608–74), poet and controversialist. He early won a high reputation for his scholarship and literary gifts: his *Ode on the Morning of Christ's Nativity* dates from 1629. In 1641 he joined the *Presbyterians, but his *Doctrine and Discipline of Divorce* (1643), pleading for the solubility of marriage, caused a breach. Its publication without a licence from the censor led the case to be submitted to Parliament and drew from Milton his celebrated *Areopagitica* (1644) in defence of the freedom of the press. From this time his religious views tended towards the *Independents, and from 1649 he supported the new government. In 1651 he went blind. Despite his admiration for O. *Cromwell, he disagreed with the ecclesiastical policy of his later years which ran counter to Milton's main idea of a complete disestablishment of Churches everywhere. With the fall of his religious and political hopes, he turned again to poetry. In his greatest work, *Paradise Lost* (q.v., published 1667), he undertook to 'justify the ways of God to men' and to show the cause of evil and injustice in the world. In 1671 appeared both its sequel, *Paradise Regained*, which deals with the Temptation of Christ, and *Samson Agonistes*, describing the last hours of Samson 'before the prison in Gaza'; here the blind hero partly represented Milton himself.

Milvian Bridge, Battle of the (312). The battle in which *Constantine defeated Maxentius. It enabled Constantine to establish himself with Licinius as joint Emperor and thus prepared the way for the so-called 'Edict of *Milan'.

Minims (Ordo Fratrum Minimorum). The Order of friars founded by St *Francis of Paola; the traditional date of the foundation is 1435. The main characteristic of their rule was a fourth vow of perpetual abstinence from eggs, cheese, butter, and milk, as well as meat and fish; the penitential aspects of the rule were somewhat relaxed in 1973. The Order reached its zenith in the 16th-17th cents., suffered severely in the late 18th and 19th cents., but experienced a revival in the 20th.

minister (Lat., 'servant'). A person officially charged to perform spiritual functions in the Church. Among non-episcopal bodies it is used as a general designation for any clergyman. In the liturgical formularies of the C of E it usually means the conductor of a service, who may or may not be a priest.

minor canon. A cleric attached to a *cathedral or *collegiate church to assist in rendering the daily service.

Minor Orders. The inferior ranks of the ministry, below the *Major Orders (q.v.). In the RC Church before 1972 there were four minor orders, namely *doorkeepers, *lectors, *exorcists, and *acolytes. In 1972 the minor orders, now called 'ministeria', were reduced to two, lectors and acolytes alone surviving. The rite by which minor orders are conferred consists chiefly of a commission to exercise their office and the handing over of the *instruments. The minor orders surviving in the E. Church are those of lector, *cantor, and *subdeacon.

Minor Prophets, the. In the OT the authors of the twelve shorter prophetic Books, as contrasted with the three Major Prophets—*Isaiah, *Jeremiah, and *Ezekiel. They are *Hosea, *Joel, *Amos, *Obadiah, *Jonah, *Micah, *Nahum, *Habakkuk, *Zephaniah, *Haggai, *Zechariah, and *Malachi.

Minorites. An older name for the *Franciscan 'Friars Minor'.

minster. A name applied in England to certain cathedrals (e.g. *York) and other large churches (e.g. Beverley). It originally meant a monastic establishment or its church, whether strictly a *monastery or a house of secular canons. In *Anglo-Saxon England 'old minsters', staffed by groups of clergy living in community, were the centres of vast parishes, within which new churches, each served by a single priest, served smaller areas.

Minucius Felix (2nd or 3rd cent.), author of the *Octavius*. This is a defence of Christianity in the form of a conversation between Octavius, a Christian, and Caecilius, a pagan, who is converted by the argument.

miracle. According to the traditional view, a miracle is a sensible fact produced by a special intervention of God, transcending the normal order of things, usually termed the Law of Nature. The possibility of miracles began to be questioned with the rise of modern science and its growing tendency to regard the world as a closed system. The miracles of Scripture and history were then normally regarded as facts within the sphere of natural explanation, misrepresented by credulous contemporaries. On the other hand, it is argued that if God is held to be the supreme First Cause responsible for, and not subject to, the Laws of Nature, it is likely that He should, from time to time, act directly without the intervention of secondary causes.

Whereas Protestant orthodoxy normally confines itself to belief in the miracles recorded in the Bible, Catholics claim that miracles have occurred throughout history; the reputed cures at *Lourdes are among the best known. Proof of a miracle at the intercession of the candidate is a necessary element in the current RC procedures for *beatification and *canonization.

Miracle Plays. See MYSTERY PLAYS.

Mirfield. See COMMUNITY OF THE RESURRECTION.

Mirk, John. See MYRC, JOHN.

Miserere. A common designation of Ps. 51 (Vulg. 50) derived from the initial word of the Latin version.

misericord. The projection on the underside of a hinged seat of a choir-stall, commonly said to have been designed to provide support for those incapable of standing for long periods during Divine worship.

Mishnah (Heb., 'repetition', hence 'instruction'). An early and authoritative document of rabbinic Judaism. It is attributed to Rabbi Judah ha-Nashi (d. c.AD 229). It is a redaction and collection of earlier material and forms the basis of the *Talmud of both Palestine and Babylonia. The Mishnah and Talmud have had an influence on Judaism second only to that of Scripture.

Misrule, Lord of, also known as the **Abbot (or Master) of Misrule.** In medieval times, a person selected to preside over the Christmas revels and games.

Missa Cantata (Lat., 'Sung Mass'). In the W. Church the form of Mass in which the celebrant and congregation sang the liturgical parts of the rite set to music for *High Mass, but without *deacon or *subdeacon. The term is now obsolete.

Missal. The book containing the words and ceremonial directions for the celebration of Mass. Missals began to appear in the 10th cent., combining in one book what had previously been contained in several (the *Antiphonary, *Evangeliary, etc.); their development was fostered by the practice of saying private Masses. The 1970 *Missale Romanum*, however, omits the biblical readings which were issued in a separate *lectionary.

missions. The propagation of the Christian faith among non-Christian people was one of the main tasks of the Church from the first. The command to 'make all nations my disciples' was attributed to the Risen Christ (Mt. 28: 19). Apart from the labours of St *Paul and the missionary journeys rightly or wrongly attributed to the Apostles (notably St *Thomas), unknown Christians soon carried the Gospel throughout the Roman world and beyond it. Missionaries of the *Church of the East went as far as *China. St *Patrick's work in *Ireland (5th cent.) was followed by activity in *Scotland and England, where St *Aidan's work in the north was supplemented in the south by the Roman mission of St *Augustine. *Gregory I's instruction to him not to destroy pagan temples but to turn them into Christian churches was important in the development of missionary thought. In the 8th cent. British missionaries took part in the conversion of northern and central Europe. The conquests of *Charlemagne (d. 814) were accompanied by the forcible Baptism of the vanquished. In Slavonic lands there were missions from *Constantinople as well as Rome. The *Poles, Magyars and *Russians were converted. In the Middle Ages efforts were made to convert the remaining heathen tribes of Europe, missions to the Muslims were initiated (though largely overshadowed by the *Crusades), and work was carried on among the Tartars and Chinese.

The *Counter-Reformation brought a renewal of missionary endeavour in the RC Church. New gains were sought to counteract the 'losses' in north-western Europe, and the *Dominicans, *Franciscans, *Augustinians, and the newly-founded *Capuchins and *Jesuits worked unstintingly in the Americas and in *India, *Japan, China, and in *Africa. In 1622 Gregory XV formed the Congregation of *Propaganda which struggled to liberate missionary work from Spanish and Portuguese secular interests. It subsequently had general supervision of missionary work in the RC Church. In the 19th cent. a number of modern religious orders devoted themselves specifically to missionary work, including the *Marists, the *Holy Ghost Fathers, the *Mill Hill Missionaries, the Society of the *Divine Word, and the *White Fathers. Prominence was given to charitable and educational work, and women religious

played an important part. In the early 20th cent. a different approach was foreshadowed by *Benedict XV's encyclical *Maximum illud* (1919); this was directed to the firm establishment of the Church locally, with a clergy and hierarchy of its own. The Second *Vatican Council in 1965 stressed the need to understand people and their cultures as a precondition for adapting liturgy and theology.

In the Reformed Churches there was at first little missionary activity for various reasons. The *SPCK and *SPG were founded in 1698 and 1701 respectively, but the main missionary work was still carried out by the *Moravians and the Danish-Halle missions in India. The *Evangelical Revival gave a new impetus to evangelization on a world-wide scale. The Methodist Missionary Society dates from 1786, the Baptist Missionary Society from 1792, the *LMS from 1795, the *CMS from 1799, and the *British and Foreign Bible Society from 1804. Similar organizations were being founded in America and in other parts of Europe. This phenomenal expansion of work saw the rise of other societies with specialized spheres of work, such as the *Universities' Mission to Central Africa (1859). There has also been a growth in ecumenism, until recently confined to Protestant denominations. The World Missionary Conference at *Edinburgh in 1910 aimed at world evangelism on an ecumenical basis. The International Missionary Council (founded in 1921) in 1961 joined the *World Council of Churches and became its Division of World Mission and Evangelism (now its Mission, Education and Witness unit). Since 1963 it has enjoyed the co-operation of the *Orthodox Church which, in the 20th cent. expanded from Europe and America to parts of Africa and the Far East. Another element in the missionary scene is the activity of various 'independent' Churches which are not affiliated to the World Council of Churches. At the same time, Christian missionaries from the non-Western world are trying to introduce the Gospel into W. culture and to overcome the gulf between the established Churches and secularized people.

Mit brennender Sorge (Ger., 'with burning anxiety'). The encyclical condemning Nazism which *Pius XI ordered to be read in all RC churches in Germany on Palm Sunday 1937.

Mithraism. Mithras was a god associated with light and the sanctity of oaths in India and Iran; he became the object of a distinctive cult in the Roman Empire probably *c.*AD 100. The mysteries of Mithras were celebrated by small groups of male initiates in underground temples, lined on either side by benches used for ritual meals and dominated by a representation of the god slaying the primal bull. Mithraism seems to have died out in the 4th cent.

mitre. The liturgical head-dress and part of the insignia of a bishop. In the E. Church it takes the form of a crown, decorated with medallions in enamel or embroidery. In the W. Church it is shield-shaped, usually of embroidered satin and often jewelled; two fringed lappets hang down at the back.

Mixed Chalice. Nearly all the historic Liturgies enjoin or presuppose the mixture of water with the wine in the Eucharistic chalice. The practice reflects what Christ probably did at the *Last Supper. The first BCP of 1549 directed the continuance of this usage, but the direction disappeared in 1552. Its revival in the C of E in the 19th cent. became a matter of dispute between the *Anglo-Catholics and their opponents.

mixed marriage. A marriage between Christians of different denominations or of a Christian and an unbaptized person.The term is used especially when one of the parties is a RC; such marriages still require the permission of the diocesan bishop or other competent authority.

Moberly, Robert Campbell (1845–1903), Anglican theologian. His main works were *Ministerial Priesthood* (1897), with a notable appendix on the validity of *Anglican Ordinations, and *Atonement and Personality* (1901), an original and profound study of the doctrine of the *Atonement.

Modalism. In the early Church a form of unorthodox teaching on the *Trinity which denied the permanence of the three Persons and maintained that the distinctions in the Godhead were only transitory. It was a form of *Monarchianism (q.v.).

Moderates. In the Church of *Scotland, the party in the ascendant in the second half of the 18th cent. They held a more moderate conception of doctrine and discipline than their opponents (the 'Evangelicals').

Moderator. In *Presbyterian Church courts the Moderator is the presbyter appointed *primus inter pares* to constitute the court and to preside over its proceedings. The Moderator of the *General Assembly of the Church of Scotland serves as the Church's representative.

Modern Church People's Union. An Anglican society for the advancement of liberal religious thought, especially in the C of E. Founded in 1898 as the 'Churchmen's Union', from 1928 to 1987 it was called the 'Modern Churchmen's Union'. It seeks to uphold the comprehensiveness of the C of E and to maintain the legitimacy of doctrinal restatement in accordance with the requirements of modern science.

Modern Devotion. See DEVOTIO MODERNA.

Modernism. A movement in the RC Church which aimed at bringing Catholic belief into closer relation with modern philosophy, the historical and other sciences, and social ideas. It arose spontaneously in several countries in the late 19th cent.; it was especially strong in France.

The main tenets of the movement were: (1) whole-hearted adoption of the critical view of the Bible, by then generally accepted outside the RC Church; (2) an inclination to reject the 'intellectualism' of Scholastic theology and to subordinate doctrine to practice; and (3) a teleological attitude to history, finding the meaning of the historic process in its issue rather than in its origins. Since the Church's growth took place under the guidance of the Spirit, the essence of the Gospel will lie in its full expansion rather than in its primitive kernel. This belief was often reflected in deep scepticism about Christian origins.

Leaders of the movement included A. *Loisy, M. *Blondel, L. *Laberthonnière, F. *von Hügel, and G. *Tyrrell. *Leo XIII tolerated the movement; *Pius X condemned it in 1907. While the clergy who were identified with the movement were mostly excommunicated, the laymen were left untouched.

In the wider sense the term 'Modernist'

has been used of radical critics of traditional theology in non-RC Churches, especially of the thought associated with the *Modern Church People's Union.

Moffat, Robert (1795–1883), missionary. Sent to *South Africa by the *LMS, he converted the Hottentot chief known as Africaner and gained official support. He worked first among the Bechuanas and later among the Matabele. In 1840 he persuaded D. *Livingstone, his future son-in-law, to go to Africa.

Moffatt, James (1870–1944), NT scholar. A minister of the *Free Church of Scotland, from 1927 to 1939 he taught at the *Union Theological Seminary, New York. His translation of the Bible is written in colloquial English; the NT appeared in 1913, the OT in 1924, and the whole was revised in 1935. He also edited a commentary on the NT based on his translation.

Mogila, Peter (1596–1646), Orthodox theologian and from 1632 Metropolitan of Kiev. The most important of his writings was his 'Confession'. A comprehensive survey of the faith of the Orthodox Church, it was approved by the Synod of *Jassy (1642), published in 1645, and remains a primary witness to Orthodox doctrine.

Möhler, Johann Adam (1796–1838), RC historian and theologian. He held professorships at *Tübingen and then at Munich. A leading representative of the Catholic 'Tübingen School', he emphasized the nature of the Church as a living community filled by the Spirit rather than as an institution.

Molina, Luis de (1535–1600), Spanish *Jesuit theologian and author of the *Concordia liberi arbitrii cum gratiae donis* (1588).
    The term 'Molinism' is used to describe doctrines of *grace of the kind elaborated in Molina's *Concordia*; their central tenet is that the efficacy of grace has its ultimate foundation, not within the substance of the Divine gift of grace itself, but in the Divinely foreknown fact of free human co-operation with this gift. The implications of this teaching were attacked by conservative theologians and the ensuing controversies '*De Auxiliis' were the subject of a special Congregation in Rome (1598–1607).

Molinos, Miguel de (1628–96), Spanish

*Quietist. Sent to Rome in 1663, he became a much-sought-after confessor and spiritual director. In 1675 he published his 'Spiritual Guide' (*Guía espiritual*), recommending the prayer of acquired or active *contemplation. Unlike discursive *meditation, this prayer of quietude, he held, needs no help from reason or imagination, but a total submission to the will of God and, once obstacles have been overcome, temptations can be disregarded. This imperfect contemplation is open to all under expert guidance, in contrast to infused or passive (perfect) contemplation which is entirely God's gift. Molinos was arrested by the *Holy Office in 1686, tried and condemned; he submitted in 1687 but remained in prison for the rest of his life.

Moltmann, Jürgen (1926–), German Reformed theologian. His faith and theological perspectives were influenced by his experiences as a British prisoner-of-war from 1945 to 1948. He held various academic posts; from 1967 until his retirement he was a professor at *Tübingen. He is best known for three books translated into English as *Theology of Hope* (Eng. tr., 1967), *The Crucified God* (Eng. tr., 1974), and *The Church in the Power of the Spirit* (Eng.tr., 1977), which were followed by works on *messianic theology. His understanding of God is characterized by Divine passibility (in contrast with the traditional notion of *impassibility) and social trinitarianism. The Divine Persons are seen as involved in a history of mutual relationships with the world.

Monarchianism. A 2nd- and 3rd-cent. theological movement. Its adherents, in their attempts to safeguard *Monotheism and the Unity ('Monarchy') of the Godhead, failed to do justice to the independent subsistence of the Son. There were two groups. The 'Adoptionist' Monarchians held that Jesus was God only in the sense that a power or influence from the Father rested upon His human person. The '*Modalist' Monarchians held that in the Godhead the only differentiation was a succession of modes or operations; they were also called '*Patripassians', as their doctrine implied that the Father suffered as the Son.

Monarchian Prologues. The short introductory narrative passages prefixed in many MSS of the *Vulgate to each of the Gospels. They were formerly held to be of

2nd–3rd-cent. date and from *Monarchian sources: hence the name. Most recent critics hold that they were *Priscillianist in inspiration and date from the late-4th or early-5th cent.

monastery. The house of a community of *monks or *nuns.

Monastic Breviary. The *Breviary formerly used by monks and nuns following the Rule of St *Benedict. It has been replaced by four alternative forms of the *Office provided in the *Thesaurus Liturgiae Monasticae Horarum* (1977).

monasticism. Christian monasticism is motivated by a desire to seek God through Christ by a life of *asceticism and *prayer; the Christian monk believes himself to have a personal call from God to lead the monastic life on a permanent basis. The two main forms of monastic life are the eremitical or *hermit life, and the *cenobitical or common life. It involves celibacy and a certain amount of seclusion from the world, normally including the renunciation of private property. Prayer, reading, and work form the basis of the monk's daily life. His main duty is to offer praise to God within the confines of the monastery; in cenobitic monasticism the liturgy, and particularly the Divine *Office, came to play a central part in monastic prayer. Monastic work may take any form; traditionally it includes agriculture, scholarship, and teaching.

The roots of monasticism probably lie in the ascetical movements of the early Church. Its development in Egypt (among the 'Desert Fathers') in the 4th cent. was of special importance: St *Antony and St *Pachomius are seen as the forerunners of the eremitical and cenobitic life respectively. Syria, Palestine, and Asia Minor also saw a rapid development of monasticism. In the W., E. monastic tradition became important as its literature became known in the 5th cent. John *Cassian, as well as the *Regula Magistri*, influenced St *Benedict, who wrote his Rule for cenobitic monasteries in the early 6th cent. By the 9th cent. it was dominant in W. Europe (see BENEDICTINE ORDER). The new forms of religious life which began in the W. in the Middle Ages (*canons regular and *mendicant friars) borrowed many of their institutions from monasticism. In the 16th cent. monastic life

disappeared in the Reformed Churches, but it continued in RC countries until the French Revolution and the Napoleonic conquests. A revival took place in the mid-19th cent. in many European countries, and monasticism spread to N. America and *Australia. In the 20th cent. it began to take root in Africa, Asia, and South America.

Monasticism also flourished in the Byzantine Empire. It spread with Christianity to the Slav countries; there were monasteries in Kiev in the 11th cent., and a flourishing monastic life around Moscow in the 14th. A 19th-cent. revival of Russian monasticism continued until 1917. A special place in Orthodox monasticism is held by Mt *Athos, where there are monks from all the Orthodox Churches.

See also CARTHUSIAN and CISTERCIAN ORDERS and CLUNY; also RELIGIOUS ORDERS IN ANGLICANISM.

Monasticon Anglicanum. A vast collection of monastic charters and other sources relating to English monasteries and collegiate churches in the Middle Ages, published (1655–73) by Sir William *Dugdale.

Mone, Franz Joseph (1796–1871), German historian and liturgical scholar. His *Lateinische und griechische Messen* (1850) contains the text of some early Masses which are notable for the absence of all reference to the cycle of liturgical feasts; they are commonly known as the 'Mone Masses'.

Monica, St (*c.*331–87), mother of St *Augustine of Hippo. Widowed at the age of 40, Monica became apprehensive at Augustine's waywardness and prayed earnestly for his conversion. She pursued him from Africa to Italy and from Rome to Milan, where she came under the influence of St *Ambrose and witnessed her son's conversion. Feast day, 27 Aug. (formerly, 4 May, as in the American BCP, 1979).

Monism. The philosophy which seeks to explain all that is in terms of a single reality. Materialism is a form of Monism. Monism is incompatible with the Christian belief in a radical distinction between the uncreated God and the created order.

monk. The word is popularly applied to any member of a *religious community of men living under vows of chastity, poverty, and obedience, but its proper use is confined to *hermits or members of a monastic community, whose main duty is to offer praise to God within a *monastery.

Monogenes, The. A Greek hymn, so called from its opening word, which forms part of the Byzantine Liturgy.

monolatry. Restriction of worship to one god, when other gods may be held to exist. Some OT scholars have held it to be a necessary stage in the transition from polytheism to *monotheism, and that it marked Israel's condition from the *Sinai Covenant to the time of the Prophets.

Monophysitism. The doctrine that in the Incarnate Christ there is only one nature, not two. The term covers a variety of positions, some capable of orthodox interpretation, others not. The term 'Monophysite' was first used in the aftermath of the Council of *Chalcedon (451) to describe all those who rejected the Council's Definition that the Incarnate Christ is one Person 'in two natures'. They did so on the ground that it obscured the full reality of the Incarnation and seemed to them to verge on *Nestorianism.

*Eutyches taught a heretical form of Monophysitism, namely that after the Incarnation there was only one nature in Christ, and that that nature was not 'consubstantial with us'. Moderate Monophysites taught that in the Incarnate Christ there was 'one nature out of two' (i.e. Divine and human). They were led by *Severus of Antioch. An extreme type of Monophysitism was held by the *Aphthartodocetae (q.v.).

During the 5th and 6th cents. many attempts were made to reconcile the Monophysites to the Catholics, including those by the Emps. *Zeno, *Justinian I, and *Heraclius, but separate hierarchies emerged to constitute the *Armenian, *Coptic, *Ethiopian, and *Syrian Orthodox Churches. In modern times there have been renewed contacts with both the Orthodox Churches and the RC Church, and a measure of agreement on Christology is reflected in recent statements.

Monotheism. Belief in one personal and transcendent God. According to traditional Christian teaching it was the original religion of man, but lost by most men as a consequence of the *Fall. In the 19th cent.

it was often maintained that the religious beliefs of man had progressed from *animism by way of polytheism to monotheism, but this theory is now less widely held.

Monothelitism. A 7th-cent. heresy confessing only one will in Christ. Under the auspices of the Emp. *Heraclius a formula seemingly acceptable to both *Monophysites and Chalcedonians was produced in 624; it asserted two natures in Christ but only one mode of activity or 'energy'. When *Sergius, Patr. of Constantinople, wrote to *Honorius c.634, the Pope in his reply used the unfortunate expression 'one will' in Christ, which then replaced the 'one energy'. It was taken up in the '*Ecthesis', issued by Heraclius in 638. This forbade the mention of one or two energies and admitted only one will. It was accepted by two Councils at Constantinople but rejected by successive Popes. The controversy was finally settled in 681 when the Third Council of *Constantinople proclaimed the existence of two wills in Christ, Divine and human, to be the orthodox faith.

Monsignor, usually abbreviated Mgr. In the RC Church an ecclesiastical title attached to an office or distinction ordinarily bestowed by the Pope.

monstrance. The vessel used for exposing relics or, more usually, the Eucharistic Host for veneration. It now normally consists of a disc-shaped receptacle, framed by gold or silver rays, with a glass window.

Montaigne, Michel de (1533–92), French essayist. He was a counsellor in the *Cours des Aides* at Périgueux, but on succeeding to the family estates (1568), he sold his office and in 1571 retired to the Chateau de Montaigne. He published the first two books of his *Essais* in 1580 and a third in 1585. The longest of his *Essais* is an 'Apologia' for *Raymond of Sebonde. In this he demonstrates the fallibility of the human mind and its inability to know anything. Scepticism is used to humble man's pride and defend the Faith, revealed exclusively to the RC Church, by destroying all philosophical and religious certainty based on unaided human reason, and by emphasizing each man's need of grace. The *Essais* were placed on the *Index in 1676.

Montalembert, Charles René Forbes (1810–70), French RC historian. He associated himself with the movement sponsored by F. R. de *Lamenais and H.-D. *Lacordaire, but when *Gregory XVI condemned *liberalism in 1832, he submitted and ceased to propagate his views for some time. His historical works were polished in style, but uncritical. The best-known is his *Moines d'occident* (1860–7; Eng. tr., 1896).

Montanism. A 2nd-cent. apocalyptic movement; its adherents expected a speedy outpouring of the Holy Spirit on the Church, and saw the first manifestations of this in their own leaders. Montanus began preaching in Phrygia in 156/7 or in 172. Associated with him were two women, Prisca and Maximilla.

The ascetic traits which developed were particularly prominent in an offshoot of the movement in Roman Africa, which won the allegiance of *Tertullian. It disallowed second marriages, condemned the existing regulations on fasting as too lax, and forbade flight in persecution.

Monte Cassino. The principal monastery of the *Benedictine Order, founded by St *Benedict *c.*529. It reached the peak of its prosperity in the 11th cent., when the Norman church was consecrated (1071) and the fame of the *scriptorium established.

Montes Pietatis. In the later Middle Ages, charitable institutions for lending money in cases of need. From the mid-15th cent. Italian *Franciscans established many successful *montes*, which charged a low contribution towards expenses. They were opposed by the *Dominicans on the ground that they offended the canonical prohibition of *usury, but they were approved by *Leo X in 1515.

Montesquieu, Charles Louis Joseph de Secondat, Baron de la Brède et de (1689–1755), French historian and philosopher. His *Letters persanes* (published anonymously, 1721), was a witty satire on European society, which attacked Louis XIV's government and the Catholic Church. His main work, the *Esprit des lois* (1748), defends the English principle of the division of power as the safeguard of liberty and the way to an ideal form of government. Here he regards Christianity as a powerful moral force in society which, though directly occupied only with the next life, makes for order and happiness in this.

Month's Mind. The *Requiem Mass until 1970 celebrated on the 30th day after death or burial.

Montini, Giovanni Battista. See PAUL VI.

Mont-St-Michel. On a rocky island off the north coast of France an oratory is said to have been established by St Aubert, Bp. of Avranches (8th cent.), in obedience to the commands of an apparition of St *Michael. In 966 a *Benedictine monastery was founded; a fortress was added later.

Montserrat. This mountain, near Barcelona, is surrounded by legends which locate there the Castle of the Holy *Grail. The *Benedictine monastery, whose church enshrines the famous image of 'Our Lady of Montserrat', was founded between 1025 and 1035. St *Ignatius Loyola hung up his sword there. It is a place of pilgrimage.

Moody, Dwight Lyman (1837–99), American evangelist. Becoming a *Congregationalist in 1856, Moody embarked on evangelistic work in connection with his Sunday School in Chicago. In 1870 he was joined by Ira David Sankey (1840–1908), who regularly accompanied his preaching with singing and organ-playing. They toured both America and Britain. The 'Sankey and Moody Hymn Book' (1873) incorporated many of the songs used by Sankey and other revivalists. Moody founded various institutions in the USA.

moral philosophy. The branch of philosophy which explores questions of what is good and right apart from any considerations derived from a supernatural revelation; it examines the nature, meaning, and justification of moral concepts.

Moral Re-Armament. The name by which the work of the *Oxford Group came to be known after 1938, when F. N. D. *Buchman called for 'moral and spiritual re-armament'.

moral theology. The study of moral questions and the foundations of morality in the light of Christian belief. From earliest times Christian thinkers were concerned with questions of morality, but moral theology began to emerge as a discipline independent of dogmatic theology only at the end of the 16th cent. Since the early 19th cent. Protestants have generally preferred the title 'Christian ethics' for the discipline of Christian moral enquiry.

The '*Didache' contains perhaps the earliest Christian treatise on moral theology in its teaching of the Two Ways. With the conversion of large numbers of pagans in the 4th cent., strict moral teaching became urgent. In the W. St *Augustine's adaptation of classical and *Neoplatonist thought to Christian theological purposes was the dominant patristic influence on medieval ethical thought; he established *charity (or love) as the fundamental principle of Christian morality from which other values flow. With the revival of *Aristotelianism in the 13th cent. St *Thomas Aquinas linked moral theology to *natural law, the natural and supernatural virtues, and the gifts of the Holy Spirit. At the same time, precursors of the modern *casuistry made their appearance with *Raymond de Peñafort's *Summa de Poenitentia* (*c.*1225).

At the time of the *Counter-Reformation the RC Church needed to respond to the Protestant emphasis on *grace. The period was marked by the growth of, and controversies over, different systems of casuistry, especially *Probabilism, and by numerous manuals on moral theology. This development was fostered by the increased frequency of sacramental confession. The most renowned moral theologian in modern times is St *Alphonsus Liguori. Against the harsher *Probabiliorist method, then common in France and Italy, his *Theologia Moralis* (1753–5) established the milder *Equiprobabilism. In the 20th cent. RC moral theologians sought to give greater prominence to biblical authority, to the role of moral theology in providing positive guidance in Christian living rather than instructions to confessors about minimum standards of obligation, to the social dimensions of human existence, and to *ecumenical dialogue.

Protestants have tended to dissociate themselves from attempts to produce systems of duties binding on all Christians, arguing that good works are a free response to the completed work of *justification in Christ. J. *Calvin gave more weight to the directive use of moral law than M. *Luther, and in 17th-cent. England both *Puritans and *High Churchmen were interested in moral theology, but in the 18th cent. Prot-

estant thinkers looked increasingly to *moral philosophy for guidance. In the 20th cent. K. *Barth's revolt against liberal theology helped to reinstate in Europe a distinctively theological conception of ethics, while in the *United States of America R. *Niebuhr's attack on the '*Social Gospel' movement employed an Augustinian awareness of sin to criticize the dominant optimism. Distinctions between RC and Protestant moral theology have become less sharp, and in all Churches cultural and technological change has set the agenda for many debates in moral theology, e.g. concerning *bioethics, social and economic justice, and the morality of modern *war.

Morality Play, or **Morality.** A form of drama, popular in the 15th and 16th cents., in which a moral truth or lesson was inculcated by the chief characters personifying various abstract qualities. It developed independently of the *Mystery Plays, but at the same time.

Moravian Brethren, now commonly known as the **Moravian Church.** The remnant of the *Bohemian Brethren who from 1722 settled at *Herrnhut under the patronage of N. L. von *Zinzendorf, became known as the Moravian or United Brethren. There was a strong *Pietistic element in the community, and in the early days they had close links with the *Lutheran Church. They felt they had a peculiar calling to witness to Christ among people who did not know Him, and in 1732 Moravian missionaries began work in the *West Indies, soon going also to Greenland (1733), *South Africa (1736), and Labrador (1752).

Moravians have always emphasized fellowship and service rather than credal statements. They have retained the offices of *bishops, *presbyters, and *deacons, but they do not wholly correspond with their Catholic counterparts. The Moravian Church is made up of 19 self-governing Provinces; it has a membership of *c.*600,000, of whom over a quarter are in Tanzania.

More, Hannah (1745–1833), religious writer and philanthropist. Under the influence of W. *Wilberforce, she established schools at Cheddar and in the neighbouring villages at a time when schemes of popular education were almost unprecedented; religious teaching was combined with training in spinning. Between 1793 and 1799 she wrote many tracts designed to combat the influence of the French Revolution (collected as *Cheap Repository Tracts*).

More, Henry (1614–87), *Cambridge Platonist. In various works he defended theism and immortality against the materialism represented by T. *Hobbes. He emphasized the instinctive reasonableness of Divine truth and affirmed the existence of a higher principle than reason, which he termed the 'Divine Sagacity'. It was, he held, possible to apprehend this higher truth only through the cultivation of a righteous disposition and a free intellect, though afterwards this intuitive instinct might be confirmed by the methods of reason.

More, St Thomas (1478–1535), Lord Chancellor of England. His house in Chelsea was a centre of learning and piety. His most famous work, *Utopia* (1516), describes an ideal community living by natural law, religion, and reason; it aims satirical barbs at contemporary abuses.

From 1510 More held a series of appointments, succeeding T. *Wolsey as Lord Chancellor in 1529. During the 1520s, when the *Lutheran controversy raged throughout Europe, he emerged as a zealous defender of Catholicism. He had some part in *Henry VIII's *Assertio Septem Sacramentorum* (1521). However, his reluctance to support Henry in his pursuit of a divorce rendered his political position difficult and Henry's attack on the liberties of the Church in England made it untenable. In 1532, within hours of Convocation's acceptance of Henry's demands (see SUBMISSION OF THE CLERGY), More resigned the Chancellorship. When he refused to take the oath to the Act of Succession in 1534 he was confined to the Tower. He was tried for high treason on a charge of having denied the Royal *Supremacy, convicted, and executed. Feast day, formerly 9 July; now, with St John *Fisher, 22 June; in CW, 6 July.

Morgan, William (1545–1604), translator of the *Welsh Bible. He was successively Bp. of *Llandaff (from 1595) and (from 1601) of *St Asaph. While he was still a parish priest, he translated the Bible into Welsh (published, 1588). He based the NT on a translation already published in 1567, but rendered the OT from the original languages single-handed.

Morin, Jean (1591–1659), French *Oratorian theologian. A biblical and patristic scholar, he advised *Urban VIII on the subject of *Orders during attempts to unite the E. and W. Churches. He rejected the idea that the Tradition of the *Instruments constituted the *matter of Ordination.

Morison, James (1816–93), founder of the '*Evangelical Union'. As minister of the *United Secession Church at Kilmarnock, he preached that Christ made atonement for all, and published his beliefs in a short tract. He was expelled from the United Secession Church in 1841; in 1843 he founded the 'Evangelical Union'.

Mormons. The popular name for the 'Church of Jesus Christ of Latter-day Saints'. This was founded in Manchester, New York, in 1830 by Joseph Smith (1805–44), who claimed to have been given, through a revelation, *The Book of Mormon*. In 1843 Smith had another revelation sanctioning polygamy. Brigham Young, Smith's successor as President, in 1847 moved their headquarters to Salt Lake Valley in Utah. The practice of polygamy brought them into conflict with the Federal Government until 1890 when their President advised his followers to conform to the law.

The Mormons accept a modified form of the doctrine of the *Trinity, in which Father, Son, and Holy Spirit are believed to be separate Gods united in a common godhead of purpose and perfection. Their teaching has a strong *Adventist element. They hold that after His resurrection Christ ministered briefly in America and that Zion will be built in the W. hemisphere. They lay stress on missionary activity, and each male is expected to devote two years to this work at his own expense. In 1998 Mormons claimed a membership of 10 million.

Morning Prayer. See MATTINS.

Morone, Giovanni (1509–80), cardinal. He became nuncio to Germany in 1536 and was present at the Diets of *Hagenau (1540), *Ratisbon (1541), and Speyer (1542). He showed some sympathy with the Reformers' grievances and tried to establish less embittered relations. In 1542 he was created a cardinal and nominated as one of three to preside over the forthcoming Council of *Trent. In 1557 *Paul IV imprisoned him for supposed heresy. He was cleared of all the charges under *Pius IV, who employed him during the last sessions of the Council.

Morris, William (1834–96), English artist and author. He aimed at the reintegration of life and art, the unity of which he held had been broken by the specialization and mechanization of post-medieval times. Believing that a sound social life was a prerequisite of healthy art, in 1884 he became the leader of the Socialist League. His earlier romances were modelled on G. *Chaucer; the later ones deal with either the remote past or the distant future. In 1890 he founded the Kelmscott Press.

Morrison, Robert (1782–1834), first Protestant missionary in *China. Working under the *LMS, he was sent to Canton in 1807. With great difficulty he secured lessons in Chinese, which could not then be taught to foreigners. He published a Chinese grammar, a dictionary, and a translation of the Bible.

mortal sin. The traditional designation for the most serious category of sin (called in 1 Jn. 5: 16 'sin unto death'); in the RC Church it is now also officially described as 'grave sin'. According to Catholic teaching such sin consists in a deliberate turning away from God as man's last end by seeking satisfaction in a creature; it involves the loss of sanctifying grace and eternal damnation unless it is followed by adequate repentance. To fall into this category a sin must be committed with a clear knowledge of its guilt and with full consent of the will, and must concern a 'grave matter'.

mortification. An ecclesiastical term used to describe the action of 'killing' or 'deadening' the lusts of the flesh through spiritual self-denial and the infliction of bodily discomfort. See also ASCETICISM.

Mortmain. The condition of land which could not be alienated because it was held by an ecclesiastical or other corporation. Statutes of Mortmain designed to limit the Church's power to acquire property were repeatedly enacted in the Middle Ages. In England the concept was finally abandoned in 1960.

Moschus, John (b. *c.*550; d. 619 or 634), spiritual writer. About 575 he retired to a monastery near Jerusalem; later, he travelled widely, visiting or settling at various monastic centres. His *Pratum Spirituale* contains a large collection of anecdotes on the monastic life; it became very popular as a devotional manual.

Moses, the Founder and Lawgiver of Israel. According to the *Pentateuchal narrative, he was born in Egypt and owed his life to being hidden and rescued by Pharaoh's daughter. He received a Divine commission to rescue the Hebrews from their bondage and eventually led them out of Egypt. During the journey across the desert they often rebelled against him, but by his intercession they were given *manna for food and the Ten *Commandments to guide their common life. He was granted a sight of the Promised Land and died in Moab.

Opinions on the reliability of this account range from those who regard the narrative about Moses as substantially true to those who deny his existence. Most scholars agree that some such commanding figure as Moses is presupposed by the unity of the Israelite tribes and that it is unlikely that the Hebrew people would have sought their beginnings in bondage unless such had been the fact.

Moses figures prominently in Christian tradition. At the *Transfiguration scene he appears as the Representative of the Law. He was the subject of various legends.

Moses, The Assumption of. A composite Jewish work of the 1st cent. AD, much of which has been lost. It contained a speech of *Moses prophesying the history of the Israelites and probably also an account of Moses' death and taking up into heaven.

Moses bar Kepha (*c.*815–903), *Syrian Orthodox Bp.of Mosul from *c.*863. He is said to have written commentaries on most Books of the Bible; parts of those on Gen., the Gospels, and the Pauline Epistles survive.

Moses of Chorene, author of an influential 'History of the *Armenians'. He professes to be a pupil of St *Mesrob; if this were the case he would have lived in the 5th cent., but it is more likely that his work is to be dated in the 8th cent.

motet. A type of polyphonic musical composition, occupying an interpolative place in the liturgy. Its precise role has varied, but its main use has been at the *Offertory and *Elevation in the Mass. The medieval motet was designed for performance by a group of solo voices and used a *plainsong melody as its constructional basis; from the 15th cent. it became choral in style and reached its peak with Josquin des Prés (d. 1521), O. de *Lassus, G. P. da *Palestrina and others. In the 17th cent. solo voices were used again, with instrumental accompaniment.

Mother of God. See THEOTOKOS.

Mothering Sunday. The Fourth Sunday in Lent. The name has been referred to: (1) the custom in some parts of England of visiting one's mother on this day; (2) the practice of visiting the cathedral or mother church on this day; or (3) the words in the traditional Epistle for the day, 'Jerusalem . . . which is the mother of us all' (Gal. 4: 26).

Mothers' Union, the. An Anglican organization of women which aims at upholding 'the sanctity of marriage' and developing in mothers a sense of responsibility in the training of their children. It was founded in 1876, originally as a parochial organization, by Mary Elizabeth Sumner, wife of the rector of Old Alresford, Hants. Granted a royal charter in 1926, it now operates in 150 dioceses and is growing in Africa.

Mott, John Raleigh (1865–1955), American *Methodist. He became known for his zealous propaganda on behalf of missions, and he was chairman of the committee which called the first International Conference at *Edinburgh in 1910. His interest in the *Ecumenical Movement dated from this time. He took a prominent part in the '*Faith and Order' and '*Life and Work' Conferences, and also in the foundation of the *World Council of Churches.

motu proprio (Lat., 'on his own impulse'). A letter by the Pope written on his own initiative and bearing his personal signature. It may be addressed to the Church at large, to some part of it, or to particular persons.

Moule, Handley Carr Glyn (1841–1920), Bp. of *Durham from 1901. In 1881 he became the first principal of Ridley Hall, Cambridge. He was a leading influence for *Evangelicalism at Cambridge and later at Durham.

Moulton, James Hope (1863–1917), classical, Iranian, and NT scholar. He brought to bear on NT Greek the new evidence from non-literary *papyri.

Mount Carmel; Mount of Olives. See CARMEL, MOUNT; OLIVES, MOUNT OF.

movable feasts. Annual ecclesiastical feasts which do not fall on a fixed day in the secular calendar, but vary according to certain rules. Thus *Easter Day is the first Sunday after the full moon between 21 Mar. and 18 Apr.

Mowinckel, Sigmund Olaf Plytt (1884–1965), Norwegian OT scholar. His most noteworthy work was on the Psalms. He held that the Psalms which celebrate *Yahweh's kingship are parts of the liturgies of a pre-exilic festival in which the enthronement of Yahweh was annually celebrated, and that its themes provided the pattern of the later eschatological hope. He also wrote on the *Messianic hope, *Ezra-Nehemiah, and the *Hexateuch.

Mozambique, Christianity in. Portuguese occupation of the coast of Mozambique began in 1505 and spread up the Zambesi valley. From 1577 there were *Dominican missionaries, joined in 1610 by *Jesuits. After the suppression in *Portugal of the Jesuits (1759) and other religious orders (1834), Christianity in Mozambique almost died out. Missionaries began to return in the late 19th cent., but no diocese was established until after the 1940 Vatican-Portugal Concordat. In the decade before political independence (1975) there was tension between the missionaries and the colonial government; the new Marxist government was hostile to the Church, but relations were subsequently normalized. About half the population is Christian, of whom about three quarters are RC. The Pentecostal *Assemblies of God form the largest Protestant group.

Mozarabic chant. The music of the *Mozarabic rite. The *neumes in most of the early MSS cannot now be read, but there is some evidence that the melodies resembled the *Ambrosian as much as the *Gregorian chant.

Mozarabic rite. The conventional name for the liturgical forms which were in use in the Iberian Peninsula from the earliest times until the 11th cent. Its replacement by the Roman rite was a result of the Christian reconquest of *Spain. There was resistance to its abolition in Toledo, and here it was allowed to remain in use in six parishes. F. *Ximénez de Cisneros caused a *missal and *breviary to be printed (1500 and 1502). In 1989 permission was given for the general use in the region of Toledo (and, with the permission of the *Ordinary, throughout Spain) of a new *Missale Hispano-Mozarabicum* which had been revised on the basis of the oldest MSS and with regard to the reforms of the Second *Vatican Council.

The Mozarabic rite has affinities with the *Gallican, though influences from North Africa and possibly Byzantium have also been detected. Distinctive features of the Mass include the use of the *Trisagion in Greek; an elaborate *Illatio (corresponding to the *Preface) varying each day; and the *Fraction of the Host into seven (or according to the Missal of Ximénez, nine) pieces, representing the mysteries of the life of Christ. In the *Office a distinction between the secular and monastic Office survived. The secular Office consisted only of *Vespers and *Mattins; the monastic Office, in its developed form, appears to have had twelve Offices by day and twelve by night.

mozetta. A short cape-like garment to which until 1969 a small hood was attached. It is worn by Popes, cardinals, and other dignitaries.

Mozley, James Bowling (1813–78), post-*Tractarian theologian. After the secession of J. H. *Newman in 1845, Mozley was for a time a leading member of the *Oxford Movement. His Bampton Lectures on *Miracles* (1865) were acclaimed a masterly contribution to what was then a pressing issue.

His brother, **Thomas Mozley** (1806–93) is remembered for his *Reminiscences, chiefly of Oriel College and the Oxford Movement* (1882).

Muggletonians. A small sect founded in 1652 by John Reeve and his cousin Ludowicke Muggleton. They denied the doctrine of the Trinity, and held that during the period of the Incarnation the government of heaven was left to *Elijah. The last member of the sect died in 1979.

Muhlenberg, Henry Melchior (1711–87),

'Patriarch' of the *Lutheran Church in America. Imbued at Göttingen with a broad form of *Pietism, he expressed an interest in missionary work. In response to an appeal by Lutheran congregations in Pennsylvania, in 1742 he was sent to America by the mission centre at Halle which had been established by A. H. *Francke. He was to give instruction in confessional Lutheranism, recover disaffected members, and see to the organization of the Lutheran Church. He recruited European Lutheran pastors for service in America, trained an American clergy, and in 1748 organized the Ministerium of Pennsylvania, the first permanent Lutheran synod in America.

Müller, Friedrich Max. See MAX MÜLLER, FRIEDRICH.

Müller, George (1805–98), philanthropist and preacher. When a student at Halle in 1825, he experienced a religious conversion. Moving to Teignmouth in 1830, he associated himself with the *Plymouth Brethren. He became a local preacher, abolished pew rents, refused a salary, and supported himself with offerings from his followers. In 1832 he moved to Bristol. Here he devoted himself to the care of orphan children, again relying on voluntary offerings. At the age of 70 he set out on a 17-year preaching mission to Europe, India, Australia, and China.

Müller, Julius (1801–78), German Protestant theologian. In his principal work, *Die christliche Lehre von der Sünde* (1839–44), he tried to interpret the fact of sin on the assumption of an extra-temporal fall occasioned by a free and intelligent act of decision on the part of each individual. He took a leading part in the negotiations for the Prussian Evangelical Union.

Mungo, St. See KENTIGERN, ST.

Münster, Sebastian (1488–1552), Hebrew scholar. He produced the first German edition of the Hebrew Bible (1534–5; with a literal Latin version and notes). M. *Coverdale made extensive use of it for the OT of the *Great Bible (1539).

Müntzer (or Münzer), Thomas (c.1489–1525), German radical reformer. In 1517/8 he attended lectures at *Wittenberg and probably on M. *Luther's recommendation became preacher in Zwickau in 1520. He developed a spiritual and mystical theology at odds with the literal biblical interpretation of Wittenberg. He was expelled in turn from Zwickau, Prague, and Allstedt, where as pastor (1523-4) he composed the first liturgies in German and also tracts in which he expressed reservations about *Infant Baptism. At Mühlhausen in 1525 he recast the city government as an eternal council, pledged to the Word of God, and completed the establishment of reformed worship. He placed himself at the head of the local troops in the *Peasants' War; after the defeat of the rebels he was executed. Some later *Anabaptist leaders invoked his name and theology in their cause.

Muratori, Lodovico Antonio (1672–1750), Italian historian and theological scholar. He published a vast corpus of medieval sources of Italian history, *Rerum Italicarum Scriptores* (25 vols., 1723–51), and an important collection of liturgical documents under the title *Liturgia Romana Vetus* (1748). See also the next entry.

Muratorian Canon. The oldest extant list of NT writings, discovered by L. A. *Muratori in an 8th-cent. MS at Milan. It is generally held to date from the later 2nd cent., though some scholars assign it to the 4th cent. It mentions all the NT Books except Heb., Jas., and 1 and 2 Pet.

Murillo, Bartolomé Esteban (1617–82), Spanish painter. He is known especially as the painter of the 'Immaculate Conception', which he executed more than 20 times, and he was the foremost Spanish artist of the theme of the 'Virgin and Child'. He excelled in the painting of children.

Muslim. See ISLAM.

Myconius, Friedrich (1490–1546), *Lutheran reformer of Thuringia. A member of the *Franciscan Order, he sympathized with M. *Luther's attack on *indulgences and was confined in various houses of his Order. In 1524 he fled and in the same year was appointed preacher at Gotha. Here he married, reformed the schools, and exercised a powerful moral influence. In correspondence with Luther and P. *Melanchthon, he played a leading part in the Reform Movement. His *Historia Reformationis*, written in conjunction with J. Heller, is a valuable contemporary source.

Myconius, Oswald (1488–1552), Swiss Reformer and humanist. At Zurich he persuaded the cathedral chapter to elect U. *Zwingli as people's priest, and later collaborated with him. In 1532 he succeeded J. *Oecolampadius at Basle. His undogmatic temper, expressed in his desire to reach a compromise with the *Lutherans, and his distrust of the increasing part of the secular authorities in such matters as *excommunication, aroused distrust among the stricter Zwinglians. He was the author of a Life of Zwingli and of the *Basle Confession of 1534.

Myrc, John, also spelt **Mirc** (*fl. c.*1400), religious writer. He was prior of the *canons regular of Lilleshall in Shropshire. He wrote a *Liber Festialis*, a collection of sermons for the main festivals of the Christian year; a *Manuale Sacerdotum*; and *Instructions for Parish Priests* (in English verse).

Mysteries of the Rosary. The fifteen subjects of meditation connected with the *decades of the *Rosary. They are divided into three groups known as the *Joyful, *Sorrowful, and *Glorious Mysteries (qq.v.).

Mystery (or Miracle) Plays. The terms 'mystery' and 'miracle' are applied loosely to the vernacular religious drama of the later Middle Ages, notably the English *Corpus Christi plays and the French Passion Plays. Much is uncertain about the origins of this type of drama, but the shaping influence of the Liturgy, especially that of *Holy Week and Easter, is clear. Vernacular paraphrases of the Bible and Gospel harmonies were more immediate sources. Apocryphal legends and the lives of saints were also dramatized. Performances usually took place out of doors. The plays were suppressed in the 16th cent., but some have recently been revived. See DRAMA.

mysticism, mystical theology. In modern usage 'mysticism' usually refers to claims of immediate knowledge of Ultimate Reality (whether or not this is called 'God') by direct personal experience; 'mystical theology' is used to mean the study of mystical phenomena or the science of the mystical life. Paranormal experiences, such as trances and visions, are often regarded as 'mystical', but are not usually thought essential. Protestant theologians have tended to regard mysticism with suspicion.

In recent years there has been increased interest in the subject.

Language connected with 'mystery' was common in the early Church; its use depends on the conviction that Christian doctrine and liturgy involve matters known only by revelation. The phrase 'mystical theology', however, is first used by *Dionysius the Pseudo-Areopagite. As well as 'philosophical theology', which uses clear concepts and arguments, there is a 'mystical theology' which has to do with symbols and rituals, leading us beyond intellectual notions of God to a real union with Him in the 'truly mystic darkness of unknowing'; here the height of the 'mystic words' of Scripture are apprehended and the 'mysteries of theology' are revealed in silence.

In some later Byzantine writers the third stage of spiritual progress, which Dionysius calls '*unitive', is named 'mystical', and this is taken to mean that one is now in a position to 'initiate' others into the mysteries of God.

Medieval W. interpreters of Dionysius tended to see 'mystical theology' as leading, through the *purgative and illuminative ways, to a loving union with God at the peak of our affectivity, in which all intellectual operations are left behind. There was, however, debate as to whether 'mystical theology' is to be located entirely in the will and affections, or whether it is rather the ascent of the intellect, enlightened by faith, to union with God. In later medieval writers 'mystical theology' was increasingly taken to mean an experiential knowledge of God, and some writers specified particular subjective experiences as constituting or indicating the attainment of 'mystical theology' (generally identified from the 16th cent. with *contemplation). This process reached its height in St *Teresa of Ávila and St *John of the Cross, whose influence thereafter predominates.

Since the 17th cent. there has been debate among RC theologians as to whether 'mysticism' – the phrase replaced 'mystical theology' – is to be regarded as the normal flowering of sanctifying grace, open to all Christians, or whether it should be seen as a special grace reserved for the few. Modern discussions have been dominated by the notion of 'mystical experience' and, on the one hand, by the quest for mystical elements common to different religions, and on the other, by attempts to identify a specifically Christian 'mysticism'.

Naassenes. A *Gnostic sect similar to, if not identical with, the *Ophites (q.v.).

Nag Hammadi Papyri. A collection of 13 papyrus codices found in 1945–6 near Nag Hammadi (the ancient Chenoboskion) in Upper Egypt. Written in *Coptic, they date from between the 3rd and 5th cent. AD and contain over 40 (mainly *Gnostic) works, nearly all previously unknown. The MSS, which are a primary source for our knowledge of Gnosticism, are now all in the Coptic Museum at Cairo. They include the 'Gospel of Truth' (see EVANGELIUM VERITATIS) and the Gospel of *Thomas.

Nag's Head Story. A tale apparently fabricated in the 17th cent. to discredit the validity of M. *Parker's episcopal consecration. It alleged that at the Nag's Head tavern in Cheapside J. *Scory constituted Parker and others bishops by placing a Bible on the neck of each of them in turn with the words 'Take thou authority to preach the Word of God sincerely'.

Nahum, Book of. *Minor Prophet. It predicts the fall of Nineveh (c.612 BC), which is regarded as so imminent that the Book is usually dated shortly before this event. The psalm at the beginning (1: 2–9 or 1:

2–2: 2) may come from an independent source.

Name of Jesus. Because of the close relation between name and person, the name of Jesus is used in the NT as a synonym for Christ, denoting His character and authority. The disciples perform miracles and exorcisms 'in the name of Jesus', i.e. by His power (Mk. 9: 38 ff., Acts 4: 30), and baptize in it (Acts 2: 38). Devotion to the Holy Name was popularized by the *Franciscans in the 15th cent. A feast was officially granted to them in 1530 and prescribed for the whole RC Church in 1721; it was suppressed in 1969. It had been kept on various dates in Jan. In the Anglican Communion it is sometimes observed on 7 Aug., the date assigned to it in the calendar of the BCP. The American BCP (1979) places it on 1 Jan., and various other modern Anglican liturgies use the 'Naming of Jesus' as an alternative title for the feast of the *Circumcision.

Nantes, Edict of (1598). The edict signed at Nantes by *Henry IV at the end of the French wars of religion, granting extensive rights to the *Huguenots. They were allowed free exercise of their religion (except in certain towns) and given a State subsidy for their troops, pastors, and schools. It was revoked in 1685.

Narsai (d. c.503), also **Narses**, poet and theologian of the *Church of the East. Born probably in 399, he became head of the famous school of *Edessa, but c.471 he fled to Nisibis, where the bishop, *Barsumas, asked him to found a school. A large number of his metrical homilies and some hymns survive.

narthex. In a Byzantine church, the antechamber of the nave, from which it is separated by columns, rails, or a wall. *Catechumens, candidates for Baptism, and penitents occupied the narthex.

Nasorean. See NAZARENE.

Natalitia (Lat., 'birthday'). In the early Church the word was used of the death-day of Christians, especially of martyrs, denoting their birthday into eternal life.

Nathanael. A disciple of Jesus. His call is related in Jn. 1: 43–51. He is commonly identified with St *Bartholomew.

National Apostasy, Sermon on. A sermon with this title preached by J. *Keble in 1833 is commonly regarded as the beginning of the *Oxford Movement.

National Assembly of the Church of England. See CHURCH ASSEMBLY.

National Council of the Evangelical Free Churches. The title adopted in 1896 by the National Free Church Council, formed in 1892 for mutual consultation, co-operation and witness among the Free Churches. In 1940 it was merged in the *Free Church Federal Council.

National Covenant (1638). The Covenant of Scottish *Presbyterians inaugurated at Edinburgh in answer to the attempt to impose on the Scottish Church the 1637 BCP.

National Institutions Measure 1998. A Measure reorganizing the central structures of the C of E. It established the *Archbishops' Council, transferring to it many of the functions previously undertaken by committees of the General *Synod or the *Church Commissioners.

National Society. The popular name of the Society founded in 1811 as 'The National Society for the Education of the Poor in the Principles of the Established Church'. It was one of the pioneers in the provision of elementary education in England and Wales. After the establishment by the State of Board Schools in 1870, the Society's schools (the 'National Schools') remained independent until 1902, when they began to receive financial aid from the Local Authorities; though now part of the State system, they retain some independence, including scope for specifically Church teaching. The Society's work, since 1934 embracing all classes, includes *Sunday Schools and adult education.

Nativity of Jesus Christ. See CHRISTMAS.

Nativity of St John the Baptist. A feast observed on 24 June, at least since the 4th cent., to commemorate the miraculous birth of the Baptist recorded in Lk. 1.

Nativity of the BVM. The feast, which is observed on 8 Sept., is attested in the E. in the 8th cent. It was not generally observed in the W. until the 11th cent. The choice of date is unexplained.

Natural Law. An expression used with a

variety of meanings, but in a theological context the law implanted in nature by the Creator, which rational creatures can discern by the light of reason. While the concept has been accepted in some form by ancient, medieval, and modern thinkers, there has often seemed to be little agreement about its content other than that good is to be done and evil avoided. The notion of 'human rights' (and 'animal rights'), understood as 'natural rights', has sometimes been based on the concept of Natural Law, and the growing importance of international law has led to new interest in it.

Natural Theology. The body of knowledge about God which may be obtained by human reason alone without the aid of *revelation. Reformation theologians generally rejected the competence of fallen human reason to engage in Natural Theology; this incompetence was reasserted by K. *Barth and the *Dialectical School. See also PHILOSOPHY OF RELIGION.

Naumburg Convention (1561). A meeting of princes and representatives of the German Protestant leaders at Naumburg to try to secure doctrinal unity. The *Lutherans and *Calvinists were unable to agree.

nave. The part of a church, between the main front and the chancel and choir, which is assigned to the laity.

Nayler, James (c.1618–60), *Quaker. He retired from the Parliamentary army in 1651 and in the same year he was convinced by G. *Fox of the Quaker doctrine of the *Inner (or Inward) Light. At the outset he was second only to Fox in the leadership of the movement; from the summer of 1655 to the spring of 1656 he was its chief spokesman in London. Soon afterwards he came under the influence of a group of people with *Ranting views who tried to worship him as Christ. He was credited with having raised a woman from the dead, quarrelled with Fox, and entered Bristol in the manner that the Lord entered Jerusalem. He was imprisoned until 1659.

Nazarene (or **Nasorean).** (1) In the NT Christ is called 'Jesus the Nazarene'; this is usually understood as meaning 'from *Nazareth'. (2) The 'Nazarenes' was a Jewish term for the Christians. (3) 'Nazarenes' occurs as a name used by 4th-cent. writers of groups of Christians of Jewish race in Syria, who continued to obey much of the Jewish Law. (4) The *Mandaeans are sometimes called 'Nasoreans'.

Nazarene, Church of the. See HOLINESS MOVEMENT.

Nazarenes, Gospel of the. A Gospel in Aramaic, according to *Epiphanius and *Jerome used by the *Nazarenes of Beroea. Epiphanius regarded it as an Aramaic version of Mt., while Jerome identified it with the 'Gospel according to the *Hebrews'.

Nazareth. The village in *Galilee where Christ was brought up and where He lived until the beginning of His ministry.

Nazarites. See NAZIRITES.

Nazarius, St. A martyr whose body St *Ambrose discovered in a garden outside Milan c.395 and translated to a church in the city. Feast day, with St Celsus, whose body was found in the same garden, 28 July; of Nazarius' translation, 10 May.

Nazirites (so modern translations of the Bible; AV 'Nazarites'). Israelites consecrated to the service of God who were under vows to abstain from consuming wine, to let their hair grow, and to avoid defilement by contact with a dead body (Num. 6).

Neal, Daniel (1678–1743), historian. Pastor of the *Independent congregation in Aldersgate Street, London, he was recognized as one of the best *Puritan preachers of his day. His *History of the Puritans*, 1517–1688 (1732–8), is a valuable compilation, with a strong Puritan bias.

Neale, John Mason (1818–66), *High Church Anglican author and hymn-writer. Ordained in 1842, from 1846 he was warden of Sackville College, East Grinstead. In 1855 he founded the Sisterhood of St Margaret; this community, devoted to the education of girls and the care of the sick, became one of the main *religious orders in the C of E. His ritualistic practices led to his *inhibition from 1847 to 1863.

Neale excelled as a hymn-writer. His own compositions include 'O happy band of pilgrims' and 'Art thou weary', and his translations from Latin and Greek hymns, 'Jerusalem the golden' and 'All glory, laud and honour'. His *Hymns of the Eastern Church* (1862) included many translations of Easter hymns which indirectly introduced an important E. emphasis on the Resurrection into Anglican worship. Feast day in the American BCP (1979) and CW, 7 Aug.

Neander, Joachim (1650–80), German hymn-writer. He became an adherent of the *Pietist Movement. His hymns reflect his love of the beauties of nature. Those translated into English include 'Praise to the Lord, the Almighty'.

Nectarius, St (d. 397), Bp. of *Constantinople. Though unbaptized, he was selected by *Theodosius I in 381 to succeed St *Gregory of Nazianzus. He presided over the final stages of the *Oecumenical Council then in session. Feast day, 11 Oct.

Nectarius (1605–c.1680), Patr. of *Jerusalem, 1661–9. He was an opponent of all W. theology. In 1662 he expressed approval of the 'Confession' of P. *Mogila and in 1672 he took a prominent part in the Synod of *Jerusalem.

Negative Confession. An alternative name for the *King's Confession, because it denied all doctrine not in accord with the *Scottish Confession of 1560.

negative theology. See APOPHATIC THEOLOGY.

Nehemiah. Jewish leader of the post-exilic period. The cup-bearer of the Persian king Artaxerxes, he obtained leave to visit Palestine. He arrived in *Jerusalem as governor c.444 BC and supervised the rebuilding of the city walls. About 432 BC he made a second journey to Jerusalem; he then introduced important moral and religious reforms. His work is related to that of *Ezra, though their precise relationship is unclear. See EZRA AND NEHEMIAH, BOOKS OF.

Nemesius of Emesa (*fl. c.*390), Christian philosopher and Bp. of Emesa in Syria. His treatise 'On Human Nature' is an attempt to construct on a mainly *Platonic basis a doctrine of the soul agreeable with the Christian revelation.

Neocaesarea, Council of. A Cappadocian Council of uncertain date (probably early 4th cent., before 325). Its 15 canons, mainly on disciplinary and marriage questions, became part of E. and W. canon law.

Neo-Chalcedonianism. A modern term coined to describe the position of those 6th-cent. theologians who sought to interpret the Christological teaching of the Council of *Chalcedon in the light of the Christology of St *Cyril of Alexandria, in order to combat the *Monophysite claim that the Council had betrayed Cyril. This position involved an insistence that the one *hypostasis of the Incarnate Christ is identical with the Second Person of the Trinity, and a consequent justification of the *Theopaschite formula.

neophyte (Gk., literally 'newly planted'). The word was generally used in the early Church of those recently baptized.

Neoplatonism. The philosophical system of *Plotinus (c.205–70) and his successors, who included *Porphyry, *Iamblichus, and *Proclus. Its basic characteristic is the doctrine of the three hypostases: the One, the ultimate unknowable source from which everything that exists emanates; Intelligence, the realm of perfective intuitive knowledge; and Soul, the realm of discursive thought and activity. The outward movement of emanation is met by the ascending movement of return, which manifests itself as *contemplation; everything that exists is a balance between these two forces. The contemplative movement of return seeks the One by purification, which for the intellect means a method of abstraction, and finds union with the One in a mystical experience of *ecstasy.

Thoroughgoing Neoplatonists were necessarily hostile to Christianity, but Neoplatonism influenced Christian theology, partly through its diffusive impact on the whole later Roman world. Its influence is apparent in the writings of St *Augustine, *Synesius, and *Dionysius the Pseudo-Areopagite.

Neostadiensium Admonitio (1581). The reply made by the members of the 'Reformed' (*Calvinist) Church at Heidelberg to the *Lutheran 'Formula of *Concord' (1577). It sets out the distinctive tenets of Calvinism.

Neot, St (c.9th cent.), Cornish saint. According to 11th–12th-cent. sources, he was a monk of *Glastonbury who in search of solitude retired to the place now known as St Neot in Cornwall; after his death his relics are said to have found their way to St Neots, Cambs. Feast day, 31 July.

Nepomuk, John of. See JOHN OF NEPOMUK.

nepotism. The bestowal of office or patronage on one's relations. It was a frequent charge against certain 16th-cent. Popes.

Nereus and Achilleus, Sts (perhaps 1st cent.), Roman martyrs. According to their legendary 'Acta', they were taken with St *Domitilla to the island of Terracina, where Nereus and Achilleus were beheaded and Domitilla burnt. Feast day, 12 May.

Neri, St Philip. See PHILIP NERI, ST.

Nero, Claudius (37–68), Roman Emperor from 54. Proclaimed Emperor at the age of 16, he at first ruled relatively well under the guidance of *Seneca and the Praetorian Prefect Burrus, but he soon scandalized public opinion. There were rebellions in Judaea and elsewhere; the armies deserted him and he committed suicide.

Many believed that Nero caused the fire which burnt much of Rome in 64; to divert his unpopularity on this score he punished the Christians as scapegoats (see PERSECUTIONS, EARLY CHRISTIAN). He was the Caesar to whom St *Paul appealed; it is unlikely that he personally heard the case, but according to a substantial tradition both St *Peter and Paul were executed in his reign. See also NUMBER OF THE BEAST.

Nerses, St (d. *c*.373), sixth *Catholicos of the *Armenian Church. A descendant of *Gregory the Illuminator, when he became Catholicos (perhaps *c*.363) he undertook reform. He was deposed and exiled for criticizing the dissolute life of the king. Restored by his successor, he censured the new king and was poisoned by him. Feast day, 19 Nov.

Nerses IV, St (1102–73), *Catholicos of the *Armenian Church from 1166. He strove for union between the Armenian and Byzantine Churches. Of his extensive works in verse and prose, the best known is his poem on the history of salvation, called (after its opening line) 'Jesus, only Son of the Father'. Feast day, 13 Aug.

Nestle, Eberhard (1851–1913), German biblical scholar. His edition of the Greek NT, first issued in 1898, has been widely used.

Nestorius (b. after 351; d. after 451), Patr. of *Constantinople and heresiarch. He gave his name to the doctrine ('Nestorianism') that there were two separate Persons in the Incarnate Christ, the one Divine and the other human (as opposed to the orthodox teaching that in the Incarnate Christ was a single Person, at once God and man); whether Nestorius taught this is disputed.

In 428 *Theodosius II invited Nestorius, then a monk at *Antioch, to become Patr. of Constantinople. When Nestorius' chaplain preached against the use of the term '*Theotokos' as savouring of heresy (*Apollinarianism), he supported him. Controversy developed around the propriety of the term. At a Council in Rome in 430 Pope *Celestine I condemned Nestorius' teaching, and *Cyril of Alexandria was commissioned to pronounce sentence of deposition if he would not submit. Cyril condemned Nestorius in a set of anathemas and required him to retract within ten days. Meanwhile the Emperor had called a General Council; this met at *Ephesus in 431 and deposed Nestorius (see EPHESUS, COUNCIL OF). In 436 he was banished to Upper Egypt, where he died (date unknown).

Nestorius' chief writings were letters and sermons which have mostly survived only in fragments. He also wrote a treatise known as the 'Bazaar of Heracleides'. This was written when the theological climate had changed; in it Nestorius claimed that his own beliefs were identical with those then being sustained by the orthodox (against the *Eutychians). What he taught and how far it was heretical is unclear.

In the late 5th and 6th cent. the term 'Nestorian' was applied by their opponents to all upholders of a strict Antiochene Christology; consequently the *Church of the East came to be called 'the Nestorian Church'.

Ne Temere (1907). A decree that marriages in which one or both parties are RC must be celebrated before the parish priest or the *Ordinary or a priest delegated by one of them. In 1970 *Paul VI allowed some relaxation in cases of *mixed marriages.

Netherlands, Christianity in the. Christianity penetrated the territory now known as the Netherlands in Roman times, but its effective conversion was delayed until the end of the 7th cent.; St *Willibrord and St *Boniface were chiefly responsible for its evangelization. The whole country came under the dominating influence of the see of Utrecht. In the 14th cent. the Netherlands saw the rise of the movement known as '*Devotio Moderna', which stressed both mystical piety and education.

At the Reformation *Lutherans and *Anabaptists initially gained followers, but the adherence of William the Silent to *Calvinism in 1573 underlined the role of that creed in the revolt against Spanish rule. By 1609 the Netherlands was virtually independent. The Reformed religion held sway, but there were controversies within its ranks, e.g. that surrounding J. *Arminius, whose followers were condemned at the Synod of *Dort (1618–9). Other disputes led to the Secession of 1834 when some of the stricter Calvinists set up the 'Christian Reformed Churches', and to a further secession led by A. *Kuyper in 1886.

The RC Church was subject to severe penal restrictions from 1583 to 1795. From 1580 to 1853 it was without territorial bishops. In 1697 accusations of *Jansenism were made against the RCs of the Netherlands; after the censure in 1702 of Petrus Codde, the *Vicar General, a schism developed, his followers being known as '*Old Catholics' (q.v.). In the modern Netherlands RCs form a vigorous body, comprising *c.*31 per cent of the population (of which *c.*21 per cent are Protestant, mainly Calvinist). In recent years there has been advanced thinking among Dutch RCs, leading near to conflict with the Papacy.

Netter, Thomas (*c.*1375–1430), *Carmelite theologian. He took part in the struggle against the followers of J. *Wycliffe, acting in the trial of John *Oldcastle in 1413 and several other trials. He was confessor to Henry V and spiritual adviser to *Henry VI. His main work, *Doctrinale antiquitatum fidei ecclesiae catholicae*, was designed to refute the doctrines of Wycliffe and the *Hussites. The *Fasciculi Zizaniorum* (a collection of anti-Wycliffite documents) is traditionally associated with Netter, but it is unlikely that any of it is his work.

Neumann, Therese (1898–1962), of Konnersreuth in Bavaria, visionary. In 1926 she began to have visions of the Passion and received the *stigmata. She was said to have taken no nourishment after 1927, except Holy Communion daily, and was credited with various supernatural faculties. The RC authorities have made no pronouncement on the case.

neume. In plainsong, a prolonged group of notes sung to a single syllable, or the sign used to indicate the melody.

Neutral text. The type of text of the Greek NT represented by the *Codex Vaticanus and *Codex Sinaiticus, and so called by F. J. A. *Hort because it was supposed to be less subject to corrupting influences of editorial revision than any other. It is now often known as the *Alexandrian text.

Nevin, John Williamson (1803–86), American theologian. He had abandoned the dogmas of *Presbyterianism for a more liberal theology before he became professor of theology in the 'German Reformed' Theological Seminary at Mercersburg, Pa., in 1840. In *The Anxious Bench* (1843), he attacked the prevailing methods of revivalist preaching. In 1844 P. *Schaff joined him, and the theological doctrines for which they stood became known as the '*Mercersburg Theology'. In *The Mystical Presence* (1846) Nevin defended a more sacramental conception of Christianity than is ordinarily held by Protestants.

New English Bible. See BIBLE (ENGLISH VERSIONS).

New (Jerusalem) Church. See SWEDENBORG, EMMANUEL.

Newman, Ven. John Henry (1801–90), *Tractarian leader and later Cardinal. Brought up under *Evangelical influence, he became a Fellow of Oriel College, Oxford, and in 1828 Vicar of St Mary's. He was intimately associated with the *Oxford Movement, and the leading spirit in it. He wrote 27 of the *Tracts for the Times*. In *Tract 90* (1841) he advocated an interpretation of the *Thirty-Nine Articles in a sense generally congruous with the decrees of the Council of *Trent; the tract was condemned by the Hebdomadal Board of the University and the Bp. of Oxford imposed silence on its author. Meanwhile from 1839 Newman had begun to have doubts about the claims of the C of E. From 1842 he lived at Littlemore, where he set up a semi-monastic establishment. He resigned from St Mary's in 1843; in 1845 he became a RC. He issued his *Essay on the Development of Christian Doctrine* (1845) in defence of his change of allegiance.

Having been ordained in Rome, he established the *Oratorians in Birmingham in 1849, and was in Ireland as rector of the short-lived RC university in Dublin from 1854 to 1858. His opposition to the retention of the Pope's temporal power was the occasion of his breach with H. E. *Manning. In 1864 a controversy with C. *Kingsley resulted in Newman's *Apologia pro vita sua*, which won him much sympathy. The following year he wrote *The Dream of *Gerontius* (q.v.). His *Grammar of Assent* (1870) is remarkable for its differentiation between real and notional assent, its analysis of the function of conscience in our knowledge of God and of the role of the 'illative sense', i.e. the faculty of judging from given facts by processes outside the limits of strict logic, in reaching religious certainty. In 1879 he was made a cardinal. Although unsuccessful in most of his undertakings in the RC Church in his lifetime, much of his teaching found official expression at the Second *Vatican Council. In 1991 he was declared Venerable. Feast day in CW, 11 Aug.

New Rome. A name for *Constantinople, apparently given to the city by *Constantine himself.

New Testament. The Canonical Books belonging exclusively to the Church, as contrasted with those styled *Old Testament, which it shares with *Judaism. The NT contains the four Gospels, Acts, the Pauline and 'Catholic' Epistles, and Revelation. See also CANON OF SCRIPTURE.

Newton, Isaac (1642–1727), English mathematician and natural philosopher. The most eminent physicist of his day, Newton formulated the law of gravitation, discovered the differential calculus, and correctly analysed white light. In his *Philosophiae Naturalis Principia Mathematica* (1687) he also set out his religious convictions; for him belief in God rested chiefly on the order of the universe. Though a conforming Churchman, in private he denied the doctrine of the *Trinity on the ground that such a belief was inaccessible to reason.

Newton, John (1725–1807), *Evangelical clergyman. He had been a slave-trader and then Tide Surveyor at Liverpool. He considered entering the Dissenting ministry, but on being offered the curacy of Olney, Bucks., he was ordained in 1764. Here he collaborated with W. *Cowper in the production of the *Olney Hymns* (1779). His own hymns include 'Glorious things of Thee are spoken' and 'How sweet the Name of Jesus sounds'.

New Year's Day. Christians avoided the 'Saturnalia' which marked the beginning of the Roman New Year (1 Jan.). Later they reckoned the beginning of the year on different days in different countries; in England the year began with the Feast of the *Annunciation (25 Mar.). With the introduction of the *Gregorian Calendar, 1 Jan. was accepted. In the E. *Orthodox Church New Year's Day (here 1 Sept.) is solemnized in many hymns, but in the W. it has traditionally had no liturgical significance apart from the fact that it coincided with the Feast of the *Circumcision (in the RC Church now observed as the Solemnity of the Motherhood of the BVM). In England an informal 'watch-night' service is common, especially among *Methodists.

New Zealand, Christianity in. The first Christian mission to the Maori was established in 1814 by an Anglican chaplain in New South Wales. Wesleyan *Methodists began a mission in 1822, and French RCs in 1838. By the 1840s the majority of the Maori population was attending Christian services. After the British annexation of New Zealand in 1840 there was extensive European colonization, which led to the introduction of a variety of denominations. The Anglican see of New Zealand was set up in 1841, with G. A. *Selwyn as its first bishop. In 1928 a Maori was consecrated Bp. of Aotearoa to supervise work among the Maori. Women have been admitted to the Anglican priesthood in New Zealand since 1977; the first woman bishop was consecrated in 1990. In 1992 the Anglican Province of New Zealand became the Anglican Church in Aotearoa, New Zealand and Polynesia. The RC Church established two dioceses in 1848 and a Province in 1887; the first Maori RC bishop was consecrated in 1988. In the population as a whole Anglicans are the largest body, followed by the

RCs and *Presbyterians. Among the Maori the Anglicans and RCs are followed by the Ratana Church, an indigenous body founded by the Maori healer T. W. Ratana (1870–1939).

Nicaea, First Council of (325). The first *Oecumenical Council, summoned by the Emp. *Constantine, mainly to deal with the *Arian controversy. After an Arian creed submitted by *Eusebius of Nicomedia had been rejected, *Eusebius of Caesarea presented the Baptismal Creed of his own Palestinian community, and this, supplemented by the word '*Homoousios', was received by the Council as orthodox. The Creed promulgated by the Council, however, was not this, but another, probably a revision of the Baptismal Creed of *Jerusalem. With four anti-Arian anathemas attached, it was subscribed by all the bishops present, except two. It seems that *Athanasius was the leading champion of orthodoxy in this struggle. The Council also reached decisions on the *Melitian Schism in Egypt and the *Paschal Controversy, and issued 20 canons. The traditional number of bishops present (318) is probably only a symbolic figure; between 220 and 250 is more likely.

Nicaea, Second Council of (787). The seventh *Oecumenical Council, convoked by the Empress Irene to end the *Iconoclastic Controversy. The Council declared its adherence to the doctrine on the veneration of images expounded in a letter from Pope *Hadrian I, adding that such veneration is a matter of respect and honour (not the adoration due to God alone), the honour given to the image passing on to its prototype.

Nicene Creed. Two Creeds are so named:
(1) The Creed issued in 325 by the Council of *Nicaea (q.v.), known to scholars as N. It was drawn up to defend the orthodox faith against *Arianism and includes the word '*Homoousios'. Appended to it were four anti-Arian anathemas which came to be regarded as an integral part of the text.
(2) In common parlance, the 'Nicene Creed' more often means the longer formula which is in regular use in the Eucharist, in both E. and W. It is also known as the 'Niceno-Constantinopolitan Creed' and is referred to as C. From the time of the Council of *Chalcedon (451) it has been

regarded as the Creed of the Council of *Constantinople of 381; it is probable that it was not drawn up by that Council but endorsed by it. Its origin is unclear, but it was probably the Baptismal Creed of Constantinople. In the early Middle Ages, the *Filioque was added to it in the W.

Nicephorus, St (758–828), Patr. of *Constantinople. He withdrew from court life and retired to a monastery, but was recalled to Constantinople and in 806 made Patriarch, though not yet in *Holy Orders. In return, the Emp. Nicephorus demanded his reinstatement of a priest who had been deposed for blessing the adulterous marriage of the Emp. Constantine VI; after some hesitation the Patriarch gave way. When the Emp. Leo V (813–20) resumed his *iconoclastic policy, Nicephorus resisted; he was exiled in 815 and retired to his former monastery. Besides writing in the image controversy, he compiled a Byzantine history from 602 to 770. Feast day in the E. Church, 2 June; in the W., 13 Mar.

Nicephorus Callistus (c.1256–c.1335), 'Xanthopoulos', Byzantine historian. His main work, a 'Church History', covers the period from the birth of Christ to the death of the Emp. Phocas (610). It preserves material on some of the early controversies and heresies. In 1555 it was translated into Latin and furnished material for the defence of images and relics.

Niceta, St (d. c.414), ecclesiastical writer. He was Bp. of Remesiana (Beta Palanka, SE of Niš) from c.370. His *Explanatio Symboli* is a primary witness for the history of the *Apostles' Creed, containing the oldest attestation for the words 'communio sanctorum'. The ascription to him of the '*Te Deum' has not been generally accepted. Feast day, 22 June.

Nicetas Acominatos (1155/7–1217), Byzantine scholar. He rose rapidly in the Imperial service at Constantinople; when it fell in 1204 he fled to Nicaea. His writings include a 'Treasury of Orthodoxy', directed against contemporary heresies and the main source for the Councils held between 1156 and 1166, and a History of the period 1118–1206, which is especially valuable for its account of the capture of Constantinople by the Latins in 1204.

Nicetas Stethatos (c.1005–c.1085), Byzantine monk. As a young man, he entered the monastery of *Studios in Constantinople, where he knew St *Simeon the New Theologian. In 1053–4 he was involved in the controversy between Cardinal *Humbert and *Michael Cerularius which led to the mutual excommunications of 1054. His Life of Simeon is conceived as a defence of the institution of spiritual fatherhood, even in laymen, against the hierarchy. His spiritual teaching, contained in *Three Centuries of Practical, Physical and Gnostic Chapters*, is indebted to Simeon; like him he ascribes importance to the gift of tears.

Nicholas, St, Bp. of Myra. According to tradition he was imprisoned in the *Diocletianic persecution and was present at the first Council of Nicaea; the latter supposition is improbable. He is regarded as the patron saint of sailors and of Russia; also of children, bringing them gifts on 6 Dec. (his feast day; whence 'Santa Claus', a corruption of the Dutch for 'Saint Nicholas'). His symbol is sometimes 3 bags of gold, the dowry he is supposed to have given to save three girls from degradation.

Nicholas I, St (d. 867), Pope from 858. His pontificate witnessed a protracted struggle with the E. Church. He refused to sanction the Emperor's deposition of Ignatius and appointment of *Photius to the see of Constantinople, and in 863 he pronounced Ignatius restored. He also tried to win over the newly converted *Bulgars to Rome. In 867 Photius declared the Pope deposed, but was himself deprived of office later in the year. In the W. Nicholas took a firm stand in the divorce case of Lothair II of Lorraine; he asserted the supremacy of the see of Rome over Abp. John of *Ravenna, and he forced *Hincmar of Reims to accept the right of the Papacy to intervene in disputes. Feast day, 13 Nov.

Nicholas V (1397–1455), Pope from 1447. By his conciliatory spirit and diplomatic skill he obtained recognition of the Papal rights in the matter of benefices and bishoprics in the Concordat of Vienna in 1448, and in 1449 he ended the schism by receiving the submission of the antipope Felix V and that of the Council of *Basle before its dissolution. He made a serious attempt to reform abuses. He was of blameless personal life and anxious to reconcile religion with the new learning.

Nicholas of Basle (d. c.1395), heretic. He was a *Beghard who preached in the area of Basle. According to Martin of Mainz, a disciple of his burnt in 1393, Nicholas claimed to understand the Gospels better than the Apostles, assumed ecclesiastical functions, and professed to release his followers from their obedience to the Church into a state of primal innocence. It is not clear that his views were as radical as Martin's confession implies. After evading the *Inquisition for many years, he was burnt at Vienna.

Nicholas Cabasilas, St. See CABASILAS, ST NICHOLAS.

Nicholas of Cusa (1401–64), German philosopher. In 1433 he took part in the Council of *Basle as an advocate in a dispute concerning the see of Trier; he also worked for the reconciliation of the *Hussites and procured the acceptance of the *Calixtines by the Council. He originally favoured the *Conciliar Movement, but he became estranged from its supporters and from 1437 devoted himself wholly to the cause of the Pope. *Nicholas V made him a cardinal and in 1450 appointed him Bp. of Brixen (in the Tyrol) and Papal legate for the German-speaking countries. He worked for reform until a conflict with Duke Sigismund forced him to leave his diocese. He spent his last years in Rome.

In intellectual outlook Nicholas was a forerunner of the Renaissance. His main work, *De Docta Ignorantia*, was a defence of his two celebrated principles, 'docta ignorantia' and 'coincidentia oppositorum'. 'Docta ignorantia' was the highest stage of intellectual apprehension accessible to the human intellect, since Truth, which is absolute, one, and infinitely simple, is unknowable to man. Knowledge by contrast is relative, multiple, complex, and at best only approximate. The road to Truth therefore leads beyond reason and the principle of contradiction; it is only by intuition that we can discover God, the 'coincidentia oppositorum', wherein all contradictions meet.

Nicholas of Flüe, St (1417–87) 'Brother Klaus', Swiss ascetic. In 1467 he obtained the consent of his wife to leave her and their 10 children, to lead the life of a hermit in the Ranft valley. He is said to have lived there for 19 years with no food save the Eucharist. The accounts of his visions have attracted interest in modern times. Feast day, 21 Mar.; in Switzerland (of which he is Patron Saint), 25 Sept.

Nicholas Hereford (d. c.1420), *Lollard writer. At Oxford he became a supporter of J. *Wycliffe and by 1382 he was preaching Wycliffite doctrines. For this he was condemned and twice imprisoned. He seems to have recanted c.1391, in 1394 became a canon of *Hereford, and in 1417 a *Carthusian monk. His name has been associated with the earlier of the Wycliffite translations of the Bible into English.

Nicholas of Lyre (c.1270–1349), biblical exegete. A native of Lyre (in the diocese of Evreux), he had become a *Franciscan and moved to *Paris by c.1300. He was essentially a research scholar. He concentrated on the literal meaning of the Bible, writing analyses, or *Postillae*, on each verse or section of a chapter. They reflect his knowledge of the Hebrew text and of rabbinic exegesis. His *Postillae Litterales* and *Postillae Morales* were together long regarded as the definitive commentary on the Bible.

Nicholas of Oresme. See ORESME, NICHOLAS.

Nicholas of Tolentino, St (c.1245–1306), *Augustinian friar. His life was pious, but uneventful. Fragments of his body, interred at Tolentino, are reputed to bleed before great calamities. Feast day, 10 Sept.

Nicholas, Henry (1502–c.1580), or **Hendrik Niclaes**, founder of the *Familists (q.v.). A rich cloth-merchant, he associated with the *Anabaptists in Amsterdam. About 1539 he believed that he had Divine communications commanding him to found a new sect, the 'Family of Love'. In 1540 he went to Emden, where he wrote a number of books, including the 'Glass of Righteousness'; in 1560 the authorities took steps against his sectarian activities and he fled to Kampen, Rotterdam, and finally Cologne. He thought that he would heal the schisms in Christendom, but his books were condemned by Protestants and Catholics alike.

Nicodemism. The term Nicodemite, derived from *Nicodemus, who visited Jesus by night, generally denotes a secret or timid adherent. J. *Calvin applied it to those converts to Protestantism in Catholic France who outwardly continued RC practices. In modern times Nicodemism covers all forms of religious simulation.

Nicodemus. The learned Jew who visited Jesus by night and evoked the discourse on Christian rebirth narrated in Jn. 3: 1–15. He is later shown helping *Joseph of Arimathaea give Him burial (Jn. 19: 39).

Nicodemus, Gospel of. See PILATE, ACTS OF.

Nicodemus of the Holy Mountain, St (c.1749–1809), Greek monk of Mount *Athos and spiritual writer. His main publications were the *Philocalia* (q.v.) and a commentary on E. canon law entitled the *Pidalion* or 'Rudder' (1800). He also published Greek editions of RC writers, including the *Spiritual Exercises* of St *Ignatius Loyola. Feast day in the E., 14 July.

Nicolaitans. Sectaries mentioned in the NT at Rev. 2: 6 and 2: 14 f., where they appear as the advocates of a return to pagan worship. It is possible that the name is allegorical and no such sect existed, though a *Gnostic sect of the name is mentioned by some early Fathers. Later the term was applied to married priests by the upholders of clerical *celibacy.

Nicole, Pierre (1625–95), French theologian, controversialist, and moralist. He formed a close friendship with A. *Arnauld, in collaboration with whom many of his works were written, including the *Logique ou l'Art de penser* (commonly known as the *Logique de Port-Royal*, 1662). A number of his works deal with the *Jansenist controversy, but they are more moderate in tone than most Jansenist works. He also wrote against the *Calvinists and the *Quietists. His main work, the *Essais de morale* (1671–8) reflected his pessimistic view of fallen man and generally advocated both outward and inward withdrawal from the world, though he accepted that those with positions in the world could live a serious Christian life.

Nicolò de' Tudeschi. See PANORMITANUS.

Nicomedes, St, early Christian martyr. It appears that he was buried in one of the

Roman *catacombs; nothing is known of the circumstances or date of his death. Feast day, 15 Sept. (in the BCP calendar, 1 June, the date of the dedication of a church in Rome).

Niebuhr, Helmut Richard (1894–1962), American theologian. The brother of Reinhold *Niebuhr, he taught at Yale from 1938 until his death. He analysed the correlations between religious beliefs and social groupings in the United States.

Niebuhr, Reinhold (1892–1971), American theologian. From 1928 to 1960 he was Professor of Applied Christianity at the *Union Theological Seminary, New York. He sought to return to the categories of the biblical revelation and was critical of both liberal theology and metaphysics; he reinstated the doctrine of *original sin. He believed that Christianity had a direct prophetic vocation in relation to culture and for a generation his 'Christian realism' exercised an influential critique on American social and political institutions.

Niemöller, Martin (1892–1984), German *Lutheran pastor. His anti-Nazi activities in 1937 led to his arrest and confinement in a concentration camp. Offered release on certain conditions, he refused, and he became the symbolic figure of Protestant opposition to National Socialism. After the Second World War he took a leading part in the 'Declaration of Guilt' at Stuttgart.

Nietzsche, Friedrich Wilhelm (1844–1900), German philosopher. He was a professor at Basle from 1869 to 1879, when he resigned because of ill-health. In 1889 he lost his reason.

Nietzsche was a prophet rather than a systematic thinker. He held that life is the will to power; but power, not as exercised collectively by the masses, but the power of the great individual, the superman. To make this superman possible, the present values which are derived from Christianity must be abolished, since they are the portion of the weak and disinherited 'herd' who, by proclaiming humility, pity, and the like as virtues, have put themselves into power to the detriment of the strong.

Nigeria, Christianity in. The first Christian contact with peoples now included in Nigeria came with *Portuguese missions in the 1470s. The modern Christian phase dates from the 1840s. Between 1843 and 1845 the *CMS and Wesleyan *Methodists entered Yoruba country at the request of Yoruba former slaves who had been converted in *Sierra Leone and returned home. In 1846 a *Presbyterian mission from Jamaica was established in Calabar. More significant was the establishment at Abeokuta of CMS missionaries, joined in 1850 by American *Baptists. From 1857 S. A. *Crowther headed a mission to the Niger and Benue riverine peoples, establishing Churches in the Niger Delta and among the Igbo. RC work resumed in 1868 when the Society of *African Missions arrived in Lagos. Among the Southern Nigerian people Christianity spread widely. After 1918 indigenous Churches stressing prophecy and healing developed a model of the Church distinct from that introduced by the missionaries. Since the Nigerian Civil War (1967–70) there have been many new *charismatic Churches and evangelistic movements.

Northern Nigeria is mainly Muslim. The CMS and RC missions, however, extended their work to the North and two Protestant agencies were specifically devoted to the area: the Sudan Interior Mission, from which the Evangelical Churches of West Africa derive, and the Sudan United Mission, from which the eight Churches in the Fellowship of Churches of Christ in Nigeria derive. Christians form a significant minority in Northern Nigeria.

Night Office. A name for *Mattins.

Nihilianism. The doctrine that Christ, in His human nature, was 'nothing', His essential Being being contained in His Godhead alone. It was condemned in 1170 and 1177.

Nikon (1605–81), Patr. of Moscow from 1652 to 1658. He sought to revise the Russian liturgy by bringing the prescriptions of the service books into conformity with Greek usage and to eradicate corruptions. He settled such details as the making of the sign of the cross with three fingers instead of two and the use of the threefold *Alleluia. In 1658 he fell from imperial favour and resigned. He tried to regain his position, but at the Council of Moscow in 1667 he was deposed and banished, though his liturgical reforms were sanctioned.

Nil Sorsky, St (1433–1508), Russian monk and mystic. On a visit to Mount *Athos he adopted the contemplative life of *Hesychasm. Returning to Russia, he introduced a new form of the ascetic monastic life, that of the small group (*skit*) guided by a spiritual father (*staretz*), for which he wrote a Rule. Feast days, 7 Apr. and 7 May.

Nilus the Ascetic, St (d. *c*.430), also (erroneously) called 'Nilus of Sinai'. According to the traditional account, he was an official in the court at *Constantinople, who became a hermit on Mt *Sinai. It appears, however, that he was a native of Ancyra, that he studied at Constantinople, and that he then founded and became superior of a monastery near Ancyra. From here he conducted a large correspondence. His writings deal mainly with ascetic and moral subjects. His ideal of the spiritual life was a 'Christian philosophy' based on a 'moderated poverty'. Feast day, 12 Nov.

nimbus. See HALO.

Nine Fridays. See FIRST FRIDAYS.

Nineveh, Fast of. A pre-*Lenten fast of two or three days observed in the *Church of the East, the *Syrian Orthodox, and *Coptic Churches in the third week before Lent, and in the *Armenian Church immediately before Lent.

Ninian, St (5th or 6th cent.), British missionary. *Bede reports that before St *Columba (in Scotland 563–97) converted the N. Picts, Ninian had been active among the S. Picts. He describes him as a bishop, 'a Briton who had received orthodox instruction at Rome', and states that he built a church dedicated to St *Martin of Tours at a place called 'Ad Candidam Casam' (At the White House), now Whithorn, where he was buried. His tomb became a place of pilgrimage. Feast day, 16 Sept.

Nisan. The opening month of the Jewish year, roughly corresponding to April. It was the month in which the *Passover was held, the Passover lamb being slain on the 14th day of Nisan.

Nitrian Desert. The region west of the Nile delta, celebrated as a centre of early Christian monasticism.

Nitzsch, Karl Immanuel (1787–1868), German *Lutheran theologian. In the face of contemporary unbelieving rationalism, he rejected a purely speculative interpretation of Christianity and emphasized the immediacy of religious feeling which, he held, produces the foundations of religious knowledge. He promoted the Evangelical Union of the Prussian Churches (1817).

Noah (or Noe). According to the story in Gen. 6–9, Noah and his family were saved in an *ark of gopher-wood, when the rest of mankind was destroyed in the *Flood.

Noailles, Louis Antoine de; Nobili, Robert de. See DE NOAILLES, LOUIS ANTOINE; DE NOBILI, ROBERT.

Nobis quoque peccatoribus (Lat., 'To us sinners, also'). The opening words of one of the sections of the *Canon of the Mass.

Noble Guard. The bodyguard of 77 men of noble rank who formerly attended the Pope at public functions. They were instituted in 1801 and disbanded in 1970.

Nocturn. A division of the traditional night *office (*Mattins) of the W. Church.

Noetics. An early 19th-cent. group of dons at Oriel College, Oxford. They criticized religious orthodoxy and sought to increase the comprehensiveness of the C of E.

Noetus (*c*.200), heretic. He was probably the first to teach *Patripassian doctrines—that it was God the Father who in the Incarnation was born, suffered, and died. He also rejected the *Logos doctrine and accused his opponents of ditheism. He was condemned at Smyrna *c*.200.

Nolascans. An alternative name for the *Mercedarians.

Nominalism. The theory of language which emphasizes the nature of universal concepts as names given by humans. In the controversy on *universals in the 11th and 12th cents., a form of Nominalism was evolved by *Roscelin and P. *Abelard. It was directed against the *Realists who held that universals, such as genus and species, had a separate existence apart from the individuals in which they were embodied. Roscelin carried the denial of the unity of species to the point where he was accused of Tritheism. Abelard described universals as 'names' (nomina) as opposed to 'things' (res), but he does not seem to have denied that the resemblances among individual things justified the use of universals for establishing knowledge.

A different form of Nominalism appeared in the 14th cent.; it is usually associated with *William of Ockham. He asserted that the universal is not found at all in reality, but only in the human mind; universals are only a way of knowing individual things. In its application to theology Nominalism simplifies God's Being to such a degree that the reality of the Three Persons, which depends on formal distinctions and relations, can be accepted only on authority of faith. Nor can reason demonstrate that the First Cause of the Universe is the One God. It thus withdrew almost all the data of faith from the realm of reason and so paved the way for the disintegration of *Scholasticism.

Nomocanon. In the E. Church, a collection of ecclesiastical canons and Imperial laws, arranged according to subject-matter.

Nonconformists' Chapels Act 1844. In the face of disputes between *Presbyterians and *Unitarians, the Act laid down that where no particular religious doctrine or mode of worship was prescribed by the trust deed, the usage of the previous 25 years was to be taken as evidence of what might properly be done in meeting houses. It was repealed in 1960.

Nonconformity. Refusal to conform to the doctrines, polity, or discipline of any Established Church. The word is now used of all dissenters from the C of E, especially those of Protestant sympathy; these include the *Presbyterians (in England) and the *Congregationalists (now mainly united in the *United Reformed Church), the *Methodists, *Quakers, and *Baptists.

None. The last of the 'Little Hours' of the Divine *Office. See also TERCE, SEXT, NONE.

Nonjurors. Members of the C of E who after 1688 scrupled to take the Oaths of Allegiance and Supremacy to William and Mary on the ground that by doing so they would break their earlier oaths to *James II and his successors. They numbered 9 bishops (including Abp. W. *Sancroft and T. *Ken) and c.400 priests, who were deprived of their livings, as well as prominent laymen. Since the bishops were deprived by

Act of Parliament, with no canonical sentence, the Nonjuring clergy regarded them as their lawful bishops; to perpetuate the succession two further bishops were secretly consecrated in 1694. By the end of the 18th cent. most of the Nonjurors had been absorbed into the Established Church.

Norbert, St (c.1080–1134), founder of the *Premonstratensians. He underwent a conversion in 1115. He became famous as an itinerant preacher in N. France and in 1120 he founded the Order of the Premonstratensians in the valley of Prémontré. He was appointed Abp. of Magdeburg in 1126; his zeal for reform made him many enemies. Accompanying the Emp. Lothair II to Rome in 1132–3, he supported Innocent II against the antipope, Anacletus, and prevented the outbreak of fresh quarrels about *investiture. Feast day, 6 June.

Noris, Henry (1631–1704), English theologian. He was Custodian of the *Vatican Library and from 1695 a cardinal. His *Historia Pelagiana* (1673), a history of the *Pelagian controversy, followed by a defence of the *Augustinian doctrine of grace, aroused much opposition.

Norris, John (1657–1712), the last '*Cambridge Platonist'. Influenced by N. *Malebranche, he combined Cartesianism with Platonic mysticism. His *Essay towards the Theory of the Ideal or Intelligible World* (1701–4) contained penetrating criticisms of J. *Locke's *Essay* (1690).

'North End'. The position sometimes adopted at the Communion table by the celebrant of the Eucharist in the C of E. It is now confined to pronounced *Evangelicals, who claim that it rules out any ascription to the celebrant of a priestly or mediatorial function.

North India, Church of. The Church inaugurated in 1970 by the union of six Christian bodies, including *Anglicans, *Congregationalists and *Presbyterians, *Baptists, *Disciples of Christ, and some *Methodists. The C of E entered into full communion with it in 1972.

Norway, Christianity in. From the mid-10th cent. Christianity seems to have been gradually introduced, sometimes at the point of the sword; after the death of St *Olav (1030) there is no record of 'heathen'

opposition. Nicholas Breakspear (the future Pope *Hadrian IV) made Nidaros (Trondheim) an archbishopric with jurisdiction over the other Norwegian dioceses and elsewhere. The Reformation was imposed in 1537 by the Danes who annexed Norway. *Lutheranism became the State religion, no other being recognized until 1845, when Norway had been (since 1814) united with *Sweden. From the mid-19th cent. a Low Church *Pietism was influential. Religious dissent spread (*Methodists, *Baptists, *Pentecostals, and after the Second World War, *Jehovah's Witnesses and *Mormons). The RC Church was introduced in 1843; since 1945 its position has been enhanced by intellectual converts and immigrant refugees.

Norwich. The conversion of East Anglia dates from the 7th cent. In 672 *Theodore, Abp. of Canterbury, divided the diocese between the North Folk and the South Folk, making Elmham a new diocese for Norfolk. In 1094/5 the see was transferred to Norwich by Herbert of Losinga (Bp. 1091–1119), who in 1096 founded the Cathedral of the Holy and Undivided Trinity and constituted it a monastic church under the *Benedictine Rule. The limits of the diocese were almost unchanged until 1837; it now corresponds roughly with the county of Norfolk. The cathedral is mainly a Norman building with a 15th-cent. spire and fine 15th- and 16th-cent. vaulted roofs. The position of the bishop's throne behind the altar is unique in England.

notaries. Specially appointed persons who confirm and attest the truth of deeds or writings in order to render them authentic. In the Middle Ages their appointment lay with the Pope or his delegates, and their work was and remains international. The modern English notary, who is an ecclesiastical officer, is nominated by the judge of the provincial courts of *Canterbury and *York.

Notes of the Church. The four characteristic marks of the Church, first enumerated in the so-called *Nicene Creed, i.e. one, holy, catholic, and apostolic. At the time of the *Reformation RC theologians began to utilize them to discern the true Church among the rival Christian Communions. The *Tractarians employed them to demonstrate the Catholicity of the C of E.

Noth, Martin (1902–68), German OT scholar. His earlier work was concerned with the social and political structure of early Israel. He also engaged in *Traditio-Historical Criticism. Of special importance was his contention that Jos., Jgs., 1 and 2 Sam., and 1 and 2 Kgs. form a '*Deuteronomistic History', to which the bulk of Deut. is a preamble rather than the concluding section of the *Pentateuch.

Notker. Two monks of St *Gall, both masters of the monastic school:

(1) **Notker Balbulus** (c.840–912), 'the Stammerer'. He is famous for his literary work, especially his compilation of *Sequences, the *Liber Hymnorum*. He is also probably the author of the *Gesta Caroli Magni*, a carefully constructed series of *exempla* or moral tales about *Charlemagne, by a 'monk of St Gall'. Feast day, 6 Apr.

(2) **Notker Labeo** (c.950–1022), 'Notker the German'. To help his pupils in their study of Latin school texts and the Bible, he took the unprecedented step of composing a number of bilingual Latin-German versions. He was the most notable German vernacular writer of his time.

Notker (c.940–1008), Bp. of Liège from 972. He owed his position to the Emp. Otto I and throughout his life he defended German interests in Italy and Lorraine. He was a benefactor of the Liège schools, to which he attracted celebrated scholars.

Notre-Dame, Paris. The cathedral church of Paris. Built in early French Gothic style, it was begun in 1163 and consecrated in 1182. The west front was added in 1200–20.

Novatianism. A rigorist schism in the W. Church. Novatian was a Roman presbyter and author of a treatise on the doctrine of the *Trinity. Apparently because he was disappointed by the election of *Cornelius as Pope (251), he joined the rigorist party which deprecated concessions to those who had compromised in the *Decian persecution, and he was consecrated rival Bp. of Rome. He suffered martyrdom in 257–8. The Novatianists, though doctrinally orthodox, were excommunicated. They survived into the 5th cent.

Novello, Vincent (1781–1861), Church musician. He was organist of the Portuguese Embassy chapel in London and of the RC church in Moorfields. He is remembered for his editions of sacred music and for his introduction of such works as the Masses of J. Haydn and W. A. Mozart and the music of G. P. da *Palestrina in England.

Novena. In the W. Church, a period of nine days' devotion, by which it is hoped to obtain some special grace.

novice. A probationary member of a religious community. A novice is under the authority of the superior, and wears the dress and follows the rule of the community. A novice may be dismissed or may leave at any time without incurring ecclesiastical penalties.

Nowell, Alexander (c.1507–1602), Dean of *St Paul's from 1560. He wrote three 'Catechisms'—the 'Large', the 'Middle', and the 'Small'. The last-named, published in 1573, so closely resembles the *Catechism of the 1549 BCP that it has been argued that Nowell wrote that as well.

Nubia, Christianity in. In the Nile Valley, from the First Cataract south to the area around Khartoum (the region formerly known as Nubia), there was a considerable Christian community from the late 6th to at least the 15th cent. There may have been Christians in north Nubia in the 4th cent., but the formal introduction of Christianity dates from the arrival of missionaries sent by the Emp. *Justinian and his wife *Theodora in 543. The rulers of the three kingdoms in the area were converted, soon to be followed by the greater part of the population; by c.580 all three kingdoms were officially Christian. The Nubian Churches were *Monophysite, and bishops were appointed by the Patr. of *Alexandria. In 1172 the Fatimid dynasty in Egypt, which had been tolerant of Christianity and on good terms with Nubia, was overthrown. Both Church and State in Nubia declined. In the 15th cent. there were still Christian kings and bishops in parts of Nubia, but by the early 16th cent. Muslim political control was complete and the Christian community faded away. For modern Christianity, see SUDAN, CHRISTIANITY IN.

nullity. In law, nullity generally means the absence of legal validity from an act or contract, owing to the omission of an integral requirement, or the presence of a fatal flaw.

RC canon law has elaborate rules and a world-wide system of ecclesiastical tribunals to decide on the nullity of marriages. A purported marriage can be declared null if certain formalities were not complied with, if a *diriment impediment was present, or if the consent of either party was substantially defective. Provided that at least one party acted in good faith, even after a declaration of nullity the children are considered legitimate.

In England, since 1857 the civil courts have exercised jurisdiction in matrimonial causes, and the C of E has generally submitted. By the Matrimonial Causes Act 1973 a marriage may be declared null if it is either void from the beginning (e.g. within the *prohibited degrees) or voidable (e.g. not consummated through either incapacity or wilful refusal, defective consent or mental disorder). While C of E clergy were urged by a 1957 Act of Convocation not to solemnize marriages during the lifetime of the partner of a marriage dissolved by *divorce, this bar in practice never applied in cases of annulment.

Number of the Beast. The number 666 (or, according to some MSS, 616) in Rev. 13: 18. As in both Greek and Hebrew each letter of the alphabet represented a figure as well as a letter, every name could be represented by a number corresponding to the sum of its letters. Many explanations have been given of the cryptogram. The most probable is that '*Nero Caesar' is intended.

Numbers, Book of. The bulk of this OT Book narrates the experiences of the Israelites under *Moses during their wanderings in the desert. Its English title is explained by its two records of a census (1–4 and 26).

numinous. A word coined by R. *Otto to denote the elements of a non-rational and amoral kind in what is experienced in religion as the 'holy'. The numinous is held to include feelings of awe and self-abasement as well as an element of religious fascination.

nun. In popular usage, a member of any religious community of women living under vows of poverty, chastity and obedience. In RC canon law the term is restricted to members of enclosed orders who live in houses which outsiders are not usually permitted to enter and which the members are rarely permitted to leave.

Nunc Dimittis. The Song of *Simeon (Lk. 2: 29–32), so named from its initial words in the *Vulgate version. In the E. it is said at *Vespers. In most W. breviaries its use is ordered at *Compline, whence it passed into *Evening Prayer in the BCP and modern Anglican liturgies.

nuncio. A permanent diplomatic representative of the *Holy See accredited to a civil government, who also acts as a link between Rome and the Church in the State to which he is accredited.

Nuptial Mass. The wedding Mass which includes the celebration of the marriage and contains the nuptial blessing. Since 1966 a Nuptial Mass has been permitted at a *mixed marriage, in which both parties are baptized, though the non-RC partner generally may not receive Communion.

Nuremberg Declaration (1870). The statement of belief issued by a group of 14 German Catholic professors and teachers which met at Nuremberg in protest against the decrees of the First *Vatican Council on the Papal claims. It was later signed by others. The signatories formed the nucleus of the *Old Catholic Movement (q.v.).

Oak, Synod of the (403). A synod held in a suburb of Chalcedon called 'The Oak'. It condemned St John *Chrysostom on a number of fabricated charges.

Oakeley, Frederick (1802–80), *Tractarian clergyman. From 1839 to 1845 he was in charge of the Margaret Chapel, London, on the site of the present All Saints', Margaret Street; the chapel became a centre of Tractarian worship in London. He became a RC in 1845; from 1852 he was a canon of the diocese of Westminster.

O-Antiphons (also known as the **Greater Antiphons).** The *antiphons, each beginning 'O ...', which are sung before and after the *Magnificat at *Vespers, according to the Roman use, on the seven days preceding Christmas Eve.

Oates, Titus (1649–1705), conspirator. He spread stories of alleged RC intrigues to assassinate *Charles II and place his brother *James on the throne. The panic lasted from 1678 to 1681, and many people were executed on his false testimony.

oath. Several Christian bodies, e.g. the *Baptists and *Quakers, interpret Mt. 5: 33–7 as forbidding all oaths, but the general Christian teaching is that an oath, though not desirable, may be required by human weakness and is admissible for reasons of serious necessity. It must be concerned only with what one knows to be true, its object must be morally good, and in order to be valid it must be taken with the intention to swear. See also ALLEGIANCE, OATH OF.

Obadiah, Book of. *Minor Prophet and the shortest Book in the OT. It foretells the punishment of the Edomites (the traditional foes of the Jews) in the coming Day of the Lord. Most modern scholars divide it into a number of sections which are variously dated from the 9th to the 5th cent. BC.

obedience. The moral virtue which inclines a man to carry out the will of his lawful superior. While absolute obedience is due to God alone, obedience to men is limited by the bounds of authority and by the claims of conscience. It is the subject of one of the *vows taken by *religious.

obedientiary. An almost obsolete name of the permanent officials in a monastery.

Oberammergau, in Upper Bavaria. In 1633 the villagers vowed that if God would rid them of the plague, they would at ten-year intervals enact a play recalling Christ's Passion and Resurrection. The play, first performed in 1634, since 1680 has usually been staged in the decimal years. It has been rewritten several times. It takes over 5 hours, with up to 850 people on the stage, plus 100 musicians and some animals.

oblate. In the early Middle Ages the term was applied especially to children dedicated to a monastery by their parents and placed there to be brought up. Later it was widely used of laity who lived at a monastery or in close connection with it, but who did not take full religious vows. It has been adopted in the title of some religious communities in the RC Church.

Oblates Regular of St Benedict. An association of women in Rome living under a modified form of the *Benedictine Rule. They give themselves to prayer and good works, but without vows or giving up their property; they make revocable promises of obedience. They were founded by St *Frances of Rome in 1425.

oblations. In Christian usage the term is applied both to the bread and wine offered for consecration in the Eucharist, and also to any other kind of gift presented by the faithful at Mass for the use of the clergy, the sick, the poor, etc.

Obligation, Feasts of. See FEASTS OF OBLIGATION.

O'Bryan, William. See BIBLE CHRISTIANS.

obscurantism. Active opposition, especially from supposedly religious motives, to intellectual enlightenment.

Observantines, also **Observants.** Those members of the *Franciscan Order who wanted to 'observe' the Rule of St *Francis with no relaxation. The movement started in Italy in 1368 as a protest against the decline in religious life and discipline and drew its inspiration largely from the *Spiritual Franciscans and early Papal pronouncements about the Rule. In 1517 the Observantines were separated from the *Conventuals and declared the true Order of St Francis. In the 16th cent. they were divided into the Reformed, the *Recollects, and the *Discalced, but in 1897 these were all incorporated into a single Order of Friars

Minor. A fourth group, the *Capuchins, broke away completely in 1528.

Occasional Conformity Act. The commonly used name for the Toleration Act 1711, part of which was designed to restrain Nonconformists who had received Communion in the C of E in order to qualify for Government posts from subsequently attending dissenting places of worship. Any who were found to have done so were to forfeit £40 and lose their office. This part of the Act was repealed in 1719.

Occasional Offices. In the BCP those offices which are used only as occasion demands, e.g. *Baptism and *Matrimony.

Occasional Prayers. In the BCP a collection of 11 prayers for use upon 'several [i.e. appropriate] occasions' before the final prayers of the *Litany or of Morning and Evening Prayer. In modern Anglican liturgies the number of such prayers is greater.

Occasionalism. The philosophical theory of the relation of mind to matter which denies that finite things have efficient causality, and postulates that God always intervenes to bring about a change in matter when a change occurs in the mind, and vice versa. Among its chief exponents were A. *Geulincx and N. *Malebranche.

occurrence. The falling of two feasts (or other commemorations) on the same day in the ecclesiastical year, e.g. the coincidence of Christmas Day with a Sunday. In the W. Church, the feast of the higher rank is kept in such cases.

Ochino, Bernardino (1487–1564), Protestant Reformer. He was an *Observantine Franciscan and then a *Capuchin, in each case holding high office. He became a *Lutheran in 1541. He was cited before the *Inquisition, but escaped to *Geneva. In 1547 T. *Cranmer invited him to England. Here he wrote against the Papacy and against the Calvinist doctrine of *predestination. In 1555 he became a pastor at Zurich, but he was later expelled from office, being found unsound on the doctrine of the Trinity and on monogamy.

Ockham, William of. See WILLIAM OF OCKHAM.

O come, all ye faithful. See ADESTE FIDELES.

O'Connell, Daniel (1775–1847), Irish states-man. Trained as a lawyer, he quickly gained influence as a Catholic leader. In 1823 he formed the *Catholic Association with the object of securing Catholic emancipation by legal means. In 1828 he became MP for Clare. The following year the Roman Cath-olic Emancipation Act (see CATHOLIC RELIEF ACTS) was passed. O'Connell now led his own parliamentary party, while also con-ducting successive movements to repeal the Union. He acted impartially while he was Lord Mayor of Dublin (1841–2), but in 1843 resumed his agitation, holding a series of 'monster meetings'; he was arrested and in 1844 condemned to a year's imprison-ment, but freed on appeal to the House of Lords. He created modern Irish consti-tutional nationalism.

Octateuch. The first eight books of the OT.

Octave. In Christian liturgical use, the eighth day after a feast, reckoning inclu-sively. The term is also used of the whole period of eight days, during which the observance of certain major feasts came to be continued. In the RC Church only *Christmas and *Easter are now so observed.

Octoechos. A liturgical book in the E. Church which contains the variable parts of the services when these are not taken wholly from one of the other service books—the *Triodion, the *Pentecostarion, or the *Menaion.

Oda, St (d. 959), mistakenly also 'Odo', Abp. of *Canterbury from 942. He is said to have been the son of a Dane and originally a pagan. He was active in raising the morals and discipline of his clergy. Feast day, 4 July.

Odes of Solomon. See SOLOMON, ODES OF.

Odilia, St (d. c.720), patroness of Alsace. She is said to have been born blind and later miraculously received sight. Having been granted by her father the castle at Hohenburg (now the Odilienberg) in the Vosges Mountains, she founded a nunnery which she ruled as Abbess; it became a centre of pilgrimage; the water of the well is said to cure diseased eyes. Feast day, 13 Dec.

Odilo, St (961/2–1049) Abbot of *Cluny from 994. Under him the Order was extended and also strengthened by his plan of centralization, whereby most of the reformed monasteries were made directly dependent on Cluny. He was esteemed by Popes and Emperors, and the '*Truce of God' for S. France and Italy was largely his work. He introduced the commemoration of *All Souls' Day (2 Nov.), which soon spread from Cluny to the whole W. Church. Feast day, 2 Jan. (by the *Benedictines, 11 May).

odium theologicum (Lat., 'theological hatred'). A proverbial expression for the ill-feeling to which theological controversy often gives rise.

Odo, St (c.879–942) second Abbot of *Cluny. In 909 he entered the monastery of Baume, where he was soon in charge of the monastery school. He succeeded St Berno as Abbot of Cluny in 927. He was largely instrumental in raising the monastery to the high position which it held in the next centuries. Under him the monastic church was completed and the influence of Cluny over other monasteries greatly extended. Feast day, 18 Nov. (by the *Benedictines, 11 May).

Odo, St (d. 959). See ODA, ST.

Odo (b. c.1030 or c.1035; d. 1097), Bp. of Bayeux from 1049/50. A half-brother of *William I, the Conqueror, he was present at the Battle of Hastings and probably commissioned the Bayeux Tapestry. In 1067 he was made Earl of Kent. After the failure of his rebellion under William II, he left England. He set out on the First *Crusade in 1096, but died at Palermo. Though much engaged in temporal affairs, he had a good reputation as a bishop.

Oecolompadius, Johannes (1482–1531), Reformer. In 1515 he helped J. *Froben with the printing of *Erasmus' Greek-Latin NT (1516) and wrote the notes at the end of it. He entered a monastery in 1520 but left it in 1522 to throw in his lot with the Reformers. On his return to Basle his influence led to the adoption by the city of Reformation principles, which were accepted by the Canton of Berne in 1528. He is thought to be the first Reformer to have advocated lay participation in Church government.

Oecumenical Councils. Assemblies of

bishops and other ecclesiastical representatives of the whole world whose decisions on doctrine, discipline, etc. are considered binding on all Christians. According to RC canon law, the Pope alone has the right to convene a Council, to preside over it (in person or through deputies), and to approve its decrees. Under certain conditions, the college of bishops gathered in an Oecumenical Council is held to possess infallible teaching authority.

Seven Councils are held both in E. and W. to be oecumenical, namely those of *Nicaea I (325), *Constantinople I (381), *Ephesus (431), *Chalcedon (451), *Constantinople II (553), *Constantinople III (680-1), and *Nicaea II (787). The RC Church reckons the following Councils as also possessing oecumenical authority: Constantinople IV (869-70), *Lateran I (1123), Lateran II (1139), Lateran III (1179), Lateran IV (1215), *Lyons I (1245), *Lyons II (1274), *Vienne (1311-2), *Constance (1414-7), *Basle-*Florence (1431-45), Lateran V (1512-7), *Trent (1545-63), *Vatican I (1869-70), and *Vatican II (1962-5).

Oecumenical Patriarch. The style borne by the Abps. or Patrs. of *Constantinople.

Oecumenius (6th cent.), author of the oldest extant Greek commentary on Rev., to whom tradition has assigned the designations 'Rhetor' and 'Philosopher'. The commentary accepts Rev. as a divinely inspired canonical Book.

Oengus, St (8th-9th cent.), Irish saint, commonly, but perhaps erroneously, called the *Culdee, author of a Félire or verse *martyrology. He apparently spent the latter part of his life in the community at Clonenagh, Co. Laoise, and in a nearby hermitage. At some point he joined the fraternity of Tallaght, near Dublin. Here he collaborated with St Máel Rúain (d. 792) on the compilation of the Martyrology of Tallaght, the oldest Irish martyrology and a major source of his own. Both martyrologies in their extant form can be dated c.800 or c.830. Feast day, 11 Mar.

Offa (d. 796), King of the Mercians from 757. He gradually secured dominion, either directly or as overlord, over other parts of England south of the R. Humber. His dealings with *Hadrian I led to a visit by two Papal legates to England in 786 and the creation of a new archbishopric at *Lichfield in 787 (suppressed in 803); in 787 his son was anointed king—the first recorded consecration of an English king.

Offertory. In the Eucharist: (1) The worshippers' offering of bread and wine (and water) to be consecrated. (2) The anthem formerly sung in the Roman rite at the time of the act of offering. It came normally to consist of only an antiphon, now often replaced by a hymn or other chant.

Office, Divine. The daily public worship of the Church, also called in the RC Church, the 'Liturgy of the Hours'. Its recitation at stated times differentiates it from other liturgical services.

The practice of saying prayers at fixed times was general among the Jews, and was doubtless taken over by the early Christians. From the first it seems that parts of the Psalter were used in Christian prayer. The early monks ('Desert Fathers') used long sections of the Psalter, different groups of monks sometimes taking over from one another. This practice influenced the organization of the Office by St *Basil in the E. and *Cassian in the W. The monastic Offices of the hours of the night and day came into existence, namely *Mattins and *Lauds, *Terce, *Sext, *None, *Vespers and *Compline. *Prime apparently originated near *Bethlehem and was adopted by Cassian. In cathedrals and non-monastic churches there was a simpler pattern of morning and evening prayer. From the 5th cent. the great basilicas of Rome were served by monastic communities; these added to morning and evening prayer both the other Day Hours and the Night Office or *Vigils. By the 8th cent. the cycle of Day Hours and Mattins had become the general pattern for all clergy, secular and monastic. The Papal Curia developed a shorter Office. Because of the prestige of the Curia, by the 12th cent. this was regarded as the Office of the Roman Church. St *Francis of Assisi adopted it for his friars and its use spread throughout Europe.

In principle the whole Psalter was to be recited each week, and the readings were to include most of the Bible, but the proliferation of saints' days and other factors meant that by the end of the Middle Ages the Office was in confusion. In 1568 *Pius V issued a new *Breviary, which was shortened and simplified by *Pius X in 1911. A complete reordering of the Office was achieved in the *Liturgy of the Hours* issued by *Paul VI in 1971. This provides for an *Office of Readings (q.v.), Lauds, a midday Office (see TERCE, SEXT, NONE), Vespers, and Compline, now to be said before retiring. Besides the Bible, there are readings from the Fathers and later writers. All RC priests and deacons aspiring to the priesthood, and all religious whose rule requires it, are bound to the daily recitation of the Office. Some religious orders have their own Offices, and some are also bound to recite a Night Office. See MONASTIC BREVIARY.

In the C of E at the Reformation the traditional Offices were combined into Morning and Evening Prayer (Mattins and *Evensong). In parts of the Anglican Communion there has been some modern restructuring of the Office, e.g. provision for Noonday Prayer in the American BCP (1979).

Office, Holy. See HOLY OFFICE.

Office Hymns. *Hymns appear as part of the Monastic *Office in the Rule of St *Benedict, though they were not generally used in the Roman liturgy until the 12th cent. The 1971 *Liturgy of the Hours* places a hymn before the Psalms in all Offices; provides two sets of hymns; and allows conferences of bishops to introduce others.

Office of Readings. The Office which in 1971 replaced *Mattins. It may be said at any time of the day. The main elements are a hymn, Psalms, and two Readings, of which only the first is from the Bible.

Official Principal (also **Official).** In Anglican ecclesiastical law, the person to whom a bishop formerly entrusted the exercise of his coercive jurisdiction. Since 1963 the office has been combined with that of *chancellor in a single judge.

According to RC canon law, every diocesan bishop has to appoint (in addition to his *Vicar General) an *officialis* or judicial vicar, who constitutes a single tribunal with the bishop, but cannot judge cases which the bishop reserves to himself.

oils, holy. See CHRISM.

Olav, St (995?–1030), **Olav Haraldsson**, patron saint of *Norway and King from 1016 to 1028. He was baptized shortly

before he became King; his support of Christianity was decisive in the long run, but the harshness of his methods provoked resistance and he had to flee to Russia. He was killed in battle. Feast day, 29 July.

Old Believers. The section of the *Russian Orthodox Church which refused to accept the liturgical reforms of the Patr. *Nikon. They were excommunicated in 1667 and persecuted. As no bishops seceded, they were left without a hierarchy and split into two sections: the one, called 'Popovtsy', sought means of establishing their own priesthood; the other, the 'Bezpopovtsy', denied its necessity. In 1846 a deposed bishop joined the Popovtsy and established a hierarchy. The anathemas imposed on the Old Believers in 1667 were lifted by the Russian Orthodox Church in 1971, but the schism has not been healed.

Old Catholics. A group of small national Churches, consisting of Christians who have separated from the RC Church.

(1) The Old Catholic Church in the *Netherlands, sometimes called the Church of Utrecht. This owes its origin to the Papal handling of the *Jansenist controversy and particularly to the deposition in 1702 of Petrus Codde, the Vicar Apostolic of the area. The Chapter of Utrecht, acting independently of Rome, in 1723 elected Cornelius Steenoven Abp. of Utrecht; he was consecrated by D. M. Varlet, Bp. of Babylon, who had fallen foul of the Roman authorities but whose consecration had been regular. On Steenoven's death, Varlet consecrated his successor in 1725.

(2) The German, Austrian, and Swiss Old Catholic Churches. This group of Churches was created from those who refused to accept the dogmas of the *infallibility and universal ordinary jurisdiction of the Pope as defined by the *Vatican Council of 1870, and seceded from the RC Church soon afterwards. They received their episcopal succession from the Church of Utrecht.

(3) Small groups of Slav origin. National Church movements among the Poles in the USA (1897) and the Croats (1924) resulted in the establishment of separate Churches.

The doctrinal basis of the Old Catholic Churches is the 'Declaration of *Utrecht', agreed upon in 1889. Old Catholic bishops have several times taken part in the consecration of Anglican bishops.

The term 'Old Catholic' is also used of RCs in England of older (especially *recusant) background in contrast to converts and immigrants.

Oldcastle, Sir John (*c*.1378?–1417), *Lollard leader. In 1413 he was accused of heresy before *Convocation and upheld Lollard opinions. He was given 40 days to recant, escaped from the Tower of London, and led a conspiracy for a Lollard rebellion, which, however, collapsed. When captured he was executed.

Oldham, Joseph Houldsworth (1874–1969), missionary statesman and leader of the *Ecumenical Movement. He was secretary of the World Missionary Conference which met in *Edinburgh in 1910 and of its Continuation Committee. Called upon by the missionaries to pursue with the Government the question of indentured labour in East Africa, he voiced a missionary opinion in the debate on the political future of colonial territories. In 1934 he became Chairman of the Research Commission of the Universal Christian Council for '*Life and Work'; he thus had a leading part in the *Oxford Conference of 1937 and that at Utrecht in 1938 which set up the provisional committee of the *World Council of Churches.

Old Latin Versions. The Latin versions of the Scriptures in use in the Church before they were superseded by the *Vulgate. The existence of Latin translations of the Bible in S. Gaul and N. Africa is attested before the end of the 2nd cent. The MSS of the Old Latin differ among themselves and it was largely in order to remedy the resulting inconvenience that St *Jerome undertook the Vulgate.

Old Roman Catholic Church. A small community tracing its episcopal orders to A. H. *Mathew.

Old Roman chant. The musical repertory accompanying a form of the Roman rite in five MSS. It is usually thought to be a precursor of the *Gregorian chants, but both may derive from a simpler original.

Old Roman Creed. An earlier and shorter form of the *Apostles' Creed, which by the end of the 2nd cent. was the official baptismal creed of the Church of Rome.

Old Syriac Version. The Syriac translation of the NT which circulated in the Syriac-speaking Church before the construction of the *Peshitta version in the 5th cent. Only two MSS are known, both of the Gospels, but the existence of a Syriac text of Acts is attested by a commentary on it.

Old Testament. A term denoting the collection of Canonical Books which the Church shares with *Judaism, together with (in Catholic and Orthodox Churches) certain other Jewish Books not now accepted as canonical by the Jews (the *Apocrypha). Like the NT, the OT Books are regarded as inspired in the Church, which from the time of *Marcion has defended them against attack.

Olier, Jean-Jacques (1608–57), founder of the Society and Seminary of *Saint-Sulpice (q.v.). Threatened with the loss of his sight, on a pilgrimage to *Loreto he was cured and converted to a deeply religious life. Ordained in 1633, he established a seminary at Vaugirard; when he became parish priest of Saint-Sulpice in Paris in 1642, he transferred the seminary there. He divided his parish into eight districts, with a priest in charge of each; schools, catechism classes, homes for women and charitable organizations were established. He built up a community of secular priests, pursuing a common aim, but without religious vows. His spiritual writings are centred on the need for self-abasement, turning from a devotion to Christ's humanity to His divinity.

Oliver Plunkett, St. See PLUNKETT, ST OLIVER.

Olives, Mount of. The highest point in the range of hills E. of *Jerusalem. It appears that Christ often went there. The traditional site of the *Ascension was marked by a church known as the 'Imbomon' before 378. Another 4th-cent. church, the 'Eleona', was built over the grotto where Christ was believed to have discoursed on the Last Things (Mk. 13).

Olivetan (*c*.1506–38), Protestant Reformer. His real name may have been Pierre Robert. A cousin of J. *Calvin, from 1532 to 1535 he preached Reformation doctrines to the *Waldenses in Neuchâtel, and for the purposes of his mission he translated the Bible into French (published 1535).

Olivetans (The Congregation of Our Lady of Mount Olivet). A monastic *Congregation of *Benedictine monks founded in 1319 by Giovanni Tolomei at Monte Oliveto, near Siena. Their houses include the Abbey of *Bec.

Olivi, Petrus Joannis (c.1248–98), *Spiritual Franciscan. As leader of the rigorists in the *Franciscan Order, he was accused of heresy in the General Chapter of Strasbourg in 1282 and his works were censured in 34 propositions in 1283. At the General Chapter of Montpellier (1287), however, he established his orthodoxy, which was confirmed at Paris in 1292. After his death the Spiritual Franciscans accorded him exaggerated veneration, and though at the Council of *Vienne (1311) certain propositions believed to be his were repudiated, his name was not mentioned.

Oman, John Wood (1860–1939), *Presbyterian theologian. From 1907 to 1935 he taught in Cambridge. Holding the uniqueness and independence of the religious consciousness as an immediate, self-authenticating awareness of the Supernatural, he nevertheless insisted that it should not be isolated from other spheres of experience. In *The Natural and the Supernatural* (1931) he set out a philosophic justification of his position.

Omar, Mosque of. See DOME OF THE ROCK.

ombrellino. In the W. Church, a small umbrella-like canopy sometimes carried over the Blessed Sacrament when it is moved from place to place informally.

omophorion. A long scarf used in the E. Church by bishops at the Liturgy and at other rites performed by them.

Oneida Community. A Christian communist society established at Oneida, NY, in 1848, and also known as the **Perfectionists**. It became prosperous and in 1881 was formed into a joint-stock company.

Onesimus, St. The Phrygian slave on whose behalf St *Paul wrote his Epistle to *Philemon. According to tradition, he suffered martyrdom. Feast day in the W., 16 Feb.; in the E., 15 Feb. (also 22 Nov.).

Ontological Argument. A classical argument for God's existence, holding that the concept of God entails the real existence of God. It was first elaborated by St *Anselm (q.v.).

Ontologism. A philosophical system favoured by certain Catholic philosophers in the 19th cent. The ontologists asserted that God Himself is the guarantee of the validity of human ideas; that all human knowledge, itself a mode of truth, implies an immediate intuition of uncreated Truth; and that the idea of being, which is the first and simplest idea of all, is an immediate perception of absolute Being. A set of seven 'Errores Ontologistarum' was condemned by the *Inquisition in 1861.

Ophites and **Naassenes.** *Gnostic sects who attached special importance to the serpent; it is not clear whether they were connected. Since the serpent induced *Adam and *Eve to eat of the tree of knowledge (Gen. 3), it might be expected that it would have an honourable place among the Gnostics, but some sects saw it as a hostile power.

Optatus, St (*fl.* 370), Bp. of Milevis in N. Africa. Nothing is known of him apart from his treatise 'Against Parmenian the Donatist'. His argument turns on the lack of 'catholicity' among the *Donatists, but he also attacks their claim to 'holiness'. An appendix ('dossier') of important historical documents has received much attention from modern scholars. Feast day, 4 June.

option. The right formerly possessed by an archbishop, when about to consecrate a bishop, of choosing within the latter's see a benefice to which he would act as patron at the next vacancy. The word is also used of the right of members of certain Cathedral or Collegiate chapters to secure at choice a particular benefice or title.

Opus Dei (Lat., 'the work of God'). A *Benedictine designation for the Divine *Office.

Opus Dei is also the name of a RC organization devoted to fostering the application of Christian principles to daily living in all walks of life. It was founded in 1928 in Madrid by the St Josemaría Escrivá (1902–75), who also set up a branch for women (1930) and in 1943 the Society of the Holy Cross for priests. In 1982 the *Personal

Prelature of the Holy Cross and Opus Dei was established, giving the organization considerable independence of local bishops. It maintains a number of educational establishments, notably the University of Pamplona.

opus operatum. See EX OPERE OPERATO.

Oracles, Sibylline. See SIBYLLINE ORACLES.

Orange, Councils of. Two synods were held at Orange in S. France in 441 and 529. The 25 dogmatic *capitula* of the latter upheld many of St *Augustine's doctrines on the nature of *grace against the *Semi-pelagianism previously current in the region, though the Council repudiated any predestination of man to evil.

Orangism. The movement defending Protestantism in *Ireland, maintained by the Orange Association (founded 1795).

orarion. In the E. Church, the deacon's stole.

Oratorians. (1) **The Oratory of St *Philip Neri** is a congregation of secular priests living in community without vows, approved in 1575. The name derives from the oratory of S. Girolamo, Rome, where they held their 'Exercises'. Their chief task is to lead men to God through prayer, preaching, and the Sacraments. They lay stress on attractive services, especially on good music; the modern *oratorio grew out of the *laudi spirituali* sung in their devotional exercises. They were introduced into England by J. H. *Newman in 1848.

(2) **The French Oratory** was founded in 1611 by P. de *Bérulle. Though formed on the Italian model, it differs mainly in that it is a centralized organization. One of its chief activities is the training of priests in *seminaries run on the lines laid down by the Council of *Trent. Dissolved in the French Revolution, the Oratory was re-established in 1852.

oratorio. The musical setting of a religious libretto for soloists, chorus, and orchestra (or other accompaniment) without (in modern practice) the use of dramatic action, scenery, or costume. Oratorio apparently derives from the dramatic services of St *Philip Neri (d. 1595) at the *Oratory in Rome. The English oratorio, with its emphasis on the chorus, was essentially the creation of G. F. *Handel (q.v.).

oratory. The term, used in antiquity of both churches and private chapels, has come to be restricted to places of worship other than the parish church. RC canon law distinguishes both oratories and private chapels from churches, to which all the faithful have access for divine worship. In general, all sacred celebrations can be carried out in an oratory, whereas permission is required for them in a private chapel.

'The Oratory' is used absolutely for the *Oratorians (q.v.) or 'Congregation of the Oratory' and for churches belonging to it, e.g. Brompton Oratory in London.

ordeals. A method of judicial proof used in early medieval Europe in cases where sworn testimony and the evidence of witnesses was thought insufficient to establish guilt or innocence. The accused was subjected to some physical test, such as walking on heated ploughshares; success or failure was demonstrated by the physical consequences, such as a 'clean' wound or a septic one. The ordeal was normally administered by the Church, and the blessing of a priest was required for its administration. It was seen as providing God's verdict on the accusation. The Fourth *Lateran Council (1215) prohibited the participation of the clergy in the ceremony, which was abandoned quickly in some countries and slowly disappeared completely.

Ordericus Vitalis (1075–?1142), Anglo-Norman historian. In 1085 he entered the *Benedictine house of St-*Évroul(t) in Normandy. He wrote an Ecclesiastical History, beginning with the birth of Christ. The latter part is a prime source for the political and ecclesiastical history and the customs of his time.

Orders and Ordination. The ministry of the Church traces its origins to the Lord's commissioning of the Twelve (Mt. 10: 1–5 etc.) and the Seventy (Lk. 10: 1) to the work of the kingdom. It received a new power and wider responsibility after Pentecost (Acts 2: 1–13). In the newly founded Churches patterns of local ministry varied, but the charismatic ministry of *prophets and teachers recognized by St *Paul (1 Cor. 12: 28) soon gave way to 'elders', i.e. *presbyters. Acts represents Paul as himself appointing them (14: 23) and at 20: 28 takes *bishops to be broadly equivalent. A monarchical episcopate is advocated and represented at *Antioch by St *Ignatius (d. c.103). However, the gradual transition from apostolic leadership and a variety of charismatic and non-charismatic ministries to the stronger Church order that provides a focus of unity is only partially visible to the historian. 1 Tim. 3–4 is the first evidence of a definite order of bishops and *deacons. It also adumbrates or envisages ordination: the local presbyters lay *hands on Timothy and the Spirit is understood to be conveyed by the rite. The account in Acts 6: 1–6 of the appointment of the Seven echoes this passage. All these hints of later practice preserve the sense of God's choosing ministers. By the mid-3rd cent. considerable evolution of the system is evident. At Rome under *Cornelius (251–3) there were, besides the bishop, 46 presbyters, 7 *deacons, 7 *subdeacons, 42 *acolytes and 52 *exorcists, *readers, and *doorkeepers. By the later Middle Ages the prevalent view was that there were seven Orders, and in the W. a distinction was made between the three *Major and four *Minor Orders (qq.v.). According to Catholic theology the gift of Order is a Sacrament, and it is held to impart an indelible *character. In the Middle Ages the Minor Orders were commonly regarded as included within the Sacrament of Orders, but RC theologians now reject this view.

It is traditionally held that only a baptized and confirmed male person can be validly ordained. However, in modern times many provinces in the Anglican Communion have admitted *women to the deaconate and priesthood and some to the episcopate also. The candidate must be of good moral character and nowadays convinced that he has a Divine call ('vocation') to the office. He must be of due age (see AGE, CANONICAL) and generally needs a '*title' to the cure of souls. Traditional theology also holds that the Sacrament of Orders can validly be conferred only by a duly consecrated bishop.

Ordination has always taken place in the context of the Eucharist. The rite, which long remained simple in the E., had become elaborate in the W. by the end of the Middle Ages. In the RC Church much simplified rites of Ordination were introduced in 1968. The bishop now lays hands on each candidate for the diaconate in silence and then says the Ordination prayer over them all. After each candidate has

been vested in *dalmatic and *stole, the bishop gives him the book of the Gospels with a charge to proclaim and live by it. In the case of candidates for the priesthood the bishop is joined by other clergy in the laying-on of hands, and a different formula is used in the Ordination prayer. The bishop then anoints the hands of each candidate with *chrism and delivers to him the paten and chalice with bread and wine offered by the people. In the ordering of bishops, the co-consecrators join with the consecrating bishop in saying that part of the consecratory prayer held to be necessary for *validity; while this prayer is being said, the book of the Gospels is held over the head of the candidate. The consecrating bishop then anoints his head, delivers the Gospels to him, puts a *ring on his finger and a *mitre on his head, and gives him a pastoral staff or *crosier. For rites in the C of E, see ORDINAL.

In the W. the *Ember seasons were the normal times for the ordination of priests and deacons. In recent years the feast of St *Peter has replaced *Trinity Sunday.

See also ANGLICAN ORDINATIONS.

Ordinal. (1) In the Middle Ages, a book to acquaint the priest with the Office to be recited in accordance with variations in the ecclesiastical year.

(2) In the C of E, 'The Form and Manner of Making, Ordaining, and Consecrating of Bishops, Priests, and Deacons'. There have been four English Ordinals, in 1550, 1552, 1559, and 1662, the first being based on the *Sarum Pontifical. Here, in the Consecration of Bishops the medieval ceremonies of anointing and the delivery of the *ring and *mitre were omitted. In the Ordering of Priests the tradition of the *Instruments was dropped in 1552, but all the Ordinals include in the formula accompanying the laying-on of hands the words 'Receive the Holy Ghost' and 'Whose sins thou dost forgive, they are forgiven; whose sins thou does retain, they are retained'. Subsequent attempts at revision throughout the Anglican Communion have been conservative, though, like the RC rite, modern Anglican liturgies often omit any reference to the power to forgive sins.

Ordinary. In canon law, an ecclesiastic in the exercise of the jurisdiction annexed to his office. In the RC Church the term is closely defined; it includes diocesan bishops and those who, even temporarily, are set over a diocese or particular Church, *vicars general and episcopal vicars, and for their members major superiors of clerical religious *institutes. Its meaning in the BCP is not precisely determined, though it usually refers to the bishop.

Ordinary of the Mass (Lat. *Ordo Missae*). Until recently the term was used to describe the invariable or almost invariable parts of the Mass, as distinguished from the parts which varied with the ecclesiastical calendar. The 1970 *Missale Romanum* applies the term 'Ordo Missae' to the whole service.

Ordination. See ORDERS AND ORDINATION.

Ordines Romani. Ancient collections of ceremonial directions for the performance of the Roman rite. The earliest of them date from the 8th to the 10th cents. and are of importance for the history of liturgy.

Oresme, Nicholas (*c.*1320–82), mathematician, natural philosopher, and economist. He was closely associated with the University of *Paris and the French court; from 1377 he was Bp. of Lisieux. He gave powerful arguments in favour of the Earth spinning daily on its own axis, but said that he did so as a ploy against those who would use reason to attack the truths of Christianity. For the French court he produced several philosophical works in the vernacular, including translations of, and commentaries on, works of *Aristotle.

Organic Articles (1802). The provisions of Napoleon regulating public worship and the relations of Church and State in France.

organs. The organ was a purely secular instrument until the 10th cent., when it began to appear in major churches. Its role is largely unknown until *c.*1400, when the alternating of organ verses with *plainsong or polyphony sung by the choir became an established custom in both the *Mass and *Office. This continued as a common practice, especially in France, until the 19th cent., but in *Lutheran churches in Germany it gave way to the development of the organ chorale. From the early 17th cent. the organ provided simple accompaniment for some choral music; its present pre-

dominant role of leading congregational singing developed gradually from the 17th cent. In the second half of the 20th cent. electronic organs for economic reasons replaced pipe organs in many churches, but are a poor substitute.

Oriental Orthodox Churches. A modern name for those Churches (*Armenian, *Coptic, *Ethiopian, and *Syrian Orthodox) which rejected the Christological teaching of the Definition of *Chalcedon. It distinguishes these Churches from the Eastern *Orthodox Church and avoids the term *Monophysite.

orientation. The construction of a church so that its longer axis runs east to west. In the early *basilicas of Rome the altar was at the west end; elsewhere more usually at the east. Though orientation is derived historically from a pagan habit of praying towards the sunrise, Christians have seen in its adoption symbolic reference to Christ as the Rising Sun.

Origen (*c.*185–*c.*254), biblical critic, theologian, and spiritual writer. Born in Egypt, he was brought up as a Christian and recognized by *Demetrius, Bp. of *Alexandria, as head of the *Catechetical School (q.v.). When trouble broke out in Alexandria in 215, he went to Palestine; his preaching here as a layman was regarded as a breach of Alexandrian ecclesiastical discipline and he was recalled. In 230 he went to Palestine again and was ordained priest by the bishops who had invited him to preach on his previous visit. In consequence Demetrius deprived him of his chair and deposed him from the priesthood. Origen went to *Caesarea (231), where he established a school which became famous. In 250, in the *Decian persecution, he was imprisoned and tortured.

Origen wrote much, but many of his works have perished and most of the others survive only in fragments or in Latin translation. His main work on biblical criticism was his '*Hexapla' (q.v.). He also wrote commentaries on most Books of the Bible and many homilies. The original Greek of some of these was recovered in the 20th cent. His chief theological work is the *De Principiis*, which covers a wide range of doctrinal topics. His two ascetical works, 'Exhortation to Martyrdom' and 'On Prayer', were much read in antiquity. He also wrote an apologetic work against *Celsus (q.v.).

As a biblical scholar, Origen recognized a triple sense—literal, moral, and allegorical—of which he favoured the last. The point of departure of his doctrinal teaching was faith in the unity of God. This unity in its fullest sense is understood of God the Father, and for Origen the Son is divine only in a lesser sense than the Father. His philosophical speculations led him into audacious thought, though it is not always clear that he held as certain the propositions he expressed. He affirmed that creation was eternal. He maintained that all spirits were created equal, but through the exercise of their free will they developed in hierarchical order and some fell into sin and so became demons or souls imprisoned in bodies. Death does not finally decide the fate of the soul, which may turn into a demon or an angel. This ascent and descent goes on until the final *Apocatastasis (q.v.), when all creatures, even the devil, will be saved.

Origenism. The group of theories enunciated by, or attributed to, *Origen. Among his earliest opponents was *Methodius of Olympus, who rejected his teaching on the pre-existence of souls and his denial of the identity between the mortal and resurrection bodies. The 4th-cent. controversy was concerned mainly with the Trinitarian teaching of the *De Principiis*. Origen was further accused of teaching *metempsychosis and of interpreting the Scriptures only allegorically. The initial attack by St *Epiphanius was taken up by St *Jerome. In 398 *Rufinus issued his Latin translation of the *De Principiis*, which was designed to vindicate Origen's orthodoxy, but in 400 a Council at *Alexandria condemned Origenism, and Pope Anastasius I and the Bps. of Palestine and Syria adhered to the condemnation.

The controversy flared up again in Palestine in the 6th cent. The opponents of Origenism secured the support of the Emp. *Justinian, who issued an edict giving a list of Origenistic errors and their refutation. The Origenist monks at Jerusalem then split into two parties. The Second Council of *Constantinople (553) finally condemned Origen's teaching.

Original Righteousness. According to Catholic theology, God's gratuitous impartation to man of perfect rectitude in his condition before the *Fall. The state of Original Righteousness in which man was created is held to have included freedom from concupiscence, bodily immortality, and happiness.

Original Sin. In Christian theology, the state of sin in which mankind has been captive since the *Fall (q.v.). The scriptural foundation of the doctrine is the Pauline teaching that 'through one man [i.e. Adam] sin entered into the world', so that 'by the trespass of the one many died' (cf. Rom. 5: 12-21 and 1 Cor. 15: 22). St *Irenaeus began to develop the doctrine in his struggle against the *Gnostics, defending the teaching that evil came into the world through the sin of Adam, as against the *dualist systems of the heretics. The Greek Fathers generally emphasized the cosmic dimensions of the Fall—since Adam men are born into a fallen world—but at the same time they held fast to the belief that man, though fallen, is free. The precise formulation of the doctrine was left to the W. Here *Tertullian, St *Cyprian, and St *Ambrose taught the solidarity of the whole race with Adam not only in the consequences of the sin but in the sin itself, which is transmitted through natural generation. Beyond this two schools of thought developed. St *Augustine and his followers maintained that Adam's guilt was transmitted to his descendants by concupiscence, making of humanity a *massa damnata* and much enfeebling, though not destroying, the freedom of the will. St *Anselm separated Original Sin from concupiscence; he defined it as 'the privation of the righteousness which every man ought to possess' and held that it was transmitted by generation, since the whole human race was present in Adam *seminaliter*. St *Thomas Aquinas distinguished, in the state of Adam before the Fall, 'pure nature' from the supernatural gifts which perfected it. Hence Original Sin consists in the loss of those supernatural privileges which had directed man to his supernatural end and enabled him to keep his inferior powers in submission to reason. This conception leaves to the reason, will, and passions of fallen man their natural powers. According to Aquinas, Original Sin is transmitted not as the personal fault of Adam but as a state of human nature, yet constituting a fault inasmuch as all men are regarded as one great organism of which Adam was the first mover. The instrument of transmission is generation, regardless of the accompanying concupiscence.

In the 16th cent., both M. *Luther and J. *Calvin again equated Original Sin with concupiscence and affirmed that it destroyed liberty and persisted after Baptism. D. *Soto, on the other hand, in restating the doctrine of Aquinas eliminated the element of concupiscence from the definition altogether and identified Original Sin with the loss of sanctifying grace; his views were widely influential in the RC Church, though the *Jansenists inclined towards the old Augustinian pessimism. From the 18th cent. the dogma of Original Sin was attenuated by the *Enlightenment's confidence in human progress and belief in evolution, but in some form it persisted and was strongly reaffirmed in the 20th cent. by K. *Barth and his followers. Modern treatments of Original Sin tend to regard it as belonging to the nature of man rather than to the individual person; they derive it less from heredity than from the social character of man.

Ornaments Rubric. The common name for the ruling in the 1559 BCP that the ornaments of the church and the ministers should be those in use 'by the authority of Parliament in the second year of the reign of King *Edward VI'. Its meaning has been disputed since the 16th cent.

Orosius (5th cent.), Paulus Orosius, historian. A native of Braga, he migrated to Africa in 414. His *Historia adversus Paganos*, written at St *Augustine's request, attacked the pagan complaint that Rome's troubles were due to her abandonment of her gods; only after AD 378 is it of historical value.

Orsisius, St (d. c.380), ascetic and Abbot of Tabenne (an island in the Nile). He was a disciple and friend of *Pachomius. He wrote a 'Doctrina de Institutione Monachorum' (probably in Coptic), which survives in a Latin translation. Feast day, 15 June.

Orthodox Church, also termed the 'Eastern', 'Greek', or 'Greco-Russian Church'. A family of Churches, mostly situated mainly in E. Europe; each Church is independent in its internal administration, but all share the same faith and are in communion with each other, acknowledging the honorary primacy of the Patr. of *Constantinople (or *Oecumenical Patriarch).

What is known as 'the Orthodox Church' developed historically from the Church of the Byzantine Empire. It became limited on its E. side by the *Monophysite and *Nestorian schisms of the 5th–6th cents. (The *Oriental Orthodox Churches also claim the title 'Orthodox'.) From the 9th cent. there was increasing tension between Rome and Constantinople, leading to the final breach which is conventionally dated in 1054; it was in fact a gradual process. The main doctrinal points at issue were the Papal claims and the *Filioque. Bounded on the E. and W., the Orthodox Church expanded to the North. A missionary advance was inaugurated in the 9th cent. by Sts *Cyril and Methodius. *Bulgaria, *Serbia, and subsequently *Russia were converted to the Christian faith largely through the efforts of Byzantine missionaries. Since the fall of Constantinople to the Turks (1453), the Church of Russia has been the largest and most influential member of the Orthodox communion. For over five centuries Orthodoxy suffered persecution, first under the Ottoman Empire and then under Communism, but with the collapse of the Communist power c.1988, a new era of expansion began in Russia and the rest of E. Europe. Largely through immigration after 1920, Orthodoxy has been taken to the *United States of America, W. Europe, *Australia, and Africa.

The faith of the Orthodox Church is based primarily on the dogmatic definitions of the seven *Oecumenical Councils. Certain local Councils have also exercised a decisive influence on Orthodox doctrine, especially those of Constantinople in 1341 and 1351, which endorsed the teaching of *Hesychasm concerning the Divine light; and the Councils of *Jassy (1642) and *Jerusalem (1672), which clarified Orthodox teaching on the Eucharist and the nature of Church. Orthodox acknowledge the *seven sacraments, or 'mysteries' as they are termed, though no rigid distinction is drawn between them and other sacramental actions such as *burial of the dead. Baptism is by *immersion; chrismation (*confirmation) is administered by the priest immediately after Baptism, and children are taken to

Communion from infancy. In principle services are in the language of the people, but in many places an archaic form is used. The veneration of *icons plays an important part in Orthodox worship, both private and public. Intercession for the departed is emphasized in Orthodox spirituality, but the doctrine of *purgatory, as developed in RCism, is not accepted. Monasteries have been influential throughout Orthodox history; the chief monastic centre is Mount *Athos. Bishops are drawn from the celibate clergy; parish priests are generally married, but must be so before becoming deacons. Most Orthodox Churches are now represented on the *World Council of Churches; in recent years they have begun to develop friendly links with the Oriental Orthodox Churches.

Orthodoxy. As a religious system, right belief as contrasted with heresy. The word is used especially in connection with those Churches of the E. which are in communion with *Constantinople, collectively described as 'Eastern Orthodox' to distinguish them from the '*Oriental Orthodox Churches'. See also previous and following entries.

Orthodoxy, Feast of. A feast established in 843 to celebrate the downfall of the *Iconoclastic party and the restoration of images. It is now observed in the E. Church (by both Orthodox and *Uniats) on the first Sunday of Lent to commemorate the triumph of right faith over all heresies.

Orthros. The morning *office of the E. Church.

Ortlieb of Strasbourg (c.1200), founder of a sect ('Ortlibarii') condemned by *Innocent III. His teaching stressed a *pantheistic union of man with God, and his followers appealed against the Church to the inner authority of the Spirit, maintaining the eternity of the world and unorthodox doctrines of the Trinity and Incarnation.

O Salutaris Hostia (Lat., 'O Saving Victim'). The last two verses of St *Thomas Aquinas's hymn 'Verbum supernum prodiens'. In the RC Church it is often sung during the service of *Benediction.

O Sapientia (Lat., 'O Wisdom'). The opening of the first of the *O-Antiphons, included in English calendars against 16 Dec.

Osiander, Andreas (1496/8–1552), theologian. He joined the *Lutherans c.1524 and took part in the Colloquy of *Marburg in 1529 and the *Augsburg Diet of 1530. In his *De Justificatione* (1550) he opposed M. *Luther's doctrine of *justification by faith, maintaining that justification was not a mere imputation of Christ's merits, but a substantial transference of His righteousness to the believer.

Osmund, St (d. 1099), Bp. of *Salisbury from 1078. He completed the cathedral at Old Sarum, dedicated in 1091, and constituted a chapter of canons. He has been credited with a document regulating chapter life, which influenced the statutes of several cathedrals in the 13th cent., but the earliest part of this was probably not composed before 1150. The Sarum liturgical use, also attributed to him, is probably not older than Richard *Poore. Feast day, 4 Dec.; of his translation, 16 July.

Ossius. Probably the correct spelling of the name of the Bp. of Córdoba commonly known as *Hosius.

ostensory. A receptacle for showing objects of religious devotion to the people. The word is now commonly restricted to the *monstrance used for the exposition of the Blessed Sacrament.

Ostervald, Jean Frédéric (1663–1747), Swiss Reformed pastor of Neuchâtel. In 1713 he published a Eucharistic liturgy in which J. *Calvin's rite was combined with elements from the BCP and the Roman Missal. In use until the 20th cent., it is seen as the first ecumenical liturgy.

Ostian Way. The ancient road which led from Rome to the port of Ostia.

Oswald, St (c.605–42), King of Northumbria. Forced to flee to Scotland after his father's death in 616, he was converted to Christianity by the monks of *Iona. He returned in 634 and, after erecting a wooden cross on the battlefield, defeated the British king, Cadwallon, at Heavenfield, near Hexham. He began to establish Christianity in his kingdom, giving his full support to St *Aidan. He was killed in battle against the pagan Penda of Mercia and is honoured as a martyr. Feast day, 5 Aug.; in some places, 8 or 9 Aug.

Oswald, St (d. 992), Abp. of *York. he was consecrated Bp. of *Worcester by St *Dunstan in 962 and retained this see after he became Abp. of York in 972. He established many monasteries, of which the most famous was the abbey of Ramsey in Cambridgeshire. Feast day, 28 Feb.

Oswine, St (d. 651), also 'Oswin', Anglo-Saxon king. The southern part of Northumbria came under his rule on the death of his kinsman, St *Oswald, in 642. He was a devout Christian and friend of St *Aidan. He was murdered at Gilling, near Richmond, N. Yorks.; his tomb here became a place of pilgrimage. Feast day, 20 Aug.

Otfrid of Weissenburg (d. c.875), author of an Old High German biblical epic. He was a monk of Weissenburg (modern Wissembourg) in Alsace. His *Evangelienbuch*, a poem of over 7,000 lines, consists of a Life of Christ constructed from Gospel passages accompanied by theological commentary and culminating in the Last Judgement.

Otto, St (1062/3–1139), the 'Apostle of Pomerania'. He was nominated Bp. of Bamberg in 1102 and consecrated in 1106. He tried to maintain a neutral attitude in the *Investiture Controversy, though his sympathies were with the Pope. He went to Pomerania in 1124, after the Pomeranians had promised to accept Christianity as a condition of peace. He converted many of the important towns and most of the nobles. Feast day, 30 Sept.; in the *Roman Martyrology, 2 July.

Otto of Freising (c.1114/5–58), historian. The uncle of *Frederick I (Barbarossa), he became Bp. of Freising in 1138. His *Chronicon seu historia de duabus civitatibus* modified St *Augustine's conception of the two cities, seeing their union in the Church as the continuation of the Roman Empire. His *Gesta Friderici* describes the first part of Barbarossa's reign, largely on the basis of original documents.

Otto, Rudolf (1869–1937), Protestant theologian. The central theme of *Das Heilige* (1917; Eng. tr., *The Idea of the Holy*, 1923) was insistence on the part played by the *numinous in the religious consciousness.

Ouen, St (c.610–84), Bp. of Rouen from 641. He encouraged scholarship, founded monasteries, and fought *simony and other abuses. He was employed on several political missions by the Merovingian kings. Feast day, 24 Aug.

Our Father. See LORD'S PRAYER.

Overall, John (1560–1619), Bp. of *Coventry and Lichfield (1614–18) and then of *Norwich. The section on the Sacraments added to the BCP *Catechism in 1604 was drawn up by Overall on the basis of A. *Nowell's 'Small Catechism' of 1573. He also took part in the translation of the AV.

Overbeck, Franz (1837–1905), Protestant theologian. Holding that the Christian Gospel was wholly eschatological and world-negating, Overbeck came to reject historic Christianity and expounded a 'secular Church history', in which the course of ecclesiastical history was understood as a radical departure from the original revelation in Scripture. In his critique of immanental religious notions, he influenced modern *Dialectical Theology.

Overseas Missionary Fellowship (OMF). An interdenominational and international mission to E. Asia. Founded in 1865 as the *China Inland Mission (q.v.), its name was changed in 1965.

Owen, John (1616–83), *Puritan. Originally a *Presbyterian, he took up the more tolerant *Independent position. O. *Cromwell in 1651 made him Dean of *Christ Church, Oxford; he was one of Cromwell's *Triers and a member of the *Savoy Conference. After the *Restoration he preached and wrote in London.

Oxford. The ecclesiastical history of the city appears to begin with St *Frideswide (q.v.), whose father founded a convent there in the 8th cent. Throughout the Middle Ages Oxford was in the diocese of *Lincoln, but in 1542 *Henry VIII created the see of Oxford, with the suppressed Oseney Abbey as the cathedral church; in 1546 he transferred the seat of the bishopric to the college founded on the site of St Frideswide's priory (*Christ Church).

The origins of the university go back to the 12th cent., when, in addition to schools attached to parish churches, there is fragmentary evidence of independent masters teaching Arts, Theology, and Civil and Canon Law in schools in the centre of the town. In 1214 the Papal legate drew up a constitution for the schools; from this date the university developed as a corporate institution. Between 1220 and 1230 the Friars came—*Dominican, *Franciscan, *Carmelite, and *Augustinian. The colleges grew out of the boarding houses for masters and students; Merton's statutes date from 1264. In 1571 the university was incorporated and from then until 1871 subscription to the *Thirty-Nine Articles was required from all its members. Its statutes were remodelled by W. *Laud; further changes began in the 19th cent. The University had close links with the Church from the beginning and only in modern times has theology ceased to hold a dominant position.

Oxford Conference (1937). The second Conference of the '*Life and Work' branch of the *Ecumenical Movement was held at Oxford under the title of 'Church, Community, and State'. It was agreed to take steps to fuse the 'Life and Work' Movement with that of '*Faith and Order'. See also WORLD COUNCIL OF CHURCHES.

Oxford Group. The religious movement founded by F. N. D. *Buchman, who defined his aim as 'a programme of life issuing in personal, social, racial, national and supernatural change'. In 1920 he visited *Cambridge and then *Oxford, where his preaching made a great impression on a generation of post-war students. In 1928 a party from Oxford visited South Africa, and it was there that the name 'Oxford Group' was attached to them. Despite opposition it was incorporated under this title in 1939. Meanwhile, in 1938, Buchman had issued his call for 'moral and spiritual rearmament', and the name 'Moral Re-Armament' superseded the local name, which remained the official title in Britain.

Moral Re-Armament was launched in Washington, DC, in 1939. Buchman was joined by some Swiss supporters who decided to create a centre for post-war reconstruction in their country and acquired the former Caux-Palace above Montreux. This opened in 1946; it did much to heal relationships between former enemies. There are now training and conference centres in many parts of the world. The Westminster Theatre in London is the main centre in Britain; besides presenting plays, it is a workshop and distribution centre for films and videos throughout the world.

Oxford Movement. A movement (1833–45) in the C of E, centred in Oxford, which aimed at restoring *High Church principles. Several causes contributed to its growth, including the decline of Church life, the spread of 'Liberalism' in theology, and the question of Anglican identity raised by the removal of religious tests for State office in 1829. The plan to suppress ten Irish bishoprics in 1833 evoked from J. *Keble a sermon in the university church at Oxford which is usually regarded as the beginning of the movement. Its chief object was the defence of the C of E as a Divine institution, of the doctrine of the *apostolic succession, and of the BCP as a rule of faith. The *Tracts for the Times were designed for this purpose. The leaders of the movement were Keble, J. H. *Newman, and E. B. *Pusey. It gained influential support, but it was also attacked by the liberals within the university and by the bishops. After the censure by the Convocation of Oxford in 1845 of a book by W. G. *Ward, and again after the *Gorham case in 1850, there were a number of conversions to the RC Church. But the majority remained in the C of E, and, despite the hostility of the press and of the Government, the movement spread. Its influence was exercised in the sphere of worship and ceremonial, in the social sphere (the slum settlements were among its notable achievements), and in the revival of religious community life in the C of E (see RELIGIOUS ORDERS IN ANGLICANISM).

Oxyrhynchus Papyri. The collection of papyri found from 1897 onwards at Oxyrhynchus, c.10 miles W. of the Nile. It includes the MSS of '*Sayings of Jesus'.

Ozanam, Antoine Frédéric (1813–53), French scholar. In 1833 he founded the 'Society of St *Vincent de Paul', an association of laymen for personal service among the poor. He became a professor at the *Sorbonne, and he edited some early *Franciscan poetry (1852), of importance for the history of medieval spirituality. Together with H. D. *Lacordaire he founded the *Ère nouvelle* in 1848 as a mouthpiece for their ideas on Catholic socialism.

'P'. A symbol used by scholars who follow the 'documentary hypothesis' of the origin of the *Pentateuch to denote the 'Priestly source'. It is marked by a preponderance of ritual and ceremonial enactments over narrative and the avoidance of anthropomorphic ideas of God.

Pacelli, Eugenio. See PIUS XII.

Pachomius, St (c.290–346), the founder of *coenobitic Christian monasticism. He apparently served as an army conscript; after his discharge in 313, he was converted and baptized. For a time he was a disciple of the hermit Palaemon; c.320 he founded a monastery at Tabennisi in the *Thebaid, to which his fame attracted large numbers. Other foundations followed. His 'Rule' survives complete only in Latin translation. Feast day in the W., 14 May; in the E., 15 May; in the *Coptic Church, 9 May.

Pacian, St (4th cent.), Bp. of Barcelona. He defended the Catholic doctrine of the forgiveness of sins against the *Novatianists. He is noted for the epigrammatic passage in one of his letters: 'My name is Christian; my surname is Catholic'. Feast day, 9 Mar.

Pacific Islands. See SOUTH PACIFIC.

pacifism. See WAR, CHRISTIAN ATTITUDE TO.

Padre. A popular designation of a chaplain in the forces, also used of all clergy.

Paedobaptism. See INFANT BAPTISM.

Paenitemini (1966). An Apostolic Constitution which revised the rules of penitential observance in the RC Church. It reduced the number of days of *fasting and empowered episcopal conferences to substitute for the traditional *abstinence on penitential days some other form of penance, especially works of charity and piety.

Paget, Francis (1851–1911), Bp. of *Oxford from 1901. He supported the reinterpretation of *Tractarian principles by the *Lux Mundi group. His *Spirit of Discipline* (1891) contains a notable essay on '*Accidie'.

Pagnini, Santi (1470–1536), Italian *Dominican scholar. He made a completely new Latin translation of the Bible from the original languages (published 1528); in it the text is divided into verses. The translation was utilized by M. *Coverdale.

pain bénit. The blessed bread often, until recently, distributed to the people after Mass in French and Canadian churches.

Paine, Thomas (1737–1809), political reformer. Born in Norfolk, he went to America in 1774. In 1776 he issued his pamphlet *Common Sense* in favour of American independence. He returned to England in 1787 and in 1791 published the first part of his famous *Rights of Man*. After the publication of the second part (1792) he fled to Paris to escape arrest. *The Age of Reason* (1794–5) ridiculed the beliefs and institutions of Christianity as full of superstition and bad faith.

Paisy Velichkovsky, St. See VELICHKOVSKY, ST PAISY.

Pakistan, Church of. The Church inaugurated in 1970 by the union of *Anglicans, *Methodists, *Presbyterians, and *Lutherans in Pakistan.

Palamas, St Gregory. See GREGORY PALAMAS, ST.

Palatine Guard. A corps of militia in the Papal service. Formed in 1850 out of two existing bodies, it was disbanded in 1970.

Palestrina, Giovanni Pierluigi da (c.1525–94), Italian composer. He held a series of appointments in major churches in Rome and may have been associated with St *Philip Neri's *Oratory. From 1571 until his death he was choirmaster of *St Peter's. His works include the *Missa Papae Marcelli*, the famous *Improperia* (first performed in 1573), the Masses *Aeterna Christi munera* and *Assumpta est Maria*, and *motets to words from the Song of Songs. His music is suffused with a deep spirituality.

Paley, William (1743–1805), author of the *Evidences of Christianity*. His *Horae Paulinae*

(1790), written to prove the historicity of the events recorded in the NT by a comparison of the accounts of St *Paul in the Epistles and Acts, was probably his only original work. His famous *View of the Evidences of Christianity* (1794), though its arguments added little that was new, became popular from its effective presentation of the facts and its clear style. He became Archdeacon of *Carlisle in 1782.

palimpsest. A MS from which the original writing has been obliterated and the surface then used for some other (usually quite different) writing. A famous example is the *Codex Ephraemi (q.v.).

pall. (1) The small linen cloth with which the *chalice is covered at the Eucharist, in its modern form stiffened with a piece of cardboard; and (2) a cloth spread over the coffin at a funeral.

Palladius (*c*.364–420/30), historian of early monasticism. He spent several years with the monks of Egypt, and was a pupil of *Evagrius Ponticus. In 400 he became Bp. of Helenopolis in Bithynia. His *Lausiac History*, though at times credulous, is the most valuable single writing that survives for the history of early monasticism. He was also probably the author of a 'Dialogue' on the life of St *Chrysostom.

Palladius, St (5th cent.), first bishop of the Irish. According to *Prosper of Aquitaine, as a deacon Palladius persuaded *Celestine I (422–32) to send St *Germanus, Bp. of Auxerre, to stamp out the *Pelagian heresy in Britain, and was later himself sent to the Irish as their first bishop. Lives of St *Patrick from the 7th cent. portray Palladius as an unsuccessful missionary who left the way open for Patrick; his career may perhaps have been subsumed within the legend of Patrick. Feast day, 7 July.

pallium. The circular band of white material with two hanging strips and marked with six black crosses which is worn on the shoulders by the Pope and granted by him to *metropolitans (formerly also to some other bishops and archbishops) of the RC Church. It is held to signify the power which, in communion with the Roman Church, the metropolitan possesses by law in his province. It went out of use in the C of E at the Reformation, but still appears in some armorial bearings.

Pallottini Fathers. A society of RC priests, lay brothers and associates founded in 1835 by St Vincent Pallotti (1795–1850). They were previously known as the 'Pious Society of Missions' but are now generally called the 'Society of the Catholic Apostolate'. Pallotti believed that all Christians had an equal status in working for the salvation of others; *Pius XI saw him as a forerunner of *Catholic Action.

Palm Sunday. The Sunday before *Easter. The distinctive ceremonies of the day are the blessing of palms and, in the W., the procession representing the Lord's triumphal entry into *Jerusalem.

An elaborate rite for blessing the palms developed in the Middle Ages, similar in structure to the Mass. In the C of E the ceremony was abolished in 1549 and only in recent times has a special rite for Palm Sunday been officially sanctioned in the Anglican Communion. In the RC Church the rite was simplified in 1955. There is now a general blessing of palms (or other greenery) held by the people, if possible in a different building from that in which the Mass is to be celebrated; the Gospel account of Christ's entry into Jerusalem is read, and, after a short homily, clergy and people process into the church singing the traditional 'Gloria, laus' ('All glory, laud and honour' by *Theodulf of Orléans) or some other chant. The Mass which follows includes the chanting of the Passion. Modern Anglican rites follow a similar pattern. In the *Byzantine rite, palms or olive branches are blessed and distributed at *Mattins; a procession is not usual.

Palmer, William (1811–79), Fellow of Magdalen College, Oxford, from 1832. In 1840 and 1842 he visited Russia to explore the possibilities of intercommunion between the Anglican and Orthodox Churches, and he did much to foster interest in the E. Churches in Britain. He became a RC in 1855.

Pammachius, St (*c*.340–410), Roman Christian and friend of St *Jerome. After the death of his wife, he took the monastic habit and spent his possessions on works of piety, including the famous hospital for pilgrims at Portus. Feast day, 30 Aug.

Pamphilus, St (c.240–309), disciple of *Origen. He was educated at *Alexandria and directed a theological school at *Caesarea in Palestine, where he was martyred. While imprisoned in the persecution of Maximin Daza, he wrote an 'Apology for Origen', to which *Eusebius of Caesarea added a sixth book. Feast day in the E., 16 Feb.; in the W., 1 June.

panagia (Gk., 'all holy'). A favourite title of the BVM in the E. Church. The word is also used of: (1) an oval medallion depicting the BVM worn suspended on a chain by Orthodox bishops; and (2) bread which is solemnly blessed in honour of the BVM.

Pancras, St (d. 304), martyr. There is no reliable information about him. According to tradition he was a member of the Roman Church who at the age of 14 was martyred in the Diocletianic *persecution. St Pancras railway station in London is named after the dedication of the church of the parish in which it is situated. Feast day, 12 May.

panentheism. The belief that the Being of God includes and penetrates the whole universe, so that every part of it exists in Him, but (as against *pantheism) that His Being is more than, and not exhausted by, the universe. The concept has gained some popularity in recent years.

Pange Lingua. The title of two Latin hymns: the *Passiontide hymn by *Venantius Fortunatus (*Pange lingua gloriosi proelium certaminis*; 'Sing, my tongue, the glorious battle') and the *Corpus Christi hymn by St *Thomas Aquinas (*Pange lingua gloriosi corporis mysterium*; 'Of the glorious Body telling'). On the latter see also TANTUM ERGO.

Pannenberg, Wolfhart (1928–   ), German Protestant theologian. From 1968 to 1994 he was Professor of Systematic Theology in the Protestant Faculty of Theology at Munich. In 1961 he edited *Offenbarung als Geschichte* (Eng. tr., *Revelation as History*, 1968). Here he argued that Christian theology cannot protect itself against criticism by appeal to some privileged epistemology of faith. Faith, rather, is a manner of response to certain historical facts that, rationally speaking, suggest interpretation in revelatory terms. The key facts to which such appeal is made are explored in his first major work, *Grundzüge der Christologie* (1964;

Eng. tr., *Jesus—God and Man*, 1968), which is remarkable for its defence of the historicity of the *Resurrection of Christ, in the context of a positive appreciation of Jewish *apocalyptic thought. Later books maintain that Christian theology must argue with *atheism in the shared context of critical rationality. Notable features of his work include a powerful defence of reform (as opposed to revolution) in Christian social ethics, and a novel, if controversial, attempt to underpin the theology of hope with an ontology of God as the power of the future.

Pannychis. A Greek word for a *Vigil. It is used mainly of vigils for the dead.

Panormitanus (1386–1445), canonist. Nicolò de' Tudeschi became Abp. of Palermo (hence Panormitanus) in 1435. In 1433 he had been sent to the Council of *Basle by *Eugenius IV as his representative, but in 1436 he returned as the ambassador of Alfonso of Aragon, who was a contender for the throne of Naples against a nominee of Eugenius; consequently he usually supported the antipope and maintained that the Pope was inferior to a *General Council. His main writings were on canon law; they included commentaries on the *Decretals of Gregory IX, on the *Sext, and on the *Clementines.

panpsychism. The 19th-cent. doctrine that everything in the universe is endowed with a measure of consciousness. It is little favoured by Christian theologians.

Pantaenus, St (d. c.190). A convert from *Stoicism, he taught at *Alexandria from c.180 until his death. *Eusebius describes him as head of the *Catechetical School and says that he preached in 'India'. Feast day, 7 July; in the *Coptic Church, 22 June.

Pantaleon, St (d. c.305), martyr. Nothing is certainly known of him. According to one form of the legends, he was a physician to the Emp. Galerius, apostatized, was reconverted, and martyred when *Diocletian gave orders to purge the court of Christians. Feast day, 27 July; also other dates.

pantheism. The belief or theory that God and the universe are identical. The word appears to have been coined by J. *Toland in 1705, but pantheistic systems go back to early times. Mysticism, with its passionate desire for union with the Divine, has often been charged with pantheism.

Papa Angelicus (also **Pastor Angelicus**). A belief arose in 13th-cent. Italy that some Pope would revive Apostolic simplicity and zeal in the Church and inaugurate a new age. In the Prophecies of *Malachy, the 106th Pope, i.e. *Pius XII, is so designated.

Papacy. While the term strictly denotes the office of the Pope, i.e. the Bp. of *Rome, it commonly refers to the system of centralized government in the Church exercised by him, along with the claim that by Divine appointment he has universal authority over Christendom. According to RC doctrine, St *Peter was the first Bp. of Rome, and the Pope is not only his lineal successor in that office, but also inherits the unique commission given him by Christ (cf. especially Mt. 16: 18 f. and Jn. 21: 17). The Papal primacy was never formally accepted by the E. Church and it was repudiated by Protestant communions. From 756 to 1870 the Papacy was also a territorial power ruling a large part of central Italy. See also ROMAN CATHOLICISM.

'Papal Aggression'. The name popularly given to the action of *Pius IX in 1850 making England and Wales an ecclesiastical province of the RC Church with a hierarchy consisting of an archbishop and 12 *suffragans, all with territorial titles.

Papal legate; Papal States. See LEGATE, PAPAL; STATES OF THE CHURCH.

Paphnutius, St (d. *c.*360), Bp. of the Upper Thebaid. He was an Egyptian monk who suffered badly in the persecution of Maximin Daza (305–13). He is said to have dissuaded the Council of *Nicaea from ordering all clergy to put away their wives. Feast day, 11 Sept.

Papias (*c.*60–130), Bp. of Hierapolis in Asia Minor. His work survives only in quotations in *Irenaeus and *Eusebius. In the fragments on the origin of the first two Gospels he states that St *Mark, having become the interpreter of St *Peter, set down accurately, though not in order, everything that he remembered of the words and actions of the Lord; and that St *Matthew composed 'the oracles' in Hebrew, and everyone translated them as best he could.

papyrology. The science of dealing with MSS on papyrus. Papyrus is a writing material made out of the fibres of the stem of a water plant which formerly grew plentifully in the Nile. It was used in ancient Egypt and became the chief writing material in the Greco-Roman world from at least the 5th cent. BC to the 4th cent. AD, when it gave way to vellum. Papyrus MSS have survived in few areas apart from Egypt, where they were first found in 1778. See also MANUSCRIPTS OF THE BIBLE.

Parabalani. An association of men at *Alexandria, devoted to looking after the sick. From references in 5th- and 6th- cent. laws, it appears that they were clerics, exempt from public duties.

parable. In the *Synoptic Gospels, the word stands for a wide range of striking sayings, from well-known proverbs to small metaphors and elaborate *allegories. Mk. contains examples of all these, with the historical allegories of the Sower and the Wicked Husbandman dominating by size and importance. They alert the reader to the theological significance of the narrative. In Mt. parables are given a more moral thrust than those in Mk. Lk. adds famous, realistic stories, such as the *Good Samaritan and the Prodigal Son. Like Mt.'s parables they have moral purpose, but they are distinctive in not being so strongly or solely allegorical. The allegories in Jn. are not designated parables.

Parabolani. The Latin (apparently corrupt) form of Parabalani (q.v.).

Paracelsus. The name used by Theophrast Bombast von Hohenheim (1493–1541), Swiss physician. He elaborated a mystical theosophy on a *Neoplatonic basis; he held that, just as we know nature only to the extent that we are ourselves nature, so we know God only in so far as we are God.

Paraclete. A Johannine epithet of the Holy Spirit, traditionally translated 'Comforter'. Modern translations often render the word 'Helper', 'Consoler' or 'Advocate', or leave it untranslated.

Paradigm. The title given by *Form Critics to passages in the Gospels which contain narratives woven round a saying of Christ in order to drive its teaching home.

paradise. The word is probably of Persian origin, denoting an enclosed park or pleasure-ground. It is used in the LXX of Gen. 2 and 3 as the Greek rendering of the 'garden' planted by God in *Eden. In later Jewish literature it came to signify a state of blessedness, whether material or spiritual. In Lk. 23: 43 it has been variously interpreted as referring either to the intermediate state of the just before the Resurrection (*limbo) or as a synonym of the heaven of the blessed; it is used in the second sense in 2 Cor. 12: 4 and Rev. 2: 7. In popular usage it usually denotes the state of future bliss.

Paradise Lost. J. *Milton's epic describing the *Fall of man and its consequences.

Paragraph Bibles. In 1755 a NT arranged in paragraphs (as opposed to the usual AV arrangement in verses), with a revised text, was issued by J. *Wesley. An edition of the whole AV text in paragraphs was published by the *Religious Tract Society in 1838. It is the arrangement adopted in the RV and most other modern translations.

Paralipomenon. The name by which the two Books of *Chronicles are sometimes known to RCs.

parallelism. A characteristic of Hebrew poetry. There are three kinds: synonymous parallelism, consisting in the simple repetition of the same thought in slightly different words; antithetical parallelism, produced by contrasting the first member with the second (e.g. 'A merry heart doeth good like a medicine: But a broken spirit drieth the bones', Prov. 17: 22); and synthetic parallelism, in which the first member is developed or completed by a similar thought in the second or third (e.g. 'The kings of the earth stand up: And the rulers take counsel together: Against the Lord and against His Anointed', Ps. 2: 2).

Paraphrases of Erasmus, The. The commentary on the Gospels written by *Erasmus which *Edward VI's *Injunctions of 1547 ordered should be placed in every parish church.

parclose. A screen or set of railings for enclosing a *chantry altar and one or more seats for members of the family of the deceased. At the Reformation these enclosures developed into the 'family pew'.

Pardon. (1) Another name for an *indulgence (q.v.). The 'Pardoners', who hawked the right to share in an indulgence, were widely denounced. (2) In Brittany, the feast of the patron saint of a church at which an indulgence may be granted. It is often accompanied by a village fair.

Paris. The city was a centre of Christianity at an early date. According to St *Gregory of Tours, St Denis (*Dionysius (3)), its first bishop, was one of those sent out by Pope *Fabian c.250, and the Christian cemetery on the road to Sens and the episcopal buildings on the Île de la Cité date from the late 3rd to early 4th cent. *Clovis made it his capital in 507, but its importance diminished before it revived in the 11th and 12th cents. The beginnings of the university date from the 12th cent.; it received its statutes from *Innocent III in 1215. The early 13th cent. saw the foundation of colleges, which originally provided lodging and food for poor students; the most famous was the *Sorbonne. In the 13th cent. Paris was the chief centre of *Scholasticism. It played an important part in the time of the *Great Schism and of the Reform Councils, when some of its most learned men favoured the *Conciliar party. Paris became an archdiocese in 1622. During the 17th cent. it witnessed a religious regeneration brought about by the activities of St *Francis de Sales, St *Vincent de Paul, P. de *Bérulle, and P. *Olier, who counteracted *Jansenism and *Gallicanism, which numbered many adherents in the capital. In the Revolution of 1789 the old university was abolished; a new one was established in 1806 by the combination of the faculties of arts, medicine, and law, but without theology, which, since 1875, has been represented by the Institut Catholique. The Orthodox Institut St-Serge (founded in 1925) has attracted a succession of distinguished Russian scholars. See also NOTRE-DAME, PORT-ROYAL, ST-DENIS, ST-GERMAIN-DES-PRÉS, SAINTE-CHAPELLE, VICTORINES.

Paris, Matthew. See MATTHEW PARIS.

parish. In England, an area under the spiritual care of a C of E clergyman (the *incumbent), to whose religious ministrations all the inhabitants are entitled. The earliest English parishes were large territories controlled from monastic churches, mostly founded in the late 7th and 8th cents. In the 10th cent. these parishes of 'old ministers' were starting to fragment, as private manorial lords built churches on their estates and diverted to them the *tithes and parochial allegiance of their tenants. In the 12th cent. the parochial network crystallized as bishops applied the principles of canon law at a local level and restricted the rights of lay *patrons. The Third *Lateran Council of 1179 gave the bishop the right of *institution and strengthened the position of the incumbent against the patron.

From an early date the English parish was also a unit of civil administration and the creation of new parishes was controlled by Parliament. With the abolition of Church Rates in 1868 the civil importance of the parish declined. Diocesan Pastoral Committees and the *Church Commissioners now virtually control the establishment of new parishes and *team and *group ministries.

parish clerk. A church official (usually a layman), who in England assists the priest by making the responses of the congregation in the services, and also in the general care of the church. The office is ancient.

Parker, Matthew (1504–75), Abp. of *Canterbury from 1559. He received preferment originally through the patronage of *Anne Boleyn. Appointed Archbishop by *Elizabeth I, he was consecrated by four bishops who had held sees in *Edward VI's reign. He sought to preserve the settlement of 1559 from further change and to retain as far as possible the links with the past. He took part in the issue of the *Thirty-Nine Articles and of the '*Bishops' Bible', and in 1566 published his '*Advertisements', which commanded, among other things, the use of the *surplice. He had to face opposition from the *Puritans.

Parker, Theodore (1810–60), American *Unitarian preacher. In his *Discourse of Matters Pertaining to Religion* (1842) he argued that the permanent essence of Christianity was the moral influence of Jesus and that belief in *miracles was unnecessary.

Parochial Church Council. A council set up in every parish of the C of E by the Church of England Assembly (Powers) Act 1919, to give the laity a share in parochial administration.

Paroissien. The name for various prayer-books in the vernacular designed for the use of the laity which have been published in France since the 17th cent. They usually contain liturgical matter as well as private devotional exercises.

Parousia (Greek for 'presence' or 'arrival'). In its English form the word is used particularly to denote the future return of Christ in glory (later called the 'Second Coming') to judge the living and the dead, and to terminate the present world order. Primitive Christianity believed this event to be imminent, and this belief has often been revived, but the prevailing Christian tradition has opposed speculation on the time and manner of the Coming.

parson. Properly, the holder of an ecclesiastical benefice who has full possession of its rights, i.e. a *rector. This use was general until the 17th cent. The current use for any (especially C of E) clergymen has superseded the original sense.

Parsons, Robert (1546–1610), also 'Persons', *Jesuit. He left Oxford, became a RC at Louvain, and in 1575 joined the Jesuits. Chosen with St Edmund *Campion to lead the Jesuit Mission to England in 1580, he was soon (1581) forced to flee. He became a trusted counsellor of Popes and other rulers (especially *Philip II of Spain). He was rector of the *English College at Rome from 1597 and took part in the foundation of the English Colleges at Valladolid, Seville, and *St-Omer. Though he was a skilled controversialist, the most influential of his writings was a spiritual treatise, *The Christian Directory* (1582).

Particular Baptists. The group of *Baptists whose theology was essentially *Calvinistic, as contrasted with the *Arminianism of the *General Baptists. Their first community in England was established in 1633. In 1891 the General Baptists of the New Connexion joined the Baptist Union which had been formed among the Particular Baptists.

Particular Judgement. In Catholic theology, the judgement on each individual soul immediately on its separation from the body. It is thus prior to and quite distinct from the *General Judgement (q.v.).

parvis. Originally the court in front of a

cathedral or other large church, the word came also to be used of the portico of a church porch. It is sometimes erroneously applied to the room over such a porch.

Pascal, Blaise (1623–62), French scientist, polemicist, and Christian apologist. Educated at home, he came into contact with the *Jansenists in 1646 (his 'first conversion'). He continued his scientific pursuits and frequented fashionable society in Paris. In 1654 his 'definitive conversion' took place, and from 1655 he was a frequent visitor at *Port-Royal-des-Champs.

The condemnation of A. *Arnauld by the *Sorbonne in 1655 prompted Pascal's *Lettres écrites à un provincial* (commonly known as his 'Lettres provinciales', 1656–7). This attack on the *Jesuit theories of grace (*Molinism) and moral theology (*Probabilism) was intended to expose the moral character of their casuistry and to oppose to it the rigorist morality of the Jansenists. The *Pensées* were designed as a vindication of the truth of Christianity against the indifference of free-thinking contemporaries; rather than depending on philosophical reasoning, the work seeks to persuade of the unique applicability of Christianity to the human condition as the author portrays it. A selection of the material which Pascal left unfinished was published in 1670; the rest were stuck into an album regardless of sequence, and the whole has been frequently re-edited.

Pasch. A name used for both the Jewish *Passover and the Christian *Easter.

Paschal II (d. 1118), Pope from 1099. He renewed the Papal decrees against lay investiture in 1102; though he did not settle the *Investiture Controversy with the Empire, compromises had been reached with England and France by 1107. He supported the rebellion of the future Emp. Henry V against *Henry IV, but when Henry V practised investiture Paschal opposed him and in 1116 renounced the concessions extorted from him when Henry had taken him prisoner in 1111. He maintained the links between the Papacy and *Cluny and at various councils enacted important canons. On the other hand, the support which he gave to *Bohemond I's attack on the Eastern Emp. Alexius in 1107–8 caused bitter resentment.

Paschal Baylon, St (1540–92), *Franciscan lay brother. He was born on the border of Castile and Aragon; in obedience to a vision he entered the neighbouring convent of the Franciscans of the Alcantarine reform where he practised extreme mortification. He was especially devoted to the cult of the Blessed Sacrament and in 1897 *Leo XIII declared him patron of *Eucharistic Congresses and Associations. Feast day, 17 May.

Paschal Candle. In the *Paschal Vigil Service the Paschal Candle is lit from the New Fire and carried through the darkened church by the deacon, who stops three times before he reaches the altar, in each case singing 'Lumen Christi' ('Light of Christ'). Other candles are lit from the Paschal Candle. It is lit at liturgical functions from Easter until the eve of *Whitsunday and at Baptisms throughout the year in the RC Church and parts of the Anglican Communion.

Paschal Chronicle. See CHRONICON PASCHALE.

Paschal Controversies. Disputes on how to settle the date of *Easter. (1) Whether Easter should be observed on a fixed day of the lunar month (14 *Nisan) or on the following Sunday. See QUARTODECIMANISM. (2) Divergences in the different methods of determining the 'Paschal Moon' used by the *Antiochenes (who accepted the Jewish reckoning) and the *Alexandrians, who used an independent reckoning; the first Council of *Nicaea (325) decided in favour of the latter. (3) Differences between the Roman and Alexandrian methods of computation through the use of divergent 'paschal cycles' in the 4th and 5th cents. The *Anatolian cycle used at Alexandria was formally adopted in the W. by *Dionysius Exiguus (525). (4) The *Celtic Churches had their own method of computing Easter; this was a matter of dispute after the arrival of St *Augustine's mission. The Roman practice was accepted for Northumbria by the Synod of *Whitby (664) and subsequently through the whole of England.

With the introduction of the *Gregorian Calendar (1582), Easter was again observed on divergent dates in different parts of Christendom. The Orthodox Churches, even though most of them have adopted the Gregorian Calendar for fixed feasts, still calculate Easter according to the Julian

Calendar, and, as their calculation of the Paschal full moon is five days later than the astronomical full moon, their Easter sometimes coincides with the W. date, but is often one, four, or five weeks later.

Paschal lamb. The lamb sacrificed and eaten at the Jewish *Passover. By analogy Christ is regarded as a 'Paschal Lamb'.

Paschaltide, the period immediately after *Easter. It extends from Easter Sunday to *Pentecost in the RC Church. The C of E long reckoned Eastertide from Easter to the Saturday before *Trinity Sunday, but CW and other modern Anglican formularies now follow the RC practice.

Paschal Vigil Service. The main celebration of *Easter, observed during the night of *Holy Saturday/Easter Sunday. There seems at first to have been a single celebration of the Passion and Resurrection of Christ, and this was closely associated with *Baptism. From the 4th cent., with the separate observance of *Good Friday, the emphasis of the Paschal Vigil Service came to centre on the Resurrection. In the W. Church it was put back to the Saturday morning, but in 1951 in the RC Church it was restored to the late evening.

According to the current RC rite, the *Paschal Candle, lit from the New Fire blessed outside the church, is carried through a darkened church, and other candles are lit from it. The *Exultet is sung. Up to nine Bible readings follow, and then a sermon. After a procession to the *font, the baptismal water is blessed. Baptism is administered to any candidates (and *Confirmation also if a bishop or priest with a faculty to confirm is present). The congregation then renew their baptismal vows. The service concludes with the remaining parts of the Easter Eucharist. In the C of E, a form of Paschal Vigil Service, modelled on the RC rite, was authorized in 1986. In the Byzantine rite the Paschal Vigil properly begins with *Vespers on Holy Saturday, which ends with 15 readings from the OT; the Eucharist is then celebrated. These services are meant to begin late on Saturday afternoon but are usually anticipated in the morning. What is commonly thought of as the Orthodox Easter Vigil consists of Mattins (beginning at midnight) and the Liturgy of Easter Day; it is preceded by the Midnight Office.

Paschasius Radbertus, St (*c*.790–*c*.860), theologian. He was a monk, and from 843/4 to 849 abbot, of *Corbie. His works include commentaries on Lam. and Mt., but he is best known for his treatise *De Corpore et Sanguine Domini*, the first doctrinal monograph on the Eucharist. In maintaining the Presence of Christ in the Eucharist, Radbertus specified it further as the flesh born of Mary, which had suffered on the Cross and risen again, and which is miraculously multiplied by the omnipotence of God at each consecration. His teaching was attacked by *Ratramnus and *Rabanus Maurus. It is now generally accepted that he was also the author of *Cogitis me*, attributed to St *Jerome, which is important in the history of the doctrine of *Assumption of the BVM in the W. Feast day, 26 Apr.

Passion, the. The term is used absolutely of the Lord's redemptive suffering during the last days of His earthly life, and especially of His Crucifixion.

Passion, musical settings for the. From about the end of the 4th cent., Scriptural readings were recited to musical tones in church; the Gospel narratives of the Passion were thus recited in *Holy Week. The characters were early differentiated by changes of pitch, and by the 13th cent. at the latest this was emphasized by dividing the narrative between three or more singers; from the 15th cent. parts or all began to be composed polyphonically. From the end of the 17th cent. lyric poems were sung in comment and chorales were added to be sung by the congregation; an orchestra was also introduced. J. S. *Bach excelled in this *oratoria type of Passion.

Passion Plays. See DRAMA and MYSTERY PLAYS; also OBERAMMERGAU.

Passion Sunday. Traditionally the name of the fifth Sunday in *Lent. In the RC Church the special designation of this Sunday was suppressed in 1969 and the name is commonly used of *Palm Sunday (*Dominica in Palmis de Passione Domini'). See also PASSIONTIDE.

Passional. (1) The book containing lections from the Lives or Acts of the Saints read at *Mattins on their feast days. (2) That containing the narratives of the Lord's Passion from the four Gospels.

Passionists. The popular name for the members of the 'Congregation of Discalced Clerks of the Most Holy Cross and Passion of our Lord Jesus Christ', founded by St *Paul of the Cross. He drew up its rule in 1720 and erected the first house in 1737. The Passionists take a fourth vow to foster the memory of Christ's Passion.

Passions. See ACTS OF THE MARTYRS.

Passiontide. Traditionally the last two weeks of *Lent, from *Passion Sunday to *Holy Saturday. It was customary to veil all crucifixes, pictures, and images in church, and to omit the *Gloria Patri during this period. In the RC Church the title of *Passion Sunday as such was dropped in 1969 and the observance combined with *Palm Sunday. There are now no observances peculiar to the period as a whole.

Passover. The Jewish festival celebrated each spring in connection with the *Exodus. According to the account of its institution in Exod. 12, a lamb is to be slain in each household and its blood sprinkled on the lintel and doorposts of the house in memory of the fact that when the first-born in Egypt were slain, the Lord 'passed over' the houses which were so marked. Later the lambs were sacrificed in the *Temple. In the time of Christ it was the chief Jewish festival of the year, celebrated on the night of 14/15 Nisan.

Whether the *Last Supper was a Passover Meal (as the chronology of the *Synoptic Gospels would suggest) or not (as Jn.), it is clear that the Eucharist was instituted at Passover time, and Christians have seen in the death of Christ the fulfilment of the sacrifice foreshadowed by the Passover. It is probable that the earliest celebration of the Christian Easter (the *Paschal Vigil Service) grew out of the Jewish Passover rite.

pastophorion. In the E. Church, the sacristy adjacent to the *apse, used for the *reservation of the Sacrament.

Pastor. The title given by *Lutherans and some other Protestant bodies to their clergy, primarily those in charge of a church or congregation.

Pastor Aeternus (1870). The Dogmatic Constitution of the First *Vatican Council defining the primacy and infallibility of the Pope.

Pastoral Epistles, the. A designation for the Epistles to *Timothy and Titus (q.v.).

pastoral letters. Official letters of a bishop to all members of his diocese. They are distinguished from 'encyclical letters' addressed by the bishop only to his clergy.

pastoral staff. Another name for the *crosier.

pastoralia. The branch of theology concerned with the principles regulating the life and conduct of the parish priest.

Patarenes. The name first appears in the 1050s at Milan as the designation of an extreme reforming movement; it is supposed to derive from that of the ragpickers' quarter in Milan. The Patarenes played an important part in Milanese politics; they invited Roman intervention in the hitherto largely independent Ambrosian Church and opposed every manifestation of secular power over its affairs. In 1071 when the Emp. *Henry IV invested a new archbishop, the Patarenes demanded a free canonical election, propagated their movement elsewhere in Lombardy, and became *Gregory VII's allies against Henry. The movement persisted at Milan until the early 12th cent. In the 1170s the name reappeared as a general label for heretics.

paten. The dish, now usually of silver or gold, on which the bread is placed at the celebration of the Eucharist.

Pater Noster. The opening words of the Latin version of the *Lord's Prayer (q.v.).

Patmos. An island in the Aegean on which the author of *Revelation (q.v.) received his vision. According to tradition St *John the Apostle was exiled to Patmos under *Domitian (81–96) and returned to *Ephesus under Nerva (96–8). A monastery on Patmos founded by St. Christodulus in 1088 still survives.

Paton, John Gibson (1824–1907), missionary to Vanuatu (then known as the New Hebrides). A member of the *Reformed Presbyterian Church of Scotland, he arrived at Aneityum in 1858; soon afterwards he moved to the island of Tanna, but in 1862 fled to the Australian colonies. From 1866 to 1881 he was a missionary in the Presbyterian Church of Victoria on the island of Aniwa, near Tanna; from 1881 he was based in Melbourne. His autobiography (1889) did much to stimulate support for his cause.

Paton, William (1886–1943), *Presbyterian minister and writer on missionary subjects. He was Secretary of the International Missionary Council and editor of the *International Review of Missions*.

patriarch (biblical). Literally, the father or ruler of a family or tribe. The term is most commonly used of the great forefathers of Israel, *Abraham, *Isaac, and *Jacob. It is also used of the ancestors of the human race before the *Flood and of the twelve sons of Jacob. See also TESTAMENTS OF THE TWELVE PATRIARCHS.

patriarch (ecclesiastical). A title dating from the 6th cent. for the bishops of the five chief sees of Christendom: *Rome, *Alexandria, *Antioch, *Constantinople, and *Jerusalem, whose jurisdiction extended over the adjoining territories. In more recent times the title has been given to the heads of certain other *autocephalous Churches of the East (*Russia, *Serbia, *Romania, *Bulgaria, and *Georgia). In the (Latin) RC Church it is used in an honorific way for the bishops of certain sees, e.g. *Venice. See also OECUMENICAL PATRIARCH and CATHOLICOS.

Patrick, St (5th cent.), 'Apostle of the Irish'. Patrick was born in Britain and brought up as a Christian. At the age of 16 he was captured by pirates and spent six years as a herdsman in Ireland. He turned earnestly to God and received a Divine message that he was to escape. He persuaded some sailors to give him passage to Britain and returned to his kinsfolk, a changed man. He underwent training for the Christian ministry and went from Britain as 'bishop in Ireland' (his own phrase); he spent the rest of his life there, evangelizing, ordaining clergy, and instituting monks and nuns. He wrote a moving account of his spiritual pilgrimage, called his *Confession*, perhaps in response to an attack on his character. Discussions on the chronology of his life have focused on the statement of *Prosper of Aquitaine that *Celestine I (422–33) sent *Palladius to be the 'first bishop to the Irish believing in Christ'. It is argued that Patrick's mission cannot have been much later than 431; from this date of his

birth is inferred and his death put *c.*460; others argue that he lived a generation later and died *c.*490. The canons attributed to him and the '*Breastplate of St Patrick' are not his work. Feast day, 17 Mar. See also ST PATRICK'S PURGATORY.

Patrick, Simon (1625–1707), Bp. successively of *Chichester (1689) and *Ely (1691). In 1653 he was ordained a *Presbyterian minister, but the study of H. *Hammond and H. *Thorndike determined him to seek episcopal ordination in 1654. He was a prominent *Latitudinarian. He wrote extensively.

Patrimony of St Peter. The estates belonging to the Church of Rome. Once an edict of *Constantine in 321 had enabled the Church to hold permanent property, the patrimony came to include vast estates in Italy and lands in other countries. As the further patrimonies were conquered, Popes concentrated on defending the region round Rome. In 753 *Stephen II appealed for protection to *Pepin, King of the Franks. By the Donations of 754 and 756 Pepin gave the Papacy territory in the exarchate of *Ravenna, the Duchy of Rome, and elsewhere, and, renouncing the Byzantine authority, founded the Papal States independent of any temporal power. See also STATES OF THE CHURCH.

Patripassianism. A form of *Monarchianism (q.v.) which arose in the 3rd cent. Its adherents held that God the Father suffered as the Son.

patristics. The branch of theological study which deals with the writings of the *Fathers (*patres*) of the Church (q.v.). 'Patristics' normally embraces the Fathers in the more restrictive sense of the term, i.e. those who lived after the writing of most of the works that comprise the NT and before the end of the 8th cent.; this period is commonly termed the 'Patristic Age'.

patrology. A systematically arranged manual on the *patristic literature.

patron. See ADVOWSON.

patron saint. A saint who has been chosen as the special intercessor or advocate in heaven of a particular place, person, or organization. The custom of having patron saints for churches arose from the practice of building churches over the tombs of martyrs.

Patteson, John Coleridge (1827–1871), missionary. In 1855 he set out for the *South Pacific to assist in the work of the Melanesian Mission. He toured the islands in the *Southern Cross* and in 1861 he was consecrated first Bp. of Melanesia. He was murdered in 1871. His fate made a deep impression in England. Feast day in some parts of the Anglican Communion, 20 Sept.

Pattison, Mark (1813–84), Rector of Lincoln College, Oxford, from 1861. In 1832 he entered Oriel College; here he came under the influence of J. H. *Newman. Later his enthusiasm for the *Oxford Movement declined, and with it his faith in institutional Christianity. He was one of the authors of *Essays and Reviews*.

Paul, St (d. probably AD 62–5), 'Apostle of the Gentiles'. Born at *Tarsus, the future St Paul, originally 'Saul', was a Jew, said by Acts to possess Roman citizenship. He was brought up as a *Pharisee and perhaps studied at *Jerusalem under *Gamaliel (so Acts 22: 3). Coming into contact with the new 'Way' of the followers of Jesus, he persecuted the Church. Acts 9: 1–2 represents him as authorized by the High Priest to arrest converts in *Damascus. On the way there he was himself converted.

SOURCES. The account in Acts of Paul's activities has been widely challenged. The primary source for his life and missionary work are the seven letters generally agreed to be authentic: Rom., 1 and 2 Cor., Gal., Phil., 1 Thess., and Philem., all except 1 Thess. and possibly Gal. written within a few years of each other in the mid-50s. Col. and 2 Thess. are doubtful; Eph. is widely thought to stem from a gifted follower; and the *Pastorals are almost certainly later. There is no reliable evidence for his life after the period covered by Acts, beyond early witness to his martyrdom under *Nero. Some sources assume that he visited *Spain, perhaps on the basis of Rom. 15.

MISSION. Paul's conversion can be dated c.AD 33. He saw a vision of the risen Lord Jesus (1 Cor. 9: 1) on which he implies that his call and status as an *apostle rested (1 Cor. 15: 8 f.). It seems from Gal. 1: 16 that from the outset his mission was to the Gentiles, though a few have questioned this. He

went to Arabia, back to Damascus, and three years later to Jerusalem, where he came to know St *Peter and St *James, and then on to Syria and Cilicia. The next 14 years include his journey with St *Barnabas from *Antioch to Cyprus, Pamphylia, S. Galatia and back, described in Acts 13–14. They may also (contrary to Acts) include his travels with *Silas and *Timothy through Phrygia and N. Galatia (cf. Acts 16: 6), Troas, and Greece. On his second visit to Jerusalem, the so-called council allowed Paul to continue his Gentile mission on condition that he raised funds for the Jerusalem Church, but some Jewish Christians continued to oppose him.

Around AD 50–52 he spent 18 months in *Corinth; the reference in Acts 18: 12–17 to *Gallio allows this to be dated with some confidence. The next major centre of his activity was *Ephesus, where he remained for 2–3 years. He went to Macedonia and Achaia (probably Corinth) in 56–7 before his final visit to Jerusalem, with representatives of his Gentile congregations, bringing the 'collection'. The most disruptive issue that Paul faced in this period came from missionaries visiting his congregations and persuading his converts to observe the Jewish law. Gal. provides an angry, but reasoned response. For Paul the vital question was whether the Jerusalem Church would finally accept his law-free Gentile mission. His concern was well founded. However 'gladly' (Acts 21: 17) the Church in Jerusalem welcomed Paul and his Gentile party with their gift, it was apparently a proposal of James that led to his arrest. There followed trials before the *Sanhedrin and the Roman governor in *Caesarea and two years' imprisonment. On appealing to Caesar, Paul was sent to Rome as a prisoner. After shipwreck, he probably arrived in AD 60, and spent two further years under house arrest.

THEOLOGY. Paul was a phrase-maker, who wrote rhetorically powerful and theologically profound letters. His insistence that Christ rather than the Law was decisive for believers in their relationship to God made the separation of Christianity from mainstream Judaism inevitable. He maintained his earlier beliefs about God and the revelation of God in the Law and the Prophets, but the new factor was what God was doing now. Having sent His Son, God was rescuing Gentiles as well as Jews from the present evil age by transferring them into the age to come. This dawned with the resurrection of the crucified *Messiah and would soon transform the world. The decisive factor in Paul's messianic Judaism was the arrival and identity of the Messiah, 'Jesus Christ our Lord', whose death he understood as a sacrifice and whose resurrection was the first-fruits and beginning of the general resurrection inaugurating the new creation. Believers are through Baptism (symbolically) united with Him, incorporated into Him, and so are 'in Christ'. Those who have been baptized 'into' Christ have received the *Holy Spirit, who both sheds the love of God in the believer's heart and bears fruit in love, joy, peace, etc. Paul's picture of human existence outside Christ is negative: the world is under judgement and needs God's liberating intervention. Jews and Gentiles alike are in the same predicament and rescued in the same way—by faith in Christ.

INFLUENCE. Paul's hope for the ultimate inclusion of Israel was soon lost, but his refusal to submit Gentile converts to *circumcision contributed to the success of the Christian mission outside Jerusalem. The collection of his surviving letters and their inclusion in Christian Scripture gave him a different kind of influence; his rhetoric helped to shape the faith of millions who did not understand his arguments. His polemical contrast between the old and the new ways of salvation exercised a vast influence on St *Augustine's anti-*Pelagian doctrine of *grace, on M. *Luther's doctrine of *justification by faith alone, and J. *Calvin's belief in *predestination. It indirectly supported the modern tendency to make humanity the centre of theology.

A joint feast of SS Peter and Paul is observed in E. and W. on 29 June, in addition to the feast of the *Conversion of St Paul on 25 Jan. in the W. A further commemoration of St Paul on 30 June was dropped from the RC calendar in 1969.

Paul, Acts of St. An apocryphal book written in Greek and put into circulation in the 2nd cent. It was designed to glorify St *Paul's achievements and incorporates much legendary material. A number of treatises which circulated independently are now known to be parts of this work, among them the 'Martyrdom of Paul', the 'Acts of *Paul and Thecla', and possibly the 'Third Epistle of Paul to the *Corinthians' (qq.v.).

Paul, Apocalypse of St. An apocryphal apocalypse, written in Greek and in its present form dating from the 4th cent., which describes what St *Paul saw when he was taken up into the 'third heaven' (2 Cor. 12: 2). It became very popular as a source of ideas about the afterlife. It is to be distinguished from the Gnostic 'Apocalypse of Paul' found at *Nag Hammadi.

Paul, Clerks Regular of St. See BARNABITES.

Paul, Martyrdom of St. An apocryphal account of the death of St *Paul. It forms the final section of the 'Acts of *Paul'.

Paul III (1468–1549), Pope from 1534. In his personal life Alessandro Farnese was a typical Renaissance Pope, but he promoted the inner reform of the Church. He created as *cardinals men of virtue and scholarship, established commissions to draw up plans for reform, and favoured the new religious orders, especially the *Jesuits, whom he approved in 1540. In 1542 he restored the *Inquisition and he fought hard against the opposition to the General Council which finally opened at *Trent in 1545. He was less successful in his political efforts to check the spread of Protestantism; the bull he published against *Henry VIII in 1538 alienated England still further from Rome.

Paul IV (1476–1559), Pope from 1555. Giovanni Pietro Carafa was Bp. of Chieti (Theate) from 1504 to 1524, sitting in 1520 on the commission at Rome appointed to deal with the affair of M. *Luther. He resigned his bishopric to found, in conjunction with St *Cajetan, the *Theatine Order. In 1536 he became Abp. of Naples. As Pope his hatred of *Spain led him to quarrel with *Mary Tudor, and his opposition to anything savouring of Protestantism was so violent that he even had cardinals brought before the *Inquisition.

Paul V (1552–1621), Pope from 1605. When the Senate of *Venice refused to repeal the laws of 1604–5 restricting the erection of religious buildings and the donation or sale of secular property to the Church, the Pope excommunicated the Senate and put the city under an *interdict. He condemned the Oath of Allegiance required by *James I in

England. After futile attempts to re-establish the RC Church in *Russia, he saw the beginning of the *Thirty Years War in Germany. He was, however, a skilful canonist and he fostered the work of Congregations devoted to education and nursing as well as the missions, notably those in Africa and in *Canada.

Paul VI (1897–1978), Pope from 1963. Giovanni Battista Montini held office in the Papal Secretariat of State from 1922 for over thirty years, apart from a few months in Warsaw. In 1954 he became Abp. of Milan. *John XXIII made him a *cardinal and continually brought him forward at the Second *Vatican Council; when John XXIII died he was elected Pope. He promised to continue the Council and pursue the same policy as his predecessor. During the Council, he announced that he would be establishing a 'Synod of Bishops' which would have deliberative as well as consultative powers at the Pope's discretion. [For the decrees of the Council, see VATICAN COUNCIL, SECOND].

The most far-reaching reforms of his pontificate were brought about through the Commissions he appointed to put into effect the wishes of the Council. These included the publication of a new *Missal in 1970, with its accompanying *lectionary, and a new *Breviary in 1971; these involved a reordering of the Mass and *Office, both of which could now be in the vernacular. His own encyclicals generally seemed more conservative; they include *Sacerdotalis coelibatus* (1967), insisting on the need for clerical *celibacy, and *Humanae Vitae* (1968), condemning artificial means of birth control. After 1968 he faced tensions within the Church.

In 1964 on a visit to the Holy Land he embraced *Athenagoras, the *Oecumenical Patriarch of Constantinople, and at the close of the Council he took part in a historical gesture of friendship with the Eastern *Orthodox Church. He also established the *Anglican-Roman Catholic International Commission (1966). He was the first Pope to travel extensively abroad. He fixed a retirement age for bishops and clergy at 75, reduced the ceremonial pomp of the Papacy, and sold his *tiara for the benefit of the poor.

Paul of the Cross, St (1694–1775), founder

of the *Passionists. Paul Francis Danei came of an impoverished noble family. In 1720 a vision inspired him to found a religious order in honour of the Passion of our Lord; the first house was opened in 1737. He was a celebrated preacher and famous as a miracle-worker and spiritual director. Feast day, 19 Oct. (formerly, 28 Apr.).

Paul the Deacon (c.720–c.800), chronicler. Of Lombard descent, he received an exceptionally good education. He became a monk at *Monte Cassino, perhaps c.760. About 781 he visited *Charlemagne and remained in Francia for a few years. On his return he undertook his main work, the *Historia Gentis Langobardorum* covering the period from 568 to 744; it is the main source for the Lombard history of the time, being especially valuable for Franco-Lombard relations and for its vivid picture of life in that age.

Paul of Samosata (3rd cent.), heretical Bp. of *Antioch from c.260. His teaching on the Person of Christ was condemned at two, or possibly three, Synods of Antioch, and in 268 he was deposed from his see. He seems to have taught a form of *Monarchianism, according to which the Word was simply an attribute of the Father, His reason or power. In the Incarnation, he held, the Word descended on the man Jesus, who thus became 'Son of God'. His use of the term '*Homoousios' to deny that the Word was a *hypostasis separate from the Father seems to have been condemned. Later he was regarded by the opponents of *Nestorius as his predecessor. His followers, the Paulianists, long survived his death.

Paul the Silentiary. See PAULUS SILENTIARIUS.

Paul of Thebes, St (d. c.340), traditionally the first Christian *hermit. He apparently fled to the desert in the *Decian persecution (249–51). St *Antony is said to have visited him when he was 113 years old, and later to have buried him. Feast day, 15 Jan.

Paul and Thecla, Acts of Sts. An apocryphal work which is part of the 'Acts of St *Paul'. It describes how *Paul preached the benefits of chastity at Iconium and won St Thecla away from Thamyris, to whom she was betrothed. Paul was charged before the civil authorities and beaten, while Thecla was condemned to death but miraculously saved.

Paula, St (347–404), Roman matron. In 385 she and her daughter, St *Eustochium, followed St *Jerome to Palestine; she settled at *Bethlehem, founding communities for monks and nuns. Feast day, 26 Jan.

Paulicians. Members of a sect in the Byzantine Empire. Their founder seems to have been Constantine of Mananali, who established a community at Kibossa in Armenia, and was stoned *c.*684. They were severely persecuted in the 9th cent.; many accepted *Islam, and those who sought refuge in Bulgaria seem to have amalgamated with the *Bogomils in the 10th cent. They apparently ceased to exist as a separate sect in the 12th cent. They professed a *dualistic doctrine, denied the reality of Christ's body and of the Redemption, and considered His teaching to be Christ's most important work. Like *Marcion, they repudiated the OT and held Lk. and the Pauline Epistles in particular esteem.

Pauline Privilege. The privilege conceded by St *Paul (1 Cor. 7: 15) to the partner of a heathen marriage to contract a new marriage on becoming a Christian if the non-Christian partner wished to separate or put serious obstacles in the way of the convert's faith and practice. The right is incorporated in RC canon law.

Paulinus, St (*c.*730–802), Bp. of *Aquileia. He was a scholar whom *Charlemagne summoned to the Frankish court in 776 and appointed Patr. of Aquileia in 787. He took part in the suppression of *Adoptianism. He was also a skilful poet. Feast day, 28 Jan. (also 11 Jan. and 2 Mar.).

Paulinus, St (353/5–431), Bp. of Nola. He was governor of Campania before he married. He underwent a conversion and was baptized (before 390). After the death of their only son, he and his wife took vows of continence and began distributing their property. Paulinus was ordained at Barcelona in 393 or 394. The next year he and his wife left Spain to lead a monastic life near the tomb of St Felix at Nola in Campania, where Paulinus was made bishop some time between 403 and 413. With *Prudentius he ranks as the two foremost Christian

Latin poets of the patristic period. Feast day, 22 June.

Paulinus, St (d. 644), Bp. of *York. He was sent to England by *Gregory I in 601. When in 625 *Edwin, King of Northumbria, married Ethelburga of Kent, Paulinus was consecrated bishop and went with her to York. As a result of his preaching, Edwin and his chiefs accepted Christianity at the assembly of Goodmanham (627). When Edwin was defeated in 633, Paulinus returned with Ethelburga to Kent and became Bp. of *Rochester. Feast day, 10 Oct.

Paulists. The popular name for members of 'The Missionary Society of St Paul the Apostle in the State of New York', founded by I. T. *Hecker in 1858 to further the work and interests of the RC Church in the USA.

Paulus Silentiarius (6th cent.; a *silentiarius* had to maintain silence in the Imperial Palace), Christian poet. His chief work was a hymn to mark the consecration of *Hagia Sophia at Constantinople in 562; it gives a full description of the church.

Pax. See KISS OF PEACE and following entry.

pax brede (also **pax**). A small plate of ivory, metal, or wood, with a representation of some religious subject on the face and a projecting handle on the back, formerly used for conveying the *Kiss of Peace. It was kissed by the celebrant and then by others who received it in turn.

Peace of the Church, the. The term is applied to the new situation in the Church when persecution ended with the 'Edict of *Milan' (313), and to the temporary cessation of the *Jansenist conflict in 1668.

Peake, Arthur Samuel (1865–1929), biblical scholar. The son of a *Primitive Methodist minister, from 1904 he was a professor at Manchester University. He is chiefly remembered for his editorship of a *Commentary on the Bible* in one volume (1919). The so-called new edition of *Peake's Commentary*, edited by M. Black and H. H. Rowley (1962), is a completely new work.

Pearson, John (1613–86), Bp. of *Chester from 1673. He was an erudite and profound scholar. His classic *Exposition of the Creed* (1659) originated in a series of lectures at St Clement's, Eastcheap. He defended the authenticity of the Epistles of St *Ignatius against the attacks of J. *Daillé; his conclusions have been strengthened by later work.

Pearson, John Loughborough (1817–97), architect. His work was mainly ecclesiastical and in geometrical gothic style; it was characterized by refined detail, elegant proportions and noble vaulting. The best-known example is *Truro Cathedral.

Peasants' War, formerly called the 'Peasant Revolt'. A series of insurrections of the German peasants in 1524–6. The immediate causes were probably religious, social, economic, and political. M. *Luther's doctrine of the priesthood of all believers could be interpreted as postulating greater social equality than it in fact did, and the economic distress of the peasants was real. T. *Müntzer's apocalyptic visions, though not responsible for the War, served as an inspiration in the later stages. The rebels consisted of groups of serfs, farmers, townspeople, and minor clergy. They set out their grievances in the *Twelve Articles adopted at Memmingen (1525), but they had few real leaders and were brutally stamped out.

Pecham, John (c.1225–92), also 'Peckham', Abp. of *Canterbury. He was born at Patcham (formerly Pecham) in E. Sussex, studied at *Paris and then at *Oxford, where he joined the *Franciscans c.1250. He taught in Paris, Oxford, and Rome. In 1279 he was appointed Abp. of Canterbury. He immediately inaugurated a vigorous policy of reform, which brought him into conflict with some of his *suffragans.

In theology he upheld the Franciscan tradition; he opposed the teaching of St *Thomas Aquinas on the unity of form in man, even insisting on its condemnation as heretical (1286). He wrote on theological subjects; he produced a standard treatise on optics; and he was a gifted poet.

Pecock, Reginald (c.1393–1461), Bp. successively of *St Asaph (from 1444) and *Chichester (from 1450). He was accused of heresy in 1457 and, though he recanted, he was deprived of his bishopric.

His best-known work, *The Repressor*, was written to combat the *Lollards; it emphasizes the 'law of kind', 'written in mennis soulis with the finger of God', to which the Scriptures are subordinate and supplementary.

pectoral cross. A cross of precious metal worn on the breast, suspended by a chain which goes round the neck. In the C of E its use is almost exclusively confined to bishops; in the RC Church and especially in the E. Church it is more widely worn.

Peculiar. A place exempt from the jurisdiction of the bishop of the diocese in which it is situated. Royal Peculiars, which are usually churches connected with a royal castle or palace (e.g. St George's Chapel, *Windsor, and *Westminster Abbey), are exempt from any jurisdiction except that of the Sovereign. Most of the rights and privileges of the other types of Peculiar (e.g. Monastic and Cathedral Peculiars) have now been removed.

Peculiar People, the, also 'Plumstead Peculiars'. A small sect of faith-healers, founded in Rochford, near Southend, in 1838. In 1956 they took the name of the Union of Evangelical Churches.

Pedilavium. The ceremony of footwashing performed on *Maundy Thursday in memory of Christ's action before the *Last Supper (Jn. 13). When the Maundy Thursday Mass came to be celebrated in the morning, the Pedilavium remained in the evening as a separate service, confined to cathedral and abbey churches. *Pius XII's Holy Week Ordinal placed it in the restored evening Mass immediately after the homily and recommended its observance in all churches. Twelve men are led into the sanctuary, where the celebrant washes and dries the feet of each in turn. Provision for a pedilavium, which in the C of E had been dropped at the Reformation, was made in 1986 and is included in modern liturgies of some other Provinces of the Anglican Communion. In the Byzantine rite a similar ceremony, mainly confined to cathedrals and monasteries, follows the Eucharistic liturgy.

Peel parish. In the C of E, a *parish set up under the New Parishes Act 1843, passed when Sir Robert Peel was Prime Minister, or one of the subsequent Acts on the subject.

Péguy, Charles Pierre (1873–1914), French poet and philosopher. An ardent socialist and Dreyfusard, he gave up his studies at the *Sorbonne to manage a Paris bookshop, which became a centre of intellectual activity. In 1900 he founded the *Cahiers de la Quinzaine*, in which he and a group of contributors attacked the evils of the day. At one time a professed atheist, *c*.1907 he came back to the Catholic faith, but remained unreconciled to the Church because of domestic circumstances.

Pelagia, St (d. *c*.311), virgin and martyr. She was a 15-year-old girl of *Antioch who, when her house was surrounded by soldiers during one of the *persecutions, threw herself out of a window into the sea to preserve her chastity. Feast day, 9 Jun. To the name of this historical person a legend became attached of a 4th-cent. actress of Antioch who was suddenly converted and lived as an austere recluse in a grotto of the Mount of *Olives. Feast day, 8 Oct. The story of a third Pelagia, a virgin martyr of *Tarsus, seems to be a combination of the former two. This Pelagia is supposed to have been burned to death for refusing to become the mistress of the Emperor. Feast day in the E., also 8 Oct; in the Roman martyrology, 4 May.

Pelagianism. Theologically, Pelagianism is the heresy that man can take the initial steps towards salvation by his own efforts, apart from Divine *grace. Historically, it was an ascetic movement composed of disparate elements united under the name of the British theologian Pelagius, who taught in Rome in the later 4th and early 5th cents. It arose in the aristocratic circles in Rome which admired St *Jerome in the 380s. Pelagius' contribution was to supply a theology vindicating Christian asceticism against the charge of *Manichaeism by emphasizing man's freedom to choose good by virtue of his God-given nature. The denial of the transmission of *Original Sin seems to have been introduced into Pelagianism by *Rufinus the Syrian, who influenced Pelagius' supporter *Celestius.

In 409 or 410 Pelagius and Celestius left Italy for Africa, whence Pelagius soon moved to Palestine. Celestius was accused of denying the transmission of Adam's sin to his descendants and was condemned by a Council of *Carthage in 411. Soon afterwards St *Augustine began to preach and write against Pelagian doctrines. In 415 Pelagius was accused of heresy by *Orosius, who had been sent to Palestine by Augus-

tine. He cleared himself at a diocesan synod at *Jerusalem and at a provincial synod at Diospolis (Lydda), but the African bishops condemned Pelagius and Celestius at two Councils in 416 and persuaded *Innocent I to excommunicate them. Pope *Zosimus reopened the case but in 418 he confirmed his predecessor's judgement.

Pelagius himself then disappears from history. Pelagianism, however, was defended by *Julian of Eclanum, who conducted a literary debate of great bitterness with Augustine. Celestius and his followers were again condemned at the Council of *Ephesus in 431. Doctrines henceforth identified as Pelagian continued to find favour in Britain, while in Gaul the debate gave rise to *Semipelagianism (q.v.).

Pelagius. See PELAGIANISM.

pelican. The image of the pelican, wounding herself with her beak to feed her young with her blood, has been widely used to typify Christ's redeeming work, especially as mediated through the Eucharist.

penalties, ecclesiastical. In the RC Church these fall into three classes: (1) 'Censures' or 'medicinal penalties' designed to secure the correction of the offender and his reintegration into the life of the Church; these are *excommunication, *interdict, and *suspension of clerics from their office. (2) 'Expiatory penalties' designed to punish the offender and safeguard the community; these include prohibition to live in a certain area and dismissal from the clerical life. (3) 'Penal remedies' and *penances. These remedies (warning and rebuke) are intended to prevent likely wrongdoing or to deal with the serious suspicion that an offence has been committed.

Penance. Little is known of the early history of the Sacrament. By the 3rd cent. a developed system of public Penance had emerged. After the sinner had asked the bishop for Penance, he was enrolled in the order of *penitents, excluded from Communion, and committed to a course of prayer, fasting, and almsgiving; after a period whose length was determined by the gravity of the sin, the sinner was reconciled and rejoined the congregation. Penance could then be undergone only once in a lifetime and entailed lifelong continence.

A new system was developed in the W. under the influence of *Celtic or *Anglo-Saxon monk-missionaries. The Penance remained public, long, and arduous, but confession of the details of sin was private and absolution was gradually pushed back until it was granted on confession and before the Penance began. From this developed the 'private Penance' of today, with its confession, absolution, and light formal penance. The Fourth *Lateran Council (1215) required every Christian to confess his or her sins to the parish priest at least once a year. By 1500 the system of regular confession was sufficiently ubiquitous to be a major target of the Church's more radical critics. In the E. a similar development took place, though here Penance was bound up with spiritual direction, which was not confined to the priesthood, and absolution is not always mentioned. By the 15th cent. private confession to a priest, followed by a prayer for forgiveness, was a generally accepted practice among lay people.

The theology of Penance depends on the ability of the Church to intercede for sinners and the power of its ministers to absolve them. In the W. Church, however, it came to be held that post-Baptismal sin must be atoned for in part by the punishment of the sinner. Owing to the grave inconvenience occasioned by long Penances, the system of commutation grew up. A Penance of years could be compressed into a single day by the payment of money or its place taken by the repeated recitation of the Psalter in an uncomfortable position. This idea of commutation affected the development of *indulgences (q.v.).

The 1973 RC Order of Penance provides three rites, one of which allows the granting of absolution without individual confession of sins in the presence of a priest, but its use is severely restricted and those penitents who benefit from it are bound to confess their sins at a later date. In the C of E the use of Penance for those who wished for it was revived in the 19th cent. on the basis of the provisions in the BCP *Visitation of the Sick. Several modern Anglican liturgies contain a rite for the Reconciliation of a Penitent.

See also SEAL OF CONFESSION.

Penington, Isaac, the 'Younger' (1616–79), or 'Pennington', *Quaker. He was the eldest son of Sir Isaac Penington, who was

Lord Mayor of London (1642–3). In 1657 he heard George *Fox; the following year he and his wife joined the Quakers, who had hitherto had no one of his station in their ranks. After 1660 he was imprisoned five times and his property confiscated. A meeting house built on his land at Jordans, Chalfont St Giles, still survives.

Penitential Books. Books containing directions for confessors which included lists of sins with a set of graded *penances for each. They first appeared in the *Celtic Churches in the 6th cent. and spread throughout the W. Church. Efforts to provide more orderly handbooks culminated in Book 19 of the *Decretum* of *Burchard of Worms (d. 1025).

Penitential Psalms. See SEVEN PENITENTIAL PSALMS.

Penitentiary. In the RC Church a Penitentiary is a cleric charged with certain aspects of the administration of the Sacrament of *Penance and related matters.

penitents. In the ancient system of public *Penance (q.v.), penitents were segregated from the rest of the congregation by wearing special dress and worshipping apart in the church. Even after restoration to Communion, some disabilities remained.

Penn, William (1644–1718), founder of Pennsylvania. A sermon which he heard in 1666 had a decisive influence and in 1667 he attached himself to the *Quakers. His writing in defence of his newly-won faith led to his imprisonment in the Tower. During his confinement he wrote *No Cross, No Crown* (1669), a classic of Quaker practice. He became interested in founding a colony in America which would assure liberty of conscience for Quakers and others. From 1677 he and two other Quakers were trustees of West New Jersey which was given a constitution on Quaker principles, and in 1681 he joined eleven others to purchase East New Jersey. Also in 1681 he obtained by letters patent a grant of Pennsylvania, confirmed the following year. He founded the 'Free Society of Traders' to develop the colony economically, drew up a constitution which permitted all forms of worship compatible with monotheism and religious liberty, and sailed for America. Having returned to England in 1684, he expressed the Quakers' thanks to *James II for the *Declaration of Indulgence of 1687.

Pennefather, William (1816–73), *Evangelical clergyman. He was incumbent of Christ Church, Barnet (1852–64) and of St Jude's, Mildmay Park, Islington (1864–73). In 1861 he founded what was to become the Mildmay Deaconess Institution, modelled on *Kaiserswerth; it survived (as St Christopher's Deaconess House, Highbury) until 1940.

Pennington, Isaac. See PENINGTON, ISAAC.

Penry, John (1559–93), *Separatist. He came into conflict with the bishops on account of his *Puritan ideas. In 1588, when the *Marprelate Tracts appeared, he was, almost certainly unjustly, suspected of being their author and fled to Scotland. On his return in 1592 he joined the London Separatist congregation. He was hanged on an ill-founded charge of treason.

Pentateuch. A title in use among biblical scholars for the five 'Books of *Moses': *Genesis, *Exodus, *Leviticus, *Numbers, and *Deuteronomy. Traditionally these Books have been held to be written by Moses himself. In the 19th cent. the 'documentary hypothesis' was developed by J. *Wellhausen and others; according to this the Pentateuch was compiled from written documents dating from the 9th to the 5th cent. BC. Some scholars now reject the notion that previously independent documents were combined to form the Pentateuch and argue that cycles of oral tradition gradually evolved until something like the present form of the Pentateuch emerged. See also 'J', 'E', 'D', 'P', and HOLINESS CODE.

Pentecost. The Greek name for the Jewish Feast of Weeks, which falls on the 50th day after *Passover. As the Holy Spirit descended on the Apostles on this day (Acts 2: 1), the name is applied to the Christian feast celebrating this event, popularly called *Whitsunday (q.v.).

Pentecostalism. The modern Pentecostal movement is characterized by belief in the possibility of receiving the same experience and spiritual 'gifts' as did the first Christians 'on the day of Pentecost' (Acts 2: 1–4). Its adherents emphasize the corporate element in worship (often marked by great spontaneity) and lay stress on the practice of the gifts listed in 1 Cor. 12 and 14 and recorded Acts (e.g. speaking in tongues or *glossolalia, divine [*spiritual] healing, and *exorcism) and on possession of these gifts by all true believers. Most claim that the 'power' to exercise these gifts is given initially in an experience known as '*baptism in the Holy Spirit'(q.v.).

In the early 20th cent. experiences of 'Spirit baptism' were reported among various revivalist or *Holiness groups in America; those occurring in Los Angeles in 1906 attracted attention. The largest Pentecostal body in the USA is the '*Assemblies of God', an affiliation of Churches formed in 1914. Pentecostalism in Britain is dated from a visit in 1907 by a *Methodist minister who claimed to have received 'Spirit baptism'; it was reinforced by immigrants from Jamaica who established the 'New Testament Church of God' in 1953. It also spread early to other W. European countries and is now expanding in the Third World. Since c.1960 the Pentecostal movement has come to be widely represented within the main Christian denominations, where it is sometimes called 'Neo-Pentecostalism' (see CHARISMATIC RENEWAL MOVEMENT).

Pentecostarion. In the E. Church, the liturgical book which contains the variable parts of the services between *Easter and the Sunday after *Pentecost.

Pepin (or more correctly **Pippin) III** (714–68), Frankish King. A son of *Charles Martel, he succeeded to his father's office as Mayor of the Palace of the Frankish kingdom. With the assent of Pope *Zacharias, he was elected King by the nobles in 751 in place of the nominal Merovingian King and anointed by Frankish bishops. In 754 the ceremony was repeated by *Stephen II (III), for whom Pepin promised to win back the exarchate of *Ravenna and the rights and territories of the Roman republic. Having defeated the Lombards in 754 and 756, Pepin fulfilled his promise by giving the Pope the territories specified in the (no longer extant) 'Donation of Pepin'. Throughout his reign, in collaboration with Bp. *Chrodegang of Metz, he took an active part in furthering the ecclesiastical reforms begun by St *Boniface. He was succeeded by *Charlemagne. See also PATRIMONY OF ST PETER.

Percival, John (1834–1918), Bp. of *Hereford from 1895. In his latter years he sought to further the cause of reunion between the C of E and the Nonconformist Churches; he aroused much opposition by inviting Nonconformists to receive Communion in Hereford Cathedral.

Percy, John. See FISHER THE JESUIT.

perfection. The primary meaning of the term is completeness and in an absolute sense it may be attributed only to God. In the NT, however, perfection is frequently enjoined on the Christian; according to Mt. 5: 48 the perfection required of man is related to that of God ('Be ye therefore perfect, even as your heavenly Father is perfect'). From early times *martyrdom was described as perfection (or fulfilment) and the term was soon applied also to the state of virginity. From the 4th cent. *monasticism came to be regarded as the way of perfection *par excellence*, and a double standard of perfection developed: 'Religious Perfection', involving the practice of the so-called '*Counsels of Perfection', was distinguished from 'Christian Perfection' made possible by Baptism.

The idea of perfection has played a central part among the *Methodists. They regard entrance on the way of perfection as an instantaneous experience, which takes place some time after conversion, and convinces those who receive it that sin is rooted out in them.

Perfectionists. See ONEIDA COMMUNITY.

Pergamum. The town (modern Bergama in Turkey) was a centre of culture in the 2nd cent. BC. To this period belongs the invention of parchment ('pergamena carta') as a substitute for papyrus.

One of the '*Seven Churches' addressed in Rev. (2: 12–17), Pergamum is called the 'place where Satan's throne is'. As it was the first city in Asia to receive permission to worship the living ruler, the reference is presumably to Emperor-worship.

pericope. A passage from the Bible, especially one appointed to be read in the Church services. See also LECTIONARY.

pericope adulterae, i.e. Jn. 7: 53–8: 11. These verses, which narrate the Lord's compassionate dealing with the woman taken in the act of adultery, are not part of the original text of Jn., but the story seems to be primitive; the passage may belong to Lk.

Perkins, William (1558–1602), *Puritan theologian. He became prominent in the university at Cambridge as a vigorous anti-Roman theologian and supporter of Puritan principles. His writings were held in high repute throughout the 17th cent. by theologians of *Calvinist sympathies.

Perpetua, St (d. 203), African martyr. The *Passion of St Perpetua and St *Felicity* tells how Perpetua and her slave, with other African catechumens, were imprisoned and, after their Baptism, condemned to execution in the arena at Carthage. It is a contemporary document. Feast day, formerly 6 Mar., since 1969, 7 Mar.

perpetual curate. In the C of E the technical name given before 1969 to a clergyman who officiated in a parish or district to which he had been nominated by the *impropriator and licensed by the bishop. When parishes which had been *appropriated to monasteries passed at the *dissolution to *lay rectors, these rectors had to nominate to the bishop for his licence a priest to serve the cure. Curates thus licensed became perpetual. The ministers of new parishes and districts established by various 19th cent. Acts of Parliament were also perpetual curates. By the Pastoral Measure 1968 all perpetual curates became vicars in 1969.

Perrone, Giovanni (1794–1876), Italian *Jesuit. His *Praelectiones Theologicae* (1835–42) was one of the most widely used books on Catholic dogmatics in the 19th cent.

per saltum (Lat., 'by a leap'). A term used of the conferring of a particular rank of *Orders on a candidate who has not previously received the lower grades, e.g. the ordination to the priesthood of a man who is not already a deacon.

persecution. See TOLERATION and the following entry.

persecutions, early Christian. Christianity at first appeared to the Roman authorities as a form of *Judaism, which was tolerated, but Jewish agitation against the Christians revealed its separate identity. The secrecy of the early Christian rites and misunderstanding of Christian language (e.g. Jn. 6: 35) and of the *agape and *Eucharist led pagans to suppose them guilty of *flagitia*, promiscuity, incest, and cannibalism. This fact explains why *Nero in 64 could make them scapegoats for the fire in Rome. From then on persecution continued intermittently. It is attested under *Domitian, and *Pliny (q.v.) assumed that avowed Christians as such deserved death. The Emp. Trajan and his successors were unwilling to withstand public indignation against the Christians, who were alienated from ordinary social life. Persecutions, though attested in every reign of any length, were until 249 not initiated by the central government and were sporadic and ineffectual.

As the Church grew in strength and respectability, popular hostility abated, but in the mid-3rd cent. some Emperors took more seriously the conception that Rome's welfare rested on the favour of the gods. In 249 *Decius commanded all subjects to sacrifice and obtain certificates of their obedience. Those who refused were marked out as Christians and suffered accordingly. The persecution did not outlast Decius' death in 251. Valerian in 257 forbade Christian meetings and ordered the clergy to sacrifice; in 258 he subjected them to death and high-ranking laymen to other severe penalties. He was captured by the Persians in 260 and Christians resumed their meetings and received back their property. Systematic persecution was resumed in the later years of *Diocletian (q.v.). In 299 he took steps to rid the army and court of Christians, but only in 303 did he issue edicts of general persecution. These increased in severity until sacrifice was enjoined on all subjects. A fearful persecution ensued throughout the Empire, though its intensity varied in different areas. After the abdication of Diocletian and his co-Augustus in 305, it subsided in the W., but continued in the E. until *Galerius issued an edict of toleration in 311. *Constantine, on acceding to power in Gaul and Britain in 306 had granted the Christians toleration and restitution of their possessions and Maxentius had followed suit in Italy in 311; in the so-called Edict of *Milan (313) Licinius made the same concessions in the E.

The victims of persecution might be executed; they enjoyed the fame of *martyrs.

Many Christians were imprisoned for a time, or sent to the mines; survivors, who had often endured torture used to induce apostasy, acquired prestige as *confessors. Many, too, recanted, or persuaded the authorities they had done so. Controversy about whether, and on what conditions, these *lapsi*, *libellatici*, or *traditores* might be reconciled, gave rise to the *Novatian, *Melitian, and *Donatist schisms.

perseverance. In addition to its general meaning, the word is used technically in connection with the doctrine of *predestination, to mean steady continuance, after conversion, in the faith and life proper to the attainment of salvation.

personal prelature. An institution established in 1982 with the creation of *Opus Dei into a personal prelature. Erected in each case by the Holy See, a personal prelature consists of priests and deacons of the secular clergy presided over by a bishop who can ordain men under the title of service to the prelature.

Persons, Robert. See PARSONS, ROBERT.

Perth, Articles of. Five articles on such subjects as kneeling at Communion which were forced on the Church in *Scotland by *James I at Perth in 1618. In 1621 they were carried through the Scottish Parliament.

Perugino, Pietro Vannucci (*c.*1446–1523), Italian painter. In 1482 he painted the *Delivery of the Keys to St Peter* in the *Sistine Chapel. The devotional warmth of his style created great demand for his religious pictures. His greatest work is the fresco of the *Crucifixion* in Sta. Maria Maddalena dei Pazzi at Florence (completed in 1499).

Peshitta. The official text of the Bible in Syriac-speaking Christian lands from the early 5th cent. The NT may have been the work of *Rabbula, Bp. of Edessa from 412 to 435, but was probably begun before the end of the 4th cent. It did not include Rev., 2 Pet., 2 and 3 Jn., and Jude. The origins of the OT are obscure, but in part it seems to be the work of Jews.

Petavius, Dionysius (1583–1652), Denis Pétau, *Jesuit historian and theologian. His *Opus de Doctrina Temporum* (1627) was a fundamental contribution on ancient chronology. He also issued notable editions of the

works of *Synesius (1612) and St *Epiphanius (1622). As a dogmatic theologian he was
one of the first to accept the idea of doctrinal development and to concede the
imperfections of much patristic teaching
judged by later standards.

Peter, St, Prince of the *Apostles. According to Jn. (1: 35-42) he was introduced to
Christ by his brother *Andrew and given
the name 'Cephas', the Aramaic equivalent
of the Greek 'Peter' (πέτρα, 'rock'); according to Mt. (4: 18-20) and Mk. (1: 16-18) they
were called together from their fishing. In
all the lists of the Twelve [Apostles] Peter is
named first. He is present on all three occasions when only a small 'inner group' is
admitted, and he usually takes the lead as
the mouthpiece of the Apostles. After his
confession of faith at *Caesarea Philippi
that Jesus is the Christ (Mk. 8: 27-30; in Mt.
16: 16, 'the Christ, the Son of the living
God'), Mt. adds the Lord's promise, 'Thou
art Peter, and on this rock I will build my
Church', together with the keys of heaven
and the power of binding and loosing (16:
18f.). (The precise interpretation of this passage has been the subject of much controversy.) His pre-eminence is again affirmed
by the Lord at the *Last Supper (Lk. 22: 31 f.),
but his boast that he will never leave Him
is answered by Christ's prediction that
before the end of the night he will deny
Him thrice. When in the courtyard of
the High Priest he is accused of being one of
His followers, he three times denies that
he knows Him, remembers His prediction, and repents bitterly (Mt. 26: 69-75). He
goes to the Lord's tomb as soon as the
women report that it is empty (Lk. 24: 12)
and he is later favoured with a special
appearance of the risen Christ (Lk. 24: 34).
After the Ascension he immediately takes
the lead of the Apostles and throughout
the first half of Acts he appears as their
head. He opens the Church to the Gentiles by admitting Cornelius (Acts 10: 1-11:
18) and his authority is evident at the
so-called Council at Jerusalem (Acts 15:
7-11).

Little is known of his later years. The
tradition connecting him with Rome is
early and unrivalled. The later tradition
attributing to him an episcopate of 25 years
in Rome is less well supported. His death is
placed in the reign of *Nero (54-68) and
was probably in the persecution of 64.

There are historical grounds for believing
that his tomb in *St Peter's, Rome, is
authentic. The statement of *Papias that
his memoirs lie behind Mk. is accepted by
many scholars. Feast day (sometimes with
St *Paul), 29 June. For the NT Epistles, see
PETER, EPISTLES OF ST.

Peter, Acts of St. An apocryphal book,
written in Greek, c.180-190. The 'Martyrdom of St Peter', which forms part of it,
records the '*Quo Vadis?' incident and the
crucifixion of St *Peter head downwards.

Peter, Apocalypse of St. This apocryphal
apocalypse, dating from the early 2nd cent.,
describes how the Lord granted to the
Apostles a vision of their brethren in the
next world and of their rewards. An 'Apocalypse of Peter' found at *Nag Hammadi has
only the title in common.

Peter, Epistles of St. Two NT Epistles are
ascribed to St *Peter. The First Epistle was
written to Christian communities in Asia
Minor to encourage them under persecution. Its Petrine authorship has been questioned on the grounds that its literary style
is not that of a Galilean fisherman; that
passages in it reflect Pauline teaching; and
that 'persecution of the Church of Asia
Minor is not otherwise attested before c.112
(in *Pliny). What is envisaged, however,
may not be official persecution by the
State. The arguments are inconclusive.

The main message of the Second Epistle
is a warning against false and ungodly
teachers. Though it professes to be written
by Peter, there are various indications that
it is of later date, and it was received into
the *canon with considerable hesitation. It
is probably to be dated c.150.

Peter, Gospel of St. An apocryphal Gospel,
probably written in Syria in the first half of
the 2nd cent. From the surviving section, it
seems to have been a largely legendary
work.

Peter, Letter of St, to Philip. A Coptic
document found at *Nag Hammadi. The
title applies only to the first page or so of
the text, which tells of St *Philip's reply, a
gathering of the Apostles on the Mount of
*Olives, an appearance of the risen Christ,
and the ensuing conversation.

Peter, Liturgy of St. A Mass combining
elements of the Byzantine and Roman rites

which was probably drawn up for the use of Greek communities in Italy, but may have been put together only as a literary experiment. It is to be distinguished from the *Maronite Third Anaphora of St Peter.

Peter, Martyrdom of St; Patrimony of St. See PETER, ACTS OF ST; PATRIMONY OF ST PETER.

Peter, Preaching of St. A Greek treatise purporting to be the work of St *Peter, but probably dating from the 2nd cent. Intended for missionary propaganda, it emphasized the superiority of Christian monotheism to the beliefs of Greeks and Jews.

Peter of Alcántara, St (1499–1562), Spanish *Discalced Franciscan. Juan de Sanabria was born at Alcántara and in 1515 joined the *Franciscans of the sub-province of Santo Evangelio, then attached to the *Conventuals but transferred to the *Observantines in 1517. In 1519 it became the province of St Gabriel, regarded as the mother province of the Spanish Discalced Franciscans. In 1557 Peter became Commissary General of the reformed Conventuals. The relationship of the *Tratado de la oración y meditación* (c.1556) bearing Peter's name, and *Luis de Granada's *Libro de la oración y meditación* has long been debated; it seems that, while it borrows from the *Libro*, the *Tratado* is basically Peter's work. Feast day, 19 Oct.

Peter of Alexandria (d. 311), Bp. of *Alexandria from 300. He survived the persecution of *Diocletian and drew up rules for the readmission to the Church of those who had lapsed. While he was in hiding, *Melitius began to ordain priests and subsequently claimed authority over Alexandria. It seems that Peter returned when peace was restored in 311 but was beheaded soon afterwards. Feast day in the E., 24 Nov.; in the W., 26 Nov.

Peter de Bruys (d. probably soon after 1130), heretic. He rejected infant Baptism, the Mass, church buildings, prayers for the dead, the veneration of the Cross, as well as large parts of the Bible, and the authority of the Church. He gained a considerable following. His teaching was frequently condemned and he was thrown into the flames at St-Gilles, near Nîmes, by the people.

Peter of Candia; Peter Canisius, St. See ALEXANDER V; CANISIUS, ST PETER.

Peter the Chanter (d. 1197), theologian. He was one of the most influential masters at *Paris in the late 12th cent. He concentrated on practical questions of ethics, and by his discussion of concrete cases for the guidance of confessors he contributed to the doctrine of circumstances to be observed in the administration of *Penance. He strongly condemned the use of *ordeals in the administration of justice.

Peter Chrysologus, St. See CHRYSOLOGUS, ST PETER.

Peter Claver, St (1581–1654), 'Apostle of the Negroes'. A native of Catalonia, he landed in what is now Colombia in 1610 and at once began ministering to the slaves who were brought over in terrible conditions from W. Africa. Ordained priest in 1615, he is said to have instructed and baptized over 300,000 people. Feast day, 9 Sept.

Peter Comestor (d. 1178/9), biblical scholar. He became dean of the cathedral at Troyes in 1147 and by 1168 was also chancellor of *Notre-Dame; he retained both offices when he retired to the *Victorine house in Paris towards the end of his life. His best-known work, the *Historia Scholastica*, is a continuous history from the Creation to the Ascension; it uses the works of the Fathers and pagan authors to fill the gaps in the biblical narrative.

Peter Damian, St (1007–72), reformer. Born in Ravenna, in 1035 he entered the hermitage of Fonte Avella, and c.1043 was chosen prior. He became famous as an uncompromising preacher against the worldliness and simoniacal practices of the clergy and in 1057 was made Cardinal Bishop of Ostia. He was an important thinker in the spheres of theology and canon law; he defended the *validity of sacraments administered by priests guilty of *simony against the rigorist views of *Humbert of Silva Candida and he wrote a treatise against *homosexuality. Feast day, 21 Feb.

Peter the Fuller (d. 488), Patr. of *Antioch. According to an uncertain tradition, he was a monk in the house of the *Acoemetae at *Constantinople, where he practised as a fuller. Expelled because of his *Monophysite leanings, he accompanied the Emp. *Zeno to Antioch. Here he joined the *Apollinarians and opposed the bishop; in the bishop's absence in 470 he had himself made bishop, with Zeno's support. *Gennadius, Patr. of Constantinople, obtained a decree of exile against him, but in 482 he assented to Zeno's '*Henoticon' and regained his see. He is remembered for his addition to the *Trisagion of the clause 'who was crucified for us'.

Peter Gonzalez, St. See ELMO, ST.

Peter the Hermit (d. 1115), preacher of the First *Crusade. 12th-cent. sources report that he visited *Jerusalem as a pilgrim and returned with an appeal to *Urban II to send help; there may be a kernel of truth in this account. After the Council of *Clermont (1095) he raised a force which was destroyed by the Turks; he then joined the main army and entered Jerusalem with it. On his return to Europe he became prior of an *Augustinian abbey which he had helped to found.

Peter Lombard (c.1100–60), 'Master of the Sentences'. He taught at the Cathedral School in *Paris from 1143/4. In 1148 he opposed *Gilbert de la Porrée at the Council of Reims and in 1159 he was appointed Bp. of Paris. His 'Sentences' are divided into four books on (1) the Trinity, (2) the Creation and Sin, (3) the Incarnation and the Virtues, and (4) the Sacraments and the Four Last Things. Though after his death, the orthodoxy of the work was challenged, after 1215 it became for some time the standard textbook of Catholic theology. Its teaching on the *Sacraments marked an important development; Peter was among the first to insist on the number seven, to distinguish them from *sacramentals, and to clarify the conception by asserting the efficacy and causality of the sign.

Peter Martyr, St (c.1200–52), *Inquisitor. Born at *Verona (hence known also as **Veronensis**), of a predominantly *Catharist family, he was nevertheless brought up as a Catholic. He entered the *Dominican Order, probably c.1220–21. Renowned as an eloquent preacher and successful controversialist against the Cathari, he was appointed Inquisitor in

Milan and Como in 1251; he was assassinated. Feast day, 4 June (formerly, 29 Apr.).

Peter Martyr (1499–1562), an Anglicized form of 'Pietro Martire Vermigli', Reformer. Named after St *Peter Martyr, he joined the *Augustinians and in 1533 became prior of a house in Naples. He was impressed by reading works of M. *Bucer and U. *Zwingli; his sympathy with the Reformers led to accusations of error, and in 1542 he fled from Italy. In 1547 he came to England at T. *Cranmer's invitation and became Regius Professor of Divinity at Oxford (1548). He took part in a disputation on the Eucharist in 1549, was consulted over the BCP of 1552, and was one of the commissioners for the reform of canon law. On *Mary's accession, he was put under house arrest but soon allowed to go to Strasbourg; in 1556 he moved to Zurich.

Peter Mogila. See MOGILA, PETER.

Peter Mongo (d. 490), Patr. of *Alexandria. In 477 he was elected the successor of the *Monophysite *Timothy Aelurus. Both Rome and Constantinople recognized Timothy Salophaciolus as Patriarch, but on Salophaciolus' death in 482, Acacius, Patr. of *Constantinople, persuaded the Emp. *Zeno to recognize Mongo in return for his acceptance of the *Henoticon.

Peter Nolasco, St (c.1180–c.1249), founder of the *Mercedarian Order. He was probably engaged in the work of ransoming captives by the mid-1220s. The focus of this work was Catalonia. When others associated themselves with his activities, the Mercedarian Order began to take shape. The date of his death is disputed, but he was no longer head of the Order after 1245. Feast day, 28 (formerly 31) Jan., now suppressed.

Peter of Spain. See JOHN XXI.

Peter of Tarentaise, St (d. 1175), from 1142 Abp. of Tarentaise (Moutiers, in Savoy). He had been a *Cistercian monk, and he thoroughly reformed his diocese. He stood high in the confidence of the Popes and was commissioned to reconcile Prince Henry (later Henry II) of England and Louis VII of France. Feast day, 8 May.

Peter the Venerable (1092/4–1156), Abbot of *Cluny from 1122. Against opposition he carried through important reforms, especially in the financial and educational spheres. His interest in the pursuit of studies at Cluny brought him into conflict with St *Bernard, who wanted to see the monastic life confined to prayer and manual work. In 1130 Peter supported Innocent II against the antipope Anacletus II, himself a Cluniac monk, and in 1140 he gave shelter to *Abelard. He had the *Koran translated into Latin and wrote against *Islam. His other works include treatises against *Peter de Bruys and against the Jews, sermons, and some poems. Though never canonized, he is commemorated in several martyrologies on 29 Dec.

Peterborough. At a Saxon village on the site a monastery was established c.655. After the church had been destroyed by the Danes, it was rebuilt c.966 by *Ethelwold, Bp. of Winchester, who dedicated it to St *Peter; hence the village came to be called 'Peterborough'. This church having been burnt in 1116, the foundations of a new one were laid in 1117; it was completed in 1237, and in 1541 it became the cathedral of the newly constituted diocese.

Peter's Pence, also 'Rome-Scot', formerly an ecclesiastical tax in England paid to the Pope. First paid by King *Offa (d. 796), it was a levy on all but the poorest houses, commuted in the 12th cent. to an annual sum. It was abolished in 1534. After the restoration of the RC hierarchy in 1850, the bishops agreed to resume regularly constituted contributions to Rome and from the 1860s Peter's Pence was collected on an informal diocesan basis, which received official sanction in 1871.

Petrarch, Francesco (1304–74), Italian poet and humanist. In 1326 he received *minor orders. His poems on Laura (collected in the *Canzoniere*) and his epic *Africa* on Scipio Africanus won him the poet's crown in 1341. In 1347 he supported the short-lived republican movement of Cola di *Rienzo. In the following years he was employed on various political embassies. His religious nature, which was often in conflict with the sensuousness of the fame-loving poet and the passion of the scholar for pagan culture, found expression in several Latin treatises. His last great poetical work, the *Trionfi*, celebrates in allegorical form the triumph of the Divine over all things and the ultimate redemption of man from the dominion of the senses.

Petri, Olaus (1493–1552), Swedish Reformer. He studied at *Wittenberg and returned to *Sweden imbued with *Lutheran views. Gaining the favour of Gustavus Vasa, by whom he was later made chancellor (1531–3), he became the leading exponent of doctrinal change in Sweden. He published the first Swedish service book (1529) and was probably responsible for the Swedish translation of the NT (1526).

His brother **Laurentius Petri** (1499–1573) was the first Protestant Abp. of *Uppsala.

Petrobrusians. The followers of *Peter de Bruys (q.v.).

Petrock, St (6th cent.), also 'Pedrog', Cornish saint. He is said to have been the son of a Welsh chieftain who, after studying in Ireland, made his way to Cornwall and founded monasteries at Padstow and Bodmin. Feast day, 4 June.

Petronius, St (5th cent.), Bp. of *Bologna c.432–50. His (largely legendary) Life, written between 1162 and 1180, describes him as a member of the imperial family, says that he visited *Jerusalem, and on becoming bishop erected a monastery and church modelled on the Constantinian buildings at the *Holy Sepulchre. Feast day, 4 Oct.

pew. At first the customary postures for worship were standing and kneeling, and no seats were provided for the congregation. Later, as a concession to the infirm, stone seats were attached to the walls of naves. By the end of the 13th cent. many English churches seem to have been equipped with fixed wooden benches, known as pews. They were sometimes elaborately carved at the ends and back. To finance the endowment of new churches and chapels, the Church Buildings Act 1818 and subsequent Acts allowed payment for the exclusive use of certain pews; few, if any, of these 'pew rents' remain.

Pfaff Fragments of Irenaeus. Four fragments published in 1713 by C. M. Pfaff, who claimed that he had found them in the Turin library and attributed them to St *Irenaeus. A. *Harnack showed them to be a fabrication of Pfaff himself.

Pflug, Julius von (1499–1564), Bp. of Naumburg. His humanistic sympathies made him eager for peace with the Protestants, and to this end he took part in several conferences. He was ready to tolerate a married clergy and Communion in both kinds. He was elected Bp. of Naumberg-Zeitz in 1541 but could not take possession of his see until 1547. The 'Interim of *Augsburg' (1548; q.v.) was largely his work.

Phanar, the. The official residence and court of the *Oecumenical Patriarch at *Constantinople.

Pharisees (Heb. for 'separated ones'). A Jewish religious party mentioned by *Josephus and in the NT. Unlike the *Sadducees, who tried to apply the *Mosaic Law precisely as it was given, the Pharisees allowed some interpretation of it to make it more applicable to different situations. In the Gospels they appear as the chief opponents of Christ, whom they attacked e.g. for forgiving sins and breaking the *Sabbath. He denounced what the Gospels describe as their purely external observance of the Law and their self-righteousness. They seem to have been less hostile than the Sadducees to the nascent Church, with whom they shared belief in the resurrection. After the fall of *Jerusalem (AD 70) they disappear from history.

phelonion. The E. form of the *chasuble.

phenomenology, literally 'the science of phenomena'. The term is now used mainly of the philosophical doctrines of Edmund Husserl (1859–1938) and his school. According to Husserl, phenomenology is a descriptive science concerned with the discovery and analysis of essences and essential meanings. It professes to exclude all metaphysical questions, but much in Husserl's first elaboration of the science tended towards a *Platonic realism. These Platonist elements were developed by his disciples and used for the defence of a Christian metaphysic of an *Augustinian (non-Thomistic) type. Husserl himself in his later writings embraced a form of Subjective Idealism.

Phenomenology was the most influential movement in German philosophy in the period 1910–33. It fell into disrepute under the Nazis but was revived in a modified form in France and in RC circles influenced both the Jesuit philosopher Bernard Lonergan (1904–84) and Pope *John Paul II. It has also enjoyed renewed favour in America. See also EXISTENTIALISM.

Philadelphia. A city in the Roman province of Asia. It was the seat of one of the '*Seven Churches' addressed in Rev.; it is commended for its faithfulness (3: 7–13).

Philadelphians. A 17th-cent. sect. John Pordage (1607–81), rector of Bradfield, Berks., gathered round him a group of followers who shared his enthusiasm for J. *Boehme. It was organized in 1670 as the Philadelphian Society for the Advancement of Piety and Divine Philosophy. Its members were to retain their ecclesiastical allegiances. They professed a kind of nature pantheism, imbued with esoteric and pseudo-mystical teaching, and held that their souls were immediately illuminated by the Holy Spirit.

Philaret, Theodore Nikitich Romanov (c.1553–1633), Patr. of Moscow. His son was elected Tsar in 1613, but Philaret, who had been imprisoned by the Poles, was not freed until 1619. In that year he was made patriarch and virtually ruled Russia until his death. He was a zealous reformer and encouraged the study of theology.

Philaret Drozdov (1782–1867), Russian theologian and Metropolitan of Moscow from 1826. He was an exemplary bishop and exercised a profound influence in Church and State. The best-known of his writings is a Catechism published in 1823.

Philaster, St (d. c.397), more correctly 'Filaster', Bp. of Brescia. In 381 he took part in a Council of Aquileia which deposed two *Arian bishops. About 385 he wrote a treatise designed to refute 28 Jewish and 128 Christian heresies. The work suffers from clumsy arrangement and lack of proportion, but it seems to have filled a real need in the W. Feast day, 18 July.

Phileas, St (d. 306/7), Bp. of Thmuis in Lower Egypt. Of noble birth and great wealth, he was imprisoned, tried before the prefect, and executed at *Alexandria. A letter to his flock from his dungeon is preserved by *Eusebius. Feast day, 4 Feb.

Philemon. The recipient of St *Paul's brief epistle of that name. He was a Christian of Colossae or the neighbourhood, whose slave, *Onesimus, had run away and had met Paul. Paul sent Onesimus back to his master with this letter, which is a plea for his forgiveness. According to tradition Philemon was martyred. Feast day, 22 Nov.

Philibert, St (d. 684), founder and first abbot of *Jumièges. He was abbot of Rebais, near Meaux, but the refractory character of his monks led him to retire to Neustria, where he founded the abbey of Jumièges. In 674 his reproof of the Mayor of the Palace led to his expulsion. He founded another monastery on the island of Her (now Noirmoutier). Feast day, 20 Aug.

Philip, St. See PHILIPS IN THE NT.

Philip, Gospel of. One of the *Gnostic treatises found at *Nag Hammadi. It is a series of reflections on the quest for salvation, with no narrative and only a few incidents or sayings attributed to Christ.

Philip, John (1771–1851), Scottish missionary and reformer in *South Africa. In 1819 he was sent by the *LMS to South Africa on a commission of inquiry and remained there. He was a passionate defender of native rights. His campaign on behalf of the Khoi or 'Hottentot' population prepared the ground for the 1828 Ordinance 50 which extended civil rights to all races. He was responsible for bringing the Paris Evangelical Missionary Society to the Sotho people and the American Board of Missionaries to the Zulus.

Philip the Arabian (d. 249), Roman Emperor from 244. He celebrated the millennium of Rome's foundation in 248 with pomp and the customary religious observance. This fact, and his coins, tell against the tradition that he was a Christian. He seems to have tolerated Christianity.

Philip (1504–67), Landgraf of Hesse. The most able of the German princes who supported M. *Luther, he introduced the Reformation in Hesse, and in 1527 he founded the University of *Marburg as a school for Protestant theologians. Though he failed to bring about an understanding between Luther and U. *Zwingli, he united the Protestant princes and in 1531 the *Schmalkaldic League was established. His position was impaired by a bigamous marriage in 1540, and he made peace with the Emperor. He devoted his later years to the task of uniting Catholics and Protestants.

Philip II (1527–98), of Spain. In 1556 he inherited a composite monarchy which included all the Spanish kingdoms, Naples, Sicily, and Milan, the *Netherlands, and the Spanish Empire in America and the Philippines. From 1554 to 1558, as the husband of *Mary (Tudor), he was also titular king of England, though never crowned. At first his policies were largely defensive. In the Netherlands, however, his religious policies and disregard of local laws led to civil war and foreign intervention. From c.1580 his policies became more aggressive and were financed by increasing imports of American silver and foreign loans. He conquered *Portugal (1580), reconquered the southern Netherlands (modern *Belgium), organized the abortive *Armada against England (1588), and sent his armies into France. He failed in his more ambitious aims, but he defended most of his dominions, maintained Catholicism, neutralized the Turks, and had a part in forcing *Henry IV of France to abandon Protestantism.

Philip Neri, St (1515–95), 'Apostle of Rome'. Going to Rome in 1533, from 1538 he devoted himself to works of charity and spent nights in prayer in the *catacombs; in 1544 he experienced an ecstasy which is believed miraculously to have enlarged his heart. After ordination, he went in 1551 to live in a community of priests at San Girolamo, where his confessional soon became the centre of his work. He also held spiritual conferences for men and boys. Out of these activities grew the Congregation of the Oratory (see ORATORIANS). Feast day, 26 May.

Philip Sidetes (5th cent.), historian. A native of Side, in Pamphylia, he went to *Constantinople, where he was an unsuccessful candidate for the patriarchate. His 'Christian History' was a hotch-potch of information on the period from the Creation to AD 430; only fragments remain, including the assertion that *Papias had stated that *John the Apostle and his brother *James had been martyred by the Jews.

Philippians, Epistle to the. This NT letter is addressed by St *Paul to the Christian community at Philippi in Greece, the first Church which he had founded in Europe. Its authenticity is solidly attested in antiquity and almost unanimously accepted by modern scholars. It was probably written in the later part of Paul's captivity in Rome, though both its place of origin and date have been subject to discussion.

After thanking the Philippians for their partnership, Paul tells them of the success of his preaching in captivity and exhorts them to charity, self-discipline, and humility. After warnings and more exhortations, he ends with a doxology and salutations. The Epistle contains a Christological passage (2: 5–11) of great importance (see KENOTIC THEORIES). It is commonly held that these verses originally existed as a hymn.

Philippines, Christianity in the. Christianity was introduced with the Spanish conquest and occupation in the 16th cent. From the beginning of Spanish rule in 1565 until the end of the 19th cent., the RC Church was supported and largely controlled by the Spanish Crown. Missionary work among the Filipino people was undertaken by religious orders from Spain and Mexico and by the late 18th cent. most of the population was baptized. In the 1890s, resentment against the continued domination of the RC Church by Spanish clergy and against the wealth of the friars led to the emergence of a national Church independent of Rome: the Philippine Independent Church was founded in 1902. In 1961 it entered into full communion with the *Episcopal Church in the USA.

With the cession of the Philippines to the USA in 1898, the way was open for Protestant missionary activity. In 1948 several denominations merged to form the United Church of Christ in the Philippines, and in 1963 the National Council of Churches of the Philippines was established, but most Evangelical Protestants belong to sects not affiliated to the National Council. The Philippines, which became an independent republic in 1946, has the largest Christian population in Asia. Over 80 per cent of Filipinos are RC; there is a sharp division between those influenced by *Liberation Theology and the conservatives.

Philippists. The followers of the *Lutheran theologian Philip *Melanchthon.

Philip's Lent, St. In the E. Church the period from 15 Nov. to 24 Dec., the counterpart of *Advent in the W. Church.

Philips in the NT. (1) ST PHILIP THE APOSTLE.

According to Jn. (6: 7) at the feeding of the 5,000 he observed that 200 pennyworth of bread would not provide even a scanty meal; when some Greeks wished to see Jesus, they approached Philip, who was from *Bethsaida of Galilee (Jn. 12: 20 f.), and he later asked the Lord, 'Show us the Father' (Jn. 14: 8). His subsequent career is obscure. According to some traditions he was crucified. Feast day in the E., 14 Nov.; in the W. (jointly with St *James the Less), 1 May, transferred in the RC Church to 11 May and then to 3 May.

(2) ST PHILIP THE EVANGELIST was one of the 'seven men of good report' whose appointment for the service of the poor and distribution of alms is recorded in Acts 6: 1–6 (later regarded as *deacons). He preached in Samaria, baptized an Ethiopian eunuch (Acts 8), and later entertained St *Paul at Caesarea (Acts 21: 8). One tradition makes him Bp. of Tralles, in Lydia. Feast day in the E., 11 Oct.; in the W., 6 June.

(3) PHILIP THE TETRARCH. One of the sons of *Herod the Great, he was ruler from 4 BC to AD 33/4 of the 'region of Ituraea and Trachonitis' (Lk. 3: 1).

Phillimore, Robert Joseph (1810–85), English judge. He was Dean of the *Arches from 1867 to 1875. His *Ecclesiastical Law of the Church of England* (1873) long remained a standard work.

Phillpotts, Henry (1778–1869), Bp. of *Exeter from 1830. An old-fashioned *High Churchman, he was sympathetic to the *Oxford Movement. His refusal to institute G. C. *Gorham (q.v.) to the living of Brampford Speke, on the grounds of his denial of baptismal regeneration, gave rise to a famous ecclesiastical lawsuit.

Philo (c.20 BC–c.AD 50), Jewish thinker and exegete. A member of a prosperous priestly family in *Alexandria, Philo was the foremost figure among the Hellenistic Jews of his age and a fertile author. In religious outlook he was eclectic; he reproduced a variety of doctrines without welding them into a harmonious whole. His most influential achievement was his development of the *allegorical interpretation of Scripture which enabled him to discover much of Greek philosophy in the OT. Of special interest for Christian theology is the central place which he accorded in his system to the *Logos, who was at once the creative power which orders the world and the intermediary through whom men know God. Many of Philo's ideas were taken up in the Christian mystical tradition, but whether he himself should be regarded as a mystic is disputed.

Philocalia. A title meaning 'Love of what is beautiful' applied, especially to: (1) the *Philocalia* of *Origen, an anthology from his writings compiled by St *Basil the Great and St *Gregory Nazianzus in 358–9; (2) the *Philocalia* of Sts Macarius Notaras and *Nicodemus of the Holy Mountain (1782), a collection of ascetical and mystical writings dating from the 4th to the 15th cent., dealing with the teaching of *Hesychasm.

Philocalian Calendar, the. An alternative name for the '*Liberian Catalogue'.

Philomena, St. In 1802 a *loculus* was found in one of the *catacombs, closed with three tiles on which were painted the letters LUMENA/PAX TE/CUM FI, which, when rearranged, read 'Pax tecum Filumena'. The bones found in the tomb were taken to be those of a martyred Christian virgin, who was for a time widely venerated. Feast day, 11 Aug., suppressed in 1961.

Philopatris. A Greek dialogue attacking Christianity. It purports to be the work of *Lucian of Samosata, but probably dates from the 10th cent.

Philoponus, John. See JOHN PHILOPONUS.

philosophy of religion. The notion of the philosophy of religion as a distinct discipline was the creation of the *Enlightenment. Its aim is the philosophical investigation of the group of phenomena covered by the terms 'religion' and 'religious experience'. It studies the essence, content, origin, and, to some extent, the value of religion as a factor in human life, and examines the claims of religion to be true. The '*natural theology' of earlier writers could be considered as philosophy of religion in its broadest sense, but whereas natural theology was regarded as a prelude to revealed theology, the philosophy of religion takes no cognizance of this distinction. Thus it is free to examine concepts found in any religion, not just Christianity. In so far as religions make conflicting claims to truth, the exploration of what kind of a conflict is entailed has

become an increasing concern for the philosophy of religion, which thus overlaps with *comparative religion (q.v.).

Philostorgius (*c*.368–*c*.439), *Arian historian. His 'History of the Church' (*c*. 300–430) survives only in fragments and in an epitome by *Photius. It is inaccurate and biased, but is of value because of its use of excellent sources and for its description of some of the chief Arian personalities.

Philoxenian Version of the NT. The Syriac version of the NT made from the Greek in 508 for *Philoxenus. It was revised in 616 by Thomas of Harkel and for the most part the original text has been lost.

Philoxenus (*c*.440–523), Bp. of Mabbug (Hierapolis in Syria) from 485. He was one of the leading thinkers and writers of the nascent *Syrian Orthodox Church. See also the preceding entry.

Philpot, John (1516–55), Protestant martyr. At an unknown date under *Edward VI (1547–53) he became Archdeacon of *Winchester. An attack on *transubstantiation in the first Convocation of *Mary's reign (1553) was followed by imprisonment. He was burnt at *Smithfield.

Phocas, St (d. 117), Bp. of Sinope in Pontus. A martyr of this name, who was suffocated in a bath, is commemorated in the *Roman Martyrology on 14 July. He is confused with 'St Phocas the Gardener', who is said to have been martyred in the *Diocletianic persecution, and with St Phocas of Antioch. When the various traditions had been fused, the cult of St Phocas became popular, especially among seafarers.

Phoebadius, St (d. *c*.395), Bp. of Agen in S. France. He opposed *Arianism and attacked the *Sirmian formula of 357 in his *Liber contra Arianos*. In 359 he signed the formula of *Ariminum but denounced the Council when he realized its import. Feast day, 26 Apr.

phoenix. A mythical bird, which was the subject of several legends in antiquity. According to one of these, after living for 500–600 years it burnt itself to ashes and then came back to life with renewed youth. From early times Christian writers regarded it as an image of the Resurrection.

Phos Hilaron. In the E. Church, the hymn

sung at 'Hesperinos' (the counterpart of the W. *Vespers) and the central item in the Office. It is used in some modern Anglican liturgies in Evening Prayer. Translations include J. *Keble's 'Hail! gladdening Light'.

Photius (c.810–c.895), Patr. of *Constantinople. When the Emp. Michael III deposed the Patr. Ignatius in 858, Photius, still a layman, was appointed his successor. On Ignatius' refusal to abdicate, Michael and Photius sent an embassy to Pope *Nicholas I. Although Nicholas's delegates took part in the Synod at Constantinople in 861 which deposed Ignatius, at a Synod in Rome in 863 Nicholas annulled the proceedings; he declared Ignatius still Patriarch and Photius deposed. In 867 Photius in an encyclical denounced the presence of Latin missionaries in *Bulgaria as an intrusion, and gave an exposition of his objections to the *Filioque clause in the Creed. Also in 867 a Council at Constantinople pronounced sentence of deposition against the Pope. With the accession of the Emp. Basil (867), the situation changed. Ignatius was reinstated, and Photius was restored only after his death (877). At a Council in Constantinople in 879–80 the Papal legates seem to have approved Photius, but he still faced difficulties within the Byzantine Church and, when *Leo VI became emperor in 886, he resigned.

The Photian schism accentuated the conflict between the Roman claim to be the centre of unity for Christendom and the Greek conception of five patriarchates of almost equal status. Photius was also the first theologian to accuse Rome of innovating in the matter of the Filioque. He was a scholar of wide interests and encyclopaedic knowledge. His main work, the *Bibliotheca* or *Myriobiblion*, is a description of several hundred books, often with exhaustive analyses and copious extracts. In the E. Church he is venerated as a saint; feast day, 6 Feb.

phylactery. A small leather case containing vellum strips inscribed with four passages from the OT. From pre-Christian times orthodox Jews have worn them on the forehead and arm during morning prayer on most days of the year to remind them of their obligation to keep the law.

Pia Desideria. P. J. *Spener's book which aimed at fostering a religious revival in German Protestantism and was a key element in the creation of the *Pietist movement. It was written in German and published in 1675.

Piarists. An order of *clerks regular devoted to the education of the young, especially among the poor. Their name derives from the 'Pious Schools', or free public schools, of which the first was opened in Rome by St *Joseph Calasanctius in 1597. Their teachers were recognized as a congregation in 1617 and made an order in 1621.

Pica. See PIE.

Pico della Mirandola, Giovanni (1463–94), Italian nobleman, scholar, and writer on philosophy and religion. Besides being a classical scholar, he knew Hebrew, Aramaic, and Arabic. He was the first to seek in the *Kabbala a clue to the Christian mysteries; he took a generous view of the existence of truth in non-Christian religions and was an early exponent of *syncretism.

Pie, or **Pica.** The name given in England in the 15th cent. to the book of directions for saying the services. In the BCP ('Concerning the Services of the Church') it is censured for 'the number and hardness of its rules'.

Pietà. A representation of the BVM lamenting over the dead body of Christ, which she holds on her knees.

Pietism. A late-17th- and 18th-cent. movement within (primarily German) Protestantism which sought to supplant the emphasis on institutions and dogma in orthodox Protestant circles by concentrating on the 'practice of piety', rooted in inner experience and expressing itself in a life of religious commitment. The way had been prepared by various writers, but the publication of P. J. *Spener's *Pia Desideria* (1675) was a decisive moment. Spener instituted devotional circles for prayers, Bible reading, etc., but did not in essence deviate from *Lutheran doctrine or intend to separate from the Church. Anti-establishment tendencies, sometimes with *millenarian expectations, were found in the circles of 'radical Pietism'; their relationship with the mainstream Lutheran and Reformed Pietism is debated. The more moderate form won support from a large body of pastors. A clash with the orthodox became inevitable when A. H. *Francke, who had been instrumental in bringing about a revival among the students of Leipzig, attacked the Leipzig theologians. The newly-founded university of Halle then became the centre of the movement which spread throughout Protestant Germany, taking different forms in different areas. In Halle it developed into a hard-and-fast system of penance, grace, and rebirth, while at *Herrnhut it consisted mainly of personal devotion to the Redeemer. In the 18th cent. Pietism was characterized by various philanthropic activities and by its contribution to missionary enterprise. It lasted into the 20th cent.

Pighi or **Pigge, Albert** (c.1490–1542), Dutch Catholic theologian. His principal work, *Hierarchiae Ecclesiasticae Assertio* (1538), is an elaborate defence of *tradition as a source of Christian truth co-ordinate with Scripture; it defended a doctrine of Papal infallibility and denied the proposition that a Pope might personally lapse into heresy.

Pilate, Pontius. The governor ('prefect' not 'procurator') of Judaea from AD 26 to 36 under whom Christ was crucified.

Pilate, Acts of. An apocryphal work giving an account of the trial, death, and resurrection of Christ. In some MSS an independent treatise on the *Descent of Christ into Hades is attached to it; the two together are sometimes known as the 'Gospel of *Nicodemus'. The first part, the 'Acts' proper, is probably not earlier than the 4th cent. The second part purports to have been written by the sons of *Simeon. The work forms the basis of the medieval play-cycle on the *Harrowing of Hell and of the legends of St *Joseph of Arimathaea and the Holy *Grail.

Pilgrim Fathers. The English founders of the colony of Plymouth, Mass., who sailed from the Netherlands and England in the *Mayflower* in 1620.

pilgrimage. A pilgrimage is generally a journey to a holy place undertaken from motives of devotion in order to obtain supernatural help or as an act of penance or thanksgiving. However, the Greek and Latin words for a pilgrim meant a 'resident alien', and pilgrimage could be seen, not as a journey to a particular place, but as voluntary exile from one's native land. Such

an understanding culminated among Irish monks in the 6th and following centuries in the ascetic ideal of perpetual pilgrimage for the love of God; it inspired St *Columba and St *Columbanus. From Carolingian times the practice gradually lapsed, at least in the W. Meanwhile the idea of pilgrimage to special holy places had developed. The practice of visiting places connected with Christ's life on earth received a strong impetus from the visit of the Empress *Helena to *Jerusalem (326). Almost on an equal footing with pilgrimages to Palestine were those to Rome to visit the tombs of the Apostles *Peter and *Paul. From the 8th cent. the practice of imposing a pilgrimage in place of a public *penance added to the number of pilgrims, who, in the Middle Ages, were organized on a grand scale. In modern times *Lourdes has acquired unrivalled fame as a place of pilgrimage.

Pilgrimage of Grace, the. A series of risings in N. England in 1536–7. There was widespread hatred of T. *Cromwell and of government innovations in ecclesiastical matters (especially the *dissolution of the lesser monasteries, and the attacks on the Sacraments and saints' days in the *Ten Articles). In addition, there were economic and social grievances. In some areas peers and gentry took the lead. Promises of a parliament and free pardon led R. *Aske, the leader in Yorkshire, to disband his forces. After a further rising, over 200 rebels were hanged.

Pilgrim's Progress, The. The First Part of J. *Bunyan's masterpiece, written in Bedford gaol, was published in 1678; the Second Part in 1684. The persons and incidents encountered by Christian in his journey from the 'City of Destruction' to the 'Heavenly City'—'Mr Worldly-Wiseman', 'Greatheart', the 'Slough of Despond', and the 'House Beautiful'—have become part of the language of religion in England.

Pilkington, James (c.1520–76), Bp. of *Durham from 1560 (the first Protestant occupant of the see). He returned from the Continent on *Mary's death in 1558, took an active part in the revision of the BCP, and upheld the tenets of the Reformation in Cambridge. At Durham his support for the Protestant cause provoked hostility.

Pillar Saint. See STYLITE.

Pin, Louis Ellies Du. See DUPIN, LOUIS ELLIES.

Pio da Pietrelcina, St. See p. 644.

Pionius, St (d. 250), martyr. He was executed at *Smyrna during the *Decian persecution; the *Acta* describing his death are reliable documents. He was responsible for the preservation of the *Martyrium Polycarpi*. Feast day in the E., 11 Mar.: in the W., 1 Feb.

Pippin III. See PEPIN III.

Pirckheimer, Willibald (1470–1530), German humanist. His house at Nuremberg was a centre of learning. At the beginning of the Reformation he favoured M. *Luther, whose chief opponent, J. *Eck, he attacked in *Eccius Dedolatus*. But he regretted Luther's break with the Church, and in 1521 he asked to be absolved from the ban of excommunication which he had incurred as a follower of the Reformer.

Pirminius, St (d. probably 753), first Abbot of *Reichenau. He founded Reichenau (724) and other monasteries among the Alamanni in Baden and in Alsace. He is traditionally regarded as the author of the *Scarapsus* (in one MS called *Dicta Pirminii*), a work which contains the earliest evidence for the present form of the *Apostles' Creed. Feast day, 3 Nov.

Pisa, Council of. Convoked by the cardinals in 1409 to end the *Great Schism which had divided W. Christendom since 1378, it deposed both Popes *Benedict XIII and Gregory XII and elected a third, who took the name *Alexander V. Its authority is disputed. Though it did not end the Schism, it paved the way for the solution found at the Council of *Constance (1417).

piscina (Lat., 'basin'). A small bowl with a drain connected with the earth, usually in a niche in the wall on the south side of the altar; it is intended for the *ablutions of the priest's hands and of the *chalice and *paten at Mass.

Pisgah. The mountain or mountain range east of the R. *Jordan where *Moses was granted a sight of the Holy Land and the promise made that his descendants would possess it (Deut. 34: 1–4). It is usually identified with Ras Siyagha, NW of Mt Nebo.

Pistis Sophia. A 3rd-cent. Egyptian work which purports to record instruction given by Christ to certain disciples at the end of a 12-year sojourn on earth after the Resurrection. It relates the salvation of the personified 'Pistis Sophia' (i.e. 'Faith-Wisdom') from a demon named 'Self-Will'.

Pistoia, Synod of (1786). The synod met under the presidency of Scipione de' *Ricci, Bp. of Pistoia-Prato. It passed a number of *Gallican measures, and also decreed alterations in religious practices and condemned the use of Latin in Church services. The proposals aroused popular opposition as well as official displeasure. *Pius VI in 1794 condemned 85 of the Pistoian articles.

Pithou, Pierre (1539–96), theologian. Brought up as a *Calvinist, he became a RC in 1573. His treatise *Les Libertés de l'Église gallicane* (1594) formulated the leading principles of *Gallicanism for the first time.

Pius I, St (d. *c*.154), Bp. of Rome from *c*.140. According to the *Muratorian Canon, he was the brother of *Hermas. Nothing certain is known of his pontificate. Feast day, 11 July, suppressed in 1969.

Pius II (1405–64), Pope from 1458. Aeneas Sylvius or Enea Silvio de' Piccolomini was a leading humanist. At the Council of *Basle he supported the antipope Felix V against *Eugenius IV, and he advocated the *Conciliar Theory in his *Libellus Dialogorum de Concilii Auctoritate* (1440). In 1445 he was reconciled to Eugenius. He reformed his moral life and was ordained in 1446. From the fall of Constantinople in 1453 he worked for a *Crusade, and as Pope he subordinated all other interests to the war against the Turks. In his bull 'Execrabilis' (1460) he condemned the practice of appealing to a General Council. Louis XI repealed the *Pragmatic Sanction of Bourges in 1461, but many of the German princes remained in more or less open revolt against the Pope, invoking his former views in their support.

Pius IV (1499–1565), Pope from 1559. Probably his greatest achievement was the reassembling and successful conclusion of the Council of *Trent (1562–3), whose decrees he began to execute. He published a new *Index in 1564, imposed the 'Professio Fidei Tridentina' on all holders of ecclesiastical office, and reformed the *Sacred College.

Pius V, St (1504–72), Pope from 1566. He entered the *Dominican Order at the age of

14, and as Pope he continued to observe the ascetical practices of the religious life—the Papal custom of wearing a white cassock is said to derive from the colour of his Dominican habit. He worked zealously for the reform of the Church. He compelled bishops and clergy to accept the recommendations of the Council of *Trent, had the '*Roman Catechism' completed (1566), and reformed the *Breviary (1568) and *Missal (1570). In his struggle against the spread of the Reformation he made successful use of the *Inquisition in Italy, but his excommunication of Queen *Elizabeth I in 1570 aggravated the position of RCs in England. The Turks were defeated by the combined Papal, Spanish, and Venetian fleets at the Battle of *Lepanto in 1571. Feast day, 30 Apr. (formerly 5 May).

Pius VI (1717–99), Pope from 1775. In his reign Papal prestige was at a low ebb. *Febronian ideas were put into effect by Joseph II (see JOSEPHINISM), and a visit of the Pope to Vienna in 1782 was fruitless. In 1786 similar doctrines were adopted at the Synod of *Pistoia; 85 of the Pistoian articles were condemned by Pius in 1794. In 1791 he condemned the *Civil Constitution of the Clergy as schismatical and heretical and suspended all priests and prelates who had taken the civil oath; France then annexed the Papal territories of *Avignon and the Venaissin. Napoleon subsequently occupied the States of the Church; the occupation was ended only in 1797 by the surrender of territory and valuables. Pius died a prisoner at Valence.

Pius VII (1742–1823), Pope from 1800. By the *Concordat of 1801 Catholicism was restored in France, but the success of the arrangement was vitiated by the *Organic Articles, against which the Pope protested in vain. In 1808 a French army entered Rome. Pius considered himself a prisoner and refused to negotiate, and in 1809 the States of the Church were incorporated into the French Empire. Under pressure Pius, who had been taken under arrest to Fontainebleau, made extensive concessions to Napoleon in 1813, but he revoked them two months later. After Napoleon's fall he returned to Rome in 1814 and in the same year he re-established the *Jesuits. The Congress of Vienna (1815) restored the States of the Church, and new concordats

were concluded with various countries in the following years.

Pius IX, Bl (1792–1878), Pope from 1846. Elected because of his reputation as a supporter of liberal ideals, he lost popular favour and had to appeal to the European Catholic powers for help before he could return to Rome in 1850. His temporal power gradually decreased until, after the seizure of Rome by Victor Emmanuel in 1870, the Papacy was virtually deprived of all temporal sovereignty by the Law of *Guarantees (1871). There were, however, spiritual and ecclesiastical achievements. New dioceses and missionary centres were created and the hierarchy was restored in England (1850) and the *Netherlands (1853). Catholic devotion was stimulated by the definition of the doctrine of the *Immaculate Conception of the BVM in 1854. The most important event of his pontificate was the definition of Papal infallibility by the First *Vatican Council of 1869–70.

Pius X, St (1835–1914), Pope from 1903. From the beginning it was clear that he wished to be a religious rather than a political Pope. When the French government effected the separation of Church and State in 1905, Pius secured the independence of the Church in France from State interference at the price of material ruin (1906). In 1907 he condemned *Modernism and three years later introduced the anti-modernist oath. He undertook a series of difficult reforms, including the codification of *canon law (promulgated by *Benedict XV in 1917), *Breviary revision, and the restoration of *plainsong to its traditional place in the liturgy. His recommendation of daily Communion in 1905 laid the foundations of the modern *Liturgical Movement. Feast day, 21 Aug.

Pius XI (1857–1939), Pope from 1922. Achille Ambrogio Damiano Ratti made 'the restoration of all things in Christ' the chief object of his pontificate. To this end he issued a number of great encyclicals, including 'Casti Connubii' (1930), condemning *contraception, and 'Quadragesimo Anno' (1931), on social questions; and he gave his support to *Catholic Action. The *Jubilee of 1925 was the occasion of many *canonizations (including that of St *Teresa of Lisieux). The most important political event of his reign was the *Lateran Treaty

of 1929 (q.v.). His last years were overshadowed by the development of events in
Europe.

Pius XII (1876–1958), Pope from 1939.
Eugenio Pacelli entered the Papal Secretariat of State in 1901; in 1920 he became
Nuncio in Berlin, and in 1930 Papal Secretary of State. He was elected Pope six
months before the outbreak of the Second
World War. His alleged 'silence' in the face
of Nazi atrocities has been the subject of
criticism; his experience in dealing with
the German Government had probably
convinced him that a public stand would
provoke worse persecution. Throughout
the War (1939–45) he laboured to relieve
distress, especially among prisoners.

His encyclical 'Mediator Dei' (1947)
expressed sympathy with the desire to use
the vernacular in the liturgy and gave conditional support to the *Liturgical Movement. In 1951 he restored the *Paschal Vigil
Service to the evening, and in the following years he reordered the entire *Holy
Week liturgy. His relaxations of the
*Eucharistic Fast in 1953 and 1957 made
possible the widespread introduction of
*Evening Masses. Other events of his pon-
tificate included the opening of the way to a
more critical approach to biblical studies by
RC scholars (1943), the initiation of the
excavations under *St Peter's, Rome, and
the definition of the doctrine of the
*Assumption of the BVM. An instruction of
the *Holy Office in 1949 recognized that the
desire for unity of those engaged in the
*Ecumenical Movement was inspired by
the Holy Spirit and under strict conditions
allowed RC experts to join with other Christians in discussions on faith and morals.

Placebo (Lat., 'I will please'). A traditional
title for the *Vespers of the Dead, so called
from the word with which it used to open.

Placet. See EXEQUATUR.

plainsong. The traditional music of the
Latin rite, often known as Gregorian chant,
after St *Gregory the Great, although in its
surviving form it has little, if anything, to
do with him. It was paralleled in the early
Middle Ages by a number of other rites and
their music, including the *Ambrosian (or
Milanese), the ancient *Gallican, *Mozarabic, and *Old Roman. Its origins and relation to the Old Roman chant are disputed.

Plainsong itself is entirely monophonic,
though often subsequently used as the
basis for polyphonic compositions such as
*motets. Whether it has always been sung
in unmeasured time values is disputed. Its
tonal organization is based on a system of
modes, or scales corresponding to the
white notes on the piano and centred for
the most part on the notes D, E, F, or G. By
the 16th cent. the traditional plainsong had
been altered under the influence of
humanist ideals, for example by redistrib-
uting the notes so that lengthy melismas
fell on accentuated syllables. In the 19th
cent. a restoration of the medieval tradition
was pursued, largely through the work of
the monks of *Solesmes. After the Second
*Vatican Council plainsong ceased to be
the normal accompaniment of the Roman
rite, but the singing of plainsong to translated texts, used in the Anglican Communion from *Tractarian times, has
recently gained acceptance in the RC
Church.

Plantin, Christopher (c.1520–89), printer.
Brought up in France, in 1548 he settled in
Antwerp, where he soon built up the largest printing and publishing business in
Europe. His most celebrated production
was the Antwerp *Polyglot Bible (1569–72).
He and his successors printed a large number of editions of the *Missal, *Breviary,
and other liturgical books, in virtue of a
monopoly granted to him within the
dominions of the King of Spain.

Platina, Bartolomeo (1421–81), Italian
humanist. While *Vatican librarian, he
compiled his 'Lives of the Popes' (1479). The
juxtaposition of a reference to Halley's
comet and mention of the prayers and
curses of *Callistus III against the Turks in
1456 gave rise to the fable that the Pope had
excommunicated the comet.

Plato (427–347 BC), Greek philosopher. He
was a pupil of Socrates. After Socrates' execution (399), he left Athens. Some time
after 388 he returned and established a
school on the outskirts of the city near the
grove sacred to Academus (hence the
'Academy'). Apart from one brief interlude,
he seems to have spent the last 40 years of
his life at the Academy.

With the exception of a small collection
of Letters, Plato's writings are in the form
of Dialogues. Socrates is often the main

speaker, with various critics or pupils, after whom the different Dialogues are named, taking part in the discussion.

In the earlier Dialogues the main emphasis is ethical. They insist that the cultivation of mind and will, 'goodness of soul', is the chief business of life; that this is attained by a rational insight into the nature of goodness, truth, and beauty; that morality and the claims of the enlightened conscience are to be respected in political life; and that the rational moral personality is created by the 'recollection' of what the soul knows of these values. Since the soul naturally aims at what it believes to be good, wrongdoing is the pursuit of a falsely conceived good.

These doctrines are based on a metaphysic which is developed especially in the later Dialogues. This contrasts the world of sense and everyday experience with the true or higher world of 'Ideas' (or better 'Forms'). These 'Forms' are 'present to' individual entities, and by grasping the eternal Forms and participating in them the soul attains its true well-being and is lifted above the flux of 'becoming'. But the highest value, the 'Form of the Good' remains mysterious.

Plato's main discussions of theology in the narrower sense are in the *Timaeus* and Book 10 of the *Laws*. The *Timaeus* describes how the divine *Demiurge brings the world into being, how He makes it as an image of an eternal archetype, and how He enables it to share in His perfection by putting into it mind and soul. The *Laws*, Book 10, embodies the earliest known exposition of *natural theology, namely a form of the *cosmological argument based on the belief that all motions ultimately require at their head a 'perfectly good soul'. It remains obscure how Plato related the highest of the Forms to God as the Supreme Soul. In the *Timaeus* the Forms are the thoughts of God, but, since God also created the universe after the pattern of the Forms, He would seem in some sense subordinate to them. It was, however, only among the more theologically interested Platonists of a later generation that the problem became a matter of debate.

Platonism. *Plato's doctrines had a wide following in the Hellenistic age and made an impact on later Judaism. In the 3rd cent. AD a recasting of Plato's system by *Plotinus (*Neoplatonism) was developed by *Porphyry in conscious opposition to Christianity.

The beginnings of an interweaving of Platonism with Christian thought go back to *Clement of Alexandria and *Origen. More important for Christian theology was the influence of Platonic doctrines on St *Augustine, whose authority did much to secure for many Platonic notions a permanent place in Latin Christianity. Henceforth the Platonic Forms were regularly interpreted as the creative thoughts of God. The relevance of Platonism for Christian mysticism was appreciated by *Dionysius the Pseudo-Areopagite and other spiritual writers of both E. and W. The Renaissance led to a revival of interest in Plato himself, and Platonic influences have continued to play an important part in Christian philosophy, especially in England. On the Continent Protestant orthodoxy, with its distrust of natural reason, has commonly been hostile to Platonism and in the 20th cent. there was theological criticism of Greek metaphysics.

plenary indulgence. In modern RC theology an *indulgence (q.v.) which is held to remit the whole of the temporal punishment due to an individual's sins. As its efficacy is believed to depend on the perfection of the soul's disposition (of which no one can be certain), there is always an element of doubt whether a soul has profited to the full by a particular plenary indulgence. The earliest known example of the issue of a plenary indulgence was the promise of *Urban II that all *penances incurred by *Crusaders who confessed their sins should be remitted.

Plethon, Georgius Gemistus. See GEMISTUS PLETHON, GEORGIUS.

Pliny. Gaius Plinius Caecilius Secundus (*c.*61–*c.*112), Roman senator and man of letters. As governor of Bithynia and Pontus, he asked the Emp. Trajan for guidance as to how to deal with Christians. Of those accused before him of Christianity, he had executed those who had confessed or refused to sacrifice to the gods or emperor. But some had proved their apostasy by taking this test, and Pliny did not know whether the offence consisted in the name alone or in criminal acts supposed to be inherent in the Christian cult. Trajan replied that apostates should not be punished and that Christians should not be 'sought out'. See also PERSECUTIONS, EARLY CHRISTIAN.

Plotinus (c.205–70), *Neoplatonist philosopher and mystic. In 244 he established a school at Rome. His writings were published after his death by *Porphyry.

The main concern of Plotinus' thought is with the relations between unity and multiplicity. At the summit of the hierarchy of beings is the One or the Good, the first principle. Beneath it is the divine Mind, which is the world of ideas. Next comes Soul, the third member of the Plotinian Triad, and the intermediary between the intelligible and the material world. The World Soul is a particular soul, part of the hypostasis Soul on the same level as individual souls. It creates and orders the universe which other souls share in animating. All souls share in the unity of Soul and its capacity for contemplation. This is the most perfect activity, for by it souls can attain union with God. To reach this end the soul must pass not only beyond attachment to sensible things and discursive reasoning but beyond the highest intellectual contemplation. In Plotinus' system, union is reached by the natural power of reason which the soul receives in its creation, whereas in Catholic teaching it is the work of Divine grace; Plotinus nevertheless indirectly influenced Christian thought.

Plumstead Peculiars. See PECULIAR PEOPLE.

Plunkett (or Plunket), St Oliver (1625–81), RC Abp. of *Armagh from 1669. During the persecutions that began in 1673 he remained in Ireland and in the fury engendered by the *Titus Oates Plot he was arrested (1679), tried in London, and executed for treason. Feast day, 11 July.

pluralism, religious. See THEOLOGY OF RELIGIONS.

Plymouth Brethren. A Christian religious body so named because its first centre in England was established by J. N. *Darby at Plymouth in 1830. Their teaching combines elements from *Calvinism and *Pietism, and emphasis has often been laid on an expected *Millennium. They renounce many secular occupations, allowing only those compatible with NT standards (e.g. medicine). Controversies on the human nature of Christ and subsequently on Church government led to a division in 1849 between the 'Open Brethren' and the 'Exclusive Brethren'. Their numbers declined sharply in the later 20th cent.

Pneumatomachi, heretics who denied the full Godhead of the Holy Spirit. They came to the fore in 373, when *Eustathius of Sebaste became their leader. They were condemned by Pope *Damasus in 374. At its peak, c.380, the sect contained a more conservative section which, while rejecting the Divinity of the Holy Spirit, accepted the consubstantiality of the Son, and a radical party which rejected this also. The Pneumatomachi were anathematized at the Council of *Constantinople in 381 and soon disappeared.

Poimandres. The first treatise in the *Hermetic writings (q.v.). It describes a vision seen under the guidance of Poimandres, a semi-divine being, and treats of the creation of the universe and man, the union of spirit with matter after the Fall, and the method of redemption by knowledge. There are some parallels with the NT.

Poiret, Pierre (1646–1719), French Protestant spiritual writer. He was an admirer of Antoinette *Bourignon. His *Bibliotheca mysticorum* (1708) contains out-of-the-way information on minor writers on mystical subjects.

Poissy, Colloquy of. A conference held in 1561 at Poissy (near Paris) between the French bishops and the Protestant ministers led by T. *Beza. It prepared the way for the edict of 1562 which gave official recognition to French Protestants.

Poland, Christianity in. Poland received Christianity in the 10th cent., probably from Moravia. In 966 Prince Mieczysław I was baptized and in 1000 Gniezno became a metropolitan see. In the early 15th cent. some of the nobility supported the *Hussites, and in the 16th cent. the *Reformation also made headway. *Calvinism was the strongest influence, though *Lutheranism developed in German areas, and the country became a haven for exiled *Bohemian Brethren and *Socinians.

Religious tension grew but by the Confederation of Warsaw in 1573 mutual toleration was secured. In 1595 the Ruthenian Church (see UKRAINIAN CHURCHES) renounced communion with *Constantinople and submitted to Rome, and soon afterwards the *Armenians in Poland accepted *Uniat status. In the 17th cent. the RC majority made toleration almost a dead letter. The partition of Poland between Russia, Austria, and Prussia, completed in 1795, had serious consequences for the RC Church. The Russians put restrictions on RCs and in 1831 compelled the Uniat Easterns to give up their communion with Rome. With the independence of Poland in 1919 the influence of the RC Church revived, though the Orthodox retained their hold in many eastern parts. Both Orthodox and RC Churches suffered under German and Russian occupation in 1939–45, and under the Communist-controlled government established in 1945. The election of a Polish Pope in 1978 and RC opposition were factors in the collapse of the Communist regime in 1989.

Pole, Reginald (1500–58), Abp. of *Canterbury. Of the blood royal by his mother, Pole declined *Henry VIII's offer of the see of *York or *Winchester in 1530, and wrote a book censuring the King's conduct. *Paul III made him a cardinal in 1536 and in 1538 sent him on a fruitless mission to persuade Spain and France to break with England. On *Edward VI's death in 1553, Pole was appointed legate in England. He formally absolved Parliament from schism and presided over a synod of both *Convocations. In 1556 he was ordained priest and consecrated Abp. of Canterbury two days later. With the outbreak of war between Pope *Paul IV and *Philip II of Spain, Queen *Mary became the Pope's enemy and he cancelled Pole's legation.

Polish National Church. See OLD CATHOLICS (3).

Polycarp, St (traditionally *c*.69–*c*.155, but possibly slightly later), Bp. of *Smyrna. He seems to have been the leading Christian figure in the Roman province of Asia in the middle of the 2nd cent. A letter addressed to him by St *Ignatius has survived, as well as his own 'Ep. to Philippians', which has many echoes of the NT. He went to Rome to discuss the date of keeping *Easter; it was

agreed that each Church should maintain its own custom and that Asia should continue the *Quartodeciman practice. Soon after his return to Smyrna he was arrested; proclaiming that he had served Christ for 86 years, he refused to recant his faith and was burnt to death. Feast day, 23 Feb. (in the W. formerly 26 Jan.).

Polycrates (2nd cent.), Bp. of *Ephesus. He was the leading *Quartodeciman who opposed Pope *Victor in his attempts to secure that *Easter should be uniformly celebrated on a Sunday.

Polyglot Bibles. A 'Polyglot Bible' is a single Bible containing the text in several languages. Such Bibles were issued especially in the 16th and 17th cents. The most celebrated is the '*Complutensian Polyglot' (1522), which in parallel columns printed the OT in Hebrew, Latin, and Greek, and the NT in Greek and Latin.

Pomponazzi, Pietro (1462–1525), Italian Renaissance philosopher. He held that it was possible to demonstrate by natural reason the mortality of the human soul, and that the only sense in which one could legitimately speak of its immateriality and immortality was in reference to its capacity for reflective knowledge and conceiving universal concepts. He argued that these doctrines need cause no offence to Christians, since they were merely the deductions of human reason and were transcended by the supernatural revelation made to the Church.

Pomponia Graecina (1st cent.), wife of Aulus Plautius, the conqueror of Britain, thought by some to have been an early convert to Christianity.

Pontifex Maximus (Lat., 'Supreme Pontiff'). Originally a pagan title for the chief priest at Rome, from the 15th cent. it became a regular title of honour for Popes.

Pontifical. The liturgical book of the W. Church containing the prayers and ceremonies for rites used by a bishop, e.g. *Confirmation and *Ordinations; it does not, however, contain the Pontifical Mass. A Pontifical probably put together at Mainz in the 10th cent. gained acceptance throughout Europe and was received at Rome; the books based on this gave place in the 14th cent. to a clearly arranged private compilation made *c.*1293–5 by William *Durandus, Bp. of Mende. His work was the basis of the authoritative edition issued by *Clement VIII in 1596. A new Pontifical (less complete in its coverage) was issued in 1978; some additional texts for the revised rites have appeared since.

pontificals. The insignia of the episcopal order which are or may be worn by prelates when celebrating Pontifical Mass. They include, *gloves, *dalmatic, *ring, *pectoral cross, *crosier, and *mitre.

Pontius Pilate. See PILATE, PONTIUS.

Poor Clares, the 'Second Order' of St *Francis, founded by him and St *Clare between 1212 and 1214. It received its first rule in 1219; a second one in 1247, allowing some mitigations; and a third one (1253) which included the right to practise corporate as well as personal poverty. This was not accepted by all convents, and in 1263 Pope Urban IV sanctioned a milder one; those nuns who follow this are known as 'Urbanists'. In the 15th cent. St Colette restored the principle of poverty in her houses (known as *Colettines). The *Capuchin Reform of the 16th cent. added the Capuchinesses to the family of Poor Clares. Most Poor Clare convents are strictly contemplative; they are regarded as the most austere women's Order in the RC Church.

Poor Men of Lyons. The name under which the *Waldenses (q.v.) were condemned in 1184.

Poore, Richard (d. 1237), Bp. of *Salisbury from 1217 to 1228. In 1219 he removed his see from Old Sarum to its present site and in 1220 he began building the present cathedral. He drew up the Salisbury *Customary and probably gave the 'Use of Salisbury' (q.v.) its final form. The diocesan statutes which he drew up were widely influential in other dioceses. In 1228 he was translated to *Durham.

Pope (Lat. *papa*, 'father'). In the W. Church the title is now restricted to the Bp. of Rome in respect of his capacity as supreme head on earth of the universal Church; in early times it was used of any bishop. In the E. it was apparently confined to the Patr. of *Alexandria, who is still so styled, but from the 6th cent. the chancery at *Constantinople normally kept it for the Bp. of Rome.

Pope, William Burt (1822–1903), *Wesleyan theologian. He was tutor at Didsbury College, Manchester (1867–86). His *Compendium of Christian Theology* (1875) contains a sympathetic defence of the Methodist doctrine of Christian *perfection.

Popery. A hostile designation for the doctrines and practices of the RC Church.

Popery, the Declaration against. The declaration imposed by the Parliament Act 1678 requiring all Members of Parliament (except the Duke of York) to denounce *transubstantiation, the Mass, and invocation of *saints as idolatrous. A less exacting oath was substituted in 1778.

Popish Plot. The supposed plot to murder *Charles II which T. *Oates (q.v.) claimed that he had discovered in 1678.

poppy heads. In ecclesiology, the ornamental finials at the tops of bench-ends, in form somewhat resembling a fleur de lys. They became common in the 15th cent.

Porette, Margaret (d. 1310), also 'Porete', author of *The Mirror of Simple Souls*. Probably a native of Hainault, she was burnt at the stake in Paris for continuing to circulate a book already condemned as heretical. The *Mirror* had long been known and circulated as harmlessly pious, but Porette's authorship was only recognized in 1965.

Porphyry (*c.*232–*c.*303), *Neoplatonist philosopher. It is possible that he was at one time a Christian. He was convinced of Neoplatonist principles by *Plotinus, whom he met in Rome in 262.

His work 'Against the Christians' was condemned to be burnt in 448, and survives only in quotations in works written mainly to refute it. He seems to have observed a certain restraint in his remarks about Christ, whom he admired as a teacher, but he considered the apparent failure of His life proof that He was not divine. He launched bitter invective against the Apostles and leaders of the Church, which he finally condemned for its lack of patriotism in resisting the religious revival fostered by the Emps. *Decius and Aurelian. His numerous philosophical works are important for their clear exposition, development, and preservation of much that was obscurely put in Plotinus and others.

He also wrote a Life of Plotinus and edited his works.

Porta Santa. The Italian for *Holy Door.

porter. See DOORKEEPER.

Porteus, Beilby (1731–1808), Bp. of London from 1787. He was of American descent. He identified himself with the practical ideals of the rising *Evangelical school, and he promoted mission work among Negro slaves in America. He was also a keen *Sabbatarian.

Portiuncula. A small chapel in the plain below *Assisi. In it St *Francis received his vocation, and during his lifetime it was the headquarters of his Order. The chapel and the cell in which he died are now enclosed by an imposing 16th-cent. church, largely rebuilt after an earthquake in 1832. The chapel gives its name to the 'Portiuncula *Indulgence', said to have been granted by *Honorius III in 1216.

Port-Royal, Convent of, *Jansenist centre. A convent of *Cistercian nuns was founded in 1204 at Port-Royal, a marshy site SW of Paris (hence 'Port-Royal-des-Champs'). In 1602 (Jacqueline Marie) Angélique *Arnauld was appointed abbess; converted to a new view of her responsibilities in 1608, she undertook far-reaching reforms. In 1625 the community moved to a new house in Paris ('Port-Royal-de-Paris'), and in 1627 it was removed from the jurisdiction of *Citeaux. In 1635 S. Zamet, Bp. of Langres, handed over the direction of Port-Royal to *Saint-Cyran, Jansen's associate; after his death in 1643 his influence was maintained by Antoine *Arnauld, the spokesman of what came to be called Jansenism. From 1637 some of Saint-Cyran's converts came to live near the community as 'Solitaires', and by 1648 their labours had rendered Port-Royal-des-Champs habitable enough to receive some of the nuns. For a time the two houses existed with a single conventual organization, but in 1669 they were separated, Port-Royal-de-Paris being given over to the nuns who had signed the anti-Jansenist formulary of *Alexander VII, while the Jansenist majority were established in Port-Royal-des-Champs. In 1705 *Clement XI condemned those who used mental reservations in signing the formulary; the nuns refused to accept this new definition and were finally dispersed in 1709.

Portugal, Christianity in. The independent history of Portugal began in the 12th cent., when the country became free of Castile-León and a self-governing vassal of the Papacy. There was subsequently a nationalist anti-Papal movement, but in the *Great Schism anti-Castilian feeling kept the Portuguese bishops on the side of *Urban VI and his successors. The reform of the bishops and clergy at the end of the 15th cent. anticipated the Reformation, which had no influence in the country. Especially from the mid-16th cent., Portuguese missionaries were active in the territories conquered by Portugal in Africa, America, and the East; mass conversions were secured, but only in *Brazil is there much trace of this activity.

Between 1580 and 1640 Portugal was annexed by Spain, but Portuguese independence was recognized by the Papacy in 1669. In the 18th cent. the policies of the Marquis de Pombal led to the secularization of higher education and the expulsion of the *Jesuits (1759). After the triumph of the liberals in the civil war of 1832–4, Portugal was further secularized; the property of the religious orders was confiscated and no novices allowed. The RC Church was disestablished in Portugal in 1911 and in the Portuguese colonies in 1913. In 1933 the religious orders were allowed to return and a new concordat between the Portuguese government and the Vatican was signed in 1940. The importance of the Church in national life is considerable.

The Lusitanian Church of Portugal, a small episcopal body dating from c.1867, was integrated into the Anglican Communion in 1980.

Porvoo Agreement. See REUNION.

Positive Theology. The branch of theology which treats of matters of historic and particular fact, custom, or enactment, as opposed to '*Natural Theology', which deals with religious principles and laws of universal validity. In RC theology, also historical theology as contrasted with speculative theology.

Positivism. In its original and narrower sense, the system of the French thinker Auguste *Comte (q.v.), which confined intellectual inquiry to observable ('positive') facts and their relations, and eschewed all consideration of ultimate issues, including those of philosophy and theology. The term has come to be used in a wider sense for any form of philosophical outlook which rejects metaphysics, especially when the physical sciences are regarded as offering the norm of knowledge. Such an outlook was developed by the 'Vienna Circle', formed in 1922, which gave the name 'Logical Positivism' to its doctrines. This has had a lasting effect on 20th-cent. philosophy and indirectly on theology by its demand for verifiability as a criterion of any statement's being meaningful.

postcommunion. In the Roman Mass the prayer which follows after the Communion.

postil. The word, which in the Middle Ages was used of a gloss on a Scriptural text, came to be applied especially to a homily on the Gospel or Epistle for the day or to a book of such homilies.

Postlapsarianism. See SUBLAPSARIANISM.

postulant. One who is undergoing a stage of testing as a candidate for a religious order before admission to the *novitiate.

Potamius (d. after 359), the earliest known Bp. of Lisbon. He originally defended the orthodox *Nicene position, but at least for a time he aligned himself with the *Arianizing policy of the Emp. Constantius II.

Pothinus, St (c.87–177), first Bp. of Lyons. He was probably a native of Asia Minor and a disciple of St *Polycarp. He was among those martyred in 177. Feast day, 2 June.

Potter, John (c.1674–1747), Abp. of *Canterbury from 1737. As Bp. of *Oxford, he ordained J. *Wesley. He produced a fine edition of *Clement of Alexandria (1715).

Powers. According to medieval angelology, the sixth order of angels in the celestial hierarchy. The word is also used of any celestial being who exercises control or influence over other parts of creation.

Praedestinatus. A treatise probably composed at Rome during the papacy of Sixtus III (432–40), and directed against the extremer forms of the doctrine of *predestination then being taught under the influence of writings of St *Augustine.

Praemunire. The title of statutes (first passed in 1353, 1365, and 1393), which were designed to protect rights claimed by the English Crown against encroachment by the Papacy. The name can denote the statutes, the offence, the writ, and the punishment. The statute of 1353 forbade the withdrawal from England of cases which should be decided in the king's courts. All the statutes were repealed in 1967. .

Praepositinus (c.1140–c.1210), theologian and liturgist. Probably a native of Cremona, he studied at *Paris and later taught theology there. In 1194 he was invited to take charge of the cathedral school at Mainz. From 1206 to 1209 he was head of the Parisian schools as chancellor of the cathedral. His main theological work, his *Summa Theologica*, follows the pattern of *Peter Lombard's *Sentences*. His *Tractatus de Officiis*, on the liturgical year, was the main source of the standard work of William *Durandus. He was one of the ablest of the Parisian theologians of the late 12th century.

pragmatic sanction. The term was originally used in later Roman law for an arrangement defining the limits of the sovereign power of a prince, especially in the matter of the royal succession. The Pragmatic Sanction of Bourges, issued by the French clergy in 1438, was a statement of *Gallicanist principles; it upheld the right of the French Church to administer its temporal property independently of the Papacy and disallowed Papal nominations to vacant benefices. It was superseded by the Concordat of *Bologna (1516).

Pragmatism. A system of belief based on the principle that every truth has practical consequences and that these are a test of its truthfulness. It justifies and explains religions according as they satisfy psychological criteria and generate suitable values.

Prassede, St. See PRAXEDES, ST.

Praxeas (fl. c.200), a heretic against whom *Tertullian wrote a treatise. He is said to have turned the Pope (*Victor or *Zephyrinus) against the *Montanists and proclaimed himself a leader of the

'*Patripassian Monarchians', i.e. those who upheld the unity of the Godhead even at the cost of declaring that God the Father suffered. He recanted.

Praxedes, St (1st–2nd cent.), also **Prassede**, martyr. According to her (spurious) *acta*, she was a Roman virgin who sheltered Christians during the persecution under *Marcus Aurelius. Feast day, 21 July.

prayer. 'Prayer, properly speaking, is a petition which we make to God for the things which pertain to our salvation; but it is also taken in another, broader sense to mean any raising of the heart to God' (*Luis of Granada). Prayer in the sense of petition is a universal phenomenon, wherever people believe they are dependent on some higher power outside their control. Until well into the Middle Ages no other meaning was normally envisaged. The extended meaning, taking in all sorts of 'raising of the heart to God', dates from the late Middle Ages, and in some circles there has been a tendency to devalue petitionary prayer.

In antiquity prayer usually involved spoken words and gestures. The Church soon recognized that prayer need not be spoken aloud; the medieval monastic tradition increasingly stressed silent prayer, which became common among the laity also. Prayer may be offered privately by an individual or publicly in a formal act of worship. Christ taught His disciples to call God 'Father' and He taught them what to pray, though Christian tradition is unanimous in not confining prayer to the words of the *Lord's Prayer. According to *Origen, prayer should be made only to the Father through Christ, but prayer to Christ has been common from early times and subsequently prayer to the Holy Spirit was introduced. To the conceptual problem that God knows what man needs better than man does and from the beginning of time has already determined what He will do, St *Thomas Aquinas provides the classic answer: in prayer man is not trying to force God's will; he is submitting his desires to Him; he does not pray in the hope of changing God's mind, but in order to co-operate with Him in bringing about certain effects which He has foreordained; prayer is a secondary cause, itself caused by God.

The early monastic tradition stressed the need for purity in prayer: in prayer the mind must be fixed on God without distraction. To facilitate this concentration short, intense prayer was recommended. Some E. writers recommend that a single formula of prayer, preferably containing the name of Jesus, should be adopted and used all the time. In the W. the tradition of short intense prayer persisted until near the end of the Middle Ages, but from the 15th cent. longer regular periods of private prayer were sought. From the 14th cent. *contemplation and *meditation are sometimes treated as parts or forms of prayer. Thereafter various kinds of prayer came to be identified, such as 'discursive prayer', 'affective prayer', and 'contemplative prayer', and these are sometimes systematized as successive stages of prayer. Praise, thanksgiving, and confession also came to be regularly seen as parts of prayer.

Prayer to the BVM and other saints is attested early. It is theologically different from prayer to God, being properly a request for the prayers of the saints. Its legitimacy is denied by Protestants.

Prayer Book. A common designation for the Book of *Common Prayer.

prayers for the dead. See DEAD, PRAYERS FOR THE.

Preachers, Order of. See DOMINICAN ORDER.

preaching. Preaching has always been regarded as an essential part of Christian ministry, though the emphasis placed on it in different traditions has varied. In the Anglican view of ministry preaching has taken an equal place with the administration of the *sacraments. In the *Calvinist tradition it has been accepted as the principal work of a minister, and in Calvinist churches the *pulpit has been given pride of place in the centre of the building. The RC Church has at times subordinated preaching to the administration of the sacraments, but the Second *Vatican Council (1962–5) declared that the homily (or sermon) was an integral part not only of the Eucharist but also of the other sacraments, and that preaching was central to the ministry of priests and bishops.

Preaching is speech under the authority of God, and the communication of that authority is as important to preaching as speech itself. The *Prophets of the OT saw themselves as God's spokesmen, and through their work the idea of God relating to His people through His word became an important part of the OT tradition. In the NT Jn. used that tradition when the birth of Jesus Christ was described as 'the Word was made flesh and dwelt among us' (1: 14). Christ is depicted in the Gospels as one who spoke with authority; after His death and resurrection the Apostles are shown exercising a similar but dependent ministry: dependent in that the content of their preaching is witness to Him.

Since the 1st cent. the work of preaching has been mainly, though not exclusively, directed to the Church, and its purpose to strengthen the Christian community. It is closely related to Scripture and often takes the form of an exposition of a Biblical passage. Its effective performance is usually seen as demanding an educated clergy. The influence of preachers often extends far beyond their immediate hearers.

prebendary. The title of the holder of a (now normally honorary) *cathedral benefice. In the Middle Ages the endowment of most non-monastic cathedrals was divided into separate portions, known as 'prebends', each designed for the support of a single member of the *chapter, and their holders became known as 'prebendaries'.

precentor. In *cathedrals, the cleric responsible for the direction of the choral services. In those of the 'Old Foundation' he is a member of the chapter; in most of those of the 'New Foundation' he is a *minor canon or chaplain.

precept. In moral theology, a matter of obligation, as contrasted with a 'counsel', which is only a matter of persuasion. For Precepts of the Church, see COMMANDMENTS OF THE CHURCH.

preceptory. Among the Knights *Templar a community established on one of their provincial estates.

preces feriales (Lat., 'ferial prayers'). A short series of prayers consisting of *Kyrie Eleison, the *Lord's Prayer, and versicles and responses, which used to be said on *ferial (non-festal) days in the Divine *Office of the W. Church.

Precious Blood, devotion to the. The Blood of Christ, shed during the Passion, has been honoured and regarded as of redeeming virtue since the Apostolic Age, especially in connection with the Eucharist. Various churches have claimed to possess particles of it, which have been greatly venerated. Feasts in honour of the Precious Blood were celebrated by various religious orders in the 19th cent., and in 1849 the Feast was extended to the whole RC Church. It was then observed on the first Sunday of July; on 1 July from 1914 until it was suppressed in 1969.

Precisian. A name used of the *Puritans in the 16th and 17th cents.

predella. (1) The platform on the uppermost of the steps to an altar, on which the priest formerly stood when celebrating Mass; (2) the lowest piece of a *reredos.

predestinarianism. The doctrine according to which human free will and cooperation are eliminated from the process of salvation by a thorough-going application of the principle of *predestination.

predestination. The Divine decree according to which certain persons are infallibly guided to eternal salvation. It is presupposed in the Gospels, e.g. Mt. 20: 23, where Christ is reported as saying that sitting on His right and left is reserved 'for them for whom it hath been prepared of my Father'. In Rom. 8: 28–30 St *Paul traces the process of salvation of those 'that are called according to His purpose' from foreknowledge and predestination to vocation, justification, and glorification.

In the W. St *Augustine developed this teaching in the *Pelagian controversy. For him the mystery of predestination consists in the inaccessibility to the human mind of the reasons for the Divine choice, which, nevertheless, is made in perfect justice. It contains the gift of final perseverance and depends not on human acceptance, but on the eternal decree of God; it is therefore infallible, without, however, according to Augustine, violating free will. In S. Gaul his teaching was questioned by John *Cassian and other *Semipelagians, but the Augustinian position was accepted at the Council of *Orange (529). In the 9th cent. *Gottschalk, basing himself on Augustine, taught a double predestination of some to eternal blessedness and others to eternal fire. This doctrine was condemned by the

Synod of *Quiercy in 849. Medieval teaching was based on Augustine but took account of the Greek doctrine represented by St *John of Damascus. He held that God 'antecedently' wills the universal salvation of all men, but, in consequence of their sins, He wills eternal punishment for some. Various attempts to reconcile this view with the Divine omnipotence and the efficacy of *grace were made by the *Schoolmen.

Predestination emerged again as a significant issue at the *Reformation. M. *Luther revived the full Augustinian doctrine which he combined with a new stress on the depravity of man. In 1525 he maintained that in an act of Divine sovereignty both the elect and the reprobate are predestined without reference to their merits or demerits. The Formula of *Concord in 1577, however, embodied the position of the *Philippists, who, while accepting the total depravity of man after the *Fall and *justification by faith alone, denied that double predestination followed from either. This has remained *Lutheran doctrine. The doctrine of double predestination, however, became a cornerstone of the *Calvinist system. Though rejected by the *Arminians, it was imposed by the Synod of *Dort (1618–9) and by the *Westminster Assembly (1647), which declared that at least after the Fall God does not will the salvation of all men and that Christ died only for the elect. Post-Tridentine RC theologians in their formulations of the doctrine of predestination have tried to preserve the element of human consent and the reality of the Divine will that 'all men should be saved'.

See also ELECTION.

Preface. In the Eucharist of the W. Church, the words which introduce the central part of the service. It begins with the '*Sursum Corda' and ends with the '*Sanctus'. It is mainly an ascription of praise to the Creator offered in union with angels. Part of it varies with the feast observed.

prelate. The term was originally of wide connotation, but it came to be restricted to Church officials of high rank. In the C of E it is reserved for bishops; in the RC Church it is also applied to a variety of officers attached to the Roman curia. See also PERSONAL PRELATURE.

Premonstratensian Canons, also 'Norber-

tines' and, in England, 'White Canons' from the colour of their habit. An Order founded by St *Norbert at Prémontré, near Laon, in 1120. The basis of their rule is the so-called Rule of St *Augustine, with additional austerities. The Order spread over W. Europe and became powerful in *Hungary. It became nearly extinct in the early 19th cent., but has re-established its influence and is especially strong in *Belgium.

Preparation, Day of. A Jewish name for Friday, i.e. the day preceding, and therefore employed in preparation for, the *Sabbath. The title may perhaps also have been used for the day before certain other great feasts, e.g. the *Passover. All four Gospels record that the Crucifixion took place on the day of preparation.

Presanctified, Mass of the. A shortened form of the Eucharistic Liturgy without consecration, a *Host consecrated at a previous Mass being used for Communion. In the E. Church it is ordinarily celebrated on the *Wednesdays and *Fridays in *Lent and on Monday, Tuesday, and Wednesday of *Holy Week. Here the Liturgy of the Presanctified is a complex service combined with *Vespers and using a previously *intincted Host. At the *Great Entrance the consecrated elements are carried in procession and placed on the altar; after the *Lord's Prayer, the priest communicates himself and then the people. In the Latin Church the Mass of the Presanctified (no longer officially so called) is restricted to *Good Friday. After the *Veneration of the Cross, the ciborium, containing Hosts consecrated on *Maundy Thursday, is brought from the Altar of *Repose to the High Altar; the priest says various prayers and then communicates himself and the people.

presbyter. The earliest organization of the Christian Churches in Palestine resembled that of the Jewish synagogues, each of which was administered by a board of 'elders' (πρεσβύτεροι, i.e. 'presbyters'), and Acts 14: 23 has St *Paul appointing presbyters in the Churches he founded. At first the presbyters seem to have been identical with the 'overseers' (ἐπίσκοποι, i.e. 'bishops'), but from the 2nd cent. the title of bishop is normally confined to the presidents of these local councils of presbyters, and as such 'bishops' came to be distinguished from the presbyters, who were held to derive their authority by delegation from the bishops. See also BISHOP, ORDERS, and PRIEST.

Presbyterianism. A form of ecclesiastical polity in which the Church is governed by *presbyters. Its proponents in the 16th and 17th cent. regarded it not as an innovation but a rediscovery of the apostolic model found in the NT. Most Presbyterians now recognize that the early Church had episcopal and congregational elements and that Presbyterianism has no claim to be the only permissible Church polity.

The normal pattern of government of Presbyterian Churches is a hierarchy of interrelated bodies: the Session (*Kirk session), *Presbytery, Synod, and *General Assembly. These are all made up of ministers and *elders. The elders are elected representatives of the congregation, but their office is recognized as one of the four ministries of the Church, and they may participate in preaching, teaching, and administering the sacraments. Ministers are elected by the people, but their ordination is an act of the Presbytery. Most Presbyterian Churches ordain men and women both as ministers and elders. All Presbyterian Churches acknowledge the Bible as the supreme standard of faith and practice, and many still accept the *Westminster Confession and the two *Westminster Catechisms as their chief subordinate standards. The United Presbyterian Church in the *United States of America in 1967 adopted a *Book of Confessions* as its doctrinal base and this was accepted by the Presbyterian Church (USA) when that came into being in 1983. It includes various *Calvinist documents, among them the *Barmen Declaration, and a new formula of confession drawn up in 1967. A 'Brief Statement of Faith' was added in 1991. Presbyterian worship emphasizes hearing and *preaching the Word of God, but there was an increased appreciation of the sacraments in the late 20th cent., and the Lord's Supper is now commonly celebrated seven to 12 times a year.

Presbyterian Churches are found throughout the world. There are concentrations in the USA, *Scotland (the only Presbyterian State Church), *Hungary, the *Netherlands, Northern *Ireland, Switzerland, *France, the Cameroon, and *Korea. The World Presbyterian Alliance (founded in 1875) was merged in 1970 with the International Congregational Council to form the *World Alliance of Reformed Churches. In the USA there have been unions of Presbyterian Churches, notably in 1958 and 1983, the latter bringing together streams of Presbyterianism divided since the Civil War. Presbyterian Churches have also been involved in regional unions with different denominations in *Canada, the *Philippines, *Zambia, *Australia, *North and *South India, and *Pakistan. In 1972 the Presbyterian Church of England united with the greater part of the Congregational Church of England and Wales to form the *United Reformed Church.

Presbytery. (1) The sanctuary or eastern part of the chancel of a church beyond the choir. (2) The residence of (especially) RC priests. (3) According to current *Presbyterian usage, the Church court which has oversight of and jurisdiction over a particular area. A Presbyterian minister is ordained by it (the ministerial members only joining in the imposition of hands) and is subject to it, and it is responsible for the oversight of public worship.

Presentation of Christ in the Temple. In the BCP an alternative name for the feast of the *Purification of the BVM or *Candlemas (2 Feb.). It is the sole title in CW and some other modern Anglican liturgies.

Presentation of the BVM. A feast kept on 21 Nov. to commemorate the presentation of the BVM in the Temple when three years old, as related in the 'Book of *James'.

Presentation of the Lord. The title given in the RC Church since 1969 to the feast of *Candlemas.

Prester John (i.e. 'Presbyter' John), a legendary medieval Christian king of Asia. The story of a *Nestorian priest-king who had defeated the Muslims and would bring help to the Holy Land spread in Europe from the mid-12th cent. In 1177 *Alexander III wrote a letter 'to the King of the Indies, the most holy priest'; this was supposed to be addressed to Prester John, but it may have been meant for a real king of *Ethiopia, which was often confused with India. Another theory identifies Prester John with the Chinese prince, Gor Khan, who defeated the Sultan of Persia in 1141.

Price, Richard (1723–91), Nonconformist minister, moral and political philosopher. In *A Review of the Principal Questions in Morals* (1758) he defended a view of ethical action which had affinities with the teaching later expounded by I. *Kant. He held that the rightness and wrongness of an action belonged to it intrinsically and criticized the 'moral sense' view of ethics. By 1778 he was a *Unitarian.

pricket. A stand containing one or more spikes on which to fix votive candles.

pride. The first of the *seven deadly sins, being the inordinate love of one's own excellence.

Prideaux, Humphrey (1648–1724), Dean of *Norwich from 1702. His fame rested on two treatises, his *Life of Mahomet* (1697), really a tract against the *Deists, and *The Old and New Testaments connected in the History of the Jews* (1716–18), an account of the Jewish people in the last centuries BC.

prie-dieu (Fr., 'pray God'). A small prayer-desk for private use, usually constructed with a sloping ledge.

Prierias, Sylvester (1456–1527), Sylvester Mazzolini, one of the earliest opponents of M. *Luther. A native of Priero in Piedmont, he entered the *Dominican Order in 1471 and held various offices in it. In 1512 *Leo X appointed him 'Master of the Sacred Palace', Inquisitor and censor of books for Rome, and professor of Thomistic theology at the Sapienza. He was involved in the juridical process against J. *Reuchlin and Luther and in the cases of P. *Pomponazzi and *Erasmus. The procrastination of the Roman Curia mitigated against the impact of his writings against Luther.

priest. The word 'priest' is etymologically a contraction of '*presbyter' (Gk. πρεσβύτερος), but the traditional English versions of the NT render πρεσβύτερος by 'elder' and keep 'priest' and 'priesthood' for the purely sacerdotal terms ἱερεύς and ἱεράτευμα (Lat. *sacerdos* and *sacerdotium*). By the end of the Old English period 'priest' had become the current word alike for 'presbyter' and 'sacerdos' and so an ambiguous term.

The idea and institution of priesthood are found in almost all the great religions, usually connected with the concept of *sacrifice. According to the OT the priesthood before the age of *Moses was patriarchal, but Moses was ordered to consecrate *Aaron and his sons 'to minister in the priest's office' (Exod. 28: 1); later priests were held to be descendants of Aaron, but it is likely that the reality was very different. The importance of the priesthood, and especially of the *High Priest, increased with the enhanced position of the *Temple in later Judaism. His position as mediator between God and man came to be the predominant idea of the Jewish priesthood in the time of Christ. In the NT the idea of Christ as High Priest finds clear expression in Heb.

The idea of priesthood as belonging to the Christian ministry was a gradual development arising from a sacrificial understanding of the Eucharist and based on OT ideas of priesthood. The term 'priest' does not appear to have been applied to Christian ministers until the end of the 2nd cent., and then the term was commonly confined to bishops. While in the 3rd cent. presbyters were held to share in the episcopal *sacerdotium*, and could offer the Eucharist and receive penitent *lapsi*, it seems that these functions were to be exercised only in the absence of the bishop and were regarded as delegated by him. With the spread of Christianity in the country and the establishment of parish churches, the presbyters adopted more fully the priestly functions of the bishop. As the parish priest became the normal celebrant of the Eucharist and customarily exercised the power of absolution, he came to be regarded increasingly as the representative of God to the people rather than the converse. He acquired a position outside the feudal hierarchy, though he remained entirely subordinate to his bishop, and the *validity of his position depended on his *Ordination.

The tendency of medieval theology to see the priesthood of the clergy almost exclusively in relation to the Mass led to its rejection by the Reformers. The term 'priest' was retained in the BCP apparently to make clear that *deacons were not to celebrate the Holy Communion. See also ORDERS AND ORDINATION.

Priestley, Joseph (1733–1804), *Presbyterian minister and scientist. His religious beliefs became increasingly unorthodox. In his *History of the Corruptions of Christianity* (1782) he denied the impeccability and infallibility of the Lord, views which he elaborated in his *History of Early Opinions concerning Jesus Christ* (1786). In 1791 he became one of the founder members of the *Unitarian Society. From 1794 he lived in America. As a scientist he is known for his 'discovery' of oxygen in 1774 and his work on *Different Kinds of Air* (1774–86).

Primasius (6th cent.), Bp. of Hadrumetum in N. Africa. His commentary on Rev. is valuable for the light which it throws on the history of the *Old Latin text of the NT.

Primate. The title of the bishop of the 'first see', usually the chief bishop of a single state or people. The Abp. of *Canterbury is 'Primate of All England', the Abp. of *York 'Primate of England'.

Prime. The *Office traditionally appointed for the first hour of the day, i.e. 6 a.m. It has usually been held that it was introduced by John *Cassian in his monastery at *Bethlehem *c.*395; it certainly figures in the *Regula Magistri* and the Rule of St *Benedict (6th cent.). In 1964 its recitation became voluntary for the secular clergy and it has no place in the 1971 *Breviary.

Primer or **Prymer.** A devotional book popular among the educated laity from at least the 14th cent. It contained the *Little Office of the BVM, the *Seven Penitential Psalms, the 15 *Gradual Psalms, the *Litany of the Saints, and the Office for the Dead.

primicerius. A title applied to the senior in rank of several classes of officials, both ecclesiastical and secular.

Primitive Methodist Church. One of the *Methodist Churches which united in 1932. About 1800 Hugh Bourne began an evangelistic movement outside the official structure of Methodism near Mow Cop, Staffs., and here in 1807 Lorenzo Dow, an American Methodist, introduced the *Camp Meeting into English Methodism. This form of meeting, designed for those not attracted by the ordinary work of the Church, was condemned by the Wesleyan Conference, and in 1810 both Bourne and William Clowes, who had joined in evangelical work at Tunstall and later in Hull, were expelled from the Methodist Church. In 1811 their followers united under the name of Primitive Methodists. They engaged in widespread evangelism and in 1843 founded missions in *Australia and *New Zealand. In 1932 they united with the Wesleyan and *United Methodists.

Primus. The title of the presiding bishop of the Scottish Episcopal Church.

prior. The holder of an office in certain male religious orders. In an abbey, the *abbot's deputy is usually designated prior; in a priory, the prior is the superior. Among the *mendicant friars (except the *Franciscans) and in a few monastic orders, it is the general term for all superiors.

prioress. In general, the prioress fulfils the same function as the *prior in the corresponding male order. While the office of *abbess in current RC usage is restricted to the superiors of certain houses of *nuns, the title of prioress is also used in certain Religious *Institutes of women who are not nuns in the strict sense.

priory. A religious house presided over by a *prior or *prioress. It is the normal unit among most *mendicant friars; among orders following the Rule of St *Benedict, a conventual priory is autonomous, and a dependent priory depends on some other monastery.

Prisca. The name given to a Latin translation of the canons of certain Greek Councils, including those of *Nicaea and *Chalcedon. It almost certainly dates from the 5th cent.

Priscilla, St (1st cent.), also **Prisca**, an early Christian convert. She is mentioned six times in the NT and it is clear that she and her husband Aquila were prominent members of the primitive Church. There are no sufficient grounds for identifying her with the St Prisca whose relics are supposed to be enshrined in the church in Rome known as the *titulus S. Priscae* or with the Priscilla of the 'Coemeterium Priscillae', one of the oldest *catacombs. Feast day in the E., 13 Feb.; in the W., 8 July.

Priscillianism. A 4th–5th cent. heresy of uncertain origin. Priscillian was the leader of an ascetic movement in Spain, whose adherents included two bishops, *Instantius and Salvianus, and many women. Despite the condemnation at Saragossa in 380 of doctrines attributed to him (though Priscillian was not named), he became Bp. of Ávila soon afterwards. In 381 he and his followers were exiled. In Italy they got the decree of exile annulled by the secular authorities and, returning to Spain, won a large following. The new Emperor, Maximus, however, wanted the support of the Catholic bishops, and in 386 Priscillian was tried in the imperial court on a charge of sorcery, convicted, and executed. The fall of Maximus in 388 produced another change in imperial policy and Priscillianism flourished; it is possible that the shrine at *Compostela is on the site of Priscillian's burial-place. The movement did not disappear until the end of the 6th cent.

Our knowledge of Priscillianist doctrine is derived mainly from a collection of anonymous writings generally attributed to Priscillian or possibly a disciple of his. From these it appears that Priscillianism was a movement of spiritual renewal. Priscillian set great store by asceticism. He rejected the accusation of *Manichaeism, though several features of his teaching made him vulnerable to it, notably his interest in the cosmic dimensions of the ascetic struggle, his demand for celibacy coupled with his tolerance of the lower virtue of married Christians, and his taste for the occult.

privileged altar. An altar at which, according to RC canon law until 1967, a *plenary indulgence could be secured for a soul in *purgatory by the application of a Mass celebrated on it.

Privy Council, Judicial Committee of the. See JUDICIAL COMMITTEE OF THE PRIVY COUNCIL.

Probabiliorism. The system of *moral theology based on the principle that, if the licitness or illicitness of an action is in doubt, it is lawful to follow the opinion favouring liberty only when it is more probable than the opinion favouring the law. See also the following entry.

Probabilism. The system of *moral theology based on the principle that, if the licitness or illicitness of an action is in doubt, it is lawful to follow the solidly probable opinion favouring liberty, even though the opposing opinion be more probable.

Probabilist principles were developed in Spain in the 16th cent.; the teaching was given its classical form by B. *Medina and was accepted by both *Dominicans and *Jesuits. The system was, however, recognized as being open to charges of *Laxism. In 1656 a conflict broke out. The Dominicans adopted a system which came to be known as *Probabiliorism, and B. *Pascal, inspired by *Jansenism, attacked the morality of the Jesuits, with whom Probabilism has since been increasingly identified. By the early 18th cent. Probabiliorism held sway. The subsequent rehabilitation of Probabilism is due especially to the authority of St *Alphonsus Liguori, who in 1762 expounded his own theory of *Equiprobabilism, which rests at bottom on Probabilist principles. Probabilism, with Equiprobabilism, became the most generally accepted system in the RC Church until the Second *Vatican Council. It is less in evidence in the works of moral theologians writing since the Council.

probationer. In *Presbyterian Churches, one who, after examination and approval by the *Presbytery, receives a licence to preach. He may assist the minister but must not administer the Sacraments until he is ordained to a charge of his own.

Process Theology. A modern theological movement which emphasizes the processive or evolutionary nature of man and the world, and holds that God Himself is in process of development through His intercourse with the changing world. It originated in the USA, especially in the University of Chicago during the 1920s and 1930s. Its concept of God stresses His relationships with creation, His capacity to 'surpass' Himself (but in respect of other entities to remain 'unsurpassable'), His 'bi-polar' nature, and His root attribute as love rather than uncreatedness.

procession (liturgical). Processions may be festal or penitential. According to W. use they take place before the principal celebration of the Eucharist on festivals; the ancient English use was for processions to be held after *Vespers. Processions are sometimes held in the open air as acts of witness, e.g. on *Good Friday. Other traditional processions include those on *Palm Sunday, the *Rogation Days, and *Corpus Christi. In the Byzantine rite a procession is prescribed for Vespers on the eves of Sundays and great feasts. There are also processions with the *epitaphion on *Good Friday and *Holy Saturday, and a procession at the beginning of Mattins in the Midnight Easter Vigil. For processions in the Eucharistic Liturgy, see GOSPEL, OFFERTORY (1), and GREAT and LITTLE ENTRANCE.

Procession (theological). In Trinitarian doctrine, the attribute which distinguishes the Holy Spirit from the Persons of the Father and the Son. See also DOUBLE PROCESSION OF THE HOLY SPIRIT and FILIOQUE.

Processional. The book containing the text of the *litanies, hymns, and prayers formerly prescribed for use in processions.

Proclus (410 or 412–85), *Neoplatonist philosopher. He spent most of his life in *Athens, first as a student and later as head of the Academy. His writings are the main source of our knowledge of late Athenian Neoplatonism. His philosophy is a systematization of the thought of *Plotinus, combined with an appreciation of the effectiveness of the pagan religious cult as a way of establishing contact with the Divine. His works include the *Elements of Theology*, a concise summary of Neoplatonic metaphysics, and his more elaborate *Platonic Theology*.

Proclus, St (d. 446/7), Patr. of *Constantinople from 434. He won sympathy by his moderation in the cause of orthodoxy, and his popularity was enhanced by the solemn translation of the body of St *Chrysostom (438). His works include the so-called 'Tome of St Proclus' (Ep. 2) on the doctrine of the one Christ in two natures, directed against *Theodore of Mopsuestia. Feast day in the E., 20 Nov.; in the W., 24 Oct.

Procopius of Caesarea (mid-6th cent.), Byzantine historian. He wrote a 'History of the Wars' (i.e. those which he had witnessed), 'De Aedificiis' (an account of the buildings of the Emp. *Justinian), and the so-called 'Anecdota' (or 'Secret History'), issued only after his death. His works are of great historical value.

Procopius of Gaza (*c.*475–*c.*538), rhetorician and biblical exegete. He was perhaps the foremost figure of the 'School of Gaza', a group of Christian rhetoricians of the 5th–6th cent. His biblical works consist mostly of extensive extracts from older exegetes.

Proctors of the Clergy. In the C of E, the elected representatives of the clergy who, together with the *ex officio* members, constitute the Lower Houses of the *Convocations of *Canterbury and *York.

profession, religious. The taking of a public *vow promising, either explicitly or implicitly, to follow the three evangelical *counsels of poverty, chastity, and obedience inherent in the 'religious life'.

prohibited degrees. The relationships by blood or marriage which render it unlawful for two persons to marry. Blood relationships are called '*consanguinity'; relationships by marriage '*affinity'. Ecclesiastical legislation forbidding marriage between related persons is based on Lev. 18, sometimes somewhat extended. According to the 1983 *Codex Iuris Canonici*, in the RC Church all marriages with direct descendants are invalid, as are those between first cousins (though *dispensations may be given in the latter case). In the C of E the prohibited degrees are listed in the Table of *Kindred and Affinity in the 1969 *Canons (B 31).

prokimenon. Verses from the Psalter sung at the beginning of any series of readings from Scripture in the Byzantine rite. At *Vespers it is always sung after the *Phos Hilaron, even when no readings follow.

prolocutor. The title of the president of each of the Lower Houses of the *Convocations of *Canterbury and *York.

Promised Land, the. The land of *Canaan, promised to *Abraham and his descendants (Gen. 12: 7 etc.).

Promotor Fidei (Lat., 'promoter of the faith'). The foremost theologian of the Congregation for the *Causes of Saints in Rome. He used to be responsible for examining the alleged virtues and miracles of a candidate for *beatification or *canonization, with a view to preventing any rash decision (he was popularly known as 'the Devil's Advocate'). He now presides over the meetings of the theological consultors who make the final assessment of a case and prepares their report for the cardinals and bishops who advise the Pope.

Promotor Justitiae (Lat., 'promoter of justice'). The priest responsible for testing critically in the diocese in which he or she died the evidence adduced on behalf of a candidate for *beatification or *canonization in the RC Church.

Prone. The vernacular office inserted into High Mass after the *Offertory on Sundays and other feast days in the Middle Ages. It ordinarily consisted of such items as the 'bidding of the *beads' (q.v.) and expositions of the Lord's Prayer and Creed, as well as notifications of ensuing feasts and fasts and *banns of marriage.

Propaganda Fide, Congregation of. The *Roman Congregation which is concerned with missionary activity throughout the world and with the administration of territories where there is no established hierarchy. It originated in the latter half of the 16th cent. to meet the spiritual needs of the newly discovered heathen populations. In 1988 it was renamed the 'Congregation for the Evangelization of the Nations' (Congregatio pro Gentium Evangelizatione).

Proper. The part of the *Eucharist and *Offices which changes with the ecclesiastical season. The 'Proper of Saints' is the Proper for festivals of a fixed date; the 'Proper of Time' that for Sundays, *ferias, and *movable feasts. In the RC Church many saints' days share the same Proper with others; such Propers are printed once under the heading '*Common of Saints'.

prophecy. From early times Christians have believed that before the Incarnation God the Holy Spirit 'spoke by the prophets' (*Nicene Creed), and it has generally been recognized that the prophets were the inspired deliverers of God's message not only about the future but also declaring His will to their contemporaries.

At least since NT times, the Jews have applied the term 'Prophets' to a large section of the OT Canon intermediate in authority between the ancient 'Law' and the more recent 'Writings'. In this connection it was customary to distinguish (1) the 'Former Prophets', namely Jos., Jgs., 1 and 2 Sam., 1 and 2 Kgs., and (2) the 'Latter Prophets', namely Is., Jer., Ezek., and the 12 (*Minor) Prophets. But the name of prophet could be applied personally in a wider sense, e.g. to *Moses.

The beginning of Hebrew prophecy can be traced to the early days of the monarchy.

1 Sam. 9 f. attests the existence of two types of prophet: the Seer, possessed of clairvoyance, like Samuel, who was able to show Saul the whereabouts of the lost asses, and the ecstatic, associated with a local shrine, who uttered words not his own, held to be God's (1 Sam. 10: 10 f.). Gradually the ecstatic features became of less importance and the delivery of a Divine message or 'word' became the dominating feature of prophecy. A development can be traced in the message which prophets communicated. *Amos proclaimed unrelieved Divine judgement on Israel, but later prophets saw hope beyond judgement, and by the post-exilic age the prophetic message had turned to one of blessing and encouragement.

It is in the prophets of the OT that most of the passages concerning the *Messiah occur. Christ Himself saw the fulfilment of OT prophecy in His own ministry, e.g. declaring that in His coming the words of Is. 61: 1 were fulfilled (Lk. 4: 21). Similarly the Evangelists point to the fulfilment of a number of OT prophecies in the events they describe, and the appeal to OT prophecy was a constant feature of early Christian preaching. In the patristic and medieval period almost all who sought to expound Christian doctrine assumed that the inspiration of Scripture guaranteed the prophetic foreknowledge of the Christian revelation, so that OT texts might be used as arguments, e.g. for specific Christological teaching. It was only with the *Enlightenment and the rise of a critical approach to history that doubts began to be cast on the existence of any real anticipation of NT events in such texts as Is. 7: 14.

prophets (early Christian). While prophecy as a phenomenon is well attested in the early Church (1 Cor. 12–14), the position of the prophets mentioned in the NT is unclear. Sometimes they appear as a distinct order of ministers (1 Cor. 12: 28); other references suggest something less definite (e.g. Acts 11: 27), while women as well as men could prophesy (Acts 21: 9). Several early Christian writers assume the authority of prophets, but prophecy seems to have died out. 'Prophets' were prominent in *Montanism.

prophets (Old Testament). See PROPHECY.

propitiation. The general meaning of the

word is the appeasing of the wrath of the Deity by prayer or sacrifice when a sin or offence has been committed against Him. It is, however, possible that the primary meaning in the NT is the removal of an obstacle on man's part to his relationship with God. To say that the death of Christ is 'propitiatory' is to say that it is effective in restoring the relationship between God and man, damaged by sin. See also ATONEMENT.

proprietary chapel. In the C of E a chapel built by subscription and maintained by private individuals. The ministers of such chapels were normally granted episcopal licences, which could be issued only with the consent of the incumbent of the parish. Few remain.

Prose. An alternative name for the *Sequence (q.v.).

proselyte. A convert to Judaism and, in a wider sense, a convert to any faith or sect.

Proskomide. In the E. Church, the preparation of the bread and wine for the Eucharist; it takes place before the beginning of the service. See also PROSPHORA.

Prosper of Aquitaine, St (c.390–c.463), theologian. Prosper Tiro of Aquitania was living at Marseilles when the *Semipelagian controversy broke out (426). He wrote to St *Augustine, and in 431, after Augustine's death, he went to Rome to secure *Celestine I's support for Augustinian teaching. From his writings it seems that Prosper's theological views developed from the rigid Augustinianism of his earlier controversial works to a milder view which rejected predestination to damnation and affirmed the will of God to save all men, though believing in the reprobation of a great number. In the last period of his life he was closely associated with *Leo I. Feast day, 7 July.

prosphora. In the E. Church, the altar bread. Traditionally five loaves are required; they are solemnly cut up at the *Proskomide. One portion (known as the 'lamb') is used for the liturgy; the rest is not consecrated but is distributed later among the congregation. The Greek Church now generally uses one large loaf, but the Russians continue to use five smaller ones.

Protasius, St. See GERVASIUS AND PROTASIUS, STS.

Protestant Episcopal Church in the United States of America. See EPISCOPAL CHURCH IN THE UNITED STATES OF AMERICA.

Protestantism. The 'Protestatio', from which the word derives, was a statement issued by five reforming princes and 14 cities at the Diet of *Speyer in 1529. Outnumbered by the Catholic powers who wanted to halt the reforming movement, the signatories believed that to keep silent would touch 'God's honour and ... the eternal life of our souls'. The term 'Protestant' originally applied only to the *Lutherans, the *Calvinists being described as '*Reformed'. It thus originally had a more positive sense than its modern anti-Roman flavour would suggest.

Lutheranism, Calvinism, and *Zwinglianism would now all be regarded as Protestant, and there are many denominations which are in a general sense Protestant. Whether the C of E is Protestant is disputed. The word is not used in the BCP, but *Charles I affirmed his adherence to the Protestant religion, using the term as opposed to both Roman Catholicism and *Puritanism. After the Restoration it was generally extended to include Nonconformists.

Because Protestantism has become such an inclusive term, it is difficult to provide a definition of its beliefs; acceptance of the Bible as the sole source of revealed truth, the doctrine of *justification by faith alone, and the universal priesthood of believers are characteristic. Protestants reject any kind of two-tier spirituality (clerical/monastic and lay); a lay spirituality based on Bible-reading and a high standard of personal morality have been the norm. In general Protestant worship is marked by the participation of the whole congregation, by the public reading of the Bible in the vernacular, and by an emphasis on *preaching. Charismatic, *Pentecostal Christianity has been an important element in modern Protestantism.

In the 18th cent. the influence of the *Enlightenment began to dissolve some of the earlier Protestant certainties, raising questions about the literal understanding of Scripture, emphasizing reason above revealed religion, and stressing the importance of an interior and subjective religion of the spirit. From 1870 to *c.*1920 the tone of Liberal Protestantism was set by A. *Ritschl, who reacted against F. D. E. *Schleiermacher's emphasis on feeling, revived I. *Kant's moralism and metaphysical scepticism, and encouraged historical research. K. *Barth attempted a comprehensive restatement of classical dogmatic Protestantism, based on his conviction that a belief in the Trinity necessarily follows from an acceptance of the premiss that God reveals Himself.

American Protestantism grew out of the 17th-cent. *Puritanism of New England, the 18th-cent *Great Awakening, and the revivalism of the 19th cent. These elements fashioned a peculiar mixture of Calvinism and *Arminianism, which has deeply influenced American culture. Protestants were strongly motivated to reform society; they were also intent on the moral and psychological improvement of individuals. In the 20th cent. American Protestantism championed human rights abroad and individual rights at home. Its religious tolerance has bequeathed a proliferation of denominations, fostering a reductionist approach to the W. Church's historic liturgy and body of doctrine. Against the prevailing Reformed religious ethos, some immigrant groups, notably Lutherans, have struggled to employ traditional forms of worship, piety, and theology which were long held suspect by the Protestant mainstream.

Protevangelium. An alternative title for the 'Book of *James'.

prothesis. In the E. Church the word is used of: (1) the table on which the solemn preparation (*Proskomide) of the Eucharistic gifts takes place; (2) the chamber to the left of the apse of the church in which this table stands; and (3) the Proskomide itself.

Protomartyr (i.e. First Martyr). A title commonly given to St *Stephen and occasionally to the first martyrs of different countries, e.g. to St *Alban, the 'Protomartyr of England'.

protonotary apostolic. A member of the college of *notaries attached to the Papal court.

Proverbs, Book of. This poetical OT Book is divided into eight clearly defined sections, three of which are attributed to *Solomon. The Book represents a compilation of various collections of proverbs, stemming from widely different periods and places, while the separate collections contain individual sayings of even more diverse origin. While some of these may go back to Solomon, the tradition that he compiled the Book is probably best explained by the fact that he was known to have uttered proverbs and to have made his court a centre of Eastern wisdom (1 Kgs. 4: 29–34).

Providentissimus Deus (1893). An encyclical on the study of the Bible issued by *Leo XIII. Its purpose was to give guidance in the situation brought about by recent discoveries in archaeology and literary criticism. While it stressed the need to study the new evidence, it condemned the use made of it in some quarters.

province. A group of *dioceses, territorially contiguous, forming an ecclesiastical unit, so called because such groups were originally coincident with the provinces of the Roman Empire.

provincial. An official of a religious order. He exercises authority over all houses of the Order within a particular area. The office came into being with the *Mendicant Orders and was taken over by most modern orders and congregations. The provincial is normally either elected by the provincial chapter, subject to the approval of the superior-general, or is appointed by the superior-general. He holds office for a fixed period.

Provisors, Statutes of. Four English laws, passed in 1351, 1353, 1365, and 1389, intended to check the practice of Papal 'provision' or nomination to vacant benefices over the head of the ordinary patron. The practice of provision nevertheless continued until the Reformation.

provost. In modern times, the head of an ecclesiastical chapter. In England until 1999 the title was used in the newer dioceses of the head of a cathedral chapter where the cathedral is also a parish church. It is also used for the heads of certain colleges.

Prudentius, the common title of Aurelius Prudentius Clemens (348–*c.*410), Latin poet and hymn-writer. A Spaniard by birth, he had a successful career in civil administration and spent his retirement in devout exercises and Christian writing. His didactic poems exhibit distinction in abstract thought as well as in the imitation of classical models. The 'Psychomachia', an allegorical description of the struggle of the Christian soul and of the Church, influenced later writers. Extracts from his lyrical poems or 'hymns' are found in most W. *breviaries. Those in common use include 'Bethlehem, of noblest cities'.

Prudentius, Galindo (d. 861), Bp. of Troyes from c.843. He played a major part in the controversy on *predestination between *Hincmar of Reims and *Gottschalk; he defended Gottschalk's Augustinianism and denied the general saving will of God. In his *Epistola ad Hincmarum* he taught the doctrine of double predestination to damnation as well as to salvation.

Prymer. See PRIMER.

Prynne, William (c.1602–69), *Puritan controversialist. He was severely punished after the publication in 1632 of his *Histrio-mastix*, which was thought to contain veiled attacks on *Charles I and *Henrietta Maria, and he was again imprisoned in 1637 after he wrote against the 'Book of *Sports'. When the Long Parliament met in 1640 he was freed and defended the right to take up arms against the King. His ideal of the supremacy of the State over the Church put him out of sympathy with the *Independents, whom he also attacked; and he hated the notion of toleration. When he gained a seat in the House of Commons in 1648, he unexpectedly opposed the King's execution. He was imprisoned for a time under the Commonwealth. In Feb. 1660 he resumed his seat in Parliament and brought in the bill for the dissolution preparatory to *Charles II's restoration. Charles appointed him Keeper of the Tower Records, but his *Presbyterianism brought him into conflict with the reviving Anglicanism.

Psalms, Book of (Gk. ψαλμοί, 'songs, accompanied by string music'). The OT Book contains 150 Psalms, variously enumerated; for the most part the Greek and Latin (*Vulgate) versions are one number behind the Hebrew counting, which is followed in the BCP and most non-Catholic English Bibles, so, e.g. Ps. 90 AV is Ps. 89 Vulg.

The Psalms are traditionally divided into five books, namely 1–41, 42–72, 73–89, 90–106, 107–50, but there are indications of earlier groupings which point back to independently existing collections. The *Dead Sea Scrolls show that the order of the Psalms was not fixed until the Christian era. Rubrics in the *Massoretic text and in the *Septuagint make it clear that in its present form the Psalter is essentially a liturgical book; it has often been described as the 'hymn-book of the Second *Temple'. The popular belief that *David was the author of the whole Psalter can no longer be sustained. Most scholars believe that the Psalms come from a variety of authors and are of widely different dates. Many probably come from the early years of the Monarchy and in their original form may have been used for worship in the First Temple. It is unclear when the various collections were made, but they were probably all post-exilic.

Traditionally interpreted, the Psalms are held to cover the whole range of relations between God and man. This interpretation has been challenged in the last 100 years, some for instance arguing that the 'I' of the Psalms commonly refers not to an individual but to Israel as a nation.

In the Church the Psalter has been used both in public worship and in private prayer from very early times. In the Divine *Office of the RC Church, until its recent reordering, the whole Psalter was recited every week, as it still is in the E. Church (here twice a week in Lent). See also PSALTER.

Psalms, imprecatory and **metrical**. See IMPRECATORY and METRICAL PSALMS.

Psalms of Solomon. See SOLOMON, PSALMS OF.

Psalter. (1) The biblical Book of Psalms as used, in appropriate translations, in the worship of the Church.

IN THE W. CHURCH. The earliest Latin Psalters were translated from the *Septuagint. St *Jerome in his preface to the *Gallican Psalter says that he had earlier worked on a translation of the Psalms from the LXX; this work was in the past equated with the *Roman Psalter (q.v.). About 392 he made a fresh translation from the *Hexaplaric text of the LXX (the Gallican Psalter, q.v.) and *c.*400 he made a further one from the Hebrew (the 'Hebrew Psalter'). In the *Breviary the Gallican Psalter remained in use until it was replaced in 1945 by a new Latin translation made from the Hebrew text. The text in the 1971 Breviary, however, is an eclectic one which seeks to combine fidelity to the Hebrew with some of the felicities of style of the Vulgate. The vernacular versions of the Psalter used in modern RC liturgy are normally based on the Hebrew text.

The version of the Psalms in the BCP is based on M. *Coverdale's translation from the Vulgate, i.e. from the Gallican Psalter, and thus embodies many Septuagintal readings not found in the Hebrew. The version in CW is based on the Psalter of the *Episcopal Church of the USA. It is normally consistent with the Hebrew text and generally uses inclusive language.

IN THE E. CHURCH. Greek-speaking Christians use the version of the Psalms in the LXX, which formed the basis of the translation used by the Slavonic Churches. The Syrian Churches used, and in some areas still use, the version of the Psalms in the *Peshitta, which is translated from the Hebrew. In most modern Orthodox Churches, where the Psalter is used in the vernacular, there is a preference for a translation made from the LXX.

(2) The book containing the Psalms for use in worship. In the W. the Psalms were commonly arranged according to the requirements of the Divine *Office. They often contained *antiphons and other matter such as hymns. When their contents were incorporated into the Breviary, they fell out of use. In the E. Church separate Psalters remain common. Here the Psalms are divided into 20 sections (see KATHISMA) and the book contains other material, such as *canticles, *odes, hymns, and prayers.

Psalter Collects. Collects composed with reference to each of the Psalms. There are some indications that in late antiquity such collects were actually recited after their respective Psalms, but it is unlikely that whole series were ever used liturgically, except perhaps in Spain. Psalter collects are used in a limited way in some contemporary, especially RC, liturgies.

psaltery. (1) An ancient and medieval stringed instrument. (2) An obsolete term for Psalter (2).

Psellus, Michael (*c.*1019–*c.*1078), Byzantine philosopher, historian, theologian, and statesman. He held high office at the Imperial court, but fell from favour in 1072. His *Chronographia* ('History') is an important source for the period 976–1077. His other works include biblical commentaries, treatises against the Latin theologians and against the *Messalians, as well as commentaries on *Plato and *Aristotle.

Pseudepigrapha. Writings ascribed to some other than their real author, generally with a view to giving them an enhanced authority. The term is used especially of the pseudonymous Jewish works dating from the centuries immediately before and after the beginning of the Christian era, which are not included in the OT or *Apocrypha. Among them are the 'Books of *Enoch', the 'Assumption of *Moses', and the 'Psalms of *Solomon'.

Pseudo-Clementines; Pseudo-Isidorian Decretals. See CLEMENTINE LITERATURE; FALSE DECRETALS.

psychology of religion. A modern field of study in which the concepts and methods of psychology are applied to religious experience and behaviour. One of the first to investigate such possible applications of psychology was W. *James; he studied the experience of well-being or of conflict in human response to God, and the experiences of religious conversion and of saintliness and mysticism. Many of the writings of S. Freud (1856–1939) on psychoanalysis contributed to the psychological study of religion, though his critical and reductionist views of religion no longer command assent. Similarly the conclusions of C. G. Jung (1875–1961), though by contrast tending to assign an almost indiscriminate validity to religious phenomena in human experience, have in turn led to restatements of permanent value for the psychology of religion. Since the early 1960s more sophisticated methods of analysis have been developed. Religious behaviour and experience have been studied in relation to age, to cognitive style and other personal characteristics, and also with reference to pathological and drug-induced conditions. Merely psychological methods, however, cannot fully answer questions about the validity of religious behaviour and experience, even if they can account for some aspects of both in non-religious terms.

Ptolemaic system. The astronomical system elaborated by Ptolemy (2nd cent. AD), who explained the apparent motions of the sun, moon, and planets on the assumption that the earth was stationary.

Public Worship Regulation Act 1874. An Act designed to suppress the growth of ritualism in the C of E. The imprisonment of four priests for contumacy between 1877 and 1882 discredited the Act. It was repealed in 1963.

publican. The word used in the traditional English versions of the Bible to translate the Greek term τελώνης (Lat. *publicanus*), a member of one of the financial organizations which farmed the taxes in the service of the Roman government. The system led to abuses and corruption; the publicans were generally hated.

Pudens, St. A Christian of Rome, mentioned in 2 Tim. 4: 21 as sending greetings to *Timothy. Tradition makes him St *Peter's host at Rome. There are no sufficient grounds for identifying him with the Pudens (probably 3rd cent.) who gave his house (*titulus Pudentis* or *ecclesia Pudentiana*) to the Roman Church. Feast day in the E. of the former, 14 Apr.; in the W. of the latter (sometimes identified with the former), 19 May.

Pudentiana, St. She is described as an early Christian Roman virgin, but her cult probably rests on the mistaken notion that the 'ecclesia Pudentiana' in Rome, which is the church of St *Pudens, presupposed a St Pudentiana. Feast day, 19 May.

Pufendorf, Samuel (1632–94), German professor of natural and international law. Developing the system of H. *Grotius, he divided law into natural, civil, and moral, and maintained that while moral law was based on revelation and civil law on the positive enactments of the State, natural law had its basis in the instinct of society, and therefore ultimately in human reason. He also expounded the theory of Church government known as '*Collegialism'.

Pugin, Augustus Welby Northmore (1812–52), architect and *ecclesiologist. He was the chief inspirer of the 'Gothic Revival'. His works include St Chad's (RC) Cathedral, Birmingham; St Giles, Cheadle; and the chapel of St Edmund's College, Ware. He collaborated with C. Barry on the designs for the Houses of Parliament.

Pulcheria, St (399–453), E. Empress from 450. From 414 to 416 she was guardian of her brother, *Theodosius II. A stalwart supporter of orthodoxy, she induced him to condemn *Nestorius and in the *Monophysite controversy she was on the orthodox side. As Empress she arranged for a General Council to meet at *Chalcedon. Feast day, 10 Sept.

Pullen, Robert (d. 1146), theologian. He was one of the earliest known masters in the schools of *Oxford and he later taught in *Paris. He was made a cardinal in 1143/4. His main surviving work is his 'Sentences', a compilation treating a range of theological subjects, soon to be superseded by the 'Sentences' of *Peter Lombard.

pulpit. An elevated stand of stone or wood for the preacher or reader. Pulpits first became general in the later Middle Ages. Except in *cathedrals, the north side of the *nave is considered the proper place for the pulpit. The workmanship is sometimes elaborate. Pulpits are also generally found in monastic refectories.

Purcell, Henry (1659–95), English composer. In 1679 he was made organist at *Westminster Abbey and in 1682 also at the *Chapel Royal. One of his most famous ecclesiastical works is the *Te Deum* and *Jubilate* in D (1694). Although he wrote many 'full' *anthems in the older polyphonic style, including 'Hear my prayer', his outstanding contribution is to the development of the verse anthem, often with string accompaniment. Much of the music is elaborate and highly dramatic; the words are nearly always from the OT.

Purchas Judgement. The judgement given in 1871 by the *Judicial Committee of the Privy Council against the Revd John Purchas that *Eucharistic Vestments, the *Eastward Position, the *Mixed Chalice, and Wafer *Bread were illegal. The decision meant that the ritualists were held to be law-breakers, but it was widely disregarded.

purgative, illuminative, and unitive ways. The analysis of Christian development into these three 'ways' or phases derives from *Dionysius the Pseudo-Areopagite, who ascribed a rhythm of purification, illumination, and union (or perfection) both to the hierarchies of angels and to the Church on earth. Medieval W. interpreters of Dionysius turned his scheme into an account of spiritual progress in terms of the three ways, beginning with the eradication of bad habits and the cultivation of the virtues, moving on to the illumination of the mind by meditation and contemplation, and culminating in unitive love. These three ways were adopted by later writers such as St *John of the Cross and so became classic in systematic theories of Christian spirituality.

purgatory. In W. Catholic theology, the state (or place) of punishment and purification where the souls of those who have died in a state of grace undergo such punishment as is still due to forgiven sins and, perhaps, expiate their unforgiven *venial sins, before being admitted to the *Beatific Vision. In that explicit form the doctrine was not found before the 12th cent., but elements of it are much older, especially the notion that not all souls are condemned to Hell or are worthy of Heaven at the moment of death, and that prayer for the *dead (q.v.) is valuable. The E. Church came to admit of an intermediate state, but refrained from defining it.

Belief that sins might be purged in an afterlife, and that the process might be accelerated by prayer, is expressed in the 'Passion of Sts *Perpetua and Felicity' (AD 203), and St *Gregory the Great specifically taught that 'light sins' might be purged in purgatorial fire. Scriptural passages alluded to in support of this teaching include Mt. 12: 32, Jn. 14: 2, and 1 Cor. 3: 11–15. In the 12th cent. the elaboration of the theology of *penance helped to fashion the idea of purgatory as a place where penances unfinished in this world could be completed. St *Thomas Aquinas taught that in purgatory any unforgiven guilt (*culpa*) of venial sin is expiated and any punishment (*poena*) for sins, both venial and mortal, still remaining at death is borne; and that the smallest pain in purgatory is greater than

the greatest on earth, but is relieved by the certitude of salvation which establishes the holy souls in deep peace. Moreover, they may be helped by the prayers of the living. The teaching of the W. Church was defined at the Councils of *Lyons (1274) and *Florence (1439) in the hope of reconciling the Greeks, who objected to various aspects. It provided a context for the development of *indulgences.

The Reformers' opposition to the Church's teaching on purgatory was usually couched in terms of allusions to its weak support in Scripture and rejection of the mercenary aspects of later medieval religion in which purgatory was implicated, together with the way in which it seemed to extend Papal power into the afterlife. M. *Luther at one time denied the existence of purgatory, but later Lutheran Confessions do not reject all ideas of purification after death, however much they object to Papal claims to remit sins. The Council of *Trent reaffirmed the teaching of the Councils of Lyons and Florence, but confined itself to asserting the principles of purification after death and the value of prayers for the faithful departed. In the C of E Art. 22 of the *Thirty-Nine Articles condemns the 'Romish' doctrine of purgatory, but the existence of an intermediate state of purification and the value of prayers for the dead are accepted by many Anglicans and some modern Protestant theologians. Recent RC discussions of purgatory are characterized by restraint and leave open many questions, such as whether souls in purgatory can pray for the living.

Purgatory, St Patrick's. See ST PATRICK'S PURGATORY.

Purification of the BVM. The feast kept on 2 Feb. in commemoration of the BVM's purification in the Temple, recorded in Lk. 2: 21–39; it is also known as *Candlemas.

purificator. A small piece of white linen used at celebrations of the Eucharist to cleanse the *chalice after communion.

Purim. A Jewish festival celebrated in the spring. It commemorates the deliverance of the Jews from massacre under the Persian Empire (473 BC), as related in the Book of *Esther. The 'feast of the Jews' mentioned in Jn. 5: 1 was formerly thought to have been the Feast of Purim.

Puritans. The more extreme English Protestants who, dissatisfied with the religious settlement of *Elizabeth I, sought a further purification of the Church from supposedly unscriptural and corrupt forms along the *Genevan model. Although never in the majority, they were powerful and influential. At first they attacked church ornaments, *vestments, *surplices, *rochets, *organs, the *sign of the Cross, and ecclesiastical courts, and emphasized preaching, Sunday observance, and the 'tablewise' position of the *altar. From the early 1570s the more extreme Puritans attacked episcopacy itself and advocated *Presbyterianism. Elizabeth I bitterly opposed all Puritan attempts to change the C of E. On *James I's accession they presented the *Millenary Petition (1603), which led to the unsuccessful *Hampton Court Conference (1604). By 1600 some Puritans had come to advocate *Congregationalism. The Great Rebellion (sometimes called the 'Puritan Revolution') in and after 1642 led to the temporary triumph of Presbyterianism, but also to the proliferation of sects, and the term 'Puritan' ceased to be applicable after 1660.

Purvey, John (*c.*1353–*c.*1428), *Wycliffite preacher. Brought to trial in 1401 on account of his *Lollard activities, he recanted, but in 1403 he resigned his living and apparently reverted to Lollardy. His name has been linked with the revision of the Wycliffite translation of the Bible, but this association is dubious.

Pusey, Edward Bouverie (1800–82), *Tractarian leader. From 1828 he was Regius Professor of Hebrew at Oxford and canon of Christ Church. At the end of 1833 he became formally attached to the *Oxford Movement by contributing one of the *Tracts for the Times*; his prestige and erudition greatly benefited the cause. The death of his wife in 1839 left an indelible mark on his life; from that time he practised many austerities. When J. H. *Newman withdrew in 1841, the leadership of the Oxford Movement devolved largely on Pusey. His sermon on *The Holy Eucharist*, preached before the university in 1843, was condemned by the vice-chancellor and six doctors of divinity; the condemnation secured for it wide publicity and drew attention to the doctrine of the *Real Presence. In 1845 he assisted in the foundation of the first Anglican sisterhood (see RELIGIOUS ORDERS IN ANGLICANISM). In 1846 he preached another university sermon on *The Entire Absolution of the Penitent*, in which he claimed for the C of E the power of the keys and the reality of priestly absolution; this sermon was important in encouraging the revival of the practice of private confession in modern Anglicanism. As the main champion of the *High Church movement, Pusey frequently had to defend its doctrines, e.g. in the *Gorham Case, and from 1867 he took an active part in the Ritualist controversy. He wrote various works designed to promote union with the RC Church, but his hopes were disappointed when the First *Vatican Council defined Papal *infallibility in 1870. Pusey House, Oxford, was set up in his memory. Feast day in the American BCP (1979), 18 Sept.; in CW, 16 Sept.

Pyrrhonism. Properly, the system of sceptical philosophy expounded *c.*300 BC by the Greek thinker Pyrrho of Elis. In a wider sense the term is now used of any sceptical system of thought.

pyx. In official documents the term is used of any receptacle designed to contain the reserved *Host, but it is commonly applied especially to the small gold or silver-gilt box which is used for carrying the Blessed Sacrament to the sick. For this purpose it is wrapped in a small *corporal and placed in a pyx-bag hung round the priest's neck.

Q

'Q'. The symbol (usually held to come from the German *Quelle*, 'source') used by biblical critics in a strict sense for the hypothetical source of those passages in the Synoptic Gospels where Mt. and Lk. show a close similarity to each other but not to any parallel passage in Mk. The existence of such a document is challenged but has wide support. Some scholars use 'Q' or 'q' in a broader sense to denote not a common source of Mt. and Lk., but their common material. See also SYNOPTIC PROBLEM.

QAB. See QUEEN ANNE'S BOUNTY.

Quadragesima. Another name for the forty days of *Lent and, occasionally, for the first Sunday in Lent.

Quadratus, St (2nd cent.), *Apologist. About 124 in Asia Minor he wrote an apology for the Christian faith addressed to the Emp. Hadrian; a single fragment is preserved by *Eusebius. He may have been Bp. of *Athens. Feast day, 26 May.

quadrivium. The medieval name for the four sciences (music, arithmetic, geometry, and astronomy) which constituted the superior group of the *seven liberal arts.

Quakers. A popular name for the Religious Society of *Friends.

Quare Impedit. In the C of E, a form of legal action which a patron may bring in the temporal court against a bishop who refuses to institute a presentee to an ecclesiastical benefice.

Quarles, Francis (1592–1644), religious poet. He was for a time secretary to Abp. J. *Ussher and later chronologer to the city of London. He published a collection of biblical paraphrases under the title *Divine Poems* (1630) and two emblem-books: *Emblems* (1635) and *Hieroglyphikes of the Life of Man* (1638). In his later years he wrote devotional prose; his *Enchiridion* (1640), a collection of thoughts on religion and morals, achieved great popularity. Though often overladen with conceits and epithets, his poetry shows deep religious feeling.

Quartodecimanism. The custom of observing *Easter on the 14th day of Nisan (the day of the Jewish *Passover), whatever the day of the week. The tradition was rooted in Asia Minor. When St *Polycarp, Bp. of Smyrna, visited Rome *c*.155, Pope Anicetus refused to change his own practice but had no scruples about Polycarp's continuing to follow his custom. A more rigid line was taken by *Victor I (189–98), who tried to suppress Quartodecimanism. The Quartodecimans later organized themselves as a separate Church, surviving until the 5th cent.

Quattro Coronati (i.e. 'the Four Crowned Ones'). Four martyrs commemorated in the W. Church on 8 Nov., to whom a famous basilica in Rome is dedicated. There is doubt as to which saints are intended.

Queen Anne's Bounty (QAB). A fund formed by Queen *Anne in 1704 to receive the firstfruits (*annates) and tenths which had been diverted from the Crown under *Henry VIII; they were to be used to augment the livings of the poorer Anglican clergy. The fund later received considerable parliamentary grants and private benefactions. In 1948 QAB was joined with the *Ecclesiastical Commissioners to form the *Church Commissioners for England.

Quesnel, Pasquier (1634–1719), French *Jansenist. He became an *Oratorian in 1657. In 1672 he issued the first edition of the book which became famous as *Réflexions morales*. As against the formalized methods of spirituality in the manuals, the work emphasized the value of close study of the Bible in increasing devotion. His edition of the works of *Leo I (1675) was put on the *Index because of the *Gallican theories developed in the notes. In 1684 he refused to subscribe to an anti-Jansenist formula imposed by his superiors and went to Brussels; he was imprisoned but escaped to the Netherlands. His *Réflexions* were condemned in a brief by *Clement XI in 1708 and by the bull *Unigenitus (1713); among the doctrines censured were the theses that no grace is given outside the Church, that grace is irresistible, that without grace man is incapable of any good, and that all acts of a sinner, even prayer, are sins.

Quest of the Historical Jesus. See HISTORICAL JESUS, QUEST OF THE.

Quicunque Vult. An alternative name for the *Athanasian Creed.

Quiercy, Synods of. Several synods were held at Quiercy near Laon in the 9th cent. Those of 849 and 853 condemned the extreme form of *predestination taught by *Gottschalk.

Quietism. The teaching of certain 17th-cent. writers, especially M. de *Molinos (condemned in 1687) and to a lesser degree Mme *Guyon and Abp. *Fénelon; by extension the term is used loosely of any system of spirituality minimizing human activity.

The fundamental principle of Quietism is its condemnation of all human effort. Its exponents seem to have exaggerated earlier teaching, such as that of St *Teresa of Ávila, on the 'prayer of quiet'. They held that, in order to be perfect, a man must attain complete passivity and annihilation of will, abandoning himself to God to such an extent that he ceases to care even about his own salvation. This state is reached by a form of mental prayer in which the soul consciously refuses not only discursive meditation but any distinct act, and simply rests in the presence of God in pure faith. Once a man has reached this state, outward acts are superfluous and sin impossible.

Quinisext Synod. See TRULLAN SYNOD.

Quiñones, Francisco de (d. 1540), cardinal. Of noble Spanish family, he became a *Franciscan in 1498; in 1523 and 1526 he was elected Minister General of the *Observants. After the Sack of Rome (1527) he mediated between *Charles V and *Clement VII, who made him a cardinal. On the Pope's instruction he compiled a new *Breviary, published by *Paul III in 1535; it is often called the 'Breviary of the Holy Cross' after the cardinal's titular church. Though intended for private use, it was widely adopted before it was proscribed in 1558; it influenced the BCP.

Quinquagesima. In modern usage, the Sunday before *Ash Wednesday. The name

was dropped in the RC Church in 1969 and later in some modern Anglican liturgies.

Quinque Viae. The five 'ways' or arguments by which St *Thomas Aquinas sought to prove the existence of God from the effects of His Being which are known to us, namely (1) that change implies an unchanging changer; (2) that a sequence of efficient causes, and their effects, such as we find in the world, implies an uncaused first cause; (3) that the existence of things able to be generated and to perish implies the existence of what is not generable and perishable (i.e. 'necessary') and that the existence of what is necessary ultimately implies the existence of something whose existence derives from nothing but itself; (4) that the comparisons we make (more or less 'true', 'noble', etc.) imply a standard of comparison which is in itself perfect in all these qualities; (5) that the fulfilment by inanimate or unintelligible objects of an end to which they invariably tend implies a purpose or intelligence operative in nature.

quire. An old spelling of *choir.

Quirinus. The signature over which a series of 69 letters on the First Vatican Council was published in the *Augsburger Allgemeine Zeitung* in 1869–70. Their author is now known to have been J. J. L. von *Döllinger.

Qumran. The site of some ruins at the NW end of the *Dead Sea, near which the first of the *Dead Sea Scrolls was found in 1947; further finds were made in later years.

quodlibet. An academic exercise in medieval universities. Originally it was a voluntary disputation in which a master undertook to deal with any question raised by any of the participants. The answers were afterwards drawn up in writing and published. In the 14th cent. it came to be part of the exercise required of a bachelor seeking the licentiate.

Quo Vadis? According to a legend, first found in the 'Acts of St *Peter', the words 'Domine quo vadis?' ('Lord, where are you going?') were spoken by St *Peter when, fleeing from Rome, he met Christ, who replied, 'I am going to be crucified again.' Peter went back to Rome, where he was martyred.

R

Rabanus Maurus (*c.*780–856), poet, teacher, and archbishop. He entered the abbey of *Fulda as an *oblate, became master of the school (818) and abbot (824–42). In 847 he became Abp. of Mainz.

As a schoolmaster he wrote books on grammar and the reckoning of time, commentaries on nearly every Book of the Bible, and many hymns. As abbot he wrote treatises on ecclesiastical law and practice, including the *De institutione clericorum*, a manual for clergy; as archbishop he addressed specific issues of discipline (e.g. *chorepiscopi) and theology (notably in his *De praedestinatione*, against *Gottschalk). The *De rerum naturis*, written *c.*842, is an encyclopedic work. Over 50 of his letters and *c.*100 poems survive. The '*Veni Creator' has sometimes been attributed to him.

Rabbi (Heb., 'my master'). A Jewish title of respect given to honoured teachers. Soon after NT times it came to be added to the name of Jewish religious leaders as a title, e.g. 'Rabbi Johanan'. The Romans invested the rabbis with delegated judicial powers which lasted in Europe until modern times. Today in the W. rabbis are little more than ministers of religion, but in Israel they are State functionaries.

Rabbula (d. 435), Bp. of *Edessa from 412. A leading figure in the Syrian Church, he opposed *Nestorianism and in particular attacked the writings of *Theodore of Mopsuestia. It was once thought that he was responsible for producing the *Peshitta NT.

Raccolta. An officially approved RC prayer book containing all the devotions to which Papal *indulgences were attached. It was supplanted in 1968.

Racovian Catechism. The first statement of Socinian principles. Drawn up by Valentin Schmalz and Johannes Völkel on the basis of drafts by F. P. *Socinus, it was published in Polish in 1605 at Raków in S. Poland. German and Latin versions followed. It was professedly not a formal confessional creed but a body of opinions which would point believers to eternal life.

Rad, Gerhard von (1901–71), German OT scholar. His most important writings are concerned with *Deuteronomy, the analysis and interpretation of the *Hexateuch, and the theology of the OT. He did not attempt to construct a unified system of OT theology but expounded (1) Israel's confession of the *Heilsgeschichte* (lit., 'Salvation History') as proclaimed in the cult and transmitted in the historical traditions, (2) the searching criticism of the older traditions by the prophets and their proclamation that new Divine acts were about to take place, and (3) the relationship between the OT and NT in terms of a modified *typological interpretation.

Radbertus, Paschasius. See PASCHASIUS RADBERTUS.

Radegunde, St (*c.*518–87), the Queen of Clothar I, King of the Franks. His murder of her brother gave her an excuse to flee from court (*c.*550). Soon afterwards she founded a convent outside Poitiers, where she spent the rest of her life. In 569 she obtained a fragment of the true cross, which inspired *Venantius Fortunatus to write the '*Vexilla regis'. Feast day, 13 Aug.

Radewijns, Florentius. See FLORENTIUS RADEWIJNS.

Rahner, Karl (1904–84). One of the most influential RC theologians of the 20th cent. He became a *Jesuit in 1922 and held professorial chairs at Innsbruck, Munich, and Münster. He was a *peritus* (expert [adviser]) at the Second *Vatican Council.

His basic position was expounded in *Geist in Welt* (1939; Eng. tr., *Spirit in the World*, 1968). While interpreting in *existentialist terms St *Thomas Aquinas's doctrine of perception as the grasping of intelligible being through the medium of the sensible species, he sees the human subjectivity as functioning within a horizon of being whose ultimate determinant is God. From 1958 he edited, with H. Schlier, the series *Quaestiones Disputatae*, and he was one of the editors of the second edition of the *Lexikon* *für Theologie und Kirche* (1957–65 + supplements on the Second Vatican Council). His pastoral writings are direct and forceful.

Raikes, Robert (1736–1811), founder of *Sunday Schools. The owner of the *Gloucester Journal*, Raikes was moved by the neglected condition of the local children and their behaviour on Sundays; he helped to establish a Sunday School in a neighbouring parish and in 1780 he started a school in his own parish, open on weekdays and Sundays, for the teaching of Scripture, reading, and other elementary subjects. Though Raikes was not the 'inventor' of Sunday Schools, his example and publicity stimulated their rapid expansion.

Rainolds, John (1549–1607), Dean of *Lincoln (1593–8) and then President of Corpus Christi College, Oxford. At the *Hampton Court Conference (1604) he was the chief representative of the *Puritan cause. He took part in preparing the AV.

Rainy, Robert (1826–1906), scholar and ecclesiastical politician. He was ordained to the ministry in the *Free Church of Scotland in 1851; from 1874, when he became principal of New College, Edinburgh, and leader of the *General Assembly, he dominated the counsels of the Free Church and later of the *United Free Church. He exercised a liberalizing influence in theology and joined in the campaign for the disestablishment of the Church of Scotland (*c*.1875–*c*.1895). His last great achievement was the union of the Free and United Presbyterian Churches in 1900.

Rambler. A monthly RC periodical, founded in 1848, which became an organ of liberal English Catholicism. It was suppressed in 1864.

Ramsey, Arthur Michael (1904–88), Abp. of *Canterbury 1961–74. He held professorial chairs at *Durham and *Cambridge before he became Bp. of Durham in 1952. He was translated to *York in 1956. While at Canterbury, he travelled widely to visit provinces of the Anglican Communion and to promote relations with the Orthodox and the RC Churches. At home he presided over the introduction of *synodical government in the C of E, gaining for the Church substantial control over its liturgy in the *Worship and Doctrine Measure

1974. As a theologian he was a representative of the *Biblical Theology movement, but he is chiefly remembered for his writings on spirituality. He taught that *contemplative prayer was something to which all Christians could aspire.

Ramus, Petrus (Pierre de la Ramée) (1515–72), French humanist. Despite his attacks on the university curriculum at *Paris, he became a professor at the Collège Royal in 1551. On becoming a *Calvinist in 1562, he went to Germany. He returned to Paris in 1571, but he was killed in the Massacre of St *Bartholomew's Day. To *Aristotle's system, which he accused of falsifying the innate logic of the human mind, he opposed his own, a development of Ciceronian topics which he presented in typographically schematic form (the so-called 'dichotomies').

Rancé, Armand-Jean le Bouthillier de (1626–1700), reformer of *la Trappe. A godson of A. J. P. du *Richelieu, by 1636 he held five benefices *in *commendam*, including the *Cistercian abbey of la Trappe. He led a worldly life until a sudden death in 1657 caused a dramatic conversion. Divesting himself of all his benefices except la Trappe, he invited monks of the Strict Observance to take over in 1662; after a year's novitiate at Perseigne he was blessed as regular abbot in 1664. To the existing rules of the Strict Observance he added more stringent regulations, based, he insisted, on the original uses of Cîteaux. He remained within the obedience of the Cistercian Order and Strict Observance, and it was only the unique survival of la Trappe in the time of the French Revolution that led to the widespread adoption of his reform in the Order. See also TRAPPISTS.

Ranters. A grouping of people with *antinomian and *pantheistic tendencies in 17th-cent. England. They were probably a disparate collection of individuals on the fringes of radical religious sects who attracted popular suspicion by their wild behaviour and pronouncements.

Raphael, St, *archangel. In *Tobit and I *Enoch he is one of the seven archangels who stand in the presence of God. In Tobit (12: 15) he presents the prayers of holy men before God; in I Enoch (10: 7) he is said to have 'healed' the earth when it was defiled by the sins of the fallen angels. Feast day, previously 24 Oct.; in 1969 combined with St *Michael on 29 Sept.

In the C of E the Guild of St Raphael was founded in 1915 to restore the Ministry of Healing as a normal function of the Church.

Raphael (1483–1520) **(Raffaello Sanzio)**, the most famous of the Renaissance painters. In 1508 he was summoned to Rome to decorate the Vatican 'Stanze' and in 1514 appointed chief architect of *St Peter's. His works include the *Espousals of the Virgin* (1504; Brera, Milan), the *Sistine Madonna*, and the *Madonna della Sedia* (c.1513–14; Pitti, Florence).

Rapp, Johann Georg (1757–1847), founder of the *Harmony Society (q.v.).

Rashdall, Hastings (1858–1924), moral philosopher and theologian. He taught at Oxford (1888–1917) and then was Dean of *Carlisle. *The Theory of Good and Evil* (1907) expounded an ethical doctrine which he described as 'Ideal *Utilitarianism'. *The Idea of Atonement in Christian Theology* (1919) upheld an '*exemplarist' theory.

Rashi (1040–1105), Jewish biblical scholar, so called from the initials of his name, Rabbi Solomon ben Isaac. He was *rabbi in his native city of Troyes. His scientific outlook and his evaluation of the literal sense marked the beginning of a new era in OT interpretation. His commentaries were influential among both Jews and Christians.

Raskolniki (Russian, 'schismatics'). An alternative name for the *Old Believers.

Ratherius (c.887–974), Bp. of *Verona. He received the see in 931, but was soon removed; he was in possession of it again from 962 to 968. A man of refractory and ambitious character, he took a prominent part in the ecclesiastical life of his time.

Ratio Studiorum (Lat., 'the method of the studies'). The abbreviated name of the *Jesuit scheme of studies issued in 1599. It was based on the best pedagogical theory of the time, and the success of Jesuit secondary education from the 16th to the 18th cent. was largely due to it. Later the term was used, until 1975, to denote the legislation on the philosophy and theology studied by Jesuit seminarians.

rationale. The word has been used of the breastplate worn by the Jewish *High Priest, of a liturgical vestment worn by some German bishops, of a gold ornament formerly sometimes worn by bishops celebrating Mass, and in ecclesiastical contexts in a general sense of a reasoned exposition of principles, e.g. in the title of W. *Durandus, *Rationale Divinorum Officiorum*.

Ratisbon, Conference of (1541). A conference of three Catholic and three Protestant theologians convened by *Charles V at Ratisbon (Regensburg). Though doctrinal agreement was reached on some subjects, including a basis of agreement on *justification, major differences remained, and the subsequent hostility of M. *Luther, as well as political rivalries, prevented any union being effected.

Ratramnus (9th cent.), theologian. He entered the monastery of *Corbie c.825. His *De Corpore et Sanguine Domini* (843) was a reaction to the realism of *Paschasius Radbertus' earlier treatise on the Eucharist. In his *De Praedestinatione* (849–50), he clarified the patristic basis for *Gottschalk's belief in double *predestination to good or evil. His *Contra Graecorum Opposita* (c.867) is a reply to *Photius' criticism of the W. Church; in it he defends the *Double Procession of the Holy Spirit. In the 11th cent. his Eucharistic treatise was seen as incompatible with a change in the substance of the Bread and Wine and condemned in 1050. Only at the time of the Reformation was it much read; it was a major source for N. *Ridley's formulations of Eucharistic doctrine.

Rauschenbusch, Walter (1861–1918), exponent of the *Social Gospel in N. America. Serving as pastor of the Second German *Baptist Church of New York, he encountered the cost of escalating social evils. His *Pietistic background provided few resources for dealing with social questions, but he found in the Kingdom of God theology taught by A. *Ritschl and others a way to bring together his inherited evangelical and his new social convictions. His *Christianity and the Social Crisis* (1907) was an eloquent plea for the joining of Christian faith with social passion.

Ravenna. According to tradition, the first Bp. of Ravenna was St *Apollinaris. In 402 the imperial court of the W. Empire moved to Ravenna; in 493 Ravenna fell to *Theodoric the Ostrogoth, who used it as his capital and patronized the *Arian Church in the city. In 540 it was captured by the Byzantines; it served as the capital of the beleaguered Byzantine province until it fell to the Lombards in 751. Its importance elevated the status of its bishops who were placed over a newly created metropolitan province in the 5th cent. and given the title of 'archbishop' in the 6th. In the 5th and 6th cents. a number of splendid churches were built and decorated with *mosaics, which are the finest collection surviving from the period.

Raymond Nonnatus, St (*c*.1204–40), *Mercedarian missioner. He appears to have been sent to N. Africa, redeemed many slaves, and when his funds were exhausted gave himself up in ransom; for some years he lived among the Muslims, converting many to the Christian faith. He was himself ransomed by members of his Order. Feast day, 31 Aug.

Raymond of Peñafort, St (*c*.1180–1275), Spanish canonist. He became a *Dominican in 1222. His *Summa de casibus poenitentiae* profoundly influenced the development of the penitential system. In 1230 *Gregory IX charged him with the collection and arrangement of Papal decretals subsequent to *Gratian; the work was finished and promulgated in 1234. In 1238 he was elected Master General of his Order; he rearranged the Dominican statutes into the form that they essentially retained until 1924. From 1240 he devoted himself mainly to the conversion of Jews and Moors. Feast day, 7 (formerly 23) Jan.

Raymond of Sebonde (d. 1436), Spanish philosopher. He taught at Toulouse. His *Liber Naturae sive Creaturarum* or *Theologia Naturalis* (first published in 1484) achieved fame through M. de *Montaigne, who translated and defended it in 1569. Its prologue, maintaining that it is possible for human reason to discover the contents of the Christian Revelation in nature alone, was put on the *Index in 1595. The book itself, however, was highly esteemed.

reader. In the Anglican Communion, a lay person licensed to conduct religious services. The office in its present form in the C

of E dates from 1866. Readers are formally admitted to their office by a bishop, from whom they may receive a licence for a particular parish or for the diocese generally. The duties which may be assigned to them include the reading of *Morning and *Evening Prayer (except the Absolution), distributing the Bread and Wine at the Eucharist, officiating at the *Burial of the Dead, and preaching. Since 1969 women have been eligible for the office.

In the Episcopal Church of *Scotland the Canons of 1863 provided for lay readers and many provinces of the Anglican Communion have since established readers with duties similar to those exercised in the C of E. See also LECTORS.

Real Presence, the. In (especially *Anglican) Eucharistic theology an expression used to cover several doctrines emphasizing the actual presence of the Body and Blood of Christ in the Sacrament, as contrasted with others that maintain that they are present only figuratively.

Realism. (1) Any form of belief which is chary of speculation and rooted in fact. In this sense Christianity claims to be realistic. (2) The philosophical doctrine of the reality of the external world as against the idealistic view that it is constituted by consciousness. (3) In a more technical sense the doctrine that abstract concepts (*universals') have a real existence apart from the individuals ('particulars') in which they are embodied. This was developed in the Middle Ages on the basis of *Plato's metaphysic and opposed by *Nominalism.

recapitulation (Lat. *recapitulatio*, a 'summing up', 'summary'). The Greek equivalent in its verbal form is used in Eph. 1: 10, where God is said to 'sum up' all things in Christ; from this passage the term was taken over by the Fathers. The conception of recapitulation was elaborated by St *Irenaeus, who interpreted it both as the restoration of fallen humanity to communion with God through the obedience of Christ and as the summing up of the revelations of God in past ages in the Incarnation.

Recared (d. 601), King of the Visigoths. He was associated with his father in governing the country (most of Spain) from 573 and succeeded him in 586. In 587 he abandoned

*Arianism and became a Catholic. This step helped to pacify the country, since the Catholic clergy and nobles were more powerful than the Arian Visigoths.

reception. The informal process by which the whole Church gives subsequent assent to a conciliar or Papal decision. While the development of Papal *authority has led reception to be largely neglected in the RC Church, Anglicans and Orthodox have emphasized it in modern times. Recently the idea has been used in the Anglican Communion to support experimentation in the expectation that innovations might come to be 'received'.

receptionism. A form of Eucharistic teaching according to which, while the bread and wine continue to exist unchanged after consecration, the faithful communicant receives together with them the Body and Blood of Christ.

recluse. A person who lives apart from the world, especially for the purpose of religious meditation.

Recognitions, Clementine. See CLEMENTINE LITERATURE.

recollection. A term used by modern spiritual writers to denote an attitude of attentiveness to God and to oneself. The idea that the soul becomes dissipated through concern for worldly things and should 'collect itself' into itself to concentrate on its spiritual purpose goes back at least to *Plato. The noun 'recollection' (in its Spanish form) dates from the 15th cent. Some writers, such as *Teresa of Ávila, treat recollection as a kind or stage of prayer. Later the term was extended to cover almost any kind of spiritual exercise.

Recollects. Two religious Orders:
(1) The Franciscan Recollects. A reformed branch of the Franciscan *Observants, started in France at the end of the 16th cent. In 1897 they were incorporated with the other Observants.
(2) The Augustinian Recollects. A strict branch of the *Augustinian Hermits, started in Spain. Their first house was founded in 1589. They were erected into a separate province in 1602, formed a separate congregation in 1621 and in 1912 were constituted an independent Order.

Record, The. An Anglican weekly newspaper, begun in 1828. It was strongly *Evangelical. In 1949 it was amalgamated with the *Church of England Newspaper*.

rector. In the C of E, the rector was the person entitled to the whole *tithes of a parish. At first the rector was the incumbent, and it is when these two positions are still combined that the term is most familiar. Where, however, the tithes were appropriated to a monastery or other spiritual body, the clergyman in the parish was merely the rector's *vicar (substitute) or *curate. See also VICAR and LAY RECTOR.

In the RC Church the heads of *seminaries and *Jesuit houses are commonly styled rectors. Otherwise rectors are normally priests with the care of churches which are not parochial, capitular, or attached to a religious community or society.

recusancy. Refusal to submit to authority, and especially refusal to attend the services of the established C of E. Though used particularly of RC recusants, it was also applied to Protestant *Separatists. Until the Pope excommunicated *Elizabeth I in 1570, recusancy had been rare, since conservative religious elements had received no clear instruction about their attitude to the Establishment. It received a powerful impetus with the arrival of *Jesuits and other priests from the Continent c.1580. Elizabethan and Jacobean statesmen regarded it as a dangerous problem because of its tenacious roots throughout the social structure of some regions, e.g. in the North of England. The small recusant minority preserved the continuity of RC practice in England. See also ROMAN CATHOLIC CHURCH IN ENGLAND AND WALES AFTER THE REFORMATION.

Redaction Criticism. The investigation of the editorial work done by biblical writers on earlier material, e.g. of the use of the Marcan material by Matthew and Luke.

Red Hat. The flat-crowned broad-brimmed hat traditionally distinctive of a *cardinal. Although cardinals are now invested with a red *biretta instead, the expression 'red hat' is still used for the cardinal's office.

red letter day. An important feast or saint's day, often printed in red in ecclesiastical calendars. In the C of E the term is applied to the days for which the BCP provides a proper Collect, Epistle, and Gospel.

Red Mass. According to W. usage, a *Votive Mass of the Holy Spirit, so called from the red vestments in which it is traditionally celebrated.

Red Sea. The crossing of the Red Sea by the Israelites, recorded in Exod. 14 and 15, marked the end of their bondage in Egypt and was subsequently regarded as a turning-point in their destiny.

redemption. The idea of redemption is common to many religions, being based on the desire of man to be delivered from sin, suffering, and death. Christianity claims that it has become a fact through the Incarnation and Death of Christ. It is viewed by theologians under the double aspect of deliverance from sin and the restoration of man and the world to communion with God.

While the Greek Fathers stressed the restoration of man to the Divine life (see DEIFICATION), the Latins gave primacy to the expiation of our sins through the sacrificial death of Christ and worked out their theology of redemption in connection with the doctrine of *Original Sin. St *Thomas Aquinas maintained that, though it was impossible that sin should be abolished as a physical reality, it could be repaired morally by the objective merits of the Redeemer, which, applied to the repentant sinner, enabled him to co-operate with *grace towards justification and sanctification. The Reformers denied the possibility of human co-operation except by faith alone, and placed exclusive emphasis on the forgiveness of sin and justification by imputation of the righteousness of Christ. In the 16th and 17th cents. some Protestant and RC theologians, influenced by the teaching of J. *Calvin and C. *Jansen, maintained that Redemption extends only to the elect; this was pronounced heretical by *Innocent X in 1653. See also ATONEMENT.

Redemptorists. Members of the 'Congregation of the Most Holy Redeemer', founded by St *Alphonsus Liguori in 1732. This was instituted for mission work among the poor both in Europe and among the heathen, and it has refused to engage in purely educational activities.

Reformatio   Legum   Ecclesiasticarum
(Lat., 'the Reform of the Ecclesiastical Laws'), a book which was designed to provide a system of order and discipline for the C of E in place of the medieval *canon law. It was presented to Parliament in March 1553, but the death of *Edward VI prevented further progress.

Reformation, the. The term is sometimes used to describe a series of changes in W. Christendom between the 14th and 17th cents., but is usually restricted to the early 16th cent. It is said to have begun with the attacks of the *Lollards and the *Hussites upon the hierarchical structure of the Church. Until the early 16th cent. divergence from Catholic doctrine was uncommon, but there were many attacks upon the financial exactions of the Papacy and Curia and upon their worldliness and involvement in the dynastic politics of Italy. M. *Luther was breaking no new ground when he protested against the corruptions of Rome and the abuses attending the sale of *indulgences. His study of St *Augustine had led him to question devotional practices and the emphasis of late medieval theology on 'good works'; later his historical reading raised doubts about the validity of the Papal claims to supremacy. From these traditionalist origins were derived his fundamental attacks on *transubstantiation, clerical *celibacy and the religious orders, as well as his demands for the abolition of Papal power in Germany. The rulers of Saxony, Hesse, Brandenburg, Brunswick, *Denmark and *Sweden were won to the reformed beliefs before or shortly after their classic enunciation in the 'Confession of *Augsburg' (1530). These rulers reorganized and regulated the Churches within their territories according to Lutheran principles, which were also adopted by a number of the imperial cities of Germany.

Meanwhile in 1523-5 the Swiss Reformer U. *Zwingli had won the support of the civic authorities of Zurich and carried through anti-papal, anti-hierarchic, and anti-monastic reforms in the city. Zwingli's theology, more radical and less scholastic in his Eucharistic and social doctrines than Luther's, affected many of the Swiss cantons and some cities in SW Germany. After Zwingli's death (1531) leadership of the Swiss Reformation passed to *Geneva.

Here, from 1541, J. *Calvin established an elaborately organized theocracy. A coherent theological system based upon the doctrine of *predestination was provided by his *Institutes* (1536). *Calvinism for several generations became the driving force of the Reformation, especially in W. Germany, *France, the *Netherlands, *Scotland, and England. In nearly every case it was linked with political struggle.

The English Reformation was an insular process responsive to peculiar political and social forces. *Henry VIII, a convinced traditionalist in both doctrine and Church government, accomplished the overthrow of Papal supremacy and the *dissolution of the monasteries largely in pursuit of short-term political ends and the extension of royal control. Despite his opposition, reforming Continental doctrines and native heresy became more widespread. During the reign of *Edward VI, political calculation and the influence of T. *Cranmer and others led to a more wide-ranging alteration of doctrine and liturgy. After *Mary's attempt to reverse the changes, the accession of *Elizabeth I was followed by the reimposition of the earlier Protestant formularies. The English Reformation grafted elements of Reformed theology and worship on to a traditional Church structure; the continuities ensured peaceful change, and, ultimately, widespread public acceptance. See also CHURCH OF ENGLAND.

Reformed Churches. The term is sometimes taken to include all the Protestant Churches, but it is more accurately used specifically of those influenced by the theology of J. *Calvin, J. *Knox, and U. *Zwingli (popularly called *Calvinist), as contrasted with the *Lutherans.

Reformed Presbyterian Church. The small body of Scottish *Presbyterians who declined to accept the settlement of 1690 which established the Church of *Scotland. The Reformed Presbytery was formed in 1743. The majority joined the *Free Church of Scotland in 1876, but some remain as an independent body.

Refreshment Sunday. The Fourth Sunday in *Lent, so called perhaps in reference to the traditional Gospel of the day relating the feeding of the five thousand (Jn. 6: 1–14), or perhaps because of the relaxation of the Lenten discipline allowed on this day.

Regale. The right to the revenues of vacant bishoprics and abbeys and to presentation to their dependent benefices claimed by the kings of Europe during the Middle Ages. The claim was denied by the Papacy and became associated with the *Investiture Controversy. In England it is still enjoyed by the Crown over the temporalities of vacant sees (though the revenues are now restored untouched when the newly elected bishop does homage).

regeneration. The spiritual rebirth which, according to traditional theology, is effected in the soul by *Baptism.

Regensburg, Conference of. See RATISBON, CONFERENCE OF.

Regina Coeli (Lat., 'Queen of Heaven'). The *Eastertide anthem to the BVM, so called from its opening words. Its authorship is unknown, but it probably dates from the 12th cent.

Reginald of Piperno (*c*.1230–1285/95), *Dominican friar. He was known as the 'lifelong' companion of St *Thomas Aquinas. He collected Thomas's writings and it was probably under his editorship that the Supplement to the Third Part of the *Summa Theologiae* was compiled.

regionarius. A name in use in the Middle Ages for certain of the clergy of Rome.

Regium Donum (Lat., 'Royal Gift'). A grant made from public funds to the ministers of the *Presbyterian, *Baptist, and *Congregational Churches in England until 1851. It originated in sums which *Charles II ordered to be paid to Presbyterian ministers after the *Declaration of Indulgence of 1672.

Regnans in Excelsis (1570). The bull of excommunication against *Elizabeth I issued by *Pius V.

Regula Fidei. See RULE OF FAITH.

Regula Magistri. An anonymous monastic Rule written by 'the Master' in Italy SE of Rome *c*.500–25. In part it is verbally identical with the Rule of St *Benedict; the relationship of the two Rules has been the subject of controversy, but nearly all scholars now give priority to the *Regula Magistri*.

regular. A general term for members of the

RC clergy who are bound by *vows of religion and live in community, following a rule. They are distinguished from the *seculars, i.e. priests living in the world.

regular canons; regular clerks. See CANONS REGULAR; CLERKS REGULAR.

Regularis Concordia. A code of monastic observance in England, approved by a Synod of *Winchester some time between 970 and 973. According to *Aelfric, it would appear that it was the work of St *Ethelwold, though it was probably inspired by St *Dunstan, to whom it was long attributed. Its provisions generally follow the *Benedictine tradition.

Reichenau. A small island in the western arm of Lake Constance famous for its *Benedictine monastery, founded by St *Pirminius in 724. It was an important centre of culture.

Reichsbischof. The title adopted in 1933 for the head of the united German Evangelical Church.

Reimarus, Hermann Samuel (1694–1768), *Deist and biblical critic. From 1727 he was professor of Hebrew and Oriental languages at Hamburg. Between 1744 and 1767 he composed the treatise from which G. E. *Lessing published the *Wolfenbüttel Fragments* in 1774–8. The work, which Reimarus withheld from publication during his lifetime, rejected miracles and revelation, and accused the biblical writers of conscious fraud, contradictions, and fanaticism. It was published in full in 1972.

Reims. According to tradition the see was founded in the 3rd cent., but the first bishop of whom there is historical evidence was Imbetausius, who took part in the Council of *Arles (314). The power of the see increased under St *Remigius (d. c.533; q.v.), who baptized *Clovis and evangelized the surrounding districts, and under *Hincmar (d. 882). From the mid-10th cent. the Abps. of Reims successfully claimed the right to crown the French kings. The cathedral, a fine example of French Gothic, was begun in 1211 and completed in the 14th cent. The treasury contains the remains of the Sainte Ampoule (see AMPULLA).

Reims New Testament. See DOUAI-REIMS BIBLE.

reincarnation. See METEMPSYCHOSIS.

Reinkens, Joseph Hubert (1821–96), *Old Catholic bishop. He became professor of Church history at Breslau in 1850. He opposed the definition of Papal Infallibility at the First *Vatican Council and in 1871 he joined in the *Nuremberg Declaration. Excommunicated by the RC Church, he was elected the first bishop of the German Old Catholics in 1873 and consecrated by Bp. Hermann Heykamp of Deventer.

Reitzenstein, Richard (1861–1931), German classical philologist and historian of religions. In *Poimandres* (1904) he tried to show that NT phraseology and ideas were largely derived from *Hermetic sources and that the Christian Churches were modelled on Hermetic communities.

relics. In Christian usage the word is most commonly applied to the material remains of a saint after his death and to sacred objects which have been in contact with his body. The most important relic, however, has been the True Cross (or fragments of it), according to tradition discovered by St *Helena in 326. From an early date the bodies of *martyrs were venerated; clear evidence comes from the 'Martyrdom of Polycarp' (c.156–7). At Rome the cult was linked with the *catacombs, where services were held at their tombs. In opposition to the *Iconoclasts, who rejected the veneration of relics as well as of *icons, the Second Council of *Nicaea (787) anathematized those who despised relics and ordered that no church should be consecrated without them. In the W. the cult increased enormously during the *Crusades, when quantities of relics, often spurious, were brought back from the Holy Land. They were kept in *reliquaries, carried in procession, and often gave rise to superstitious practices.

The theological foundation for the cult of relics was developed in the Middle Ages. Stress was laid on the special dignity of the bodies of saints as temples of the Holy Spirit destined to a glorious resurrection, and on the sanction given by the Godhead in making them the occasion of miracles. The doctrine was confirmed by the Council of *Trent against the Reformers. See also SAINTS, DEVOTION TO THE.

Relief Acts. See CATHOLIC RELIEF ACTS.

Religionsgeschichtliche Schule. The 'History of Religion School', an influential group of German biblical scholars between 1880 and 1920 who advocated extensive use of data from the comparative study of religion in the interpretation of Christianity. They reduced dogmatic considerations to a minimum and held that religious documents have to be considered not as isolated expressions of their authors' thoughts and aspirations, but as the product of a long and often complex development of the tribe or country. At first they tried only to trace historical developments within Judaism and Christianity, but soon they came to search for parallels in Egyptian, Babylonian, and Hellenistic religious systems.

religious. The technical name for a member of a Religious *Institute of Consecrated Life (q.v.). Religious bind themselves by a public *vow to observe the evangelical *counsels of obedience, chastity, and poverty, and live a common life.

Religious Institutes. See INSTITUTES OF CONSECRATED LIFE.

religious orders in Anglicanism. The revival of religious orders in the Anglican Communion was one of the results of the *Oxford Movement. In 1841 E. B. *Pusey received the vows of Marian Rebecca Hughes, who in 1849 became the first superior of the Convent of the Holy and Undivided Trinity at Oxford, and in 1845 he founded the first community at Park Village, Regent's Park, in London which was later merged in the Society of the Holy Trinity, founded at Devonport by Priscilla Lydia *Sellon in 1848. Other communities followed in quick succession, including the Community of St Mary the Virgin at Wantage (1848), the Community of St John the Baptist at Clewer (1852), and the Community of St Margaret at East Grinstead (1855). These were all 'active' or 'mixed' communities, combining the monastic life with a life of service, and they were among the pioneers in the care of the poor in the slums of the great cities. The Deaconess Community of St Andrew, founded in 1861, was unique in combining community life with admission to the order of *deaconess. In 1907, with the foundation of the first 'enclosed' community, the Sisters of the Love of God, at Fairacres, Oxford, the 'contemplative' life was revived.

The first religious order for men was the *Society of St John the Evangelist, founded at Cowley in 1865. The *Community of the Resurrection (founded in 1892) and the Society of the Sacred Mission, which was at Kelham from 1903 to 1974, both trained ordinands. The English Order of St Benedict (from 1926 to 1987 at Nashdom) derived from the community founded on Caldey Island in 1906, most of whose members had joined the RC Church in 1913. In 1981 the Rule of St *Benedict was adopted by the community at Alton Abbey (founded at Rangoon in 1884). In 1931 an Anglican *Franciscan Order was established, and in 1938 R. C. S. Gofton-Salmond retired to a woodland property near Crawley, West Sussex, where the Community of the Servants of the Will of God follow a contemplative vocation of a semi-eremitic type.

In recent years there has been a decline in vocations; some orders have closed and some have moved to smaller buildings. A few of the smaller women's communities have become *double monasteries, and there has been increased interest in the eremitic life.

From England the revival of the religious life spread over much of the Anglican Communion. Many of the English orders have branches overseas and new communities have grown up in America, Africa, India, and Australasia.

Religious Tract Society. A society of Anglicans and Nonconformists founded in 1799 for the publication and dissemination of tracts and other evangelical literature. In 1935 it was absorbed in the *United Society for Christian Literature.

reliquary. A receptacle for *relics. Reliquaries, in various shapes, are often made of precious metals and richly decorated.

Rembrandt (1606–69) **(Rembrandt Harmensz or Harmenszoon van Rijn),** Dutch painter. The son of a wealthy miller of *Leiden, he was famous for his portraits by the time he moved to Amsterdam in 1631. His wife died in 1642, financial difficulties led to bankruptcy, and in 1654 the scandal of having a child by his servant brought him into conflict with the Reformed Church at Amsterdam. These sufferings helped to deepen and spiritualize his art and to give him an understanding of the Passion, the theme of some 90 paintings and etchings. Characteristic was his treatment of light and shade out of which his human figures appear to grow, thereby producing an impression of a happening beyond space and time.

Remigius, St (d. *c.*533), also **Remi**, 'Apostle of the Franks'. He is reputed to have been elected bishop of the metropolitan see of *Reims at the age of 22, perhaps *c.*458. His Baptism of *Clovis, with many of his subjects, marked the beginning of a close co-operation between the Church and the Frankish ruler. He directed missions to the Morini and the *Arians of Burgundy and is associated with the foundation of various bishoprics. According to legend, the *ampulla of chrism used in the coronation of French kings was brought by a dove in answer to his prayers at the Baptism of Clovis. Feast day, 1 Oct., now dropped.

Remigius of Auxerre (*c.*841–*c.*908), scholar and teacher. He was a monk of St Germanus, Auxerre. He taught there, at *Reims, and then at *Paris. He followed a comprehensive programme based on literary and moral texts, commenting on classical and Christian authors. Though not an original thinker, he did more than anyone else we know of to make sound learning available to his contemporaries and successors.

Remonstrance, the. The statement of *Arminian doctrine drawn up at Gouda in 1610. It contains the celebrated five articles, taken from J. Arminius' *Declaratio Sententiae* of 1608, which summarized the Remonstrants' doctrine and set the agenda for the ensuing controversies. It repudiated both the *Supralapsarian and *Sublapsarian form of *predestination, the doctrine that Christ died only for the elect, and the notion that, for the latter, grace was both irresistible and indefectible. The Remonstrants were condemned at the Synod of *Dort (1618–19).

Renan, Joseph Ernest (1823–92), French philosopher, theologian, and orientalist. His *Averroès et l'averroïsme* (1852) established his reputation as a scholar. In 1860 he was sent on an archaeological mission to Phoenicia and Syria; while in Palestine he wrote his *Vie de Jésus*. In this he repudiated the supernatural element in Christ's life,

ignored its moral aspect, and portrayed Him as an amiable Galilean preacher. Its publication in 1863 created a sensation. A study of *Joachim of Fiore (1866) combines serious scholarship with a romantic vision of a new 'religion of humanity'.

Renaudot, Eusèbe (1646–1720), French orientalist and liturgist. His chief theological works are his *Historia Patriarcharum Alexandrinorum Jacobitarum* (1713) and his *Liturgiarum Orientalium Collectio* (1716). The latter contains the texts of many E. liturgies and is still indispensable.

Renunciation of the Devil. The renunciation of Satan at *Baptism is attested in the *Apostolic Tradition* and has been a regular part of almost all Baptismal rites, E. and W.

reordination. The repetition of an ordination to the priesthood which has been conferred either *extra ecclesiam*, i.e. by a heretical or schismatic bishop, or *intra ecclesiam* but not canonically, e.g. by a deposed or simoniacal bishop. Though a matter of controversy from the 3rd cent., reordination was often practised before the 12th cent., when the doctrine of the *Sacraments began to receive more precise formulation. According to Catholic theology the Sacrament of *Orders is held to confer on the recipient an indelible *character, provided that it is conferred in the prescribed form and with the right *intention. The Greek Church repudiated reordination at the *Trullan Synod (692), but has continued to waver in its practice.

reparation. The making amends for damage done to another. In moral theology it is generally used in a sense similar to *restitution. In modern devotional language the term is often used for the amends made to God for offences against Him by means of prayer and penance. It plays a central part in the *Sacred Heart devotion.

repentance. The acknowledgement and condemnation of one's sins, coupled with a turning to God. It includes sorrow for the sin committed, confession of guilt, and the purpose of amendment.

Repington, Philip (d. 1424), Bp. of *Lincoln from 1404 to 1419. In early life he supported the teaching of J. *Wycliffe; in 1382 he was excommunicated, but he soon recanted. He was twice chancellor of the University of

Oxford, and soon after his accession in 1399 Henry IV made him his confessor.

Repose, Altar of. An altar to which (according to W. usage) *Hosts consecrated at the *Maundy Thursday Mass are taken and kept for Communion on *Good Friday.

Reproaches, the. A set of reproaches addressed by the Crucified Saviour to His ungrateful people, which form part of the *Good Friday liturgy of the RC Church. They are built up on OT passages, but their early history is obscure. They are sung during the *Veneration of the Cross.

reprobation. The act by which God condemns sinners to eternal punishment, and the state of this punishment. St *Augustine used expressions which could be taken as meaning that God predestines some men to sin and damnation, and in the 9th cent. *Gottschalk was accused of teaching this explicitly. This issue has been central to the controversies over *predestination (q.v.).

Requiem. A Mass offered for the dead, so named from the opening word of the *Introit which, until recently, was used at all such Masses in the Roman rite. Many of the features previously characteristic of requiems, such as the requirement to use unbleached candles, disappeared in 1970.

reredos. Any decoration put up above and behind an altar. The earliest were paintings on the walls against which altars backed. In the Middle Ages the reredos was usually made of painted wooden panels, either fixed or in the form of a triptych, or of carved stone or alabaster.

Rerum Novarum (1891). An encyclical of *Leo XIII, intended to apply traditional Catholic teaching to the conditions created by the Industrial Revolution. On the ground that society originated in the family, it proclaimed private property a natural right and condemned socialism as infringing it; it upheld the ideal of a just wage, defined as 'enough to support the wage-earner in reasonable and frugal comfort' with a family; and it maintained that the natural place of women was in the home.

Reservation. The practice of keeping the Bread (and occasionally also the Wine) consecrated at the Eucharist, primarily for the purpose of Communion. At first the faithful kept the Bl Sacrament in their homes or on their persons, but from the 4th cent. the churches became the ordinary places for reservation. The Sacrament was kept either in the sacristy or in the church itself, in an *aumbry in the wall, in a *pyx hanging over the altar, or in a *tabernacle on the altar, the last being until recently the normal modern practice in the RC Church, as it still is in the E. Church. Current RC legislation favours reservation in a separate chapel, but allows some latitude. A lamp is kept burning nearby as a sign of honour. Reservation under the Species of Bread only seems originally to have been the common practice in both E. and W., but in the E. the Host is now marked with consecrated Wine from a communion spoon and may then be artificially dried.

In the C of E the 1549 BCP provided for reservation for the Communion of the sick, but the provision was dropped in 1552. In the 19th and 20th cents. the practice was revived in some places. It is implicitly recognized in the rubrics of some modern Anglican liturgies.

reservation, mental. See MENTAL RESERVATION.

reserved sins. Bishops in the RC Church have the right to 'reserve' certain sins to their own jurisdiction. In the 1983 *Codex Iuris Canonici there are no longer any sins reserved by law, but a penalty can be reserved, so that its remission may be obtained only through specified ecclesiastical authorities, such as diocesan bishops. A few grave matters are reserved to the Pope.

residence. All clergy are under a grave obligation to reside in the place in which they are authorized to minister. Owing to frequent abuses, injunctions on the subject figure in *canons from early times; the duty is precisely specified in modern RC canon law and in the C of E canons of 1969.

responses. See VERSICLES.

responsory. A liturgical chant traditionally consisting of a series of *versicles and responses, the text usually taken from Scripture. The arrangement was designed for the alternate singing of sentences or lines by different people. At Mass there were formerly responsories at the *Gradual (now replaced by a Responsorial Psalm sung by cantor or choir and people) and at the *Offertory. In the Divine *Office there are responsories after the lessons in the '*Office of Readings' and a shorter form, the 'responsorium breve', follows the Little *Chapter in the other Offices.

restitution. In W. *moral theology, the act of 'commutative justice' by which an injury done to another person is repaired.

Resurrection, Community of the. See COMMUNITY OF THE RESURRECTION.

Resurrection of Christ. The conviction that God not only sent His Son into the world but also vindicated Him after His death upon a cross, is fundamental to the NT witness and the cornerstone of Christian faith and theology.

One of the earliest Christian creeds, quoted by St *Paul at 1 Cor. 15: 3–5 (perhaps 15: 3–7) speaks of Christ being raised (i.e. by God) 'on the third day', and appearing to Cephas (i.e. St *Peter) and to the twelve. Other appearances are listed. Paul insists (v. 11) that this belief was shared on all sides in the early Church.

The Gospels report the discovery of Christ's empty tomb either by St *Mary Magdalene alone (Jn. 20: 1–9) or with one or more other women (Mt. 28: 1; Mk. 16: 1; Lk. 24: 10). They disagree over other details: whether it was one or two angels or young men who told of Christ's resurrection, whether Christ Himself then appeared, whether He or the young man directed the disciples to *Galilee, and whether the women obeyed. Appearances in *Jerusalem and/or Galilee follow. Attempts to harmonize these traditions have not persuaded critics, but the testimony of the biblical writers to the Divine event itself is unanimous. However, because Paul (writing earlier than the Evangelists) did not mention the empty tomb, some modern critics have questioned its historicity.

The nature of Christ's risen body has been a matter of debate. Insistence on its objective reality may be found at Lk. 24: 36–43, but the Gospels generally avoid implying that He was restored to His previous earthly life; He is said, for example, to have passed through closed doors (Jn. 20: 19).

resurrection of the dead. It is a fundamental Christian belief that at the *Parousia or 'Second Coming' of Christ departed souls will be restored to bodily life and the saved will enter in this renewed form upon the life of heaven. The Christian teaching on the resurrection of the dead differs from the Greek doctrine of the natural immortality of the soul in that it implies a restoration of the whole psychophysical organism, and it holds that life after death is wholly a gift of God. At some periods it has been maintained that the resurrection will involve revivifying the material particles of the dead body, but many theologians now argue that the resurrection body will be a body of a new order, identical with the earthly body only in the sense that it will be the recognizable organism of the same personality.

retable. A structure placed at the back of an altar in the form either of a ledge on which ornaments may be set or a frame for decorated panels.

retreat. A period of days spent in silence and occupied with religious exercises. As a formal devotion, retreats were introduced in the *Counter-Reformation period; retreat houses were established in the 17th cent. In the RC Church the practice of making an annual retreat became widespread in the 19th cent.

Retz, Cardinal de (Jean-François-Paul de Gondi) (1613–79), Abp. of *Paris. He was forced into an ecclesiastical career by his family, who had held the see of Paris since 1570. In 1643 he was appointed Coadjutor-Abp. of Paris to his uncle and in 1652 made a cardinal. Soon afterwards, at the insistence of J. *Mazarin, he was imprisoned. On his uncle's death in 1654, the King made him sign a resignation of the archbishopric, but the Pope refused to accept it. Retz escaped from prison and went to Rome. After Mazarin's death, in 1661 he returned to Paris and resigned his see in exchange for the abbey of *Saint-Denis, held *in commendam*.

Reuchlin, Johannes (1454/5–1522), German humanist. About 1485 he began to study Hebrew, with the help of learned Jews, and he became interested in *Kabbalistic doctrines. His most important work, *De Rudimentis Hebraicis* (1506), which consists of a Hebrew grammar and lexicon, placed the scientific study of Hebrew on a new basis and encouraged the study of the OT in the original. His later life was troubled by controversy with the *Dominicans of Cologne, who advocated the destruction of Jewish religious books. His opposition, combined with his interest in Kabbala, led to his being involved in a long trial for heresy. He remained a loyal Catholic.

reunion. Desire for the visible unity of the Church increased in the 20th cent. as growing doctrinal agreement between the major Christian denominations was reinforced by liturgical reforms. In modern times there has also been an increased openness in the attitude of the RC Church towards members of other communions.

Reunion with the *Orthodox Church has frequently been attempted by W. Churches. After the short-lived union effected by the Council of *Florence (1439), there were other less important *rapprochements*. Some Orthodox Churches sent observers to the Second *Vatican Council, and in 1965 the mutual anathemas of 1054 between the E. and W. Churches were lifted. There have been contacts between the Orthodox and the C of E since the 18th cent. (now impeded by the ordination of *women), and Orthodox Churches are engaged in discussions with the *Old Catholics and *Reformed Churches.

Since the 17th cent. there have been aspirations for reunion between the C of E and the RC Church, notably at the time of the *Oxford and post-*Tractarian movements and of the *Malines Conversations (1921–5). There have also been several efforts to unite the English dissenting bodies with the Established Church, beginning with the abortive attempt at the Restoration to 'comprehend' *Presbyterians and Independents. The *Lambeth Conference of 1888 laid down four conditions for such a union (the *Lambeth Quadrilateral). The main difficulty which emerged in conversations between the C of E and the Free Churches concerned questions of ministry. These figured largely in the abortive *Anglican-Methodist Conversations and the proposals of the Churches' Council for Covenanting, set up in 1978, but rejected by the C of E in 1982.

Schemes for reunion between the C of E and foreign Protestant bodies have been discussed intermittently since the 16th cent. In the 20th cent. there were agreements to establish mutual Eucharistic hospitality between the C of E and various *Lutheran State Churches in Europe. The Porvoo Agreement, reached in 1992, envisaged a relationship between the Anglican Churches of Britain and Ireland and the Nordic and Balkan Lutheran Churches with a common membership and interchangeable ministry: it was ratified by all the Churches except those of Latvia and Denmark. In 2001 a similar scheme brought the Evangelical Lutheran Church in America and the *Episcopal Church into a relationship described as 'full communion'.

While numerous negotiations have proved abortive, there have been a series of Church unions since the early 19th cent. Past divisions have been healed by *Presbyterians in *Scotland in 1847, 1900 and 1929 and in the USA in 1958 and 1983, between Methodist bodies both in Britain and the USA. Across denominational boundaries, the Lutheran and Reformed Churches of Prussia were brought together in 1817 in the United Evangelical Church of Prussia, later constituted the Church of the Union, and in 1972 the Presbyterian Church of England and the greater part of the Congregational Church of England and Wales united to form the *United Reformed Church. Unions formed on a multidenominational basis include united Churches in *Canada (formed in 1925), *South India (1947), the *Philippines (1948), *Zambia (1965), *Zaire (1970), *North India (1970), *Pakistan (1970), Bangladesh (1971), and *Australia (1977). In these unions Presbyterians and Congregationalists have most often been involved; Anglicans entered only the unions on the Indian subcontinent. In Africa and Asia local unions have played an important part in indigenizing the Church, as several missionary-founded Churches have been succeeded by a single locally funded and locally led Church. In 1970 two world confessional organizations joined to form the *World Alliance of Reformed Churches, which encourages its member Churches to enter into unions. See also ANGLICAN-ROMAN CATHOLIC INTERNATIONAL COMMISSION, CONSULTATION ON CHURCH UNION, ECUMENICAL MOVEMENT, LEUENBERG CONCORD, UNIAT CHURCHES.

Reusch, Franz Heinrich (1825–1900), *Old Catholic theologian. In 1870 he opposed the *infallibility decrees of the First *Vatican Council and in 1872 he was excommunicated on his refusal to subscribe. He then took a leading part in organizing the Old Catholic Church and in arranging the *Bonn Conferences of 1874 and 1875. When the Old Catholics abandoned clerical *celibacy in 1878, Reusch protested and retired into lay communion.

revelation. In Christian theology the word is used both of the body of truth about Himself which God discloses and of the process by which His communication of it takes place. Since it is commonly held that some truths about God can be learnt through man's natural endowments (e.g. His existence, which philosophers outside the Christian tradition have claimed they could establish), while others, e.g. the doctrine of the Holy *Trinity, are not knowable except by faith, Christian philosophers have distinguished between 'truths of reason' and 'truths of revelation'. Traditionally Protestants have held that all revelation is sufficiently contained in the Bible, Catholics that part is also to be found in the unwritten traditions of the Church, but in recent times RC theologians have drawn a less sharp distinction between *tradition and Scripture and stressed their ultimate unity.

Revelation, Book of. The last Book of the NT and the only one that is an *Apocalypse. Apart from the letters to the *Seven Churches of Asia Minor, the Book consists of a series of visions.

The author is identified as 'John' in the title and at 1: 9, and called 'the theologian' ('the divine') in later MSS of the title. In the W. he was from an early date held to be St *John the Apostle, but it is unlikely that he is this John. There are a few verbal points of contact with St *John's Gospel and the Johannine Epistles; such features could suggest a common theological background for the authors of Rev. and Jn., but common authorship is precluded by wide differences in eschatology, tone, and language.

Its hostile attitude to Rome indicates that the Book cannot be earlier than the persecution under *Nero in 64. It more probably dates from a later persecution, perhaps that of *Domitian (81–96). Many of the pictures and images doutbless have a historical reference, but the aim of the Book is to give assurance about God's power and purpose, rather than information about events to come. Its political passion on behalf of the oppressed has attracted some modern readers, but its importance and potentially dangerous impact stem from its futuristic eschatology and the use made of it by *millenarians of all periods, and especially by *fundamentalist Protestants today.

Reverend. An epithet of respect applied to the clergy since the 15th cent. Since the 17th cent. it has been used as a title prefixed to their names in correspondence. Archbishops are styled 'Most Reverend'; other bishops 'Right Reverend', and deans 'Very Reverend'.

Revised Version of the Bible. See BIBLE (ENGLISH VERSIONS), 4.

revivalism. A type of religious worship and practice centring on evangelical revivals, or outbursts of mass religious fervour, and stimulated by intensive preaching and prayer meetings.

Rheims. See REIMS.

Rhenanus, Beatus (1485–1547), German humanist. He produced many editions of the classics and of the *Fathers and an excellent work on German antiquities. He wrote the earliest Life of his friend *Erasmus (published first in Erasmus' translation of *Origen). Like him, Rhenanus at first favoured the Reformers, but changed his attitude when the revolutionary character of Protestantism became apparent.

Rhodes, Knights of. See HOSPITALLERS.

Rhodo (2nd cent.), anti-*Gnostic apologist. For a time he was a disciple of *Tatian at Rome; he wrote under the Emp. Commodus (180–92).

rhythmical office. A form of the Divine *Office, popular in the Middle Ages, in which not only the hymns but also almost all the other parts except the psalms and lessons were put into metre or rhyme.

Ricci, Matteo (1552–1610), *Jesuit missionary. In 1582 he was sent to Macao, where he began to learn Chinese; in 1601 he settled in Beijing. He gained favour at court by displaying European scientific inventions and explaining astronomy; he influenced the scholarly élite by his assimilation of Confucian classics to Christian humanist ethics in various apologetic and catechetical works. Full Christian catechesis was kept for a later stage. Criticism of his method of *accommodation was one of the factors leading to the Rites Controversy about 100 years later. See CHINA, CHRISTIANITY IN.

Ricci, Scipione de' (1741–1810), ecclesiastical reformer. In 1780 he became Bp. of Pistoia-Prato. He took the lead in introducing into N. Italy *Josephinist doctrines and a higher standard of morals. He carried through a plan of reform at the Synod of *Pistoia (1786), but he met with much opposition and resigned his see in 1791.

Richard of Chichester, St (c.1197–1253), Bp. of *Chichester. He was born at 'Wych' (i.e. Droitwich) and hence is sometimes known as 'Richard of Wych'. He was elected Bp. of Chichester in 1244 and consecrated by *Innocent IV in 1245. He was a man of deep spirituality and an excellent administrator. Feast day, 3 Apr; of his translation, 16 Jun.

Richard of Middleton (born c.1249), 'Richardus de Mediavilla', *Franciscan philosopher and theologian. It is disputed whether he was English or French, and little is known of his life. He was certainly a regent master in Paris from 1284 to 1287. His chief works are a commentary on the 'Sentences' of *Peter Lombard, which is notable for its clarity and precision, *Quodlibets*, and *Quaestiones disputatae*.

Richard of St-Victor (d. 1173), *Victorine theologian and spiritual writer. Apparently a native of Scotland, he came to the Abbey of St-Victor in Paris as a young man. His most important theological work, a treatise *De Trinitate*, presents a complex argument, based on the nature of love, of necessary reasons for a triune deity. His other writings are mainly on the spiritual life and scriptural exegesis. He insisted on the importance of demonstration and argument in matters of theology and the folly of relying only on an array of authorities.

Richelieu, Armand Jean du Plessis (1585–1642), French theologian and politician. He was created a cardinal in 1622; he became President of the Council of Ministers in 1624 and from 1629 he was chief minister of France. Seeking to establish a centralized absolutism, he opposed both the feudal aristocracy and the *Huguenots; the latter were defeated at La Rochelle in 1628 and their political privileges abolished. Abroad he allied himself with the Protestant German princes and with *Gustavus Adolphus of Sweden against the Emperor, thereby impeding the progress of the *Counter-Reformation in Germany. He kept his political and religious commitments separate. He was Abbot-General of *Cluny from 1629 and encouraged reform of the *Benedictine and other religious orders, and he fostered the revival of religious practice and the training of priests.

Ridley, Nicholas (c.1500–55), Bp. of London from 1550. From c.1535 he had leanings towards the teaching of the Reformers, and c.1546 he influenced the shift in T. *Cranmer's Eucharistic views away from the *Real Presence. He helped in the composition of the 1549 BCP and in the establishment of Protestantism in the University of *Cambridge. Nevertheless in 1550–51 he played a leading role in defeating J. *Hooper's attempt to avoid wearing *rochet and *chimere at his consecration. On *Mary's accession he was deprived of his see. He was excommunicated in 1554 and burnt with H. *Latimer. In the American BCP (1979) and CW, feast day, 16 Oct.

Ridsdale Judgement. The judgement of the *Judicial Committee of the Privy Council in 1877 that the use of *Eucharistic vestments was illegal in the C of E, but that the *eastward position was permitted, provided that it did not conceal from the congregation the *manual acts. The defendant in the case was the Revd C. J. Ridsdale.

Riemenschneider, Tilman (c.1460–1531), German wood-carver and sculptor. In his altar-pieces he secured unity by focusing the design on a central point. In place of colour he achieved his effects by the play of light, the texture of his material, and the highly expressive faces of his figures.

Rienzo, Cola di (c.1313–54), Tribune of the Roman People. In 1343 he was part of a Roman embassy sent to *Clement VI to persuade him to return to Rome; his ability impressed the Pope. In May 1347 he stirred up a popular revolution, as a result of which the people made him 'Tribune of the People'. At first he ruled nominally in partnership with the Papal legate, but he became increasingly autocratic. He bathed in the font of the *Lateran Basilica and challenged the election of the Emp. Charles IV, which the Pope had engineered. The people of Rome forced him to flee in Dec. 1347. In 1350 Charles IV arrested him and sent him to Clement, who imprisoned him. Nevertheless, when in 1353 Cardinal Albornoz went to Rome to restore order, Innocent VI sent Rienzo with him, and he triumphantly entered the city in 1354. His behaviour again offended the people, who rose against him and killed him while he was trying to escape.

rigorism. In a technical sense the term is used as another name for the system of moral theology known as *Tutiorism. Non-technically it denotes the cult of extreme asceticism and self-denial and rigid keeping of the letter of the law.

Rijswick Clause. See RYSWICK CLAUSE.

Rimini, Synod of. See ARIMINUM AND SELEUCIA, SYNODS OF.

rings. The ring is considered an emblem of fidelity. Those in Christian use include:
(1) In the W., episcopal rings. Rings are first mentioned as an official part of a bishop's insignia of office in the 7th cent. They now usually contain an amethyst.
(2) Nuns' rings. In many orders a ring is conferred at solemn *profession.
(3) Wedding rings. Originating in the betrothal rings used by the Romans, they were adopted by Christians at an early date. Customs regarding their use have varied. The current RC marriage ceremony envisages the use of a ring for both parties.
(4) The 'Fisherman's Ring' is a seal-ring placed on the finger of a new Pope and broken at his death. Engraved on it is St *Peter in a boat fishing, with the Pope's name round it.
(5) The 'Coronation Ring' in England is placed on the fourth finger of the Sovereign's right hand as 'the ensign of Kingly Dignity and of Defence of the Catholic Faith'.
(6) Rosary rings. These have ten small knobs and are used for saying the *rosary.

Ripalda, Juan Martínez de (1594–1648), Spanish *Jesuit. He was one of the most famous theologians of his time. His chief work is a treatise on the supernatural, *De Ente Supernaturali* (1634–48).

Ripon. Not long before 661, Alchfrith, a son of Oswiu, King of Northumbria, founded a monastery, of which St *Wilfrid became abbot in 661; it was destroyed in 950. In the 11th cent. *Augustinian canons built a new church on the ruins. This foundation was dissolved by *Henry VIII, but was refounded as a collegiate church in 1604. In 1836 the church became the cathedral of the new diocese of Ripon.

Rita of Cascia, St (1381–1457), nun. She apparently married reluctantly, but made an exemplary wife and mother. After her husband's death she was admitted to the *Augustinian convent at Cascia in Umbria, owing (it is related) to supernatural intervention. Feast day, 22 May.

Rites, Congregation of Sacred. This Congregation was established by *Sixtus V in 1588 to carry out the decrees of the Council of *Trent on public worship. It was responsible for the direction of liturgy and everything to do with *canonization, *beatification, and the veneration of *relics, as well as for all *faculties, *indulgences, and *dispensations in liturgical matters. In 1969 it was divided into two Congregations, one for the *Causes of Saints and the other for Divine Worship. In 1988 the latter was again combined (as it had been from 1975 to 1984) with the Congregation for the Discipline of the Sacraments.

Ritschl, Albrecht (1822–89), German Protestant theologian. He was professor of theology first at Bonn and then at Göttingen. He insisted on the irreducibility of religion to other forms of experience. We apprehend by faith, not by reason, and this faith rests not on the intellectual apprehension of facts but on the making of value-judgements. He further insisted that it was to a community, not to individuals, that the Gospel was, and still is, committed. It is in and through the community that justification is primarily achieved. His writings, and especially *Die christliche Lehre von der Rechtfertigung und Versöhnung* (1870–4), exercised great influence on the theology of Germany in the late 19th cent. The so-called 'Ritschlian School' was characterized by its stress on ethics and on the 'community', and by its repudiation of metaphysics and religious experience.

ritual. Strictly, the prescribed form of words of a liturgical function. In common usage the word is also employed of the accompanying ceremonial. In the 19th cent. the term 'Ritualist' was used of those who introduced medieval or modern RC ceremonial into the C of E.

Ritual Commission. The Royal Commission created in 1867 to inquire into the differences in ceremonial practice in the C of E. Its four reports dealt with *Eucharistic vestments (1867), *incense and lights (1868), the *lectionary (1869), and Prayer Book revision and other subjects (1870). In general the Commissioners recommended that practices that had prevailed for 300 years should be the standard of Anglican usage.

Ritual Masses. The Masses provided in the 1970 Roman Missal for use on the various occasions when Sacraments or other solemn acts are included in the Eucharist, e.g. at *Baptisms, weddings, or wedding anniversaries.

Rituale Romanum. The official service book of the RC rite, containing the prayers and formulas for the administration of the Sacraments and other liturgical actions of a priest apart from the Mass and Divine Office. The first edition appeared in 1614. Revised rites appeared separately between 1969 and 1976.

Ritus Servandus. The short title of two liturgical items relating to the traditional RC rite: (1) The rules about the customs and ceremonial of the Mass formerly printed at the beginning of the Missal and now replaced by the 'Instructio Generalis' issued in 1969 and attached to the 1970 Missal; and (2) A book containing directions and prayers for *Benediction of the Blessed Sacrament and certain other extra-liturgical services. This has now been replaced by a section of the *Rituale Romanum, *De Sacra Communione . . .* (1973).

Robber Council of Ephesus (449). See LATROCINIUM.

Robert, St (*c.*1027–1111), Abbot of Molesme. He became a monk when he was 15. In 1075 he founded a monastery at Molesme in Burgundy for some hermits who had asked to be placed under his direction. When divisions appeared in the community, Robert and some of the monks left Molesme and founded the monastery of *Cîteaux. Later the monks of Molesme asked to have their abbot back; Robert returned and Molesme became a famous *Benedictine centre. Feast day, 29 Apr.

Robert Bellarmine, St; Robert of Holcot. See BELLARMINE, ST ROBERT, and HOLCOT, ROBERT.

Robert of Melun (d. 1167), *Scholastic theologian. An Englishman by birth, he studied and taught at *Paris. In 1142 he went to Melun, where he directed a school; in 1148 he took part in the condemnation of *Gilbert de la Porrée at the Synod of Reims. He became Bp. of *Hereford in 1163. His Trinitarian doctrine was influential. According to him power is to be especially attributed to the Father, wisdom to the Son, and goodness to the Holy Spirit, without, however, robbing the other two Persons of the quality predicated in a particular way of the one.

Robert of Winchelsea. See WINCHELSEA, ROBERT OF.

Robertson, Frederick William (1816–53), 'Robertson of Brighton', Anglican preacher. He had abandoned his earlier *Evangelicalism in favour of a *Broad Church type of theology before 1847, when he was appointed minister of Trinity Chapel, Brighton, a small *proprietary chapel. Here his influence as a preacher extended far and wide, embracing the working classes, at that time largely untouched by the C of E.

Robertson, William (1721–93), a pivotal figure in the Scottish *Enlightenment. Ordained in 1744, he came into prominence in the 1750s, when he helped to formulate the policies of the *Moderate party within the Church of *Scotland. In 1762 he became principal of Edinburgh University. Here he ended the imposition of religious tests for professors. As leader of the General Assembly (1752–80), he helped to revolutionize the government and ethos of the Church. Unlike the leaders of the Popular Party, who supported opposition to the Patronage Act, he insisted on obedience to civil and canon law. He also rejected the controversial theology of the 17th cent., distrusting dogmatism and Puritan other-worldliness and freeing the clergy to contribute to the secular culture of the time.

Robinson, Henry Wheeler (1872–1945), *Baptist theologian. From 1920 to 1942 he was Principal of Regent's Park College and was chiefly responsible for its move from London to Oxford. His main interests lay in the fields of OT theology and the doctrines of the Holy Spirit and redemption. His influence extended well beyond his own communion.

Robinson, John (c.1575–1625), pastor of the *Pilgrim Fathers. Though ordained in the C of E, he became a *Puritan, joining the 'gathered Church' at Scrooby Manor, Notts. In 1608 he and his congregation fled to the *Netherlands. In 1609 he settled at *Leiden and from 1617 took an interest in the plans of his community to emigrate to America, as their strict *Calvinism had brought them into conflict with the *Arminianism of which Leiden was a centre. Though he did not sail in the *Mayflower*, he encouraged the enterprise.

Robinson, John Arthur Thomas (1919–83), Anglican theologian and bishop. He spent most of his working life in *Cambridge, apart from the time (1959–69) when he was Suffragan Bishop of Woolwich. In 1963 he published a paperback, *Honest to God*, advocating new ways of interpreting traditional Christianity and conceiving of the supernatural. The ideas were not new; the strong impact they made was partly due to the lively and original way in which they were synthesized and to the fact that the writer was a bishop. His academic writings were mainly concerned with the NT.

Roch, St (c.1295–1327), healer of the plague-stricken. He is said to have stopped on a journey from France to Italy at the plague-ridden town of Aquapendente, where he cured many by the sign of the cross, and later to have performed similar miracles elsewhere. Feast day, 16 Aug.

Rochester, Kent. The see was founded by St *Augustine, who consecrated St *Justus its first bishop in 604. The cathedral, which was served in early times by secular canons, was damaged by the Mercians and by the Danes. Gundulf (Bp., 1077–1108) began a new cathedral, and in 1083

replaced the secular canons with *Benedictines; this cathedral was consecrated in 1130. In 1343 the choir was rebuilt and a central tower added (replaced 1825–7). At the *Dissolution, the priory surrendered in 1540; a secular foundation with a dean and canons was established in 1541.

rochet. A white linen vestment, resembling the *surplice but with tight sleeves, which is worn by bishops and occasionally by other ecclesiastical dignitaries. The rochet worn by Anglican bishops under the *chimere has wide lawn sleeves.

rococo. A development of *baroque architecture and decoration, which originated in France and lasted from c.1715 to 1760.

Rogation Days. In W. Christendom certain prescribed days of prayer and fasting in early summer, associated with prayer for the harvest. The 'Major Rogation' on 25 Apr. was a Christianized version of the pagan Robigalia, which involved a procession through the fields to pray for the preservation of the crops from mildew. The 'Minor Rogations', on the Monday, Tuesday, and Wednesday before *Ascension Day, derived from the processional litanies ordered by St *Mamertus of Vienne (c.470), when his diocese was troubled by volcanic eruptions. In the C of E the BCP of 1662 ordered the observance of the three (minor) Rogations as 'Days of Fasting and Abstinence'. In the RC Church the Rogation Days were replaced in 1969 by periods of prayer for the needs of mankind, the fruits of the earth, and the works of men's hands; these may be arranged at any time of year.

Rogers, John (c.1500–55), editor of '*Matthew's Bible'. He became a Protestant in the Netherlands, soon after meeting W. *Tyndale (d. 1536), and in 1537 under the name of 'Thomas Matthew' he published the first complete version of the Bible in English; his own share was confined to contributing prefaces and marginal notes. Returning to London in 1548, he was given parochial preferment and in 1551 he became a prebendary of *St Paul's Cathedral. Under *Mary he was burnt.

Rolle of Hampole, Richard (c.1300–49), English hermit and spiritual writer. He appears to have been a native of N. Yorkshire and to have studied at *Oxford. At the age of 18 he became a hermit; he spent the last years of his life near the convent of *Cistercian nuns at Hampole.

The canon of his writings contains: (1) biblical commentaries; (2) Latin treatises, including *Incendium Amoris* and *Emendatio Vitae* (both later translated into English); (3) English treatises, including *The Form of Living*, written for the recluse Margaret Kirkby; and (4) a number of English poems. His authorship of the English *Meditations on the Passion* is uncertain. The contemplative life, in his view, begins with the experience of 'the opening of Heaven's door' and is thereafter characterized by 'heat', 'sweetness', and 'angel-song'.

Rolls Chapel. A chapel which once stood on the site of the Public Record Office, London. The records (Rolls) of Chancery were formerly kept in the chapel.

Romaine, William (1714–95). *Calvinist preacher. After following the scholarly traditions of the C of E in his early years, he came under the influence of G. *Whitefield in 1755 and became one of the chief representatives of rigid Calvinism. His preaching attracted vast crowds to St George's, Hanover Square, where their presence was resented by the fashionable parishioners. In 1766 he became incumbent of St Anne's, Blackfriars, where his revivalist preaching continued to draw large congregations.

'Roman Catechism'. The *Catechismus ex Decreto Concilii Tridentini* (1566), issued after the Council of *Trent on Papal authority, is known as the 'Roman Catechism'. It is not a catechism in the ordinary sense of a work arranged in question and answer form, but is a doctrinal exposition of the Creeds, Sacraments, Ten Commandments, and Prayer (including the *Lord's Prayer), intended for the use of parish priests.

Roman Catholic Church in England and Wales after the Reformation. Although there was strong Catholic sentiment in parts of the kingdom, and some notable figures were executed rather than accept the royal *supremacy, the majority of the population acquiesced in the Reformation of the *Church of England under *Henry VIII and *Edward VI. Catholicism began to be restored under *Mary, but her persecu-tion of the Reformers created a legacy of bitterness. Under *Elizabeth I the distinction between RCs and Anglicans was made clear by the 1559 Act of *Uniformity's imposition of fines on those who did not attend the services of the C of E. Many Catholics practised their faith in secret, and at first there was little persecution. Later, political events, and the excommunication of Elizabeth in 1570, hardened attitudes. The arrival in 1574 of the first missionary priests from the Continent, followed by *Jesuits from 1580 onwards, strengthened the RC community, but was met by penal legislation and executions. In the later years of *James I's reign the penal laws against RCs were often not enforced, and their suspension was one of the conditions of *Charles I's marriage to *Henrietta Maria. *Charles II promised toleration and tried to secure it, but was forced to accept legislation which excluded RCs from Parliament and office. Although *James II came to the throne in 1685 professing personal allegiance to the RC Church, his attempts to further the interest of his fellow-Catholics led to his replacement by William and Mary. The Bill of Rights 1688 and the Act of Settlement 1700 debarred from the throne any RC or anyone who should marry a RC, and other legislation excluded RCs from the professions.

In 1685 John Leyburn was appointed the first *Vicar Apostolic. Three further Vicars were appointed in 1688 and England was divided into four districts. The need to recruit Irish and Scottish clansmen for the American War of Independence led to the first of the *Catholic Relief Acts in 1778. By 1829 nearly all disabilities were removed. The sufferings of the RC Church on the Continent in the French Revolution (from 1789) created a degree of sympathy in England, and English religious communities returned from abroad. In the 19th cent. the RC population was also increased by Irish immigrants. In 1850 a hierarchy of 12 *suffragan bishops under an archbishop was established; N. P. S. *Wiseman became Abp. of *Westminster and a cardinal. He introduced into England the *Ultramontanism which was fostered by his successor, H. E. *Manning. In 1908 England and Wales ceased to be missionary territory and in 1918 'missions' became legally constituted parishes. Card. A. *Hinsley became something of a national figure through his broadcasts in the early years of the Second World War. Nevertheless, in 1945, after a century of growth and consolidation, the RC Church was still regarded with hostility. The educational expansion following the 1944 Education Act resulted in an increase in the number of RCs in higher education and the professions. The Second *Vatican Council (1961–5) drew the whole RC Church into a new relationship with other Churches and the introduction of the vernacular in the liturgy has made the RC Church seem less 'foreign'. Membership has increased to c.4 million and under Card. G. B. *Hume the RC Church was drawn into the mainstream of national life.

Roman Catholicism. The term, which denotes the faith and practice of Christians who are in communion with the Pope, is used especially of Catholicism as it has existed since the *Reformation, in contradistinction to *Protestant bodies. Whereas in the early centuries the Church had to clarify the mysteries of the *Trinity and the *Incarnation and in the Middle Ages concentrated on the relation of God and man through *grace and the *sacraments, post-Tridentine theologians have been especially concerned with the structure and prerogatives of the Church, the position of the BVM in the economy of salvation, and the function of Pope as Vicar of Christ on earth, culminating in the dogma of *infallibility promulgated at the First Vatican Council in 1870. In the 20th cent. an attempt was made to bring the Church into closer communication with the modern world. This was especially associated with the Second *Vatican Council (1962–5), the use of the vernacular in worship, and a more liberal attitude towards Christians of other denominations.

From an external point of view RCism presents itself as an organized hierarchy of bishops and priests, with the Pope at its head. Supernatural life is normally mediated to individual Christians by members of the hierarchy in the *seven sacraments, which cover the whole life of RCs. The centre of this liturgical life is the Mass (or *Eucharist), attendance at which is obligatory on all Sundays and *Feasts of Obligation, or on the previous evening.

In post-Reformation Catholicism the religious life increased in scope and size. New orders, of whom the *Jesuits were the most influential, were founded to engage in teaching, nursing, and social work. The period since the Second World War has seen the growth of 'lay congregations', such as the 'Little Brothers' inspired by the ideals of Charles *de Foucauld; they seek to combine an element of contemplation with the discipline of earning their living, often in industrial society. The traditional religious orders have also undergone considerable reorganization. Despite some changes in emphasis, the primary aim of the RC Church remains the sanctification of its members and the conversion of souls.

See also previous entry.

Roman Catholic Relief Acts. See CATH-OLIC RELIEF ACTS.

Roman Congregations. The executive departments of the Roman *Curia responsible for the central administration of the RC Church. They were established by *Sixtus V in 1588. In the reorganization of 1967, nine congregations emerged, most of them with modified titles and redefined competence. After further changes there are again (since 1988) nine congregations, headed by the former *Holy Office. See also CAUSES OF SAINTS, PROPAGANDA FIDEI, and RITES, CONGREGATION OF SACRED.

Roman Martyrology. The official *martyrology of the RC Church. It was compiled by a commission of scholars, including C. *Baronius, and issued in 1584 to replace the various local adaptations of *Usuard's text. It has been subject to revision.

Roman Psalter. The text of the Psalms used in Italian churches until the time of *Pius V (1566–72), when it was virtually replaced, except at *St Peter's, Rome, by the '*Gallican Psalter' (q.v.). Earlier scholars equated it with the revision of the Latin Psalter which St *Jerome says that he made hastily on the basis of the LXX, but few now think that the Roman Psalter was produced by Jerome. See also PSALTER.

Romania, Christianity in. Roman Dacia, which roughly covered the W. parts of the present Romania, may have received Christianity through Roman soldiers and colonists in the 4th cent. or earlier. Under Bulgarian rule its ecclesiastical affairs were placed under *Constantinople, and its worship gradually took on an E. character. In the 19th cent. Romania gradually emerged as an independent State, and in 1885 the claim of her national Church for independence from the metropolitan jurisdiction of Constantinople was allowed. After the First World War (1914–18), Romania acquired Transylvania, where a *Uniat Church had existed since 1700, and there were RC, *Lutheran, *Calvinist, and *Unitarian minorities. In the 1923 constitution the Romanian Orthodox Church was recognized as the national Church. After Romania surrendered to Russia in 1944 the Romanian Orthodox Church was closely controlled by the Communist government until 1989, and other Churches suffered persecution. Only the *Baptists increased. Since 1989 all denominations have enjoyed greater freedom. The Uniat Church, which had been forced to join the Orthodox Church in 1948, was reconstituted in 1990.

Romanos, St (*fl. c.*540), 'Melodos', Greek religious poet, the most significant composer of the *kontakion, the metrical sermon chanted to music. A Syrian by birth, he made his way to *Constantinople, where he achieved fame. Eighty metrical sermons have come down under his name, but not all are genuine. Feast day, 1 Oct.

Romans, Epistle to the. The longest of St *Paul's letters, it was sent from *Corinth, probably *c.*AD 58. After a formal opening, Paul points to the universality of sin and concludes that man cannot be justified before God 'by the works of the law'. *Justification occurs 'by the righteousness of God', which is revealed in the Gospel of His Son, whom God 'set forth to be a propitiation [or expiation]' to reconcile sinners to God (3: 25). This free gift is appropriated by *faith. Paul rebuts the suggestion that in such a situation we might as well continue in sin that grace might abound (6: 1); in reply he points to the change in character effected by *Baptism. Discussing the destiny of the Jews, most of whom have rejected the salvation now offered to Jews and non-Jews alike, Paul emphasizes the sovereignty of God and claims that the falling away of Israel is only temporary. He then deals with the practical obligations of the Christian life. He ends with greetings, the 'grace', and a doxology.

The integrity of the text has been much discussed. There is evidence that one ancient recension ended at 14: 23 and another at 15: 33, both followed immediately by the doxology. There are also texts which omit the name 'Rome' in 1: 7 and 1: 15. A few modern scholars have contended that the long list of personal greetings in ch. 16 suggests that this chapter was designed for a Church in which Paul had friends, rather than Rome, which he explicitly states (1: 13) that he had never visited.

Rom. is a text of primary importance for the Christian theological tradition. Its teaching was especially influential in St *Augustine's anti-Pelagian writings, and it has profoundly affected the W. Christian outlook on *sin, *grace, *merit, free will, justification and *predestination. Recent attempts at rapprochement with Judaism take their start from Rom. 11, and Rom. 13: 1–6 has been a force for social and political conservatism, especially in German *Lutheranism.

Romanticism. The movement in literature and art reasserting passion and imagination in reaction from the classicism and rationalism which marked the 18th cent. Such a reaction against the *Enlightenment is found first in Germany among writers such as Goethe and F. D. E. *Schleiermacher; in England it can be seen in the works of W. *Blake, W. *Wordsworth and S. T. *Coleridge.

Romanus, St. A deacon and *exorcist of a church in *Caesarea in Palestine, who was martyred at *Antioch (*c.*304) in the *Diocletianic persecution. Feast day, 18 Nov.

Romanus, St, 'Melodus'. See ROMANOS, ST.

Rome (early Christian). An early but not well-grounded tradition asserts that St *Peter reached Rome in AD 42. When the Epistle to the *Romans was written (*c.*AD 58), a large Christian community already existed at Rome. St *Paul arrived between AD 59 and 61, and many scholars hold that his '*Captivity Epistles', as well as Mk., Lk., Acts, and 1 Pet., were written in Rome. The burning of the city under *Nero (AD 64) was the pretext for a general *persecution of the Christians. Ancient tradition held that both Peter and Paul were martyred at Rome in the 60s.

The early bishops of Rome were all Greek-speaking and mostly administrators rather than theologians. *Victor I (189–98) was the first Latin-speaking Pope, and his action in the *Quartodeciman Controversy reflects the growing importance of the see. A serious schism was caused by St *Hippolytus's dispute with *Callistus I (217–22) on disciplinary and dogmatic matters. During the persecution of *Decius (249–51) *Fabian (236–50) was martyred and the see kept vacant for 13 months. Another rigorist schism, led by *Novatian, took place under *Cornelius (251–3). Persecution broke out again under the Emp. Valerian (253–60), and in 258 *Sixtus II and all his deacons were martyred.

By this date the Roman Church was highly organized. Under Cornelius there were 46 *presbyters, seven *deacons, and numerous lesser ministers. The property of the Church included private houses in the city for worship and burial-places outside the walls (*catacombs). The administration of the property and the relief of the poor fell to the deacons, each of whom had a district and staff under him.

In the persecution which broke out under *Diocletian in 303, the Church's property was confiscated and a number of Christians fell away. With the accession of the Emp. Maxentius in 306, persecution in the W. ceased, and the next two Popes had to face opposition from the *lapsed who wanted to be readmitted to communion with little or no *penance. Under Bp. *Miltiades (311–4) the Church's property was restored and full toleration granted.

Between the mid-4th and late-5th cent. the authority of the bishops, or Popes, of Rome steadily increased. They consistently intervened on the orthodox side in the theological disputes of the time. *Julius I (337–52) and *Liberius (352–66) upheld the Nicene faith against the *Arians, *Damasus I (366–84) condemned *Apollinarianism, *Innocent I (402–17) *Pelagianism, and *Celestine I (422–32) *Nestorianism, while the '*Tome' of *Leo I (440–61) assisted the defeat of *Eutychianism at the Council of *Chalcedon (451). The Council of *Sardica (343) and the legislation of the Emps. Gratian (375–83) and *Theodosius (379–95) firmly established the Roman see as a court of appeal.

Rome declined in political significance when the capital of the Empire was moved to *Constantinople (330). In the 5th cent. Italy was invaded and Rome was sacked twice before it came under the authority of barbarian rulers in 476. The partial conquest of Italy by the Lombards, some of whom were pagan and the rest Arian, and the decline of the Byzantine power led the Popes, notably *Gregory I (590–604), to assume political authority in Rome. In the 7th cent. relations between the Papacy and the Byzantine Emperors, who were the nominal overlords of Rome, deteriorated. The beginnings of the temporal power of the Papacy may be seen in the Donation of Sutri to 'St Peter' (729) by the Lombard King Liutprand, but the growth of Lombard power caused *Stephen II (III) in 753 to appeal to the Frankish King *Pepin. The Frankish intervention led to the destruction of the Lombard kingdom, to the restoration of the Roman Duchy and the Exarchate of Ravenna not to the Byzantine Emperor but to the Papacy, and in 800 to the coronation in Rome by *Leo III of *Charlemagne as Roman Emperor.

See also PATRIMONY OF ST PETER; also LATERAN BASILICA; ST PETER'S, ROME; SANTA MARIA MAGGIORE; and ST PAUL'S OUTSIDE THE WALLS.

Romero, Oscar Arnulfo (1917–80), Abp. of San Salvador from 1977. At the time of his appointment, he was known as a conservative; as recently as 1976 he had attacked *Liberation Theology as expounded by Jon Sobrino. Partly as a result of the murder of a friend, and partly because of the general polarization caused by the worsening situation, he soon espoused the principles of Liberation Theology and became an opponent of the dictator of El Salvador, also called Romero. The majority of his clergy supported him, but nearly all the other bishops opposed him. After the overthrow of his namesake, he tried to negotiate between the three main factions in the country, but he was assassinated while celebrating Mass. Feast day in CW, 24 Mar.

Romuald, St (c.950–1027), founder of the *Camaldolese Order. A nobleman of *Ravenna, he entered the abbey of Sant' Apollinare in Classe through horror at his father's having killed a man in a duel. He later retired to the neighbouring marshes to practise more rigid asceticism. He founded various hermitages and monasteries, that at Campus Malduli becoming the centre of the Camaldolese Order. Feast day, formerly 7 Feb., now 19 June.

Roncalli, Angelo Giuseppe. See JOHN XXIII.

'Root and Branch'. The London Petition of 1640 demanded that the episcopal system 'with all its dependencies, roots, and branches, be abolished'. The Petition became known as the Root and Branch Petition; and the expression came to be used of any thoroughgoing policy.

rosary. A form of prayer in which 15 *decades of *Hail Marys are recited, each decade being preceded by the *Lord's Prayer and followed by the *Gloria Patri; the prayers are counted on a string of beads or sometimes on a *ring. Each decade is accompanied by meditation on one of a sequence of *Mysteries (q.v.). Usually only five decades or less are recited at a time.

Roscelin (d. 1125), *Scholastic philosopher and theologian. He was accused of *Trithe- ism at a Council of Soissons, c.1092, but denied having taught it. An early and out- standing defender of *Nominalism, Rosce- lin stressed that universal terms were *voces* (voices), and claimed to establish that a being can have no parts. These philo- sophical tenets led him to identify the three Persons of the Trinity as distinct things (*res*), on the ground that if they were identical in substance, the Father and the Holy Spirit would have become incarnate together with the Son.

Rose of Lima, St (1586–1617), the first canonized saint of America. She lived in Lima, Peru. A vow of virginity and her strictness of life incurred persecution from her family and friends: she also suffered from inner desolation and long illness. She is the Patroness of S. America and the *Philippines. Feast day, 23 Aug.

Rose, Golden. See GOLDEN ROSE.

Rosicrucians. Secret societies who vener- ated the emblems of the Rose (or perhaps the Dew, *ros*) and the Cross as twin symbols of the Lord's Resurrection and Redemption. In 1614 and 1615 two anonymous writings were published in Germany, the *Fama Fra- ternitatis* and the *Confessio Fraternitatis*. They were followed in 1616 by the *Chymische Hochzeit Christiani Rosenkreutz* (now ascribed

to the *Lutheran pastor J. V. Andreae) which states that a certain Christian Rosenkreutz founded a secret society devoted to the study of the hidden things of nature and an esoteric and anti-catholic kind of Christianity; the author claimed this society still existed. The books were taken seriously and various societies with alchemistic tendencies came into being under their influence.

Rosmini-Serbati, Antonio (1797–1855), Italian philosopher. His system is a form of Idealism, founded on the leading idea of indeterminate being, innate in the human soul. If analysed, this idea divides itself into a plurality of other ideas which are identi- cal with those that are in the mind of God. He distinguished between degrees of being according to their completeness, God alone being absolutely complete. The being, however, which actualizes finite nature and which is the object of human intuition, is 'something of God', though not God Himself. Some of Rosmini's works were put on the *Index in 1849, though removed before his death, but 40 propositions were mildly condemned in 1887–8.

In 1828 he founded the congregation of 'Fathers of Charity', often known as 'Ros- minians'. Its aim is the sanctification of its members, along with such works of charity as they may be called upon to perform.

Rossetti, Christina Georgina (1830–94), poetess. She was a younger sister of D. G. *Rossetti, and closely associated with the Pre-Raphaelite Brotherhood. Her works include the carol 'In the bleak mid-winter'.

Rossetti, Dante Gabriel (1828–1882), Eng- lish painter and poet, and one of the found- ers of the Pre-Raphaelite Brotherhood. In his early years he was much influenced by *Dante, and in his own poetry of this period Christian themes abound, his ideal of womanhood being expressed by the BVM and Beatrix. Of his paintings *The Girlhood of Mary Virgin* and *Ecce Ancilla Domini* (both in the Tate Gallery, London) recall something of the spiritual beauty of medi- eval pictures, but this simplicity is lacking in most of his work. From c.1863 religious motives disappear and his poetry and art are inherently sensual.

Rosvitha. An alternative form of *Hrosvit.

Rosy Sequence. Part of the hymn '*Jesu, dulcis memoria*' (q.v.) used as a *sequence for the Feast of the *Name of Jesus in the *Sarum rite.

Rota Romana. The normal RC appeal tribunal for judging cases brought before the *Holy See. It dates from the reorganization of the Papal administration in 1331; its name appears to derive from the circular table used by the judges at *Avignon. With the cessation of the temporal power of the Papacy in 1870, its duties practically ended. It was reconstituted in 1908 and has been reorganized several times. It is the court of appeal for ecclesiastical cases first heard in the diocesan and other courts, and then coming under the Roman *Curia, unless they are reserved for others; it also judges at first instance cases reserved to the Holy See or set aside by the Pope. It is the court to which certain *nullity of marriage cases are referred.

Rothmann, Bernt (or Bernhard) (c.1495–c.1535), German *Anabaptist. In 1529 he was appointed chaplain of a church in Warendorf, near Münster. After visiting P. *Melanchthon and W. *Capito in 1531, he supported the cause of the Reformation. He was backed by the Council and guilds of Münster and given the pulpit of a large church in the city. In 1532 he published a confession of faith, which was *Lutheran in most respects, but *Zwinglian on the Eucharist. His *Bekenntnisse van beyden Sacramenten* (1533), however, showed that Rothmann and his circle now rejected both Lutheranism and Zwinglianism and repudiated *Infant Baptism. They were rebaptized by followers of M. *Hoffmann and Münster became an Anabaptist city-state. Community of goods and polygamy were established. Rothmann's role is uncertain, but he wrote in defence of the 'New Jerusalem' of Münster. Münster fell to the prince-bishop in 1535; Rothmann's fate is unknown.

Rousseau, Jean-Jacques (1712–78), French author. He became a RC in 1728. In 1741 he went to Paris; here he was introduced to the circle of the *Encyclopaedists. He returned to his native city, *Geneva, in 1754, and also to *Calvinism. In the same year he wrote his *Discours sur l'origine et les fondements de l'inégalité parmi les hommes*; on the gratuitous assumption that primitive

man was a free and happy being, Rousseau alleged that human inequalities arose from the undue development of his social and proprietary instincts. In 1756 he settled near Montmorency, where he wrote his most famous works. In a chapter of *Émile, ou de l'Éducation* (1762) he summed up his religious beliefs. He advocated a *Deism which, although similar to that of the Philosophes in affirming belief in the existence of God, the soul, and a future life, found its ultimate justification in the individual's sense of a personal relationship with God through the conscience, of which He is the source and inspiration. *Du contrat social* (1762) set out his theory of a just state, resting on the general will of the people. Here 'civic religion' forbids all dogmatic intolerance and admits only those religions which do not claim to possess absolute truth.

After his death Rousseau became one of the most powerful influences in Europe. His religious impact was the deeper as he offered man a substitute for revealed religion which was not only doctrinally simple and unelaborate in its moral prescriptions, but also addressed his emotional as well as his intellectual needs.

Routh, Martin Joseph (1755–1854), president of Magdalen College, Oxford, from 1791. It was he who advised S. *Seabury, when sent to Europe to inaugurate an episcopal succession for the American (Anglican) Church, to seek it from the Scottish Episcopal Church. Routh's *Reliquiae Sacrae*, an edition of scattered pre-Nicene patristic texts, was published in 1814–18.

Rowites. The disciples of J. McLeod *Campbell, who had charge of the parish of Row, near Cardross, Dumbarton, from 1825 to 1830.

Rowntree, Joseph (1836–1925), *Quaker philanthropist. The head of the cocoa business, Rowntree and Co., he was a pioneer in the movement for securing for workpeople reasonable hours and conditions of labour, higher wages, and provision against old age and unemployment. He established three trusts to carry out some of his ideals.

Royal Chapels; Royal Declaration. See CHAPEL ROYAL and DECLARATION OF THE SOVEREIGN.

Royal School of Church Music (RSCM). An organization founded in 1927 as the School of English Church Music, and granted its present title in 1945. In 1996 it was appointed the official music agency of the C of E. Its work has consisted in advice to choirs affiliated to the School, provision of music, and the organization of choral festivals.

Royal Supremacy. See ESTABLISHMENT.

rubrics. Ritual or ceremonial directions in service-books. The word originated from the fact that they were often written in red to distinguish them from the text of the services. See also BLACK RUBRIC and ORNAMENTS RUBRIC.

Rucherat (or **Ruchrat), John.** See JOHN OF WESEL.

Rufinus, Tyrannius or **Turranius** (c.345–411), monk, historian, and translator. Born near *Aquileia, he went to Egypt c.373 and for some years studied at *Alexandria under *Didymus the Blind. In 381 he was in *Jerusalem. He had a part in founding a *double monastery on the Mount of *Olives. He returned to Italy in 397.

Though he was also an original writer, Rufinus is important mainly as a translator of Greek theological works into Latin at a time when knowledge of Greek was declining in the W. His free rendering of *Origen's *De Principiis*, the only complete text now surviving, was intended to vindicate Origen's orthodoxy. It involved Rufinus in bitter controversy with St *Jerome who criticized the tendentious character of the rendering. Other works he translated include some of Origen's biblical commentaries, the *Clementine *Recognitions*, and *Eusebius' *Ecclesiastical History*, to which he added two further books. His commentary on the *Apostles' Creed gives the earliest continuous Latin text of the 4th-cent. form of the Creed, as used at Aquileia and Rome.

Rufinus (*fl.* 399–401?), commonly called the Syrian, author of a *Liber de Fide*, described in the only known MS as the work of Rufinus, priest of the province of Palestine. The fact that this work is hostile to *Arianism, *Origen, and the doctrine of *Original Sin has led to identification of its author with the Rufinus *natione Syrus*, said by *Marius Mercator to have corrupted the theology of

*Pelagius, and with the deceased priest mentioned by *Celestius in his trial at *Carthage in 411.

Rule, Golden. See GOLDEN RULE.

Rule of Faith *(Regula Fidei).* One of the names used to describe the outline statements of Christian belief which circulated in the 2nd-cent. Church. Other names were the 'rule of truth', the 'law of faith', or the 'norm of truth'. Unlike *creeds, which came later, these formularies varied in wording.

Rule of St Benedict; Rule of the Master. See BENEDICT, RULE OF ST; *REGULA MAGISTRI*.

ruler. A name formerly applied to those who presided in cathedrals over the singing in choir.

Rumania, Christianity in. See ROMANIA, CHRISTIANITY IN.

Runcie, Robert Alexander Kennedy (1921–2000), Abp. of *Canterbury, 1980–91. He had been Principal of Cuddesdon Theological College (1960–69) and Bp. of *St Albans (1970–80). At his invitation *John Paul II visited Canterbury in 1982, the first Pope to come to Britain since the Reformation. With Runcie's support, legislation allowing women to be made *deacons in the C of E was passed in 1986. At the *Lambeth Conference of 1988 he worked to avoid a split in the Anglican Communion over the ordination of *women.

Rupert of Deutz (c.1075–1129/30), theologian. At an early age he entered a monastery in Liège. In his *Liber de divinis officiis* he used language about the Eucharist which provoked the accusation that he taught the doctrine later known as *Impanation. In 1116 a fellow monk returned from a period of study under *Anselm of Laon reporting that he taught that God willed that evil should happen. Rupert was scandalized and wrote a rejoinder, *De voluntate Dei*. This created a storm and he had to retire to the monastery of Siegburg. The Abp. of Cologne secured his election as Abbot of Deutz (near Cologne) in 1120. His later writings included a commentary on the Song of Songs in which he interprets the bride as the BVM. The 16th-cent. Reformers tried to find support in his works for their own doctrines, especially on the Eucharist.

rural dean. In the C of E, the head of a group of parishes in a given area ('rural deanery'). The office is ancient, but its duties were gradually taken over by the *archdeacons. It was revived in 1836. The rural dean is president of the ruridecanal chapter, i.e. the incumbents and clergy licensed under seal in the deanery, and co-chairman of the deanery synods set up by the *Synodical Government Measure 1969.

Ruskin, John (1819–1900), English art critic and social reformer. His fame was established by the first volume of his *Modern Painters* (1843–60). In this and later writing he expounded his spiritual interpretation of art; he held that the art and architecture of a people are the expression of its religion and morality. His *Stones of Venice* (1851–3) included the famous chapter on 'The Nature of Gothic' which influenced the growth of the Gothic Revival in architecture. After 1860 he devoted himself to social and economic problems. His early *Evangelicalism gave place to a vague *Theism, and his ideas for social reform included a plan for a completely dependent State Church with state-salaried officials and a minimum of dogma. In 1870 he was elected the first professor of fine arts in Oxford. Here his social programme was among the influences leading to the establishment of university settlements.

Russell, Charles Taze (1852–1916), founder in 1881 of Zion's Watch Tower Tract Society, the forerunner of the organization now popularly known as *Jehovah's Witnesses (q.v.). A draper in Pennsylvania, he was active in the *Congregational Church before he encountered *Adventism. He came to reject the doctrine of eternal punishment, to believe that the Second Coming of Christ had taken place in 1874, and to expect the end of the world in 1914. His publications attracted others who regarded him as their Pastor, though he was never ordained. He began publishing the magazine *Zion's Watch Tower* in 1879. Under his presidency the Watch Tower Bible and Tract Society (as it was renamed in 1896) developed into a flourishing business, despite his involvement in various scandals.

Russia, Christianity in. Christian missionaries first preached extensively in Russia in the 9th and 10th cents. Prince *Vladimir was baptized c.988 and established Christi-anity as the official religion in his dominions. At the *Great Schism of 1054 the Russian Church took the E. side. Monastic life began in the first half of the 11th cent. with the coming from Mount *Athos of the monk Antony, who established himself near Kiev. After the reforms initiated in the 14th cent. by St *Sergius of Radonezh it extended all over Russia. The monasteries supplied bishops, while the secular clergy were commonly married.

Russia rejected the union achieved at the Council of *Florence (1439). As the Church in Constantinople for a time accepted the Florentine union, in 1448 a Council of Russian bishops elected a Metropolitan of Moscow without reference to the Greek ecclesiastical authorities; in this way the Russian Church became *autocephalous. In 1461 the Russian Church was divided between two Metropolitans, centred at Moscow and Kiev; the former was entirely Russian and rigidly Orthodox, the latter more exposed to W. influence. In 1589 the Patriarchate of Moscow was created. Before that, in 1551, the famous Council of the Hundred Chapters had been called to reform the clergy.

Since the Council of Florence RCs had been severely repressed in the Moscow Tsardom, but Russians in the metropolis of Kiev fell within the territory of *Poland and Lithuania and were under pressure from their RC overlords. Many Russian Orthodox in this area recognized the Papacy at the Synod of *Brest-Litovsk in 1596.

Within the Russian Church the liturgical reforms of *Nikon, Patr. of Moscow (1652–67), precipitated the schism of the *Old Believers, which greatly weakened the Church in Russia. The Emp. Peter the Great (1672–1725), anxious to subjugate the Church to his authority, abolished the office of Patriarch, and in his 'Spiritual Regulation' of 1721 replaced it with the *Holy Synod, whose members were nominated by the Emperor.

In 1917–18 a council of bishops, priests, and laity met in Moscow and initiated a thorough reorganization of all aspects of Church life, in particular restoring the Patriarchate, to which *Tikhon was elected. The Revolution of 1917, however, completely disrupted its work. Though public worship was not forbidden by law, it became difficult after Lenin's decree of 1918 removed the right of the Church to own property and made the teaching of religion to anyone under 18 a criminal offence. Clergy were arrested, monasteries and theological seminaries closed, and the Church's public role ceased. When Patr. Tikhon died in 1925, no successor could be elected. After the German invasion of Russia in 1941, Sergius, Metropolitan of Moscow, supported the war effort and the government allowed the reopening of some 20,000 Orthodox Churches and other concessions, including the election of Sergius as Patriarch. With the defeat of Germany in 1945 and increasing tension with the W., anti-religious propaganda resumed. The Orthodox Church retained a limited degree of freedom, but there was widespread persecution of the *Lutheran and RC Churches in the newly acquired western territory, including the Balkan states. There was a further wave of persecution in 1959–64 and pressure remained severe until the accession of President Gorbachev in 1985. In 1988, to mark the millennium of the conversion of the East Slav lands to Christianity, a Council of the Russian Orthodox Church was held at Zagorsk, near Moscow. The government promised concessions in return for help in rebuilding society. The restored Danilov monastery became the headquarters of the Moscow Patriarchate, while in the Balkan states RC and Lutheran cathedrals began to reopen. In 1990 a new code on religious freedom was adopted, but it proved short-lived. In 1997 the Duma passed a new law which gave primacy to the Russian Orthodox Church, Islam, and Judaism as traditional Russian religions, while introducing new restrictions on RCs, Protestants, and all minorities.

See also BAPTISTS and UKRAINIAN CHURCHES.

Ruth, Book of. This OT Book tells the story of Ruth, a Moabitess, who married a Hebrew in Moab. After her husband's death, she returned with her mother-in-law to Judah; Boaz, a kinsman of her former husband, took her under his protection and married her. Though the incident is set in the later days of the Judges (before 1000 BC), the Book is not earlier than the Exile (6th cent. BC). The genealogy at the end (4: 18–22) indicates one of the apparent aims of the author, namely to record the Moabite strain in *David's ancestry. Ruth is thus an ancestress of Christ (Mt. 1: 5–16).

Ruthenian Churches. See UKRAINIAN CHURCHES.

Rutherford, Joseph Franklin (1869–1942), 'Judge Rutherford', second head of the organization popularly known as *Jehovah's Witnesses (q.v.). Of *Baptist family, he practised law in Missouri. In 1906 he joined the Bible Students of C. T. *Russell and soon became the organization's legal counsel. Elected its President in 1917, he moulded it into a *theocratic organization resilient enough to withstand persecution in many countries during the Second World War.

Rutherford, Mark, pseudonym of **William Hale White** (1831–1913), author. A civil servant for most of his life, he won recognition as a religious writer by *The Autobiography of Mark Rutherford* (1881).

Rutherford, Samuel (c.1600–61), Scottish *Presbyterian minister. In 1639 he became professor of divinity at St Mary's College, St Andrews, and in 1647 principal. He was one of the Scottish Commissioners at the *Westminster Assembly in 1643. His *Lex Rex* (1644), attacking monarchical absolutism, brought him repute as a constitutional theorist; it was publicly burnt at the Restoration (1660). In *A Free Disputation against Pretended Liberty of Conscience* (1649) he defended religious persecution on the ground that advocacy of toleration put conscience in the place of God and the Bible.

Ruysbroeck, or more correctly **Ruusbroec, Bl Jan van** (1293–1381), Flemish mystic. He retired to a hermitage at Groenendaal, near Brussels, with two other priests in 1343. They were joined by others and in 1350 the group became a community of *Canons Regular, with Ruysbroeck as prior until his death. Groenendaal became prominent in the religious movement later known as *Devotio Moderna*. Ruysbroeck wrote almost entirely in the vernacular of the country, Middle Dutch. His works (with their titles in English) include *The Spiritual Espousals*, *The Mirror of Eternal Salvation*, *The Seven Steps of the Ladder of Spiritual Love*, and *The Sparkling Stone*. Feast day, 2 Dec.

Rycaut, Paul (1628–1700), traveller and author. He was secretary to the British Embassy at *Constantinople and then consul to the Levant Company at *Smyrna. His essay on *The Present State of the Greek and*

Armenian Churches (1679) remains an important source of information.

Ryder, Henry (1777–1836), the first *Evangelical to be made a bishop in the C of E. He was the younger son of Lord Harrowby. At first he stood aloof from the Evangelicals, but he was won over and became one of their most prominent leaders. He was Bp. of Gloucester (1815–24) and then of Coventry and *Lichfield. He introduced reforms into his diocese; he preached more often than most bishops, and he worked hard to reach the masses, building a number of new churches.

Rylands St John. Part of a page of a *papyrus codex, now in the John Rylands University Library of Manchester, which has the text of Jn. 18: 31–3 on one side and 18: 37–8 on the other. Probably dating from the first half of the 2nd cent., it is both the earliest known MS of any part of the NT and also the earliest distinct evidence for the existence of St *John's Gospel.

Ryle, John Charles (1816–1900), first Bp. of Liverpool from 1880. A strong *Evangelical, he defended his convictions in a number of tracts which had a wide circulation.

Ryswick (or **Rijswick) Clause.** The clause inserted into the Treaty of Ryswick between the Emp. Leopold and Louis XIV of France (1697), modifying the rule that the religious frontiers should revert to their position at the time of the Treaty of Nijmegen (1679) in favour of the Catholic communities in those places where they had been re-established by Louis in the interval.

Sá, Manoel de (c.1530–96), Portuguese *Jesuit. In 1595 he published *Aphorismi Confessariorum*, a manual of *casuistry in dictionary form. It was put on the *Index in 1603 for allowing confession and absolution to be made by letter, but the corrected edition of 1607–8 was much esteemed.

Sabaoth. A Hebrew word meaning 'armies' or 'hosts' which is left untranslated in older translations of the NT and in the traditional version of the *Te Deum.

Sabas, St (439–532), monk. A native of Cappadocia, in 478 he founded a large *lavra between *Jerusalem and the *Dead Sea. He reluctantly accepted ordination to the priesthood (not then usual among monks) in 490, and in 492 the Patr. of *Jerusalem made him superior of all the hermits in Palestine. Feast day, 5 Dec.

Sabas, St, Patron of Serbia. See sava, st.

Sabatier, Auguste (1839–1901), French Protestant theologian. He propagated the theories of F. D. E. *Schleiermacher and A. *Ritschl in France, applied the methods of historical criticism to the NT, and, especially by his interpretation of Christian dogma as the symbolism of religious feelings, he exercised a profound influence not only on French Protestantism but also in Catholic theological circles, thus helping to prepare for the *Modernist movement.

Sabatier, Paul (1858–1928), *Calvinist pastor and student of St *Francis. He held two pastoral cures, but was forced by ill health to give up this work; he devoted the rest of his life to his research. His *Vie de S. François* (1893; Eng. tr., 1894) depicts Francis' mission as a renewal of the medieval Church in the light of the 'pure Gospel'; it is brilliant in presentation and penetrating in its psychological understanding. His later work brought to light much new material, though some of his contentions about the primitive sources have turned out to be mistaken.

Sabbatarianism. Excessive strictness in the observance of the Divinely ordained day of rest. Although there is evidence of a similar rigidity in the observance of *Saturday among the *Anabaptists of E. Europe in the 16th cent., the strict observance of *Sunday is a peculiar development of the English and Scottish Reformation, unknown on the Continent. Its origins are connected with the publication of N. Bound's *True Doctrine of the Sabbath* (1595), which advocated strict enforcement on OT lines. The ensuing controversy assumed political importance when *James I issued his 'Book of *Sports' (1618), allowing various sports on Sunday. When this was reissued by *Charles I in 1633, it aroused a storm of protest. The Puritan Sabbath was imposed by various Acts of Parliament, but somewhat relaxed at the Restoration. Under the influence of the *Evangelical Revival rigorism reappeared at the end of the 18th cent.; the Lord's Day Observance Act, drawn up by Bp. B. *Porteus in 1781, forbade the opening on Sunday of places of entertainment or debate to which admission was gained by payment. Relaxation has been progressive since the latter part of the 19th cent. See also SUNDAY.

Sabbath. The seventh day of the Jewish week. It served the double purpose of being a day set apart for the worship of God (Exod. 31: 13-17) as well as for the rest and recreation of man and cattle (Deut. 5: 14). The prohibition of work was regulated by minute prescription. In NT times activities such as healing and plucking ears of corn were sometimes considered forbidden, but debate about the precise definition of the work that was prohibited continued to rabbinic times. One of the *Pharisees' chief grievances against Christ was that He declared the Sabbath to have been made for man and not vice versa (Mk. 2: 27). Though the primitive Church continued to keep the seventh day as a day of rest and prayer, the fact that the Resurrection took place on the first day of the week soon led to the substitution of that day (*Sunday) for the Jewish Sabbath on Saturday.

Sabbatical Year. The one year in seven which the OT ordered to be observed as a 'Sabbath', i.e. requiring the land to remain fallow and debtors and Israelite slaves to be freed. See also JUBILEE, YEAR OF.

Sabbatine Privilege. An indulgence granted to the *Carmelite Order. On the basis of a bull ascribed to *John XXII (1322) members of the Order and its confraternities were promised unfailing salvation and early release from *purgatory if certain conditions were met. The Privilege has been confirmed by modern Popes, but the original bull is regarded as spurious.

Sabellianism. An alternative name for the Modalist form of *Monarchianism (q.v.), so called after Sabellius, who was perhaps a 3rd-cent. theologian of Roman origin.

Sabina, St. According to her *acta*, she was a widow of Umbria, who was converted by her servant and martyred at Rome *c.*126. It is unlikely that such a saint existed. The *acta* were perhaps fabricated to account for the Church of Sta Sabina on the Aventine Hill at Rome. Feast day, 29 Aug.

Sacheverell, Henry (1674-1724), *High Church cleric and pamphleteer. In 1705 he was elected chaplain of St Saviour's, Southwark (now *Southwark Cathedral). He preached two sermons in 1709 upholding the doctrine of non-resistance and emphasizing the dangers to the Church of the Whig government's policy of toleration and allowing *Occasional Conformity. The House of Commons condemned the sermons as seditious and Sacheverell was impeached, but the sentence imposed was so light as to be a triumph for the accused, and he became a popular hero.

Sacrament. The word is derived from the Latin *sacramentum*, which was used to translate the Greek μυστήριον ('mystery') in the Latin NT; sacraments are thus the means by which Christians partake in the 'mystery of Christ'. This participation is accomplished through certain symbolic acts (e.g. the washing of *Baptism, the meal of the *Eucharist).

The scope of the word has varied. St *Augustine, who defined it as a 'visible form of invisible grace', applied it to such *formulae* as the Creed and the *Lord's Prayer, and this wide connotation was usual in the first millennium. In the 12th cent. W. theology narrowed the meaning by regarding institution by Christ as an essential characteristic. In *Peter Lombard's *Sentences* the *seven sacraments which have become traditional in the W. are enumerated, i.e.

Baptism, *Confirmation, the Eucharist, *Penance, Extreme *Unction, *Orders, and *Matrimony. Other symbolic rites came to be called '*sacramentals' (q.v.). Despite the importance of the notion of Dominical institution, in several cases no occasion of such institution by Christ is apparent; such institution had to be held to be implicit. In modern times there has been more emphasis on the Church as the fundamental sacrament of Christ in which the commonly enumerated sacraments are implicit.

In the Middle Ages a distinction was made between the 'matter' and 'form' of the sacraments, the matter being the material element (e.g. the bread and wine in the Eucharist) and the form the consecratory words ('This is my Body', 'This is My Blood'). Despite problems, the distinction became the norm in W. theology until the mid-20th cent. According to such an approach, the right matter and the right form, used with the right *intention, are necessary for the *validity of the sacrament; where these are present, the performance of the act is sufficient to ensure that the sacrament will normally convey grace, since the validity of the sacrament is, according to Catholic theology, independent of the worthiness of the minister. Nevertheless, they do not convey grace if the recipient is not rightly disposed. In the rites authorized since the Second Vatican Council (1962–5) there has been increased emphasis on the 'word'; a Bible reading and homily form a normal part of sacramental celebration. The 'word' is thus more than the 'form' of the sacrament; rather it effects an encounter with the Word of Christ by which the mind and heart are opened to the incoming grace of God. Three of the sacraments, Baptism, Confirmation, and Orders, are held to implant an abiding mark or *character on the soul and therefore cannot be repeated. In Protestantism, though the technicalities of sacramental theology are less developed, great importance is attached to Baptism and the Eucharist or Lord's Supper, and their reception is taken very seriously. See also the entries on the separate Sacraments; also 'BAPTISM, EUCHARIST, AND MINISTRY'.

sacrament house. A shrine-like receptacle for the *reservation of the Blessed Sacrament. Except in *Scotland, sacrament houses came to take the form of a small tower, with the central part often done in open-work. From the 16th cent. they were largely displaced by *tabernacles.

sacramentals. According to RC theology, sacred signs with spiritual effects, resembling the *sacraments. When the number of the latter was restricted to seven in the W. Church in the 12th cent., analogous religious practices, not held to be instituted by Christ, were called 'sacramentals'. In contrast to the sacraments, which are held to convey grace primarily through the power of the rite itself (*ex opere operato*), sacramentals do so *ex opere operantis ecclesiae*, that is through the intercession of the Church. They include the blessing of holy oils and saying *grace at meals.

Sacramentarians. The name given by M. *Luther to those theologians who maintained that the Bread and Wine of the Eucharist were the Body and Blood of Christ only in a 'sacramental', i.e. metaphorical, sense. The word came to be applied to all who denied the *Real Presence of Christ in the Eucharist.

Sacramentary. In the W. Church, the liturgical book used by the celebrant at Mass until the 13th cent. It contained the *Canon of the Mass and the proper *Collects, *Prefaces, and other prayers for use throughout the year, but not the *Epistles, *Gospels, nor those parts of the service which were sung. Sacramentaries also contained *Ordination formularies, blessings, and other prayers used by bishops and priests. They were gradually replaced by *Missals and *Pontificals.

Sacred College. The former and still commonly used designation of the college of *cardinals, though 'sacred' has now been dropped from the official title.

Sacred Heart. Devotion to the physical heart of Jesus can be traced back to the Middle Ages, but it was long confined to mystics. In the 16th cent. it extended to many given to the ascetic life. An elaborate theological foundation was provided by St John *Eudes, but it was the visions of St *Margaret Mary Alacoque in 1673–5 which gave definite shape to the object of the devotion and its practices. Its most prominent feature was *reparation for the outrages committed against the Divine Love, especially in the Blessed Sacrament. It became a popular RC devotion, though the Mass and Office for the feast were not authorized until 1765; it is observed on the Friday in the week after *Corpus Christi.

Sacred Heart of Mary. Devotion to the heart of the BVM was fostered in the 17th cent. by St John *Eudes, who linked it with the cult of the *Sacred Heart of Jesus. In 1805 *Pius VII allowed the observance of a feast, which in 1944 was made universal, to be kept on 22 Aug.; in 1969 it became an optional '*memoria'.

sacrifice. Sacrifice is fundamentally the offering to the Deity of a gift, especially a living creature. It is a widespread feature of religion. Early in the OT there is the record of the sacrifices of Cain and *Abel (Gen. 4: 3–5), while the demand for the sacrifice of *Isaac (Gen. 22) underlies the need for the offering to be a costly one. Sacrifices were also associated with the making of *covenants, such as that of God with Israel at *Sinai (Exod. 24: 4–8). After the settlement in Canaan, sacrificial observances became more elaborate; from the 7th cent. BC they were restricted to the *Temple at Jerusalem. The chief annual sacrifices were those of the *Paschal Lamb at *Passover and those of the Day of *Atonement.

In the NT Christ appears to have tolerated the current practice of sacrifice, but He quoted with approval the teaching of Hosea subordinating 'sacrifice' to 'mercy' (Mt. 9: 13, 12: 7; cf. Hos. 6: 6). At the Institution of the Eucharist, He pointed to the sacrificial quality of His death (cf. Mk. 10: 45), speaking of the shedding of His Blood in a New Covenant. The Fathers developed the ideas of the NT, stressing the uniqueness of His sacrifice in that He was: (1) a voluntary victim; (2) a victim of infinite value; and (3) Himself also the Priest. In the Middle Ages the relationship of Christ's sacrifice with the Eucharist was elaborated. Christian theology also commonly asserts that the individual's conscious obedience to the will of God may be a form of sacrifice.

sacrilege. Violation or contemptuous treatment of a person, thing, or place publicly dedicated to the worship of God. It is held to be a grave sin.

sacring bell. A bell, also known as a 'Sanctus bell', rung at Mass to focus the people's attention, e.g. at the *Elevation.

sacristan. The term is used for either (1) a *sexton, or (2) the sacrist or official who has charge of the contents of a church, including the vestments and sacred vessels.

sacristy. A room (or suite of rooms) annexed to a church or chapel for keeping the sacred vessels and for the vesting of priests and other clerics.

Sadducees. A Jewish politico-religious sect, opposed to the *Pharisees. Though never numerous, they included men of high standing, and they exercised political influence; at the time of Christ they were important in *Jerusalem. They rejected the traditional interpretations accepted by the Pharisees and accepted the written Law only. Thus they rejected belief in the resurrection of the body and the existence of angels and spirits. They appear to have taken a leading part against Christ and repeatedly attacked the Apostles.

Sadoleto, Jacopo (1477–1547), cardinal from 1536. In 1537 he became a member of the special commission for the reform of the Church and the preparation of a General Council. He tried to win back both P. *Melanchthon and the city of *Geneva to the RC faith. He was one of the most trusted advisers of *Paul III.

Sahdona (7th cent.), spiritual writer. About 635/40 he became Bp. of Mahoze in the *Church of the East, but was expelled from that Church because of his teaching on the Person of Christ. His 'Book of Perfection' is a masterpiece of Syrian spirituality.

Sahidic. A dialect of *Coptic.

St Albans. A church has existed at Verulamium on the site of the reputed martyrdom of St *Alban at least since the time of *Bede; c.794 King *Offa endowed a monastery. In 1077 Paul of Caen, the first Norman abbot, began to rebuild it. At the Reformation the church was bought from *Edward VI (1553) for use as a parish church. In 1877 a diocese of St Albans was created and the abbey became the cathedral church.

St Asaph. The church at St Asaph in *Wales was in origin a monastic settlement, traditionally held to have been founded by St *Kentigern in the late 6th cent. According to a 12th-cent. Life, he was succeeded by St *Asaph, from whom the church later took its name. It became a territorial diocese in the 12th cent. The present cathedral is largely the work of Bp. Redman (c.1480); the choir was rebuilt c. 1770; and the whole restored by G. G. *Scott (1869–75).

Saint-Cyran, Abbé de (1581–1643), Jean Duvergier de Hauranne, commendatory Abbot of Saint-Cyran from 1620, and one of the authors of *Jansenism. He was a close friend of C. O. *Jansen, and, attracted to St *Augustine's writings, he sought to reform Catholicism on Augustinian lines, largely in the hope of defeating Protestantism with its own weapons. From 1623 he was associated with the *Arnauld family and with *Port-Royal; as spiritual counsellor of the convent from 1633 he came to exercise great influence.

St Davids. According to tradition a monastery was founded by St *David (6th cent.) in Menevia, which was thereafter called St Davids. On the death of the last native Welsh bishop in 1115, King Henry I forced on the clergy as their bishop Bernard, chaplain to Queen Matilda, who was prepared to recognize the authority of the Abp. of *Canterbury. Various attempts in the 12th and early-13th cent. to secure metropolitan status for St Davids were unsuccessful. Meanwhile the shrine of St David became a popular place of pilgrimage. The present cathedral was begun by Bp. Peter de Leia (1176–98).

St-Denis. The abbey of St-Denis, 4 miles north of *Paris, was founded c.625 and contained the reputed shrine of St Denis (see DIONYSIUS, ST [3]). It became the regular burying-place of the kings of France and enjoyed royal favour. It was dissolved and sacked at the Revolution (1792–3); the buildings are now a 'national monument'.

St Gall. See GALL, ST.

St-Germain-des-Prés. An abbey in *Paris, founded in the 6th cent. St *Germanus of Paris dedicated the church (557/9), and it later assumed his name. In the 17th cent. it adopted the *Maurist reform and became famous as a centre of scholarship. Most of its buildings were destroyed in the French Revolution, but its MSS were saved.

St-Omer. The *Jesuit college of St-Omer in Artois was founded by R. *Parsons c. 1592 for the education of the English RC laity. When the Jesuits were expelled from France in 1762, they moved their school to Bruges, and later to *Stonyhurst.

St Patrick's Purgatory. A place of pilgrimage on Station Island, Lough Derg, Co. Donegal, where Christ is supposed to have revealed to St *Patrick an entrance to *purgatory and the earthly paradise. The first recorded visit dates from the mid-12th cent.; various knights made pilgrimages in the 14th and 15th cents., and from the 16th cent. pilgrims of all classes were drawn by Patrick's promise of a *plenary indulgence to all who visited the sanctuary in penitence and faith.

St Paul's Cathedral, London. A church was built c.607 by *Ethelbert, King of Kent, as a cathedral for St *Mellitus, first Bp. of London. It was rebuilt in stone by St *Erconwald between 675 and 685. This Saxon building was burnt in 1087. A Norman cathedral was begun in the same year and completed in 1240. In the NE part of the Close stood 'St Paul's Cross', a national centre for religious and political proclamations, sermons, and disputations; it was destroyed in 1643. The cathedral, already ruinous, was burnt in the Great Fire of 1666. The present cathedral, designed by Sir Christopher *Wren, combines classical style with a traditionally Gothic ground-plan. It was completed by 1710.

St Paul's outside the Walls, Rome (San Paolo fuori le Mura). The *Liber Pontificalis states that the original building was erected over the relics of St *Paul by *Constantine. The rebuilding of a large basilica was certainly planned in the late 4th cent. and completed by the Emp. Honorius (395–402/3). This was destroyed by fire in 1823, only the triumphal arch and its mosaics surviving. The present church, which conforms to the plan of the earlier basilica, was consecrated in 1854.

St Peter's, Rome. The present 16th-cent. building replaced an older basilican structure, erected by *Constantine (d. 337) on the supposed site of St *Peter's crucifixion. *Nicholas V (1447–55) planned to replace it by a new church in the form of a Latin cross. Work, begun under *Julius II in 1506, was continued by a succession of archi-tects, who all made changes in the design. The building was finished in 1614 and con-secrated in 1626.

The traditional burial-place of St Peter is the *confessio* under the high altar. Excav-ations carried out since 1940 have revealed the existence of a Christian shrine dating from the 3rd cent., if not earlier.

Saint-Simon, Claude Henri de Rouvroy (1760–1825), exponent of French socialism. In a number of works he argued that only the industrial classes work for the moral and physical welfare of mankind and that they should be preferred to those who had hitherto been privileged. His *Nouveau Chris-tianisme* (1825) maintains that the only Divine principle in Christianity is that men must behave towards each other as brothers; religion should therefore provide amelioration of the lot of the poorest, with dogma and cult as negligible accessories.

His teaching had little following in his lifetime but was influential later in the 19th and the early 20th cents.

St Sophia. See HAGIA SOPHIA.

Saint-Sulpice, Society of. The congrega-tion of secular priests founded by J.-J. *Olier in the parish of St-Sulpice, *Paris, in 1642, with the aim of forming a zealous clergy, especially suited to be directors of seminar-ies. The Society spread to *Canada in 1657 and it soon gained great influence on the ecclesiastical life of France; it still trains many of those destined for the French priesthood. It has provinces in Canada and the USA and missions in the Far East, Cen-tral Africa, and Central and South America.

St-Victor, Abbey of. See VICTORINES.

Sainte-Chapelle, *Paris. The chapel was built by St *Louis IX of France to house the *Crown of Thorns. Begun c.1245, it was consecrated in 1248. Part of the Palais de Justice, it was finally secularized in 1906.

saints, devotion to the. The practice of venerating and invoking the saints has long been an element in Catholic and Orthodox devotion. Its justification rests on the beliefs that the saints are close to God (because of their holiness) and accessible to man (whose nature they share), and in the efficacy of intercessory prayer.

In the NT the gift of special privileges for certain people in the next world is held to be indicated in Christ's promises to the Apostles (Mt. 19: 28), while support for the idea that the dead may intercede for the living is found in the parable of Dives and Lazarus (Lk. 16: 19–31). But it is to the implications of the Pauline doctrine of the Church as the Body of Christ, rather than to specific texts, that the advocates of devo-tion to the saints appeal.

There is clear evidence of devotion to *martyrs in the 'Martyrdom of *Polycarp' (c.156), and this was furthered by the grow-ing cult of their *relics. From the 4th cent. the ranks of those accounted saints were enlarged by the addition of '*confessors' and virgins, on the ground that a life of renunciation and holiness might equal the devotion of those who had died for Christ. Theologians sought to rebut the charge of idolatry by distinguishing between the worship of God, expressed by the word '*latria', and the cult of honour and imita-tion due to saints, expressed in the term '*dulia'.

Liturgical developments followed popu-lar devotion and the current of patristic teaching. The mention of saints in the Mass is attested by St *Augustine, and from the 8th cent. the Lives of saints were read at *Mattins. Councils often found it necessary to curb the excesses and superstition of popular devotion. Among the Reformers all cult of the saints was repudiated, especially by the *Zwinglians and *Calvinists, on the ground that it was not explicitly recom-mended in Scripture. In the C of E its legit-imacy is debated. The attitude of the E. Church is akin to that of Rome.

See also BEATIFICATION and CANONIZA-TION.

sakkos. In the E. Church an embroidered liturgical vestment worn by bishops. It is similar in form to the *dalmatic in the W.

Salesians. Of the many Orders known under this name, the chief is the 'Society of St *Francis de Sales', founded near Turin in 1859 by St John *Bosco for the Christian education of boys and young men of the poorer classes, especially with a view to their ordination. In 1846 he began to gather boys together in what he termed 'festive oratories' and night schools. A congrega-tion of priests and teachers under the pat-ronage of Francis de Sales came into being to develop the work and in 1859 began to live by a rule drawn up by Bosco.

Salisbury. Herman, Bp. of Ramsbury, who united the dioceses of Ramsbury and *Sherborne in 1058, transferred the see to Old Sarum in 1075. His successor, St *Osmund, completed a cathedral, constituted a chapter, and drew up offices, which perhaps formed the basis of the Sarum Rite (see the next entry). Richard *Poore moved the see to New Sarum or Salisbury in 1219 and in 1220 laid the foundation of the new cathedral, completed in 1266. The spire, built between 1334 and 1350, is the highest in England.

Salisbury or **Sarum, Use of.** The medieval modification of the Roman rite used in the cathedral church at Salisbury, traditionally ascribed to St *Osmund. The *Customary, i.e. the cathedral statutes and customs and a complete directory of services, was compiled by Richard *Poore (d. 1237). The 'New Use of Sarum' was a 14th-cent revision. In the later Middle Ages the Sarum Use was followed in many other dioceses; it provided the main material for the First (1549) BCP.

Salmanticenses. The customary name for the authors of the *Cursus theologicus Summam d. Thomae complectens*, a group of Discalced *Carmelites who taught at Salamanca between 1600 and 1725. The *Cursus* is a huge commentary on the *Summa Theologiae* of St *Thomas Aquinas.

Salome. (1) A woman who followed Christ to Jerusalem. Matthew appears to identify her with the mother of St *James and St *John, the sons of Zebedee (Mt. 27: 56; cf. Mk. 15: 40). She is sometimes identified with the sister of the BVM (Jn. 19: 25). See MARYS IN THE NT (4).

(2) The name given by *Josephus to the daughter of Herodias who is mentioned without a name at Mt. 14: 6 and Mk. 6: 22.

Salonica. See THESSALONICA.

salos (Gk., 'silly', 'mad'). One who practised a peculiar form of asceticism in the E., presenting himself as a holy fool in society. The best known is the 6th-cent. Simeon, whose Life was written by Leontius of Neapolis. The practice gained popularity and later extended to the Russian Church.

salt. Because of its preservative quality salt was a sign of purity and incorruptibility, especially among the Semitic peoples. It served to confirm contracts and friendship, and its use was prescribed for every oblation (Lev. 2: 13). The offering of blessed salt to *catechumens formerly formed part of the RC rite of *Baptism. Salt may also be used in the preparation of *Holy Water.

saltum, per. See PER SALTUM.

Salvation Army. An international Christian organization for evangelistic and social work. It was founded by W. *Booth in 1865 and received its present form and title in 1878. It is organized on a military basis, with a 'General' at its head. Its religious teaching is largely in harmony with traditional *evangelical belief, but it rejects all Sacraments and stresses the moral side of Christianity. Open-air meetings with brass bands play an important part in its method of presenting religion to the people.

Salve Regina (Lat., 'Hail, [Holy] Queen'). One of the oldest Marian *antiphons, sometimes recited in the W. Church at the end of the canonical hours, and a widely used prayer to the BVM. Its authorship is unknown. The earliest MS evidence is usually dated at the end of the 11th cent.

Salvian (c.400-c.480), 'of Marseilles', ecclesiastical writer. After the birth of a daughter, he and his wife adopted a life of asceticism. Already a priest by 431, he seems to have spent over 40 years at Marseilles. His *De Gubernatione Dei*, by contrasting the vices of decadent Roman civilization with the virtues of the victorious barbarians, uses the latter as a witness to God's judgement on society and as an incentive for Christians to purity of life and faith in Providence.

Samaria. The capital of the kingdom of *Israel, i.e. of the 'Ten [northern] Tribes', founded by King Omri (c.880 BC) and c.721 captured by the Assyrians, who resettled the territory with pagans from other parts of their empire (2 Kgs. 18: 9-12 and ch. 17). According to Jewish tradition, the Samaritans known to later Judaism and the NT were the descendants of these settlers. Of the OT they accepted only the *Pentateuch, in a slightly divergent form (the Samaritan Pentateuch). The hostility of the Jews to the

Samaritans was proverbial. See also GOOD SAMARITAN.

Samaritans, the. See SUICIDE.

Samson (probably 11th cent. BC), Hebrew hero and traditionally the last of the great 'judges'. According to the account in Jgs. 13: 2–16: 31, he was endowed with prodigious strength and wrought havoc among the Philistines; when he fell victim to his passion for Delilah and revealed to her the secret of his strength, the Philistines put out his eyes, but he was granted his revenge in pulling down the pillars of the temple where 3,000 Philistines were assembled. Recent scholarship thinks of the Samson stories as originally independent tales, perhaps covering various local heroes. His faith is commended in Heb 11: 32.

Samson, St (c.486-after 557), Bp. of Dol in Brittany. Born in S. Wales, he was ordained by St *Dubricius and entered a monastery on Caldey Island. He retired to a cave near the R. Severn and attended a synod at which he was made a bishop. Instructed in a vision to leave his monastery, he went to Brittany; there he founded the monastery of Dol, which became a centre of missionary activity. He attended the councils of Paris in 553 and 557. Feast day, 28 July.

Samuel, Books of. The two OT Books of Samuel were originally a single Book, which was divided for convenience by the compilers of the LXX, who also grouped the Books of Samuel with those of *Kings under the single title of the '[Four] Books of the Reigns'. The English title follows the Hebrew. After relating the history of the prophet Samuel, the writer describes the reigns of Saul (c.1025–c.1010 BC) and *David (c.1010–c.970). Modern scholars concentrate their attention on the religious and theological standpoint of the compilers of the Books, which they regard as an important constituent of the so-called *Deuteronomistic History.

sanatio in radice (Lat., 'healing at the root'). In canon law the process whereby an invalid 'marriage' is validated retrospectively, i.e. from the moment it was solemnized.

sanbenito. The penitential garment which the medieval and later the Spanish *Inquisition ordered to be worn by those who had been sentenced for heresy. It was normally yellow, but in the case of those to be handed over to the secular authorities, it was black, decorated with flames, etc.

Sánchez, Thomas (1550–1610), Spanish *Jesuit. He became famous for his *Disputationes de sancto matrimonii sacramento* (1602), a comprehensive work on the moral and canonical aspects of matrimony which enjoyed high authority in the 17th cent.

Sancroft, William (1617–93), Abp. of *Canterbury from 1678 to 1690. His primacy was distinguished by a major effort to renew the strength of the C of E, both politically and spiritually. On the accession of the RC *James II (1685), he altered the *Coronation rite so that the Communion could be omitted. He led the *Seven Bishops who opposed the *Declaration of Indulgence in 1688, but he nevertheless refused to recognize William of Orange as king and was deprived of his archbishopric as a *Nonjuror. He supported schemes to perpetuate the Nonjuring succession and in 1692 he formally delegated his archiepiscopal authority to William Lloyd, the deprived Bp. of *Norwich.

Sancta Sophia. See HAGIA SOPHIA.

Sanctorale. The section of a *Missal, *Lectionary, or *Breviary which contains the variable parts of the Mass or Offices peculiar to the festivals of particular saints.

sanctuary. The part of a church containing the altar (or, if there are several altars, the high altar). In Byzantine churches it is enclosed by the *iconostasis.

sanctuary, right of. In medieval England this was of two kinds, ecclesiastical and secular. The former developed out of the usage that a criminal who had taken refuge in a church might not be removed from it, but was allowed to take an oath of abjuration before the coroner and proceed to a seaport. Secular and jurisdictional sanctuary relied upon a royal grant, and might be held to apply to any franchise where the lord had *jura regalia* and the king's writ did not run. This institution is frequently confused with ecclesiastical sanctuary, since criminals commonly repaired to a church in a franchise, especially in the ecclesiastical liberties such as *Durham. In 1540 the privilege of sanctuary was restricted to seven cities. In 1623 sanctuary for crime was abolished, though it lingered for civil processes until 1723.

Sanctus. The hymn of praise which follows the *Preface in the Eucharist and begins with the words 'Holy, holy, holy' (Is. 6: 3). It was apparently not part of the earliest Eucharistic rite, but its use in the Eucharist in most E. and some W. churches is attested by 350.

Sanctus bell. See SACRING BELL.

sandals, episcopal. Low shoes with leather soles and the upper part of embroidery which before 1984 could be worn by bishops in the W. Church at solemn Pontifical Masses and other functions (such as Ordinations) performed during them.

Sandemanians. See GLASITES.

Sanders, Nicholas (*c.*1530–81), also 'Sander', RC controversialist and historian. He fled from England in 1559. In 1565 he went to Louvain, where he became professor of theology and engaged in the controversy aroused by J. *Jewel's *Apology*. In 1572 he became consultor to *Gregory XIII on English affairs, and in 1579 he went to *Ireland as Papal agent to stir up an insurrection. His unfinished *De Origine ac Progressu Schismatis Anglicani* (publd. 1585) is now admitted to be accurate in some of its controverted statements.

Sanderson, Robert (1587–1663), Bp. of *Lincoln from 1660. He took a leading part in the *Savoy Conference of 1661 and drafted the preface to the 1662 BCP. His *Nine Cases of Conscience* (1678) was a notable contribution to moral theology.

Sanhedrin. The Jewish supreme council and court of justice at *Jerusalem in NT times. Its origin is obscure, but such a council in operation is attested before Roman times. It apparently included both priests and laymen, *Sadducees and *Pharisees, and the NT implies that it was presided over by the *High Priest. It is debated whether it had the right to try capital cases, but such a right is presupposed in the tradition that it passed sentence of death on Christ.

Sankey, Ira David. See MOODY, DWIGHT LYMAN.

Santa Claus. An American corruption of the Dutch form of St *Nicholas, Bp. of Myra.

Santa Maria Maggiore, Rome. The church was founded by Pope *Liberius (352–66); the present structure was erected under Sixtus III (432–40). According to a medieval tradition the site was indicated by the BVM, who one August night left her footprints in a miraculous fall of snow.

Santa Sophia. See HAGIA SOPHIA.

Santiago de Compostela. See COMPOSTELA.

Santiago, Order of. A military order under the patronage of St *James the Apostle, founded in 1170 for the protection of pilgrims and the expulsion of the Moors. It was modelled on the *Templars, but its knights were allowed to marry.

sarabaites. A class of ascetics in the early Church who lived either in their own houses or in small groups and acknowledged no monastic superior.

Saracens. A term probably originally applied to the nomads of N. Arabia, who claim descent from Ishmael (*Abraham's son). From at least the 9th cent. it came to be used of all Muslims, especially those against whom the *Crusaders fought.

Saravia, Hadrian a (*c.*1532–1613), Protestant theologian. As a youth he entered the *Franciscan Order at St-Omer, but left it on his conversion to Protestantism in 1557. He was consulted over the drafting of the *Belgic Confession (1561). In 1584 he became professor of theology at *Leiden, but his support for the Governor General (the Earl of Leicester) in 1587 led to his dismissal and flight to England, where he held a succession of benefices. In his chief theological work, *De Diversis Ministrorum Evangelii Gradibus* (1590), he supported episcopacy, basing his position on an appeal to the 'ius divinum'. He was among the earliest Protestants to urge the duty of preaching the Gospel to the heathen. He was one of the translators of the AV of the Bible.

sarcophagus. A stone coffin, usually adorned with bas-relief. Until the Byzantine period sarcophagi were much used by both Christians and pagans. Those of the early Christians were often adorned with pagan designs, but from the 4th cent. some Christian subjects were depicted.

Sardica (or Serdica), Council of (modern Sofia). A Council summoned *c.*343 mainly to settle the orthodoxy of St *Athanasius. The E. bishops refused to take part on the ground that Athanasius, whom the E. had deposed, was being regarded by the W. as a member of the synod; the W. bishops therefore met by themselves. They confirmed the restoration of Athanasius and passed some famous disciplinary canons; these included provisions constituting the Bp. of Rome a court of appeal for accused bishops in certain circumstances.

Sardis, a city in Lydia, Asia Minor. The Christian community there is one of the '*Seven Churches' addressed in Rev. (3: 1–6). In Late Antiquity it was a prosperous city; in the Middle Ages a significant centre and a bishopric, but by the 17th cent. there was only a Turkish village with no priest or church building.

Sarpi, Paolo (1552–1623), *Servite jurist and theologian. A native of *Venice, he rose to high office in the Servite Order. In the struggle between Venice and *Paul V (1606–7), he defended the interests of the Republic. He was excommunicated in 1607 but he continued to exercise his priestly functions until his death. His *Historia del Concilio Tridentino* (first published in London in 1619) is based on authentic material but represents the Council of *Trent as solely a conspiracy against the reform of the Church.

Sarum; Sarum rite. See SALISBURY; SALISBURY, USE OF.

Satan. In the Judaeo-Christian tradition, the supreme embodiment of evil, also called the *devil (q.v.).

satisfaction. An act of reparation for an injury; in Christian theology usually the payment of a penalty due to God on account of sin. St *Anselm gave the term theological currency in reference to the *Atonement by interpreting Christ's death as a vicarious satisfaction for the world's sins.

In Catholic theology satisfaction is held to be a necessary element in the sacrament of *Penance. With the attenuation of penances and the practice of giving absolution before satisfaction was made, the distinction between forgiveness of the fault and the satisfaction due to it after forgiveness was worked out clearly; the classic example adduced was the penance inflicted on *David after Nathan had pronounced God's forgiveness (2 Sam. 12: 13–14). Thus *satisfactio operis* came to be regarded as a necessary means of avoiding punishment in *purgatory after the sin itself had been remitted by sacramental absolution.

SATOR. See INSCRIPTIONS, EARLY CHRISTIAN.

Saturday. The Jewish '*Sabbath' (q.v.) and the day of the week on which Christ's body rested in the tomb. In the W. Saturday was regarded as a fast day by the 3rd cent., but, except in *Lent and on the *Ember Days, the Saturday fast was finally abolished in 1918. On the other hand, in most E. Churches from the 4th cent. Saturday was distinguished by a celebration of the Liturgy, which in Lent is still confined to Saturday and Sunday. The connection of Saturday with the BVM in the W. is a medieval development. In the E. Church Saturday is associated with the commemoration of the departed. See also HOLY SATURDAY.

Saturninus (2nd cent.), Syrian *Gnostic. He held that the origin of things was to be sought in a Father unknown to all, who created a series of angels and other supernatural beings who in turn created man. Man was a powerless entity who wriggled on the ground until a Divine spark set him on his feet. The God of the Jews was one of the creator angels, and the Supreme Father sent the Saviour to destroy this God and to redeem such as were endowed with the Divine spark.

Sava, St (*c.*1175–1235), also **Sabas**, patron of *Serbia. In 1191 Rastko, a son of the Serbian king, went secretly to Mount *Athos and became a monk under the name Sava. In 1206 he returned to Serbia, where as archimandrite of the monastery of Studenica he took an active part in the religious and political life of the country. In 1219 he established an independent Serbian Church, of which he was consecrated the first archbishop by the Patr. of Nicaea. Feast day in the Serbian Church, 14 Jan.

Savigny, Abbey of, in Normandy. In 1093

Vitalis of Mortain established a hermitage in the Forest of Savigny. Some of the hermits felt a call to follow the Rule of St *Benedict in its primitive strictness, and the abbey was established in 1115. It rose to high repute and daughter houses were founded. In 1147 all the houses were integrated into the *Cistercian Order.

Savonarola, Girolamo (1452–98), Italian preacher and reformer. He entered the *Dominican Order in 1475 and in 1491 became prior of San Marco in Florence. About this time he adopted an apocalyptic style of preaching, prophesying an impending Divine chastisement of the corruption of Church and society and claiming to receive special revelations from God. Wanting to go beyond the existing Dominican reform, he secured the independence of San Marco from the Reformed Congregation of Lombardy in 1493, thus launching a new Congregation to which other priories were added. Politically he called for social and moral reform, and established a kind of theocratic democracy in Florence. He supported Charles VIII of France in his Italian campaign of 1494–5, seeing in him God's instrument for reform. In 1495 *Alexander VI summoned him to Rome; he pleaded that he could not leave Florence. In 1497 he was excommunicated but held that the excommunication was invalid and continued to preach. In 1498 he wrote to the major Christian princes asking them to convene a Council. Popular opinion turned against him and, abandoned by the Florentine authorities, he was arrested, condemned for schism and heresy, and hanged. Steps are being taken to secure his canonization.

Savoy Conference (1661). A conference of 12 bishops, 12 *Presbyterian ministers, and 9 assessors from each party which met in G. *Sheldon's lodgings at the Savoy in London to review the BCP. The Presbyterians sought means to enable them to remain within the Established Church, but in reply to their *Exceptions to the BCP the bishops made only 17 trivial concessions.

Savoy Declaration (1658). A statement of *Congregational principles and polity, drawn up at a conference held in the Chapel of the Savoy in London by representatives of 120 Churches. It consists of a Preface, a Confession of Faith closely akin to

the *Westminster Confession, and a Platform of Discipline declaring that all necessary power is vested in each individual Church.

Sawtrey, William (d. 1401), *Lollard. A priest of Lynn, Norfolk, in 1399 he was summoned by his bishop to answer charges of heresy. In 1401 he was charged before Abp. T. *Arundel and burnt, on the ground that he had relapsed into heresies which he had abjured two years earlier.

Saxon Confession (1551). The Protestant Confession of Faith drawn up for the Council of *Trent by P. *Melanchthon at the request of the Elector Maurice of Saxony.

Sayers, Dorothy Leigh (1893–1957), novelist, religious playwright, and apologist. The daughter of an Anglican clergyman, she wrote detective stories (the last published in 1937), two plays for the *Canterbury Festival in 1937 and 1939, and a radio dramatization of the life of Christ, *The Man Born to be King*, broadcast in 1941–2. This caused controversy through its representation of Christ by an actor and because the dialogue in which he took part was in modern English. She combined professional competence with fresh insights into the meaning of the Christian faith. Her major work was an annotated verse translation of *Dante's *Divine Comedy*.

Sayings of Jesus. The name given by the first editors to the texts preserved in two *Oxyrhynchus papyri (nos. 1 and 654). These texts, together with those in no. 655, if not part of the Greek original of the Gospel of *Thomas, are closely related to it.

Scala Sancta (also known as the **Scala Pilati).** A staircase of 28 marble steps near the *Lateran church at Rome. Tradition asserts that they were the steps descended by Christ after His condemnation to death and brought to the W. by St *Helena from the palace of *Pilate at Jerusalem.

Scaliger, Joseph Justus (1540–1609), French scholar. He became a *Calvinist in 1562. From 1593 he was a professor at *Leiden. His editions of Latin authors marked an advance in the field of *textual criticism. His most famous work, *De Emendatione Temporum* (1583), established the modern science of chronology.

scapular. A garment consisting of a piece of cloth worn over the shoulders and hanging down in front and behind. It is usually 14–18 inches wide with its two ends reaching almost to the feet, and forms part of the regular monastic *habit. A similar garment of much smaller dimensions (known as the 'smaller scapular') is worn by people living in the world who have become affiliated to religious orders; important privileges have become attached to wearing the smaller scapular in the RC Church.

Scaramelli, Giovanni Battista (1687–1752), *Jesuit spiritual writer. In his 'Ascetic Directory' (*Direttorio ascetico*, 1752), which has long been regarded as a classic, he examines the nature of Christian perfection and the means of attaining it.

Scete. The southern part of the *Nitrian Desert, celebrated as a centre of monasticism in the 4th and 5th cents.

Schaff, Philip (1819–93), theologian and Church historian. He became a professor first of the German Reformed Seminary at Mercersburg, Pennsylvania (1844), and then in the *Union Theological Seminary, New York (1870). He edited an American adaptation of J. J. Herzog's huge *Realencyclopädie für protestantische Theologie und Kirche* and a series of translations of patristic texts, and he compiled a valuable collection of credal documents, *The Creeds of Christendom* (1877). He was an exponent of the '*Mercersburg Theology'.

Scheeben, Matthias Joseph (1835–88), RC theologian. From 1860 he was professor of dogma at the seminary at *Cologne. In various works he emphasized the rights of supernatural faith against the rationalist and naturalist tendencies of 18th- and 19th-cent. theology. At the time of the First *Vatican Council he was an opponent of J. J. I. von *Döllinger and a passionate defender of Papal *Infallibility.

Scheffler, Johannes. See ANGELUS SILESIUS.

Schelling, Friedrich Wilhelm Joseph von (1775–1854), German philosopher. In his early years he acknowledged only one reality, the infinite and absolute Ego, of which the universe was the expression. This abstract pantheism was soon modified in favour of his conception of 'Naturphiloso-

phie', according to which nature was an absolute being which works unconsciously, though purposively. The problem of the relation of nature to spirit then gave rise to his 'Identitätsphilosophie': both nature and spirit are but manifestations of one and the same being, absolute identity being the ground of all things. In his attempt to reconcile Christianity with his philosophy he distinguished three elements in God: (1) the blind primeval necessary being; (2) the three potentialities of the Divine Essence, namely unconscious will (material cause), rational will (efficient cause), and unity of the two (final cause of creation); and (3) the Three Persons who evolve from the three potentialities by overcoming the primeval being. He exercised a profound influence on German thought, and on P. *Tillich.

Schelstrate, Emmanuel (1649–92), Belgium Church historian and canonist. He became Prefect of the *Vatican Library. His treatise on the *disciplina arcani* (1685) developed the view that the secrecy demanded by Christ, the Apostles, and their successors explained the relative weakness of the evidence for the doctrines of the Person of Christ and the Sacraments in the primitive Church.

Schillebeeckx, Edward Cornelis Florentius Alfons (1914–), Dutch RC theologian. He became a *Dominican in 1934. He was a professor at Louvain (1947–58) and then at Nijmegen (1958–82). He attended the Second *Vatican Council not as a *peritus*, but as adviser to the Dutch bishops.

His book *Jezus* (1974; Eng. tr., *Jesus*), with its interpretation of the Lord as an eschatological prophet, caused an uproar in Rome. It was followed by *Gerechtigheid en liefde* (1977; Eng. tr., *Christ*, 1980). The increasing conservatism of the RC Church led him to postpone the completion of his planned trilogy, and in *Kerkelijk ambt* (1980; Eng. tr., *Ministry*, 1981) he called for changes in the RC theology of ministry on the basis of the pattern of the first millennium and modern needs. This concern cast a shadow over the last volume of his trilogy, *Mensen als verhaal van God* (1989; Eng. tr., *The Church*, 1990), in which a vision of the future influenced by *liberation theology and inter-faith dialogue is darkened by experience of the hierarchical Church.

schism. Formal and wilful separation from

the unity of the Church. It is distinguished from heresy in that the separation involved is not doctrinal in basis. RC theologians account those out of communion with the Pope in a state of schism, though the Second *Vatican Council Decree on Ecumenism stated that those baptized in other Christian communities were established 'in a certain, albeit imperfect, communion with the Catholic Church'. The term 'schism' is often used by Anglican and Protestant theologians of divisions within the Church, e.g. of that between Anglicanism and Roman Catholicism.

Schlatter, Adolf (1852–1938), Protestant theologian. He held that the only sound foundation of systematic theology lay in biblical exegesis, and he wrote commentaries on every Book in the NT. He also opposed all idealistic interpretations of the Christian faith. He thus anticipated the *Dialectical Theology of K. *Barth.

Schleiermacher, Friedrich Daniel Ernst (1768–1834), German theologian. He was Reformed preacher at the Charité in Berlin, professor of theology at Halle (1804–7), and later preacher at the Dreifaltigkeitskirche in Berlin and Dean of the Theological Faculty of the newly founded university. In 1799 he published his famous *Reden über die Religion* (Eng. tr., *Religion: Speeches to its Cultured Despisers*, 1893), in which he tried to win the educated classes back to religion. Contending that religion was based on intuition and feeling and independent of all dogma, he saw its highest experience in a sensation of union with the infinite. In *Der christliche Glaube* (1821–2) he defines religion as the feeling of absolute dependence which finds its purest expression in monotheism; the variety of forms which this feeling assumes in different individuals and nations accounts for the diversity of religions, of which Christianity is the highest, but not the only true one. His emphasis on feeling as the basis of religion was a reaction both from contemporary German rationalism and from the ruling formalist orthodoxy. His influence on Protestant thought has been immense.

Schmalkaldic Articles (1537). The doctrinal statement drawn up by M. *Luther at the behest of Friedrich, Elector of Saxony, for presentation to the projected General Council summoned by *Paul III. An assembly of Lutheran princes and theologians at Schmalkalden in Thuringia approved the Articles, as well as a more conciliatory appendix by P. *Melanchthon.

Schmalkaldic League. The alliance concluded at Schmalkalden in 1531 between several German Protestant princes and cities in opposition to *Charles V's 'Recess of Augsburg' (1530) which suppressed their religious autonomy. It united *Lutherans and *Zwinglians.

Schola Cantorum (Lat., 'a school of singers'). In the worship of the early Church all music was rendered by the clergy and congregation, but gradually the practice of having a body of trained singers was introduced. At *Rome the Schola was established on a sound footing by *Gregory the Great (d. 604). The custom spread over W. Christendom.

Scholastica, St (*c.*480–*c.*543), sister of St *Benedict. She is said to have established a convent at Plombariola, a few miles from *Monte Cassino. Feast day, 10 Feb.

Scholasticism. A method of scholarly inquiry which proceeds by way of questioning ancient and authoritative texts, first by drawing up lists of contradictory statements in these texts and then applying to them the rules of logic to reveal their underlying agreement, thus attaining what the scholastics saw as the inner truth to which in the end all these texts bore witness. The method was originally a teaching device developed in the schools and universities of W. Europe from the late-11th cent.; it flourished until the 16th cent.

The texts used by medieval scholars to develop the art of logical argument were largely works of *Boethius. *Charlemagne and *Alcuin provided a framework of monastic and cathedral schools in which learning could be cultivated and material collected; by 1050 important collections of logical material were at hand. In the late-11th to 12th cents., the scholastic method was developed in the schools. *Anselm of Laon and his brother, for their lectures on Scripture, collected authoritative statements from the Fathers and attached them to the matching texts of the Bible, beginning the *Glossa Ordinaria. When two Fathers differed in their interpretation, their contradictory statements were compared in the classroom and became the subject of a *quaestio*. The technique was perfected by Peter *Abelard in his *Sic et Non*. By simply collecting authorities without attaching them to the appropriate biblical passages, Abelard showed the way for later generations to separate systematic questioning from lecturing on Scripture. In the prologue he also enumerated two key doctrines of Scholasticism: (1) that questioning is the key to the perception of truth, (2) that differences which arise in questioning can usually be resolved by determining the meaning of terms used by different authors in varying ways. By the end of the 12th cent. *Alan of Lille had devised a complete set of rules for the proper use of language and logic in theology.

In the 13th cent. the universities developed the teaching methods of the schools. *Paris was the first to separate speculative questioning from lectures on the Bible. *Peter Lombard's *Sentences* were chosen as the textbook for the new lecture course. Besides ordinary lectures, special days in the university calendar were set aside for disputations, in which either the master broached a controversial subject or someone in the audience could ask him anything. It was in these *quaestiones disputatae* and *quodlibetales* that the scholastic method could be exploited most fully, because the master was free to explore all sides to a question. The final stage in the development of the scholastic method in the 13th cent. was reached with the *Summae*, freely composed works in which the sequence of questions was dictated not by the text used in the classroom but by the internal progress of the argument.

The main controversy of the 13th cent. revolved on the contents of *Aristotle's natural philosophy and his Arab and Jewish commentators. Despite the efforts of St *Thomas Aquinas and others to prove that there was no fundamental contradiction between secular learning and theology, doubts about a possible reconciliation between faith and reason grew as knowledge of Aristotle's natural philosophy increased. In the 14th cent. the scope of the scholastic technique became more narrowly defined. Problems of the present superseded preoccupation with ancient books and the connection between the text and question became a mere formality. *Duns Scotus was the first theologian to

limit the universal validity of logic by stating that the structure of the world represented only one possible manifestation of God's power, which was bound by nothing but His will and the law of contradiction. *William of Ockham went further; he severed the link between logic and reality, maintaining that logic is not about reality as represented by words, but just about words, and he thought logic of little use in theology. Scholasticism was attacked by the humanists, and in the 16th cent. most European universities replaced the medieval arts course with the study of Greek and Latin literature.

scholia. Notes inserted in the margins of ancient MSS. They were introduced by Christian scholars into MSS of biblical and ecclesiastical texts. They were often collected and published as a kind of commentary.

School of English Church Music. See ROYAL SCHOOL OF ENGLISH CHURCH MUSIC.

Schoolmen. The teachers of philosophy and theology at the medieval European universities, then usually called 'schools'. See SCHOLASTICISM.

schools, cathedral and **Sunday.** See CATHEDRAL SCHOOLS, SUNDAY SCHOOLS.

Schopenhauer, Arthur (1788–1860), German philosopher. His chief work was *Die Welt als Wille und Vorstellung* ('1819' [really 1818]; Eng. tr., *The World as Will and Idea*, 1883–6). He held that the ultimate Reality was Will. Though he claimed to be at one with the Christian mystics in teaching that the extinction of the will by pity and mortification of the passions was the sovereign remedy for the evils of existence, his whole philosophy was one of Pessimism; it was one of the chief anti-Christian systems in 19th-cent. Germany.

Schütz, Heinrich (1585–1672), German composer. Most of his surviving music was written for the *Lutheran Church, both for Latin and German texts. He is famous for his *Passion music.

Schwabach, Articles of (1529), the first of the *Lutheran Confessions. The 17 Articles were based on those considered and, with one exception, adopted at the Colloquy of *Marburg.

Schwartz, Eduard (1858–1940), classical

philologist and *patristic scholar. He held a succession of professorships in Germany. His main work, the *Acta Conciliorum Oecumenicorum* (1914–40), was a grandly planned edition of the Greek Councils; it provided, for the first time, a critical edition of the 'Acts' of *Ephesus (431) and *Chalcedon (451). His collection of papers on St *Athanasius (1904–11) was also important.

Schweitzer, Albert (1875–1965), German theologian, physician, and organist. In *Das Messianitäts- und Leidensgeheimnis* (1901; Eng. tr., *The Mystery of the Kingdom of God*, 1914) he expounded the idea that the Lord's teaching centred in His conviction of the imminent end of the world. The book caused a stir, and in 1902 Schweitzer was made a lecturer at Strasbourg University. In *Von Reimarus zu Wrede* (1906; Eng. tr., *The Quest of the Historical Jesus*, 1910), he developed an interpretation of Christ's life on the basis of 'thoroughgoing eschatology'; he held that the Lord shared with His contemporaries the expectation of a speedy end of the world and, when this proved a mistake, concluded that He Himself must suffer in order to save His people from the tribulations preceding the last days. In 1911 he took a degree in medicine and in 1913 he went to Lambaréné in Gabon (then French Equatorial Africa) to care for the sick and engage in missionary work. Having been interned in France in 1917, he went back to Strasbourg in 1918. His *Kulturphilosophie* (1923) summed up his views on ethics as 'reverence for life'. In 1924 he returned to Lambaréné; his hospital there was his main concern for the rest of his life, though he continued his theological writing. He exercised considerable influence on Continental as well as on English and American Protestant theology.

Schwenckfeldians. The followers of the Silesian Reformation theologian Caspar Schwenckfeld (1490–1561). Schwenckfeld, who was a mystic by temperament, was impressed by the writings of J. *Tauler and M. *Luther, but soon found that he could not give unreserved assent to many of the Protestant doctrines. He also came to hold a doctrine of the deification of Christ's humanity, and in 1540 he issued an account of his beliefs on this subject. A few years later he withdrew from the Lutheran Church. After his death a small band of disciples, calling themselves the 'Confessors of the Glory of Christ', continued to propagate his teaching. A branch, established in Philadelphia in 1734, survives.

scientia media (Lat., 'mediate knowledge'). A term coined by L. *Molina in his attempt to reconcile God's foreknowledge with human free will. It designates the knowledge which God has of 'futuribilia', i.e. of things which are not, but which would be if certain conditions were realized, and thus are intermediate between mere possibilities and actual future events. According to Molinist teaching, this mediate knowledge is independent of the decree of the Divine Will.

Scillitan Martyrs, the. Seven men and five women of Scillium in N. Africa who were executed in 180 for refusing to renounce Christianity and swear by the 'genius' of the Emperor. Feast day, 17 July.

SCM. See STUDENT CHRISTIAN MOVEMENT.

Scone, Perthshire. An ancient religious centre and once the capital of a Pictish kingdom. An abbey of *Augustinian canons was settled here c.1115, and from 1153 the kings of Scotland were crowned at Scone. The Stone of Destiny, taken from Scone to *Westminster Abbey in 1296, was transferred to Edinburgh Castle in 1996; it was traditionally believed to be that on which *Jacob laid his head at *Bethel (Gen. 28: 11).

Scory, John (d. 1585), Anglican bishop. He was a *Dominican before the *Dissolution of the Monasteries. He became Bp. of *Chichester in 1552. Under *Mary he was deprived of his see; he recanted but left England. He returned in 1558 and in 1559 he became Bp. of *Hereford. He assisted at M. *Parker's consecration and is thus held to be one of the channels by which the episcopal succession was preserved in the C of E.

Scotism. The system of Scholastic philosophy expounded by *Duns Scotus.

Scotland, Christianity in. The earliest evidence of Christianity is a number of inscribed monuments of the 5th and 6th cents. in SW Scotland. By the later 6th cent. St *Columba and other Irish saints were active in the Kingdom of Dalriada (N. Scotland). *Iona was largely responsible for the conversion of the Northumbrian kingdom of Bernicia, but the Columban Church lost influence here after King Oswiu adopted the Roman Easter in 664 and Northumbrian influence among the Picts led to their adopting the Roman practice in 710. The union of Pictland and Dalriada in the 9th cent. and the gradual settling of the frontier with the English led to the creation of the Scottish kingdom. The English and Anglo-Norman connections of Queen *Margaret (d. 1093) and her sons brought new Church leaders who transformed the structure of the Scottish Church. A territorial episcopate with clearly defined boundaries was supported by royally-imposed teind (*tithe). Attempts by the Abp. of *York to extend his metropolitan authority over the Scottish sees led in 1192 to a compromise unique in the history of the W. Church, whereby all of them except Galloway (which remained under York) were exempted from any superior authority except that of Rome; the Popes regarded themselves as Scotland's metropolitans. In the Middle Ages the Scottish Church was normally under royal control, and King and Pope seldom disagreed.

The first wave of the Reformation in Scotland was *Lutheran, the second *Calvinist. After the return of John *Knox in 1559, the Reformed Church of Scotland was established on Presbyterian lines in 1560. For more than a century, however, the fortunes of Scottish Presbyterianism ebbed and flowed owing to the determination of the Stuart kings to make the Kirk episcopal. The imposition of the Prayer Book brought the conflict between the Kirk and *Charles I to a head in 1637. In 1638 the Presbyterian *National Covenant was subscribed and Episcopacy was swept away. In 1643 the alliance between the Scottish Covenanters and the Long Parliament was cemented by the *Solemn League and Covenant, which was to impose Presbyterianism throughout the British Isles. The *Westminster Assembly then produced a number of documents which were formally accepted as standards by the Church of Scotland. After the Restoration (1660) Episcopacy was re-established, but at the Revolution the Church of Scotland became Presbyterian again in 1690 and has remained so.

The Church of Scotland was weakened by a number of secessions in the 18th cent.

and by the *Disruption of 1843, when nearly a third of its ministers and members left the Establishment and founded the *Free Church of Scotland. Later there were unions between different Presbyterian Churches in Scotland, notably in 1847 (Secession and Relief to form *United Presbyterian), 1900 (United Presbyterian and Free to form *United Free), and in 1929 (United Free and Church of Scotland under the name of the latter). After the 1929 reunion, the majority of the population belonged to the Church of Scotland, which is Presbyterian, national, endowed, and with its spiritual independence enshrined in Act of Parliament. From those who adhered to Episcopacy after 1690 arose the Episcopal Church of Scotland (since 1979 called the Scottish Episcopal Church). It is an autonomous Province of the *Anglican Communion. It is governed by a General Synod, of which one House is comprised of the seven diocesan bishops. They elect one of their number as *Primus, who is their chairman, but metropolitical authority resides with the College of Bishops, not an individual. The RC Church retained its hold on the descendants of those in parts of the Highlands who were never much influenced by the Reformation and on those of Irish extraction in the industrial Lowland areas. In recent years it has attracted a wider following and now comprises about 20 per cent of the population, roughly the same proportion as the Church of Scotland.

Scott, George Gilbert (1811–78), architect. Brought up as an *Evangelical, he was drawn by A. W. N. *Pugin and B. *Webb to study the principles of Gothic art. In 1844 he won a competition for a *Lutheran church in Hamburg. He designed many churches in Britain and was entrusted with work of restoration at *Westminster Abbey and the cathedrals at *Ely, *Hereford, *Salisbury, and *Chester. His 'restorations' met with resistance because of his preference for his own designs to existing work.

His grandson, **Giles Gilbert Scott** (1880–1960), designed the Anglican cathedral at *Liverpool.

Scott, Thomas (1747–1821), biblical commentator. His *Commentary on the Bible*, issued in weekly numbers between 1788 and 1792, had a huge circulation. It sought to find the message in each section of the the Bible and refused to shirk difficulties.

Scottish Confession. The first Confession of Faith of the reformed Church of Scotland. A typically *Calvinist document, it was adopted by the Scottish Parliament in 1560 and remained the confessional standard until it was superseded by the *Westminster Confession in 1647.

Scottish Episcopal Church. See SCOTLAND, CHRISTIANITY IN.

Scottus Erigena. See ERIGENA, JOHN THE SCOT.

Scotus, Duns. See DUNS SCOTUS.

screens. Partitions of wood, stone, or metal, often with painted or sculptural decoration, dividing a church into two or more parts. Chancel- or choir-screens, separating the *choir from the *nave, may be high or quite low; when surmounted by a cross ('rood'), they are termed 'rood-screens'. See also ICONOSTASIS.

scriptorium. The room set apart for scribes to copy MSS.

Scrope, Richard le (c.1346–1405), Abp. of *York from 1398. Though he assisted in forcing the abdication of Richard II in 1399 and took part in the enthronement of Henry IV, he grew discontented with the latter's government and favoured the Earl of Northumberland's revolt, to which his reputation for holiness gave weight. He led an army against the royal troops, but was tricked into surrender and irregularly sentenced to death. Miracles were believed to have taken place at his tomb.

scruples. In *moral theology, unfounded fears that there is sin where there is none.

scrutiny. The formal testing of *catechumens before their *Baptism in the early Church. The 1972 RC Order for Adult Baptism includes three 'scrutinies' of catechumens; these comprise a homily, prayers, and laying on of hands after the Gospel in the Eucharist on certain Sundays in Lent. The word is used also for the examination of candidates for Holy *Orders.

Sea, Forms of Prayer to be used at. In the BCP, a small collection of prayers and anthems for use in various circumstances at sea.

Seabury, Samuel (1729–96), first bishop of the *Episcopal Church in the USA. Ordained priest by the Bp. of *Lincoln in 1753, he worked in New Brunswick and later near New York. He was elected bishop in 1783. As his inability to take the Oath of Allegiance (now that the United States were independent) precluded his consecration by English bishops, he was consecrated in Scotland (at Aberdeen) in 1784. An able organizer and administrator, he secured for the Episcopal Church in America a structure and liturgy in which the native High Church tradition could develop. Feast day in the American BCP (1979) and CW, 14 Nov.

Seal of Confession. The absolute obligation not to reveal anything said by a penitent in the Sacrament of *Penance.

Sebaldus, St, patron saint of Nürnberg. His date (9th–11th cent.) is disputed, but he is probably to be placed within the eremetical movement of the 11th cent., and seems to have lived in the woods near Nürnberg. His tomb is attested as a place of pilgrimage from 1072. Feast day, 19 Aug.

Se-Baptists (Lat., *se baptizare*, 'to baptize oneself'). A name sometimes given to the followers of John *Smyth (q.v.).

Sebaste, the Forty Martyrs of. Forty Christian soldiers of the '*Thundering Legion' who were martyred at Sebaste in Lesser Armenia, c.320, by being left naked on the ice of a frozen pond, with baths of hot water on the banks as a temptation to apostatize. The place of one who gave way was taken by a heathen soldier of the guard, who was immediately converted. Feast day, in the E., 9 Mar.; in the W., formerly 10 Mar.

Sebastian, St, Roman martyr, who is believed to have suffered in the *Diocletianic persecution. According to legend, he was sentenced by Diocletian to be shot by archers, recovered, and presented himself before the Emperor, who caused him to be clubbed to death. Feast day, 20 Jan.

Secker, Thomas (1693–1768), Abp. of *Canterbury from 1758. After qualifying in medicine, he was won over from Dissent to the C of E and ordained priest in 1723. Through the favour of Queen Caroline, he achieved rapid preferment. He stood for tolerance and good sense in general. He favoured the dispatch of bishops to the American colonies.

Second Adam. A title of Christ, the new head of redeemed humanity, as contrasted with the 'first *Adam', the original member and type of fallen man. The conception goes back to St *Paul, whose expression, however, is not the 'second' but the 'last Adam' (1 Cor. 15: 45).

Second Coming. See PAROUSIA.

Secret. The name long given to a prayer recited by the celebrant at Mass after the offering of the bread and wine. Until 1964 it was customarily said silently; the name probably derived from this circumstance.

Secrets of Enoch, Book of the. A name sometimes given to 2 *Enoch.

sectary. The term was applied in the 17th and 18th cents. to Nonconformist Protestants in England. It is now occasionally used of those whose zeal for their own religious body is considered excessive.

secular arm. In *canon law, the State or any lay power when intervening in ecclesiastical cases. Resort by individuals to lay authorities to interfere with or hinder the process of ecclesiastical jurisdiction was until recently punished in the RC Church by excommunication. On the other hand, the Church was unwilling in her own tribunals to impose penalties involving mutilation or death; when stern measures were felt necessary, especially for heresy, after trial by an ecclesiastical judge the condemned prisoner was handed over to the secular authorities for punishment.

secular clergy. Priests living in the world, as distinct from the '*regular clergy', i.e. members of religious orders.

Secular Institute. See INSTITUTES OF CONSECRATED LIFE.

secularism. The term was coined *c.*1850 to denote a system which sought to order and interpret life on principles taken solely from this world, without recourse to belief in God and a future life. It is now used in a more general sense of the tendency to ignore, if not to deny, the principles of supernatural religion.

sede vacante (Lat., 'the see being vacant'). The period during which a diocese is without a bishop.

sedia gestatoria. The portable throne on which until recently the Pope used to be carried on certain solemn occasions.

sedilia (Lat., 'seats'). The seats for the celebrant, deacon, and subdeacon, on the south side of the chancel. In medieval England they were usually stone benches built into a niche in the wall. On the Continent of Europe and in modern England wooden seats were more common. Since 1964 a chair for the celebrant in the centre of the sanctuary has largely replaced sedilia.

Sedulius (5th cent.), poet. In his early years he devoted himself to pagan literature. Later (perhaps after conversion to Christianity), he was ordained priest and lived in a religious community. His great poem, *Paschale Carmen*, traces the life of Christ from His conception to His Ascension, at all points emphasizing the miraculous.

Sedulius Scottus (9th cent.), poet, teacher, and biblical critic. Born and educated in *Ireland, he went to France between 840 and 851, and then followed the itinerant royal court. His occasional poems show the range of his patrons. His *De Rectoribus Christianis* may arise from a formal position as tutor to the future King Lothair II; his extensive grammatical commentaries testify to his work as a teacher. His other works include commentaries on Mt. and the Pauline Epistles, the latter drawing on the genuine commentary of *Pelagius.

see. The official 'seat' or 'throne' (*cathedra) of a bishop. It normally stands in the *cathedral of the diocese; hence the place where the cathedral is located is also known as the bishop's see. See also HOLY SEE.

Seekers. A loose grouping of defectors from the C of E and particularly from the *Puritan congregations in early-17th cent. England. They believed that no true Church had existed since the spirit of *Antichrist became uppermost in the Church, and that God would in His own time ordain new Apostles or Prophets to found a new Church; they did not think it right to hasten on this process.

Seeley, John Robert (1834–95), historian and author of *Ecce Homo* (1865; q.v.).

Segneri, Paolo (1624–94), Italian *Jesuit. He was a great preacher. His sermons combined vigorous and ordered argument with powerful emotional appeal.

Seises, Dance of the. The religious dance performed in Seville Cathedral during the celebrations of *Corpus Christi and the Immaculate *Conception of the BVM.

Selden, John (1584–1654), author of *The History of Tithes*. A moderate *Puritan, he became a member of the *Westminster Assembly in 1643. In his *History of Tithes* (1618) he upheld the legal, but denied the Divine, basis of the obligation to pay *tithes.

Seleucia, Synod of. See ARIMINUM AND SELEUCIA, SYNODS OF.

Sellon, Priscilla Lydia (1821–76), a restorer of *religious orders in Anglicanism. In 1848, hearing a public appeal by H. *Phillpotts, Bp. of Exeter, she abandoned a plan to leave England in order to work among the destitute of Plymouth, Devonport, and Stonehouse. She was joined by others and created a community life (the 'Devonport Sisters of Mercy'). In 1856 she united her community with the Sisters of the Holy Cross at Osnaburgh Street, Regent's Park, in London, and assumed the title of Abbess of the combined sisterhood of the 'Society of the Most Holy Trinity' (later centred at Ascot Priory, Berks). Feast day in CW, 20 Nov.

Selwyn, George Augustus (1809–78), first Bp. of *New Zealand from 1841 to 1867. He was a *Tractarian in his convictions. He had a marked effect on the future of the New Zealand Church, for whose constitution he was largely responsible. Feast day in the American BCP (1979) and CW, 11 Apr.

Semiarianism. The teaching of the theologians who gathered round *Basil of Ancyra from c.356 and upheld a doctrine of Christ's Sonship intermediate between that of orthodoxy and *Arianism. Over against the term '*Homoousios' ('of the same substance'), they took as their watchword 'Homoiousios' ('of like substance'), but the whole tendency of the group was towards orthodoxy.

Semi-Doubles. Feasts in the RC Calendar of an intermediate rank, which was abolished in 1955.

seminary. In ecclesiastical usage, a school or college devoted to the training of the clergy, especially used of such institutions in the RC Church. The Council of *Trent ordered the establishment of a seminary in every diocese. The 1983 *Codex Iuris Canonici* provides for minor and major seminaries: the former to assist a young man in his spiritual formation while he engages in the same course as other young men; the latter to form men spiritually, academically, and pastorally for the priesthood.

Semipelagianism. Doctrines on human nature upheld in the 5th cent. by a group of theologians who, while not denying the necessity of *grace for salvation, maintained that the first steps towards the Christian life were ordinarily taken by the human will and that grace supervened only later. The position was roughly midway between the views of St *Augustine and *Pelagius. These teachings were first given expression c.425 by representatives of the monastic movement in S. Gaul, including John *Cassian. Though opposed by St *Prosper of Aquitaine, Semipelagianism continued to be the dominant teaching on grace in Gaul for several generations. After the condemnation of Semipelagianism (and Pelagianism) by a Council at *Orange in 529, the Augustinian doctrine on grace was generally accepted in the W.

Semi-Quietism. The doctrines of Abp. *Fénelon and others who, though not sufficiently unorthodox to come under the censures attaching to *Quietism, manifest certain quietist tendencies.

Semler, Johann Salomo (1725–91), *Lutheran theologian and biblical critic. He was one of the first German theologians to apply the critico-historical method to the study of the Bible, and he reached many novel and often unorthodox conclusions. He held, however, that Christian ministers should be required to make external profession of all traditional doctrine.

Sempringham, S. Lincs. The mother-house of the Order founded by St *Gilbert of Sempringham (q.v.).

Seneca, Lucius Annaeus (c.4 BC–AD 65), Roman moralist and tragic poet. He embarked on a senatorial career, was banished to Corsica (41–9), and then became tutor to the future Emp. *Nero. After Nero's accession in 54, Seneca was the chief adviser of state, but he lost favour, retired from public life in 62, and in 65 was forced to take his own life. He wrote several tragedies, essays couched as letters, and various treatises. He was a professed *Stoic and his writings are one of the chief sources of our knowledge of Stoicism.

There is an apocryphal correspondence between Seneca (8 letters) and St *Paul (6 letters). Their manner and style show that they cannot be the work of either writer.

Sens, Councils of. Many provincial Councils were held at Sens. That of 1140 condemned P. *Abelard for heresy.

Sentences. Short expositions of the main truths of Christian doctrine. The Latin word *sententia* originally meant any exposition of thought, but in the Middle Ages it took on a new technical meaning in relation to exegesis. Collections of *Sentences* then became systematized compilations of opinions; the most famous was that of *Peter Lombard. By the 13th cent. *sententia* denoted an accepted theological proposition.

Separatists. A title applied to the followers of R. *Browne and later to the *Congregationalists and others who separated from the C of E.

Septuagesima. The third Sunday before *Lent and hence the ninth Sunday before *Easter. In the RC Church it was suppressed in 1969; it previously marked a stage towards the Lenten fast, with purple vestments being worn from that day until *Holy Week. The name passed into the BCP but has been dropped in some modern Anglican liturgies.

Septuagint ('LXX'). The most influential of the Greek versions of the OT. Jewish tradition ascribes its origin to the initiative of Ptolemy Philadelphus (285–246 BC), who wanted a translation of the Hebrew Law and engaged 72 translators (hence the title 'Septuagint') for the work. The name was gradually attached not just to the *Pentateuch but to the whole OT. It seems to be the work of a number of translators, working in different places over a long period; it was probably complete by 132 BC. It differs from the Hebrew Bible both in the order of

the Books and in the fact that it contains those Books known as the *Apocrypha in English Bibles. The text also differs in some places.

In the early Church the LXX was regarded as the standard form of the OT, from which the NT writers normally (but not invariably) quoted, and it was the basis of the '*Old Latin' versions. St *Jerome's *Vulgate first provided Christians with a Latin text of the OT translated directly from the original and did much to dispel the belief that the LXX was verbally inspired. It is still the canonical text of the OT in the E. Orthodox Church.

Sequence. A chant sung on certain days until 1970 after (now before) the *Alleluia of the Mass. Originally the word seems to have denoted a purely melodic extension of the word 'Alleluia', sung to its final vowel; in the 9th cent. a syllabic text was provided for the melody; the word was later applied to the resulting musical-textual entity and eventually to the text alone. The first author to make a systematic collection of such texts was *Notker Balbulus (d. 912); later authors include *Hildegard of Bingen and *Adam of St-Victor. In medieval times numerous sequences were in use; now only five remain: '*Victimae paschali', '*Veni, Sancte Spiritus', 'Lauda Sion' (at *Corpus Christi), '*Dies Irae', and '*Stabat Mater', of which only the first two need be used.

Seraphic Order, the. Another name for the *Franciscan Order.

Seraphim. The six-winged creatures which *Isaiah saw standing above the throne of God (Is. 6: 2–7). Christian exegetes have held them to be a category of *angels, counterparts to the *Cherubim.

Seraphim of Sarov, St (1759–1833), Russian monk and *staretz. At 19 he entered the monastery of Sarov in the Oka region of E. Russia. From 1794 to 1825 he lived in seclusion, first as a hermit close to the monastery and then enclosed in a small cell within the monastic building. In 1825 he opened the door of his cell; he then devoted himself to the work of spiritual direction, receiving visitors from all over Russia. He stressed the importance of joy and cheerfulness in the spiritual life. Feast day, 2 Jan.

Serapion, St (d. after 360), Bp. of Thmuis in

the Nile delta from c.339. He had been a monk and companion of St *Antony. St *Athanasius chose him for a difficult mission to the Emp. Constantius and addressed to him a series of letters on the Divinity of the Holy Spirit. Serapion wrote against the *Manichees, and a *Sacramentary which has come down under his name was probably his compilation. Feast day, 21 Mar.

Serbia, Church of. Systematic missionary work in Serbia was first undertaken by the Byzantines in the second half of the 9th cent., and by 891 Christianity was the official religion. The attachment of the Serbs to E. Christianity did not become definite until the early 13th cent. An *autocephalous Serbian Church was established by St *Sava in 1219. In 1346 the head of the Serbian Church assumed the title *Patriarch, with his seat at Peć; the Serbian Patriarchate was recognized by *Constantinople in 1375. In the Ottoman period the Serbs passed increasingly under Greek ecclesiastical control and the Patriarchate of Peć was suppressed in 1766. The Serbian Church became autocephalous again in 1879, and in 1920 the Patriarchate was restored, with its seat now in Belgrade.

Serdica. See SARDICA.

Sergius (d. 638), Patr. of *Constantinople from 610 and exponent of *Monothelitism. In an attempt to reconcile the *Monophysites with the adherents of *Chalcedonian orthodoxy, he began to teach that there were two natures in Christ but only one 'activity' (ἐνέργεια). On being opposed by St *Sophronius of Jerusalem, he issued the 'Psephos' (633), which forbade mention of either one or two 'activities' in Christ. He also appealed to Pope *Honorius I, and together they agreed that there was only one 'will' in Christ. This doctrine was promulgated by *Heraclius I in the '*Ecthesis', written by Sergius (638). The '*Acathistus' has sometimes been ascribed to him.

Sergius, St (d. 701), Pope from 687. He resisted the attempt of the Emp. Justinian II to secure his support for the *Trullan Synod (692), and he introduced into the Mass the singing of the *Agnus Dei. Feast day, 8 Sept.

Sergius, St (c.1314–92), Russian monastic reformer and mystic. With his brother he founded the famous monastery of the Holy Trinity at Sergievo, near Moscow, thereby re-establishing in Russia the community life which had been lost through the Tartar invasion. He exercised great influence over all classes in Russia, and founded 40 monasteries. Feast day, 25 Sept.

Sergius Paulus. The proconsul of *Cyprus who, according to Acts 13: 4–12, invited St *Paul and St *Barnabas to preach before him and 'believed'.

Seripando, Girolamo (1492/3–1563), *Augustinian friar. He rose to high office in his Order, being General of it from 1539 to 1551. He played a significant part in the Council of *Trent. Anxious to avoid a complete break with the *Lutherans, he took a moderate position on *justification, adopting the theory of '*double justice', but he failed to win support. He became Abp. of Salerno in 1554 and a cardinal in 1561.

sermo generalis. The ceremony at which the final decision in trials of heretics by the *Inquisition was pronounced. After a short sermon, sentences were pronounced: those found innocent were acquitted; those who recanted were sentenced to the penances prescribed by canon law; and unrepentant heretics were handed over to the secular authorities for punishment. This took the form of *burning at the stake. The term *auto de fe is also used.

Sermon on the Mount. The compilation of Christ's sayings in Mt. 5–7 provides an epitome of His moral teaching. It includes the *Beatitudes and the *Lord's Prayer.

Servant Songs. Four passages in *Deutero-Isaiah (Is. 42: 1–4; 49: 1–6; 50: 4–9; and 52: 13–53: 12) describing the person and character of the 'servant of the Lord'. Whether the writer referred to the nation of Israel or to an individual is disputed. By Christians the passages have been interpreted as a prophecy of Christ.

server. In the W. Church, a minister of the sanctuary, especially at the *Eucharist. The server makes the responses, brings the bread and wine to the altar, and washes the celebrant's hands. Until 1994 only males could act as servers in the RC Church.

Servetus, Michael (c.1511–53), physician and anti-Trinitarian writer. In 1531 he published a treatise attacking the current formulation of the doctrine of the Trinity; it shocked his Protestant friends. After studying medicine, in 1542 he was appointed physician to the Abp. of Vienne. He entered into correspondence with J. *Calvin in 1546, sending him the manuscript of his main work, *Christianismi Restitutio*, which was to appear anonymously in 1553. In this he not only rejected the traditional doctrine of the Trinity but developed unorthodox views on the Incarnation. With Calvin's collaboration, Servetus' authorship was denounced to the *Inquisition. He was imprisoned but escaped to *Geneva; here he was arrested and burnt as a heretic nearby. This event gave rise to heated controversy among Protestants as to whether heretics should be condemned to death.

servile work. Work which is forbidden on Sundays and Holy Days. Various attempts have been made to define it. The term does not figure in the 1983 *Codex Iuris Canonici*. For current RC requirements, see SUNDAY.

Servites. A religious order founded by seven wealthy Florentine city councillors who abandoned their positions to devote themselves to the service of the BVM, traditionally in 1233. They adopted the Rule of St *Augustine, with some additions from the *Dominican constitutions. The Order developed rapidly after 1304.

Servus Servorum Dei (Lat., 'the servant of God's servants'). A title of the Pope used in official documents.

session. See KIRK SESSION.

Settlement, Act of, 1700. The Act, passed in 1701, vested the succession to the Crown in the Electress Sophia of Hanover, the granddaughter of *James I. It thus set aside the hereditary rights of the descendants of *Charles I. It also extended the provisions of the Bill of Rights (which had debarred RCs and anyone who should marry a RC from the Crown) by ordaining positively that future sovereigns should 'join in Communion' with the C of E.

Seven Bishops, Trial of the. When *James II in 1688 ordered that his *Declaration of Indulgence should be read in all churches, Abp. W. *Sancroft and six other bishops protested. They were imprisoned and tried on a charge of seditious libel, but the jury acquitted them.

Seven Churches. The Churches in Asia Minor to which the letter incorporated in Rev. (1–3) was addressed, namely *Ephesus, *Smyrna, *Pergamum, *Thyatira, *Sardis, *Philadelphia, and *Laodicea.

Seven Deacons. A title given to the 'seven men of honest report' who, according to Acts 6: 1–6, were appointed to administer the temporal concerns of the Church. Traditionally their appointment was regarded as instituting the order of *deacon.

seven deadly sins. They are *pride, covetousness, lust, envy, gluttony, anger, and sloth (*accidie).

seven liberal arts. The group of sciences which formed the staple of secular education in the earlier Middle Ages, consisting of the elementary *trivium (grammar, rhetoric, and dialectic) and the more advanced *quadrivium (music, arithmetic, geometry, and astronomy). Not until the student had completed his studies in the liberal arts was he held competent to proceed to theology.

Seven Penitential Psalms, the. Psalms 6, 32, 38, 51, 102, 130, and 143.

Seven Sacraments, the. *Baptism, *Confirmation, *Eucharist, *Penance, Extreme *Unction, *Orders, and *Matrimony. It was through the *Sentences* of *Peter Lombard (c.1150) that the belief gained credence that these seven *Sacraments constituted a set different in kind from all other religious rites. Their sevenfold number was defined at the Council of *Trent and is also generally accepted in the E. Church.

Seven Sleepers of Ephesus. Seven Christian young men who are said to have been walled up in a cave during the *Decian persecution (c.250) and to have been awakened under the Emp. *Theodosius II (d. 450). Feast day, 27 July.

Seven Sorrows of the BVM. According to the former RC *Breviary, they were: (1) at the prophecy of *Simeon; (2) at the flight into Egypt; (3) at the loss of the Holy Child; (4) on meeting Christ on the way to Calvary; (5) at standing at the foot of the Cross; (6) at the taking down of Christ from the Cross; (7) at His burial. Before 1969 they were commemorated on the Friday after *Passion Sunday and on 15 Sept. (now the feast of Our Lady of Sorrow).

seven virtues, the. They are *faith, *hope, *charity (*love), justice, prudence, *temperance, and fortitude.

Seven Words from the Cross. The seven sentences which the Gospels record as spoken by Christ on the Cross. They are: (1) 'Father, forgive them; for they know not what they do' (Lk. 23: 34); (2) 'Today shalt thou be with me in paradise' (Lk. 23: 43); (3) 'Woman, behold they son! . . . Behold thy mother!' (Jn. 19: 26 f.); (4) 'My God, my God, why hast thou forsaken me?' (Mt. 27: 46); (5) 'I thirst' (Jn. 19: 28); (6) 'It is finished' (Jn. 19: 30); (7) 'Father, into thy hands I commend my spirit' (Lk. 23: 46).

Seventh-day Adventists. One of the groups of *Adventists who originally expected the Second Coming of Christ in 1844. Later that year they began to observe the seventh day of the week as the *Sabbath, though the name 'Seventh-day Adventists' was not adopted until 1861. In England their beginnings as an organized community go back to a mission at Southampton in 1878. They are a staunchly Protestant body, believing that the Bible provides the unerring rule of faith and practice and that the return of Christ is imminent, though they set no date for this event. They practise adult Baptism by total immersion, require strict temperance, and observe the Sabbath from sunset on Friday to sunset on Saturday.

Seventh Day Baptists. From about the 1640s some English *Baptists regarded the Fourth *Commandment as requiring the observance of *Saturday, rather than *Sunday, as the day of rest and worship. The movement spread to North America, where a group of them severed their membership of the Baptist Church in Newport, Rhode Island, in 1671. Seventh Day Baptists, though small in number, still survive.

Severian (*fl. c.*400), Bp. of Gabala in Syria. An opponent of St John *Chrysostom, he took part in the events leading to his exile in 403. He is important chiefly as a biblical exegete of the *Antiochene school.

Severinus, St (d. 482), 'Apostle of Austria'. He was in early life a monk in the East.

After the death of *Attila in 453, he came to Noricum Ripense, then overrun by barbarian invaders; he rallied the Church, founded two monasteries, and organized relief work. Feast day, 8 Jan.

Severus (*c.*465–538), *Syrian Orthodox Patr. of *Antioch. At *Constantinople he secured the support of the Emp. Anastasius (491–518) for the persecuted *Monophysite monks, and in 512 he was made Patr. of Antioch in place of the deposed Flavian II. On Justin I's accession (518) he was deposed. He was the leading theologian of the moderate Monophysites. His writings survive mainly in Syriac translation.

Severus, Gabriel and **Sulpicius.** See GABRIEL SEVERUS and SULPICIUS SEVERUS.

Sexagesima. The second Sunday before *Lent and hence the eighth before *Easter. The name was suppressed in the RC Church in 1969, and no longer figures in some modern Anglican liturgies.

Sext. (1) In *canon law the sixth book of *decretals, promulgated by *Boniface VIII in 1298. It contains the decretals issued since the publication of the five books by *Gregory IX (1234). (2) The *Office appointed to be said at noon, i.e. the sixth hour. See TERCE, SEXT, NONE.

sexton. Traditionally the sexton was the assistant to the *parish clerk. His main duties were cleaning the church, ringing the bell, and digging graves. In the C of E he is now appointed by the minister and *Parochial Church Council, who determine the nature of his duties and terms of employment (can. E 3 of 1969).

Shaftesbury, Anthony Ashley Cooper (1801–85), Seventh Earl of Shaftesbury, social reformer. His main concern was with the improvement of the conditions of the working classes, and he was largely responsible for the Factory Act of 1874. He was a fervent *Evangelical. For many years he was president of the *British and Foreign Bible Society. He was also first president of the *CPAS, and he took a deep interest in the work of the *CMS and *YMCA.

Shakers, also 'The United Society of Believers in Christ's Second Appearing' or 'The Millennial Church', a communistic body which originated in 1747 in a group known as 'Shaking Quakers' in Bolton, Lancs.; their connection with the main body of *Quakers is unclear. The first leaders were succeeded by Ann Lee, known as 'Mother Ann', who was regarded as 'The female principle in Christ', Jesus being the 'Male principle'; in her the Second Coming was fulfilled. In 1774 she led a small band to the USA; they settled near Albany, NY, and in the 1780s were joined by members of existing *revivalist movements.

The name 'Shaker' derived from the shaking by which under the stress of spiritual exaltation they were possessed during their meetings; this later developed into ritual dances. Organized in large 'families' within each community, they practise community of goods under a hierarchical form of government. A minute discipline is exercised over dress and personal behaviour. The principle of 'simplicity' is exemplified in Shaker artefacts which are now admired for their aesthetic qualities. Since 1992 only one community has remained.

Shakespeare, John Howard (1857–1928), British *Baptist. Becoming secretary of the Baptist Union in 1898, he made it an influential organization. He was largely responsible for founding the Baptist World Alliance (1905) and the Federal Council of the Evangelical Free Churches (1919; see FREE CHURCH FEDERAL COUNCIL).

Sharp, James (1618–79), Abp. of St Andrews from 1661. He was rewarded by appointment to this office for his collaboration with General G. Monck in 1660 and his secret work for the restoration of episcopacy. As Archbishop he took severe measures to abolish Presbyterianism, and he aroused bitter resentment by his support for the oppressive policy of the Earl of Lauderdale. He was murdered.

Sharp, John (1645–1714), Abp. of *York from 1691. As Dean of *Norwich he refused to read the *Declaration of Indulgence in 1688. In 1689 he took the oaths to William and Mary, but announced that he would not accept any bishopric vacated by a *Nonjuror during the lifetime of the former occupant. His episcopate was marked by a high standard of duty.

Shaxton, Nicholas (c.1485–1556), Bp. of *Salisbury. He was a member of the committee appointed by Cambridge University in 1530 to consider *Henry VIII's divorce. He developed pronounced Protestant views. In 1535 he was made Bp. of Salisbury, but he resigned in 1539 in protest against the *Six Articles. In 1546 he was charged with heretical views on the Eucharist, but recanted. Under *Mary he became a suffragan to the Bp. of *Ely.

Sheer Thursday. An old name for *Maundy Thursday.

Sheldon, Gilbert (1598–1677), Abp. of *Canterbury from 1663. In 1660 he became Bp. of London and Master of the Savoy, and in 1661 the *Savoy Conference met at his lodgings. As Archbishop he worked for the re-establishment of W. *Laud's religious principles. He carried through the arrangement whereby the *Convocations ceased to tax the clergy (1664).

Shema, the. The confession of faith to be recited by Jewish men morning and evening. It consists of three biblical passages (Deut. 6: 4–9, 11: 13–21, Num. 15: 37–41), preceded and followed by blessings.

Shenoute (d. probably 466), Abbot of Athribis in Egypt from c.388. His community of monks and nuns grew very large. His government was severe and he added many austerities to the more humane rule of St *Pachomius. In 431 he accompanied St *Cyril of Alexandria to the Council of *Ephesus, where he played an important part in opposing *Nestorius. His writings (in Coptic) deal mainly with monastic concerns and exhortations to virtue. Feast day in the Coptic Church, 1 July.

Sheol. In the OT, the underworld, the place of departed souls. It is translated in the AV variously as 'hell', 'grave' or 'pit'; more recent translations usually leave it untranslated as a proper noun. The notion reflects an undeveloped and shadowy belief in the future life which was superseded by more defined beliefs of later Judaism.

Shepherd of Hermas, The. The treatise of *Hermas (q.v.), so named from the angel who, in the form of a shepherd, is represented as having communicated to Hermas some of its contents.

Sheppard, Hugh Richard Lawrie (1880–1937), popularly 'Dick Sheppard', vicar of St Martin-in-the-Fields, London, from 1914 to

1926. His religious enthusiasm and personal attractiveness won the affection of innumerable people in all stations of life, especially after the growth of *broadcasting. From 1929 to 1931 he was Dean of *Canterbury. In his last years he was an ardent Pacifist.

Sherborne. St *Aldhelm established the seat of the Bp. of W. Wessex here in 705 and founded a church and school. In 978 Bp. Wulfsige introduced the Rule of St *Benedict. The see was united with Ramsbury in 1058 and in 1075 moved to Old *Sarum. At the *Dissolution of the Monasteries in 1536 the abbey became the parish church. A bishopric of Sherborne, suffragan to *Salisbury, was founded in 1928.

Sherlock, William (1641–1707), Dean of *St Paul's. In the Revolution of 1688 he originally sided with the *Nonjurors. His *Vindication of the Doctrines of the Trinity and of the Incarnation* (1690) provoked a violent controversy, in which he was accused of teaching *Tritheism. In the same year he took the oath of allegiance to William and Mary, and in 1691 he became Dean of St Paul's. He is now best remembered for his *Practical Discourse concerning Death* (1689).

Shewbread. The twelve loaves which, according to the practice of the Jewish *Temple, were placed beside the altar of incense. When they were removed for renewal at the end of each week, only the priests might eat them. Modern Bible translations often prefer the terms 'Bread of the Presence' or 'bread of offering'.

shibboleth. A word used by Jephthah as a test to distinguish the Gileadites from the Ephraimites, whose pronunciation of it as 'sibboleth' betrayed their identity (Jgs. 12: 4 ff.). In modern usage it denotes a sectarian or party catchword.

Shorthouse, Joseph Henry (1834–1903), author of *John Inglesant* (1881). The son of *Quaker parents, Shorthouse was baptized in the C of E in 1861. The delicacy and charm with which John Inglesant's spiritual pilgrimage is portrayed, its sympathetic understanding of the religious life of the 17th cent., and its vivid delineation of the community at *Little Gidding made the book a powerful *apologia* for Anglicanism.

shrine. The word can designate a *reli-

quary (q.v.), but is now commonly used of a sacred image of special importance usually kept in a church, or of any holy place, especially one connected with *pilgrimages.

Shroud, Holy. See HOLY SHROUD.

Shrove Tuesday. The day immediately before *Ash Wednesday, so named from the 'shriving', i.e. confession and absolution, of the faithful on that day.

Sian-Fu Stone. See SIGAN-FU STONE.

Sibylline Oracles. A collection of oracles imitating the pagan 'Sibylline Books'. The oracles, written in hexameters, are preceded by a prose prologue affirming that they are utterances of Greek Sibyls of various periods. Their genuineness was accepted by many of the Fathers, who drew from them arguments in defence of Christianity. Modern critics assign them to Jewish and Christian authors; for, though genuine Greek oracles are inserted in some places, the tendency of the whole is monotheistic and Messianic. The dates of the Jewish portions range from the *Maccabean period to the time of the Emp. Hadrian (117–38); the Christian additions seem to date from the 2nd cent. onwards.

Sicard (*c.*1155–1215), Bp. of Cremona from 1185. His *Chronicon*, a history of the world to 1213, is a primary authority for the Crusade of *Frederick I. His *Mitrale* throws light on contemporary liturgical practice. He also wrote a *Summa* on the Decretum of *Gratian.

Sicilian Vespers, the. A massacre of the French in Sicily in 1282, the signal for which was the tolling of the bell for *Vespers.

Sick, Visitation of the. See VISITATION OF THE SICK.

Sickingen, Franz von (1481–1523), German knight. Under the influence of U. von *Hutten he embraced the Reformation, defended J. *Reuchlin, and offered his castles as places of refuge for Protestants. In 1522 he led an army against the Abp. of Trier and was mortally wounded.

sidesmen. In the C of E, persons who may be elected by the annual parochial church meeting to promote true religion in the parish and assist the *churchwardens.

Sidetes, Philip. See PHILIP SIDETES.

Sidgwick, Henry (1838–1900), moral philosopher. At Cambridge he supported the movement for abolishing religious tests. His *Methods of Ethics* (1874), a study of moral philosophy on mainly *hedonistic lines, had considerable influence.

Sidonius Apollinaris, St (*c*.430–*c*.486), statesman and bishop. About 450 he married a daughter of the future Emp. Avitus (455–6) and entered upon a successful political career. In 470/71, when possibly still a layman, he was elected Bp. of Clermont, partly to defend the country against the Goths. He was imprisoned when Clermont was occupied by the Visigoths in 475, but he was freed and reinstated in his diocese in 476. His poetry, which he ceased to write on becoming bishop, shows great technical skill; his letters are a valuable historical source. Feast day, 21 or 23 Aug.

Sierra Leone. Before 1896 the name denoted a small area around Freetown. Here in 1787 associates of the *Clapham Sect bought land for a self-supporting Christian settlement of poor Blacks. This soon collapsed but was refounded in 1792 with Black soldiers from America who had supported Britain in the War of Independence. They brought a vigorous Church life, *Methodist, *Baptist, and the Countess of *Huntingdon's Connexion. In 1808 Sierra Leone became a British colony and the landing place for intercepted slave cargoes from all over W. Africa. Most of them entered the new model of society offered by the missionaries (especially the *CMS) and the 1792 settlers. A Christian, literate, English-speaking Krio community resulted. Sierra Leonians travelled extensively in W. Africa, taking Christianity with them. The incorporation of the British Protectorate in 1896 changed Sierra Leone's demographic basis; the Krio community was eclipsed and the hinterland became dominant as the independent State emerged in 1961. Missions to the hinterland had begun in the 1790s, with increasing American involvement from the mid-19th cent., but the response was slow. Today the United Methodist Church and the RC Church are the leading Christian bodies in the hinterland.

Sigan-Fu Stone. An early monument of the *Church of the East at Sigan-Fu (Sian-

fu, Hsi-an-fu, or Xian) in NW *China. Set up in AD 781, it records the arrival in 635 of a missionary from Tuts'in and recounts the fortunes of the Church to date. It is the main witness to the growth of Christianity in the Far East before the 13th cent.

Sigebert of Gembloux (*c*.1030–1112), chronicler. He was a monk of the abbey of Gembloux. His main works are the *De Viris Illustribus* (an ecclesiastical literary history), the *Liber Decennalis*, which seeks to fix the dates of Christ's Incarnation and Passion in the overall chronology of the world, and the *Chronicon* (from 381 to 1111), which uses some first-hand material from 1024 onwards. He opposed the reforms of *Gregory VII as inopportune.

Siger of Brabant (*c*.1240–*c*.1284), *Averroist philosopher. By 1266 he was teaching in *Paris. He was involved in the condemnation of 13 errors by the Bp. of Paris in 1270 and in that year St *Thomas Aquinas wrote his *De Unitate Intellectus contra Averroistas*, which was directed chiefly against him. In 1276 he was cited for heresy by Simon du Val, Inquisitor of France; it is not known whether he was acquitted or had already fled the kingdom.

Siger's most substantial works were commentaries and *quaestiones* on *Aristotle's *Metaphysics* and works on natural philosophy which had recently been included in the curriculum at Paris. He regarded it as his task not to conceal Aristotle's views, even if these were contrary to revealed truth. The chief doctrines in question were the eternity of the world and the unity of the intellect in the human race, which involved the denial of personal immortality and of rewards and punishments in a future life. Critics accused him of holding that some tenets might be true in theology and false in philosophy; this he would have disputed, though it is not clear from his writings how far he resolved the status of philosophical truths.

sign of the Cross. From early times the sign of the Cross has been used to sanctify actions in daily life, as an encouragement in temptation and trial, and as a means of mutual recognition in times of persecution. It is also employed in *Baptism and *Confirmation, and its use was extended to the liturgical blessing of people and things. It is now made by drawing the right hand from forehead to breast, then from shoulder to shoulder, returning to the centre.

Silas, St. St *Paul's companion on his first visit to Greece is called Silas in Acts 15: 22–18: 5. Paul calls him 'Silvanus' in 2 Cor. 1: 19 (as does 1 Pet. 5: 12) and associates him with himself in writing to the Thessalonians. Feast day, 13 July; in the Greek Church, 30 July.

silence, the argument from. The deduction from the absence of any known reference to a subject in the extant writings of an author that he was ignorant of it.

Siloam, Pool of. A pool or reservoir at *Jerusalem, mentioned in both the OT and the NT. It is almost certainly the modern *Birket Silwān*.

Silvia of Aquitaine. A relative of the Roman prefect Rufinus. She was at one time thought to be the author of the 'Pilgrimage of *Egeria' (q.v.).

Simeon. (1) In the OT, one of the Hebrew patriarchs, the ancestor of the tribe of that name. (2) The aged and devout Jew who took the infant Christ in his arms in the *Temple at *Jerusalem, spoke the words now known as the '*Nunc Dimittis', and prophesied that a sword would pierce the soul of the BVM (Lk. 2: 25–35).

Simeon, the New Theologian, St (949–1022), Byzantine mystic and spiritual writer. In 981 he became abbot of St Mamas in *Constantinople, but because of the fierce opposition aroused by some aspects of his teaching, he went into exile in Asia Minor in 1009. He assigned a central place to the vision of the Divine Light and exercised a formative influence on the rise of *Hesychasm. His appellation 'the New Theologian' probably implies comparison with St *Gregory of Nazianzus, known in the E. as 'Gregory the Theologian'. Feast day in the E., 12 Mar.

Simeon of Durham (c.1060–c.1130), chronicler. A monk of *Durham, he wrote a history of the see (to 1096) and was probably the author of a general history of England.

Simeon of Mesopotamia (5th cent.), a leader of the *Messalians, sometimes identified with the Simeon to whom some MSS attribute the writings of Pseudo-Macarius. See MACARIUS/SIMEON.

Simeon Metaphrastes, St (*fl. c.*960), Byzantine hagiographer. He owes his fame to his collection of saints' Lives ('Menologion'). A few of the Lives were simply copied from earlier collections, but most of them were worked over ('metaphrased'; hence his name) to make their style acceptable to the taste of the time. The continuation of the Chronicle of *George Hamartolus to 948 is ascribed in some Greek MSS and in the Old Church Slavonic translation to Simeon Logothetes, who has often been identified with Simeon Metaphrastes, but the identification is now disputed. Feast day in the E., 9 or 28 Nov.

Simeon Stylites, St (c.390–459), the first of the *Stylites or pillar ascetics. After some time as a monk, he spent several years as a hermit in N. Syria and then mounted a pillar, at first low but gradually increased to a height of 40 cubits (c.20 metres); he lived on the top of it until his death. This novel form of austerity attracted pilgrims and was widely imitated. Feast day in the E. Orthodox Church, 1 Sept.; among the *Syrian Orthodox, 27 July; in the W., 5 Jan.

Simeon of Thessalonica, St (d. 1429), Abp. of *Thessalonica. Little is known of his life, but he was an influential author. His main work, a 'Dialogue against all Heresies and on the One Faith', consists of a short treatise on doctrine and a longer one on the Liturgy and Sacraments. Besides other works long known, a collection of treatises with polemical interests has recently been discovered. Feast day, 15 Sept.

Simeon, Charles (1759–1836), leader of the *Evangelical Revival. From 1783 he was vicar of Holy Trinity, Cambridge. At first he met with hostility, but his pastoral zeal broke down opposition and he exercised much influence among Evangelical undergraduates and ordinands. He was one of the founders of the *CMS (1799). He also founded a body of trustees (the Simeon Trustees) for securing and administering Church patronage in accordance with his principles. Feast day in CW, 13 Nov.; in American BCP (1979), 12 Nov.

Similitudo Dei (Lat., 'likeness of God'). The element in man's being as originally constituted which he lost through the *Fall. See IMAGE OF GOD.

Simon, St, 'the Less', Apostle. St *Luke describes him as 'Simon the zealot' (Acts 1: 13). This could imply that he had been a member of the *Zealots, if that party existed at the time. The apocryphal 'Passion of Simon and *Jude' relates the preaching and martyrdom of the two Apostles in Persia. In the W. they are always coupled in the ecclesiastical calendar and in dedication of churches. Feast day in the E., 10 May; in the W. (with St Jude), 28 Oct.

Simon of Cyrene. A passer-by who was compelled by the Roman soldiers to carry Christ's cross on the way to the crucifixion (Mt. 27: 32 etc.). In modern times he has been claimed as patron by groups of people working among outcasts.

Simon Magus. According to Acts 8: 9-24, a sorcerer, who practised in *Samaria, was converted to Christianity and baptized; he was rebuked by St *Peter for trying to obtain spiritual powers for money (hence the term '*simony'). The Fathers of the 2nd-3rd cent. who opposed *Gnosticism regarded Simon as its founder. St *Hippolytus ascribes to him a short treatise, the *Apophasis Megale*. There is, however, dispute about Simon Magus' relationship to Gnosticism and, in particular, to the 2nd cent. sect of Simonians to whom, rather than to Simon himself, the *Apophasis* is probably to be ascribed.

Simon Peter, St. An alternative designation for St *Peter, who was originally called Simon.

Simon Stock, St (*c.*1165–1265), English *Carmelite. He may have been elected Prior General at a chapter held in London in 1254; he did not (as was previously thought) hold that office in 1247 when *Innocent IV approved changes in Carmelite practices. According to tradition, in 1251 he received a vision of the BVM which gave rise to the 'Scapular devotion', a devotion based on the belief that all who wore the small Carmelite *scapular would be saved. Feast day, 16 May.

Simon of Sudbury (d. 1381), Abp. of *Canterbury from 1375. He seems to have been reluctant to take proceedings against J. *Wycliffe until ordered by the Pope to do so, and then he was not extreme in his measures. In 1380 he became Chancellor and was responsible for the imposition of a poll tax. He was killed by the mob.

Simon, Richard (1638–1712), biblical scholar. From 1662 to 1678 he was a member of the French *Oratory. His *Histoire critique du Vieux Testament* (1678), arguing from the existence of duplicate accounts of the same incident and variations of style, denied that *Moses was the author of the *Pentateuch. He is generally regarded as the founder of OT criticism.

Simons, Menno. See MENNONITES.

Simons in the NT. Besides (1) Simon *Peter the Apostle, (2) *Simon 'the Less', (3) *Simon Magus, and (4) *Simon of Cyrene, the NT mentions (5) Simon, one of the *Brethren of the Lord; (6) Simon the Pharisee, in whose house Christ was anointed by 'a woman which was a sinner' (Lk. 7: 36–50); (7) Simon the leper, in whose house at *Bethany Christ was anointed by an unnamed woman (Mk. 14: 3–9); and (8) Simon, a tanner, with whom St Peter lodged at Joppa (Acts 9: 43).

simony. The term, which is derived from *Simon Magus (see Acts 8: 18–24), denotes the purchase or sale of spiritual things. The canons of the early Church show that simony became frequent after the age of the persecutions; there has been repeated legislation against it, especially in connection with ecclesiastical preferment.

Simple Feasts. Feasts of the lowest rank in the pre-1960 RC calendar.

Simplicianus, St (d. 400), Bp. of Milan from 397. He was instrumental in bringing about *Victorinus' conversion and had some part in that of St *Augustine. A phrase of Augustine's may imply that he prepared St *Ambrose for Baptism. Feast day, 16 (sometimes 13) Aug.

Simplicius, St (d. 483), Pope from 468. During his pontificate, which was marked by the deposition of the last western emperor (476), followed by the rule of an *Arian as King of Italy, and by the spread of the *Monophysite heresy, he advanced the jurisdictional claims and the prestige of the Roman see. In the E. he successfully intervened in defence of the *Chalcedonian formula against its Monophysite critics. Feast day (local), 2 or 10 Mar.

simultaneum. The term was originally used in 16th-cent. Germany for the authorization of two or more religious communions in the same territory; it came to be restricted to the right of two religious congregations differing in their faith to use a single ecclesiastical building. Provisions for this practice were made in the Peace of *Ryswick (1697).

sin. The purposeful disobedience of a creature to the known will of God. In the OT it is represented as a constant factor in the experience both of God's people and of the world from the first transgression of *Adam and *Eve. *Ezekiel and *Jeremiah proclaim the personal responsibility of each man for his sins. The Psalms are marked by penetrating insights into the personal and emotional effects of sin. In the NT the Lord's teaching makes it clear that its roots lie in a man's character (Mt. 5: 21–5; 15: 18–20). St *Paul explains sin as a breach of the *natural law written in the conscience of man (Rom. 2: 14–16) and asserts its universality.

Later theology has added little to what is implicit in the Bible. An influential factor in the development of this theology was St *Augustine's rejection of the *Manichaean doctrine that evil was a substance and the created universe inherently wicked, in favour of the *Platonic view that sin is in essence a privation of good. The development of the *penitential system in the Middle Ages tended to foster an external view of sin. Rejecting this, M. *Luther preached *justification by faith alone. Under the secularizing influence of the *Enlightenment attempts were made to remove sin from its religious setting and to interpret it as moral evil; in the 19th cent. the notion of sin was largely eliminated from much popular religious teaching. In the 20th century there was renewed emphasis on the gravity of sin (e.g. in *Dialectical Theology).

See also ATONEMENT, FALL, ORIGINAL SIN, PENANCE, and REDEMPTION.

Sinai. The mountain in the desert between Egypt and Palestine where the Law was given to *Moses (Exod. 19: 1 ff.). The region of the traditional Sinai (now Jebel Musa) was an early centre of Christian monasticism; the monastery dedicated to St *Catherine of Alexandria claims to have been built on the site to which her body was miraculously transported.

The Church of Sinai is the smallest independent Church of the Orthodox Communion. It is ruled by the 'Archbishop of Mount Sinai', who is abbot of the monastery of St Catherine. See also CODEX SINAITICUS.

Sinodos. An Ethiopic collection of canons, the first two sections of which are often called the 'Sinodos Alexandrina'. This contains four documents: the *Apostolic Church Order, the *Apostolic Tradition, parts of Book 8 of the *Apostolic Constitutions, and the *Apostolic Canons.

Sion. See ZION.

Sion College, London. Thomas White (d. 1624) left £3,000 for a 'college' for the clergy of London, with almshouses attached. The College, transferred from London Wall to the Victoria Embankment in 1886, functioned mainly as a library until 1996, when it was decided to sell the building and divide most of the books between *Lambeth Palace Library and *King's College, London.

Si quis (Lat., 'If anybody'). The notice until 1976 issued on behalf of a candidate for a benefice, holy orders, etc., in the C of E, requiring any objectors to come forward.

Siricius, St (c.334–99), Bp. of *Rome from 384. His pontificate marked a stage in the development of Papal authority. His letter to Himerius, Bp. of Tarragona (385), advocating relatively lenient treatment of penitents, is the first Papal *decretal; and the disciplinary canons of a synod held in Rome in 386 were sent to the African Church. Feast day, 26 Nov.

Sirmium, Blasphemy of. The doctrinal formula issued by the Council of Sirmium (modern Sremska Mitrovica) in 357, setting out the teaching of the extreme *Arians. All mention of the term 'substance' in Trinitarian speculation was forbidden, and the subordination of the Son to the Father was asserted. It takes its name from St *Hilary of Poitiers's description of it.

Sisters of Mercy. (1) A name widely used in the 19th cent. for members of any (especially Anglican) religious community engaged in nursing or similar work. (2) A RC sisterhood founded in Dublin in 1827.

Sistine Chapel. The principal chapel of the *Vatican Palace, so called because it was built for *Sixtus IV (1471–84).

Sistine Madonna. An altarpiece by *Raphael, now in Dresden. It depicts the BVM and Child floating on the clouds of heaven, between St *Sixtus II and St *Barbara.

Sitz im Leben (Ger., 'place in life'). A term used mainly in biblical criticism, to signify the circumstances (often in the life of a community) in which a particular story, saying, etc., was either created or preserved and transmitted.

Six Articles. The Articles imposed at *Henry VIII's bidding by the Religion Act 1539 to prevent the spread of Reformation doctrines and practices. They maintained *transubstantiation and *Communion in one kind, enforced clerical *celibacy, upheld *monastic vows, and defended private *Masses and *auricular confession.

Six Points, the. The *Eastward Position, *Eucharistic Vestments, *Mixed Chalice, *Altar Lights, Unleavened *Bread at the Eucharist, and *Incense. Their introduction into the C of E followed a campaign, set on foot c.1870, to restore these and similar ceremonial usages. See also PURCHAS JUDGEMENT, LINCOLN JUDGEMENT.

Sixtus II, St (d. 258), or 'Xystus', Pope from 257. He resumed relations with St *Cyprian and the Churches of Africa and Asia Minor broken off by his predecessor (*Stephen I) over the *validity of Baptism by heretics. He suffered martyrdom and was highly venerated. Feast day, 7 (formerly 6) Aug.

Sixtus IV (1414–84), Pope from 1471. A *Franciscan, he became General of the Order in 1464. With him the *nepotism of the Renaissance Popes reached its worst stage, implicating the Papacy in political intrigues with Italian cities and leading to confusion in the Papal finances. He founded the Sistine Choir and built the *Sistine Chapel.

Sixtus V (1521–90), Pope from 1585. His pontificate was devoted to far-reaching reforms in the government of the Church and of the Papal States, ruthlessly implemented. He put the Papal finances on a sound footing by the sale of certain offices,

the setting up of more '*montes', and additional taxes. He fixed the number of *cardinals at 70 and established the *Roman Congregations. He built the *Lateran Palace and the *Vatican Library, and supplied Rome with drinking water. He also inaugurated an edition of the *Vulgate.

slavery. A state of servitude by which one person becomes the property of another. Although there is no specific condemnation of slavery in the NT, the spiritual equality of men and the charity demanded are incompatible with it. From *Constantine onwards Imperial legislation followed Christian sentiment and many mitigations were introduced; slavery was gradually transformed into the milder institution of serfdom, which disappeared at the end of the Middle Ages. After the fall of *Constantinople in 1453, however, the Turks reduced large numbers of Christians to servitude, and in America the Spanish, Portuguese, and British settlers made slaves of the Indians and introduced slaves from Africa, despite the resistance of missionaries and the condemnations of successive Popes. In the 18th cent. the movement against slavery was taken up by the *Quakers and then by philanthropists such as W. *Wilberforce. The slave trade was made illegal in 1808 and slavery abolished in the British Empire in 1833. In the USA a constitutional amendment in 1865 prohibited slavery for ever.

Sleidanus, Johannes (1506–56), historian of the German Reformation. He adopted Protestant views (the exact date is not known), and in 1545 was commissioned by the *Schmalkaldic League to write the history of the Protestant cause in Germany. His *De Statu Religionis et Reipublicae Carolo V Caesare Commentarii* (1555; Eng. tr., 1560) is now valued chiefly for the many official documents preserved in it.

Slessor, Mary (1848–1915), missionary of the *United Presbyterian Church. In 1876 she sailed for the Calabar coast of W. Africa. Here she gained influence among the native population and ended many tribal abuses (e.g. twin murder and human sacrifice). In 1905 she was invested with the powers of a magistrate. In CW, feast day, 11 Jan.

Smalkaldic Articles, League. See SCHMALKALDIC ARTICLES, LEAGUE.

Smaragdus (d. after 825), abbot of St-Mihiel. He took part in the Council of Aachen in 809 and formulated its conclusions in a letter sent by *Charlemagne to Pope *Leo III. He wrote a number of theological and ascetical works, including an 'Expositio' on the Rule of St *Benedict.

Smart, Peter (1569–c.1652), *Puritan. As a prebendary of *Durham cathedral he resisted the introduction of High Church ornaments and in 1628 preached against J. *Cosin, one of the promoters of the advanced ceremonial. He was brought before the Durham *High Commission; on refusing to pay the fine imposed by the *York High Commission, to which the case had been referred, he was degraded and imprisoned. He was released in 1640 and in 1641 restored to his preferments. He took the *Solemn League and Covenant in 1643 and was given various sequestered benefices.

'Smectymnuus'. The professed writer of a book published in 1641 defending the *Presbyterian theory of Christian ministry in reply to J. *Hall's *Humble Remonstrance*. The name was made up of the initials of the five authors.

Smith, John (?1570–1612). See SMYTH, JOHN.

Smith, John (1618–52), *Cambridge Platonist. Under the influence of B. *Whichcote, he became one of the leading Cambridge Platonists, upholding spiritual religion against the acrimonious theological disputes of the age.

Smith, William Robertson (1846–94), Scottish theologian and Semitic scholar. He was at the centre of the storm provoked by the *Higher Criticism of the OT. His articles in the *Encyclopaedia Britannica* were criticized by a committee of the General Assembly of the *Free Church of Scotland as undermining belief in the inspiration of Scripture, and in 1881 he was removed from his chair at the Free Church College in Aberdeen. He spent the rest of his life in Cambridge. His lectures on *The Old Testament in the Jewish Church* (1881) popularized J. *Wellhausen's theory of the structure and date of the *Pentateuch and the development of Israelite religion; in *The Prophets of Israel* (1882) he expounded on this basis the life and teaching of the early Prophets.

Smithfield in London was noted as the site of executions, especially in the Reformation period. It is now a meat market.

Smyrna. A city of Roman Asia, now Izmir, on the W. coast of Turkey. The Christian community was one of the '*Seven Churches' addressed in Rev. (2: 8–11); it was warned of coming persecution. St *Polycarp was martyred here. The city long continued to have a substantial Christian population.

Smyth, or Smith, John (? 1570–1612), the reputed founder of the *General Baptists. Ordained in the C of E, he became a *Puritan preacher at *Lincoln and later (by 1607) was a *Separatist pastor in Gainsborough. He led a company of exiles to Amsterdam c.1608 and there, after baptizing himself (hence his title, the '*Se-Baptist'), in 1609 he established the first modern *Baptist Church. He came increasingly under *Mennonite influence.

sobornost. A Russian term with no exact English equivalent. In modern Russian theology it denotes a unity of many persons within the organic fellowship of the Church, each person maintaining his full freedom and personal integrity. It is claimed as a special characteristic of the *Orthodox Church, contrasted with the emphasis on juridical authority in the RC Church and the individualism of the Protestant communions.

Social Gospel. The most conspicuous movement representing the social aspects of Christianity in American and Canadian Protestantism in the late 19th and early 20th cents. Washington Gladden (1836–1918), a *Congregational minister and prolific author who defended the right of working people to form unions, is known as the 'father' of the Social Gospel. Josiah Strong (1847–1916) organized interdenominational gatherings that promoted the movement while he was secretary of the (American) Evangelical Alliance; W. *Rausenbusch became its foremost prophet. It was influential in the Congregational, *Episcopal, *Baptist, *Methodist, and *Presbyterian Churches. Based largely on liberal theology, the movement had a high view of human nature and its potentiality, stressed the idea of progress, was reformist in tone, and had a somewhat utopian caste. It passed its zenith after the First World War, but left an important legacy in the thought of many Churches.

Socialism, Christian. See CHRISTIAN SOCIALISM.

Society for Promoting Christian Knowledge; Society for the Propagation of the Gospel; Society of Jesus. See SPCK; SPG; JESUITS.

Society of St John the Evangelist (SSJE). An Anglican society of mission priests and laymen, popularly known as the '*Cowley Fathers'. It was founded in 1865 by R. M. *Benson and is the oldest Anglican religious community for men.

Society of the Holy Cross. An *Anglo-Catholic society of clergy founded in 1855 by C. F. *Lowder and others. It aimed to promote a stricter rule of life among the clergy, missions to the poor, and the publication of works in defence of Catholic faith and practice.

Socinianism. See the following entry and UNITARIANISM.

Socinus. The Latinized name of two Italian religious teachers.

(1) Lelio Francesco Maria Sozini (1525–62). Trained as a lawyer at *Bologna, he found his main interests in theology and was received by the Reformers in various countries. At *Geneva he was challenged on the doctrine of the Trinity, but satisfied H. *Bullinger and settled at Zurich.

(2) Fausto Paolo Sozzini (1539–1604), his nephew. In 1562 he published at Lyons a work on St John's Gospel denying the essential divinity of Christ; by 1563 he also rejected the natural immortality of man. He returned to Italy in 1563 and was in the service of the daughter of the Grand Duke of Tuscany until 1574, outwardly conforming to Catholicism. From 1579 he lived in Poland, where he did much to spread moderate *Unitarian doctrines among the upper classes. See also RACOVIAN CATECHISM and UNITARIANISM.

Socrates (c.380–450), 'Scholasticus', Greek historian. His 'Church History' was designed as a continuation of *Eusebius's work and extends from the abdication of *Diocletian (305) to 439. It is generally objective and lucidly written, if colourless.

sodality. In the RC Church a guild established to further some religious purpose by common action or mutual assistance.

Söderblom, Nathan (1866–1931), *Lutheran Bp. of *Uppsala from 1914. He supported the *Ecumenical Movement and was the leading figure in the *Stockholm Conference on '*Life and Work' (1925); his aim was to organize practical co-operation between the Churches, especially on social questions, without consideration of doctrinal differences.

In *The Nature of Revelation* (1903; Eng. tr., 1933) he defended the position of *Higher Criticism; he criticized the dogma of the two natures in Christ as unacceptable to modern man, and he maintained that God's revelation is restricted neither to the Bible nor to the Church, but continues throughout history.

Sodom and Gomorrah. According to Gen. 19: 24 f. two cities which were destroyed by fire from heaven because of their wickedness. The association of Sodom with *homosexual practice rests only on Gen. 19: 1–14, where the men of Sodom attempt to exploit Lot's hospitality to two angels by seeking to assault them sexually.

Sodor and Man. The present Anglican diocese of Sodor and Man consists of the Isle of Man. Tradition credits St *Patrick with the establishment of episcopal authority there in the 5th cent. After the arrival of Norwegian rulers in the 8th cent., Man was associated by them with the islands west of the Scottish mainland as part of the Southern Isles ('Sodor'). A single see was established in 1134; after 1154 it was part of the province of Nidaros (Trondheim) in Norway. In the mid-14th cent. the English Crown assumed control of the Isle of Man; parallel lines of bishops emerged there and in the Scottish section of the diocese. Since 1542 the diocese of Sodor has been in the province of *York, but has its own Convocation. The termination 'and Man' was apparently added in error by a 17th-cent. legal draughtsman.

Soissons, Councils of. The two chief Councils were those of c.1092, which condemned *Roscelin for teaching *Tritheism, and 1121, which condemned Peter *Abelard's *Theologia Summi Boni*.

soleas. In the E. Church the platform immediately in front of the *iconostasis.

Solemn League and Covenant. The agreement between the Scots and the English Parliament in 1643. Its professed aims were the maintenance of the *Presbyterian Church of Scotland, the reformation of the Church of England, uniformity of the Churches in the British Isles, the preservation of the rights of Parliaments and the liberties of the kingdoms, and defence of the just power of the King. For a time the proceedings of the *Westminster Assembly took a Presbyterian turn, but after 1644 the Independents came to power and the Covenant was a dead letter in England.

Solemnitas (Lat., commonly rendered in English 'Solemnity'), the name given since 1969 in the RC Church to feasts of the greatest importance.

Solesmes. The seat of a famous *Benedictine monastery in France. It was founded in 1010, but in modern times its history goes back to Dom Prosper *Guéranger, who settled there with five other priests in 1833. It became a centre of the *Liturgical Movement, taking a notable part in the revival and development of liturgical music.

Solifidianism. The doctrine of *justification by faith alone (*per solam fidem*).

Solomon (d. *c*.930 BC), King of Israel from *c*.970 BC, when he succeeded his father *David. The impression given in 1 Kgs. 1–11 is of an oriental despot, honoured for his wealth and wisdom. This reputation was responsible for the later attribution to him of the Books of *Proverbs, the Song of *Solomon, *Ecclesiastes, and *Wisdom. His reign marked the zenith of ancient Israel's prosperity; the *Temple was part of a grandiose building scheme intended to make *Jerusalem a worthy capital of the kingdom. To finance his projects he imposed a system of levies and forced labour; the resulting discontent led, after his death, to the secession of the ten northern tribes. See also the following entries.

Solomon, Odes of. This *pseudepigraphical work contains 42 hymns of a lyrical character. They are probably Christian in origin. Their composition is variously dated between the 1st and 3rd cent., the late 2nd cent. being most likely. They were probably written in Syria, but whether their original language was Greek or Syriac is disputed.

Solomon, Psalms of. A Jewish *pseudepigraphical collection of 18 Psalms. Though extant only in Greek (and a Syriac translation of the Greek), they were almost certainly written in Hebrew. They date from the post-*Maccabean age, probably from the years 70–40 BC. The last two Psalms predict the coming of a *Messiah of the house of *David.

Solomon, Song of (also called **Song of Songs** or **Canticles),** OT Book. It seems to be an anthology of love poems, ascribed to *Solomon and his beloved (the 'Shulamite') and their friends. It probably dates from as late as the 3rd cent. BC, though individual poems may be much earlier.

In the *Talmud the Book is regarded as an allegory of God's dealings with Israel. Christians have seen in it a description of God's relations with the Church or with the individual soul.

Solomon, Wisdom of. See WISDOM OF SOLOMON.

Solovyov, Vladimir (1853–1900), Russian philosopher and theologian. Until 1881 he shared the antipathy of many Slavophils for the RC Church; he later changed his attitude and carried on negotiations with J. G. *Strossmayer for a reunion of the Orthodox and RC Churches. His *La Russie et l'Église universelle* (1889) met with strong opposition in Russia, and he was forbidden by the Holy Synod to write on religious questions. In 1896 he received Communion in a RC church in Moscow, an act, he believed, of adhesion to the universal Church. In his philosophical system he admitted *Gnostic elements and upheld the existence of a female principle, 'Sophia' (*Wisdom) or the world-soul. His influence did much to bring Russian intellectuals to a definitely religious and Christian view of the world.

Somaschi. An order of clerks regular founded in 1532 by St *Jerome Emiliani at Somasca in N. Italy.

Somerset, Duke of (*c*.1506 [or perhaps *c*.1500]–1552), Protector of England from 1547 to 1549. Edward Seymour was a brother of Jane Seymour, third wife of *Henry VIII. He was a leading figure in the

Council when his nephew succeeded as *Edward VI. As Protector he pressed on the reforming cause in the English Church. He was deprived of office in 1549 and executed on a charge of conspiracy.

Son of Man. In the NT, a designation of Jesus, with one exception (Acts 7: 56), used only by Himself. In the Aramaic of NT times, it seems that the phrase could be used almost as a paraphrase for 'I', and in some cases parallel passages in another Gospel have 'I' or 'Me'. In the OT the corresponding Hebrew expression is often a synonym for 'man', i.e. a human being. In Dan. 7: 13, however, 'one like a son of man' occurs in the context of the final establishment of God's *kingdom, and is used as a symbol representative of God's elect. In Dan. it denotes some angelic being; the identification with an individual leader or *Messiah is not found until the Similitudes of *Enoch and 2 Esdras, in passages probably too late to have influenced the Gospels. The element of mystery about the phrase in the Gospels confirms the view that it was not an established Messianic title before the time of Jesus. Later readers of the Gospels have seen 'Son of Man' as denoting the humility of Christ's incarnate manhood as contrasted with the majesty of His Divinity denoted by 'Son of God', and as emphasizing His universalist role in contrast with the nationalist conceptions associated with the title 'Son of David'.

Song of Songs. See SOLOMON, SONG OF.

Song of the Three Children (or 'Song of the Three Young Men'). A short 'Book' of the *Apocrypha. In the LXX and *Vulgate (where it is inserted after Dan. 3: 23) the Song is part of the story of the three Hebrew exiles thrown into the furnace by Nebuchadnezzar. It includes the canticle of praise known as the *Benedicite.

Songs of Ascent or **Songs of Degrees.** See GRADUAL PSALMS.

Songs of Praise. A 'national' hymnal designed for use by Christians of all denominations, first published in 1925. Theologically its standpoint was markedly liberal, and became even more so in the second edition of 1931.

Sophronius, St (*c.*560–638), Patr. of *Jerusalem from 634. From 633 he was the chief opponent of *Monothelitism. He negotiated the surrender of Jerusalem to the Arabs in 638. Feast day, 11 Mar.

Sorbonne. The most famous college of the old University of *Paris. It was founded *c.*1257 by Robert de Sorbon, confessor of *Louis IX, for the education of students aspiring to the theological doctorate. From 1554 it was the regular meeting place of the Theological Faculty and the name was popularly applied to that Faculty. It was suppressed in 1793 but re-established as the Theological Faculty of the University in 1808. The faculty was abolished in 1885, but the name 'Sorbonne' continued in use for the University of Paris as a whole. Since the latter's reorganization into 13 separate universities in 1969, the name has been attached to those connected with the original site, e.g. Paris I ('Panthéon-Sorbonne').

Sorrowful Mysteries, the Five. The second *chaplet of the *Rosary, consisting of the Agony in Gethsemane, the Scourging, the Crowning with Thorns, the Carrying of the Cross, and the Crucifixion.

soteriology. The section of Christian theology which treats of the saving work of Christ for the world.

Soto, Dominic de (1494–1560), Spanish *Dominican. He was professor of theology at Salamanca. In 1545 *Charles V chose him as Imperial Theologian for the Council of *Trent, at which he expounded the *Thomistic doctrine on grace and free will.

Soubirous, Bernadette. See BERNADETTE, ST.

soul. The idea of a distinction between the soul, the immaterial principle of life and intelligence, and the body, is ancient. There is little specific teaching on the subject in the Bible, beyond an underlying assumption of some sort of afterlife (see IMMORTALITY), but Greek thought developed various ways of understanding the relation of soul and body. They included the *Platonic idea that the immortal soul is the true self, imprisoned for a time in an alien body. A modified Platonic view came to be accepted in the post-Nicene period; this saw the soul as the true self, immortal but not pre-existent. According to St *Thomas Aquinas, the soul is an individual spiritual substance, the 'form' of the body; body and soul together constitute the human entity, though the soul may be severed from the body and lead a separate existence, as happens after death. The separation, however, is not final, as the soul was made for the body. As it is purely spiritual, the soul is not a product of the generative powers of man, but each individual soul is a new creation of God. In modern times the doctrine of the soul, if considered at all, is thought of in relation to the whole biblical doctrine of man.

Source Criticism. See HIGHER CRITICISM.

South Africa, Christianity in. The first Christian missionaries to Africa south of the Zambezi were Portuguese. Their effect was very limited, and Christianity was really introduced by the Dutch, who began to settle in 1652. In the Napoleonic Wars the British occupied the Cape and they retained the colony in 1814.

The existence of a large White community led to the establishment of a settled Church, but, apart from a *Moravian mission to the Cape in 1737, there was practically no attempt to convert the Africans before the end of the 18th cent. The *LMS arrived in 1799 and provided many of the most famous missionaries, including J. *van der Kemp, J. *Philip, and R. *Moffat. *Methodists arrived in 1814; they came to have the largest number of African adherents in the country. Particularly influential was the Church of *Scotland mission centred around the educational institution at *Lovedale in Ciskei. The Great Trek (1837) resulted in the establishment as the State Church in the Transvaal of the Hervormde Kerk, separate from the Dutch Reformed Church, and a further separation led to the creation of a free Gereformeerde Kerk. RC missions have grown since the latter part of the 19th cent. The multiplication of missions led to the creation of the *ecumenical General Missionary Conference in 1904; this evolved into the South African Council of Churches.

Racially discriminatory government policies brought tension with the Churches. The Dutch Reformed Church, whose theology in the 20th cent. for a time backed a policy of 'separate development', left the *World Council of Churches after the Sharpeville crisis of 1960. The other Churches were all opposed to the policies of the State and their work in Black education was virtually halted in 1954. With the establishment of the Christian Institute in Johannesburg in 1963, Christian opposition to racialism became more systematic; it was increasingly led by Black Christians such as Desmond *Tutu.

African Independent Churches are numerous and include at least 30 per cent of African Christians. Some derive from schisms from a mainstream Church whose doctrine and order they retain; others have developed their own rituals, especially of healing, and were often founded by a 'prophet' figure. The most famous is the Amanazaretha, founded by Isaiah Shembe in Zululand.

The Church of the Province of Southern Africa (so called since 1982) is an independent province of the *Anglican Communion. The archiepiscopal see at Cape Town was founded in 1847. The Province has been strongly influenced by the *Tractarian movement.

South India, Church of. The Church inaugurated in 1947 by a union of: (1) the (*Anglican) Church of *India, Burma, and Ceylon; (2) *Methodists; and (3) the South India United Church, which had been formed by an earlier union of *Presbyterian, *Congregationalist, and Dutch Reformed bodies. The union was achieved by the acceptance of ministers possessing congregational, presbyteral, and episcopal ordination into a united ministry, without requiring the reordination of any, combined with the introduction of an episcopate in the historic succession (from Anglicanism) and its maintenance for the future, and the assurance that all subsequent ordinations would be episcopal.

The 1948 *Lambeth Conference gave the union a measure of qualified approval and in 1955 a state of 'limited intercommunion' between the C of E and the Church of South India was achieved. This was extended in 1972. The Church of South India, though not part of the *Anglican Communion, is a member of the Anglican Consultative Council, the *Lambeth Conference, and the Primates' Meeting.

South Pacific, Christianity in. The *LMS sent evangelists who started work in Tahiti in 1797 and rapidly extended it. Many other bodies have played a smaller part in attempts to evangelize the Pacific Islanders, notably Wesleyan *Methodists, *Presbyterians, and *Lutherans. Among RCs the work was entrusted particularly to the Picpus Society, whose members included Father *Damien, and the *Marists. Anglican work began under G. A. *Selwyn, first Bp. of *New Zealand, and the diocese of Melanesia (founded in 1861) formed part of the Province of New Zealand until it became an independent Province in 1975. The Anglican mission in Papua, founded from Australia in 1891, developed into the Province of Papua New Guinea, formed in 1977.

Difficulties of communication and the savagery of many of the inhabitants made the task of missionaries in the South Pacific a hard one, though most of the people now profess Christianity. In the 20th cent. there was much *ecumenical activity. The United Church of Papua New Guinea and the Solomon Islands, inaugurated in 1968, brought together Methodists and the Papua Ekalesia, which had grown out of the work of the LMS. Another trend in the late 20th cent. was the creation of self-governing Churches and the advance towards indigenous leadership. See also PATON, J. G., and PATTESON, J. C.

Southcott, Joanna (1750–1814), self-styled prophetess. A dairymaid and then a domestic servant, in 1791 she joined the *Methodists and in 1792 proclaimed that she was the 'woman clothed with the sun' of Rev. 12. By 1814 she was expecting to give birth to a messianic child. Meanwhile she had been 'sealing' in large numbers those who hoped to be among the 144,000 elect. R. T. *Davidson, when Abp. of Canterbury, was pressed to summon the bishops to open a box of her prophecies.

Southwark. The Anglican diocese was created in 1905. The church of the priory of St Mary Overie ('over the water from the City of London'), founded in 1106, became the cathedral. It had been the parish church of St Saviour, Southwark, since the *dissolution of the priory in 1539, but had been largely rebuilt in the 19th cent.

The RC diocese dates from the restoration of the hierarchy in 1850; it was made an archdiocese in 1965.

Southwell. St *Paulinus is said to have founded a collegiate church here c.630. A college of secular canons was dissolved by *Henry VIII in 1540, refounded in 1585, and again dissolved in 1841. In 1884 the largely Norman church became the cathedral of the new diocese.

Southwell, St Robert (c.1561–95), *Jesuit poet. A native of Norfolk, he was sent on the English mission in 1586. He was betrayed in 1592, and after three years' imprisonment he was hanged and quartered as a traitor. He was among the *Forty Martyrs of England and Wales canonized in 1970. Most of his poems were probably written in prison. Designed to encourage Catholics under persecution, they express deep religious feeling and became popular with both Catholics and Protestants.

Sozomen (early 5th cent.), Church historian. A lawyer at *Constantinople, he determined to continue *Eusebius of Caesarea's 'Church History' to his own day. His work covers the period 323 to 425. He drew on *Socrates, but reports some subjects, e.g. the spread of Christianity among the *Armenians, Saracens, and Goths, more fully.

Spain, Christianity in. Tradition ascribes the evangelization of Spain to St *Paul and St *James, but the earliest record of Spanish ecclesiastical organization is a letter of St *Cyprian of 254. The spread of Christianity by the end of the 3rd cent. is attested by Spanish martyrdoms in the *persecution under *Diocletian and the disciplinary measures of the Council of *Elvira (c.306). In the 5th cent. most of Spain fell under the rule of *Arian Visigoths. The conversion of the people to Catholicism, officially proclaimed by King *Recared in 589, inaugurated a period of brilliance in religious and cultural life. In the 8th cent. the Visigothic kingdom was conquered by the forces of *Islam. Though officially tolerated, Christians suffered occasional persecution. Christian principalities emerged in N. Spain in the 8th and 9th cents. as nuclei of opposition to Islamic rule. They slowly expanded south, and by c.1250 most of the Iberian peninsula had come under Christian rule. From c. 1050 Franco-Papal influences were strong; they may be seen in the foundation of *Cluniac and *Cistercian monasteries and the disappearance of some distinctively Spanish usages such as the *Mozarabic rite, proscribed in 1080. Both the *Dominican and *Franciscan Orders, which were popular in Spain, experienced a movement for reform which resulted in branches of *Observants. Thus the Franciscans, under the Observant Abp. of Toledo, F. *Ximénez de Cisneros, were in a good position to take advantage of the opportunities offered in the mission field by the discovery of America. The Spanish *Inquisition, which, in answer to popular hostility to Jews and converted Muslims, was established by *Ferdinand and *Isabella in Andalusia in 1480, spread to the rest of Castile, though not to Aragon until the 16th cent.

The adhesion of Spain to the Papacy in the 16th cent. was of prime importance. The influence of Spanish bishops at the Council of *Trent did much to shape the *Counter-Reformation. In Spain groups of *Alumbrados and Protestants were suppressed, and the great mystics and spiritual writers, St *Teresa of Ávila, St *John of the Cross, Luis de *Leon, and *Luis of Granada, faced ecclesiastical hostility.

In the early 18th cent. the position of the Spanish Church, as the one serious threat to royal absolutism, was uneasy, and relations between the Spanish Court and the Papacy, broken off during the War of Spanish Succession (1701–15), were not restored until 1753. The *Jesuits were expelled in 1767. Hostility between the Church and liberalism continued in the 19th cent., a period of unrest, conflict, and alternating extremes. In the 1830s Church assets were expropriated, convents and monasteries dissolved, and churches destroyed, but the constitution of 1876 recognized Catholicism as the State religion, subsidized clergy stipends and the upkeep of RC Churches, and limited the activities of other religious bodies. When the monarchy fell in 1931, the Second Republic separated Church and State. In 1936 *anticlerical violence resulted in the killing of almost 7,000 priests and religious and the destruction of churches and other ecclesiastical buildings. After General Franco's victory in 1939 the Republic's laicizing changes were swept away and the old closeness of Church and State re-established. Until the 1960s the alliance was unchallenged. Then criticism among the clergy mounted and by the time of Franco's death in 1975 the Church had distanced itself far enough from the dicta-torship to find a secure place in the new order enshrined in the 1978 constitution. Spain now has no State religion, and Protestantism no longer involves any legal disabilities.

Spalatin, Georg (1484–1545), humanist and Reformer. Georg Burkhardt was born at Spalt (hence his name), near Nürnberg. In 1509 he became tutor to the sons of the Prince Elector, *Frederick III of Saxony. In 1511 he was sent to *Wittenberg, where he had studied; here he became acquainted with M. *Luther. It was mainly through Spalatin's influence that the hesitating Elector was won over to the ideas of the Reformer. In 1525 Spalatin went to Altenburg, where he carried through the change from Catholicism to *Lutheranism.

SPCK. The 'Society for Promoting Christian Knowledge'. It was founded by T. *Bray and others in 1698 'to promote and encourage the erection of charity schools in . . . England and Wales; to disperse, both at home and abroad, Bibles and tracts of religion', and generally to promote Christian knowledge. Much of its original educational and missionary work was taken over by the *National Society and the *SPG. It now operates in three divisions: SPCK Worldwide, which by funding helps to make books available overseas; publishing; and bookselling.

species. A Latin word meaning 'form' or 'kind', employed in *scholastic theology to designate the material elements used in the sacraments, especially the bread and wine in the Eucharist, and in that sense taken over into theological English.

Speier, Diets of. See SPEYER, DIETS OF.

Spencer, Herbert (1820–1903), the chief exponent of *agnosticism in 19th-cent. England. He divided reality into the knowable (the province of science) and the unknowable (that of religion). He asserted that man could not only be conscious of the unknowable, but that knowledge itself was finally dependent upon the unknowable, and that the Absolute is the fundamental reality behind all things. Nevertheless the Absolute could not be known in the strict sense of the word.

Spencer, John (1630–93), English Hebraist. In his *De Legibus Hebraeorum Ritualibus et* *earum Rationibus* (1685) he sought to trace the connection between the religious rites of the Hebrews and those of other Semitic peoples. He thus has a claim to be the founder of the study of *comparative religion.

Spener, Philipp Jakob (1635–1705), early leader of German *Pietism. Influenced by the works of J. *Arndt and the English *Puritans, and by J. de Labadie (see LABAD-ISTS), he became convinced of a call to revivify the *Lutheran Church with evangelical fervour. At Frankfurt, where he was appointed minister in 1666, he introduced 'Collegia Pietatis', devotional meetings which gathered twice a week in his house; and he issued his *Pia Desideria* (1675). While he remained loyal to the Lutheran tradition, the personal and interior turn of his religion made him critical of a sterile and polemical form of orthodoxy. He also tried to give the laity an active part in Church life. In 1686 he went to Dresden as court preacher. He came into conflict with the theology faculty of the University of Leipzig and in 1691 migrated to Berlin. His movement, by then known as 'Pietism', spread, and in 1694 the University of Halle was founded, largely under his influence.

Speyer, Diets of. (1) The Diet of 1526 consolidated reforming influences in Germany. It decreed that each Prince should order ecclesiastical affairs in his own State in accordance with his conscience.

(2) The Diet of 1529 was controlled by a Catholic majority. It passed legislation to end all toleration of *Lutherans in Catholic districts. Five Princes and 14 cities made a formal 'protest'; henceforward the Reformers were known as '*Protestants'.

SPG. The 'Society for the Propagation of the Gospel in foreign parts'. It was founded in 1701 by T. *Bray and others to provide the ministrations of the C of E for British people overseas and to evangelize the non-Christian races subject to the Crown. In 1965 it joined with the *UMCA to form the United Society for the Propagation of the Gospel (*USPG).

Spinckes, Nathaniel (1653–1727), *Nonjuror. He was a prebendary and rector of St Martin's, *Salisbury, when he was deprived on refusing to take the oath of allegiance to William and Mary in 1690. In 1713 he was consecrated bishop by G. *Hickes, assisted by two Scottish bishops, but he took no title. In the dispute about the *Usages, he advocated retention of the BCP as it was. A man of learning, he was revered for his personal piety.

Spinoza, Benedictus de (also **Baruch)** (1632–77), Dutch Jewish philosopher. In 1656 he was expelled from the Synagogue and had to leave Amsterdam. In various places he earned his living by grinding lenses. Most of his writings were published posthumously, including his main work, the *Ethica ordine geometrico demonstrata* (1677).

The foundation of Spinoza's system is his idea of God as a single all-embracing substance, which contains within itself the reason for its existence. This substance is infinite, with an infinite number of attributes, of which only two, thought (*cogitatio*) and extension (*extensio*) are known to man. All individual things are modes of these two attributes, being either bodies or ideas. The human mind is part of the Divine impersonal intellect which works according to necessity. Spinoza thus denies free will, the permanence of personality, and immortality. The highest human activity is the loving contemplation of God which becomes possible in so far as one can master the passions and live in accordance with reason. His studies on the Bible have made him one of the fathers of modern historical biblical criticism.

Spiridion, St. See SPYRIDON, ST.

Spirit. In Christian theology the word denotes: (1) The intelligent and immaterial part of man or the human *soul in general, whether united with the body in life or separated from it in death, and especially that aspect of it which is concerned with religious truth and action and is directly susceptible to Divine influence. (2) An order of being which is superhuman in the sense that it is not subject to the limits of time, space, and a bodily frame. (3) One of the creatures belonging to this order, whether good or evil, i.e. angels or demons. (4) The Third Person of the *Trinity (see HOLY SPIRIT).

Spiritual Exercises, The. The famous treatise of St *Ignatius Loyola, originating from his experiences at Manresa in 1522–3 and substantially completed by 1541. It is a manual for those giving *retreats, and provides a structured programme of mainly imaginative prayer lasting, in its full form, for about a month. Themes from it are often taken for shorter retreats.

Spiritual Franciscans. Before St *Francis's death two groups of *Franciscans could be distinguished: (1) those who wanted to mitigate the rule of poverty and remodel the Order, and (2) those later known as 'Zealots' or 'Spirituals', who wished to maintain the original way of life. The latter group became more apparent as the Franciscan rule was progressively modified. A compromise, based on St *Bonaventure's contention that property left to the friars belonged to the Church and that the friars could use what was necessary for their life and work, was embodied in a decretal of Pope Nicholas III in 1279. It proved unacceptable to the Spirituals but was reaffirmed in 1312. In the face of continued intransigence, *John XXII enjoined them to obey authority on pain of excommunication and burnt four of them as heretics (1318). Soon afterwards the Franciscan Order was threatened with schism over what was originally a separate issue, the theoretical question of the poverty of Christ and the Apostles, which John declared to be heretical in 1323. In the face of persecution the number of Spirituals declined, but the movement gave an impetus to the rise of more rigorous groups in the Franciscan Order, first the Friars of the Strict Observance (*Observantines) and later the *Capuchins.

spiritual healing. Though occasionally used as a synonym for psychotherapy, the phrase is properly confined to attempts to heal the whole personality by prayer and sacramental means. Among the methods in general use are *Unction and the laying on of *hands. The patient is generally encouraged also to make use of medical skill, though some hold that spiritual means alone should suffice. Spiritual healing (often called 'faith healing' or 'divine healing') has a prominent part in modern *Pentecostalism and in the *Charismatic Renewal Movement.

spiritual works of mercy. Traditionally there are seven: converting the sinner; instructing the ignorant; counselling the doubtful; comforting the sorrowful; bearing wrongs patiently; forgiving injuries; praying for the living and the dead. See also CORPORAL WORKS OF MERCY.

Spiritualism. A system of (often superstitious) beliefs and practices intended to establish communication with the spirits of the dead. Necromancy is an element common to most primitive and many higher religions; an early example is recorded in 1 Sam. 28: 8. In its modern form Spiritualism dates from the occult experiences of the American Fox family in 1848; it spread to England and the Continent. It professes to make contact with the souls of the departed chiefly by means of mediums, accompanied by table-turning, automatic writing, and other devices. The practice of Spiritualism is condemned by all parts of the Church.

The Christian Spiritualist Churches profess acceptance of the leadership of Jesus Christ, but their understanding of Him differs from that of the orthodox Churches.

spirituality. A vague term now used to refer both to people's subjective practice and experience of their religion, and to the spiritual exercises and beliefs which individuals have regarding their personal relationship with God. It is usual to regard *prayer, *meditation, *contemplation, and *mysticism as major factors in spirituality.

spirituals. American religious folk songs. They originated (as 'spiritual songs') in the White *revivalist Churches of the 18th cent. and their *camp meetings in the 19th cent. The Black form ('Negro spirituals'), though apparently derived from the White style, acquired its own character, with texts identifying the sufferings of Christ with the Blacks' own condition of slavery, and an emphasis on the desire for release from the troubles of the world. Other forms of *Gospel music developed out of both styles in the late 19th cent.

sponsor. A godparent (q.v.).

spoon, liturgical. In the E. rites a spoon is used for giving Communion, a portion of the consecrated Host being dipped in the chalice and the two species being conveyed on the spoon to the communicant. In the RC Church the use of a spoon for administering the consecrated Wine was sanctioned in 1965.

Sports, Book of. A declaration defining the recreations permissible on *Sunday, first issued in 1617 by *James I for the use of magistrates in Lancashire, and extended in 1618 to the whole country. It was reissued by *Charles I in 1633. It permitted archery and dancing and was designed to counteract *Sabbatarianism.

Spottiswoode, John (1565–1639), Abp. of St Andrews and historian. Originally a strict *Presbyterian, he became an adherent of the royal policy and the chief agent of *James I in suppressing the political influence of the Kirk. He was consecrated Abp. of Glasgow in 1610; in 1615 he was translated to St Andrews. At the General Assembly of the Kirk in 1618 he made himself Moderator without election and imposed the Five Articles of *Perth. In 1635 *Charles I made him Chancellor; as such he gave reluctant support to the introduction of the BCP in Scotland. When the *National Covenant was signed in 1638 he fled to Newcastle. His *History of the Church of Scotland* [to 1625] (1655) is well documented; it reflects the author's position.

Spurgeon, Charles Haddon (1834–92), *Baptist preacher. In 1854 he went to Southwark; his sermons drew such crowds that a new church, the Metropolitan Tabernacle in Newington Causeway, was built. He estranged some members of his community by his rigid opposition to liberal methods of biblical exegesis, and in 1887 he withdrew from the Baptist Union.

Spy Wednesday. The Wednesday before *Good Friday, so named as the day on which *Judas Iscariot arranged to betray Christ (Mt. 26: 14–16).

Spyridon (also Spiridion), St (d. c.348), Bp. of Tremithus in *Cyprus. He was a peasant who, according to tradition, had suffered in the *Diocletianic persecution. As bishop he is said to have attended the Council of *Nicaea; he was certainly present at that of *Sardica (c.343). There are many legends attached to his life. Feast day in the E., 12 Dec.; in the W., 14 Dec.

Sri Lanka (formerly known as Ceylon), Christianity in. According to *Cosmas Indicopleustes, there were Christians of the *Church of the East in Sri Lanka in the 6th cent., but they seem to have died out. From 1505 Sri Lanka came within the Portuguese seaborne trading empire; the first RC priests arrived in Colombo in 1518. In 1543 missionary work was begun by *Franciscan friars, joined in the 17th cent. by other Orders. The Christian community grew rapidly. In 1658 the Portuguese were driven out by the Dutch; they tried to suppress the RC Church, brought missionaries from the *Netherlands and supported the Dutch Reformed Church. In 1796 the Dutch were displaced by the British and in 1802 Ceylon became a Crown colony. Under British rule missionary work was undertaken by English societies: *Baptist, Wesleyan *Methodist, the *CMS and *SPG. Since political independence in 1948, all the Churches have had to face the challenge of a revived Buddhism, which was recognized as the State religion in 1972. Christians comprise about 8 per cent of the population; nine tenths of them are RC.

SSJE. See SOCIETY OF ST JOHN THE EVANGELIST.

Stabat Mater dolorosa. A Latin hymn of unknown date describing the Sorrows of the BVM at the Cross. It came into liturgical use in the later Middle Ages. The many English translations include 'At the Cross her station keeping'.

stability. Part of the commitment made by monks and nuns following the Rule of St *Benedict. It is variously interpreted as meaning staying in one place, staying with one community, or perseverance in the monastic life.

Stainer, Sir John (1840–1901), organist and composer. In 1872 he became organist at *St Paul's Cathedral, where he carried out reforms in the music, which became famous under his direction. From 1889 to 1899 he was Professor of Music at Oxford. His main works were oratorios and cantatas, among them *The Crucifixion* (1887).

stalls. The fixed seats on both sides of the choirs of cathedral and certain other churches. They are usually separated by high projecting arms, often richly carved, and sometimes surmounted by canopies. The seats can frequently be turned back, disclosing a bracket called a *misericord.

stake. A post to which persons were bound

for execution, especially by *burning; hence the punishment of death by burning.

Stanford, Sir Charles Villiers (1852–1924), composer and teacher. From 1883 he was Professor of Composition at the Royal College of Music in London, and from 1887 also Professor of Music at Cambridge. His many settings of Anglican services gave Victorian Church music freshness. He also wrote the anthems 'The Lord is my shepherd' and 'Ye choirs of new Jerusalem'.

Stanislaus, St (1030–79), Patron of *Poland. Bp. of Cracow from 1072, he came into conflict with King Bolesław II, whom he repeatedly reproved for scandalous conduct. Eventually he excommunicated the King and, according to tradition, Bolesław himself killed him while he was offering Mass. Feast day, 11 Apr. (formerly, 7 May; at Cracow, 8 May).

Stanley, Arthur Penrhyn (1815–81), *Broad Churchman. As Dean of *Westminster from 1864, he tried to make the Abbey a national shrine for all, irrespective of creed. He offended conservative Churchmen by inviting all the scholars who had produced the RV, including a *Unitarian, to receive Communion in the Abbey. Despite the atmosphere of unorthodoxy that hung about him all his life, he was an influential figure.

Stanton, Arthur Henry (1839–1913), *Anglo-Catholic priest. In 1862 he was ordained to the title of St Alban's, Holborn, where he remained as curate for 50 years. He won the confidence of men in one of the roughest parts of London, but, like many Anglo-Catholic priests at that time, he met with official opposition.

Stapeldon, Walter de (c.1261–1326), Bp. of *Exeter from 1308. He helped to rebuild Exeter Cathedral and founded Stapeldon Hall, which became Exeter College, Oxford. He was murdered by the London mob for his association with the misgovernment of Edward II.

Stapleton, Thomas (1535–98), RC controversialist. He became a prebendary of *Chichester under *Mary in 1558, but fled to Louvain on *Elizabeth I's accession. He taught in the universities at Douai and Louvain and became Dean of Hilverenbeck. He was an able and erudite controversialist.

Star of Bethlehem. The star seen by the wise men at the birth of Christ which 'went before them till it came and stood over where the young child was' (Mt. 2: 1–11). Various attempts have been made to connect it with astronomical phenomena.

staretz. In the Russian Church, a person who is sought out as a spiritual guide because of his exceptional personal holiness. He has no formal position in the ecclesiastical hierarchy.

Starovery. Another name for the *Old Believers (q.v.).

State Prayers. In the BCP, the prayers for the Sovereign and Royal Family towards the end of *Mattins and *Evensong.

State Services. In the C of E, the services appointed to commemorate days of national rejoicing and deliverance. There were formerly a number of such services printed at the end of the BCP, but since 1859 only that commemorating the Sovereign's accession has been retained.

States of the Church. Those parts of Italy and the territory of *Avignon and Venaissin in France which at one time acknowledged the temporal sovereignty of the Papacy. Some of these lands were also known as the '*Patrimony of St Peter' (q.v.).

In 1791 the Papal territories in France were lost to the new republic, and by 1861 the Papacy was left with Rome alone, the rest having been absorbed into the kingdom of Italy. In 1870 Rome itself was lost and the Pope withdrew into the *Vatican. By the Law of *Guarantees (1871) Italy allotted to the Pope a pension and declared the basilicas and palaces of the Vatican and the *Lateran and the Papal villa at *Castel Gandolfo to be extraterritorial. The *Lateran Treaty in 1929 contained an agreement on much the same lines and constituted the 'Vatican City' a separate State.

Station Days. Certain days on which the Pope formerly celebrated Mass in one of the so-called 'station churches' in Rome. There is early evidence for the observance of *stationes*, but apart from the fact that such observance involved fasting, it is unclear what it consisted of. At Rome from the 4th cent. the solemnity was enhanced by processions of clergy and people from one church, called *collecta*, to the station church, where the Pope was to offer Mass. According to tradition it was *Gregory I who assigned its special church to each of the station days. The Papal station Masses fell into disuse, especially during the exile of the Popes at *Avignon, but traces of the custom survive in the *indulgences attached to visits to the station churches.

Stations of the Cross. A series of 14 pictures or carvings which depict incidents in the last journey of Christ from *Pilate's house to His entombment. They are commonly arranged round the walls of a church; it is a popular devotion to visit the stations in order, reciting prayers and meditating on each incident.

Statuta Ecclesiae Antiqua (Lat., 'The Ancient Statutes of the Church'). A document comprising a profession of faith, disciplinary canons, and a ritual for *Ordination. It was compiled in S. Gaul in the second half of the 5th cent.

Stein, St Edith (1891–1942), *Carmelite nun. Of Jewish family, she studied under E. Husserl and became a leading figure in the *Phenomenological School. She became a RC in 1922 and tried to interpret Phenomenology from a *Thomist standpoint. She joined the Carmelites in 1934. She was put to death by the Nazis in a gas chamber at Auschwitz. Feast day, 9 Aug.

Steiner, Rudolf (1861–1925), founder of *anthroposophy. In 1902 he became the leader of a German section of the *Theosophical Society, but, rejecting the eastern associations of the main body, in 1913 he founded the Anthroposophical Society as an independent association. His aim was to develop the faculty of spirit cognition inherent in ordinary people and to put them in touch with the spiritual world from which materialism had estranged them.

'Stephanus' (Estienne). A family of scholar-printers.

ROBERT ESTIENNE (1503–59), Printer to Francis I, King of France, is famous for his *Thesaurus Linguae Latinae* (1532) and for his editions of the Bible, including the OT in Hebrew and the NT in Greek. His annotations to his Bibles provoked attacks by the *Sorbonne, and in 1551 he moved to Gen-

eva. The verse divisions which he introduced in his 1551 NT are still in use.

HENRI ESTIENNE (1528–98), Robert's eldest son, published editions of the *Fathers. His *Thesaurus Linguae Graecae* (1572) was indispensable to generations of Greek scholars.

Stephen, St (d. *c.*35), protomartyr and traditionally the first *deacon. He was one of those who, according to Acts 6: 5, were appointed by the Apostles to 'serve tables' in *Jerusalem. It is reported that he also took part in preaching and performed miracles (Acts 6: 8 ff.), thus incurring the hostility of the Jews. After delivering a long discourse (Acts 7: 2–53) before the *Sanhedrin, he was stoned, apparently without formal trial. He died asking forgiveness for his persecutors (Acts 7: 60). Feast day in the W., 26 Dec.; in the E., 27 Dec.

Stephen I, St (d. 257), Pope from 254. He intervened in disputes in Gaul and in Spain. He later became involved in a bitter controversy with St *Cyprian over the *validity of Baptism by heretics, which Cyprian held to be null and void. Feast day, formerly 2 Aug.

Stephen II (III) (d. 757), Pope from 752. (He is sometimes counted the third of his name, 'Stephen II' having died four days after his election.) When the Lombard king besieged Rome, the Pope turned in vain to the Byzantine Emperor for help; he then crossed the Alps to ask for assistance from the Frankish king, *Pepin. From him, Stephen obtained the much-discussed 'Donation' of Quiercy (now often called the 'Donation of Pepin', 754). It was possibly in Stephen's curia that the '*Donation of Constantine' was produced. See also PATRIMONY OF ST PETER.

Stephen III (IV), (d. 772), Pope from 768. He held a synod at the *Lateran which excluded laymen from Papal elections, confirmed the veneration of images, and anathematized the *iconoclastic synod of 754. He allied himself with the Lombards.

Stephen, St (975–1038), first king of *Hungary. He became a Christian in 985 and on his accession to the Hungarian throne in 997 he set out to Christianize the country. In 1001 he obtained from the Pope a royal crown; it was apparently later returned to

Rome and is no longer thought to form part of the Hungarian crown preserved at Budapest. Feast day (now optional), 16 Aug. (formerly 2 Sept.), but in Hungary 20 Aug., the day of the translation of his relics, is his main festival.

Stephen Harding, St (d.1134), abbot of *Cîteaux. A monk of Molesme, he was part of the community that went to Cîteaux in 1098. He became abbot in 1109. The monastery was in danger of extinction when St *Bernard and 30 followers joined the community in 1112. The sudden increase in numbers soon necessitated other foundations. In order to maintain the original austerity and uniform government, Stephen drew up the nucleus of the *Carta Caritatis, which established the system of regular visitations and General Chapters in the *Cistercian Order. Feast day, 26 Jan. (formerly 17 Apr. and 16 July).

Stercoranists. Persons who asserted that the Blessed Sacrament is digested and evacuated by the recipient. Although they are written of as a sect, there appears to be no evidence that such a sect existed.

Stern, Henry Aaron (1820–85), missionary to the Jews. He was born of Jewish parents in Hesse-Cassel. Having embarked on a commercial career he went to London, where he received Christian Baptism in 1840. He was later ordained. He worked among Jews in various parts of the Middle East, and in *Ethiopia did notable work among the Falashas, the so-called 'Black Jews'. His later years were spent in missionary activity in London.

Sternhold, Thomas (d.1549), versifier of the Psalms. He entered the service of *Henry VIII and became a court favourite. Probably in 1549 he published a first (undated) edition of his metrical version, containing 19 Psalms; it was dedicated to *Edward VI. A third edition, with 37 Psalms, appeared posthumously in 1549; it contained a further seven Psalms by 'J. H.' (John Hopkins, probably a Suffolk clergyman, d. 1570). The collection, in the complete edition printed by J. *Day in 1562, became known as 'Sternhold and Hopkins'.

Sterry, Peter (? 1613–72), *Puritan. He was a member of the *Westminster Assembly and from 1649 one of O. *Cromwell's chaplains. After Cromwell's death he devoted himself to literary pursuits. His theology was a mixture of *Calvinism and *Neoplatonism.

stewardship. The management of property by a servant on behalf of its owner, and particularly in modern times, the organized pledging of a specific amount of money to be given regularly to the Church, often called 'Christian stewardship'. While the idea of stewardship goes back at least to the NT, it was the need to fund missionaries which brought about the 'Stewardship Awakening' in the 19th cent. in the USA. An important element was the idea that everyone, not just the rich, could be benefactors of religion. American Protestant Churches developed the 'Every Member Canvass', and many established denominational agencies to assist parishes' annual stewardship programmes. The system was refined by commercial fund-raising agencies such as the Chicago-based Wells Organization, founded in 1946 by Herbert Wells. This introduced triennial stewardship programmes, first to *Australia (1954) and then to other Commonwealth countries, including England. The programmes featured elaborate brochures and parish dinners, as well as individual solicitation by Church members who had already made a significant financial pledge. They stressed both the Church's need for money and the need of individuals to promise regular financial support as part of their personal Christian stewardship. They often resulted in large increases in parish income, but after the initial success many Churches wanted to reduce the cost and eliminate the peer-pressure inherent in the Wells method. They then set up their own departments of stewardship. From the 1920s stewardship theology was applied to all aspects of life, often defined as time, talents, and treasure.

sticharion. The liturgical tunic worn in the E. Church, comparable to the *alb in the West.

sticheron. In the E. Church a brief liturgical hymn which is attached to a verse of a Psalm or other scriptural passage.

Stigand (d. ?1072), Abp. of *Canterbury. He became Bp. of *Winchester in 1047. When he was appointed Abp. of Canterbury in

1052, he retained the see of Winchester as well. He did not secure Papal recognition until 1058, and then from Benedict X, who was himself deposed in 1059. Although Stigand's dubious status at Canterbury provided a pretext for *William I's invasion in 1066, he was honoured by the Conqueror until the throne was secure. In 1070 William had him deposed by Papal legates and he died in custody.

stigmatization. The reproduction of the wounds of the Passion of Christ in the human body. Stigmata may be either invisible, when the pain is experienced without any exterior sign, or visible, in which case they normally consist of wounds or blood blisters on hands, feet, and near the heart, also on the head or shoulders and back. They do not become septic and resist ordinary treatment. The first person known to have received the stigmata is St *Francis of Assisi; later cases have been numerous, predominantly among women. The attitude of the RC Church has been guarded.

Stillingfleet, Edward (1635–99), Bp. of *Worcester from 1689. He held *Latitudinarian views. His *Irenicum* (1659) advocated a union between *Episcopalians and *Presbyterians, treating forms of Church government as inessential. In 1664 he replied to the *Jesuit account of the controversy between W. *Laud and J. *Fisher in his *Rational Account of the Grounds of the Protestant Religion*. His *Origines Britannicae* (1685) deals with the sources of the British Church.

Stock, St Simon. See SIMON STOCK, ST.

Stockholm Conference (1925). The Universal Christian Conference on *Life and Work which met in Stockholm to promote Christian influences on political, social, and economic life.

Stoicism. A Graeco-Roman school of philosophy founded at *Athens by Zeno of Citium (335–263 BC). The system is a form of materialistic *pantheism. God is the immanent all-pervading energy by which the natural world is created and sustained. He is also the world reason or '*Logos' which manifests itself in the order and beauty of the world. To the Stoic the good man is the wise man, and his wisdom consists in conformity to nature, i.e. in living according to the law of the universe embodied in the Divine reason.

stole. A liturgical vestment consisting of a long narrow strip of coloured material. Its origin is doubtful. In the W. Church it has become the distinctive vestment of the *deacon, who wears it like a sash over his left shoulder, its ends being fastened together under the right arm. It is, however, also a regular vestment of the priest, who now always wears it round the neck with its ends falling down in front, as does the bishop. Besides being used at the Eucharist, it is worn when administering the Sacraments and generally when preaching. Its colour depends on that of the other vestments and the occasion, e.g. when hearing confessions the priest wears a purple stole. In the C of E, where the use of the stole disappeared at the Reformation, it was revived in the middle of the 19th cent. The 1969 Canons allow its use at the Eucharist and the Occasional Offices.

Stone, Barton W. See CAMPBELL, ALEXANDER.

Stonyhurst College. An English RC public school. Conducted by the *Jesuits, it traces its origin to the foundation of a college for English boys at *St-Omer in 1592. It moved to Stonyhurst Hall in Lancashire in 1794.

Storch, Nicolas (d. after 1536), *Anabaptist. He became leader of the *Zwickau Prophets during T. *Müntzer's stay in the city (1520–21). After the defeat of the rebels in the *Peasants' War, he emerged as a leader of an Anabaptist sect in N. Franconia. In 1536 he was rumoured to be again in Zwickau. His teaching was spiritualist, with a chiliastic expectation of the imminent purification of the Church.

stoup. A basin near the entrance of a church containing *holy water with which the faithful may sprinkle themselves. Stoups are of various forms, either let into the wall or standing on a socle, and are often richly decorated.

Strabo, Walafrid. See WALAFRID STRABO.

Stratford, John (c.1275/80–1348), Abp. of *Canterbury from 1333. As Bp. of *Winchester, in 1327 he advised Edward II to abdicate and in 1330 Edward III made him Chancellor. When Edward returned from an unsuccessful expedition in 1340, a series of charges were brought against Stratford. He stood firm and obtained recognition of the principle that peers should be tried only by their equals in Parliament. He then retired from political life.

Strauss, David Friedrich (1808–74), German theologian. His famous *Leben Jesu* (1835) applied the 'myth theory' to the life of Christ. It denied the historical foundation of all supernatural elements in the Gospels, which were assigned to an unintentionally creative legend (the 'myth'), developed between the death of Christ and the writing of the Gospels in the 2nd cent. The growth of primitive Christianity was to be understood in terms of the *Hegelian dialectic. The book led to Strauss's dismissal from his post at Tübingen, but it exercised a deep influence on subsequent Gospel criticism.

Street, George Edmund (1824–81), architect. Before 1849, he worked under G. G. *Scott. He became a leader in the Gothic revival, was diocesan architect of *Oxford, *York, *Ripon, and *Winchester, and designed a number of churches and ecclesiastical institutions.

Streeter, Burnett Hillman (1874–1937), NT scholar. From 1905 to 1933 he was a Fellow of Queen's College, Oxford (Provost from 1933 to 1937) and from 1915 to 1934 also a canon of *Hereford. His researches into the *Synoptic Problem helped to establish among English Churchmen belief in the priority of Mk. and the existence of '*Q'. In *The Four Gospels* (1924) he set out his conclusions on the Gospels as a whole and expounded his thesis on the '*Caesarean text'.

Strigel, Victorinus (1524–69), Reformation theologian. In 1548 he became professor and rector of the new school at Jena. Here, in opposition to the strict *Lutheranism of M. *Flacius, he expounded more moderate and conciliatory doctrines and defended a form of *synergism.

Strossmayer, Joseph Georg (1815–1905), RC Bp. of Djakovo in Croatia from 1850. He promoted the cause of pan-Slavism, worked for reunion with the Orthodox Church of *Serbia and *Russia, and spent large sums on education, regardless of the denomination of the beneficiaries. At the

First *Vatican Council (1869–70) he opposed the definition of Papal infallibility and caused a 'scene' by his ill-timed defence of Protestantism.

Strype, John (1643–1737), English Church historian. His works deal mainly with the Reformation period. They include *Memorials of Thomas Cranmer* (1694) and *Annals of the Reformation in England* (1709–31). The wealth of documentation on which they are based renders them valuable, despite bad arrangement and frequent errors.

Stubbs, John (c.1543–90), also 'Stubbe', *Puritan writer. In 1579 he published *The Discovery of a Gaping Gulf*, attacking *Elizabeth I's proposed marriage with Francis, Duke of Anjou. Stubbs, his publisher and printer were all sentenced and the first two had their right hands cut off. He was subsequently commissioned by Lord Burghley to write a reply (1587, now lost) to W. *Allen's *Defence of the English Catholics* (1584).

Stubbs, William (1825–1901), historian and bishop. He was Regius professor of modern history at Oxford (1866–84) and then Bp. of *Chester (1884–9) and of *Oxford (1889–1901). He was the greatest British historian of his time. Many of his works deal with ecclesiastical sources.

Studd, Charles Thomas (1862–1931), missionary. He was influenced by his father's conversion at a mission of D. L. *Moody and I. D. Sankey in 1877, and he volunteered for missionary work in *China. As one of the 'Cambridge Seven' his intention aroused great interest and laid the seeds of the Student Volunteer Movement. He worked successively in China, *India, and Central Africa.

Studdert Kennedy, Geoffrey Anketell (1883–1929), Anglican priest. As Chaplain to the Forces (1916–19), he won the affectionate title of 'Woodbine Willie', from a brand of cigarettes which he distributed. In 1922 he was appointed Rector of St Edmund, King and Martyr, Lombard Street. He continued his mission-preaching, travelling and working in association with the *Industrial Christian Fellowship. He held unconventional views on various theological matters. Feast day in CW, 8 Mar.

Student Christian Movement (SCM). The British section of a world fellowship of students desiring 'to understand the Christian faith and live the Christian life'. It developed out of several independent movements at Cambridge and elsewhere in the later 19th cent. As a body drawing its membership from all Christian communions (since the Second *Vatican Council including RCs), it cultivated an outlook akin to that of the *Ecumenical Movement, many of whose leaders had earlier been associated with it. After the Second World War it failed to find a role in the new universities and allied itself with ephemeral radical movements; by the 1990s it had virtually disappeared. The publishing house which it had developed became independent of the SCM in 1989.

Studios. A monastery at *Constantinople, founded probably before 454 by Studios, who in that year became a consul. Its monks were notable defenders of *Chalcedonian orthodoxy. In 799, monks from the Saccudium monastery, led by St *Theodore, reinforced the community. He introduced a new rule, based on that of St *Basil; manual work played a larger part and discipline was strict, but emphasis was laid on patristic learning. Studios became a model for E. monasticism, and influenced the monks of Mount *Athos.

studium generale. From the mid-13th cent., a higher educational establishment of more than local significance, notably (1) a university attracting students from different regions and, usually, different countries, and (2) an international college run by a religious Order, such as the *Dominicans, along university lines and often in association with a university.

Stundists. Certain Russian evangelical sects which emerged in the Ukraine c.1858-62, under the influence of *Lutheran and *Reformed pastors and *Mennonite preachers. They became increasingly *Baptist in orientation; their descendants form part of the 'All Union Council of Evangelical Christians and Baptists' established in Russia in 1944.

Sturm, Johannes (1507–89), Reformer and educationalist. Having become a Protestant under M. *Bucer's influence, he moved from Paris to Strasbourg in 1537. Here he took an active part in furthering the Reformation. His interest in education did much to make the city one of the chief educational centres in Europe.

Stylite. In the early Church a solitary who lived on the top of a pillar. The pillars varied in height and the platforms on the top were generally provided with a parapet against which the Stylite would lean for sleep. Food was usually provided by disciples or admirers. There are many examples of such ascetics from the 5th to the 10th cents., and a few to modern times.

Suárez, Francisco (1548–1617), Spanish *Jesuit. He taught in Rome and at Alcalá; in 1597 *Philip II summoned him to the University of Coimbra. He is accounted the greatest theologian of his order.

His *Disputationes Metaphysicae* (1597) became a standard textbook; it abandoned *Aristotle's sequence of thought to give an independent systematic treatment of the subject. Writing a series of major works on *grace, he proposed in the system known as *Congruism a solution to the problem of the relation between human freedom and Divine grace on *Molinist lines. According to Suárez, God does not cause man's free acts, but, foreseeing them by His special knowledge (called *scientia media*), He brings about the salvation of the elect by giving them those graces of which He foresees they will make good use in certain given circumstances. This teaching provoked opposition but it became the prevalent doctrine among non-Thomist RC theologians. His *De Legibus* (1612), on the principles of natural and international law, has influenced jurists and legislators in Europe and America.

subcintorium. An ecclesiastical vestment resembling the *maniple. In the Middle Ages it was worn by bishops and occasionally by priests, but its use came to be restricted to the Pope and has now been dropped entirely. Its purpose was to secure the *stole to the *girdle.

subdeacon. In the RC Church, until the office was suppressed in 1972, a person in the lowest of the *Major Orders. The office existed by the 3rd cent.; until the 13th cent. it was regarded as a *Minor, not a Major, Order.

A subdeacon was one of the three sacred ministers at *High Mass, where his functions included that of chanting the

*Epistle. In modern times, however, his part was often taken by a person in deacon's or priest's orders. In the C of E the subdiaconate was given up in the 16th cent. It survives as a Minor Order in the E. Church.

Subiaco. A town *c.*40 miles east of Rome, famous as the site of the grotto where St *Benedict settled on his retirement from the world. He founded 12 monasteries in the area, two of which still exist.

Subiaco Congregation. An international monastic *Congregation of *Benedictine monks formerly known as the Cassinese Congregation of the Primitive Observance. It originated in 1851 within the *Cassinese Congregation; it was renamed in 1967.

subintroductae. In the early Church, women who lived associated with men in spiritual marriage. The practice was forbidden by early 4th cent. councils.

Sublapsarianism, also known as 'Infra' or 'Post-lapsarianism'. The form of the *Calvinistic doctrine of *predestination that holds that it was only after the *Fall that God decreed the election or non-election of individuals to salvation.

submersion (also 'total immersion'). The form of *Baptism in which the water completely covers the candidate's body. Though *immersion is now also common, submersion is practised in the Orthodox and several other E. Churches, and it is one of the methods provided in the 1969 RC rite for the Baptism of Infants. It is widely supposed to have been the custom in the early Church.

Submission of the Clergy. The act whereby the English *Convocations in 1532 surrendered to the demands of *Henry VIII. Its effect was to make the King supreme in ecclesiastical causes. In 1534 it was incorporated into the Submission of the Clergy Act 1533, which coupled it with restraint of appeals to Rome.

subordinationism. Teaching about the Godhead which regards either the Son as subordinate to the Father or the Holy Spirit as subordinate to both. It was a characteristic tendency in much teaching of the first three cents., but by the standards of orthodoxy established in the 4th cent. it came to be regarded as heretical. The issue was dealt with in the conflicts with *Arianism and then with the *Pneumatomachi.

substance. (1) In philosophy the word has played an important part since the time of *Aristotle, whose distinctions were taken over by the *Schoolmen. In general, *substantia* was the permanent, underlying reality as contrasted with its changing and perceptible accidents.
(2) In the Christian doctrine of the Godhead, the word is used to express the underlying Being, by which all Three Persons are One.
(3) In the medieval teaching on the *Eucharist, the substance of the Eucharistic species was contrasted with their '*accidents' (q.v.). See TRANSUBSTANTIATION.

Subunists. The party in 15th-cent. Bohemia which defended the practice of Communion in one kind against the *Utraquists.

Suburbicarian Dioceses. The seven dioceses in the immediate vicinity of Rome. The '*Cardinal Bishops' take their episcopal titles from these sees, but since 1962 they have not had pastoral charge of them. Their bishops probably had the right to take part in Papal elections as early as the 11th cent.

succentor. In *cathedral churches of the 'Old Foundation', the title usually given to the deputy of the *precentor. He is generally a *minor canon.

succession, apostolic. See APOSTOLIC SUCCESSION.

Sudan, Christianity in. The ancient Church of *Nubia, in Northern Sudan, died out in the 16th cent. Christianity returned to the Upper Nile in the 19th. In 1846 a *Vicariate Apostolic of Central Africa was created, and RC missionaries (including D. *Comboni) worked to establish the Church in Khartoum and up the Nile. Missionary work came to an end in the Mahdist rising of 1881, but began again when an Anglo-Egyptian condominion over Sudan was established in 1899. No direct evangelization was allowed in the mainly Muslim North, but in the South the *Verona Fathers returned and were joined by the *CMS and American *Presbyterian Mission. All education in the South was in the hands of missionaries. In 1946 government policy changed: the South was to be integrated with the Muslim North in preparation for independence, which came in 1956. In 1957 Church schools were nationalized, and the remaining missionaries expelled in 1964. Although the churches were deprived of clergy outside the main towns, Church membership increased as Southerners found a Christian identity over against the Muslim North. The *World Council of Churches and the All Africa Conferences of Churches largely brokered the 1972 Addis Ababa Agreement between the Sudanese government and the South Sudan Liberation Movement. It was, however, steadily abandoned by the government, hostilities were resumed in 1985, and in the 1990s civil war and famine rendered the position of the Christians desperate.

Sudbury, Simon. See SIMON OF SUDBURY.

Suetonius, Roman writer and until 121/2 secretary to the Emp. Hadrian. He is apparently one of the first pagan writers to mention Christianity.

suffragan bishop. The phrase denotes (1) any bishop in relation to his *archbishop or *metropolitan and (2) an assistant bishop appointed to help the bishop of the diocese. In the later Middle Ages such appointments were frequent and were made by the Pope. In England the Suffragan Bishops Act 1534 made provision for the appointment of suffragan bishops, but the office lapsed in 1592. In 1870 two suffragan bishops were consecrated under this Act, and in 1888 provision was made for lengthening the list of places from which suffragan bishops could take their titles. Since 1978 the Diocesan and General Synods have been involved in the creation of new suffragan sees.

Suger (c.1081–1151), Abbot of *St-Denis from 1122. Though of humble origins, for much of his life Suger was an influential adviser to the French Crown; during Louis VII's absence on the Second *Crusade he was one of the regents. His Life of Louis VI is a primary historical source. His new church at St-Denis, of which he left an account, was a crucial step in the development of Gothic architecture.

Suicer, Johann Kaspar (1620–84), Swiss Reformed theologian. His *Thesaurus*

Ecclesiasticus e Patribus Graecis (1682) is a work of great erudition and value.

suicide. The intentional taking of one's own life is not specifically condemned in the Bible apart from the general prohibition of killing, but nearly all the biblical suicides are associated with God's disfavour, and normal Jewish practice in the 1st cent. AD apparently included the shameful burial of suicides after dusk. Roman law opposed any moral condemnation of suicide. Christian authority took the opposite position, but gradually. From the late 4th cent. the Fathers condemn suicide forcibly and at length, St *Augustine seeking to dissuade Christian women from preferring suicide to rape. At about the same time posthumous sanctions appear in the context of Egyptian monasticism, and by the 6th cent. canon law denied suicides normal burial and prayers. Most medieval secular law augmented the canonical penalties with its own, e.g. putting suicide among the crimes involving loss of property. The sanctions were applied with varying degrees of rigour, but the status of suicide as a secular crime continued in England until 1961. The modern erosion of sanctions can be traced to the simple view, derived from Roman law and tradition, that suicide is intrinsically innocent, and to the more complex view that, while suicide is wrong, it is proper to feel pity for the suicide and hope for God's mercy on his behalf. RC canons no longer expressly exclude suicides from Christian burial, while those of the C of E allow burial with a special form of service. The *Catechism of the Catholic Church*, while condemning suicide, states positively that 'The Church prays for those who have taken their own lives'. Unless dispensed, attempted suicide remains a bar to RC ordination.

The Samaritans, a voluntary organization founded in 1953, gives help anonymously to those tempted to suicide.

See also DEAD, PRAYERS FOR THE, and DYING, CARE OF THE.

Suidas (c.AD 1000), 'lexicographer'. The idea that the Greek Lexicon which goes under this name was the work of a certain 'Suidas' is probably mistaken; the word apparently means an armoury of information. The Lexicon, completed c.1000, contains items of historical importance.

Sulpice, St. See SAINT-SULPICE, SOCIETY OF.

Sulpicius Severus (c.360–?c.430), historian and hagiographer. He was an advocate in Aquitaine before his conversion to asceticism (c.394). He then established a community on an estate in SW Gaul, where he lived a gentlemanly version of the religious life. His Life of St *Martin of Tours portrays him as a man of God, attested by miracles. Later Sulpicius added 3 letters and the *Dialogues*, in which Martin's thaumaturgical powers are compared with those of the Egyptian ascetics. He also wrote a *Chronicle*, which summarizes OT and Christian history to AD 400; it is an important source for the *Priscillianist movement.

Summa. Originally a title of reference books on various subjects, the term came to denote a compendium of theology, philosophy, or canon law. These compendia were used as handbooks in the Schools, much like the earlier *Sentences.

Summa Theologiae. The chief dogmatic work of St *Thomas Aquinas, known until recently as the 'Summa Theologica'. The three parts treat of God, of man's return to God, and of Christ as the way of man to God. The final sections, on the Sacraments and the Last Things, were left unfinished, the missing parts being supplied on the basis of Thomas's 'Commentary on the Sentences'.

Sumner, John Bird (1780–1862), Abp. of *Canterbury from 1848. Though unsympathetic towards R. D. *Hampden's theology, he did not oppose his appointment as Bp. of *Hereford, and took part in his consecration. In the controversy over the *Gorham Case he denied that Baptismal Regeneration was a fundamental doctrine of the C of E. In 1852 he presided over the Upper House of *Convocation when it met for business for the first time in 135 years.

Sundar Singh, Sadhu (1889–c.1929), Indian Christian and mystic. Born of wealthy Sikh parents, he was converted and baptized in the C of E in 1905. He donned the robe of a Sadhu (i.e. 'holy man') in an attempt to present Christianity in a Hindu form. He travelled widely in India and tried to evangelize Tibet. In CW, feast day, 19 June.

Sunday. Sunday replaced the Jewish *Sabbath mainly in commemoration of Christ's Resurrection on this day. Already in NT times St *Paul and the Christians of Troas assembled on the first day of the week 'to break bread' (Acts 20: 7), and in Rev. (1: 10) it is called 'the Lord's day'.

The observance of Sunday as a day of rest began to be regulated by ecclesiastical legislation early in the 4th cent., and in 321 *Constantine forbade townspeople to work on Sundays, though permitting farm labour. From the 6th to the 13th cent. ecclesiastical legislation became stricter, also enforcing attendance at Mass; it was supported by the infliction of severe penalties by the civil authorities. From the 13th cent. *dispensations became common. According to current RC canon law, the faithful are normally obliged to hear Mass on Sunday or on the previous evening and to abstain from 'work or business that would inhibit the worship to be given to God, the joy proper to the Lord's Day, or the due relaxation of mind and body'.

The Protestant Churches did not at first introduce special Sunday legislation, but the abuse of Sunday led to a reaction in some places and the development of *Sabbatarianism (q.v.). In the 19th cent. Sunday was still mainly devoted to the duties of piety, but the secularization of life in the 20th cent. reduced its religious observance. Increased leisure in the Western world has been accompanied by pressure to abolish restrictions on both recreational and commercial activities on Sundays.

Sunday letter. In ecclesiastical calendars that one of the seven letters A to G, allotted to the days of the year in rotation (1 Jan. = A, etc.) which coincides with the Sundays in a given year.

Sunday Schools. Schools, mainly for children, in which instruction, now primarily religious, is given on Sunday; they are usually held in conjunction with a parish or congregation. Although there are isolated earlier examples of schools for poor children on Sundays, the movement owed its success to R. *Raikes, who, along with the local incumbent, engaged four women in 1780 to instruct the children of Gloucester in reading and the (BCP) *Catechism on Sundays. His example was followed both in Europe and America. In England two national societies were founded on an interdenominational basis: the Sunday School Society (1783) to give financial support to individual schools, and the Sunday School Union (1803) to help provide books and materials. Most schools, however, were locally supported and after the early 1800s interdenominational co-operation was replaced by denominational rivalry. The desire of Anglicans to introduce more specifically C of E teaching led to the formation in 1843 of the Sunday School Institute (incorporated into the *National Society in 1936). In 1966 the (National from 1921) Sunday School Union became the National Christian Education Council.

supererogation, works of. In RC *moral theology, acts which are not enjoined as of strict obligation, and are therefore not simply good as opposed to bad, but better as opposed to good. Thus the '*Counsels of Evangelical Perfection' are held to be not of duty but of supererogation.

superintendents. In the reformed Church of Scotland, officials appointed under the *First Book of *Discipline* (1560) to oversee districts roughly corresponding to the old dioceses. While they enjoyed some superiority over other ministers, they differed from diocesan bishops in being admitted to office by fellow-presbyters, in not possessing exclusive powers of ordination, and in being subject to the control and censure of other ministers.

In the *Lutheran Churches, officials of the same name were created from an early date for similar reasons and with similar functions; they were appointed by, and responsible to, the civil power. See also GENERAL SUPERINTENDENT.

In English *Methodism, in J. *Wesley's lifetime, senior travelling preachers with the title of 'Assistant', supervised a 'Circuit' (localized group of societies). Since the 1790s these ministers have been called 'Superintendents'. In American Methodism, the title of Superintendent or General Superintendent was originally applied to the two supervising ministers of the whole Church, but was soon replaced by that of 'Bishop'. Since 1908 District Superintendents have supervised Districts within the American regional Conferences.

superior. One who has authority over others by virtue of his ecclesiastical rank.

The term is commonly used of the heads of certain religious orders or congregations.

Supper, Last. See LAST SUPPER.

Suppression of the Monasteries. See DISSOLUTION OF THE MONASTERIES.

Supralapsarianism (or 'Antelapsarianism'). The form of the *Calvinistic doctrine of *predestination which maintains that God decreed the election and non-election of individuals even before the *Fall.

Supremacy, Acts of. The Supremacy of the Crown Act 1534 confirmed to *Henry VIII and his successors the title of 'the only supreme head in earth of the Church of England'. It was repealed under *Mary. *Elizabeth I's Act of Supremacy 1558, passed in 1559, declared the Queen to be 'the only supreme governor of this realm ... as well in all spiritual or ecclesiastical things or causes as temporal'.

Surin, Jean-Joseph (1600–65), French *Jesuit mystic and spiritual writer. In 1634 he was sent to Loudun to exorcize some *Ursulines believed to be possessed by the devil. He acted as spiritual director to the superior, and she recovered. Surin experienced some 20 years of mental trials, alternating between believing himself damned (with an attempt at *suicide) and to be receiving Divine graces; modern scholars suspect manic depressive illness. He seems, however, to have had some genuine mystical experiences. His writings advocate the practice of the presence of God and the prayer of contemplation in which the soul, abandoned to the direction of the Holy Spirit, loses itself in the love of God.

surplice. A loose white liturgical garment, with wide sleeves. It developed from the *alb, allowing room for warm clothes underneath. From the 12th cent. it came to be the distinctive dress of the lower clergy and to be used by priests outside Mass. It is now worn by all clerics, and is also used by laymen, e.g. in choir. Its use in the C of E was a matter of controversy in the reign of *Elizabeth I, but is now accepted. See VESTIARIAN CONTROVERSY.

surplice fees. The fees which are payable to the incumbent of a parish for marriages and burials, whoever performs the service.

surrogate. In ecclesiastical usage, the

clergyman or other person appointed by the bishop as his deputy to grant licences for marriages without *banns.

Sursum Corda (Lat., 'Lift up your hearts'). In the Eucharist the words addressed by the celebrant to the congregation immediately before the *Preface.

Susanna, Book of. A short Book of the *Apocrypha, reckoned in the *Vulgate as Dan. 13. It tells of the false accusation of adultery brought against Susanna, her condemnation, and her final deliverance by the sagacity of Daniel. In the Church the incident symbolizes the saved soul.

Susanna, St (3rd cent.), Roman martyr. According to legend, she was put to death for refusing to marry a pagan relative of *Diocletian. Feast day, 11 Aug.

Suso, Bl Henry. See HENRY SUSO, BL.

suspension. In the RC Church, one of the censures or 'medicinal' *penalties which may be imposed upon a cleric. It prohibits the exercise of some or all the functions of *Orders, the powers of governance, and the rights and functions attaching to an office. In the C of E it is one of the five censures which under the *Ecclesiastical Jurisdiction Measure 1963 may be imposed on a cleric after conviction for an offence not involving doctrine, ritual, or ceremonial.

Suvermerian. A word applied by the Saxon Reformers to certain Swiss Protestant extremists.

swastika. A symbol in the form of a cross of equal arms, each of which is bent at right angles. It was probably in origin a charm for attracting good luck and averting misfortune; it is found on vases dating from c.4000–3000 BC. In modern times it was adopted as the official symbol of the National Socialist Party in Germany.

Sweden, Christianity in. About 830 St *Anskar established a Church near Stockholm, but this did not survive. A more lasting mission was initiated by St Sigfrid, a monk from England, who baptized King Olov Skötkonung c.1000. The conversion of the country was virtually complete by the early 12th cent. In 1104 Asker, Bp. of *Lund, became Abp. of the newly constituted Nordic province, and in 1164 *Uppsala became an archbishopric independent of Lund (then in *Denmark).

The Reformation was gradual and closely associated with political events. Gustav Vasa, King of Sweden 1523–60, was in need of funds and anxious to curb the power of the bishops. Under his protection Olaus *Petri was appointed city clerk at Stockholm in 1524, and in 1527 at the Diet of Västerås the 'superfluous' revenue of the bishops, cathedrals, and monastic houses was vested in the King. In 1531 Olaus Petri's brother Laurentius was consecrated Abp. of Uppsala without Papal sanction, though the *apostolic succession was maintained through the participation of Petrus Magni, Bp. of Västerås. Soon the monasteries disappeared and the bishops became State officials, but only in 1593 did the Swedes adopt the *Augsburg Confession, so committing themselves to *Lutheran dogma.

Towards the end of the 17th cent. *Pietism became an influence in Sweden, and to combat it the Conventicle Proclamation of 1726 restricted meetings for religious purposes. E. *Swedenborg tried to combine rationalism and mysticism to form a new moral religion. The 1860 Dissenter Act provided freedom of worship and allowed the formation of Christian denominations. In 1878 P. P. *Waldenström broke with the Church of Sweden and founded a free Lutheran Church, the *Svenska Missionsförbundet* (Swedish Mission Covenant Church), which now has its own ministers and sacraments. In the early 20th cent. there was a revival of theological scholarship, led by N. *Söderblom, Abp. of Uppsala, who played a leading part in the *Ecumenical Movement. The majority of the population still belongs to the Church of Sweden, which was disestablished in 2000. The next largest denomination is the RC Church, followed by the *Orthodox, the Swedish Mission Covenant Church, and the *Pentecostals.

Swedenborg, Emanuel (1688–1772), Swedish scientist and mystical thinker. While employed at the Swedish Board of Mines (1716–47), he anticipated various later scientific hypotheses and discoveries; he was also increasingly concerned to show by scientific analysis that the Universe had a fundamentally spiritual structure. In 1743–5 he became conscious of direct contact with the spiritual world and felt that he was commissioned to make known his doctrines to the world at large. The agency was to be the New Church, organized not as a body separate from the existing Churches, but as a spiritual fraternity of all those, of whatever ecclesiastical allegiance, who accepted his doctrines. The basis of his system was a 'doctrine of correspondence' between the physical and spiritual worlds. He envisaged the spiritual world as containing various groupings of deceased human beings which made up a single great human being. He accepted Christ as the greatest manifestation of humanity, but rejected the doctrine of the *Atonement.

Among the earliest disseminators of his teaching were two C of E clergymen, but the formal creation of a separate body, known as the New Jerusalem Church, was the work of five ex-Wesleyan preachers in London in 1787. In the USA the first congregation was formed in Baltimore in 1792. There are also bodies of Swedenborgians in mainland Europe, *Africa, *Australia, *Canada, *Japan, and South America. They claim world membership of c.65,000.

Swift, Jonathan (1667–1745), Dean of St Patrick's, *Dublin, from 1713, and satirist. In politics he was a Whig, but he wrote against the *Occasional Conformity Bill in 1708, and he used his satirical power for religious ends in his *Argument to Prove the Inconvenience of Abolishing Christianity* (1708). He is popularly remembered as the author of *Gulliver's Travels* (1726).

Swiss Brethren. A group of *Anabaptists who reintroduced believers' Baptism as the basis of Church fellowship at Zollikon (near Zurich) in 1525. The name originally designated congregations in the German-speaking areas of Switzerland, but it came to be used also of similar groups in the Austrian Tyrol, S. Germany, and Alsace. Their religious tenets were formulated in the Schleitheim Confession or 'Brotherly Union of a Number of the Children of God' (1527). Though they survived in Switzerland, most migrated to Germany, the *Netherlands, and the *United States of America, where they form part of the *Mennonites.

Swiss Guard. The military guardians of the Papal Palace. The corps, instituted by

*Julius II (1503–13), consists of about 100 men, recruited from all the Swiss cantons.

Swithun, St (d. 862), also 'Swithin', Bp. of *Winchester from 852. Little is known of his life. Originally buried 'humbly' outside the walls of the minster, in 971 his body was translated to a shrine in the cathedral; in 1093 his relics were again translated but disappeared when his shrine was destroyed at the Reformation (1538). The popular belief that the weather on St Swithun's day (15 July) will be that for the next 40 days may have arisen from a similar attribution to the feast of SS. Processus and Martinian, which coincides with the anniversary of Swithun's death (2 July).

Sword of the Spirit. A RC social movement inaugurated by Card. A. *Hinsley in 1940. Its aims were supported by the Abps. of *Canterbury and *York and the Moderator of the Free Churches, but the initial collaboration between RCs and other groups was restricted in 1941. In 1965 it became the Catholic Institute for International Relations.

Syllabus Errorum. A set of 80 theses, already condemned in earlier pronouncements of *Pius IX and promulgated as erroneous in 1864. They covered a wide area, including pantheism, rationalism, the Church and its rights, civil society and its relation to the Church, the temporal power of the Pope, and modern liberalism. The covering letter seemed to make the Syllabus dogmatically binding. Its issue aroused a storm of protest.

Sylvester I, St, Bp. of Rome from 314 to 335. Little is known of him. Later legend asserts that he baptized *Constantine (cleansing him from physical leprosy) at the Baptistery of the *Lateran and established the Lateran church as the cathedral of Rome on land given him by the Emperor. He is also the reputed recipient of the *Donation of Constantine. Feast day in the W., 31 Dec.; in the E., 2 Jan.

Sylvester II (c.940–1003), Pope. Gerbert is important both as a scholar and as a Churchman. It appears that in the school at *Reims he was the first master in Europe to use a substantial part of the logical works of *Aristotle and *Boethius as a practical system of education, and he wrote extensively on mathematics. He became Abp. of

Reims in 991, of *Ravenna in 998, and Pope in 999. He owed these promotions to the Emp. Otto III, and his choice of name was in conscious imitation of *Sylvester I, who had long been regarded as the pattern of Papal co-operation with the Emperor. As Pope, he opposed *simony and upheld clerical *celibacy, and did much to strengthen the Church in E. Europe. He established archbishoprics in Gniezno (Poland) and Esztergom (Hungary) and recognized St *Stephen of Hungary as king.

Sylvestrines. A monastic *Congregation which follows the Rule of St *Benedict. It was founded in 1231 by St Sylvester Gozzolini; it joined the Benedictine Confederation in 1973.

Symeon. See SIMEON.

Symmachus (probably later 2nd cent.), translator of the Greek version of the OT reproduced in the 4th column of *Origen's *Hexapla. He preferred a readable style and palatable rendering to verbal accuracy, and he modified the anthropomorphic expressions of the Hebrew text.

Symmachus, St (d. 514), Pope from 498. He was opposed by a rival candidate, who secured the support of *Theodoric, but in 507 Theodoric withdrew his opposition. In the latter part of his pontificate Symmachus devoted himself to the defence of the Catholic faith against the *Henoticon of *Zeno and against the *Manichaeans, whom he expelled from Rome. He sent the *pallium to *Caesarius of Arles, the first bishop outside Italy to receive the privilege. He introduced the singing of the *Gloria in excelsis at Mass on Sundays and the feasts of martyrs (but only by bishops). Feast day, 19 July.

synagogue. The Jews may have introduced synagogues as regular meeting places for worship during the Babylonian exile (6th cent. BC), when they could no longer take part in the *Temple worship at Jerusalem, but the first clear evidence of synagogue building comes from Egypt in the Hellenistic period. The worship of the synagogue has always been non-sacrificial; it consists chiefly of readings from Scripture, with prayers, canticles, and sometimes a sermon. Christ took part in synagogue worship and often preached or taught in the synagogue. According to the account in

Acts, it was St *Paul's normal practice first to preach in the synagogue in the places he visited and turn to the Gentiles only after the Jews had failed to respond to his message.

Synapte. In the E. Church, a prayer in the form of a *litany used in the Liturgy and other services.

Synaxarion. (1) In the E. Church, a short account of a saint or feast appointed to be read at the early morning service (*Orthros); (2) the book containing these passages ('The Greater Synaxarion'); (3) another book which merely enumerates the feasts to be observed, with a reference to the appropriate biblical lessons ('The Lesser Synaxarion').

synaxis. An assembly for public worship. In the E. Church the term includes the Eucharist; in the W. it was used in early times especially of the 'aliturgical synaxis', or non-Eucharistic service, consisting of Psalms, readings from the Bible, and prayers.

syncellus. In the Byzantine Church, an ecclesiastic who lived continually with a bishop, especially in the capacity of a domestic chaplain and in order to bear witness to the purity of the bishop's moral life. Later the word was used of a dignitary associated as counsellor with a prelate who subsequently succeeded to his office.

syncretism. The attempt to combine opposing doctrines and practices, especially in reference to philosophical and religious systems. The term came into prominence in the 17th cent. when it was applied to the teaching of G. *Calixtus (q.v.).

synergism. The teaching of P. *Melanchthon that in the act of conversion the human will can co-operate with the Holy Spirit and God's grace.

Synesius (c.370–c.413), Bp. of Ptolemais. A native of Cyrene, he was descended from an ancient family. In 403/4 he married a Christian. Having won the confidence of his fellow-countrymen by a successful embassy to the Imperial court, c.410 he was chosen Bp. of Ptolemais in Cyrenaica. After some hesitation, he was consecrated, without engaging to give up either his wife or his philosophical doctrines. Before he became a bishop he wrote a number of philosophical treatises, none of which betray anything distinctively Christian. He also wrote nine hymns; the tenth in the collection, the well-known 'Lord Jesus, think on me', is the work of a copyist. His letters are a major source for the study of provincial Church life.

Synod. See COUNCIL. For the General Synod of the C of E, see the following entry.

Synodical Government. The system of government of the C of E introduced by the Synodical Government Measure 1969, which took effect in 1970. A General Synod took over all the powers of the *Church Assembly and some of those of the *Convocations. It is comprised of a House of Bishops consisting of the members of the Upper Houses of the Convocations of Canterbury and York, a House of Clergy consisting of the two Lower Houses of the Convocations, somewhat reduced in size, and a House of Laity elected by members of the Houses of Laity of the deanery synods. Matters concerning doctrinal formulas, church services, and the administration of the Sacraments can be approved only in terms proposed by the House of Bishops. Diocesan conferences were replaced by diocesan synods, each consisting of the Bishop, the House of Clergy, and the House of Laity. Members of the two latter are elected by the respective Houses of the deanery synods. In 1980 a House of Bishops was constituted; it consists of the diocesan Bishop, every *suffragan bishop, and such other bishops working in the diocese as the diocesan Bishop may invite. The former ruridecanal conferences were replaced by deanery synods. The base of the system remains the electoral roll of each parish from which elections are made to the deanery synod and the *parochial church council.

Synodicon. (1) An act of a synod or a collection of such acts. (2) A liturgical text used in the E. Church on the Feast of *Orthodoxy. Composed c. 843 by Patr. Methodius I, it has frequently been modified.

Synoptic Problem. The problem of the relationship between the three 'Synoptic Gospels' (Mt., Mk., Lk.) posed by the amount of subject matter which they share and the many similarities in wording and order. In modern times most scholars have held (1) that Mk. was the earliest of the Synoptic Gospels and that it was used as a source by Mt. and Lk., and (2) that for the non-Marcan material common to Mt. and Lk., their authors drew independently on a lost common source (or sources) known as '*Q' (q.v.). This 'two-document hypothesis' (that Mt. and Lk. are based on Mk. and 'Q') was developed mainly in Germany in the 19th cent., was given classic expression by B. H. *Streeter, and came to be almost universally accepted. In the second half of the 20th cent. a few scholars challenged the priority of Mk. and several denied the existence of 'Q'.

synteresis. A technical term used by *Scholastic theologians for our knowledge of the first principles of moral action.

Syriac. A branch of *Aramaic which was spoken in *Edessa and its neighbourhood from shortly before the beginning of the Christian era. It was used extensively in the early Church because of the active Christian communities in these parts. Most of the surviving literature is Christian and a number of Greek patristic works survive only in Syriac translation. It has remained the language of the liturgy in the *Church of the East and the *Syrian Orthodox Church. When Arabic became the current vernacular, Syriac became an artificial language. See also the following entry.

Syriac Versions of the Bible. These are of special value to textual critics because of their early date and the natural accuracy of Syriac scholars. The chief versions of the OT are: (1) The *Peshitta, perhaps made in part by Jews for the Jewish community at *Edessa, probably in the early 2nd cent. Apart from Proverbs (where the *Targum derives from the Peshitta), this version was used only by Syriac-speaking Christians, for whom it is still the authorized version. (2) The Syro-Hexapla, a close rendering of the LXX text in *Origen's *Hexapla, made at *Alexandria c.616–17 by Paul, *Syrian Orthodox Bp. of Tella in Mesopotamia.

The Gospels were known in a Syriac version of *Tatian's *Diatessaron and in a translation of the four Gospels separately, known as the *Old Syriac Version. The latter is probably not earlier than 200 and is independent of, and later than, the Syriac

Diatessaron. It is generally held to be the basis of the Peshitta (q.v.). There were two further versions of the NT: the *Philoxenian in 508, and the *Harklean in 616.

Syrian Catholics. A small body of *Uniats descended from the *Syrian Orthodox. The present Church traces its existence to the accession of Mar Michael Garweh, who had become a RC, to the archbishopric of Aleppo in 1783.

Syrian Orthodox Church. One of the *Oriental Orthodox Churches. It emerged as a separate body in the aftermath of the Council of *Chalcedon (451), whose Christology it refused to accept. An independent hierarchy under the Patr. of *Antioch was built up in the 6th cent. Numbers were reduced in the 14th cent. by Mongol invasions, in the 18th cent. by the establishment of a separate *Uniat patriarchate (see SYRIAN CATHOLICS), and at the turn of the 20th cent. by massacres at the hands of the Turks. They may now number c.200,000 in the Middle East, 100,000 in Europe and N.

and S. America, and perhaps a million in South *India (*Malabar Christians). Since the 1960s large numbers have emigrated to W. Europe. Their liturgical language is Syriac. They are also known as *Jacobites or *Monophysites (qq.v).

Syrian text of the NT. The name given by B. F. *Westcott and F. J. A. *Hort to an edition of the Greek text of the NT which they held was made in or near Antioch in Syria c.300, and of which *Lucian of Antioch was the probable author.

Syro-Chaldeans. An alternative name for the *Chaldean Christians.

Syro-Hexapla. See SYRIAC VERSIONS OF THE BIBLE.

syzygy. A word used by the *Gnostics for a pair of cosmological opposites, e.g. male and female. It was held that the universe had come into being through the interaction of such opposites.

Tabernacle (Jewish), also called the 'tent of meeting'. The portable shrine said to have been constructed under *Moses' direction during the wilderness wanderings. Theologically it was held to embody the presence of God in the midst of His people. The writer of Heb. used the imagery of the Tabernacle to explain the meaning of Christ's atoning work (cf. Heb. 1: 9–10: 25).

Tabernacle (Christian). The word now denotes the box placed on the altar which contains the vessels in which the Blessed Sacrament is reserved in RC churches. See also RESERVATION.

Tabernacles, Feast of. One of the great feasts of the Jewish year.

table, Communion. See COMMUNION TABLE.

Tablet. A RC weekly founded in 1840.

Taborites. The extreme party of the *Hussites, so called from their fortified stronghold south of Prague to which they gave the OT name of Mount Tabor (Jgs. 4: 6–14). They gained the ascendancy after the death of King Wenceslaus (1419) and, under their leader Žižka, began to spread the 'Kingdom of God' by force of arms. They split into two parties after Žižka's death (1424): the more moderate joined the Catholics after the Compactata of Prague (1433; see UTRAQUISM); the radicals were defeated at Lipany in 1434 and lost influence, though some elements of their tradition were inherited by the *Bohemian Brethren.

Tacitus, Cornelius (c. 55-after c. 113), Roman historian. In his *Annals* (15. 44), he describes

*Nero's persecution of the Christians of Rome as scapegoats for the fire in the city (AD 64). The passage is the earliest non-Christian reference to the Crucifixion.

Tait, Archibald Campbell (1811–82), Abp. of *Canterbury from 1868. At Oxford in 1841 he was one of the four tutors who protested against *Tract 90* (see TRACTARIANISM), and as Bp. of London (1856–68) he withdrew the licence of Alfred Poole, curate of St Barnabas, Pimlico, for hearing confessions. He publicly deprecated *Essays and Reviews* (1860), but in 1864 he sided with the majority on the *Judicial Committee of the Privy Council in favour of two of the essayists. As Archbishop he used his gifts of statesmanship to secure the best possible terms for the disestablished Church of *Ireland. The *Public Worship Regulation Act 1874 was mainly his creation.

Taizé Community. An ecumenical monastic community founded in 1940 by Roger Schutz-Marsauche (b. 1915). His aim was to open up ways of healing the divisions between Christians and through the reconciliation of Christians to overcome conflicts within humanity. Acquiring a house in Taizé in SE France, he began by sheltering Jews and other refugees. The first brothers took life-vows in 1949. They were all Protestants, but since 1969 they have been joined by RCs. Since 1958 the community has welcomed young people at Taizé in huge numbers. Weekly intercontinental meetings are centred on three set times of prayer each day in the Church of Reconciliation. Each year the brothers lead a 'European Meeting' where thousands of young people are welcomed for several days by parishes of a major city.

Talbot, Edward Stuart (1844–1934), Anglican bishop. The first Warden of Keble College, Oxford (1870–88), and then Vicar of Leeds (1888–95), he became Bp. of *Rochester in 1895. His main work here was the division of the diocese and the creation of the see of *Southwark, of which he became bishop in 1905. From 1911 to 1923 he was Bp. of *Winchester. He promoted moderate *High Church principles throughout his life.

Talbot House ('*Toc H') was founded in memory of his son, Gilbert Talbot (1891–1915).

Tall Brothers. Four monks who led the *Origenist movement in Egypt at the end of the 4th cent. In 399 they made their way from the *Nitrian Desert to *Alexandria and later went to *Constantinople, where St John *Chrysostom supported them.

Talleyrand-Périgord, Charles Maurice de (1754–1838), Prince of Benevento. In 1789 he was made Bp. of Autun. He joined the cause of the Revolution and became a member of the Constitutional Assembly, taking the oath to the *Civil Constitution and consecrating persons prepared to do likewise to fill the vacated bishoprics. In 1791 he was constrained to resign his see and in 1792 he was excommunicated. He became Foreign Minister in 1796, took charge of the provisional government of France in 1814, and was French Ambassador to England from 1830 to 1834.

Tallis, Thomas (c.1505–85), composer. He was organist at Waltham Abbey before its dissolution in 1540, and soon afterwards became a Gentleman of the *Chapel Royal. His main compositions are vocal works; they are mostly set to Latin words but include a number of settings for the Anglican service, responses and anthems which, in their simplicity of form, reflect T. *Cranmer's desire for intelligible word-setting.

Talmud. The Jewish compilations which embody the *Mishnah, or oral teaching of the Jews, and the Gemara, or collection of discussions on the Mishnah. The two main forms of the Talmud, the Palestinian and the Babylonian, both date from the 5th cent. AD, but include earlier material.

Tambaram Conference. The missionary conference, convened by the International Missionary Council, which met at Tambaram, near Madras, in 1938.

Tametsi. The *Tridentine decree of 1563 prescribing the formal mode of celebrating matrimony. It aimed at repressing *clandestinity. It took effect only after it had been officially published in a parish, and it was not normally published in Protestant countries. It was superseded in 1908 by the provisions of *Ne Temere.

Tanner, Thomas (1674–1735), English antiquary, from 1732 Bp. of *St Asaph. His *Notitia Monastica* (1695) is an erudite account of the medieval religious houses in England and Wales. His *Bibliotheca Britannico-Hibernica* (published by D. *Wilkins in 1748) gives an account of British writers to the beginning of the 17th cent.; it long remained a standard work.

Tantum ergo. The last two verses of St *Thomas Aquinas's hymn '*Pange lingua gloriosi', often used at *Benediction in the RC Church. One English translation begins 'Therefore we, before Him bending'.

Tarasius, St (d. 806), Patr. of *Constantinople from 784. He sought to restore good relations with the W. Church and persuaded the Empress Irene to convoke a General Council in concert with Pope *Hadrian I; it met at *Nicaea in 787 under his presidency. He was attacked for laxity by *Theodore of Studios. Feast day, 25 Feb.

Targum. The *Aramaic interpretative translations of the OT made when Hebrew had ceased to be the normal medium of speech among the Jews.

Tarsicius, St (3rd-4th cent.), martyr. According to tradition, he was killed by a mob in *Rome while carrying the Blessed Sacrament rather than surrender it to profanation. Feast day, 15 Aug.

Tarsus. Pompey made this ancient city of Asia Minor the capital of the Roman province of Cilicia in 67 BC. It became the seat of a *Stoic philosophical school and was the birthplace of St *Paul.

Tasso, Torquato (1544-95), Italian poet. He entered the service of Card. Luigi d'Este in 1565, but he was able to devote much of his time to his great epic, *Gerusalemme liberata*, a poem on the first *Crusade, completed in 1574. He later suffered from religious scruples and persecution mania; he died shortly before receiving the crown of the Poet Laureate intended for him by *Clement VIII.

Tate, Nahum (1652-1715), and **Brady, Nicholas** (1659-1726), authors of the *New Version of the Psalms* (1696). Both were Irish Protestants. Tate became Poet Laureate in 1692. Brady, who had been ordained by 1688, was chaplain to William III, Mary, and Queen *Anne. The *New Version* is a versification of the Psalter according to the artificial taste of the period. It gradually supplanted the rendering of T. *Sternhold and J. Hop-

kins and was widely used until the early 19th cent.

Tatian (2nd cent.), *Apologist and rigorist. Of Middle Eastern origin, he became a Christian in Rome between 150 and 165. About 172 he returned to the E., where he is said to have founded the *Encratites. His *Oratio ad Graecos* is a defence of the antiquity and purity of Christianity, combined with an attack on Greek civilization. His chief claim to fame is his *Diatessaron* (q.v.).

Tattam, Henry (1789-1868), English Coptic scholar. He recovered from the *Nitrian Desert several important Coptic and Syriac MSS, including a 5th cent. codex of the *Old Syriac text of the Gospels.

Tauler, John (d. 1361), German spiritual teacher. He was probably born near the end of the 13th cent. He joined the *Dominican Order at Strasbourg. He was famous as a preacher and director of nuns. Apart from his sermons and one letter, the ascription to him of other works is now rejected. His spirituality is notable for its balance between inwardness (detachment, the birth of God in the soul, and living in the 'ground' of the soul) and the external practice of the virtues and pious exercises. He had a lasting influence on later German piety, both Catholic and Protestant.

Tausen, Hans (1494-1561), Reformer, the 'Danish Luther'. He was a *Hospitaller, but came under the influence of M. *Luther when studying at *Wittenberg. On his return to *Denmark he was imprisoned for teaching novel doctrines. On his release, he discarded his religious habit and, becoming chaplain to King Frederick I (1526), he married and used Danish in Church services. In 1529 he secured the support of the Danish National Assembly. He and his supporters drew up a Confession of 43 Articles, but this was later replaced by the more moderate *Augsburg Confession. In 1535 Tausen published a Danish translation of the Pentateuch. In 1542 he was made Bp. of Ribe.

Taverner's Bible. The English translation of the Bible issued in 1539 by Richard Taverner. It was a revision of *Matthew's Bible.

tax-collector, tax-gatherer. Terms used in modern English versions of the Bible to replace *publican (q.v.).

Taylor, James Hudson (1832–1905), founder of the *China Inland Mission. A medical man who felt called to be a missionary, he sailed for China in 1853 under the auspices of the Chinese Evangelization Society. He returned to England in 1860 and in 1865 founded the interdenominational China Inland Mission. He went back to China, conforming as far as he could to Chinese habits of life, and carrying missionary work into the heart of the country.

Taylor, Jeremy (1613–67), Anglican bishop and writer. He was chaplain to *Charles I, rector of Uppingham, and then chaplain in the Royalist army. After a short imprisonment he retired in 1645 to Wales, where he lived as chaplain to Lord Carbery at Golden Grove. In 1660 he was appointed Bp. of Down and Connor and vice-chancellor of *Dublin University, and in 1661 he received the further see of Dromore. His fame rests mainly on his devotional writings, especially *The Rule and Exercise of Holy Living* (1650) and *The Rule and Exercise of Holy Dying* (1651). They are characteristic expressions of Anglican spirituality in their insistence on a well-ordered piety which stresses temperance and moderation. His theological works are less felicitous. Feast day in some Anglican Churches, 13 Aug.

Taylor, John (1694–1761), Dissenting minister. His *Hebrew Concordance* (1754–7) was designed to serve also the purposes of a lexicon and marked an advance in the study of Hebrew roots. His *Scripture Doctrine of Original Sin* (1740), which circulated widely in both America and Britain, undermined the foundations of the *Calvinist system and helped to prepare the way for the *Unitarian Movement in American Congregationalism.

Teaching of the Twelve Apostles, The. The full title of the work commonly known as the *Didache (q.v.).

team ministry. In the C of E since 1968, where a pastoral scheme has been made, the cure of souls in the area of a benefice or plurality may be shared by a team consisting of the incumbent of the benefice, known as the team rector, and one or more other ministers, with the title of vicar and the status of an incumbent of a benefice.

Te Deum. A Latin hymn to the Father and the Son, in rhythmical prose. Verses 22 ff. are petitions, appended to the original at an early date. The ascription of the hymn to Sts *Ambrose and *Augustine is rejected by modern scholars. Its use in the *Office is mentioned in the Rule of St *Benedict. The BCP includes in *Mattins the English translation 'We praise thee, O God'. Modern Anglican liturgies retain its use at Morning Prayer, at least on some occasions, often without the concluding verses, and the central section figures in some *burial services.

Te Igitur (Lat., 'Thee, therefore'), the first words of the prayer which was long regarded as the opening section of the *Canon of the Mass, and hence also the name of the first section of the Canon.

Teilhard de Chardin, Pierre (1881–1955), French *Jesuit theologian and scientist. He worked for many years in China, where he gained a reputation as a palaeontologist; his last years were spent in America. His theological works appeared only after his death, beginning with *Le Phénomène humain* (1955; Eng. tr., *The Phenomenon of Man*, 1959). They made a powerful impression as a new synthesis of science and religion. The universe is seen as an evolutionary process in which the movement is always towards systems of greater complexity. Correlated with this movement towards complexity is the movement towards higher levels of consciousness. The whole process has included several critical moments or thresholds at which leaps to new levels have been made. Such thresholds were the emergence of life on earth and then the emergence of rational self-consciousness in man. This latter emergence has special significance, since it means that evolution no longer takes place in accordance with the laws of nature only, but that man now takes part in directing it. The whole process moves towards a fulfilment in which all things will be gathered up in God.

Teilo, St (6th cent.), patron saint and Bp. of *Llandaff. He is credited with having been consecrated bishop at *Jerusalem while on a pilgrimage to Palestine and (a less unlikely tradition) with having visited St *Samson at Dol. He is also said to have succeeded St *Dubricius in the see of Llandaff in 495. Feast day, 9 Feb.

teinds. The Scottish equivalent of *tithes.

Telemachus, St. According to *Theodoret, Telemachus was an E. monk who, seeking to end the gladiatorial shows at Rome, in 391 entered the arena to separate the combatants and was killed by the spectators. Feast day, 1 Jan.

teleology. The science of ends or final causes, and especially the doctrine that the universe embodies design and purpose. This doctrine forms the basis of the modern argument from design (known as the 'physico-theological' or the 'teleological argument') for the existence of God. In its classic form it sets out from the observation that every biological species is apparently designed to serve its own needs and argues therefrom to an intelligent Creator.

Telesio, Bernardino (1509–88), Italian humanist. In 1566 he founded a scientific academy at Naples. His doctrines were based on an extreme empiricism, but he built up a speculative system in which the *Aristotelian doctrine of matter and form was replaced by one of matter and force.

Telesphorus, St (d. *c.*137), Bp. of Rome from *c.*127. He is the only 2nd-cent. Pope whose martyrdom is well attested. Feast day in the E., 22 Feb.; in the W., 2 or 5 Jan., suppressed in 1969.

temperance. Restraint of the appetites and passions in accordance with reason. It is one of the four *cardinal virtues. For the Christian, temperance in its physical aspects is linked with the need for self-control of the body, regarded as a 'temple of the Holy Spirit'.

The 'temperance societies', founded to foster abstinence from alcohol, date from the 19th cent. The first American temperance society was founded at Saratoga, NY, in 1808, but the formation of a nationwide movement was largely due to L. *Beecher. The United States Temperance Union, created in 1833, in 1836 became the American Temperance Union (to accommodate the Canadian societies). There were divisions as to whether the aim should be temperance or total abstinence, but the latter was accepted. The manufacture, sale, and transportation of intoxicating liquor was forbidden in the USA from 1919 to 1933. The prohibition was unpopular and discredited the leaders of the temperance societies. More recently societies (including the International Temperance Society founded in 1947) have concerned themselves with problems associated with alcohol, tobacco, and drugs. Similar temperance societies were founded in Britain, where coffee taverns were established as alternatives to public houses, but their influence was never so great as those in America.

Templars (or Knights Templar). The 'Poor Knights of Christ and of the Temple of Solomon', one of the two chief Military Orders of medieval Christendom. The original nucleus consisted of Hugh de Payens, a knight of Champagne, and eight companions who *c.*1119 bound themselves by a solemn vow to protect pilgrims on the public roads of the Holy Land. They were given quarters on the site of Solomon's *Temple. At the Council of Troyes (1129) approval was given to their Rule, said to have been drawn up by St *Bernard. They soon increased in influence and wealth, acquiring property in every part of Christendom. They were also granted extensive privileges by the Papacy. In the *Crusader States of the 12th and 13th cents. the professional forces of the Templars and the *Hospitallers played an important role in campaigns.

The integrity and credit of the Order led to its being trusted as a banking house. Its wealth led to its ruin after the fall of Acre (1291). Philip IV of France coveted its riches; aided by a renegade Templar he brought charges of sodomy, blasphemy, and heresy against the Order, and *Clement V reluctantly suppressed it at the Council of *Vienne in 1312. The Templars' innocence is now generally admitted.

Temple, the. Although tradition ascribes the idea of a national Israelite shrine at *Jerusalem to *David, the first Temple dates from the reign of *Solomon (*c.*970–*c.*930 BC). The building became the central sanctuary of the nation and here alone could sacrificial worship be offered. It was destroyed by the Babylonians *c.*586 BC; its rebuilding (the 'Second Temple') was undertaken *c.*520. The Temple buildings were reconstructed by *Herod the Great. This was the Temple standing in Christ's time. With the destruction of Jerusalem in AD 70, the Temple worship ceased.

Temple, Frederick (1821–1902), Abp. of *Canterbury from 1897. He was Headmaster of Rugby (1857–69), Bp. of *Exeter

(1869–85), and Bp. of London (1885–97). At London he played a part in the *Lincoln Judgement (1890) and he became involved in conflict with the *High Church party. His primacy was marked by the 'Responsio' of the Abps. of Canterbury and *York in 1897 to '*Apostolicae Curae', the *Lambeth Conference of 1897, and the issue of the *Lambeth Opinions of 1899–1900.

Temple, William (1881–1944), Abp. of *York (1929–42) and of *Canterbury (from 1942). He was a son of F. *Temple. In 1923 he became a member (from 1925, Chairman) of the Commission which in 1938 produced the report on *Doctrine in the Church of England*. As Abp. of York he became prominent in national life, especially through his concern with social, economic, and international questions. He presided over the *Malvern Conference in 1941. He also supported the *Faith and Order and *Life and Work Movements. His time at Canterbury was overshadowed by the 1939–45 War; he joined with Card. A. *Hinsley and the Moderator of the Free Church Council in issuing a statement of principles to guide a post-war settlement. In CW, feast day, 6 Nov.

Temporale. The section of a *Missal, *Lectionary, or *Breviary which supplies the variable parts of the services for the ecclesiastical year, except in so far as they are provided for in the *Sanctorale.

temptation. The etymology of the word suggests a neutral meaning of 'trying' or 'proving'. This primary sense is retained in the idea of God's tempting *Abraham (Gen. 22: 1). It may also be the meaning of the word in the traditional version of the *Lord's Prayer. In most passages of the NT and in present-day usage, however, it has the implication of incitement to sin. In this sense temptation seems to be part of man's experience, even before the *Fall. The inclination to wrongful action is not sinful before consent. According to Jas., temptation is inherent in free will, but God does not permit it beyond what the soul can bear. The traditional sources of temptation are the world, the flesh, and the devil.

Temptation of Christ. In the account of the temptation of Christ in the wilderness, three particular temptations are described in Mt. 4: 1–11: (1) to use His power as Son of God to turn stones into bread to satisfy His hunger; (2) to cast Himself down from a pinnacle of the Temple, i.e. to put God to an arbitrary test and to stage a spectacular miracle; and (3) to obtain from the devil power over all the kingdoms of the world by falling down and worshipping him, i.e. to desert His true mission for the sake of power unworthily obtained. In Lk. 4: 1–13 the last two temptations are related in the reverse order.

tempus clausum (Lat., 'closed time'). The seasons in the Christian year in which, because of their solemn or penitential character, marriages might not normally be celebrated with solemnity or at all. The periods in question varied at different times. The restriction no longer figures in RC canon law, but survives in the E. Church.

Ten Articles (1536). The first Articles of faith issued by the C of E in the Reformation period. Adopted by *Convocation at the desire of *Henry VIII, they were superseded in 1537 by the '*Bishops' Book'.

Ten Commandments, the. See COMMANDMENTS, THE TEN.

Ten Thousand Martyrs. The *Roman Martyrology commemorates two such groups: (1) on 22 June there is a reference to a legendary record of 10,000 soldiers crucified on Mount Ararat; (2) on 18 Mar. there is an entry which seems to relate to a group who suffered at the beginning of the *Diocletianic persecution (303).

Ten Tribes, the. On *Solomon's death (c.930 BC), ten of the twelve Hebrew tribes separated to form the kingdom of Israel, while two formed the kingdom of Judah. When Israel was conquered by the Assyrians c.721, many of the people were deported to Assyria (2 Kgs. 17: 1–6).

Ten Years' Conflict (1834–43). The struggle in the Church of *Scotland which culminated in the *Disruption. Lay patronage had long been a grievance in Scotland, and in 1834 the *General Assembly passed the Veto Act obliging presbyteries to reject a patron's presentee if he was vetoed by a majority of the 'male heads of families'. Disappointed patrons and presentees appealed to the Court of Session in Edinburgh and ultimately to the House of Lords, both of which condemned the Veto Act as *ultra vires*. The 'Non-intrusionists', led by

T. *Chalmers, concluded that the State connection was no longer in the interests of religion and in 1843 over a third of the ministers of the Church withdrew to form the *Free Church of Scotland.

Tenebrae. The popular name for the special form of *Mattins and *Lauds provided for the last three days of *Holy Week. Until 1955 it was sung by anticipation on the three preceding evenings. The name (literally, 'darkness'), probably derived from the ceremony of extinguishing the lights in church one by one during the service.

Tenison, Thomas (1636–1715), Abp. of *Canterbury from 1695. He revived the Archbishop's Court and took a prominent part in founding the *SPG. He fell into disfavour under Queen *Anne because of his pronounced Whig and *Low Church views.

Terce, Sext, None. The *Offices said at the third, sixth, and ninth hours respectively. They each consist of a hymn, three Psalms (or one Psalm divided into three parts) with *antiphons, a short reading from the Bible, a *versicle and response, and a concluding prayer. Since 1971 only one of these Offices is required, and the time of day at which it is said dictates which should be chosen.

Teresa, Mother (1910–97), founder of the Missionaries of Charity. Agnes Gonxha Bojaxhiu was born in Macedonia of Albanian parents. In 1928 she joined the Sisters of Loretto, taking the name of *Teresa (of Lisieux). She was sent to Calcutta to teach in a school which catered for the well-to-do. She felt drawn to the very poor and was allowed in 1948 to leave her Order. Dressed in a sari, she went to live in the slums of Calcutta, teaching the children of the poor and caring for the destitute. Others joined her and in 1950 her new Order, the Missionaries of Charity (Sisters), was approved. The foundation of the Missionary Brothers of Charity (1963) and the International co-Workers of Mother Teresa (1969) followed. Her devotion (especially to the dying) caught the imagination of the world; in India she was given a State funeral.

Teresa of Ávila, St (1515–82), the commonly used name of **St Teresa of Jesus**, Spanish mystic. She entered the *Carmelite convent of the Incarnation ('Mitigated Observance') at Ávila in 1535, but it was not until 1555 that she was finally converted to a life of perfection. Her mystic life began soon afterwards with Divine locutions, her first ecstasy, and an intellectual vision of Christ. Despite opposition, in 1562 she founded the convent of St Joseph at Ávila, where the primitive rule was observed. Here she began *The Way of Perfection* (for her nuns), having recently completed her *Life*, a spiritual autobiography. From 1567 she was engaged in establishing houses of the primitive rule ('Discalced Carmelites') for both nuns and friars, helped by St *John of the Cross. At the same time her own religious life deepened until it reached the state of 'spiritual marriage' (1572). She wrote *Foundations*, *The Interior Castle*, several smaller works, and some poetry. Her influence as a spiritual writer was epoch-making, because she was the first to point to the existence of states of prayer intermediate between discursive meditation and ecstasy and to give a scientific description of the entire life of prayer from meditation to the so-called mystic marriage. She combined mystic experience with ceaseless activity. Feast day, 15 Oct.

Teresa of Lisieux, St (1873–97), *Carmelite nun. The daughter of a devout watchmaker, she obtained permission to enter the Carmelite convent at Lisieux at the age of 15. She was professed in 1890 and from 1893 was assistant novice-mistress. She died of tuberculosis.

The spread of her fame was largely due to the decision of the prioress of Lisieux to circulate to all Carmelite houses a revised version of Teresa's autobiography, *L'Histoire d'une âme*. Miracles were reported and by 1907 an account of these was appended to the autobiography. She was canonized in 1925. Her cult had a wide appeal to ordinary people because her life showed that the attainment of sanctity was possible not only through extreme mortification but through continual renunciation in small matters. She is popularly known as 'The Little Flower' from the subtitle of her autobiography. Feast day 1 (formerly 3) Oct.

Teresian reform. The reform of the *Carmelite Order begun by St *Teresa of Ávila.

Terminism. (1) The doctrine held by some *Pietists, that God has ordained a definite period or term in the life of every individual at the end of which he loses his opportunity of achieving salvation. (2) An alternative name for *Nominalism.

Territorialism. The theory that the civil authority has the right to determine the religious doctrines of its subjects.

Tersanctus. An alternative name for the *Sanctus.

Tersteegen, Gerhard (1697–1769), German Protestant devotional writer. He underwent a conversion in a circle of *Pietists at the age of 20 and retired into solitude, earning his living as a ribbon-weaver. From 1728 he devoted himself entirely to directing souls and devotional meetings. Besides translating into German French *Quietist works, he published poems and hymns, and a set of biographies of Catholic mystics. His piety was highly individualistic. Today he is known chiefly for his hymns. Those translated into English include 'Lo, God is here!'.

Tertiary. A member of a *Third Order.

Tertullian, Quintus Septimius Florens (c.160–c.225), African Church Father. Brought up in Carthage as a pagan, he may have practised as a lawyer. He was converted to Christianity before 197. The chronology of his life and works is disputed.

Tertullian wrote a large number of apologetic, theological, and ascetic works. In his *Apologeticum* (c.197) he appeals for toleration of Christianity, attacking pagan superstition, rebutting charges against Christian morality, and claiming that Christians are no danger to the State but useful citizens. In moral and disciplinary works addressed to Christians he emphasizes the separation from pagan society which is needed to escape contamination from its immorality and idolatry. Many occupations and social institutions are barred, and in the last resort martyrdom must be accepted. He may be the editor of the *Passion of St *Perpetua and St Felicity*. His theological works are mainly polemical in origin and form. In the early *De Praescriptione Haereticorum* he disposes of all heresy in principle: the one true Church alone possesses the authentic tradition and has the authority to interpret Scripture; it has no need to argue. Against *Marcion he defended the identity of the God of the Old and New Testaments and that of Jesus Christ with the *Messiah of prophecy. Against ''*Praxeas' he tried to expose the unscriptural and unhistorical implications of *Modalism and to formulate a positive doctrine of the *Trinity. In *De Anima*, which advocated *Traducianism, he prepared the way for the pessimistic doctrine of the *Fall and *Original Sin which came, through St *Augustine, to dominate Latin theology. The rigorist strain in Tertullian, and the opposition which it evoked, took him into *Montanism, and his rigorism is evident in his extant Montanist works.

Test Act. The Popish Recusants Act 1672, passed in 1673, required all holders of office under the Crown to receive Communion according to the usage of the C of E, to take the Oaths of Supremacy and Allegiance to the Sovereign, and to make the *Declaration against Transubstantiation. It remained in force until 1829.

Testament, Old and **New.** See OLD TESTAMENT and NEW TESTAMENT.

Testament of Our Lord in Galilee, also known as the **Epistle of the Apostles.** An *apocryphal document, written c.150, in the form of an *encyclical sent out by the Apostles. It purports to record conversations between them and the Risen Christ.

Testaments of the Twelve Patriarchs. A *pseudepigraphical writing which professes to relate the message that each of the twelve sons of *Jacob gave to his descendants on his deathbed. It is unclear whether the work was Christian in origin or Jewish (in which case the obviously Christian passages are explained as interpolations). If Jewish, it probably dates from the 2nd cent. BC; if Christian, from c. AD 200.

Testamentum Domini. A short early Christian treatise professing to be in the words of Christ. It contains detailed regulations on matters of ecclesiastical order and church building, and a liturgy. It probably dates from the 4th–5th cent., was a private compilation, and does not represent the official practice of any Church.

Tetragrammaton. The technical term for the four-lettered Hebrew name of God יהוה (i.e. YHWH or JHVH). Because of its sacred character, from c.300 BC the Jews tended to avoid uttering it when reading

Scripture and substituted 'Adonai' (i.e. the Hebrew word for 'Lord'), whence the rendering Κύριος of the LXX, *Dominus* of the *Vulgate, and 'the LORD' in most English Bibles. When *vowel points were put into Hebrew MSS those of 'Adonai' were inserted into the letters of the Tetragrammaton, and since the 16th cent. the bastard word 'Jehovah', obtained by fusing the vowels of the one word with the consonants of the other, has become established. The original pronunciation is commonly thought to have been 'Yahweh' or 'Jahveh'; both these forms (nowadays mostly the former) are found in scholarly works.

Tetrapolitan Confession. A Protestant Confession of Faith drawn up by M. *Bucer and W. *Capito at the Diet of *Augsburg in 1530 and presented to *Charles V in the name of four S. German cities.

Tetrateuch. A name given to the first four Books of the *Pentateuch (Gen.–Num.). It is argued that these Books were compiled from the same sources and on the same editorial principles, and that the main dividing line in the earlier part of the OT is to be placed at the end of Num.; Deut. is then regarded as the first volume of a '*Deuteronomistic History' extending it to 2 Kgs.

Tetzel, Johann (*c.*1464–1519), German *Dominican. After preaching the *indulgence for the campaign of the *Teutonic Order in Livonia, in 1516 he was appointed to preach the one for the rebuilding of *St Peter's, Rome. Following the instructions given to the team of which he was part, he maintained the controversial thesis that indulgences could be obtained for the benefit of souls in *purgatory by payment of money, even by those not themselves in a state of grace. His preaching prompted M. *Luther to issue his 95 theses in 1517.

Teutonic Order. The Order of German knights grew out of a nursing community founded near Acre in 1190. In 1198 it was converted into a military order with the rule of the *Templars; in 1245 it received a rule of its own. The Order, made up of knights, priests, and lay brothers, was active and richly endowed in Palestine and Syria, but soon sought to advance the frontiers of Christendom elsewhere. Duke Conrad of Masovia invited the knights to subdue the heathen Prussians and in 1226

*Frederick II conferred princely powers on the Grand Master and gave almost limitless rights over future conquests to the Order. In 1231 the knights crossed the Vistula and from 1236 the Order also expanded in Livonia, but from the later 13th cent. it gave itself increasingly to the administration of its territories. When Lithuania accepted Latin Christianity and entered into a personal union with the Polish kingdom in 1386, the knights' crusading task lost its meaning. In 1525 the Grand Master, *Albert of Prussia, resigned his office, embraced *Lutheranism, and secularized his territory for dynastic ends. The Order survived under the protection of the Habsburgs in Austria. From *c.*1840 it again found its vocation in hospital work, especially in military hospitals, and in schools.

Textual Criticism. The critical study of the text of a writer whose work has come down from the period before the invention of printing. Few scribes can copy a text exactly; consequently the more often a text is copied and the greater the number of resulting MSS, the greater the variation there is likely to be between them. The task of the textual critic is to compare and evaluate the differences in the MSS (known as different 'readings') in order to reconstruct the history of the text through its various stages and ultimately to establish the original text as it left the hands of its author.

The majority of the extant Hebrew MSS of the OT have few variations. This situation is probably due to the establishment of the so-called *Massoretic text early in the Christian era and to its being subsequently copied with the greatest care. The *Septuagint Greek MSS, however, not only display differences among themselves, but in a number of instances they agree in differing from the Hebrew. Critics have deduced that the LXX translation was made from a different (and probably earlier) text than that which has survived in the Massoretic text. This deduction has been confirmed by the discovery of the *Dead Sea Scrolls.

In the NT there are numerous variations between the Greek MSS, some of them considerable, such as that involving the end of the Gospel of *Mark (q.v.). Study has shown that three main types of text are to be distinguished; the evidence of the ancient versions (Latin, *Syriac, *Coptic, etc.) and quotations in the Fathers have made it possible to localize and date these types. They are: (1) an *Alexandrian type, which must go back to an early 2nd-cent. archetype; (2) a *Western type (so called because its chief witnesses are the Latin versions and Fathers), which can be traced to c.AD 150; and (3) a type associated with *Antioch and *Constantinople (the so-called 'Koine', *Byzantine, or *Syrian text), which appears to be a systematic revision undertaken towards the end of the 3rd cent. This type of text is found in the majority of extant Greek MSS of the NT and was the text of the first printed editions.

The works of early and medieval Christian writers have sometimes survived in one MS, sometimes in many. Here the problems confronting the textual critic and the methods used in dealing with them are similar to those encountered in the NT.

Modern editors of texts, whether biblical or otherwise, print as the text of their edition either the text of a single MS or a text which they have themselves constructed from the total material available; in either case it is usual to accompany the text with a statement of variant readings found in other MSS or elsewhere (e.g. in versions and quotations). This is normally printed at the foot of the page and is known as a '*critical apparatus'.

The belief that textual criticism has radically altered the text lying behind the traditional translations of the Bible has been one of the factors prompting the production of modern versions. At least in the NT, the resulting changes are less fundamental than is often supposed.

Textus Receptus (Lat., 'the Received Text'). The Greek text of the NT ordinarily contained in printed editions until the later decades of the 19th cent. It is in substance the *Byzantine text contained in the majority of MSS. See TEXTUAL CRITICISM.

Thaddaeus, St. Mentioned in Mt. 10: 3 and Mk. 3: 8 (some MSS read *Lebbaeus), he is usually identified with the Apostle *Jude (q.v.); sometimes with *Addai (q.v.).

theandric activity. A term popularized by *Dionysius the Pseudo-Areopagite to devote the characteristic activity of the God-man.

Theatines, religious order. The 'Clerks Regular of the Divine Providence' were founded in Rome in 1524 by St *Cajetan and Gian Pietro Carafa (Bp. of Chieti, or 'Theate'; later *Paul IV). The Order aimed at the reform of the Church from within; it played an important part in the *Counter-Reformation, having spread to Spain and Central Europe.

Thebaid, the. The upper part of the Nile valley (named after its capital, Thebes). From the 3rd cent. it was the cradle of Christian monasticism.

Theban Legion, the. The Christian legion from the *Thebaid which is said to have been massacred during the *Diocletianic persecution. See MAURICE, ST.

Thecla, St, virgin. The tradition about her derives from the 'Acts of Sts *Paul and Thecla' (q.v.). Feast day in the W., 23 Sept. (suppressed in 1969); in the E., 24 Sept.

Theism. In current usage the word denotes a philosophical system which accepts a transcendent and personal God who not only created but also preserves and governs the world, the contingency of which does not exclude miracles and the exercise of human freedom. In various forms it is the view common to orthodox Christian philosophers, to *Judaism, and to *Islam.

Themistians. See AGNOETAE.

Theobald (d. 1161), Abp. of *Canterbury from 1139. He was the candidate of King Stephen. The disappointed *Henry of Blois, Bp. of Winchester and Papal legate until 1143, became a rival power in the English Church. When Theobald defied the King and attended the Council of Reims in 1148, his property was seized and he was exiled; for a short time *Eugenius III placed England under an *interdict. In 1149 Theobald was made a Papal legate and in 1151 he held an important legatine Council in London. In 1152 he refused to crown Stephen's son Eustace and had to flee to Flanders. Soon recalled, in 1153 he reconciled Stephen and Henry of Anjou and on Stephen's death (1154) he crowned Henry king and recommended to him Thomas *Becket as chancellor. He did much to give the English Church a new identity and purpose.

theocracy (literally 'government by God').

The Greek term was coined by *Josephus to denote the political organization of the Jewish people. Before the institution of kingship in Israel, God was regarded as the supreme ruler of the Hebrews, whose laws constituted both religious and civil obligations; even after the election of a king, the kings were vice-regents of God. A more complete theocracy was created after the Exile, when the monarchy disappeared. A theocratic form of government was known to many ancient peoples and is intrinsic to *Islam. An attempt to realize the theocratic ideal was made by J. *Calvin at Geneva.

Theodicy. That part of natural theology which is concerned to defend the goodness and omnipotence of God against objections arising from the existence of evil in the world. The word is sometimes used as a synonym for *Natural Theology.

Theodora I (*c.*500–47), wife of *Justinian I, crowned as co-regnant Empress in 527. She exercised great influence on the theological controversies of the time. Her sympathies were with the *Monophysite party, and it was probably mainly because of her that Justinian sought to conciliate the Monophysites, especially in the dispute over the *Three Chapters.

Theodore the Lector (6th cent.), historian. His 'Tripartite History' is composed of extracts from the Histories of *Socrates, *Sozomen, and *Theodoret. His own Church History continued to the time of Justin I (d. 527); only fragments remain.

Theodore of Mopsuestia (*c.*350–428), *Antiochene exegete and theologian. From 392 he was Bp. of Mopsuestia (in southern Turkey). In his biblical commentaries he used critical, philological, and historical methods, rejecting the Alexandrian use of allegorical interpretation. His teaching on the Incarnation was condemned at the Councils of *Ephesus (431) and *Constantinople (553), but the recovery of some of his works preserved in Syriac has shown that he has sometimes been unjustly judged; his Christological terminology is imprecise. See also THREE CHAPTERS, THE.

Theodore of Pharan. See the following entry.

Theodore of Raïthu (*fl.* after 550; perhaps 7th cent.), monk of the monastery of Raïthu on the Gulf of Suez. He may later have been Bp. of Pharan and as such been involved in the early stages of the *Monothelite controversy as a proponent of monenergism. He wrote a *Praeparatio* defending the Christological formulas of St *Cyril of Alexandria (d. 444) and of the Council of *Chalcedon (451) alike and attacking the doctrines of *Severus of Antioch and *Julian of Halicarnassus.

Theodore of Studios, St (759–826), monastic reformer. He became Abbot of Saccudium (in NW Asiatic Turkey) in 794. In 796 he opposed the adulterous marriage of the Emp. Constantine VI; he was banished but recalled a year later. In 799 he and most of his community went from Saccudium, which was exposed to Saracen raids, to the old monastery of *Studios (q.v.) at Constantinople; under Theodore it became the centre of E. monasticism. When Leo V became Emperor in 813, he revived an *Iconoclastic policy and exiled Theodore, its most vigorous opponent. After Leo's assassination in 820, Theodore was recalled, but as image worship was prohibited in Constantinople, he spent most of his time on the peninsula of Tryphon. His writings include a 'Short' and a 'Long Catechesis', an Exposition of the Liturgy of the *Presanctified, and several spiritual orations. He is widely venerated in the E. Feast day, 11 Nov.

Theodore of Tarsus, St (*c.*602–90), Abp. of *Canterbury from 668. He was an Asiatic Greek, recommended to Pope *Vitalian by *Hadrian, who accompanied him to Britain. Theodore set about reforming the government of the Church by dividing dioceses and extending the episcopate. In 672 or 673 he summoned, and presided over, the first important synod of the whole English Church at *Hertford and in 679 he held another synod at *Hatfield. A number of his writings have recently been identified. The 'Penitential' attributed to him reflects his views. Feast day, 19 Sept.

Theodoret (*c.*393–*c.*460), Bp. of Cyrrhus in Syria from 423. He soon became involved in the Christological controversy between *Nestorius and *Cyril of Alexandria. In a polemical work against Cyril, he maintained a duality in Christ and accepted the title of *Theotokos only in a figurative sense. Though he abandoned this position in a later confession of faith in 448, he was nevertheless deposed by the Council held at Ephesus in 449 (the *Latrocinium) and forced into exile. The new Emp. Marcian summoned him to the Council of *Chalcedon (451), where he reluctantly anathematized Nestorius. He apparently spent his last years peacefully administering his diocese. A century later his writings against Cyril were the subject of the '*Three Chapters Controversy' and were condemned at the Council of *Constantinople (553).

His surviving works include a fine Christian apology (the *Graecarum Affectionum Curatio*); the *Eranistes*, which is a treatise against the *Monophysites; and a Church History continuing the work of *Eusebius to 428, as well as exegetical works which are among the finest specimens of the *Antiochene School.

Theodoric (*c.*455–526), King of the Ostrogoths from 475 and ruler of Italy from 493. He spent his early years as a hostage in *Constantinople. In 487 he was commissioned by the Emp. *Zeno to overthrow Odoacer, then ruling Italy. He defeated and killed Odoacer and then ruled virtually independently. Although he and his followers were *Arians, he allowed the Catholic Church to keep its churches, property and privileges.

Theodosian Code. A collection of Roman imperial constitutions of general application from the time of *Constantine to that of *Theodosius II. Assembled and edited on Theodosius' instructions, it was promulgated in 438. It was still accepted as authoritative in the W. even after it had been superseded in the E. by *Justinian.

Theodosian Collection. The compilation of documents in the *Verona Chapter MS LX (58) subscribed with the name of Theodosius the Deacon. It contains important material not found elsewhere.

Theodosius I (the 'Great'), Roman Emperor from 379 to 395. In secular affairs he defeated and pacified the Goths. Ecclesiastically he founded the orthodox Christian State; *Arianism and other heresies became legal offences, sacrifice was forbidden, and paganism almost outlawed.

Theodosius II (401–50), E. Roman Emperor from 408. He is significant in ecclesiastical history for summoning the Council of *Ephesus (431) and enacting the *Theodosian Code. Politically he was incompetent.

Theodotion (probably 2nd cent.), translator or reviser of the Greek version of the OT placed in *Origen's *Hexapla next after the LXX; some of the excerpts here attributed to him may be the work of earlier revisers. This is especially likely in the text of Dan., which was used in the Church from the 4th cent. in preference to the LXX.

Theodotus (2nd cent.), *Gnostic. He was a follower of *Valentinus, known from fragments of his work preserved by *Clement of Alexandria.

Theodotus, the Cobbler or Leather-seller (2nd cent.), Adoptionist *Monarchian. He held that Jesus was a man who had been anointed with the Holy Spirit at His Baptism and thus became Christ. He was excommunicated by Pope *Victor.

Theodotus (d. *c.*445), Bp. of Ancyra (modern Ankara). At first a supporter of *Nestorius, he became one of his most determined adversaries, taking a prominent part on the Cyrilline side at the Council of *Ephesus (431). His surviving works include sermons for *Christmas and the *Purification, which are early witnesses to the existence of these feasts.

Theodulf (*c.*750–821), Bp. of Orléans, poet, and textual critic. A Visigothic refugee from the Islamic invasion of *Spain, he was welcomed at the court of *Charlemagne and by 798 he was Bp. of Orléans. In 818 he was deposed from all his offices for alleged conspiracy against *Louis I.

His writings reflect the intellectual concerns of the imperial court at Aachen. His treatise *De Spiritu Sancto* is a collection of patristic excerpts on the *Double Procession of the Holy Spirit; the *De ordine baptismi* is one of several responses to Charlemagne's letter to his bishops asking how they understood Baptism. The '*Caroline Books' (now attributed mainly to Theodulf) concern the use of visual images in private devotion and in the liturgy. One of his hymns, 'All glory, laud, and honour', became the *Palm Sunday processional of the W. Church. His most distinctive achievement was his scholarly revision of the *Vulgate.

Theognostus (3rd cent.), *Alexandrian

ecclesiastical writer. *Philip Sidetes states that he was head of the *Catechetical School, but no other ancient authority gives him such a position. He elaborated a system of theology on *Origenist lines in his *Hypotyposes*, of which an account is preserved by *Photius.

theologia crucis (Lat., 'theology of the cross'). The name given by M. *Luther to the theological principle that our knowledge of the Being of God must be derived from the study of Christ in His humiliation and the suffering He underwent on the cross. He opposed it to a *theologia gloriae* ('theology of glory') which would maintain that a true knowledge of God can be obtained from the study of nature.

Theologia Germanica. An anonymous spiritual treatise written in German by a priest of the *Teutonic Order in the later 14th cent. It counsels radical poverty of spirit and renunciation of self as the way of union in and with God.

Theological Colleges (Anglican). In these Colleges candidates receive their final preparation for ordination. Edinburgh Theological College, founded in 1810, is the oldest surviving theological college in the Anglican Communion. Later in the century colleges were opened in the majority of English dioceses, but in recent years many have closed or been amalgamated, and some have joined with colleges of other denominations.

theological virtues. The virtues of *faith, *hope, and *charity (or *love) which are grouped together by St *Paul as the bases of the Christian life. They are contrasted with the natural or *cardinal virtues.

theology, literally the 'science of God'. Among the Greek Fathers the word came to denote either the doctrine of the *Trinity (i.e. of God's Being as opposed to His dealings with the created order) or prayer (as it is only in prayer that God is truly known). In the W. it came to mean the science of the Divinely revealed religious truths. Its theme is the Being and Nature of God and His creatures and the whole complex of the Divine dispensation from the *Fall of Adam to the *Redemption through Christ and its mediation to man by His Church, including the so-called natural truths of God, which

are accessible to mere reason. Its purpose is to investigate the contents of belief by faith and understanding.

theology of religions. The interpretation of how God (or ultimate Divine reality) may be operative for salvation through religions other than Christianity. Belief in Jesus Christ as God's final agent of salvation fostered the view that He either fulfilled or was destined to replace the religious aspirations within other traditions. This attitude was qualified by puzzlement about the availability of salvation before the coming of Christ and in places where the Gospel had not penetrated.

The 2nd- and 3rd-cent. *Apologists held a positive view of other religions based on the doctrine of the universal presence of the Divine *Logos, manifest in Greek religions, ancient Judaism, and even in Buddhists and Brahmins. After *Constantine, the maxim 'no salvation outside the Church', hitherto applied to Christian heretics and schismatics, was extended to pagans and Jews, because it was assumed that in the Roman Empire all would be able to hear the Christian message. The Fourth *Lateran Council (1215) and the Council of *Florence (1442) endorsed the belief that salvation was confined to the Church. The encounter with peoples beyond the known world in the late-15th and 16th cents. rekindled debate about the culpability of such people in respect of salvation; some *Dominicans and some *Jesuits argued that salvation outside the Church was possible by virtue of a 'baptism of desire' or 'implicit faith'. In the 18th and 19th cents. some missionaries (both Protestant and RC), though believing in the superiority of Christianity, came to doubt that exclusivist views were an adequate response to the ethical aspirations and depth of spirituality in other religions. The beginnings of the inter-faith movement are sometimes traced to the first conference of the World's Parliament of Religions held in Chicago in 1893. In the second half of the 20th cent. Christians met other faiths with increased respect. The Second *Vatican Council encouraged RCs to value what is holy, good, and true in other religions, and in 1979 the *World Council of Churches established a Sub-Unit on Dialogue with People of Living Faiths and Ideologies. Dialogues have stressed elements common to different religions as well as the symbolic nature of theological concepts, and have utilized such notions as the 'cosmic Christ' or 'normative Christ', which is thought to be somehow effective for other believers within their own traditions.

Theopaschites. Those in the 5th and 6th cents. who held that, in view of the unity of the Incarnate Christ, it could be said that God had suffered. The first controversy on the subject arose when *Peter the Fuller added the phrase 'who was crucified for us' to the *Trisagion, which he and other *Monophysites regarded as a Christological hymn; the addition was condemned by the Catholics who regarded it as addressed to the Trinity. The second centred on the formula 'One of the Trinity suffered in the flesh', first defended by a group of Scythian monks at *Constantinople in 519. It was rejected by the Patr. of Constantinople and (with some hesitation) by Pope *Hormisdas, but upheld by the Emp. *Justinian and Pope John II. The Second Council of *Constantinople in 553 anathematized those who denied that Christ, who was crucified in the flesh, was one of the Trinity.

Theophan (in Russian, **Feofan) the Recluse, St** (1815–94), bishop and spiritual writer. George Vasilievich Govorov became a monk in 1841, taking the name Theophan. He was consecrated Bp. of Tambov in 1859, translated to Vladimir in 1863, and retired in 1866; he spent the rest of his life in the monastery of Vyshi. He did much to make the fruits of the 18th-cent. *Hesychast revival known in Russia and popularized the use of the *Jesus Prayer among the Russian Orthodox. Feast day, 10 Jan.

Theophany. An appearance of God in visible form, temporary and not necessarily material.

Theophilanthropists. A *Deistic sect founded in France at the end of the 18th cent. The three articles of its creed were belief in God, virtue, and immortality. It was given by the Directory the use of 10 churches in Paris, but it soon lost ground when Catholicism was re-established by the *Concordat of 1801.

Theophilus (later 2nd cent.), Bp. of *Antioch and *Apologist. The purpose of his 'Apology' was to set before the pagan world the Christian idea of God and the superiority of the doctrine of *Creation over the immoral myths of the Olympian religion. He was the first theologian to use the word '*Triad' of the Godhead.

Theophilus (d. 412), Patr. of *Alexandria from 385. In the early years of his patriarchate he took an active part in suppressing the remnants of paganism in the city. Originally a supporter of *Origenism, he became an opponent of the Origenist monks. When the *Tall Brothers were sheltered at *Constantinople by St John *Chrysostom, Theophilus used this opportunity to secure Chrysostom's deposition at the Synod of the *Oak in 403. The Copts and Syrians celebrate his feast on 15 and 17 Oct. respectively.

Theophylact (b. c.1050/60; d. after 1125), Byzantine exegete. About 1090 he was made Abp. of Ohrid in the country of the Bulgarians. His main work is a series of commentaries on several OT Books and the whole of the NT except Rev. They are lucid in thought and expression and closely follow the text, while at the same time insisting on practical morality.

theosophy. The Greek term θεοσοφία, denoting knowledge of Divine things, is found in magical papyri and was taken up by the *Neoplatonists; it was brought into Latin by John Scottus *Erigena. In the 17th cent. it was revived in both Latin and vernacular forms to denote the kind of speculation, based on intuitive knowledge, which is found in the Jewish *Kabbala. In modern times it has been used of the supposed hidden essence of all religions; it is believed to be an empirical philosophy handed down by wise men of all cultures and religious traditions. It is held that knowledge of the truth, obtained by direct perceptions, results from the development of powers latent in all men. The primary tenet of theosophy is that all existence is a unity; the essence of everything, physical and spiritual, is one life. Theosophical philosophy denies the existence of a personal God, personal immortality, and the validity of the Christian revelation.

The Theosophical Society was founded in New York in 1875 by Mme H. P. Blavatsky and Col. H. S. Olcott. They moved to India in 1879; soon afterwards the headquarters of the Society were established at Adyar, near Madras. On the death of Col. Olcott in 1907, Mrs Annie Besant was elected President of the Society, which subsequently spread through most of the world.

theotokion. In the E. Church a stanza of liturgical hymnography referring to the BVM.

Theotokos, the 'one who gave birth to God', a title of the BVM. The word became a popular term of devotion. In 429 it was attacked by the *Nestorians as incompatible with the full humanity of Christ, and 'Christotokos' was proposed in its place. It was defended by St *Cyril of Alexandria and upheld at the Councils of *Ephesus (431) and *Chalcedon (451). Its orthodoxy was then generally accepted.

Therapeutae. A pre-Christian monastic community of Egyptian Jews described by *Philo. Nothing is known of their history.

Theresa, St; Thérèse, St. See TERESA OF ÁVILA, ST; TERESA OF LISIEUX, ST.

thermarion. In the E. Church a vessel for the warm water used in the Eucharist for mixing with the wine after its consecration and in the washing of altars at their dedication.

Thessalonians, Epistles to the. The First of these two NT Epistles was probably written by St *Paul at *Corinth, *c*.51. In it he assures his converts that at the Second Coming of Christ those who have died in the Lord will rise first and then, together with the living, be united with Him; he declines to pronounce on the time and circumstances of these events, except that the day of the Lord will come 'like a thief in the night' (5: 2). The Second Epistle reminds the Thessalonians, who, believing in the immediately impending *Parousia, were neglecting their ordinary duties, that the apostasy and the 'Son of Perdition' must come first, but teaches that there is still something or someone 'that restraineth' (2: 6–7). This may refer to the Roman Empire under Claudius; in the traditional view it refers to a supernatural power.

The authenticity of the First Epistle is generally accepted. That of the Second is rejected by many scholars, mainly because of the differences in the eschatological teaching of the two Epistles and because of their different tone.

Thessalonica. The city in Greece now called Thessaloniki but long known as Salonica, was founded *c*.315 BC. Under the Romans it became the virtual capital of the province of Macedonia. In AD 50 or 51 St *Paul visited the city and founded a Christian community (Acts 17), which was renowned for its orthodoxy and steadfastness. See also the previous entry.

Theudas. The leader of an unsuccessful insurrection mentioned in a speech attributed to *Gamaliel in Acts 5: 36. *Josephus describes an insurrection by a leader of this name in AD 45 or 46, but there are difficulties in reconciling the two references.

Thierry of Chartres (*c*.1100–*c*.1155), philosopher and teacher. A Breton by birth, he made his name as a teacher in *Paris *c*.1125–41, becoming Chancellor of *Chartres, probably in 1141. He took part in the examination of *Gilbert de la Porrée at Reims in 1148.

Thierry's most original work was in the application of the liberal arts to Christian doctrine. His analysis of *Boethius' *Opuscula Sacra* offered a more conservative interpretation of the Trinity than that proposed by Gilbert de la Porrée. For Thierry the doctrine of the Trinity might be deduced from a consideration of the unity, the Father, which leads to equality, the Son, and thence to the bond between the two, the Holy Spirit. The *De Sex Dierum Operibus* (*On the Six Days of Creation*) is a bold interpretation of Gen. 1 in the light of his study of *Plato and *Aristotle; he assigned the four Aristotelian causes to the Persons of the Trinity, the Father being the efficient cause, the Son the formal, and the Holy Spirit the final cause, whereas divinely created matter was the material cause.

Third Orders. Religious organizations affiliated usually to one of the *Mendicant Orders, so called to distinguish them from the First and Second Orders, now normally of professed men and women respectively. Their origins lie in the practice, developed in the 12th cent., of voluntarily adopting the status of *penitent. In the 13th cent. various attempts were made to clarify the canonical position of these penitents and to gather them into regular institutions; many attached themselves to the *Franciscans and *Dominicans. In 1284 the Master of the Dominican Order established a

Dominican Order of Penance subject to his own jurisdiction, and soon afterwards the Franciscans were given official responsibility for the groups of penitents under their care, who became known as the Third Order of St Francis. In the late 13th cent. informal communities of men and women established houses and attached themselves to the Mendicants. In the 15th cent. some of them began to take religious vows. From these communities developed the Third Orders Regular, whose members are sometimes known as Regular Tertiaries. They differ little from the First and Second Orders of their respective societies. Members of Third Orders who do not take religious vows are known as Secular Tertiaries. They lead a normal life in the world; they usually have to make a novitiate, observe a rule, and say certain prescribed prayers.

Third Rome. A name used by Russian Christians for Moscow.

Thirlwall, Connop (1797–1875), Bp. of *St Davids from 1840. He learnt Welsh, restored Church life in his diocese, and took part in the ecclesiastical questions of his day in a liberal spirit. He supported the removal of the civil disabilities of the Jews (1848) and urged the disestablishment of the Church of *Ireland (1869). He and A. C. *Tait were the only bishops in the C of E who refused to issue an interdict against Bp. J. W. *Colenso preaching in their dioceses.

Thirty-Nine Articles. The set of doctrinal formulas finally accepted by the C of E. The first text was issued by *Convocation in 1563; they received their final form in 1571. They are not a statement of Christian doctrine in the form of a creed; rather they are short summaries of dogmatic tenets, each dealing with some point raised in contemporary controversy. Various interpretations have been put on some of them, and probably this licence was intended by their framers. Until 1865 the clergy were required to accept each and every one of them, but then a more general assent was substituted, and since 1975 the Articles have only to be accepted as one of the historic formularies of the C of E which bear witness to the faith revealed in Scripture and set forth in the catholic creeds.

Thirty Years War (1618–48). A series of religious and political wars fought in Central Europe. The causes included the decay of the *Holy Roman Empire and the continued religious unrest after the Peace of *Augsburg (1555). The Bohemian Protestants rebelled in 1618 and set up Frederick V of the Palatinate in opposition to the Emp. *Ferdinand II. They were defeated by the armies of the Catholic League. In 1623 war broke out again in Lower Saxony. After victories by the Imperial generals in 1626, the Peace of Lübeck was concluded in 1629. In the same year Ferdinand ordered the restitution of all ecclesiastical property unlawfully appropiated since 1552; the execution of this edict roused much opposition. In 1630 *Gustavus Adolphus of Sweden landed in Pomerania; he was encouraged by Card. *Richelieu, who was pursuing an anti-Habsburg policy. In 1632 Gustavus won the battle of Lützen, but was killed himself. The Imperial and Bavarian troops gained a decisive victory at Nördlingen (1634), which led to the Treaty of Prague between the Emperor and most of the Protestant estates (1635). The Swedes, however, continued to fight and were openly joined by France. The French position became increasingly advantageous and in 1644 negotiations were opened, leading to the Peace of *Westphalia (1648). By this the ecclesiastical state of the Empire was restored to what it had been in 1624, except for the secularization of much ecclesiastical property which was distributed among the powers in compensation for their part in the war. The decrees of the Peace of Augsburg were reaffirmed and extended to the *Calvinists.

Tholuck, Friedrich August Gottreu (1799–1877), German Protestant theologian. His influential work, *Die Lehre von der Sünde und dem Versöhner* (1823) did much to check the spread of Rationalism in Germany. He was a representative of the *Vermittlungstheologie (q.v.), combining piety with wide disregard for dogma.

Thomas, St, Apostle. He is mentioned as one of the Twelve in all four Gospels. In Jn. he appears in three episodes, namely offering to die with the Lord on the way to Bethany (11: 16), interrupting the Last Discourse with the question 'We know not where you are going, how can we know the way?' (14:

5), and doubting the Resurrection (20: 24–8). After Christ's appearance he confesses his faith in the words 'My Lord and my God' and is thus the first explicitly to confess His Divinity. According to one tradition he evangelized the Parthians, according to another he preached in *India. Feast day: 3 July in the RC Church, CW, and the Syrian Church; 21 Dec. in the BCP and some modern Anglican liturgies (and formerly in the RC Church); 6 Oct. in the Greek Church. See also the following entries.

Thomas, Acts of. An apocryphal book recounting the missionary activities of the Apostle St *Thomas. Gundaphorus, an Indian king, sent a merchant to Syria to obtain a skilled architect. The merchant met Jesus, who recommended Thomas; Thomas agreed to go back with him. Gundaphorus and many others were converted. Thomas was eventually killed for persuading Mygdonia to cease marriage relationships with her husband. The Acts contain two hymns, including the famous 'Hymn to the Redeemer' (108–13; now usually called the 'Hymn of the Pearl') and two hymnic invocations relating to Baptism (27) and the Eucharist (50). The work was *Gnostic in origin, apparently dates from before the middle of the 3rd cent., and was probably written in Syriac.

Thomas, Apocalypse of. An apocryphal eschatological treatise, probably written by a *Manichaean at the end of the 4th cent.

Thomas, Book of. One of the *Coptic documents found at *Nag Hammadi in 1945–6. It professes to contain 'secret words' spoken by Jesus to St *Thomas; its main themes are ethics and eschatology.

Thomas, Gospel of. An apocryphal Gospel of which a *Coptic version was found at *Nag Hammadi in 1945–6. The Greek original perhaps dates from c.150, the Coptic from c.350. It professes to be the work of St *Thomas. It is not, like the canonical Gospels, historical in form, but consists of a series of pithy sayings and parabolic discourses of Christ; it is possible that it may preserve a few of the Lord's words not found in the canonical Gospels. The work is apparently of *Gnostic provenance.

Thomas, Infancy Gospel of. An apocryphal writing which professes to record miracles performed by Christ in His childhood. The alleged miracles are primarily displays of power, without theological point or moral justification.

Thomas Aquinas, St (c.1225–74), philosopher and theologian. At the age of 5 he was given to the abbey of *Monte Casino, in the expectation that he would become abbot. When the troops of *Frederick II occupied the abbey in 1239, Thomas went to Naples, where he joined the *Dominican Order. He was sent to *Paris. Here he came under the influence of St *Albertus Magnus, with whom he went to *Cologne (1248–51). Returning to Paris, he lectured on various texts, wrote against *Avicebron, and began the *Summa contra Gentiles*, which was apparently designed for the use of Dominican missionaries in their dealings with non-Christians. In Italy (1259–68) he taught in various Dominican houses, composed a liturgy for the Feast of *Corpus Christi, and began the *Summa Theologiae*, which was originally designed as a handbook for friars not bound for university study. Back in Paris, he held one of the Dominican chairs in the University from 1268 to 1272. He was involved in controversy with the secular masters over the rights of the mendicants and also with *Siger of Brabant, as well as with conservative theologians opposed altogether to the use of *Aristotle in theology. In 1272 he went to Naples to set up a Dominican *studium*. A mysterious traumatic experience in 1273 ended his teaching and writing.

He left a huge body of writings, including biblical commentaries, commentaries on works of Aristotle, academic disputations, and works of spirituality, as well as his *Summae*. Athough he accorded primacy to revelation, he recognized an autonomy proper to human reason and clearly delineated the spheres of faith and reason. He held that knowledge necessarily begins with sense perception. This conviction that valid arguments start with facts of the natural world gave his proofs for the existence of God their characteristic form (for these see QUINQUE VIAE). Also running through his thought are the antitheses between potency and act (God being 'pure act', between matter and form, and between essence and existence.

Thomas declared theology, distinct from philosophy, to be a science, in as much as it is an ordered body of knowledge, even though it depends for its first principles on a higher knowledge that it cannot itself test or prove, namely the knowledge which God reveals. The fundamental truths revealed by God are the Trinity of Persons in the Godhead and the Incarnation of the Word as a Person of human nature. But he held that revelation was also necessary for truths which reason can attain unaided, such as the existence of God, since without revelation such 'truths would be known only to a few . . . and with an admixture of error'. He treated theology as a single discipline which embraces the whole life of the Church, including worship, morals, and spiritual practice. Seeing God as the only subsistent being, the necessary being who cannot not exist, Thomas was able to resolve the dichotomy between immanence and transcendence, positing God's intimate presence at the centre of every creature as the cause of its being. He emphasized the role of Christ's humanity in the Incarnation and its causal relation to the work of redemption. This work is continued through the sacraments, which are an extension of His humanity. Thomas held the Eucharist was the highest of the sacraments, and that as the ultimate purpose of *Orders was the Eucharist, the priesthood was the highest order and the episcopate therefore not a separate order. He utilized the Aristotelian philosophy of *substance and *accidents to develop a systematic understanding of *transubstantiation.

Various of his teachings were attached before and after his death; a formal condemnation by the Abp. of Paris in 1277 was averted only by the intervention of the Roman Curia. By the time of the Council of *Trent the RC Church had accepted the substance of his teaching as an authentic expression of doctrine. Feast day, 28 Jan. (formerly 7 Mar.).

Thomas Becket, St; Thomas de Cantilupe, St. See BECKET, ST THOMAS; CANTILUPE, ST THOMAS DE.

Thomas of Celano (c.1190–1260), the earliest biographer of St *Francis. He wrote two Lives, one in 1228 and the other in 1246-7, and the *Tractatus de Miraculis S. Francisci* in 1250-3; in modern times their historicity has been challenged. He also wrote the 'Legend' of St *Clare and, according to an uncertain tradition, the *Dies Irae*.

Thomas Christians. See MALABAR CHRISTIANS.

Thomas Gallus (d. 1246), mystical theologian. A canon of St-Victor in Paris (see VICTORINES), in 1219 he was sent to help establish a new foundation at Vercelli. He wrote commentaries on individual works of *Dionysius the Pseudo-Areopagite and a synopsis of his whole system, making his work known in the West. He seems to have been the first to link Dionysius' *apophatic theology with the idea that the deepest part of the human personality is the non-intellectual mystical faculty for apprehending God.

Thomas of Hereford, St. See CANTILUPE, ST THOMAS DE.

Thomas a Jesu (1564–1627), Spanish spiritual writer. Díaz Sánchez de Ávila entered the *Carmelite Order in 1587. His writings on missionary theory contributed to the foundation of the Congregation 'De *Propaganda Fide'. His works on mysticism present the teaching of St *Teresa in the form of *Scholastic treatises.

Thomas à Kempis (c.1380–1471), ascetical writer and probably the author of the '*Imitation of Christ'. Thomas Hemerken was born at Kempen, near Krefeld, educated by the *Brethren of the Common Life, and in 1399 entered the house of the *Canons Regular at the Agnietenberg, near Zwolle (a daughter-house of *Windesheim), taking the habit in 1406. All his writings are pervaded by a devotional spirit. Feast day in the American BCP (1979), 24 July.

Thomas of Marga (9th cent.), historian of the *Church of the East. He was Bp. of Marga in Iraq and later Metropolitan of Beth-Garmai. His *Book of Governors*, written c.840, is an important source for the monastic history of the Church of the East.

Thomas More, St. See MORE, ST THOMAS.

Thomism. The systematized expression of the doctrines of St *Thomas Aquinas.

Thompson, Francis (1859–1907), RC poet. He was intended for the priesthood but later unsuccessfully studied medicine. In 1885 he went to London and spent three years in almost complete destitution. His first volume of *Poems* (1893) includes 'The Hound of Heaven', with its arresting description of the pursuit of the soul by God. His poetry has affinities with that of the *Metaphysical Poets of the 17th cent.

Thoresby, John (d. 1373), Abp. of *York from 1352. He was Chancellor of England (1349–56) and guardian of the kingdom in 1355. It was mainly through him that the old dispute over the respective privileges of *Canterbury and York was settled.

Thorn, Conference of (1645). A conference of Catholic, *Lutheran, and *Calvinist theologians at Thorn (Toruń), convened on the proposal of the king of Poland to bring about reunion. No result was achieved.

Thorndike, Herbert (1598–1672), Anglican theologian. He was ejected from his living in 1643 and from his fellowship of Trinity College, Cambridge, in 1646. In 1661 he became a Prebendary of *Westminster. His chief work is *An Epilogue to the Tragedy of the Church of England* (1659). In this he looks for a united Christendom on the basis of the first six *General Councils, conceding a certain superiority to the Pope with prescriptive rights over the W. Church. In the section on the Eucharist, he holds that the mystical but objective Presence of the Body and Blood of Christ is added to the substance of bread and wine by the consecration, which, however, is effected not by the words of *Institution, but by the use of prayer.

Thorvaldsen, Bertel (1770–1844), Danish sculptor. His most famous religious work is the group of Christ and His Apostles in the Frue Kirke at Copenhagen; the figure of the Transfigured Christ, His hands extended in blessing, has often been imitated.

Three Chapters, the. The three subjects condemned by *Justinian in an edict of 543–4, namely (1) the person and works of *Theodore of Mopsuestia; (2) the writings of *Theodoret against *Cyril of Alexandria; and (3) the letter of *Ibas of Edessa to Maris. As all three were considered sympathetic to *Nestorius, Justinian hoped the edict would conciliate the *Monophysites. The E. Patriarchs assented, but Pope *Vigilius at first refused to approve the edict on the ground that it opposed the decrees of the Council of *Chalcedon. After the Fifth General Council at *Constantinople in 553 had condemned the Three Chapters, the Pope accepted the Council's decision.

Three Denominations, the. A title applied to the *Presbyterian, *Congregational and *Baptist Churches. Their ministers in London formed an association for joint political action in 1727. See also REGIUM DONUM.

Three Hours' Service. A service held on *Good Friday during the hours of the Lord's Passion from noon to 3 p.m. It usually consists of seven sermons (normally on the *Seven Words from the Cross), interspersed with hymns and prayers.

Three Witnesses, the. See JOHANNINE COMMA.

Thundering Legion. When in the Danubian campaigns of *Marcus Aurelius a sudden rainstorm saved the Roman army from drought and defeat in 172, Christians attributed this to the prayers of the Christian members of the 'Legio XII Fulminata'. The mistranslation 'thundering' for 'thunderstruck' led to an elaboration that a thunderbolt had destroyed the enemy.

thurible. A metal vessel for the ceremonial burning of *incense. The container is usually suspended on chains from which it can be swung during the incensation.

thurifer. A person who carries the *thurible at religious ceremonies and services.

Thursday, Holy or **Maundy.** See MAUNDY THURSDAY.

Thyatira, a city in NT times in N. Lydia; the modern Akhisar, now in W. Turkey. It is one of the 'Seven Churches' addressed in Rev. (2: 18–29); here it is upbraided for tolerating a 'Jezebel' who teaches Christians 'to commit fornication and to eat things sacrificed to idols' (2: 20). In the 3rd cent. it was a stronghold of *Montanism.

In 1922 the head of the newly-founded Orthodox Exarchate of W. Europe was given the title 'Metropolitan of Thyatira' by the Patr. of *Constantinople. In 1963 the Exarchate was divided and since 1968 the spiritual leader of the Greek Orthodox community in Britain has been styled 'Abp. of Thyatira and Great Britain'.

tiara, Papal headdress. It attained its present shape, like a beehive, in the 15th cent. It was worn by, or carried in front of, the Pope at important non-liturgical functions, such as Papal processions, and at solemn acts of jurisdiction, such as dogmatic definitions, but it has not been used since the death of *Paul VI (1978).

Tiele, Cornelis Petrus (1830–1902), Dutch theologian. As professor of religious history at *Leiden University (1877–1901), he exercised great influence on the development of the study of comparative religion.

Tikhon, St (1866–1925), Basil Ivanovitch Belavin, the first Patriarch of the *Russian Church since 1700. In 1917 he became Metropolitan of Moscow, and later in the year the Panrussian Council elected him Patriarch. His courage and humility gave him moral authority. In 1919 he anathematized all who persecuted the Church but he imposed neutrality on the clergy in the civil war between the Reds and the Whites. He resisted the State confiscation of Church property in the famine of 1921–2 and was placed under arrest. In 1923 he signed a declaration professing loyalty to the Soviet Government; he was then allowed to live in a monastery in Moscow and to officiate in the capital. Feast day, 9 Oct.

Tikhon of Zadonsk, St (1724–83), Russian spiritual writer. In 1761 he was appointed assistant bishop in the Novgorod diocese, and in 1763 Bp. of Voronezh. He resigned in 1767, settling at the Zadonsk monastery in central Russia in 1769. He was much influenced by the West, but possessed a deep understanding of the ascetic and mystical tradition of E. Orthodoxy. Feast day, 13 Aug.

Tillich, Paul (1886–1965), Protestant theologian. He held university positions in Germany, but left the country in 1933. He settled in the USA and was a professor in turn at the *Union Theological Seminary, New York, at Harvard, and at Chicago.

Tillich was a prolific writer and exercised great influence. His aim was to bridge the gap between Christian faith and modern culture. To do this he employed the 'method of correlation', according to which the content of the Christian revelation is stated as answering the questions arising out of the cultural situation. He interpreted this in terms of *existentialism, ontology, and Jungian psychology. Probably the most important of his works is his *Systematic Theology* (1951–64).

Tillotson, John (1630–94), Abp. of *Canterbury from 1691. He attended the *Savoy Conference (1661) as a watcher on the Nonconformist side. In 1689 he was made Dean of *St Paul's. His archiepiscopate was undistinguished. His policy was based on dislike of the RC Church and a desire to include all Protestant dissenters, except *Unitarians, within the C of E.

Timothy, St. St *Paul's companion on his second missionary journey and later apparently one of his most intimate friends. He was entrusted with missions to *Thessalonica (1 Thess. 3: 2) and to *Corinth (1 Cor. 4: 17). Tim. 1: 3 suggests that he became Paul's representative at *Ephesus, and *Eusebius saw him as the first bishop of that city. He is said to have been martyred in 97. Feast day 26 (formerly 24) Jan; in the Greek and Syrian Churches, 22 Jan.

Timothy and Titus, Epistles to. The term 'Pastoral Epistles', under which these three NT Epistles attributed to St *Paul are generally known, dates from the 18th cent. Since the early 19th cent., there has been increasing agreement that the situation reflected in the Epistles is that of a period later than the lifetime of St Paul, though they contain earlier traditions; their Pauline authorship is generally denied.

The chief subject is the organization of a Christian ministry able to combat false doctrines, which seem to have included elements of Jewish speculation and an asceticism incompatible with belief in God's creation. Their witness to the development of Church organization is important, but ambiguous. '*Bishops' appear to be synonymous with 'elders' in Tit. 1: 5–7, but the reference to 'the bishop' (singular) in 1: 7 may indicate a development in the direction of the monarchical bishop found in the writings of St *Ignatius. Similarly, it is not clear whether 'deacon' is used as a nontechnical term meaning 'helper, assistant' or whether it denotes a grade in the order of ministry. In each case, interest centres on the moral qualifications of the officials, not on their function.

Timothy (d. 518), Patr. of *Constantinople from 511. After some hesitation he defended *Monophysite doctrine, and at a synod in 515 he condemned the *Chalcedonian teaching. Introduction of the regular use of the *Nicene Creed in the Liturgy at Constantinople is ascribed to him.

Timothy (6th or 7th cent.), priest of *Hagia Sophia. He wrote a treatise on the reception of heretics into the Church, dividing them into categories requiring *Baptism, *Confirmation (Chrismation) only, and those who needed simply to renounce their errors.

Timothy Aelurus (d. 477), Patr. of *Alexandria. He became patriarch in 457, but because of his *Monophysite views he was unacceptable to the majority of the bishops and was banished by the Emp. Leo I in 460. In exile he wrote much to propagate Monophysitism, but also anathematized *Eutyches because, unlike Eutyches, he held that the human nature of Christ was of the same substance as that of other human beings. He was recalled to Alexandria by the Emp. Basiliscus in 475 and died before another decree of banishment by the Emp. *Zeno could be carried out. Feast day in the *Coptic Church, 31 July.

Tindal, Matthew (1655–1733), a leading *Deist. His *Christianity as Old as the Creation* (1730) sought to show that there is an unchangeable law of nature common to all rational creatures; to this the Gospel was not designed to add or take away anything, but to free man from superstition.

Tindal, William. See TYNDALE, WILLIAM.

Tintern Abbey, in the Wye valley. It was founded in 1131 for *Cistercian monks from the Abbey of L'Aumône. The magnificent abbey church was built in the 13th cent. The ruins inspired a poem of W. *Wordsworth.

Tintoretto (1518–94), Venetian painter, so called from his father's occupation as a dyer. His main religious work was done for the Scuola di San Rocco, a charitable body in *Venice. He painted a series of 64 huge canvases to cover the walls and ceilings of their Lower Hall and the rooms of the upper floor of the Hall (1576–88). The Lower Hall has scenes from the life of the BVM and pictures of St *Mary Magdalene and St *Mary of Egypt; the upper floor scenes from the life and passion of Christ. They concentrate on the dramatic moment, have sharp perspectives and contrasts of light and shade, as well as strong colours.

tippet. A broad black scarf worn by Anglican clergy in choir over the *surplice. It evolved, it seems, from the long ends of the academic hood which hung down from the shoulders in front, and was not originally confined to the clergy.

Tischendorf, Constantin (1815–74), NT textual critic. From 1859 he was professor of theology at Leipzig. He visited many libraries in search of MSS, the most famous of his finds being the *Codex Sinaiticus (q.v.). Between 1841 and 1869 he published eight editions of the Greek NT with full *critical apparatus; the last edition remains a standard work of reference.

Tissot, James Joseph Jacques (1836–1902), French Bible illustrator. He was a portrait and genre painter, known for his caricatures for *Vanity Fair*. After an experience of conversion he devoted himself to illustrating the Life of Christ. In his *Vie de Notre-Seigneur Jésus-Christ* (1896) he depicted the scenes of the Gospel in a fresh and unconventional style. His illustrations of the OT are inferior in quality.

tithes. The tenth part of all fruits and profits due to God and thus to the Church for the maintenance of its ministry. The payment of tithes is ordered in the OT (Lev. 27: 30–2); it is, however, only implied in the NT (Mt. 5: 17–19), which places more emphasis on voluntary giving (e.g. 2 Cor. 9: 6–7). The early Church depended on offerings. In the 4th cent. payment of a tenth part of all produce of the land began to be taught as a Christian duty and in the following cents. this gradually became established. In England it was legally enforced by King *Athelstan's Ordinance *c*.930. Tithes were at one time subject to canonical division between the bishop, the clergy, the fabric of the church, and the relief of the poor, but eventually their disposal was left to the clergy who received them. At first the owner of the land could pay the tithe to what clergy he liked, but as the parochial system developed the tithes of each parish were allotted to its own '*parson'.

In England, as a result of various Acts from 1836 onwards, payment of tithe ceased in 1988. In Scotland tithes (called *teinds) were collected until 1925; in

Ireland they were abolished in 1871. They have never been part of the law in the USA.

For the distinction between C of E *rectors and *vicars, which derived from their entitlement to tithes, see RECTOR and VICAR. See also STEWARDSHIP.

Titian (probably 1487/90–1576), **Tiziano Vecellio** or **Vecelli**, Venetian painter. From 1516 he was the acknowledged head of the Venetian school. His famous *Assumption* (completed in 1518 for the High Altar of Santa Maria dei Frari in Venice) is of high craftsmanship, but lacks religious feeling. On the other hand, his *Crowning with Thorns* (c.1542; Louvre) and *Ecce Homo* (1543; Vienna) are fraught with tragic emotion. The compositions of his later years increasingly emphasize dramatic effect.

title. At least since the 3rd cent. the term has been used to designate the older churches of Rome. As several clergy were attached to each *titulus*, all of whom were provided with revenues for their maintenance, allocation to a 'title' at *ordination came to mean the provision of maintenance. Hence the term has acquired the general sense of a definite spiritual charge or office with guarantee of maintenance, without which a bishop may not ordinarily ordain a person, unless he is prepared to support him (or her) until he can prefer him (or her) to a 'living'.

Titus, St. A *Gentile disciple of St *Paul. He first appears on the journey to the so-called council of the Apostles at *Jerusalem (Gal. 2: 1) and was later sent on missions to *Corinth (2 Cor. 8: 6, 16 f., and 23). According to Tit. 1: 5 he was left behind in Crete to organize the Church there; *Eusebius says he became its first bishop. Feast day in the Greek and Syrian Churches, 25 Aug.; in the W. Church, formerly 4 Jan., then 6 Feb., now with St *Timothy, 26 Jan. For the Epistle to Titus, see TIMOTHY AND TITUS, EPISTLES TO.

Titus (4th cent.), Bp. of Bostra. He wrote a long treatise against the *Manichaeans. In the first part he gives the Christian solution to the problem of evil based on the ideas of Divine Providence and human free will; in the second he defends the OT and denounces the Manichaean falsifications of the NT.

Tobit, Book of. This Book of the *Apocrypha was written in Aramaic or Hebrew, probably c.200 BC. It relates the story of Tobit, a pious Jew who had been taken captive to Nineveh and in his old age became poor and blind. He prayed and, remembering a debt due from a friend in Media, he sent his son Tobias there with a companion who later revealed himself as the angel *Raphael. With the angel's assistance Tobias rescued a kinswoman from the power of a demon and married her. Raphael recovered the debt and then enabled Tobias to heal Tobit of his blindness.

Toc H. A Christian fellowship which originated in Talbot House, a soldiers' club opened in Belgium in 1915 under the Rev. P. T. B. Clayton and named after Lt. Gilbert Talbot, son of E. S. *Talbot. In 1920 Toc H (the army signallers' method of pronouncing T H) was refounded in London and spread rapidly. It engages in a variety of Christian social service.

Toland, John (1670–1722), *Deistical writer. In *Christianity not Mysterious* (1696) he asserts that neither God Himself nor His revelation is above the comprehension of human reason, and he attributes the mysteries of Christianity to the intrusion of pagan conceptions and the machinations of priestcraft. The book aroused great indignation. Further scandal was caused by a passage in his *Life of Milton* (1698), which was believed to cast doubt upon the authenticity of the NT; in his reply Toland said that he was referring to the apocryphal writings. Though not an original thinker, Toland was influential.

Toledo, Councils of. Many Councils were held at Toledo. The 'First' (400) was directed against *Priscillianism; at the 'Third' (589) *Recared renounced the *Arian Creed; and the 'Fourth' (633) issued important liturgical regulations.

Toledo, rite of. An alternative name for the *Mozarabic rite (q.v.).

tolerati (Lat., 'tolerated'). The technical term formerly used in *canon law for those *excommunicated persons with whom the faithful were allowed to have some measure of intercourse.

Toleration Act 1688. This Act, passed in 1689, granted freedom of worship to

Dissenters on certain conditions. RCs and disbelievers in the Trinity did not benefit.

Toleration, Edict of (313). See MILAN, EDICT OF.

toleration, religious. Christianity, which claims to be the only true religion, is in principle intolerant of other religions and *heresy within its ranks has been repeatedly anathematized. In practice, however, Christian Churches and Christian rulers have often suffered or 'tolerated' a non-Christian presence and Christian diversity, their power being insufficient to coerce infidels or dissenters into conformity.

Christians in the pagan world of late antiquity did not always suffer intolerance from non-Christians (see PERSECUTIONS, EARLY CHRISTIAN), but they almost always practised it among themselves. From the time of *Constantine, with the close connection between ecclesiastical authority and the civil power, persistence in unorthodoxy became an offence against civil as well as canon law. Throughout the Middle Ages mainstream ecclesiastical opinion followed St *Augustine's demand for the punishment of heretics and schismatics. The leading Protestant Reformers (M. *Luther, J. *Calvin, T. *Beza, and H. *Bullinger) seem at first sight to argue for individual liberty of conscience, but they prove to be resolute defenders of the right and duty of the ecclesiastical and civil powers to co-operate in the extirpation of heresy; they demanded freedom to worship in their own way but pursued dissenters with relentless zeal.

In 17th cent. England, *Baptists, *Congregationalists, and *Quakers insisted on their religious independence of Church and State. Experiments in practical toleration took place in North America: the founders of Maryland and Rhode Island saw no responsibility for religious coercion resting on the civil power. S.*Castellio's assertion that belief in a merciful God entailed acceptance of the liberty of the individual Christian was developed further by J.*Milton, while J.*Locke argued that the Church was a voluntary organization having the right to expel dissenters but no right to hound them thereafter. Intellectuals of the *Enlightenment used arguments in favour of toleration in attacks not only on ecclesiastical authority but on Christianity itself.

In the 19th cent. heterogeneous defenders of religious toleration by the State in many countries secured its embodiment in law. After much debate within the RC Church in the 20th cent., the Second *Vatican Council's 'Declaration on Religious Freedom' (*Dignitatis Humanae*, 1965) declared that 'in the sphere of religion no one' should be 'compelled to act against his *conscience' and that the right to religious freedom is founded on the dignity of the human person. The RC Church thus adopted a position similar to that long held elsewhere in the Christian world.

See also CONSCIENCE and THEOLOGY OF RELIGIONS.

Tolstoy, Leo (1828–1910), Russian novelist and social reformer. After the publication of his two most famous novels, *War and Peace* (1864–9) and *Anna Karenina* (1873–7), he renounced literary ambition, though he continued to write on moral and religious subjects. He became critical of the formalism of the Orthodox Church, which excommunicated him in 1901. He tried to live simply, renouncing his property and the happiness of family life. His religious teaching in its latest phase claimed to be a following of the Gospel with the miraculous and other irrelevancies set aside. He rejected the divinity of Christ and believed that men's greatest good consisted in loving one another.

Tome of Damasus. A collection of 24 canons endorsed by a Roman synod (probably in 377) and sent by Pope *Damasus to Paulinus, then recognized in Rome as the legitimate Bp. of *Antioch. Twenty-three of them are dogmatic, anathematizing the main Trinitarian and Christological heresies of the 4th cent. The ninth, condemning the *translation of bishops, was directed against *Melitius of Antioch.

Tome of Leo. The letter sent by *Leo I to *Flavian, Patr. of *Constantinople, on 13 June 449. It expounds the Christological doctrine of the Latin Church, and was directed especially against *Eutyches. It was given formal authority at the Council of *Chalcedon (451).

tongues, gift of. See GLOSSOLALIA.

tonsure. The shaving of all or part of the head, traditionally a distinctive feature of monks and clerics in the RC Church. It has no place in the 1972 rite of *Admission to Candidacy for Ordination of Deacons and Priests; monks now follow various customs in the matter.

Toplady, Augustus Montague (1740–78), Anglican clergyman and hymn-writer. In 1758 he adopted extreme *Calvinist opinions; these are elaborated in *The Historic Proof of the Doctrinal Calvinism of the Church of England* (1774). He is chiefly remembered for his hymns, which include 'Rock of Ages'.

Torah. The English equivalent of a Hebrew word usually translated 'Law'. It was pre-eminently the function of the priests to give 'torah' or instruction on the Will of God, and the word came also to be used of written collections of such priestly decisions, and so of the *Pentateuch as containing the *Mosaic legislation, as well as of individual laws within that legislation.

Torgau Articles. A memorandum summarizing the disciplinary and ceremonial demands of M. *Luther, P. *Melanchthon, J. *Bugenhagen, and J. *Jonas which was handed to the Diet of *Augsburg (1530).

They are to be distinguished from the Torgau Book of 1576 produced by a group of theologians called to reconcile the Swabian-Saxon Confession and the Maulbronn Formula. J. *Andreae's summary of it was incorporated in the Formula of *Concord (q.v.).

Torquemada, Juan de (1388–1468), Spanish *Dominican theologian. From 1432 to 1437 he attended the Council of *Basle and he took an active part in the negotiations with the Bohemians and the Greeks. He was created cardinal in 1439, and for the rest of his life had a large share in ecclesiastical Papal policy. He wrote on canon law and on the nature of the Church.

Torquemada, Tomás (1420–98), Spanish Inquisitor. Of Jewish ancestry, he entered the *Dominican Order at an early age and was an enthusiast for its reform. For many years he was (at least titular) confessor to *Ferdinand V and *Isabella. In 1482 he was appointed an inquisitor of the newly-established Spanish *Inquisition; he became its first Inquisitor General in 1483. He issued a series of instructions for the practice of the Inquisition; under him it became a powerful force used particularly in the repression of nominally converted Jews. He also influenced the decision made in 1492 to expel Jews from Spain.

Tosefta (Heb., 'supplement'). A collection of early Jewish traditions of the same character as, and contemporary with, the *Mishnah, but not incorporated in it.

total depravity. A term used, especially in *Calvinism, to express the extreme wretchedness of man's condition as the result of the *Fall.

total immersion. See SUBMERSION.

Touching for the King's evil. See KING'S EVIL, TOUCHING FOR THE.

tract (liturgical). A chant formerly sung or recited on certain penitential days in place of the *Alleluia after the *Gradual at Mass. It was suppressed in 1969.

tract (propagandist) A pamphlet, usually with a religious or moral purpose. The religious controversies of the 16th and 17th cents. stimulated the production of tracts, e.g. the *Marprelate Tracts. On the *Tracts for the Times*, see the following entry.

Tractarianism. A name for the earlier stages of the *Oxford Movement, derived from the *Tracts for the Times* (1833–41) issued under its aegis. Their purpose was to disseminate Church principles 'against Popery and Dissent'. Their form gradually changed from brief pamphlets to learned treatises. The storm provoked by J. H. *Newman's *Tract 90* (on the *Thirty-Nine Articles) brought the series to a close. Other authors included E. B. *Pusey and J. *Keble.

Tractatus Origenis (Lat., 'Tractates of Origen'). A collection of homilies formerly ascribed to *Origen; they are probably by *Gregory, Bp. of Elvira.

tractoria. Originally a 'letter of summons', the word was also applied to letters containing the decisions of Councils.

Tracts for the Times. See TRACTARIANISM.

Traditio-Historical Criticism, also called 'History of Traditions Method'. In biblical criticism, the study of the development of texts and motifs (often with particular reference to oral transmission), the circumstances in the life of the community in which they were created, and its cultural background. See also FORM CRITICISM.

Traditio Symboli (Lat., the 'delivery' or 'handing over of the Creed'). In the early Church candidates for *Baptism were subjected to a long course of instruction; the latter part of this consisted of explanations of the Creed, known as the 'delivery' or *traditio*, by which the candidates 'received the Creed' into their own keeping. At their Baptism they were required to recite and profess the Creed, thus 'returning it' (*redditio symboli*) to the presiding bishop. The ceremony has been restored in the 1972 RC Order for Adult Baptism.

tradition. In the early Fathers tradition means the revelation made by God and delivered by Him to His people through the prophets and apostles. It denotes something 'handed over', not something 'handed down'. From the 3rd cent. it was sometimes expressly identified with the Gospel record contained in Scripture.

In a more modern sense tradition means the continuous stream of explanation and elucidation of the primitive faith, illustrating the way in which Christianity has been presented and understood in past ages. It is the accumulated wisdom of the past. In the Reformation period the relation of unwritten tradition and Scripture became a matter of controversy. As against the Protestant belief in the sole sufficiency of the Bible, the Council of *Trent appeared to lay down that Scripture and unwritten traditions were to be received as of equal authority. The Second *Vatican Council minimizes the distinction, stating that Scripture and tradition 'flow from the same divine wellspring, merge into a unity and tend to the same end'.

Tradition of the Instruments. See INSTRUMENTS, TRADITION OF THE.

Traditionalism. In its strict sense, a theory proposed by a group of 19th-cent. RC thinkers, according to which all metaphysical, moral, and religious knowledge is based on a primitive revelation of God to man handed down in an unbroken tradition. Denying to human reason the power of attaining by itself to any truths, it makes an act of faith in a revealed tradition the origin of all knowledge. It was condemned in a number of decrees and ruled out as a possible Catholic system at the First *Vatican Council (1870).

The term is used less strictly by liberal theologians of what they consider unduly conservative beliefs.

traditors. The name given in Africa to Christians who surrendered the Scriptures when their possession was forbidden in the *Diocletianic *persecution.

Traducianism. The theory that the human soul is transmitted by parents to their children. The term is sometimes restricted to the crudely materialistic view that this happens in the physical act of generation. For St *Augustine, Traducianism suggested a simple explanation for *Original Sin, though he could not decide between it and *Creationism. In its crude form, Traducianism is incompatible with the spiritual nature of the soul.

Traherne, Thomas (c.1637–74), Anglican clergyman and *Metaphysical poet. His poetry is remarkable for a penetrating sense of the glory of nature and childhood. His poems were not published until 1903; they were followed in 1908 by *Centuries of Meditations*, reflections on ethics and religion which proved more attractive than his verse. Recently various other works have been recovered, including *Commentaries of Heaven* and *Select Meditations*.

transenna. In ecclesiastical architecture, a wall, usually of marble, pierced with holes in a regular pattern. Transennae were often used to surround the tomb of a martyr.

Transfiguration, the. The appearing of the Lord in glory during His earthly life, related in the Synoptic Gospels (Mt. 17: 1–13; Mk. 9: 2–13, and Lk. 9: 28–36) and alluded to in 2 Pet. 1: 16–18. This vision of Christ transfigured, with *Moses and *Elijah, was witnessed by Sts *Peter, *James, and *John, and is described by the Evangelists as a historical event; some critics have suggested that it is a misplaced *Resurrection appearance. The Feast of the Transfiguration, observed on 6 Aug., originated in the East. In the W. *Callistus III ordered its general observance in commemoration of the victory over the Turks at Belgrade on 22 July 1456, news of which reached him on 6 Aug.

translation. In ecclesiastical usage: (1) the transference of the relics of a saint either from their original place of burial into an altar tomb or shrine or from one shrine to another; (2) the transference to a different day of a feast when the season (e.g. *Holy Week) prohibits its observance, or when a feast of higher rank occurs on the same day; (3) the transference of a cleric from one ecclesiastical office to another, especially of a bishop from one see to another.

transubstantiation. In the theology of the Eucharist, the conversion of the whole substance of the bread and wine into the whole substance of the Body and Blood of Christ, only the *accidents (i.e. the appearance of the bread and wine) remaining. The word was in use in the latter part of the 12th cent., and at the *Lateran Council of 1215 the Eucharistic elements were said to be 'transubstantiated' into the Body and Blood of Christ, but the elaboration of the doctrine was not achieved until the acceptance of *Aristotelian metaphysics later in the 13th cent., when it found classic formulation in the teaching of St *Thomas Aquinas. It was reaffirmed at the Council of *Trent. The *Anglican-Roman Catholic International Commission in 1971, reaching agreement on Eucharistic doctrine, stated that the term 'transubstantiation' affirmed the fact of the 'mysterious and radical change' rather than explaining how the change takes place.

Trappists. Since the French Revolution, the popular name for the reformed *Cistercians belonging to the foundations originating from the exiled community of *la Trappe. See CISTERCIAN ORDER.

Travers, Walter (c.1548–1635), *Puritan. Ordained to serve the English congregation at Antwerp, in 1581 he became afternoon lecturer at the Temple in London and would have become Master in 1584 if he had not declined to receive *Orders in the C of E. In 1594 he became Provost of *Trinity College, Dublin. His main works were the *Ecclesiasticae Disciplinae, et Anglicanae Ecclesiae . . . Explicatio* (1574) and the *Disciplina Ecclesiae Sacra* (written in 1587 and circulating in MS until an Eng. tr., A *Directory of Church Government*, was printed in 1645); both defended the *Presbyterian form of Church government as of Dominical institution; they were the most important English exposition of the Presbyterian case.

Traversari, Ambrogio (c.1386–1439), scholar and theologian. He entered the *Camaldolese Order in 1400. As well as bringing to light many patristic MSS, he translated the works of various Greek Fathers into Latin. He defended Papal supremacy at the Council of *Basle and provided material for the discussion of the *Filioque at the Council of *Florence; he was responsible for the Greek version of the Decree of Union (1439).

Treacle Bible. A popular name for the '*Great Bible' (1539), from its rendering of Jer. 8: 22: 'There is no more *triacle* [AV: 'balm'] in Gilead'.

Tre Fontane. The traditional site of St *Paul's martyrdom, south of Rome. According to legend, his head, severed from his body, rebounded from the ground at three points, from which issued the three springs which give the place its name.

Tremellius, John Immanuel (1510–80), Hebrew scholar. The son of a Jew, he was converted to Catholicism in 1540; in 1541 *Peter Martyr persuaded him to become a Protestant. He was King's Reader of Hebrew at Cambridge from 1549 to 1553. He translated the OT and NT into Latin from Hebrew and Syriac respectively.

Trench, Richard Chenevix (1807–86), Abp. of *Dublin from 1863 to 1884. He strongly opposed W. E. *Gladstone's proposals for disestablishing the Church of *Ireland. His books on the *parables (1841) and *miracles of Christ (1846) created fresh interest in the Gospels in some quarters.

Trent, Council of (1545–63). Reckoned by RCs the 19th *Oecumenical Council, it embodied the ideals of the *Counter-Reformation and established a solid base for the renewal of discipline and spiritual life in the RC Church. The spread of Protestantism and the need for moral and administrative reforms had led to widespread demands for a General Council. Summoned by *Paul III in 1537, it eventually met at Trent in 1545.

PERIOD I (1545–7). The Council reaffirmed the *Nicene Creed as the basis of faith; it upheld the validity of both Scripture and unwritten *traditions as sources of religious truth, the sole right of the Church to interpret the Bible, and the authority of the *Vulgate; and it defined the theology of the *Sacraments in general. Its decrees on *Original Sin and on *justification and *merit struck at the root of the Protestant system.

PERIOD II (1551–2). Reconvoked by *Julius III, the Council reached important decisions on the *Eucharist, on *Penance, and on Extreme *Unction. *Transubstantiation was affirmed and the *Lutheran, *Calvinist, and *Zwinglian Eucharistic doctrines repudiated.

PERIOD III (1562–3). When the Council reassembled under *Pius IV, all hope of conciliating the Protestants had gone. The doctrine of *concomitance and the adequacy of Communion in one kind was affirmed, and there were various definitions on the sacrificial character of the Mass. Other decrees dealt with *Orders and *Matrimony, established *seminaries in each diocese, and regulated the appointment of bishops. Various works recommended or initiated by the Council were handed over to the Pope for completion. These included the revision of Vulgate, publication of the '*Roman Catechism', and reform of the *Breviary and *Missal.

Trental. A set of 30 *Requiem Masses for the repose of a soul, whether said on a single or on successive days.

Triad. A word first used of the *Trinity in the Godhead by *Theophilus of Antioch.

Tridentine. Having reference to the Council of *Trent.

Triduum Sacrum (Lat., 'the sacred three days'). The last three days of *Holy Week, i.e. *Maundy Thursday, *Good Friday, and *Holy Saturday.

Triers and Ejectors. In 1640 a committee of Parliament was formed to eject 'scandalous' ministers [i.e. those with *Laudian or '*Arminian' sympathies]. Local committees were later formed to eject those who would not accept the *Solemn League and Covenant. A national commission of Triers was appointed by O. *Cromwell in 1654 to approve public preachers and lecturers before their admission to office.

Trimmer, Sarah (1741–1810), author. She interested herself in the establishment of *Sunday Schools. Her Abridgements of the OT and NT (both 1793) were designed as textbooks for charity schools. The History of the Robins (1786) was long a favourite children's book for the upper classes; her numerous school books were intended for the instruction of the poor.

Trinitarian. In modern usage, a person who believes in the doctrine of the *Trinity, as contrasted with a *Unitarian.

Trinitarians (Order of the Most Holy Trinity). The Order was founded in 1198 by St *John of Matha and St Felix of Valois (d. 1212); its members are sometimes called 'Mathurins'. They devoted themselves to the ransoming of captives. In 1596 a reform was started in Spain; these Barefooted Trinitarians alone survive and engage in education, nursing, and pastoral work.

Trinity, doctrine of the. The central Christian dogma that the one God exists in three Persons and one substance, Father, Son, and Holy Spirit. The God who reveals Himself to mankind is one God equally in three distinct modes of existence, yet remains one through all eternity.

Though the word 'Trinity', in its Greek form τριάς, was first used by *Theophilus of Antioch (c. AD 180), Christian theologians have seen adumbrations of the doctrine in the Bible. The appearance of three men to *Abraham (Gen. 18) was held to foreshadow the revelation of the threefold nature of God. Besides the reference to the three Persons in the baptismal formula in Mt. 28: 19, there are held to be Trinitarian overtones in other NT passages, such as the Pauline benediction in 2 Cor. 13: 14.

Finding appropriate concepts to develop the doctrine was difficult and many 2nd- and 3rd-cent. Christians adopted views which were later considered unorthodox. These included the so-called 'economic Trinity', in which the distinctions between the Persons depended solely on their functions (or 'economies') towards the created universe; also various *subordinationist propositions. At the Councils of *Nicaea (325) and *Constantinople (381) the doctrine was defined in outline by negative rather than positive pronouncements, affirming against *Sabellianism the real distinction of the Divine Persons, and against *Arianism and *Macedonianism their equality and co-eternity. The Persons differ only in origin, in that the Father is ungenerated, the Son is generated by the Father, and the Holy Spirit proceeds from the Father. Some E. Fathers understood the Spirit to proceed from the Father through the Son; others are less explicit or deny any '*double procession'. From the time of *Photius, belief in the procession of the Spirit from the Father alone was characteristic of E. theology.

In the W. the doctrine developed somewhat differently. Latin theologians started, not from the difference of the Persons, as did many of the Greeks, but from the unity of the substance. The procession of the Spirit was attributed both to the Father and the Son. St *Augustine compared the generation of the Son to an act of thinking on the part of the Father (an idea based on *Tertullian) and explained the Spirit as the mutual love of the Father and the Son. This so-called 'psychological theory of the Trinity' was developed by the Schoolmen.

The Trinitarian doctrine elaborated by the Schoolmen was challenged in the 17th cent. by *Socinianism and *Unitarianism, but has remained the central strand of W. theology. In the 20th cent. J. *Moltmann developed a distinctive doctrine of the social Trinity, reviving the patristic theory of *circumincession to express the self-differentiation of God as the crucified God.

Trinity College, Dublin. The (one) college in the university of *Dublin, founded in 1591. Until 1873 membership was confined to Anglicans.

Trinity Sunday. The first Sunday after *Pentecost or *Whitsun. Its observance as a celebration embracing God in all three Persons was universally enjoined in the W. in 1334. Sundays are reckoned after Trinity in the *Sarum Missal and in the BCP and not after Pentecost as was usual in the Roman rite until 1969.

Triodion. In the *Byzantine rite, the liturgical book containing the variable parts of the services from the 4th Sunday before Lent until the Saturday before Easter.

triple candlestick. In the W. rite until 1955 a triple candlestick was used in the *Paschal Vigil Service to hold the three candles which were lit during the procession to the altar. In the E. Church a triple candlestick (and a double candlestick) are used for epis-

copal blessings at the Liturgy, the bishop holding one in each hand.

Trisagion (Gk., 'thrice holy'). The refrain 'Holy God, Holy and strong, Holy and immortal, have mercy upon us'. It is a characteristic feature of Orthodox worship, chanted at most services. In the Roman rite it is sung as part of the *Reproaches on Good Friday. See also THEOPASCHITES.

Tritheism. The heretical teaching about the *Trinity which denies the unity of substance in the Divine Persons. The name is used especially of the teaching of a group of 6th-cent. *Monophysites, including *John Philoponus. He taught that the common nature shared by the three Persons is an intellectual abstraction, and that though the Father, Son, and Holy Spirit have a common nature and substance, they are as individuals distinct substances or natures and are distinct in their properties. This teaching was condemned as tritheism at the Council of *Constantinople (680–81). *Roscelin and *Gilbert de la Porrée were both accused of tritheism and condemned.

Trithemius, Johannes (1462–1516). Abbot of Sponheim from 1483 to 1506. He rapidly brought about the reform of the monastery, collecting a library of MSS which made it famous.

Trito-Isaiah. The last eleven chapters of Isaiah (56–66) or the author(s) of them. They are dated after 520 BC.

triumphant, the Church. The body of Christians in heaven.

trivium. The medieval name for grammar, rhetoric, and dialectic, which made up the inferior group of the *seven liberal arts.

Troeltsch, Ernst (1865–1923), theologian and philosopher. He held professorships at Heidelberg (1894–1915) and then at Berlin. His originality as a theologian lay in his application of sociological theory to theology. He was also among the first seriously to consider the truth of other world religions alongside Christianity.

troparion. A generic term used in the E. Church for a stanza of religious poetry.

trope. In the W. Church, a phrase or sentence, with its music, introducing, or interpolated into, any of the chants of the

Mass and some of those of the Divine *Office. Tropes for the *Proper flourished particularly in the 11th cent. and then went out of use; those for the *Ordinary continued until they were forbidden by the Council of *Trent.

Trophimus, St. (1) According to Acts 20: 4 and 21: 29 he was an Ephesian Gentile who accompanied St *Paul on part of his third missionary journey and to *Jerusalem, where rumours that Paul had taken him into the *Temple were the chief ground for a riot. Feast day, with others, 14 Apr. (2) The first Bp. of Arles. Feast day, 29 Dec.

Truce of God. In medieval times, a suspension of hostilities ordered by the Church on certain days and during some seasons, e.g. in *Lent.

Trullan Synod. The synod of E. bishops held in 692 to pass disciplinary canons to complete the work of the Fifth (553) and Sixth (680–1) General Councils (hence its other name of 'Quinisext' or Fifth-Sixth Council). It sat in the domed room ('trullus') of the imperial palace at *Constantinople. Its decrees were rejected by the Pope.

Truro. The Anglican diocese of Truro, covering Cornwall, was created in 1877. Until Anglo-Saxon times the Cornish Church had been independent; in 931 it was finally incorporated in the English Church and Cornwall became an English diocese. In 1027 it was annexed to the see of *Crediton and in 1050 the see of the united diocese was fixed at *Exeter.

Truth, Gospel of. See EVANGELIUM VERITATIS.

Tübingen. The university, founded in 1477, became a centre of *Lutheran orthodoxy when Württemberg was made Protestant by Duke Ulrich in 1534–5. The 18th-cent. 'Tübingen School' of theology was characterized by a 'biblical supranaturalism' which put the guarantee of Christ and the Apostles in the place of the orthodox Protestant doctrine of the inspiration of Scripture and regarded the Bible as the exclusive source and law book of Christianity, from which the tenets of the faith were to be derived by deductive methods. In the 19th cent. another school of theology was founded by F. C. *Baur (see TÜBINGEN SCHOOL). A Catholic faculty of theology was opened in 1817; it has been characterized by a combination of historical and speculative methods, and by its emphasis on the need to relate modern thought to the data of faith.

Tübingen School. A school of German NT theologians founded by F. C. *Baur. It tried to apply G. W. F. *Hegel's conception of development to primitive Christianity: the early Church was divided into 'Petrinists' (Jewish Christians) and 'Paulinists' (Gentile Christians), the cleavage between them being healed only in the later 2nd cent. ('Catholicism'). Most NT Books were regarded as a product of the 2nd-cent. synthesis and therefore as of practically no historical value for the period to which they refer. The influence of the school was at its peak in the 1840s; its position has been generally abandoned. For the Catholic Tübingen School, see the previous entry.

Tuckney, Anthony (1599–1670), *Puritan. He became vicar of Boston, Lincs., in 1633. In 1643 he was nominated to the *Westminster Assembly, where he took a leading part in drawing up its doctrinal formularies. He held high academic office at Cambridge until the *Restoration.

Tulchan Bishops. A term contemptuously applied to the titular bishops introduced into the Reformed Church of *Scotland after a concordat in the Assembly of Leith (1572). It derives from the Gaelic *tulachan*, 'little hillock', used to describe the device of stuffing a calf's skin with straw to deceive a cow into giving milk: a reference to the bishops' diversion of revenues.

Tulloch, John (1823–86), Scottish theologian. From *c.*1875 he was the most prominent member of the Church of Scotland and in 1878 he was elected *Moderator. He tried to awaken a spirit of liberal orthodoxy and to defend the Church's comprehensiveness in doctrine.

tunicle. In the W. rite the outer liturgical garment of the *subdeacon. It seems to have developed from the ordinary overcoat of the later Roman Empire. It became obsolete with the suppression of the office of subdeacon in the RC Church.

Tunkers, also known as Dunkers, Dunkards, and German Baptists, a Protestant body, so named from their distinctive baptismal rite. Originating in Germany in 1708, they were forced by persecution to emigrate to America (1719–29). In the 1880s they divided into three bodies: (1) the conservative Old German Baptist Brethren; (2) the majority, who continued to be known as German Baptist Brethren until 1908, when the title 'Church of the Brethren' was adopted; and (3) the more liberal 'Brethren Church', which divided into two in 1939. They all profess no creed other than the NT, reject infant Baptism, insist on total immersion, accompany the Lord's Supper with an *agape, and refuse to take oaths or bear arms.

Tunstall, Cuthbert (1474–1559), Bp. of London (1522–30) and then of *Durham. In the divorce of *Henry VIII he was one of the counsel of the Queen. Subsequently he was sympathetic to Catholic doctrine, but lacked strength of purpose, first opposing the Royal Supremacy and then accepting it. Under *Edward VI his position became more difficult and he was deprived of his bishopric in 1552; he was reinstated under *Mary in 1554. On *Elizabeth I's accession he refused to take the Oath of Supremacy and declined to consecrate M. *Parker (1559). He was deprived of his see and kept a prisoner in *Lambeth Palace.

Tur 'Abdin (literally 'mountain for the servants [of God]'). An area in SE Turkey noted for the survival of a number of early *Syrian Orthodox monasteries and parish churches still in use.

Tutiorism (also called **Rigorism).** The system of *moral theology according to which, in cases of doubt, the 'safer opinion' (i.e. that in favour of the moral principle) must be followed unless there is a degree of probability amounting to moral certitude in the 'less safe opinion' (i.e. that against the principle). It was condemned in 1690.

Tutu, Desmond Mpilo (1931–), Abp. of Cape Town, 1986–96. A Black South African, he came under the influence of E. U. T. *Huddleston and was ordained priest in 1961. He had been Dean of Johannesburg (1975–6), Bp. of Lesotho (1976–8), Secretary of the South African Council of Churches (1978–85), and Bp. of Johannesburg (1985–6) before he became Abp. of Cape Town. He came to international prominence in 1975 when, a few weeks before riots broke out in

Soweto, he warned the Prime Minister of South Africa of his fear that violence would envelop the land, and later called for sanctions against South Africa. He campaigned against the apartheid regime, organizing political rallies under the cover of church services. After 1990 he worked for reconciliation, engineering a meeting between Nelson Mandela and Chief Buthelezi; he was Chairman of the Commission for Truth and Reconciliation (1995–8).

Twelfth Night. The evening before the twelfth day (*Epiphany) after *Christmas, formerly kept as a time of merry-making.

Twelve Articles. The main charter of the *Peasants' War adopted at Memmingen in 1525. The Peasants' demands included the right to appoint their own pastors, control over *tithes, and the abolition of serfdom. M. *Luther expressed agreement with the Articles, though he opposed the attempt to achieve these ends by revolt.

Twelve Great Feasts, the. In the E. Church, the 12 chief feast days in the liturgical year: *Epiphany (6 Jan.), *Presentation of Christ in the Temple (2 Feb.), *Annunciation of the BVM (25 March), *Palm Sunday, *Ascension Day, *Pentecost, *Transfiguration (6 Aug.), *Dormition of BVM (15 Aug.), *Nativity of BVM (8 Sept.), *Holy Cross (14 Sept.), *Presentation of BVM in the Temple (21 Nov.), and *Christmas Day (25 Dec.). *Easter Day stands in a class by itself.

Tychicus, St. According to Acts 20: 4, he was a native of Asia who accompanied St *Paul on his third missionary journey. He is mentioned several times in the NT. Feast day in the E., 8 Dec.; in the W., 29 Apr.

Tychon, St. See TIKHON, ST.

Tyconius (d. c.400), *Donatist theologian. He seems to have been an important layman; he was attacked for his catholicizing views and condemned by a Donatist Council at Carthage c.380, but refused to join the Catholic Church. His chief work was his *Liber Regularum*, which propounded seven rules for interpreting Scripture. They were incorporated by St *Augustine in his *De Doctrina Christiana* and thus influenced medieval exegesis.

Tyndale, or **Tindale, William** (? 1494–1536), translator of the Bible and Reformer. When

C. *Tunstall, Bp. of London, refuse[...]
port his project for translating the [...]
into English, Tyndale went to Germany.
The printing of his first translation of the
NT began at *Cologne in 1525 and was
completed at Worms the same year. Tyndale spent most of the rest of his life in
Antwerp, where he repeatedly revised the
NT. He also published translations of the
Pentateuch (1530) and Jonah (1531) and left
Jos.–2 Chron. in MS. His translations, made
from the Greek and Hebrew, were the basis
of both the AV and RV. He moved away
from M. *Luther's teaching on *justification by faith alone towards the idea of
double justification by faith and works; his
Eucharistic teaching came to resemble that
of U. *Zwingli. He was burnt for heresy.
Feast day in some Anglican Churches, 6
Oct.

types. In theology the foreshadowing of
the Christian dispensation in the events
and persons of the OT. Just as Christ could
refer to *Jonah as the symbol of His *Resurrection, so St *Paul found in the Israelites' crossing of the Red Sea the 'type' of
Baptism (1 Cor. 10: 1–6). Typology was much
used in the early Church.

typicon. In the E. Church a liturgical manual indicating how the services are to be
recited throughout the ecclesiastical year.
The term is also used of the Rule of a
monastic house.

Typos, the. The Imperial edict issued by
Constans II in 647 or 648 to supersede the
*Ecthesis. It forbade anyone to assert either
*Monothelite or *Dyothelite beliefs, and
required that teaching should be limited to
what had been defined in the first five
*Oecumenical Councils.

tyrannicide. The murder of a tyrant whose
rule has become insupportable. Some
Christians hold that it is unjustifiable on

nic[...]
the opp[...]
justified, a[...]
considerable a[...]
milder means of re[...]

Tyre and Sidon. The two [...]
Phoenicians, on the coast of [...] OT
times they carried on a lucrative [...] The
inhabitants of the region are mentioned
among those attracted to Christ (Lk. 6: 17)
and He visited the district (Mk. 7: 24).

Tyrrell, George (1861–1909), English
*Modernist theologian. He became a RC in
1879 and a *Jesuit in 1880. In 1896 he was
sent to Farm Street, the main Jesuit church
in London; here he was a sought-after confessor and made a name through his devotional writing. His friendship with F. *von
Hügel led to his acquaintance with the
writings of the Continental Modernists;
this contributed to his hostility towards
*Scholasticism and his stress on the anti-intellectual and experiential aspects of
religion. An article on hell, entitled 'A Perverted Devotion', in 1899 caused his
retirement to the Jesuit house in Richmond, N. Yorks. He asked in vain for secularization in 1905, but he was expelled from
the Society of Jesus in 1906 after the publication of an anonymous 'Letter to a Professor' in which he contrasted living faith
with dead theology. He was excommunicated when two letters in *The Times* (1907)
protested against the issue of *Pius X's
encyclical 'Pascendi'. His posthumous
work, *Christianity at the Cross-Roads* (1909)
questioned whether Christianity was the
final religion, and held out hope of a universal religion of which Christianity was
but the germ.

Ubaghs, Gerhard Casimir (1800–75), the chief representative of the *Traditionalist *Ontologism of Louvain. He combined Traditionalist belief that knowledge of metaphysical and moral truths is based on a primitive Divine teaching handed on by oral tradition, with the Ontologist doctrine of the direct contemplation of God by the intellect in the 'objective ideas'. His teaching was censured in 1864; he soon submitted.

Ubertino of Casale (1259–c.1330), *Spiritual Franciscan. He became a *Franciscan in 1273. In 1305 he wrote his main work, *Arbor vitae crucifixae Jesu Christi*, a mystical writing with a strong apocalyptic vein. He was summoned to *Avignon by *Clement V in 1310 to defend the Spirituals in the controversy on poverty, and in 1322 *John XXII asked his opinion on the question of 'theoretical poverty', then a matter of dispute between the *Dominicans and the Franciscans. He fled from the *Curia in 1325; in 1328 he was probably among the Franciscans who accompanied Louis of Bavaria to Rome, and in 1329 he seems to have preached against John XXII at Como.

ubiquitarianism. The doctrine held by M. *Luther and many followers that Christ in His human nature is everywhere present. Luther used it to uphold his belief in the real presence of Christ in the *Eucharist.

Udall, John (c.1560–92), *Puritan pamphleteer and Hebrew scholar. In 1588 he published anonymously a widely read pamphlet on *The State of the Church of England*, and he was suspected of complicity in the *Marprelate Tracts. In 1590, refusing to clear himself on oath, he was found guilty of the authorship of *A Demonstration of the Truth* ... [1588], but the sentence of death was not executed. His *Key of the Holy Tongue* (1593) included a Hebrew dictionary.

Udall, Nicholas (c.1505–56), Reformer and dramatist. His *Lutheran sympathies probably forced him to leave Oxford in 1529. He became Headmaster of Eton in 1534, but was dismissed in 1541. In 1547 he was appointed to assist Princess (later Queen) *Mary in translating the *Paraphrases* of *Erasmus. He received preferment under *Edward VI and remained in favour under Mary, becoming Headmaster of Westminster in 1555. His works include translations of Erasmus' *Apophthegms* (1542) and of *Peter Martyr's treatise on the Eucharist (c.1550) and *Ralph Roister Doister*, a Christmas comedy written for a London school, long lost but recovered in the 19th century.

Uganda, Christianity in. The first Christian missionaries were sent to the kingdom of Buganda by the *CMS in 1877; the RC mission was inaugurated by the *White Fathers in 1879. Despite rivalry between the missions, the early preaching was welcomed by many at the court of King Mutesa. Under his successor both Churches suffered persecution: over 40 Christians were martyred between 1885 and 1887, the RCs being canonized in 1964. In the conflict that preceded the establishment of the British Protectorate in 1894, missionaries were expelled. A young leadership was established, the laity came to play a major role in Church life, and mass conversions took place. British rule enabled evangelization to spread from Buganda throughout the Protectorate of Uganda. An impressive network of schools was established and by the latter part of the 20th cent. 75 per cent of the population professed Christianity.

Uganda was notable for the speed with which a local clergy developed, both Anglican and RC. In 1939 an entire Vicariate Apostolic, Masaka, was handed over to African priests under the first Black African RC bishop in modern times.

Ukrainian Churches. These comprise both the Orthodox Churches of the Ukraine and certain *Uniat Churches, mostly in the west of the Ukraine, Slovakia, *Hungary, and *Poland, with colonies in North America. The latter were formerly known as the Ruthenian Churches. Their ancestors, who were Slavonic converts of St *Vladimir, formed part of the *Russian Church until the destruction of Kievan Russia by the

Monguls in 1237–40 and the absorp[...]
the Ukraine by Lithuania and Poland[...]
1595 the Metropolitan of Kiev and 5 other
bishops petitioned for communion with
Rome, achieved by the Union of *Brest-
Litovsk. After the partitions of Poland
(1772–95) most of the Ruthenians, except
those of Galicia, passed under the sovereignty of Russia and their Churches were
gradually suppressed in favour of the
Orthodox Church. The Ruthenians of Galicia came under the sovereignty of Austria.
They enjoyed toleration as, in theory, did
the Uniat Ruthenians (now usually called
Ukrainians) in the independent Poland
constituted after 1918. At the time of the
Russian Revolution the Orthodox Church
in the Ukraine was declared a self-
governing exarchate of the Russian Orthodox Church; it became an autonomous
Church in 1941. In 1946 the Ukrainian Uniat
Church in the Soviet Union and in Poland
was suppressed and forced to declare a
union with the Orthodox Church of the
Ukraine. The Uniats maintained a clandestine existence and in 1989 the Uniat
Church in the Ukraine was restored. There
are now three Churches of the Byzantine
rite in the Ukraine: the Greek-Catholic
Ukrainian Church (the 'Uniats'), the
Ukrainian 'Autonomous' Orthodox
Church, and the Ukrainian 'Unified' (previously 'Autocephalous') Orthodox Church
(created in 1919 in association with a
reform movement in Russia, never recognized by other Orthodox Churches, but
favoured by the political authorities).

A further Ukrainian community (the
Podcarpathian Ruthenians) was created
when a majority of the Ruthenian population south of the Carpathians was brought
into communion with Rome in 1646 by
the Union of Užhorod. Since 1945 this
community has been split between the
Transcarpathian Ukraine, Slovakia, and
Hungary.

There are Ukrainian communities of all
jurisdictions in the USA, *Canada, *Brazil,
and *Argentina.

UIODG (or IODG), the initial letters of *(ut)
in omnibus Deus glorificetur* ('that God may be
glorified in all things'), a motto of the
*Benedictine Order.

Ullathorne, William Bernard (1806–89),
RC Bp. of Birmingham. A monk of *Down-

became [...]
with Card. [...]
the fusion of th[...]
converts and with [...]
modern congregations[...]
can Council he occupied [...]
position.

Ulphilas (c.311–83), Apostle of the Goths.
About 341 he was consecrated bishop by
*Eusebius (formerly Bp. of Nicomedia),
then Bp. of *Constantinople. He then
returned as a missionary to the Goths,
among whom he was born. He translated
the Bible into *Gothic. Through his connection with Eusebius he was led into
*Arianism; it was through his influence that
the Goths were long attached to that heresy.

Ulrich, St (c.890–973), Bp. of Augsburg
from 923. He is the first person known to
have been formally *canonized by a Pope;
John XV pronounced him a saint in 993.
Feast day, 4 July.

Ulrich, St (d. 1154). An alternative form of
Wulfric, St.

Ultramontanism. A tendency in the RC
Church which favours the centralization of
authority in the Papal *Curia as opposed to
national and diocesan independence. It
developed in the 17th and 18th cents. when
national and centrifugal movements such
as *Gallicanism, *Jansenism, and *Josephinism became discredited either as
involved in definite heresy or as countenancing the liberal anti-Christian movements of which the French Revolution was
the logical expression. The main stages of
the triumph of Ultramontanism were the
revival in 1814 of the *Jesuit Order, which
was the mainstay of curial as opposed to
local authority; the publication in 1864 of
the *Syllabus Errorum, in which Catholicism and liberalism were held to be
incompatible; and the declaration of the
First *Vatican Council in 1870 that the Pope
is infallible when he makes a solemn pronouncement on faith or morals.

UMCA. The (Anglican) Universities' Mission to Central Africa. It was founded in

Malawi, the
1864 to the island of
the centre of the slave trade.
this was abolished in 1873, work was
re-established on the mainland; it extended
through Tanzania, Malawi, and *Zambia. In
1965 the UMCA joined with the *SPG to
form the *USPG.

Unam Sanctam (1302). The bull issued by
*Boniface VIII in his quarrel with Philip IV
of France, declaring that there was 'One
Holy Catholic and Apostolic Church' outside which there was 'neither salvation nor
remission of sins'. It contained nothing
new, but it brought to a point the growing
claims of the Papacy and marks the zenith
of medieval Papal ecclesiastical polity.

uncial script. A form of majuscule script
(similar to modern 'capitals') used for
books in Greek and Latin from about the
4th to the 8th cent. AD.

Uncreated Light. In the *Hesychast system the mystical light of God's visible Presence which the soul was held to be capable
of apprehending by submitting to a process
of ascetic purification and devotion.

unction. Anointing with oil, with a
religious significance, usually by a bishop
or priest, e.g. at the *Coronation of a monarch. In the RC and E. Orthodox Churches
unction is used at both *Baptism and
*Confirmation, but the word is most
commonly applied to the Sacrament of the
Unction (or Anointing) of the Sick, long
known in the W. as Extreme Unction.

In the NT anointing of the sick is mentioned in Mk. 6: 13 and Jas. 5: 14 f. There are
various references in the Fathers, and from
the time of *Peter Lombard (d. 1160) it has
been reckoned one of the *Seven Sacraments. Until c.800 recovery from illness
was expected to result. In the W., however,
the rite became connected with the penitential system and was commonly post-
poned until death was approaching; bodily
recovery was not ordinarily looked for. The
1972 RC Ordo again lays emphasis on healing. After prayer and the laying on of
hands, the patient is anointed on the forehead and hands; normally oil blessed by the
bishop on *Maundy Thursday is used. In
the E. Church the rite, called *Euchelaion*
(from the Greek words meaning 'prayer'
and 'oil'), is administered in church by a

number of priests. The primary end is
said to be physical cure, but it is often
received as a preparation for Communion
by those who are not ill. In the C of E
a form of unction was included in the
Order for the *Visitation of the Sick in
1549, but was dropped in 1552. Provision
for anointing the sick is included in
most modern Anglican liturgies, including
CW.

Underhill, Evelyn (1875–1941), English
exponent of the mystical life. In 1907 she
underwent an experience of religious conversion; she was drawn to the RC Church
but felt unable to join it and turned to the
study of the mystics. The comprehensive
approach of her book on *Mysticism* (1911)
made it a standard work. In 1911 she came
under the influence of F. *von Hügel; in
1921 she became a communicant member
of the C of E, and from 1924 she conducted
retreats. *Worship* (1936) embodies her
general outlook in a broad review of the
subject. Feast day in the *Episcopal Church
in the USA and in CW, 15 June.

Uniat (or Eastern Catholic) Churches.
The Churches of E. Christendom in communion with Rome, which retain their
respective languages and rites in accordance with the terms of their union; these
usually provide for *Communion in both
kinds, *Baptism by immersion, and marriage of the clergy. They used to retain their
own *canon law, but in 1990 a code for all
the Uniat Churches was promulgated. The
main groups are the *Maronites, *Syrians,
*Malankarese, of the Antiochene rite; the
*Armenians; the *Chaldeans and *Mala-
brese of the Chaldean rite; the *Copts and
*Ethiopians, of the Alexandrian rite; and
of the Byzantine rite, the *Ukrainians,
*Hungarians, *Romanians, *Melchites, and
some Bulgars, Serbs, and Greeks.

Uniformity, Acts of. (1) The Uniformity
Act 1548, passed in 1549, imposed the
exclusive use of the First Book of *Common
Prayer in all public services and laid down
penalties for holders of benefices who
failed to comply. (2) The Uniformity Act
1551, passed in 1552, ordered the use of the
Second BCP. Absence from church on Sundays and Holy Days without reasonable
cause was punishable by ecclesiastical censures, and attendance at other forms of
service by imprisonment. (3) The Act of

Uniformity 1558, passed in 1559, ordered the use of the 1552 BCP, with slight modifications. Absence from church was now punishable by a fine. (4) The Act of Uniformity 1662 required that all ministers should publicly assent to the 1662 BCP and ordered its exclusive use. Ministers not episcopally ordained were to be deprived. Some 2,000 *Presbyterian ministers who refused to conform were ejected from their livings. This Act has been modified by subsequent legislation, most notably by the Church of England (*Worship and Doctrine) Measure 1974.

Unigenitus. (1) *Clement VI's bull 1343 approving the teaching that *indulgences owe their efficacy to the Pope's dispensation of the accumulated *merit of the Church. (2) *Clement XI's constitution of 1713 condemning 101 propositions from P. *Quesnel's *Réflexions morales*.

Union Theological Seminary, New York. An institution for the training of ministers founded in 1836 by the independent action of 'New School' Presbyterians for 'men of moderate views' of any denomination.

Unitarianism. A type of Christian thought and religious observance which rejects the doctrines of the Trinity and the Divinity of Christ in favour of the unipersonality of God.

Modern Unitarianism dates from the Reformation era. It attracted adherents among those of extreme reforming views, especially among the sects. Early Unitarians included M. *Servetus and B. *Ochino. Organized communities became established in the 16th-17th cents. in *Poland, where F. *Socinus was their leader from 1579 until his death (1604) and where the *Racovian Catechism was issued in 1605, in *Hungary, and in England. The followers of J. *Biddle held conventicles in London in 1652-4. A century later Unitarian principles were defended by J. *Priestley, and in 1773 T. *Lindsey seceded from the C of E and for the first time formed a Unitarian denomination. Penal Acts remained in force against Unitarians until 1813. In the 18th cent. Unitarian views were also widely accepted by Dissenting congregations, especially among the English *Presbyterians. In the 19th cent. great influence was exercised by J. *Martineau, who insisted that 'Unitarian' could be only the name of the belief of

individuals, not the restrictive title of a denomination. The early 20th cent. saw a swing towards more radical Unitarianism in some quarters. Since 1925 the Unitarians in England have been a distinctive and organized denomination, though its numbers have dwindled in modern times.

In America the beginnings of definitive Unitarianism date from the late 18th cent. In the early 19th cent. Unitarianism was also adopted in *Congregational Churches. By the end of the 19th cent. American Unitarianism had become a liberal or rationalist movement, accepting scientific methods and ideas and recognizing the truth of non-Christian religions. In 1961 the American Unitarian Association (founded in 1825) joined with the Universalist Church of America to form the Unitarian Universalist Association.

Unitas Fratrum. The Latinized title of the *Bohemian Brethren and their successors, the *Moravian Brethren.

United Church of Christ. A Church in the USA formed in 1957 by the union of nearly all members of the Evangelical and Reformed Church with about 85 per cent of the *Congregational Christian Churches. Both bodies were themselves the results of earlier unions, the former containing *Lutheran and *Calvinist elements.

United Free Church of Scotland. The Church formed in 1900 by the union of the *United Presbyterian Church and the *Free Church of Scotland. The greater part joined the Established Church of Scotland in 1929, but a minority remains outside this union.

United Methodist Church. (1) In England, the branch of Methodism formed in 1907 by the union of the *Methodist New Connexion, the *Bible Christians, and the *United Methodist Free Churches (qq.v.). It was itself embodied in the *Methodist Church (q.v.) in 1932. (2) In the USA, the Church formed in 1968 by a union of the Methodist Church and the Evangelical United Brethren Church. It is the main Methodist Church in the country.

United Methodist Free Churches. One of the bodies which made up the *United Methodist Church in 1907. It was an amalgamation of small communities which had broken away from Wesleyan *Methodism for constitutional, not doctrinal, reasons. The Protestant Methodists were formed in 1827; the immediate cause of their secession was the erection of an organ at Brunswick Chapel, Leeds. The Wesleyan Methodist Association was formed in 1835 as the result of a dispute about the foundation of a Theological Institution for the training of ministers; it was joined by the Protestant Methodists in 1836. The Wesleyan Reformers came into being after three ministers had been expelled from the 1849 Conference when they refused to answer questions about some anonymous pamphlets known as Fly Sheets. The Wesleyan Methodist Association and the bulk of the Wesleyan Reformers joined in 1857 to form the United Methodist Free Churches.

United Presbyterian Church. The Church formed in Scotland in 1847 by the union of the *United Secession Church and the Relief Synod, a body formed in 1761 after difficulties over the patronage system. In 1900, apart from a small minority (the *Wee Frees) it joined the *Free Church of Scotland to form the *United Free Church of Scotland.

United Reformed Church. The Church formed in 1972 by the union of the greater part of the *Congregational Church of England and Wales with the *Presbyterian Church of England. In 1981 most of the *Disciples of Christ in Britain joined it; as some of these congregations were in Scotland, the Church took the name 'United Reformed Church in the United Kingdom'.

United Secession Church. The Church formed in Scotland in 1820 by the fusion of the 'New Lichts' of the *Burghers and Antiburghers. It 1847 it was embodied in the *United Presbyterian Church.

United Society for Christian Literature. A society formed in 1935 by the fusion of the *Religious Tract Society, the Christian Literature Society for India and Africa (founded 1858), and the Christian Literature Society for China (founded 1884).

United Society for the Propagation of the Gospel. See USPG.

United States of America, Christianity in. The colonial settlement of North America produced a pattern of religious diversity reflecting the fragmented state of European Christianity. In 1565 on the Florida peninsula the Spanish founded St Augustine, the oldest Christian settlement on what would become the United States. Later they established other RC missions in the SW part of the continent. RC missionaries also accompanied French fur-traders into the upper regions of North America. English land companies chartered by the Crown organized the first successful settlements at Jamestown (1603) in Virginia and at Plymouth (1620) and Massachusetts Bay (1630) in New England. In Virginia the C of E was legally established; in New England *Puritanism was initially the official religion. Maryland was founded in 1634 by a RC nobleman; Roger *Williams organized Rhode Island for dissenters. William *Penn, a *Quaker, received a charter for Pennsylvania (1681), which became a haven for the oppressed. The Dutch and Swedish brought the Dutch Reformed and *Lutheran Churches to New Netherland (1626) and New Sweden (1638). By the end of the 17th cent. regional patterns were evident. The C of E was dominant in the southern English colonies; in Puritan New England Reformed ideas, as modified by *covenant theology, held sway; in the middle colonies *Presbyterians, Quakers, RCs, Lutherans, Jews, and *Baptists lived side by side. In the Spanish and French regions of North America, RCism remained the established Church.

The most significant event of the 18th cent. was the *Great Awakening, a series of religious revivals originating in isolated Dutch Reformed, *Congregational, and Presbyterian congregations in the 1720s and 1730s. In the early 1740s a surge of religious activity swept through the English colonies. The 'New Light Movement', arising out of the Great Awakening, featured the need for a 'new birth', a describable spiritual experience of transforming grace. This provided grounds for an assault upon the traditional authority of the clergy and the integrity of the parish system by supporting lay exhorters and itinerant preachers. It also gave increased religious opportunities to women and new impetus to Christianize Blacks and Indians.

After the American Revolution (1776–83), the Anglicans secured their first American bishop with the consecration in 1784 of Samuel *Seabury and the Protestant *Episcopal Church became an autonomous organization, no longer dependent on the C of E. The Methodists decisively broke with Anglicanism when J. *Wesley appointed a Superintendent for America in 1784. In the same year the RCs ceased to be dependent on the *Vicars Apostolic in England; in 1790 they acquired a bishop of their own when John *Carroll was consecrated. The Constitution, with its Bill of Rights (1791), guaranteed religious liberty and the First Amendment proscribed religious establishments, thus laying the foundation of the system of religious pluralism.

In the early 19th cent. the evangelical Churches experienced a new surge of *revivalism at the time when thousands of migrants were leaving the seaboard areas for the transappalachian regions. The Second Great Awakening (1800–35) affected the whole republic. After 1820 an increasing stream of immigrants from N. and W. Europe added to the religious diversity. The arrival of nearly a million Irish, most fervently RC, before 1860 transformed the RC Church which by then was the largest single denomination. There were also new religious movements. Some were imported, such as the *Harmonists. More were indigenous, often centred on charismatic leaders who claimed special revelations and chose unconventional patterns of life. They included the *Shakers, the *Oneida Community, the 'Christians' (later *Disciples of Christ) and the *Mormons.

The question of racial *slavery divided American Christians. Some argued for freeing the slaves, others that slavery had biblical sanction and was a means to Christianization. In the North, free Blacks organized independent *Black Churches. By the time of the Civil War (1861–5) Presbyterians, Methodists, and Baptists had split over the issue. The intellectual revolution symbolized by the publication of Charles Darwin's *Origin of Species* (1859) was reflected in theological conflict. Conservative Protestants, later identified as *Fundamentalists, rejected the new science in the name of tradition and became embroiled in ecclesiastical controversies. Protestant Liberalism, also known as the 'New Theology' or Progressive Orthodoxy, attempted a reconciliation of science and tradition in support of an optimistic perspective on human nature and progress, emphasizing the immanence of God. At the same time, the expanding

urban environment, with its stresses and uncertainties, fostered the growth of new religious movements. These included *Christian Science, *Seventh-day Adventism, and *Jehovah's Witnesses. *Holiness and *Pentecostal Churches arose in both urban and rural locations in response to a perceived loss of spiritual vitality.

In the early 20th cent. the religious and cultural hegemony exercised by Protestantism in the 19th cent. was eroded. This was partly due to the rapid expansion of the RC, Greek and Russian Orthodox, Jewish and sectarian communities, and to the theological divisions within Protestantism, especially the Modernist-Fundamentalist struggle. A growing effort to overcome divisions among Protestant denominations led to the formation by liberal Protestants of the Federal Council of Churches in 1908; the American Council of Christian Churches (1941) and the National Association of Evangelicals (1942) were formed as alternative federations of conservative Protestant Churches. Ecclesiastical mergers among Presbyterians, Methodists, and Lutherans took place around the middle of the 20th cent. After the Second World War (1939–45) large numbers of immigrants from E. Europe and the Middle East brought members of Orthodox Churches other than the Greek and Russian who had come earlier.

The beginning of the second half of the 20th cent. was one of prosperity for organized religion. The RC Church became a powerful force in American life, and in 1960 John Kennedy (a RC) was elected President. Conservative Evangelicalism experienced a resurgence, and Billy *Graham rose to fame by his effective use of the media. In the 1960s there was a general shift towards a more secular life-style. The Second *Vatican Council (1962–5) brought changes and upheavals in the RC Church. Most Protestant Churches suffered loss of membership, though the more conservative ones (notably the Southern Baptists) continued to grow, as did the sectarian communities. Religious issues have come to play a prominent part in politics, with the Religious Right supporting prayer and Bible reading in State schools, as well as opposing *abortion, equal rights for women and *homosexuals, and the teaching of evolution. Television preachers have disseminated these ideas (see BROADCASTING, RELIGIOUS). *Feminist and *Liberation theology have cut across denominational lines. Christianity no longer exercises the hegemony in American life that it did until the middle of the 20th cent.

unitive way. The third and last stage of the spiritual life. See PURGATIVE, ILLUMINATIVE, AND UNITIVE WAYS.

Univers, L'. A French newspaper which, under the editorship of L. *Veuillot, became an organ of extreme *Ultramontane views.

Universalism. (1) The teaching of some of the later Hebrew prophets that God's purpose covered not only the Jewish race but at least some people of other nations. (2) Another name for Apocatastasis (q.v.).

universals. Abstract concepts, representing the common elements belonging to individuals of the same genus or species. The medieval doctrine of universals derived from Greek philosophy. According to their answer to the question whether universals were things ('res') or only names ('nomina'), philosophers subscribed to the system of *Realism or *Nominalism (qq.v.).

Universities' Mission to Central Africa. See UMCA.

Unknowing, The Cloud of. See CLOUD OF UNKNOWING, THE.

unleavened bread. See BREAD, LEAVENED AND UNLEAVENED.

Upper Room, the. See CENACULUM.

Uppsala. Uppsala became the head of an ecclesiastical province, separate from *Lund, in 1164, and from the mid-15th cent. until the Reformation the Archbishop was styled 'Primate of Sweden'. The university, founded in 1477, in the 19th cent. became the home of a liberal and 'Low Church' theology as contrasted with the orthodoxy of Lund.

Urban II (c.1035–99), Pope from 1088. He was a monk of *Cluny, called to Rome by *Gregory VII. On his election he was faced by an antipope, who was backed by the Emp. *Henry IV, and he could not at first enter Rome. In 1089 he held a Council at Melfi which promulgated canons against *simony, lay *investiture, and clerical marriage, and in 1095 he held two Councils at

Piacenza and *Clermont, also concerned with the reform of the Church. At Clermont the '*Truce of God' was proclaimed a law of the Church; Philip of France, who had put away his queen and remarried, was anathematized; and Urban launched the First *Crusade. He also tried to heal the E. schism. Feast day, 29 or 30 July.

Urban V (1309/10–70), Pope from 1362. He was a *Benedictine monk and in many ways the best of the *Avignon Popes. He seriously tried to reform the Church, especially with regard to the distribution of benefices. In 1367, urged by the Emp. Charles IV, he moved to Rome, where he was enthusiastically received by the people. In 1369 he received the E. Emp. John V Palaeologus into communion. Later in 1369 Perugia revolted and war broke out between England and France; despite the admonitions of St *Bridget, Urban returned to France in 1370. Feast day, 19 Dec.

Urban VI (1318–89), Pope from 8 Apr. 1378. He was elected on the death of *Gregory XI under pressure from the Roman populace, who demanded an Italian. Though he had previously been noted for his austerity and aptitude for affairs, his pontificate became a series of grave imprudences. In Aug. 1378 the French cardinals declared his election void as performed under duress, and in Sept. they elected the antipope Clement VII, thus beginning the *Great Schism.

Urban VIII (1568–1644), Pope from 1623. Though Maffeo Barberini was essentially a 'political' Pope, he encouraged religious life by canonizing a number of saints and approving new orders such as the *Visitation (1626), and he fostered missionary efforts by founding the Urban College of *Propaganda (1627). His decrees on *canonization still have a place in the present law and his revision of the *Breviary remained in force until 1912. He also revised the *Missal and *Pontifical and reduced the number of *Feasts of Obligation. Under him G. *Galilei was condemned for the second time (1633) and the *Augustinus of C. O. *Jansen declared heretical (1642). From 1625 he favoured the policy of Card. *Richelieu against the Habsburgs and deprived the Catholic League of subsidies, but he tried to prevent the alliance of France and Sweden.

Urbi et Orbi (Lat., 'to the City [i.e. of Rome] and for the World'). A phrase used especially of the solemn blessing which the Pope imparts from time to time from the balcony of *St Peter's, Rome.

Urbs Beata Hierusalem. A 6th–7th-cent. hymn celebrating the Heavenly Jerusalem in terms suggested by Rev. 21. The many English translations include J. M. *Neale's 'Blessed City, heavenly Salem'.

Urbs Sion Aurea. A set of extracts from a work of *Bernard of Cluny in use as the well-known hymn 'Jerusalem the golden'.

Urgeschichte (Ger., 'prehistory'). A term used in *Dialectical Theology for events which, from the standpoint of faith, are seen to be God's direct supernatural revelation to man, though viewed from the human angle they appear merely as historical occurrences.

Urim and Thummin. Probably originally 'lots', used in early Hebrew divination to interpret the will of God to the people. There are several references in the OT.

Ursacius (fl. 335–71), Bp. of Singidunum (Belgrade). With *Valens (q.v.), a leader of the *Arians in the West.

Ursinus, Zacharias (1534–83), *Calvinist theologian. He taught at Breslau before he went to Heidelberg in 1561. At the behest of the Elector *Frederick III, with K. Olivian, he drew up the *Heidelberg Catechism (q.v.). On Frederick's death he went to Neustadt, where he wrote the *Admonitio Christiana* (see NEOSTADIENSIUM ADMONITIO).

Ursula, St. The legend of St Ursula and her 11,000 virgins grew out of the veneration of some nameless virgins martyred at *Cologne, attested in the 4th–5th cent. By the 8th–9th cent. several thousand virgins were said to have perished. Still later Ursula, whose name was attached to their leader, was described as a British princess who, with 11,000 virgins, went on a pilgrimage to Rome, and on their way back were massacred at Cologne by the Huns. Feast day, 21 Oct., suppressed in 1969.

Ursulines. The oldest teaching order of women in the RC Church. It was founded at Brescia in 1535 by St *Angela Merici. The original members lived in their own houses; community life and simple vows were introduced in 1572. In 1612 *Paul V allowed the Ursulines of Paris solemn vows and strict enclosure. The work of the Order then developed into the institutional form of schools for girls, especially in France. Most houses were autonomous, but in 1900 a number of convents belonging to different congregations formed the 'Roman Union'. Later unions include that of Eastern Quebec, formed in 1953. Since the Second *Vatican Council, the Ursulines (no longer strictly enclosed) have been able to undertake a wider range of pastoral work.

Usagers. The section of the *Nonjurors who in 1719 accepted the Communion Service drawn up by J. *Collier and others. They were so named from the four 'usages' which the new rite contained: the '*mixed chalice', prayers for the *dead, a prayer for the descent of the Holy Spirit on the elements (*Epiclesis), and an oblatory prayer.

use. In the study of liturgy, a local modification of the standard (especially Roman) rite. In the W. such uses arose partly through the absorption of *Gallican features by the Roman rite as it spread through Europe, and partly through local developments in the Roman rite itself. They were often used over a wide area, e.g. the use of *Salisbury. Most local uses were abolished by the Council of *Trent.

USPG. The United Society for the Propagation of the Gospel, formed in 1965 when the *SPG and the *UMCA amalgamated.

Ussher, James (1581–1656), Abp. of *Armagh from 1625. A scholar of vast learning, he was an authority on a wide range of subjects, including biblical chronology and the early history of Ireland. He distinguished the seven genuine letters of St *Ignatius from the later spurious ones, whose existence had previously discredited the whole collection. After the Irish rebellion in 1641 he remained in England.

Usuard, Martyrology of. The most widely circulated of the medieval *martyrologies and the basis of the '*Roman Martyrology'. Its compiler, Usuard (d. c.875), was a monk of the Abbey of *St-Germain-des-Prés at Paris. He seems to have based his work on the somewhat earlier Martyrology of *Ado of Vienne (d. 875).

usury. The exaction of interest was forbidden in the OT in the case of Jewish debtors. In the patristic age clerics were forbidden to lend at interest and in the Middle Ages this prohibition was extended to lay Christians, though Jews were exempted by the Fourth *Lateran Council (1215). It was justified by the medieval view of money as solely a means of exchange. With the rise of capitalism, money came to be regarded not as a barren means of exchange but as capital productive of wealth. Since the exaction of a moderate rate of interest for loans has been tolerated by the Church (and State), the term 'usury' has tended to be restricted to excessive rates.

Utica, the Martyrs of. A group of early African martyrs of uncertain date who suffered at the Massa Candida ('White Farm'). The name of the place, misunderstood as 'White Lump', gave rise to the legend that they were thrown alive into slaking quicklime and their bodies reduced to a mass of white powder. According to St *Augustine, the massacre took place at Utica, 35 miles from Carthage. Feast day, 24 Aug.

Utilitarianism. The doctrine in ethics which identifies the good with happiness and maintains those actions to be right which bring the greatest happiness to the greatest number.

Utraquism. The doctrine that the laity, like the clergy, should receive Communion under the forms of both bread and wine. It was maintained by the followers of John *Huss. Communion in both kinds was conceded to the laity of Bohemia by the Compactata of Prague (1433). Formally cancelled by *Pius II in 1462, the practice ended after the defeat of the Bohemian revolt in 1620.

Utrecht, Declaration of. The profession of faith which is the doctrinal basis of the *Old Catholic Church. It was drawn up at Utrecht in 1889. While professing adherence to the beliefs of the primitive Church, it is mainly concerned with controverting specific doctrines of the RC Church, including the decrees on the Papacy of the First *Vatican Council, the dogma of the *Immaculate Conception of the BVM, and the *Syllabus Errorum.

Vacancy-in-See Committee. When a diocese in the C of E becomes vacant, the Vacancy-in-See Committee of the diocese draws up a statement of the needs of the diocese, discusses possible candidates, and elects four representatives to sit on the *Crown Appointments Commission.

Vaison, Councils of. Two important Councils were held at Vaison in SE France. (1) That of 442 provided, *inter alia*, that clergy should receive the *chrism at Easter from their own bishops, and it regulated the adoption of children. (2) That of 529 issued five canons of liturgical import.

Valdés, Juan de (?1490–1541), Spanish religious writer. He fled from the Spanish *Inquisition to Italy in 1531. From 1534 he lived in Naples, where he became the spiritual centre of a group of prominent people anxious for reform and revival in the Church. Though outwardly he remained a Catholic, his conception of personal religion and interiority was largely Protestant in character and later had a wide appeal for the Reformed traditions; after his death various of his friends left the RC Church. He wrote a number of religious works and translated the Hebrew Psalter into Catalan.

His brother, **Alfonso de Valdés** (?1490–1532) was a noted humanist. His *Diálogo de Mercurio y Carón* (1529), which attacks religion that has become a matter of empty, outward forms, was long erroneously attributed to Juan.

Valdes, Peter. See WALDENSES.

Valence, Councils of. Three important Councils were held at Valence in Dauphiné. (1) That of 374 issued four disciplinary canons. (2) That of c.530 was directed against *Pelagianism and *Semipelagianism. (3) That of 855 discussed *predestination. It upheld 'double predestination' and rejected the view that the redemptive work of Christ extended to all mankind.

Valens (4th cent.), Bp. of Mursa (modern Osijek). With *Ursacius, he was an *Arian leader in the W. Pupils of *Arius, they became bitter enemies of St *Athanasius. They attacked him or adopted a more compromising position in accordance with changes in the policy of the Emp. Constantius.

Valentine, St. The commemoration formerly observed on 14 Feb. appears to refer to two Valentines: a Roman priest martyred on the Flaminian Way c.269, and a Bp. of Terni who was taken to Rome and martyred. The association of St Valentine's day with courtship is not connected with any tradition concerning either saint of the name.

Valentinus (d. c.165), *Gnostic theologian and founder of the Valentinian sect. Apparently a native of Egypt, he came to Rome c.136 and is said to have hoped to be elected Bishop, was passed over, seceded from the Church, and went to the E. Later he returned to Rome, where he died.

Several texts from *Nag Hammadi derive from the Valentinian school (including the *Evangelium Veritatis and the Gospel of *Philip), but none can confidently be ascribed to Valentinus. His system is known only in the form developed and modified by his disciples. The spiritual world or 'pleroma' comprises 30 'aeons' emanated by the Primal Ground of Being. The visible world owes its origin to the fall of Sophia, the last of these aeons; this fall is variously described, but results in the emergence of her offspring the *Demiurge or creator, identified with the God of the OT. The Valentinian myth is intended to explain the human predicament by showing how a divine element has become imprisoned in this alien world. Redemption is effected by another aeon, Christ, who unites with the man Jesus (either at his conception or at his baptism) to bring mankind the saving knowledge ('gnosis') of its origin and destiny. This gnosis, however, is given only to the 'spiritual' or 'pneumatics', i.e. the Valentinians, who through it are destined to return to the pleroma; other Christians can attain by faith and good works to a form of salvation, but only in the lower realm below the pleroma; the rest of mankind are doomed to eternal perdition.

Valerian, St (d. after 450), Bp. of Cemele (now Cimiez) in S. Gaul. He was present at the Councils of Riez (439) and *Vaison (442), and he upheld the jurisdictional claims of the see of Arles against *Leo I. Theologically he seems to have inclined to *Semipelagianism. Feast day, 23 July.

validation of marriage. A marriage null by reason of defective consent or some *diriment impediment can be validated in canon law (1) by simple renewal of consent or (2) by *dispensation, depending on the circumstances of the original defect.

validity. A term used in W. sacramental theology to denote that a *Sacrament is genuine if certain formal conditions have been fulfilled. It is distinguished from fruitfulness (or efficacy) and regularity. Thus a Sacrament, even if celebrated irregularly (e.g. outside the unity of the Church), and even if unfruitful in that the participants will not receive *grace through the Sacrament, may still be a real (or valid) Sacrament, conferring e.g. membership of the Church (in the case of *Baptism) or Holy *Orders (in the case of Ordination). The formal conditions are that the minister of the Sacrament be himself validly ordained (if necessary), that the essential part of the Church's liturgy be used (see FORM), and that there be a proper *intention on the part of the minister to do what the Church intends in celebrating the Sacrament. The concept was developed in the W. in connection with the problem of the Church's attitude to Sacraments conferred in heresy or schism. It was repudiated by most Protestants at the Reformation.

Valla, Lorenzo (c.1406–57), Italian humanist. His famous work demonstrating the spuriousness of the '*Donation of Constantine' (1440) contained a bitter attack on the temporal power of the Papacy. He also ridiculed the dialectical method of *Scholasticism and denied the possibility of understanding the harmony of God's omnipotence with human free will. His *De Elegantiis Linguae Latinae* (first version, 1441) long remained a standard work on humanist Latin. His audacious views had a deep influence on Renaissance scholars and his writings were held in high esteem by the Reformers.

Vallumbrosans. A monastic *Congregation, formerly a separate order, so named from the mother house at Vallombrosa, *c.*20 miles from Florence. The Order was founded *c.*1036 by St *John Gualbert. The mother house was burnt by the soldiers of *Charles V in 1527, plundered by Napoleon's troops in 1808, suppressed by the Italian government in 1866, but restored in 1949. The Vallumbrosans joined the *Benedictine Confederation in 1966.

Valor Ecclesiasticus. The official valuation of ecclesiastical and monastic revenues made in 1535, popularly known as the 'King's Books'. It was necessitated by the legislation of *Henry VIII appropriating ecclesiastical revenues to the Crown.

van der Kemp, Johannes Theodorus (1747–1811), Dutch missionary. After a spiritual conversion following the death of his wife and daughter in 1791, he was ordained in the Church of *Scotland and went as leader of three missionaries sent by the *LMS to *South Africa in 1799. His preaching was probably heard by Ntsikana (*c.*1760–1820), the visionary Xhosa prophet. Van der Kemp finally settled among the Khoi (Hottentots, later known as 'Cape Coloured'), whose cause he championed.

Van Espen, Zeger Bernhard (1646–1728), Belgian canonist. His most important work is *Jus Ecclesiasticum Universum* (1700). He defended *Gallican theories and was an ardent upholder of secular power against religious authority.

van Eyck, Hubert (d. 1426) and **Jan** (d. 1441), Flemish painters. Jan became court painter to Philip, Duke of Burgundy, in 1425, and probably in 1430 settled in Bruges. The Ghent Altarpiece, for which the brothers are renowned, is a huge polyptych of 12 oak panels arranged in two layers, the outer panels painted on both sides. They depict the Adoration of the Lamb, Christ enthroned, and other subjects. A quatrain on the frame asserts that it was begun by

Hubert and finished by Jan in 1432, but Hubert's connection with it has sometimes been denied. From the 16th cent. the van Eycks were believed to have invented oil painting; this is clearly untrue, but they (or Jan, as no work is known which is certainly Hubert's) made technical advances which permitted unprecedented realism of detail and richness of colour.

Van Mildert, William (1765–1836), Bp. of *Durham from 1826. The last bishop with palatine rank, he was one of the founders of Durham University.

Vane, Henry (1613–62), English politician. In the Long Parliament he was a bitter opponent of W. *Laud and of Strafford, and he was one of the commissioners chiefly responsible for the *Solemn League and Covenant. In 1652 he became President of the Council of State, but latterly lost influence. At the *Restoration he was arrested and was executed in 1662.

Vangeon, Henri-Léon. See GHEON, HENRI.

Västerås, Ordinance of (1527). The regulations passed by the Diet of Västerås which carried through the Protestant Reformation in *Sweden.

Vatican. The main residence of the Popes in Rome since their return from *Avignon in 1377. Little of the existing building is earlier than the 15th cent. Extensive rebuilding was planned by *Nicholas V in 1447 and the palace was completed by *Clement VIII (d. 1605). Under the Law of *Guarantees (1871) the Vatican, with the *Lateran and the Papal villa at *Castel Gandolfo, was granted extraterritoriality. The Vatican Museum houses valuable collections of early Christian art and antiquities; the Vatican Library contains important MSS. For the basilica, see ST PETER'S, ROME.

Vatican Council, First (1869–70), reckoned by RCs the 20th *Oecumenical Council. Convoked by *Pius IX in 1868, it was intended to deal with a wide variety of subjects. It opened in Dec. 1869 and began by discussing the schema 'De Fide'. A revised constitution on Faith, 'Dei Filius', was promulgated on 24 Apr. 1870. It contains four chapters on God the Creator, on Revelation, on Faith, and on Faith and Reason. It was decided to turn next to the questions of Papal *infallibility and the primacy of the

Pope. In the debate on the primacy the minority particularly objected to the definition of the Pope's jurisdiction as ordinary, immediate, and truly episcopal. They also tried to get his infallibility linked more closely with that of the Church. The constitution '*Pastor Aeternus', accepted on 18 July, disappointed the extremists on both sides. It clearly stated the infallibility of the Pope, but restricted it to those occasions when, speaking ex *cathedra, he defines a doctrine regarding faith or morals. The outbreak of war between France and Prussia on 19 July and the Italian occupation of Rome brought the Council to an end.

The definitions of the Council aroused serious opposition only in Germany and Austria. In these countries small minorities organized themselves as '*Old Catholics', and in Germany Bismarck's opposition to the consolidation of Papal power issued in the *Kulturkampf.

Vatican Council, Second (1962–5), reckoned by RCs the 21st *Oecumenical Council. The decision to hold a Council was apparently due entirely to *John XXIII; it was intended to renew the life of the Church and to bring up to date its teaching, discipline, and organization, with the unity of all Christians as the ultimate goal. Observers from the main Churches not in communion with the RC Church were invited to the Council. After the First Session (Oct.–Dec. 1962), Pope John died. *Paul VI on his election announced that he intended to continue the Council. The Second Session (Sept.–Dec. 1963) promulgated a Constitution on the Liturgy and a decree on the Instruments of Social Communication. The Third Session (Sept.–Nov. 1964) promulgated a Dogmatic Constitution on the Church and decrees on Ecumenism and the Eastern Catholic Churches; and the Pope proclaimed the BVM to be the 'Mother of the Church'. The Fourth Session (Sept.–Dec. 1965) promulgated decrees on a variety of subjects, including the Bishops' Pastoral Office, the Appropriate Renewal of the Religious life, and the Apostolate of the Laity, and the Declaration on the Relationship of the Church to Non-Christian Religions. The Pope formulated the norms of the new episcopal synod which was to help him govern the Church and announced the beginning of the reform of the *Curia.

The consequences of the Council have been far-reaching. The most obvious has been the almost complete replacement of Latin by the vernacular in the liturgy; nearly all the liturgical texts have been revised, and *Communion in both kinds gradually extended to the laity. Public worship in the RC Church is now closely akin to that in other W. Churches. Relationships with other Churches are now warm; there are regular dialogues with *Orthodox, *Anglican, *Lutheran, *Methodist and other Churches, and co-operation in various areas of work. The 'Constitution on the Church in the Modern World' inaugurated a shift in the Church's concern towards social and political issues, especially in the Third World. The development of a permanent married *diaconate has changed the shape of the Church's ministry, especially in North America. Inevitably, the changes have produced tensions within the RC Church. For legislation implementing decisions of the Council, see PAUL VI.

Vaudois. See WALDENSES.

Vaughan, Charles John (1816–97), Dean of *Llandaff from 1879. In 1860 he became Vicar of Doncaster. Here he began preparing graduates for ordination; by the time of his death over 450 young men, known as 'Vaughan's Doves', had gone through his training. His sympathy with Nonconformity won him influence in S. Wales, and he took part in the foundation of the University College at Cardiff (1883–4).

Vaughan, Henry (1622–95), poet. He practised medicine in Brecon and from c.1650 at Newton-by-Usk. A religious experience, due partly perhaps to the death of a brother and a serious illness, issued in a collection of spiritual poems, Silex Scintillans (1650–55). They are marked by an atmosphere of intense and sustained religious fervour. Vaughan is often numbered among the '*Metaphysical Poets'.

Vaughan, Herbert (1832–1903), Abp. of Westminster from 1892, made Cardinal in 1893. Descended from an old English RC family, in 1866 he founded St Joseph's College, *Mill Hill (q.v.). From 1872 to 1892 he was Bp. of Salford. The most notable events of his archiepiscopacy were his obtaining permission from the authorities at Rome for RCs to attend the ancient English universities, the building of *Westminster Cathedral, the discussions over *Anglican Ordinations, and his activities in connection with the Education Bill of 1902.

Vaughan Williams, Ralph (1872–1958), English composer. Apart from active service in the 1914–18 War, his life was devoted to music. He composed works of every kind, including nine symphonies and six operas. He wrote hymn tunes, among them the notable *Sine nomine* ('For all the saints'), a superb Mass in G minor, *canticle settings and anthems, the *Te Deum* in G for C. G. *Lang's enthronement at Canterbury and a *Festival Te Deum* for the coronation of George VI. He was music editor of the *English Hymnal* and helped in the preparation of *Songs of Praise* and the *Oxford Book of Carols*.

Vecchioni. Members of an ancient guild at Milan. Until recent times four of them made public offerings of bread and wine on behalf of the laity at solemn celebrations of the Liturgy in Milan cathedral.

Vedast, St (d. 539), also 'Vaast'. He was deputed to prepare *Clovis I for Baptism. About 499 he was consecrated Bp. of Arras, where he established Christianity; he was also put in charge of the diocese of Cambrai. Feast day, 6 Feb.

veil. (1) Christian headdress. The veil, which was worn by Roman matrons, from the 3rd cent. was given by the bishop to consecrated virgins as a symbol of their spiritual marriage to Christ; it later came to be considered the most important part of the religious *habit of women.

(2) Liturgical cloths for covering various objects, e.g., the *chalice veil, *humeral veil (qq.v.), and the veil used for the *ciborium when containing the sacred species. In the W. Church it is customary to veil all crucifixes and pictures during *Passiontide and later throughout Lent. In current RC practice such veiling is not obligatory and is confined to *Holy Week.

Velichkovsky, St Paisy (1722–94), Ukrainian monk and spiritual writer. In 1746 he became a monk on Mt. *Athos, where he attracted other Slavs and Romanians; his community grew so large that he transferred it to Moldavia. At Dragomirna, and later at Neamţ, he organized a huge monastery modelled on the life on Mt

Athos. Through his writings and training of disciples, he started a spiritual revival which continued the *Hesychast tradition and is still of influence in the E. Orthodox world. Feast day, 15 Nov.

Venantius Fortunatus (c.530–c.610), Latin poet. Born near *Venice, c.565 he went on a pilgrimage to the tomb of St *Martin of Tours; he settled at Poitiers, of which he became bishop towards the end of the 6th cent. He wrote much occasional verse, a metrical Life of St Martin of Tours, and prose Lives of St *Hilary of Poitiers, St *Germanus of Paris, and Queen *Radegunde, as well as the hymns which stand out as the true expression of his genius; they include '*Vexilla Regis' and '*Pange lingua gloriosi'.

Venerable. (1) In the RC Church, a title bestowed on a dead person when a certain stage in the process or *canonization has been reached. It is also used of other persons of marked holiness of life, especially the 'Venerable *Bede'. (2) In the C of E, the title of an *archdeacon.

Veneration of the Cross. A ceremony of the Latin rite for *Good Friday, also called **Creeping to the Cross**, in which clergy and people solemnly venerate a crucifix, usually at the entrance to the sanctuary.

Veni Creator. A Latin hymn to the Holy Spirit, probably composed in the Frankish Empire in the 9th cent. It has been used at Vespers in *Whitsuntide since the 10th cent.; it is also used at the ordination of priests and bishops. English translations include 'Come, Holy Ghost, our souls inspire'.

Veni Sancte Spiritus. The *Sequence for *Whitsunday, now usually attributed to Stephen *Langton. English translations include 'Come, Thou Holy Paraclete'.

Veni, veni, Emmanuel ('O come, O come, Emmanuel'). The hymn is a versification of the *O-Antiphons (q.v.), but the origin of both the words and the music is obscure.

venial sin. In RC *moral theology, a sin which, though it disposes the soul to death and is the greatest of all evils except *mortal sin (q.v.), does not wholly deprive the soul of sanctifying grace.

Venice. The see of Venice goes back to the

bishopric founded in 774 on the isle of Olivolo, later known as Castello. Owing to disputes between the see of Olivolo and the patriarchate of Grado, to which it belonged, both were suppressed in 1451 and replaced by the patriarchate of Venice.

The most famous church is San Marco, originally the chapel of the Doges. Destined to receive the relics of St *Mark, it was completed in 883. Burnt down in 976, it was rebuilt (1063–71) on the model of the Basilica of the Apostles at Constantinople. Its plan forms a Greek cross of equal arms, the centre and each arm being surmounted by a dome. It became the cathedral of the patriarchate in 1807.

Venite. Ps. 95 [Vulg. 94], so called from the opening word of its Latin version. From the time of St *Benedict it has been used in the first *Office of the day in the W. Church. It passed into *Mattins in the BCP.

Venn, Henry (1725–97), *Evangelical. He was vicar of Huddersfield from 1759 to 1771. He later influenced C. *Simeon. His *Complete Duty of Man* (1763) was popular among Evangelicals. In CW, feast day, 1 July.

Venn, Henry (1796–1873), missionary statesman. A grandson of Henry *Venn, he was a leading *Evangelical and secretary to the *CMS from 1841 to 1872. He wanted overseas Churches to be 'self-supporting, self-governing and self-extending'. In CW, feast day, 1 July.

verger. Strictly the official who carries a mace or verge before a dignitary. The term is now commonly used for one who takes care of the interior fabric of a church.

Vergil, Vergilius. See VIRGIL, VIRGILIUS.

Vermigli, Pietro Martire. See PETER MARTYR.

Vermittlungstheologie. A school of 19th-cent. German Protestant theologians who tried in various ways to combine the traditional *Protestantism of the Reformation Confessions with modern science, philosophy, and historical scholarship.

Vernazza, Battista (1497–1587), *Augustinian canoness and mystic. A disciple of St *Catherine of Genoa, she was long thought to have been the final redactor of her works, but this suggestion has been discredited.

Verona. The first historically attested Bp. of Verona is Lucilius, who took part in the Council of *Sardica (343). Its patron is St *Zeno. An important synod was held at Verona in 1184; it introduced the episcopal *inquisition. The 12th-cent. cathedral houses *Titian's painting of the Assumption; the chapter library has a notable collection of manuscripts.

Verona Fathers. The popular name for the Comboni Missionaries of the Heart of Jesus, a society of priests and lay brothers dedicated to missionary work. D. *Comboni founded the Verona Fathers in 1867 and the Verona Sisters (now called the Comboni Missionary Sisters) in 1871.

Veronica, St. A woman of *Jerusalem who is said to have offered her head-cloth to Christ to wipe the blood and sweat from His face on the way to *Calvary; He returned it with His features impressed upon it. The legend is first found in its present form in the 14th cent. The incident occupies a regular position in the *Stations of the Cross. Feast day, 12 July.

versicle. A short sentence, often taken from the Pss., which is said or sung antiphonally in Christian worship. It is answered by a 'response' on the part of the congregation or the other half of the choir.

Vesperale. (1) A liturgical book containing the Psalms, hymns, etc., used at *Vespers, with their chants. Those of *Compline are commonly added. (2) In the W. Church, the cloth spread over the altar when not in use to keep the white linen altar-cloths clean.

Vespers. The evening service of both the E. and W. Church and one of the oldest parts of the Divine *Office (q.v.). In its present form in the W. Church, a hymn is followed by two Psalms, a NT *canticle, a short Bible reading, a *responsory, the *Magnificat with *antiphon, prayers, and a blessing. Vespers, with *Lauds, is the most important of the Day Offices and is often chanted with solemnity. The service of *Evensong in the BCP was partly formed on the model of Vespers, with additions from *Compline. In the E. Church the central point of Vespers ('Hesperinos') is the singing of the *Phos Hilaron. This is preceded by Psalms, litanies and *troparia, and is followed by Bible readings (on feast days and in Lent), more litanies, prayers and troparia, and the *Nunc Dimittis.

Vespers, the Sicilian. See SICILIAN VESPERS, THE.

Vestiarian Controversy. A dispute about clerical dress which began under *Edward VI and under *Elizabeth I became one of the foundations of the *Puritan party. The question became acute in 1550, when John *Hooper, nominated Bp. of *Gloucester, at first refused to be consecrated in the *surplice and *rochet prescribed in the *Ordinal. M. *Parker's *Advertisements* (1566) required the use of a surplice in parish churches and a *cope in cathedral and collegiate churches. 37 London clergy refused compliance and were deprived. Disturbances followed but eventually most clergy acquiesced.

vestments. The distinctive dress worn by the clergy when performing the services of the Church. It originated in the ordinary clothes of the world of antiquity and developed into a specifically priestly costume between the 4th and 9th cents., largely because the laity abandoned the use of long tunics and cloaks. By the 10th cent. the main liturgical vestments and their use had been established in the W. From the 10th to the 13th cent. minor changes were made. The *surplice was substituted for the *alb on many occasions, the *chasuble came to be almost reserved to the celebration of Mass, and the *tunicle became the distinctive vestment of the *subdeacon. Bishops also received additional vestments such as *sandals, *mitre, and *gloves. The main vestments in the E. Church are similar to those of the W., though the tunicle, *dalmatic, and some others are not represented, and there is no equivalent of the *epigonation and *epimanikion in the W. See also COPE, EUCHARISTIC VESTMENTS, and ORNAMENTS RUBRIC.

vestry. A room in or attached to a church in which the vestments, vessels, and other requisites for Divine worship are kept and in which the clergy robe. From the fact that it was here that parishioners formerly met to transact the business of the parish, the word came to be used both of the parochial body (the incumbent or curate in charge, the persons rated for the relief of the poor of the parish, and the occupiers of the property so rated), and of the actual meeting. After 1894 the vestries of the C of E gradually lost most of their powers. In the *Episcopal Church of the USA every parish has a 'vestry', consisting of the incumbent, two wardens, and a number of 'vestrymen'; it is responsible for the financial administration of the parish and exercises control over the appointment of the incumbent (subject to the bishop's approval).

Veuillot, Louis (1813–83), *Ultramontane French journalist. In 1843 he became editor of *L'*Univers*, a newspaper which gained an international significance through his defence of the Church. In his original stand for the freedom of Catholic teaching he was widely supported by French Catholics; much less so when he defended the temporal power of the Papacy and advocated Papal *infallibility.

Veuster, Joseph de. See DAMIEN, FATHER.

Vexilla Regis. A Latin hymn by *Venantius Fortunatus celebrating the victory of Christ on the Cross. It is sung at *Vespers in *Holy Week. The translation, 'The royal banners forward go', is due to J. M. *Neale.

Via Dolorosa. The route in *Jerusalem which Christ is held to have followed from *Pilate's judgement-hall to *Calvary.

via media (Lat., 'the middle way'). A term used by J. H. *Newman and other *Tractarians for the Anglican system as a middle road between 'Popery' and 'Dissent'.

Vianney, St Jean-Baptiste Marie. See CURÉ D'ARS, THE.

Viaticum (Lat., 'provision for a journey'). The Holy Communion given to those likely soon to die to strengthen them with grace for their journey into eternity.

vicar. In the C of E, every incumbent is now either a *rector or a vicar. Originally all were rectors. In medieval times, the *tithes of a parish were often *appropriated to other bodies, such as monasteries, who were then obliged to appoint and endow a vicar to perform the parochial duties. As parish priest a vicar holds the same status as a rector, and the forms of *institution and *induction are identical. See also PERPETUAL CURATE.

Vicar Apostolic. The name given to a RC

ecclesiastic who has been entrusted with the pastoral care of certain people in an area, generally in missionary countries, which has not yet been constituted a *diocese. He is usually a titular bishop.

Vicar of Christ. A title of the Pope dating from the 8th cent.

Vicar General. An official whom a bishop deputes to represent him in the exercise of his jurisdiction. In early times his functions were mostly performed by the *archdeacons, but by the late 13th cent. the office was established and its duties defined.

In the C of E the office is ordinarily committed to the *Chancellor of the diocese. Each archbishop also has a Vicar General who holds a court for the confirmation of bishops, where the validity of the election and the qualifications of the candidate may be challenged.

Vicelin, St (c.1090–1154), 'Apostle of Holstein'. Ordained priest in 1126, he was sent by the Bp. of Bremen as a missionary to the pagan Wagrians. From 1127 he worked in Holstein. After the unfortunate Crusade against the Wends in 1147 had destroyed his labours, he was consecrated Bp. of Oldenburg in 1149, but, declining to be *invested by the Count of Saxony, was not recognized by him. Feast day, 12 Dec.

Vico, Giovanni Battista (1668–1744), Italian jurist and philosopher. His main work was his *Principii di una scienza nuova d'intorno alla natura comune delle nazioni* (1725; commonly known as the *Scienza nuova*). Responding to R. *Descartes' attack on the value of historical study, Vico drew a distinction between the aims and methods of natural science and those of history; the realm of nature, he argued, being a divine and not a human creation, is largely obscure to human beings, whereas history, which describes the behaviour of human beings, is a human creation and therefore open to human understanding; 'the world of civil society has certainly been made by men, and its principles are therefore to be found in the modifications of our human mind'. Language and the nature of ritual and myth are, he held, the keys to understanding society; through the use of metaphor, they reveal its values.

Victimae Paschali (Lat., 'To the Paschal Victim'). The Easter *Sequence in the W. Church, written by *Wipo.

Victor I, St (d. 198), Pope from 189. In order to settle the *Quartodeciman controversy, he ordered synods to be held throughout Christendom. He threatened *Polycrates of Ephesus and other bishops of Asia Minor with excommunication if they refused to give up their practice of keeping Easter on 14 Nisan instead of the following Sunday. He carried out the threat, but the fact that the Churches of Asia Minor remained in communion with Rome suggests that he took back the sentence. Feast day, 28 Jul., suppressed in 1969.

Victor, St (d. 554), Bp. of Capua from 541. His most celebrated work is a harmony of the Gospels, made on the basis of the *Vulgate text. Feast day, 17 Oct.

Victor (late 5th cent.), Bp. of Vita in N. Africa. About 488, in exile, he wrote a history of the persecution of the Catholic Church in Africa by *Arian Vandals in the period 429–84. Part of it is based on contemporary material and his own experience.

Victoria, Tomás Luis de (1548–1611), Spanish composer. He studied in Rome and joined St *Philip Neri's *Oratorians before returning to Spain in 1587 to become chaplain to the Dowager Empress Maria (sister of *Philip II) and 'maestro' of the choir of the Madrid convent in which she lived. His compositions consist entirely of sacred music; imbued with strong mystical feeling, they rank among the greatest works of the Renaissance. They include music for *Holy Week, including the motet 'O vos omnes'.

Victorines. The *canons regular of the former abbey of St-Victor at Paris. The house was founded by *William of Champeaux and built in 1113. The Victorines numbered among their ranks famous scholars, mystics, and poets, including *Adam of St-Victor, *Hugh of St-Victor, *Richard of St-Victor, and *Walter of St-Victor.

Victorinus, St (d. c.304), Bp. of Pettau, the modern Ptuj, in Slovenia. He is the earliest known exegete of the Latin Church, but nearly all his works are lost, probably because of the *millenarianist tendencies which caused them to be condemned as apocryphal by the '*Decretum Gelasianum'. Of his commentaries only that on Rev. survives. The treatise *De Fabrica Mundi* is almost certainly his. Feast day, 2 Nov.

Victorinus Afer, Caius (or **Fabius) Marius** (4th cent.), rhetor and theologian. A native of Africa, he taught in Rome. He became a Christian, resigned his rhetorship in 362 (an event which excited comment and influenced St *Augustine), and wrote theological works against the *Arians. The obscurity of his writing is largely due to the fact that he was translating philosophical Greek into Latin in an attempt to utilize a form of 4th-cent. *Neoplatonic metaphysics to elucidate and defend the Nicene doctrine of the Trinity.

Victricius, St (*c*.330–*c*.407), Bp. of Rouen from *c*.386. He renounced his military profession on becoming a Christian. As bishop he defended the faith against pagans and heretics and undertook missionary work in Flanders, Hainault, and Brabant. About 396 he was called to Britain to settle an ecclesiastical dispute. He was the recipient of a famous letter of *Innocent I on disciplinary matters. Feast day, 7 Aug.

Vidi Aquam (Lat., 'I saw water'). The anthem traditionally sung in the W. Church in Eastertide during the sprinkling of the congregation at Mass, in place of the *Asperges sung during the rest of the year.

Vieira, António (1608–97), Portuguese theologian. Brought up in Brazil, he joined the *Jesuits there in 1623. Returning to Lisbon in 1641, he soon won influence at court. In 1652 he was sent to refound the missions to the Maranhão and Grão Pará which had lapsed in 1649; he converted the Nheengaíbas on the island of Marajó. His attempts to uphold the freedom of the Amerindians against the colonists led to difficulties, and in 1661 he had to return to Portugal. He was arraigned before the *Inquisition and imprisoned. In 1669 he went to Rome and in 1675 obtained a brief exempting him from the jurisdiction of the Portuguese Inquisition. In 1681 he went back to Brazil for the rest of his life.

His sermons are masterpieces of Baroque pulpit oratory. He was a man of political acumen, but was also strongly influenced by Messianic and *millenarian beliefs.

Vienne, Council of (1311–12). Accounted the 15th *Oecumenical Council by RCs, it was summoned by *Clement V primarily to deal with the question of the *Templars, who were being accused of heresy and immorality. The majority at the Council at first held that the evidence against the Templars was insufficient, but when Philip IV of France appeared with an army before Vienne, the Pope suppressed the Order.

Vietnam, Christianity in. Christianity was first preached in what is now Vietnam by Spanish *Franciscans and Portuguese *Dominicans in the 16th cent. A mission in Cochin China was founded in 1615 by *Jesuits who had been driven out of *Japan. Alexander de Rhodes (1591–1660), a French Jesuit and outstanding linguist, tried to create a Church adapted to Vietnamese culture. In 1658 apostolic *vicariates were created for the north and south of Vietnam; the first Vietnamese priests were ordained in 1668 and an indigenous order of women was formed in 1690. By the late 18th cent. the Christian community numbered 300,000. Waves of severe persecution encouraged French intervention and in 1884 Cochin China became a French colony. The number of RCs increased, and the first Vietnamese bishop was appointed in 1933. After the defeat of the French in 1954 the country was divided. There was a large migration of RCs from the Communist North to the South, where the RC Church held an influential position as a bulwark against Communism. After the fall of President Thieu in 1975 and the withdrawal of United States forces, foreign missionaries were expelled. In 1980 7 per cent of the population was Christian, predominantly RC. Protestant activity began in 1911, but made little impact.

Vigil (Lat. *vigilia*, 'wakefulness', 'watch'), a service held at night, and by extension used of the day before a festival. From an early date the *Paschal Vigil Service comprised a lengthy series of readings and culminated in a Eucharist at dawn. When, in the 4th cent., *Baptism was also administered at Whitsun, a similar Vigil emerged. By this time there is also evidence of regular weekly Vigils, on Saturday night to Sunday morning or perhaps from early on Sunday morning; such Vigils were popular services of prayer which reached their climax in the reading of the Gospel account of the Resurrection. Vigils on other occasions also became popular. In some places the Vigil took the form of an extension to *Vespers; in others the morning Office was extended backwards into the early hours.

From the 8th cent. it became common to anticipate the Vigil on the evening of the previous day, and the Vigil was gradually put back to the morning of that day. Many feasts came to have a Vigil, which was little more than a special Mass on the previous day. The RC calendar of 1969 retained only the Easter Vigil, but special texts are provided for an evening Mass on the days before certain feasts and there are some texts for the Vigils of Sundays and festivals in the 1971 *Breviary.

Belief that the *Parousia would take place at midnight may have influenced the early monks of Egypt. When they came to live in communities, they spent much of the night in prayer and psalmody. The urban based ascetics apparently assembled for prayer and the recitation of Psalms before the public services at dawn. The Psalms came to be interspersed with readings. The monastic Offices and those of the non-monastic churches influenced each other. The Rule of St *Benedict refers to the night Office as 'vigiliae'.

In the E. Church the Vigil service (consisting of *Vespers, *Apodeipnon, Midnight Office, and *Orthros) has retained its importance. In monasteries major Vigils are celebrated solemnly and at length.

Vigilantius (fl. c.400), presbyter of Aquitaine. A visit to St *Jerome at *Bethlehem ended in a quarrel, and Vigilantius attacked Jerome as an *Origenist. Jerome replied with his *Contra Vigilantium* (406).

Vigilius (d. 555), Pope from 537. In the *Three Chapters Controversy he at first refused his assent to *Justinian's condemnation of the writings of *Theodore of Mopsuestia, *Theodoret, and *Ibas of Edessa. After he had been brought to Constantinople, he repudiated the Three Chapters in his 'Iudicatum' of 548, though not without reservations in favour of the Council of *Chalcedon. His capitulation met with great opposition in the W. and the Pope retracted the 'Iudicatium'. In 553 he refused to preside at the Second Council of *Constantinople, but after the Council had

condemned the Three Chapters, he eventually accepted its decision. The case was cited at the First *Vatican Council by opponents of Papal *infallibility.

Vilatte, Joseph René (1854–1929), bishop. Elected bishop by the newly formed Christian (*Old) Catholic Church in Wisconsin in 1889, he was consecrated in Sri Lanka in 1892 by Antonio Alvarez, a former Latin rite priest who had been consecrated a *Syrian Orthodox metropolitan in India. Vilatte consecrated a number of bishops. See EPISCOPI VAGANTES.

Vincent, St (4th cent.), protomartyr of *Spain. According to tradition he was a deacon and suffered in the *Diocletianic *persecution. Feast day in the W., 22 Jan.; in the E., 11 Nov.

Vincent of Beauvais (c.1194–1264), author of the vast popular encyclopedia, the *Speculum Maius*. A *Dominican, he may have been associated with the foundation of the Order's house at Beauvais in 1225; he was subprior there in 1246. Later in 1246 he was appointed lector to the *Cistercian abbey of Royaumont, near Paris, where he came into close contact with *Louis IX. The *Speculum Maius*, conceived and partly written by c.1244, was envisaged as a two-part compendium. It developed as Vincent collected material, and was completed c.1259 in three sections, the *Speculum Naturale*, the *Speculum Doctrinale*, and the *Speculum Historiale*. A supposed fourth part, the *Speculum Morale*, is not authentic.

Vincent Ferrer, St (1350–1413), Spanish *Dominican mission preacher. Until 1390 much of his time was devoted to academic work. *Benedict XIII employed him in his curia (1394–8). Vincent worked to end the *Great Schism and abandoned Benedict because of his intransigence. From 1399 he toured much of Europe as a preacher, generally accompanied by a group of followers who helped by hearing confessions, giving instruction, and leading processions of *flagellants. Feast day, 5 Apr.

Vincent of Lérins, St (d. before 450), author of the *Commonitorium*. After a period in secular employment, he became a monk at *Lérins. It is generally thought that he opposed the teaching of St *Augustine on *predestination and was probably the object of one of *Prosper of Aquitaine's controversial writings. His own *Commonitorium* was designed to provide a guide to the determination of the Catholic faith; it embodies the famous '*Vincentian Canon'. Despite his emphasis on tradition, he held that Scripture was the final ground of Christian truth, and that the authority of the Church was to be invoked only to guarantee its right interpretation. Feast day, 24 May.

Vincent de Paul (or **Depaul), St** (1581–1660), founder of the *Lazarists and of the 'Sisters of Charity'. Captured by pirates, he spent two years as a slave in Tunisia. From 1613 to 1626 he was attached to the household of the Count de Gondi, General of the galleys; as chaplain of the galleys from 1619 he did much to relieve the lot of the prisoners. In 1625 he founded the Congregation of the Mission (Lazarists, q.v.). In 1633, with St Louise de Marillac, he founded the 'Sisters of Charity', the first congregation of women who were not enclosed and took no final vows; they were devoted to the care of the sick and poor. Feast day, 27 Sept. (formerly 19 July).

The 'Society of St Vincent de Paul', founded in 1833, is a lay association for the service of the poor.

Vincentian Canon. The threefold test of Catholicity laid down by St *Vincent of Lérins, namely 'what has been believed everywhere, always, and by all'. By this triple test of ecumenicity, antiquity, and consent, the Church is to differentiate between true and false tradition.

vincible ignorance. The converse of *invincible ignorance (q.v.).

Vineam Domini Sabaoth (1705). A Constitution of *Clement XI against the *Jansenists. It claimed that the Pope could determine questions of fact as well as doctrine and that such decisions must be accepted 'by the heart' of the believer and not merely received 'with respectful silence'.

Vinegar Bible. A popular name for the edition of the AV printed in 1716–17, in which the headline of Lk. 20 reads 'The Parable of the Vinegar' instead of 'The Parable of the Vineyard'.

Vinet, Alexandre Rudolf (1797–1847), Swiss Reformed theologian. He was professor of pastoral theology at Lausanne from 1837 to 1847, when he attached himself to the newly constituted Free Church in Canton Vaud. He defended liberty of worship and the separation of Church and State. His conception of Christianity was individualistic, the seat of religion being the conscience and dogma important only in so far as it issued in moral action.

Vio, Thomas de. See CAJETAN, THOMAS DE VIO.

Viret, Pierre (1511–71), Reformer of W. Switzerland. He was ordained by G.*Farel in 1531 and helped him establish the Reformation in *Geneva and in Canton Vaud. He was in charge of the Lausanne Church from 1537 to 1559, when he was expelled because of a quarrel over Church discipline. He later played a leading part in the affairs of the French Reformed Church.

virger. An alternative form of *verger.

Virgil (70–19 BC), Roman poet. Publius Vergilius Maro was the son of a rich citizen of Mantua. He abandoned rhetoric and politics to study philosophy, to which he intended to devote himself when he had completed the *Aeneid*. He wrote ten pastorals, known as the *Eclogues* (i.e. occasional poems); the *Georgics*, on Italy and its agricultural wealth; and the unfinished *Aeneid*, an epic on the foundation of Rome by the exiled Trojan, based on Homer.

Virgil's language and style were widely influential. *Constantine tried to appropriate the Fourth ('Messianic') *Eclogue* as a prophecy of Christ, born of a virgin (1. 6: *iam redit et virgo*; this was one of the factors that led to the alteration in the spelling of his name). Despite protests against the facile Christianization of Virgil, and although during the last period of serious pagan opposition at Rome the pagans regarded Virgil as a philosophical authority, later Christian writers accorded him a unique place among pagan authors.

Virgilius of Salzburg, St (*c.*700–84), 'Apostle of Carinthia'. A learned Irishman, he went to the Continent in 743 and for some years governed the diocese of Salzburg without becoming bishop. St *Boniface, who disapproved of this arrangement, in 748 accused him to Pope *Zacharias for heretical views about the spherical shape of the earth and the existence of the antipodes. Virgilius was, however, consecrated to the see of Salzburg in 755 or 767. He secured the conversion of the Alpine Slavs and in 774 dedicated the first cathedral at Salzburg. Feast day, 27 Nov.

Virgin Birth of Christ. The belief that Jesus Christ had no human father, but was conceived by the BVM by the power of the Holy Spirit, is clearly stated in the narratives of Christ's Infancy recorded in the Gospels (Mt. 1 f. and Lk. 1 f.), and has been a consistent tenet of orthodox Christian theology. In the last century it has been challenged by some liberal theologians on such grounds as a general suspicion of everything miraculous and the belief that the LXX of Is. 7: 14, as an inexact rendering of the Hebrew, gave rise to, or at least promoted, the legend; the absence of reference to the Virgin Birth in other parts of the NT; and the contention that it would have been more congruous with the full Humanity of Christ for His Birth to be like that of other men. None of these points is unanswered. In any case, the acceptance of Christ's Divine Sonship is not theologically dependent on His not being the son of *Joseph; the doctrine of the Virgin Birth is distinct from that of the *Incarnation.

In current RC usage, the term 'Virgin Birth' has a wider connotation, covering both virginal conception, as described above, and the belief, attested since the 2nd cent., that the BVM gave birth as a virgin, i.e. that she remained *virgo intacta*.

Virgin Mary, the Blessed. See MARY, THE BLESSED VIRGIN.

virtualism. A form of *Eucharistic doctrine according to which, while the bread and wine continue to exist unchanged after consecration, the faithful communicant receives together with them the virtue or power of the Body and Blood of Christ.

virtues, cardinal and **theological.** See CARDINAL VIRTUES and THEOLOGICAL VIRTUES.

Visigothic rite. An alternative name for the *Mozarabic rite.

Visitandine Order. See VISITATION ORDER.

Visitatio Liminum Apostolorum. See AD LIMINA APOSTOLORUM.

visitation, episcopal. Episcopal visitations are designed for the periodic inspection of those temporal and spiritual affairs of a diocese under the bishop's control. In the later Middle Ages, when the work was already conducted by commissaries of the bishop, elaborate legal forms for the presentation of offenders were developed. In the C of E the Abps. of *Canterbury and *York have the right to visit the dioceses of their respective provinces.

Visitation of Our Lady. The feast which commemorates the BVM's visit to *Elizabeth recorded in Lk. 1: 39–56. It originated in the 13th cent. It was kept on 2 July until in the RC Church it was moved to 31 May in 1969, the date now adopted in various modern Anglican liturgies.

Visitation Order, also known as **Visitandines**, the 'Order of the Visitation of the BVM'. Founded in 1610 by St *Francis de Sales and St *Jane Frances de Chantal, it was designed to include women unable to bear the austerities of the older orders and devoted itself to the cultivation of humility, gentleness, and sisterly love. Enclosed since 1618, the Order has remained primarily contemplative.

Visitation of the Sick. The 'Order for the Visitation of the Sick' in the BCP provides for prayers, exhortations, and blessing in the presence of the sick person; it includes an exhortation to confession with a form prescribed for priestly absolution (which formed the basis for the 19th-cent. revival of the Sacrament of *Penance in the C of E). The 'Communion of the Sick' provides for a celebration of the *Eucharist in the sickroom. Modern Anglican liturgies include prayers for healing and provide for the laying on of *hands, *unction, and Communion either from the Reserved Sacrament or a celebration in the presence of the sick person.

The 1972 RC 'Order for Anointing the Sick and their Pastoral Care' provides a comparable rite consisting of prayers, Bible readings, Psalms, and a blessing, with laying on of hands. In cases of serious illness this is followed by unction and Communion, and when death approaches by *Viaticum and the *Commendatio animae*.

See also UNCTION.

Vitalian (d. 672), Pope from 657. In the early part of his pontificate he kept on good terms with the E. and in 663 he received the E. Emp. Constans II in Rome. Later his name was removed from the *diptychs at Constantinople for his adhesion to '*Dyothelite' views. Feast day, 27 Jan.

Vitalis, St. St *Ambrose relates that in 393 he attended the exhumation at *Bologna of the bodies of Sts Agricola and Vitalis (his slave) and that both had suffered death together. The cult of Vitalis spread rapidly. Feast day of Vitalis and Agricola, 4 Nov. (of Vitalis and his wife, Valeria, 28 Apr.)

vitandi (Lat., 'persons to be avoided'). The technical term formerly used of those *excommunicated persons with whom the faithful were debarred from having any intercourse. The category no longer figures in RC canon law.

Vitoria, Francisco de (1483–1546), Spanish *Dominican. From 1526 he held the Prime Chair in Theology at the University of Salamanca. By substituting the *Summa Theologiae* of St *Thomas Aquinas for *Peter Lombard's *Sentences* as the theological textbook, he inaugurated a new school at Salamanca, which became the chief university in Europe for the study of Scholasticism in the 16th cent. He is now often seen as the 'Father of International Law'. He discussed the morality of the conquest of the Indies and was critical of the Spanish methods of colonization in America. He also laid down the conditions of a just *war and held that no war would be permissible if it brought serious evil to Christendom and the world at large.

Vitus, St (d. perhaps 303), martyr. According to a late legend he was born in S. Italy of pagan parents and secretly brought up as a Christian by his nurse and her husband, all three being martyred under *Diocletian. He is invoked against sudden death, hydrophobia, and the convulsive disorder known as St Vitus' dance. Feast day, 15 June.

Vladimir, St (d. 1015), Apostle of the Russians and Ukrainians. Brought up as a pagan, he took Kiev from his elder brother and then subjugated large areas of White Russia. He helped the Byzantine Emp. Basil II to quell a revolt and c.989 he married the Emperor's sister Anne. Henceforth he was an ardent promoter of Christianity, which he imposed by force. Feast day, 15 July.

Voetius, Gisbert (1589–1676), Dutch Reformed theologian. He was a member of the Synod of *Dort (1618–19). He had been influenced at *Leiden by F. *Gomar, and from the first he opposed *Arminianism and defended an uncompromising *Calvinistic predestinarianism. In 1634 he became professor of theology and oriental languages at Utrecht. He did much to promote the rise of Dutch *Pietism.

Voltaire, pseudonym of François-Marie Arouet (1694–1778), the most celebrated of the French 'Philosophes'. Throughout his life he opposed the Catholic Church, though he warmly defended *Deism. His *Lettres Philosophiques* (1734) was publicly burnt in Paris, and he fled to Champagne. In 1758 he bought an estate on the Swiss border and lived as a country gentleman. Here he turned to positive social action, taking up the cause of victims of religious intolerance. He attacked atheism not, as is sometimes maintained, because he regarded belief in the existence of God and personal immortality as necessary simply for the government of the masses, but out of a pragmatic conviction that without these beliefs human existence would be one of meaningless anarchy.

voluntary. A piece of organ music, played usually at the beginning or end of a religious service.

Voluntaryism. The doctrine that the Church should be independent of the State.

von Harnack, Adolf; von Hofmann, Johann Christian Konrad. See HARNACK, ADOLF; HOFMANN, JOHANN CHRISTIAN KONRAD VON.

von Hügel, Baron Friedrich (1852–1925), RC theologian and philosopher. He had a cosmopolitan education and settled in England in 1867. He found himself in growing accord with the cultural and liberalizing tendencies in the RC Church and several of the leaders of the *Modernist Movement became his friends. In 1908 he published *The Mystical Element of Religion as studied in St Catherine of Genoa and her Friends.* It was followed by an article on Jn. in the 11th edition of the *Encyclopaedia Britannica* (1911), *Eternal Life* (1912), *Essays and Addresses on the Philosophy of Religion* (1921–6), and *The Reality of God* (1931; part of a course of *Gifford

Lectures which he was unable to deliver). He was concerned with the relation of Christianity to history, the place of human culture in the Christian life, and the significance of *eschatology. He saw the Institutional, the Intellectual, and the Mystical as the three abiding elements in religion. He became one of the chief religious influences in cultured circles in England, more so outside the RC Church than within it.

Vonier, Anscar (1875–1938), *Benedictine theologian. Elected Abbot of *Buckfast in 1906, he immediately undertook to rebuild the abbey church. In *A Key to the Doctrine of the Eucharist* (1925) he emphasized the corporate nature of the liturgy at a time when this was not usually appreciated.

Vorstius, Conradus (1569–1622), Konrad von der Vorst, *Arminian theologian. In 1610 he accepted an invitation to succeed J. Arminius at *Leiden. In the same year he issued an expanded edition of a work originally published in 1606, *Tractatus Theologicus de Deo*; this attracted attention because of its rationalist tendencies. Strict *Calvinists led by F. *Gomar pronounced it heretical and *James I instructed the British ambassador at The Hague to oppose Vorstius' appointment. Vorstius had to retire from Leiden in 1612. He increased suspicion by translating certain works of F. *Socinus; at the Synod of *Dort (1618–19) he was condemned as a heretic and banished from the territory of the States-General.

Voss, Gerhard Jan (1577–1649), Dutch humanist theologian. He was a professor at *Leiden University and then at the newly founded Athenaeum at Amsterdam. His *Historia Pelagiana* (1618) and other works were solid contributions to learning. He was among the first to argue that the *Apostles' Creed was not the work of the Apostles but of the early Roman Church and he decisively disproved the traditional authorship of the *Athanasian Creed.

Votive Masses. In the past Latin Missals have provided Votive Masses for a wide variety of occasions and objects, such as the restoration of peace and in honour of the Lord's Passion. In the 1970 Roman Missal there are 15. The Solemn Votive Masses ('for a grave cause') have been replaced by 46 Masses and Prayers for Various Needs

and Occasions, while the *Ritual Masses (q.v.) provide for particular needs.

vowel points. *Hebrew was originally written without vowel signs. When the language was no longer spoken and there was a danger of the traditional pronunciation being forgotten, a system of 'vowel points' was introduced. These are dots or strokes superimposed on the consonantal text.

vows. Solemn and voluntary promises to perform something not otherwise required but believed to be acceptable to the person to whom they are made. In the OT vows are sometimes explicitly dependent upon the performance of certain favours by God; others appear to have been made unconditionally. The obligation to fulfil a vow could be seen as absolute, as appears in the case of Jephthah's daughter (Jgs. 11: 30–9). In the NT, however, Christ condemned the Jewish rule which enabled a man to escape his duty to his parents on the pretext of a vow (Mk. 7: 9–13).

According to Catholic moral theology a vow to be valid must be made freely by a person who has sufficient use of reason, be within the bounds of possibility of performance, and tending to some future good. With the development of *monasticism, the threefold vow to follow the evangelical *counsels of perfection, taken on entering the religious life, came to occupy special prominence. Since c. the 13th cent., *canon law has distinguished between 'simple' and 'solemn' vows. In the religious life the main distinction is now between temporary and perpetual vows.

Vulgate. The Latin version of the Bible most widely used in the W. It was mainly the work of St *Jerome, and its original purpose was to end the differences of text in the *Old Latin MSS. In 1546 the Council of *Trent pronounced it the only authentic Latin text of the Scriptures.

Jerome began his work, at the request of Pope *Damasus in 382, with a revision of the Gospels which was completed in 384. It is unlikely that he revised the rest of the NT. In revising the OT he began with the Psalms. About 392 he completed the '*Gallican Psalter', using as his basis Origen's *Hexaplaric text of the LXX. He then decided that a satisfactory version of the OT could be made only with a fresh translation directly from the Hebrew. This translation occupied him intermittently for some 15 years and included a new translation of the *Psalter (the 'Hebrew Psalter'), which never became popular. Both old and new versions of Scripture were used for some time, but the excellence of Jerome's work was gradually recognized. When (probably in the 6th cent.) the various Books were collected into a single Bible (the Vulgate as we know it), it consisted of Jerome's translation from

the Hebrew of the Jewish canonical Books except the Psalter; the Gallican Psalter; Jerome's translation of Tobit and Judith; Old Latin translations of the rest of the *Apocrypha; Jerome's revision of the Gospels; and a revised text of Acts, Epistles, and Rev. All that can be said with certainty about the revision of the latter part of the NT is that the earliest evidence for its existence occurs in quotations in the writings of *Pelagius and his circle.

Wadding, Luke (1588–1657), *Franciscan historian. An Irishman, he joined the Franciscan Order in Spain. In 1618 he was sent to Rome to promote the definition of the *Immaculate Conception. He served on a number of Papal commissions. His chief works were the *Annales Ordinis Minorum* (1625–54), a monumental collection of material on the Franciscan Order to 1540, with its subsidiary *Scriptores Ordinis Minorum* (1650), and his edition of the works of *Duns Scotus (1639).

Wailing Wall, in *Jerusalem, known in Jewish tradition as the 'Western Wall'. It was originally part of the *Temple structure erected by *Herod the Great and has been venerated by Jews since the destruction of the Temple in AD 70.

wake. The name was originally applied to the all-night vigil kept before certain holy days, but it came to refer to the feasting and merrymaking on the holy day itself and then to a fair held annually on the festival of the local patron saint.

Wake, William (1657–1737), Abp. of *Canterbury from 1716. From 1717 to 1720 he engaged in negotiations with *Gallican leaders, notably L. E. *Dupin, on a plan for reunion between the C of E and the French Church. Wake sympathized with Nonconformists and advocated changes in the BCP to meet their difficulties.

Walafrid Strabo (*c.*808–49), i.e. 'Walafrid the Squinter', poet and biblical exegete. He studied under *Rabanus Maurus, became tutor to the Emperor's son Charles (the future Charles the Bald) in 829, and in 839 abbot of *Reichenau. His works include a poem on gardening, saints' Lives in verse and prose, and a liturgical treatise, *De Exordiis*. He abridged Rabanus' commentaries on the Pentateuch and perhaps commented on the Psalms and Catholic Epistles, but the belief that he wrote the *Glossa Ordinaria* to the Bible is unfounded.

Walburga, St (*c.*710–79), sister of St *Willibald and St Wynnebald (d. 761). She went from England to help St *Boniface in his missionary work in Germany; on Wynnebald's death she assumed direction of his *double monastery at Heidenheim. Feast days, 25 Feb. and 1 May.

Walden, Roger (d. 1406), Abp. of *Canterbury. He rose to high office in the royal service, becoming Treasurer of England in 1395. On T. *Arundel's banishment in 1397 Richard II secured Walden's *provision to the see of Canterbury by the Pope. When Arundel returned with the future Henry IV (1399), Walden's property was plundered and his register destroyed. He became Bp. of London in 1405.

Waldenses, also **Vaudois.** Since the 12th cent. the name 'Waldenses' has been applied to several groups of heretics. In the 16th cent. one group adopted *Calvinism and formed a 'Waldensian' Protestant Church, the 'Chiesa Evangelica Valdese'.

The earliest sources attribute the foundation of the 'Waldensian' heresy to one Valdes; the form Waldo and the addition of Peter to his name are later. Valdes was a rich citizen of Lyons; c.1170–3 he underwent a conversion, gave his wealth to the poor and began to live on alms and preach. His way of life was approved by *Alexander III in 1179, so long as he and his followers refrained from preaching except at the invitation of the clergy. In 1180 Valdes subscribed a profession of orthodox belief, but soon afterwards he and his followers broke the Church's ban on unofficial preaching and in 1182/3 they were excommunicated and expelled from Lyons. At the Council of Verona (1184) they were included with the *Cathars and others in the general condemnation of heretics. At this stage the movement was characterized by itinerant lay preaching, voluntary poverty, and works of charity.

The movement was split by a series of schisms. One group, known as 'Poor Lombards', established in and around Milan and Piacenza, in 1205 broke with the group centred in Lyons. The 'Lyonnais' themselves split in 1207 when Valdes' former follower Durand of Osca led some of them back to Catholic obedience. Others returned to Catholicism in 1210. By the 1220s there were Waldenses in what is now Germany. It seems that they confined their preaching to known sympathizers, distrusted the Catholic clergy and the sacraments offered by them, had doubts about prayer for the *dead and *purgatory, and insisted on their right to preach. By the 1290s there were Waldenses in the SW Alps, Austria, and elsewhere. From the 14th cent. a more attenuated form of heresy characterized the various groups: they entertained doubts about the Church's rites but in many cases continued to participate in them. Soon after the outbreak of the *Hussite schism in Bohemia, contact was established between the German Waldenses and the Bohemian heretics. The Waldenses of the SW Alps, who had by 1500 spread to parts of Provence, Calabria, and Apulia, quickly took an interest in the Protestant *Reformation, but not until between c.1555 and c.1564 did they form distinct Protestant Churches with settled pastors sent by J. *Calvin from *Geneva, a Genevan confession and ordinance. With the advent of Protestantism, the Waldenses lost their separate identity except in the parts of the Alpine valleys which fell under the Dukes of Savoy. From 1561 they were usually tolerated but sometimes persecuted. In 1848 the Chiesa Evangelica Valdese was given full civil rights in Piedmont-Savoy. Its worship is still based on 16th cent. Genevan Protestantism.

Waldenström, Paul Peter (1838–1917), Swedish Free Churchman. He put forward a theory of the *Atonement which was inconsistent with *Lutheran orthodoxy: man had to be reconciled to God, not God to man, and God sent His Son, not in wrath but in love. Waldenström founded the largest sectarian movement in *Sweden.

Wales, Christianity in. The early history of Christianity in Wales is obscure; continuity from late Roman times has been suggested. In the 6th cent. there were several outstanding Welsh saints (e.g. *David, *Deiniol, and *Dubricius); according to their Lives, they founded large monasteries. Some of these were also the seat of a bishop, and three of them (*St Asaph, *St Davids, and *Bangor), together with the later foundation of *Llandaff, eventually emerged as territorial bishoprics. The Welsh Church remained conservative, but eventually adopted the Roman date for Easter from 768. After the Norman conquest the Welsh sees were gradually subjected to the supremacy of *Canterbury, and in the 12th cent. diocesan and parochial boundaries began to be defined. The system of *tithes was instituted, and by the end of the 13th cent. a judicial and administrative organization was in being. Latin monasticism also was introduced by the Norman invaders. In the later Middle Ages, however, the Welsh Church suffered to a special degree from inertia, and the religious houses were seriously undermanned. The breach with Rome and the *dissolution of the monasteries aroused little opposition; the greatest upheaval was caused by *Mary Tudor's brief attempt to impose clerical *celibacy. *Elizabeth I appointed resident, active, Welsh-speaking bishops, who enforced the 1559 settlement, and a *Welsh Bible and Prayer Book were authorized by an Act of 1563.

The beginnings of Nonconformity in Wales are represented by the foundation of a 'gathered' Church at Llanfaches in 1639. The influence of the established Church declined; the Welsh sees were poor and often held by absentees hopeful of translation, and lay *impropriation of tithes ensured that most parish clergy were poor and ill-educated. *Methodism, preached by H. *Harris, spread rapidly, though its adherents remained within the Church until the *Calvinistic Methodists broke away in 1811. The Church failed to adapt to the large increase in population, Nonconformity grew, and religious differences echoed social and political divisions. The disestablishment of the Church of *Ireland (1869) and the Englishness of the Church in Wales led to demands for disestablishment. An Act of 1914 eventually disestablished the Welsh Church; it took effect in 1920. A separate province was created; the bishops are nominated by electors representing various elements in the Church, and one of the diocesans is elected Archbishop of Wales. The Church in Wales is no longer *Eglwys Loegr* (the 'English Church'); services are conducted in Welsh as well as in English, and after 1920 it increased in numbers and influence. Welsh Nonconformity lost a unifying objective and Welsh nationalism turned to secular objectives. The Calvinist Methodists are still the most numerous of the Free Churches; the *Baptists and *Independents remain strong, but in the *United Reformed Church and among the Wesleyans there has been a marked decline in numbers. The RCs are a small but vigorous community, recruited largely from Irish immigrant stock in the SE; there is a RC Abp. of Cardiff and Bps. of Menevia (whose cathedral is in Swansea) and Wrexham. There is a Greek Orthodox community in Cardiff.

See also ROMAN CATHOLIC CHURCH IN ENGLAND AND WALES SINCE THE REFORMATION.

Wall, William (1647–1728), Anglican theologian. His *History of Infant Baptism* (1705), designed to combat the arguments of the *Baptists, has remained the English classic work on the subject.

Walsingham, Norfolk. A replica of the Holy House at *Nazareth, said to have been built in the 11th cent., made Walsingham an important place of pilgrimage in the Middle Ages. The shrine was destroyed in 1538. A statue of the BVM, placed in the parish church in 1922, became the nucleus of a new shrine; a separate building to house it (the Holy House) was erected in 1931. In 1934 the medieval Slipper Chapel was opened as a RC shrine.

Walter, Humbert; Walter de Stapledon. See HUMBERT WALTER; STAPLEDON, WALTER DE.

Walter of St-Victor (d. after 1180), prior of St-Victor, Paris (see VICTORINES). His *Contra Quatuor Labyrinthos Franciae* was an attack on the dialectical method, directed against P. *Abelard, *Peter Lombard, Peter of Poitiers (d. 1205), and *Gilbert de la Porrée.

Walton, Brian (1600–61), editor of the 'London *Polyglot Bible'. The *Biblia Sacra Polyglotta*, in six volumes, was completed in 1657. Nine languages are repesented, but no individual Book of the Bible is printed in more than eight versions. The work, which has not been superseded, is especially useful because of its lucid arrangement. Walton was appointed Bp. of *Chester in 1660.

Walton, Izaak (1593–1683), English author. He retired from business in 1644 and spent most of the rest of his life in the households of eminent ecclesiastics such as G. *Morley, whose Steward he was. His *Compleat Angler* (1653) combines being a practical handbook with an idealized picture of country life. Though his Lives of J. *Donne (1640), H. Wotton (1651), R. *Hooker (1665), G. *Herbert (1670), and R. *Sanderson (1678) have been influential as Anglican hagiography, it is clear that he sometimes conflated, transposed, and invented speeches and events.

Wandering Jew, the. A Jew who, according to legend, taunted Christ on His way to crucifixion and was doomed to wander over the earth until the Last Day. The legend appeared in a pamphlet published in 1602.

war, Christian attitude to. It has always been recognized that in a world wholly governed by Christian principles war would be ruled out; nevertheless, since Christians are members of a secular society in which the use of force is necessary to maintain the authority of law, it has been widely, though not universally, held that war and Christian participation in it are on occasion morally justified and even praiseworthy. In early times, when forms of civil government were pagan, some ecclesiastical enactments seemed to forbid Christians from taking part in military service, but there were Christians in the army from the 2nd cent. onwards. From the time of *Constantine, Christians were less troubled by scruples about participation in war. The *Crusades are the classic example of warfare undertaken for supposedly religious ends. Medieval moral theologians came to distinguish between wars in which a Christian could or could not legitimately take part. St *Thomas Aquinas lays down three conditions for a 'just war': that it must be on the authority of the sovereign; that the cause must be just; and that the belligerents should have a rightful intention. F. de *Vitoria (d. 1546) adds that the war must be waged by 'proper means'.

In modern times 'Absolute Pacifism', that is the doctrine that warfare is in all circumstances forbidden by the Gospel, has been upheld by various groups of people, including leading Churchmen. It has also been argued that participation in a 'just war' is no longer possible, since the means (weapons of mass destruction and especially nuclear weapons) are never 'proper'. The main stream of Christian thought, however, has not supported modern pacifist movements, on the ground that there are even worse evils than physical destruction.

war, participation of the clergy in. Since the Middle Ages clerics in *major orders have been expressly forbidden to take a direct part in the shedding of blood. Where, however, the power of the State compels them to undertake military duties, they are permitted to conform. The C of E has commonly upheld the medieval discipline, though ecclesiastical penalties have not been imposed on the few clerics who have entered the services.

Warburton, William (1698–1779), Bp. of *Gloucester from 1759. His *Divine Legation of Moses* (1737–41) professed to uphold the Divine origin of the Mosaic Law against the *Deists by the singular argument that it contained no doctrine of eternal life: since the doctrine of future rewards and punishments is essential to the well-being of humanity, its absence in the OT can only be explained by Divine inspiration. He preached against the slave trade as early as 1766.

Ward, Mary (1585–1645), foundress of the Institute of the Blessed Virgin Mary. She was a member of the *Poor Clares at *St-Omer (1606–9), and then, with five other Englishwomen began what would become a religious *congregation modelled on the *Jesuits. Her project involved freedom from enclosure, from *Office in choir, and from episcopal jurisdiction; these innovations were unacceptable and the Institute was suppressed in 1631. She eventually secured the approval of *Urban VIII and resumed her activities on an informal basis. Her Institute survives in three branches, each with its own General Superior.

Ward, Reginald Somerset (1881–1962), Anglican priest and spiritual director. He worked mainly in London parishes until 1915; he then devoted himself to spiritual direction, supported financially by an anonymous group of friends. He exerted considerable influence in the C of E, especially on the clergy, among whom the use of a spiritual director and the sacrament of *Penance became widespread.

Ward, Seth (1617–89), Bp. successively of *Exeter (from 1662) and *Salisbury (from 1667). He had earlier been Savilian Professor of Astronomy at Oxford and was one of the original members of the Royal Society. He was a determined opponent of dissenters and a vigorous supporter of the *Conventicles and *Five Mile Acts.

Ward, Wilfrid (1856–1916), RC critic. The son of W. G. *Ward, he wrote Lives of his father in two books and of N. P. S. *Wiseman and J. H. *Newman. Under his direction the *Dublin Review* (of which he became editor in 1906) rose to distinguished rank.

Ward, William George (1812–82), theologian and philosopher. A fellow of Balliol College, Oxford, he pushed *Tractarian principles to extremes, and in 1845 he was deprived of his degrees for heresy. He became a RC, supporting the *Ultramontane party.

Warham, William (c.1456–1532), Abp. of *Canterbury from 1503. From 1504 to 1515 he was also Lord Chancellor. In 1527 he was T. *Wolsey's assessor in the secret inquiry into the validity of *Henry VIII's marriage, and in 1530 he signed the petition to the Pope asking him to grant the King the divorce. When, in 1531, the English clergy were bidden to acknowledge Henry as the Supreme Head of the Church in England, Warham introduced the amendment 'so far as the law of Christ will allow'. In 1532 he formally though ineffectually protested against all Acts of Parliament prejudicial to the Pope.

Wartburg. The castle in Thuringia where M. *Luther was hidden after being seized (with his own connivance) on his way home from the Diet of *Worms in 1521.

Washington Cathedral. The cathedral church of St *Peter and St *Paul, Washington, DC, is the seat of the Bp. of Washington in the *Episcopal Church in the United States of America. It is known as the 'National Cathedral', but has no extra-diocesan status. A vast cruciform building in 14th-cent Gothic style, it was begun in 1907 and completed in 1990.

Watch Tower Bible and Tract Society. See JEHOVAH'S WITNESSES.

Waterland, Daniel (1683–1740), Anglican theologian. He took part in the theological controversies of his time, especially those on the Divinity of Christ and the Trinity, on *Deism, and on the *Eucharist. The Eucharist was, he held, a commemorative and representative service, which possessed a sacrificial aspect from the remembrance of Christ's death, and the sacramental Presence was to be understood as the virtue and grace of the Lord's Body and Blood communicated to the worthy receiver. This intermediate position was long widely accepted in the C of E.

Watson, Richard (1737–1816), Bp. of *Llandaff from 1782. He was given a bishopric as a known opponent of the American War, but his proposals for radical ecclesiastical reform, including a redistribution of Church revenues, combined with his sympathy for the American colonists and—initially—for the French Revolution, prevented any further advancement.

Watts, Isaac (1674–1748), hymn-writer. He was pastor of the *Independent congrega-tion at Mark Lane, London; from 1703 his health deteriorated and he resigned in 1712. In his later years he seems to have inclined towards *Unitarianism. His hymns reflect his strong and serene faith; they did much to make hymn-singing a powerful devotional force, especially in Nonconformity, where the use of music in worship had been regarded with suspicion. They include 'When I survey the wondrous Cross' and 'Our God, our help in ages past'. In CW, feast day, 25 Nov.

Waynflete, William. See WILLIAM OF WAYNFLETE.

Wazo (980/90–1048), Bp. of Liège from 1042. He defended the rights of the Emp. Henry III against Henry I of France, but in the incipient conflict between the Papacy and the Empire he upheld the superiority of the spiritual authority.

Wearmouth and Jarrow. The twin *Benedictine abbeys between the Tyne and the Wear, founded respectively in 674 and 682 by St *Benedict Biscop, soon became a centre of learning and culture; they became widely known through the writings of *Bede.

Webb, Benjamin (1819–85), ecclesiologist. While still an undergraduate, with J. M. *Neale he founded the *Cambridge Camden Society (q.v.). He was a strictly moderate ceremonialist and never wore the Eucharistic vestments.

Wednesday. From early times Wednesday was, together with *Friday, a Christian fast day; it long remained so in *Embertide, and still is in the E. Church. It is said to have been chosen as a fast day because it was the day of the week on which *Judas Iscariot and the chief priests planned the betrayal of Christ (cf. Mk. 14: 1; 14: 10 f.).

Wee Frees. A popular name for the minority of the *Free Church of Scotland which remained outside the *United Free Church.

week. The week as a liturgical institution derived from the Jewish observance of the *Sabbath. The conception of a day of rest dedicated to God was taken over by the Christians, but transferred to the first day of the week (*Sunday) in honour of the *Resurrection. The Jewish fasts of Tuesday and Thursday were translated to *Wednesday, the day of the Betrayal, and *Friday, the day of the Crucifixion. Thursday as a day of rejoicing on account of the *Ascension and of the Institution of the *Eucharist came into prominence in the early Middle Ages, and *Saturday began to be dedicated to the BVM. See also HOLY WEEK.

Weigel, Valentin (1533–88), *Lutheran mystical writer. His works consisted largely of attacks on the 'Bibliolaters' and of cosmological speculations incompatible with dogmatic Lutheranism. His ideas influenced J. *Boehme.

Weiss, Johannes (1863–1914), German NT scholar. His *Die Predigt Jesu vom Reiche Gottes* (1892) was the first attempt at a consistent *eschatological interpretation of the Gospel, defending the thesis that the central purpose of Christ's mission was to proclaim the imminence of a transcendental Kingdom of God, in which He Himself was to be manifested as the Messiah. He elaborated this view in later works. He also expounded for the first time the principles of *Form Criticism in an article, 'Literaturgeschichte des NT', in *Religion in Geschichte und Gegenwart* (1912).

Wellhausen, Julius (1844–1918), German Biblical critic and orientalist. His thesis on the relative dating of the component documents of the *Pentateuch (q.v.) aimed at establishing the development of Hebrew religion from a nomadic stage through that of the Prophets to the religion of the Law. His analysis of the Pentateuch became the established orthodoxy in OT scholarship; though challenged from the 1930s, it still has supporters. In his later years he turned to a critical study of the NT on similar lines, but here his conclusions met with less ready acceptance.

Wells. A minster existed in Wells by the third quarter of the 8th cent., perhaps as early as 705. About 909 this church became the cathedral of the newly created diocese of the Somerset people. After the see was removed to *Bath (between 1088 and 1091), the establishment at Wells fell into neglect, but Bp. Robert of Lewes (1136–66) refounded the chapter and endowed the deanery and 22 prebends. The present cathedral was begun c.1180 and the main structure consecrated in 1239. The 13th-cent. west front has 293 medieval figures and reliefs. The most striking interior feature is the inverted arches (14th cent.), by which the piers of the tower are strengthened. See also BATH AND WELLS.

Welsh Bible and Prayer Book. The NT first appeared in Welsh in 1567; this served as the basis for the complete Bible published by W. *Morgan (q.v.) in 1588. A revision was issued in 1620. It remained in general use until a fresh translation was published in 1988.

A Welsh translation of the English BCP of 1559 was issued in 1567; one lesson was still read in English. A full translation of the 1662 BCP appeared in 1664. A new 'Book of Common Prayer for use in the Church of Wales', issued in 1984, provides for services in Welsh and English.

Wenceslas, St (c.907–29 [or possibly 935]), Bohemian prince. Taking over the government from his mother, probably c.922, he worked for the religious and cultural improvement of his people. Murdered by his brother, he was venerated as a martyr. The content of J. M. *Neale's 'Good King Wenceslas' is imaginary. Feast day, 28 Sept.

Werburg, St (d. c.699), less correctly 'Werburgh', abbess. The daughter of a Mercian king, she entered the abbey of *Ely, where she became abbess. She was later instigated by King Ethelred to reform the nunneries of his kingdom. In 875 her body was removed to *Chester. Feast day, 3 Feb.

Wesley, Charles (1707–88), brother of John *Wesley. A member of the Oxford *Methodists, he was ordained in 1735. He came under *Moravian influence and experienced conversion in 1738. He engaged in itinerant preaching until 1756; he then settled in Bristol and from 1771 in London. He opposed all moves tending to separation from the C of E, especially John's ordinations. He was a gifted and indefatigable hymn-writer; all his collections professed to be the joint work of the two brothers. His hymns include 'Jesu, Lover of my soul' and 'Love divine, all loves excelling'. Together with John, he is commemorated in CW on 24 May; in the American BCP (1979) on 3 May.

Wesley, John (1703–91), founder of the *Methodist Movement. He was a son of the Revd Samuel Wesley, rector of Epworth, Humberside. At Oxford he gathered around him a group which became known as the '*Holy Club' or 'Methodists'. In 1735 he set out on a missionary journey to Georgia, but he alienated the colonists and fled home (1737). He came under *Moravian influence, underwent a conversion experience in 1738, and determined to devote his life to evangelistic work. Finding the churches closed to him, he followed G. *Whitefield in preaching out of doors. He broke with the Moravians in 1740 and with Whitefield in 1741. He then developed his own organization with the help of lay preachers and extended his activity to cover the whole of the British Isles by 1751. He travelled extensively. From 1744 he held conferences of lay preachers which became annual events and for which a legal constitution was provided in 1784. From the 1760s the Methodist system gradually developed also in America. The needs of this field induced Wesley in 1784 to ordain T. *Coke as *Superintendent or Bishop, and to instruct him to ordain F. *Asbury as his colleague. Wesley still wanted the Movement to remain within the C of E, but an increasingly independent system grew up.

Theologically Wesley combined the teaching of *justification by faith alone with an emphasis on the pursuit of holiness to the point of 'Christian *perfection'. Intellectually he combined a strong belief in the supernatural with appeals to Scripture, reason, and the *Fathers of the Church, and to experience. He valued liturgical prayer and Eucharistic devotion, as well as extempore worship. He is commemorated (with Charles) in CW on 24 May; in the American BCP (1979) on 3 May.

Wesley, Samuel Sebastian (1810–76), composer and organist. A grandson of Charles *Wesley, he was organist at *Hereford and *Exeter Cathedrals, Leeds Parish Church, and *Winchester and *Gloucester Cathedrals. Though not outstanding as a choir-master, he wrote some fine Church music, including the anthems 'The Wilderness', 'Blessed be the God and Father', and 'Thou shalt keep him in perfect peace'.

Wesleyan Methodists. See METHODIST CHURCHES.

Wessel (c.1419–89), Dutch theologian, also known as **Gansfort**. He taught at *Paris and later visited Italy. German Protestants

regard him as a 'Reformer before the Reformation' since in his attitude to the Papacy, to the authority of the Church, and to the superstitious tendencies of his age, he shared many of the views of M. *Luther.

Wessenberg, Ignaz Heinrich von (1774–1860), *Febronianist reformer. Though he was only a subdeacon, in 1802 K. von Dalberg, Coadjutor Prince-Bishop of Constance, appointed him his *vicar general. Besides initiating various reforms, he aimed at the creation of a National German Church, largely independent of the Papacy. At Rome his *Josephinistic principles aroused opposition and Dalberg had to depose him. On Dalberg's death (1817) the Chapter elected Wessenberg as vicar and administrator of the diocese. In open disobedience to the Pope he acted as administrator until 1827, when the diocese of Constance was incorporated into that of Freiburg. He retired into private life in 1833.

West Africa, Christianity in. The first Europeans arrived on the coast of W. Africa at the end of the 15th cent., but for the most part they were involved in the slave trade rather than in evangelization. In the 19th cent. there was sustained missionary activity by Churches of every denomination. *Anglicans, *Methodists, and *Baptists were active in *Sierra Leone and, with *Presbyterians, in *Nigeria, while Methodists also set up missions in *Ghana, Gambia, and Dahomey. The RC Church enjoyed a favoured position in the *Congo, and RC missions were established in almost every part of West Africa. In French territory, French Evangelicals also were active; they included A. *Schweitzer.

The independence which most W. African States achieved after the Second World War was matched by the establishment of national Churches by Protestant bodies and the replacement of the older *vicariates by hierarchies in the RC Church. In 1951 the Anglican dioceses in the area, except Liberia, were formed into the Church of the Province of West Africa. In 1979 a separate Nigerian Province was formed out of part of it, but in 1982 the diocese of Liberia was joined to it. See also AFRICA, CHRISTIANITY IN.

West Indies, Christianity in the. The earliest evangelization was carried out by

RC missionaries who came with the Spanish colonists in the late 15th cent. The aboriginal population was, however, largely exterminated and replaced by slaves from West Africa. In the 17th cent. there was colonization by other nations. In the French islands, the *Code Noir* of 1685 prescribed that all slaves should be instructed and baptized into the Catholic religion, but the cruelty with which they were treated led to antagonism. In the islands ruled by the British, the C of E was established, but until the 19th cent. it did little to evangelize the slaves. Missionary work was, however, undertaken by the *Moravians, *Methodists, *Baptists, and (from 1824) by the *Presbyterians. In the Danish territories a royal ordinance of 1755 provided that God's Word should be preached to the slaves and their children baptized like other people's; *Lutheran missions were subsequently established. In 1808 the Bp. of London recommended that Sunday Schools should be set up for the education of Negro children; in 1824 the bishoprics of Jamaica and Barbados were established. Between 1868 and 1870 the C of E was disestablished everywhere except in Barbados, and in 1883 the Church in the West Indies was constituted an independent Province of the Anglican Communion.

In those areas which were originally Spanish or French the RC Church retained its predominance, and when Trinidad and Tobago were ceded to Britain in 1802 no change was made in the status of the RC Church. In 1820 a bishopric was created for the Port of Spain; this post, now an archbishopric, was filled by a West Indian in 1971. Other Churches have also gradually developed indigenous ministries. Since the mid-20th cent. *Pentecostalism has flourished. The two largest groups of Pentecostals are the Church of God and the New Testament Church of God. Most of the Negroes accepted some form of Christianity, but the Oriental immigrants have largely retained their own religions.

Westcott, Brooke Foss (1825–1901), Bp. of *Durham from 1890. While he was Regius Professor of Divinity at Cambridge, he prepared, with F. J. A. *Hort, the celebrated edition of the Greek NT, published in 1881; it was followed by his great commentaries on Jn. (1881), on the Epp. of Jn. (1883), and on Heb. (1889). In his diocese he made social problems his special concern, and he mediated in the coal strike of 1892. In CW, feast day, 27 July.

Western text of the NT. A type of the Greek NT marked by a distinctive cluster of variant readings, so named because the chief witnesses to it were thought to be of Western provenance. It is now acknowledged that this type of text is not confined to the W., and the term is used as a proper name rather than a geographical term.

Westminster Abbey. According to a legend, probably of 13th-cent. origin, an abbey was founded in Thorney Island in 616 and miraculously consecrated by St *Peter. Rebuilding and restoration of the abbey were undertaken by *Edward the Confessor. Erection of the present church in Gothic style began in 1245; the eastern part was complete in 1269 and the nave finished c.1505. The western towers, designed by C. *Wren, were completed by 1745.

The *Benedictine foundation of Edward the Confessor became one of the richest abbeys in England. In 1540 the monastery was dissolved and a *collegiate church established; the abbey became a Royal *Peculiar, independent of the see of London. In 1540 a bishopric of Westminster was established; it was suppressed in 1550. Since the time of *William I the abbey has been the place of Coronation of the sovereign; it has retained a unique position as a centre of the national life.

Westminster Assembly. The synod appointed by the Long Parliament in 1643 to reform the English Church. It consisted of 30 lay assessors and 121 clergymen of widely different views; when the *Solemn League and Covenant was adopted it was increased by five clerical and three lay Commissioners from *Scotland.

The Assembly began by revising the *Thirty-Nine Articles, but with the appearance of the Solemn League and Covenant it turned to the production of a new formula, the *Westminster Confession (q.v.). It also prepared the Directory of Public *Worship (q.v.) and the two *Westminster Catechisms (q.v.). Although only partially and temporarily accepted in England, these documents came into general use throughout the *Presbyterian world.

Westminster Catechisms. Two Catechisms compiled by the *Westminster

Assembly and approved by Parliament and the *General Assembly of the Church of *Scotland in 1648. The Larger Catechism is a popular restatement of the teaching of the *Westminster Confession. The Shorter Catechism opens with the well-known Question and Answer: 'What is the chief end of man?' 'Man's chief end is to glorify God and to enjoy Him for ever.'

Westminster Cathedral. The cathedral of the RC Abp. of Westminster, begun in 1895 and opened in 1903. It was designed in early 'Christian Byzantine' style and executed mainly in red brick. Its domed campanile is 284 ft. high.

Westminster Confession. The profession of *Presbyterian faith drawn up by the *Westminster Assembly. It was approved by Parliament in 1648, having been ratified by the *General Assembly of the Church of *Scotland in the previous year. It immediately established itself as the definitive statement of Presbyterian doctrine in the English-speaking world.

Westminster Directory. See WORSHIP, DIRECTORY OF PUBLIC.

Weston, Frank (1871–1924), Anglican Bp. of Zanzibar from 1908. Joining the *UMCA in 1898, he learned to live among Africans and to understand their point of view. He took the lead in opposing the proposals of the *Kikuyu Conference of 1913. In 1920 he largely inspired the appeal for Christian Unity put out by the *Lambeth Conference.

Westphalia, Peace of (1648). Two treaties which ended the *Thirty Years War (q.v.).

westward position. In some early Roman churches the celebrant of the Eucharist appears to have stood on the far side of the altar, facing the people. This position (normally facing westward) was superseded by the *eastward position but has gradually been restored in the RC Church and is used in many C of E churches.

Wette, Wilhelm Martin Lebrecht de. See DE WETTE, WILHELM MARTIN LEBRECHT.

Wettstein, Johann Jakob (1693–1754), NT critic. From 1733 he was a professor at Amsterdam. His edition of the Greek NT (1751–2) included in the critical apparatus many important variants hitherto unrecorded and also the *sigla* for denoting the MSS in common use since then.

Weymouth New Testament. An English version of the NT published in 1903 under the title *The New Testament in Modern Speech*. It was the work of R. F. Weymouth (1822–1902), a *Baptist schoolmaster.

Wharton, Henry (1664–95), medievalist. In 1688 he became domestic chaplain to Abp. W. *Sancroft. He took the Oaths of Allegiance and Supremacy to William and Mary in 1689, but continued to enjoy Sancroft's confidence. The first two volumes of Wharton's main work, the *Anglia Sacra* (1691), provided the first comprehensive collection of sources for the pre-Reformation history of the English sees whose cathedrals were served by *regulars, including editions of medieval chronicles. A third volume, covering the cathedrals served by the *secular clergy, was unfinished; it was published incomplete in 1695.

Whately, Richard (1787–1863), Anglican Abp. of *Dublin from 1831. At Oxford he was one of the best-known of the '*Noetics', an anti-*Erastian, and an anti-*Evangelical. His writing influenced J. H. *Newman, who at one time assisted him. Later Whately opposed the *Tractarians. In Dublin he was active in the political life of *Ireland and did valuable work as a Commissioner of National Education.

Whichcote, Benjamin (1609–83), *Cambridge Platonist. He became Provost of King's College, Cambridge, in 1644. He was ejected at the Restoration, but after accepting the Act of *Uniformity in 1662, he held important cures in London.

Whichcote was averse to the pessimistic view of human nature prevalent among the *Puritans and exalted man as a child of reason. He saw in reason the test of Scripture, maintained that some matters on which good men disagreed were insoluble, and pleaded for freedom of thought.

Whiston, William (1667–1752), mathematician and theologian. In 1703 he succeeded I. *Newton as Lucasian Professor of Mathematics at Cambridge; his *Arianizing views led to his expulsion from the university in 1710, and in 1747 he joined the *General Baptists. He is remembered for his translation of *Josephus (1737).

Whitaker, William (1547/8–95), *Puritan.

In 1580 he became Regius Professor of Divinity at Cambridge and in 1586 Master of St John's College. A strict *Calvinist, he exercised a wide influence by his devotion to learning and his impartiality. He was mainly responsible for drafting the *Lambeth Articles.

Whitby, Synod of (664), a council held by King Oswiu of Northumbria to establish unity of practice in the date of observing *Easter (see PASCHAL CONTROVERSIES) and the style of the *tonsure within his territory. Oswiu decided to follow the tradition of St *Peter. Northumbria adopted the Roman practice and those clergy who would not change withdrew to *Iona and later to Ireland. Despite the view of historians, there is little reason to think that the Synod had much influence outside Northumbria.

Whitchurch, Edward (d. 1561), printer. He became an adherent of the Reformed doctrines and in 1537 he associated himself with R. *Grafton to circulate *Matthew's Bible (printed at Antwerp). In 1538 he and Grafton gave financial assistance to M. *Coverdale in printing his NT at Paris and in 1539 they published the *Great Bible in London. Under *Edward VI Whitchurch printed the BCP of 1549 and 1552.

White Fathers. The Society of Missionaries of Africa, founded by Abp. C.-M. A.-*Lavigerie at Algiers in 1868. It is composed of secular priests and coadjutor brothers living in community without vows, but bound by solemn oath to lifelong work in the African mission. They wear a white tunic and cloak, with a rosary round the neck. They are the most numerous group of RC missionaries at work in Africa.

White Friars. The *Carmelite friars, so called from their white cloaks and *scapulars.

White Ladies. A popular name, from their white habits, for (1) the Sisters of the Presentation of Mary, a teaching order founded in France in 1796 and since 1853 also established in Canada; (2) the *Magdalens; and (3) the *Cistercian nuns.

White Monks. The *Cistercian monks, so called from their habits of undyed wool.

White Sisters. (1) The Congregation of the Missionary Sisters of Our Lady of Africa was founded by Abp. C.-M. A.-*Lavigerie in 1869 to help the *White Fathers. (2) The Congregation of the Daughters of the Holy Ghost, called White Sisters from their white habits, was founded in Brittany in 1706. Its chief objects are education and nursing. Largely driven out of France by the legislation of 1902, they established houses in Belgium, England, and the USA, and have missions in Cameroon, *Nigeria, and *Chile.

White, Francis (c.1564–1638), Bp. successively of *Carlisle, *Norwich, and *Ely. An *Arminian, he licensed R. Montagu's *Appello Caesarem* for printing in 1625 and in 1626 attacked *Calvinist teaching at the York House conference. He was also a prominent anti-Papist disputant and in 1622 he was engaged by *James I to support W. *Laud in presenting the Anglican case in a formal dispute with the *Jesuit 'John *Fisher'.

White, John (1867–1951), Scottish Church leader. An original member from the Church of *Scotland of the committee appointed in 1909 to negotiate a possible union with the *United Free Church of Scotland, he was the dominant leader of the movement which led to the union of 1929. He was instrumental in promoting legislation in Parliament which preserved the status of the Church of Scotland as the *established Church but gave it freedom to govern its affairs independently of Parliament and the courts.

White, Joseph Blanco (1775–1814), theological writer. Born in Spain of Irish parents, he was ordained to the RC priesthood in 1800. He suffered religious doubt, came to England, and became an Anglican; he was well known among the *Tractarians. He finally became a *Unitarian.

White, William Hale. The real name of 'Mark *Rutherford' (q.v.).

Whitefield, George (1714–70), *Methodist evangelist. At Oxford he came under the influence of John and Charles *Wesley. In 1738 he followed them to Georgia, returning later that year to obtain priest's orders and collect money for an orphanage. His spectacular preaching (especially at open-air meetings from 1739) attracted a remarkable response, despite opposition from the ecclesiastical authorities. In 1741 his *Calvinist theology led him to break with the Wesleys and build a 'Tabernacle' in Moorfields, London. His loose *Calvinistic Methodist Connexion was overseen mostly by others, as Whitefield was determined to act as an 'Awakener' to all the Churches. Under the patronage of Lady *Huntingdon, he gained a hearing from the aristocracy. He was the most striking orator of the Evangelical Revival; in America he helped to stimulate the *Great Awakening.

Whitgift, John (probably 1532–1604), Abp. of *Canterbury from 1583. He had held high office at Cambridge, where his opposition to T. *Cartwright brought him to the notice of *Elizabeth I. In 1583 he issued the 'Eleven Articles', one of which required subscription to articles of loyalty to the existing settlement. He used the Ecclesiastical Commission to repress *Puritanism (e.g. the *Marprelate Tracts), and he resisted the attempts of the extreme Puritans in 1584–9 to impose upon the Church a *Presbyterian form of government. A determined advocate of episcopacy and ritual uniformity, theologically he was a *Calvinist (*Lambeth Articles).

Whitsunday. The feast of the descent of the Holy Spirit upon the Apostles on the 50th day after *Easter (see PENTECOST). It ranks, after Easter, as the second greatest festival in the Church. In the W. the vigil of Pentecost soon became a secondary date for *Baptisms, with a ceremony resembling that of the *Paschal Vigil Service, and the name 'Whitsunday' is said to derive from the white robes worn by the newly baptized on that day. In the RC Church the Sundays between Whitsunday and *Advent were, until 1969, reckoned as 'Sundays after Pentecost'; in the E. Church the Sundays outside the period Lent-Eastertide are still so reckoned, though the feast itself is kept as that of the Holy Trinity, the Monday following being designated of the Holy Spirit. For current divisions of the ecclesiastical year see YEAR, LITURGICAL.

Whittier, John Greenleaf (1807–92), American *Quaker poet, associated with the anti-*slavery movement. Verses from some of his poems have become well known as hymns, among them 'Dear Lord and Father of mankind' and 'Immortal love, for ever full'.

Whittingham, William (c.1524–79), Dean of *Durham. His *Calvinistic views forced him to flee from England during *Mary's reign. He followed J. *Knox to *Geneva and in 1559 succeeded him as minister, apparently without receiving any ordination. In 1563 he was made Dean of Durham. His iconoclasm and failure to conform to the BCP led E. *Sandys, Abp. of York, to try to deprive him on the ground that he had not been validly ordained, but he died before the proceedings were concluded.

Whole Duty of Man, The. A devotional manual published c.1658 and formerly widely used. It has been attributed to H. *Hammond, J. *Fell, and R. *Allestree.

Whyte, Alexander (1836–1921), Scottish Evangelical. Minister of the *Free (later *United Free) Church of Scotland's church of St George's, Edinburgh (1870–1916) and principal of New College, Edinburgh (1909–18), he was regarded as the finest preacher in late-Victorian Scotland. He welcomed the biblical criticism of W. R. *Smith and the beginning of the *Ecumenical Movement in the *Edinburgh Conference of 1910.

Wichern, Johann Hinrich (1808–81), founder of the German *Innere Mission. In 1833 he founded an institute in Hamburg, the Rauhes Haus, to provide for the spiritual and material needs of neglected children. From 1844 he edited a periodical which became the central organ of all charitable undertakings in the German Protestant Churches; at his suggestion these were co-ordinated in the central organization of the Innere Mission at the first congress of the Evangelical Churches in 1848. He later undertook the reform of Prussian prisons.

Wiclif, John. See WYCLIFFE, JOHN.

widows. In NT times widows had an acknowledged claim to the charity of their fellow-Christians. They soon acquired a recognized status in the Church, the early history of which is closely linked with that of *deaconesses.

Wied, Hermann von. See HERMANN OF WIED.

Wilberforce, Samuel (1805–73), Bp. of

*Oxford (1845–69) and then of *Winchester. A son of W. *Wilberforce, he encouraged the building of churches and the formation of Anglican sisterhoods, and he founded Cuddesdon Theological College (1854). His effective methods of pastoral administration were widely imitated. He promoted legislation to provide synodical structures for the colonial Church and to enable the appointment of missionary bishops. At Winchester he initiated the revision of the AV.

Wilberforce, William (1759–1833), philanthropist. He was converted to *Evangelicalism and dissuaded from taking Holy *Orders by advice that he could best serve Christianity in Parliament. He became a prominent member of the *Clapham Sect and leader of the Evangelical party. His main concern was the abolition of the slave trade; after many vicissitudes the Bill to effect this became law in 1807. Later he supported the movement for the complete abolition of slavery, achieved in 1833. He helped in the foundation of the *CMS and the *British and Foreign Bible Society, advocated the introduction of English missionaries into *India, and championed the cause of *Sunday observance. Feast day in the American BCP (1979) and CW, 30 July.

Wilfrid, St (634–709), Bp. of *York. He was educated at *Lindisfarne, but he became dissatisfied with the *Celtic way of religious life and as Abbot of *Ripon he introduced the *Benedictine Rule. At the Synod of *Whitby (664) he was largely responsible for the victory of the Roman party. Soon afterwards he was consecrated Bp. of York at Compiègne. On his return he found his see occupied by St *Chad, but he was put in possession of it by *Theodore, Abp. of Canterbury, in 669. When Theodore divided the diocese of York in 678, Wilfrid went to Rome to appeal. He was eventually reinstated in his see, which he held from 686 to 691. Disputes with the king forced him to flee from York and a synod held in 703 called upon him to resign; after a further successful appeal to Rome, he resigned in favour of St *John of Beverley. He brought England into closer touch with the Papacy and succeeded in replacing Celtic usages in the north of England by the Roman liturgy. Feast day, 12 Oct.

Wilkes, Paget (1871–1934), missionary. In 1897 he sailed for *Japan under the *CMS. Here he formed the idea of a Japanese Evangelistic Band which, free of ecclesiastical organization, would be directed towards aggressive evangelism; in 1903 the 'One by One Band' of Japan was established, with its centre at Kobe. Wilkes spent all his active life in Japan.

Wilkins, David (1685–1745), editor of the 'Concilia'. He was Librarian of *Lambeth Palace. His *Concilia Magnae Britanniae et Hiberniae* (1737) long remained a standard source for British and Irish ecclesiastical councils.

Wilkins, John (1614–72), Bp. of *Chester from 1668. His chief interests lay in the furthering of science and philosophical linguistics, and when the Royal Society received its charter in 1662 he became its first Secretary. At Chester he advocated the toleration of dissenters. He was a strong upholder of natural theology and maintained that the conflicting contentions of fanatics were the main cause of unbelief.

Willehad, St (d. 789), Bp. of Bremen. A native of Northumbria, between 765 and 774 he set out for missionary work in Frisia. In 780 *Charlemagne sent him to preach to the Saxons at Wigmodia near the North Sea. His work was interrupted by an insurrection in 782, but he later resumed his activities and in 787 was consecrated first Bp. of Bremen. Feast day, 8 Nov.

William I (?1028–87), Duke of Normandy and King of England ('the Conqueror'). The illegitimate son of Duke Robert I, William won and kept firm control over Normandy. Here he presided over an ecclesiastical revival. In 1066, with the blessing of *Alexander II, he conquered England. His relations with Rome remained generally co-operative. There was no conflict over lay *investiture, which William continued to practise. The episcopate in England was largely Normanized and, with Abp. *Lanfranc, the King saw to the implementation of Papal legislation on *simony, clerical immorality, and diocesan administration.

William of Auvergne (c.1180–1249), philosopher and theologian. He became Bp. of *Paris in 1228. He was a protector of the *Mendicant Orders and exercised influence at the court of *Louis IX. His prolific writings mainly form a vast philosophico-theological encyclopedia, the *Magisterium Divinale ac Sapientale*. He used *Aristotelian language and principles of scientific procedure, but remained wary of many Aristotelian doctrines.

William of Auxerre (d. 1231), *Scholastic theologian. He taught at *Paris. He was a member of the Commission appointed by *Gregory IX to examine and amend the physical treatises of *Aristotle, and was himself among the first to make use of Aristotle's newly discovered works, especially in his *Summa Aurea*.

William of Champeaux (c.1070–1121), *Scholastic philosopher. He taught at the cathedral school in *Paris, whence he was driven (1108) by *Abelard's ridicule of his exaggerated *Realism. He retired to the priory of St-Victor, apparently modified his doctrines, and by his lectures there laid the foundations of the *Victorine school. In 1113 he became Bp. of Châlons.

William of Conches (c.1080–c.1154), philosopher. A pupil of *Bernard of Chartres, he sought to encourage the study of the profane sciences and literature in the interests of a Christian humanism. His writings, of which the *Philosophia Mundi* and *Dragmaticon* were the most popular, deal mainly with natural philosophy.

William of Malmesbury (c.1090–c.1143), historian. He appears to have spent most of his life in the monastery at Malmesbury. His *Gesta Regum Anglorum* (1120) and *Gesta Pontificum Anglorum* (1125) deal respectively with the secular and ecclesiastical history of England. His *Historia Novella* continues the *Gesta Regum* to the year 1142.

William of Moerbeke (d. 1286), translator of Greek philosophical and scientific works. He was in Greece, as a Dominican, in 1260. By 1267 he was at Viterbo and until 1279 was attached to the Curia as Papal penitentiary. In 1278 he was consecrated Abp. of Corinth. By 1283 he was again attached to the Papal court. He translated into Latin or revised existing translations of works of *Aristotle, of *Proclus (whose *tria opuscula* survive only in his translations), and of other Greek philosophers and ancient commentators on Aristotle.

William of Norwich, St (1132–44), supposed victim of a Jewish ritual murder. An apprentice at *Norwich, he was enticed from his home on the Monday in *Holy Week 1144 and on *Holy Saturday his body was found with marks of violence. He was alleged to have been crucified by Jews during the Passover. Feast day at Norwich, 26 Mar.; elsewhere, 25 Mar.

William of Ockham (c.1285–1347), philosopher, theologian, and polemicist. A native of Ockham in Surrey, he joined the *Franciscan Order and taught at *Oxford. In 1323 he was denounced at *Avignon for teaching dangerous doctrines. He was summoned there and a commission censured 51 propositions from his writings, but no formal condemnation followed. In 1327 the Minister General of the Franciscans instructed Ockham to examine the Papal constitutions in the dispute on Franciscan poverty; Ockham concluded that *John XXII had taken up heretical positions. In 1328 he fled from Avignon and joined Louis of Bavaria. Excommunicated and expelled from his Order, he wrote polemical works against the Pope and in favour of the Imperial policy.

Ockham was a vigorous, critical, and independent thinker, and he contributed to the development of formal logic. He eliminated the notion, then generally accepted, of the existence of *universals. Only individual things exist, and they are directly apprehended by the mind. On the theological side much of his thinking was determined by his resolute attempt to do away with anything that limited God's omnipotence. He considered that the doctrine of eternal ideas in the Divine mind, in accordance with which the world was created and ordered, limited God's freedom. But God's omnipotence cannot be philosophically proved; it has to be accepted on faith through revelation. He also criticized the traditional proofs of God's existence as not philosophically demonstrable.

Ockham's radical criticism of the prevailing belief in the reality of universals, his grounding of human knowledge in intuitive cognition, and his rethinking of the relation of theology to philosophy prepared the ground for a more scientific approach to reality. His philosophical and theological influence pervaded the university world from c.1340; he was acknowledged as a mentor by G. *Biel and M. *Luther and universally as the inspirer of *Nominalism. His political theories played an important part in the development of the *Conciliar Movement. In CW, feast day, 10 Apr.

William of St-Thierry (1075/80–1148), theologian and spiritual writer. About 1120 he was elected Abbot of the *Benedictine abbey of St-Thierry, near *Reims. He formed a close friendship with St *Bernard, and in 1135 he resigned his abbacy and joined a group of *Cistercians who were establishing a house at Signy in the Ardennes.

William's early works were largely didactic and include a treatise in which he tried to synthesize the teaching of the E. and W. Fathers on the relation of the body and the soul. In 1138 he wrote to Bernard urging him to refute Peter *Abelard's views on the Trinity and Redemption. He himself wrote against Abelard and against *William of Conches. His other works include two commentaries on the Song of Songs, his *Meditativae Orationes*, and his famous *Epistola ad Fratres de Monte Dei de Vita Solitaria*, known as the 'Golden Letter' and often attributed to Bernard.

William of Tyre (c.1130–probably 1186), historian. Born in Palestine, probably of European parents, in 1167 he was appointed Archdeacon of Tyre by Amaury, King of Jerusalem, with an enhanced stipend on condition that he wrote the official history of the reign. In 1175 he was consecrated Abp. of Tyre. His *Historia Rerum in Partibus Transmarinis Gestarum* covers the period from 1095 (Preaching of the First *Crusade) to 1184. It is the primary authority from 1127. Although his sympathies lay with Raymond of Tripoli and the native crusaders, his work is marked by insight, tolerance, and a careful sifting of evidence from a wide range of sources.

William of Waynflete (c.1395–1486), Bp. of *Winchester from 1447. He had been headmaster of Winchester College and then provost of the newly founded Eton College. In 1448 he obtained licence to found a hall in Oxford to foster the study of theology and philosophy; in 1457-8 it was refounded as Magdalen College. He was a favourite of *Henry VI, took a prominent part in public affairs, and was Chancellor from 1456 to 1460. He acquiesced in the accession of Edward IV, though he renewed his support of Henry in 1470-71.

William of Wykeham (1324–1404), Bp. of *Winchester from 1367. He also became Chancellor in 1367, but, being blamed for the disasters of the French war, he was driven from office in 1371. He then devoted himself mainly to his diocese and to his plans for academic foundations. At Oxford he founded a college dedicated to St Mary, but soon known as New College, and at Winchester he established a school for 70 poor scholars. As a member of the commission of regency appointed in 1386 and as Chancellor from 1389 to 1391, he tried to exercise a moderating influence.

William of York, St (d. 1154), Abp. of *York. William FitzHerbert was elected Abp. of York in 1141, but, as he was accused of *simony by the *Cistercians, *Theobald, Abp. of *Canterbury, refused to consecrate him. Pope Innocent II allowed him to be consecrated in 1143, probably by *Henry of Blois. His difficulties reflect the power struggle of Henry of Blois and St *Bernard. When William went to Rome for the *pallium in 1147, *Eugenius III (a Cistercian) suspended him, and after his relatives had attacked *Fountains Abbey, where the rival candidate was abbot, William was deposed. Pope Anastasius IV restored him in 1153 and gave him the pallium. He entered York in 1154, but died within a month, possibly by poison. He was regarded as a martyr. Feast day, 8 Jun.; of his translation, 8 Jan., until 1478 when it was transferred to the first Sunday after the *Epiphany.

Williams, Charles Walter Stansby (1886–1945), poet and theological writer. As well as poems, he wrote novels largely devoted to supernatural themes, a play for the *Canterbury festival of 1936, and *The Descent of the Dove* (1939), an unconventional and penetrating study of the Church. He had a concept of romantic love in which the image of the beloved is revealed to the lover, and a literal understanding of substitution, of which the *Atonement was the culminating example. He did much to commend Christianity in a Catholic and sacramental form to many who would have been unmoved by conventional apologetic.

Williams, John (1582–1650), Abp. of *York. Under *James I he received many benefices, including the bishopric of *Lincoln (1621), and was made Lord Keeper. He was disliked by *Charles I and W. *Laud, but in the Long Parliament he headed a party of compromise and, recovering royal favour, was translated to York in 1641. He was a royalist in the Civil War but allowed to retire to Wales.

Williams, John (1796–1839), missionary. In 1816 he was accepted by the *LMS, which had chosen the *South Pacific for its earliest work. He sailed for the Society Islands in 1817 and in 1818 settled on Raiatea. In 1839 he landed at Dillon's Bay, Erromanga, in Vanuatu, where he and his companion were killed, becoming Protestant 'martyrs'. News of his death aroused missionary enthusiasm in England.

Williams, Ralph Vaughan. See VAUGHAN WILLIAMS, RALPH.

Williams, Roger (c.1603–83), champion of religious *toleration. Though apparently ordained in the C of E, he sailed for N. America in 1630 in search of religious liberty. When he found restrictions on religious freedom in Boston, he set up a schismatic Church. In 1635 he was ordered to leave Massachusetts and took refuge among the Indians outside the state, founding a settlement which he called 'Providence' (1636). Here he established the first *Baptist Church in America. He returned to England to secure a charter for the colony (later called 'Rhode Island'). Its constitution included wide religious latitude, and when the *Quakers came to America in 1656 Williams granted them political toleration, though he attacked their doctrines.

Williams, Rowland (1817–70), Anglican clergyman. His essay on Biblical criticism in *Essays and Reviews* (1860) led to a prosecution for heterodoxy; the Court of *Arches sentenced him to a year's suspension, but the sentence was annulled by the *Judicial Committee of the Privy Council in 1864.

Willibald, St (700–86), Bp. of Eichstätt. In 722 he set out from England on a pilgrimage to Rome; he went on to the E. Mediterranean. After he had spent 10 years at *Monte Cassino, in 740 Gregory III sent him to Germany. St *Boniface ordained him priest in 741/2 and soon afterwards bishop. He joined in a confraternity agreement with other bishops and abbots in 762 and consolidated the Church in Franconia. Feast day, 7 July.

Willibrord, St (658–739), 'Apostle of Frisia'. A Northumbrian, he spent 12 years in an Anglo-Saxon religious community in *Ireland. In 690 he went as a missionary to W. Frisia. On a visit to Rome in 693 he gained Papal support for his mission, and on a second visit in 695 he was consecrated Abp. of the Frisians. *Pepin gave him a site for his cathedral outside Utrecht, and in 698 he founded the monastery of *Echternach. His work extended to *Denmark, Heligoland, and Thuringia. Feast day, 7 Nov.

The Society of St Willibrord, founded c.1910, exists to foster relations between the C of E and the *Old Catholic Churches.

Wilsnack. A former place of pilgrimage in Germany. After a fire in the church in 1383 three consecrated *hosts were said to have been found unharmed, but marked with drops of blood. The alleged miracle drew crowds of pilgrims. In 1552 Wilsnack became Protestant and the miraculous hosts were burnt.

Wilson, Daniel (1778–1858), a leading *Evangelical. He was minister of St John's, Bedford Row, in London (1812–24) and then vicar of Islington (1824–32). He founded the annual Islington Clerical Conference (1827) and the *Lord's Day Observance Society (1831). In 1832 he accepted the bishopric of Calcutta. In *India he improved the provision of churches and chaplains, excluded the caste system from the churches of southern India, and devoted much of his fortune to the building of St Paul's cathedral in Calcutta (consecrated 1847).

Wilson, Thomas (1663–1755), Bp. of *Sodor and Man from 1698. Taking advantage of the freedom of the Manx Church from Acts of the English Parliament, he enforced discipline by his Ecclesiastical Constitutions of 1704, which inflicted public penance for slander, perjury, immorality, and other offences; their administration involved him in acrimonious legal disputes, as did his suspension of his archdeacon for heresy (1722). His devotional works long enjoyed a wide circulation.

Winchelsea, Robert of (c.1245–1313), Abp. of *Canterbury from 1293. He was Rector of the Faculty of Arts in *Paris in 1267 and Chancellor of the University of *Oxford by 1288. His theological teaching was mainly concerned with the doctrine of the Trinity.

As Archbishop, he was a staunch upholder of ecclesiastical rights and soon became involved in a struggle with Edward I, mainly over taxation of the clergy. When Bertrand Got, a former royal clerk, became Pope as *Clement V in 1305, the King was able to secure Winchelsea's suspension in 1306. After Edward I's death in 1307 he returned to his see, but was soon in opposition to Edward II and the Pope and associated with baronial grievances. He was assiduous in pursuit of his pastoral duties and attempts were made to secure his canonization.

Winchester. About 648 King Cenwealh of Wessex founded a church at Winchester; a bishop was appointed in 660, possibly when the bishopric of Wessex was transferred there from *Dorchester. The refoundation of the former Roman city by King *Alfred, coupled with the fame of St *Swithun (Bp. 852–62), assisted the growth of the see. St *Ethelwold (Bp. 963–84) replaced the secular canons with *Benedictine monks. He and his successor rebuilt the cathedral on a vast scale. The cathedral (the Old Minster), with the New Minster (founded in 901–3) and Nunnaminster (founded before 902), formed the greatest ecclesiastical centre in Anglo-Saxon England. These buildings have not survived. A new cathedral on an adjacent site was built in Norman style by Walkelin (Bp. 1070–98). Apart from the transepts, this building was gradually transformed from Norman to Gothic. *Henry of Blois (Bp. 1129–71) brought from the site of the Old Minster the remains of the Saxon kings and bishops now in mortuary chests round the presbytery. The west front and Perpendicular nave were the work of William Edington (Bp. 1346–64) and *William of Wykeham. The stone screen was probably completed by 1476. At the *Dissolution (1539) the last Prior became the first Dean of the new foundation. The see of Winchester ranks fifth among the English bishoprics, and the bishop at present always has a seat in the House of Lords.

Windesheim, near Zwolle, in the Netherlands. A house of *Augustinian Canons was established in 1387 by six of G. *Groote's disciples under the direction of *Florentius Radewijns. Under the second prior, Johannes Vos (1391–1424), it formed, with three

other Dutch monasteries, the 'Congregation of Windesheim'. The Canons of Windesheim were the chief monastic representatives of the '*Devotio Moderna'. Their members included *Thomas à Kempis and G. *Biel.

Windsor, St George's Chapel. The 'Royal Free Chapel of Windsor' was constituted by Edward III to take charge of the shrine of the Order of the Garter (founded c.1348); it received its statutes in 1352. The present Perpendicular chapel, with its elaborate stone vaulting, dates from 1475–1508.

Windthorst, Ludwig (1812–91), German Catholic politician. He held high office in Hanover. After the union of Hanover with Prussia in 1866, he became a member of the N. German Diet and later of the German Reichstag. In 1871 he helped to found the *Centre Party; he was its leader until his death. He took part in the *Kulturkampf and had a large share in the negotiations for the repeal of the *May Laws.

wine. Wine is frequently mentioned in the Bible and appears to have been in everyday use in Palestine in NT times. It has traditionally been held to be one of the essential materials for a valid *Eucharist. The words of administration imply that the consecrated wine conveys to the communicant the Blood of Christ, though RC theologians have held that both the Body and the Blood are present in each of the Eucharistic species (see CONCOMITANCE). From early times it has been customary to mix water with the wine at the Eucharist. In the C of E the admixture was not ordered from 1552, but it was generally revived in the 19th cent. (see MIXED CHALICE). A conscientious abstinence from wine has led to the use of unfermented grape-juice by Nonconformists; the matter has sometimes been an issue in *ecumenical discussions.

Winifred, St (d. c.650), patron saint of N. Wales. According to late legends, she was a fair maiden sought in marriage by Prince Caradog of Hawarden; refusing his advances, she was wounded (or killed) by him, but miraculously healed (or restored to life) by her uncle, St *Beuno. A spring marked the scene, at the present Holywell, Flintshire; here she established a nunnery and became abbess. Feast day, 3 Nov.

Wipo (d. after 1046), poet and royal biographer. He was chaplain to the Emps. Conrad II and Henry III. His best-known work is the '*Victimae paschali laudes' (q.v.). His *Gesta Chuonradi Imperatoris* is one of the main sources for the reign of Conrad II (1024–39).

wisdom. In the OT wisdom, whether human or Divine, occupies a prominent place. Human wisdom is both practical and speculative. Divine wisdom is manifested in creation and in God's guidance of nations and individuals (Wisd. 10–19). It is more than a mere quality and tends increasingly to become a *hypostasis, so especially in Prov. 8 and Wisd. 7: 22 f. The so-called 'Wisdom Literature' is generally reckoned to include Job, Prov., Eccles., Ecclus., and Wisd. (qq.v.). The combination of practical advice with speculation about Divine wisdom is characteristic of this type of literature, as is the attribution of wisdom to an ancient ruler, such as *Solomon. In the NT St *Paul calls Christ 'the wisdom of God' (1 Cor. 1: 24). He also echoes the OT view of wisdom as a gift of the Spirit (Is. 11: 2) at 1 Cor. 12: 8. Among the Fathers most use 'Wisdom' as a synonym for the Incarnate Word or *Logos, but some equate 'Wisdom' with the Third Person of the Trinity. In *Gnostic thought, which saw in Wisdom a Divine emanation and a cause of the creation and redemption of the world, the conception played a central part. In modern times it has become a subject of speculation in connection with the Deity in the thought of Russian authors such as V. *Solovyov and S. *Bulgakov, and it has a major role in *Feminist Theology.

Wisdom of Solomon. A Book of the *Apocrypha. The first part (1: 1–6: 8) describes the different destinies awaiting the righteous and the wicked; the second part (6: 9–9: 18) contains the meditation on Wisdom which gives the Book its name; the last part (10–19) reviews the history of Israel to the *Exodus, with an excursus on idolatry in 13–15. The ascription of the Book to *Solomon is a literary device. It was most probably written by an *Alexandrian Jew in the 1st or 2nd cent. BC.

The Book has greatly influenced Christian thought. It may have been directly used by NT writers. Later the terms used of the Divine Wisdom are freely applied to Christ. See also the previous entry.

Wiseman, Nicholas Patrick Stephen (1802–65), cardinal. In 1828 he became rector of the *English College, Rome. He returned to England in 1840 as president of Oscott College, Birmingham, and Coadjutor to the *Vicar Apostolic of the newly-created Central District. When the hierarchy was restored in England and Wales in 1850, he became first Abp. of *Westminster and a cardinal. He was criticized by RCs as well as Protestants for his *Ultramontane views and his attempts to impose Italian devotional practices in England, but he did much to organize and advance the cause of the RC Church in the country. He held three provincial synods, encouraged RCs to support parliamentary candidates disposed to remove disabilities from RCs, and tried to foster a genuine Catholic culture in England.

Wishart, George (c.1513–46), Scottish Reformer. He fled to England when charged with heresy in 1538 and travelled on the Continent. Returning to Scotland in 1543, he began active propaganda on behalf of the Reformed doctrines, assisted by J. *Knox. He was arrested and burnt.

witchcraft. The alleged exercise of magical powers through the gift of supernatural beings other than God and His angels. The narrative of the witch of Endor (1 Sam. 28: 7–25) and the condemnations of witchcraft in the OT (Exod. 22: 18) and NT (Gal. 5: 20) have sometimes been adduced as proofs of its existence.

Before 1100 witchcraft in W. Europe consisted chiefly in the performance of pagan rituals divorced from their religious context. In the 12th cent. learned, ritual magic, derived from Hellenistic and Arabic sources, reached the W.; the Church viewed this more seriously and condemned all rites involving the invocation of spirits. Nevertheless, witches and sorcerers were arrested only if accused of conspiring to cause criminal damage; they were then tried in the bishops' courts and, if found guilty, punished by the civil magistrates in accordance with secular law. From 1398 the Inquisition was given jurisdiction over such cases.

Although witchcraft trials increased from the late 14th cent., they did not reach their height until between 1580 and 1630, and in some countries not until the early 18th cent. Probably *c.*500,000 people were executed for the alleged crime, but the pattern of prosecutions varied. In the Mediterranean countries there were few prosecutions. In the *Netherlands the death penalty ceased to be applied *c.*1600, and in France after 1624 acquittals were common. In England the worst persecutions occurred in 1645–6. Witch-hunting on any scale had ended everywhere by 1750 and legislation dealing with witchcraft was repealed in this period. The last legal execution for witchcraft took place in Switzerland in 1782.

Witelo (born *c.*1230), Polish mathematician and natural philosopher. At the Papal court at Viterbo, he joined a scientific circle including *William of Moerbeke, to whom he dedicated his main work, the *Perspectiva.* Treating of both mathematical optics and the physiological and psychological aspects of vision, it is largely based on the work of the Arabic scholar Alhazen (Ihn al-Haytham).

Wittenberg, the cradle of the *Reformation. M. *Luther became a professor at its university in 1508. In 1517 he affixed his 95 theses against *indulgences to the door of the Schlosskirche, and in 1522 Protestant public worship was celebrated for the first time in the parish church here.

Wittenberg, Concord of (1536). An agreement on *Eucharistic doctrine drawn up by P. *Melanchthon and accepted by a representative body of *Lutheran and *Zwinglian theologians at Wittenberg. The Swiss Zwinglians, however, refused to accept it.

Wittgenstein, Ludwig (1889–1951), philosopher. Born in Vienna, he went to Cambridge in 1912 but returned home in 1914 to join the Austrian army. His *Tractatus Logico-Philosophicus,* completed in 1918, was published (under a different title) in 1921. Thinking all philosophical problems were solved, he worked in remote schools in Austria (1920–26); he was drawn back to philosophy by discussions with members of the Vienna Circle who had founded logical positivism partly on what he considered to be a misunderstanding of his *Tractatus.* He returned to Cambridge in 1929, becoming Professor of Philosophy in 1939. His later writings were published posthumously, beginning with *Philosophical Investigations* (1953). In them he discussed the relationship between thought or language and the world, the nature of meaning and understanding, states of consciousness, and the will. Some philosophers of religion have developed themes from his work which others have labelled 'Wittgensteinian fideism', namely the doctrine that only participants in religious forms of life can play the appropriate language-games, so that religion remains immune to criticism from outside. How far such views are grounded in Wittgenstein's work is disputed.

Wolfenbüttel Fragments. The title under which G. E. *Lessing issued seven extracts (1774–8) from an unpublished work in which H. S. *Reimarus had attacked historic Christianity.

Wolff, Christian (1679–1754), German philosopher. He became a professor at Halle in 1706. In an attempt to systematize the principles of G. W. *Leibniz, he developed a comprehensive system of philosophy. His confidence in reason offended the *Pietists who, in 1723, persuaded Frederick I to expel him. He spent his exile at *Marburg. He was recalled on the accession of Frederick the Great (1740). His system was taught in most German universities in the later 18th cent.

Wolsey, Thomas (1472/4–1530), cardinal. He held a number of benefices under Henry VII and under *Henry VIII he rose rapidly. He became Abp. of *York in 1514 and a cardinal in 1515. Three months later he was made Lord Chancellor, with almost royal authority. In foreign policy he skilfully held the balance of power between the Empire and France. In 1521, though he favoured friendship with France, he had to sign a secret treaty with the Emp. *Charles V, who nevertheless failed to use his influence to get Wolsey elected Pope. At home he made enemies, especially by his ruthless methods of raising money for the French war. When in 1527 Henry began to take steps to obtain his divorce, Wolsey tried to further his wishes. His plan to induce the Pope to cede to himself authority to decide the case failed; Wolsey, unable to obtain the Papal dispensation necessary for the divorce, was blamed by *Anne Boleyn and incurred the King's displeasure. In 1529 he pleaded guilty to a *praemunire*, resigned the Great Seal, and gave up his property to the King. He spent his last months in his diocese. In 1530 he was arrested on a charge of treason; he died on the way to London.

women, ordination of. Though there were women of standing among Christ's followers, and in the early Church women exercised roles of leadership in the emerging communities, it is not known how these roles relate to the three-fold ministry of *bishops, *priests, and *deacons that was in place by the 2nd cent. The references to women fulfilling priestly functions in heretical bodies indicate that in orthodox circles such behaviour was regarded as an outrage. There is evidence for a distinct order of *deaconesses (q.v.) in the patristic period, but it is not clear that they should be seen as women in deacon's orders; their relationship to *widows and virgins is obscure, and the order disappeared in the W. by the 11th cent. and in the E. slightly later.

The first Churches to admit women to official ministry were those who had abandoned the three-fold order of bishop, priest, and deacon at the *Reformation and which had little or no centralized hierarchical structure. It was not, however, until the 19th cent. that the ordination of women became a serious concern. In most denominations unofficial ministries (e.g. as preachers) preceded the admission of women into the ranks of ordained clergy.

The office of deaconess was revived at *Kaiserswerth in Germany in 1836. In 1862 A. C. *Tait 'set aside' Elizabeth Ferard as the first deaconess in the C of E. In the *Episcopal Church in the United States of America the office of deaconess was established by canon in 1889. *Methodist deaconess institutes were established in America in 1888 and in England in 1890.

The earliest ordination of a woman as a minister in a recognized denomination took place in the First *Congregational Church in Butler and Savannah, Wayne County, New York, in 1853. Later in the 19th cent. women were ordained in the USA by the Universalist Association, the *Disciples of Christ, some *Baptists, Methodists, and *Presbyterians. In England the first woman was ordained to pastoral charge of a local

Baptist church in 1918, and in 1925 the Baptist Union of Great Britain and Ireland formally accredited women as ministers. Other Nonconformist Churches followed during the 20th cent. Since the first *Lutheran ordination of a woman in the *Netherlands in 1929, many Lutheran Churches have admitted women to their ordained ministry, though some still do not do so.

In the Anglican Communion Florence Tim Oi Li was ordained priest in 1944 by the Bp. of Hong Kong to serve Christians cut off by war or revolution in China. His action was condemned by the *Lambeth Conference of 1948. That of 1968, however, affirmed that deaconesses 'should be regarded as within the order of deacons', opening the way for canonical regulations on the subject in each Province. In the Episcopal Church in the USA legislation to this effect was passed in 1970, and in the C of E in 1986. In 1976, after several irregular ordinations of women to the priesthood in the Episcopal Church, the General Convention allowed the ordination of women both to the priesthood and the episcopate. The C of E allowed the ordination of women as priests in 1993. Women have been regularly ordained as priests in a number of Provinces.

The United Methodist Church (USA) in 1980 ordained the first bishop in any major denomination. The first woman to be ordained to the episcopate in the historic succession was consecrated as Suffragan Bishop of Massachusetts in the Episcopal Church in the USA in 1989; the first diocesan bishop was consecrated in *New Zealand in 1990. The Lutherans ordained two women as bishops in 1992.

The RC Church, the E. *Orthodox and *Oriental Orthodox Churches maintain an ordained ministry which is exclusively male, holding such to be of the essence of Orders.

Woodard, Nathaniel (1811–91), founder of the 'Woodard Schools'. As a curate in East London he became convinced of the need for public schools which would provide a middle-class education on a definitely Anglican basis. In 1848 he outlined his ideas in his *Plea for the Middle Classes* and established the St Nicolas Society for realization of his plans. He received wide moral and financial support, especially from *High

Churchmen, and many schools were founded, among them Lancing (1848) and Hurstpierpoint (1850). He became a Canon of Manchester in 1870.

Woolman, John (1720–72), American *Quaker preacher. From 1743 he led a long campaign against *slavery, travelling among the Quaker communities in America in support of Negro rights. His *Journal*, beginning in 1756, records his 'Life, Gospel-Labours and Christian Experience'.

Woolston, Thomas (1670–1733), *Deistical writer. In 1721 he was deprived of a Fellowship in Cambridge and announced his intention of founding a new sect. He wrote in support of A. *Collins and maintained that the Virgin Birth and the Resurrection were allegories.

Worcester. The diocese was founded *c*.680 for the tribe of the Hwicce when the diocese of Mercia was divided. The first cathedral was richly endowed by the Mercian kings. The secular canons who served it were replaced by *Benedictine monks under St *Oswald, who also built a new cathedral (completed in 983). After this had been destroyed by the Danes, it was rebuilt (1084–9) by St *Wulfstan; it was restored and reconsecrated in 1218. It has been much altered. The choir is Early English and the nave Perpendicular in style. The monastery was suppressed in 1540 and a secular chapter was in place by 1542.

Worcester House Declaration (1660). See DECLARATIONS OF INDULGENCE.

Word of God. See LOGOS.

Wordsworth, John (1843–1911), Bp. of *Salisbury from 1885. A grand-nephew of W. *Wordsworth, he was one of the best Latin scholars of his day. From 1878 he worked on a critical edition of the *Vulgate NT (Mt. to Rom., 1889–1911; minor edition of the whole NT, 1911). As bishop he was an invaluable adviser to Abp. E. W. *Benson and an enthusiastic worker in the cause of reunion, especially with the *Swedish and *Old Catholic Churches. To this end he published two books on the validity of *Anglican Ordinations. In 1897 he composed the Latin *Responsio* sent by the Abps. of *Canterbury and *York in reply to '*Apostolicae curae'.

Wordsworth, William (1770–1850), Eng-

lish poet. In 1798 he and S. T. *Coleridge published *Lyrical Ballads*, which contains the famous 'Lines written . . . above Tintern Abbey'. Wordsworth's aim in this collection was to bring out the deeper spiritual meaning in everyday persons and events. His later works include *The Prelude*, his spiritual autobiography to 1805, and *Poems in Two Volumes* (1807), containing the 'Ode to Duty' and 'Ode. Intimations of Immortality'. Nature was the great inspiration of his art.

World Alliance of Reformed Churches. The World Alliance of Reformed Churches (Presbyterian and Congregational) was formed in 1970 by the amalgamation of the (*Presbyterian) World Alliance of Reformed Churches (founded in 1875) with the International Congregational Council (founded in 1891).

World Council of Churches. The 'fellowship of Churches which accept our Lord Jesus Christ as God and Saviour', formally constituted at *Amsterdam in 1948. The organization arose from the fusion of two earlier movements, '*Life and Work' and '*Faith and Order'. A provisional organization was established at Utrecht in 1938, but because of the Second World War the formal constitution was delayed until 1948. Representative Assemblies, held at intervals of six to eight years, meet in different parts of the world. From them are elected members of the Central Committee, the Council's highest governing body. The headquarters of the Council is in *Geneva. In a reorganization in 1992 its work was gathered into four programme units.

Apart from the RC Church and the *Unitarians, the Council includes Churches from all the main Christian denominations, including nearly all the Eastern *Orthodox Churches. Since 1961 the RC Church has sent observers to Assemblies; in 1968 it became a full member of the Faith and Order Commission and was thus involved in the production of the 1982 report on '*Baptism, Eucharist and Ministry'.

World Evangelical Fellowship. See EVANGELICAL ALLIANCE.

Worms, Concordat of (1122). The agreement between *Callistus II and the Emp. Henry V which ended the *Investiture

Controversy. The Emperor renounced all investiture by ring and staff. The Pope conceded that in the German kingdom (only) elections of bishops and abbots should take place in the presence of the Emperor, who should grant the regalia by investiture with the sceptre before consecration; in other parts of the Empire consecration was to precede investiture with the regalia.

Worms, Conference of (1540–41). A meeting designed to reunite the Catholics and Protestants in Germany. After an agreed formula had been reached on *original sin, discussions were ended in view of the forthcoming Reichstag at *Ratisbon.

Worms, Diet of (1521). The Imperial Diet at which M. *Luther defended his doctrines before *Charles V. Immediately after the Diet, Luther's teaching was formally condemned in the Edict of Worms.

Worms, Synod of (1076). The synod convened by *Henry IV of Germany to secure the deposition of *Gregory VII at the start of the *Investiture Controversy. It charged Gregory with many crimes. Gregory excommunicated Henry soon afterwards.

Worship, Directory of Public (1645). The 'Directory for the Public Worship of God' was compiled by the *Westminster Assembly on *Presbyterian principles; it was designed to replace the BCP. In *Scotland it was accepted by the *General Assembly and became one of the standards of Presbyterianism. An Ordinance requiring its use in England was passed by Parliament but was not long enforced.

Worship and Doctrine Measure. The Church of England (Worship and Doctrine) Measure 1974 gives the General *Synod power to regulate all matters of worship, provided that the forms in the BCP 'continue to be available for use'. It also allows the Synod to determine the obligations and forms of *assent to the doctrine of the C of E required of clergy and lay officers.

Wounds, the Five Sacred. Though the Passion narratives of the Gospels expressly record only the opening of the Lord's side, the piercing of His hands and feet, a normal practice in contemporary crucifixions, is attested in the Resurrection appearances. Devotion to the Five Wounds developed in the Middle Ages. It was fostered by the *stigmatization of St *Francis of Assisi. The preference soon given to the wound in the side led to the cult of the *Sacred Heart.

wrath of God, the. An anthropomorphic phrase for the Divine attitude to sin. The expression often occurs in the Bible. In the NT the wrath of God is particularly connected with the Judgement on the Last Day.

Wrede, William (1859–1906), German NT scholar. He pioneered the 'history of traditions' approach to the Gospels in *Das Messiasgeheimnis in den Evangelien* (1901; Eng. tr., 1971). In this work, which gave its name to the whole discussion of the so-called *Messianic Secret (q.v.), Wrede challenged the view that Mk. was an unadorned record of historical fact and maintained that Jesus did not claim to be the Messiah, the Gospel story being a reading back of later beliefs into the narrative. In his *Paulus* (1905; Eng. tr., 1907) he argued that St *Paul had radically transformed Christ's teaching.

Wren, Christopher (1632–1723), architect of *St Paul's Cathedral. He was Savilian Professor of Astronomy at Oxford and a founder of the Royal Society. After the Great Fire of 1666 in London, he was one of the rebuilders of the city. Besides St Paul's Cathedral, built between 1675 and 1710, Wren was responsible for building 52 London city churches, as well as secular buildings. As a church designer his great achievement was to produce models specifically suited to the Anglican rite, allowing 'all to hear the Service, and both to hear distinctly, and see the Preacher'.

Wroth, William (1570 or 1576–1641), Welsh Nonconformist pastor. He became rector of Llanfaches, west of Chepstow, in 1611 or 1617, and, after a sudden conversion in 1620, became famous as a *Puritan preacher. In 1639, after he had ceased to hold his living, he established at Llanfaches the first separatist Church in Wales.

Wulfric, St (d. 1154), anchorite. After a conversion attributed to an interview with a beggar, who told him the contents of his purse and prophesied a life of sanctity for him, c.1125 he was enclosed in a cell at Haselbury Plucknett in Somerset. He became famous for his prophecies and miracles. Feast day, 20 Feb.

Wulfstan (d. 1023), Bp. of London from 996

to 1002, and Abp. of *York from 1002. (He held the see of *Worcester as well as that of York from 1002 to 1016.) He was a prominent royal counsellor and a distinguished writer in Old English. His many homilies are practical expositions of essential doctrine; his 'Institutes of Polity, Civil and Ecclesiastical' is mainly concerned with the duties of the different ranks and classes of society. He composed much of the legislation issued after 1008 by Kings Ethelred II and Canute and drafted or influenced various private law-codes.

Wulfstan, St (c.1009–95), Bp. of *Worcester. He spent some 25 years in a monastery at Worcester, and in 1062 accepted the bishopric reluctantly. He administered his diocese effectively and, together with *Lanfranc, suppressed the slave trade between England and Ireland. Feast day, 19 Jan.

Württemberg Confession. A Protestant confession of faith compiled for presentation to the Council of *Trent in 1552.

Wycliffe, John (c.1330–84), philosopher, theologian, and reformer. He was Master of Balliol (c.1360–1) and Warden of Canterbury Hall, Oxford (1365–7). He was also rector of Fillingham (1361–8), of Ludgershall (1368–84), and of Lutterworth (1374–84), but until 1381 he lived mainly in Oxford. He was in the service of the Black Prince and of John of Gaunt after 1371, and so protected against ecclesiastical censures.

Wycliffe's early reputation was as a philosopher. He reacted against the prevalent Oxford scepticism, which divorced the spheres of natural and supernatural knowledge; in his *Summa de Ente* he argued that individual beings derived from God through a hierarchy of universals and were therefore in essence changeless and indestructible. His repugnance at the religious institutions of his time led him to elaborate a concept of the Church which distinguished its eternal, ideal reality from the visible, 'material' Church, and denied to the latter any authority which did not derive from the former. In his *De Civili Dominio* he argued that secular and ecclesiastical authority depended on grace and that therefore the clergy, if not in a state of grace, could lawfully be deprived of their endowments by the civil power. He later maintained that the Bible was the sole criterion of doctrine, that the authority of the Pope was ill-founded in Scripture, and that the monastic life had no biblical foundation. He attacked the doctrine of *transubstantiation as philosophically unsound and as encouraging a superstitious attitude to the Eucharist.

Wycliffe gradually lost support in Oxford. His Eucharistic teaching was condemned by the University in 1381, and in 1382 Abp. W. *Courtenay condemned a wide range of his doctrines and the persons of his followers, though not Wycliffe himself. Wycliffe retired to Lutterworth. After his death his doctrines were again condemned in 1388, 1397, and at the Council of *Constance in 1415. The extent of his influence in England is unclear, but from c.1380 his philosophical and theological writings exercised a major influence on Czech scholars, notably J. *Huss. The 16th-cent. Reformers appealed to Wycliffe, but his preoccupations were largely different from theirs. Feast day in CW, 31 Dec.

Wycliffites See LOLLARDS.

Wynfrith, St. See BONIFACE, ST.

Xavier, St Francis. See FRANCIS XAVIER, ST.

Ximénez de Cisneros, Francisco (1436–1517), Cardinal Abp. of Toledo. He was *vicar general in the diocese of Siguenza before he became an *Observantine friar in Toledo. He attracted crowds of penitents and retired to a remote monastery. In 1492 he reluctantly became confessor to Queen *Isabella; his advice was sought on matters of state as well as on spiritual matters. He became Abp. of Toledo in 1495; the office carried with it the High Chancellorship of Castile. On Isabella's death (1504) he managed to establish concord between *Ferdinand and his son-in-law, Philip of Burgundy, who succeeded to the throne of Castile. On Philip's death (1506), Ximénez virtually ruled Castile until Ferdinand returned from Naples, bringing for him a cardinal's hat (1507). When Ferdinand died in 1516, Ximénez was regent during the minority of *Charles V; he died, possibly by poison, on his way to meet Charles, who had landed in Asturias and virtually dismissed him from office. A great patron of learning, from his private income he founded the university of Alcalá and commissioned the *Complutensian Polyglot.

Xystus. See SIXTUS II.

Yah, an abbreviation of *Yahweh, used in poetical passages in the OT.

Yahweh. The Hebrew proper name for God. It probably represents the original pronunciation of the *Tetragrammaton (q.v.).

year, liturgical. In the W. Church the Christian year is based on the *week and on the festivals of *Easter and *Christmas. It begins with the period leading up to *Christmas. The ASB reckoned nine Sundays before Christmas, but in most calendars the year starts with the First Sunday in *Advent. Sundays have traditionally been numbered through Advent, after Christmas and after *Epiphany, through *Lent, after Easter, and after *Whitsunday or *Trinity Sunday. According to the calendar introduced into the RC Church in 1969, after Epiphany the 'Sundays of the Year' are numbered consecutively, excluding the period from the beginning of Lent to Whitsunday. In the E. *Orthodox Church the liturgical year has much the same shape as in the W., except that it begins on 1 Sept. (the beginning of the tax year in the Byzantine Empire), and the Sundays outside the period of Lent-Eastertide are numbered 'after Pentecost'. The period Lent-Eastertide embraces the ten weeks before Easter to the Sunday after Pentecost.

YMCA ('Young Men's Christian Association'). An interdenominational association founded in London in 1844 by George Williams. At its centre are Christians who wish to share their faith with others, but those of different or no religious faith are welcomed. Women and girls have been accepted as members since 1964. It provides hostels, sports and leisure facilities, vocational training for the unemployed, drug counselling, and camps for children and youth groups. In the past it worked extensively with the Armed Forces. YCare, the overseas development agency of the YMCAs of Great Britain and Ireland, was founded in 1984.

yoga. A Sanskrit word meaning 'bind together'. In a technical sense it denotes an Indian system of religious philosophy aiming at the union of the soul with the Divine Spirit by means of concentration to the exclusion of all sense-perception. This has influenced Christian devotion. The word is used loosely of a modern system of health culture with ascetic aspects.

Yom Kippur. The Hebrew name for the Day of *Atonement.

Younge, Charlotte Mary (1823–1901), novelist. When in 1836 J. *Keble became vicar of Hursley, she came under his influence. She determined to apply her talent as a storyteller to spreading the faith in fiction. Besides successful novels, she wrote Lives of J. C. *Patteson and Hannah *More.

York. York was the military headquarters of the Romans in northern Britain. A Bp. of York is recorded in 314. The Christian community was destroyed in the Saxon invasions. St *Paulinus, who was consecrated Bp. of York in 625, baptized the Northumbrian King *Edwin in 627 and received the *pallium in 631. After another pagan invasion in 633, Paulinus fled to *Rochester, and York came under the care of the bishops of *Lindisfarne. The see was restored in 664 with the consecration of St *Wilfrid; in 735, under *Egbert, it was raised to archiepiscopal dignity and its archbishops became primates of the Northern episcopal Province. Under the first Norman Archbishop, Thomas of Bayeux (1070–1100), the struggle for precedence between Canterbury and York began. It was finally settled by Pope Innocent VI (1352–62), who decided that the Abp. of Canterbury was to have precedence and the title 'Primate of All England', and that the Abp. of York should be styled 'Primate of England'.

Medieval York was important as a regional capital, and in the Middle Ages and later the Abps. of York took part in governing the North of England. At the height of its prosperity there were over 40 parish churches and nine religious houses in the city. No church can be traced back to Roman times, though Roman materials were reused in several. The Saxon cathedral, which may have been on the site of St Michael-le-Belfrey, was destroyed during the rebellion of 1069. A Norman church preceded the present York Minster, built on the same site between c.1227 and 1472. There were four restorations in the 19th cent. The foundations of the Central Tower and West Front, which rest on Roman rubbish, were strengthened between 1967 and 1972. Serious damage caused by a fire in 1984 has been repaired.

Young Men's (and **Women's) Christian Association.** See YMCA and YWCA.

yule. *Christmas and its attendant festivities.

YWCA ('Young Women's Christian Association'). A charitable body devoted to the needs of young women. In 1855 Miss Emma Robarts started a Prayer Union and Lady Mary Jane Kinnaird opened a hostel for nurses in London; the two organizations united in 1877. The YWCA is entirely separate from the YMCA.

Zabarella, Francesco (1360–1417), Italian canonist. Created cardinal by *John XXIII in 1411, he conducted the negotiations with the Emp. Sigismund for the Council of *Constance. His conduct at the Council helped to heal the schism. His writings on canon law long remained standard works.

Zacchaeus. A *publican, he climbed a tree to see Christ, and was called by name to come down and give Him lodging in his house (Lk. 19: 1–10).

Zachariah. The father of St *John the Baptist (Lk. 1 and 3: 2). A Jewish priest, he is said to have received a vision in the *Temple promising him a son who would be 'filled with the Holy Spirit'; he celebrated the birth of the child in the *Benedictus. Feast day, 5 Nov.

Zacharias, St (d. 752), Pope from 741. The last Greek Pope, he induced the Lombard King Liutprand to return four cities and all her patrimonies to the Church and to abandon his attack on *Ravenna. His relations with the Frankish kingdom were cordial, and in 751 he sanctioned the deposition of the last Merovingian in favour of *Pepin. He denounced the *Iconoclastic policy of the Emps. *Leo III and Constantine V. Feast day in the E., 5 Sept.; in the W., formerly 15 Mar.

Zacharias Scholasticus (d. after 536), *Monophysite writer. He became a lawyer at *Constantinople c.492 and later was Bp. of Mitylene on the island of Lesbos. His main work was a Church history, valuable for the period 450–91. He also wrote Lives of *Severus of Antioch, Peter the Iberian, and others, and works against the *Neoplatonists and the *Manichees.

Zahn, Theodor (1838–1933), German NT and patristic scholar. His standpoint was that of sober conservatism and his work was marked by erudition and thoroughness. His long series of studies on the NT *canon contained pioneer work. He also wrote on *Marcellus of Ancyra, *Hermas, St *Ignatius, and on the Acts of *John.

Zaire. See CONGO, DEMOCRATIC REPUBLIC OF THE.

Zambia, Christianity in. Missionary work began relatively late in the area of central Africa known as Zambia since it became independent in 1964. In 1886 the French Evangelical Missionary Society began work among the Lozi. About the same time the *LMS established a mission in the north of the country and Scottish *Presbyterians came in the east. The main RC missions were *White Fathers in the north and *Jesuits in the south. An early attempt in the 1930s to unite denominational missions resulted in the formation of the African United Church (the United Missions in the Copperbelt) and in the establishment of the Mindola Ecumenical Foundation. In 1965 the United Church of Zambia, comprising *Congregationalists, *Methodists, and the Paris Mission, was inaugurated. Other major denominations are the Anglican, African Reformed (founded by the Dutch Reformed Church in *South Africa), and *Jehovah's Witnesses. Most Zambians are members of one of the Churches, the RC being the largest.

Zanchi, Girolamo (1516–90), *Calvinist theologian. He became an *Augustinian Canon in 1531 and was sent to Lucca; here from 1541 he came under the influence of *Peter Martyr. He was successively a professor at Strasbourg, preacher at the Reformed Church in Chiavenna in North Italy, and a professor at Heidelberg; he left for Neustadt when the Palatinate became *Lutheran in 1576. He collaborated with Z. *Ursinus on a Reformed Confession.

Zealots. A Jewish party of revolt. According to *Josephus they were one of the factions which inspired the fanatical resistance to the Romans in *Jerusalem which led to its destruction in AD 70. They have commonly been identified with (1) the followers of Judas of Gamala who led a revolt in AD 6, and (2) the Sicarii, who refused to surrender to the Romans at Masada. There is, however, doubt about these identifications. The epithet 'zealot' applied to St *Simon 'the Less' in Lk. 6: 15 may mean that he belonged to the Zealot party, or may describe his character.

Zechariah. The Hebrew form of the name rendered *Zachariah in Greek, widely used in modern English translations of the Bible.

Zechariah, Book of. *Minor Prophet. Chs. 1–8, deriving mainly from Zechariah himself, date from 519–517 BC. An introductory prophecy is followed by eight visions. In one of these (4: 1–14) Zerubbabel, the contemporary head of the royal house of Judah, is exhorted to complete the restoration of the *Temple and is perhaps identified with the Davidic prince (see MESSIAH). In chs. 7–8 Zechariah asserts the need for righteousness rather than fasting, and prophesies the future glory of Judah when the Gentiles seeking God should voluntarily join themselves to the Jews. Chs. 9–14 contain two anonymous prophecies reflecting the circumstances of a later age.

Zeno, St (d. c.375), Bp. of *Verona from c.362. He was an African. His sermons (*Tractatus*) have affinities with the writings of *Tertullian and *Cyprian; they did not come into circulation until the early Middle Ages. Feast day, 12 Apr.

Zeno (c.450?–91), E. Emperor from 474. His reign was marked by a series of disastrous wars, and his *Henoticon (482) did nothing to bring about the desired union of the *Monophysites with the orthodox.

Zephaniah, Book of. *Minor Prophet. The Book announces the approaching judgement of all peoples in the Day of the Lord, but holds out the hope of future conversion among foreign nations and of a faithful remnant among the Jews. The prophecy claims to have been delivered in the reign of Josiah (d. *c.*608 BC); it probably belongs before 621 BC. The opening words of the '*Dies irae' are taken from the *Vulgate version of 1: 15 f.

Zephyrinus, St (d. 217), Pope from 198. Little is known of him. St *Hippolytus charged him with laxity in enforcing discipline and failure to suppress the heresies (especially *Sabellianism) then prevalent in Rome. Feast day, 26 Aug., dropped in 1969.

Zerbolt, Gerhard. See GERHARD ZERBOLT.

Zernov, Nicolas (1898–1980), Russian scholar and ecumenist. He left Russia in 1921 and in 1934 settled in England. From 1947 to 1966 he was Spalding Lecturer in Eastern Orthodox Culture in Oxford. In 1959 he founded a house in Oxford to bring together Christians of E. and W. traditions, with a library, residential accommodation for students, and a place of worship for the Russian Orthodox community; later a church was built (consecrated in 1973) which is shared between the Greek and Russian Orthodox parishes. In his writings he made the world of Russian Orthodoxy familiar in the W.

Zimbabwe, Christianity in. There were *Jesuit and *Dominican missionaries at court in the 16th and early 17th cents. Missionary activity, eliminated in the late 17th cent., was resumed in the later 19th cent. by the *LMS and by Jesuits, but little progress was made until the conquest of the country by Cecil Rhodes. After 1890 the Churches grew rapidly; *Methodists (British and American), *Lutherans, *Anglicans, and RCs had missions. John White, who was President of the Missionary Conference (1924–8), and others did much to defend African rights. Since Zimbabwe became independent in 1980, relations between the Church and the government have mainly been good. Most Zimbabweans are linked with some Church; the largest single one is the RC. There are many Independent Black-founded Churches.

Zinzendorf, Nikolaus Ludwig Graf von (1700–60), founder of the Herrnhuter 'Brüdergemeine' or *Moravian Brethren. From 1722 he received on one of his estates Protestant emigrants from Austria, many of them descendants of the *Bohemian Brethren. He left his civil post in 1727 and devoted himself to the spiritual care of this colony, called *Herrnhut. He was attacked by orthodox *Lutherans as an innovator and exiled from Saxony from 1736 to 1747. He founded communities in the Baltic Provinces, the *Netherlands, England, the *West Indies, and North America.

He was opposed both to the spirit of the *Enlightenment and to traditional Protestant orthodoxy. Believing that 'God fulfils Himself in many ways', he hoped to work pervasively within the Protestant Churches, but circumstances forced his movement to adopt a separate organization. In 1737 he received episcopal orders from a Moravian bishop in England. For a time he influenced *Evangelicals, notably J. *Wesley, but exception was taken to his teaching on the relation between *justification and sanctification and to the emotionalism of his 'religion of the heart'. Through F. D. E. *Schleiermacher, his emphasis on the place of feeling in religion influenced 19th-cent. theology.

Zion. The citadel of *Jerusalem, taken by *David from the Jebusites (2 Sam. 5: 6–7). The name came to signify Jerusalem itself (Is. 1: 27) and, allegorically, the heavenly city (Heb. 12: 22).

Zita, St (*c.*1215–72), the patroness of domestic servants. At the age of 12 she entered the service of the Fatinelli family at Lucca, where she remained all her life. She was fervently religious. Feast day, 27 Apr.

Zonaras, Johannes (12th cent.), Byzantine canonist and historian. He held high office in the Imperial administration before he retired to a monastery. His 'Epitome of History' preserves material which would otherwise be lost; it extends to 1118 and covers events which Zonaras had witnessed. He also wrote a commentary on Greek canon law.

Zoroastrianism (also known as **Mazdaism).** The system of religious doctrine ascribed to Zoroaster which became the dominant religion in Iran. After the conversion of Iran to *Islam, Zoroastrians went to *India, where they are called Parsis.

Zoroaster is traditionally held to have lived in the 6th cent. BC, but his dates are disputed. There is also disagreement as to the degree of continuity between his teaching and later dualistic Zoroastrianism. According to this, the world was made by one 'Wise Lord' with the help of his holy spirit and other spirits. Opposed to the Wise Lord is an uncreated Evil Spirit, supported by other evil spirits. The created world is the arena for a conflict between good and evil. At death each individual is judged according to his words and deeds on the 'bridge of decision'; those who fail fall into hell. In the last days of the world, the World Saviour will come in glory and in a final battle good will triumph over evil. Zoroastrianism is sometimes held to have influenced Christianity. See also AVESTA.

Zosimus (d. 418), Bp. of Rome from 417. His pontificate was marked by blunders. Having reopened the case of *Pelagius and his supporters, he was forced by an Imperial edict to come into line with the views of St *Augustine and the African Church and condemn Pelagianism. He was again outmanoeuvred when, citing as *Nicene a canon which belonged to the Council of *Sardica, he tried to quash the sentence passed on *Apiarius by the Bp. of Sicca. Feast day, 26 Dec.

Zosimus (later 5th cent.), Greek historian. His history of the Roman Empire, extending to 410, is a primary source for the secular history of the 4th cent. Because of its pagan viewpoint, it serves as a corrective to the better-known accounts of ecclesiastical affairs in Christian writers.

zucchetto. A small round skull-cap used by certain RC ecclesiastics.

Zurich Consensus. See CONSENSUS TIGURINUS.

Zwickau Prophets. A group of early *Anabaptists who tried to establish a community of the elect at Zwickau, an industrial town in S. Saxony. N. *Storch was one of their leaders who visited *Wittenberg in 1521 and impressed P. *Melanchthon and N. von *Amsdorf. Their influence survived at Zwickau into the 1530s.

Zwingli, Ulrich (or **Huldreich)** (1484–1531), Swiss Reformer. Ordained priest in 1506, as pastor at Glarus he devoted himself largely to humanistic studies. In 1516 he moved to *Einsiedeln, where the pilgrimage abuses quickened his desire for reform. In 1518 he was elected People's Preacher at the Old Minster in Zurich. The rupture with ecclesiastical authority came gradually. The real beginning of the Reformation in Switzerland was Zwingli's sermons commenting on the NT in 1519; they were followed by attacks on *purgatory, invocation of *saints, and *monasticism. His first Reformation tract appeared in 1522. Johann *Faber, sent to Zurich to deal with the situation, was silenced in a public disputation in 1523, when Zwingli upheld 67 theses. The sole basis of truth was the Gospel; the authority of the Pope, the sacrifice of the Mass, times and seasons of fasting, and clerical *celibacy were rejected. The city council supported Zwingli and the Minster Chapter was made independent of episcopal control. Zwingli then began to develop his characteristic theology ('Zwinglianism'). In 1522 he still accepted a traditional view of the Eucharist, but by 1524 he upheld a purely symbolic interpretation. In a series of writings against M. *Luther from 1525 onwards he urged (against Luther's doctrine of *consubstantiation) that it is only the communicant's faith that makes Christ present in the Eucharist; there is no question of any physical presence. Zwingli also distinguished more clearly than Luther between the human and Divine nature in Christ; he refused to admit the Lutheran distinction between the Law and the Gospel; and, unlike Luther, he believed that the magistrate had the right to legislate in religious matters. The movement spread to other parts of Switzerland. It met with resistance in the five Forest Cantons. In 1531 they made a sudden attack on Zurich and Zwingli was killed in battle.

Chronological List of Popes and Antipopes

Antipopes are indicated by indenting the names to the right in [ ]

until c.64	St *Peter	432–40	Sixtus III
	*Linus	440–61	*Leo I
	*Anacletus	461–8	Hilarus
fl. c.96	*Clement I	468–83	*Simplicius
	Evaristus	483–92	Felix III (II)
	Alexander I	492–6	*Gelasius I
c.117–c.127	Sixtus I	496–8	Anastasius II
c.127–c.137	*Telesphorus	498–514	*Symmachus
c.137–c.140	Hyginus	[498–9, 501–6 Laurentius]	
c.140–c.154	*Pius I	514–23	*Hormisdas
c.154–c.166	Anicetus	523–6	John I
c.166–c.175	Soter	526–30	Felix IV (III)
c.175–89	Eleutherius	530–2	Boniface II
189–98	*Victor I	[530 Dioscorus]	
198–217	*Zephyrinus	533–5	John II
217–22	*Callistus I	535–6	*Agapetus I
[217–c.235 *Hippolytus]		536–7	Silverius
222–30	Urban I	537–55	*Vigilius
230–5	Pontian	556–61	Pelagius I
235–6	Anterus	561–74	John III
236–50	*Fabian	575–9	Benedict I
251–3	*Cornelius	579–90	Pelagius II
[251–257/8 *Novatian]		590–604	*Gregory I
253–4	Lucius I	604–6	Sabinianus
254–7	*Stephen I	607	Boniface III
257–8	*Sixtus II	608–15	Boniface IV
259–68	*Dionysius	615–18	Deusdedit or Adeodatus I
269–74	Felix I	619–25	Boniface V
275–83	Eutychianus	625–38	*Honorius I
283–96	Caius	640	Severinus
296–304	Marcellinus	640–2	John IV
c.307–308/9	Marcellus I	642–9	Theodore I
310	Eusebius	649–55	*Martin I[1]
310/11–314	*Miltiades	654–7	Eugenius I
314–35	*Sylvester I	657–72	*Vitalian
336	Mark	672–6	Adeodatus II
337–52	*Julius I	676–8	Donus
352–66	*Liberius	678–81	*Agatho
[355–65 Felix II]		682–3	Leo II
366–84	*Damasus I	684–5	Benedict II
[366–7 Ursinus]		685–6	John V
384–99	*Siricius	686–7	Cono
399–401	Anastasius I	[687 Theodore]	
402–17	*Innocent I	[687 Paschal]	
417–18	*Zosimus	687–701	*Sergius I
418–22	*Boniface I	701–5	John VI
[418–19 Eulalius]		705–7	John VII
422–32	*Celestine I	708	Sisinnius

[1] After Martin's banishment his successor was elected and consecrated.

708–15	Constantine
715–31	*Gregory II
731–41	Gregory III
741–52	*Zacharias
752	Stephen II
752–7	*Stephen II (III)
757–67	Paul I
[767–9	Constantine]
[768	Philip]
768–72	*Stephen III (IV)
772–95	*Hadrian I
795–816	*Leo III
816–17	Stephen V
817–24	Paschal I
824–7	Eugenius II
827	Valentine
827–44	Gregory IV
844–7	Sergius II
[844	John]
847–55	*Leo IV
855–8	Benedict III
[855	*Anastasius Bibliothecarius]
858–67	*Nicholas I
867–72	Hadrian II
872–82	John VIII
882–4	Marinus I
884–5	Hadrian III
885–91	Stephen VI
891–6	*Formosus
896	Boniface VI
896–7	Stephen VII
897	Romanus
897	Theodore II
898–900	John IX
900–3	Benedict IV
903	Leo V
[903–4	Christopher]
904–11	Sergius III
911–13	Anastasius III
913–14	Lando
914–28	John X
928	Leo VI
928–31	Stephen VIII
931–5	John XI
936–9	Leo VII
939–42	Stephen IX
942–6	Marinus II
946–55	Agapetus II
955–64	*John XII
963–5	Leo VIII[1]
964	Benedict V

965–72	John XIII
973–4	Benedict VI
[974, 984–5	Boniface VII]
974–83	Benedict VII
983–4	John XIV
985–96	John XV
996–9	Gregory V
[997–8	John XVI]
999–1003	*Sylvester II
1003	John XVII
1003/4–9	John XVIII
1009–12	Sergius IV
1012–24	Benedict VIII
[1012	Gregory VI]
1024–32	John XIX
1032–44	Benedict IX
1045	Sylvester III
1045	Benedict IX [for the second time]
1045–6	Gregory VI
1046–7	Clement II
1047–8	Benedict IX [for the third time]
1048	Damasus II
1048–54	*Leo IX
1055–7	Victor II
1057–8	Stephen X
[1058–9	Benedict X]
1059–61	Nicholas II
1061–73	*Alexander II
[1061–72	Honorius II]
1073–85	*Gregory VII
[1080, 1084–1100	Clement III]
1086–7	Victor III
1088–99	*Urban II
1099–1118	*Paschal II
[1100–1	Theodoric]
[1101	Albert]
[1105–11	Sylvester IV]
1118–19	Gelasius II
[1118–21	Gregory VIII]
1119–24	*Callistus II
1124–30	Honorius II
[1124	Celestine II]
1130–43	Innocent II
[1130–8	Anacletus II]
[1138	Victor IV]
1143–4	Celestine II
1144–5	Lucius II
1145–53	*Eugenius III
1153–4	Anastasius IV
1154–9	*Hadrian IV

[1]His pontificate is dated from the deposition of his predecessor, but its legitimacy is contested.

1159–81	*Alexander III	1471–84	*Sixtus IV
[1159–64	Victor IV¹]	1484–92	Innocent VIII
[1164–8	Paschal III]	1492–1503	*Alexander VI
[1168–78	Callistus III]	1503	Pius III
[1179–80	Innocent III]	1503–13	*Julius II
1181–5	Lucius III	1513–21	*Leo X
1185–7	Urban III	1522–3	*Hadrian VI
1187	Gregory VIII	1523–34	*Clement VII
1187–91	Clement III	1534–49	*Paul III
1191–8	*Celestine III	1550–5	*Julius III
1198–1216	*Innocent III	1555	Marcellus II
1216–27	*Honorius III	1555–9	*Paul IV
1227–41	*Gregory IX	1559–65	*Pius IV
1241	Celestine IV	1566–72	*Pius V
1243–54	*Innocent IV	1572–85	*Gregory XIII
1254–61	Alexander IV	1585–90	*Sixtus V
1261–4	Urban IV	1590	Urban VII
1265–8	Clement IV	1590–1	Gregory XIV
1271–6	*Gregory X	1591	Innocent IX
1276	Innocent V	1592–1605	*Clement VIII
1276	Hadrian V	1605	Leo XI
1276–7	*John XXI²	1605–21	*Paul V
1277–80	Nicholas III	1621–3	Gregory XV
1281–5	*Martin IV	1623–44	*Urban VIII
1285–7	Honorius IV	1644–55	*Innocent X
1288–92	Nicholas IV	1655–67	*Alexander VII
1294	*Celestine V	1667–9	Clement IX
1294–1303	*Boniface VIII	1670–6	Clement X
1303–4	Benedict XI	1676–89	*Innocent XI
1305–14	*Clement V	1689–91	*Alexander VIII
1316–34	*John XXII	1691–1700	Innocent XII
[1328–30	Nicholas V]	1700–21	*Clement XI
1334–42	*Benedict XII	1721–4	Innocent XIII
1342–52	*Clement VI	1724–30	*Benedict XIII
1352–62	Innocent VI	1730–40	Clement XII
1362–70	*Urban V	1740–58	*Benedict XIV
1370–8	*Gregory XI	1758–69	*Clement XIII
1378–89	*Urban VI	1769–74	*Clement XIV
[1378–94	Clement VII]	1775–99	*Pius VI
1389–1404	Boniface IX	1800–23	*Pius VII
[1394–1417	*Benedict XIII]	1823–9	Leo XII
1404–6	Innocent VII	1829–30	Pius VIII
1406–15	Gregory XII	1831–46	*Gregory XVI
[1409–10	*Alexander V]	1846–78	*Pius IX
[1410–15	*John XXIII]	1878–1903	*Leo XIII
1417–31	*Martin V	1903–14	*Pius X
[1423–9	Clement VIII]	1914–22	*Benedict XV
[1425–30	Benedict XIV]	1922–39	*Pius XI
1431–47	*Eugenius IV	1939–58	*Pius XII
[1439–49	Felix V]	1958–63	*John XXIII
1447–55	*Nicholas V	1963–78	*Paul VI
1455–8	*Callistus III	1978	*John Paul I
1458–64	*Pius II	1978–	*John Paul II
1464–71	Paul II		

¹ No account was taken of the previous antipope, who had resisted for a very short time.
² No Pope bearing the name of John XX ever existed.

Supplementary information for 2003 reprint

Common Worship. Authorization of the ASB generally ended in 2000; it is being replaced by new services collectively called *Common Worship*. The main book, subtitled *Services and Prayers for the Church of England* (2000), provides a *Calendar, with many new names, Morning and Evening Prayer for Sundays, Night Office or *Compline (in both contemporary and traditional language), two Orders for the Eucharist (each in contemporary and traditional language), Thanksgiving for the Gift of a Child, *Baptism, *Collects and Postcommunions, a *Lectionary for Sundays and greater feasts, and the *Psalter. In the Eucharist, Order One is based on the two main rites of the ASB; Order Two is closer to the 1662 BCP as commonly used in modern times. Order One contains eight alternative *Eucharistic Prayers, of which two are prescribed for use in Order One in traditional language. There are numerous supplementary texts and alternatives. The main book is supplemented by *Initiation Services* (1998), which contains rites for Baptism and Confirmation (with or without the Eucharist) and Reception into the C of E, *Pastoral Services* (2000), which provides for Ministry to the Sick, Marriage (including An Order for Prayer and Dedication after a Civil Marriage), Emergency Baptism, and Funerals (including the Burial of Ashes and an Outline Order for a Memorial Service), *Daily Prayer* (preliminary edition, 2002), which provides for the *Office on weekdays, and a Lectionary. A book called *Times and Seasons* (with *Propers for the whole year), and a new *Ordinal are expected.

Pio da Pietrelcina, St (1887–1968), *Capuchin, popularly known as 'Padre Pio'. Francesco Forgione was born at Pietrelcina in S. Italy, and became a Capuchin friar in 1903 taking the name of Pio da Pietrelcina. He was ordained priest in 1910, and from 1916 spent virtually all his life in the friary at San Giovanni Rotondo (near Foggia), where he is buried. Despite long periods of official suspicion and restrictions on his ministry, he attained a world-wide following due to the holiness of his life, the spiritual direction he gave, particularly during *confessions, and for the mystical phenomena and *stigmatization (from 1918) attributed to him. He founded a hospital in San Giovanni Rotondo and established a widespread network of 'Groups of Prayer'. He was canonised in 2002. Feast day, 23 Sept.

Oxford Paperback Reference

The Kings of Queens of Britain
John Cannon and Anne Hargreaves

A detailed, fully-illustrated history ranging from mythical and pre-conquest rulers to the present House of Windsor, featuring regional maps and genealogies.

A Dictionary of Dates
Cyril Leslie Beeching

Births and deaths of the famous, significant and unusual dates in history – this is an entertaining guide to each day of the year.

'a dipper's blissful paradise ... Every single day of the year, plus an index of birthdays and chronologies of scientific developments and world events.'

Observer

A Dictionary of British History
Edited by John Cannon

An invaluable source of information covering the history of Britain over the past two millennia. Over 3,600 entries written by more than 100 specialist contributors.

Review of the parent volume
'the range is impressive ... truly (almost) all of human life is here'
Kenneth Morgan, *Observer*

OXFORD

Oxford Paperback Reference

The Concise Oxford Companion to English Literature
Margaret Drabble and Jenny Stringer

Based on the best-selling *Oxford Companion to English Literature*, this is an indispensable guide to all aspects of English literature.

Review of the parent volume
'a magisterial and monumental achievement'

Literary Review

The Concise Oxford Companion to Irish Literature
Robert Welch

From the ogam alphabet developed in the 4th century to Roddy Doyle, this is a comprehensive guide to writers, works, topics, folklore, and historical and cultural events.

Review of the parent volume
'Heroic volume ... It surpasses previous exercises of similar nature in the richness of its detail and the ecumenism of its approach.'

Times Literary Supplement

A Dictionary of Shakespeare
Stanley Wells

Compiled by one of the best-known international authorities on the playwright's works, this dictionary offers up-to-date information on all aspects of Shakespeare, both in his own time and in later ages.

OXFORD

Oxford Paperback Reference

The Concise Oxford Dictionary of Quotations
Edited by Elizabeth Knowles

Based on the highly acclaimed *Oxford Dictionary of Quotations*, this paperback edition maintains its extensive coverage of literary and historical quotations, and contains completely up-to-date material. A fascinating read and an essential reference tool.

The Oxford Dictionary of Humorous Quotations
Edited by Ned Sherrin

From the sharply witty to the downright hilarious, this sparkling collection will appeal to all senses of humour.

Quotations by Subject
Edited by Susan Ratcliffe

A collection of over 7,000 quotations, arranged thematically for easy look-up. Covers an enormous range of nearly 600 themes from 'The Internet' to 'Parliament'.

The Concise Oxford Dictionary of Phrase and Fable
Edited by Elizabeth Knowles

Provides a wealth of fascinating and informative detail for over 10,000 phrases and allusions used in English today. Find out about anything from the 'Trojan house' to 'ground zero'.

OXFORD

Oxford Paperback Reference

The Concise Oxford Dictionary of World Religions
Edited by John Bowker

Over 8,200 entries containing unrivalled coverage of all the major world religions, past and present.

'covers a vast range of topics ... is both comprehensive and reliable'
The Times

The Oxford Dictionary of Saints
David Farmer

From the famous to the obscure, over 1,400 saints are covered in this acclaimed dictionary.

'an essential reference work'
Daily Telegraph

The Concise Oxford Dictionary of the Christian Church
E. A. Livingstone

This indispensable guide contains over 5,000 entries and provides full coverage of theology, denominations, the church calendar, and the Bible.

'opens up the whole of Christian history, now with a wider vision than ever'
Robert Runcie, former Archbishop of Canterbury

OXFORD